RELIGIONS IN THE UK

A MULTI-FAITH DIRECTORY

RELIGIONS IN THE UK

A MULTI-FAITH DIRECTORY

edited by
Paul Weller

researched by
Eileen Fry & Paul Weller

Published by the University of Derby in association with
The Inter Faith Network for the United Kingdom

ISBN 0 901437 68 9

Published by University of Derby in association with
The Inter Faith Network for the United Kingdom
(Registered Charity number 296773).

University of Derby, Mickleover, Derby, DE3 5GX.

In association with
The Inter Faith Network for the United Kingdom,
5-7 Tavistock Place, London, WClH 9SN.

Typeset by Debbie Martin and Indexed by David Bush,
University of Derby

Printed by Butler & Tanner Limited, Selwood Printing Works,
Caxton Road, Frome, Somerset, BA11 1NF

CONTENTS

Page references for sections within each chapter can be found in the left hand column at the start of each major chapter and in the same column at the start of each set of the UK and of the Regional and Local organisation listings. More detailed page references for sub-sections can be found in the Topic Index (in the case of the textual materials) and in the Local Guide Index (in the case of the listings).

Y0058604

PREFACE

Religions in the UK: A Ground-Breaking Project

The initial 1993 edition of *Religions in the UK* was the first comprehensive directory of national and local religious organisations and places of worship covering all the United Kingdom's major faith communities. It was widely welcomed as a new resource for living in a multi-faith society. Religious community representatives, journalists, academics and educators, those working in community relations and service provision, are among the many for whom it has already become a standard reference book.

The New, Improved 1997 Edition

This new edition of the directory, like the first, is designed to assist and encourage the development of inter-religious contacts and dialogue in the UK and to facilitate the participation in public life of the world religious traditions which have significant communities in this country. It develops and updates the first edition in ways suggested by users of the first edition who participated in a reader survey.

The 1997 edition contains listings for around a thousand more organisations than the first and gives greater detail about many of those which are listed. Alongside the basic contact information included in the first edition, for many organisations some or all of the following additional information is included in the present edition: EMail addresses, languages used, local and national affiliations, social groupings or traditions and movements within the particular religion concerned. Standardised information is given on a range of activities undertaken by organisations and some religious newspaper and magazine listings have been included in the chapter on "Finding Out More: Some Other Relevant Publications and Resources".

The preparation of a new edition has also given an opportunity to review the descriptions of each religious community to achieve greater detail and clarity and even more balance and accuracy. We have also tried to make the directory simpler to use, with improved layout and better indexes.

The Partnership Behind the Directory

Religions in the UK has been produced the result of co-operation between the Religious Resource and Research Centre of the University of Derby and The Inter Faith Network for the UK.

The Religious Resource and Research Centre is a designated research centre of the University of Derby which developed out of a joint initiative, begun in 1990, by the University and the Church of England Diocese of Derby. Its research focuses on personal, social, and values issues relating to religious plurality.

The Inter Faith Network was founded in 1987. It works alongside its eighty member organisations to increase mutual understanding and respect between the faith communities of the world religions represented in the UK today. It also works more widely within society to promote an appreciation of the importance of religious identity and of inter-faith understanding.

The Consultative Process

The materials about each religious community are the product of a lengthy, extensive and careful process of consultation and debate which has involved both religious practitioners and academic experts as listed in the "Acknowledgements" chapter. An important principle of effective inter-faith dialogue is that partners in dialogue should be free to define themselves.

The editorial process for this directory has tried to take into account as fully as possible the perspectives and sensitivities of all the religious communities included. At the same time, the drafting process has benefited from the expertise and advice of a number of academics working in the relevant fields.

The Challenge of the Task

Describing such a range of religious communities and traditions within a single volume is a challenging and sensitive task. Similarly, it is a complex and extensive operation to gather data on thousands of their organisations. We have aimed for the highest degree of accuracy possible, but if there are omissions and accidental inaccuracies, we apologise and ask readers to let us know.

We believe, however, that a high level of comprehensiveness and accuracy has been achieved and that *Religions in the UK* will continue to be a standard reference work and resource for building a shared society characterised by increasing mutual understanding and respect.

In particular it is our hope that this edition of the directory will prove to be of particular value in the context of inclusive planning for Millennium events, so that as wide a participation as possible might be facilitated to celebrate both the distinctive contribution of each religious tradition and community, and also of what can be shared together for the good of all within our common society.

Dr Paul Weller
Editor, "Religions in the UK" and Director, Multi-Faith Directory Research Project

Religious Resource and Research Centre, School of Education and Social Science, University of Derby

THE UNIVERSITY OF DERBY

Religious Studies Subject Area
Division of Social Science

The Religious Studies Subject Area is a part of the Division of Social Science within the University's School of Education and Social Science. Religious Studies is offered from Foundation level through undergraduate and taught postgraduate study to doctoral research. Its Divisional location means that it shares some programmes of study with the other two subject areas within the School, namely, Counselling and Psychotherapy, and Sociology. The School also offers Religious Education within the BEd PGCE programme of the Division of Education.

- **Religious Studies in the Foundation Programme**
  Religious Studies is available as one of the subjects on offer within the University's Foundation programme for students with non-standard academic backgrounds.

- **Religions: Culture & Belief, Joint & Minor in Combined Subject BA/BSc (Hons)**
  At undergraduate level. Religions: Culture and Belief is available within the University's Combined Subject BA/BSc degrees, as a minor or joint programme that can be taken in combination with other subjects.

- **BA (Hons) Social, Cultural & Religious Studies**
  A specialist undergraduate degree which draws upon Religious Studies and Sociology modules to provide a distinctive and inter-disciplinary programme of study in the study of religion.

- **MA in Religion Within a Plural Society**
  The programme has been offered since 1992 under its original name of the MA in Religious Pluralism. It offers an opportunity to engage critically with both the social and the religious issues posed by religious plurality within the context of secularity.

- **MA in Pastoral Studies**
  A programme of study for those involved with, and interested in, pastoral care, including those in religious leadership roles and those in secular care organisations who wish to take account of the religious needs of the individuals and communities with whom they work.

- **MPhil and PhD Research**
  Supervision is offered for full and part-time research in religion. Centre staff have particular research interests in inter-faith dialogue; missiology; religions and ethnicity; religions, state and society; religion and the social sciences; Islam in Britain; religions and education; Sikhism in the modern world; religion in India.

Further information available from: School of Education & Social Science, University of Derby, Mickleover, Derby DE3 5GX. Tel: 01332-622231, Fax: 01332-622746, http://www.derby.ac.uk

THE UNIVERSITY OF DERBY

Religious Resource and Research Centre

The Religious Resource and Research Centre is a designated Research Centre of the University of Derby. It has also acted as a central service unit within the University, advising on matters of religious belief and practice. As an academic unit the Centre researches into the religious dimensions of social and individual life with a special focus upon religious and social issues related to religious plurality; pastoral care in a plural context; and issues of values. The spirit and practice of dialogue are fundamental to the Centre's activities which it conducts in co-operation with a wide range of academic disciplines, religious communities and other insitutions.

- **Multi-Faith Directory Research Project**
  The project which lies behind this directory commenced in 1991 and is a joint project between the Centre and the Inter Faith Network for the United Kingdom, of which the Centre is an affiliated organisation.

- **Religions and Statistics Research Project**
  The project aims critically to evaluate the nature, purpose, validity and reliability of the current and future collection of statistics on United Kingdom religious communities. It is currently engaged in a programme of testing the acceptability of a possible question on religious affiliation for the 2001 census.

- **MultiFaith Net**
  The University is currently planning the possibility of developing a MultiFaith Net as a World Wide Web site offering areas to religious information and resource and providing a virtual space for inter-faith dialogue. It is intended that MultiFaith Net (http://www.multifaithnet.org/) will be available as a subscription-based service, including a special comprehensive subscription offering specified forms of electronic access to this edition of *Religions in the UK: A Multi-Faith Directory*.

- **Multi-Faith Centre**
  The University is planning the building of a Multi-Faith Centre to cater for student and staff needs for religious worship and meeting. The University understands its plans for this Centre, the design for which has been informed by a group drawn from seven world religious traditions, as an expression of its commitment to promote inter-faith dialogue.

- **Religious Services**
  A multi-faith Steering Committee provides the organisational framework for the work of the University's team of Religious and Cultural Advisers, among whom are Hindu, Jewish, Muslim and Sikh Advisers and an Ecumenical Team of Christian Chaplains which is recognised as a Local Ecumenical Partnership and includes Christian Chaplains from the Anglican, Free Church and Roman Catholic traditions of Christianity.

Further information available from: Religious Resource and Research Centre, University of Derby, Mickleover, Derby DE3 5GX. Tel: 01332-622222 ext. 2102, Fax: 01332-514323, EMail: P.G.Weller@derby.ac.uk.

THE INTER FAITH NETWORK
FOR THE UK

The Inter Faith Network was set up in 1987. It works with its member bodies to combat inter religious prejudice and intolerance and to help make Britain a country marked by mutual understanding and respect between religions where all can practise their faith with integrity

The Network:
- Provides information on faith communities and on inter faith affairs
- Advises the public and private sectors on multi faith projects and inter faith issues
- Publishes materials designed to help people working in the religious and inter faith sectors
- Fosters inter faith co-operation on social issues
- Holds regular national meetings of its member bodies where social and religious questions of concern to the different faith communities can be examined together and sets up multi faith working groups, seminars and conferences to pursue these where appropriate
- Links 80 member organisations including representative bodies from the different faith communities; national inter faith organisations; local inter faith groups; academic institutions and bodies concerned with multi faith education.

The Network has also worked with other organisations, such as the Commission for Racial Equality and the Inner Cities Religious Council, on a number of its projects.

Its partnership with the Religious Resource and Research Centre at the University of Derby lies behind *Religions in the UK: A Multi Faith Directory*.

1997 is the Tenth Anniversary year of the Network. Member bodies and a number of other organisations around the UK are arranging events to mark the occasion and to draw attention to the general importance of working to build good inter faith relations in all contexts.

Further information available from: The Inter Faith Network, 5/7 Tavistock Place, London, WC1H 9SN, Tel 0171-388-0008, Fax 0171-387-7968.

MEMBER ORGANISATIONS OF
THE INTER FAITH NETWORK FOR THE UK

FAITH COMMUNITY REPRESENTATIVE BODIES

Afro West Indian United Council of Churches
Arya Pratinidhi Sabha (UK)
Bahá'í Community of the United Kingdom
Board of Deputies of British Jews
Buddhist Society
Churches' Commission for Inter-Faith Relations
  (Council of Churches for Britain & Ireland)
Council of African & Afro-Caribbean Churches (UK)
Friends of the Western Buddhist Order
Imams & Mosques Council (UK)
Islamic Cultural Centre, Regent's Park, London
Jain Samaj Europe
Jamiat-ul-Ulama Britain (Association of Muslim
  Scholars)
Maha Bodhi Society of Sri Lanka (UK)
National Council of Hindu Temples
Network of Buddhist Organisations (UK)
Network of Sikh Organisations (UK)
Roman Catholic Committee for Other Faiths of the
  Bishops' Conference of England & Wales
Sikh Missionary Society
Swaminaryan Hindu Mission
UK Action Committee on Islamic Affairs
Vishwa Hindu Parishad (UK)
World Ahl ul-Bayt (AS) Islamic League
World Islamic Mission (UK)
Zoroastrian Trust Funds of Europe

NATIONAL INTER FAITH ORGANISATIONS

Calamus Foundation
Council of Christians & Jews
International Association for Religious Freedom
  (British Members' Group)
London Society of Jews & Christians
Maimonides Foundation
Northern Ireland Inter Faith Forum
Standing Conference of Jews, Christians & Muslims
  in Europe
Westminster Interfaith
World Conference on Religion & Peace
  (UK & Ireland Chapter)
World Congress of Faiths

LOCAL INTER FAITH GROUPS:

Birmingham Council of Faiths
Birmingham Fellowship of Faiths
Bradford Concord Inter Faith Society
Bristol Interfaith Group

Cambridge Inter-Faith Group
Cardiff Interfaith Association
Cleveland Inter Faith Group
Coventry Inter Faith Group
Derby Open Centre Multi-Faith Group
Dudley Council of Faiths
Edinburgh Interfaith Association
Glasgow Sharing of Faiths Group
Gloucestershire Inter Faith Action
Harrow Inter-Faith Council
Kirklees & Calderdale Inter-Faith Fellowship
Leeds Concord Inter-Faith Fellowship
Leicester Council of Faiths
Manchester Inter Faith Group
Medway & Maidstone Inter-Faith Group
Merseyside Inter Faith Group
Newham Association of Faiths
Nottingham Inter-Faith Council
Oxford Round Table of Religions
Peterborough Inter-Faith Council
Reading Inter-Faith Group
Redbridge Council of Faiths
Richmond Inter-Faith Group
Rochdale Interfaith Action
Suffolk Inter-Faith Resource
Tyne & Wear Racial Equality Council Inter Faith
  Panel
Walsall Inter Faith Group
Waltham Forest All Faiths Group
Wellingborough Multi-Faith Group
Wolverhampton Inter-Faith Group

EDUCATIONAL AND ACADEMIC BODIES

Bharatiya Vidya Bhavan
Centre for the Study of Islam & Christian-Muslim
  Relations, Selly Oak, Birmingham
Centre for the Study of Judaism & Jewish-Christian
  Relations, Selly Oak, Birmingham
Community Religions Project, University of Leeds
Institute of Jainology
Islamic Foundation, Leicester
National Association of SACREs
Religious Education Council
Shap Working Party on World Religions in Education
Standing Conference on Inter-Faith Dialogue in
  Education
Study Centre for Christian-Jewish Relations (Sisters
  of Sion)
University of Derby Religious Resource & Research
  Centre

USER'S GUIDE

INTRODUCTION

This chapter explains the layout of the directory and what the reader will find in its texts and listings.

RELIGIONS COVERED BY THE DIRECTORY

The directory contains basic information about the Bahá'í, Buddhist, Christian, Hindu, Jain, Jewish, Muslim, Sikh and Zoroastrian communities in the UK. It also covers inter-faith activities, organisations, groups and resources.

There are many other kinds of formal and informal religious belief and practice in the UK, but it is not possible to be totally comprehensive within the constraints of a single volume. However, the chapter on "Some Other Religious Communities and Groups" provides information on some of these and gives signposts for further information. For information on New Religious Movements, readers are referred to the specialist information service, INFORM, at Houghton Street, London, WC2A 2AE, Tel: 0171-955-7654.

INTRODUCTIONS TO THE RELIGIOUS COMMUNITIES IN THE UK

The materials about each tradition have been prepared with the help of religious practitioners and academic specialists to provide a starting place for the interested enquirer. More detailed information about each religion can be found in the books and articles suggested in the sections on "Further Reading"; from religious community organisations themselves; and from the education and information organisations listed in the chapter on "Finding Out More: Some Other Relevant Publications and Resources".

The introductory chapters to the faith communities generally follow a standard format for ease of reference. Slight variations in approach and internal balance reflect the views of the religious community consultants on how their community and its tradition can best be presented to the general reader. However normally, the main sections in each chapter are:

In the UK

Basic historical, ethnic, linguistic and statistical information.

Origins and Development

The historical origins of the religious community in terms of its significant or founding figure or figures and an outline of some of the principal features of its global and historical development.

Sources of Beliefs and Practices

The teachings, scriptures and religious structures which are seen as authoritative within the community.

Key Beliefs

The religion's central understandings of the nature of the human and the divine or the ultimate, as well as its basic understandings of the purpose of existence.

Traditions

The principal traditions of interpretation in the religious community.

Life

How adherents are initiated into the religion and something of the way in which the religion shapes their everyday life in terms of ethics, family, food and similar matters.

Worship

Information on the buildings in which the religion's worship takes place and outlines of some of the forms of worship which occur within them.

Calendar and Festivals

The dating system of the religion, the rhythm of its year, and its major days of religious observance.

Organisation

Organisational patterns of the community in the UK and descriptions of the roles of its religious personnel.

Further Reading

Details of a number of useful general introductions to the religion, together with a number of books and articles which particularly focus on the life of that religion in the UK.

CALENDARS AND FESTIVALS

The directory cannot list specific dates for every festival since many religious traditions operate according to calendars which differ from that used in public life in the UK and some do not determine the dates of their festivals far in advance. A calendar of festivals is produced annually by the Shap Working Party on World Religions in Education (available from the National Society's RE Centre, 36 Causton Street, London, SW1P 4AU and see the display page at the end of the chapter "Finding Out More: Some Other Relevant Publications and Resources"). Many faith communities also publish their own calendars.

In this directory, dates are given as CE (Common Era) rather than AD (Anno Domini) and BCE (Before Common Era) rather than BC (Before Christ), reflecting the increase in this usage. Thus, instead of 1997AD, one will find 1997CE.

TRANSLITERATION, TRANSLATION AND DIACRITICAL MARKINGS

The religious traditions covered in this directory all have scriptures and other important texts which were not originally written in English. For some religions, languages other than English remain the main medium for their religious discourse and practice. In the directory, such terms are given in italics in the original language in a transliterated form, together with an English approximation of their meaning as a translation.

Italics have also been used for English language terms which have a meaning or overtone which might not be clear to English speakers from outside the tradition concerned. Personal names are not italicised, but the names of scriptures and of particular books within them are.

Apostrophes, inverted apostrophes, acute, grave and circumflex accents are used in the transliterations but not other less well known diacritical markings of the kind often used in scholarly texts. In the descriptions of the communities an attempt has been made to ensure consistency of transliteration and translation. In the organisational listings, however, the reader will find variety since the directory has largely followed the spellings and transliterations supplied by the organisations themselves.

USING THE ORGANISATION LISTINGS

After the introduction to each religion a listing is given of its organisations and places of worship, together with their contact details and other information. With the exception of the Christian listings, these are laid out in alphabetical order, in the following sequence:

UK-Wide Organisations

UK-wide organisations within each religion are listed in alphabetical order.

National, Regional and Local Organisations and Places of Worship

Local organisations and places of worship are set out within the chapter on each religion, by nation of the UK and then by regional area. National bodies in each of the nations are listed at the beginning, and then within each region,

bodies covering the whole region or a county within it are listed first, followed by bodies operating at a city, town, or local level which are listed in alphabetical order of town or city. Within each town or city, bodies are listed in alphabetical order of their names. Listings for **London** are, however, divided by borough on the basis of information provided by organisations or the project's best judgement on their location and then ordered alphabetically by their organisation name. Nations and regions appear in the following order:

England

The structure of these entries is divided into the regions which follow below. The geographical location of organisations within these regions of England is indicated by the following names of counties and other areas appearing within organisation addresses.

North East
Durham, Northumberland, Tyne and Wear

Yorkshire
East Riding of Yorkshire, North Yorkshire, South Yorkshire, West Yorkshire.

North West
Cheshire, Cumbria, Greater Manchester, Isle of Man, Lancashire, Merseyside.

East Midlands
Derbyshire, Leicestershire, Lincolnshire, Northamptonshire, Nottinghamshire.

West Midlands
Hereford and Worcester, Shropshire, Staffordshire, Warwickshire, West Midlands.

East Anglia
Cambridgeshire, Norfolk, Suffolk.

London
London Boroughs.

South East
Bedfordshire, Berkshire, Buckinghamshire, Channel Islands, East Sussex, Essex, Hampshire, Hertfordshire, Isle of Wight, Kent, Oxfordshire, Surrey, West Sussex.

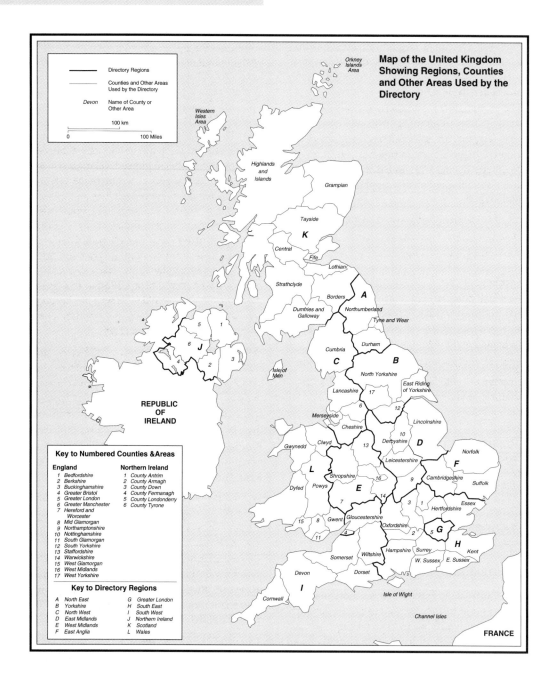

The directory groups organisations according to twelve regions marked A–L on the map above. These are limited by thick lines. The areas contained by each directory region are marked by name where space allows and by numbers elsewhere. Keys to the numbered areas are to the left of the map. The Isle of Man is in the North West region and the Channel Isles are in the South East.

South West

Cornwall, Devon, Dorset, Gloucestershire, Greater Bristol, Somerset, Wiltshire.

Northern Ireland

The structure of the entries is not further divided into regions. Christian listings are included on an all-Ireland basis, reflecting Church organisational structures. Location in Northern Ireland is indicated by the names of the following counties appearing in the addresses:

County Antrim, County Armagh, County Down, County Fermanagh, County Londonderry and County Tyrone.

Scotland

The structure of the entries is not further divided into regions. Location in Scotland is indicated by the following regions appearing in each address:

Borders, Central, Dumfries and Galloway, Fife, Grampian, Highlands and Islands, Lothian, Strathclyde, and Tayside.

Wales

The structure of the entries is not further divided into regions. Location in Wales is indicated by use of the following areas appearing in each address:

Clwyd, Dyfed, Gwent, Gwynedd, Mid Glamorgan, Powys, South Glamorgan, and West Glamorgan.

Christian Listings

The Christian listings differ from those in other chapters due to the sheer number of Christian organisations and places of worship in this country. UK-wide Christian organisations are laid out in alphabetical order within the following sections:

- Organisations known as ecumenical instruments and other groupings of Churches operating at a UK-wide level.

- Churches operating at the level of the UK which are either directly or indirectly

(through their affiliation to a full member organisation) part of an ecumenical instrument and some other Christian Churches.

- Networks, agencies and other bodies which are either directly or indirectly part of an ecumenical instrument.

There are no local listings for the Christian community. Rather, regional level organisations are listed. These appear by nation of the UK and then by region. Within each region, regional ecumenical instruments appear in alphabetical order of their name, followed by regional Church structures also in alphabetical order of names. Finally, information is given on local Evangelical Fellowships and some other bodies, also in alphabetical order. Christian listings for London are not broken down by borough because most Church regional bodies cover more than one London borough.

The national and regional Church and ecumenical bodies can give more information about local Christian organisations and places of worship. The vast majority of Christian Churches produce their own national handbooks and directories. Many also have publications covering regional and local areas, as do a number of regional and local ecumenical instruments.

In addition to Churches and places of worship, there are many hundreds of Christian voluntary organisations. The *UK Christian Handbook* and the *Irish Christian Handbook* (see section on "Directories of Religious Organisations" in the chapter on "Finding Out More: Some Other Relevant Publications and Resources") give information on many that are active in the UK and in Ireland.

In addition, details of English and Welsh Christian and other religious buildings certified as places of worship and/or for the solemnisation of marriage can be obtained from the General Register Office of the Office for National Statistics' *Official List of Certified Places of Worship, parts I-IV*. There are no comparable lists for Scotland and Northern Ireland.

UNDERSTANDING THE ORGANISATION LISTINGS

Every organisation listing gives a name and an address or telephone number for the organisation or place of worship. For most organisations and places of worship there is also additional contact information. Further information given about such matters as activities and the particular traditions, movements, or social groupings within a faith community varies according to the detail provided by the organisations.

It is important to note that the information, or lack of it, in these fields reflects the choices made by listed organisations. The directory has not imposed information editorially, even where this is widely known or could be deduced from other information supplied. In particular, with regard to the affiliations field, organisations may have more affiliations than are listed here, but what appears reflects the information prioritised by the organisations themselves.

National organisations have also had the option to add a note on matters which they feel it is particularly important for the directory user to know. Where this opportunity has been taken up, then these self-descriptions follow, to a maximum of around thirty words (or fifty words in the case of Resource organisations).

The fields of information used are as follows:

Name
Name of the organisation or place of worship.

Address
Unless otherwise indicated, the address is normally that of the organisation's offices in a public building or of the place of worship. Where it is known that a home address (of, for example, a Secretary) has been given as the postal contact address, this is indicated by "(h)" after the address.

Telephone
Normally that of an organisation's offices in a public building or that of a place of worship.

Some places of worship and organisations do not have an office telephone, or the regular contact person for that organisation is not generally present at the place of worship. In such cases, the entry may well be the home telephone number of the contact person. If we have been informed of this, "(h)" appears after the number.

Fax
Normally that of an organisation's office or of a place of worship.

Contact
The person designated as the principal contact to handle incoming enquiries. This may be an individually named person or an office-holder such as a Chairperson, President or Secretary. Office holders may change (sometimes annually) but former officers will usually refer callers to the relevant new person.

Position
A description of the position which the contact holds in the organisation.

EMail
An Email address is given if one is available.

Internet
Where the organisation has a Home Page on the Internet, then this Internet address is given.

Activities
The following range of standard entries indicate what the nature and main activities of organisations and places of worship are: **worship** (place of worship); **resource** (educational resource organisation); **media** (deals with the media); **umbrella** (body to which other organisations are affiliated); **visits** (welcomes pre-arranged visits by groups of visitors); **youth** (activities organised for young people); **elderly** (activities organised for the elderly); **women** (activities organised for women); **newsletter** (publication of regular newsletter or journal); **books** (publication of books); **inter-faith** (participation in inter-faith activities).

Other Languages

Up to four languages other than English are listed, if spoken by significant numbers within the organisation or at the place of worship, and appear in the order of most widespread use.

Affiliations

The name of one local or regional body, up to two national bodies, and one international body within its own religious tradition to which the organisation or place of worship is affiliated.

For most religions, there is also the heading:

Traditions

The name of the major broad grouping within the religion with which the organisation or place of worship identifies.

For a number of religions, there are also the headings:

Social Groups

The name of any particular social group or groups with which the organisation or place of worship most closely identifies.

Movements

The name of any specific movements with which the organisation or place of worship most closely identifies.

HOW THE ORGANISATION LISTINGS WERE COMPILED

We offered free inclusion in the directory, thus ensuring that its coverage is as wide as possible. The variety of information contained in each organisation's entry reflects both the questions asked of organisations in different religious traditions and the choices made by particular organisations about the kind of information which they wished to have published.

To understand the range of information provided in different entries on organisations and places of worship, it is important to explain something of the process by which they came to be included in their present form. The assistance of all those listed in the "Acknowledgements" chapter at the end of the directory helped the project in its aim of constructing a grid of interlocking information sources in order to ensure that as many organisations as possible would be identified and checked. Information was gathered and checked in the following ways:

- A questionnaire was drawn up with advice from a range of the directory's consultants including variations, where necessary, to tailor it to different religious traditions.

- The questionnaires were piloted with a sample of organisations and the results of the pilot were used to modify the original designs.

- Postal contact was made with each organisation on which the project had any information, with a request to complete and return the form in a Freepost envelope provided or to reply stating that it did not wish to be included in the directory.

- Follow-up letters were sent to the organisations and places of worship which did not respond to the original request to complete the questionnaire and, in the case of many organisations, attempts were also made to telephone organisations which did not initially respond by post.

- Details were cross-checked with local inter-faith groups in various localities, with project consultants from within the religious communities and from higher education institutions, as well as with some local Racial Equality Councils.

- Additional forms were sent out during the course of the project as new information on additional organisations and places of worship came to light.

- A draft entry was sent to every listed organisation in early 1997, giving a final opportunity to update and correct its draft entry or to ask for it to be omitted.

Level of Accuracy

Users will appreciate that not all organisations reply to correspondence and questionnaires, not all are contactable by telephone, and that contact details can and do change with the passage of time. As a result, the absolute accuracy of all entries cannot be guaranteed. But as will be seen, the project has gone to considerable lengths to ensure that the entries are as up to date and accurate as possible.

Apparent Omissions

We have also sought to respect the wishes of organisations which have requested that we do not include details about their existence, even where this information might be available elsewhere in the public domain. The small number of such requests may be the reason why some organisations known to directory users do not appear in the directory.

Duplicate Entries

There may also be some cases in which the directory includes two sets of details referring to the same organisation. This can occur in those instances where, despite its best efforts, the directory project has been unable to confirm positively which is the correct and/or preferred contact point. In these cases, both possible contact points are included rather than neither.

KEYS TO TERMS USED IN ORGANISATION TITLES

At the end of most of the introductory chapters on the religious communities, a guide is included to the meaning of the key terms used in the names of organisations listed.

These guides are not glossaries of generally significant terms in each religion. Rather, they are provided to help the directory user in understanding the meaning or significance of the names of the listed organisations. In many cases, the names can indicate something about those whom the organisation holds in great esteem, or perhaps something about the nature of the group or its place in the overall spectrum of that community's life.

To track down further information on particular concepts which are italicised within the "Keys to Terms Used in Organisation Titles", the reader should refer to the "Significant Word Index" at the end of the directory, which lists significant words together with their references throughout the text.

FINDING OUT MORE: SOME OTHER RELEVANT PUBLICATIONS AND RESOURCES

The final chapter on "Finding Out More: Some Other Relevant Publications and Resources" points the directory user to additional sources of published information as well as to organisations which provide information on religious life in the UK and which can give further information on the religious communities. Within this chapter there is also a section that includes details of some newspapera and magazines which provide coverage of a variety of religious communities.

INDEXES

There are four indexes:

The "Topic Index" gives page references for each major section and sub-section of the introductions to each religion and the other descriptive material in the directory. It enables the directory user to find broad topic areas.

The "Significant Word Index" indexes the incidence of italicised words throughout the directory together with a number of other significant words such as the names of religious personalities and leaders.

The "UK and National Organisation Index" is an alphabetical listing of all the religious organisations listed in the directory and operating at a UK and/or national level together with national inter-faith organisations and groups and resource organisations.

The "Local Guide Index" lists all the towns and cities in the directory and indicates the page ranges where organisations and places of worship located in these towns and cities can be found.

FURTHER READING AND HELP

At the end of most chapters there is a section on further reading to assist directory users in following up additional relevant information.

Questions about the directory can be directed to the Religious Resource and Research Centre of the University of Derby at the Mickleover Campus, Western Rd, Derby DE3 5GX, Tel: 01332-622222 ext 2102; Fax: 01332-514323; EMail: P.G.Weller@derby.ac.uk. (More details on the Centre and the University can be found in the display panels on pp. 9-10).

Further advice and information about inter-faith relations and making contact with religious communities and their organisations can be obtained from The Inter Faith Network for the UK at 5-7 Tavistock Place, London WC1H 9SN, Tel: 0171-388-0008; Fax: 0171-387-7968. (More details on the Network can be found in the display panels on pp. 11-12).

RELIGIOUS LANDSCAPE OF THE UK

THE VARIETY OF RELIGIONS

Religions in the United Kingdom exhibit a considerable degree of vigour and diversity despite the effects of secularisation on personal and social life. The UK is now more religiously diverse than any other country of the European Union.

There are no precise statistics for most communities, but it is clear that, of the world religious traditions with a following in the UK, Christians form the largest religious community followed by Muslims, then Hindus, Sikhs and Jews; then Buddhists; and then Jains, Bahá'ís and Zoroastrians.

Members within each of these religious communities share in common many beliefs and practices, but within most communities there are also significant differences of tradition, organisation, ethnicity and language. For example, over the centuries, Christianity itself has developed into richly diverse forms. This diversity to some extent reflects doctrinal difference and dispute, but it also reflects the varied national and religious histories of the different component parts of the United Kingdom of Great Britain and Northern Ireland.

In addition to diversity within traditions, in some cases the boundaries between different religious traditions can be somewhat fluid. For example, within the religious practice of many ethnically Chinese people, traditions of Taoism, Confucianism and also Buddhism can often be found in intermingled forms.

Alongside those who belong to the major world religions in the UK, there are those who espouse other forms of religious expression. Among these are groups often popularly referred to as "sects" or "cults" but which, in academic usage, have normally come to be described as "New Religious Movements" (NRMs), as well as those who understand themselves as Pagans. Another area of religious life, often described as "New Age" spirituality, is characterised by a concern for ecology and personal growth and draws upon spiritual practices and traditions from a variety of sources.

As well as people who have an active involvement in the corporate life of their religious communities, the UK also has a significant proportion of people whose religious belief and practice is often described as "folk religion" or "residual Christianity". Such people may turn to an active involvement in Christian religious life only, or mainly, at times of crisis or personal significance such as birth, marriage and death, or at festivals such as Christmas. Other faith communities also have followers whose religious observances are of this kind.

In relation to all communities there are also some individuals and groups who acknowledge their connection with a particular tradition but find themselves in conflict with its official representatives over one or other single issue or across a whole range of ways of understanding the significance of their inherited or adopted tradition.

Not everyone, of course, is religious. There are also many who, whilst they may uphold strong ethical and moral values, do not profess any form of religious belief. These include humanists, some of whom may be either agnostics or atheists. Not all those who are non-religious are antagonistic towards religion, but some do have deeply felt concerns about allowing too prominent a role for religion in public life and certainly about any official privileging of religion in general or any one religion in particular.

As the following brief summary shows, whilst Christianity remains the UK's principal religious tradition in terms of the size of its following and of its historical and contemporary significance, there is a very wide spectrum of belief and practice in the UK.

THE HISTORICAL DEVELOPMENT OF A RELIGIOUSLY PLURAL COUNTRY

For much of the history of these islands (as elsewhere in the world) it has been difficult to distinguish between political and religious loyalties. There have often been attempts to impose varying degrees of uniformity in the public profession of belief and in religious worship, sometimes through physical force and sometimes through the use of the law.

Despite this, religious diversity has always been present. Pagan traditions were present here from before the arrival of Christianity and have continued to the present day. From the time of the Roman conquest onwards, alongside varieties of Christian belief and practice, individuals and groups of people belonging to other religious traditions have come as visitors, or to live here, with much more extensive settlement taking place during the last half century.

A small Jewish community was established after the Norman conquest in 1066, but the community was expelled in 1290 and was not re-admitted until the period of the Commonwealth, following the English Civil War of the 17th century. In the following centuries, Britain's international role expanded through trade, with the development of colonialism and imperialism. In this period, numbers of individual Hindus, Muslims and others came either as slaves, or as servants or *ayahs*.

The Nineteenth and Early Twentieth Centuries

During the nineteenth century, there were rapid advances in religious toleration and the abolition of many civil disabilities related to religion. This facilitated both the development and the public visibility of diverse forms of religious life, including an expansion of the influence of Nonconformist Christian traditions and the re-emergence of Roman Catholic Christianity after centuries of restricted existence. Catholic Christianity was also strengthened in Great Britain by the migration from Ireland of many Catholic workers to fill jobs, especially in the construction industries.

Also, in the nineteenth century, many civil disabilities were removed from the Jewish community. Between 1881 and 1914, the Jewish community was strengthened by a combination of economic migration in the face of restricted social and economic possibilities and escape from the anti-Jewish pogroms occurring within the Russian Empire.

Zoroastrians began to settle in some numbers in England during the nineteenth century. The majority of them were of Indian origin and known as Parsees. The Parsee Zoroastrians were the first group with South Asian origins to make an impact, as a community, on the social and political life of the UK. The first three Asian Members of Parliament, who were elected in the latter part of the nineteenth century, were Parsees. The first of these was the Liberal, Dadabhai Naoroji, who became an MP in 1892.

Also in the nineteenth century a local Muslim presence developed in particular geographical areas, such as the Yemeni Muslims who settled in South Shields and other communities centred around seaports such as Cardiff and Liverpool. Individual Hindu and Sikh traders and settlers were also to be found.

In the opening years of the twentieth century a nascent Buddhist community emerged. Initially, this community was mainly composed of indigenous followers who had become interested in the tenets of Buddhism through reading the texts translated and prepared by 19th century Western academics.

Following the First World War there was further settlement by Muslims and people of other religions from all over the Empire who had been demobilised from the British forces. Together with the movement of families from the original seaport areas of settlement this led to the establishment of small Muslim communities in a larger number of localities.

Bahá'ís have been present in England since 1899 and, in the early twentieth century when Shoghi Effendi (who became Bahá'í Guardian of the Faith and Interpreter of Scripture) lived in London, a Bahá'í community began to develop.

From 1933 onwards, the arrival of escapees from Nazi persecution and the Holocaust in Germany and other Nazi-occupied European countries led to a further strengthening of the Jewish community in the UK.

Post-Second World War

The religious diversity of the UK increased rapidly after the Second World War, with the settlement of some groups of demobilised members of the armed forces of the Empire, among whom were Hindus, Muslims, Sikhs and African-Caribbean Christians. There was also migration to the UK of significant numbers of people from Poland and Italy which led to a further strengthening of the Roman Catholic Christian community as well as to its ethnic diversification.

In the 1950s, new settlers from the New Commonwealth included many migrants from the Caribbean islands who, in response to what they often felt was at best a frosty reception, and at worst discrimination from indigenous Christians, developed new forms of Christian Church life. But it was the migration of significant numbers of people from India, Pakistan, Bangladesh and Hong Kong and, later, in the 1960s and 1970s, of South Asians from Tanzania, Uganda and Kenya, that led to the present breadth of religious diversity in the UK, enabling the establishment here of significant communities of Hindus, Jains, Muslims and Sikhs.

During the 1970s and 1980s refugee settlement further strengthened, in particular, the Buddhist community, following the Chinese take-over of Tibet; the Orthodox tradition of Christianity following conflict in Cyprus; the Bahá'í and Zoroastrian communities following the Iranian Revolution; and the Muslim community in the wake of conflicts in Somalia, Bosnia and the Middle East.

Those who migrated in the early post-war period focused first on the basic need to find somewhere to live, and on getting a job so that they could send remittances back to their families in their home countries. In this phase of settlement, ethnic associations flourished rather than groups organised on a distinctively religious basis, resulting in forms of organisation centred around groupings based on the country of origin.

As immigration restrictions tightened, male migrants were increasingly joined by spouses and children. This laid the basis for the development of a range of social, cultural and religious communities and institutions which would maintain and transmit their religious traditions. Mandirs, gurdwaras and mosques were founded and became an increasingly established part of community life.

The Muslim community is the largest of those which became established here, primarily on the basis of post-Second World War New Commonwealth immigration. It was in the 1950s and 1960s that the Hindu community became more fully established when significant numbers settled and a community emerged. It was further strengthened in the 1970s by Hindus migrating from East African states as a consequence of the Africanisation policies introduced at this time.

As with the Muslim and Hindu communities, the origins of the Sikh presence in the UK can also be traced to individuals and small groups of settlers in the nineteenth and early twentieth centuries. However, the majority of Sikhs migrated in the post-Second World War period. The Sikh community in the UK is now the largest outside of India.

Some Jains migrated directly from India in the 1950s. Others came in the 1970s and 1980s, also as a result of the Africanisation policies in East Africa.

The twentieth century has also seen the growth of a plethora of New Religious Movements, some of which understand themselves as related to one or more of the world religious traditions, but others of which see their role in more universalist terms.

In addition there is a growing movement of people who understand themselves as Pagans and identify with one or other of the major Pagan traditions. Many of these understand themselves as, in some sense, heirs to early Pagan traditions. Others have been drawn to contemporary Paganism predominantly by ecological concerns and commitments.

Religion, Ethnicity and Language

Religion is an important aspect of the identity of a significant number of individuals and groups. For some it is the most important. However, other aspects of identity are represented by ethnicity and language. These are often linked with religious identity because of the history of when and where religious traditions developed. Thus, for example, the majority of people in the UK with Pakistani antecedents are also Muslim, and nearly all Sikhs have some antecedents in the Punjab.

However, the patterns of overlap between religion and ethnicity are not always straightforward and the majority of the UK's religious communities are ethnically diverse, having origins in various parts of the world. So, for example, the Christian community includes, among others, people of African, African-Caribbean, Chinese, East and Central European and South Asian backgrounds.

Similarly, there are Muslims with South Asian, Middle Eastern and Far Eastern roots, just as there are Hindus with ethnic origins in the Caribbean and in Fiji as well as in India. Also, just as one religious tradition may embrace many ethnicities, so one national or regional origin can be shared by several religions. Someone with roots in Gujarat, for example, might be Christian, Hindu, Jain or Muslim.

Shared language can also be an important factor in the relationship between religion and ethnicity. For example, in Wales there are local Christian communities for whom Welsh is the first language of both worship and everyday life. This is also true of Gaelic for smaller numbers of Christians in Scotland. Punjabi is a common language among many Sikhs.

In specific local areas, members of faith communities may share ethnic, cultural and linguistic backgrounds. In some cases the bulk of the community may, for example, be Muslims from Pakistan or, in others, Muslims from Bangladesh, or Muslims from particular regions and even villages within these regions. For example, in Preston the Muslim community is largely Gujarati and so is the local Hindu community.

Such local homogeneity may diminish in the future with greater population mobility. At the same time, evidence from the 1991 Census indicates that, broadly speaking, the geographical spread and concentration of the minority ethnic communities was much the same in 1991 as in 1981, although with a slight increase in the concentration within metropolitan areas.

Geographical Distribution of Religions

Both longer-term religious and national history and more recent patterns of migration and settlement have affected the religious composition of each local and regional area. Therefore some areas have a more multi-faith character, and others have concentrations of people of particular religions or traditions within these religions.

In England, the largest single Christian Church is the Church of England, whilst in Scotland it is the Church of Scotland (which is Presbyterian in tradition). In Wales, the Free Churches collectively are larger than any other Christian tradition, as are the Protestant Churches in Northern Ireland, although the Roman Catholic Church is the largest single Church there.

Even within the four nations, however, a range of groups and denominations within Christianity can be found in varying strengths in different regional and local areas. Throughout England, Scotland and Wales, Roman Catholic Christians are predominantly concentrated in urban areas and, in England, the Church of England has a more widespread presence in rural areas than any other Christian Church.

England has the widest and proportionately greatest variety of religious communities, followed by Scotland and Wales, and then Northern Ireland. Throughout the UK the greatest diversity is to be found in cities, metropolitan boroughs and some towns, and religious, ethnic and linguistic diversity is, not surprisingly, at its greatest concentration in the cosmopolitan capital city of London.

Seaports such as Liverpool and Cardiff often have the oldest local minority religious communities because international trade led to the settlement there of seafarers from other countries. Many old industrial towns and cities of the English Midlands and North, such as Leicester and Bradford, have communities which were established as a result of migration from particular areas of Commonwealth countries in response to the invitation to work in British industries during post-World War II labour shortages.

Bahá'í and Buddhist groups can be found scattered throughout the UK. Other communities, however, are often more geographically concentrated. The largest Hindu communities are in Greater London (especially Wembley and Harrow), Birmingham, Coventry and Leicester. Many Jains live in and around Greater London and in Leicester. Jain communities are also found in Coventry, Luton, Manchester, Northampton and Wellingborough. Zoroastrians are found mainly in the London area, but also in the North West of England.

The densest Jewish population is in the Greater London area and the largest provincial Jewish populations are in Manchester, Leeds and Glasgow. There are also other sizeable Jewish communities in Birmingham, Bournemouth, Brighton, Liverpool and Southend. The largest Muslim communities are to be found in the West Midlands, West Yorkshire, Lancashire, Greater London and in Scotland's central belt. The most substantial Sikh communities are to be found in Birmingham, Bradford, Cardiff, Coventry, Glasgow, Leeds, Leicester, Greater London (especially Southall) and Wolverhampton.

PLACES OF WORSHIP

The historical development and present diversity of the religious profile of the UK is mirrored in its religious architecture. One way in which the religious landscape has quite literally changed is in the presence and range of a variety of different religious buildings. Church steeples and towers are a familiar part of both the urban and rural landscape of the UK. Synagogues have had a long historical presence, but increasingly gurdwaras, mandirs, mosques and viharas are also becoming part of the skyline in a significant number of areas.

Places of worship have an important role as actual or potential community resources within local neighbourhoods. They embody the sources and goals of their religious traditions, thus signifying the established presence and the geographical belonging of these traditions of faith to both national and local society.

Apart from the pre-Christian Pagan traditions and the Christian community, the Jewish community was the first to establish places of worship in Britain. The oldest synagogue in current use is the Bevis Marks Synagogue in London, which was built in 1701. As other communities began to emerge, places of worship within their traditions also began to be established. For example, the first purpose-built mosque was established in Woking in 1899 and the first Sikh gurdwara in Putney, London, in 1911.

It was in the wake of the major post-Second World War migrations that the pattern and distribution of places of worship began to change significantly. Gradually, during the 1960s, as migrants decided to settle in the UK and to bring their families rather than just working here, the provision of worship facilities began to emerge as a community concern. People began to look for premises in which to meet. Often lacking the economic means to buy or build new facilities, they either adapted existing private dwellings for religious purposes or, faced with prejudice and misunderstanding from the wider population, initially turned to those Christian places of worship which were sympathetic, in order to seek hospitality for their gatherings for worship.

This phase coincided with the continuing numerical decline in attendance at the traditional Christian Churches which was resulting in the closure of many Christian buildings, particularly in those inner city areas where traditional Christianity had become weak. As a result, minority religious organisations quite often sought to purchase formerly Christian places of worship.

This gave rise to considerable debate within the Christian community. For some Christians it seemed tangible evidence of the displacement of Christianity's social significance. In addition, for many minority ethnic groups within the Christian Church, such sales were met with puzzlement. The Churches with predominantly black Christian membership and leadership could not understand why such redundant buildings were not either given or sold on favourable terms to them as fellow Christians, since they also needed places of worship and often lacked the economic means to build new ones.

In addition to purchasing redundant church buildings, minority religious groups began to convert dwelling-houses and to purchase old warehouses, cinemas and other public buildings and, in a few cases, to construct their own buildings. At this stage, it was often the case that groups which would normally have remained separate on grounds of ethnicity, caste or sect found that, in the new situation, and under pressure of smaller total numbers and the consequent limitations of economic resources, they needed to join together to create premises for common use within the community.

At a later stage, rediversification into sectarian and ethnically based groups has sometimes occurred with increasing relative security and prosperity in areas with the greatest numerical concentrations. Conversely, pressing economic factors have also been influential in bringing about rationalisation and ecumenical sharing of buildings within the Christian community, especially in the inner urban areas.

SIZE OF THE RELIGIOUS COMMUNITIES

Statistical Problems

Readers will naturally expect a directory entitled *Religions in the UK* to offer figures on the size of religious communities in the UK. However, whilst Census data on religious adherence is collected in Northern Ireland, it is not currently collected in England, Wales and Scotland. In England and Wales there has been no official Census dealing with religion since the 1851 Census of Public Worship. Data on religious affiliation and practice has only been collected in particular contexts for a variety of specific purposes, such as in prisons, the armed forces and the health service.

In the course of considering the range of questions to be included in the 2001 decennial Census, the Office for National Statistics has consulted both data users and religious communities on the desirability of including a question on religious identity. In the light of this consultation, it has been decided to include a question on religious affiliation in the trial of possible Census questions due to take place in selected areas in June 1997. On the basis of its results, the acceptability and practicality of the inclusion of such a question in the 2001 Census will be further considered.

In the absence of a question on religion in the past decennial Census (apart from in Northern Ireland) there are very great problems with statistics on UK religious communities. For the UK as a whole and for England, Wales and Scotland separately, the only figures which are currently available are estimates based upon extrapolations from data on ethnic background gathered by the 1991 Census; data based upon the collection of information on the religious affiliation of schoolchildren; data from other sample studies; or figures supplied by organisations from within the religious communities themselves. All of these are subject to limitations.

Where Census data has been used, the resulting religious figures are open to some question because they have been extrapolated from the limited categories of ethnicity offered in the Census and there is no complete match between the categories of ethnic groups and religious communities. As already pointed out, for example, whilst the majority of people in the UK with Pakistani antecedents might reasonably be expected to be members of the Muslim community, some at least will be members of other religious traditions

At local level in England and Wales, a profile is beginning to be built up of the religious affiliation of schoolchildren, based upon data collected in response to the then Department of Education and Science's Circular of July 1989 on "Ethnically-Based Statistics on School Pupils." This required the recording of information on the religious affiliation of schoolchildren alongside data on ethnicity, gender and language, using the classifications of Christian, Hindu, Jewish, Muslim, Sikh, Other (please specify), No religion and Unclassified for recording this data. From this data, in some local authority areas, extrapolations are being made to estimate the proportion of religious communities in the population as a whole.

However, the results derived from this exercise need to be treated with caution even before any extrapolations can be made to the population as a whole. This is because answering the question is voluntary; answers are supplied by parents rather than by the children themselves; and the data thus far collected has been patchy in its coverage, with a comparatively high non-response rate particularly, it appears, from among the white population.

Data from this and other sample studies is always open to question. The smaller the sample, the more difficult it is to take account of varied factors related to the geographical, occupational and other spreads and concentrations of groups. This, in turn, makes more questionable any national projections based upon sample surveys.

There can also be difficulty when religious communities supply their own statistical data. It is not always clear how such data is arrived at, or whether the data encompasses all members of a community or only active participants. The criteria for establishing what are "active" and "community" memberships can vary, both within and between different religious communities. Some communities count all family members associated in any way with that faith, whilst others only count committed adults. This makes comparison of communities, using internally generated figures, a complex and problematic matter.

Indeed, regardless of sources, where figures for faith communities are quoted, it is very important to establish whether these relate to active or community membership. For example, the Christian Research Association's *UK Christian Handbook, 1996/97* offers a 1994 figure (the last year for which firm figures are given by the Handbook) of around 7,000,000 Church members in the UK (including non-Trinitarians). Nevertheless, it also acknowledges that probably about 40,000,000 people would, in some sense, categorise themselves as Christians (including non-Trinitarians).

The approximate estimates given below are generally figures for *community* membership rather than *active* membership. In other words, they reflect figures for those who in some way identify with a particular religious tradition, including children and adults, *whether or not* they are actively involved in any organisation within the religion concerned.

The degree of sensitivity about religious statistics was illustrated by some of the responses to the statistics given in the 1993 edition of the directory. This led the University of Derby's Religious Resource and Research Centre to initiate, in 1994, a Religions and Statistics Research Project. This has begun its work by evaluating the nature, purpose, validity and reliability of the current and possible future collection and use of statistics on UK religious communities, and by examining whether any kind of consensus is emerging on these issues. The research is examining the attitudes of religious organisations themselves, and of voluntary and statutory service-providers at local and national levels in the fields of race, health, education, and social services.

UK Figures in This Directory

The Multi-Faith Directory Research Project did not have the resources to undertake any new research on religious statistics for the UK and, as stressed above, in the current state of knowledge and research there are inevitably speculative elements involved in all estimates in this field.

Since statistics are so sensitive a matter, religious communities will naturally be concerned if they believe that their numbers have been underestimated. The directory project has been carried out in consultation with individuals from within the religious communities, as well as with external academic researchers, and reference is also made within a number of chapters to internal religious community assessments which suggest the possibility of a significantly higher figure than the numerical estimates which are offered by the directory.

The UK *community* membership figures below are the product of a survey of such research as has been conducted on religious statistics in the UK, combined with consultation with members of the Reference Group of the University of Derby's Religions and Statistics Research Project and directory consultants from within the various faith communities, as listed in the "Acknowledgements" chapter.

The *community* (as opposed to active membership) figures offered by the directory are, as follows, in alphabetical order:

Bahá'ís	6,000
Buddhists	30,000 – 130,000
Christians	40,000,000
Hindus	400,000 – 550,000
Jains	25,000 – 30,000
Jews	300,000
Muslims	1,000,000 – 1,500,000
Sikhs	350,000 – 500,000
Zoroastrians	5,000 – 10,000

These figures for the size of *communities* in the UK should be read in the light of the following notes:

Bahá'ís
The figure for the Bahá'í community reflects the detailed records of Bahá'í membership kept at national level.

Buddhists
The higher of the Buddhist figures offered is based on the inclusion, for this purpose, of approximately 100,000 of the ethnically Chinese people under the classification of Buddhist. Given the often overlapping and intermingling complexity of Buddhist, Taoist and Confucian belief and practice found among many ethnic Chinese families and individuals this is not unproblematic. Nevertheless, it would also be misleading not to acknowledge in any way the role and significance of Buddhism within this community. At the same time, there are very real difficulties in estimating the number of indigenous Buddhists since these cannot be estimated on the basis of any kind of abstraction from ethnicity figures.

Christians
The figure for the Christian community is based upon work by the Christian Research Association and depends upon a very broad interpretation of the identification with the Christian tradition of many indigenous people in the overall population.

Hindus
The range of figures for the Hindu community reflects, in part, differences of judgement concerning the balance between the Hindu and non-Hindu components of the population group classified as Indian in the 1991 Census. In addition, for some Hindus, the drawing of sharp boundaries in relation to religious traditions originating in the Indian subcontinent is not thought to be appropriate. Such Hindus may tend to classify as Hindu most people of Indian origin, regardless of particular religious tradition, and because of this might suggest a

figure significantly higher than even the top of the range offered here.

Jains
The range of figures for the Jain community reflects differing internal and external estimations of the size of the Jain community in the UK.

Jews
The figure for the Jewish community is produced from within the community by the Community Research Unit of the Board of Deputies of British Jews. It is based upon work of considerable detail and scope which, as research, is open to methodological scrutiny for the validity and reliability of its results.

Muslims
The range of figures for the Muslim community reflects different evaluations of the proportion of Indian-origin people listed by the 1991 Census who might be expected to be Muslims on the basis of projections made from the distribution of Muslims in the population of India, as well as debate about the likely numbers of Muslims in other, smaller, ethnic and national groupings.

Sikhs
The range of figures for the Sikh community also reflects different evaluations of the likely relative proportion of different religious groups among those ethnically categorised as Indian in the 1991 Census.

Zoroastrians
The range of figures for the Zoroastrian community reflects the range of estimations proposed by different researchers into the community in the UK.

Statistics for Northern Ireland

More precise figures can be given for religious affiliation in Northern Ireland, since these can be based upon data derived from the religious question in the 1991 Census for Northern Ireland which allows for self-definition of respondents. The following cumulative totals can be derived from the published Census tables: Bahá'ís 319; Buddhists 270; Christians 1,397,006; Hindus 742; Jains are not listed (and are therefore presumably less than 10, at least 10 adherents being the criteria for separate listing); Jews 410; Muslims 972; Sikhs 157; Zoroastrians 10.

Figures for Christian Traditions

Only in the chapter on "Introducing the Christian Community" does the directory attempt to give figures for traditions and movements within a religion. In this case, the figures which the directory uses are taken from the *UK Christian Handbook 1996-97*, Christian Research Association, London, 1996. They refer to statistics for 1994 which is the last year for which the Handbook offers figures that are not qualified by footnotes which indicate that they are based predominantly upon estimates.

The figures for Anglicans, Roman Catholics, Presbyterians, Methodists, Baptists, Orthodox, Pentecostalists and House Church members are *community* figures, whilst those for Brethren, Congregationalists, Salvationists, Lutherans, Unitarians and Moravians are *active membership* figures since the Handbook does not offer separate community figures for these traditions. It should also be noted that the *UK Christian Handbook* category of Presbyterian, in this context, includes figures for the United Reformed Church. Figures relating to a selection of the principal Christian traditions are, in alphabetical order, as follows:

Anglicans	26,200,000
Baptists	600,000
Brethren	80,397
Congregationalists	69,976
House Churches	300,000
Lutherans	14,025
Methodists	1,300,000
Moravians	4,013
Orthodox	500,000
Pentecostalists	400,000
Presbyterians	2,600,000
Roman Catholics	5,700,000
Salvationists	58,962
Unitarians	8,000

There are, of course, also other groups not covered by these broad categories of tradition. These include the Society of Friends (Quakers) and others, and around another 160,000 people are distributed among these traditions as community members of the Brethren, Congregationalist, Salvation Army, Lutheran, Unitarian and Moravian traditions (for whom only membership figures are given above), bringing the overall Christian community membership total to approaching 40,000,000.

Some Other Widely Used UK Figures

Despite the problems associated with religious statistics, a number of figures are given in official publications and thus are widely used. In *Britain 1997*, published by the Central Office of Information, figures for *community membership* are given, and are set out here in alphabetical order: Bahá'ís 6,000; Hindus 320,000; Jews 300,000; Muslims 1,000,000-1,500,000 (or 1,500,00 – 2,000,000 based on internal estimates); and Sikhs 400,000-500,000. *Britain 1997* gives no community membership figures for Buddhists, Christians, Jains or Zoroastrians.

A non-governmental, but widely used source of quoted figures is the Christian Research Association's *UK Christian Handbook 1996/ 1997*. This gives the following overall *community membership* figures for 1994 which, as with the community figures for Christianity referred to above, is the last date for which the Handbook offers figures unqualified by footnotes which indicate that they are predominantly based upon estimates. The 1994 figures are, in alphabetical order: Christians 38,200,000; Hindus 400,000; Jews 300,000; Muslims 1,200,000; Others 300,000; and Sikhs 500,000.

Social Trends 27, published by the Central Statistical Office, uses figures for adult *active membership* which are based upon estimates for 1995 provided by the Christian Research

Association (see note on the Association's community membership figures above). These figures are, in alphabetical order: Christians 7,000,000; Hindus 100,000; Jews 100,000; Muslims 600,000; Others 100,000; and Sikhs 400,000. It is probable that the *Social Trends* figure for "Others" includes Bahá'ís, Jains and Zoroastrians which are separately covered in the directory. The figure given for Christians includes non-Trinitarians.

Global Figures

The conditions and qualifications which apply to community figures for religions in the UK apply even more so in the case of global estimates of the size of the religious traditions contained within this directory's individual chapters on these religions. Global figures can only give a very rough indication of relative size and they inevitably lack any real precision.

Those included here draw upon the work of David Barrett, who has done research over a number of years on this topic. His most recent estimates covering the religions included in this directory were published in the January 1997 edition of the *International Bulletin of Missionary Research*, and are, in alphabetical order:

Buddhists	328,233,000
Christians	1,955,026,000
Hindus	806,099,000
Jews	14,180,000
Muslims	1,154,302,000
Sikhs	20,159,000

(No separate figures given for Bahá'ís, Jains or Zoroastrians)

STATISTICS ON PLACES OF WORSHIP

"Certified Buildings" in England and Wales

Statistics on the size of religious communities remain controversial and sensitive. Somewhat less controversial are statistics on places of worship although, even here, matters are not straightforward.

While no parallel figures are kept for Scotland and Northern Ireland, an indication of some kind of the numbers of places of worship in England and Wales can be derived from tables found in the Annual Register of Statistics of the Registrar General in the Office for National Statistics. This is not published, but contains cumulative totals relating to three kinds of buildings:

- Buildings of all religious bodies that are "certified" as places of worship (this excludes buildings of the Church of England or the Church in Wales which are technically not "certified" buildings, but "recorded").

- "Recorded" churches and chapels of the Church of England and the Church in Wales.

- Buildings of religious bodies that are registered for the lawful solemnisation of marriages (with all such registered buildings also being "certified" or being buildings of the Church of England or the Church in Wales).

The categories in which running totals are kept in the Annual Register of Statistics do not exactly match the nine world religious traditions with which this directory is principally concerned. However, the following tables give the total number of "certified" and "recorded" buildings that can be derived from the Office for National Statistics' Classification of Denominations and Production of Annual Statistics, as at 30th June 1996.

TABLE 1

Certified and Recorded Christian (Trinitarian, non-Trinitarian and Christian-Related), Jewish, Muslim, Sikh and "Other (Eastern)" Places of Worship in England and Wales

on 30th June in the specified Years

	1972	1975	1980	1985	1990	1996
Christian & Related Churches	47638	47139	45378	45129	44922	44699
Jewish Synagogues	320	348	335	351	355	361
Muslim Mosques	79	90	193	314	452	562
Sikh Gurdwaras	40	59	90	129	149	178
Other (Eastern) Bodies	222	217	219	264	305	349

TABLE 2

Approximate Numbers of Places of Worship in the UK in the Buddhist, Hindu, Jain, Jewish, Muslim and Sikh Traditions

As derived from the listings in *Religions in the UK: A Multi-Faith Directory*, University of Derby, 1997.

	UK	England	Scotland	Wales	Northern Ireland
Buddhist	117	98	7	8	4
Hindu	161	150	4	3	4
Jain	3	3	0	0	0
Jewish	311	301	8	2	0
Muslim	660	612	23	23	2
Sikh	202	185	11	5	1

The numbers of places of worship in the directory cannot be known with certainty where organisations have not made clear if they are a place of worship. However, these figures represent an informed judgement based upon the evidence in the directory.

The Buddhist figure includes details of centres, *viharas*, monasteries and other publicly accessible Buddhist buildings.

The Bahá'ís do not have one of their *Houses of Worship* in the UK, but *Religions in the UK* contains details of a number of Bahá'í Centres as publicly accessible buildings.

The Zoroastrians do not have any *Fire Temples* in the UK, but Zoroastrian House in London has a room which is used for worship.

TABLE 3

Recorded (Church of England and Church in Wales) and Certified (all others) Christian Trinitarian, non-Trinitarian and "Related" Places of Worship in England and Wales

on 30th June in Relevant Years

	1972	1975	1980	1985	1990	1996
Christian & Related	47683	47139	45378	45129	44922	44699
composed of: **Trinitarian**						
Anglican	17046	16901	16721	16614	16563	16496
Roman Catholic	3502	3585	3630	3673	3693	3701
Traditional Free Church	21059	20237	18655	18117	17668	17174
Non-Trinitarian						
Jehovah's Witnesses	652	723	759	809	872	913
Society of Friends	368	368	355	358	365	364
Unitarian	192	199	186	186	178	180
Other						
"Other Christian"	4864	5126	5072	5372	5583	5871

TABLE 4

Recorded and Certified Places of Worship by Region in England and Wales

on 30th June in 1996

	Trinitarian Christian	Non-Trinitarian	"Other Christian"	Jewish Synagogues	Muslim Mosques	Sikh Gurdwaras	Other Eastern
Northern	2180	89	342	11	14	5	12
Yorks & Humb★	3334	163	487	15	117	25	28
North West	3402	190	783	60	123	10	51
East Midlands	3436	110	428	5	31	15	32
West Midlands	3147	133	630	9	122	48	41
East Anglia	2490	68	211	2	7	4	7
London	2489	124	863	200	71	31	75
South East	6557	287	1062	43	55	30	76
South West	5120	177	575	10	6	7	19
Wales	5216	116	490	6	16	3	8
TOTALS	37371	1457	5871	361	562	178	349

★ Yorkshire and Humberside was abolished in the recent local government review. However, this region was used by the Annual Register of Statistics in 1996.

The legislative framework for "certification" is the *Places of Worship Registration Act* passed in 1855. "Certification" is not compulsory but it has benefits. Provided the worship held in the building is accessible to the general public it can bring exemption from local taxation - an exemption which extends to associated buildings of the place of worship even if used for purposes other than religious worship. It is also the basis for an application to become a registered building for the solemnisation of marriages. In addition, certification frees a place of worship from the need to register itself under the 1960 *Charities Act*.

For a place of worship to become "certified", the Registrar needs to be satisfied that the organisation is religious and that its buildings are being used for "religious worship." This is done by submitting to the local Superintendent Registrar of Births, Marriages and Deaths two copies of a document signed by an owner, occupier, minister or member of a building's congregation, declaring an intention to use this building for the purposes of worship and naming the religious tradition concerned.

The Superintendent Registrar forwards this to the Registrar General who grants certification through the Superintendent Registrar if satisfied that the certified place is to be used "wholly or predominantly" for worship by an identifiable and settled group. Churches of the established Church of England and the Anglican Church in Wales do not need to apply to be "certified", they are automatically "recorded".

Since places of worship are not required to be certified and because house-based places of worship are rarely certified, the total numbers of those which are certified does not give a completely accurate picture of the actual numbers of places of worship for each tradition.

In addition, especially for the earlier years in which records were kept, the number of classified buildings is likely to have reflected an under-reporting. Not all the minority traditions knew the procedures for certification and since many of their early places of worship were house-based they were therefore less likely to apply for certification.

In recent years the relationship between the actual numbers of places of worship and the numbers certified and recorded has undoubtedly become closer as increasing numbers of buildings in minority religious traditions have sought certification. However, since there is no complete correspondence between the numbers of certified and recorded places of worship (see Table 1) and the actual numbers of places of worship, the directory also presents its own figures for the numbers of places of worship in other than Christian traditions (see Table 2).

The figures in Table 2 are based on the specific research done for this directory which covers Scotland and Northern Ireland as well as England and Wales. But it is important to make clear that these figures also have limitations and qualifications. For example, they exclude a number of places of worship in each religious group which did not wish to be included in the directory, and they also reflect a degree of ambiguity where organisations have not made clear whether it would be appropriate to classify them as places of worship.

Trends

Table 1 contains figures derived from the General Register Office's annual statistics. Each of these tables has columns of figures in Table 1, beginning with the earliest cumulative figures held by its office in Southport - namely, those for 1972 and then records figures at five yearly between 1975 and 1990, together with the figures for 1996.

Table 2 contains data that has been derived from the present directory. This table varies in several places from the 1996 cumulative figures of the General Register Office for the reasons described in the previous section.

The General Register Office's figures conflate all other religions than Christian (and a number of Christian-related bodies appearing separately), Jewish, Muslim and Sikh, into a cumulative category of "Other (Eastern) Bodies". The *Religions in the UK* figures, however, distinguish between Bahá'í, Buddhist, Hindu, Jain and Zoroastrian places of worship, according to notes set out at the foot of Table 2.

From the General Register Office's cumulative totals over a period of years it is possible to discern certain trends in the provision of places of worship. The overall number of certified and recorded Christian Trinitarian, non-Trinitarian and Christian-related churches has shown a pattern of decline over the period surveyed, albeit one that is slowing down. Over the same period, Muslim mosques, Sikh gurdwaras, and places of worship of "Other (Eastern) Bodies" have more or less consistently increased. This is also true of Jewish synagogues, perhaps surprisingly in view of the community's overall slight demographic decline.

However, these bald national figures hide a number of variations which are more clearly visible in Table 3. For example, the main decline in the numbers of certified and recorded Christian places of worship has actually been among the Trinitarian Christian traditions, with the exception of the Roman Catholic tradition which has seen some small increase over the same period.

The more traditional non-Trinitarian Unitarians have, until the most recent figures, also reflected the pattern of decline found among the Anglican and traditional Free Churches. The Society of Friends have remained broadly stable, with only some slight downward and upward movements recorded over the period. However, the number of certified places of worship in the "Related" Jehovah's Witnesses tradition has grown significantly, making the total trend among the Non-Trinitarian Churches one of growth.

The "Other Christian" category has also seen a significant expansion of the number of its certified places of worship. This sector includes the Pentecostalist and Independent churches

as well as the other burgeoning black-led or black-majority Churches. At the same time, it should be noted that there will be many places of worship within the "House Church" movement which are not certified.

Table 4 illustrates regional variations in the distribution of "recorded" and "certified" places of worship which are of considerable significance because they reflect the geographical concentrations of people within the minority religious traditions.

Thus the 1996 concentrations of over 100 mosques in each of Yorkshire and Humberside, the North West and the West Midlands, reflect the main areas of Muslim settlement. The dominant concentration of 200 synagogues in the London area underlines the importance of London for the Jewish community in England, while the 60 and 43 synagogues in the North West and the South East, respectively, demonstrate the clear provincial centres of the Jewish community. The 48 gurdwaras in the West Midlands testify to the large Sikh settlement in that area.

As has been noted, however, the "Other (Eastern) Bodies" category includes all those other traditions that are separately featured in *Religions in the UK* - namely, Bahá'ís, Buddhists, Hindus, Jains and Zoroastrians, and it is therefore difficult to read much of significance from the regional variations in this category.

RELIGIONS IN PUBLIC LIFE

Religion, State and Society in the UK

Christianity, especially in its established forms, still plays a pre-eminent role in the public religious life of the UK.

The Church of England has a special constitutional position with regard to the UK state as a whole which marks it out from other Churches. As an expression of the current relationship between the state and this Church, twenty-four of its bishops and its two archbishops sit in the House of Lords as of right and the Prime Minister's Office and the monarch are involved in their appointment.

The Church of England also has a special role in public ceremonial on both ordinary occasions (such as the daily prayers offered by an Anglican Chaplain in the House of Commons) and special ones (such as the prayers at the Cenotaph on Remembrance Day). Its ecclesiastical law is treated as a part of the public law of England, being passed through parliamentary processes and receiving the Royal Assent. In addition, its ecclesiastical courts currently have the legal power to call as witnesses individuals of any faith or none.

However, despite this special relationship with the state, in contrast with the national Churches of some other European countries, the Church of England is not funded by the state in any direct way. Also, within the various parts of the UK there is a range of different arrangements for defining the relationships between religious bodies, the state and society.

England

In England, the Church of England is the form of religion "by law established" and other Christian denominations do not have any formal link with the state. The reigning monarch is its Supreme Governor (and not, as is sometimes popularly, but incorrectly stated, its "Head").

The monarch has the title "Defender of The Faith" which, although its origins pre-date the Reformation, has since been understood in terms of upholding the particular character and role of the Church of England. This has recently become a matter of public debate following suggestions by the Prince of Wales that the more general term "Defender of Faith" might be more appropriate to the religiously plural nature of contemporary society.

Scotland

Since the 1603 accession of James VI of Scotland to the English Crown as James I and the union of the Parliaments in 1707, Scotland has had close links with England. But, at the same time, in many ways Scotland has remained distinct, especially in its systems of law and education. This distinctiveness has also applied in matters of religion.

The Presbyterian Church of Scotland (rather than the Anglican tradition's Episcopal Church of Scotland) is the established Church in Scotland. It has had a strong historical role as a national Church and, in the absence of devolved political representation in Scotland, the Kirk (as it is known in Scotland), which is governed by a hierarchy of elected clerical and lay Kirk Sessions, Presbyteries, Synods and the General Assembly, has sometimes been seen as a surrogate Scottish parliament.

The Scottish form of establishment no longer places legal restrictions upon the Church of Scotland's self-government, nor does the British Prime Minister or Secretary of State for Scotland have any role in the appointment of its leadership. Similarly, despite its established status and its prominent role within Scottish history, the Church of Scotland has no right, corresponding to that of the Church of England, for its leaders to have seats in the House of Lords. The Church of Scotland does, however, maintain a formal link with the Crown which is symbolised by the Lord High Commissioner's presence at the Church's General Assembly, which meets each May in Edinburgh.

Wales

Following the 1920 disestablishment of the Anglican Church in Wales, there is now no established form of religion there. Wales does not have a single denominational focus for national identity, but the Nonconformist Free Churches have played a particular and significant role in Wales' social, political and cultural life, especially in preserving and promoting the use of the Welsh language. In recent decades, the Church in Wales has also been promoting its Welsh identity and the use of the Welsh language in its liturgical life.

Ireland (Northern Ireland and the Republic of Ireland)

Northern Ireland and the Republic of Ireland have a much higher level of professed religious belief and participation than England, Wales and Scotland. There is no officially established form of religion in either the North or the Republic. The episcopal Church of Ireland (which is part of the global Anglican Communion) was disestablished in 1871. In Northern Ireland, although the Roman Catholic population is the largest single denomination, it is outnumbered two to one by the combined Protestant groupings of which the Presbyterians (organised in a number of different denominations) are the largest.

In the Republic of Ireland, the Roman Catholic Church originally had a special position within the 1937 constitution of the Republic which meant that its teachings had a significant formative effect upon legislation in the Republic, particularly in areas of personal, social and sexual morality. However, in 1972 its "special position" clause in the Irish Republic's constitution was abolished.

Despite the existence of the political border between Northern Ireland and the Republic of Ireland, the Churches of the island of Ireland are organised on an all-Ireland basis with regional and local bodies existing within a common organisational framework both north and south of the border.

At the same time, religion has been a dimension of the conflict which has become known as "The Troubles". The Roman Catholic community in the North has been closely identified with broad nationalist aspirations, whilst the continuing demographic decline of Southern Protestants has reinforced Northern Protestants' concerns about their minority position in the whole island of Ireland.

Religious Diversity and Public Life

The historical position of the Church of England and the Church of Scotland in public life is reflected in their access to, and influence on, social institutions such as hospitals, prisons, schools, universities and local government. With regard to the Church of England, some of the implications of this for a society increasingly conscious of its religiously plural composition have been investigated by the University of Warwick Department of Sociology's 1994-96 research project on "The Church of England and Other Faith Communities in a Multi-Faith Society", funded by the Church of England Central Board of Finance and the Leverhulme Trust. This project has reported on publicly-funded chaplaincy provision in the health and prison services as well as the role of civic religion in local life.

Over the past century, other Christian denominations have also played an increasing role in both state occasions and civic events and structures. Now, other religious communities are also beginning to have a greater public presence, with their representatives increasingly being involved in such structures and attending such functions and services. This reflects a growing recognition of the increasingly multi-faith nature of religious life in the UK.

Over the years many governmental, public and voluntary bodies have developed arrangements for consultation with both the Christian and Jewish communities. Because of their presence over a long period of time, these communities have developed the kind of broadly representative bodies which can facilitate this consultation at a variety of local, regional and national levels. These bodies are professionally staffed and funded by their congregations and by donors from within their communities.

Similar patterns of consultation with other religious communities are not yet so developed. This is partly because some communities have not yet been able to develop representative bodies which have found a general acceptance within their communities and which external bodies can easily consult. This has been the case particularly at national level, since many of these communities have had to put their initial energies into establishing and building up their local grassroots organisations. It is also partly due to the fact that, often, these communities do not have full time paid professional representatives. This makes it difficult for them to participate in structures which tend to assume that consultations will be serviced and sustained by the communities in question.

Despite the difficulties involved in evolving mechanisms for consultation, in 1992 the Government established the Inner Cities Religious Council (ICRC) within the Department of the Environment with representatives on it of five major faith communities. The communities involved are the Christian (black-majority Churches included), Hindu, Jewish, Muslim and Sikh, which are the traditions with the strongest numerical presence in the inner cities.

The Council is chaired by a Department of the Environment Minister. It is a forum for faith leaders and government which is particularly concerned with the urban regeneration issues which influence, and are influenced by, faith communities. It holds regional conferences open to all faiths and has offered free consultancy to local groups which are concerned to develop economic and social activities.

The increasing religious diversity of the UK has been gradually reflected in changing patterns in the coverage of religion in the media and also, in particular, in the changes to religious broadcasting on radio and television. This has played an important part in helping the population at large to learn more about the various faith communities in this country.

The BBC has recently established a Multi Faith Bureau to widen its coverage of the different faiths and The Central Religious Advisory Committee which advises the British Broadcasting Corporation and the Independent Television Commission, now has membership drawn from a number of different religious communities.

The Inter Faith Network for the UK has worked, since its formation in 1987, to promote the wider participation of the UK's faith communities in public life. In a whole range of areas there are increasing signs that organisations and bodies which have previously only liaised with the Christian and Jewish communities are now beginning to make efforts to consult more widely.

At the same time, though, there remains some significant concern among minority religious communities that developments in the direction of consultation are not fast enough or sufficiently widespread. Religious leaders and other representatives of minority religious communities can still find it hard to gain access to many public and social institutions on the same basis that is available to most Christian leaders and representatives.

RELIGION AND THE LAW

Religions and the Legal Systems of the UK

The legal framework for the practice of religion in the UK is clearly of importance to all religious communities since it has a bearing on the degree to which religions can operate in accordance with their own traditions. In general terms, the legal system for England and Wales differs from that of Scotland. Northern Ireland, in turn, has many provisions which are different from those which exist in the rest of the UK. These differences affect the relationship between religion and the law in the various parts of the UK.

Unlike some other European countries, the UK has no formal list of religions officially recognised by the state. From time to time, however, although there are no clear criteria, the courts have to decide whether a particular organisation or movement is a "religion" in order, for example, to interpret a legal provision in relation to charity law. In the past, indicators of religious status have been taken to include monotheistic belief, but even this is not a firm requirement since, for instance, it is clearly problematic with regard to Buddhism.

Recognition and the Legal Protection of Religious Identity

The status of religious belief and practice is a complex matter. At times in the UK's history, the law has been used to uphold certain forms of belief and suppress others. For example, the position of the Church of England as the established church in England has been buttressed, not only by custom, but also by laws such as the *Corporation* and *Test Acts* of 1661 and 1673, which limited the holding of office under the Crown to communicant members of the Church of England.

Most of the provisions of the *Corporation* and *Test Acts* were repealed in 1828 and 1829, removing important legal restrictions on the participation of Roman Catholic and Non-conformist Christians in public life. Many of the legal restrictions on the full participation of the Jewish community in wider social and political life were, however, not fully removed until 1858.

A number of restrictions still remain with respect to people within traditions other than Anglican Christianity. For example, an heir to the Throne is specifically precluded from marrying a Roman Catholic. In addition, there is legal uncertainty over whether the office of Lord Chancellor can be held by someone who is of another than Christian religion.

Although most forms of overt legal religious discrimination have now been lifted, the degree to which the present law accommodates the full practice of all religious traditions is being continually tested. For example, Sikhs had to engage in a lengthy struggle before being allowed exemption from a 1972 *Road Traffic Act* requirement for motorcyclists to wear safety helmets. The *Road Traffic Act* 1988, re-enacting the *Motor-Cycle Crash Helmets (Religious Exemption) Act* 1976, now exempts a follower of the Sikh religion "while he is wearing a turban" from the crash helmet requirements applicable to others.

A similiar exemption was granted by the *Employment Act* 1989 to allow turbaned Sikhs to work on construction sites without a helmet or hard hat as required by new safety regulations. More recently, however, concerns have emerged among the Sikh community that European legislation may override some of these gains.

Another example is the exemption for Jewish and Muslim methods of animal slaughter from the general legislation contained in the *Slaughterhouses Act* 1974 and the *Poultry Act* 1967. Both Acts contain provisions to allow Jews and Muslims to follow the requirements of their religious traditions with regard to the slaughter of animals for Jewish and Muslim consumption, waiving, for example, the general requirement for pre-stunning an animal prior to slaughter.

Family, marriage and burial law have also been the subject of some legal and social debate involving the religious communities, raising questions about the relationship to religious law and practice of social legislation on matters such as marriage, divorce and inheritance. There has also been debate about the extent to which employers can or should provide time and facilities at work for the performance of obligatory prayers and days off for the observance of religious festivals.

Until now, the response of the legal system to increased religious diversity has generally been of an *ad hoc* and pragmatic nature rather than seeking to provide generally applicable new frameworks for law. It has therefore often been concerned with defining permissible exceptions to generally applicable laws.

There is a continuing debate about the extent to which the law should protect people against forms of direct discrimination connected with religious identity. Much of the legislation and social policy that is designed to deal with social identities based upon race and ethnicity does not sit easily with the rise of religious self-definition.

At the time of writing there are specific legal provisions in Northern Ireland against religious discrimination and for the prosecution of incitement to religious hatred, but not in the rest of the UK. The possible avenues of redress which are available where discrimination has a religious dimension are summarised in the Inner Cities Religious Council's pamphlet on *Challenging Religious Discrimination: A Guide for Faith Communities and their Advisers.*

In Northern Ireland, the *Prevention of Incitement to Hatred Act (Northern Ireland)* 1970 makes it an offence intentionally to stir up hatred against, or rouse the fear of, any section of the public on the grounds of religious belief, colour, race or ethnic or national origins. This covers the publication or distribution of written or any other matter which is threatening, abusive or insulting as well as the use of words of a similar nature in a public place or in a public meeting. Therefore, although its provisions have only rarely been used, the scope of this law is not only concerned with incitement directed to, or against, religious groups but is also concerned with incitement against any group when such incitement is carried out on religious grounds.

There are some provisions in the common law of England and Wales against blasphemy and blasphemous libel. However, as the testing of these provisions in the courts during the controversy over the book *The Satanic Verses* in the late 1980s and early 1990s demonstrated, these laws only give protection to the Christian religion and, sometimes, more particularly to the doctrines and practices of the Church of England.

In England, Scotland and Wales there are provisions against discrimination occurring in relation to a member of an "ethnic group". In terms of the law, one of the factors which is taken as indicative of the existence of an ethnic group is that of a long, shared group history of which religion may be a dimension. Jews have therefore been judged to be an "ethnic group", as also have Sikhs following the case of *Mandla v. Dowell Lee* in 1983. Muslims, as such, however, fall outside the scope of the *Race Relations Act* because they are correctly viewed as being a religious, and not a racial or ethnic group. As members of a universal faith community they are not viewed as having a shared history in the same sense as Jewish or Sikh people.

"Indirect" discrimination is the most that Muslims can claim under the present law (by pursuing a case as an Asian or an Arab or as a Yemeni or Pakistani, relying on a racial or national identity, and complaining that certain practices or procedures have had a disproportionately adverse effect because they unjustifiably interfere with religious observance). A white Muslim and, indeed, white members of other religious traditions do not, therefore, have protection under the present law.

It is the lack, other than in Northern Ireland, of legal protection of religious identity which has led to increasing calls for legislation to be passed addressing specifically religious discrimination and identity. In its *Second Review of the Race Relations Act 1976*, published in 1992, the Commission for Racial Equality stated that it considered the present blasphemy laws to be unsatisfactory and recommended that consideration be given to making incitement to religious hatred an offence under English law, as well as to incorporating international obligations against religious discrimination into domestic law. This would bring the law in the rest of the UK into line with that of Northern Ireland. In late 1995, the Commission announced that it was setting up a special project team to explore the different aspects of legal protection for religious, as distinct from racial, identity.

RELIGIOUS COMMUNITIES AND EDUCATION

As in other aspects of life in the UK, there are both commonalities and important differences with respect to the relationship between religion and education in the various nations of the UK, although England and Wales share much of the same legislative framework.

Religiously Based Schools in England and Wales

Religious communities have always had a natural interest in education. The Church of England became a provider of education before either national or local Government. When, early in this century, educational provision came under government administration, the Church of England's denominational schools became part of a national education framework as a result of an agreement between it and the state embodied in the 1902 *Education Act*.

The continuing Anglican denominational schools preserved some degree of autonomy as "voluntary aided" or "voluntary controlled" schools. Both categories of school receive public funding, but a proportion of the financial responsibility for "voluntary aided" schools rests with the sponsoring religious body. These schools also have more autonomy with respect both to admissions policies as well as arrangements for Religious Education and Collective Worship. "Voluntary controlled" schools are much more fully integrated into the local authority system.

The Anglican and Roman Catholic (and to a much lesser extent the Methodist) Churches now have "voluntary aided" and "voluntary controlled" schools in England and Wales, as has the Jewish community, and as do some of the Christian Churches in Northern Ireland.

A significant sector of the Muslim community has expressed a concern that discrimination may be prevalent in this field because, although the Government has said that there is no reason in principle why Muslim and other faith community schools should not be given public funding in cases which meet the existing criteria, the authorities have not, as yet, designated any Muslim schools as voluntary aided schools. Such schools have also not been accepted for the new "grant maintained" status (by which schools receive funding direct from national government, rather than through the Local Education Authority).

The majority of children in the UK attend "county" schools rather than religiously-based (or "denominational") schools whether voluntary aided, controlled or private. Educators have therefore had to confront issues arising from the growth of religious diversity in the catchment area of many schools.

Religious Education in England and Wales

Unlike in many other countries, in UK schools there are legal requirements for Religious Education and Collective Worship. In England and Wales the 1944 *Education Act* made "Religious Instruction" mandatory and required that syllabuses should be drawn up ("agreed") at a local level. The Act merely specified that the content of the "instruction" should not be of a "denominational" character, although the unwritten assumption of that time was that the content would be Christian.

Gradually, however, a shift began to happen which was reflected in a change of subject name to "Religious Education." The task of Religious Education was increasingly no longer seen as "instructing" or "nurturing" pupils in a particular religious tradition but as educating them *about* religion.

With changes in the composition of society and the development of new faith communities, "multi-faith syllabuses" were developed which were designed to help children to understand the diversity of religious traditions.

By the late 1970s the majority of maintained schools were teaching this kind of broader based Religious Education and many "denominational" schools had also introduced material about different religions into their Religious Education curriculum.

The 1988 *Education Reform Act* (which applies to England and Wales but not to Scotland and Northern Ireland) introduced a requirement that any new Religious Education syllabus must "reflect the fact that the religious traditions in Great Britain are in the main Christian whilst taking account of the teaching and practices of the other principal religions represented in Great Britain." The precise meaning and implications of these new statutory provisions have been widely debated since the 1988 legislation was enacted.

In July 1994 "model syllabuses" were published by the Schools Curriculum and Assessment

Authority (SCAA) which advises the Government on the content of the school curriculum. SCAA worked with both the teaching professions and representatives of various religious communities in producing syllabuses, which do not have statutory force, but which are intended as advisory guidance to local authority Agreed Syllabus Conferences.

A variety of religious traditions are represented on every local authority's Agreed Syllabus Conference which has responsibility for drawing up the syllabus of Religious Education to be used by publicly funded schools in the relevant area. Voluntary aided schools do not have to include other religious traditions within their Religious Education syllabuses, although they often mirror the county syllabus to a greater or lesser extent.

All Agreed Syllabuses now have to be reviewed on a five yearly basis. Local religious organisations are also represented, alongside teacher and local authority representatives, on SACREs (Standing Advisory Councils for Religious Education), which monitor the delivery of Religious Education and collective worship within the publicly funded sector of education in their area.

Many within the minority religious communities have been concerned that the emphasis given to Christianity in Religious Education and collective worship in recent legislation has shifted the balance back from the broader approaches which had been developing during the 1970s and 1980s.

Collective Worship in England and Wales

The 1988 Act included complex provisions on school collective worship in England and Wales. In recent years many schools had moved away from exclusively Christian acts of worship seeing these as inappropriate for a plural school community containing children with different religious commitments and with none.

The 1988 legislation provides that the majority of acts of "Collective Worship" should be

"wholly or mainly of a broadly Christian character". As in the case of Religious Education, the existing right of parents to withdraw their children from collective worship was maintained and fresh provisions were introduced under which what is known as a "determination" might be issued by a local authority to allow alternative arrangements for whole school collective worship to take place.

In January 1994 the Department for Education issued a circular on *Religious Education and Collective Worship* which sets out the provisions of the 1988 Act (and supplementary provisions enacted in 1993) and gives guidance on their application. Considerable concern was expressed by many educators and religious community leaders that the circular went beyond legislative requirements with regard to collective worship.

This concern relates to the need to respect the integrity of pupils from different faith backgrounds or those without any religious faith commitment; the need to encourage the development, in an undivisive way, of the whole school as a community; and the practicalities of the capacity of schools to meet the current requirements for Collective Worship. The Religious Education Council, the National Association of SACREs and The Inter Faith Network are currently co-sponsoring a consultative process designed to see what degree of consensus exists on whether educationally appropriate provision can be made for collective worship in schools in contemporary society.

Religion and Education in Scotland

From the years of the Reformation in Scotland until 1872, the established Church of Scotland shared responsibility for education with the civic authorities. It is this partnership which undergirded the 1696 *Education Act's* requirement that there should be a school established, and a school-master appointed, in every parish "by advice of the Heritor and Minister of the Parish". These schools were, in effect, Presbyterian in outlook. But eventually, during the first half of the 19th century, the Scottish Episcopal Church and the Roman Catholic Church established their own denominational schools.

In 1872, another *Education Act* transferred responsibility for education in Scotland wholly to the state. However, the right to continue religious instruction was secured in a Preamble to this Act, subject to the operation of a conscience clause which gave "liberty to parents, without forfeiting any other of the advantages of the schools, to elect that their children should not receive such instruction." Under the 1918 *Education Act* Roman Catholic schools, which had not been transferred in 1872, became part of the state system, thus establishing in Scotland a system of denominational schools which continues to be publicaly funded.

Historically, therefore, it has been the custom for religious observance to be practised and instruction in religion provided in Scottish schools. This tradition has been reflected in more recent *Education Acts* which allow education authorities to continue this provision. Indeed, it is unlawful for an education authority to discontinue religious observance or instruction unless the proposal to do so has been the subject of a poll of the local government electors in the area concerned and has been approved by the majority of those voters.

Every school run by the education authority must be open to pupils of all denominations and faiths, and the law continues to provide a "conscience clause" whereby parents may withdraw their children from any instruction in religious subjects and from any religious observance in the school. It also continues to be laid down that no pupils must be placed at a disadvantage as regards their secular education at the school, either because they have been withdrawn from such classes or because of the denomination to which they or their parents belong.

Guidance on the provision of Religious Education and observance in both primary and secondary schools has been issued by the Education and Industry Department of the Scottish Office and local authorities formulate their own policies based on these guidelines. The Scottish Office states that Religious Education in all schools should be based on Christianity, this being the main religious tradition in Scotland, but the syllabus should also take account of the teaching and practices of other religions. Religious Education should enable the individual to explore questions concerning the meaning of life. It should aim to promote understanding and respect for others' belief, which is recognised as being particularly important in schools where there are significant numbers of children from faiths other than Christianity.

Government guidelines indicate that religious observance in non-denominational schools should be of a broadly Christian nature, but the form it takes varies very much from school to school, and takes account of the presence of the pupils of different faiths and of none. There is one publicly-funded Jewish Primary school. However, denominational schools in Scotland are mainly Roman Catholic schools. These provide their own particular form of worship.

Religion and Education in Northern Ireland

In the wake of the *Education Reform Act (England and Wales)*, 1988, a new statutory Core Syllabus for Religious Education in Northern Ireland was drawn up by the four largest Christian Churches in the Province (Roman Catholic, Presbyterian, Church of Ireland and Methodist). This historic achievement provided a commonly agreed programme of Religious Education from both sides of the traditional Catholic-Protestant divide. However, it is characterised by an exclusively Christian content.

Beyond this Christian content, schools are free to include teaching relating to religions other than Christianity within their total Religious Education programme. A formal set of non-statutory guidelines (which include a limited amount of material relating to Judaism and

Islam) has been produced to assist teachers both in implementing the Core Syllabus, and in moving beyond it. However, this guidance package, being entirely optional, is unlikely to make a significant difference to the traditional styles and content of the Religious Education generally available in Northern Ireland's schools. A World Religions paper is available as an option in the Northern Ireland GCE A Level examination in Religious Studies, but this has not proved to be a particularly popular choice on the part of Northern Ireland schools.

THE CHALLENGE OF THE FUTURE

Alongside difficulties related to their minority religious status, the ethnic profile of many religious minorities means they have also had to contend with discrimination and disadvantage on the basis of their racial or ethnic origins. At the same time, in contrast to many other European Union countries, the majority of the religious minorities with roots in recent migrations who settled in the UK either had, or were entitled to take up, British citizenship.

There remains a gap between the formal, legal position and the personal and social realities of experienced discrimination and disadvantage. Nevertheless, the formal and legal position of the minority religious communities in the UK has put them in a stronger position to build their own organisations and engage in community development than in some other European countries where their second or third generation counterparts still retain the status of migrant rather than citizen, with all of its accompanying legal and psychological consequences.

Since the mid-1960s, the ideal of multi-culturalism has been the basis of a general political consensus underlying the equal opportunity policies of central and local government and other significant social institutions. On the basis of this policy, significant social institutions have engaged in concerted attempts at positive action to address the needs of those citizens who have widely been referred to as the "ethnic minorities."

However, religion was initially only rarely considered in terms of the implications of the new plurality. As this chapter has indicated, there has been recent change in this regard, reflecting a greater recognition of the increasing differentiation of personal and social identities on the basis of religion. In a cultural milieu in which ethnicity, nationality, class and lifestyle have been seen as the major determining factors of individual and corporate identity, for people and organisations to define themselves primarily in terms of their religious identity and values represents a significant challenge to the prevailing social ethos.

The increasing religious diversity of UK society is raising new questions and possibilities. The challenge facing everyone including the religious communities themselves, is to evolve the common visions and structures necessary for sustaining an integrated but richly diverse community, without either assimilation or fragmentation. The shape of our common future will depend upon whether the religious communities, social organisations and the state can rise to this challenge and draw upon the distinctiveness and resources of all sectors of society for the benefit of the common good.

FURTHER INFORMATION

The following list is of public bodies mentioned in this chapter. These do not include the full spectrum of bodies involved in multi-faith aspects of life in the UK. The reader will also find it helpful to look in the listings for the chapter on "Inter-Faith Activity" in the UK.

BBC Multi Faith Bureau
PO Box 76, Bush House, London, WC2B 4PH
Tel: 0171-257-2713
Contact: David Craig

Central Religious Advisory Committee
Religious Broadcasting Officer, Independent Television Commission, 33 Foley Street, London, W1P 3LB
Tel: 0171-255-3000
Contact: Rachel Viney

Commission for Racial Equality
10-12 Allington Street, London, SW1E 5EH
Tel 0171-828-7002

Inner Cities Religious Council
Floor 4, K10, Eland House, Bressenden Place,
London, SW1E 5DU
Tel: 0171-890-3704

Registrar General
Office for National Statistics, 1 Drummond Gate,
London, SW1V 2QQ
Tel: 0171-233-9233

School Curriculum & Assessment Authority
Newcombe House, Notting Hill Gate, London
W11 3JB
Tel: 0171-229-1234

Department for Education & Employment
Sanctuary Buildings, Great Smith Street, London,
SW1P 3BT
Tel: 0171-925-5000

**Scottish Office Education & Industry
Department**
Victoria Quay, Edinburgh, Lothian, EH6 6QQ
Tel: 0131-556-8400

Welsh Office Education Department
Cathays Park, Cardiff, South Glamorgan, CF1 3NQ
Tel: 01222-825111

Department of Education for Northern Ireland
Rathgael House, Balloo Road, Bangor,
County Down, BT19 7PR
Tel: 01247-279279

FURTHER READING

Archbishops' Commission, *Church and State 1970*, (reprinted), Church Information Office, London, 1985.

Badham, P (ed), *Religion, State and Society in Modern Britain*, Edwin Mellen Press, Lampeter, 1989.

Badham, P, "Religious Pluralism in Modern Britain", in Gilley, S and Sheils, W (eds), *A History of Religion in Britain: Practice and Belief from Pre-Roman Times to the Present*, Blackwell, Oxford, 1984, pp. 488-502.

Ballard, R (ed), *Desh Pardesh: The South Asian Presence in Britain*, Hurst and Co, London, 1994.

Barker, E, *New Religious Movements: A Practical Introduction*, HMSO, London, 1989.

Barley, C; Field, C; Kosmin, B; and Nielsen, J, *Religion: Reviews of United Kingdom Statistical Sources*, Volume XX, Pergamon Press, Oxford, 1987.

Barot, R (ed), *Religion and Ethnicity: Minorities and Social Change in the Metropolis*, Kok Pharos, Kampen, 1993.

Beckford, J and Gilliat, S, *The Church of England and Other Faiths in a Multi-Faith Society*, Warwick Working Papers in Sociology, University of Warwick, Coventry, 1996.

Berman, D, *A History of Atheism in Britain: From Hobbes to Russell*, Croom Helm, London, 1988.

Bishop, P, "Victorian Values? Some Antecedents of a Religiously Plural Society", in Hooker, R, and Sargant, J (ed), *Belonging to Britain: Christian Perspectives on a Plural Society*, Council of Churches for Britain and Ireland, London, nd, pp. 31-52.

Bradney, A, "Separate schools, ethnic minorities and the law", in *New Community*, Volume XIII, No 3, Spring 1987, pp. 412-420.

Bradney, A, *Religions, Rights and Laws*, Leicester University Press, Leicester, 1993.

Brown, A, *Festivals in World Religions*, Longmans, Essex, 1986.

Bruce, S, *Religion in Modern Britain*, Oxford University Press, Oxford, 1995.

Buchanan, C, *Cut the Connection: Disestablishment and the Church of England*, Darton, Longman and Todd, London, 1994.

Charlton, R and Kay, R, "The politics of religious slaughter: an ethno-religious case study", in *New Community*, Volume XII, No 3, Winter 1985-86, pp 409-503.

Commission for Racial Equality, *Britain a Plural Society: Report of a Seminar*, Commission for Racial Equality, London, 1990.

Commission for Racial Equality, *Schools of Faith: Religious Schools in a Multi-Cultural Society*, Commission for Racial Equality, London, 1990.

Cox, E and Cairns, J, *Reforming Religious Education: The Religious Clauses of the 1988 ERA*, Kogan Page, London, 1989.

Davie, G, *Religion in Britain Since 1945: Believing Without Belonging*, Blackwell, Oxford, 1994.

Edwards, D, "A Brief History of the Concept of Toleration in Britain", in Horton, J and Crabtree, H (eds), *Toleration and Integrity in a Multi-Faith Society*, University of York Department of Politics, York, 1992, pp 41-49.

Froh, M, *Roots of the Future: Ethnic Diversity in the Making of Britain*, Commission for Racial Equality, London, 1996.

Fryer, P, *Staying Power: The History of Black People in Britain*, Pluto, London, 1984.

Gilbert, A D, *The Making of Post-Christian Britain: A History of the Secularization of Modern Society*, Longman, Essex, 1980.

Gill, S; D'Costa, G; and King, U (eds), *Religion in Europe: Contemporary Perspectives*, Kok Pharos, Kampen, 1994.

Gilley, S and Sheils, W (eds), *A History of Religion in Britain: Practice and Belief from Pre-Roman Times to the Present*, Blackwell, Oxford, 1994.

Gunter, B and Viney, R, *Seeing Is Believing: Religion and Television in the 1990s*, John Libbey and Co, London, 1994.

Halstead, M, *The Case for Muslim Voluntary-Aided Schools: Some Philosophical Reflections*, Islamic Academy, Cambridge, 1986.

Hastings, A, *Church and State: The English Experience*, University of Exeter Press, Exeter, 1991.

Hooker, R, and Sargant, J (eds), *Belonging to Britain: Christian Perspectives on a Plural Society*, Council of Churches for Britain and Ireland, London, nd.

Horton, J, "Religion and Toleration: Some Problems and Possibilities", in Horton, J and Crabtree, H (eds), *Toleration and Integrity in a*

Multi-Faith Society, University of York Department of Politics, York, 1992, pp 62-70.

Horton, J and Crabtree, H (eds), *Toleration and Integrity in a Multi-Faith Society*, University of York Department of Politics, York, 1992.

Hulmes, E, *Education and Cultural Diversity*, Longman, Harlow, 1989.

Inter Faith Network for the UK and Commission for Racial Equality, *Law, Blasphemy and the Multi-Faith Society*, Commission for Racial Equality, London, 1990.

Inter Faith Network for the UK, *Places of Worship: The Practicalities and Politics of Sacred Space in Multi-Faith Britain*, Inter Faith Network for the UK, London, 1995.

Inter Faith Network for the UK, *Britain's Faith Communities: Equal Citizens?*, Inter Faith Network for the UK, London, 1996.

James, C, *Immigration and Social Policy in Britain*, Tavistock Publications, London, 1977.

Lynch, J, "Cultural Pluralism, Structural Pluralism and the United Kingdom," in Commission for Racial Equality, *Britain a Plural Society: Report of a Seminar*, Commission for Racial Equality, London, 1990, pp 29-43.

MacIntyre, J, *Multi-Culture and Multi-Faith Societies: Some Examinable Assumptions*, Farmington Occasional Papers, No 3, Oxford, 1978.

Modood, T, "Establishment, multiculturalism and British citizenship", in *Political Quarterly*, Volume LXV, January 1994, pp. 53-59.

Murphy, T, "Toleration and the Law", in Horton, J and Crabtree, H (eds), *Toleration and Integrity in a Multi-Faith Society*, University of York Department of Politics, York, 1992, pp. 50-61.

Nicholls, D, *Church and State in Britain Since 1820*, Routledge and Kegan Paul, London, 1967.

Nielsen, J, *Islamic Law: Its Significance for the Situation of Muslim Minorities in Europe*, Research Papers on Muslims in Europe, No 35, September 1987.

Parekh, B, "Britain and the Social Logic of Pluralism", in Commission for Racial Equality, *Britain a Plural Society: Report of a Seminar*, Commission for Racial Equality, London, 1990, pp 58-78.

Parsons, G (ed), *The Growth of Religious Diversity: Britain From 1945, Volume I: Traditions*, Routledge/Open University, London, 1993.

Parsons, G (ed), *The Growth of Religious Diversity: Britain From 1945, Volume II: Issues*, Routledge/Open University, London, 1994.

Pearl, D, *Family Law and the Immigrant Communities*, Jordan's, London, 1986.

Poulter, S, *English Law and Ethnic Minority Customs*, Butterworth's, London, 1986.

Poulter, S, *Asian Traditions and English Law: A Handbook*, Trentham Books, Stoke-on-Trent, 1990.

Poulter, S, "Cultural Pluralism and its Limits: a Legal Perspective", in Commission for Racial Equality, *Britain a Plural Society: Report of a Seminar*, Commission for Racial Equality, London, 1990, pp. 3-28.

Rex, J, *The Concept of a Multi-Cultural Society*, University of Warwick Centre for Research in Ethnic Relations, Coventry, 1985.

Rex, J, "Religion and Ethnicity in the Metropolis", in Barot, R (ed), *Religion and Ethnicity: Minorities and Social Change in the Metropolis*, Kok Pharos, Kampen, 1993, pp. 17-26.

Ryan, M, *Another Ireland: An Introduction to Ireland's Ethnic-Religious Minority Communities*, Stranmillis College, Belfast, 1996.

Smart, N, "Church, Party and State" in, Badham, P (ed), *Religion, State and Society in Modern Britain*, Edwin Mellen Press, Lampeter, 1989, pp. 381-395.

Social Policy Group of the British Council of Churches Committee on Relations with People of Other Faiths and the Race Relations Unit, "Religiously-based voluntary schools", in *Discernment: A Christian Journal of Inter-Religious Encounter*, Volume VI, No 2, 1992, pp 32-40.

Thomas, T (ed), *The British: Their Religious Beliefs and Practices*, Routledge, London, 1988.

Verma, G, "Pluralism: Some Theoretical and Practical Considerations", in Commission for Racial Equality, *Britain a Plural Society: Report of a Seminar*, Commission for Racial Equality, London, 1990, pp. 44-57.

Vertovec, S (ed), *Aspects of the South Asian Diaspora, Volume II, part 2: Papers on India*, Oxford University Press, Delhi, 1991.

Visram, R, *Ayahs, Lascars and Princes: The Story of Indians in Britain 1700-1947*, Pluto Press, London, 1986.

Watson, B, "Integrity and Affirmation: an Inclusivist Approach to National Identity", in Hooker, R, and Sargant, J (ed), *Belonging to Britain: Christian Perspectives on a Plural Society*, Council of Churches for Britain and Ireland, London, nd, pp. 135-148.

Weller, P, "The Rushdie affair, pluraility of values and the ideal of a multi-cultural society", in *National Association for Values in Education and Training Working Papers*, Volume II, October 1990, pp. 1-9.

Weller, P, "A Christian Perspective on Integrating religious, social and political values in a multi-cultural society", in *World Faiths Encounter*, November 1995, pp. 28-37.

Weller, P, "Values, visions and religions: pluralist problematics in a secular and multi-faith context", in *Cutting Edge*, No. 9, February 1994, pp.15-17.

Wilson, B, "Old Laws and New Religions", in Cohn-Sherbok, D (ed), *The Canterbury Papers; Essays on Religion and Society*, Bellew Publishing, London, 1990, pp. 210-224.

Wolffe, J (ed), *The Growth of Religious Diversity: Britain From 1945, A Reader*, Hodder and Stoughton, London, 1993.

York, M, *The Emerging Network: A Sociology of New Age and Neo-Pagan Movements*, Rowman and Littlewood, London, 1995.

MAKING CONTACTS, ORGANISING EVENTS AND CONSULTATIONS

INTRODUCTION

You may be using this Directory to get some pointers regarding how to organise events, projects or consultations which seek to draw together members of different religious communities. There are no hard and fast guidelines as to how to do this successfully but this chapter may offer some useful ideas. It also includes guidance on arranging visits to places of worship.

MAKING CONTACT

The Importance of the Introductory Materials

The directory lists most of the key religious organisations and groups in the United Kingdom. You may already be knowledgeable about the religions from which they come. If not, the directory's introductory material about these traditions should give an idea of the basic aspects of each religion, especially as it is represented in the United Kingdom.

Although much is held in common within particular religious communities, within most there are a number of different traditions of interpretation and it is helpful to have a sense of these when you plan to make contact with particular groups. Members of religious communities will not expect you to be an expert in their traditions, but they will appreciate your efforts at least to understand where they fit within the general pattern of their religion. The introductory chapters on each of the religious communities contained in the directory are designed to help you to understand the diversity within each community, as well as to appreciate their common beliefs and practices.

Understanding the context will also be helpful to you if you are planning a multi-faith event or consultation, because you will probably be hoping to ensure a certain level of representativeness. Knowing from which part of a religion a possible speaker or participant comes can help you ensure balance and avoid later difficulties.

For consultation purposes it is also worth bearing in mind that within any given religious community, many ethnic and national backgrounds are likely to be represented.

Some Things to be Aware of When Making Contact

You will usually find that contacts for the various religious organisations are happy to explain more about their community and to help with your enquiries. However, this partly depends on the time they have available. If you need information or are organising an event, allow ample time for getting hold of the contact people and arranging a time to speak with them.

Sometimes people who are not fluent in your first language, and in whose first language you may not be fluent, will answer the telephone and it will be necessary to ring back later or ask for an alternative contact number. You may also find that you need to ring an organisation several times because contact people for the various religious communities are usually extremely busy and often voluntary. *Imams, vicars*, temple secretaries, women's group leaders and others have hectic schedules and may have full-time employment in addition to their work for the organisation you are contacting.

If you are making an arrangement for someone to come and speak or contribute to a consultation it is often helpful to write as well as phone and also to check on the day before the event that the person is still planning to come or has found a suitable substitute (if necessary).

Possible Areas of Sensitivity

There are certain areas of sensitivity of which it is helpful to be aware when making contact. Sometimes, the previous experiences or the beliefs of the person you are talking to may make them suspicious of, or even hostile towards, multi-faith or inter-faith encounter. Where minority communities or their members have been the target of conversion campaigns by other religious groups, there may

be particular wariness about inter-religious encounter. It is very important to explain what the context of your enquiry is and to be clear and open about your purpose.

ARRANGING A MULTI-FAITH EVENT

If you are organising a multi-faith event, the following checklist may be helpful.

Avoid Clashes with Religious Festivals

Check that the event you are planning does not clash with one of the key festivals or special days of a group that you are hoping to involve. The annual Shap Calendar of Festivals (available from the Shap Working Party, c/o The National Society's Religious Education Centre, 36 Causton Street, London, SW1P 4AU, Tel: 0171-932-1190) is a vital resource for this. Many commercial diaries now also include main festival dates.

If you are in any doubt about the significance of the festival (in other words, whether it is one that means those observing it are unlikely to be able to attend other events), then contact the relevant community to double-check details.

Fridays are difficult for observant Muslims, and especially for *imams*, because of the importance of the Friday midday prayer. If possible, avoid scheduling afternoon events during the period of *Ramadan* when practising Muslims fast from before dawn until sunset. From noon midday on Friday until sunset on Saturday can be problematic for observant Jews in relation to events involving travel and what could be construed as "work" (though interpretations of this vary within different parts of the community).

For church-going Christians, and for members of other faiths who meet regularly on Sundays, for example Sikhs, that day can be difficult. However, because of the practical difficulty for many people of not being able to take time off during the working week, weekend events may prove necessary. If you are planning a weekend event, it is important to check with members of these religions how they personally feel about attending on these days or about their participation during particular parts of the event's timetable.

Allow Plenty of Planning And Organising Time

Planning time of at least two to three months is advisable for local events and, for national events, a lead time of at least six months will probably be needed. Good speakers and participants are obtainable from all religious communities, but are likely to have quite full diaries and need to be booked well in advance (except for response to political or social emergencies). Participant lists also take time to draw up and, if the event involves people needing to take time off work or to arrange child care, adequate notice is needed.

Choose an Appropriate Venue

It is important not to use a venue which does not make some participants feel ill at ease. For example, if you are a local inter-faith group just starting up and without a strong sense of each other's views and sensitivities, it may not be wise initially to meet at one community's place of worship. A meeting at a member's house or on "neutral" ground, such as a local school or village hall, might be the best way to begin.

If you hold meetings at the premises of a faith community it is important to discover where the "sacred" area of their religious building is. There may be other parts, such as a social meeting hall, which are not so imbued with religious and symbolic significance and which might therefore be more appropriate for inter-faith meetings. This is because participants of different religions may feel more comfortable about meeting in these other areas (for example in the community centre attached to a *mandir*). They may not, however, feel comfortable about any visit which would involve them in entering the sacred space where they might feel obliged to offer respect to another's sacred symbols (or might be worried about causing offence in declining to do so for religious reasons).

In a *gurdwara*, *mandir* or a *mosque*, for example, the sacred area is clearly definable by the point beyond which you should not go without removing your shoes. In Christian *churches*, the matter may be less clear-cut because, particularly in modern and adapted buildings, meetings without a specifically religious purpose sometimes take place even in what is the *church* itself, as distinct from its *church* hall. The introductory materials on each religious community and the chapter on "Visiting Places of Worship and Hosting Visits" provide further background on sacred buildings, their contents and significance.

Religious Observance During an Event

Members of all the different religious traditions may wish to retire for prayer or meditation at certain points during the day and time should be left within the schedule for this after consultation with members of the religious traditions involved. However, practising Muslims pray five times a day at specific times. For Muslims, it is important also to provide a room for prayer, a sheet for covering the floor for prayer, as well as a bowl and jug of water and a towel for ablutions before prayer. If there is a toilet or bathroom nearby with washing facilities this is usually sufficient.

Shared Religious Observance During an Event

Any shared religious observance should be approached with great care. The least controversial option is a shared silent meditation or wordless prayer. If you are in any doubt about the feelings of the participants it is wise to go for this choice. When spoken prayers or readings are used there is always the danger that people find themselves voluntarily or involuntarily joining in what appears to be lowest common denominator worship of a deity who is not recognisably the deity which they themselves worship.

Non-theists (such as Buddhists or Jains) can be put into an awkward situation by assumptions that all religions acknowledge a deity. Likewise, for traditions where the divine is understood wholly or partly in feminine or impersonal terms, the constant use of masculine or personal terms may prove alienating. Given these possibilities of misunderstanding and offence, it is always necessary to proceed with caution.

However, there are occasions when people may very much wish to pray together, or when civic life calls for communal celebration or mourning. In such contexts a widely used option is what is sometimes called "serial worship". In serial worship, members of different religions pray or offer a reading relevant to the theme to which others listen but in which they do not join. Rather, prayer is offered individually by members of the gathering in a way which respects the integrity of their own tradition.

Because the Church of England is the established Church in England, its *churches* and especially *cathedrals* have often been the venue for this kind of civic or communal worship. There are both opportunities and difficulties associated with this which are discussed in the booklet *Multi-Faith Worship?*, Church House Publishing, London, 1992.

Catering for Multi-Faith Events

Many religious traditions have certain dietary requirements as a result of their beliefs. These are explained in more detail in the appropriate introductory material on each religion. Generally speaking, the easiest way to cater for a multi-faith event is to make it absolutely vegetarian. It is helpful to label food where its contents are not immediately apparent.

No animal fat should be used in any vegetarian cooking and when cheese is used it should be marked "vegetarian" on the packet indicating that it has not been made with rennet which is a meat product of cows. Puddings should not include gelatine (unless it is of a vegetarian variety). Cakes and biscuits should include no animal fat or gelatine. Some butter substitutes contain rendered beef fat, so labels need careful checking.

Within the vegetarian dishes, make sure that at least some contain no eggs or milk products like cheese, and that some of these non-egg dishes also contain no garlic or onions (since all these may be unacceptable to some Hindus, observant Jains and also some other groupings). Observant Jains avoid eating all root vegetables that produce numerous sprouts from the skin (such as potatoes).

Within Judaism, the *kosher* rules are widely observed but with differing interpretations. Check in advance how your Jewish participants interpret them. Normally, it is sufficient to provide vegetarian food and disposable plates, cups and cutlery. However, for the very *Orthodox*, it is necessary to provide separate meals which have been prepared in a *kosher* kitchen. *Kosher* foods include *kosher* wine, bread and cheese as well as meats. Such food and drink is marked with a *hechsher* (seal) which certifies it to be *kosher*. Ask your local *synagogue* for advice on vendors. Also ask for advice on any meals to be served during the festival of *Pesach/Passover* when special requirements apply.

Muslims will wish that, ideally, their food be prepared in a kitchen where the utensils and contents have not been in contact with *haram* (forbidden) food. However, most Muslims are primarily concerned to ensure that any meat served is *halal* (permitted and slaughtered according to the *Shar'iah*), and are generally happy to eat vegetarian food that has no animal fat used in its production.

Buddhist monks frequently do not eat after midday. In an all day event it may therefore be important to provide substantial refreshments for them earlier in the morning. Some Christians fast on *Ash Wednesday* and limit the range of foods consumed during *Lent*. Some Jains do not eat after sunset. During *Ramadan*, most Muslims do not eat between sunrise and sunset. Many Sikhs are vegetarian, but Sikhs who do eat meat are not permitted to eat *halal* meat.

Different traditions have varying approaches to the consumption of alcohol. In Islam it is considered *haram* (forbidden) and there are warnings against the dangers that can arise from associating with those who drink alcohol. For Hindus and Jains it is considered undesirable. Sikhs who have taken *amrit* are also expected to avoid alcohol. For most Christians alcohol is not prohibited, although some groups advocate abstinence. Within Judaism there is likewise no prohibition and responsible use of alcohol is not frowned upon. Practice varies among Buddhists although alcohol is viewed as dangerous in so far as it can hinder *mindfulness*. Bahá'ís are not allowed to consume alcohol, even as an ingredient in cooked foods or sauces.

Because of the diversity of practice within religions, alcohol is often not served at a specifically inter-faith event. If you do provide alcohol at a function, it is wise to provide only wine and to set it at some distance from the non-alcoholic drinks. Fruit juices and mineral water should always be provided as an alternative. Coffee and tea, as stimulants, are avoided by observant members of certain traditions. It is therefore important to provide fruit juice, water or herbal tea as alternatives to morning and afternoon coffee and tea.

Gender Relations

It is important to be aware of differing attitudes to the roles and relationships of men and women. These may vary even within one religious tradition according to how a group interprets that tradition and according to the cultural background in which their tradition has been practised.

For example, a *Chasidic* Jewish family will have a somewhat different dynamic from a *Reform* Jewish one and *Anglican* Christians may differ radically one from another concerning what they believe the *Bible* and tradition teaches about the roles of Christian men and women. Within Islam, interpretations of the *Qur'an* and *Shar'iah* by the different legal schools mean that there is a legitimate diversity of interpretation. However, modesty is an important concept in Islam for both women and men. Some interpret this to mean that single sex events should be the norm. Others interpret it to mean that a careful, formal and modest manner should characterise meetings between people of different sexes in public contexts.

Within almost every religious tradition there are those who believe that women should not exercise a public leadership role and there are those who believe they can do so. This can occasionally lead to some awkwardness when seeking women to participate in multi-faith events and panels.

Generally speaking the best rule is to proceed with courtesy and care in requests for speakers and to try to accommodate requests for such things as hotel rooms in separate parts of the building for men and women, or perhaps to consider offering additional travel expenses to allow a person's husband, wife or family member to travel with them for reasons of propriety.

Consider Arranging a Crèche

The provision of a crèche will support family participation. If no crèche facilities are available it can be difficult for young couples to come to events, and impossible for many women.

ARRANGING MULTI-FAITH CONSULTATIONS OR PANELS

You may be working to gain multi-faith contributions on particular issues, such as disability, inner city regeneration or sex education. If you are working locally or nationally to set up such a consultation, there are some questions worth asking at the outset:

What Kind of Input Is Actually Wanted?

Depending on the project, you may be seeking to bring together:

- Religious experts (scholars or knowledgeable *clergy* or *laity*).
- Religious community leaders (who are not necessarily scholars or religious teachers themselves).

- Representative or "average" members of particular faith communities (including women and young people).
- Members of religious communities with expertise on a particular topic.

Often you will need a mixture of different kinds of participants. For example, suppose you want to determine what different religions have to say about the care of the elderly. You might want an expert to give an overview of what the sacred texts and historical traditions have said. You might also want members of religious commitees who are older citizens and have thought about what their religion means in the context of their own ageing. Alternatively, you could involve carers who are putting their faith into practice in caring for the elderly. There are many options and it is important to decide what you are hoping to gain from the encounter.

What Should the Composition of a Panel/Consultants be?

The scope, timetable and financing of any project will clearly define some of the constraints. However, there are certain questions which it is important to ask at the outset:

- From which religions is an input sought?
- Do we want all the religions represented in the UK to be present, or just those with a substantial presence?
- Should the panel or consultants reflect the national religious composition of the UK, or of the geographical areas in which ones organisation is most involved? (Jains, for example, might be a small grouping nationally but are particularly important in a city such as Leicester).
- Do we want input from: both men and women; people of varying ages; and lay people as well as clergy?

Questions about which religion you are seeking to involve can only be answered in the context of your particular project. People often overlook the smaller religious communities, but if you are working on an issue such as medical ethics you may, for example, want to make a special effort to include a tradition which has a particular contribution to make to the discussion, even if that tradition is numerically not a large one in the UK. For some purposes a "representative group" is sought. The diversity within and between most religious communities makes this difficult to achieve. It takes a while to establish who are the key figures in a religious tradition in a particular area of the country. It is also not always easy to find out who is genuinely representative and what their capacity is to relay information back to that community or to provide accurate information about what that community itself needs.

If you are seeking to involve religious "leaders", the nature of these may vary very widely between traditions, as will the understanding of who or what is a religious leader. The role of an *imam*, for example, is not strictly comparable to that of a *vicar*. The job of a Sikh *granthi* is likewise very different.

Different community structures have given rise to different types of personnel. Information on some of these roles can be found in the directory's introduction to the various communities. Care should be taken not to assume that religious leaders in other communities will conform to the pattern of the Christian Churches. With regard to all religious traditions, women and men under forty rarely appear in consultations where the membership draws solely upon religious leaderships.

PRODUCING GUIDELINES

Producing Information Packs

This will depend on what kind of information is needed. If it is basic information about different religions that you need, many good resources already exist. It may not be necessary to arrange for consultants from different religions to come and help produce an entirely new pack.

If the information is designed to help service provision, and you are drawing together religious community members who include people unused to consultancy work, give clear guidance on what kind of information and assistance is needed. Even those who have previously been involved in consultancy work will benefit from a clear idea of what you are seeking.

Some national religious organisations may have staff available to respond to written requests for information or invitations to participate in various events. Many do not, and this is also true at local level. If you write asking for information and receive no reply within a couple of weeks, you may need to follow up the letter with a phone call.

Avoiding Stereotypes

It is important, in sensitive ways, to ask the groups or individuals with whom you are dealing, what they believe and consider important. Religion is not monolithic and it is unhelpful and dangerous to operate with a stereotypical concept of, for example, a Bahá'í, a Christian or a Jew (even where this is based on much research). If you are producing pamphlets or guidance for service providers working with people of a variety of religions, this cannot be stressed strongly enough. Make sure that the reader understands that there can be a wide variety of interpretation, and degrees of strictness in observance.

Some people born into religious communities may not even consider themselves any longer to be members of that community. There are some atheists, agnostics and humanists who would find it unacceptable to be asked to say what their religious background is. Likewise, there may be people who belong to a tradition by birth, and for whom religion is still important, but who do not set particular store by ceremonial or ritual observance and may also not observe the usual dietary regulations. In all cases, it is best to allow people to define their own religious identity.

MILLENNIUM RELATED PROJECTS

The year 2000 marks a key event in the Christian calendar: 2,000 years according to traditional dating, since the birth of Jesus. Modern dating methods suggest that it is more likely that he was born 4 years earlier, but the Christian calendar does not reflect this change so 2000 will be the focus for the celebrations (as will be New Year's Day 2001 which is when the "third millennium" technically begins). The Christian Churches will be marking the entry to the third *Millennium* in a range of ways.

Each major faith has its own calendar dating system marking the years according to key dates in its own tradition, as the chapters on individual religious communities explain. However, because the Christian tradition has strongly shaped the history and life of England, Ireland, Scotland and Wales, the public calendar of the UK is based on the Christian dating system. This makes it 2000 for the public life of the country as a whole and so the *Millennium* is a shared occasion as well as a Christian one: a time to think together about the shape of our society and the future for generations to come.

The Christian Churches and other faith communities are already in consultation with each other and with the various national bodies involved in *Millennium* planning. Guidelines are likely to be available by late 1997 on planning with sensitivity and awareness for *Millennium* events and projects in multi-faith contexts.

For information about the Christian context of the *Millennium* and the Churches' plans, contact the national ecumenical bodies listed in the chapter on the Christian community. A number of these have individuals or committees working on the *Millennium*. A key point of contact is Revd Stephen Lynass, Churches Together in England *Millennium* Secretary and Archbishops' Officer for the Millennium, Millennium Office, Church House, Great Smith Street, London SW1P 3NZ (0171-222-9011). For further information about inter faith issues and the *Millennium*, contact The Inter Faith Network.

FURTHER HELP

If you need further advice and information on the points discussed in this chapter, The Inter Faith Network (5-7 Tavistock Place, London, WC1H 9SN, Tel 0171-388-0008, Fax 0171-387-7968) may be able to help. It can put you in touch with individuals and organisations who might be able to advise or assist.

If you are wanting to get involved in inter-faith activity locally or nationally the Network can make suggestions. Information and advice can also be obtained from the other organisations listed in the chapter on "Inter-Faith Activity in the UK".

VISITING PLACES OF WORSHIP AND HOSTING VISITS

INTRODUCTION

In the introductory materials on each religious community you will find a description of what you may see if visiting the places of worship of that religious tradition. You will also find a description of the personnel you are likely to meet and explanations of some of the key concepts found in the religious tradition concerned.

If you are making a visit to a place of worship, the likelihood is that a person of that religion will be helping to arrange the visit for you. Usually people are delighted to show others their place of worship. It is a sharing of what they hold very dear.

VISITING PLACES OF WORSHIP

Before going to another's place of worship it is as well to think over how you feel about such matters as joining in their service, or receiving food that has been offered to the deities of other religions and has been blessed. It is quite possible to visit others' places of worship without this kind of participation so long as you explain your reservations courteously in advance.

The religious community you are visiting would not want you to feel ill at ease. Likewise, they would not wish to be made ill at ease themselves by criticisms of their ways of worship or of their religion. Questions are always welcomed but negative comparisons with the visitor's own customs are unlikely to promote a friendly relationship!

Whether you make your visit alone, or as a group, it is important to follow the guidelines for clothing and behaviour so as not to cause offence. For groups, it is important not to talk loudly, thus disturbing any who may be at prayer. If any of your group have special needs, let the place you are visiting know in advance so that they can prepare to help. For example, although the normal custom of the place of worship in question may be to sit on the floor or to stand for worship, chairs can often be provided for elderly, infirm or disabled visitors.

Ask before taking any photographs as this is not always allowed.

VISITING A BAHÁ'Í PLACE OF WORSHIP

There are no formal buildings for Bahá'í worship in the UK. Gatherings are held at the Bahá'í Centre in London and various regional Bahá'í centres, as well as in members' homes or meeting rooms. Interested members of other religious traditions are welcome to attend *Unity Feasts* and other meetings for worship and prayer, as well as *Holy Day* celebrations. Those wishing to attend a Bahá'í meeting should contact the secretary of the *Local Assembly* to make suitable arrangements.

Clothing in Bahá'í Places of Worship

There are no special requirements, although it is appropriate to dress tidily and modestly.

Entering the Bahá'í Meeting

You may find a place wherever you feel comfortable.

Bahá'í Worship

A *Unity Feast* begins with devotional readings, prayers or songs. You may join in or not, as you wish. During prayers, a reverent silence is requested. There is no sacred food or *sacrament*. The Feast closes with a period during which people meet each other and share refreshments.

VISITING A BUDDHIST TEMPLE

Buddhist places of devotion vary considerably in style and practice. Such places may be a part of a *vihara* (a place where monks live), or may be found in a centre. In either case, the actual place of devotion is the *shrine room*. The *shrine room* will contain a *Buddharupa* (statue of the *Buddha*) in a central position, commonly with an incense holder, flowers and candles by its side.

Clothing in a Buddhist Place of Worship

There are no particular requirements with regard to clothing except that it should be modest and, practically, it can help for it to be loose fitting because of the normal practice of sitting on the floor.

Entering a Buddhist Shrine Room

Before entering the *shrine room*, one should remove one's shoes as a mark of respect. Inside the room, seating is generally on the floor and it is appropriate to adopt a quiet and meditative demeanour. One may see Buddhists, on entering a temple or *shrine room* prostrating themselves three times before the shrine, but visitors would not be expected to do this. In some traditions it is considered disrespectful to sit with one's legs or feet pointed in the direction of the shrine, or with one's back turned to the *Buddha*.

Buddhist Worship

The *shrine room* is primarily a place for meditation and teaching. It is also the place for the performance of *puja*, which is a way of expressing one's devotion by means of offering flowers, lights, incense, food or other gifts. There is no expectation that a visitor will participate in this although one may do so, if one wishes.

VISITING A CHRISTIAN CHURCH

Clothing in a Christian church

There is a wide variation between different types of *churches*, but as a general rule it is wise to dress tidily and avoid particularly revealing clothing. This is perhaps most strongly true in *Orthodox* as well as conservative *Catholic* and *Protestant churches*. Men traditionally remove their hats when entering *church*. If you are a male visitor of another religious tradition who normally keeps his head covered for religious reasons, it is worth explaining this fact to your hosts. In some very conservative Christian *churches* women are expected to cover their heads.

Entering a church

Most *churches* have *pews* (benches with raised backs) or rows of seats, although in *Orthodox churches* people generally stand for worship.

Where there are *pews* or seats, find a seat and sit quietly. Christians will not generally expect visitors to bow or show other forms of special outward respect to the *altar* (or to any of the statues or *icons* that may be found respectively in *Catholic* or *Orthodox churches*). In some *Orthodox* and *Eastern Catholic churches*, women sit on the left and men on the right.

Christian Worship and Sacred Food

Visitors are generally welcome to join in the prayers and hymns of the service if they wish. During services, the congregation may kneel, stand or sit depending on the part of the service. Visitors who are not Christians usually sit and stand with the rest of the congregation and also kneel if they feel comfortable doing so.

If you attend a *Eucharist/Mass/Communion* service and you are not a *communicant* Christian you will not be expected to take bread or wine (and in many *churches*, may not be allowed to do so). If you go to a *Protestant* church where the bread and wine of the *Communion* service is passed around the seated congregation, let the plate and cup pass by to the person next to you.

If you are in a church where people are going up to the altar to take *Communion*, remain in your seat. Some *priests* or *ministers*, however, will invite non-*Communion* takers to come forward and receive a *blessing* from the *priest*. If you would like this, stand or kneel with your head bowed, keeping your hands folded together or holding a book or service paper so that the priest can see that you wish a *blessing*, rather than to receive *Communion*. But it is important to be aware that the form of any *blessing* will be specifically Christian, including the invocation of the name of Jesus or of God the Son.

VISITING A HINDU MANDIR

Clothing in a Hindu Mandir

Clothing should be modest for both men and women. Shoes are removed before going into the *mandir* and put on the racks provided. Clean and presentable socks, stockings, or tights are therefore a good idea. Sometimes women are

requested to cover their heads and they should also keep in mind that, since they will be sitting on the floor, short dresses and skirts may be unsuitable.

Entering a Hindu Mandir

Walk in quietly and find a place to sit on the floor (usually carpeted). In some *mandirs* men and boys sit on one side of the room and women and girls on the other. Sit with crossed legs or with your legs pointing to one side. It is considered disrespectful to sit with your legs forward with the feet pointing towards the sacred area at the front of the *mandir*. In some *mandirs* guests may be expected to stand as a sign of respect during *arti*.

Hindu Worship and Sacred Food

There is no expectation that you should join in the formal prayer and worship unless you wish to do so. When Hindus go to the *mandir*, they usually take an offering such as food or money to give to the deities. If you are not a Hindu, this would not be expected although it would be welcomed. If offering food, it should not be cooked food and especially not if it violates the principle of *ahimsa* (not-harming). Fresh fruit or nuts would be appropriate.

Food becomes sacred when given to the deity, usually prior to the ceremony called *arti*. After it becomes sacred it is called *prasada*. Often the blessed food takes the form of sweets or fruit offered on a tray. You will be offered one piece which you can either eat or take home. If you take a piece, take it in cupped hands with the right hand uppermost. If you are uncomfortable for religious reasons about being given some of this sacred food to eat, let the offerer know with a quiet "No thank you". If possible, explain to your hosts in advance that you will be declining for reasons of your own personal religious position, and not out of any disrespect for them.

A Note for Women

In some *mandirs* women will be expected not to enter the temple during menstruation.

VISITING A JAIN TEMPLE

Clothing in a Jain Temple

Clothing should be modest for both men and women, but need not be formal. Head coverings are not necessary for either sex. Shoes are removed before going into the temple and put on the racks provided. Clean and presentable socks, stockings, or tights are therefore a good idea. All leather objects should be left outside when entering the temple.

Entering a Jain Temple Area

No eating or chewing is allowed in the temple area. When Jains enter the temple they bow to the image in the temple and chant a *mantra*. This will not be expected of a visitor, from whom a reverent silence is appropriate. Walk in quietly and find a place to sit on the floor (usually carpeted). Sit with crossed legs, or with your legs pointing to one side. It is considered disrespectful to sit with your legs forward with the feet pointing towards the sacred area at the front of the temple or to stand or sit with your back to the image.

Jain Worship

There will be no expectation that you join in the prayer unless you particularly wish to do so. In Jain temples, there is no custom of offering sacred food to devotees or visitors.

A Note for Women

In some Jain temples women will be expected not to enter the temple during menstruation.

VISITING A JEWISH SYNAGOGUE

Clothing in a Synagogue

Dress should be modest, with arms and legs covered, but need not be formal. Women should wear a skirt or dress of reasonable length and not trousers. In an *Orthodox synagogue*, married women should cover their heads. Men and boys should cover their heads when visiting any *synagogue*.

Entering a Synagogue

You should not bring non-*kosher* food into a *synagogue*.

Check before entering whether men and women usually sit separately at the *synagogue* in question. In many *Orthodox synagogues* women sit in a separate balcony or gallery area during worship.

If the community is standing quietly in prayer, then visitors should wait at the back until the prayer has finished since this prayer should not be interrupted. *Sabbath* services in *Orthodox synagogues* can be up to two to three hours long, so visitors are advised to take this into account when planning for their arrivals and departures.

Synagogue Worship and Sacred Food

There is no expectation that you should join in the worship unless you particularly wish to do so. *Orthodox* services, and many *Masorti* services, are conducted in Hebrew, but prayerbooks with translations are generally available in bookcases at the back of the *synagogue*. *Reform* services have a high proportion of English, and *Liberal* services are mostly in English.

You will not be expected to make particular gestures of respect toward any objects. No sacred food is distributed during the service but *kiddush* (the Hebrew for *sanctification*) may take place after the service and visitors will be invited to join in this *blessing* which is said or sung over wine and bread in order to give thanks to God for these. The wine and bread will then be shared and will be offered to visitors as a sign of hospitality, although there is no compulsion to take them. Young children are usually given fruit juice.

VISITING A MUSLIM MOSQUE

Clothing in a Mosque

Clothing should be modest for both men and women. For women this means an ankle length skirt or trousers, which should not be tight or transparent, together with a long sleeved and high necked top. A headscarf is usually essential for women. Shoes are removed before going into the prayer hall and put on the racks provided. Clean and presentable socks, stockings, or tights are therefore a good idea.

Entering a Mosque

Where women attend the *mosque*, men and women usually enter the prayer hall by separate entrances. You may be greeted by the Arabic greeting *"As salaam-u-'alaikum"* which means "Peace be upon you". The answer, if you like to use it, is *"Wa 'alaikum-us-salaam"*, or "Peace be upon you too". Do not expect to shake hands with people of the opposite sex to yourself. Before entering the prayer hall or prayer room, Muslim men and women perform *wudu* or ablutions if they have not already done so earlier. This is not necessary for the non-Muslim visitor who will not be joining in the prayer.

Entering a Mosque Prayer Hall

Go quietly into the hall, and sit on the floor, avoiding pointing your feet in the direction of the *Qibla* (the wall with the niche or alcove in it indicating the direction of Makka), unless a medical condition makes this the only possible posture. If you go as a group, and prayers are taking place, sit together toward the rear of the hall.

Worship in a Mosque

When *salat* (Arabic) or *namaz* (Persian/Urdu), one of the five daily prayers is in progress, non-Muslim visitors are welcomed but simply to observe and not join in. If you arrive at such a time, find a place near the rear wall and sit quietly observing the prayer. No sacred food will be offered to you at a *mosque*, nor will you be expected to make any physical gesture of respect to holy objects (except removing your shoes and acting respectfully in the prayer hall).

A Note for Women Visiting a Mosque

The main place of prayer is often used only by the men and a separate area is provided for women. Where men and women pray in the same hall, they remain in separate groups. Muslim women are expected not to come to the *mosque* during their menstrual period. Many Muslim women pray at home and therefore do not frequently attend the *mosque*. However, if you are a non-Muslim woman visiting a *mosque* you are likely to be as courteously welcomed and shown around as would be a non-Muslim man.

A Note for Parents of Children Visiting a Mosque

Children under the age of seven are not normally brought to *mosques*, in accordance with the request of the Prophet, except on the occasion of *Eid-al-Fitr* or *Eid-al-Adha*.

VISITING A SIKH GURDWARA

Clothing in a Gurdwara

This should be modest for both men and women. Women should wear a long skirt or trousers. Head covering is essential for both women and men. A large clean handkerchief is adequate for men, and women are expected to use scarves. The *gurdwara* will usually have some head coverings available for those who have not brought them, but not necessarily enough for a large group of visitors. Because shoes are removed before going into the *gurdwara* clean and presentable socks, stockings, or tights are therefore a good idea.

Entering a Gurdwara Prayer Hall

No tobacco or alcohol or drugs should ever be taken into the buildings of the *gurdwara* (not just the prayer hall). If you are a smoker, remember to leave your cigarettes outside.

Shoes should be removed before entering the prayer hall and may also need to be left off before entering the *langar* hall. In addition to covering your head, you may be asked to wash your hands (which Sikhs do before entering to pray).

As you go in, you will see the *Guru Granth Sahib* (the Sikh sacred scripture) placed on a low platform, covered by a canopy. When Sikhs enter they touch the floor before this with their forehead and offer a gift such as food or money.

Visitors may also bow in similar fashion as a mark of respect or, if they are uncomfortable with this for religious reasons, they may if they wish simply give a slight bow or stand for a few moments before the *Guru Granth Sahib* in silence as a mark of respect. No gift would be expected from a visitor although, of course, it would be deeply appreciated. If you do wish to make one, leave it with the others on the floor in front of the *Guru Granth Sahib*.

Seating is on the floor (usually carpeted). Men and women usually sit in separate groupings. Sit in a position which avoids your feet being pointed toward the *Guru Granth Sahib*, or your back being turned toward it. Both those positions are considered disrespectful. A cross-legged meditational stance is the usual practice, but simply tucking one's legs in is acceptable.

Worship and Sacred Food in a Gurdwara

If you arrive during worship, you will normally be expected to join the worshippers, but you do not have to join in unless you would particularly like to do so. At the end of the worship you may be offered *karah prashad* (holy food). This is a sweet mixture that has been blessed during the service and is given to all to signify that all are equal and united in their humanity and that there are no *caste* distinctions.

To receive the *karah prashad* (from the right hand of the person distributing) hold your hands out cupped, with right hand on top of left. You can then transfer the food to your left hand and lift it to your mouth with the fingers of your right hand. The *karah prashad* is buttery in texture and you may therefore need to wipe your hands after receiving it. Often, paper napkins are distributed for this purpose.

If you are uncomfortable, for religious reasons, about being given some of this sacred food to eat, let the offerer know with a quiet "No thank you". If possible, explain to your hosts in advance that you are declining for reasons of your own personal religious position and not out of any disrespect to them. The same applies to *langar* (the food served in the communal kitchen at the *gurdwara*) since this has also been blessed.

Because the food served in the *langar* has been blessed, head covering is usually maintained in the *langar* hall. The *langar* is a meal to which outsiders are cordially welcomed. However, it is advisable to ask only for what you are likely to eat rather than to leave any.

VISITING A ZOROASTRIAN PLACE OF WORSHIP

There are no Zoroastrian fire temples in the United Kingdom. There is, however, a room for Zoroastrian worship in Zoroastrian House in London. People from outside the Zoroastrian community may, on occasion, be invited to attend a *jashan* (festival). Non-Zoroastrians are requested not to enter the prayer room known as the *setayeshgah*.

HOSTING VISITS TO PLACES OF WORSHIP

If you are a member of a religious community, it is sometimes easy to forget how strange and complicated the proceedings in your place of worship may seem to outsiders. Making visitors feel at ease is important. If you are hosting a visit to a place of worship by people of other traditions it is helpful to think in advance about a few questions:

- What kind of service or worship or celebration would it be most appropriate for them to attend? Explain carefully in advance the nature of the event to those attending.

- Can the suggested size of the group be accommodated comfortably whilst regular worship is taking place, or would it be better to offer a guided tour outside of the times of regular worship ?

- Will you expect visitors to join in the worship in any way ? If so, have you considered how some aspects of your worship may present difficulties of conscience for some visitors and how you will deal with such instances ?

- Will visitors be expected to express respect in any particular way to any holy item within the place of worship? If so, you will need carefully to explain what is involved.

- Are there any rules of clothing or of hygiene, or expectations concerning the handling of food which visitors must observe? If so, make sure that these are clearly explained.

- If there are any guidelines for general behaviour within your place of worship it would be helpful to tell your visitors in advance.

- If your place of worship is regularly visited by people of other religious traditions and those of no religious commitment, you may find it helpful to create a short fact sheet about the building, its worshippers, the main forms of worship which take place and any requirements which you may have for guests who visit or attend worship.

FURTHER HELP

If you need further advice and information on the points discussed in this chapter, The Inter Faith Network (5-7 Tavistock Place, London, WC1H 9SN, Tel 0171-388-0008, Fax 0171-387-7968) may be able to help. It can put you in touch with individuals and organisations who might be able to advise or assist.

If you are wanting to get involved in inter-faith activity locally or nationally the Network can make suggestions. Information and advice can also be obtained from the other organisations listed in the chapter on "Inter-Faith Activity in the UK".

INTER-FAITH ACTIVITY IN THE UK

THE MEANING OF "INTER-FAITH"

"Multi-faith", "inter-faith" and "inter-religious" are now commonly used terms. Although often used interchangeably their different usages may illustrate some of the different perspectives adopted by those involved in inter-faith relations. The precise meanings can vary and often derive from the way in which they are used in different contexts.

The choice of terms may simply reflect personal preference. However, when a society or an event or project is described as "multi-faith" it usually means that it includes a variety of religious groups. While the use of "*multi-faith*" often highlights variety, use of the term "*inter-*faith" often points more to the relationships *between* religions and the people who belong to them. So, for example, in an inter-faith group, people of different faiths come together to share their views or work together on particular projects.

Some people are concerned that closer interaction between people of different religions will lead to a blurring of their distinctive religious identity. This fear can be heightened when "interfaith" appears as a single word. Although this may not be the intention of those who use it, the unhyphenated "interfaith" can sometimes conjure up a vision of some new syncretistic religion which takes elements from various religions and puts them together in a new pattern.

In practice, this fear tends to be misplaced since the experience of the vast majority of people involved in inter-faith activity is that it strengthens rather than weakens their sense of their own religious identity, while at the same time it encourages greater understanding and respect for that of other people.

The term "inter-religious" is occasionally used interchangeably with "inter-faith". Sometimes this is because of a preference for the term "religion" rather than "faith" on the grounds that "religion" is a wider term which more readily covers non-theistic as well as theistic traditions. "Inter-religious" can sometimes be used in ways that denote the simple state of encounter between different religions in a religiously plural context whereas "inter-faith" tends to be used in circumstances which involve conscious "dialogue" between the religions and faiths.

THE GROWTH OF ORGANISED INTER-FAITH ENCOUNTER AND ACTIVITY

There has been contact between people of different religions in almost every century. However, as an organised development, inter-faith activity in modern times began with the World Parliament of Religions held in Chicago in 1893. This brought religious leaders such as Swami Vivekananda and Paramahansa Yogananda to the attention of the Western world.

In the UK, one of the earliest significant initiatives was the Religions of the Empire Conference. This was held in 1924 in conjunction with the British Empire Exhibition and was organised by Sir Denison Ross. The explorer and mystic Sir Francis Younghusband took a prominent part in it and, in 1936, convened the World Congress of Faiths. This subsequently established itself as an inter-faith organisation which still continues its work today.

Like all promoters of new initiatives, those who pioneered the development of inter-faith relations were initially viewed with some suspicion by other members of their own communities. However, while inter-faith organisations have traditionally welcomed people with a wide variety of perspectives, the majority of those involved in inter-faith activity today are committed members from the mainstream of their religious communities. For this reason, suspicion is gradually lessening as more and more people within the different faiths are realising the importance of working to prevent conflict and misunderstanding and to encourage respect and co-operation.

In the last three decades the development and spread of organised inter-faith activities in Britain has accelerated, largely in response to the immigration, during the 1950s, 1960s and 1970s, of people from diverse religious backgrounds. In the earliest days, one of the main needs was simply for information about one another's beliefs and practices and a good deal of inter-faith activity was oriented towards this aim. This remains a continuing need, but at the same time inter-faith activity has expanded and developed in a variety of ways with differing goals, participants and forms of organisation as people from various communities of faith have responded to the challenges presented by a multi-faith society.

There can be a variety of overlapping motives for inter-faith activity: a desire for social harmony and friendship; a wish on the part of the participant groups to secure greater social and religious acceptance; an imperative within one's own religion to respect and work with others; a wish to share one's own faith with others; a desire for better understanding and appreciation of another religious tradition or, in some cases, a hope that the different religions will eventually grow closer together.

Some inter-faith organisations are primarily based on individual membership (eg the World Congress of Faiths) whilst others link institutions and organisations (eg The Inter Faith Network for the UK). A certain amount of inter-faith work is specifically geared to social and political issues (eg that of the World Conference on Religion and Peace) while in other cases the focus is on prayer and worship or meditation (eg the Week of Prayer for World Peace).

Inter-faith activity can involve all the major religions or it can revolve around particular relationships. So, for example, the World Congress of Faiths organises events for many faiths whereas the Council of Christians and Jews focuses principally on the special issues which arise in the relations between Christians and Jews in the light of their shared, and often difficult, past history.

The Jain-Jewish Association is an example of a new bilateral initiative, based in this case on a newly formed relationship rather than historic ties. In the context of wider participation by a range of religious traditions in multi lateral relationships, new bilateral initiatives have also begun to emerge as participants have become increasingly conscious of particular bilateral agendas which need to be addressed separately and in greater depth.

NATIONAL INTER-FAITH INITIATIVES

The Inter Faith Network: An Institutional Link

The Inter Faith Network for the United Kingdom was established in 1987. It now links around eighty organisations including: representative bodies from within the nine principal world religious traditions profiled in this directory (eg the Network of Sikh Organisations and the National Council of Hindu Temples); national inter-faith organisations (eg the Council of Christians and Jews and the World Congress of Faiths); local inter-faith groups (eg the Wolverhampton Inter-Faith Group and the Leeds Concord Inter-Faith Fellowship); and educational bodies, study centres and academic bodies concerned with the study of religions and the relationships between them (eg the Religious Education Council for England and Wales and the Community Religions Project of Leeds University).

The aim of the Network is "to advance public knowledge and mutual understanding of the teachings, traditions and practices of different faith communities in Britain, including an awareness both of their distinctive features and of their common ground and to promote good relations between persons of different religious faiths."

It provides information and advice on inter-faith matters and on establishing contact with religious communities in Britain. It holds regular national and regional meetings and has organised seminars and conferences on a variety of issues and projects, including the quest for shared values in a multi-faith society; young people and inter-faith relations; the role of the media in reporting on the religious life of Britain; and planning, registration and other issues relating to places of worship in a multi-faith society.

The Network also works to encourage wider participation of the full range of religious communities in Britain's public life. The Network's association with the Multi Faith Directory Research Project is an expression of its aim to encourage and facilitate contact between different religious communities and their members.

The Network is a forum for information, exchange and encounter. Its aim is to promote mutual understanding rather than to represent the views and positions of its member organisations to others. On occasion, however, its officers have issued statements in relation to important issues and events which have a direct bearing on inter-religious relations in the UK, such as the Gulf War.

In 1991 the Network produced a formal *Statement on Inter-Religious Relations*, drafted by a multi-faith working group and endorsed by all of its member organisations. This was the first broadly based multi-lateral statement of its kind in Britain and one of the first in the world.

In 1993 it issued a short code of conduct on *Building Good Relations Between People of Different Faiths and Beliefs*, also drafted by a multi-faith working group and endorsed by all its member organisations. It also produced a longer document entitled *Mission, Dialogue and Inter-Religious Encounter*. The Code is reproduced in an annexe to this chapter. In 1995, translations of it into Bengali, Gujarati, Hindi, Punjabi and Urdu were published.

World Congress of Faiths

As already noted, the World Congress of Faiths (WCF) was founded in 1936 on the initiative of

Sir Francis Younghusband who, whilst on a military-diplomatic mission to Tibet in 1903, had a mystical experience of the unity of all peoples. He convened a "Congress" of people of different religious traditions from Britain and from overseas which met at University College, London, in July 1936 and led to the setting up of the World Congress of Faiths.

The World Congress of Faiths aims to create understanding and a sense of unity and friendship between members of the world's faiths. The Congress's founder, Sir Francis Younghusband, deliberately chose to use the word "faiths" in order to include humanists and followers of what today are known as "New Religious Movements" within the ambit of the organisation rather than restricting membership to the generally accepted world religious traditions alone. The organisation is based on individual rather than organisation membership and is open to "seekers" as well as to those who are firmly rooted in a particular religious tradition.

The WCF sponsors a range of conferences and lectures and also publishes the journal, *World Faiths Encounter* and the newsletter *One Family*. In conjunction with the International Association of Religious Freedom and Westminster College, Oxford, it has established an International Interfaith Centre in Oxford. The Centre's aims are to act as a centre for: education and research; the gathering of information about worldwide inter faith activities; support for those involved in inter-faith work and the study of religions; and for learning about spirituality in the world's religions.

International Association for Religious Freedom

The International Association for Religious Freedom (IARF) has a claim to be the oldest inter-faith organisation in the world. It dates back to the 1900 International Council of Unitarian and other Liberal Religious Thinkers and Workers. Its roots lie in the Unitarian and Free Christian movements and it began as a grouping of religious believers committed to "free" or liberal religious values, rather than as a body campaigning for religious liberty. Its current agenda is reflected in its present name, adopted in 1969, which does not link it specifically either to the *Unitarian* or to the wider Christian tradition.

Today, the IARF's membership includes organisations from a range of religious communities (eg a number of Japanese Buddhist organisations and the Ramakrishna Mission) alongside those of *Unitarian* and wider Christian backgrounds who continue to contribute significantly to its work. The aims of its British Chapter are: "to support the international organisation in encouraging free, critical and honest affirmation of one's own religion: religion which liberates and does not oppress; the defence of freedom of conscience and the free exercise of religion in all nations." The international headquarters of the organisation were moved from Frankfurt to Oxford in 1993.

World Conference on Religion and Peace

Following a long history of attempts to convene a world inter-faith conference for peace, the World Conference on Religion and Peace (WCRP) met in Kyoto, Japan, in 1970.

At this event it was agreed to form an organisation which would engage in at least four programmes designed to: (a) initiate inter-religious seminars and conferences at all levels in order to create a climate for the peaceful resolution of disputes among and within nations without violence; (b) encourage the establishment of national and regional committees for peace; (c) develop an inter-religious presence at the United Nations and other international conferences, through which the influence of religion could be directly exerted to resolve conflicts; (d) encourage the further development of the science of inter-religious dialogue for peace.

A European Committee of the WCRP was formed in 1975 following the 1974 meeting of WCRP International's Louvain Assembly in Belgium. The United Kingdom and Ireland Chapter was also formed at this time. As its name suggests, the WCRP is centrally concerned with the resources for peace which the traditions and communities of the various religions can offer. Its work also involves bringing about inter-religious dialogue aimed at overcoming conflict rooted in religious differences. It has an international assembly every six years. The international body has consultative status in the United Nations Economic and Social Council.

The Council of Christians and Jews

Apart from Christianity, Judaism is the world religious tradition which has had the longest substantial and settled presence in the UK. Not surprisingly, organisations that are specifically concerned with Christian-Jewish relations have an especially strong historical and contemporary profile in the UK.

In 1942, partly as a response to the situation of Jews in Nazi Europe, a Council of Christians and Jews (CCJ) was formed. From the outset it secured significant support from within the religious and political establishment of the UK.

Its present constitution sets out its aims as: "to educate Christians and Jews to appreciate each other's distinctive beliefs and practices and to recognise their common ground; to eradicate the roots of discrimination and prejudice, especially anti-semitism, but also all forms of intolerance and racial or religious hatred; to promote the fundamental ethical teachings which are common to Christianity and Judaism." There are now 55 local branches around the country which are linked to the national Council.

In 1946 an international conference of Christians and Jews was held at Lady Margaret Hall in Oxford and it was decided to plan for an International Council of Christians and Jews

(ICCJ). Its tasks became all the more urgent as the full truth emerged concerning the Holocaust of European Jewry in the Nazi death camps.

For various reasons the Council did not formally meet until 1975 in Hamburg, Germany, although from 1962 onwards an International Consultative Committee of organisations concerned with Christian-Jewish co-operation was in existence. The CCJ in this country is a member organisation of the ICCJ, which holds regular international conferences and seminars.

Other Christian-Jewish Initiatives

An early attempt at the organised promotion of better Christian-Jewish relations was the establishment, in 1927, of the London Society for Jews and Christians. This emerged from an initiative of the Social Service Committee of the Liberal Jewish Synagogue and the Society continues to hold regular meetings today.

There are other organisations and institutions which focus on Christian-Jewish relations including the Study Centre for Christian-Jewish Relations in London run by the Roman Catholic Sisters of Sion and the Centre for the Study of Judaism and Jewish-Christian Relations at Selly Oak, Birmingham.

Other National Inter-Faith Organisations

In 1971 the Standing Conference of Jews, Christians and Muslims in Europe was formed due to the concern of European Christian and Jewish leaders that their communities should have greater mutual knowledge, particularly given the increasingly significant Muslim presence in Europe. There is a common agenda for dialogue among these three religions in Europe arising from their common Abrahamic, monotheistic and historical inheritance. The main activity at present of the Standing Conference is the organisation of regular gatherings in Bendorf, Germany.

The Calamus Foundation, established in 1990, also focuses primarily on the encouragement of greater understanding between Christians, Jews and Muslims. The Centre for the Study of Islam and Christian-Muslim Relations at Selly Oak, Birmingham was established in 1976.

Two new bilateral organisations are the Maimonides Foundation, established in 1993, which focuses on relations between Jews and Muslims and the Jain-Jewish Association, which was formed in 1995.

LOCAL INTER-FAITH ACTIVITY

In the last three decades inter-faith organisations and initiatives have sprung up in towns and cities throughout Britain. This directory records over 80 such groups in the UK. Many, but not all, are members of The Inter Faith Network. Those which are members are not branches of the Network but are independent entities in their own right and in many cases were in existence before the Network was established. They have a variety of histories, self-understandings and methods of working.

The Network organises regular regional meetings for representatives of local inter-faith groups, both those in membership of the Network and those who are not, in order to facilitate the sharing and exchange of local experience. It also supports and encourages the launching of new local inter-faith initiatives.

The variety of approaches taken by local groups is reflected in their names. Some adopt the word "group" in their titles (eg the Derby Multi-Faith Group). This generally signifies a more informal form of organisation and an individual membership rather than an attempt to be a corporate and representative body.

On the other hand, there are those which call themselves a "council" (eg the Leicester Council of Faiths and the Birmingham Council of Faiths). These tend to be more formally structured and attempt to maintain a balanced representation from among the principal religious traditions. They often have a role in representing the concerns of their local religious communities to the local authorities and other public bodies.

Some of the local organisations (eg the Tyne and Wear Racial Equality Council Inter Faith Panel and the Medway Inter-Faith Group) originate in the work of local Racial Equality Councils. Consequently, these groups have a particular concern for the promotion of better community relations and an anti-racist stance figures significantly in their self-understanding.

Other local groups place a particular emphasis on individual fellowship and meeting (eg the Birmingham Fellowship of Faiths) and may also include in their membership people who are spiritual seekers. Still others have an accent on common action in pursuit of agreed social goals (eg Rochdale Interfaith Action which has had a particular concern for immigration issues).

There are also groups which have been formed in areas with less local religious diversity but which aim to promote a greater understanding within their area of inter-faith issues (eg the Beaminster One World Fellowship).

In practice, however, most local inter-faith groups or councils embrace a variety of motivations and explore various ways to relate more effectively and relevantly to the needs and challenges of their religiously diverse local communities.

FAITH COMMUNITIES AND INTER-FAITH RELATIONS

For all religions, the existence of other religious traditions raises many profound questions. At a practical level, living together in a multi-faith society means that communities need to develop positive ways to interact and cooperate. Therefore for both theological/philosophical and practical reasons faith communities in the UK have been giving increasing attention to relationships with people belonging to other religious traditions.

For example, the Council of Churches for Britain and Ireland has within it a Commission for Inter-Faith Relations, and a number of its member Churches have their own committees which focus on inter-faith issues. Some of these bodies are concerned with particular bi-lateral relations, for example the Roman Catholic Church's Committee for Roman Catholic-Jewish Relations. These various bodies have produced material on issues which arise for Christians in a multi-faith society in both theological and social terms.

Within the Sikh community, a Sikh Council for Inter Faith Relations was formed in 1987. Other religious communities are developing ways of relating at a national level to the other religious groups alongside whom they live. For example, the Leopold Muller Inter Faith Centre at The Sternberg Centre in North London is a new resource for developing inter-faith relationships involving the Reform tradition within Judaism. In some areas, local inter-faith activity has been generated by an initiative for outreach on the part of a particular religious community (eg Westminster Interfaith of the Roman Catholic Archdiocese of Westminster).

For some religious groupings the search for religious unity is central to their self-understanding. They therefore have a particular emphasis on relations between different religions although their view of this relationship will naturally be grounded in their particular tradition's perspective. These groupings include, for example, the Bahá'ís.

Among those groups often described as New Religious Movements, the Brahma Kumaris and the Unification Church have been particularly concerned to promote the search for religious unity. A variety of groups associated with the "New Age" movement also put particular emphasis on the unity of humanity and its spiritual dimension and reflect this in their activities.

SCOPE OF INTER-FAITH ACTIVITIES

Although the scope of inter-faith activity has broadened in recent years, there is perhaps less participation from women and from young people than might be expected, especially in events or activities organised on a representative basis and particularly where these have been at national level.

Where women are concerned, this is partly because in the majority of faith communities it is men, rather than women, who are in the positions of power and leadership, and partly because within some religious communities there are reservations about joint activity involving both men and women.

At the local level, though, women have often been the driving force in developing inter-faith activity. The Inter Faith Network (on the first occasion together with the Women's National Commission) has arranged two conferences to bring women together from different communities to discuss matters of mutual concern.

There has also been a tendency for the majority of key figures in inter-faith work to be in the older age group. Various efforts have been made to involve young people in inter-faith events. Sometimes these have been arranged by youth organisations and sometimes by local inter-faith groups. In the context of some emerging conflicts on higher education campuses, a pressing need is the development of appropriate inter-faith structures to bring together students from different cultural and religious backgrounds, including international as well as home students, and to enable institutions to adapt their policies and practices to meet the challenges posed by religious diversity.

Another grouping which is under-represented in dialogue in the UK are the religious leaders (as distinct from community leaders) and scholars of faith traditions other than the longer established Christian and Jewish communities. This is in part because, for the newer communities, the more pressing concern has until recently been to establish themselves in the new context of this country. Inter-faith relations have appeared of secondary importance, although there are signs that this is beginning to change. In the past, the problem has also been that many of the significant figures among the religious leaders and scholars of these communities have not been comfortable using the shared language of English in contexts where nuances of language can be significant.

SPECIAL ISSUES

Prayer and Worship Together

Inter-faith prayer and worship has always been a more controversial and difficult activity than common action towards agreed social goals or engagement in theological dialogue. There are people in all religious communities who have reservations about participating in shared worship or prayer while others will feel that they can take part on particular occasions without compromising their integrity.

Members of other religious communities have sometimes been invited simply to be present as guests of a particular community at a special event as, for example, at the enthronement of the current Archbishop of Canterbury. On other occasions there has been a conscious effort to bring people of different religions together for "inter-faith worship" or "inter-faith prayer".

There have been moves to include representatives of different religious communities at national events, such as the Commonwealth Day Observance now held annually at Westminster Abbey, or in civic services at local level. Special meetings have been held to pray together at times of crisis, for example when Christians, Muslims and others met at the time of the Gulf War to pray together for peace. Special events have been organised to express concern for refugees, political prisoners, the homeless or the environment, such as the annual Amnesty International multi-faith human rights service.

Such gatherings have taken various forms. A distinction has sometimes been drawn between "being together to pray", and "praying together". In the first situation each participant prays from within his or her own tradition. The second situation involves the use of prayers in common. On some occasions those present have been invited to listen respectfully to prayers and readings from different traditions, delivered in turn by their members. Sometimes the focus has been on shared silence. At other times, those present have been invited to share what is said or sung, whilst taking care that what is contributed does not contradict or offend the beliefs or practice of the participants.

It has often proved easier to organise events where people of various traditions are present at the service of another tradition and perhaps offer a reading or prayer, but where the service basically remains within the framework of the normal pattern of prayer and worship practised by the host group.

The Week of Prayer for World Peace is an annual event which seeks to engage people of all religious traditions in common prayer for peace. It was initiated in 1974 and is observed during the week in October which precedes One World Week. One World Week itself is sponsored by the Christian Churches and by development agencies, although people of other religious traditions also participate in it, especially at local level. Specifically religious events are organised across the UK in connection with both weeks.

During 1994-96 a research project on "The Church of England and Other Faith Communities in a Multi-Faith Society" (based at the University of Warwick Department of Sociology) explored the area of "civic religion". It looked at how arrangements are made by civic and religious authorities for activities which place the life of villages, towns and cities in a religious setting. These include annual services for the local emergency services and judiciary, the recital of prayers at the opening of local Council meetings and the decoration of public places at times of religious festivals, and the project noted some trends towards greater multi-faith participation.

Inter-Religious Social and Political Co-operation

Increasingly, religious individuals and groups are forming multi-faith coalitions to pursue particular social and political goals, such as help or support for the homeless, the disabled and refugees. In the mid-1980s a Faith Alliance produced a Manifesto for Human Rights and Racial Justice that was signed by various leading British religious figures.

There has also been a noticeable growth of inter-religious activities within organisations that are not themselves constituted on the basis of a religious commitment but which want, in recognition of the more religiously plural nature of British society, to engage people from various religious traditions in support of their organisations' goals. Many of the organisations involved in this development are concerned with issues of peace and justice and of the environment.

For example, the United Nations Association Religious Advisory Committee has, for many years, produced briefing papers and other materials to support religious communities in observance of worship and vigils for United Nations Day.

The Amnesty International Religious Bodies Liaison Panel has furthered Amnesty's aims among the religious communities by holding an annual conference, producing relevant materials on religions and human rights, and seeking the support of religious communities and leaders, both nationally and locally, for Amnesty campaigns. Among the Panel's publications have been pamphlets about religions and the death penalty, and about arguments for human rights from the world's religions.

Faith Asylum Refuge was formed in 1993 to promote inter-faith concern for refugees and asylum seekers and in 1996 the Central London Interfaith Refugee Network was established.

The Fellowship of Reconciliation, whose international organisation dates back to 1919, has both national and international branches. It is a pacifist organisation with Christian roots, which has now established a Multi-Faith Non-Violence Group. Various Gandhian organisations are active for peace, and invite participation from all religious traditions in line with the openness which Gandhi himself displayed. The World Wide Fund for Nature is very active in ecology and inter-religious concerns and has sponsored inter-faith events concerned with ecology and produced books and booklets on ecology and the world religions. Out of its work has come a new organisation, the Alliance of Religions and Conservation.

There also have been moves by public authorities at national level to promote inter-faith cooperation. One of the most significant has been the establishment by the Department of Environment in 1992 of the Inner Cities Religious Council. This has membership from the Christian, Hindu, Jewish, Muslim, and Sikh communities and is designed to foster partnership between Government and faith communities in tackling urban social and economic problems. Its regional conferences have brought together people from different faith communities to explore ways in which they can work together as well as with local public agencies. Some local authorities, such as Birmingham, have also set up consultative machinery involving their local faith communities.

The Quest for Common Values

As the UK, like many other countries, grows more culturally and religiously diverse, concerns are sometimes expressed that the process is leading to the fragmentation of social unity. These concerns link with an anxiety that, alongside the strains imposed by economic change, there is an erosion of traditional sources of moral authority underpinning both civic and personal values.

Within a plural society agreement is unlikely to be reached on the authority of the sources to which various religious groupings and others look for their values. But there has been an increasing interest in exploring the extent to which there might be a set of common or shared values which can provide a sufficient degree of coherence in terms of morality in the public sphere.

In a global context, these issues have been explored and developed in the recent *Declaration Toward a Global Ethic* of the World Parliament of Religions, held in Chicago, USA, in 1993 to mark the centenary of the first Parliament of the World's Religions, also held in Chicago. The Declaration affirms "a minimum fundamental consensus concerning binding values, irrevocable standards and fundamental moral attitudes" among the religions.

It affirms that the principles of a Global Ethic, to which both religious people and humanists might be able to subscribe, are as follows: no new global order without a new global ethic; a fundamental demand: every human being must be treated humanely; four irrevocable directives - commitment to a culture of non-violence and respect for life, commitment to a culture of solidarity and a just economic order, commitment to a culture of tolerance and a life of truthfulness, and commitment to a culture of equal rights and partnership between men and women; a transformation of consciousness.

In the UK, there is a multi-faith project sponsored by the International Interfaith Centre in Oxford and the Global Ethic Foundation of Tübingen, Germany, to prepare material on the Global Ethic for teenagers, designed for use in Religious and Moral Education.

The Values Education Council of the UK was established in 1995 and links a range of religious and secular bodies concerned with the relationship between education and values. In the same year, the School Curriculum and Assessment Authority convened a National Forum for Values in Education and the Community to explore whether an agreed statement could be developed as a framework for moral education in schools. Approaching the year 2000, the ecumenical Christian body Churches Together in England have called for a wide ranging debate involving people of all religions and none about "common values", as

people reflect on the changes that are hoped for in society.

As the new century approaches, the quest for common values appears likely to become an increasingly significant dimension of inter-faith dialogue and relations in the UK since this debate is seen as being of crucial importance to the development of a shared and stable framework for a plural society.

The Inter Faith Network's 1991 *Statement on Inter-Religious Relations in Britain* said, "Our religious traditions offer values and insights of great worth to society, and provide a framework of meaning within which individuals can interpret their experience......Both within and between our communities there are significant differences in the ways in which we translate these values and ideals into ethical judgements concerning specific personal and social issues. But a recognition of the extent to which we share a range of common values and ideals can contribute to a wider sense of community in our society."

TOWARDS THE FUTURE

In its beginnings over 100 years ago, modern inter-faith activity was often seen as a "fringe" activity undertaken by people who were less central to their own religious tradition. But it is increasingly being seen as an important and necessary part of the life and witness of all religious communities in a multi-faith society.

New initiatives are constantly emerging at all levels and many secular bodies are also developing their consultative processes and their activities to take account of Britain's increased religious diversity. There is a clear desire to work together to build a better society founded on a shared citizenship.

The Inter Faith Network's Code of Practice, on *Building Good Relations with People of Different Faiths and Beliefs* (see the facing page), provides a framework within which religious communities can find helpful and constructive ways of living and working together for the positive benefit of all, with mutual integrity.

BUILDING GOOD RELATIONS WITH
PEOPLE OF DIFFERENT FAITHS AND BELIEFS

In Britain today, people of many different faiths and beliefs live side by side. The opportunity lies before us to work together to build a society rooted in the values we treasure. But this society can only be built on a sure foundation of mutual respect, openness and trust. This means finding ways to live our lives of faith with integrity, and allowing others to do so too. Our different religious traditions offer us many resources for this and teach us the importance of good relationships characterised by honesty, compassion and generosity of spirit. The Inter Faith Network offers the following code of conduct for encouraging and strengthening these relationships.

As members of the human family, we should show each other respect and courtesy. In our dealings with people of other faiths and beliefs this means exercising good will and:

- Respecting other people's freedom within the law to express their beliefs and convictions
- Learning to understand what others actually believe and value, and letting them express this in their own terms
- Respecting the convictions of others about food, dress and social etiquette and not behaving in ways which cause needless offence
- Recognising that all of us at times fall short of the ideals of our own traditions and never comparing our own *ideals* with other people's *practices*
- Working to prevent disagreement from leading to conflict
- Always seeking to avoid violence in our relationships

When we talk about matters of faith with one another, we need to do so with sensitivity, honesty and straightforwardness. This means:

- Recognising that listening as well as speaking is necessary for a genuine conversation
- Being honest about our beliefs and religious allegiances
- Not misrepresenting or disparaging other people's beliefs and practices
- Correcting misunderstanding or mis-representation not only of our own but also of other faiths whenever we come across them
- Being straightforward about our intentions
- Accepting that in formal inter-faith meetings there is a particular responsibility to ensure that the religious commitment of all those who are present will be respected

All of us want others to understand and respect our views. Some people will also want to persuade others to join their faith. In a multi-faith society where this is permitted, the attempt should always be characterised by self-restraint and a concern for the other's freedom and dignity. This means:

- Respecting another person's expressed wish to be left alone
- Avoiding imposing ourselves and our views on individuals or communities who are in vulnerable situations in ways which exploit these
- Being sensitive and courteous
- Avoiding violent language, threats, manipulation, improper inducements, or the misuse of any kind of power
- Respecting the right of others to disagree with us

Living and working together is not always easy. Religion harnesses deep emotions which can sometimes take destructive forms. Where this happens, we must draw on our faith to bring about reconciliation and understanding. The truest fruits of religion are healing and positive. We have a great deal to learn from one another which can enrich us without undermining our own identities. Together, listening and responding with openness and respect, we can move forward to work in ways that acknowledge genuine differences but build on shared hopes and values.

The Inter Faith Network, 5-7 Tavistock Place, London, WC1H 9SN. Tel: 0171-388-0008

FURTHER READING

Ahmed, Ishtiaq et al, "Bradford: between co-existence and dialogue", in *World Faiths Encounter*, No 1, March 1992, pp. 32–42.

Amnesty International, *Arguments for Human Rights from the World's Religions*, Amnesty International, London, nd.

Amnesty International, *Helping Amnesty's Work: Ideas for Religious Bodies*, Amnesty International, London, nd.

Amnesty International, *Religions and the Death Penalty: The Case for Abolition*, Amnesty International, London, nd.

Andrews, A, "The Inter-Faith movement in the UK", in *The Indo-British Review: A Journal of History*, Volume XX, No 1, pp. 123-130.

Anees, M A; Abedin, S Z; Sardar, Z, *Christian-Muslim Relations: Yesterday, Today, Tomorrow*, Grey Seal, 1991.

Bayfield, T and Braybrooke, M, *Dialogue With a Difference: The Manor House Group Experience*, SCM Press, London, 1992.

Beales, C, "Partnerships for a change: the Inner Cities Religious Council", in *World Faiths Encounter*, No 8, July 1994, pp. 41-46.

Beaver, M et al, "Bedford: town of unexpected contrasts", in *World Faiths Encounter*, No 3, November 1992, pp. 28-33.

Bennett, C, "'Within God's gracious purposes: a review of fifteen years of ecumenical interfaith collaboration in Britain, 1977-1992", in *Discernment: A Christian Journal of Inter-Religious Encounter*, Volume VI, No 3, 1993, pp. 3-16.

Beverluis, J (ed), *A Sourcebook for the Community of Religions*, The Council for a Parliament of the World's Religions, Chicago, 1993.

Braybrooke, M, *Time to Meet: Towards a Deeper Relationship Between Jews and Christians*, SCM, London, 1990.

Braybrooke, M, *Children of One God: A History of the Council of Christians and Jews*, Valentine Mitchell, London, 1991.

Braybrooke, M, *Pilgrimage of Hope: One Hundred Years of Interfaith Dialogue*, SCM Press, London, 1992.

Braybrooke, M (ed), *Stepping Stones to a Global Ethic*, SCM Press, London, 1992.

Braybrooke, M, "Interfaith in Europe", in Gill, S; D'Costa, G; and King, U (eds), *Religion in Europe: Contemporary Perspectives*, Kok Pharos, Kampen, 1994, pp. 201-213.

Braybrooke, M, *Faith in a Global Age: The Interfaith Movement's Offer of Hope to a World in Agony. A Personal Perspective*, Marcus Braybrooke, Oxford, 1995.

Braybrooke, M, *A Wider Vision: A History of the World Congress of Faiths*, One World, Oxford, 1996.

Brockington, J, *Hinduism and Christianity*, Macmillan, London, 1992.

Brockway, A, *The Theology of the Church and the Jewish People*, World Council of Churches, Geneva, 1988.

Brown, S, *Meeting in Faith: Thirty Years of Christian-Muslim Conversations Sponsored by the World Council of Churches*, World Council of Churches, Geneva, 1989.

Cole, W O and Sambhi, P Singh, *Sikhism and Christianity: A Comparative Study*, Macmillan, London, 1993.

Council of Churches for Britain and Ireland, *In Good Faith: The Four Principles of Interfaith Dialogue*, Council of Churches for Britain and Ireland, London, 1992.

Cohn-Sherbok, D, *World Religions and Human Liberation*, Orbis, New York, 1992.

Coward, H (ed), *Hindu-Christian Dialogue: Perspectives and Encounters*, Orbis, New York, 1990.

Cragg, K, *Troubled by Truth: Life Studies in Inter-Faith Concern*, Pentland Press, London, 1992.

D'Costa, G (ed), *Faith Meets Faith: Interfaith Views on Interfaith*, BFSS Religious Education Centre, 1988.

Hare, W L (ed), *Religions of the Empire: A Conference on Some Living Religions Within the Empire*, Duckworth, London, 1925.

Houston, G W, *The Cross and the Lotus: Christianity and Buddhism in Dialogue*, Motilal Banarasidass, New Delhi, 1985.

Hussain, A and Martin, S, "Religious belief and human rights", *World Faiths Encounter*, No 8, July 1994, pp. 33-40.

Ingram, P O and Streng, F J, *Buddhist-Christian Dialogue: Mutual Renewal and Transformation*, University of Hawaii Press, Honolulu, 1986.

Inter Faith Network for the United Kingdom, *Statement on Inter-Religious Relations*, Inter Faith Network for the UK, London, 1991.

Inter Faith Network for the United Kingdom, *Building Good Relations With People of Different Faiths and Beliefs*, Inter Faith Network for the UK, London, 1993.

Inter Faith Network for the United Kingdom, *Mission, Dialogue and Inter-Religious Encounter*, Inter Faith Network for the UK, London, 1993.

Inter Faith Network for the United Kingdom, *The Quest for Common Values: Conference Report*, Inter Faith Network for the United Kingdom, London, 1997.

Islamic Foundation, *Christian Mission and Islamic Da`wah: Proceedings of the Chambesy Dialogue Consultation*, The Islamic Foundation, Leciester, 1982.

Jack, H A, *A History of the World Conference on Religion and Peace*, New York, 1993.

King, U, "Hindu-Christian dialogue in historical perspective", in *The Indo-British Review: A Journal of History*, Volume XX, No 1, pp. 169-176.

Küng, H (ed), *Yes to a Global Ethic*, SCM Press, London, 1996.

Küng, H and Ching, J, *Christianity and Chinese Religions*, SCM Press, London, 1993.

Küng, H and Kuschel, K-J (eds), *A Global Ethic: The Declaration of the Parliament of the World's Religions*, SCM Press, London, 1993.

Lefebure, L, *The Buddha and the Christ: Explorations in Buddhist and Christian Dialogue*, Orbis, New York, 1993.

Marty M and Greenspahn, F, *Pushing the Faith: Proselytism in a Pluralistic World*, Crossroad, 1991.

Millard, D, (ed.), *Faiths and Fellowship: The Proceedings of the World Congress of Faiths, held in London, July 3rd-17th, 1936*, J M Watkins, London, 1937.

Moayyad, H, (ed), *The Baha'i Faith and Islam: Proceedings of a Symposium, McGill University, March 23rd-25th, 1984*, Association for Bahá'í Studies, Ottawa, 1990.

Momen, M, *Hinduism and the Bahá'í Faith*, George Ronald, Oxford, 1990.

Novak, D, *Jewish-Christian Dialogue: A Jewish Justification*, Oxford University Press, Oxford, 1989.

O'Neill, M, *Women Speaking Women Listening: Women in Interreligious Dialogue*, Orbis, New York, 1990.

Palmer, M; Nash, A; and Hattingh, I, (eds), *Faith and Nature: Our Relationship With the Natural World Explored Through Sacred Literature*, Century, London (undated).

Potter, J and Braybrooke, M (eds), *All in Good Faith: A Resource Book for Interfaith Prayer*, One World Publications, Oxford, 1997.

Seager, R M, *The World's Parliament of Religions: The East-West Encounter, Chicago, 1893*, Indiana University Press, Indianapolis, 1995.

Simpson, B and Weyl, R, *The International Council of Christians and Jews*, International Council of Christians and Jews, Heppenheim, Germany, 1988.

Swidler, L; Cobb Jr, J; Knitter, P; Hellwig, M, *Death or Dialogue: From the Age of Monologue to the Age of Dialogue*, SCM Press, London, 1990.

Taylor, J H and Gebhardt, G (eds), *Religions for Human Dignity*, World Conference on Religion and Peace, Geneva, 1986.

Townshend, G, *Christ and Bahá'u'lláh*, George Ronald, Oxford, 1957.

Weller, C F (ed), *World Fellowship: Addresses and Messages by Leading Spokesmen of all Faiths, Races and Countries*, Liversight Publishing Company, New York, 1935.

Weller, P, "'Inheritors Together': the Interfaith Network for the United Kingdom", in *Discernment: A Christian Journal of Inter-Religious Encounter*, Volume III, No 2, Autumn, 1988, pp. 30-34.

Weller, P, "The Inter Faith Network for the United Kingdom", in *The Indo-British Review: A Journal of History*, Volume XX, No 1, pp. 20-26.

Weller, P, "Inter-Faith roots and shoots: an outlook for the 1990s", in *World Faiths Encounter*, No 1, March, 1992, pp. 48-57.

Wigoder, G, *Jewish-Christian Relations Since the Second World War*, Manchester University Press, Manchester, 1990.

Yates, G, (ed), *In Spirit and in Truth, Aspects of Judaism and Christianity: A Jewish Christian Symposium*, Hodder and Stoughton, London, 1934.

INTER FAITH UNITED KINGDOM ORGANISATIONS

The organisations listed in this section are either organisations operating at a United Kingdom level formed by individuals and groups in two or more religious traditions; or are sections of secular organisations, formed in order to engage the religious communities more effectively on a multi-faith basis in meeting the organisations' aims and objectives; or are organisations based within a single religion but with a specific brief for inter-faith relations.

All organisations included in these listings have "inter-faith" as one of their activities, so this is not recorded in their activities field in each individual case, but is presupposed for all.

Alliance of Religions and Conservation
c/o International Consultancy on Religion, Education and Culture, Manchester Metropolitan University, Manchester, Greater Manchester, M20 2RR
Tel: 0161-434-0828   **Fax:** 0161-434-8374
Contact: Mr Martin Palmer
Position: Secretary General
Activities: Resources, newsletters
ARC is designed to help religious communities and environmental organisations work together on faith based conservation projects which respect and build upon the teaching of the world religions. It currently has projects in India, China, Europe, Africa, Thailand, Canada and the Middle East.

Amnesty International Religious Liaison Panel
99-119 Rosebery Avenue, London, EC1R 4RE
Tel: 0171-814-6200   **Fax:** 0171-833-1510
Contact: Asad Rehman

Association for Pastoral Care & Counselling
1 Regent Place, Rugby, Warwickshire, CV21 2PJ
Tel: 01788-550899   **Tel:** 01509-263047 (h)
Fax: 01788-562189
Contact: Michael Wright
Position: Chair
Activities: Newsletters
Promotes understanding and standards in counselling in faith communities. A division of The British Association for Counselling, it draws on the insights and experience from different religious traditions. Seeks to include and learn from all the faiths.

Calamus Foundation, The
18j Eaton Square, London, SW1 9DD (h)
Tel: 0171-235-0302 (h)   **Fax:** 0171-245-6821
EMail: 100537.2412@compuserve.com
Contact: Mrs Saba Risaluddin
Position: Trustee
Affiliations: Inter Faith Network for the UK
Informal membership group. A Muslim-led, multi-religious organisation, dedicated to building bridges of understanding between followers of the Abrahamic faiths and the faith traditions of the Indian subcontinent.

Churches' Commission for Inter-Faith Relations
Church House, Great Smith Street, London, SW1P 3NZ
Tel: 0171-222-9011   **Fax:** 0171-799-2717
Contact: Revd Canon Dr Christopher Lamb

Position: Secretary
Activities: Umbrella
Traditions: Ecumenical
Other Languages: Welsh
Affiliations: Inter Faith Network for the UK
CCIFR is the main agency of the British Churches
in their relationship with other faith communities.

Council of Christians & Jews
Drayton House, 30 Gordon Street, London,
WC1H 0AN
Tel: 0171-388-3322 **Fax:** 0171-388-3305
Contact: Mr Paul Mendel
Position: Director
Activities: Newsletters
Affiliations: Inter Faith Network for the UK
An organisation which aims to educate Christians
and Jews to appreciate each other's distinctive beliefs
and practices, to recognise their common ground
and to combat all forms of discrimination, prejudice
and intolerance between people of different religion.

Holy Island Project
c/o Samye Ling Tibetan Centre, Eskdalemuir,
Langholm, Dumfries and Galloway, DG11 2LU
Tel: 01387-373232 **Fax:** 01387-373223
EMail: holy.@rokpa.u-net.com
Contact: Nicholas Jennings
Position: Resource Director
Activities: Worship, visits, newsletters
Affiliations: Alliance of Religion and
Conservation

Inner Cities Religious Council: Department of the Environment
Floor 4/K10, Eland House, Bressandale Place,
London, SW1E 5DU
Tel: 0171-890-3703 **Fax:** 0171-890-3709
Contact: Secretary
Activities: Newsletters
Members from Christian, Hindu, Jewish, Muslim
and Sikh communities. Forum for discussion of
policy issues between Government and faith
communities. Sponsors regional conferences and
consultancy fieldwork support to faith communities.

Inter Faith Network for the United Kingdom
5-7 Tavistock Place, London, WC1H 9SN
Tel: 0171-388-0008 **Fax:** 0171-387-7968
Contact: Mr Brian Pearce
Position: Director
Activities: Umbrella, newsletters, books

The UK's national inter-faith body, linking over 80
faith community, inter faith and educational bodies.
It promotes good relations between the faiths in this
country and gives information and advice on inter
faith issues. For more details see the display pages
pp. 11-12.

International Association for Religious Freedom (British Chapter)
Upper Chapel, Norfolk Street, Sheffield,
South Yorkshire, S1 2JD
Tel: 0114-276-7114 **Tel:** 0114-233-1218 (h)
Contact: Revd Geoffrey Usher
Position: Chairman
Affiliations: Inter Faith Network for the UK

International Association for Religious Freedom (International Secretariat)
2 Market Street, Oxford, Oxfordshire, OX1 3EF
Tel: 01865-202744 **Fax:** 01865-202746
EMail: iarf@interfaith.center.org
Contact: Revd Robert Traer
Activities: Umbrella, newsletters
IARF affirms freedom of religion or belief through
interfaith co-operation. Founded in 1900 the IARF
includes Buddhists, Christians, Hindus, Jews,
Muslims, Shintoists, Sikhs, Unitarians, Universalists
and members of indigenous traditions from Africa,
Asia, Europe and North America.

International Fellowship of Reconciliation Multi Faith Nonviolence Group
249b Ladbroke Grove, London, W10 6HP
Tel: 0181-964-0995 (h)
Contact: Ms Faith Kenrick
Position: Secretary
Activities: Newsletters
Produces leaflets on 8 religions' views on peace,
available from The Old School, Clopton, Kettering,
Northamptonshire.

International Institute of Peace Studies & Global Philosophy
c/o Intercultural Studies, Institute for Education,
University of London, 20 Bedford Way, London,
WC1H 0AL
Tel: 0171-652-1925 **Tel:** 01386-750965 (h)
Fax: 0171-652-1925
Email: tdaffern@sas.ac.uk
Contact: Dr Thomas C Daffern
Position: Director
Activities: Umbrella, newsletters
The IIPS & GP provides access to a large network of

research and information on peace education activities world-wide. It organises meetings, seminars, lectures and publishes the academic journal "Love, Justice & Wisdom".

International Interfaith Centre

2 Market Street, Oxford, Oxfordshire, OX1 3EF
Tel: 01865-202745 **Fax:** 01865-202746
EMail: iic@interfaith.center.org
Contact: Sandy Martin
Position: Co-ordinator
Activities: Newsletters, books
A registered charity for education and research into worldwide inter-faith activity and a support network for those engaged in this work. Arranges conferences and lectures, publishes a newsletter and offers advice and information on inter-faith activity.

Jain-Christian Association

20 St James Close, London, NW11 9QX (h)
Tel: 0181-455-5573
Position: Chairman

Jain-Jewish Association

The Sternberg Centre for Judaism, 80 East End Road, London, N3 2SY
Tel: 0181-455-5573
Contact: Dr Natubhai Shah
To promote fellowship and understanding among the members of the Jain and Jewish communities; to have dialogue and promote non-violence, peace and respect for the sanctity of life.

Maimonides Foundation

BCM Box 6764, London, WC1N 3XX
Tel: 0171-222-1992 **Tel:** 0171-222-5853
Fax: 0171-233-0161
EMail: ipcaa@dircon.co.uk
Contact: Douglas Krikler
Position: Executive Director
Affiliations: Inter Faith Network for the UK
An organisation which promotes contact and understanding between Jews and people of different faiths in the UK and abroad through dialogue and the exchange of culture, in particular between Jews and Muslims.

Multifaith & Multicultural Mediation Service

c/o Institute of Education, University of London, 20 Bedford Way, London, WC1H 0AL
Tel: 01386-750965
EMail: tdaffern@sas.ac.uk

Contact: Dr Thomas Daffern
Position: Co-ordinator
A voluntary service working with the International Institute of Peace Studies & Global Philosophy, the Gandhi Foundation and WCRP (UK & Ireland) providing trained mediators dedicated to finding peaceful resolutions to conflicts involving religion, spirituality and ethnicity.

Religious Advisory Committee of the United Nations Association

92 Willifield Way, London, NW11 6YJ (h)
Tel: 0181-458-3532 (h)
Contact: Betty Scharf
Position: Honorary Secretary
An inter-faith committee of different faiths who believe in a common religious obligation to seek peace and in the principles and potential of the UN as an instrument of peace. We act as a channel between the UN Association of Great Britain and Ireland and religious communities in Britain.

Sikh Council for Interfaith Relations UK

43 Dorset Road, London, SW19 3EZ (h)
Tel: 0181-540-4148 (h)
Contact: Mr Indarjit Singh OBE
Position: General Secretary
Aims to develop and focus interest on interfaith dialogue in the Sikh community; to promote a greater understanding of Sikhism among non-Sikhs; producing suitable literature and disseminating information on interfaith dialogue with meetings and seminars.

United Inter-Faith Ministry of God (Asaholah)

107 Ormside Street, Ilderton Road, Peckham, London, SE15 1TF
Tel: 0171-635-9374 **Tel:** 0171-771-1958 (h)
Fax: 0171-639-7218
Contact: Revd. Isaac Yumi Akinkunmi
Position: Minister & Chief Co-ordinator
Activities: Umbrella, newsletter, books
It started work in West Africa to create religious understanding and stop conflicts, especially between the Christians and Muslims. Regular symposia and lectures are organised and visits are arranged to religious centres.

Week of Prayer for World Peace

60 Childcross Road, Gillingham, Kent, ME8 7SN
Tel: 01634-363631
Contact: Revd Jonathan Blake

World Conference on Religion & Peace

37 Grange Road, Bushey, Hertfordshire, WD2 2LQ
Tel: 01923-211168 **Tel:** 01923-241349 (h)
Fax: 01923-211169
EMail: 101471.413@compuserve.com
Contact: Jehangir Sarosh
Position: Co-chair
Activities: Youth, newsletters, books
An international, "religions working together" organisations with (global) regional/national and local chapters. It is a recognised Non-Governmental Organisation at the United Nations.

World Congress of Faiths

2 Market Street, Oxford, Oxfordshire, OX1 3EF
Tel: 01865-202751 **Fax:** 01865-202746
Contact: Diana Hanmer
Position: Secretary
Activities: Resource, inter-faith
Affiliations: Inter Faith Network for the UK
The World Congress of Faiths offers the opportunity to get to know people of other faiths in a practical way by listening and talking to people of other religions. Membership costs £20 per annum which includes the journal "World Faiths Encounter".

World Peace 2000

World House, P O Box 6, Woking, Surrey, GU22 0NW
Tel: 01483-727170
EMail: childred@aol.com
Internet: http://www.worldpeace2000.com
Contact: Christopher Hildred
Position: Founder
Activities: Resource, media, umbrella, visits, youth, elderly, women, newsletters
World Peace 2000 was created to give every kind and caring person of good-will in the world the opportunity to do something really positive for world peace. Our aim is World Peace.

Wyndham Place Trust

Keeley House, 22 Keeley Road, Croydon, Surrey, CR0 1TE
Tel: 0181-686-7171 **Fax:** 0181-680-5895
Contact: Mrs Fiona Shipley
Position: Executive Secretary
Activities: Books

Promotes among people of religious faith, concern for peace, world order and rule of law. Undertakes research and education with people of many vocations, specialisations, political and religious opinions.

Late Entries

Faith Awareness Programmes of Christians Aware

6 Osterley Park Road, Southall, Middlesex, UB2 4BL
Tel: 0181-571-1833
Contact: Sister Karuna Margaret Nourse

Three Faiths Forum

Star House, Grafton Road, Kentish Town, London, NW5 4BD
Tel: 0171-485-2538 **Fax:** 0171-485-4512
Contact: Sidney Shipton
Position: Co-ordinator

INTER-FAITH REGIONAL AND LOCAL ORGANISATIONS

Most of the organisations included in this section are groups which are not based in any one single religious community, but involve two or more religious traditions however, also included are a small number of organisations based in one religion but concerned with inter-faith relations.

ENGLAND

NORTH EAST
City, Town or Local Bodies

Gateshead Interfaith Forum
Gateshead, Tyne & Wear, c/o Upland House, View Lane, Stanley, County Durham, DH9 0DZ
Tel: 01207-280095
Contact: Jan Massey
Position: Chair

Hindu-Sikh Friendship Society
13 Ilford Road, West Jesmond, Tyne & Wear, Newcastle upon Tyne, Northumberland, NE2 3NX
Tel: 0191-2843494 **Tel:** 0191-2852888 (h)
Contact: Davender Kumar Ghai
Position: Chair
Activities: Youth, elderly, women

Tyne & Wear Racial Equality Council Interfaith Subcommittee
4th Floor, MEA House, Ellison Place, Newcastle upon Tyne, Tyne and Wear, NE1 8XS
Tel: 0191-232-7639
Contact: Simon Banks
Position: Director
Activities: Umbrella
Affiliations: Inter Faith Network for the UK

YORKSHIRE
City, Town or Local Bodies

North Kirklees Interfaith Council
3 Ebury Street, Batley, West Yorkshire, WF17 0LW (h)
Tel: 01924-450706
Contact: Mrs Joy Gunter
Position: Secretary
Activities: Umbrella

Bradford Concord Interfaith Society
c/o Bradford Interfaith Education Centre, Listerhills Road, Bradford, West Yorkshire, BD7 1HD
Tel: 01274-731674 **Tel:** 01274-410841 (h)
Contact: Bob Exon
Position: Convenor
Affiliations: Inter Faith Network for the UK

Kirklees & Calderdale Inter-Faith Fellowship
244 Alder Street, Fartown, Huddersfield,
West Yorkshire, HD2 1AX
Tel: 01404-516373
Affiliations: Inter Faith Network for the UK

Hull Inter-Faith Forum
c/o Hull and East Riding Race Equality Council,
120-122 George Street, Hull, East Riding of
Yorkshire, HU1 3AA
Tel: 01482-227601 **Fax:** 01482-225166
Contact: Mrs K Pilling
Position: Coordinator
Activities: Umbrella, newsletters

Harrogate Interfaith Concord
24 Woodpark Drive, Knaresborough,
North Yorkshire, HG5 9DL (h)
Tel: 01432-862726 (h)
Contact: Catherine Margaret Margham
Position: Secretary
Activities: Newsletters

Leeds Concord (Inter-Faith Fellowship)
19 Gledhow Park Drive, Leeds, West Yorkshire,
LS7 4JT (h)
Tel: 01532-629140 (h)
Contact: Dr Peter Bell
Position: Secretary
Affiliations: Inter Faith Network for the UK

Cleveland Interfaith Group
4 Brindle Close, Marton, Middlesbrough,
North Yorkshire, TS7 8PS (h)
Tel: 01642-313281 (h)
Contact: Stuart Nimmo
Position: Secretary

Sheffield Christian Muslim Dialogue
c/o 525 Abbeydale Road, Sheffield,
South Yorkshire, S1 1FU (h)
Tel: 0114-250-8695 (h)
Contact: Qari Hamid
Position: Organising Committee Member

Sheffield Interfaith
c/o The Chaplaincy, Sheffield Hallam University,
City Campus, Sheffield, South Yorkshire, S1 1WB
Tel: 0114-253-2132 **Tel:** 0114-242-5013
Fax: 0114-253-2187
EMail: s.howes@shu.ac.uk
Contact: Revd Sandra Howes
Position: Secretary
Activities: Newsletters

York Interfaith Group
c/o York Peace Centre, 15a Clifford Street, York,
North Yorkshire, Y01 1RG
Tel: 01904-655116 **Fax:** 01904-655116
Contact: Mr Charlie Bridge
Position: Contact Person
Activities: Newsletters

NORTH WEST
Regional and County Bodies

**Northwest Standing Conference on Inter-Faith
Dialogue in Education**
1 Saint Paul's Close, Clitheroe, Lancashire,
BB7 2NB (h)
Tel: 01200-424719 (h)
Contact: Colin Scott
Position: Secretary

City, Town or Local Bodies

Hyndburn Inter-Faith Forum
St Peter's Vicarage, 151 Willows Lane, Accrington,
Lancashire, BB5 0LN
Tel: 01245-382173
Contact: Revd David Lyon

Bolton Inter Faith Fellowship
Bank Street Chapel Vestry, Crown Street, Bolton,
Lancashire, BL1 2RU
Tel: 01204-528633 (h)
Contact: Tony McNeile

Pendle Inter Faith Group
40 Chatburn Park Drive, Brierfield, Lancashire,
BB9 5QA
Tel: 01282-698048
Contact: Revd Sally Thomas
Position: Convenor

**Northwest Standing Conference on Inter-Faith
Dialogue in Education**
1 Saint Paul's Close, Clitheroe, Lancashire,
BB7 2NB (h)
Tel: 01200-24719 (h)
Contact: Colin Scott
Position: Secretary

Merseyside Inter-Faith Group
c/o 23 Hunter's Lane, Wavertree, Liverpool,
Merseyside, L15 8HL (h)
Tel: 0151-733-1541 (h)

Contact: Revd Canon Michael M Wolfe
Position: Contact
Affiliations: Inter Faith Network for the UK

Manchester Inter-Faith Group
St Margaret's Rectory, Rufford Road, Manchester,
Greater Manchester, M16 8AE (h)
Tel: 0161-226-1289 (h)
Contact: Revd Robert Boulter
Affiliations: Inter Faith Network for the UK

Preston Inter-Faith Forum
University of Central Lancashire, 33–35 St Peter's
Square, Preston, Lancashire, PR1 2HE
Tel: 01772-892615 **Tel:** 01772-784283 (h)
Contact: Revd Peter James Thomas
Position: Convenor
Activities: Umbrella

Rochdale Interfaith Action
c/o 445 Bury Road, Rochdale, Lancashire,
OL11 5EU (h)
Contact: Mr Stanley Hope
Position: Member
Affiliations: Inter Faith Network for the UK

EAST MIDLANDS
City, Town or Local Bodies

Derby Open Centre Multi-Faith Group
Derby Open Centre, 43 Peartree Road,
Normanton, Derby, Derbyshire, DE23 6PZ
Tel: 01332-360737
Contact: Project Director
Activities: Youth, women
Affiliations: Inter Faith Network for the UK

Environ Trust Ltd
Parkfield, Western Park, Leicester, Leicestershire,
LE3 6HX
Tel: 0116-222-0222 **Fax:** 0116-255-2343
Contact: Ian Roberts
Position: Executive Director
Activities: Newsletters

Leicester Council of Faiths
Pilgrim's House, 10, Bishop Street, Leicester,
Leicestershire, LE1 6AF
Tel: 0116-271-9185 (h)
EMail: afj2@tutor.open.ac.uk
Contact: The Administrator

Activities: Umbrella
Affiliations: Inter Faith Network for the UK

Leicester Inter Faith Council
6 Half Moon Crescent, Oadby, Leicester,
Leicestershire, LE2 4HD (h)
Tel: 0116-2712339 (h)
Contact: David Russell
Position: President
Activities: Resource, umbrella, visits

Rainbow Project
147 Narborough Road, Leicester, Leicestershire,
LE3 0DB

Lincoln Inter Faith Group
2 Thornton Close, Washingborough, Lincoln,
Lincolnshire, LN4 1HQ (h)
Tel: 01522-790838 (h)
Contact: Revd Frank Maples Amery
Position: Convenor

Loughborough Council of Faiths
c/o 129 Ashby Road, Loughborough,
Leicestershire, LE11 3AB (h)
Tel: 01509-263047 **Fax:** 01509-267826
Contact: David Paterson
Position: Contact Person

Loughborough Inter-Faith Group
c/o 66 Nottingham Road, Loughborough,
Leicestershire, LE11 1EU (h)
Tel: 01509-261651 **Tel:** 01509-261688 (h)
Fax: 01509-267826
Contact: Daphne Beale
Position: Contact Person

Nottingham Inter-Faith Group
400 Woodborough Road, Nottingham,
Nottinghamshire, NG3 4FJ (h)
Contact: Mr John Hay
Position: Secretary
Affiliations: Inter Faith Network for the UK

Wellingborough Multi-Faith Group
Victoria Centre, Palk Road, Wellingborough,
Northamptonshire, NN8 1HR
Tel: 01933-277400
Contact: Cynthia June Bailey
Position: Centre Manager
Activities: Youth, elderly, women, newsletters
Affiliations: Inter Faith Network for the UK

WEST MIDLANDS
City, Town or Local Bodies

Birmingham Council of Faiths
c/o 23 Evelyn Road, Sparkhill, Birmingham,
West Midlands, B11 (h)
Tel: 0121-771-2363 (h)
Contact: Mr Suresh Pala
Position: Chairperson
Activities: Newsletters
Affiliations: Inter Faith Network for the UK

Birmingham Fellowship of Faiths
35 Manilla Road, Selly Park, Birmingham,
West Midlands, B29 7PZ (h)
Contact: Caroline Wallace
Position: Secretary
Affiliations: Inter Faith Network for the UK

Coventry Inter Faith Group
St Barnabas Vicarage, 55 St Paul's Road, Coventry,
West Midlands, CV6 5DE (h)
Tel: 01203-688264 (h)
Contact: Revd Supriyo Mukherjee
Affiliations: Inter Faith Network for the UK

Dudley Council of Faiths
c/o Russells Hall Hospital, Dudley, West Midlands,
DY1 2HQ
Tel: 01384-456111, Ext. 2781
Tel: 0121-426-4580 **Fax:** 01384-244051
Contact: Revd Mark Stobert
Position: Secretary
Affiliations: Inter Faith Network for the UK

South Warwickshire Interfaith
43 Mill Street, Harbury, Leamington Spa,
Warwickshire, CV33 9HR (h)
Tel: 01926-613402 (h)
Contact: Mrs Rosemary Harley
Position: Secretary

North Staffordshire Faiths in Friendship
c/o The Archdeacon of Stoke-on-Trent, 39 The
Brakens, Stoke-on-Trent, Staffordshire, ST15 0ET
Tel: 01782-663066 (h) **Fax:** 01782-711165
Contact: The Venerable Denis Ede
Position: Convenor

Walsall Inter-Faith Group
193 Lichfield Road, Rushall, Walsall, West Midlands,
WS4 1EA (h)

Tel: 01922-21703 (h) **Fax:** 01922-21703
EMail: M.2.Wilkins@zoo.co.uk
Contact: Margaret Wilkins
Position: Secretary
Affiliations: Inter Faith Network for the UK

West Bromwich Fellowship of Faiths
Churchfields High School, Church Vale,
West Bromwich, West Midlands, B71 4DR
Tel: 0121-588-8452 **Tel:** 01203-337571 (h)
Fax: 0121-588-8436
Contact: Edwin Smith
Position: Convenor

Wolverhampton Inter-Faith Group
The Inter-Faith Centre, 43 Princess Street,
Wolverhampton, West Midlands, WV4 6AL
Tel: 01902-27601 **Tel:** 01902-341948 (h)
Fax: 01902-27601
Contact: Mrs Ivy Gutridge
Activities: Umbrella, newsletters, books
Affiliations: Inter Faith Network for the UK

EAST ANGLIA
Regional and County Bodies

Suffolk Inter-Faith Resource (SIFRE)
Suffolk Inter-Faith Centre, c/o University College
Suffolk, Bolton Lane Annexe, Ipswich, Suffolk,
IP4 2BT
Tel: 01473-233447 **Fax:** 01473-289360
Contact: Mrs Cynthia Capey
Position: Co-ordinator
Activities: Resource, youth, newsletters, books
Languages: Punjabi, Bengali, Cantonese, Arabic
Affiliations: Inter Faith Network for the UK

City, Town and Local Bodies

Cambridge Inter-Faith Group
6 Corbett Street, Cottenham, Cambridge,
Cambridgeshire, CB4 4QX (h)
Contact: John Betteridge
Position: Chairperson/Treasurer
Affiliations: Inter Faith Network for the UK

Suffolk Inter-Faith Resource (SIFRE)
Suffolk Inter-Faith Centre, c/o University College
Suffolk, Bolton Lane Annexe, Ipswich, Suffolk
IP4 2BT
Tel: 01473-233447

Contact: Mrs Cynthia Capey
Position: Chair/Co-ordinator
Activities: Resources, youth, newsletters, books
Languages: Punjabi, Bengali, Cantonese, Arabic
Affiliations: Inter Faith Network for the UK

Cambridge University Inter-Faith Group
c/o Queen's College, Cambridge, Cambridgeshire

Peterborough Inter-Faith Council
150a Broadway, Peterborough, Cambridgeshire,
PE1 4DG (h)
Tel: 01733-891294 (h)
EMail: xgv92@dial.piper.com
Contact: Paul Brocklehurst
Position: Secretary
Activities: Newsletters, inter-faith
Affiliations: Inter Faith Network for the UK

GREATER LONDON
Regional or Area Bodies

Central London Interfaith Refugee Network
Clirnet, 5 Leicester Place, London, WC2H 7BP
Tel: 0171-328-9574 (h)   **Fax:** 0171-209-4862
Contact: Ms Catherine Gregory
Position: Co-ordinator
Activities: Umbrella

Faith, Asylum, Refuge
48 Great Peter Street, London, SW1P 2HB
Tel: 0171-222-1313
Contact: Mr Michael Feeney
Position: Director

London Society of Jews & Christians
28 St John's Wood Road, London, NW8 7HA
Tel: 0171-285-5181   **Tel:** 0171-267-0276 (h)
Fax: 0171-266-3591
Contact: Rabbi David J Goldberg
Position: Co-chair
Affiliations: Inter Faith Network for the UK

South London Inter-Faith Group
82 Toynbee Road, West Wimbledon, London,
SW20 8SR (h)
Tel: 0181-542-9618 (h)
Contact: Eric Ulric Bramsted
Position: Secretary
Activities: Newsletters, inter-faith

Westminster Interfaith
2 Church Avenue, Southall, Middlesex, UB2 4DH
(h)
Tel: 0181-843-0690 (h)   **Fax:** 0181-843-0690
Contact: Daniel Faivre
Position: Co-ordinator
Activities: Newsletters, books
Affiliations: Inter Faith Network for the UK

Borough or Local Bodies

BRENT

Brent Interfaith Council
49 Keslake Road, Queen's Park, London,
NW6 6DH (h)
Tel: 0181-968-3898   **Fax:** 0181-968-5735
Contact: Revd Fergus Capie
Position: Chair
Activities: Umbrella

CAMDEN

Hampstead Interfaith Group
63b Belsize Park Gardens, Hampstead, London,
NW3 4JN
Tel: 0171-722-9010
Contact: Mrs Eva Tucker
Position: Organiser

CROYDON

Croydon Interfaith Group
Croydon College, Croydon, Surrey, CR9 1DX
Tel: 0181-760-5874   **Tel:** 0181-679-8941 (h)
EMail: sedgml@croydon.ac.uk
Contact: Ms Lynne Sedgmore
Position: Chair
Activities: Umbrella

EALING

Westminster Interfaith
2 Church Avenue, Southall, Middlesex, UB2 4DH
(h)
Tel: 0181-843-0690 (h)   **Fax:** 0181-843-0690
Contact: Daniel Faivre
Position: Co-ordinator
Activities: Newsletters, books
Affiliations: Inter Faith Network for the UK

GREENWICH

Greenwich Multi-Faith Forum
Town Hall, Wellington Street, London, SE18
Tel: 0181-854-8888   Tel: 0181-855-4688 (h)
Contact: Councillor Sajid Jawid
Position: Sponsor

HARROW

Harrow Inter-Faith Council
19 Culverlands Close, Green Lane, Stanmore,
Middlesex, HA7 3AG
Tel: 0181-954-6526 (h)
Contact: Miss Pat Stevens
Position: Secretary
Affiliations: Inter Faith Network for the UK

LEWISHAM

Lewisham MultiFaith Forum
42 Alkham Road, London, N16 7AA

MERTON

Wimbledon Interfaith Group
55 Dora Road, Wimbledon, London, SW19 7EZ
(h)
Tel: 0181-946-2651 (h)
Contact: John Elderton
Position: Secretary

NEWHAM

Newham Association of Faiths
Froud Centre, 1 Toronto Avenue, London, E12 9JF
Tel: 0181-534-1092
Contact: Secretary
Affiliations: Inter Faith Network for the UK

REDBRIDGE

Redbridge Council of Faiths
c/o 10 Clarendon Gardens, Cranbrook, Ilford,
Essex, IG1 3JN (h)
Tel: 0181-554-3928 Tel: 0181-554-3928 (h)
Contact: Mr Peter Baker
Position: Chair
Activities: Umbrella
Affiliations: Inter Faith Network for the UK

RICHMOND-UPON-THAMES

Richmond Inter-Faith Group
c/o Richmond Unitarian Church, Ormond Road,
Richmond, Surrey, TW10 6TH
Tel: 0181-398-3706 (h)
Contact: Revd Anne McClelland
Position: Secretary
Affiliations: Inter Faith Network for the UK

WALTHAM FOREST

Waltham Forest All Faiths Group
17 Lee Close, London, E17 5QG
Tel: 0181-527-0818 (h)   Fax: 0181-523-1885
EMail: 101612.1047@compuserve.com
Contact: Mr John Hall
Position: Treasurer
Activities: Youth, elderly, women, newsletters
Affiliations: Inter Faith Network for the UK

WESTMINSTER, CITY OF

Central London Interfaith Refugee Network
Clirnet, 5 Leicester Place, London, WC2H 7BP
Tel: 0171-328-9574 (h)   Fax: 0171-209-4862
Contact: Ms Catherine Gregory
Position: Co-ordinator
Activities: Umbrella

Faith, Asylum, Refuge
48 Great Peter Street, London, SW1P 2HB
Tel: 0171-222-1313
Contact: Mr Michael Feeney
Position: Director

SOUTH EAST
City, Town or Local Bodies

Basingstoke Association of Faiths & Cultures
16 Horwood Gardens, Basingstoke, Hampshire,
RG21 3NR (h)
Tel: 01256-50187 (h)
Contact: Mrs Zarin Hainsworth Fadaei
Position: Chairperson
Activities: Youth, elderly

Bedford Inter Faith Group
4 Oberon Court, Shakespeare Road, Bedford,
Bedfordshire, MK40 2EB
Tel: 01234-262178

Contact: Bryan Walker
Position: Chairman

Brighton & Hove Inter Faith Contact Group
PO Box 2882, Brighton, East Sussex, BN1 5PU
Tel: 01273-565199
Contact: Mr Peter Sharrock
Position: Acting Secretary

Medway & Maidstone Inter-Faith Group
16 Horsted Avenue, Chatham, Kent, ME4 6JL
Tel: 01634-812605
Contact: Mrs Pat Evenden
Position: Secretary
Affiliations: Inter Faith Network for the UK

Mid Essex Inter Faith Group
16 Mayberry Walk, Colchester, Essex, CO2 8PS (h)
Tel: 01206-765379 (h)
Contact: Angela Tidswell
Position: Secretary
Activities: Umbrella

Wycombe Sharing of Faiths
35 Trees Road, Hughenden Valley, High
Wycombe, Buckinghamshire, HP14 4PN (h)
Tel: 01494-564445 (h)
Contact: Anne Bowker
Position: Chair

Luton Inter Faith Forum
c/o Grassroots, Luton Industrial College, Chapel
Street, Luton, Bedfordshire, LU1 2SF
Tel: 01582-416946 **Fax:** 01582-32032
EMail: 106570.2524@compuserve.com
Contact: Mr Shanthi Hettiarachchi
Position: Interfaith Worker
Activities: Umbrella, newsletters

Maidenhead Community Consultative Council
c/o Community Consultative Council, 14 Delmont
Park Road, Maidenhead, Berkshire, SL6 6HT
Tel: 01628-21414
Contact: Mike Bruton

Milton Keynes Inter Faith Forum
11 Fairways, Two Mile Ash, Milton Keynes,
Buckinghamshire, MK8 8AL (h)
Tel: 01908-560714 (h)
Contact: Mr E Friedman

Oxford Round Table of Religions
The Old Rectory, Middleton Stoney, Oxfordshire,
OX6 8RZ (h)
Tel: 01869-343317 (h) **Fax:** 01865-559781
Contact: Mr Chandra Kumar Vadivale
Position: Liaison Officer
Affiliations: Inter Faith Network for the UK

West Kent Interfaith Group
Jarosa, North End Lane, Downe, Orpington, Kent,
BR6 7HQ (h)
Tel: 01689-861004 (h)
Contact: Kenneth Knight
Position: Co-ordinator

Reading Inter-Faith Group
Reading, Berkshire, c/o 41 Groveland Road,
Newbury, Berkshire, RG14 1ST (h)
Contact: Jo Fageant
Position: Chair/Treasurer
Affiliations: Inter Faith Network for the UK

Watford Inter-Faith Association
17 Swiss Avenue, Watford, Hertfordshire,
WD1 7LL (h)
Tel: 01923-231224 (h)
Contact: Mrs Mary Fudge
Position: Secretary

SOUTH WEST
Regional or County Bodies

Gloucestershire Inter Faith Action Group
Barton Stredsworth Community Centre, Conduit
Street, Gloucester, Gloucestershire, GL1 2LX
Tel: 01452-530337 **Tel:** 01452-539586 (h)
Fax: 01452-530337
Contact: Mr Gulam Musa
Position: Secretary
Activities: Umbrella, youth, elderly, newsletters

City, Town or Local Bodies

Bath Inter-Faith Group
45 Brooklyn Road, Bath, Somerset, BA1 6TF (h)
Tel: 01225-422252 (h)
Contact: Mrs Shelagh James
Position: Honorary Secretary

Beaminster One World Fellowship
56 The Green, Beaminster, Dorset, DT8 3SD (h)
Tel: 01308-862004 (h)
Contact: Mary Moorhead
Position: Secretary

Bournemouth Interfaith Group
27a Abinger Road, Boscombe, Bournemouth,
Dorset, BH7 6LX (h)
Tel: 01202-428819 **Tel:** 01202-428819 (h)
Contact: Mr Tony Harrington
Position: Treasurer
Activities: Newsletters

Bristol Inter Faith Group
The Orchard, Broad Oak Hill, Dundry, Bristol,
Greater Bristol, BS18 8NB (h)
Tel: 01179-640595 **Tel:** 01454-772138 (h)
Contact: Mrs June Ridd
Activities: Resources
Affiliations: Inter Faith Network for the UK

Exeter Interfaith Group
Exeter, c/o 1 Ivy Lane, Teignmouth, Devon,
TQ14 8BT (h)
Tel: 01626-773856 (h)
Contact: David Potter
Position: Honorary Secretary

Gloucestershire Inter Faith Action Group
Barton Stredsworth Community Centre, Conduit
Street, Gloucester, Gloucestershire, GL1 2LX
Tel: 01452-530337 **Tel:** 01452-539586 (h)
Fax: 01452-530337
Contact: Mr Gulam Musa
Position: Secretary
Activities: Umbrella, youth, elderly, newsletters

Plymouth Interfaith Group
8 Masefield Gardens, Plymouth, Devon,
PL5 3HU (h)
Tel: 01752-706552 (h)
Contact: Kathryn Colling
Position: Secretary

West Somerset Inter Faith Group
Four Acre, Broom Street, near Porlock, Somerset,
TA24 8JR (h)
Tel: 01598-741377 (h)
Contact: John Gamlin
Position: Honorary Secretary

Swindon Interfaith Group
2 Brecon Close, Swindon, Wiltshire, SN3 1JT (h)
Tel: 01793-534923 (h)
Contact: Mrs Margaret Griffiths
Position: Secretary

NORTHERN IRELAND

Bodies Operating at the Northern Irish Level

Northern Ireland Inter Faith Forum
Religious Studies Department, Stranmillis College,
Stranmillis Road, Belfast, County Antrim,
BT9 5DY
Tel: 01232-612637 **Fax:** 01232-664423
Contact: Revd Maurice Ryan
The Forum was set up in May 1993 to promote
friendship and understanding across Northern
Ireland's ethnic-religious minority communities, and
between them and the Christian Churches. The
Forum has a membership of around 50.

SCOTLAND

Bodies Operating at the Scottish Level

Churches' Agency for Inter-Faith Relations in Scotland (CAIRS)
326 West Princes Street, Glasgow, Strathclyde,
G4 9HA
Tel: 0141-339-8174
EMail: ismyth@stac.ac.uk
Contact: Sister Isabel Smyth
Position: Secretary
Activities: Umbrella, inter-faith
Traditions: Ecumenical
CAIRS exists to promote good interfaith relations in
Scotland and to encourage dialogue and the
dissemination of information about the different
faiths in Scotland. It is an agency of Action of
Churches Together in Scotland.

Scottish Inter Faith Consultative Group
Flat 1/1, 326 West Princes Street, Glasgow,
Strathclyde, G4 9HA
Tel: 0141-339-8174
Contact: Sister Isabel Smyth
Position: Secretary

City, Town or Local Bodies

Dundee Inter-Faith Group
International Women's Centre, 49 Lyon Street,
Dundee, Tayside, DD4 6RA
Tel: 01382-462058
Contact: Annette Miller
Position: Community Education
Activities: Women

Edinburgh Inter Faith Association
17 Falklands Gardens, Clerwood, Edinburgh,
Lothian, EH12 6UW (h)
Tel: 0131-539-1583 (h)
Contact: James Russell
Position: Secretary
Activities: Umbrella, youth, newsletters
Affiliations: Inter Faith Network for the UK

Glasgow Sharing of Faiths Group
46 Greenhills Road, Rutherglen, Glasgow,
Strathclyde, G73 2SS
Tel: 0141-643-0424
Contact: Michael Malik
Affiliations: Inter Faith Network for the UK

WALES

Bodies Operating at the Welsh Level

Cardiff Interfaith Association
c/o Community Education Centre, The Parade,
Cardiff, South Glamorgan, CF2 3AB
EMail: l.m.khan@op1mail.cardiff.gov.uk
Contact: Lorraine Khan
Position: Chair
Activities: Newsletters
Affiliations: Inter Faith Network for the UK

Newport Interfaith Group
Maes y Glyn Farm, Llanover Road, Blaenavon,
Gwent, NP4 9HU (h)
Tel: 01495-791618 (h)
Contact: Mrs Geraldine Layton
Position: Secretary

Swansea Inter-Faith Group
The Gables, 48 King Edward Road, Swansea,
West Glamorgan, SA1 4LN (h)
Tel: 01792-648366 (h)
Contact: Mr Trevor McGairl
Position: Co-chair

INTRODUCING THE BAHÁ'Í COMMUNITY

BAHÁ'ÍS IN THE UNITED KINGDOM

History

Bahá'ís have been present in the UK since 1899, when Miriam Thornburgh-Cropper, the first Bahá'í to live in London, started to attract others to this new faith. She had been inspired by her visit to the Holy Land to meet *'Abdu'l-Bahá*, eldest son and successor of *Bahá'u'lláh*, the founder of the faith. The growth of the faith was greatly stimulated by the visits of *'Abdu'l-Bahá* to a number of cities in England and Scotland during 1911-13. By then groups of Bahá'ís were holding regular meetings in London, Bournemouth and Manchester.

Up until 1939 most Bahá'í activity was centred in England, but in the years following the Second World War the Bahá'í Faith was also established in Scotland, Wales and Ireland. Now there are around 6,000 Bahá'ís in the UK, connected to 200 *Local Groups* and 180 *Local Spiritual Assemblies*.

Origins

Most Bahá'ís in the UK are of indigenous ethnic origin and the majority are converts from other religions or are former agnostics or atheists. There are also Bahá'ís whose family roots are in Iran, most of whom have arrived since the Iranian Revolution. Most Bahá'ís in the UK pray and read their scriptures in English. Some of Iranian descent also use Persian and Arabic.

ORIGINS AND DEVELOPMENT OF THE BAHÁ'Í FAITH

The Báb

The Bahá'í Faith began in Persia on 23rd May 1844, with the declaration of a new religion, distinctive from the *Shi`a* Islam found there. Four people were central to the development of the Bahá'í Faith: the *Báb*, *Bahá'u'lláh*, *'Abdu'l-Bahá* and Shoghi Effendi.

The person known to Bahá'ís by the title of the *Báb* (the *Gate* or *Door*, 1819-1850) was born in

Shiraz, Persia. The *Báb* was originally known by the personal name of Ali-Muhammad and was a descendant of the Prophet Muhammad. In 1844 the *Báb* proclaimed himself the *Messenger of God* and heralded the coming of *One Greater* who would bring a new age of civilisation characterised by world peace. He was executed in Persia on 9th July 1850 under the charge of heresy against Islam. Many of his early followers, known as *Bábis*, were also persecuted after his death.

Bahá'u'lláh

Husayn Ali (1817-1892), known to Bahá'ís by the title of *Bahá'u'lláh* (the *Glory of God*) was born in Tehran, Persia. In 1863, he claimed to be the *Greater One* whose coming the *Báb* had foretold. He said he was the bringer of divine revelation who was to fulfil the promises made by the previous *Messengers* of other religions. *Bahá'u'lláh* was banished from Persia, and later exiled to Palestine by the Ottoman Turkish authorities in 1868. He died in Akka in 1892 and was buried at nearby Bahji which is the holiest shrine of the Bahá'í world and provides a physical focus of its global unity.

'Abdu'l-Bahá

After the death of *Bahá'u'lláh* his son *'Abdu'l-Bahá* (*Servant of the Glory* - also known among Bahá'ís as the *Master*), was appointed in *Bahá'u'lláh's Will* as the authorised interpreter of Bahá'í teachings. *'Abdu'l-Bahá* was born in 1844 and died in Haifa in 1921.

Shoghi Effendi

On the death of *'Abdu'l-Bahá*, his grandson Shoghi Effendi (1897-1957), as appointed in *'Abdu'l-Bahá's Will*, became the *Guardian of the Faith* and *Interpreter of Scripture*. Shoghi Effendi died whilst on a private visit to London, where there was already an established community of Bahá'ís. With his death authority passed to the elected body called the *Hands of the Cause of God*. This was a group of twenty-seven people appointed by Shoghi Effendi to be the *Chief Stewards of the Faith*.

Universal House of Justice

In 1963 the *Universal House of Justice* was established as a guiding body for the Bahá'í community. It is now based at the Bahá'í World Centre in Haifa in Israel and is re-elected every five years.

Recent Decades

Over the past thirty years, the Bahá'í Faith has experienced major expansion, especially in India, Africa, South America, the Pacific and more recently in Eastern Europe. Globally, in 1995, 5,500,000 Bahá'í followers were located in 234 countries and dependent territories.

SOURCES OF BAHÁ'Í BELIEFS AND PRACTICES

Bahá'í Scriptures

Bahá'ís believe their scriptures to be the revealed message of God. These scriptures consist of the *Writings* of the three central figures of the Bahá'í Faith: the *Báb*, *Bahá'u'lláh*, and *'Abdu'l-Bahá*. They include all documents hand-written by them; all documents signed by them; and records of their spoken words, authenticated either directly or indirectly by the speakers. The *Kitáb-i-Iqán* (*The Book of Certitude*) contains the key doctrinal beliefs and *Bahá'u'lláh's Hidden Words* is a frequently used collection of ethical aphorisms.

Most of the *Writings* of *Bahá'u'lláh* and *'Abdu'l-Bahá* are in the form of letters known as *Tablets* and are written in Persian or Arabic. The collection and classification of Bahá'í sacred *Writings* as well as of their authoritative interpretations by Shoghi Effendi still continues today. There are now over 60,000 original documents or copies kept at the Bahá'í World Centre in Haifa and the Bahá'í scriptures have been translated into over 820 languages. Foremost among these scriptures is *Bahá'u'lláh's* 1873 *Kitáb-i-Aqdas* (*Most Holy Book*) which is considered the basis for Bahá'í moral principles and institutions.

KEY BAHÁ'Í BELIEFS

A Summary

A summary of key Bahá'í beliefs can be found in the various collections of the talks which 'Abdu'l-Bahá gave in America. The key Bahá'í beliefs are belief in one God; the unity of mankind; independent investigation of truth; the common foundation of all religions; the essential harmony of science and religion; equality of opportunity for men and women; elimination of prejudice of all kinds; universal compulsory education; a universal auxiliary language; abolition of extremities of poverty and wealth through international legislation; the establishment of universal peace by world government which will have international courts of justice and an international military force; and, finally, the concept of *progressive revelation*.

Progressive Revelation

Unity and its establishment in the world is a central theme of the Bahá'í religion. Its followers share a conviction that there has only ever been one religion and one God though people have called God by different names. This conviction was continually emphasised by 'Abdu'l-Bahá.

God is seen as being beyond gender and as infinite and unknowable in Divine Essence, yet revealed to humanity through a series of *Messengers* sent to different places at different times. Moses, Krishna, Zoroaster, Buddha, Christ and Muhammad are all believed by Bahá'ís to be *Messengers* from God and are described by Bahá'u'lláh as *Manifestations of God*. Bahá'ís believe that every people on earth have, at some point in their history, been recipients of a *Divine Manifestation* or *Prophet*.

There is therefore a progressive view of revelation in which each recognised *Messenger* is believed to have passed on divine law informing society how to live and behave. All *Messengers* are also believed to have promised a time when a great *Messenger* would come and bring peace to the world and Bahá'ís believe that *Bahá'u'lláh* was that *Messenger*.

Oneness of Humankind

Bahá'ís believe that the future of the world lies in a single world order existing for the benefit of everyone regardless of race, religion, class or gender. This will involve the abolition of prejudices; equality for men and women; abolition of the extremes of wealth and poverty; universal compulsory education; and a world commonwealth with a world parliament.

It is within this context that the Bahá'í commitment to a universal auxiliary language should be understood. This does not entail a commitment to any particular language to serve this purpose - the choice of such a language is to be left to the people of the world to choose, through their representatives. But its introduction and use is seen as both an aid to practical communication and as a force to help develop even further the world unity which is seen as necessary for the survival and prosperity of humanity.

It is believed that once the unity of humankind has been firmly established world peace will follow. The establishment of Bahá'í communities and groups throughout the world is seen as contributing to this process and, indeed, as modelling a new world order.

Nature and Goal of Human Life

Bahá'ís believe that the basic purposes of human life are to know and worship God, developing spiritual qualities which enable individuals to fulfill their God-given potential and to become better people.

Bahá'ís believe that each human being has a separate rational soul which is related to, but also distinct from, the human body and persists after death. The world is understood as a place where this soul can develop. The analogy is often used of the world as a womb, in which the foetus is growing arms, legs, eyes and other organs whose purpose will only become clear when it moves into the next phase of existence by being born into the world. Similarly, human beings, in this life, are seen as developing positive spiritual qualities, the true importance of which will only be appreciated in the next world. To the extent that spiritual qualities have been developed in this world, to that extent will the soul to able to progress in the next world.

Heaven is seen as a state of nearness to God and hell as being remoteness from God, each of which follows as a consequence of efforts, or the lack of them, to develop spiritually. The Bahá'í teachings emphasise that death is a "messenger of joy" and deal with the subject of the life to come in great depth. Bahá'u'lláh states that there are many worlds of God through which our souls will pass on their journey towards Him.

Education and Spirituality

The importance of education is a central theme in the Bahá'í understanding of one's place in the world. There is no dichotomy between what are often called the secular and the spiritual dimensions of life. Religion and science are viewed as being complementary ways of discovering truth: science through investigation and religion through revelation.

Ethics and Spirituality

Bahá'í ethics are understood as being both individual and social. As already indicated in terms of the analogy of the womb, the development of positive spiritual qualities is seen as the individual task of every human being. At the same time, humankind is understood to be social with the relationships between individuals also being part of the task of spiritual development. Hence Bahá'í ethics include both individual and social dimensions, as explained in the following section.

BAHÁ'Í LIFE

Joining the Community

A person becomes a member of the Bahá'í community by applying to a Bahá'í administ-

rative body such as a *Local Spiritual Assembly* (see below). An Assembly will accept them if it is satisfied that they truly believe the tenets of the Bahá'í Faith and are basically informed about the central figures of the Faith, the existence of laws they must follow, as well as the *administrative system* with which they must live in conformity. Being a part of the Bahá'í worldwide *Administrative Order* gives individual Bahá'ís confidence that they can contribute in the best way to the goals of the Bahá'í religion.

Teaching and Pioneering

Bahá'ís are forbidden to proselytise in the sense of holding out the promise of reward or the threat of punishment (whether material or spiritual) in order to make converts. However, Bahá'ís are always eager to share their vision and beliefs with enquirers and hold out a welcome to people who wish to join the Bahá'í community. This sharing of vision and belief is known among Bahá'ís as *teaching*. Many are also involved in what is known as *pioneering*, which is spreading the Faith by means of moving where there are currently few or no Bahá'ís.

Women and Men

Men and women have equal status in the Bahá'í community. Any distinctions in gender roles are culture-specific rather than religious and there is a strongly held view that both men and women should receive education of equal standard. If for any reason education is not available to all, then women, as the first educators of the next generation, should have priority.

Diet

There are no specific dietary laws in the Bahá'í Faith, although vegetarianism is commended as a healthier and more natural lifestyle and one which it is anticipated will become the norm for human beings in the future. However, the consumption of alcohol is strictly forbidden (including its use in cooking and sauces) as is the taking of habit-forming drugs, and smoking is discouraged.

Voluntary Sharing

Bahá'u'lláh advocated voluntary sharing rather than an externally imposed equalisation of wealth. Sharing is a matter of free choice and therefore is seen as more desirable.

TRADITIONS IN THE BAHÁ'Í FAITH

The Bahá'í community is tightly structured and organised. At each stage in the development of the Bahá'í religion there have been those who have split off from the community because they disputed the succession and leadership set out in the *Wills* of *Bahá'u'lláh* and *'Abdu'l-Bahá,* and who have tried to establish an alternative movement under the Bahá'í name.

These groups are referred to by Bahá'ís as *Covenant-breakers,* since the *Covenant* which binds Bahá'ís together is seen to consist of the unity of the line of authority from *Bahá'u'lláh* through to the *Universal House of Justice.* The consequence of such *Covenant-breaking* is expulsion.

Covenant-breaking is understood by Bahá'ís to be fundamentally different from simply leaving the religion or behaving in a way that falls short of Bahá'í ideals, since it is seen as disobeying the *Wills* of *Bahá'u'lláh* and *'Abdu'l-Bahá.* Bahá'ís are forbidden to have social relationships with those who have attempted to establish alternative authorities and groups. None of the groups viewed as *Covenant-Breakers* have gained a major following and some of the people involved in them have subsequently gone on to practice other religions or philosophies.

Within the community, Bahá'ís are not organised into any identifiably distinct traditions of interpretation or practice. It is a part of the Bahá'í self-understanding that their religion is unique among the world's religions in that it has not only survived a century and a half without splitting into sects, but it is believed that it will continue to be united in the future.

BAHÁ'Í WORSHIP

Daily Prayers

Every Bahá'í over the age of fifteen must recite daily one of three prayers known as the "obligatory" prayers. These three prayers differ in length and must be recited in differing ways. The three prayers are: a short prayer which should be recited once every twenty-four hours between noon and sunset; a medium length prayer which should be recited three times in a day - morning, noon and evening; and a long prayer which should be recited once every twenty-four hours. In addition to reciting one of these obligatory prayers, Bahá'ís are required to read extracts from the scriptures every morning and evening. When praying, Bahá'ís turn in the direction of Bahji, near Akka in Israel, which is the burial place of *Bahá'u'lláh.*

Regular Worship

The Bahá'í religion has no set worship services and no ordained priesthood. Devotional programmes are simple and consist of prayers, meditations, and the reading of sections from the sacred scriptures of the Faith and of other world religions. Music is encouraged and in the *Houses of Worship* (see below) this is provided by an unaccompanied choir.

Firesides

Most Bahá'í gatherings take place in people's homes. Small regular meetings in homes for discussion are known as *Firesides.* Outsiders who have expressed an interest in the Faith may be present at these. *Firesides* usually begin and end with prayers and include information and discussion. Other meetings, for example *Nineteen-Day Feasts* (see below), may be held in local Bahá'í Centres.

Houses of Worship

Across the world there are seven purpose-built *Houses of Worship* (Sydney in Australia; Wilmette near Chicago in the USA; Frankfurt in Germany; Panama City in Central America; New Delhi in India; Apia in Western Samoa;

and Kampala in Uganda). *Houses of Worship* are at present of continental rather than national or local significance. There are regular services at the *Houses of Worship* which are open to all. The oldest surviving *House of Worship* is the one at Wilmette, otherwise known as the *Mother Temple of the West*, which was dedicated in 1953. A considerable number of sites for the development of future *Houses of Worship* have been purchased.

They were built at the request of *Bahá'u'lláh*, who gave them the name *Mashriqu'l-Adhkar* (*Dawning Place of God's Praise*), and they are built to 'Abdu'l-Bahá's specifications. Each is nine sided and surmounted by a dome, standing in large gardens with fountains, trees and flowers. In addition to the place of worship itself, there are also buildings for educational, charitable and social purposes, for example old people's homes and orphanages. *Bahá'u'lláh* believed that this would ensure that Bahá'í worship would always be closely associated with the beauty of nature and art as well as with practical work for the amelioration of poor social conditions, the promotion of general education and the conduct of administration.

BAHÁ'Í CALENDAR AND FESTIVALS

Calendar

Bahá'ís follow a solar calendar which was inaugurated by the *Báb* and consists of nineteen months each containing nineteen days. The Bahá'í era (denoted by the letters "BE") dates from the declaration of the *Báb* in 1844. Thus, 1997–98 CE is 155 BE. The *Báb* named the months after what he considered to be God's attributes. For example, the first two months of the Bahá'í year as translated into English are called *Splendour* and *Glory*. Each day begins at sunset. *Nineteen-Day Feasts* are held on the first day of each Bahá'í month. The year is fixed and begins at the March equinox.

Festivals

The following are notable occasions in the Bahá'í calendar (dates are given according to their location in the *Gregorian* calendar):

Feast of Naw-Rúz (20th or 21st March depending on the Spring Equinox)
This is the Bahá'í *New Year* and the first of the nine Bahá'í holy days. On this day the nineteen day fast of the month of *Alá* (see below) finishes. This is a particularly joyful time of celebration.

Feast of Ridván (21st April – 2nd May)
This is the most important day in the Bahá'í calendar, described by *Bahá'u'lláh* as "the Lord of Feasts". It commemorates *Bahá'u'lláh's Declaration* of his mission. Celebrations take place and the feast commemorates the twelve days *Bahá'u'lláh* spent in Ridván garden before leaving Baghdad and during which his *Declaration* took place. On the first day of *Ridván* the *Local Spiritual Assemblies* are elected in Bahá'í communities.

Ninth Day of Ridván (see above).

Twelfth Day of Ridván (see above).

Anniversary of the Declaration of the Báb (23rd May)
This date also coincides with the birthday of *Abdu'l-Bahá*. Celebrations take place relating to the *Báb's* revelation of his mission to his first disciple, Mulla Husayn, in 1844.

Anniversary of the Ascension of Bahá'u'lláh (29th May)
A solemn day of prayer and discussion commemorating *Bahá'u'lláh's* passing away, in 1892 in Akka, after being released from prison there.

Martyrdom of the Báb (9th July)
A solemn day of prayer and discussion.

Anniversary of the Birth of the Báb (20th October)
The *Báb* was born in Shiraz, Persia, in 1819.

Anniversary of the Birth of Bahá'u'lláh (12th November)
Bahá'u'lláh was born in Tehran, Persia, in 1817.

Day of the Covenant (26th November)
This day is dedicated to *'Abdu'l-Bahá*.

Ascension of Abdu'l-Bahá (28th November)
A day of marking the *Ascension* of *'Abdu'l-Bahá*.

Intercalary Days (Ayyam-i-Ha)
(26th February - 1st March)
These days, in preparation for *The Fast* (see below) are days of celebration, charity and parties.

Period of the Fast (2nd - 21st March)
This is the Bahá'í month of *Alá* in which Bahá'ís abstain from food and drink from sunrise to sunset. The *Fast* is not binding for children under fifteen years or adults over seventy, nor for travellers or those who are too old or too weak (for example because of illness or giving birth). It is considered a time for reflection on spiritual progress and for detachment from material desires. During the *Feast of Ridván* Bahá'ís are forbidden to work during its first, ninth and twelfth days. On all the other festival days throughout the year, Bahá'ís should not work at all, except for the *Day of the Covenant* and the *Ascension of 'Abdu'l-Bahá* on which they may work.

Consultation on community affairs takes place every nineteen days, preferably at the beginning of each Bahá'í month, at a gathering called a *Nineteen-Day Feast*. The *Nineteen-Day Feast* is the fundamental basis of the Bahá'í administration. Its celebration is obligatory for all Bahá'í communities, whether large or small, but attendance is not strictly obligatory for individual Bahá'ís. Suggestions from the consultation are submitted to the *Local Spiritual Assemblies* through the *Assembly's* secretary.

Only Bahá'ís may attend the business part of *Nineteen-Day Feasts* which have three purposes: devotional (prayers and readings), business (consultation on the affairs of the community other than personal matters) and social. *Local Spiritual Assemblies* also do work to spread knowledge of the Faith in their locality by regularly holding events such as open meetings and lectures.

BAHÁ'Í ORGANISATIONS

The Consultative Principle

Bahá'í organisations work on the basis of the principle of consultation. This entails gathering information from a wide range of sources and perspectives; being frank but courteous about one's views; owning as the idea of the group an idea put forward by an individual; and striving for unanimity. However, if unanimity cannot be achieved then a majority vote may be taken although, in this case, all must be united behind the final decision of the majority.

Local Spiritual Assemblies

The key Bahá'í organisations are administrative bodies called *Spiritual Assemblies* which are to be found at local and national levels. They are run by elected officers. The pattern of this administrative order was laid down by *'Abdu'l-Bahá* based on what could be established from *Bahá'u'lláh's* writings.

To form a *Local Spiritual Assembly* a community must have a minimum of nine members over twenty-one years of age. *Local Spiritual Assemblies* are given responsibility for making decisions on all matters of common action on the part of the community. They also serve a social function by arranging meetings and holding Bahá'í property in trust.

Each year, on the first day of *Ridván*, nine people (including both men and women) are elected to serve on the *Local Assembly*. All Bahá'ís of twenty-one years or more who reside in the *Assembly's* area of jurisdiction have the right to vote and to serve on the *Assembly* if elected. There are no prior candidatures or nominations and canvassing is forbidden. Strict secrecy in the personal duty of election is understood to be Divinely ordained even amongst members of the same family.

Local Groups

A Bahá'í *Local Group* is formed where there are not sufficient numbers to meet the criteria for forming a *Local Spiritual Assembly*.

National Level

There are national centres for administration which may also serve as teaching centres and publishing houses. In 1995, there were one hundred and seventy-three of these *National Spiritual Assemblies* worldwide. The first Bahá'í National Assembly for the UK was elected in 1923 and was one of the first to be established anywhere in the world. Most have their own headquarters buildings known as *Haziratu'l-Quds* (the *Sacred Fold*). In 1937 the National Assembly of the Bahá'ís of the UK set up the Bahá'í Publishing Trust to publish and sell Bahá'í literature.

International Level

At an international level, the *Universal House of Justice*, based in Haifa, Israel, is the supreme governing body of the Bahá'ís. Since 1972, it has had a formal constitution and it maintains authority over all other Bahá'í institutions. The nine members of the *House* are elected every five years by all the *National Spiritual Assemblies.* One of the main functions of the *House of Justice* is to legislate on matters not expressly revealed in the teachings.

In 1948 the Bahá'í International Community was established. Under the supervision of the *Universal House of Justice* it is linked to the United Nations as a non-governmental organisation. Through this organisation the Bahá'í community participates in conferences on social issues such as human rights and supports organisations like UNICEF and WHO. The Bahá'í International Community was accredited with Class II consultative status with the United Nations ECOSOC in 1970 and with UNICEF in 1976.

Personnel

Bahá'ís have no priesthood or professional clergy and contact with Bahá'í organisations can be made through the secretaries of *Local Assemblies* or, on a national basis, with the administrative staff of the Bahá'í Community of the UK.

FURTHER READING

Bahá'í International Community, *The Bahá'ís: A Profile of the Bahá'í Faith and its Worldwide Community*, Bahá'í International Community, New York, 1992.

Bahá'í Publishing Trust, *Bahá'í Prayers*, Bahá'í Publishing Trust, London, 1975.

Bahá'í Publishing Trust, *Principles of Bahá'í Administration*, Bahá'í Publishing Trust, London, (4th edition), 1976.

Balyuzi, H M, *Bahá'u'lláh: The King of Glory*, George Ronald, Oxford, 1963.

Balyuzi, H M, *Abdu'l-Bahá*, George Ronald, Oxford, 1971.

Balyuzi, H M, *The Báb*, George Ronald, Oxford, 1973.

Collins, W, *Bibliography of English-Language Works on the Bábi and Bahá'í Faiths, 1844-1985*, George Ronald, London, 1990.

Finch, T, "Unclipping the Wings: A Survey of Secondary Bahá'í Literature in English on Bahá'í Perspectives on Women", in *The Bahá'í Studies Review*, Volume IV, No 1, 1994, pp. 9-26.

Gouvion, C and Jouvion, P, *The Gardeners of God: An Encounter with Five Million Bahá'ís*, One World, Oxford, 1995.

Hainsworth, P, *Bahá'í Focus on Human Rights*, Bahá'í Publishing Trust, London, 1985.

Hainsworth, P, *Bahá'í Focus on Peace*, Bahá'í Publishing Trust, London, 1986.

Hatcher, W S and Martin, J D, *The Bahá'í Faith: The Emerging Global Religion*, Harper and Row, San Francisco, 1984.

Momen, M, *The Bábi and Bahá'í Religions, 1844-1944: Some Contemporary Western Accounts*, George Ronald, Oxford, 1981.

Smith, P, *The Bábi and Bahá'í Religions: From Messianic Shi'ism to a World Religion*, Cambridge University Press, 1987.

Smith, P and Momen, M, "The Bahá'í Faith 1957-1988: A Survey of Contemporary Developments", in *Religion*, Volume XIX, 1989, pp. 63-91.

BAHÁ'Í UNITED KINGDOM ORGANISATIONS

Along with details of Bahá'í UK organisations, this section includes details of Bahá'í *Local Groups* listed under the entry for the Bahá'í Community of the United Kingdom. A *Local Group* can be formed where there are a number of Bahá'ís in a locality but the criteria for forming a *Local Spiritual Assembly* are not met. One criterion is that there should be at least nine Bahá'ís over the age of twenty-one.

Bahá'í Community of the United Kingdom
27 Rutland Gate, London, SW7 1PD
Tel: 0171-584-2566 **Fax:** 0171-584-9402,
Contact: Information Officer
Details of Bahá'í Local Groups follow, all of which can be contacted through the national office:

ENGLAND

North East
Alnwick Bahá'í Local Group
Blyth Valley Bahá'í Local Group
Castle Morpeth Bahá'í Local Group
Chester-Le-Street Bahá'í Local Group
Derwentside Bahá'í Local Group
Langbaurgh Bahá'í Local Group
Sunderland Bahá'í Local Group

Yorkshire
Barnsley Bahá'í Local Group
Beverley Bahá'í Local Group
Calderdale Bahá'í Local Group
East Yorkshire Bahá'í Local Group
Great Grimsby Bahá'í Local Group
Hambleton Bahá'í Local Group
Harrogate Bahá'í Local Group
Holderness Bahá'í Local Group
Kingston-upon-Hull Bahá'í Local Group
Middlesbrough Bahá'í Local Group
Rotherham Bahá'í Local Group
Ryedale Bahá'í Local Group
Scarborough Bahá'í Local Group
Scunthorpe Bahá'í Local Group
Selby Bahá'í Local Group

North West
Allerdale Bahá'í Local Group
Blackburn Bahá'í Local Group
Blackpool Bahá'í Local Group
Bolton Bahá'í Local Group
Bury Bahá'í Local Group
Carlisle Bahá'í Local Group
Congleton Bahá'í Local Group
Crewe and Nantwich Bahá'í Local Group
Eden Bahá'í Local Group
Ellesmere Port and Neston Bahá'í Local Group
Fylde Bahá'í Local Group
Isle of Man Bahá'í Local Group
Knowsley Bahá'í Local Group
Lancaster Bahá'í Local Group
Oldham Bahá'í Local Group
Ribble Valley Bahá'í Local Group

Rossendale Bahá'í Local Group
South Lakeland Bahá'í Local Group
Tameside Bahá'í Local Group
Vale Royal Bahá'í Local Group
Warrington Bahá'í Local Group
West Lancashire Bahá'í Local Group
Wigan Bahá'í Local Group
Wyre Bahá'í Local Group

East Midlands
Amber Valley Bahá'í Local Group
Broxtow Bahá'í Local Group
East Northamptonshire Bahá'í Local Group
Gedling Bahá'í Local Group
Hinckley and Bosworth Bahá'í Local Group
Newark and Sherwood Bahá'í Local Group
North East Derbyshire Bahá'í Local Group
North West Leicestershire Bahá'í Local Group
Oadby and Wigston Bahá'í Local Group
Rushcliffe Bahá'í Local Group
South Northamptonshire Bahá'í Local Group
Wellingborough Bahá'í Local Group

West Midlands
Bridgnorth Bahá'í Local Group
Bromsgrove Bahá'í Local Group
Cannock Chase Bahá'í Local Group
Cheltenham Bahá'í Local Group
Dudley Bahá'í Local Group
Gloucester Bahá'í Local Group
Leominster Bahá'í Local Group
Lichfield Bahá'í Local Group
Newcastle-under-Lyme Bahá'í Local Group
North Shropshire Bahá'í Local Group
Oswestry Bahá'í Local Group
Redditch Bahá'í Local Group
Solihull Bahá'í Local Group
South Shropshire Bahá'í Local Group
South Staffordshire Bahá'í Local Group
Stafford Bahá'í Local Group
Tamworth Bahá'í Local Group
Tewkesbury Bahá'í Local Group
Walsall Bahá'í Local Group
Wolverhampton Bahá'í Local Group

East Anglia
Babergh Bahá'í Local Group
Breckland Bahá'í Local Group
East Cambridgeshire Bahá'í Local Group
East Lindsey Bahá'í Local Group
Forest Heath Bahá'í Local Group
Great Yarmouth Bahá'í Local Group
Huntingdon Bahá'í Local Group

Lincoln Bahá'í Local Group
North Norfolk Bahá'í Local Group
Peterborough Bahá'í Local Group
St Edmondsbury Bahá'í Local Group
South Kesteven Bahá'í Local Group
Spelthorne Bahá'í Local Group
West Lindsey Bahá'í Local Group

Greater London
Barking and Dagenham Bahá'í Local Group
Islington Bahá'í Local Group
Tower Hamlets Bahá'í Local Group
Waltham Forest Bahá'í Local Group

South East
Adur Bahá'í Local Group
Arun Bahá'í Local Group
Ashford Bahá'í Local Group
Basildon Bahá'í Local Group
Beverley Bahá'í Local Group
Braintree Bahá'í Local Group
Brentwood Bahá'í Local Group
Broxbourne Bahá'í Local Group
Cherwell Bahá'í Local Group
Chiltern Bahá'í Local Group
Crawley Bahá'í Local Group
Dacorum Bahá'í Local Group
Dover Bahá'í Local Group
Eastleigh Bahá'í Local Group
Fareham Bahá'í Local Group
Gravesham Bahá'í Local Group
Guernsey Local Group
Harlow Bahá'í Local Group
Hart Bahá'í Local Group
Havant Bahá'í Local Group
Horsham Bahá'í Local Group
Jersey Bahá'í Local Group
Maidstone Bahá'í Local Group
Medway Bahá'í Local Group
Mid-Bedfordshire Bahá'í Local Group
Mole Valley Bahá'í Local Group
New Forest Bahá'í Local Group
Newbury Bahá'í Local Local Group
North Hertfordshire Bahá'í Local Group
Portsmouth Bahá'í Local Group
Rushmoor Bahá'í Local Group
St Alban's Bahá'í Local Group
Southampton Bahá'í Local Group
South Bedfordshire Bahá'í Local Group
South Buckinghamshire Bahá'í Local Group
Southend-on-Sea Bahá'í Local Group
Spelthorne Bahá'í Local Group
Swale Bahá'í Local Group

Test Valley Bahá'í Local Group
Thurrock Bahá'í Local Group
Tonbridge and Malling Bahá'í Local Group
Tunbridge Wells Bahá'í Local Group

South West
Bath Bahá'í Local Group
Caradon Bahá'í Local Group
Christchurch Bahá'í Local Group
East Devon Bahá'í Local Group
Kennet Bahá'í Local Group
Kerrier Bahá'í Local Group
Mid-Devon Bahá'í Local Group
North Cornwall Bahá'í Local Group
North Devon Bahá'í Local Group
North Dorset Bahá'í Local Group
Penwith Bahá'í Local Group
Purbeck Bahá'í Local Group
Restormel Bahá'í Local Group
Salisbury Bahá'í Local Group
Sedgemoor Bahá'í Local Group
South Somerset Bahá'í Local Group
Wansdyke Bahá'í Local Group
West Dorset Bahá'í Local Group
West Wiltshire Bahá'í Local Group
Weymouth and Portland Bahá'í Local Group
Wimborne Bahá'í Local Group

NORTHERN IRELAND

Armagh Bahá'í Local Group
Banbridge Bahá'í Local Group
Cookstown Bahá'í Local Group
Fermanagh Bahá'í Local Group
Larne Bahá'í Local Group
Magherafelt Bahá'í Local Group
Moyle Bahá'í Local Group
Newry and Mourne Bahá'í Local Group
Strabane Bahá'í Local Group

SCOTLAND

Argyle and Bute Bahá'í Local Group
Bearsden and Milngavie Bahá'í Local Group
Berwickshire Bahá'í Local Group
Clackmannan Bahá'í Local Group
Clydebank Bahá'í Local Group
Clydesdale Bahá'í Local Group
Cunninghame Bahá'í Local Group
Dumbarton Bahá'í Local Group
Dunfermline Bahá'í Local Group
East Kilbride Bahá'í Local Group

East Lothian Bahá'í Local Group
Eastwood Bahá'í Local Group
Ettrick and Lauderdale Bahá'í Local Group
Falkirk Bahá'í Local Group
Hamilton Bahá'í Local Group
Kilmarnock and Loudoun Bahá'í Local Group
Kincardine and Deeside Bahá'í Local Group
Kirkcaldy Bahá'í Local Group
Lochaber Bahá'í Local Group
Midlothian Bahá'í Local Group
Monklands Bahá'í Local Group
Moray Bahá'í Local Group
Motherwell Bahá'í Local Group
Mull Bahá'í Local Group
Roxburgh Bahá'í Local Group
Stirling Bahá'í Local Group
Sutherland Bahá'í Local Group
Tweedale Bahá'í Local Group
West Lothian Bahá'í Local Group

WALES

Alyn and Deeside Bahá'í Local Group
Blaenau Gwent Bahá'í Local Group
Colwyn Bahá'í Local Group
Cynon Valley Bahá'í Local Group
Delyn Bahá'í Local Group
Dinefwr Bahá'í Local Group
Glyndwr Bahá'í Local Group
Meirionnyd Bahá'í Local Group
Montgomery Bahá'í Local Group
Newport Bahá'í Local Group
Presli Bahá'í Local Group
Radnor Bahá'í Local Group
Rhondda Bahá'í Local Group
Rhuddlan Bahá'í Local Group
Rhymney Valley Bahá'í Local Group
South Pembrokeshire Bahá'í Local Group
Torfaen Bahá'í Local Group
Ynys Mon Bahá'í Local Group
Vale of Glamorgan Bahá'í Local Group

Bahá'í Publishing Trust
6 Mount Pleasant, Oakham, Leicestershire,
LE15 6HU
Tel: 01572-722780 **Fax:** 01572-724280

Bahá'í Service for the Blind
14 Chishill Road, Heydon, Royston,
Hertfordshire, SG8 8PW
Tel: 01763-838309 (h)
Contact: Virginia Barnes

BAHÁ'Í LOCAL SPIRITUAL ASSEMBLIES

Bahá'í *Local Spiritual Assemblies* can be formed when there are at least nine Bahá'ís over the age of twenty-one in a locality. All Bahá'í *Local Spiritual Assemblies* engage in the kind of activities described in "Introducing the Bahá'í Community of the United Kingdom". However, some have highlighted particular activities in their entries.

ENGLAND

NORTH EAST
City, Town or Local Bodies

Spiritual Assembly of the Bahá'ís of Durham
Cross House, 1 St John's Road, Nevilles Cross, Durham City, County Durham, DH1 4NU
Tel: 01913-847152 (h)
Contact: Mr Husayn Bayat
Position: Secretary

Spiritual Assembly of the Bahá'ís of Gateshead
Gateshead, Tyne & Wear, c/o 30 High Ridge, Birtley, Chester-le-Street, County Durham, DH3 1BE (h)
Tel: 0191-410-5927 (h) **Fax:** 0191-414-4687
EMail: ken@kenfinn.demon.co.uk
Contact: Mr Tony Woolmington
Position: Secretary
Activities: Visits, youth, women, inter-faith
Other Languages: Persian, Arabic

Spiritual Assembly of the Bahá'ís of Tynedale
Burnlaw, Whitfield, Tynedale, Hexham, Northumberland, NE47 8HF (h)
Tel: 01434-345391 (h)
Contact: Lorna Silverstein
Position: Chairperson
Activities: Resource, inter-faith

Local Spiritual Assembly of the Bahá'ís of Newcastle upon Tyne
Newcastle upon Tyne, Tyne and Wear, c/o Bahá'í Information Office (UK)
Tel: 0171-584-2566 **Fax:** 0171-584-9402
Contact: Information Officer

Spiritual Assembly of the Bahá'ís of North Tyneside
6 Belsay Avenue, Whitley Bay, Tyne and Wear, NE25 8PZ (h)
Tel: 0191-251-9775 (h)
Contact: Joyce Froughi
Position: Secretary

YORKSHIRE
City, Town or Local Bodies

Spiritual Assembly of the Bahá'ís of Bradford
Moor House, 607 Allerton Road, Allerton, Bradford, West Yorkshire, BD15 8AB (h)

Tel: 01274-544758 (h)
Contact: Robert Arthur Hallam
Position: Chairperson
Activities: Inter-faith
Other Languages: Persian, French, Urdu

Spiritual Assembly of the Bahá'ís of Doncaster
29 Strafforth House, Harrogate Drive, Denaby
Main, Doncaster, South Yorkshire, DN12 4NG (h)
Tel: 01709-770034 (h)
Contact: Mr Reginald Bailey
Position: Secretary
Other Languages: Farsi

Spiritual Assembly of the Bahá'ís of Kirklees
65 Grosvenor Road, Dalton, Huddersfield, West
Yorkshire, HD5 9JB (h)
Tel: 01484-429490 (h)
EMail: graham@jenks.demon.co.uk
Contact: Mr Khosro Deihim
Position: Secretary
Activities: Resource, media, visits, youth, elderly,
women, newsletters, books, inter-faith
Other Languages: Persian

Spiritual Assembly of the Bahá'ís of Leeds
PO Box MT14, Leeds, West Yorkshire, LS17 7UR
Other Languages: Persian

Spiritual Assembly of the Bahá'ís of Sheffield
2 Endowood Road, Sheffield, South Yorkshire,
S7 2LZ (h)
Tel: 01142-2363758 (h)
Contact: Mrs R P Croft
Position: Secretary
Activities: Newsletters, books, inter-faith
Other Languages: Persian, Turkish, Esperanto

Spiritual Assembly of the Bahá'ís of Craven
1 Hothfield Terrace, Carleton Road, Skipton, North
Yorkshire, BD23 2AX (h)
Tel: 01756-795256 (h)
Contact: Mrs Madeline Hellaby
Position: Secretary

Spiritual Assembly of the Bahá'ís of Wakefield
Virginia Cottage, 164 Shay Lane, Walton, Wakefield,
West Yorkshire, WF2 6NP (h)
Tel: 01924-254160 (h)
Contact: Elizabeth Mitchell
Position: Secretary
Activities: Resource, visits
Other Languages: Persian, Swedish, German

Spiritual Assembly of the Bahá'ís of York
West View, 112 Clifton, Clifton, York, North
Yorkshire, Y03 6BA (h)
Tel: 01904-641657 (h)
Contact: Mrs Patricia Castle
Position: Secretary
Activities: Inter-faith
Other Languages: Farsee

NORTH WEST
City, Town or Local Bodies

Spiritual Assembly of the Bahá'ís of Burnley
Bahá'í Centre, 9 Colne Road, Burnley, Lancashire,
BB10 1LD
Tel: 01282-832973 **Tel:** 01282-424356 (h)
Contact: Marion Pollitt
Position: Secretary
Activities: Worship, resource, visits, youth, women,
newsletters, books, inter-faith
Other Languages: Farsi

Spiritual Assembly of the Bahá'ís of Chester
1 Windermere Avenue, Chester, Cheshire,
CH2 2PS (h)
Tel: 01244-321800 (h)
Contact: Miss Margaret Lord
Position: Secretary

Spiritual Assembly of the Bahá'ís of Liverpool
Bahá'í Centre, 3 Langdale Road, Liverpool,
Merseyside, L15 3LA
Tel: 0151-733-4700 (h)
Contact: Eddie Ashton

*Spiritual Assembly of the Bahá'ís of
Macclesfield*
112a Dean Drive, Macclesfield, Cheshire,
SK9 2EY (h)
Tel: 01625-524044 (h) **Fax:** 01625-524044
Contact: Mrs H Clack
Position: Secretary
Activities: Resource, media, youth, elderly,
women, inter-faith
Other Languages: Iranian

*Spiritual Assembly of the Bahá'ís of
Manchester*
Bahá'í Centre, 360 Wilmslow Road, Fallowfield,
Manchester, Greater Manchester, M14 0AB
Tel: 0161-224-6490
Contact: Martin Perry

Position: Centre Manager
Activities: Worship, resource, visits, youth, newsletters, books, inter-faith
Other Languages: Farsi, Arabic, Portugese, French

Spiritual Assembly of the Baháʼís of Pendle
99 Carr Road, Nelson, Lancashire, BB9 7SS (h)
Tel: 01282-832973 **Tel:** 01282-691364 (h)
Contact: Mrs Dorothy MacInnes
Position: Secretary
Activities: Worship, resource, visits, youth, newsletters

Spiritual Assembly of the Baháʼís of Preston
20 Fulwood Hall Lane, Fulwood, Preston, Lancashire, PR2 8DB (h)
Tel: 01772-700539 (h)
EMail: malcolm@doclands.demon.co.uk
Contact: Dr Malcolm Craig
Position: Chair
Activities: Inter-faith
Other Languages: Arabic, Persian

Spiritual Assembly of the Baháʼís of St Helens
St Helens, Merseyside, c/o 18 Park Road North, Newton-Le-Willows, Merseyside, WA12 9TE (h)
Tel: 01925-222372 (h)
Contact: Mrs Pauline Samson
Position: Chairperson
Activities: Youth, inter-faith

Spiritual Assembly of the Baháʼís of Trafford
41 Bankfield Road, Sale, Cheshire, M33 5QD (h)
Tel: 0161-962-0817 (h)
Contact: Mrs Shohreh Ashraf-Cooper
Position: Secretary

Spiritual Assembly of the Baháʼís of Salford
100 Kersal Road, Kersal, Salford, Greater Manchester, M7 0QL (h)
Contact: Sidney Rawlings
Position: Chair
Activities: Worship, visits, youth, inter-faith
Other Languages: Persian

Spiritual Assembly of the Baháʼís of Sefton
Sefton, Merseyside, c/o Baháʼí Information Office (UK)
Tel: 0171-584-2566 **Fax:** 0171-584-9402
Contact: Information Officer

Spiritual Assembly of the Baháʼís of Stockport
Stockport, Greater Manchester, c/o Manchester

Baháʼí Centre (Manchester)
Tel: 0161-224-6490
Contact: Secretary

Spiritual Assembly of the Baháʼís of Wirral
21 Downes Green, Spital, Wirral, Merseyside, L63 9LX (h)
Tel: 0151-334-0740 (h)
Contact: John Netherwood
Position: Secretary
Activities: Resource, visits, youth, elderly, women, newsletters, books, inter-faith
Other Languages: Persian

EAST MIDLANDS
City, Town or Local Bodies

Spiritual Assembly of the Baháʼís of Chesterfield
12 Boythorpe Crescent, Boythorpe, Chesterfield, Derbyshire, S40 2NX (h)
Tel: 01246-211753 (h)
Contact: Mr Jonathan Atkinson
Position: Secretary
Activities: Inter-faith
Other Languages: Farsi, Arabic, Basic Esperanto

Spiritual Assembly of the Baháʼís of Daventry
18 Peartree Close, Arbury Park, Daventry, Northamptonshire, NN11 5XB (h)
Tel: 01327-871113 (h)
Contact: Mr S Dehghani
Position: Secretary
Activities: Resource, visits, youth, women, newsletters, books, inter-faith

Spiritual Assembly of the Baháʼís of Derby
27 Ferrers Way, Darley Abbey, Derby, Derbyshire, DE22 2BA (h)
Tel: 01332-557463 (h)
Contact: Mrs N Taleb
Position: Secretary
Activities: Resource, media, visits, youth, elderly women, newsletters, inter-faith

Spiritual Assembly of the Baháʼís of Kettering
69 Havelock Street, Kettering, Northamptonshire, NN16 9QA
Tel: 01536-519080 (h)
Contact: Mrs Teresa Attwood
Position: Secretary

Spiritual Assembly of the Bahá'ís of Leicester
22 Percival Street, Leicester, Leicestershire,
LE5 3NP (h)
Tel: 0116-251-3273 (h)
Contact: Mr Roderic Maude
Position: Secretary
Activities: Inter-faith
Other Languages: Persian

Spiritual Assembly of the Bahá'ís of Charnwood
1 Outwoods Drive, Loughborough, Leicestershire,
LE11 3LR (h)
Tel: 01509-232212 (h)
Contact: Mrs Parvaneh Brookshaw
Position: Chair
Activities: Youth, elderly, women

Spiritual Assembly of the Bahá'ís of Northampton
15 Spyglass Hill, Northampton, Northamptonshire,
NN4 0US (h)
Tel: 01604-769825 (h)
EMail: 101361.3645@compuserve.com
Contact: Mrs Susan Phillips
Position: Secretary

Spiritual Assembly of the Bahá'ís of Nottingham
57 Ashchurch Drive, Wollaton, Nottingham,
Nottinghamshire, NG8 2RB (h)
Contact: Secretary
Activities: Visits, youth, newsletters, inter-faith
Other Languages: Persian, Arabic, German, Punjabi

Spiritual Assembly of the Bahá'ís of Rutland
67 Kings Road, Oakham, Leicestershire,
LE15 6PB (h)
Tel: 01572-724179 (h)   **Fax:** 01572-724280
EMail: george@haibooks.co.uk
Contact: George M Ballentyne
Position: Secretary
Other Languages: Persian

WEST MIDLANDS
City, Town or Local Bodies

Spiritual Assembly of the Bahá'ís of Birmingham
11 Selwyn Road, Edgbaston, Birmingham, West
Midlands, B16 0SH (h)
Tel: 0121-454-2387 (h)

Contact: Mrs Vicki Warwick
Position: Treasurer
Activities: Resource, media, umbrella, youth,
elderly, women, newsletters, inter-faith
Other Languages: Persian, African, Urdu

Spiritual Assembly of the Bahá'ís of Coventry
72 Abbey Cottages, Binley, Coventry, West
Midlands, CV3 2EL (h)
Tel: 01203-444636 (h)
Contact: Margaret Hughes
Position: Secretary
Activities: Inter-faith
Other Languages: Iranian

Spiritual Assembly of the Bahá'ís of Hereford
4 Windermere Road, Hereford, Hereford and
Worcester, HR4 9PR (h)
Tel: 01432-277903 (h)
EMail: pete@anisa.demon.co.uk
Contact: Mrs Zarin Hulme
Position: Secretary
Activities: Visits

Spiritual Assembly of the Bahá'ís of Nuneaton & Bedworth
120 Higham Lane, Nuneaton, Warwickshire (h)
Contact: Mr John Neal
Position: Media Officer
Tel: 01203-350268
EMail: Jarvid@vossough.softnet.co.uk
Activities: Visitors, women, inter-faith
Other Languages: Persian

Spiritual Assembly of the Bahá'ís of Rugby
29 Rokeby Court, 295 Dunchurch Road, Rugby,
Warwickshire, CV22 6RS
Tel: 01788-522724 (h)
Contact: Mrs Penelope Viola
Position: Secretary

Spiritual Assembly of the Bahá'ís of Shrewsbury & Atcham
7 Darwin Street, Mountfields, Shrewsbury,
Shropshire, SY3 8QE (h)
Tel: 01743-360886 (h)
Contact: Mr John Bardsley
Position: Secretary

Spiritual Assembly of the Bahá'ís of Stoke-on-Trent
154 Pacific Road, Trentham, Stoke-on-Trent,
Staffordshire, ST4 8UD

Tel: 01782-643926
Contact: Information Officer

Spiritual Assembly of the Bahá'ís of Stratford on Avon

Stratford-upon-Avon, Warwickshire, c/o 6 Welsh Road West, Southam, Leamington Spa, Warwickshire, CV33 0JN
Tel: 01926-817291 (h)
Contact: Mrs Ann Vickers
Position: Secretary

Spiritual Assembly of the Bahá'ís of The Wrekin

54 Castlecroft, Stirchley, Telford, Shropshire, TF3 1UE (h)
Contact: Kerry Day
Position: Secretary

Spiritual Assembly of the Bahá'ís of Warwick

Warwick, Warwickshire, c/o 18 Blakelands Avenue, Leamington Spa, Warwickshire, CV31 1RJ (h)
Tel: 01926-312342 (h)
EMail: rocky@mercia.demon.co.uk
Contact: Rocky Grove
Position: Chairman
Activities: Books, inter-faith
Other Languages: Farsi, French

EAST ANGLIA
City, Town or Local Bodies

Spiritual Assembly of the Bahá'ís of Waveney

23 The Green, Henham, Beccles, Suffolk, NR34 8AJ (h)
Tel: 01502-578466 (h)
Contact: Mrs Rosemary Morgan
Position: Secretary
Activities: Worship, resource, inter-faith
Other Languages: Persian

Spiritual Assembly of the Bahá'ís of Cambridge

PO Box 277, Cambridge, Cambridgeshire, CB4 2HY
Tel: 01223-513351 (h)
EMail: msp@cambustion.co.uk
Contact: Dr Mark Peckham
Activities: Resource, visits, youth, newsletters, inter-faith
Other Languages: Persian, French, Arabic

Spiritual Assembly of the Bahá'ís of Ipswich

34 Eustace Road, Ipswich, Suffolk, IP1 5BT (h)
Tel: 01473-741792 (h)
Contact: Elizabeth Stewart
Position: Secretary
Activities: Worship, newsletters, books, inter-faith
Other Languages: Farsi

Spiritual Assembly of the Bahá'ís of Norwich

23 Mount Pleasant, Norwich, Norfolk, NR2 2DH (h)
Tel: 01603-250184 (h)
Contact: Mrs Natasha Wilkinson
Position: Secretary

Spiritual Assembly of the Bahá'ís of South Norfolk

27 Bridge Street, Loddon, Norwich, Norfolk
Contact: Josephine Fillery
Position: Secretary

Spiritual Assembly of the Bahá'ís of South Cambridge

Cambridge, Cambridgeshire, c/o Picots, 14 Chishill Road, Heydon, Royston, Hertfordshire, SG8 8PW
Tel: 01763-838309 (h)
Contact: Mrs Virginia Barnes
Position: Secretary

GREATER LONDON
Borough or Area Bodies

BARNET

Spiritual Assembly of the Bahá'ís of Barnet

99 Marshall Close, New Southgate, London, N11 1TG
Tel: 0181-361-7093
Contact: Mrs Jaleh Alaee
Other Languages: Persian, French, German

BRENT

Spiritual Assembly of the Bahá'ís of Brent

PO Box 392, Wembley, Middlesex, HA9 8AW
Tel: 0171-584-2566
Contact: Mr Farid Alexander Afnan
Position: Secretary
Activities: Resource, inter-faith
Other Languages: Farsi, Arabic, French, Spanish

CAMDEN

Spiritual Assembly of the Bahá'ís of Camden
6 West Heath Close, London, NW3 7NJ (h)
Tel: 0171-435-0825 (h)
Contact: Mrs Mehrjahan
Position: Secretary

CROYDON

Spiritual Assembly of the Bahá'ís of Croydon
45 Midhurst Avenue, Croydon, Surrey, CR0 3PS (h)
Tel: 0181-664-8869 (h)
Contact: Mr Abbas Erfani
Position: Secretary

EALING

Spiritual Assembly of the Bahá'ís of Ealing
Ealing, c/o Bahá'í Information Office (UK)
Tel: 0171-584-2566 **Fax:** 0171-584-9402
Contact: Information Officer

ENFIELD

Spiritual Assembly of the Bahá'ís of Enfield
51 St Georges Road, Enfield, EN1 4TYQ (h)
Tel: 0181-363-7931 (h)
Contact: Mr Gerrard Francis-Smith
Position: Chairman
Activities: Youth, women, inter-faith
Other Languages: Farsi, Arabic, Malay, Turkish

GREENWICH

Spiritual Assembly of the Bahá'ís of Greenwich
200 Conway Road, Plumstead, London, SE18 1BE
Tel: 0181-316-5627 (h)
Contact: Mr Farhad Raoufian
Position: Secretary

HACKNEY

Spiritual Assembly of the Bahá'ís of Hackney
80 Mount Pleasant Hill, Clapton, London, E5 9NF (h)
Tel: 0181-806-1312 (h)
Contact: Cedric L Osbourne
Position: Secretary
Activities: Worship, resource, media, visits, youth, newsletter, books, inter-faith
Other Languages: Persian, Turkish, French, German

HAMMERSMITH AND FULHAM

Spiritual Assembly of the Bahá'ís of Hammersmith & Fulham
Hammersmith and Fulham, c/o Bahá'í Information Office (UK)
Tel: 0171-584-2566 **Fax:** 0171-584-9402
Contact: Information Officer

HARINGEY

Spiritual Assembly of the Bahá'ís of Haringey
21 Alfloxton Avenue, London, N15 3DD
Tel: 0181-888-7436 (h)
Contact: Miss Teresa Parsons
Position: Secretary

HARROW

Spiritual Assembly of the Bahá'ís of Harrow
8 Limedene Close, Uxbridge Road, Pinner, Middlesex, HA5 3PX (h)
Fax: 0181-868-4690,
Contact: Mrs Homa Saadat
Position: Secretary
Activities: Resource, newsletters, books, inter-faith
Other Languages: Persian

HAVERING

Spiritual Assembly of the Bahá'ís of Havering
Havering, c/o Bahá'í Information Office (UK)
Tel: 0171-584-2566 **Fax:** 0171-584-9402
Contact: Information Officer
Activities: Inter-faith
Other Languages: Persian

HILLINGDON

Spiritual Assembly of the Bahá'ís of Hillingdon
107 Ploe Hill Road, Hillingdon, Middlesex, UB10 0QD
Tel: 0181-848-1314 (h)
Contact: Mrs Mehrnoosh Vahdat-Hagh
Position: Secretary

HOUNSLOW

Local Spiritual Assembly of the Bahá'ís of Hounslow
PO Box 189, Hounslow, Middlesex, TW5 9YA
Contact: Secretary
Other Languages: Farsi, French, Arabic

KENSINGTON AND CHELSEA

Spiritual Assembly of the Bahá'ís of Kensington & Chelsea
Newhaven, 26b Lonsdale Road, Notting Hill Gate, London, W11 2DE (h)
Tel: 0171-727-0254 (h)
EMail: carmen@bahai.compulink.co.uk
Contact: Carmen Henry
Position: Secretary
Activities: Worship, resource, media, umbrella, visits, youth, elderly, women, newsletters, books, inter-faith
Other Languages: Persian, Welsh, Arabic, Czech

KINGSTON-UPON-THAMES

Spiritual Assembly of the Bahá'ís of Kingston-upon-Thames
6 The Mall, Surbiton, Kingston-upon-Thames, Surrey, KT6 4EQ
Tel: 0181-390-4886 (h)
Contact: Dianne Dean
Position: Secretary
Activities: Resource, newsletters, inter-faith
Other Languages: Persian/Farsi, Arabic, French

LAMBETH

Spiritual Assembly of the Bahá'ís of Lambeth
33 Winslade Road, Brixton, London, SW2 5JL (h)
Contact: Marc King
Position: Chairperson
Activities: Visits, inter-faith
Other Languages: Farsi, Italian, Kiswahili, Creole

LEWISHAM

Spiritual Assembly of the Bahá'ís of Lewisham
38 Manor Lane Terrace, Lewisham, London, SE13 5QS
Tel: 0181-852-9324 (h)
Contact: Mrs Semiramis Sohrabian-Bailey
Position: Secretary

MERTON

Spiritual Assembly of the Bahá'ís of Merton
237 Cannon Hill Lane, Raynes Park, London, SW20 9DB (h)
Tel: 0181-542-7126 (h)
Contact: Mr & Dr Howlett

Position: Members
Activities: Resource, media, youth, women, newsletters, books, inter-faith

NEWHAM

Spiritual Assembly of the Bahá'ís of Newham
105a Osborne Road, Forest Gate, Newham, London, E7 0PP (h)
Tel: 0181-522-1585 (h)
Contact: Mr & Mrs Hedayati
Position: Chair & Vice Chair
Activities: Inter-faith
Other Languages: Persian

REDBRIDGE

Spiritual Assembly of the Bahá'ís of Redbridge
c/o 5, Long Green, Chigwell, Essex, IG7 4JB
Contact: Mrs Roya Rostami
Position: Secretary
Activities: Youth, newsletters, books, inter-faith
Other Languages: Farsi, French, Italian

RICHMOND-UPON-THAMES

Spiritual Assembly of the Bahá'ís of Richmond upon Thames
49 Ferry Road, Barnes, London, SW13 9PP (h)
Tel: 0181-748-3505 (h)
Contact: Mrs Christine Nicholas
Position: Secretary

SOUTHWARK

Spiritual Assembly of the Bahá'ís of Southwark
38 Kirwyn Way, Bethwin Road, Southwark, London, SE5 0YA (h)
Tel: 0171-703-2515 (h)
Contact: Mrs Sadat Hedayati
Other Languages: Farsi

SUTTON

Spiritual Assembly of the Bahá'ís of Sutton
Flat 2, 110 Benhill Road, Sutton, Surrey, SM1 3RS (h)
Tel: 0181-661-6375 (h)
Contact: Farshid Khalili
Position: Secretary
Activities: Inter-faith
Other Languages: Persian

WANDSWORTH

Spiritual Assembly of the Bahá'ís of Wandsworth
1043 Garratt Lane, London, SW17 0LN
Tel: 0181-682-3394 (h)
EMail: jim@tooting.u-net.com
Contact: Jim Jenkins
Position: Secretary

WESTMINSTER, CITY OF

Spiritual Assembly of the Bahá'ís of Westminster
Flat D, 30 Claverton Street, London, SW1V 3AU (h)
Tel: 0171-584-2566
Contact: Dominick Browne
Position: Secretary
Activities: Visits, youth, elderly, women, newsletters, books, inter-faith
Other Languages: Iranian, Arabic, French

SOUTH EAST
City, Town or Local Bodies

Spiritual Assembly of the Bahá'ís of South Oxfordshire
Guildown House, Burcot, Abingdon, Oxfordshire, OX14 3DW (h)
Tel: 01865-407887 (h) **Fax:** 01491-681122
EMail: hughfixsal@compuserve.com
Contact: Philip Koomen
Position: Secretary
Activities: Worship, resource, visits, youth, women, newsletters, books, inter-faith
Other Languages: German, French, Dutch, Persian

Spiritual Assembly of the Bahá'ís of the Vale of White Horse
45 The Warren, Abingdon, Oxfordshire, OX14 3XB (h)
Tel: 01235-522641 (h) **Fax:** 01235-463004
EMail: roger.kingdon@aeat.co.uk
Contact: Dr Roger Kingdon
Position: Secretary
Activities: Resource, inter-faith
Other Languages: Persian, Hindi

Spiritual Assembly of the Bahá'ís of Aylesbury Vale
5 Lisburn Path, Aylesbury, Buckinghamshire, HP20 2BQ (h)
Tel: 01296-25087 (h)

Contact: Mrs Jacqueline Harle
Position: Secretary

Spiritual Assembly of the Bahá'ís of Basingstoke & Deane
16 Horwood Gardens, Cranbourne, Basingstoke, Hampshire, RG21 3NR
Tel: 01256-50187 (h)
Contact: Mrs Zarin Hainsworth-Fadaei
Position: Secretary
Activities: Youth, inter-faith
Other Languages: Dutch, Persian

Local Spiritual Assembly of the Bahá'ís of Bedford
19 Costin Street, Bedford, Bedfordshire, MK40 1RD (h)
Tel: 01234-219143 (h)
Contact: Mrs Maureen Potter
Position: Secretary

Spiritual Assembly of the Bahá'ís of Bexley
Bexley, Kent, c/o Flat 4, 1 Lesney Park Road, Erith, Kent, DA8 3DQ (h)
Tel: 01322-349233 (h)
Contact: Martin Jeremy Lockyer
Position: Secretary
Activities: Inter-faith
Other Languages: Farsi

Spiritual Assembly of the Bahá'ís of Bracknell Forest
55 Quadrant Court, Martins Lane, Bracknell, Berkshire, RG12 4EW (h)
Tel: 01344-426581 (h)
Contact: Mr Gerald King
Position: Secretary

Spiritual Assembly of the Bahá'ís of Brighton & Hove
Bahá'í Centre, 19 Stanford Avenue, Brighton, East Sussex, BN1 6GA
Tel: 01273-505895
Contact: Secretary
Activities: Worship, resource, media, visits, youth, women, inter-faith

Spiritual Assembly of the Bahá'ís of Thanet
39 Weatherly Drive, Nicholls Avenue, Broadstairs, Kent, CT10 2EE (h)
Tel: 01843-868896 (h)
Contact: Miss Parissa Azizi
Position: Secretary

Spiritual Assembly of the Bahá'ís of Bromley
43, Ravensbourne Road, Bromley, Kent,
BR1 1HW (h)
Tel: 0181-290-1989 (h)
Contact: I. Aqdasi
Position: Secretary
Activities: Worship, resource, media, visits, youth,
elderly, women, newsletters, inter-faith
Other Languages: Arabic, Persian, German

Spiritual Assembly of the Bahá'ís of Hertsmere
Carmel, 11b King George Avenue, Hertsmere,
Bushey, Hertfordshire, WD2 3NT (h)
Tel: 0181-950-2561 (h)
Contact: Miss Farang Moshtael
Position: Secretary
Other Languages: Persian

Spiritual Assembly of the Bahá'ís of Canterbury
5 Rhodaus Close, Canterbury, Kent, CT1 2RE (h)
Tel: 01227-768458 (h)
Contact: Arthur Weinberg
Position: Secretary
Activities: Resource, youth, inter-faith

Spiritual Assembly of the Bahá'ís of Chelmsford
128 Redmayne Drive, Chelmsford, Essex,
CM2 9XE (h)
Tel: 01245-284663 (h)
Contact: Mrs Mitra Murray
Position: Secretary

Spiritual Assembly of the Bahá'ís of Chichester
100 Chatsworth Road, Chichester, West Sussex,
PO19 2YJ (h)
Tel: 01243-539715 (h)
Contact: Mrs Katherine Massoumian
Position: Secretary

Spiritual Assembly of the Bahá'ís of Colchester
16 Mayberry Walk, Colchester, Essex, C02 8PS (h)
Tel: 01206-765379 (h)
Contact: Mrs Angela Tidswell
Position: Secretary
Activities: Inter-faith

Spiritual Assembly of the Bahá'ís of Eastbourne
Eastbourne, East Sussex, c/o Bahai Information
Office (UK)
Tel: 0171-584-2566   **Fax:** 0171 5849402
Contact: Information Officer

Spiritual Assembly of the Bahá'ís of Epping Forest
35 Allnutts Road, Epping, Essex, CM16 7BE
Tel: 01992-570149 (h)
Contact: Mrs Gillian Clark
Position: Secretary

**Spiritual Assembly of the Bahá'ís of Epsom &
Ewell**
46 Pitt Place, Church Street, Epsom, Surrey,
KT17 4PY (h)
Tel: 01372-739651 (h)
Contact: Mr Hossein Shirinzadeh
Position: Secretary

Spiritual Assembly of the Bahá'ís of Shepway
31 Morrison Road, Folkestone, Kent, CT20 1PQ
Tel: 01303-243907 (h)
Contact: Mr & Mrs Defremont
Position: Secretary

Spiritual Assembly of the Bahá'ís of Gillingham
Gillingham, Kent, c/o 39 Moor Park Close,
Rainham, Kent, ME8 8QS (h)
Tel: 01634-389364 (h)
Contact: Mrs Sharon Forghani Ashrafi
Position: Secretary
Activities: Resource, visits, youth, inter-faith
Other Languages: Persian

Spiritual Assembly of the Bahá'ís of Waverley
11 Nursery Road, Farncombe, Godalming, Surrey,
GU7 3JU (h)
Tel: 01483-415773   **Tel:** 01483-274979 (h)
EMail: 101520.2510@compuserve.comm
Contact: Mrs Carolyn Neogi
Position: Secretary
Activities: Resource, youth, women, newsletters,
books, inter-faith
Other Languages: Farsi, Arabic, French, Bengali

Spiritual Assembly of the Bahá'ís of Guildford
12 Lapwing Grove, Merrow Park, Guildford, Surrey,
GU4 7DZ (h)
Tel: 01483-568926 (h)
EMail: 106131.1062@compuserve.com
Contact: Mr Edgar Boyett
Position: Secretary
Other Languages: Persian

Spiritual Assembly of the Bahá'ís of Hastings
57 Milward Road, Hastings, East Sussex,
TN34 3RP (h)

Tel: 01424-430783 (h) **Fax:** 01424-430783
EMail: 100645.3173@compuserve.com
Contact: Mike McCandless
Position: Vice Chairman
Activities: Visits, inter-faith
Other Languages: Farsi, French

Spiritual Assembly of the Bahá'ís of Welwyn & Hatfield
2 Richmond Court, Hatfield, Hertfordshire,
AL10 8XS (h)
Tel: 01707-270254 (h) **Fax:** 01707-270254
Contact: Mr Nersey Rastan
Position: Secretary
Activities: Inter-faith

Spiritual Assembly of the Bahá'ís of Mid Sussex
4 The Spinney, Haywards Heath, West Sussex,
RN16 1PL (h)
Tel: 01444-450091 (h)
Contact: Dr Farhang Tahzib
Position: Secretary

Spiritual Assembly of the Bahá'ís of Wycombe
11 Wellfield, Hazlemere, High Wycombe,
Buckinghamshire, HP15 7TJ (h)
Tel: 01494-814551 (h)
Contact: Shahram Alaee
Position: Secretary
Activities: Visits, inter-faith
Other Languages: Iranian

Spiritual Assembly of the Bahá'ís of Hove & Portslade
6 Princes Avenue, Hove, East Sussex, BN3 4GD (h)
Tel: 01273-705155 (h)
Contact: Miss Mojgan Hajatdoost-Sani
Position: Secretary

Spiritual Assembly of the Bahá'ís of Lewes
Warren Peace, Swanborough, Lewes, East Sussex,
BN7 3PQ (h)
Tel: 01273-480660 (h)
Contact: Lynda and Russell Hill
Position: Secretary

Spiritual Assembly of the Bahá'ís of Luton
47 Bracklesham Gardens, Luton, Bedfordshire,
LU2 8QJ
Tel: 01582-480859 (h) **Fax:** 01582-415956
EMail: Karl.Beech@smlawpub.co.uk
Contact: Karl Beech

Position: Vice Chairman
Activities: Inter-faith
Other Languages: Persian

Spiritual Assembly of the Bahá'ís of Windsor & Maidenhead
40 Osney Road, Maidenhead, Berkshire, SL6 7UQ
Tel: 01628-37801 (h)
Contact: Mrs J Gammage
Position: Secretary

Spiritual Assembly of the Bahá'ís of Milton Keynes
38a Bradwell Road, Loughton, Milton Keynes,
Buckinghamshire, MK5 8AJ (h)
Tel: 01908-671734 (h)
Contact: Malihe Sanatian
Position: Secretary
Activities: Worship, youth, inter-faith
Other Languages: Persian, Spanish

Spiritual Assembly of the Bahá'ís of Oxford
185 Banbury Road, Oxford, Oxfordshire,
OX2 7AR
Tel: 01865-311940 (h)
Contact: Ms Juliet Mabey
Position: Information Officer
Activities: Worship, women, youth, visits, inter-faith
Other Languages: Arabic, Persian, French

Spiritual Assembly of the Bahá'ís of Reading
84 Waverley Road, Reading, Berkshire,
RG30 2PY (h)
Tel: 01734-590233 (h)
Contact: James William Talbot
Position: Secretary
Other Languages: Persian

Spiritual Assembly of the Bahá'ís of Reigate & Banstead
6 Woodlands Road, Redhill, Surrey, RH1 6HA (h)
Tel: 01737-765325 (h)
Contact: Mr Martin Kay
Position: Secretary

Spiritual Assembly of the Bahá'ís of Shepway
Judeda, 74 Cedar Crescent, St Mary's Bay, Romney
Marsh, Kent, TN23 0XJ
Tel: 01303-873663 (h)
Contact: Mrs Siân Johnson
Position: Secretary
Other Languages: French

Spiritual Assembly of the Bahá'ís of Runnymede
c/o Royal Holloway College (English Department,
University of London, Egham, Surrey, TW20 0EX)
Tel: 01784-433380 (h)
EMail: s.kumaran@rhbnc.ac.uk
Contact: Mrs Seyedi
Position: Secretary

Spiritual Assembly of the Bahá'ís of Isle of Wight
Welcome Inn, 7 John Street, Ryde, Isle of Wight,
PO33 2RE (h)
Tel: 01983-615623 (h)
Contact: Clair Pope
Position: Secretary

**Spiritual Assembly of the Bahá'ís of East
Hertfordshire**
1 The Stables, Great Hyde Hall, Sawbridgeworth,
Hertfordshire, CM21 9JA (h)
Tel: 01279-724894 (h)
Contact: Mr Weston G Huxtable
Position: Secretary

Spiritual Assembly of the Bahá'ís of Sevenoaks
The Middle House, Morants Court, Dunton
Green, Sevenoaks, Kent, TN14 6HD (h)
Tel: 01732-462328 (h)   **Fax:** 01732-462849
EMail: loishains@gn.apc.org
Contact: Mrs Lois Hainsworth
Position: Secretary

Spiritual Assembly of the Bahá'ís of Slough
121a Goodman Park, Slough, Berkshire, SL2 5NR
Contact: R Thorpe
Position: Secretary
Activities: Inter-faith

Spiritual Assembly of the Bahá'ís of Stevenage
60 Buckthorn Avenue, Stevenage, Hertfordshire,
SG1 1TU (h)
Tel: 01438-220483 (h)
Contact: Mr Oliver Christopherson
Position: Secretary
Activities: Youth, inter-faith
Other Languages: Farsi

Spiritual Assembly of the Bahá'ís of Elmbridge
Willowstream, Wheatleys Ait, The Creek, Sunbury,
Middlesex, TW16 6DA (h)
Tel: 01932-761120 (h)
Contact: Norma Scott

Spiritual Assembly of the Bahá'ís of Wealden
8 Campbell Close, Uckfield, East Sussex,
TN22 1DR (h)
Tel: 01825-761443 (h)
EMail: bahai-wealden@nur.win-uk.net
Contact: Mr Paul Booth
Position: Secretary
Activities: Resource, visits, newsletters, inter-faith
Other Languages: Persian, Welsh

Spiritual Assembly of the Bahá'ís of Three Rivers
PO Box 489, Watford, Hertfordshire, WD1 5LA
EMail: hozi@moose.co.uk
Contact: Mr Hootan Zahrai
Position: Secretary
Activities: Resource, visits, youth, women, inter-
faith
Other Languages: Persian

Spiritual Assembly of the Bahá'ís of Watford
55 Hare Crescent, Leavesden, Watford,
Hertfordshire, WD2 7EE (h)
Tel: 01923-671135 (h)
Contact: Mrs Irandokht Ghobad
Position: Secretary
Activities: Visits, inter-faith
Other Languages: Persian

Spiritual Assembly of the Bahá'ís of Winchester
Ty Croeso, 21 Hyde Close, Winchester, Hampshire,
SO23 7DT (h)
Tel: 01962-865924 (h)
Contact: Mrs Barbara Lewis
Position: Secretary
Activities: Worship, visits, youth, elderly, women,
newsletters, inter-faith
Other Languages: Italian, German, Persian

Spiritual Assembly of the Bahá'ís of Woking
8 Thorsden Close, Woking, Surrey, GU22 7QX (h)
Tel: 01483-740607 (h)
Contact: Miss Ladan Lamakan
Position: Secretary

Spiritual Assembly of the Bahá'ís of Wokingham
Wokingham, Berkshire, c/o 37 Watmore Lane,
Winnersh, Berkshire, RG41 5JS (h)
Tel: 01734-794558 (h)
Contact: Mr R Friend
Position: Vice-Chair
Activities: Resource

Spiritual Assembly of the Bahá'ís of Tandridge
Overdale, Park View Road, Woldingham, Surrey,
CR3 7DJ (h)
Tel: 01883-652288 (h)
Contact: Shadram Braunstein
Position: Secretary

Spiritual Assembly of the Bahá'ís of West Oxfordshire
2 Glovers Close, Woodstock, Oxfordshire,
OX20 1NS
Tel: 01993-812401 (h)
Contact: Dr Stephen Vickers
Position: Secretary

Spiritual Assembly of the Bahá'ís of Worthing
11 Dorchester Gardens, Grand Avenue, Worthing,
East Sussex, BN11 5AY (h)
Tel: 01903-504213 (h)
EMail: coorousmo@controls.eurotherm.co.uk
Contact: Mrs Mojdeh Mohtadi
Position: Secretary

SOUTH WEST
City, Town or Local Bodies

Spiritual Assembly of the Bahá'ís of Bournemouth
59 Christchurch Road, Bournemouth, Dorset,
BH1 3PA (h)
Tel: 01202-391420 (h)
Contact: Mrs Najla Loughlin
Position: Secretary

Spiritual Assembly of the Bahá'ís of Bristol
49 Maplestone Road, Bristol, Greater Bristol,
BS14 0HQ (h)
Tel: 01275-837566 (h)
Contact: Mr and Mrs Eames
Position: Secretary

Spiritual Assembly of the Bahá'ís of South Gloucestershire
27 Pentland Avenue, Thornbury, Bristol, Greater
Bristol, BS12 2YB (h)
Tel: 01454-413917 (h)
Contact: Mrs Janet Dedman
Position: Secretary

Spiritual Assembly of the Bahá'ís of North Somerset
Woodsmoke, Glen Avenue, Sandy Lane, Abbots
Leigh, Bristol, Greater Bristol, BS8 3SD (h)

Tel: 01275-372040 (h)   **Fax:** 01275-375474
EMail: Wades@cix.compulink.co.uk
Contact: John & Carolyn Wade
Position: Secretary
Activities: Resource, visits, youth, inter-faith
Other Languages: Persian, Spanish

Spiritual Assembly of the Bahá'ís of North Wiltshire
4 Fishers Brook, Calne, Wiltshire, SN11 9HB (h)
Tel: 01249-815168 (h)
Contact: Ms Eira Fillis
Position: Secretary
Activities: Worship, resource, media, visits, youth,
women, inter-faith
Other Languages: Persian, Arabic, Welsh, Tamil

Spiritual Assembly of the Bahá'ís of Teignbridge
c/o 32 New Exeter Street, Chudleigh, Devon,
TQ13 0DA
Tel: 01626-853479 (h)
Contact: Ms Helen Babb
Position: Secretary

Spiritual Assembly of the Bahá'ís of Exeter
29 Wear Barton Road, Countesswear, Exeter, Devon,
EX2 7EH (h)
Tel: 01392-873817 (h)
Contact: Mrs Sharareh Rouhipour
Position: Secretary

Spiritual Assembly of the Bahá'ís of South Hams
Tranquillity, 9 Greenbanks Close, Slapton,
Kingsbridge, Devon, TQ7 2PZ
Tel: 01548-580887 (h)
Contact: Mr John Pirkis
Position: Secretary
Activities: Resource, visits, youth, elderly, women,
inter-faith

Spiritual Assembly of the Bahá'ís of Wychavon
2 Allesborough Drive, Pershore, Worcester,
Worcestershire, WR10 1JH (h)
Tel: 01386-553831 (h)
Contact: Mr Adam Thorne
Position: Secretary
Activities: Resource, visits, youth, elderly, women,
inter-faith
Other Languages: Persian

Spiritual Assembly of the Bahá'ís of Plymouth
21 Dale Road, Mutley, Plymouth, Devon,
PL4 6PH (h)

Tel: 01752-267882 (h)
Contact: Miss Arezoo Farahzad
Position: Secretary
Activities: Visits, youth, women, inter-faith
Other Languages: Iranian

Spiritual Assembly of the Bahá'ís of Poole
8 Scarf Road, Poole, Dorset (h)
Tel: 01202-382377 (h)
Contact: M Tempest

Spiritual Assembly of the Bahá'ís of Carrick
Kuffi, Wheal Friendly, St Agnes, Cornwall, TR5 0SR
Tel: 01872-553184 (h)
Contact: Mrs Diane Profaska
Position: Secretary

Spiritual Assembly of the Bahá'ís of Thamesdown
16 Tower Road, Peatmoor, Swindon, Wiltshire,
SN5 5BG (h)
Tel: 01793-873877 (h) **Fax:** 01793-873877 (h)
EMail: 101336.2736@compuserve.com
Contact: Mrs Neda Rezvani-Krishnan
Position: Secretary
Activities: Youth, inter-faith
Other Languages: Persian

Spiritual Assembly of the Bahá'ís of Taunton Deane
63 Augustine Street, Taunton, Somerset,
TA1 1QH (h)
Tel: 01823-279198 (h)
Contact: Mrs Hazel Fleming
Position: Secretary

Spiritual Assembly of the Bahá'ís of Torbay
56a Sherwell Lane, Chelston, Torquay, Devon,
TQ2 6BE (h)
Tel: 01803-690330 (h)
Contact: Mrs Carole Huxtable
Position: Secretary

Spiritual Assembly of the Bahá'ís of Mendip
26 Wood Closer, Wells, Somerset, BA5 2GA (h)
Tel: 01749-67546 (h)
Contact: Gordon Mackenzie
Position: Secretary

NORTHERN IRELAND

City, Town or Local Bodies

Spiritual Assembly of the Bahá'ís of Antrim
P 0 Box 19, Antrim, County Antrim, BT41 2AU

Tel: 01849 467165 (h)
Contact: Mrs Valerie Coyle
Position: Secretary

Spiritual Assembly of the Bahá'ís of Ballymena
89 Ballybollen Road, Ahoghill, Ballymena, County
Antrim, BT42 2RF (h)
Tel: 01226-40287 (h)
Contact: Mrs Mojeh Haghighi Shirazi
Position: Secretary
Other Languages: Persian, Italian

Spiritual Assembly of the Bahá'ís of North Down
25 Windsor Gardens, Bangor, County Down,
BT20 3DD (h)
Contact: Mrs Greta Galbraith
Position: Secretary

Spiritual Assembly of the Bahá'ís of Belfast
442 Springfield Road, Belfast, BT12 7DW
Tel: 01232 321752 (h)
Contact: Mrs Pippa Cookson
Position: Secretary

Spiritual Assembly of the Bahá'ís of Carrickfergus
Carrickfergus, County Antrim, c/o Bahá'í
Information Office (UK)
Tel: 0171-584-2566 **Fax:** 0171-584-9402
Contact: Information Officer

Spiritual Assembly of the Bahá'ís of Castlereagh
Castlereagh, c/o Bahá'í Information Office (UK)
Tel: 0171-584-2566 **Fax:** 0171-584-9402
Contact: Information Officer

Spiritual Assembly of the Bahá'ís of Coleraine
63 Elms Park, Coleraine, County Londonderry,
BT52 2OF (h)
Tel: 01265-58435 (h)
Contact: Mrs Viny Robinson
Position: Secretary
Activities: Inter-faith

Spiritual Assembly of the Bahá'ís of Lisburn
41 Sheepwalk Road, Stoneyford, Lisburn, County
Antrim, BT28 3XQ (h)
Tel: 01846-648708 (h)
Contact: Dr Orang Agahi

Spiritual Assembly of the Bahá'ís of Londonderry
PO Box 95, Londonderry, County Londonderry,
BT47 1FS
Fax: 01504-265932 **EMail:** isp@iol.ie
Contact: Dr I S Palin
Position: Secretary

Other Languages: English, Persian, Russian, Esperanto

Spiritual Assembly of the Bahá'ís of Craigavon
3 Church Road, Portadown, County Armagh, BT63 5HT (h)
Tel: 01762-394217 (h)
Contact: Mrs Wendy Anne Byrne
Position: Secretary
Activities: Resource, visits, women, inter-faith
Other Languages: Persian

Spiritual Assembly of the Bahá'ís of Newtonabbey
11d Ardmillan Drive, Rathcoole, Newtownabbey, County Antrim, BT37 9AZ
Contact: Mr Peter Black
Position: Secretary

Spiritual Assembly of the Bahá'ís of Ards
7 Chapel Island Park, Newtownards, County Down, BT23 3BG
Contact: Miss Shahla Gushtasbi
Position: Secretary

Spiritual Assembly of the Bahá'ís of Omagh
57 Tattysallagh Road, Tattysallagh, Omagh, County Tyrone, BT78 5BR
Tel: 01662-898912 (h)
Contact: Mrs Dana Cahill
Position: Secretary
Activities: Resource, visits, youth, elderly, inter-faith
Other Languages: English, Persian, German, Irish

SCOTLAND

City, Town or Local Bodies

Spiritual Assembly of the Bahá'ís of Aberdeen
190 Ruthrieston Circle, Aberdeen, Grampian, AB1 7LU (h)
Tel: 01224-571444 (h)
Contact: Audrey Mellard
Position: Treasurer
Activities: Youth, newsletters, books, inter-faith
Other Languages: Persian, Arabic, All European

Spiritual Assembly of the Bahá'ís of Gordon
9 Davidson Crescent, Alford, Grampian
Tel: 01975-563640 (h)
Contact: A Goodwin
Position: Secretary

Spiritual Assembly of the Bahá'ís of Skye & Lochalsh
25 Lower Breakish, Breakish, Isle of Skye, Highlands and Islands, IV42 8QA (h)
Tel: 01471-822317 (h) **Fax:** 01471 822317
EMail: Chrisaha.demon.co.uk
Contact: Christopher Manvell
Position: Treasurer
Activities: Visits, youth, newsletters, books, inter-faith
Other Languages: Gaelic, German

Spiritual Assembly of the Bahá'ís of North East Fife
The Old Mill, Dura Den, By Cupar, Fife, KY15 5TJ (h)
Tel: 01334-653319 (h)
Contact: Mrs Pamela Sabet
Position: Secretary
Activities: Inter-faith

Spiritual Assembly of the Bahá'ís of Nithsdale, Dumfries & Galloway
95 Georgetown Road, Dumfries, Dumfries and Galloway, DG1 4DG (h)
Tel: 01387-262730 (h)
Contact: Mrs Jacqueline Mehrabi
Position: Secretary
Activities: Worship, resource, visits, youth, women, newsletters, books, inter-faith
Other Languages: Farsi

Spiritual Assembly of the Bahá'ís of Dundee
51 Park Road, Dundee, Tayside, DD3 8LB (h)
Tel: 01382-827418 (h)
EMail: L.Sabeti@dundee.ac.uk
Contact: Mr Farhad Varjavandi
Position: Secretary
Activities: Resource, visits, youth, newsletters, inter-faith

Spiritual Assembly of the Bahá'ís of Edinburgh
26 North Fort Street, Edinburgh, Lothian, EH6 4HD (h)
Tel: 0131-554-2446 (h)
Contact: Graham Barnes
Position: Secretary
Activities: Worship, visits, youth, elderly, women, inter-faith

Spiritual Assembly of the Bahá'ís of Glasgow
2/03, 11 Laurel Place, Glasgow, Strathclyde, G11 7RE (h)

Tel: 0141-334-3465 (h)
Contact: Mr John Huxtable

Spiritual Assembly of the Bahá'ís of Inverness
6a Green Drive, Inverness, Highlands and Islands,
IV2 4EX (h)
Tel: 01463-236763 (h)
Contact: Thomas Douglas Mackenzie
Position: Secretary
Activities: Inter-faith
Other Languages: Persian

***Spiritual Assembly of the Bahá'ís of Ross &
Cromarty***
Sunnyside, Charleston, North Kessock, Inverness,
Highlands and Islands, IV1 1YA
Tel: 01463-731849 (h)
Contact: Mr Rolf Schmidt
Position: Secretary

***Spiritual Assembly of the Bahá'ís of Perth &
Kinross***
Kinross, c/o Bahá'í Information Office (UK)
Tel: 0171-584-2566 **Fax:** 0171-584-9402
Contact: Information Officer

Spiritual Assembly of the Bahá'ís of Stewartry
1 Town Walls Close, Kirkcudbright, Dumfries and
Galloway, DG6 4JZ (h)
Tel: 01557-330575 (h)
Contact: Mr James Kentley
Position: Secretary
Activities: Inter-faith

Spiritual Assembly of the Bahá'ís of Orkney
Bahá'í Centre, 3 Old Scapa Road, Kirwall, Orkney
Isles, Highlands and Islands, KW15 1BB
Tel: 01856-761624 (h) **Fax:** 01856 -761624
EMail: rosemary@laughlin.demon.co.uk
Contact: Mrs Rosemary McLaughlin
Position: Secretary
Activities: Worship, visits, newsletters

***Spiritual Assembly of the Bahá'ís of Annandale &
Eskdale***
Riggfoot, Lochmaben, Lockerbie, Dumfries and
Galloway, DG11 1LU
Tel: 01387-811989 (h)
Contact: Mrs Susan Haddow
Position: Secretary

Spiritual Assembly of the Bahá'ís of Uist
16 Dunrossil Place, Lochmaddy, North Uist,
Highlands and Islands, PA82 5AB (h)
Tel: 01876 500285 (h)
Contact: Mrs Jean Payne
Position: Secretary

Spiritual Assembly of the Bahá'ís of Shetland
46 Staney Hill, Lerwick, Shetland, Highlands and
Islands, ZE1 0QW (h)
Tel: 01595-695749 (h)
Contact: Mandy Hepburn
Position: Secretary

***Spiritual Assembly of the Bahá'ís of Lewis &
Harris***
Stornoway, Isle of Lewis, Highlands and Islands (h)
Tel: 01865-706105 (h)
Position: Appointed representative
Activities: Inter-faith
Languages: Gaelic, Persian

***Spiritual Assembly of the Bahá'ís of Banff &
Buchan***
Greeness Croft, Fyvie, Turriff, Grampian, AB53
8QX (h)
Tel: 01651 891356 (h)
Contact: Mrs Lorraine Ransome Fozdar
Position: Secretary

WALES

City, Town or Local Bodies

Spiritual Assembly of the Bahá'ís of Cardiff
14 Alfreda Road, Cardiff, South Glamorgan,
CF42EH (h)
Tel: 01222-625316 (h)
Contact: Mrs Tish Roskams
Position: Secretary

Spiritual Assembly of the Bahá'ís of Ceredigion
Ceredigion, c/o Bahai Information Office (UK)
Tel: 0171-5842-566 **Fax:** 0171-584-9402
Contact: Information Officer

Spiritual Assembly of the Bahá'ís of Dwyfor
Garreg Grow, Garn Dolbenmaen, Gwynedd,
LL51 5UQ (h)
Tel: 01766-530640 (h)
Contact: Mr Martin Wortmann
Position: Secretary

Spiritual Assembly of the Bahá'ís of Carmarthenshire
Gathen House, Llanelli, Dyfed, SA15 2RP (h)
Tel: 01554-754974 **Fax:** 01554-776013
Contact: Secretary
Activities: Resource, visits, youth, elderly, women, newsletters, books, inter-faith
Other Languages: Welsh

Spiritual Assembly of the Bahá'ís of Conwy
Ty Laon, 15 Drws-y-Nant, Llansanffraid, Glan Conwy, Gwyned, LL28 5EQ (h)
Tel: 01492-573268 (h)
Contact: Mrs Joan Birch
Activities: Worship, inter-faith

Spiritual Assembly of the Bahá'ís of Brecknock
Tan-y-Coed, Llanwrtyd Wells, Powys, LD5 4TB (h)
Tel: 01591-3363 (h)
Contact: Mrs Robina Nicholson
Position: Secretary

Spiritual Assembly of the Bahá'ís of Caerphilly
Caerphilly, Mid Glamorgan, c/o 20 Stonerwood View, Pantside, Newbridge, Gwent, NP1 5DF
Tel: 01495-247963 (h)
Contact: Mrs and Mrs Bartlett
Position: Chair and Secretary
Activities: Inter-Faith
Other Languages: Persian, Arabic

Spiritual Assembly of the Bahá'ís of Monmouth
Pinelands, The Narth, Monmouth, Gwent, NP5 4AG
Tel: 01600-860413 (h)
Contact: Mrs Roya Azordegan
Position: Secretary

Spiritual Assembly of the Bahá'ís of Swansea
63 Lloyd Road, Treboeth, Swansea, West Glamorgan, SA5 9EU (h)
Tel: 01792 413252 (h)
Contact: Mrs Josie Akhurst
Position: Secretary

Spiritual Assembly of the Bahá'ís of Arfon
Gian Gors, Waunfawr, Gwynedd, LL55 4SD (h)
Tel: 01286-650632 (h)
Contact: Dafydd Owen
Position: Secretary
Activities: Worship, youth, inter-faith
Other Languages: Welsh

INTRODUCING THE BUDDHIST COMMUNITY

BUDDHISTS IN THE UNITED KINGDOM

A wide variety of Buddhist organisations, *viharas*, monasteries, centres and more informal groups are to be found in the UK today. They reflect both the variety of ethnic groups and the different schools of Buddhism.

Buddhist activity is not as focused upon religious buildings as that of some other religious traditions. Nevertheless, the directory records approximately 117 *viharas*, monasteries and other Buddhist centres in the UK and many other groups meet in private houses or in hired halls.

Beginnings in the UK

The nineteenth century saw the development of the western academic study of Buddhism. As scholars produced an increasing number of English translations of Buddhist texts, more and more individuals developed an interest in Buddhism as a philosophy, a way of life, and a religion.

In 1881 the Pali Text Society was founded, which further fostered this development. In 1899, Gordon Douglas, the first English person to be ordained as a Buddhist monk, took his vows in Colombo, Sri Lanka and became Bhikkhu Asoka. He did not, however, return to Britain. In 1898 another Englishman, Alan Bennett, went to study Buddhism in Sri Lanka. In 1901, whilst in Burma, he was ordained as a monk, taking the name Ananda Metteyya.

In 1907, a Buddhist Society of Great Britain and Ireland was formed to receive a Buddhist mission which eventually arrived in 1908, led by Ananda Metteyya. The Society did not, however, become firmly established and in 1924 Christmas Humphreys founded the Buddhist Centre of the Theosophical Society which incorporated its remnants. In 1926, this new foundation became the Buddhist Lodge of the Theosophical Society and, in 1943, it was constituted as a new and independent organisation, known as The Buddhist Society. Christmas Humphreys remained as its President until his death in 1983.

In 1926, Humphreys had welcomed the Sinhalese Anagarika Dharmapala who had previously visited Britain in 1893, 1896 and again in 1904 on a mission. Subsequently, a branch of the Maha Bodhi Society was founded in London followed, in 1928, by the first monastery for Sinhalese monks.

Up until the 1960s, Western engagement with Buddhism was often of an individual, and sometimes rather theoretical, kind. In recent times, however, increasing numbers of Westerners have begun to practise Buddhist meditation and apply Buddhist ethical norms, seeing them as vehicles for bringing about change in their lives and ultimate awakening.

Migration

Individuals and small groups of migrants with Buddhist beliefs have arrived throughout the century from Sri Lanka, Thailand and Burma. Indian (mostly *Ambedkarite* - see below) Buddhists and the Hong Kong Chinese came mainly with the New Commonwealth migrations of the 1950s and 1960s. The number of Buddhists in the UK has been further expanded by refugees including those following the *Dalai Lama's* 1959 flight from Chinese-occupied Tibet; Vietnamese Buddhist refugees who arrived in the late 1960s and early 1970s; and more recently by Sri Lankan refugees from the Sri Lankan civil war.

Buddhists in the UK speak English and a variety of languages reflecting their countries of origin. Most teaching is conducted in English. The Buddhist scriptures are preserved in Pali (in the case of the *Southern Canon*, which forms the basis of the *Theravada* tradition - see section below on "Traditions in Buddhism") and Chinese, Japanese, Sanskrit and Tibetan (in the case of the *Mahayana* scriptures - see section below on "Traditions in Buddhism").

There is an estimated world Buddhist population of around 328,233,000. There might be as many as around 130,000 Buddhists in the UK. However, as noted in this directory's chapter on "The Religious Landscape of the UK", this figure is based on the inclusion, under the classification of Buddhist, of a significant number of approximately 100,000 ethnically Chinese people. Given the often overlapping and intermingling complexity of Buddhist, Taoist and Confucian belief and practice found among many ethnic Chinese families and individuals this is not unproblematic, but it would also be misleading not to acknowledge the role of Buddhism among the Chinese in the UK.

ORIGINS AND DEVELOPMENT OF BUDDHISM

Gautama Buddha/Gotama Buddha

Buddhism does not believe in a personal deity. It makes no claims to possess a divinely revealed book and it has no central organisational authority. The teachings of Buddhism are the inheritance of Siddhartha Gautama/Siddhattha Gotama's search for truth. (Here and throughout the chapter, key names and concepts are introduced in both their Sanskrit and Pali forms. Thereafter, only Sanskrit is used in the main body of the text).

According to Buddhist tradition, Siddhartha Gautama was born in Lumbini, in what is today Nepal, possibly in the fifth century BCE, and then grew up nearby in Kapilavatthu. As a prince, his early life was rich and comfortable. Eventually, however, he asked his charioteer to take him to see life in the city. Here he saw for himself, for the first time, the suffering of a sick person and an old man as well as seeing a corpse, but he also saw the serenity of a mendicant.

This experience awakened in him a wish to understand and alleviate suffering. So, at the age of twenty-nine, he began a spiritual search which lasted for six years until it reached its culmination in his *Enlightenment* under the Bo Tree (now known as the *Bodhi Tree*), at the place in North India now known as *Bodh Gaya*.

During Gautama's period of searching, he studied with two important teachers of his time, but he was still dissatisfied and decided to continue alone. He underwent extremes of self-denial and self-mortification. But these, too, did not satisfy him and he finally decided on a less ascetic approach. He ate some food and regained his strength. At this point five ascetics who had previously joined up with him left him in disapproval. He then sat down under the Bodhi Tree in a determined attempt to break through to that which he was seeking.

It is said that on the night of the full moon in May he finally attained the state of *nirvana/nibbana* (see section on "Key Buddhist Beliefs" below). He then sought out the five ascetics who had previously been with him. With them as his first followers, the *samgha/sangha* (Buddhist community) was born, in the Deer Park near Benares. At the age of eighty he passed away at Kushinagara and entered into what Buddhists describe as his *parinirvana/parinibbana* (final entry to *nirvana*).

Transmission

The form of the Buddhist tradition that spread south is known as the *Theravada* tradition. It was brought to Sri Lanka in 250BCE and spread to those countries now known as Thailand, Cambodia, Laos and Burma as well as to the southern part of Vietnam. Between the first and seventh century of the Common Era Buddhism spread slowly north-eastwards into Central Asia and into what is now China, Korea, Japan, the northern part of Vietnam and (in the seventh and eighth centuries) northwards into Tibet.

The forms of Buddhism traditionally associated with these countries are therefore often known as the *Northern Transmission*, or the *Mahayana* tradition. In India itself, after the first millenium CE Buddhism almost died out (apart from in what is now Bangladesh) until its revival this century, through the attraction of the *Ambedkarite* (named after the Indian social reformer Dr Ambedkar) movement for the Indian scheduled *castes*, popularly referred to as *untouchables*.

SOURCES OF BUDDHIST BELIEFS AND PRACTICES

The Buddha

The historical *Buddha* is revered as the uncoverer of the teachings or *dharma/dhamma* which exist independently of him. He himself claimed only to have rediscovered "an ancient way leading to an ancient city". Therefore, the emphasis is upon the *Buddha* as guide and upon the *dharma* rather than on the person of Gautama. Strictly speaking, therefore, Gautama is not viewed as the founder of the *dharma*.

Buddhists are those who claim to have found these teachings to be valid for themselves. In the early stages of Buddhist training one can learn the details of the teachings, but in the end every individual must discover them in their own experience and not simply as what they have been taught.

The Three Refuges

Buddhists speak of "going for refuge" or "taking refuge" in the *triratna/tiratana* (*Three Jewels*). This is an affirmation of their commitment as Buddhists and to the sources of Buddhist life: "I take refuge in the *Buddha*; I take refuge in the *dharma* (the *Buddha's* teachings); I take refuge in the *samgha/sangha* (the *Buddha's* community)."

Buddha

Siddhartha Gautama was acknowledged by his followers to be a *Buddha* or *Enlightened* one (from *Budh* meaning to be enlightened or awakened). In the *Mahayana* Buddhist tradition, Siddhartha Gautama is also known as *Shakyamuni/Sakyamuni* (the silent sage of the Shakya/Sakya people). In the *Theravada* tradition references to the *Buddha* are usually to the historical figure of Gautama, who is venerated as the one who initiated the transmission of the teaching in the current era.

Both the *Mahayana* and *Theravada* tradition also assume the existence of numerous *Buddhas* before and after him as well as of the *Buddha-nature* in all beings of which the historical *Buddha* is but one manifestation. Going to the

Buddha for refuge not only means accepting the *Buddha* as the ultimate spiritual guide and example for one's life, but also appreciating one's own *Buddha-nature* and potential for enlightenment. Many Buddhist homes and temples contain *rupas* (statues) or pictures of the *Buddha* as aids to devotion and meditation.

Dharma

Dharma has no single meaning. It is quintessentially expressed in the so-called *Four Noble Truths* (see section below on "Key Buddhist Beliefs"). Going for refuge to the *dharma* is understood to involve focusing one's energies to understand, practise and realise the *dharma* in one's own life, thus also bringing about understanding of others and expressing goodwill towards them.

Samgha

Historically, for many Buddhists, *samgha* has been understood as the community of celibate Buddhist *monks* and *nuns*. However, in some Japanese groups and movements there are no *monks* and *nuns*. Many *Tibetan Buddhists* are guided by married *lamas*, and *monks* and *nuns* have no particular status in the Friends of the Western Buddhist Order. Among other Buddhists in the *Mahayana* tradition, and particularly in some parts of *western Buddhism*, the *samgha* is understood primarily as the totality of followers of the *Buddha* who have had a significant transformative experience of transcendental insight. For some Buddhists, the meaning of the *samgha* can be taken to embrace all who potentially possess the *Buddha-nature*, in other words all sentient beings.

The Southern Canon

Several *canons* of scripture help explain the *dharma*. Most were eventually committed to writing from an original oral transmission. The southern, Pali language *canon* contains some of the oldest material which is ascribed to the Buddha and his disciples and in general is acceptable to all Buddhist schools. This *canon* is also known as the *Tipitaka*, meaning the *Three Baskets*, since its palm leaf manuscripts were originally kept in three different baskets - the *Vinaya-pitaka* (*Basket of [Monastic] Discipline*); the *Sutta-pitaka* (*Basket of Discourses*); and the *Abhidhamma-pitaka* (*Basket of Further Teachings*).

The Northern Canon

The *Mahayana* canon is extensive. Its wide variety of texts include many which were written down in Sanskrit and then translated into Tibetan and Chinese, plus some which were originally written in these languages. Some texts, known in the Far East as the *Agama*, are held in common with the Pali canon. The term *sutra/sutta* is used of the texts and refers to the idea of a single "thread" running through the discourse.

Among the more widely known *Mahayana sutras* are the *Saddharma-pundarika* (the *Lotus of the True Dharma*), the vast collection of the *Prajna-paramita sutras* (the *Perfection of Wisdom*), the long *Mahayana Parinirvana Sutra*, and the compilation known as the *Flower Ornament Sutra*.

These *sutras* were gathered into *canonical* collections of writings. The Chinese *canon* is known as the *Ta-ts'ang-ching* (*Great Scripture Store*) and its standard modern edition consists of fifty-five volumes with forty-five supplementary volumes. In Japan, this standard compilation is known as *Taizokyo*. The equally vast Tibetan *canon* consists of the *bKa'gyur* (pronounced "*Kangyur*" and meaning "the *Translation of the Word of the Buddha*") which is ninety-eight volumes long, and the *bsTan'gyur* (pronounced *Tengyur* and meaning "*Translation of Treatises*"). This, in its Peking edition, is in two hundred and twenty-four volumes and it can also be found in Japan in its original wood-block print copies.

Jataka Stories

In addition to the *canonical* texts, both *Theravada* and *Mahayana* Buddhists refer to the over five hundred *Jataka* stories said to have been told by the *Buddha* to his followers about his former lives. They form the basis of much popular teaching and reflection in some eastern countries where Buddhism is the predominant tradition and serious practioners also attest that their seeming simplicity contains unexpected depths.

KEY BUDDHIST BELIEFS

Four Noble Truths

The *Catur Aryasatya/Cattari Ariyasaccani (Four Noble Truths)* are at the heart of Buddhism. These truths are: *duhkha/dukkha* (unsatisfactoriness), *samudaya* (the origin of unsatisfactoriness), *nirodha* (the cessation of unsatisfactoriness) and *marga/magga* (the way leading to contentment).

Duhkha (Unsatisfactoriness)
Duhkha has often been translated as "suffering". However, suffering is only one of its meanings and it is better understood in terms of "unsatisfactoriness", a word that also implies imperfection and impermanence. In his first teaching, the Buddha said: "Birth is *duhkha*, ageing is *duhkha*, sickness is *duhkha*, death is *duhkha*; sorrow, lamentation, grief and despair are *duhkha*; association with what one dislikes is *duhkha*; separation from what one likes is *duhkha*; not to get what one wants is *duhkha*. "

Duhkha is one of the *Three Signs of Being* or characteristics of existence, the other two are *anitya/anicca* (impermanence), and *anatman/anatta* (no-self). One cannot expect to find permanent happiness from impermanent causes. *Anitya* (impermanence or change) means all conditioned phenomena are impermanent and are "coming to be and ceasing to be". Change is a constant characteristic of all things. *Anatman* is the teaching that there is no permanent or immortal self.

An "everyday self" is recognised but is seen as an ever-changing composite of five *skandhas/khandhas* (aggregates) which are themselves forever changing. They are: *rupa* (material form), *vedana* (feelings), *samjna/sanna* (perceptions), *samskaras/sankharas* (mental configurations), and *vijnana/vinnana* (discriminatory consciousness).

Samudaya (Origin of Unsatisfactoriness)
The origin of *duhkha* is seen by Buddhists to lie in *trishna/tanha*. This is a powerful thirsting or craving which, of its very nature, can never be satisfied and goes on reproducing itself. It manifests itself as desire for, and attachment to, material things and mental objects; including a thirst for continued existence and its opposite desire for non-existence. Such craving or thirst results in *duhkha* and in behaviour which will lead to undesired rebirth. This rebirth is not understood as the transmigration of a soul, which would be inconsistent with the teaching of *anatman*. Rather, the habits which are reinforced by craving are to bring about a "rebecoming", instead of a continuation of a soul.

Nirodha (Cessation of duhkha)
The transcendence of *trishna* (craving) leads to the cessation of *duhkha* and is known as *nirvana*. The full meaning of *nirvana* cannot adequately be described. In literal terms it means the "quenching" or "extinction" of the thirst and craving that results in *duhkha*. It does not therefore mean, as it has often been misunderstood to mean, a state of annihilation. The "quenching" and "extinction" to which it refers is rather that of the fires of greed, hatred, ignorance and craving which cause *duhkha*. It is seen as deliverance from *samsara* (see below), which is the world in which *duhkha* holds sway. Buddhists affirm that this deliverance can be realised in this life, as in the case of Gautama *Buddha* himself.

Marga (The Way)
The first three *Noble Truths* analyse the human condition and affirm the possibility of transcending *duhkha*. The fourth, more fully known as the *Arya Ashtangika Marga/Ariya Atthangika Magga* (The *Noble Eightfold Path* - see section below on "Buddhist Life"), is a way of life to be practised and leads out of *samsara*. This path is often known as the *Middle Way*, the course between and beyond the excesses of self-indulgence and self-denial.

Dependent Origination

Dependent origination is a sequence or consequence according to which all phenomena arise in dependence upon interrelated causes. In relation to sentient beings, it is often seen in terms of a chain with twelve links, each link/cause depending upon the previous one and leading to the next.

Karma and Vipata

Karma/Kamma (literally meaning "deed") is understood in Buddhism as a law of consequences inherent in the nature of things. Technically, *karma* is the deed and *vipata* the consequence, but popularly *karma* refers to both deeds and consequences. All deliberate actions have their consequences and whether a particular action has useful or negative *karmic/kammic* effects depends predominately upon the intentions.

Samsara

Samsara (the wheel of birth and death) is not the reincarnation or transmigration of a soul because, as we have seen, Buddhism does not posit the continuing existence of such a substantial or permanent soul or self. This is because the individual is understood to be a cluster of various aggregates held together by desire. Buddhists therefore usually speak of a "rebirth" or "rebecoming" of these aggregates rather than of the transmigration of an entity.

This rebirth is possible on a number of levels (not just the human) and throughout aeons. The "wheel" of birth and death is divided into six realms or states illustrative of these possibilities. Depending on the *karma* accumulated in one lifetime the rebirth or rebecoming will be of different kinds. The principal concern is ultimately not to gain a better future rebirth, but to escape altogether from this wheel of rebirth and death and to attain *nirvana*.

Being born as a human being is viewed as a precious opportunity since it is believed that from the human state there is no better chance that deliverance can be achieved. In *Mahayana* Buddhism, having escaped from the wheel of birth and death the enlightened being may compassionately return to the world, without being *karmically* bound to it, in order to assist others to awaken.

Shunyata/Sunnata

Shunyata (*Voidness* or *Emptiness*) is a concept of great importance in the *Mahayana* tradition where the idea of *anatman* or no-self has undergone further development. In the *Mahayana* view, all that exists is devoid of any abiding essence, and "empty" of any ultimate characteristics. To understand this is to recognise the ultimately fluid and inter-connected nature of all phenomena. The deep realisation of *shunyata* is believed to end fear.

Bodhi

Bodhi literally means "awakening" and refers to *Enlightenment*. This is the state of *Buddhahood* or spiritual perfection which is the goal of the Buddhist spiritual life. It comes about with the perfection of *prajna/panna* (wisdom) and *karuna* (compassion). It brings a complete seeing into the ultimate nature of existence and a totally self-less and compassionate response to all beings and situations.

TRADITIONS IN BUDDHISM

The central teachings are common to all the traditions and schools, but they contain differences in emphasis, as well as some differences in practice. The principal traditions are the *Theravada* (*Way of the Elders*) or the *Southern Transmission*, found principally in South East Asia, and the *Mahayana* (often translated as the *Great Vehicle* - from *maha* meaning "great" and *yana* meaning "vehicle") or *Northern Transmission*, with its two main branches of the *Far Eastern* and *Tibetan Buddhism*.

Within each of the major traditions there are also many different schools which emphasise particular beliefs and practices. In the West there are, also, newer developments which do not fully identify with any one traditional branch of Buddhism. Some of these are working to evolve new western styles of Buddhism.

Theravada

The ideal of the *Theravada* tradition is that of the *arahat*, an individual who has found release from the cycle of birth and death. Its hallmarks are renunciation, self-reliance and a focus upon the historical *Buddha*. This tradition is based upon the Pali *canon* and is today mainly represented in the Buddhism of the South Asian countries of Sri Lanka, Burma, Laos, Cambodia and Thailand, as well as in southern Vietnam. It is therefore sometimes known as the *Southern Transmission*. Variations within the *Theravada* tradition reflect the different cultural contexts in which the tradition has taken shape rather than the existence of distinctive schools as such.

In some books on Buddhism the *Theravada* is sometimes referred to as the *Hinayana* (Little Vehicle). However, the origins of the term *Hinayana* are to be found in a disparaging contrast with the *Mahayana* (*Great Vehicle*). More properly *Hinayana* historically refers to spiritual tendencies which existed in India and were criticised by followers of the *Mahayana* as being rigid and limited, rather than to the later developed forms of *Theravada* Buddhism found in Sri Lanka and the *Southern Transmission*. The correct term for *Theravada* is *Shravakayana* (*Vehicle of the Heavens*).

Mahayana

In addition to the concept of *shunyata* and a belief in many simultaneously present *Buddhas*, the particular characteristics of the *Mahayana* tradition include an emphasis on the ideal of the *Bodhisattva*. A *Bodhisattva* among humans is one who vows to practice the Buddhist path totally in order to help and liberate both themselves and all beings (eg Avalokiteshvara and Majushri). A *Bodhisattva-Mahasattva* is a fully perfected *Bodhisattva*, greater than any other being except a *Buddha*. They live permanently in the realm of "transcendence" and from this position strive constantly for the welfare of others. Hence the *Mahayana* is sometimes referred to as the *Bodhisattvayana* (the way of the *Bodhisattva*).

Mahayana is a generic name for a wide movement embracing many different groups in the northern countries of China, Japan,

Vietnam, Korea and Tibet. It is sometimes known as the *Northern Transmission* because it came via the Northen Silk Road and therefore reached these countries first. All have in common the same basic principles but each grouping has developed in a different cultural setting or is often associated with one or more of the great sutras and has thus evolved variations in practice.

Due to repeated persecutions most of these groups became extinct in China by the 15th century, but many were introduced to Japan and some are still extant there as the *Tendai*, *Pure Land*, *Shingon* and *Zen* schools, with one temple of the *Kegon* school. In China itself, an amalgamation of the groups took place within the broader *Ch'an* tradition (see below).

Tibetan Buddhism

There are four main lineages in *Tibetan Buddhism* which began in earnest during the reign of King Trisong Detsen (755-797CE) when it is thought that Padmasambhava (according to tradition born in what is now Kashmir), brought Buddhism to Tibet. He is particularly revered by the oldest of the *Tibetan Buddhist* schools, the *Nyingmapa* (literally meaning "the old ones"), many of whose *Lamas* today identify with the *Rime* (non-sectarian) movement that began in the nineteenth century. The teachings recorded in *The Tibetan Book of the Dead* come from this school.

The *Sakyapa* school traces its tradition back to the Indian saint Virupa but is not so numerically significant in the UK. The *Kagyupa* school traces its origins to Marpa, who is believed to have brought teachings into Tibet after having been a disciple of the Indian *tantric* master Naropa. This school especially reveres Milarepa, after whom the school divided into four further sub-schools. It tends to stress the attainment of direct experience and encourages three year isolation retreats to achieve this. The *Gelugpa* school has a more gradual approach based on an initial development of ethical and intellectual understanding. The *Dalai Lama* is the head of the *Gelupa* school and a particularly revered figure.

Ch'an (Chinese) and Zen (Japanese) Buddhism
Ch'an is an abbreviated form of the Chinese word *Ch'an-na*, which is derived from the Sanskrit word *dhyana* which refers to the state of mind during meditation in which the distinctions between subject and object is transcended. *Zen* is a shortened form of *zenna*, which derives from a Japanese pronounciation of the word *Ch'an-na*.

Although meditation is important in all Buddhist schools, *Zen* stresses the practice of *zazen* (sitting meditation) in developing awareness. *Zen* affirms that direct insight into true reality is possible through this practice, hence the Japanese name of *satori* or *kensho*, meaning "seeing into one's true nature".

Shikantaza (or just sitting) was introduced into China by the Indian monk Bodhidhamma in the 6th century CE, when other Buddhist schools had already been established. The *Rinzai* lineage developed in the 9th century. What was to become *Soto Zen* was introduced into Japan in the 8th century by Dosen Risshi. The *Rinzai* lineage found its way to Japan in the 12th century CE.

Soto Zen emphasises *Shikantaza* ("or just sitting"), which is sometimes known as *Serene Reflection Meditation*. In the *Rinzai* tradition, *zazen* is combined with the use of *koan* (questions employed by a *Zen Master* designed to engender and test genuine insight).

Pure Land Buddhism
Pure Land Buddhists are devoted to Amitabha, a cosmic *Buddha* who vowed to bring liberation to all. In *Japanese Buddhism* (where Amitabha is known as Amida) the school has two main branches - the *Jodo Shu* (*Pure Land School*) and the *Jodo Shinshu* (*True Pure Land School*, often simply known as *Shin*).

Both schools are products of an emphasis in Buddhist teaching on adaptation of the *dharma* to the world in forms that are most suitable for people. They therefore offer a path which people can follow in difficult times, teaching dependence upon the infinite merit of Amida *Buddha* and his *tariki* ("other power").

The difference between the *Jodo Shu* and the *Jodo Shinshu* is that the latter emphasises complete abandonment of all *jiriki* (self-effort). As a central part of their practice both recite the *Nembutsu*, which is an invocation of the *mantra* *Namu-Amida-butsu* (hail to Amida *Buddha*).

Nichiren Buddhism
The *Nichiren* tradition draws upon the teachings of the Japanese teacher Nichiren (1222-1282CE), who saw the *Lotus Sutra* as the highest form of Buddhist teaching, the essence of which could be found in its title. Nichiren taught that recitation of the *sutra's* name was all that was necessary for liberation. Recitation of the *mantra* having the name of the sutra, *Namu myoho renge-kyo* (*Veneration to the Lotus of the Good Law*), was therefore introduced as a key practice within this tradition.

BUDDHIST LIFE

The Five Precepts

The *Five Precepts* (or *Panca Silani*) are the basic rules of living for lay Buddhists. They express the intention to refrain from: harming living beings; taking what is not given; sexual misconduct and misuse of the senses; harmful speech; and drink or drugs which cloud the mind. For the lay Buddhist this is the basis of *samyakkarmanta/samma kammanta* (Right Action), which is one aspect of the *Noble Eightfold Path*. Ordained Buddhists take additional vows (see section below on "Buddhist Organisations").

Noble Eightfold Path

In Buddhist teaching the *Noble Eightfold Path* (*Arya Astangika Marga*) is the fourth of the *Four Noble Truths* and is the way to overcome *duhkha*. The eight aspects of the *Path* are traditionally grouped into three. The first two are concerned with wisdom, the next three with morality, and the final three with concentration and meditation. All aspects of the *Eightfold Path* are, however, interdependent.

Right Understanding

Samyagdrishti/samma ditthi (right understanding) is the corrected viewpoint, acquired through familiarity with the Buddhist teachings, that all life is impermanent.

Right Intention

Samyaksamkalpa/samma sankappa (right intention) is the changed motivation which develops with corrected vision.

Right Speech

Samyagvac/samma vaca (right speech) emerges from right understanding and intention and causes no injury to oneself or others and thus avoids lying, abuse, slander and gossip.

Right Action

Samyakkarmanta/samma kammanta (right action) consists of refraining from what is harmful and involves, among other things, cultivating the *Five Precepts* and practising what is beneficial for oneself and others.

Right Livelihood

Samyagajiva/samma ajiva (right livelihood) includes right daily conduct and behaviour and not earning one's living in ways which are inconsistent with the *Five Precepts* and the *Noble Eightfold Path*.

Right Effort

Samyagvayama/samma vayama (right effort) requires constant attentiveness and effort to sustain and generate good, as well as to refrain from what is harmful.

Right Mindfulness

Samyaksmriti/samma sati (right mindfulness) is rooted in the body and its activity; feelings; states of mind; and mental contents. Whatever enters a mind that is aware will be found to be subject to the *Three Signs of Being*.

Right Concentration

Samyaksamadhi/samma samadhi (right concentration) is nurtured through the practice of meditation.

Paramitas

In the *Theravada* tradition, the main emphasis is on the *Four Noble Truths* and the practice of the *Noble Eightfold Path*. In *Mahayana* the stress is on the traditional practice of the *paramitas*, and especially the first six of these. *Paramitas* is usually translated as "perfections". The six specially emphasised *paramitas* are: giving; keeping the moral precepts; patience; strength to persevere; meditation (see below), and wisdom (the genuine insight which results from this practice and has compassion as its natural accompaniment).

Meditation

Meditation plays a central role in the practice of the Buddhist teachings. Through meditation, faith (as confidence), concentration, mindfulness, energy and wisdom are cultivated as the five foundations of the developing spiritual life. Meditation is also rooted in right action. There are numerous methods of meditation within the various branches of Buddhism and they all require training and practice. There are, however, two basic forms which underlie the variety of methods. These are *shamatha/samatha* (tranquillity meditation) and *vipashyana/ vipassana* (insight meditation).

Shamatha meditation is concerned with promoting states of mind characterised by calm, concentration and mindfulness in order to integrate the emotions and develop positive energies. Common forms of *shamatha* meditation are awareness or mindfulness of breathing and the practice of positive good will, radiating "loving-kindness" to the whole world.

Vipassana meditation is concerned with the clarity of seeing things as they really are and in realising the *Three Signs of Being* (see under the *Four Noble Truths*). This realisation is seen as breaking the bondage of *samsara* and thus as bringing liberation from *duhkha*.

There are a variety of ways in which meditation may be aided. *Rupas* (material forms) of Gautama *Buddha* are a reminder of his life and teaching. The *Tibetan Buddhist* tradition has a rich artistic heritage and teaches visualisation of many *Buddhas* and *Bodhisattvas*.

Mantras, when chanted, are believed to resonate in ways that have a deep efficacy. *Mandalas* are sacred diagrams in the shape of circles, squares or angles that depict the teachings of Buddhism. In *Tibetan Buddhism* they are either permanently constructed, such as those painted on *thang-ka* (scrolls) or are temporarily made from different coloured sands or other such materials. *Mudras* are hand gestures which, like *mantras*, are believed to have a spiritual effect.

In *Zen* Buddhism great attention is paid to sitting meditation as well as to practice of the precepts and meditation in daily life. The state of mind cultivated is known as "empty heart", which is not one of thoughtlessness, but of an "at-one-ness" which has passed beyond the distinction of subject and object. When practised this state prevails not only when sitting in meditation but also in the activities of daily life, including all kinds of work.

Vegetarianism

Buddhism emphasises the avoidance of intentional killing. However, there is a variety of practice with regard to the eating of meat. Many *Tibetan Buddhists* do eat meat and, in *Theravada* Buddhism, *monks* and *nuns* are allowed to eat meat if they have not seen, heard or suspected that the animal has been specifically killed for them. In particular they are able to accept meat if it is offered to them as alms, which is the only way in which they are able to obtain food.

Chinese Zen has become strictly vegetarian, whereas in *Japanese Zen* the same rules apply as in *Theravada*, although meat is never served in monasteries. In general, even where Buddhists are not fully vegetarian, what are perceived as the higher forms of life are often avoided. In Chinese forms of Buddhism garlic and onions are also avoided since they are thought to heat the blood and so make meditation more difficult. The precept of right livelihood certainly excludes the "trade in flesh" entailed in being a butcher, hunter or fisher.

BUDDHIST WORSHIP

Buildings for Devotional Practice

Buddhist buildings of various types can be found in the UK, each reflecting the different traditions, schools and ethnic groupings of the Buddhists who use them. Styles range from the stark simplicity of meditation halls through to the elaborate ornateness of some temples.

Some places for devotion may be in residential houses with a room acting as the central shrine or meditation room. Others are extensive purpose-built buildings such as the Samye Ling Tibetan Centre in Scotland and the Thai Buddhapadipa Theravada Temple in Wimbledon. Some are relatively small structures such as the Peace Pagodas in Milton Keynes and Battersea Park in London.

Despite this variety there are a number of common features. A Buddhist temple or monastery usually contains at least a *Buddharupa* (statue of the *Buddha*) and a *stupa/thupa*, which is a characteristic form of Buddhist architecture (representing the mind of the *Buddha*) originally built over relics of the *Buddha* or other saints or other typically holy objects. The temple is commonly a place where teaching, religious observance and meditation takes place, and it may have adjacent accommodation for resident *monks* or *nuns*. It can thus physically focus the three refuges of Buddhism – the *Buddha*, the *dharma* and the *samgha*.

Shrines and Buddharupas

Most Buddhists also have a small shrine in their homes. The *Buddharupa* is usually found in a central position within the shrine area. In front of the *Buddharupa* will usually be an incense holder and the *rupa* will be flanked by flowers and candles. *Puja*, which involves the offering of food, flowers, incense and water, together with chanting, is carried out by all schools within Buddhism as a devotional observance alongside meditation, although it takes different forms in each school. Such observance expresses *shraddha/saddha* (faith) in the *Buddha*.

This is not blind faith, but confidence based on knowledge and awareness.

The offering of incense is symbolic of devotion. Candles symbolise the light that the *Buddha's* teaching brings to the world. There are vases of cut flowers as a reminder of impermanence and sometimes a Buddhist text wrapped in silk cloth. Tibetan Buddhists offer bowls of water to represent water for bathing, washing the feet, rinsing the mouth and drinking, as well as food, flowers, incense and light. In the *Zen* tradition, offerings of fruit, tea and water are made.

BUDDHIST CALENDAR AND FESTIVALS

Calendar

Buddhist religious festivals are based on the lunar calendars of the countries concerned. However the actual festivals and their dates and meanings vary according to Buddhist tradition and the national/ethnic origins of the group concerned. Because of these national/ethnic variations and the lunar cycle, individuals cannot easily predict the exact dates of particular festivals. Some, as in Japan, have fixed dates by the Western calendar. But many other Buddhists rely for moon dates on printed calendars, such as the one produced at the Tibetan Medical Centre in Dharamsala, India, which is consulted by Tibetan *Buddhists* all over the world.

Festivals

Uposatha Days
Are observed at full moon and new moon and also on the days half way through the lunar fortnight. The full moon and new moon observances are the most important. On these days *monks* and devout lay Buddhists engage in more intense religious activities. The way in which these days are observed varies considerably among Buddhists, but their observance usually includes a visit to a monastery to make offerings of food to the *monks* and to pay one's respect to *Buddha* images and shrines.

Parinirvana (15th February)
Far Eastern *Mahayana* Buddhists mark the final passing away of Gautama *Buddha* at Kushinagara, India, at the age of eighty.

Buddha's Birthday (8th April in Japan)
Far Eastern *Mahayana* Buddhists celebrate this as a festival of flowers, reflecting the *Buddha's* birth in a garden. Sweet tea or water is ceremonially poured over a statue of the infant *Buddha*.

Wesak or Buddha Day (May)
Known as *Wesak* in Sri Lankan Buddhism and *Vaisakha Puja* in *Theravada* Buddhism, generally this festival occurs on the full moon day in May. It commemorates the Birth, *Enlightenment* and *Parinirvana* (passing away) of the *Buddha*, all of which, according to the *Theravada* tradition, occurred on the full moon day in May. Far Eastern *Mahayana* Buddhists celebrate these three events on different dates (see above). In the West, the day is generally known as *Buddha Day* and it is usually observed in common by Buddhists of all schools.

Poson (June)
Is the Sri Lankan name for the month and the festival which mark the conversion of Sri Lanka to Buddhism through the Venerable Mahinda, son of the Emperor Asoka, who brought the *dharma* to what is now Sri Lanka in c.250BCE.

The Rains Retreat
(June/July - September/October)
The retreat is known in South Asian countries as *Vassa* and is an annual feature of the *Theravada* monastic calendar which *monks* and *nuns* observe for three months. During this period *monks* and *nuns* should remain in one place except for emergencies. In the *Northern Transmission* and in the West, dates vary in accordance with the climate. The *Zen* school has two such retreats each year, each one for three months. Special services are held on the opening and closing days.

Asalha (Dharmachakra Day) (July/August)
This is the anniversary of the *Buddha's* first sermon to the five ascetics in the Deer Park near Benares in India. It is celebrated by *Theravadins* and the Friends of the Western Buddhist Order. The discourse was called the first *Turning of the Wheel of the Law*, which is the meaning of *Dharmachakra*. The day also marks the beginning of the *Rains Retreat*.

Kathina Day (October/November)
This is celebrated by *Theravadins* and follows the *Rains Retreat* either on its final day or within one month. On this day, the laity present *monks* and *nuns* with a cloth which is made into a robe for a monk on the same day. The precise date of observance varies according to the end of the rainy season in the various countries.

Samgha Day (November)
Is celebrated by the Friends of the Western Buddhist Order and sometimes by other *Western Buddhists* as an expression of the spiritual community of all Buddhists.

Enlightenment Day (8th December)
This is celebrated by Far Eastern *Mahayana* Buddhists. In India, *Mahayana* Buddhists observe this by celebrating under the *Bodhi Tree* in *Bodh Gaya*.

New Year
Although it is generally celebrated by Buddhists as a major festival, apart from the incorporation of some elements of Buddhist practice into its observance, *New Year* is not a specifically religious festival for Buddhists. The Sri Lankan and Thai *New Year* fall in mid-April and, in Thai tradition, *New Year* also involves a water festival. It is of greater importance in the *Mahayana* countries with their colder and darker winters. The Chinese *New Year* falls at the end of January or the beginning of February. In Japan, the western *New Year* date has been adopted.

Padmasambhava Day
There is a *Padmasambhava Day* in every Tibetan Lunar month, it is celebrated among *Nyingmapa*

Tibetan Buddhists in honour of Padmasambhava as the founder of Buddhism in Tibet.

Some *Mahayana* Buddhists also have festival days for various *Bodhisattvas* and for the founders of particular temples and monasteries. In Japanese schools of Buddhism, the Spring and Autumn equinoxes are celebrated as times of change and for remembrance of the dead.

BUDDHIST ORGANISATIONS

Due to the lack of firm statistics on the Buddhist community and the question of how to categorise large numbers of the ethnically Chinese population, it is difficult to give any precise indication of the relative proportions of the various traditions and groups within the Buddhist community.

Theravada Organisations

The *Theravada* community in the UK includes many ethnically European followers. There are also substantial groups of people with personal or ancestral roots in the traditional *Theravada* countries such as Sri Lanka, Burma and Thailand. Another group are the *Ambedkarites*, followers of Dr Ambedkar who led a social movement in India among low and "scheduled caste" Indians, many of whom converted to Buddhism from Hinduism.

A Sri Lankan *vihara* which opened in London in 1928 operated until 1940. In 1954, the London Buddhist Vihara was established with Sri Lankan teachers. A Thai Buddhist *vihara* of the traditional Thai style, known as the Buddhapadipa Temple, was opened in South West London in 1966 by the King and Queen of Thailand. Ananda Metteya's mission had been funded by the Burmese Buddhists who had also given substantial assistance to the Buddhist Society and, in 1978, the Burmese community opened a *vihara* - the West Midlands Buddhist Centre/Birmingham Buddhist Vihara.

In 1956 the English Sangha Trust was set up to establish a Western Theravada Sangha and in 1962 it founded the Hampstead Buddhist Vihara. In 1979, the Venerable Sumedho, an

American-born monk, founded the Chithurst Forest Monastery with a group of western *monks* and *nuns* trained in the Thai forest tradition. This now has branches in Northumberland (1981) and in Devon (1984), and in 1985 the Amaravati Buddhist Monastery was established near Hemel Hempstead. This Western Theravada Sangha should be distinguished from the Friends of the Western Buddhist Order (see below).

Mahayana Buddhist Organisations

The *Mahayana* tradition in Britain is represented by diverse religious and ethnic groups.

Tibetan Buddhist Organisations

In 1959 there was a great diaspora of Tibetan *Lamas* following the Lhasa uprising against Chinese rule and the flight into exile of the *Dalai Lama*. European Buddhists offered help to Tibetan refugees such as Chogyam Trungpa, a one time Abbot of the Surmang group of monasteries in Tibet, who came to study in Oxford in 1963. In 1967 he and Akong Rinpoche, the former Abbot of the Drolma Lhakhang Monastery, founded the first Tibetan Buddhist Centre in the West at Johnstone House in Dumfriesshire. It was named Samye Ling, after the first Buddhist monastery in Tibet. There are now many other *Tibetan Buddhist* centres in the UK.

The *Kagyupa* and *Gelugpa* schools are numerically the strongest *Tibetan Buddhist* traditions in Britain. An example of a centre in the former school is the Samye Ling monastery in Eskdalemuir, Scotland built in traditional Tibetan style. The Jamyang Centre in London, begun in 1978 by pupils of Lama Thubten Yeshe and the Lam Rim centres in Bristol and Wales are examples of *Gelugpa* centres. The *New Kadampa* tradition emerged from the *Gelugpa* school and has centres and groups throughout the UK under the leadership of Geshe Kelsang Gyatso. Four Sakyampa centres have been established with the *Dechen* community directed by the English Lama Nyakpa Jampa Thaye.

Zen Buddhist Organisations

The Japanese Buddhist Dr D T Suzuki attended the 1936 World Congress of Faiths in London and, although some of his work was concerned with *Pure Land* and other forms of *Mahayana* Buddhism, he is considered to have introduced *Zen* to the West, and specifically the *Rinzai* school. Both *Rinzai* and *Soto* schools can be found in Britain together with the Korean *Son* and the Chinese *Ch'an*.

Rinzai *Zen* is practised at The Buddhist Society and at Shobo-an, a training temple founded in 1984 in North London by the Venerable Myokyo-ni. There are other *Zen* organisations in London and in the rest of the country, the largest of which is the Throssel Hole Priory, founded in Northumberland in 1972 by Revd Master Ptnh Jiy-Kensett, a training monastery and retreat centre, which practises *Soto Zen*.

Pure Land Buddhist Organisations

Shin Buddhism has been the most influential *Pure Land* school in Britain. The Shin Buddhist Association of Great Britain was founded in 1976 and the Pure Land Buddhist Fellowship in 1977.

Shingon Mahayana Buddhism

Shingon is a Sino-Japanese form of esoteric Buddhism based on the *Mahavairocara* (*Great Sun*) *Sutra* and the *Kongocho* (*Diamond Peak*) *sutra*. The first Shingon Association in the west was founded in 1958 and the Kongoryuji Temple in Norfolk is a centre for *Shingon* Buddhism.

Some Other Japanese Buddhist Groups

Soka Gakkai International of the UK and a range of other similar Japanese groups tend to have a lay orientation and non-ascetic approach to Buddhist practice. Soka Gakkai is a lay movement which came to Britain during the 1980s. It is based on faith in the power of the *mantra* Nam-myoho-renge-kyo (as distinct from the *Namu-myoho-renge-kyo mantra* of some other schools); on study of Buddhist teaching as presented by Nichiren and his successors; and the twice daily practice of reciting the *mantra*, which is the Japanese name of the *Lotus Sutra*, in front of the *Gohonzon* (a scroll on which the *mantra* is written).

Other Japanese groups include Rissho Kosei-Kai, founded by Revd Nikkyo Niwano and Mrs M Nagakuma, and the Nipponzan Myohoji Order, founded by Nichidatsu Fuji. This latter Order is well-known for its campaign for peace and the Peace Pagodas it built in Milton Keynes (1980) and Battersea in London (1985). It is based on the recitation of the *mantra*, Namu-myoho-renge-kyo.

Friends of the Western Buddhist Order

In 1967, the Venerable Sangharakshita, an Englishman who was ordained into the three major traditions of Buddhism while living in India, returned to the UK and established the Western Buddhist Order later supported by the Friends of the Western Buddhist Order (FWBO). This is a new Buddhist movement which draws upon all the traditions of Eastern Buddhism whilst maintaining a strong engagement with Western culture.

It seeks to find new ways of living out the basic principles of Buddhism through the commitment of its members to the *Three Jewels* shared by all Buddhists. Many people involved in the FWBO live in single-sex residential communities and work in co-operative right-livelihood businesses, but there are also those who live monastic lives in retreat centres and others who have ordinary jobs.

Social Action Groups

A number of Buddhist groups have emerged in recent years to address social issues from the perspective of Buddhism. These include the Network of Engaged Buddhists and groups with specific focii such as the Buddhist Hospice Trust.

Personnel

The *samgha* or community of *monks* and *nuns* is central in traditional Buddhism. *Monks* are known as *bhikshu/bhikkhus* and *nuns* as *bhikshuni/bhikkhunis*, which literally means "almsmen" and "almswomen", reflecting the originally mendicant lifestyle of the *samgha*. The

original role of the *samgha* was to work for their own spiritual development and to share the *dharma* with others, but Buddhist *monks* have often also called upon them to officiate in priest-like ways at rites of passage, and they have also often become involved in tasks related to education and health care.

The *Theravada samgha* can be recognised by their shaved heads and orange or ochre robes. They do not personally possess money and do not eat after mid-day. They differ from Christian *monks* and *nuns* in that they do not take vows of obedience and the vows that they do take are not necessarily binding upon them for life. Indeed, among Thai and Burmese Buddhists it is typical for young men temporarily to take on the *sharmanera* (lower) ordination as a kind of rite of passage into adulthood.

Those who take the lower ordination are called upon to live by the *Ten Precepts*. These include the *Five Precepts* together with the refraining from misuse of the senses being extended to total chastity. In addition, it entails refraining from eating at unseasonable times; dancing, singing and visiting musical shows; and wearing garlands, perfumes and unguents, finery and adornments; high or luxurious beds; and the handling of gold, silver or money in general.

After higher ordination, *monks* and *nuns* live according to the full monastic code known as the *vinaya* which entails extensive additional obligations set out in the 227 disciplinary rules for *monks* and 348 for *nuns*. The ordination of women as *nuns* was, in the *Buddha's* day, a revolutionary innovation and the *Buddha* only instituted the *bhikshuni* order after the pleading of his widowed foster mother and at the request of the monk Ananda.

The order was founded on the basis that the *nuns* followed additional special rules, intended for their protection. Generally, Buddhism argues for the equality of men and women in their spiritual potential and on several occasions Gautama defended the equality of the sexes in this regard. In the highest realms of rebirth a person or entity is not conceived of as having any gender.

The *bhikshuni* order survived only in *Northern Buddhism*. In *Tibetan Buddhism* there was controversy over the validity of their ordination, which did not come from the Indian line but was introduced in the twelfth century. In other *Mahayana* schools, the spiritual equality of women and men is recognised and women receive full ordination and follow the same precepts as men.

Today, in the *Theravada* tradition, *nuns* may again be ordained and the total number of *nuns* worldwide in all traditions has been increasing throughout this century. In recent times, especially in the West, a *Theravada nuns' samgha* has been re-established. The *Northern*, and especially the *Far Eastern*, *Transmission*, have always included *nuns*, who live on a similar basis to *monks*. Their codes of living differ according to the different schools to which they belong.

In the Tibetan tradition a *Lama* (teacher) is often a *monk* or a *nun*, but does not need to be so, and there are lay people who are skilful teachers and are revered as *Lamas*. In the *Far Eastern Mahayana* schools, except for the *Pure Land School*, both *monks* and *nuns* shave their heads at first ordination and live in monastic communities. Robes, rules and practices differ from school to school, but all are dedicated to the *Bodhisattva Way*, wishing to be of benefit to all living beings. In the *Mahayana* tradition, a lay person of either gender may take a *Bodhisattva* commitment and may be recognised as being of higher spiritual attainment than either a *monk* or a *nun*.

In the Japanese schools, the teachers are generally *monks* and *nuns* or *ministers*, although in Britain there are also a number of lay ministers who have a limited role in teaching. In the *Rinzai* school, *koans* are only taught by teachers authorised to do so. In all Japanese schools a priesthood - as distinct from *monks* and *nuns* - was introduced after the Meiji Restoration of 1868, when the Japanese Government encouraged temple incumbents/ *abbots* to marry (although *nuns* remained celibate). Today, there are training monasteries with celibate *monks* or *nuns* and a celibate *Zen Master*, and temples with ordained *priests* who may be married and train postulants for entry into a monastery.

In the Western Buddhist Order members are ordained either as *Dharmacharis* (males) or as *Dharmacharinis* (females). Some members of the Order live monastic lifestyles whilst others have families. Within the Order these differences in lifestyle are not seen as being differences in status. All members of the Order follow *Ten Precepts* (a different list from the ten *shramanera* precepts of the *Theravada* monastic tradition) which lay down basic ethical principles governing actions of body, speech and mind.

FURTHER READING

Almond, P C, *The British Discovery of Buddhism*, Cambridge University Press, Cambridge, 1988.

Batchelor, S, *The Awakening of the West: The Encounter of Buddhism and Western Culture*, Aquarian Press, London, 1994.

Batchelor, S, "Buddhism and European Culture", in Gill, S; D'Costa G; King, U (eds), *Religion in Europe: Contemporary Perspectives*, Kok Pharos, Kampen, 1994, pp 86-104.

Bechert, H and Gombrich, R, *The World of Buddhism*, Thames and Hudson, London, 1984.

Buddhist Society, The, *The Buddhist Directory*, The Buddhist Society, London, 1997.

Connolly, P and Erricker, C, *The Presence and Practice of Buddhism*, West Sussex Institute of Higher Education, 1985.

Conze, E, *Buddhist Scriptures*, Penguin, Harmondsworth, 1959.

Conze, E, *A Short History of Buddhism*, Allen and Unwin, 1980.

Dalai Lama, H H, *The World of Tibetan Buddhism*, Wisdom Publications, Boston, 1995.

Gombrich, R, *Theravada Buddhism: A Social History from Ancient Benares to Modern Colombo*, Routledge and Kegan Paul, London, 1988.

Goonewardene, A, *Introducing Buddhism*, Paper 2; *Life of the Buddha*, Paper 4; *Life of the Buddha*, Paper 5; *Geographical Development of Buddhism In Outline*, Part I, Paper 6, *Geographical Development of Buddhism in Outline*, Part II, Paper 7; *The Buddhist Councils*, Paper 8; *The Schools and Traditions of Buddhism (in outline) and Their Common Features*, Paper 9; *The Fundamental Buddhist Philosophy of the Four Noble Truths and the Noble Eightfold Path*, Buddhism for Schools and Colleges Series, Papers 10 and 11, The Buddhist Society, London, 1989-1993.

Green, D, "Buddhism in Britain: Skilful Means or Selling Out?", in Badham, P (ed), *Religion, State and Society in Modern Britain*, Edwin Mellen Press, Lampeter, 1989, pp 277-291.

Harvey, P, *An Introduction to Buddhism: Teachings, History, and Practices*, Cambridge University Press, Cambridge, 1990.

Humphreys, C, *Sixty Years of Buddhism in England 1907-1967: A History and a Survey*, The Buddhist Society, London, 1968.

Kasulis, T, *Zen Action, Zen Person*, UPH, 1981.

Myokyo-ni, *The Zen Way*, The Zen Centre, London, 1978.

Myokyo-ni, *Gentling the Bull*, The Zen Centre, London, nd.

Pauling, C, *Introducing Buddhism*, Windhorse Publications, Glasgow, 1993.

Powell, A, *Living Buddhism*, British Museum, London, 1989.

Rahula, Venerable Walpola, *What the Buddha Taught*, Gordon Fraser, Bedford, 1959.

Robinson, R and Johnson, W, *The Buddhist Religion*, 3rd edition, Wadsworth, 1982.

Saddhatissa, Venerable H, *The Buddha's Way*, Allen and Unwin, London, 1971.

Sangharakshita, Venerable, *New Currents in Western Buddhism*, Windhorse Publications, Glasgow, 1990.

Snelling, J, *The Buddhist Handbook: A Complete Guide to Buddhist Teaching and Practice*, Rider, London, 1987.

Snelling, J, *The Elements of Buddhism*, Element Books, Dorset, 1990.

Subhuti, *Buddhism for Today*, Element Books, London, 1983

Suzuki, Shunryu, *Zen Mind, Beginner's Mind*, Weatherhill, New York, 1970.

Williams, P, *Mahayana Buddhism: The Doctrinal Foundations*, Routledge and Kegan Paul, London, 1989.

Wisdom Publications, *The International Buddhist Directory*, Wisdom Publications, London, 1984.

BUDDHIST UNITED KINGDOM ORGANISATIONS

Together with a number of Buddhist bodies set up to operate beyond local and regional boundaries, this list of UK-wide Buddhist organisations also includes a number of monasteries or centres. Whilst these are based in particular localities (and some may also therefore be found listed in the Regional or Local section of this chapter), they are included in this section because they are also points of reference for wider networks which look to them for guidance and support.

In this chapter only, the standard activity descriptor "worship" appears as "worship/ meditation" since many Buddhists feel that the word "worship" is not an appropriate word for them.

Amaravati Buddhist Monastery
Great Gaddesden, Hemel Hempstead, Hertfordshire, HP1 3BZ
Tel: 01442-842455 **Fax:** 01442-843721
Contact: Secretary
Activities: Worship/meditation, newsletters, books
Traditions: Theravada
Movements: Vipassana
Other Languages: Thai, French
Facilities include a retreat centre where scheduled retreats are led by members of the Sangha. For information: send SAE to the Secretary; to book a retreat send SAE to the Retreat Manager.

Amida Trust
Quannon House, 53 Grosvenor Place, Jesmond, Newcastle-upon-Tyne, Tyne and Wear, NE2 2RD
Tel: 0191-281-5592
EMail: amida@amida.demon.co.uk
Internet: http://www.angelfire.com/tx/at/USA/
Contact: Caroline Brazier
Position: Co-ordinator
Activities: Worship/meditation, resource, newsletters, books
Traditions: Zen
Affiliations: Network of Buddhist Organisations
The Trust has an international membership and promotes practical projects in Buddhist culture, practice, community, and compassionate action, including a psychotherapy training programme, a retreat house in France, and a variety of service and aid activities.

Angulimala, The Buddhist Prison Chaplaincy Organisation
The Forest Hermitage, Lower Fulbrook, Warwick, Warwickshire, CV35 8AS
Tel: 01926-624385 **Fax:** 01926-624385
EMail: phra.khem@zetnet.co.uk
Traditions: Multi-Traditional
Unfortunately, resources do not always stretch to responding to requests for help with school projects and the like.

ApTibet (Appropriate Technology for Tibetans)
117a Cricklewood Broadway, London, NW2 3JG
Tel: 0181-450-8090 **Fax:** 0181-450-9705
EMail: aptibet@gn.apc.org
Contact: David Savage
Position: Administration and Fundraising Manager

An environmental NGO which works at grassroots level with Tibetan refugees in India, saving lives and empowering them to build a sustainable future for themselves.

Aukana Trust
9 Masons Lane, Bradford-on-Avon, Wiltshire, BA15 1QN
Tel: 01225-866821 **Fax:** 01225-865262
EMail: aukana@globalnet.co.uk
Internet: http://www.aukana.org.uk
Contact: Robert Mann
Position: Assistant Teacher
Activities: Books
Traditions: Theravada
Movements: Vipassana
The Aukana Trust runs a meditation centre, the House of Inner Tranquillity, plus two monasteries, one for monks and one for nuns.

British Shingon Buddhist Association Shingon Mushindokai
Kongoryuji Temple, 29 London Road, East Dereham, Norfolk, NR19 1AS
Tel: 01362-693692 **Fax:** 01362-693692
EMail: 100713.543@compuserve.com
Contact: Shifu Nagaboshi Tomio
Position: Shifu
Activities: Worship/meditation, newsletters, books
Movements: Shingon
Other Languages: Japanese
Affiliations: Network of Buddhist Organisations; European Buddhist Union
The Association provides study and retreat facilities for members. It sponsors training and teacher training in healing and remedial sciences according to Buddhist tradition.

British Buddhist Association
11 Biddulph Road, London, W9 1JA
Tel: 0171-286-5575 **Fax:** 0171-286-5575
Contact: A Haviland-Nye
Position: Director
Activities: Worship/meditation, resource
Traditions: Western, Non-denominational
Promotes educational, religious and meditation aspects of the Buddha's teaching at evening and weekend sessions both in London and at country retreats. It is non-sectarian and seeks to express devotion in ways suitable to Western practitioners.

Buddha Dharma Association
12 Featherstone Road, Southall, Middlesex, UB9 5AA
Tel: 0181-571-5131 **Tel:** 0181-575-2348 (h)
Fax: 0181-575-3134
Contact: Harbans Virdee
Position: Assistant Secretary
Activities: Worship/meditation, visits, youth, elderly, women, newsletters, books, inter-faith
Traditions: Theravada
Movements: Ambedkarite, Maha Bodhi
Other Languages: Hindi, Punjabi, Maharashti
Affiliations: London Buddhist Vihara; Federation of Ambedkarite and Buddhist Organisations, UK

Buddhapadipa Temple
14 Calonne Road, Wimbledon, London, SW19 5HJ
Tel: 0181-946-1357 **Fax:** 0181-944-5788
Contact: Secretary
Activities: Worship/meditation
Traditions: Theravada
Movements: Samatha, Vipassana
Other Languages: Thai, Pali
The five Dhammaduta monks who are resident at the Temple spread the teachings of the Buddha in the theory and practice of Buddhism, Insight Meditation, and the practice of daily meditation and retreats.

Buddhism Psychology & Psychiatry Group
B8 Notre Dame Mews, Northampton, Northamptonshire, NN1 2BG
Tel: 01604-604608 **Fax:** 01604-604531
EMail: 100577,150@compuserv.com
Contact: Dr Kedar Nath Dwivedi
Position: Chair
Activities: Resource
Traditions: Multi-Traditional
A membership group and forum for sharing experience, interests and ideas regarding links and parallels between Buddhism and modern psychology, psychiatry and allied professions.

Buddhist Co-operative
5 Hindmans Road, Dulwich, London, SE22 9NF
Tel: 0181-693-9951 **Tel:** 01992-504705 (h)
Contact: Dr Zenida McDonald
Position: Librarian

Activities: Resource, visits, youth, elderly, women, newsletters, books, inter-faith
Traditions: Zen, Multi-Traditional
Movements: Ch'an, Rinzai Zen
Other Languages: Malaysian, Mandarin
Affiliations: Malaysian Buddhist Association; European Buddhist Order, Amsterdam, Holland
Aims to promote the study of Buddhist Economics and teach the Art of Useful Unemployment. The essence of Buddhist economics is Right Livelihood. Works with prisoners and hospital patients. Publishes the "Buddhist Economist" magazine.

Buddhist Hospice Trust
5 Grayswood Point, Norley Vale, Roehampton, London, SW15 4BT (h)
Tel: 0181-789-6170 (h)
Contact: Ray Wills
Position: Honorary Secretary
Activities: Resource, newsletters, books, inter-faith
Traditions: Multi-Traditional
Affiliations: Network of Buddhist Organisations

Buddhist Publishing Group
Sharpham Coach Yard, Ashprington, Totnes, Devon, TQ9 7UT
Tel: 01803-732082 **Fax:** 01803-732037
EMail: buddhist.publishing@dial.pipex.com
Contact: Richard Charles St.Ruth
Position: Partner
Activities: Books
Traditions: Multi-Traditional
Affiliations: Network of Buddhist Organisations
A non-sectarian organisation, producing a quarterly magazine "Buddhism Now" and a variety of Buddhist books, selling through mail order. It holds a summer school in Leicester offering a programme of talks and meditation from various Buddhist schools.

Buddhist Society
58 Eccleston Square, London, SW1V 1PH
Tel: 0171-834-5858 **Fax:** 0171-976-5238
Contact: Mr Ronald Maddox
Position: General Secretary
Activities: Worship/meditation, resource, umbrella, visits, newsletters, books, inter-faith
Traditions: Multi-Traditional
Affiliations: Network of Buddhist Organisations; World Federation of Buddhists; Inter Faith Network for the UK

Open to all who feel able to subscribe to its aims, the Society was founded in 1924 by Christmas Humphreys. It aims to publish and make known the principles of Buddhism and to encourage the study and practice of these principles.

Clear Vision Trust
Manchester Buddhist Centre, 16-20 Turner Street, Manchester, Greater Manchester, M4 1DZ
Tel: 0161-839-9579 **Fax:** 0161-839-4815
EMail: clearvision@c-vision.demon.co.uk
Contact: Padmasri
Position: Education Development Officer
Activities: Resource, media
Traditions: Western
Movements: Ambedkarite; Friends of the Western Buddhist Order
Affiliations: Manchester Budhist Centre; Friends of the Western Buddhist Order
Clear Vision is a charitable trust set up to promote Buddhism through the visual media. We produce teaching resources for schools, provide inservice training for teachers, have a photo archive and extensive video material on Buddhism.

Dharmachakra Tapes
3 Coral Park, Henley Road, Cambridge, Cambridgeshire, CB1 3EA
Fax: 01223-566568
Contact: Shatigarbha
Position: Manager
Activities: Resource, media
Traditions: Western
Movements: Friends of the Western Buddhist Order
Produces audiotapes.

Dharma School
The White House, Ladies Mile Road, Patcham, Brighton, East Sussex, BN1 8TB
Tel: 01273-502055 (h) **Fax:** 01273-556580
Contact: Medhina
Position: Head of School
Activities: Resource, visits, inter-faith
Traditions: Multi-Traditional
Movements: Theravadin Forest Sangha
Affiliations: Theravadin Forest Sangha; Network of Buddhist Organisations
The Dharma School Trust was established in 1992 to provide high quality primary and secondary education. It currently runs a pre-school nursery

and primary school for children aged 3-11 and is Buddhist in the values it imparts. Open to children of all backgrounds.

Dr Ambedkar Memorial Committee of G.B.
Buddha Vihara, Upper Zoar Street, Pennfields, Woverhampton, West Midlands, WV3 0JH
Tel: 01902-715094 **Tel:** 01902-730664 (h)
Fax: 01902-341186
Contact: Mr Mohan Lal
Position: Secretary
Activities: Worship/meditation, resource, visits, youth, elderly, women, newsletters, books, inter-faith
Traditions: Theravada
Movements: Ambedkarite, Vipassana
Other Languages: Punjabi, Hindi, Sinhalese, Thai

Federation of Ambedkarite & Buddhist Organisations UK
Milan House, 8 Kingsland Road, Shoreditch, London, E2 8DA
Tel: 0171-729-6341 **Fax:** 0171-729-6341
Contact: Mr C Gautam
Position: General Secretary
Activities: Media, umbrella, newsletters, books, inter-faith
Traditions: Theravada
Movements: Ambedkarite, Vipassana
Other Languages: Hindi, Punjabi, Gujarati, Urdu
The Federation has been set up to propogate Ambedkar's thought and Buddhist ideas throughout the world. The Federation represents the amalgamation of many groups in the UK.

Friends of The Western Buddhist Order
c/o London Buddhist Centre, 51 Roman Road, Bethnal Green, London, E2 0HU
Tel: 0171-981-1225 **Fax:** 0181-980-1968
EMail: lbc@alanlbc.demon.uk
Activities: Worship/meditation, visits, newsletters
Traditions: Western
Movements: Friends of the Western Buddhist Order
Affiliations: Network of Buddhist Organisations; European Buddhist Union; Inter Faith Network for the UK
The Friends of the Western Buddhist Order seeks to apply the central principles of Buddhism in the context of the modern world through its thirty UK centres and retreat centres. The London Buddhist Centre can direct enquiries to the most appropriate source in the Friends of the Western Buddhist Order.

Friends of the Western Buddhist Order (Communications)
c/o St Mark's Studio, Chillingworth Road, London, N7 8QJ
Tel: 0171-700-3077 **Fax:** 0171-700-3077
EMail: Liaison@fwbo.demon.co.uk
Contact: Kulamitra and Vishvapani
Position: Liaison and Press
Activities: Media, newsletters, inter-faith
Traditions: Western
Movements: Friends of the Western Buddhist Order
Affiliations: Network of Buddhist Organisations; Angulimala Buddhist Prison Chaplaincy; European Buddhist Union
The Communications Office handles contact with the media and other religious groups.

Institute of Oriental Philosophy European Centre
Taplow Court, Taplow, Maidenhead, Berkshire, SL6 0ER
Tel: 01628-776719 **Fax:** 01628-773055
EMail: JamieC@compuserve.com
Contact: Jamie Cresswell
Position: Manager
Activities: Resource
Languages: Japanese
Traditions: Nichiren
Affiliations: Network of Buddhist Organisations; SGI-UK
A research and study centre based on a growing library (8,000 books) on Buddhism and related religions/philosophies. It holds lectures, seminars and symposia and carries out research into all areas of Buddhism and religion in a multidisciplinary and cross-traditional manner.

International Ambedkar Institute UK
90 Pennine Way, Kettering, Northamptonshire, NN16 9AX (h)
Tel: 01536-522057
Contact: Nagan Srinivasan
Activities: Resource
Traditions: Theravada
Movements: Ambedkarite

Other Languages: Kannada, Hindi, Punjabi, Urdu
Affiliations: Federation of Ambedkarite and Buddhist Organisations in the UK

International Buddhist Progress Society UK
Fo Kuang Temple, 84 Margaret Street, London, W1N 7HD (h)
Tel: 0171-636-8394 (h) **Fax:** 0171-580-6220
Contact: Venerable Chueh Yann
Position: Director
Activities: Worship/meditation, resource, visits, youth, women, newsletters
Traditions: Mahayana
Movements: Ch'an, Pure Land
Other Languages: Chinese, English, Cantonese
Affiliations: Hsi Lai Temple Los Angeles, USA
Regular Sunday service 10.30am-12.00noon. Organises at least two big events each year and a one day retreat in the Temple.

International Zen Association, UK
91-93 Gloucester Road, Bishopston, Bristol, Greater Bristol, BS7 8AT
Tel: 0117-942-4347
Position: Secretary
Activities: Worship/meditation, umbrella, visits, newsletters, inter-faith
Traditions: Zen
Movements: Soto Zen
Other Languages: French
Affiliations: Association Zen Internationale, France
National headquarters, with Zen sitting groups throughout the country. These are open to the public. Also organises Zen retreats regularly.

Jodo Shu Foundation of Great Britain
48 Laburnum Crescent, Kettering, Northamptonshire, NN16 9PJ (h)
Tel: 01536-517782 (h)
Traditions: Zen
Movements: Jodo Shu

Karuna Trust
St Mark's Studio, Chillingworth Road, London, N7 8QJ
Tel: 0171-700-3434 **Fax:** 0171-700-3535
EMail: 100420.3457@compuserve.com
Contact: Peter Joseph
Position: Director
Traditions: Multi-Traditional

Movements: Friends of the Western Buddhist Order
Affiliations: North London Buddhist Centre; Friends of the Western Buddhist Order
The Karuna Trust is a Buddhist-inspired charity supporting long term development work in India. Projects are run in the areas of education, health, and skill-training to reach out to all communities affected by poverty and discrimination.

Lam Rim Buddhist Centre
Pentwyn Manor, Penrhos, Raglan, Gwent, NP5 2LE
Tel: 01600-780383 (h)
Contact: Venerable Geshe Damcho Yonten
Position: Spiritual Director
Activities: Worship/meditation, resource, umbrella, visits, youth, elderly, women, inter-faith
Traditions: Tibetan
Movements: Gelugpa
Other Languages: German, Tibetan
Affiliations: Network of Buddhist Organisations; Drepung Loseling Monastery, South India

Lights In The Sky
39a Lough Road, London, N7 8RH
Tel: 0171-607-9480 **Tel:** 0181-800-7821 (h)
Fax: 0171-607-9480
EMail: surya@intonet.co.uk
Contact: Suryaprabha
Position: Director
Activities: Resource, media
Traditions: Western
Movements: Friends of the Western Buddhist Order
Other Languages: Spanish
Affiliations: North London Buddhist Centre, Friends of the Western Buddhist Order (Central)
We make videos and films of interest to (Western) Buddhists, though they also suit a wide audience. We have training facilities and modern computer-based editing. Work to commission also undertaken.

Linh-Son Buddhist Association in the UK
89 Bromley Road, Catford, London, SE6 2UF
Tel: 0181-461-1887
Contact: Secretary
The Vietnamese Buddhist Temple serves the Chinese as well as the Vietnamese community. It is under the guidance of the Venerable Thich Huyen Vi and, in England, the Venerable Thich Tri Camh (resident).

Longchen Foundation

30 Beechey Avenue, Old Marston, Oxford,
Oxfordshire, OX3 0JU (h)
Tel: 01865-725569 **Fax:** 01865-725569
EMail: LCF@Compuserve.com
Contact: Caroline Cupitt
Position: Administrator
Activities: Resource, newsletters, books
Traditions: Tibetan
Movements: Nyingmapa
Affiliations: Network of Buddhist Organisations
The Longchen Foundation is a circle of Buddhist
teachers and students belonging to the Mahayana
tradition of Buddhism. The principal teachers are
Rigdzin Shikpo (formerly Michael Hookham)
and Sherpen Hookham.

Manjushri Mahayana Buddhist Centre

Conishead Priory, Priory Road, Ulverston,
Cumbria, LA12 9QQ
Tel: 01229-584029 (h) **Fax:** 01229-580080
EMail: manjushri@tep.co.uk
Contact: Kelsang Kunkyen
Position: Assistant Branch Co-ordinator
Activities: Worship/meditation, visits, youth,
elderly, women, newsletters, books
Traditions: Western
Movements: New Kadampa
Visitors are welcome, whether for a weekend
course or retreat, to participate in our regular
programme, or just for a few quiet days in pleasant
surroundings

Network of Buddhist Organisations UK

The Old Courthouse, 43 Renfrew Road,
Kennington, London, SE11 4NA
Tel: 0171-582-5797 **Fax:** 0171-582-5797
Contact: Paul Seto
Position: Honorary Secretary
Activities: Resource, umbrella
Traditions: Multi-Traditional
Affiliations: Inter Faith Network for the UK
A representative body that shares the experience
and resources of many of the various Buddhist
teaching, charitable, educational and cultural
organisations and individual practitioners in the
UK.

Network of Engaged Buddhists (UK)

Plas Plwca, Cwmrheidol, Aberystwyth, Dyfed,
SY23 3NB (h)
Tel: 01970-880603 (h)

Contact: Ken Jones
Position: Secretary
Activities: Resource, newsletters, inter-faith
Traditions: Multi-Traditional
Affiliations: International Network of Engaged
Buddhists
The Network is a fellowship of people trying to
combine inner peace seeking and outward social
concern in ways which support and enrich both
endeavours. It publishes a journal, "Indra's
Network", and organises retreats and workshops.

New Kadampa Tradition

NKT Office, Conishead Priory, Ulverston,
Cumbria, LA12 9QQ
Tel: 01229-584029 **Fax:** 01229-580080
EMail: kadampa@dircon.co.uk
Internet: http://www.users.direcon.
co.uk/~kadampa
Contact: James A Belither
Position: Secretary
Activities: Umbrella
Traditions: Tibetan, Western
Movements: New Kadampa
Association of independent Mahayana Buddhist
Centres united by the common spiritual path
transmitted through a lineage of Indian and Tibetan
masters including, in particular, Atisha and Je
Tsongkhapa.

Nipponzan Myohoji

The London Peace Pagoda, c/o Park Office,
Albert Bridge Road, London, SW11 4NJ (h)
Tel: 0171-228-9620 (h) **Fax:** 0181-871-7533
Contact: Revd G Nagase
Position: Resident Monk
Activities: Worship/meditation, visits, inter-faith
Traditions: Nichiren
Movements: Nipponzan Myhohoji
Other Languages: Japanese

Office of Tibet

Tibet House, 1 Culworth Street, London,
NW8 7AF
Tel: 0171-722-5378 **Fax:** 0171-722-0362
EMail: tibetlondon@gn.apc.org
Internet: http://www.gn.apc.org/tibetLondon/
Contact: T Samdup
Position: Press and Information
Activities: Newsletters, inter-faith
Traditions: Tibetan
Movements: Multi-Movements

Other Languages: Tibetan

Established in 1981, the Office of Tibet in London is the official agency of the Dalai Lama. It represents Tibetan affairs in the UK and supervises arrangements for his visits, whilst looking after the welfare of Tibetans living in the UK and Northern Europe.

Peace Pagoda (Nipponzan Myohoji)

Willen, Milton Keynes, Buckinghamshire, MK15 0B

Tel: 01908-663652

Contact: Revd S Handa

Position: Monk in Charge

Activities: Worship/meditation, resource, visits, inter-faith

Traditions: Nichiren

Movements: Nipponzan Myhohoji

Other Languages: Japanese, Dutch

Traditional Japanese temple and gardens still under construction. Visitors and helpers welcome but please phone or write beforehand. We join in/organise frequent peace walks in troubled areas of the world.

Pure Land Buddhist Foundation of Great Britain

48 Laburnham Crescent, Kettering, Northamptonshire, NN1 69PJ

Tel: 01536-517782 (h)

Traditions: Pure Land

Reiyukai

Unit 24, Saint Mary's Works, Duke Street, Norwich, Norfolk, NR3 1QA

Tel: 01603-630857 **Tel:** 01603-465189 (h)

Fax: 01603-760749

Contact: Julian Wilde

Position: UK Secretary

Activities: Worship/meditation, resource, umbrella, visits, youth, elderly, newsletter, inter-faith

Traditions: Nichiren

Other Languages: Japanese, Thai

RIGPA Fellowship

330 Caledonian Road, London, N1 1BB

Tel: 0171-700-0185 **Fax:** 0171-609-6068

EMail: 100742,3523@compuserve.com

Contact: Katie Sharrock

Position: Director

Activities: Visits, newsletters, books, inter-faith

Traditions: Tibetan

Movements: Nyingmapa

Affiliations: Network of Buddhist Organisations; European Buddhist Union

The Rigpa Fellowship offers a complete introduction to Buddhism through graduated courses in meditation, compassion and Buddhist wisdom based on the teachings of Sogyal Rinpoche, its spiritual director.

Sakyadhita: International Association of Buddhist Women (UK)

16 Nun Street, Lancaster, Lancashire, LA1 3PJ (h)

Tel: 01524-844719 (h) **Fax:** 0181-802-0628

EMail: J.C.Milton@Lancaster.ac.uk

Contact: Jasmin Bassett

Position: UK Representative

Activities: Resource, women, newsletters

Traditions: Multi-Traditional

Affiliations: Network of Buddhist Organisations; European Buddhist Union

It works locally and globally for mutual support and education; researches into women's issues; bi-annual international conference. Male supporters welcome. International HQ in Honolulu, Hawai, USA.

Sakya Thinley Rinchen Ling

121 Sommerville Road, St. Andrews, Bristol, Greater Bristol, BS6 5BX

Tel: 0117-924-4424

Contact: David Armstrong

Position: Co-ordinator

Activities: Worship/meditation, visits, youth, newsletters, books, inter-faith

Traditions: Tibetan

Movements: Sakyapa

Affiliations: Bristol and Bath Buddhist Coalition; Network of Buddist Organisations

The centre belongs to the Dechen community, an association of Sakya and Kagyu Centres founded in Europe under the direction of Karma Thinley Rinpoche and Lama Jampa Thaye.

Samatha Trust

The Samatha Centre, Greenstreete, Llangunllo, Powys, LD7 1SP

Tel: 01547-550274

Contact: David Hall

Position: Secretary

Activities: Visits, newsletters, books

Traditions: Theravada

Movements: Samatha

The Trust was founded in 1973 with the aim of encouraging and supporting this traditional form of Buddhist practice. Classes are held around the country and residential courses at the Centre.

Samye Ling Tibetan Centre (Rokpa Trust)

Samye Ling Tibetan Centre, Eskdalemuir, Langholm, Dumfries and Galloway, DG13 0QL
Tel: 01387-373232 **Fax:** 01387-373222
EMail: samye@rokpa.u-net.com
Internet: http://www.samye.org/
Contact: Nicholas Jennings
Position: Committee Member
Activities: Worship/meditation, umbrella, visits, newsletters, books, inter-faith
Traditions: Tibetan
Movements: Kagyupa
Other Languages: Tibetan
Affiliations: ROKPA International
Founded in 1967, Samye Ling has branches throughout Europe and Africa. It established Rokpa Foreign Aid, the Holy Island Project and the Tara College of Tibetan Medicine.

Sang-ngak-cho-dzong

PO Box 2318, Bridport, Dorset, DT6 5PY
Tel: 01308-425808 **Fax:** 01308-425808
EMail: nrp@pobox.com
Contact: O.Sel Nyima
Position: Administrative Secretary
Activities: Resource, umbrella, newsletters, books
Traditions: Tibetan
Movements: Ngakphang
Affiliations: Network of Buddhist
Organisations; European Buddhist Union
Sang-ngak-cho-dzong was founded to establish the Ngakphang tradition of non-celibate, non-monastic practitioners. It's spiritual directors are holders of the Aro gTer lineage which emanates from a succession of enlightened women.

Sayagyi U Ba Khin Memorial Trust

International Meditation Centre, Splatts House, Heddington, Calne, Wiltshire, SN11 0PE
Tel: 01380-850-238 **Fax:** 01380-850-833
EMail: 100330.3304@compuserve.com
Internet: http://www.webcom. com.imcuk/
Contact: Mr E Klima
Position: Manager
Activities: Newsletters

Traditions: Theravada
Movements: Sayagyi U Ba Khin Tradition
Other Languages: German, Italian, French, Burmese
Affiliations: International Meditation Centre Yangon
Ten-day residential courses in Anapana and Vipassana Theravada Buddhist meditation teachniques held once a month at the above centre, beginning on Friday evenings and ending on Monday mornings, under guidance of Mother Sayamagyi and Sayagyi U Chit Tin.

Shambhala Meditation Centre

27 Belmont Close, Clapham, London, SW4 7AY
Tel: 0171-720-3207 **Tel:** 0171-652-6568 (h)
Contact: Deborah Coats
Position: Co-ordinator
Activities: Worship/meditation
Traditions: Tibetan
Movements: Kagyupa, Nyingmapa
Other Languages: German, Spanish, French
Affiliations: Shambhala International
Founded by Chogyam Trungpa Rinpoche - Tibetan meditation master and author of several books, including "Shambhala: The Sacred Path of the Warrior". The Centre is now directed by Sakyong Mipham Rinpoche.

Shedrup Ling Buddhist Centre

15 Parkfield Road, Aigburth, Liverpool, Merseyside, L17 8UG
Tel: 0151-727-0108
Internet: http://www.eclipse.co.uk/~rs1042
Contact: Sarah Ashmore
Position: Centre Manager
Activities: Worship/meditation, resource, media, visits, newsletters, books, inter-faith
Traditions: Tibetan
Movements: Kagyupa
Other Languages: Spanish, German
Affiliations: Network of Buddhist Organisations
Shedrup Ling belongs to the Dechen Community, an association of Kagyu and Sakya centres founded in Europe under the direction of Karma Thinley Rinpoche and Lama Jampa Thaye.

Shen Phen Thubten Choeling

The Nurses Cottage, Long Lane, Peterchurch, Hereford and Worcester, HR2 0TE (h)
Tel: 01981-550247 (h) **Fax:** 01981-550030
Contact: Elaine Brook

Position: Centre Director
Traditions: Tibetan
Movements: Gelugpa
Other Languages: French, Spanish, Nepalese, Tibetan
Affiliations: The Foundation for the Preservation of the Mayahana Tradition
Provides a place for individual and group retreat, enabling participants to deepen their experience of meditation within an awareness of a way of life that practises non-harming.

Society for the Advancement of Buddhist Understanding

Joule Road, West Point Business Park, Andover, Hampshire, SP10 3UX
Tel: 01264-353123, Ext: 217 **Fax:** 01264-354883
Contact: Kazutoshi Sato
Position: Director
Traditions: Multi-Traditional
Other Languages: Japanese
Represents Bukkyo Dendo Kyokai in Japan. It does not promote any particular denominational or sectarian doctrine but propagates a modern understanding of the Buddhist spirit to reach out to strive towards global peace and harmony.

Soka Gakkai International UK

Taplow Court, Taplow, Maidenhead, Berkshire, SL6 0ER
Tel: 01628-773163 **Fax:** 01628-773055
Contact: Mr Robert Samuels
Position: Executive Assistant
Activities: Resource, visits, youth, elderly, women, newsletters, books, inter-faith
Traditions: Nichiren
Movements: Soka Gakkai
Affiliations: The Network of Buddhist Organisations
Monthly discussion meetings, where guests are warmly welcomed, are held in the homes of members at some 300 venues throughout the UK. Details of these are available through Taplow Court.

Sri Lankan Sangha Sabha UK

c/o London Buddhist Vihara, Dharmapala Building, The Avenue, Chiswick, London, W4 1UD
Tel: 0181-995-9493 **Fax:** 0181-994-8130
Contact: Most Venerable Medagama Vajiragnana
Position: President
Traditions: Theravada

The organisation links a number of Sri Lankan Buddhist centres in the country, including the London Buddhist Vihara which is the national focal point for this community.

Taraloka Buddhist Retreat Centre for Women

Cornhill Farm, Bettisfield, Nr Whitchurch, Shropshire, SY13 2LD (h)
Tel: 01948-710646 **Tel:** 01948-710654 (h)
EMail: 100073.3502@compuserve.com
Contact: Saddhanandi
Position: Secretary
Activities: Resource, visits, women
Traditions: Multi-Traditional
Movements: Friends of the Western Buddhist Order
Affiliations: Friends of the Western Buddhist Order; European Buddhist Union
Established eleven years ago, our aim is to help women of all ages and from all walks of life to contact and realise their potential. We hold a year-round programme of events, including retreats for those completely new to Buddhism and meditation.

Throssel Hole Buddhist Abbey

Carrshield, Hexham, Northumberland, NE47 8AL
Tel: 01434-345204 **Fax:** 01434-345216
Contact: The Guestmaster
Activities: Worship/meditation, resource, visits, youth, newsletters, books, inter-faith
Traditions: Zen Buddhism
Movements: Soto Zen
Other Languages: Dutch, German, French
Affiliations: Network of Buddhist Organisations
Training monastery for male and female monks and lay retreat centre founded in 1972 by the late Revd Master Jiyu-Kennett (1924-1996). Main emphasis on Serene Reflection Meditation, Precepts and training in daily life.

Vajraloka Buddhist Meditation Centre for Men

Tyn-y-Ddol, Treddol, Corwen, Clwyd, LL21 0EN
Tel: 01490-460406
Contact: Vidyananda
Position: Secretary
Activities: Worship/meditation
Traditions: Western
Movements: Friends of the Western Buddhist Order

Vajraloka is a meditation retreat centre run by members of the Western Buddhist Order. Retreats are for men relatively new to meditation through to much more experienced practioners.

Western Ch'an Fellowship

c/o 24 Woodgate Avenue, Bury, Lancashire, BL9 7RU (h)
Tel: 0161-761-1945 (h)
Contact: Simon Child
Activities: Worship/meditation, resource, newsletters, inter-faith
Traditions: Zen, Ch'an
Movements: Ch'an, Lin Chi lineage
Affiliations: Institute of Chung Hwa Culture, New York, USA; Maenllwyd Retreat Centre, Wales

Windhorse Publications

11 Park Road, Moseley, Birmingham, West Midlands, B13 SAB
EMail: Compuserve 100331, 3327
Contact: Alan Sabatini
Position: Treasurer
Activities: Resource, books
Traditions: Western
Movements: Friends of the Western Buddhist Order

BUDDHIST REGIONAL AND LOCAL CENTRES AND ORGANISATIONS

There are a variety of forms of Buddhist local organisations listed in this directory. These include *viharas*, where monks live; centres with residential Buddhist communities, lay and/or monastic; as well as groups which meet in the homes of members or in hired premises. Some UK organisations also appear in these listings where these are also rooted in a locality.

In this chapter, groups which appear as Regional or County bodies are centres and groups which are based in one geographical location, but which have a more wide-ranging function. Branches of these centres are listed under the town or city in which they are located but without full entry details.

In this chapter only, the standard activity descriptor "worship" appears as "worship/ meditation" since many Buddhists feel that the word "worship" is not an appropriate word for them.

ENGLAND

NORTH EAST
Regional or County Bodies

Atisha Buddhist Centre
9 Milton Street, Darlington, County Durham, DL1 4ET (h)
Tel: 01325-365265 (h)
EMail: atisha@rmpk.co.uk
Contact: Becky Rooley
Position: Education Co-ordinator
Activities: Worship/meditation, resource, visits, newsletters
Traditions: Western
Movements: New Kadampa

City, Town or Local Bodies

Barnard Castle Mahayana Buddhist Centre
Barnard Castle, County Durham, c/o Atisha Buddhist Centre (Darlington), County Durham
Tel: 01325-365265 (h)
EMail: atisha@rmpk.co.uk

Ratanagiri: Harnham Buddhist Monastery
Belsay, Northumberland, NE20 0HF
Tel: 01661-881612 **Fax:** 01661-881019
Contact: Ajahn Munindo Bhikkhu
Position: Abbot
Activities: Worship/meditation, newsletters
Traditions: Theravada
Movements: Vipassana

Atisha Buddhist Centre
9 Milton Street, Darlington, County Durham, DL1 4ET (h)
Tel: 01325-365265 (h)
EMail: atisha@rmpk.co.uk
Contact: Becky Rooley
Position: Education Co-ordinator
Activities: Worship/meditation, resource, visits, newsletters
Traditions: Western
Movements: New Kadampa

Durham Buddhist Meditation Group
Woodlea, 13 North Crescent, North End, Durham City, County Durham, DH1 4NE (h)
EMail: Peter.Harvey@sunderland.ac.uk
Contact: Professor Peter Harvey

Position: Meditation Teacher
Traditions: Theravada
Movements: Samatha
Affiliations: Samatha Trust

Durham University Buddhist Society
St Cutherbert's Society, 12 Saddle Street, Durham
City, County Durham, DH1 3JU
Contact: Judy Tice

Hexham Buddhist Group
10 Tynedale Terrace, Hexham, Northumberland,
NE46 3JE (h)
Tel: 01434-602759 (h)
Contact: Robert Bluck
Activities: Worship/meditation, visits
Traditions: Theravada
Affiliations: Harnham Buddhist Monastery

Throssel Hole Buddhist Priory
Carrshield, Hexham, Northumberland,
NE47 8AL
Tel: 01434-345204 **Fax:** 01434-345216
Contact: The Guestmaster
Activities: Worship/meditation, resource, visits,
youth, newsletters, books, inter-faith
Traditions: Zen
Movements: Soto Zen
Other Languages: Dutch, German
Affiliations: Network of Buddhist Organisations

Compassion Mahayana Buddhist Centre
34 Rothwell Road, Gosforth, Newcastle upon
Tyne, Tyne and Wear
Tel: 0191-284-6315
Contact: Judith C Simpkins
Position: Education Programme Co-ordinator
Activities: Worship/meditation, visits, newsletters
Traditions: New Kadampa, Mahayana
Movements: New Kadampa
Affiliations: Madhyamaka Centre, Pocklington,
York; Manjushri Mahayana Buddhist Centre,
Cumbria

Newcastle Buddhist Centre
Friends of the Western Buddhist Order, 12 Pilgrim
Street, Newcastle upon Tyne, Tyne and Wear,
NE1 6QG
Tel: 0191-261-1722
Contact: Dharmachari Nandavajra
Position: Teacher and Trustee

Traditions: Western
Movements: Friends of the Western Buddhist
Order

Newcastle Serene Reflection Meditation Group
18 First Avenue, Heaton, Newcastle upon Tyne,
Tyne and Wear, NE6 5YE
Tel: 0191-265404 (h)
Contact: Dave Hurcombe
Position: Lay Minister
Traditions: Zen
Affiliations: Throssel Hole Buddhist Priory

Newcastle Theravadin Buddhist Group
Newcastle upon Tyne, Tyne and Wear, c/o 221
Eastbourne Avenue, Gateshead, Tyne and Wear,
NE8 4UL (h)
Tel: 0191-478-2726 (h) **Fax:** 0191-478-2726
EMail: andy@adaptvix.compulink.co.uk
Contact: Andrew Hunt
Position: Contact Person
Traditions: Theravada

Newcastle University Buddhist Society
Department of Plant Biology, The University,
Newcastle upon Tyne, Tyne and Wear
Tel: 0191-232-8511, Ext: 3899
Contact: Gilliam Craig
Traditions: Zen
Movements: Soto Zen

Sunderland Mantra Buddhist Centre
Sunderland, County Durham, c/o 78 Rothwaite
Close, Bakers Mead, Hartlepool, County Durham,
TS24 8RE

University of Sunderland Buddhist Meditation Group
Sunderland, County Durham c/o Woodlea,
13 North Crescent, North End, Durham City,
County Durham, DH1 4NE (h)
EMail: peter.harvey@sunderland.ac.uk
Contact: Professor Peter Harvey
Position: Meditation Teacher
Traditions: Theravada
Movements: Samatha
Affiliations: Samatha Trust

YORKSHIRE
Regional or County Bodies

Gyaltsabje Buddhist Centre
13 Sharrow View, Nether Edge, Sheffield, South
Yorkshire, S7 1ND
Tel: 0114-250-9663 **Fax:** 0114-250-9663
EMail: 101327.2405@compuserve.com
Contact: Kelsang Rinchen
Position: Education Co-ordinator
Activities: Worship/meditation
Movements: New Kadampa

Madhyamika Buddhist Centre
Kilnwick Percy Hall, Pocklington, York, North
Yorkshire, YO4 2UF
Tel: 01759-30832 **Fax:** 01759-305962
Contact: Joanne Bird
Position: Education Co-ordinator
Activities: Worship, meditation, visits, resource
Traditions: Tibetan
Movements: New Kadampa
Affiliations: New Kadampa Tradition

City, Town or Local Bodies

Barnsley Mahayana Buddhist Centre
Barnsley, West Yorkshire, c/o Gyaltsabje Buddhist
Centre (Sheffield), South Yorkshire
Tel: 0114-250-9663 (h) **Fax:** 0114-250-9663
EMail: 101327.2405@compuserve.com.

Beverley Mahayanna Buddhist Centre
Beverley, East Riding of Yorkshire, c/o Khedrubje
Centre (Hull, East Riding of Yorkshire)
Tel: 01482-229899

Bradford Buddhist Group
15 Silverhill Drive, Bradford, West Yorkshire,
BD3 7LF
Contact: George Abramson

Bradford Dhammapala
7 Eastcroft, Wyke, Bradford, West Yorkshire,
BD12 9AS
Tel: 01274-670865
Contact: Ann Voist
Traditions: Theravada

Kagyu Changchub Choling
c/o Interfaith Education Centre, Listerhills Road,
Bradford, West Yorkshire, BD7 1HD

Tel: 01274-731674 **Tel:** 01943-602956 (h)
Fax: 01274-731621
Internet: http://www.eclipse.co.uk/~rs1042
Contact: Tenzin Phuntsok
Position: Co-ordinator
Activities: Newsletters, books
Traditions: Tibetan
Movements: Kagyupa
Affiliations: Network of Buddhist Organisations

Doncaster Mahayana Buddhist Centre
Doncaster, South Yorkshire, c/o Gyaltsabje Centre
(Sheffield, South Yorkshire)
Tel: 0114-250-9663 (h) **Fax:** 0114-250-9663
EMail: 101327.2405@compuserve.com

Guisborough Mahayana Buddhist Centre
Guisborough, North Yorkshire, c/o Atisha Centre
(Darlington, County Durham)
Tel: 01325-365265 (h)

Harrogate Buddhist Group
137 Bramham Drive, Oakdale Court, Harrogate,
North Yorkshire, HG3 3TZ
Tel: 01423-500174 (h)
Traditions: Multi-Traditional

Harrogate Serene Reflection Meditation Group
7 Rudbeck Close, Harrogate, North Yorkshire,
HG2 7AG
Tel: 01423-885490 **Tel:** 01423-885490 (h)
Contact: Marjorie Patricia Oldham
Position: Lay Minister
Activities: Worship/meditation
Traditions: Zen
Movements: Soto Zen
Other Languages: English, French
Affiliations: Throssel Hole Priory; Order of
Buddhist Contemplatives

Kagyu Dechen Dzong
28 Harlow Moor Drive, Harrogate, North
Yorkshire, HG2 0JY (h)
Tel: 01423-522233 (h)
Contact: Howard Peter Quinn
Position: Co-ordinator
Activities: Newsletters, books
Traditions: Tibetan
Movements: Kagyupa
Affiliations: Network of Buddhist Organisations

Huddersfield Serene Reflection Meditation Group
19 Grasmere Road, Calmlands, Meltham,
Huddersfield, West Yorkshire, HD7 3EF

...749 **Tel:** 01484-681300
...: Throssel Hole Buddhist Priory

...pani Buddhist Centre
...rian Jackson Centre, New North Parade,
Huddersfield, West Yorkshire
Tel: 01535-661817 **Tel:** 01484-865007 (h)
Contact: Jim Sheridan
Traditions: Tibetan
Movements: Gelugpa

Hull Buddhist Group
42 Blenheim Street, Princes Avenue, Hull, East
Riding of Yorkshire, HU5 3PS (h)
Tel: 01482-446301 (h)
Contact: Sandie Pinnock
Position: Core Group Member
Traditions: Multi-Traditional

Khedrubje Centre
43 Hutt Street, Hull, East Riding of Yorkshire,
HU3 1QL
Tel: 01482-229899
Contact: Malcolm Ward
Position: Acting Director
Traditions: Tibetan
Movements: New Kadampa

Losang Dragpa Centre
312 Skipton Road, Beechcliffe, Keighley, West
Yorkshire, BD20 6AT
Tel: 01535-661817
Contact: Rosie Wallwork
Position: Administrative Director

Jampa Ling Centre
28 Princess Drive, Knaresborough, North Yorkshire,
HG5 0AG
Tel: 01423-866431 (h) **Fax:** 01423-866431 (h)
Contact: Dennis Hallam
Position: Co-ordinator
Traditions: Tibetan
Movements: New Kadampa
Affiliations: Madhyamaka Centre, Pocklington;
Manjushri Centre, Ulverston

Leeds Buddhist Centre
c/o 3 Knowlemount, Leeds, West Yorkshire,
LS6 2PP
Tel: 0113-230-2700
Contact: Jinaraja
Movements: Friends of the Western Buddhist
Order

Leeds Buddhist Group
28 Wellstone Drive, Leeds, West Yorkshire, LS13 4DZ
Tel: 0113-256-4330 **Tel:** 0113-256-4330 (h)
Contact: Kenneth Brown
Activities: Resource, inter-faith
Traditions: Multi-Traditional

Leeds Mahayana Buddhist Centre
12 Granby Terrace, Leeds, West Yorkshire, LS6 9JT
Tel: 01532-784085 (h)
Contact: Ms Mandy Coutier
Position: Co-ordinator
Traditions: Tibetan
Movements: New Kadampa

Leeds Network of Engaged Buddhists
91 Clarendon Road, Leeds, West Yorkshire, LS2 9LY
Tel: 0113-244-4289 **Fax:** 0113-244-4289
EMail: Interbeing@compuserve.com
Contact: Ms Alex White
Position: Secretary/Editor
Activities: Newsletters, books
Traditions: Engaged Buddhism
Affiliations: Network of Buddhist Organisations;
Buddhist Peace Fellowship

Leeds University Buddhist Society
c/o Students Union, Leeds University, Leeds, West
Yorkshire
Contact: Secretary
Traditions: Western
Movements: Friends of the Western Buddhist
Order

Ratnasambhava Centre
3 St Michael's Terrace, Headingley, Leeds, West
Yorkshire, LS6 3BQ
Tel: 01532-784764
Contact: Polly Belchetz
Position: Co-ordinator
Traditions: Tibetan
Movements: New Kadampa

Yorkshire Dales Mahayana Centre
"Buckles", Caldbergh, Leyburn, West Yorkshire

Middlesbrough Mahayana Buddhist Centre
Middlesbrough, North Yorkshire, c/o Atisha
Buddhist Centre (Darlington, County Durham)
Tel: 01325-365265 (h)

Northallerton Mahayana Buddhist Centre
Northallerton, North Yorkshire, c/o Atisha Buddhist
Centre (Darlington, County Durham)
Tel: 01325-365265
Contact: Denis Calderon
Position: Director
Traditions: Western
Movements: New Kadampa

Richmond Mahayana Buddhist Centre
Richmond, South Yorkshire, c/o Akshobya
Buddhist Centre (Nottingham, Nottinghamshire)
Tel: 0115-985-7356 **Tel:** 0115-962-5158 (h)
Fax: 0115-985-7356

Gyaltsabje Buddhist Centre
13 Sharrow View, Nether Edge, Sheffield, South
Yorkshire, S7 1ND
Tel: 0114-250-9663 **Fax:** 0114-250-9663
EMail: 101327.2405@compuserve.com
Contact: Kelsang Rinchen
Position: Education Co-ordinator
Activities: Worship/meditation
Movements: New Kadampa

Sheffield Buddhist Centre
499 Glossop Road, Sheffield, South Yorkshire,
S10 2QE
Tel: 0114-268070
Contact: Dharmachari Susiddhi
Position: Chair
Activities: Worship/meditation, visits, women
Traditions: Western
Movements: Friends of the Western Buddhist
Order

Sheffield Buddhist Group
197 Edmund Road, Sheffield, South Yorkshire, S2
Traditions: Theravada, Zen

Sheffield Buddhist Group
76 Wath Road, Sheffield, South Yorkshire, S7 1HE
Traditions: Theravada, Zen

Sheffield Zen Buddhist Meditation Group
c/o 115 Rustlings Road, Sheffield, South Yorkshire,
S11 7AB
Tel: 0114-268-6826
Contact: John Darwin
Position: Contact Person
Traditions: Zen
Movements: Soto Zen

Affiliations: Throssel Hole Priory,
Northumberland

Kashyapa Buddhist Centre
15 Selborne Terrace, Shipley, West Yorkshire,
BD18 3BZ (h)
Tel: 01274-590279 (h)
Contact: Graham Hart
Position: Director
Activities: Newsletters, books
Traditions: Western
Movements: New Kadampa
Affiliations: Manjushri Mahayana Buddhist
Centre, Cumbria

Wakefield Mahayana Buddhist Centre
Wakefield, West Yorkshire
Tel: 01535-661817
Contact: Anni Kelsang Chodzom
Traditions: Tibetan
Movements: New Kadampa

Madhyamika Buddhist Centre
Kilnwick Percy Hall, Pocklington, York, North
Yorkshire, YO4 2UF
Tel: 01759-30832 **Fax:** 01759-305962
Contact: Joanne Bird
Position: Education Co-ordinator
Activities: Workship, meditation, visits, resource
Traditions: Tibetan
Movements: New Kadampa
Affiliations: New Kadampa Tradition

York Madhyamaka Buddhist Centre
37 East Mount Road, The Mount, York, North
Yorkshire, Y02 2BD
Tel: 01904-613071
Contact: Mike Hume
Position: Co-ordinator
Activities: Worship/meditation, resource, visits,
youth
Traditions: Tibetan
Movements: New Kadampa
Affiliations: New Kadampa Tradition

NORTH WEST
Regional and County Bodies

Lancashire Buddhist Centre
Second Floor, 78-80 King William Street,
Blackburn, Lancashire, BB1 7DT

Tel: 01254-260779
EMail: Pramodana Compuserve 1D 10037, 3204
Contact: Pramodana
Position: Chairman
Activities: Worship/meditation, resource, visits, women, inter-faith
Traditions: Western
Movements: Friends of the Western Buddhist Order

Amitayus Centre
173 Ruskin Road, Crewe, Cheshire, CW2 7JX
Tel: 01270-664050 (h) **Fax:** 01270-650209
EMail: amitayus@netcentral.co.uk
Contact: Peter Willets
Activities: Worship/meditation, resource, visits, newsletters
Traditions: Tibetan, Western
Movements: New Kadampa

Duldzin Mahayana Buddhist Centre
25 Aigburth Drive, Sefton Park, Aigburth, Liverpool, Lancashire, L17 4JH
Tel: 0151-726-8900 **Fax:** 0151-726-8905
Contact: Mr Robert Crayford
Position: Administrative Director
Activities: Resource
Traditions: Western
Movements: New Kadampa

Manjushri Mahayana Buddhist Centre
Conishead Priory, Priory Road, Ulverston, Cumbria, LA12 9QQ
Tel: 01229-584029 (h) **Fax:** 01229-580080
EMail: manjushri@tcp.co.uk
Contact: Kelsang Kunkyen
Position: Assistant Branch Co-ordinator
Activities: Worship/meditation, visits, youth, elderly, women, newsletters, books
Traditions: Western
Movements: New Kadampa

City, Town and Local Bodies

Barrow-in-Furness Mahayana Buddhist Centre
Thyme Cottage, 58-60 Northscale, Barrow-in-Furness, Cumbria
Tel: 01229-472563 (h)
Contact: Jack Roskell
Traditions: Tibetan
Movements: New Kadampa

Mahasi Dhamma Fellowship
73 Royden Road, Billinge, Lancashire

Birkenhead Mahayana Buddhist Centre
Birkenhead, Merseyside, c/o Dulzin Centre (Liverpool, Merseyside)
Tel: 0151-726-8900   **Fax:** 0151-726-8905

Lancashire Buddhist Centre
Second Floor, 78-80 King William Street, Blackburn, Lancashire, BB1 7DT
Tel: 01254-260779
EMail: Pramodana Compuserve 1D 10037, 3204
Contact: Pramodana
Position: Chairman
Activities: Worship/meditation, resource, visits, women, inter-faith
Traditions: Western
Movements: Friends of the Western Buddhist Order

Tushita Buddhist Centre
c/o 14 Sunnybower Close, Blackburn, Lancashire, BB1 5QU
Tel: 01254-55601
Contact: Enid Duckworth
Position: Director
Activities: Worship/meditation, visits
Traditions: Tibetan
Movements: New Kadampa
Affiliations: New Kadampa Tradition

Bolton Mahayana Buddhist Centre
Friends Meeting House, Silverwell Street, Bolton, Lancashire
Tel: 0161-724-0302 (h)
Contact: Jamie Wincott
Position: Branch Co-ordinator
Activities: Worship/meditation, resource
Traditions: Tibetan
Movements: New Kadampa
Affiliations: Tara Centre, Etwall

Burnley Mahayana Buddhist Centre
Burnley, Lancashire, c/o 3 School Lane, Laneshawbridge, Colne, Lancashire
Tel: 01282-864389
Contact: Freda Simms
Position: Co-ordinator
Traditions: Tibetan
Movements: New Kadampa

Manchester Serene Reflection Meditation Group
62 Heap Bridge, Bury, Lancashire, BL9 (h)
Tel: 0161-797-0251 (h)
Contact: Harry James Melling
Position: Lay Minister
Activities: Worship/meditation
Traditions: Zen
Movements: Soto Zen
Affiliations: Throssel Hole Priory

Western Ch'an Fellowship
24 Woodgate Avenue, Bury, Lancashire,
BL9 7RU (h)
Tel: 0161-761-1945 (h)
EMail: wcf@child.demon.co.uk
Contact: Simon Child
Traditions: Zen, Ch'an
Movements: Ch'an, Lin Chi lineage

Uma Buddhist Centre
Ravenslea, Stoneraise, Durda, Carlisle, Cumbria,
CA5 7AX (h)
Tel: 01228-711267 (h)
Contact: Barry Strotton
Position: Co-ordinator
Traditions: Tibetan
Movements: New Kadampa, Gelugpa

Chester Friends of the Western Buddhist Order Group
Chester, Cheshire, c/o Vajraloka Buddhist
Meditation Centre (nr Corwen, Clwyd)
Tel: 01978-755521
Contact: Secretary
Traditions: Western
Movements: Friends of the Western Buddhist
Order

Chester Zen Group
23 Hamilton Street, Hoole, Chester, Cheshire,
CH2 3JG
Tel: 01224-351012 (h)
Contact: Ms Sylvia Young
Traditions: Zen
Movements: Soto Zen

Opagme Buddhist Centre - Chester
Chester, Cheshire, c/o Amitayus Centre (Crewe,
Cheshire)
Tel: 01270-664050 (h) **Fax:** 01270-602090
EMail: amitayus@netcentral.co.uk

Kagyu Dzong
36 Charles Street, Colne, Lancashire, BB8 OLZ (h)
Tel: 01282-864537 (h)
Contact: John Rowan
Position: Co-ordinator
Movements: Kagyupa
Affiliations: Network of Buddhist Organisations

Amitayus Centre
173 Ruskin Road, Crewe, Cheshire, CW2 7JX
Tel: 01270-664050 (h) **Fax:** 01270-650209
EMail: amitayus@netcentral.co.uk
Contact: Peter Willets
Activities: Worship/meditation, resource, visits,
newsletters
Traditions: Tibetan, Western
Movements: New Kadampa

Isle of Man Buddhist Group
38 Oakhill Close, Glen Park, Douglas, Isle of Man
Tel: 01624-28999
Contact: Mike Kewley
Traditions: Theravada

Wirral Buddhist Group (Karme Choling)
Hillside, 70 Oldfield Road, Heswall, Merseyside,
L60 9HF (h)
Tel: 0151-342-2026 (h)
Contact: Lawrence Mair
Position: Chairman
Traditions: Tibetan
Movements: Kagyupa
Affiliations: Network of Buddhist Organisations

Buddhist Group of Kendal (Theravada)
c/o Fellside Alexander School, Low Fellside,
Kendal, Cumbria, LA9 4NJ
Tel: 01539-733045 **Tel:** 01952-828596 (h)
Contact: J Gomes
Position: Secretary
Traditions: Theravada

Kendal Mahayana Buddhist Centre
26 Lound Road, Kendal, Cumbria, LA9 7EA
Tel: 01539-731984
Contact: Lynne Irish
Position: Co-ordinator
Traditions: Tibetan
Movements: New Kadampa

Ch'an Association
41 Rutland Avenue, Lancaster, Lancashire, LA1 4EX
Tel: 01524-388778

Contact: Richard Hunn
Traditions: Zen
Movements: Ch'an

Chenrezig Centre
21 Portland Street, Lancaster, Lancashire, LA1 1SZ
Tel: 01524-68437
Contact: Richard Lupsom
Traditions: Tibetan
Movements: New Kadampa

Lancaster Buddhist Meditation Group
51 South Road, Lancaster, Lancashire
Tel: 01524-62484
Contact: Hilary Schofield
Activities: Women
Traditions: Tibetan

Lancaster Serene Reflection Meditation Group
c/o 7 Portland Street, Lancaster, Lancashire,
LA1 1SZ
Tel: 01524-34031
Contact: Paul Taylor
Position: Lay Minister
Activities: Worship/meditation
Movements: Soto Zen
Affiliations: Throssel Hole Buddhist Priory

Lancaster University Buddhist Society
c/o The Students Union, Lancaster University,
Lancaster, Lancashire, LA1 4YX
Contact: Secretary
Activities: Worship/meditation, umbrella, visits
Traditions: Multi-Traditional

Duldzin Mahayana Buddhist Centre
25 Aigburth Drive, Sefton Park, Aigburth,
Liverpool, Lancashire, L17 4JH
Tel: 0151-726-8900 **Fax:** 0151-726-8905
Contact: Mr Robert Crayford
Position: Administrative Director
Activities: Resource
Traditions: Western
Movements: New Kadampa

Friends of the Western Buddhist Order (Liverpool)
Liverpool Meditation Centre, 37 Hope Street,
Liverpool, Merseyside, L1 9EA
Tel: 0151-709-5489
Contact: Dharmachari Mangala
Position: Chairman
Activities: Worship/meditation, resource, umbrella,
visits

Traditions: Western
Movements: Friends of the Western Buddhist
Order
Affiliations: Friends of the Western Buddhist
Order

Kagyu Osel Choling
c/o 24 Birkey Lane, Formby, Liverpool, Merseyside,
L37 4BU
Tel: 01704-872169 (h)
EMail: http://www.eclipse.co.uk/~rs1042
Contact: June Burton
Activities: Umbrella, newsletters, books
Traditions: Tibetan
Movements: Kagyupa
Affiliations: Network of Buddhist Organisations

Kampo Gangra Shedrup Ling
30a Brompton Avenue, Liverpool, Lancashire,
L17 3BU
Tel: 0151-733-2336 (h)
Contact: Geoff Ashmore

Kanzeon Zen Sangha
21a Aigburth Drive, Liverpool, L17 4JQ (h)
Tel: 0151-728-7829 (h) **Fax:** 0151-709-0398
Contact: David Dohi Scott
Activities: Worship/meditation
Traditions: Zen
Movements: Rinzai Zen, Soto Zen
Affiliations: Kanzeon Zen Sangha, Main Temple,
Salt Lake City, Utah, USA

Liverpool Serene Reflection Meditation Group
22 Bridge Road, Mossley Hill, Liverpool,
Merseyside, L18 5EG (h)
Tel: 0151-724-3030 (h)
Contact: Lynne Heidi Stumpe
Position: Lay Minister
Activities: Worship/meditation
Traditions: Zen
Movements: Soto Zen
Affiliations: Throssel Hole Priory

Samatha Group
60 Gladstone Avenue, Liverpool, Merseyside,
L16 2LQ

Buddhist Society of Manchester
Manchester, Greater Manchester, c/o 3 Grosvenor
Square, Sale, Cheshire, M33 1RW
Tel: 0161-973-7588
Contact: David Johnson

Position: Secretary
Traditions: Theravada
Movements: Vipassana

Manchester International Zen Association, UK
Room 16 Mill Street Venture Centre, 491 Mill
Street, Openshaw, Manchester, Greater Manchester,
M11
Tel: 0161-231-2344 (h)
Contact: Alan Smith
Position: Zen monk
Activities: Worship/meditation, newsletters
Traditions: Zen
Movements: Soto Zen
Other Languages: English, French

Kagyu Ling
1 Totnes Road, Chorlton, Manchester, Greater
Manchester, M21 8XF
Tel: 0161-860-7347
Contact: Angela Brady
Position: Administrator
Traditions: Tibetan
Movements: Kagyupa
Affiliations: Dechen Community

Manchester Buddhist Centre (Friends of the Western Buddhist Order)
16-20 Turner Street, Manchester, Greater
Manchester, M4 1DZ
Tel: 0161-834-9232 (h)   **Fax:** 0161-839-4815
EMail: 106044.1377@compuserve.com
Contact: Aparajita
Position: Secretary
Activities: Worship/meditation, resource, visits,
newsletters, inter-faith
Traditions: Multi-Traditional
Movements: Ambedkarite, Friends of the Western
Buddhist Order
Affiliations: Network of Buddhist Organisations;
European Buddhist Union

Manchester Samatha Association
Manchester Centre for Buddhist Meditation, 21
High Lane, Chorlton-cum-Hardy, Manchester,
Greater Manchester, M21 9DJ
Tel: 0161-283-7548
Contact: Costel Harnasz
Activities: Worship/meditation, visits, newsletters
Traditions: Theravada
Movements: Samatha
Affiliations: The Samatha Trust

Manchester Soto Zen Group
Above Global Foods Delicatessan, 903 Stockport
Road, Levenshulme, Manchester, Greater
Manchester, M19 3PN

Manchester University Buddhist Society
Students' Union, Oxford Road, Manchester,
Lancashire, M13 9PL
EMail: MBCX4DJC@stud.man.ac.uk
Contact: Daniel Coleman
Position: Treasurer
Traditions: Theravada
Movements: Samatha
Affiliations: The Samatha Trust

Manchester Vairochana Buddhist Centre
37 Whitelaw Road, Chorlton-cum-Hardy,
Manchester, Greater Manchester, M21 1HG
Tel: 0161-881-0663
Contact: Jeff Simm
Position: Co-ordinator
Traditions: Tibetan
Movements: New Kadampa

Tibetan Buddhist Centre
Top Flat, 3 Hague Road, Manchester, Greater
Manchester, M20
Tel: 0161-434-1972 (h)
Contact: David Stoh

Northwich Mahayana Buddhist Centre
30 The Woodland, Wincham, Northwich, Cheshire,
CN9 6PL (h)
Tel: 01565-733714 (h)   **Fax:** 01565-733280
Contact: John Davies
Position: Branch Assistant
Activities: Visits
Traditions: Tibetan
Movements: New Kadampa
Affiliations: Tara Centre, Etwall

Kagyu Choling
c/o 6 Faversham Brow, Oldham, Lancashire,
OL1 2XS (h)
Tel: 0161-872-3831 (h)
Internet: http://www.eclipse.co.uk/~rs1042
Contact: Jonathan Macaskill
Position: Co-ordinator
Activities: Newsletters, books,
Traditions: Tibetan
Movements: Kagyupa
Affiliations: Network of Buddhist Organisations

Oldham Mahayana Buddhist Centre
c/o 6 Church Street, Lees, Oldham, Lancashire

Penrith Mahayana Buddhist Centre
Penrith, Cumbria, c/o Manjushri Buddhist Centre
(Ulverston)
Tel: 01229-584029   **Fax:** 01229-580080
EMail: manjushri@tcp.co.uk

Preston Serene Reflection Meditation Group
7 Ballet Hill Cresent, Bilsborrow, Preston,
Lancashire, PR3 0RX (h)
Tel: 01995-640623 (h)
Contact: Iain Robinson
Position: Lay Minister
Activities: Worship/meditation
Traditions: Zen
Movements: Soto Zen
Affiliations: Throssel Hole Priory

Vajravarahi Buddhist Centre
66 West Cliff, Preston, Lancashire, PR1 8HU
Tel: 01772-259094 (h)
Contact: Kelsang Pagpa
Position: Co-ordinator
Activities: Worship/meditation
Traditions: Tibetan
Movements: New Kadampa
Affiliations: New Kadampa Tradition

Rossendale Samatha Group
c/o Weavers' Cottage, Fall Barn Fold, Rawtenstall,
Lancashire
Contact: Margaret Bailey
Traditions: Theravada
Movements: Samatha
Affiliations: The Samatha Association

St Helens Mahayana Buddhist Centre
St. Helens, Lancashire, c/o 131 Grove Street, Edge
Hill, Liverpool, Merseyside

Stockport Mahayana Buddhist Centre
c/o 25 Locksley Close, Heaton Norris, Stockport,
Cheshire, SK4 2LW

Manjushri Mahayana Buddhist Centre
Conishead Priory, Priory Road, Ulverston,
Cumbria, LA12 9QQ
Tel: 01229-584029 (h)   **Fax:** 01229-580080
EMail: manjushri@tcp.co.uk
Contact: Kelsang Kunkyen

Position: Assistant Branch Co-ordinator
Activities: Worship/meditation, visits, youth,
elderly, women, newsletters, books
Traditions: Western
Movements: New Kadampa

Wigan Mahayana Buddhist Centre
Wigan, Lancashire, c/o Manjushri Buddhist Centre
(Ulverston)
Tel: 01229-584029   **Fax:** 01229-580080
EMail: manjushri@tcp.co.uk

EAST MIDLANDS
Regional and County Bodies

Tara Buddhist Centre
Ashe Hall, Ash Lane, Etwall, Derbyshire,
DE65 6HT
Tel: 01283-732338   **Fax:** 01283-733416
EMail: tara@rmplc.co.uk
Contact: Miss Lorraine Quin
Position: Assistant Administrative Director
Activities: Worship/meditation, resource, umbrella,
visits
Traditions: Mahayana (Kadampa)
Movements: New Kadampa
Other Languages: Spanish
Affiliations: New Kadampa Tradition

East Midlands Buddhist Association
9 Una Avenue, Braunstone, Leicester, Leicestershire,
LE3 2GS
Tel: 0116-282-5003 (h)
Contact: Venerable K U Jinaratana
Position: Head of the Vihara
Traditions: Theravada
Movements: Maha Bodhi
Other Languages: Sinhalese
Affiliations: Network of Buddhist Organisations

Akshobya Buddhist Centre
52 Mayo Road, Nottingham, Nottinghamshire,
NG5 1BL
Tel: 0115-985-7356   **Tel:** 0115-962-5158 (h)
Fax: 0115-985-7356
Contact: Marcella Eldi De Persis
Position: Administrative Director
Activities: Worship/meditation, resource
Traditions: Tibetan
Movements: New Kadampa
Affiliations: Manjushri Centre, Ulvaston

City, Town and Local Bodies

Belper Mahayana Buddhist Centre
Belper, Derbyshire, c/o Tara Buddhist Centre
(Etwall, Derbyshire)
Tel: 01283-732338 **Fax:** 01283-733416
EMail: tara@rmplc.co.uk

Boston Mahayana Buddhist Centre
Boston, Lincolnshire, c/o Akshobya Buddhist
Centre (Nottingham, Nottinghamshire)
Tel: 0115-985-7356 **Fax:** 0115-985-7356

Ensapa Buddhist Centre, Chesterfield
Chesterfield, Derbyshire, c/o Gyaltsabje Buddhist
Centre (Sheffield, South Yorkshire)
Tel: 0114-250-9663   **Fax:** 0114-250-9663
EMail: 101327.2405@compuserve.com.

Chekhawa Centre, Derby
Derby, Derbyshire, c/o Tara Buddhist Centre
(Etwall, Derbyshire)
Tel: 01283-732338 **Fax:** 01283-733416
EMail: tara@rmplc.co.uk

Midlands International Buddhist Association UK
319 Osmaston Park Road, Derby, DE4 8DA

Tara Buddhist Centre
Ashe Hall, Ash Lane, Etwall, Derbyshire,
DE65 6HT
Tel: 01283-732338 **Fax:** 01283-733416
EMail: tara@rmplc.co.uk
Contact: Miss Lorraine Quin
Position: Assistant Administrative Director
Activities: Worship/meditation, resource, umbrella,
visits
Traditions: Mahayana (Kadampa)
Movements: New Kadampa
Other Languages: Spanish
Affiliations: New Kadampa Tradition

Glossop Mahayana Buddhist Centre
Glossop, Derbyshire, c/o Tara Buddhist Centre
(Etwall, Derbyshire)
Tel: 01283-732338 **Fax:** 01283-733416
EMail: tara@rmplc.co.uk

Grantham Mahayana Buddhist Centre
Grantham, Lincolnshire, c/o Akshobya Buddhist
Centre (Nottingham, Nottinghamshire)
Tel: 0115-985-7356 **Fax:** 0115-985-7356

Kettering Mahayana Buddhist Centre
Kettering, Northamptonshire, c/o Akshobya
Buddhist Centre (Nottingham, Nottinghamshire)
Tel: 0115-985-7356 (h)   **Fax:** 0115-985-7356

East Midlands Buddhist Association
Leicester Buddhist Vihara, 9 Una Avenue,
Braunstone, Leicester, Leicestershire, LE3 2GS
Tel: 0116-2825003 (h)
Contact: Venerable K U Jinaratana
Position: Religious Advisor
Activities: Worship/meditation, resources, visits,
newsletters, books, inter-faith
Traditions: Theravada (Sri Lankan)
Movements: Vipassana, Samatha
Other Languages: Sinhalese
Affiliations: Network of Buddhist Organisations;
Maha Bodhi, Serene Reflection Meditation

Leicester Buddhist Group
Leicester, Leicestershire
Tel: 0121-449-5279
Traditions: Western
Movements: Friends of the Western Buddhist
Order

Leicester Buddhist Society
Leicester, Leicestershire, c/o 6 Half Moon Crescent,
Oadby, Leicestershire, LE2 4HD (h)
Tel: 0116-712339 **Tel:** 0116-271339 (h)
Contact: David Russell
Position: Chairperson
Traditions: Multi-Traditional

Nagarjuna Buddhist Centre
27 Knighton Road, Stoneygate, Leicester,
Leicestershire, LE2 3HL
Tel: 0116-270-0785 (h)
Contact: Kelsang Lekpel
Position: Co-ordinator
Activities: Worship/meditation, visits, youth,
elderly, women, newsletters
Traditions: Mahayana
Movements: New Kadampa
Affiliations: New Kadampa Tradition

Lincoln Jampa Centre
Lincoln, Lincolnshire, c/o Gyaltsabje Centre
(Sheffield, South Yorkshire)
Tel: 0114-250-9663 (h) **Fax:** 0114-250-9663
EMail: 101327.24.05@compuserve.com

Loughborough Mahayana Buddhist Centre
Loughborough, Leicestershire, c/o Akshobya
Buddhist Centre (Nottingham, Nottinghamshire)
Tel: 0115-985-7356   **Fax:** 0115-985-7356

Mansfield Mahayana Buddhist Centre
Mansfield, Nottinghamshire, c/o Akshobya
Buddhist Centre (Nottingham, Nottinghamshire)
Tel: 0115-985-7356   **Fax:** 0115-985-7356

Melton Mowbray Mahayana Buddhist Centre
Melton Mowbray, Leicestershire, c/o Nagarjuna
Centre, 649 Welford Road, Leicester, Leicestershire,
LE2 6FQ

Newark Mahayana Buddhist Centre
Newark, Nottinghamshire, c/o Akshobya Buddhist
Centre (Nottingham, Nottinghamshire)
Tel: 0115-985-7356   **Fax:** 0115-985-7356

Akshobya Buddhist Centre
52 Mayo Road, Nottingham, Nottinghamshire,
NG5 1BL
Tel: 0115-985-7356   **Tel:** 0115-962-5158 (h)
Fax: 0115-985-7356
Contact: Marcella Eldi De Persis
Activities: Worship/meditation, resource
Traditions: Tibetan
Movements: New Kadampa
Affiliations: Manjushri Centre, Ulvaston

**Friends of the Western Buddhist Order
(Nottingham)**
Nottingham Buddhist Centre, 9 St Mary's Place,
St Mary's Gate, Nottingham, Nottinghamshire,
NG1 1PH
Tel: 0115-956-1008 (h)
Contact: Dharmachari Vimalaprabha
Position: Secretary
Activities: Worship/meditation, visits, women
Traditions: Western
Movements: Friends of the Western Buddhist
Order
Affiliations: Friends of the Western Buddhist
Order

Mahayana Buddhist Centre
64 Russell Street, Nottingham, Nottinghamshire,
NG7 6GZ
Tel: 0115-484848, Ext: 3813

Nottingham & District Buddhist Society
26 Millicent Road, West Bridgford, Nottingham,
Nottinghamshire, NG2 7PZ (h)
Contact: Alan MacCormick
Position: Secretary
Traditions: Western
Movements: Soto Zen

Nottingham Serene Reflection Meditation Group
Flat 10, Windsor House, Redcliffe Gardens,
Mapperley Park, Nottingham, Nottinghamshire,
NG3 5AX (h)
Tel: 0115-960-3450 (h)
Contact: Edward Fullick
Position: Main Organiser
Activities: Worship/meditation
Traditions: Zen
Movements: Soto Zen
Other Languages: French, Italian, Hungarian
Affiliations: Throssel Hole Priory Buddhist
Monastery, Northumberland; Shasta Abbey, Mount
Shasta, CA, USA

**Nottingham University Mahayana Buddhist
Centre**
Nottingham, Nottinghamshire, c/o Akshobya
Buddhist Centre (Nottingham, Nottinghamshire)
Tel: 0115-985-7356   **Fax:** 0115-985-7356

Western Ch'an Fellowship Nottingham Branch
c/o 8, Park Terrace, The Park, Nottingham,
Nottinghamshire, NG1 5DN (h)
Tel: 0115-924975 (h)
Contact: Ms Hilary Richards
Position: Regional representative
Traditions: Ch'an
Affiliations: Institute of Chung Hwa Buddhist
Culture, New York, USA

Peterborough Mahayana Buddhist Centre
Peterborough, Cambridgeshire, c/o Akshobya
Buddhist Centre (Nottingham, Nottinghamshire)
Tel: 0115-985-7356 (h)   **Fax:** 0115-985-7356

Spalding Mahayana Buddhist Centre
Spalding, Lincolnshire, c/o Akshobya Centre
(Nottingham, Nottinghamshire)
Tel: 0115-985-7356 (h)   **Fax:** 0115-985-7356

WEST MIDLANDS
City, Town or Local Bodies

Baba Saheb Ambedkar Buddhist Association
13 Booth Street, Handsworth, Birmingham, West
Midlands, B21 0NG
Tel: 0121-523-8254 **Tel:** 0121-358-5766 (h)
Contact: Mr Devinder Kumar Chander
Position: General Secretary
Activities: Worship/meditation
Movements: Ambedkarite

Birmingham Buddhist Centre
135 Salisbury Road, Moseley, Birmingham, West
Midlands, B13 8LA
Tel: 0121-449-5279
EMail: 101776,456@compuserve.com
Contact: Vajragupta
Position: Chairman
Activities: Worship/meditation, resource, visits,
women, newsletters, books
Traditions: Western
Movements: Friends of the Western Buddhist
Order; Network of Buddhist Organisations;
European Buddhist Union
Affiliations: Network of Buddhist Organisations;
Friends of the Western Buddhist Order; European
Buddhist Union

Birmingham Buddhist Vihara
47 Carlyle Road, Edgbaston, Birmingham, West
Midlands, B16 9BH
Tel: 0121-454-6591 (h) **Fax:** 0121-454-6591
Contact: Venerable Dr Rewata Dhamma
Position: Spiritual Director
Activities: Worship/meditation, visits, newsletters,
books, inter-faith
Traditions: Theravada
Movements: Vipassana
Other Languages: Burmese, Hindi

Birmingham Karma Ling Tibetan Buddhist Centre
41 Carlyle Road, Edgbaston, Birmingham, West
Midlands, B16 9BH
Tel: 0121-454-2782 **Fax:** 0121-456-3587
EMail: b.k.ling@jbhotcat.demon.co.uk
Contact: Alun Davies
Position: Trustee
Activities: Worship/meditation, resource, visits,
newsletters, inter-faith
Traditions: Tibetan

Movements: Kagyupa
Other Languages: Tibetan

Birmingham Serene Reflection Meditation Group
Tel: 01384-290084
Affiliations: Throssel Hole Buddhist Priory

*Buddhavihara Temple (Dr Ambedkar Buddhist
Society)*
5 Hampton Road, Aston, Birmingham, West
Midlands, B6 6AN
Tel: 0121-515-1518 **Fax:** 0121-240-1468
Contact: Venerable Panyasiri
Position: Abbot
Activities: Worship/meditation, resource, visits
Traditions: Thai Theravada
Movements: Ambedkarite, Vipassana
Other Languages: Thai, Punjabi

Buddhist Vihara
13 Booth Street, Handsworth, Birmingham, West
Midlands

Indian Buddhist Society UK
Nanda House, 9 Carlisle Road, Edgbaston,
Birmingham, West Midlands, B16 9BH
Tel: 0121-455-7728
Contact: Hind Rattan Sansari Lal
Position: Secretary
Traditions: Multi-Traditional

Samantabhadra Centre
25 Carlyle Road, Edgbaston, Birmingham, West
Midlands, B16 9BQ
Tel: 0121-454-5146 **Fax:** 0121-454-5146
Contact: Patricia Hill
Position: Administrative Director
Activities: Worship/meditation, resource, visits
Traditions: Tibetan
Movements: New Kadampa

Soto Zen Zazen Group
Buddhist Vihara, 13 Booth Street, Handsworth,
Birmingham, West Midlands
Tel: 0121-429-4080
Contact: Venerable Kassapa

Sugata Centre
Coventry, West Midlands, c/o 27 Knighton Road,
Stoneygate, Leicester, Leicestershire, LE2 3HL
Tel: 0116-270-0785 (h)
Contact: Kelsang Lekpel
Position: Co-ordinator

Activities: Worship/meditation, visits, youth, elderly, women, newsletters
Traditions: Mahayana
Movements: New Kadampa
Affiliations: New Kadampa Tradition

Fa Yue Buddhist Monastery
Cottage Street, Brierley Hill, Dudley, West Midlands, DY5 1RE (h)
Tel: 01384-484552 **Fax:** 01384-481209
Contact: Sik Hin Hung
Position: Supervisor
Activities: Worship/meditation, visits
Traditions: Zen, Chanting
Movements: Ch'an, Chinese Mahayana Tradition
Other Languages: Cantonese, Mandarin

Hanley Mahayana Buddhist Centre
Hanley, Staffordshire
Tel: 01270-664050
Contact: Peter Willets
Position: Co-ordinator
Traditions: Tibetan
Movements: New Kadampa

Karma Naro
Buddhist Centre, Middle Wenallt, Llanigon, Hay-on-Wye, Hereford and Worcester
Tel: 01497-847377
Contact: Kurt Schaffhauser
Traditions: Tibetan
Movements: Kagyupa

Lichfield Mahayana Buddhist Centre
Lichfield, Staffordshire, c/o Tara Buddhist Centre (Etwall, Derbyshire)
Tel: 01283-732338 **Fax:** 01283-733416
EMail: tara@rmplc.co.uk

Redditch Mahayana Buddhist Centre
Redditch, Worcestershire, c/o Tara Buddhist Centre (Etwall, Derbyshire)
Tel: 01283-732338 **Fax:** 01283-733416
EMail: tara@rmplc.co.uk

Buddhist Group, Shrewsbury
74 Abbey Foregate, Shrewsbury, Shropshire

Shrewsbury Buddhist Group
Shrewsbury, Shropshire, c/o Amitayus Buddhist Centre (Crewe, Cheshire)
Tel: 01270-664050 (h)   **Fax:** 01270-650209
EMail: amitayus@netcentral.co.uk

Sakya Ling Buddhist Centre
146 Neville Road, Shirley, Solihull, West Midlands, B90 2QX (h)
Tel: 0121-745-2550
Internet: http://www.eclipse.co.uk/~rs1042
Contact: Secretary
Activities: Visits, newsletters, books, inter-faith
Traditions: Tibetan
Movements: Sakyapa

Sharawa Buddhist Group
Stafford, Staffordshire, c/o Amitayus Centre (Crewe, Cheshire)
Tel: 01270-664050 (h)   **Fax:** 01270-6502090
EMail: amitayus@netcentral.co.uk

Stafford Buddhist Society
47 Burton Manor Road, Stafford, Staffordshire, ST17
Contact: Peter Morrell

North Staffordshire Zazen Group
21 Longton Road, Stoke-on-Trent, Staffordshire, ST4 8ND (h)
Tel: 01782-657851 (h)
Contact: John Forse
Traditions: Zen
Movements: Soto Zen

Tamworth Mahayana Buddhist Centre
Tamworth, Staffordshire, c/o Tara Buddhist Centre (Etwall, Derbyshire)
Tel: 01283-732338 **Fax:** 01283-733416
EMail: tara@rmplc.co.uk

Telford Buddhist Group
c/o Wrekin Council Shop, 21 Gladstone House, Hadley, Telford, Shropshire, TF1 4NF
Tel: 01952-222334
Contact: Mr D D Ahir
Position: Community Advisor
Activities: Resource, inter-faith
Traditions: Multi-Traditional
Movements: Ambedkarite
Other Languages: Punjabi, Hindi, Urdu
Affiliations: Network of Buddhist Organisations

Telford Serene Reflection Meditation Group
Telford Buddhist Priory, Old Meadow, 49 The Rock, Ketley, Telford, Shropshire, TF3 5BH
Tel: 01952-615574 **Fax:** 01952-615574
Contact: The Prior
Traditions: Zen

Movements: Soto Zen
Affiliations: Throssel Hole Priory: Order of Buddhist Contemplatives

Wat Pah Santidhamma - The Forest Hermitage
Lower Fulbrook, nr Sherbourne, Warwick, Warwickshire, CV35 8AS
Tel: 01926-624385 **Tel:** 01926-624564
Fax: 01926-624385
EMail: phra.khem@zetnet.co.uk
Contact: The Abbot
Traditions: Theravada, Thai Forest Tradition

Buddha Vihara
Upper Zoar Street, Pennfields, Wolverhampton, West Midlands, WV3 0JH
Tel: 01902-730664 **Fax:** 01902-341186
Contact: Mr Mohan Lal
Position: General Secretary
Activities: Worship/meditation, resource, visits youth, elderly, women, newsletters, books, inter-faith
Traditions: Theravada
Movements: Ambedkarite
Other Languages: Punjabi, Hindi, Thai

Wolverhampton Centre for Mahayana Buddhism
60 Elmdon Road, Oxley, Wolverhampton, West Midlands, WV10 6XJ
Tel: 01902-788741 (h)
Contact: William Giddings
Position: Organiser
Traditions: Tibetan
Movements: New Kadampa

Worcester Buddhist Group Nitartha School
33 Broughton Avenue, St John's, Worcester, Hereford and Worcester (h)
Tel: 01905-420555 (h)
Contact: Dave Rowley

Worcester Longchen Buddhist Group
111 Victoria Avenue, Worcester, Hereford and Worcester

EAST ANGLIA
City, Town or Local Bodies

Friends of the Western Buddhist Order
Friends Meeting House, St. Johns Street, Bury St. Edmunds, Suffolk, IP33 1SJ
Tel: 01842-861201 (h)

Contact: Ray McMurray
Position: Secretary
Activities: Worship/meditation, newsletters
Traditions: Western
Movements: Friends of the Western Buddhist Order

Water Hall Retreat Centre
Bury St Edmund's, Suffolk, c/o London Buddhist Centre (London, Tower Hamlets)
Tel: 0181-981-1225 **Fax:** 0181-980-1960
EMail: lbc@alanlbc.demon.uk

Cambridge Amaravati Group
17 Acorn Avenue, Bar Hill, Cambridge, Cambridgeshire, CB3 8DT (h)
Tel: 01954-780551 (h) **Fax:** 01954-789695
Contact: Gillian Wills
Position: Contact Person
Traditions: Theravada
Movements: Thai Forest Tradition
Affiliations: Buddhist Organisations in Cambridge; Sangha of Amaravati and Chithurst Monasteries

Cambridge Asvagosha Centre
Cambridge, Cambridgeshire, c/o Heruka Centre (London, Barnet)
Tel: 0181-455-7563 **Fax:** 0181-905-5280
EMail: Heruka@rmplc.co.uk

Cambridge Buddhist Centre: Friends of the Western Buddhist Order
25 Newmarket Road, Cambridge, Cambridgeshire, CB5 8ES
Tel: 01223-460252
Contact: Gill Thomas
Position: Centre Manager
Activities: Worship/meditation, resource, visits, women, inter-faith
Traditions: Multi-Traditional
Movements: Friends of the Western Buddhist Order
Other Languages: Spanish, German, French
Affiliations: Education Committee for Buddhists in Cambridgeshire; Network of Buddhist Organisations; European Buddhist Union

Cambridge Buddhist Society
32 Greens Road, Cambridge, Cambridgeshire, CB4 5EF (h)
Tel: 01223-366079 (h)
Contact: Simon and Mary Rose Baugh

Position: Secretaries
Activities: Inter-faith
Traditions: Multi-Traditional
Movements: Kagyupa, Samatha
Affiliations: Nezang Meditation group (Tibetan); The Samatha Association (Theravada)

Cambridge Samatha Association
322 Mill Road, Cambridge, Cambridgeshire, CB1 3NN (h)
Tel: 01223-240293 (h)
Contact: Alan Hines
Position: Contact Person
Activities: Worship/meditation
Traditions: Theravada
Movements: Samatha
Affiliations: Samatha Trust

Cambridge Serene Reflection Meditation Group
28 Windermere Close, Cherry Hinton, Cambridge, Cambridgeshire, CB1 4XW
Tel: 01223-411018
Affiliations: Throssel Hole Buddhist Priory

Cambridge University Buddhist Society
c/o Faculty of Oriental Studies, University of Cambridge, Cambridge, Cambridgeshire, CB3 9DA
Tel: 01223-840196   **Tel:** 01223-249732 (h)
EMail: reml001@cam.ac.uk
Contact: Dr Rachel Harris
Position: Senior Treasurer
Activities: Resource
Traditions: Multi-Traditional

Cambridge University Meditation & Buddhism Society
25 Newmarket Road, Cambridge, Cambridgeshire, CB5 8EG
Tel: 01223-460252
Contact: Dharmachari Ratnaprabha
Position: Teacher
Activities: Resource, youth
Traditions: Multi-Traditional
Movements: Friends of the Western Buddhist Order
Affiliations: Cambridge Buddhist Centre

Nezang Buddhist Meditation Group
5 Sedley Taylor Road, Cambridge, Cambridgeshire, CB2 2PW
Tel: 01223-240090 (h)
Contact: Lama Ato Rinpoche

Position: Buddhist Teacher
Traditions: Tibetan

Cromer Buddhist Group
Cromer, Norfolk, c/o Hacienda, Tower Lane, Sidestrand, Norfolk
Tel: 0126-378359
Contact: Sonny Mann
Position: Contact
Traditions: Western
Movements: Friends of the Western Buddhist Order

East Bilney Shingon Buddhism
Hillside Barn, Church Road, East Bilney, Dereham, Norfolk, NR20 4HN

Kongoryuji Temple
London Road, East Dereham, Norfolk, NR19 1AS
Fax: 01362-693962
Contact: Secretary
Activities: Worship/meditation, resource
Traditions: Shingon Esoteric Buddhism
Other Languages: Croatian/Serbian, Japanese, Sanskrit, French
Affiliations: Network of Buddhist Organisations; Mushindokai; European Buddhist Union

Shingon Mushindokai
77 The Broadway, Grantchester, Cambridgeshire

Friends of the Western Buddhist Order (Ipswich)
c/o Evolution, 5 The Thoroughfare, Town Centre, Ipswich, Suffolk, IP1 1BX
Tel: 01473-211516
EMail: evolutioni@ad.com
Contact: Dharmachari Jnanamitra
Position: Chairman
Activities: Resource
Traditions: Western
Movements: Friends of the Western Buddhist Order
Affiliations: Friends of the Western Buddhist Order

Ipswich Mahayana Buddhist Centre
Ipswich, Suffolk, c/o Akshobya Buddhist Centre (Nottingham, Notinghamshire)
Tel: 0115-985-7356 (h)   **Fax:** 0115-985-7356

Amoghasiddhi Centre
Norwich, Norfolk, c/o Akshobya Centre (Nottingham, Nottinghamshire)
Tel: 0115-985-7356   **Fax:** 0115-985-7356

Norfolk Mushindokai
7 Margetson Avenue, Thorpe St Andrew, Norwich,
Norfolk, NR7 0DG (h)
Tel: 01603-702515 (h)
Contact: Denise Anne Madden
Position: Secretary
Activities: Worship/meditation, resource, youth,
newsletters, books
Traditions: Shingon Shu Sect
Movements: Shingon
Affiliations: Kongoryuji Temple; British Shingon
Buddhist Association; British Mushindokai;
European Buddhist Union

Norwich Buddhist Centre
41a All Saints Green, Norwich, Norfolk, NR1 3LY
Contact: Secretary
Traditions: Western
Movements: Friends of the Western Buddhist
Order

Norwich Mahayana Buddhist Centre
Norwich, Norfolk, c/o Akshobya Buddhist Centre
(Nottingham, Nottinghamshire)
Tel: 0115-985-7356 **Fax:** 0115-985-7356

**Norwich Serene Reflection Buddhist Meditation
Group**
68 Mornington Road, Norwich, Norfolk, NR2
3ND
Tel: 01603-502876 (h)
Contact: Geoffrey Goates OBC
Position: Lay Minister
Activities: Resource, inter-faith
Traditions: Zen
Movements: Soto Zen
Affiliations: Throssel Hole Buddhist Priory; Order
of Buddhist Contemplatives

Padmaloka Buddhist Retreat Centre for Men
Lesingham House, Surlingham, Norwich, Norfolk,
NR14 7AL
Tel: 01508-888112
Contact: Retreat Organiser
Traditions: Western
Movements: Friends of the Western Buddhist
Order

Reiyukai
Unit 24, Saint Mary's Works, Suke Street,
Norwich, Norfolk, NR3 1QA
Tel: 01603-630857 **Tel:** 01603-465189 (h)

Fax: 01603-760749
Contact: Julian Wilde
Position: UK Secretary
Activities: Worship/meditation, resource,
umbrella, visits, youth, elderly, newsletter, inter-
faith
Traditions: Nichiren
Other Languages: Japanese, Thai

University of East Anglia Buddhist Society
Students Union, University of East Anglia,
Norwich, Norfolk, NR4 7TJ
EMail: T.Miller ea.uk
Contact: Tansy Miller
Position: Secretary
Traditions: Western
Movements: Friends of the Western Buddhist
Order
Affiliations: Friends of the Western Buddhist
Order

BUFA (Buddhism for All)
Lorien, High Street, Shipdam, Thetford, Norfolk,
IP25 7PA (h)
EMail: 10670.3007@compuserve.com
Contact: Muriel Frankl
Position: Organiser
Traditions: Multi-Traditional

GREATER LONDON
Regional or Area Bodies

Heruka Buddhist Centre
13 Woodstock Road, Golders Green, London,
NW11 8ES
Tel: 0181-455-7563 **Fax:** 0181-905-5280
EMail: Heruka@rmplc.co.uk
Contact: John McBretney
Position: Administrator
Activities: Worship/meditation, resource, visits,
newsletters
Traditions: New Kadampa

Kongoruji London
58 Mansfield Road, London, NW3
Contact: Shifu T Dukes

London Buddhist Arts Centre
Eastbourne House, Bullards Place, Bethnal Green,
London, E2 0PT
Tel: 0181-983-4473 **Fax:** 0181-983-4473

EMail: postboxbac@demon.co.uk
Contact: Srivati
Position: Director
Activities: Youth
Traditions: Western
Movements: Friends of the Western Buddhist Order

London Buddhist Centre

51 Roman Road, Bethnal Green, London, E2 0HU
Tel: 0181-981-1225   **Fax:** 0181-980-1968
EMail: lbc@alanlbc.demon.uk
Contact: Dharmachari Karmabandhu
Position: Centre Manager
Activities: Worship/meditation, visits, newsletters
Traditions: Western
Movements: Friends of the Western Buddhist Order
Other Languages: French, German, Polish, Spanish
Affiliations: Friends of the Western Buddhist Order

London Buddhist Vihara

Dharmapala Building, The Avenue, Chiswick, London, W4 1UD
Tel: 0181-995-9493   **Fax:** 0181-994-8130
Contact: Most Venerable Vajiragnana
Position: President
Activities: Worship/meditation, visits
Traditions: Theravada
Movements: Anagarika Dharmapala Trust
Other Languages: Sinhalese, Hindi
Affiliations: Network of Buddhist Organisations

London Dhamma Group

32 King Henry's Road, London, NW3
Tel: 0171-586-5416 (h)
Traditions: Theravada

London Serene Reflection (Soto Zen) Meditation Group

5 Belsize Crescent, Belsize Park, London, NW3 5QY (h)
Tel: 0171-431-6734 (h)   **Fax:** 0171-431-6734
Contact: Julie & Andrew Browne
Position: Lay Ministers
Activities: Worship/meditation
Traditions: Zen
Movements: Soto Zen
Affiliations: Reading Buddhist Priory; Throssel

Hole Priory; Shasta Abbey

London Soto Zen Group

Sunra Natural Health Centre, 26 Balham Hill, Clapham South, London, SW12

London Zen Group

Highbury Roundhouse Community Centre, 71 Ronalds Road, Islington, London, N5
Tel: 09731-47853
Contact: Mary Butler
Position: Simple Member
Traditions: Zen
Movements: Soto Zen
Other Languages: French
Affiliations: International Zen Association UK; International Zen Association

London Zen Society

10 Belmont Street, London, NW1 8HH
Tel: 0171-485-9576
Contact: Junando
Position: Resident Monk

North London Buddhist Centre

St Mark's Studios, Chillingworth Road, London, N7 8QJ
Tel: 0171-700-3075
Internet: http://www.urgyen.demon.co.uk/nlbc
Contact: Yashomitra
Position: Chairman
Activities: Worship/meditation, visits, women, newsletters
Traditions: Western
Movements: Friends of the Western Buddhist Order

South London Buddhist Centre

8 Trouville Road, London, SW4 8QL
Tel: 0181-673-5570
Contact: Dharmachari Dharmaruchi
Traditions: Western
Movements: Friends of the Western Buddhist Order

Borough or Local Bodies

BARNET

Heruka Buddhist Centre

13 Woodstock Road, Golders Green, London, NW11 8ES
Tel: 0181-455-7563   **Fax:** 0181-905-5280

EMail: Heruka@rmplc.co.uk
Contact: John McBretney
Position: Administrative Director
Activities: Worship/meditation
Traditions: New Kadampa

North Finchley Mahayana Buddhist Centre
North Finchley, London, c/o Heruka Centre
(London, Barnet)
Tel: 0181-455-7563 **Fax:** 0181-905-5280
EMail: Heruka@rmplc.co.uk

West Hampstead Mahayana Buddhist Centre
West Hampstead, London, c/o Heruka Centre
(London, Barnet)
Tel: 0181-455-7563 **Fax:** 0181-905-5280
EMail: Heruka@rmplc.co.uk

BRENT

Britain Myanmar Buddhist Trust
1 Old Church Lane, Kingsbury, London, NW9
8TG
Tel: 0181-200-6898
Contact: Sein Tun Aung
Position: Secretary
Activities: Worship/meditation, resource, youth,
elderly, women, books
Traditions: Theravada
Movements: Samatha, Vipassana
Other Languages: Myanmar

Sri Saddhatissa International Buddhist Centre
309-311 Kingsbury Road, London, NW9 9PE (h)
Tel: 0181-204-3301 (h)
Contact: Venerable Galayaye Piyadassi
Position: Head of Centre
Activities: Worship/meditation, resource, umbrella,
visits, youth, elderly, women, newsletters, books,
inter-faith
Traditions: Theravada
Movements: Maha Bodhi
Other Languages: Sinhala, Hindi, Chinese

Western Ch'an Fellowship
23 Nightingale Road, London, NW10 4RG (h)
Tel: 0181-961-7802 (h)
Contact: Bruce Stephenson
Position: Regional representative
Activities: Worship/meditation, newsletter
Traditions: Ch'an
Movements: Soto Zen, Rinzai Zen
Affiliations: Western Ch'an Fellowship

CAMDEN

Dzogchen Community
29 Jeffrey's Street, Camden Town, London, NW1
Tel: 0181-485-3108 (h)
Traditions: Tibetan

Hampstead Buddhist Group
Burgh House, New End Square, Hampstead,
London, NW3 1LT
Tel: 0181-452-4174
Contact: Susan Jordan
Position: Secretary
Traditions: Theravada, Thai Tradition
Movements: Vipassana
Affiliations: Buddhist Monastery, Hemel
Hempstead; Other Forest Sangha Monasteries

Kongoruji London
58 Mansfield Road, London, NW3
Contact: Shifu T Dukes

London Dhamma Group
32 King Henry's Road, London, NW3
Tel: 0171-586-5416 (h)
Traditions: Theravada

London Serene Reflection (Soto Zen) Meditation Group
5 Belsize Crescent, Belsize Park, London, NW3
5QY (h)
Tel: 0171-431-6734 (h) **Fax:** 0171-431-6734
Contact: Julie & Andrew Browne
Position: Lay Ministers
Activities: Worship/meditation
Traditions: Zen
Movements: Soto Zen
Affiliations: Reading Buddhist Priory; Throssel
Hole Priory; Shasta Abbey

London Soto Zen Group
23 Westbere Road, London, NW2 3SP
Tel: 0171-794-3109 (h)
Contact: Mr Duncan Sellers
Traditions: Zen
Movements: Soto Zen

London Zen Society
10 Belmont Street, London, NW1 8HH
Tel: 0171-485-9576
Contact: Junando
Position: Resident Monk

Vajradhatu Dharma Study Group
1 Compayne Gardens, London, NW6
Tel: 0181-968-3813
Traditions: Theravada

CROYDON

**Friends of the Western Buddhist Order (Surrey)
Croydon Buddhist Centre**
96-98 High Street, Croydon, Surrey, CRO 1ND
Tel: 0181-688-8624 **Fax:** 0181-649-9375
EMail: 100660, 3575@compuserve.com
Contact: Dharmachari Ratnabodhi
Position: Secretary
Activities: Worship/meditation, resources
Traditions: Western
Movements: Friends of the Western Buddhist
Order

Thames Meditation Society
Thames Buddhist Vihara, 49 Dulverton Road,
Selsdon, Surrey, CR2 8PJ
Tel: 0181-675-7120 **Fax:** 0181-657-7120
Contact: Venerable P Somaratana Thera
Position: Head of Vihara
Activities: Worship/meditation, visits, newsletters,
inter-faith
Traditions: Theravada
Movements: Maha Bodhi
Other Languages: Sinhala

EALING

London Buddhist Vihara
Dharmapala Building, The Avenue, Chiswick,
London, W4 1UD
Tel: 0181-995-9493 **Fax:** 0181-994-8130
Contact: Most Venerable Vajiragnana
Position: President
Activities: Worship/meditation, visits
Traditions: Theravada
Movements: Angarika Dharmapala Trust
Other Languages: Sinhalese, Hindi
Affiliations: Network of Buddhist Organisations

ENFIELD

Buddhist Realists' Vihara
85 Highworth Road, New Southgate, London,
N11 2SN

HACKNEY

Rokpa Trust, London Project
67 Parkholme Road, Dalston, Hackney, London,
E8 3AQ
Tel: 0171-254-5004 **Fax:** 0171-249-4134
Contact: John Ramos-Gonzalez
Position: Volunteer (Senior)
Activities: Worship/meditation, elderly, women
Traditions: Tibetan
Movements: Kagyupa
Other Languages: English

HAMMERSMITH AND FULHAM

Shingon Mushindokai
50 Collingbourne Road, Shepherds Bush, London,
W12

HARINGEY

Muswell Hill Mahayana Buddhist Centre
Muswell Hill, London, c/o Heruka Centre
(London, Barnet)
Tel: 0181-455-7563 **Fax:** 0181-905-5280
EMail: Heruka@rmplc.co.uk

HARROW

Harrow Zazenkai
8a Butler Avenue, Harrow, Middlesex, HA1 4EH

HILLINGDON

Ruislip Meditation & Retreat Centre
12 Meadow Close, Ruislip, Middlesex, HA4 8AP
(h)
Tel: 01895-624147 (h)
Contact: Jasmine Koller
Position: Sangha "Leader"
Activities: Worship/meditation, resource, inter-
faith
Traditions: Multi-Traditional
Movements: Nyingmapa, Vipassana
Other Languages: Finnish, Italian

ISLINGTON

London Zen Group
Highbury Roundhouse Community Centre,
71 Ronalds Road, Islington, London, N5
Tel: 09731-47853

Contact: Mary Butler
Position: Simple Member
Traditions: Zen
Movements: Soto Zen
Other Languages: French
Affiliations: International Zen Association UK; International Zen Association

North London Buddhist Centre
St Mark's Studios, Chillingworth Road, London, N7 8QJ
Tel: 0171-700-3075
Contact: Yashomitra
Position: Chairman
Activities: Worship/meditation, visits, women, newsletters
Traditions: Western
Movements: Friends of the Western Buddhist Order

Sakya Chogyal Sechen Dzong
47 Davenant Road, Holloway, London, N19 3NW
Tel: 0171-281-5348
Contact: Stephen Mulligan
Position: Administrator
Traditions: Tibetan
Movements: Sakyapa
Affiliations: Network of Buddhist Organiastions

KINGSTON-UPON-THAMES

Kingston Buddhist Group
Kingston-upon-Thames, Surrey
Tel: 0181-541-0617
Contact: Penny Kuner

Yon-Hwa-Sa (Lotus House)
18 Rosebery Road, Kingston-upon-Thames, Surrey, KT1 3LN
Tel: 0181-549-6092
Contact: Venerable Jisu Sunim
Activities: Worship/meditation

LAMBETH

Jamyang Meditation Centre
The Old Court House, 43 Renfrew Road, Kennington, London, SE11
Tel: 0171-820-8787 (h)   **Fax:** 0171-820-8605
EMail: Jamyang@cix.compulink.co.uk
Contact: Venerable John Feuille
Position: Co-ordinator

Activities: Worship/meditation, visits, youth, newsletters
Traditions: Tibetan
Movements: Gelugpa
Affiliations: Network of Buddhist Organisations; Foundation for the Preservation of the Mahayana Tradition

Rissho Kosei-Kai
Flat 6, 83 Sudbourne Road, London, SW2 5AF
Contact: Ms Jill Sullivan
Traditions: Nichiren
Movements: Rissho Kosei-Kai

South London Buddhist Centre
8 Trouville Road, London, SW4 8QL
Tel: 0181-673-5570
Contact: Dharmachari Dharmaruchi
Traditions: Western
Movements: Friends of the Western Buddhist Order

LEWISHAM

Linh-Son Buddhist Association in the UK
89 Bromley Road, Catford, London, SE6 2UF
Tel: 0181-461-1887
Contact: Secretary

MERTON

Buddhapadipa Temple
14 Calonne Road, Wimbledon Parkside, London, SW19 5HJ
Tel: 0181-946-1357
Contact: Sermsak Narinwong
Position: Chairman
Activities: Worship/meditation, resource, visits, youth, elderly, women, newsletters, books
Traditions: Theravada
Other Languages: Thai

Santosa Buddhist Group
c/o The Quaker Meeting House, 40 Spencer Hill Road, London, SW19
Tel: 0181-549-6375
Contact: Mike Pearce
Position: Group Co-ordinator
Activities: Worship/meditation
Traditions: Theravada
Affiliations: Amaravati and Chithurst Buddhist Monasteries

Sub-Committee for the Buddhist Mission in the UK

The Buddhapadipa Temple, Wimbledon, London, SW19 5HJ
Tel: 0181-946-1357

NEWHAM

Ambedkar International Mission

Buddha Vihara, 84 Dacre Road, Plaistow, London, E13 0PR
Tel: 0181-470-1879 **Fax:** 0181-470-8898
Contact: Bhikkhu Nagasena
Position: Patron/Chairman
Traditions: Theravada
Movements: Ambedkarite
Activities: Worship/meditation, visits, youth, elderly, women, inter-faith
Other Languages: Punjabi, Hindi, Thai, Sinhalese
Affiliations: Buddhist Cultural Institute; Thames Meditation Society; Vipassana Association; Sublime Life Mission, Thailand

Buddhist Cultural Institute

88 Ruskin Avenue, East Ham, London, E12 6PW
Tel: 0181-472-4701 (h) **Fax:** 0181-472-4701 (h)
Contact: Venerable Makuddala Gnanissara
Position: Head of Institute
Activities: Worship/meditation, visits, youth, inter-faith
Traditions: Theravada
Other Languages: Sinhalese

RICHMOND-UPON-THAMES

Richmond Mahayana Buddhist Centre

Richmond, c/o Heruka Centre (London, Barnet)
Tel: 0181-455-7563 **Fax:** 0181-905-5280
EMail: Heruka@rmplc.co.uk

Samatha Association

34 Royal Road, Teddington, Middlesex, TW11 0SB
Tel: 0181-977-2476
Contact: Paul Beck

Tisarana Vihara Association

357 Nelson Road, Whitton, Twickenham, Middlesex, TW2 7AG
Tel: 0181-898-6965 **Fax:** 0181-898-6965
Contact: Venerable U Nyakina
Position: Spiritual Instructor
Activities: Worship/meditation, visits, youth, elderly, women, newsletters, books

Traditions: Theravada
Movements: Vipassana, Buddhist Psychology
Other Languages: Hindi, Myanmar

SOUTHWARK

Kongo Raiden Zen Order

c/o 16 Moreton House, Otto Street, London, SE17
Traditions: Zen

Padma Cho Ling

68 Blenheim Grove, Peckham, London, SE15 4QL
Tel: 0171-732-0183
Contact: Mr Stephen Hodge

TOWER HAMLETS

Amrita Dzong

Unit 21F Perseverance Works, 38 Kingsland Road, London, E2
Contact: David Mayor
Position: Acting Secretary

Bodywise Natural Health

119 Roman Road, London, E2 0QN

London Buddhist Arts Centre

Eastbourne House, Bullards Place, Bethnal Green, London, E2 0PT
Tel: 0181-983-4473 **Fax:** 0181-983-4473
EMail: postboxbac@demon.co.uk
Contact: Srivati
Position: Director
Activities: Youth
Traditions: Western
Movements: Friends of the Western Buddhist Order

London Buddhist Centre

51 Roman Road, Bethnel Green, London, E2 0HU
Tel: 0181-981-1225 **Fax:** 0181-980-1968
EMail: lbc@alanlbc.demon.uk
Contact: Dharmachari Karmabandhu
Position: Centre Manager
Activities: Worship/meditation, visits, newsletters
Traditions: Western
Movements: Friends of the Western Buddhist Order
Other Languages: French, German, Polish, Spanish
Affiliations: Friends of the Western Buddhist Order

WANDSWORTH

London Soto Zen Group
Sunra Natural Health Centre, 26 Balham Hill, Clapham South, London, SW12

WESTMINSTER, CITY OF

Covent Garden Meditation Centre
71d Endell Street, London, WC2
Tel: 0181-981-1225
Traditions: Western
Movements: Friends of the Western Buddhist Order

Friends of the Western Buddhist Order (West London)
West London Buddhist Centre, 94 Westbourne Park Villas, London, W2 5PL
Tel: 0171-727-9382
EMail: Compuserve 100305, 642
Contact: Dharmachari Mokshara
Position: Chair
Activities: Worship/meditation, religious
Movements: Friends of the Western Buddhist Order
Affiliations: Network of Buddhist Organisations; European Buddhist Union

Leicester Square Mahayana Buddhist Centre
Leicester Square, London, c/o Heruka Centre (London, Barnet)
Tel: 0181-455-7563 **Fax:** 0181-905-5280
EMail: Heruka@rmplc.co.uk

SOUTH EAST
Regional and County Bodies

Essex Buddhist Society
c/o 134 Long Riding, Basildon, Essex
Tel: 01268-419095 (h)

Bedfordshire Buddhist Society
3 Pear Tree View, Elstow, Bedford, Bedfordshire, MK42 9YN
Tel: 01234-357381
Contact: Tony Cook
Position: Chairperson

Bodhisattva Centre
11 Vernon Terrace, Brighton, East Sussex, BN1 3JG
Tel: 01273-732917 **Fax:** 01273-732917
EMail: bodhisattva@fastnet.co.uk
Contact: Kelsang Rabten
Position: Education Co-ordinator
Activities: Worship/meditation, resource, umbrella, visits
Traditions: Tibetan
Movements: New Kadampa

Hampshire Buddhist Society
21 Langton Road, Bishop's Waltham, Southampton, Hampshire, S032 1GF (h)
Contact: Honorary Secretary
Activities: Inter-faith
Traditions: Theravada, Zen
Movements: Rinzai Zen, Vipassana
Affiliations: Chithurst Buddhist Monastery; Zen Centre, London; Network of Buddhist Organisations; European Buddhist Union

Hampshire Buddhist Society (Zen Group)
32 Norfolk Road, Shirley, Southampton, Hampshire, SO15 5AS (h)
Contact: Steve and Roberta Mansell
Activities: Worship/meditation
Traditions: Zen
Movements: Rinzai Zen
Affiliations: Hampshire Buddhist Society; Buddhist Society, London; Zen Centre, London; Daitoku-Ji Temple, Kyoto

Surrey Buddhist Centre Meditation Group
Wold Cottage, Goose Lane, Mayford, Woking, Surrey, GU22 0NW
Tel: 01483-727170 **Tel:** 01483-768759 (h)
Contact: Chris Hidred
Traditions: Multi-Traditional

Surrey Buddhist Meditation Group
143 York Road, Woking, Surrey, GU22 7XS (h)
Tel: 01483-761398 (h)
Contact: Rocana
Position: Co-ordinator
Traditions: Theravada
Affiliations: Cittaveka Chithurst Buddhist Monastery

City, Town and Local Bodies

Aylesbury Meditation Group
9 Recreation Ground, Wingrave, Aylesbury, Buckinghamshire, HP22 4PH (h)

Tel: 01296-681161 (h)
Contact: Christa Wright
Traditions: Multi-Traditional
Movements: Kagyupa, Theravadin Forest Tradition

Essex Buddhist Society
c/o 134 Long Riding, Basildon, Essex
Tel: 01268-419095 (h)

Pure Land Buddhist Fellowship
Hawthorn, Hillcrest Avenue, Basildon, Essex, SS16 6EQ
Tel: 01268-419095 (h)
Contact: Nick Cook

Bedford Mahayana Buddhist Centre
Bedford, Bedfordshire, c/o 171 Luton Road, Harpenden, Hertfordshire (h)
Tel: 01982-768984 **Tel:** 01759-304863 (h)
Contact: Kelsang Pagpa
Position: Teacher
Activities: Visits, youth, elderly
Traditions: Tibetan
Movements: New Kadampa
Affiliations: Mahasiddha Mahayana Buddhist Centre, Luton

Bedfordshire Buddhist Society
3 Pear Tree View, Elstow, Bedford, Bedfordshire, MK42 9YN
Tel: 01234-357381
Contact: Tony Cook
Position: Chairperson

Dr Ambedkar Mission Society Bedford
19 Henderson Way, Kempston, Bedford, Bedfordshire, MK42 8NN (h)
Tel: 01234-302236 (h)
Contact: Arun Kumar
Position: General Secretary
Activities: Resource, elderly, women, books, inter-faith
Traditions: Theravada
Movements: Ambedkarite
Other Languages: Punjabi, Hindi
Affiliations: Federation of Ambedkarite and Buddhist Organisations of the UK

Shantideva Centre
52 Elizabeth Close, Bracknell, Berkshire, RG12 3SZ (h)
Tel: 01344-487205 (h)
Contact: Richard Worrall

Bodhisattva Centre
11 Vernon Terrace, Brighton, East Sussex, BN1 3JG
Tel: 01273-732917 **Fax:** 01273-732917
EMail: bodhisattva@fastnet.co.uk
Contact: Kelsang Rabten
Position: Education Co-ordinator
Activities: Worship/meditation, resource, umbrella, visits
Traditions: Tibetan
Movements: New Kadampa

Brighton Buddhist Centre
15 Park Crescent Place, Brighton, East Sussex, BN2 3HF
Tel: 01273-698420
Contact: Khemanandi
Position: Chairwoman
Activities: Worship/meditation, resource, visits, women, newsletters, inter-faith
Traditions: Western
Movements: Friends of the Western Buddhist Order
Other Languages: French

Evolution Arts & Health Centre
2 Sillwood Terrace, Brighton, East Sussex, BN1 2LR
Tel: 01273-729803 **Tel:** 01273-685424 (h)
Contact: Indrabodhi
Position: Director
Activities: Resource, visits
Traditions: Western
Movements: Friends of the Western Buddhist Order
Affiliations: Brighton Buddhist Centre; Friends of the Western Buddhist Order; TBMSG

Maitrikara
24 Freshfield Street, Queen's Park, Brighton, East Sussex, BN2 2ZG (h)
Tel: 01273-675803 (h) **Fax:** 01273-675803
Contact: Larry Gethin
Position: Chair
Activities: Worship/meditation
Traditions: Tibetan
Movements: Nyingmapa
Affiliations: Network of Buddhist Organisations; Centre de'Etudes de Chanteloube

Sussex University Buddhist Meditation Society
17 Trinity Street, Brighton, East Sussex, BN2 3HN (h)

Tel: 01273-685424 (h)
Contact: Jayaraja
Position: Treasurer
Activities: Resource
Traditions: Western
Movements: Friends of the Western Buddhist
Order
Affiliations: Brighton Buddhist Centre; Friends of
the Western Buddhist Order; Karuna Trust

(Canterbury) East Kent Mahayana Buddhist Centre

Canterbury, Kent, c/o Bodhisattva Centre
(Brighton, East Sussex)
Tel: 01273-732917 **Fax:** 01273-732917
EMail: bodhisattva@fastnet.co.uk

Chatham Friends of the Western Buddhist Order

Chatham, Kent, c/o London Buddhist Centre
(London, Tower Hamlets)
Tel: 0181-981-1225 **Fax:** 1081-980-1960
EMail: lbc@alanlbc.demon.uk
Contact: Dharmachari Karunabandhu
Activities: Worship/meditation
Traditions: Western
Movements: Friends of the Western Buddhist
Order

Chichester Mahayana Buddhist Centre

Chichester, West Sussex, c/o Bodhisattva Centre
(Brighton, East Sussex)
Tel: 01273-732917 **Fax:** 01273-732917
EMail: bodhisattva@fastnet.co.uk

Chichester Serene Reflection Meditation Group

Chichester, West Sussex, c/o Highfield, Dairy Lane,
Walberton, Arundel, West Sussex, BN18 0PT (h)
Tel: 01243-551315 (h)
Contact: Chris Barker
Position: Secretary
Traditions: Zen
Movements: Soto Zen
Affiliations: Reading Buddhist Priory; Throssel
Hole Priory Northumberland; Order of Buddhist
Contemplatives

Colchester Buddhist Group

c/o 2 Ships Cottages, Wheatsheaf Lane, Wrabness,
Manningtree, Essex, CO11 2TB (h)
Tel: 01255-870500 (h) **Fax:** 01206-762557
EMail: Compuserve 100620, 2103
Contact: Kelvin Youngs

Position: Secretary
Activities: Worship/meditation, resource,
newsletters, inter-faith
Traditions: Western
Movements: Friends of the Western Buddhist
Order
Other Languages: German, Finnish, Greek

Epping Mahayana Buddhist Centre

Epping, Essex, c/o Heruka Centre (London,
Barnet)
Tel: 0181-455-7563 **Fax:** 0181-905-5280
EMail: Heruka@rmplc.co.uk
Contact: John McBretney
Position: Administrator
Traditions: Tibetan
Movements: New Kadampa

Guildford Mahayana Buddhist Centre

Guildford, Surrey, c/o Bodhisattva Centre
(Brighton, East Sussex)
Tel: 01273-732917 **Fax:** 01273-732917
EMail: bodhisattva@fastnet.co.uk

Harlow Buddhist Group

192 The Hornbeans, Harlow, Essex, CM20 1PL
Tel: 01279-427768
Contact: Dharmachari Shantinayaka
Position: Secretary
Traditions: Western
Movements: Friends of the Western Buddhist
Order

Harlow Buddhist Society

Dana House, 385 Longbanks, Harlow, Essex,
CM18 7PG
Tel: 01279-436564 **Tel:** 01279-303287 (h)
Contact: Dennis Wood
Position: Secretary
Activities: Worship/meditation, visits
Traditions: Theravada

Hastings Buddhist Meditation & Study Group

Cincla Cottage, Pett Level, Hastings, East Sussex,
TN35 4EE (h)
Tel: 01424-813176 (h)
Contact: Alan Dipper
Position: Chair
Traditions: Zen

Amaravati Buddhist Monastery

Great Gaddesden, Hemel Hempstead,
Hertfordshire, HP1 3BZ

Tel: 01442-842455 **Fax:** 01442-843721
Contact: The Abott
Activities: Worship/meditation, newsletters, books
Traditions: Theravada
Movements: Vipassana
Other Languages: Thai, French, German

Rivendell Retreat Centre

Clillies Lane, High Hurstwood, East Sussex, TN22 4AA
Tel: 01825-732594 (h)
EMail: Ratnachuda. Compuserve 101714,614
Contact: Dharmachari Ratnachuda
Traditions: Western
Movements: Ambedkarite, Friends of the Western Buddhist Order

Leigh Buddhist Group

c/o Twycross Villa, 5 North Street, Leigh-on-Sea, Essex
Contact: Ms Barbara Walters
Traditions: Theravada

South East Essex Buddhist Group

21 Woodlands Park, Leigh-on-Sea, Essex, SS9 3TX (h)
Tel: 01702-559241 (h) **Fax:** 01268-696839
Contact: Robert Howell
Position: Co-ordinator
Traditions: Theravada
Movements: Forest Tradition (Amaravti)
Other Languages: French
Affiliations: Amaravati Buddhist Centre; Chithurst Forest Monastery; Wat Nanachet, Ubon, Thailand

Luton Mahayana Buddhist Centre

Luton, Bedforshire, c/o Madhyamika Buddhist Centre (Pocklington, North Yorkshire)
Tel: 01759-304832 **Fax:** 01759-305962

Maidstone Mahayana Buddhist Centre

Maidstone, Kent, c/o Bodhisattva Centre (Brighton, East Sussex)
Tel: 01273-732917 **Fax:** 01273-732917
EMail: bodhisattva@fastnet.co.uk

Mid Kent & Medway Buddhist Group

c/o Friends Meeting House, Union Street, Maidstone, Kent
Tel: 01622-751202 (h)
Contact: Joan Hamze
Activities: Worship/meditation
Traditions: Theravada

Friends of the Western Buddhist Order Milton Keynes

Milton Keynes, Buckinghamshire, c/o Cambridge Buddhist Centre (Cambridge, Cambridgeshire)
Tel: 01223-460252

Milton Keynes Serene Reflection Meditation Group

Milton Keynes, Buckinghamshire, c/o 6 Chandos Road, Buckingham, Buckinghamshire, MK18 1AH (h)
Tel: 01280-813962 (h)
Contact: Mr Hilaire MacCarthy
Position: Lay Minister
Activities: Worship/meditation, inter-faith
Traditions: Zen
Movements: Soto Zen
Affiliations: Throssel Hole Priory

Friends of the Western Buddhist Order (Oxford)

46 Derwent Avenue, Headington, Oxford, Oxfordshire, OX3 0AP
Tel: 01865-61973
EMail: Odec@gn.apc.org
Contact: Shantiprabha
Position: Chairperson
Activities: Youth, elderly, women, inter-faith
Traditions: Western
Movements: Friends of the Western Buddhist Order

Mushindokai (Oxford) Shingon Shu

48 Western Road, Grandpont, Oxford, Oxfordshire, OX1 4LG (h)
Tel: 01865-245095 (h)
Contact: Christopher Jones
Position: Sempai
Activities: Worship/meditation, resource, newsletters, books
Traditions: Shingon (Chen Yen) Buddhism
Movements: Shingon-Shu
Affiliations: Association of Buddhist Groups in Oxford; Mushindokai (GB) Kongoryuji Temple, Norfolk; Network of Buddhist Organisations; European Buddhist Union

Oxford Prasangika Centre

Oxford, Oxfordshire, c/o Heruka Centre (London, Barnet)
Tel: 0181-455-7563 **Fax:** 0181-905-5280
EMail: Heruka@rmplc.co.uk

Oxford Theravadin Group
Trinity College, Oxford, Oxfordshire, 0X1 3BH
Tel: 01865-279867 **Tel:** 01865-557876 (h)
Fax: 01865-279911
Contact: Dr Peter Carey
Position: Convenor
Traditions: Theravada
Activities: Worship/meditation
Traditions: Multi-Traditional
Movements: Samatha, Vipassana
Other Languages: Pali
Affiliations: Amaravati Buddhist Monastery,
Hemel Hempsted; Network of Buddhist
Organisations

Oxford University Buddhist Society
Manor Barn, 5 Elsfield Manor, Elsfield, Oxford,
Oxfordshire, 0X3 9SP
Tel: 01865-351369 (h)
Contact: Mr Charles Shaw
Traditions: Multi-Traditional

Samatha Association Oxford Group
8 Earl Street, Oxford, Oxfordshire, OX2 0JA (h)
Tel: 01865-726312 (h)
Contact: Colin George
Position: Facilitator
Activities: Worship/meditation
Traditions: Theravada
Movements: Samatha
Affiliations: Samatha Association, Powys

Stillness in Action
Orchard House, 11 Church Street, Beckley, Oxford,
Oxfordshire, OX3 9UT

Thrangu House
76 Bullingdon Road, Oxford, Oxfordshire, OX4
1QL
Tel: 01865-241555 **Fax:** 01865-790096
Contact: Ani Yeshe Palmo
Position: Secretary
Activities: Worship/meditation, visits
Traditions: Tibetan
Movements: Kagyupa
Affiliations: Network of Buddhist Organisations

Cittaviveka
Chithurst Buddhist Monastery, Chithurst, nr
Petersfield, Hampshire, GU31 5EU
Tel: 01730-814986 **Tel:** 01730-821479 (h)
Fax: 01730-817334

Contact: Dr Barry Durrant
Position: Secretary
Activities: Worship/meditation, visits
Traditions: Theravada
Other Languages: German
Affiliations: Network of Buddhist Organisations;
World Fellowship of Buddhists

Petersfield Buddhist Group
8 St Peter's Road, Petersfield, Hampshire, GU32
3HX
Tel: 01730-63040 (h)
Contact: A S Brettell
Position: Spiritual Director
Traditions: Zen
Movements: Soto Zen

Gaden Thubten Ling
71 Duncan Road, Southsea, Portsmouth,
Hampshire, PO5 2QU
Tel: 01705-815519
Traditions: Tibetan
Movements: Gelugpa

Portsmouth Buddhist Group
71 Duncan Road, Southsea, Portsmouth,
Hampshire, PO5 2QU
Tel: 01705-815519

Reading Buddhist Priory
176 Cressingham Road, Reading, Berkshire, RG2
7LW
Tel: 0118-986-0750 **Fax:** 0118-986-0750
Contact: The Prior
Activities: Worship/meditation
Traditions: Zen
Movements: Soto Zen
Affiliations: Throssel Hole Priory

Reading Mahayana Buddhist Centre
Reading, Berkshire, c/o 23 Elizabeth Close,
Bracknell, Berkshire, RG12 3LZ

Reigate Mahayana Buddhist Centre
Reigate, Surrey, c/o Bodhisattva Centre (Brighton)
Tel: 01273-732917 **Fax:** 01273-732917
EMail: bodhisattva@fastnet.co.uk

St Albans Mahayana Buddhist Centre
St Albans, Bedfordshire, c/o Madhyamika Buddhist
Centre (Pocklington, North Yorkshire)
Tel: 01759-304832 **Fax:** 01759-305962
Contact: Joanne Bird

St Margaret's-at-Cliffe Mahayana Buddhist Centre
St. Margaret's-at-Cliffe, c/o Bodhisattva Centre
(Brighton, East Sussex)
Tel: 01273-732917 **Fax:** 01273-732917
EMail: bodhisattva@fastnet.co.uk

Dharma Trust, The
Marpa House, Rectory Lane, Ashdon, Saffron
Walden, Essex, CB10 2HN
Tel: 01799-584415 **Fax:** 01799-584415
Contact: Secretary
Traditions: Tibetan
Movements: Kagyupa

Sevenoaks Mahayana Buddhist Centre
Sevenoaks, Kent, c/o Bodhisattva Centre (Brighton,
East Sussex)
Tel: 01273-732917 **Fax:** 01273-732917
EMail: bodhisattva@fastnet.co.uk

Southend-on-Sea Mahayana Centre
Southend, Essex, c/o Heruka Centre (London)
Tel: 0181-455-7563 **Fax:** 0181-905-5280
EMail: Heruka@rmplc.co.uk

Hampshire Buddhist Society
21 Langton Road, Bishop's Waltham, Southampton,
Hampshire, S032 1GF (h)
Contact: Honorary Secretary
Activities: Inter-faith
Traditions: Theravada, Zen
Movements: Rinzai Zen, Vipassana
Affiliations: Chithurst Buddhist Monastery;
Network of Buddhist Organisations; European
Buddhist Union

Hampshire Buddhist Society (Zen Group)
32 Norfolk Road, Shirley, Southampton,
Hampshire, SO15 5AS (h)
Contact: Roberta and Steve Mansell
Activities: Worship/meditation
Traditions: Zen
Movements: Rinzai Zen
Affiliations: Hampshire Buddhist Society; The
Buddhist Society; The Zen Centre, London;
Daitoku-Ji Temple Kyoto

Southampton Friends of the Western Buddhist Order Group
1 Lumsden Mansions, Shirley Road, Southampton,
Hampshire, SO1 3JB

Thekchen Mahayana Buddhist Centre
76 Whitworth Crescent, Bitterne Park,
Southampton, Hampshire, SO18 1GA
Tel: 01703-557077 **Fax:** 01703-457092
EMail: thekchen.centre@virgin.net
Contact: Kelsang Thogme
Position: Education Programme Co-ordinator
Activities: Worship/meditation, resource,
visits, youth, elderly, inter-faith
Traditions: Mahayana, Kadampa
Movements: New Kadampa Tradition (NKT)
Other Languages: German, French

Southsea Zen Group
Southsea, Hampshire, c/o 36 Castle Road,
Portsmouth, Hampshire, PO5 3DE
Tel: 01705-754490 (h)
Contact: Mr Peter Lavin
Traditions: Zen
Movements: Soto Zen

Royal Tunbridge Wells Mahayana Buddhist Centre
Tunbridge Wells, Kent, c/o Bodhisattva Centre
(Brighton, East Sussex)
Tel: 01273-732917 **Fax:** 01273-732917
EMail: bodhisattva@fastnet.co.uk

Tunbridge Wells FBWO Group
Tunbridge Wells, Kent, c/o Rivendell Retreat
Centre, Chillies Lane, High Hurstwood, Uckfield,
East Sussex, TN22 4AA

University of Kent Buddhist Society
19 Manor Road, Whitstable, Kent
Contact: c/o Zamantha Walker

Shantideva Centre (Windsor)
4 The Drive, Langley, Windsor, Berkshire, SL3 7DB
Tel: 01753-586703
Contact: Diedre Lofters
Position: Co-ordinator
Traditions: Tibetan
Movements: New Kadampa

Surrey Buddhist Centre Meditation Group
Wold Cottage, Goose Lane, Mayford, Woking,
Surrey, GU22 0NW
Tel: 01483-727170 **Tel:** 01483-768759 (h)
Contact: Chris Hidred
Traditions: Multi-Traditional
Movements: Multi-Movements

Surrey Buddhist Meditation Group
143 York Road, Woking, Surrey, GU22 7XS (h)
Tel: 01483-761398 (h)
Contact: Rocana
Position: Co-ordinator
Traditions: Theravada
Affiliations: Cittaviveka Chithurst Buddhist
Monastery

SOUTH WEST
Regional and County Bodies

Bristol Buddhist Centre
9 Cromwell Road, St Andrews, Bristol, Greater
Bristol, BS6 5HD
Tel: 0117-924-9991 **Tel:** 0117-924-8572 (h)
EMail: 100636.3412@compuserve.com.uk
Contact: Alan Ashley
Position: Centre Administrator
Activities: Worship/meditation, resource, visits,
youth, women, newsletters
Traditions: Western
Movements: Friends of the Western Buddhist
Order

Devon Buddhist Monastery
Odle Cottage, Uppottery, nr Honiton, Devon,
EX14 9QE
Tel: 01404-891251 **Fax:** 01404-891251
Contact: The Guestmaster
Activities: Worship/meditation, resource, visits,
youth, inter-faith
Traditions: Theravada
Movements: Samatha, Soto Zen
Affiliations: Amaravati Buddhist Monastery,
Hemel Hempstead

Amitabha Buddhist Centre
St Audries House, West Quantoxhead, Taunton,
Somerset, TA4 4DU
Tel: 01984-633200 **Tel:** 01984-63395 (h)
Fax: 01984-633807
EMail: amitabha@rmplc.co.uk
Contact: Adam Waterhouse
Position: Press Person
Tradition: New Kadampa
Affiliations: New Kadampa Tradition

Sharpham College For Buddhist Studies &
Contemporary Enquiry
Sharpham College, Sharpham House, Ashprington,
Totnes, Devon, TQ9 7UT

Tel: 01803-732521 **Fax:** 01803-732037
EMail: 101364.537@compuserve.com
Contact: Martine Batchelor
Position: Coordinator
Activities: Resource
Traditions: Multi-Traditional
Movements: Non-denominational

Town, City and Local Bodies

Dammanaat Foundation UK
Spindles, Westabrook Farm Lane, Rew, Ashburton,
Devon, TQ13 7EJ

Bath Buddhist Group
12 Station Road, 12 Station Road, Lower Weston,
Bath, North Somerset, BA1 3DY
Tel: 01225-337918 (h)
Contact: Rosie Ray
Traditions: Multi-Traditional
Movements: Multi-Movement

Bath Mahayana Buddhist Centre
Bath, North Somerset, c/o Ambitabha Centre
(Taunton, Somerset)
Tel: 01225-633200 **Tel:** 01984-633935 (h)
Fax: 01984-633807
EMail: amitabha@rmplc.co.uk

Bournemouth Area Buddhist Group
2 Wollstonecraft Road, Boscombe, Bournemouth,
Dorset, BH5 1JQ (h)
Tel: 01202-304207 (h)
Contact: Nigel Ivor Watkins
Position: Chairman
Traditions: Multi-Traditional

Dromtonpa Centre, Bournemouth
Bournemouth, Dorset, c/o Amitabha Centre,
(Taunton, Somerset)
Tel: 01984-633200 **Tel:** 01984-633935 (h)
Fax: 01984-633807
EMail: amitabha@rmplc.co.uk

Bristol Buddhist Centre
162 Gloucester Road, Bishopston, Bristol, Greater
Bristol, BS7 8NT
Tel: 0117-924-9991
EMail: 100636.3412@compuserve.com.uk
Contact: Alan Ashley
Position: Centre Administrator
Activities: Worship/meditation, resource, visits,
youth, women, newsletters

Traditions: Western
Movements: Friends of the Western Buddhist Order

Bristol Ch'an Group
c/o 13 Limerick Road, Bristol, Greater Bristol, BS6 7DY (h)
Tel: 0117-924-5332 (h)
Contact: Tim & Caroline Paine
Activities: Worship/meditation, resource, newsletters, inter-faith
Traditions: Zen
Movements: Ch'an
Affiliations: Network of Buddhist Organisations; Institute of Chung Hwa Buddhist Culture New York, USA; Western Ch'an Fellowship

Bristol Mahayana Buddhist Centre
c/o 16 Muller Avenue, Horfield, Bristol, Greater Bristol, BS4 9HX
Tel: 0117-940-9722 (h)
Movements: New Kadampa

Bristol Samatha Meditation Group
26 Morgan Street, Bristol, Greater Bristol, BS2 9LQ
Tel: 01272-411902
Contact: Rupert Gethim
Traditions: Theravada
Movements: Samatha

Bristol Serene Reflection Meditation Group
Bristol, Greater Bristol, c/o Lothlorien, Newchurch West, Earlswood, Chepstow, Gwent, NP6 6AU
Tel: 01291-650581
Affiliations: Throssel Hole Buddhist Priory

Bristol Theravada Meditation Group
Bristol, Greater Bristol
Tel: 01272-684089 (h)
Contact: Nirodha
Position: Meditation Teacher
Traditions: Theravada

Bristol University Buddhist Society
c/o Department of Theology, Bristol University, Tyndalls Park Road, Bristol, Greater Bristol
Tel: 01272-303030
Contact: Rupert Gethin

Dharma Therapy Trust
12 Victoria Place, Bedminster, Bristol, Greater Bristol, BS3 3BP
Tel: 0117-963-9089 **Tel:** 0117-968-4784 (h)

Fax: 0117-968-4784
Contact: Mike Austin
Position: Trustee
Traditions: Tibetan
Movements: Gelugpa

Ladakh Project
International Society for Ecology & Culture, 21 Victoria Square, Clifton, Bristol, Greater Bristol, BS8 4ES
Tel: 0117-973-1575

Lam Rim Bristol Buddhist Centre
12 Victoria Place, Bedminster, Bristol, Greater Bristol, BS3 3BP
Tel: 0117-963-9089 **Fax:** 0117-968-4784
Contact: Mike Austin
Position: Trustee
Activities: Worship/meditation, visits, inter-faith
Traditions: Tibetan
Movements: Gelugpa
Affiliations: Network of Buddhist Organisations

Akanishta Buddhist Centre
Cheltenham, Gloucestershire, c/o Amitabha Centre (Taunton, Somerset)
Tel: 01984-633200 **Tel:** 01984-633935 (h)
Fax: 01984-633807
EMail: amitabha@rmplc.co.uk

Cheltenham Tibetan Buddhist Group
c/o 16 Clarence Square, Cheltenham, Gloucestershire, GL50 4JN
Tel: 01242-523748 **Tel:** 01242-523748 (h)
Contact: Anthony Davies
Position: Organiser
Traditions: Tibetan
Movements: Kagyupa
Affiliations: Karmapakshi Centre Bath; Dhagpo-Kagu-Ling, St Leon, Sur Vézère, France

Exeter Soto Zen Serene Reflection Meditation Group
Exeter, Devon, c/o 8 Elder Grove, Crediton, Devon, EX17 1DE (h)
Tel: 01363-777922 (h)
Contact: Adrienne Pitman OBC
Position: Lay Minister
Traditions: Zen
Movements: Soto Zen
Affiliations: Throssel Hole Priory, Hexham, Northumberland; Reading Buddhist Priory; Mount Shasta Buddhist Monastery, California, USA

Exeter Zazenkai
14 Monkswell Road, Exeter, Devon, EX4 7AX (h)
Tel: 01392-221147 (h)
Contact: Tony Doubleday

Kanzeon Sangha
14 Monkswell Road, Exeter, Devon, EX4 7AX (h)
Tel: 01392-221147 (h)
Contact: c/o Tony Doubleday
Position: Co-ordinator

Namgyal Ling
3 Hillside Avenue, Exeter, Devon, EX4 4NW (h)
Tel: 01392-258021
Internet: http://www.eclipse.co.uk/dechen/
Contact: Martyn Samuel
Position: Secretary
Activities: Resource, newsletters, books
Traditions: Tibetan
Movements: Sakyapa
Affiliations: Dechen Community

Pure Land Buddhist Centre, Exeter
Exeter, Devon, c/o Ambitabha Centre (Taunton, Somerset)
Tel: 01984-633200 **Tel:** 01984-633935 (h)
Fax: 01984-633807
EMail: amitabha@rmplc.co.uk
Contact: Adam Waterhouse

Karma Pakshi Centre
8 Catherine Street, Frome, Somerset, BA11 1DB (h)
Tel: 01373-451289 (h)
Contact: Chris Hollingworth
Position: Secretary
Activities: Worship/meditation
Traditions: Tibetan
Movements: Kagyupa
Affiliations: Dhagpo Kagyu Ling, SW France

Sakya Khandro Ling
69 Chilkwell Street, Glastonbury, Somerset, BA6 8DD (h)
Tel: 01458-834619 (h)
Internet: http://www.eclipse.co.uk/~rs1042
Contact: Jeremy Sampson
Position: Chair
Activities: Newsletters, books
Traditions: Tibetan
Movements: Sakyapa
Affiliations: Network of Buddhist Organisations

Devon Buddhist Monastery
Odle Cottage, Uppottery, nr Honiton, Devon, EX14 9QE
Tel: 01404-891251 **Fax:** 01404-891251
Contact: The Guestmaster
Activities: Worship/meditation, resource, visits, youth, inter-faith
Traditions: Theravada
Movements: Samatha, Soto Zen
Affiliations: Amaravati Buddhist Monastery, Hemel Hempstead

Gaia House
West Ogwell, Newton Abbot, Devon, TQ12 6EN
Tel: 01626-333613
Contact: The Managers
Activities: Worship/meditation, visits
Traditions: Multi-Traditional
Movements: Vipassana
Affiliations: Network for Buddhist Organisations

Yeovil Buddhist Meditation Group
Meadowcroft, 2 Hamdon View, Norton-Sub-Hamdon, Somerset
Tel: 01935-88316
Contact: David Greenhorne

Whitecross Buddhist Centre
Gilly Lane, Whitecross, Penzance, Cornwall, TR20 8BZ
Tel: 01736-740759 (h)
Contact: Karrin Kempinsky
Position: Trustee
Activities: Worship/meditation, religious
Traditions: Zen
Movements: Soto Zen, Vipassana

Plymouth Buddhist Group
By The Down, Sampford Spiney, Yelverton, Plymouth, Devon, PL20 6LE
Tel: 01822-616803
Contact: Mr C Louden

Plymouth Mahayana Buddhist Centre
Plymouth, Devon, c/o Ambitabha Centre (Taunton, Somerset)
Tel: 01984-633200 **Tel:** 01984-633935 (h)
Fax: 01984-633807
EMail: amitabha@rmplc.co.uk

Wellbeing Centre Buddhist Society, The
The Self Heal Trust, Old School House, Churchtown, Illogan, Redruth, Cornwall, TR16 4SW

Tel: 01209-842999 **Tel:** 01209-717543 (h)
Contact: Eric Parsons
Position: Group Leader
Activities: Resource, youth, elderly, women, newsletters
Traditions: Theravada
Movements: Thai Forest tradition
Affiliations: Truro Buddhist Group; Devon Buddhist Vihara; Network of Buddhist Organisations

South Dorset Buddhist Group
3 New Close Gardens, Rodwell, Weymouth, Dorset, DT4 8RG (h)
Tel: 01305-786821 (h)
Contact: Barbara Cohen Walters (Sati sati)
Position: Leader
Activities: Worship/meditation, youth, inter-faith
Traditions: Theravada
Movements: Thai Forest Tradition
Other Languages: Pali
Affiliations: The Devon Vihara, nr Honiton, Devon; Amaravati Buddhist Monastery, Hemel Hempstead

Salisbury Mahayana Buddhist Centre
Salisbury, Wiltshire, c/o Ambitabha Centre (Taunton, Somerset)
Tel: 01984-633200 **Tel:** 01984-633935
Fax: 01984-633807
EMail: amitabha@rmplc.co.uk

Salisbury Serene Reflection Meditation Group
19 Kelsay Road, Salisbury, Wiltshire
Tel: 01722-29854
Contact: Derek Evens
Traditions: Zen
Movements: Soto Zen

Saltash Buddhist Group
7 Tavy Road, Saltash, Cornwall, PL12 6DE (h)
Tel: 01752-846096 (h)
Contact: Dharmachari Jayaratna
Activities: Worship/meditation
Traditions: Western
Movements: Friends of the Western Buddhist Order
Affiliations: Bristol Buddhist Centre; Friends of the Western Buddhist Order

Western Ch'an Fellowship
Winterhead Hill Farm, Shipham, Somerset, BS25 1RS (h)

Tel: 0161-761-1945
Contact: Simon Child
Position: Secretary
Activities: Resource, umbrella, newsletters, inter-faith
Traditions: Zen
Movements: Ch'an
Other Languages: French, German, Greek
Affiliations: Bristol Ch'an Group; Western Ch'an Fellowship; Chung Hwa Institute of Buddhist Culture, New York and Taiwan

Saraswati Buddhist Group
The Market House, St James Street, South Petherton, Somerset, TA13 5BN (h)
Tel: 01460-241339 (h)
EMail: tatewist@macline.co.uk
Contact: Shan Tate & Andy Wistreich
Traditions: Tibetan
Movements: Gelugpa
Affiliations: Network of Buddhist Organisations

Western Ch'an Fellowship
Rowleys, 19 Well Hill, Minchinhampton, Stroud, Gloucestershire, GL6 9JE
Tel: 01453-731757

Swindon Buddhist Fellowship
Emoh Ruo, 1 Wharf Road, Wroughton, Swindon, Wiltshire, SN4 9LE (h)
Tel: 01793-812409 (h)
Contact: Irwin Brohier
Position: Lay Guide
Activities: Resource, inter-faith
Traditions: Theravada
Movements: Maha Bodhi, Vipassana

Swindon Buddhist Meditation Group
16 Rosebery Street, Swindon, Wiltshire, SN1 2EU (h)
Tel: 01793-487402 (h)
Contact: John Senior
Activities: Worship/meditation
Traditions: Multi-Traditional
Movements: Ch'an, Kagyupa
Affiliations: Western Ch'an Fellowship

Swindon Mahayana Buddhist Centre
Swindon, Wiltshire, c/o Ambitabha Centre (Taunton, Somerset)
Tel: 01984-633200 **Tel:** 01984-633935 (h)
Fax: 01984-633807
EMail: amitabha@rmplc.co.uk

Amitabha Buddhist Centre
St Audries House, West Quantoxhead, Taunton,
Somerset, TA4 4DU
Tel: 01984-633200 **Tel:** 01984-633935 (h)
Fax: 01984-633807
EMail: amitabha@rmplc.co.uk
Contact: Adam Waterhouse
Position: Press Person
Tradition: New Kadampa
Affiliations: New Kadampa Tradition

Shingon Mushindokai
78 Killams Crescent, Killams Park, Taunton,
Somerset, TA1 3YB

Taunton Buddhist Group
96 Eastgate Gardens, Tancred Street, Taunton,
Somerset, TA1 3RD
Tel: 01823-321059
Contact: Martin Sinclair

Barn, The
The Barn, Lower Sharpham, Barton, Ashprington,
Totnes, Devon, TQ9 7DX (h)
Tel: 01803-732661 (h)
Contact: The Managers
Position: Manager
Activities: Resource
Traditions: Multi-Traditional
Movements: Vipassana
Affiliations: Sharpham Trust

Sharpham College For Buddhist Studies And Contemporary Enquiry
Sharpham College, Sharpham House, Ashprington,
Totnes, Devon, TQ9 7UT
Tel: 01803-732521 **Fax:** 01803-732037
EMail: 101364.537@compuserve.com
Contact: Martine Batchelor
Position: Coordinator
Activities: Resource
Traditions: Multi-Traditional
Movements: Non-denominational

Truro Buddhist Group
Resugga Farm, St Erme, Truro, Cornwall, TR4 9BL (h)
Tel: 01872-79519 (h)
Contact: Jane Browne
Position: Leader
Activities: Inter-faith
Traditions: Theravada

Movements: Thai Forest Tradition
Affiliations: The Wellbeing Centre Buddhist Group; The Devon Vihara; Network of Buddhist Organisations

NORTHERN IRELAND

City, Town or Local Bodies

Tashi Khyil Tibetan Buddhist Centre
54 Derryboye Road, Crossgar, County Down,
BT30 9LJ (h)
Tel: 01238-541581 (h) **Fax:** 01238-542486
EMail: hmd@hugh.demon.co.uk
Contact: Lynn McDaid
Position: Treasurer
Traditions: Tibetan
Movements: Gelugpa
Affiliations: Jampa Ling Tibetan Buddhist Centre, Republic of Ireland; Network of Buddhist Organisations

Potala Buddhist Centre
c/o 3 Iona Terrace, Derry, County Londonderry,
BT47 1EY
Tel: 01232-42232
Contact: Kelsang Drolkar
Movements: New Kadampa

Tilopa Buddhist Centre
3 Iona Terrace, Waterside, Derry, County
Londonderry, BT47 1EY (h)
Tel: 01504-42232 (h)
Contact: Kelsang Drolkar
Position: Resident Teacher
Activities: Worship/meditation, visits
Traditions: New Kadampa
Movements: New Kadampa

Asanga Institute Centre
23 Woodcroft Park, Holywood, County Down,
BT18 OPS (h)
Tel: 01232-427720 (h)
Contact: Paddy Boyle
Position: Chair
Activities: Worship/meditation, visits, inter-faith
Traditions: Theravada
Movements: Vipassana
Affiliations: Amaravati Buddhist Centre, Hemel Hempstead

SCOTLAND

SCOTTISH NATIONAL BODIES

Vajrasattva Buddhist Centre
c/o 58 Cardoness Street, Dumfries, Dumfries and
Galloway, DG1 3AJ
Tel: 01387-254852   **Fax:** 01387-254852
Contact: Mrs Jill McKean
Position: Educational Co-ordinator
Activities: Worship/meditation, resource,
Traditions: Tibetan, Western
Movements: New Kadampa
Affiliations: New Kadampa Tradition

Western Ch'an Fellowship (Scotland)
Kingarth, 16 Kirkland Street, Peebles, Borders,
EH45 8EU (h)
Tel: 01721-721146 (h)
Contact: Frank Tait
Position: Meditation Teacher
Activities: Worship/meditation, resource,
newsletter
Movements: Ch'an

City, Town or Local Bodies

Aberdeen Mahayana Buddhist Centre
Aberdeen, Grampian, c/o Madhyamika Buddhist
Centre (Pocklington, North Yorkshire)
Tel: 01759-304832   **Fax:** 01759-305962

Aberdeen Serene Reflection Meditation Group
33 Bredero Drive, Banchory, Aberdeen, Grampian,
AR3
Tel: 01330-824339 (h)
Contact: Bob McGraw
Position: External Contact
Traditions: Zen
Movements: Soto Zen
Affiliations: Throssel Hole Buddhist Priory

Ayr Mahayana Buddhist Centre
Ayr, Strathclyde, c/o Varjrasattva Centre (Dumfries)
Tel: 01387-254852   **Fax:** 01387-254852

Tharpland Retreat Centre
Glenkiln, Parkgate, Dumfries, Dumfries and
Galloway, DG1 3LY

Vajrasattva Buddhist Centre
c/o 58 Cardoness Street, Dumfries, Dumfries and
Galloway, DG1 3AJ

Tel: 01387-254852   **Fax:** 01387-254852
Contact: Mrs Jill McKean
Position: Educational Co-ordinator
Activities: Worship/meditation, resource,
Traditions: Tibetan, Western
Movements: New Kadampa
Affiliations: New Kadampa Tradition

Dundee Mahayana Buddhist Centre
Dundee, Tayside, c/o Madhyamika Buddhist Centre
(Pocklington, North Yorkshire)
Tel: 01759-304832   **Fax:** 01759-305962

Buddhist Organisations in Edinburgh
12 Saxe Coburg Street, Edinburgh, Lothian,
EH3 5BN
Tel: 0131-337-6349 (h)
Contact: Ms Jody Higgs
Traditions: Multi-Traditional

**Edinburgh Buddhist Centre Friends of the Western
Buddhist Order, Edinburgh**
55a Grange Road, Edinburgh, Lothian, EH9 1TX
Tel: 0131-662-4945
EMail: 101722.106 compuserve
Contact: Dharmachari Tejamitra
Position: Chairman
Activities: Worship/meditation, visits, women,
inter-faith
Traditions: Western
Movements: Ambedkarite; Friends of the Western
Buddhist Order
Affiliations: Edinburgh Buddhist Groups; Friends
of the Western Buddhist Order

Edinburgh Dharma Study Group
34 Corstorphine Road, Edinburgh, Lothian,
EH12 6HP (h)
Tel: 0131-337-6349 (h)
Contact: Rod Burstall
Position: Secretary
Traditions: Tibetan
Movements: Kagyupa

Edinburgh Mahanaya Buddhist Centre
Edinburgh, Lothian, c/o Madhyamika Buddhist
Centre (Pocklington, North Yorkshire)
Tel: 01759-304832   **Fax:** 01759-305962

Edinburgh Serene Reflection Meditation Group
c/o The Salisbury Centre, 2 Salisbury Road,
Edinburgh, Lothian, EH16 5AB
Tel: 0131-667-5438   **Tel:** 0131-662-1865 (h)

Contact: Rawdon Goodier
Position: Lay Minister
Activities: Worship/meditation
Traditions: Zen
Movements: Soto Zen
Affiliations: Throssel Hole Priory; Order of
Buddhist Contemplatives

Edinburgh Theravada Buddhist Group

Salisbury Centre, 2 Salisbury Road, Edinburgh,
Lothian, EH16 5AB
Tel: 0131-667-5438 **Tel:** 0131-332-7987 (h)
Contact: Jody Higgs
Activities: religious, visits, inter-faith
Traditions: Theravada
Affiliations: Buddhist Organisations in Edinburgh;
Ratanagiri Harnham Buddhist Monastery

Samye Dzong Edinburgh

250 Ferry Road, Trinity, Edinburgh, Lothian,
EH5 3AN
Tel: 0131-552-1431 **Fax:** 0131-552-1431
Contact: Mr Ian Tullis
Position: Chairman
Activities: Worship/meditation, resource, visitors,
newsletters, inter-faith
Traditions: Tibetan
Movements: Kagyupa
Affiliations: Edinburgh Buddhist Groups; Samye
Ling Tibetan Centre

Wellspring Buddhists

13 Smith's Place, Edinburgh, Lothian, EH6

Samye Ling Tibetan Centre (Rokpa Trust)

Samye Ling Tibetan Centre, Eskdalemuir,
Langholm, Dumfries and Galloway, DG13 0GL
Tel: 013873-73232 **Fax:** 013873-73222
EMail: 100645.700@compuserve.com
Contact: Nicholas Jennings
Position: Committee Member
Activities: Worship/meditation, umbrella, visits,
newsletters, books, inter-faith
Traditions: Tibetan
Movements: Kagyupa
Other Languages: Tibetan
Affiliations: ROKPA International

Glasgow Buddhist Centre

329 Sauchihall Street, Glasgow, Strathclyde,
G2 3HW
Tel: 0141-333-0524 **Fax:** 0141-333-0524

Contact: Shakyasinha
Position: Centre Administrator
Activities: Worship/meditation, visits, women
Traditions: Western
Movements: Friends of the Western Buddhist
Order
Affiliations: Friends of the Western Buddhist
Order (Central); Madhyamaloka, Birmingham

Glasgow Mahayana Buddhist Centre

Glasgow, Strathclyde c/o Manjushri Buddhist
Centre (Ulverston, Cumbria)
Tel: 01229-584029 (h) **Fax:** 01229-580080
EMail: manjushri@tep.co.uk

Glasgow Theravada Buddhist Group

c/o 3 Corrie Grove, Muirend, Glasgow, Strathclyde,
G44 (h)
Tel: 0141-637-9731 (h)
Contact: James Scott
Position: Secretary
Traditions: Theravada
Movements: Vipassana
Other Languages: Senghalese
Affiliations: Edinburgh Theravada Buddhist
Group; "Ratanagiri" Harnham Buddhist Monastery,
Belsay, Northumberland; Amaravati Buddhist
Monastery, Great Gaddesden, Hemel Hempstead

Glasgow Zen Group (IZAUK)

4 Vinicombe Street, Glasgow, Strathclyde,
G12 8BG (h)
Tel: 0141-339-3888 (h)
Contact: John Fraser
Position: Secretary
Traditions: Zen
Movements: Soto Zen
Affiliations: International Zen Association

Samye Dzong

23 Bruce Road, Pollockshields, Glasgow,
Strathclyde, G41 5EE
Tel: 429-1875 (h)
Contact: Karma Samten
Position: Secretary
Activities: Worship/meditation, visits
Traditions: Tibetan
Movements: Kagyupa
Affiliations: Kagyu Samye Ling Tibetan Centre

Dhanakosa Buddhist Retreat Centre

Dhanakosa Buddhist Retreat Centre, Ledcreich,
Balquhidder, Lochearnhead, Central, FK19 8PQ

Tel: 01877-384213 (h) **Fax:** 01877-384213
EMail: 100731.2301@compuserve.com
Contact: Dharmachari Bodhipaksa
Position: Manager
Activities: Worship/meditation, women
Traditions: Western
Movements: Friends of the Western Buddhist
Order

Motherwell Mahayana Buddhist Centre
43 Douglas Street, Motherwell, Strathclyde,
ML1 3JQ (h)
Tel: 01698-263263 (h) **Fax:** 01698-261323
EMail: NKT@metanode.demon.co.uk
Contact: Irene Burns
Position: Co-ordinator
Activities: Worship/meditation, resource, media,
visits, newsletters, books
Traditions: Tibetan
Movements: New Kadampa
Affiliations: Mahakaruna Centre Edinburgh; New
Kadampa Tradition

Western Ch'an Fellowship (Scotland)
Kingarth, 16 Kirkland Street, Peebles, Borders,
EH45 8EU (h)
Tel: 01721-721146 (h)
Contact: Frank Tait
Position: Meditation Teacher
Activities: Worship/meditation, resource,
newsletter
Movements: Ch'an

Stirling Mahayana Buddhist Centre
Stirling, Grampian, c/o Manjushri Buddhist Centre
(Ulverston, Cumbria)
Tel: 01229-584029   **Fax:** 01229-580080

WALES

Regional or County Bodies

Dharmavajra Buddhist Centre
13 St James's Gardens, Uplands, Swansea, West
Glamorgan, SA1 6DX
Tel: 01792-458245 (h)
Contact: Graham Peter Rutt
Position: Admininistrative Director
Activities: Worship/meditation, visits
Traditions: Tibetan, Western
Movements: New Kadampa

Other Languages: Welsh
Affiliations: New Kadampa Tradition

City, Town or Local Bodies

Aberystwyth Buddhist Group
Plâs Plwca, Cwmrheidol, Aberystwyth, Dyfed,
SY23 3NB (h)
Tel: 01970-880603 (h)
Contact: Kenneth Henry Jones
Position: Chair
Traditions: Multi-Traditional
Affiliations: Ch'an Fellowship, Kanzeon Sangha,
International Network of Engaged Buddhists

Bangor Buddhist Fellowship
62 Carneddi Road, Bethesda, Bangor, Gwynedd (h)
Tel: 01248-601109 (h)
Traditions: Multi-Traditional

Bangor Mahayana Buddhist Centre
Bangor, Gwyndd, c/o Kalpa Bhadra Buddhist Centre
Tel: 01492 540414
Contact: Nigel David Spaull
Position: Administrative Director
Traditions: Tibetan
Movements: New Kadampa
Other Languages: Welsh

Cardiff Buddhist Centre
P 0 Box 679, Cardiff, South Glamorgan, CF2 2XN
Tel: 01446-745541
Contact: Dharmacharis Surana and Pramudita
Position: Teachers
Activities: Worship/meditation, women
Traditions: Western
Movements: FWBO

Cardiff Buddhist Community
97a Albany Road, Cardiff, South Glamorgan,
CF2 3LP

Cardiff Serene Reflection Meditation Group
114 Parc-y-Fro, Creigiau, Cardiff, South
Glamorgan, CF4 8SB (h)
Tel: 01222-890034 (h)
Contact: George Norwell
Position: Lay Minister
Activities: Worship/meditation, resource, visits
Movements: Soto Zen
Affiliations: Throssel Hole Priory Buddhist
Monastery; Order of Buddhist Contemplatives,
Shasta Abbey, California, USA

Dorje Dzong
100 Mardy Street, Cardiff, South Glamorgan,
CF1 7QU
Tel: 01222-374196 (h)
Contact: Leighton Cooke
Position: Director
Traditions: Tibetan

Friends of the Western Buddhist Order
P0 Box 679, Cardiff, Soth Glamorgan, CP2 2XN
Tel: 01446-745541
Contact: Surana

Lam Rim Buddhist Group
Milarepa House, 51 Ferry Road, Grangetown,
Cardiff, South Glamorgan, CF1 7DW
Tel: 01222-373927 (h)
Contact: Judith Harte
Traditions: Tibetan

Western Ch'an Fellowship
19 Velindere Road, Cardiff, South Glamorgan,
CF4 7JE
Tel: 01222-691146
EMail: streetec@cardiff.ac.uk

Carmarthen Mahayana Buddhist Centre
Carmarthen, Dyfed, c/o Dharmavajra Centre
(Swansea, West Glamorgan)
Tel: 01792-458245 (h)

Kalpa Bhadra Buddhist Centre
89 Llanerch Road West, Colwyn Bay, Clwyd,
LL28 4AS
Tel: 01492 540414
Contact: Nigel David Spaull
Position: Administrative Director
Activities: Resource, visits
Traditions: Tibetan
Movements: New Kadampa
Other Languages: Welsh
Affiliations: Kadampa Buddhism

Vajrakuta Dharma Study Centre
Blaenddol House, Corwen, Clwyd, LL21 0EN
Tel: 01490-460648
Contact: Samamati

Gwent Zazen Group
6 Ruskin Close, Silver Birches, Fairwater,
Cwmbran, Gwent, NP44 4QX
Tel: 01633-874882 (h)

Contact: Mr Kevin Davies
Traditions: Zen

Buddhist Meditation Class
The Green Oak, Llanfyllin, Powys

Llangollen Buddhist Group
Llangollen, Clwyd, c/o Vajraloka Buddhist
Meditation Centre (nr Corwen)
Tel: 01490-460406
Contact: Secretary
Traditions: Western
Movements: Friends of the Western Buddhist
Order

Carmarthenshire Womens Meditation Group
Penrhiw, Cwrt-Y-Cadno, Pumsaint, Llanwrda,
Dyfed, SA19 8YB (h)
Tel: 01558-650690 **Fax:** 01558-650690
Contact: Sumana
Position: Teacher/Organiser
Traditions: Theravada
Movements: Maha Bodhi
Affiliations: The London Buddhist Vihara

Kagyu Tegchen Choling
Woodland Cottage, Leeswood Hall Estate, Mold,
Clwyd, CH7 4LB (h)
Tel: 01352-750671
Contact: Lyn Williams
Position: Secretary
Activities: Newsletters, books
Traditions: Tibetan
Movements: Kagyupa
Affiliations: Network of Buddhist Organisations

Newport Mahayana Buddhist Centre
Newport, Gwent, c/o Ambitabha Centre (Taunton,
Somerset)
Tel: 01225-633200 **Tel:** 01984-633935 (h)
Fax: 01984-633807
EMail: amitabha@rmplc.co.uk

Je Tsongkhapa Centre
c/o 75 Lancaster Drive, Llantwit Fadre, Pontypridd,
Mid Glamorgan, CF38 2NS (h)
Tel: 01443-204616 (h)
Contact: Alison Smith
Position: Administrative Director
Activities: Resource, visits, newsletters
Traditions: Tibetan
Movements: Gelugpa, New Kadampa
Affiliations: New Kadampa Tradition

Dharmavajra Buddhist Centre

13 St James's Gardens, Uplands, Swansea, West
Glamorgan, SA1 6DX
Tel: 01792-458245 (h)
Contact: Graham Peter Rutt
Position: Admininistrative Director
Activities: Worship/meditation, visits
Traditions: Tibetan, Western
Movements: New Kadampa
Other Languages: Welsh
Affiliations: New Kadampa Tradition

Kandro Gar Buddhist Society

13 Oakland Road, Mumbles, Swansea, West
Glamorgan, SA3 4AQ
Contact: Tony Court
Traditions: Tibetan
Movements: Nyingmapa

Tiratanaloka Women's Retreat Centre

Aberclydach House, Tallybont-on-Usk, Powys,
LP3 7YS

Llangollen Friends of the Western Buddhist Order

45 Heol Maelor, Coedpoeth, Wrexham, Clwyd,
LL11 3LY

KEY TO TERMS USED IN BUDDHIST ORGANISATION TITLES

Note: This is not a complete glossary of significant Buddhist terms. It is a guide to the meaning and/or background of some of the words used in the titles of Buddhist organisations listed in this directory. More information on the italicised words can be tracked down elsewhere in the key and/or in the section on "Introducing the Buddhist Community" by using the directory's "Significant Word Index".

Akshobya: Sanskrit, literally meaning "immovable". As a monk Akshobyhya is said to have taken a vow never to harbour anger towards a living being. He succeeded in this and became a *Buddha* thus symbolising the defeat of passions. Iconographically he is often seen riding a blue elephant.

Amaravati: The name of a South Indian city which was an important centre for Buddhist art and learning in the third century CE and had a *stupa* containing some relics of the *Buddha*. Its Pali meaning is "the deathless realm".

Ambedkar: Bhimrao Raniji Ambedkar (1891-1956) was a jurist who converted from Hinduism to Buddhism in 1956 together with five hundred thousand of the so-called "untouchables", members of the "scheduled *castes*" of Indian society who felt discriminated against by virtue of their *caste* position. He founded the Buddhist Society of India and his movement emphasised the social implications of Buddhism, rejecting *caste* and other similar distinctions.

Ambedkarite: That which pertains to the movement founded by Dr Ambedkar.

Amida: Amida is the Japanese version of the name of the *Buddha* of Infinite Light who symbolises mercy and wisdom. Also found as Amidha.

Amitabha: Sanskrit name of Amidha, the *Buddha* of Infinite Light (see above).

Amitayus: Sanskrit word, meaning "infinite life". Amitayus is the name in the *Mahayana* tradition for a manifestation of the *Buddha* who is depicted as holding a container in which is the nectar of immortality.

Amoghasiddhi: Means *Buddha* of "purified compositional factors".

Amrita: Sanskrit for "immortal", relating to water of life.

Angulimala: The name of a murderer who became a disciple of the *Buddha* and eventually an *Arahant*.

Asanga: The name of the founder of the *Yogachara* (or *Yogacara*) (school) which began in the fourth century CE. *Yogachara* is Sanskrit and literally means "application of *yoga*". According to this school, everything that exists is "mind only".

Asvagosha: The name of a first or second century CE Buddhist poet who was the author of a poetic life of the *Buddha*.

Atisha: A Buddhist scholar (980/90-1055CE) who founded the *Kadampa* school of *Tibetan Buddhism*.

Aukana: The name of a place in Sri Lanka, where there is a colossal and ancient *Buddha* image.

Baba: Hindi term meaning "father" or "daddy" (in the familiar form) and used in modern Indian languages as a title of respect. For example, Dr. Ambedkar, the founder of the *Ambedkarite* movement is known as *Baba Saheb*.

Bodhi: Sanskrit and Pali for "awakening", a synonym for *Enlightenment*.

Bodhisattva: A being on the way to full *Buddhahood*, one in whom the *bodhicitta* (the will to *Enlightenment* for the sake of all beings) has arisen.

Buddhapadipa: Pali for "*Buddha's* lamp".

Buddhavihara: From *Buddha*, meaning "awakened one", and *vihara* (see below) which is Sanskrit/Pali for "resting place". It is used of the residence of monks. The first *viharas* were simply houses placed at the disposal of the *Buddha* for his growing *sangha* (see below).

Ch'an: A shortened form of *Ch'an-na*, which is a Chinese school of *Mahayana* Buddhism that developed in the sixth and seventh centuries CE and stresses the possibility of sudden and direct enlightenment (see also entry for *Zen* below).

Changchub: Tibetan for *Bodhi* (see above).

Chekhawa: The name of an early *Tibetan Buddhist* teacher of the *Kadampa* school.

Chenrezig: Tibetan literally meaning "looking with clear eyes". It is a Tibetan word for Avalokiteshvara, the *Bodhisattva* of Compassion who is viewed as the founder of the Tibetan people. The Tibetan leader, the *Dalai Lama*, is viewed as an incarnation of Chenrezig.

Chogyal: Tibetan, literally meaning "*dharma*-King".

Choling: Variant Romanisation of *chooling* (see above).

Chooling: Tibetan, literally meaning "*dharma*-place".

Cittaviveka: Pali and Sanskrit for "mental discrimination". It also carries the sense of "silent mind", an attitude of great equanimity.

Dechen: Tibetan meaning "great bliss". The name of a Buddhist community.

Dhamma: Pali version of the Sanskrit *dharma* (see below), meaning "cosmic law", "righteousness", "ethics". It also is used for "truth" or the "teaching" of the *Buddha*.

Dhammapala: Pali literally meaning "guardian of the teaching". In *Mahayana* Buddhism, the *dharmapalas* (Sanskrit) protect one from dangers and bad influences for one's spiritual development. Dharmapala is also the name of a Sinhalese Buddhist (1865-1933) who founded the Mahabodhi Society in 1891, the objective of which was the restoration of the Mahabodhi monastery in Bodh-gaya. In 1925, he founded the Maha Bodhi Society of Great Britain.

Dhanakosa: Sanskrit, meaning "treasury of wealth" or "treasure chest".

Dharma: Sanskrit form of Pali *dhamma* (see above).

Dharmachakra: The wheel of the *dharma*, which was said to have been set turning by the *Buddha's* first sermon.

Dharmavajra: Sanskrit, meaning "diamond of the *dharma*" or "thunderbolt of the *dharma*".

Dorje: Tibetan for "diamond" or "thunderbolt", literally meaning "lord of stones". In *Tibetan Buddhism* diamonds are symbolic of clarity of insight on the path to *Enlightenment*. It is the equivalent to the Sanskrit *Vajra*.

Dragpa: Tibetan meaning "wrathful".

Dromtonpa: An important *Kadampa* teacher in the *Tibetan Buddhist* tradition and principal pupil of Atisha.

Duldzin: Tibetan, meaning "holder of morality".

Dzogchen: Tibetan for "great perfection". This is the description of the central teaching which the *Nyingmapa* school of *Tibetan Buddhism* consider to be the most definitive and secret teaching of the *Buddha*. In this, purity of mind is understood to always be present and only to need realising.

Dzong: Tibetan meaning "bastion".

Fa Yue: Meaning "*dhamma* rain".

Gaden: Tibetan name for the *Pure Land* (see *tushita* below) of *Buddha* Maitreya.

Gar: Tibetan for "tent".

Gyaltsabje: Tibetan meaning "Lord Regent". Name of one of the two principal disciples of Tsongkhapa in the 14-15th centuries CE (see also *khedrubje* below).

Heruka: A wrathful *Buddha* form in *Tibetan Buddhism.*

Jampa: Tibetan title for Manjushri and Maitreya.

Jamyang: Jamyang is a Tibetan variant form of the name of Manjushri (see below).

Je: Tibetan, meaning "foremost". It is used as a very respectful title for eminent *lamas.*

Jodo: From *Jodo-shin-shu* which is Japanese, literally meaning "The School of the *Pure Land*". The school was of Indian origin and was prevalent in China, but in this form it is extant as a school of *Japanese Buddhism* founded by Shinran. It is a lay school which emphasises the help of *tariki*, meaning "other power", in attaining the goal of the *Pure Land*. This is believed to be achieved through trusting in Amidha *Buddha* for help.

Kadampa: Tibetan, literally meaning "oral instruction". The original *Kadampa* School was founded by Atisha. It is now used in the name of the *New Kadampa* tradition.

Kagyu: Tibetan meaning "transmission of expertise", it is the name of one of the four principal schools of *Tibetan Buddhism*. It places an emphasis on the direct transmission of teaching from teacher to disciple. *Karma Kagyu* is a grouping within the wider school.

Kalpa: Is an age or aeon of time in Buddhist thought.

Kandro: Tibetan literally meaning "those who fly through space". It refers to female spiritual beings (in Sanskrit called *dakhini*) some of which are quite worldly and others of which are enlightened.

Kanzeen: The Abbot of the *Kanzeen Sangha* is the person under whose instruction this group practises *Zen* Buddhism.

Kanzeon: The Japanese for Avalokiteshvara, the *Bodhisattva* of Compassion within *Mahayana* Buddhism.

Karma: Sanskrit for "deed", but encompassing a wide range of meanings including mental, verbal and physical actions, their consequences, the totality of the actions and consequences connected with an individual, and also cause and effect in terms of morality.

Karme: Tibetan for *karma* (see above).

Karuna: Sanskrit and Pali for "compassionate action".

Kashyapa: The name of one of the *Buddha's* leading disciples.

Kempo: The title for Tibetan Masters of Philosophy usually entailing nine years of intensive study.

Khandro: Variant Romanisation of *kandro* (see above).

Khedrubje: One of the two main disciples of Tsongkhapa in the 14th-15th century CE (see also Gyaltsabje above).

Khyil: Tibetan meaning "centre". It combines with *khor* to make a *khyil khor*, otherwise known as a *mandala.*

Kongoryuji: Kongoruji is the "Thunderbolt Dragon".

Lam: Tibetan meaning "path".

Ling: Tibetan meaning "place".

Liu: Chinese meaning "six" and also a name.

Longchen: Tibetan for "vast openness".

Losang: Losang Dragpa was the personal name of Tsongkhapa and it means "good mind".

Lotus: The lotus flower is the water lily which is a symbol of the Buddhist understanding of the nature of living beings.

Madhyamika: In the context of Buddhist organisational names, the middle way relates to the Buddhist school known as the *Madhyamika* which comes from the Sanskrit *madhyama* meaning "the middle", and which was founded by the teachers Nagarjuna and Aryadeva.

Madhyamaka: Means, in Sanskrit, "the teaching of the *Middle Way*" as put forward by the *Madhyamikas* in relation to their position in the Buddhist debate on the existence or non-existence of things, rather than the broader usage of the term "*Middle Way*" as describing Buddhism itself. In this debate the "middle way" focuses instead on *shunyata* (emptiness) and hence is also known by the alternative name of the *Shunyatavada* (meaning, "Teaching of *Emptiness*").

Maha: Sanskrit meaning "great".

Mahasi: Burmese, meaning "great teacher".

Mahasiddha: Tibetan for "great master of perfect capabilities", which refers to those who have achieved paranormal powers through their mastery of the *Tantras*.

Mahayana: Sanskrit literally meaning "great vehicle" and describing the form of Buddhism which developed stressing the ideal of the *Bodhisattva*.

Maitreya: Sanskrit meaning "loving one". He is viewed as the embodiment of universal compassion, who is expected to come as the next and last in line of earthly *Buddhas*.

Maitrikara: Meaning "love", or "compassion-maker".

Manjushri: Sanskrit for "he who is noble and gentle". In all *Mahayana* Buddhist schools it is the name of the *Bodhisattva* of Wisdom. In *Tibetan Buddhism*, and especially with the *Gelugpa* school, Manjushri is a particularly important figure. Great scholars are believed to be his *tulku* (incarnations). In wrathful aspect, Manjushri is depicted in *Tibetan Buddhism* as Yamantaka (meaning "Subduer of the Lord of Death") and appears as a fearsome looking bull-headed deity.

Marpa: The name of the "man from Mar" (1012-1097 CE), a *yogi* from Southern Tibet and the *Master* of Milarepa who is the principal founder in the *Kagyupa* school's transmission. Marpa represents the ideal of the married householder who committed himself to the *dharma*. He was the translator into Tibetan of many Sanskrit texts.

Mushindokai: Mushin is Japanese for "empty heart" and is a *Zen* Buddhist expression for freedom from any notions and opinions.

Naro: Tibetan for Naropa, the name of a Buddhist teacher.

Nezang: Tibetan, meaning "good place".

Nichiren: Japanese from *Nichiren-shu* meaning "the School of the Lotus of the Sun", named after its founder Nichiren (1222-1282 CE). Based upon the *Lotus Sutra*, the title of which is believed to summarise Buddhism and is recited in the formula *namu myoho renge-kyo*, meaning "veneration to the sutra of the lotus of the good law". It is believed that through recitation of this formula, *Buddhahood* can be attained. The school and organisations based within

it have an emphasis on the earthly *Buddha* realm and Buddhist sociopolitical action. *Nichiren sho-shu* ("True School of Nichiren") venerates Nichiren as a *Buddha*. The Soka Gakkai, Rissho Koseikai and Nipponzan Myohoji (see below) organisations are based on the idea of this *Nichiren* school.

Nipponzan Myohoji: The name of a Japanese Buddhist revival movement which takes its name from its main Temple. It is also known as the Movement of the Wondrous Law of the *Lotus Sutra*. It was founded in 1917 by Fuji Nichidatsu and sought to base itself on the teachings of Nichiren. Nichidatsu became a radical pacifist and the movement advocates world peace and builds peace *pagodas* throughout the world and its servants beat drums for peace.

Nitartha: Sanskrit meaning "of which the meaning is expounded". Refers to teaching which is to be taken literally, as distinct from teaching expressed obliquely or metaphorically.

Opagme: Tibetan for Amitabha (see above).

Osel: Tibetan, meaning "clear light".

Padma: Sanskrit for "lotus".

Padmaloka: From the Sanskrit *padma* (see above), meaning "lotus" and the Sanskrit *loka*, meaning "universe". The lotus is a water lily and in Buddhism it is a symbol of the true nature of things unstained by the mud of *samsara* and ignorance. In Buddhist art, the lotus appears as a throne for the *Buddha* and in the *Pure Land* school of *Mahayana Buddhism* it is the major symbol for Buddhist doctrine.

Pah: Thai, meaning "forest".

Pakshi: The name of the second *Karmapa*, who is the spiritual authority in the *Karma Kagyu* school.

Pali: The language in which the *Theravada* scriptures and commentaries are written and which is considered to be the language closest to that spoken by the *Buddha* himself.

Phen: Tibetan for "benefit".

Potola: The Potola is the name of the Palace of the *Dalai Lama* in Lhasa, Tibet, where Chenrezig is said to rest.

Prasangika: One of the two main sub-schools of the *Madhyamika* philosophy, the word is Sanskrit, meaning "using logical entailment".

Pure Land: The *Pure Lands* are seen in *Mahayana* Buddhism as transcendent paradises ruled over by *Buddhas*. In folk belief they are geographical locations, but fundamentally they stand for states of mind on the way to *Nirvana*.

Ratanagiri: Pali for "Jewel Mountain", the name of a Buddhist site in India.

Ratnasambhava: Sanskrit literally meaning "Jewel-Born One". He is one of the transcendent *Buddhas* and is usually seen iconographically as riding a lion or horse or making the gesture of granting a wish.

Reiuykai: An organisation founded in Japan in 1924 by Kakutaro Kubo (1892-1944).

Rigpa: Tibetan meaning" enlightened intelligence".

Rim: Meaning "sequence" and relating to a "staged" or "graduated" form of spiritual discipline.

Rissho Kosei Kai: Japanese meaning "Society for the Establishment of Justice and Community for the Rise (of the *Buddha*)". It is a movement which seeks to base itself upon the teachings of Nichiren. It was founded in 1938 by Niwano Nikkyo and Naganuma Myoko. It emphasises the salvific power of the *Lotus Sutra* and the socio–political dimensions of Buddhism.

Rokpa: Tibetan, meaning "help".

Saddhatissa: The name of a Sinhalese Buddhist monk of the Maha Bodhi Society and author of many books on Buddhism.

Sakya: The equivalent of Shakya, the Sanskrit name of the noble clan from which Siddhartha Gotama, the historical *Buddha*, came. At that time, the clan ruled one of India's sixteen states which covered part of present-day Nepal.

Sakyadhita: Pali, meaning "daughter of the Sakya", in other words, "daughter of the *Buddha*". Traditionally it is a term which is used of nuns.

Samantabhadra: Name of a *Bodhisattva* in *Mahayana* Buddhism, meaning "all-good" or "auspicious all-round".

Samatha: Sanskrit for "living in tranquillity", a meditation tradition found in all Buddhist schools. In the *Gelugpa* school of *Tibetan Buddhism, samatha* meditation is seen as a precondition for *vipashyana* (insight).

Samye: Tibetan meaning "beyond concept". It was the name of the first major Buddhist monastery of Tibet and is now used in the title of the Samye Ling Buddhist Monastery in Scotland.

Sangha: Sanskrit and Pali meaning "group". In Buddhism it refers to the Buddhist community as a whole and to the community of Buddhist *monks, nuns* and *novices*.

Sang-ngak-cho-dzong: Means, literally, "secret *mantra dharma* bastion".

Santidhamma: Means "peace of the *dharma*" (see above).

Santosa: Pali, meaning "satisfaction" or "contentment".

Sarana: Pali and Sanskrit for "refuge". Appears in the *trisarana* (*tri* is Sanskrit, meaning "three") or threefold refuge of Buddhism - to take refuge in the *Buddha*, the *dharma* (see above) and the *sangha* (see above).

Saraswati: The name of the Goddess of Learning and eloquence in both Buddhist and Hindu traditions.

Sayagyi: Burmese, meaning "revered teacher".

Shambala: The name of what is believed to be a hidden, perfect realm in the world where *Tantric* teachings were given and preserved. It is also used as the name of a coming millenial utopia.

Shantideva: A monk of the seventh to eighth centuries associated with the *Madhyamika* school of *Mahayana* Buddhism.

Shedrup: Tibetan for "established in wisdom/knowledge".

Shen: Tibetan, meaning "others".

Shin: The short form of *Shin-shu*, the Japanese Buddhist school founded by Shinran (1173-1262 CE) which focuses on venerating Amidha Buddha with the formula of the *nembutsu*. It believes in the necessity for complete trust in the *tariki* ("other power") of Amidha Buddha which it is believed can even overcome an accumulation of negative *karma*. It is a lay group and has no monks, unlike the *Jodo Shu* school.

Shingon: Japanese for "School of the True Word", founded by Kukai (774-835 CE) which places great importance on the so-called "three secrets" of body, thought and speech.

Shu: Japanese for "school" as in *Jodo Shu*, "the School of the Pure Land" in which reciting the name of Amidha Buddha (the *nembutsu*) is seen as a method of strengthening trust in him. The school was brought to Japan by Enin (793-864 CE). The present Japanese school was founded by Honen (1133-1212 CE) and uses the formula of recitation "*namu amidha butsu*", meaning "veneration to Buddha Amidha". The *Jodo Shu*, unlike the *Jodo-Shinshu*, has a monastic life.

Thrangu: Part of the name of the Venerable Thrangu Rinpoche, a contemporary *Tibetan Buddhist* teacher.

Ti: Pali, meaning "three", as in *tisarana* (see below).

Tisarana: Pali, meaning "*Triple Gem*" of the *Buddha*, *dharma* and *sangha*.

Soka Gakkai: Literally meaning "Society for the Creation of Values", it is a modern Buddhist movement founded by Makiguchi Tsunesabwo in Japan in 1930. It is in the *Nichiren* tradition of Buddhism.

Soto: The name of one of the largest Japanese *Zen* Buddhist schools, brought to Japan from China in the thirteenth century by the Japanese Master Dogen. It has a focus on the practice of *zazen* (see below), meaning "sitting meditation".

Tantric: That which pertains to *Tantra*, a Sanskrit word referring to a type of scriptures. In *Tibetan* Buddhism it is a term which refers to the *Vajrayana* as a major tradition of Buddhism and also to various texts and their associated systems of meditation. There are various *Tantras* according to the spiritual capabilities of the practioners.

Tara: Sanskrit for "saviour". Tara is said to be an emanation from the *Bodhisattva* Avolokiteshvara. She embodies the feminine aspect of compassion, although she is seen in both peaceful and wrathful depictions as well as in various colours, the Green Tara and the White Tara forms being the most frequently seen.

Taraloka: The name of a women's retreat centre, meaning literally "the place of Tara".

Tashi: Chinese for "great master" – the equivalent of *daishi* in Japanese. It is an honorific title.

Thekchen: Tibetan, meaning "*Mahayana*".

Theravada: Pali meaning "teaching of the elders of the order". *Theravada* Buddhism sees itself as the closest to original Buddhism.

Theravadin: That which pertains to the *Theravada* tradition.

Thinley: Tibetan for "enlightened activity".

Thubten: Tibetan, literally meaning "Sage's teaching", in other words, the teaching of the *Buddha*.

Tilopa: The name of an Indian *siddha* (an *Enlightened* figure of power), particularly important in the *Kagyu* School.

Tiratanaloka: Meaning "world/place of the *Three Jewels*", in other words, the *Buddha*, the *dharma* (see above) and the *sangha* (see above).

Tsongkhapa: The name of the sixteenth century founder of the *Gelugpa* tradition of *Tibetan Buddhism*.

Tushita: The place where Maitreya (see above) is presently thought to be residing. In the *Mahayana* tradition of Buddhism, it is commonly thought of as a "*Pure Land*".

Vairochana: Sanskrit literally meaning "he who is like the sun". One of the transcendent *Buddhas* iconographically depicted making the *mudra* of wisdom. In some developments of *Mahayana* Buddhism, he came to be seen as the *Adi-Buddha* or primordial *Buddha*.

Vajra: Sanskrit meaning "diamond" and, in the Hindu tradition also "thunderbolt", the weapon of the Hindu god Indra. In Buddhism it relates to indestructibility and is found as part of the name of the *Vajrayana* tradition of Buddhism (see entry above on *dorje*).

Vajradhatu: From the Tibetan *vajra* (see above), meaning "diamond", and the Sanskrit and Pali *dhatu*, meaning "realm" or "region". It is the name of a famous *mandala* meaning "the Diamond Realm".

Vajrakuta: Meaning "Diamond/Thunderbolt peak".

Vajravarahi: Literally meaning "Thunderbolt/Diamond Sow". In *Tantric* Buddhism, and particularly in Tibet, the name refers to an important female, pig-headed, yidam and consort of Chakrasamvara.

Vajraloka: From the Tibetan *vajra* (see above), meaning "diamond" and the Sanskrit *loka* meaning "universe". It is the name of a Friends of the Western Buddhist Order meditation centre in Wales.

Vajrapani: Sanskrit meaning, "with a thunderbolt in his hand". It refers to the holder of a *vajra*, originally regarded as a deity who guarded the *Buddha* and later as a *Bodhisattva* of wrathful appearance, usually associated with a dynamic activity of protecting, or of removing obstacles.

Vajrasattva: Sanskrit meaning "Diamond Being". He is depicted in white and is associated with purification. The *mantra* associated with him is used in all schools of *Tibetan* Buddhism.

Vihara: Sanskrit/Pali for "resting place". It is used of the residence of monks. The first *viharas* were simply houses placed at the disposal of the *Buddha* for his growing *sangha* (see above).

Vipassana: Pali (Sanskrit is *vipasyana* or *vipashyana*) for "insight" or "clear sight" which is related to the "three signs of being". It is a meditation discipline which, together with *samatha* (calming of the mind), is seen as being necessary for *Enlightenment*.

Wat: The name describing Thai Buddhist temples.

Yoga: Sanskrit for "joining" or "discipline". In a religious context, it refers to a particular religious practice or discipline usually involving bodily postures, breathing and meditation. The *Tantric* practices of *Tibetan Buddhism* are known as *yoga* and its saints, such as Milarepa, are called *yogis*.

Zazen: Japanese *za* means "sitting" and when put together with the word *zen*, meaning "meditation", refers to a basic practice of *Zen*. *Zazen* is free of any object of meditation but consists of a state of alert attention in which *Enlightenment* can be achieved.

Zazenkai: Japanese for "*zazen* meeting", an occasion where followers of *Zen* meet to practise and hear teaching in the tradition.

Zen: A Japanese abbreviation of the word *zenna*, which represents the Japanese way of reading the Chinese *ch'an-na* (or, in its short form, *ch'an*). In turn, the Chinese version relates to the Sanskrit *dhyana*, which refers to the state in which dualism of mind is overcome. In the *Theravada* tradition, this is known by the Pali word *jhana*, meaning the highest form of concentration. *Ch'an* was developed in China in the 6th and 7th centuries CE out of the meeting between *Mahayana* Buddhism and Taoism. It focuses on the possibility of a direct and immediate breakthrough to *Enlightenment*.

INTRODUCING THE CHRISTIAN COMMUNITY

CHRISTIANS IN THE UNITED KINGDOM

Christianity is the largest and longest established of the world religious traditions in the UK. Around 40,000,000 people in the UK regard themselves as Christian, out of the world wide Christian following of approximately 1,955,026,000. In its various forms, Christianity has shaped the past and present life of the British Isles and helped mould legal structures, public institutions, and the social and intellectual tradition.

This strong presence and influence is reflected in the number of places of worship around the country. In England and Wales, for example, at the last count there were 44,699 registered places of Christian worship (figures are not available for the overall UK). Because there are so many Christian places of worship, this directory lists only Christian bodies at regional and national level, from whom more detailed information about local churches and Christian organisations can be obtained.

Beginnings in the United Kingdom

Christianity was introduced into Britain by missionaries from continental Europe during the first centuries of the Common Era. Over the next four hundred years it developed in parts of Wales, Ireland, Scotland and northern England. It did so in a form known as *Celtic* Christianity, which had its own distinctive ethos and was somewhat independent of the organisational structures of Western *Christendom* that had begun to develop around the *Bishop* of Rome (the *Pope)*.

In 597 CE, Augustine, an emissary of *Pope* Gregory the Great of Rome, arrived in Kent. Canterbury became the base for his missionary work. Gregory became *Archbishop* of Canterbury and was given authority by the *Pope* over the *bishops* in the rest of Britain, an authority which they acknowledged at the *Synod* of Whitby in the seventh century CE. The *Catholic* form of Christianity gradually displaced *Celtic* Christianity, although in Wales and Ireland *Celtic* forms of Christianity continued independently for some centuries.

Western Christianity gradually became consolidated under the jurisdiction of the *Pope*, and Christians in the different parts of these islands remained part of what was known as the *Catholic* (meaning universal) tradition until the time of the *Reformation*.

Protestant Reformation

During the sixteenth and seventeenth centuries Western *Christendom* underwent major religious and political upheavals. This period is referred to as the *Reformation*, because of the attempts made by *Protestants* (initially those reformers who protested against certain *Roman Catholic* practices) in a number of European countries to remodel the Christian Church in a way which, they believed, reflected more truly the earliest forms of Christianity to which the *New Testament* scriptures witnessed. Key reformers were Martin Luther and John Calvin.

In England and Wales, various changes took place in the Church which reflected these movements. After King Henry VIII's political break with the *Papacy*, the Church of England was brought into being as the established form of religion in England. The Church of Scotland, embodying a *Calvinist*, *Presbyterian* (see below) form of Church government, became the established religion in Scotland. Those Christians remaining loyal to the *Papacy* were forced underground and systematically persecuted during the seventeenth century and subjected to legal disabilities and penalties until the nineteenth century. In addition to the new Churches of England and Scotland, other forms of *Protestant* Christianity came into being during the sixteenth, seventeenth and eighteenth centuries. They were also subjected to numerous restrictions and penalties until the nineteenth century. These movements are often known as *Nonconformist* because of their refusal to conform to ways of worship and organisation required in the Churches established by law.

Denominational and Ethnic Diversity

Christianity in the UK is ethnically and denominationally very diverse. Groups of Christian immigrants have, over the centuries, brought their own distinctive traditions with them. These groups have included the French *Reformed Huguenots*, Irish and Italian *Roman Catholics* and, more recently, Greek, Russian and other Eastern *Orthodox* (see below) Christians, as well as members of the *Pentecostal, Holiness* and *Spiritual* Churches of mainly African-Caribbean membership. Also included are groups from Africa, Asia and Latin America, and who now form a small but growing and increasingly significant proportion of the practising Christian community, especially in England.

There are also groupings of Chinese Christians from Hong Kong and of Asian Christians with ethnic origins in the Indian sub-continent, Korea and elsewhere. One of the fastest growing sections of Christianity in the UK is the so-called *New Church* or *House Church* Movement which is *Evangelical* in flavour, and is so named because it began predominantly at meetings in the houses of its members.

Numbers and Geography

Although some 40,000,000 people in the UK regard themselves as Christian, the combined active membership of the various Christian Churches stands at around six and a half million. Active and participative membership varies considerably between the four nations of these islands, with this being at its greatest in Northern Ireland and Scotland.

Concepts of membership, and therefore the basis upon which these statistics are calculated, vary significantly from Church to Church. The active strength of different *denominations* also varies between the four nations. In England, the Church of England is the largest single Church, whilst in Scotland the largest single Church is the Church of Scotland (*Presbyterian*), and in Northern Ireland, the *Roman Catholic* Church. In Wales, the *Free Churches* collectively are larger than any other tradition as are the *Protestant* Churches in Northern Ireland.

This pattern is, however, the subject of considerable variation in terms of numerical growth and decline. Thus the *Independent* and *Orthodox* Churches and, in some parts of the UK, the *Baptist* and *Pentecostal* Churches, have been growing steadily in terms of active membership while parallel to this there has been a significant decline in the active membership, measured by Church attendance, of the *Roman Catholic*, *Anglican* and *Presbyterian* Churches. This has contributed in recent decades to an overall decline of active Church membership in the UK.

ORIGINS AND DEVELOPMENT OF CHRISTIANITY

Early Years

Christianity began around two thousand years ago as a radical renewal movement within Judaism. It is rooted in the life and teaching of Jesus of Nazareth. The early Jesus movements were linked strongly to Jewish life, but as the tradition spread it came to include also *Gentiles*, or those of a non-Jewish background. It developed a separate life but retained a complex and often problematic link to the Jewish tradition. For a long period Christians suffered localised opposition, coupled with sporadically intense persecution throughout the Roman Empire, especially under the Emperors Decius and Diocletian. However, Christianity gradually gained a wider following and, following the conversion of the Roman Emperor Constantine in the early fourth century CE, it eventually became the official religion of the Roman Empire.

The Roman Empire became divided into Eastern and Western parts which followed distinct Christian traditions. Although the Churches in the East and the West had much in common, differences of doctrine and practice began to emerge within the different jurisdictions. Following the great *Schism*

between these Churches in 1054, by the twelfth century these differences had resulted in the distinctive forms of Eastern and Western *Christendom* which underlie, respectively, the various forms of Eastern *Orthodox* and *Roman Catholic* Christianity.

Eastern and Western Christendom and Protestant Reformation

After the rise of Islam in the seventh century CE, the Churches of Eastern *Christendom* in the Middle East and in North Africa became separate religious minorities. By contrast, in Western *Christendom*, Christianity was the dominant religious tradition, largely supplanting indigenous pagan traditions. In the Middle Ages, Western Christendom was commonly understood as a socio-political unity with two poles of authority: the state power of the *Holy Roman Emperor* or an individual country's monarch, and the ecclesiastical and spiritual authority of the *Pope* (the *Bishop* of Rome, the senior *bishop* of the Church).

There was a continued tension between these secular and spiritual poles until, in the sixteenth century, Western *Christendom* fragmented, with many territories becoming *Protestant* and no longer acknowledging *papal* jurisdiction in the spiritual sphere. Many *Protestant* Churches developed as national Churches having a close relationship with the states in which they were set.

The Protestant Reformation and the Missionary Movement

With growing European awareness of the world beyond Europe, both *Protestant* and *Roman Catholic* Christians increasingly became convinced of a need to spread the message of Christianity to the countries where European colonies were being established. The *missionary* movement began with the *Roman Catholic missions* of the sixteenth and seventeenth centuries to China, Goa, Japan and the New World. It reached its peak during the latter part of the nineteenth century and the first half of the twentieth century, with the development of the Protestant *Christian missions* that led to Christian Churches of many denominations being established on every continent.

This process in turn contributed to the development of the *ecumenical* movement (see below) towards unity in faith, prayer and action among the Christian Churches of the world. Many individual Christian *missionaries* were undoubtedly motivated by genuine Christian convictions about their responsibility for spreading the Christian message, but the relationship between the *missionary* movement and European colonialism and imperialism has, with hindsight, been criticised by the more recently founded Churches in other continents and by many of the European Churches themselves. However, the *missionaries* made a significant impact, and today the global focus of Christianity has shifted significantly from Europe and North America to Africa and Latin America.

SOURCES OF CHRISTIAN BELIEFS AND PRACTICES

Scriptures

The Christian scriptures comprise what Christians have traditionally called the *Old Testament* and the *New Testament* (*testament* meaning *covenant*). Together they form what is known among Christians as the *Bible*. From the earliest years of Christianity Christians have believed that one God speaks through both the Jewish law, the prophets and the writings as recorded in the Hebrew Scriptures (commonly known among Christians as the *Old Testament*), and through Jesus as testified to in the *Gospels*, *Epistles* and other writings (which collectively came to be known among Christians as the *New Testament*).

The Christian *Old Testament* is similar in content to the Jewish *Tanakh* (see chapter on "Introducing the Jewish Community"), though different in its internal order after the first five books. The *New Testament* is a collection of texts dating from the first and early second centuries which describe the impact of Jesus upon his followers who became known as "Christians" together with beliefs about him, the story of the formation of early Christian communities, and the elaboration of the ethical implications of Christian belief.

The *canon* (normative contents) of the Christian *New Testament* emerged out of a process of debate concerning the authenticity and authority of a wider range of writings which were in circulation among the early Christian communities. The *canon* was finalised by a Church Council held in Carthage in 397 CE, although there remains some difference among Christians today concerning the place of a number of Greek texts collectively known as the *Apocrypha* (literally, "the hidden things") which are not included in the Hebrew language version of the *Old Testament*.

Roman Catholics and some other Christians understand these books to be fully a part of the scriptures, whilst others see their religious value as of less centrality. The status of these texts is, however, different from that of texts which emerged much later in history, such as the forged *Gospel of Barnabas*, which is not accepted by Christians as authentic in any sense.

In the *New Testament* the four *Gospels* (the English term from the Saxon word *Godspell*, meaning *Good News*) tell the story and describe the significance of Jesus, emphasising particularly his public life, death and *resurrection*. They are named after four early followers of Jesus: Matthew, Mark, Luke and John. They are followed by the *Book of the Acts of the Apostles*, which describes the spread of early Christianity; the *Epistles*, in which the leaders of the early Church address problems and issues arising in the Christian communities; and finally the *Book of Revelation*, which records a series of visions.

The scriptures are central to the life of all Christians. Some Christians understand them as being the literal words of God without error or human distortion, whilst others see them as human testimony, guided by the Spirit of God in all central matters of belief and practice and bearing witness to Jesus as the revelation of God in human nature.

The Creeds

Creeds are summary statements of orthodox beliefs hammered out during vigorous controversies throughout the first centuries of CE. The most commonly used and important are the *Apostles' Creed* and the *Nicene Creed*. There are, however, some Christian denominations which dislike the use of credal formulae, notably Unitarians, members of the Society of Friends and some Baptists.

Tradition

For *Orthodox, Roman Catholic* and *Anglican* Christians, *Tradition* is the third key source of belief and practice. It embraces the authoritative understandings and interpretations of basic Christian beliefs contained in the scriptures and the *creeds* of the Church. The texts of the *Patristic* period (the period of the early *Church Fathers*) are of great importance for many Christians, and particularly for those within the *Orthodox* Churches, as authoritative interpretations of scripture. Also important for belief and practice, although less authoritative, are the writings of the great Christian *saints* (see below).

Reason, Conscience and Experience

Human reason, individual conscience and religious experience are also recognised sources of belief and practice when exercised in the context of the scriptures, the *creeds, Tradition* and the teaching of the denomination or the local church. Christians differ, however, on the scope for individual interpretation.

The Church

On the basis of its scriptures, and for many Churches also drawing on *Tradition*, the Church provides guidance to Christian individuals and Christian communities. The community of those who follow Jesus is known as the *Church* (from the Greek, *kuriakon*, meaning "belonging to the *Lord*").

The Greek word *ekklesia* (translated as Church) originally referred to the whole community of believers and is still today used to denote the universal Christian community. Nevertheless, the English word Church has also come to be used in a variety of other ways. Sometimes (and usually when it begins with a capital letter) it is used to refer to particular national bodies or world communions such as the Methodist Church or the Russian Orthodox Church. At other times it refers to the buildings in which Christian worship takes place (as when people refer to "the church on the corner of the street") or the local Christian group which is found there. In these latter instances, the word usually begins with a small "c".

KEY CHRISTIAN BELIEFS

Jesus

The common focus of Christianity is upon the person of Jesus of Nazareth. Christian groups differ to some extent in their interpretations of his teaching, life, death and *resurrection* (being raised from the dead), but these matters are at the heart of the teaching and way of life of all of them.

The earliest Christian confession of faith appears to have been the expression "Jesus is *Lord*". In other words, he was seen as the criterion by which all of life was to be evaluated, and not simply as the *Saviour* of those who followed him. By this title of *Lord*, used also in Jewish tradition of God, the universal significance of Jesus is asserted.

The name *Christians* was originally a nickname given to the early followers of Jesus, who confessed him to be the *Christ*. The English word *Christ* comes from the Greek *Christos* which is, in turn, a translation of the Hebrew *Mashiach*. Although this word often appears together with Jesus as if Jesus Christ is a personal name, Jesus is the personal name and *Christ* is a title given to him by the early Christians, who believed that Jesus fulfilled the expectations of the Jewish people for the *Messiah* (the *Anointed One* - a coming deliverer). Other titles used of Jesus in the *New Testament* scriptures include *Son of Man, Son of God, Saviour* and *Word of God*.

Christians turn to the four *Gospels* and the *Book of the Acts of the Apostles* for an account and explanation of the origins of Christianity, the story of Jesus and its significance. These documents indicate that Jesus was born in Bethlehem, approximately two thousand years ago; that he grew up in the town of Nazareth in the region known as Galilee; that when he was about thirty years old he began to teach, heal and travel through Judaea, Samaria and Galilee with a group of *disciples* (learners) from among whom he chose twelve *apostles* (messengers - from the Greek *apostoloi*); that in his work, as well as associating with the ordinary people of his nation, he deliberately also associated with the disreputable and with social and religious outcasts, in order to demonstrate the love of God for all kinds of people.

The *Gospels* also indicate that Jesus called people to turn to God, repent of their sins and receive forgiveness, teaching that the self-righteous are less likely to be accepted by God than the outcasts. They indicate that although Jesus was a faithful Jew, he also came into conflict with the Jewish authorities of his day and that he was put to death by *crucifixion* by the Roman occupiers of the country, (a form of execution usually applied to political rebels which entailed hanging its victims upon a cross made of wood until they died by asphyxiation).

The *Gospels* recount that three days later his tomb was found empty; that he was met by one of his women followers and his disciples reported meeting with him, talking with him and eating with him; and that eventually these disciples believed that he had been *resurrected* from the dead and had *ascended* to be with God the Father.

The *Acts of the Apostles* describe the early Christian community's experience of the *Holy Spirit* being sent down on gathered followers and also give an account of the spread of the new faith. These texts and the *Epistles* (from the Greek *epistole*, meaning "letter") reveal the significance of Jesus for the earliest Christians and show something of Christianity's development in a variety of different locations throughout the eastern Mediterranean area. The *Epistles*, in particular, portray Jesus as the key to God's activity in the world, and they attempt to apply his teaching to daily life.

God, Incarnation and Revelation

Christians are *monotheists*. They believe that there is one God who has been revealed as Father and as the Creator, Sustainer and Redeemer of all that is. They also believe that whilst this one God has been manifested in many different places and times, and in particular through the history and faith of the Jewish people, God's nature has been shown most clearly in the life, teaching, death and *resurrection* of Jesus of Nazareth.

Indeed, it is traditionally believed that God himself was present in Jesus, born as a Jew, and that in and through Jesus, God identified fully with humanity. This is called the *incarnation* (from the Latin for "enfleshed"). The classical definition of the 451CE *Council of Chalcedon* contains the paradoxical statement that Jesus was both fully human and fully divine. This expresses the belief that Jesus was fully human in all respects except for *sin* (falling short of the will of God) and yet also that God was fully present in Jesus' human vulnerability.

It is because of belief in the *incarnation* that, in Christian understanding Jesus' teachings, such as the well-known *Sermon on the Mount*, cannot ultimately be separated from his life, death and *resurrection* as the embodiment and expression of the nature of God. Through Jesus, understood as the revelation of God made flesh, the nature of God is pre-eminently seen as being that of self-giving love (signified by the use of the Greek word *agape*, one of three Greek words rendered in English by the word "love").

Salvation

Jesus is therefore seen as the pivotal historical locus of God's activity. This activity is first of all seen as creative. God is understood as the origin of all things, both seen and unseen, which were created as good. But God's activity is also seen as *salvific* (putting right that which has gone wrong), because the world and human beings within it are understood to have become fundamentally flawed and to be in need of God's healing. This flawedness has been understood in a variety of ways within Christianity across a range of understandings from the effect of *original sin* passed down the generations from the *sins* of the first humans, Adam and Eve, to the falling away from God of each individual human.

Whatever the cause, humans are believed by Christians to fall short of God's intention for them. Human beings are created in the *image of God*, but the image in each has become clouded over or damaged and is in need of restoration, so that they can come back into right relationship with God. It is believed by Christians that God takes the initiative in this restorative forgiveness and acceptance and this activity of God is known as *grace.*

God's healing *salvific* activity is understood by Christians to be most fully demonstrated in Jesus' life and teaching, which serve as a pattern for human life, and in God's participation in Jesus' death and *resurrection*. The *Gospels* show Jesus' death as the inevitable consequence of his faithful announcement of the message of the coming *Kingdom of God*. Very early on, many Christians also came to interpret the death and *resurrection* of Jesus as in some sense a *sacrifice* paid on behalf of human sin, to bring about an *atoned* ("at-oned") and restored relationship with God (a key theme in the writings attributed to St Paul).

It was also believed that God somehow, in the *crucifixion* of Jesus, plumbed the depths of human experience: death itself, the last enemy of human life. Death was then conquered in the *resurrection* and it is this conquest that Christians celebrate at *Easter*. In traditional belief, because of Jesus' conquest of death, no lesser powers can bind or enslave any who put their trust in him, and death itself will be overcome after this life by those who partake, through faith, in his *resurrection*.

Many Christians also hold to the traditional biblical idea that Jesus will return a second time to judge humanity and bring about a complete renewal of all creation: not just of human beings. For some *Evangelical* Christian groups, this idea of a *Second Coming* is connected with a belief that it is possible to interpret world events in the light of such biblical texts as the *Book of Revelation* to discern when Jesus will come again.

Judgement and Eternal Life

Christians believe that human beings have only one life and that they will be judged on how they have lived this life. The exact shape of beliefs about judgement has varied over time, but some biblical texts describe a *Last Judgement* which will be followed by immortal union with God or by punishment. In the *Catholic* tradition, a state called *Purgatory*, or the place where sins are purged, is seen as preparatory for entry to heaven. On the whole, contemporary western Christianity tends to emphasise the importance of Christian faith and love in this world and to focus less on the penal aspect of the afterlife than has been the case in some centuries.

The Holy Trinity

Jesus is seen as the most complete expression and revelation of God, but the Christian vision and experience of God does not focus on the person of Jesus alone. The Christian conviction about the ultimately unfathomable nature of God came to be expressed in the Christian doctrine or *Mystery* of the *Holy Trinity.*

The Christian doctrine of the *Trinity* should not be understood as *tritheism* (belief in three individual gods) since the oneness of God is emphatically affirmed by Christians. Rather, it is intended to express belief in a dynamic interrelationship of community, interdependence and unity within the nature of the one God. God's nature and activity are said to be expressed in what the original Greek doctrine referred to as three *hypostases* (often, somewhat misleadingly, translated into English as three *persons*, although *hypostasis* does not refer to an independent individual in the modern sense of the word person).

Although expressed in highly complex language in its doctrinally developed form, by this doctrine Christians give expression to their experience that it is by the Holy Spirit of God, in and through God revealed and active in Jesus, that they worship God as the Father, the Creator and Redeemer of all things. Some Churches also see the union of believers in mutual love as reflecting the life of the *Trinity*.

The Virgin Mary

The Virgin Mary, the Mother of Jesus, is a focus of devotion for millions of Christians. Hundreds of Church buildings within the *Roman Catholic*, *Anglican* and *Orthodox* traditions are named after her. However, Christians have varying views about the place which Mary has within Christian life and doctrine. Most Christians believe that Jesus had no human father but was conceived by the Virgin Mary through the Holy Spirit; therefore she is to be honoured for her role of being the Mother of Jesus and the first and best example of Christian faith and obedience. The *Roman Catholic* and *Orthodox* traditions, however, emphasise this unique role more than the *Protestant* Churches do.

Orthodox tradition calls Mary *Theotokos* (Greek for God-bearer) since it is through her that the incarnation is believed to have taken place. She is therefore held to have a special role as a link between the spiritual and material worlds. Among *Roman Catholics* Mary is known as the

Queen of Heaven. In both the *Orthodox* and *Roman Catholic* traditions, Christian believers address prayers to Mary, asking her to intercede with Jesus on behalf of those who pray to her.

Some in the *Anglican* tradition also share in the veneration of Mary as the most honoured of human beings. Very few *Protestant* Christians pray to Mary. The official teaching of the *Roman Catholic* Church proclaims a belief that Mary, by the singular grace of God and through the merits of Christ's saving work, was conceived without *original sin*. This is known as the doctrine of the *Immaculate Conception*.

The Saints

In some branches of Christianity, individual Christian men and women who have led particularly holy and exemplary lives manifesting the grace and power of God are venerated as *saints* (from the Latin *sanctus*, meaning holy) and are looked to for help and support. This is particularly true of both *Orthodox* and *Roman Catholic* Christianity where veneration of the saints underlines the universal Christian sense that the Church is composed of all Christian people, both present and past.

Many Church buildings are named after individual *saints*. *Saints* are also often associated with particular places of Christian pilgrimage. In the early Christian Church, the scriptures referred to all Christian believers as the *saints* (meaning the "set apart ones") as distinct from the more specialised and restrictive use of the term which developed in the course of Church history.

TRADITIONS IN CHRISTIANITY

Globally, the largest Christian traditions are the *Roman Catholic*, *Orthodox*, *Protestant* and *Pentecostal*. The *Anglican* tradition of Christianity understands itself as both *Reformed* and *Catholic* in tradition. These traditions share many of the key beliefs described above, but they also have their own distinctive teachings, ethos and emphases.

Roman Catholic

The *Catholic* Church embraces around half the Christians in the world. It understands itself as "one, holy, *catholic* and *apostolic*"; that is to say, as one united church which is sanctified by God, which is universal in scope (Catholic from the Greek, *katholos*), and in an authentic and unbroken line of transmission of the Christian faith from the earliest apostles until the present time. It is often referred to by non-Catholics as the *Roman Catholic* Church.

Its *bishops* are believed to be in direct *apostolic* line of succession from the first leaders of the Church who were appointed by Jesus, and particularly from the *Apostle* Peter. The *Pope* is understood by *Roman Catholics* to be Peter's successor and the *Vicar of Christ* by virtue of his office as the *Bishop of Rome*. The *bishops* are nominated by the *Pope* and consecrated by other *bishops* who are in communion with the *Pope*, and are responsible for the teaching and discipline of the Church as well as for ordaining *priests* to serve local Christian communities, and thus for maintaining what is known as the *Apostolicity* of the Church.

In *Roman Catholic* teaching the scriptures, as interpreted according to tradition, are given the supreme authority within the Church. But it is believed that the teaching authority of the Church, known as the *magisterium*, resides in the collective role of all the *bishops* gathered in *Ecumenical Councils* such as were held in the early centuries of Christianity.

Since the time of the *Reformation, Roman Catholics* have recognised three further *Ecumenical Councils* - the Council of Trent (1545-1563), Vatican I (1870) and Vatican II (1962-65). At the same time, a supreme authority is given to the *Pope* as the *Bishop of Rome* and the head of the *College of Bishops*, and the right, under certain conditions, to make infallible declarations on matters of faith and morals.

The *Roman Catholic* commitment to *Catholicity* refers to the universality and the unity-in-diversity of that Church in all geographical contexts and also throughout space and time. There is therefore a great sense of belonging to a living tradition reflecting the diversity of humanity and yet kept in unity particularly by celebration of the *eucharist* (see below) as the focus of unity. Participation in *sacramental Communion* at the *Roman Catholic Mass* generally requires full initiation into the Roman Catholic Church in the sense of being in communion with the *bishops* and the *Pope*, who are seen as maintaining the Church's *Apostolicity*.

Orthodox

The Churches of the *Orthodox* tradition of Christianity understand themselves as representing the tradition and practice of the undivided Church before the separation of Eastern and Western *Christendom*. *Orthodoxy* thus claims to represent a more original form of Christianity than others.

The *Orthodox* give central importance to the doctrine of the *Holy Trinity*. It is this which lies behind the so called *filioque* controversy between *Orthodoxy* and Western Christendom. This is the debate over whether, within the *creeds* of the Church, it should be said with reference to *Trinitarian* doctrine that, the Spirit proceeds "from the Father", the source of all Godhead (which is the *Orthodox* credal form) or "from the Father and the Son" (which is the Western credal form).

The Western formulation expresses the understanding that the Spirit of God is always manifested in terms of the character and person of Jesus. The *Orthodox* are concerned that such a formulation may subordinate the role of Spirit to that of Jesus. They also see the Western addition, made without the authority of an *Ecumenical Council*, as an illegitimate act by one section of the Church.

The *Orthodox* tradition places a great emphasis on prayer, on spirituality and on celebration of the *Liturgy*. In Church government, it has so-called *autocephalous* (Greek, meaning independently governed) Churches with their own *patriarchs* (senior *bishops*) or *Archbishops*, although all *Orthodox* Churches recognise the *Patriarch of Constantinople* as the *Ecumenical Patriarch* who is first in order of seniority. In global terms, the numerical strength of the *Orthodox* Churches is to be found primarily in Eastern Europe, the Mediterranean and the Middle East.

Protestant

Protestant is the name given to the Christian groupings whose particular character derives from the sixteenth and seventeenth century division in the Church in Europe generally referred to as the *Reformation* (see above).

They vary in belief and practice, particularly about Church organisation and government. There are also significant differences between those *Protestant* Christian traditions which have seen a close relationship with the state and/or the nation in a positive light (for example, in Scotland the *Reformed* Church of Scotland) and those traditions, generally known as the *Free* Churches, which have advocated the separation of the Church and the state.

In general, the *Protestant* tradition declares the supremacy and authority of the scriptures in matters of belief and Church government. However, it also emphasises the role of the individual believer, under the guidance of the Holy Spirit, in reading and interpreting the text of the *Bible*. It places emphasis upon personal faith in Jesus as the means to *salvation*. In some *Protestant* traditions, such as *Methodism*, this has also been supplemented by a focus on the need for a strong personal experience of conversion, understood as a complete change of life orientation.

Most *Protestant* Churches also place particular emphasis upon *preaching* (the proclamation of the Word of God believed to be revealed in scripture). Through this, God is understood to offer eternal life in Christ and by the Holy Spirit to enable Christian hearers to deepen their faith and live in a more Christlike way.

Anglican

The *Anglican* tradition is a worldwide Christian tradition composed of autonomous Churches which, historically, are daughter Churches of the Church of England and look to the *Archbishop of Canterbury* for international leadership. Like the Church of England, as a consequence of the distinctive course of events of the *Reformation* in England and Wales, these Churches understand themselves as being both *Reformed* and *Catholic* in tradition.

The *Catholic* element is part of the *Anglican* emphasis on its continuity with the past and in *apostolic succession* to the earliest church. The *Protestant* element was rooted in the correction of matters which, at the time of the *Reformation*, were judged to be abuses and distortions of *Catholic* Christianity.

Anglicanism strives for balance in all things. In doctrine, this is expressed by affirming scripture, tradition and human reason as God-given instruments for interpreting revelation. In matters of authority, reason is seen as a necessary interpreter of scripture and tradition, and in matters of church order individual and *parochial* (the level of the local *parish*) freedom is combined with an *episcopal* (the order of *bishops*) Church structure. In recent decades most *Anglican* Churches have developed *synodical* democratic structures where key issues in the life of the Church are debated by both lay and ordained elected representatives.

There is also an attempt to balance a developed *liturgical* life and private devotion with a focus on scripture and social responsibility. There is concern, too, for comprehensiveness, which is envisaged as embracing a breadth of Christian belief and practice containing several identifiable theological and liturgical streams of life. These streams are known as the *Evangelical* (sometimes called *Low Church*), the *Anglo-*

Catholic (sometimes called High Church), the Liberal (or Broad Church) and the Charismatic (see below for an explanation of these terms).

Pentecostal

The Pentecostal tradition has historical roots in Protestantism but there are also good reasons for regarding it as a distinctive tradition of Christianity that has come to global prominence in the course of the twentieth century. The Pentecostal tradition shares with the wider Protestant tradition a commitment to the primacy of the scriptures for individual and Church life, as well as the necessity of personal faith in, and commitment to, Jesus. However, Pentecostalism goes further to assert that there is no gap between the power and love of God that was available to the first Christian believers as recorded in the scriptural book of the Acts of the Apostles, and that which is available to Christians today.

Pentecostalists believe in the necessity of actually experiencing this power and love as well as believing in it. An event which they describe as the experience of baptism in the Spirit is seen as the occasion in and through which individuals can gain access to the spiritual gifts of God. In classical Pentecostal practice, the outward sign of this baptism in the Spirit has been seen as the ability to engage in glossolalia (speaking in tongues). This involves the individual producing sounds, directed in praise and worship to God, which are not the words of the person's day-to-day language. However, although this has become particularly identified with Pentecostalism, the tradition's own emphasis is upon all the spiritual gifts of God, including the gifts of prophecy and healing.

Restorationist and House Church Movements

During the 1970s and 1980s, European Christianity has seen the growth of the so-called Restorationist and House Church movements, organised separately from the traditional Christian denominations. Christians in these movements often feel that the older Churches have stifled the real spirit of Christianity in outmoded structures. They therefore seek to develop forms of organisation and networking which they believe to be more consistent with those that were found among the earliest Christian communities.

Quakers and Unitarians

As well as the traditions outlined above, there are also some groups which do not fit neatly into any of these categories but which have an historical and, in many cases, a contemporary connection with the Protestant tradition.

Among these are the Quakers (officially known as the Religious Society of Friends) and the Unitarian and Free Christian Churches. Both of these traditions have historical roots in Protestant Christianity. At the same time, both are non-credal traditions, believing that credal statements about orthodoxies of belief or church order are restrictive of true religion. Indeed, some of the members of these traditions would not wish to be identified as specifically Christian in any way which they believe implies separation from people of other religions or, sometimes, also from humanists.

Churchmanship

Within many of these major traditions of Christianity there are streams or tendencies of what often used to be called churchmanship, which refer to Christians in all the major traditions who have particular emphases within their Christian understanding and life. Among the principal tendencies are the following:

Anglo-Catholic
Anglo-Catholics are Anglican Christians who emphasise the Catholic inheritance of the Anglican tradition in various aspects of theology, doctrine and worship.

Charismatic
Charismatic Christianity is a movement that is historically related to the Pentecostal branch of Christianity, but which is now present in all

other major branches of Christianity. It is characterised by an emphasis on the direct experience of the Holy Spirit being available to Christian believers today, including the possibility that the Holy Spirit can produce miraculous works in the contemporary world. *Charismatic* Christians do not, however, necessarily adopt particular items of *Pentecostal* theology or practice, such as the emphasis on *speaking with tongues* as a necessary evidence of *baptism* in the Spirit.

Evangelical

Evangelicals are Christians who draw upon the inheritance of the *Reformation* particularly as it developed in the eighteenth and nineteenth centuries. They try to live according to the Christian scriptures viewed as the supreme authority for Christian life, and understood as revealed and inspired without human error or distortion.

Because their personal decision to follow Jesus is so central, they feel strongly called to bring others into the Christian Church by means of *evangelism* (meaning *Good News* - from the Greek word *euangelion*). *Evangelism* means sharing the good news of what Christians believe God has done in and through Jesus. Whilst *Evangelical* Christians are centrally concerned with this, other Christians also engage in *evangelism*, since bearing *witness* to Jesus is understood to be obligatory for all Christians (see section on "Christian Life" below).

Liberal

Liberal Christians are those Christians in all traditions and denominations who place an emphasis upon the necessity for a contextualised understanding and practice of Christianity and believe that rationality and contemporary relevance are crucially important for the meaning and communication of the Christian message.

The Ecumenical Movement

Particularly during the twentieth century, the *Ecumenical Movement* (from the Greek *oikumene*, meaning the whole inhabited earth) has developed. This represents a desire among Christians of all traditions to fulfill the prayer of Jesus for the unity of the Church and so to build a universal Christian fellowship which transcends or embraces all divisions and boundaries and shares resources for witness and ministry. This global movement has sometimes found expression in the search for common Church structures and organisations and in attempts to form united Churches out of two or more formerly separate Churches as, for example, in the UK with the United Reformed Church (see below).

More recently, the organised *Ecumenical Movement* has also sought to achieve closer co-operation and working relationships in common projects between Christians who remain in separate Churches, as in the work of the Council of Churches for Britain and Ireland. At the European level many *Protestant* and *Orthodox* Churches belong to the Conference of European Churches (CEC). At an international level many *Anglican*, *Protestant* and *Orthodox* Churches belong to the World Council of Churches (WCC) and *Roman Catholics* participate fully in its Faith and Order Commission.

CHRISTIAN LIFE

Jesus commanded his disciples to "love one another as I have loved you", and so Christian believers are called upon to live according to the pattern of Jesus' life which was characterised by sacrificial and self-giving love or *agape* (the Greek word for this form of love).

Sin and Grace

Without the assistance of the power of God, Christianity sees human beings as being gripped by self-centredness and powers beyond their control, a condition described as enslavement to *sin*. The release which believers experience when they put their trust in God through Jesus is known as *salvation*. This means a progressive liberation from all that enslaves human beings in terms of self-centredness.

In the Christian life there is a dynamic tension between the belief that one is already, in principle, freed from the power and guilt of *sin*, whilst in this life never being entirely free from it. This is expressed in the Christian scriptures by the concept of *salvation* appearing in all three tenses: past, present and future.

The activity by which God is believed to draw people into his purposes is referred to as *grace*. This is a word that expresses dependence upon the free and unmerited gift of God's power in contrast to reliance upon human goodness or self-sufficiency, and Christians are called to put their trust in God's name.

This trust is described by the word *faith*, which is understood to be evoked and sustained through the power of God known as the Holy Spirit, who is God at work in and among believers. Christians believe that they can draw upon this power of God through their practice of prayer, and they are supported in this by participation in *fellowship* with other Christian believers within the Church.

Baptism

The rite of *baptism* (from the Greek *baptizo*, meaning to dip or immerse) in water accompanied by prayer and conducted in the name of the Holy Trinity marks a person's entry into the Christian Church. In many older church buildings the *baptismal font* (usually a standing receptacle which holds the water used in *baptism*) is near the door of the Church, to show symbolic entry. The waters of *baptism* are understood as a sign of the remission of *sins* and entry into new life in Jesus.

In the *Anglican, Roman Catholic, Reformed*, and *Orthodox* Churches the *baptismal* rite is generally administered to babies or infants. They are presented for *baptism* by their parents who, together with friends or relatives designated as godparents, make promises on behalf of the infant. In the *Anglican, Roman*

Catholic and *Reformed* Churches, a small amount of water is poured on the child's head. Some then *anoint* with oil. In the *Orthodox* Churches, the baby is immersed three times in the *baptismal* waters and is then *chrismated* (anointed with oil) and admitted to full *Communion*.

In some traditions infant *baptism* is popularly known as *christening*, from the ancient practice of giving candidates for *baptism* a Christian name to indicate their new identity as believers and members of the Church.

In other Christian traditions, such as the *Baptist* and *Pentecostal* movements, it is believed that *baptism* should only be administered to those (generally teenagers and adults) who are capable of a personal confession of Christian faith. In these traditions *baptism* is also generally by complete immersion in the *baptismal* waters. Such Churches usually have specially constructed sunken *baptistries* (tanks) designed for this purpose.

There are a few Christian traditions, such as the Society of Friends and the Salvation Army, which do not practise water *baptism*, since their emphasis is on a spiritual and inner *baptism* rather than on outward signs such as the rite of *baptism*.

Confirmation and Membership

In the *Roman Catholic* tradition, *confirmation* with *Holy Communion* completes initiation into the Church, making possible the fuller life given at *baptism*. The Christian believer bears public witness to Jesus and is believed to receive the Holy Spirit of God in a special way. Among those who have grown up within the Church, *confirmation* often takes place in the early teenage years.

In the *Anglican* tradition, and also in some parts of the *Protestant* tradition, *confirmation* is understood in a similar way but with an emphasis on believers affirming their faith and making their own the promises made on their behalf at their *baptism* as infants.

In *episcopal* Churches, *confirmation* is usually administered by a *bishop* by the laying-on of hands on the head of the candidates, accompanied by prayer. In the *Roman Catholic* tradition, anointing with *chrism* also takes place. In the *Orthodox* tradition, the *chrismation* with oil blessed by the *bishop*, which immediately follows after *baptism*, is the equivalent of *Confirmation*.

In Churches of the *Reformed* tradition *confirmation* or what is sometimes called *reception into membership* is usually administered by the *minister*. This is done within a solemn service at which *baptised* individuals (usually at least in their mid-teens) confess their own faith and commitment and are welcomed as full members of the world-wide Church and of the local worshipping community. Thereafter, those who have been welcomed play their part in the decision-making processes within their Church, their names being entered on the roll, or list, of Church members.

Christian Witness

Christians believe that Jesus' last command was to preach the Gospel and make disciples, and Christian Churches in the UK are currently (1991-2000) committed to a Decade of Evangelism/Evangelisation (the former word in more common use amongst *Protestant* Christians and the latter word among *Roman Catholics*). The commitment to spread the message of Christianity is undergirded by the conviction that the Christian message is (as *euangelion*, the Greek of the word *Gospel* suggests) *Good News* to announce to people, concerning which it would be selfish to remain quiet.

Some Christians see their responsibility to bear *witness* in terms of participating in organised *evangelistic* activities known as *missions*, or in belonging to *missionary* organisations that are specifically concerned with presenting the claims of the Christian message, both in this country and in other parts of the world. Other Christians see the call to *witness* more in terms of the way in which they attempt to go about their day-to-day activities in conformity with the life and teaching of Jesus.

Ethics and Discipleship

Discipleship, for Christians, involves following the example or "way" of Jesus. For all Christians, the example of Jesus and the teachings of the *Bible* are key sources for decision and practice. In this context, the *Decalogue* or *Ten Commandments* (shared with Judaism) have been a key reference in Christian ethical reflection, as have Jesus' Beatitudes and the rest of his *Sermon on the Mount*.

For Christians in the *Protestant* tradition, individual conscience is also particularly important in deciding how to apply the teachings of the *Bible*. In the *Roman Catholic* tradition, the role of conscience is affirmed and there is a strong emphasis on informing the individual conscience by the scriptures and the corporate teaching of the Church. This teaching is expressed, in particular, through its bishops and, supremely, through the *Ecumenical* and other Councils of the Church and the official pronouncements of the *Pope* (known as *Encyclicals*). These are often very specific in the guidance they give to individual believers and some aspects of this guidance are reinforced through the application of measures of Church discipline.

Christianity has a strong tradition of social concern. Jesus reinforced the *Old Testament* command to love one's neighbour as oneself and he enjoined his disciples to "love as I have loved you". In his teaching concerning the *Last Judgement* of human beings he pointed out that in serving or neglecting the hungry, the sick and the imprisoned, his followers would be serving or neglecting Jesus himself. In the light of such teaching, Christians have been behind the foundation of many philanthropic and educational initiatives in the UK.

But in the twentieth century, alongside a commitment to charitable works, the Christian Churches have increasingly come to understand that they have a calling to oppose structural and institutionalised injustice. In the contemporary *Ecumenical Movement*, Christian ethics and *discipleship* are expressed by a commitment to what is known as the JPIC process - Justice, Peace and the Integrity of Creation, no one aspect of which can be fully achieved without the other two.

Dietary Issues

Christians do not generally have any universally agreed dietary regulations although some Christians observe, in various ways, the discipline of abstaining from certain foods during the season of *Lent* (see the section on Calendar and Festivals). Some Christians also fast at other, individually chosen times, in order to focus on prayer or as an act of solidarity with the poor, donating the money which they would have otherwise spent on food to a Christian justice and development charity such as Christian Aid, Tear Fund or the Catholic Fund for Overseas Development (CAFOD). There are also some, especially those within the *Protestant* traditions, who refrain, on principle, from drinking alcohol.

Monks, Nuns and Religious

The majority of Christians lead ordinary lives at work in the world and within family life, but from the earliest years of Christianity some have felt called to form special groups in which they could aim to share a more complete devotion to Jesus, and to the pattern of his life and work. Some groups are known as *Orders*, and those within them, generally called *monks* (men) and *nuns* (women), have taken what are known as "solemn vows" of poverty, chastity and obedience.

There are also *Congregations* whose members are known as *Religious*. There are also *Religious Brothers* who are not necessarily *monks*, but make vows to live in community. *Monks*, *nuns* and *religious* can be found in the contemporary *Roman Catholic*, *Orthodox* and *Anglican* Churches. The particular pattern of life of a group of *monks*, *nuns* or *Religious* varies according to the self-understanding of the *Order* or *Congregation* of which they are a part. This, in turn, is based upon the life and teachings of its founder. Some emphasise prayer and meditation and retreat from the world, whilst for others practical service in the world is basic to their calling.

Among the more well-known *Orders* that have grown up in Western Christianity are the *Society of Jesus* (Jesuits, founded by St. Ignatius of Loyola and noted for teaching and missionary work); the *Benedictines* (founded by St. Benedict and with an emphasis on prayer, work and the reading of holy books); the *Dominicans* (after the spirit of St Dominic and who are known for intellectual study and rigour); the *Carmelites* (known for silent prayer and meditation); and the *Franciscans* (who follow the rule of St. Francis of Assisi).

Many other organisations and groups exist within and with the blessing of the Churches, having developed as responses to particular contemporary needs or in order to strengthen and renew Christian life. These include *ecumenical* communities such as Iona in Scotland and Lee Abbey in Devon, England.

CHRISTIAN WORSHIP

Holy Communion

For the majority of Christians *Holy Communion*, or the *Eucharist*, is the most characteristic and central act of Christian worship. Some Christians, such as the Religious Society of Friends (the Quakers) and the Salvation Army do not celebrate *Holy Communion*. *Communion* means sharing (from the Latin *communio*) and refers to the sharing of bread and wine and of the life of the Church. Christians believe that the act was instituted by Jesus himself at what is known as the *Last Supper* when he blessed, or gave thanks over bread and wine, declaring it to be his body and his blood and then shared this with his disciples before his *crucifixion*.

Holy Communion is also known as the *Eucharist* (from the Greek word *eucharistetitia*, meaning thanksgiving); among *Roman Catholics* as the *Mass* (probably originating from Latin words spoken at the end of the service *ite, missa est* the meaning of which has variously been translated as "It is offered" or "Go, you are sent forth"); among the *Orthodox* Churches as the *Divine Liturgy* (from the Greek word *leitourgia*, meaning service); and among some *Protestant* Churches as the *Sacrament of the Lord's Supper* or the *Breaking of Bread*.

The content, interpretation and frequency of this event vary considerably among Christians of different traditions. *Roman Catholic* churches celebrate the *Mass* daily, as do some *Anglican* churches (especially those in the *Anglo-Catholic* tradition), whilst others have one or more weekly celebrations. Some *Protestant* Churches have only monthly or quarterly celebrations, using other forms of worship at other times. The elements of the *Eucharist* also differ from Church to Church. *Roman Catholics* normally use a flat wafer of unleavened bread.

This is also an *Anglican* practice, although in an increasing number of *Anglican* churches ordinary bread is used. *Anglicans* normally receive wine also, whereas in *Roman Catholic* churches there is a variety of practice, with some offering *Holy Communion* under the appearance of both bread and wine and also under one element only. *Orthodox* Christians receive from a long spoon a small piece of bread dipped in wine. In some *Protestant* Churches pieces of bread are taken from a single loaf and each individual receives an individual cup of wine (which may be non-alcoholic). In most churches, however, the wine is alcoholic and is drunk from a common cup.

In *Roman Catholic*, *Orthodox* and *Anglican* Churches the congregation usually go up to the front of the church to receive communion either from the *priest* or, in the *Anglican* and *Roman Catholic* Churches, also from lay *eucharistic ministers*, who are authorised to assist the *priest* in the distribution of the sacrament. In some *Protestant* Churches the bread and wine are taken out to the congregation by lay officers of the church or are passed from member to member.

The *Protestant* traditions generally see *Holy Communion* as a remembrance of Jesus' death and *resurrection* in obedience to his command to do so in remembrance of him, as recorded in the *New Testament*, with God's act of atonement in Jesus being symbolised by the bread and wine which represent his body and blood. There is also an emphasis on the spiritual nourishment received by believers, individually and collectively, with a sense of reliance upon the indwelling Spirit of God expressed by the idea of spiritually feeding on *Christ* by *faith*.

Among *Roman Catholics*, the *Orthodox* and many *Anglicans* in the *Anglo-Catholic* tradition, the elements of the bread and wine are seen as, in a real sense, "re-presenting" the body and blood of Christ so that, by sharing in them, the faithful can actually have *communion* with the risen Jesus. The *Eucharist* is understood as the memorial or making present of Christ's sacrifice in his saving death and resurrection, so that by taking part in the celebration, the faithful are united with Christ's once-for-all work of *salvation*. Among *Roman Catholics*, *First Communion* is usually taken by children after a period of preparation at around the age of seven or eight and is of great personal and family significance.

Preaching

All the Christian denominations in the UK give an important place to preaching or expounding the scriptures within worship. But among the Churches of the *Reformation* and among Churches established following the *Evangelical Revival* of the seventeenth and eighteenth centuries, the preaching of the Word is often given greater prominence than the celebration of the sacrament of *Holy Communion*.

Preaching is normally a particular responsibility of ordained *ministers*, but most Churches also authorise appropriately trained and designated lay preachers to share in the leading of worship, including the ministry of preaching based upon the scriptures. In the *Roman Catholic* Church only *bishops*, *priests* and *deacons* may normally preach at *Mass*.

Prayer

In both public and private prayer the *Lord's Prayer* is important. It is the prayer which Jesus is recorded in the *Gospels* as having taught his first *disciples*, and is therefore a pattern for all Christian prayer. In addition to participating in corporate prayer and worship, many individual Christians have private and personal disciplines of prayer, scriptural study and meditation.

Church Buildings

Most Christian buildings for worship are referred to as churches, but in some *Protestant* branches of Christianity, especially among the *Free Churches*, this word is generally reserved for describing the people who make up the community of the Church. In these cases, in England and Wales (though not generally in Scotland or Ireland) the word *chapel* may be used to describe the building, instead of church. However, the word *chapel* is also used among *Roman Catholics* and *Anglicans* to denote a small church without a parish building or a small part of a larger building.

Some Christians do not meet in recognisably religious buildings but in private homes or in hired public meeting places such as schools, as with the *House Church* movement which is a growing form of Christian life in the UK.

From the outside, Christian places of worship vary in appearance. Many old churches, however, have a range of recognisable features such as a tower or spire which makes them into landmarks in both town and countryside. Very old buildings of this kind are generally now of the *Anglican* Christian tradition, although a large number of them pre-date the *Reformation*. By contrast, some Christian places of worship have the external appearance of a simple square or rectangular hall. Many churches of all kinds have stained glass windows frequently depicting scriptural characters, stories or events.

Once inside a building there is again a very wide variety in terms of what might be found. At one end of the spectrum, *Baptist* or *Methodist chapels* can often have an interior bare of religious symbols except perhaps for a wooden *cross* on the wall, although a number of local churches now have colourful banners hanging from their walls. Attention is focused on the *pulpit* (the raised enclosed platform, usually at one end of the building, from which the preacher addresses the congregation) with a simple table in front of it from which the service of *Holy Communion* (see above) is led.

In most *Protestant* and *Catholic* churches there are seats for the worshippers, but in *Orthodox* Churches most of the congregation stand during the service. A place of worship in the *Orthodox* tradition may have brightly coloured frescoes and also many religious pictures called *icons*, whose purpose is to bring close to the worshipper the spiritual realities which they depict in *iconographic* form.

As well as an elevated *pulpit*, there may be a modest *lectern* (reading desk). Instead of a simple table for *Communion*, the *Orthodox* Church will have an *altar* which is hidden from general view behind a screen known as an *iconostasis*. This is a screen which is covered in *icons* and has doors in the middle through which the priest passes to bring out the bread and wine from the *altar* to the congregation.

In *Roman Catholic* and *Anglican* Churches in the *Catholic* tradition the main focal point is the *altar*. Another focal point is the *tabernacle,* a secure container in which is placed the consecrated bread from the *Eucharist*. The presence of the consecrated bread is indicated by a lightened lamp or candle. There will also be statues of the Virgin Mary and perhaps of *saints* as well. These statues help the worshippers to focus their devotion. They are not, in themselves, objects of worship.

In *Orthodox*, *Roman Catholic* and *Anglo-Catholic Anglican* churches, services of worship may be accompanied by the use of incense. Organs and other musical instruments, sometimes including guitars, are used to accompany singing in *Anglican*, *Protestant* and *Roman Catholic* churches, but not in *Orthodox* churches. Choirs are to be found in most Christian traditions, but vary greatly in style between the traditional and formal *Cathedral* choirs and the more informal and contemporary *Gospel* choirs of the *Pentecostal* tradition.

The main church building of *Anglican*, *Roman Catholic* and *Orthodox Dioceses* is known as a *Cathedral* or, in the case of some *Anglican* churches, a *Minster*. Such buildings act as focal points for their respective *Dioceses* since they are where the *bishop* has his *cathedra* or seat. Church of England *Cathedrals*, in particular, are very often also seen as places where events of civic and social importance are held, as well as being important parts of the country's architectural and spiritual heritage and thus also as tourist attractions.

CHRISTIAN CALENDAR AND FESTIVALS

The Christian Calendar

The Christian calendar dates world history in relation to what was believed to have been the year of the birth of Jesus, although it is now generally accepted that this took place a number of years earlier than was originally thought. This makes the coming *Millennium* the third *Millennium* for Christians.

Because of the Christian belief in the *incarnation*, the birth of Jesus is seen as being the pivotal point of world history. It is in this context that the letters "AD" (from the first letters of the Latin words *Anno Domini*, meaning "In the Year of our Lord") and "BC" (for "Before Christ") came to be used for dating world history, although outside of internal Christian community usage this notation is now more generally becoming replaced, as in this directory, by the letters CE (for Common Era) and BCE (for Before the Common Era).

Sunday

Christianity inherited its seven day week from Judaism. Sunday (the first day of the Jewish week) is usually observed as the day of assembly for Christian worship because, as it was the day of the week on which Jesus is believed to have been raised from death, it marks *resurrection* and new beginning. However, the so-called *Sabbatarian* or *Seventh Day* Churches believe that the commandment to the Jews to keep the seventh day (Saturday) holy is still binding on Christians after the coming of Jesus.

The understanding of Sunday observance varies considerably among Christians. Many *Roman Catholics* attend *Vigil Sunday Mass* on Saturday evening since, following the Biblical tradition, the day is seen as commencing the previous evening. Some *Protestants* refrain from employment or secular recreation throughout Sunday, concentrating on participation in morning and evening worship.

The Church Year and Festivals

The Christian *liturgical* year begins with *Advent* in November. The *liturgical* year marks key events and commemorates figures connected with the Christian story and is particularly important for *Roman Catholics*, the *Orthodox* and *Anglicans*. Most *Protestant* Churches of the *Reformed* and *Congregational* traditions observe only Sundays, *Holy Week*, *Easter*, *Pentecost*, *Advent* and *Christmas* (see below).

In some small Christian groupings even these days are seen as, at best, of marginal importance. At worst they are seen as a corruption of pure Christianity, introduced largely to incorporate some elements of pre-Christian tradition in order to wean Christians away from the traditional celebrations at these times of year.

There are three cycles of festivals within the Christian year. The Christmas cycle has dates which are fixed within the *Gregorian* calendar. Then comes the *Easter* cycle, the dates of which vary for reasons explained below under *Easter*. Finally, there is a third cycle of festivals and commemorations of *saints* and *martyrs* of the

Church, which are observed on fixed dates. A number of *Orthodox* Churches follow the so-called *Julian* calendar which, in the present century, is thirteen days behind the date of the calendar which is in common social use in the UK.

The Roman Catholic Church has also prescribed certain days as *holy days of obligation*. On these days believers are expected to attend *Mass*. In England, Scotland and Wales, this includes all Sundays together with *Christmas Day*, *Ascension Day*, the *Assumption of the Blessed Virgin Mary*, *All Saints' Day*, the feast days of *Saints Peter and Paul*, *Corpus Christi* (a celebration of thanksgiving for the institution of the *Eucharist*) and *Epiphany*.

Advent (November-December)

Advent means "coming" and it refers to the coming of Jesus into the world and to his *Second Coming* at the end of time. The season is observed by Western Christians as a solemn preparatory season for *Christmas*, traditionally beginning on the fourth Sunday before *Christmas*.

Immaculate Conception of the Blessed Virgin Mary (8th December)

Roman Catholics celebrate the belief that Mary the Mother of Jesus was herself conceived free of *original sin* in order that she might be sinless for the bearing of Jesus.

Christmas (25th December)

Celebrates the birth of Jesus, the precise date of which is unknown, but the *Catholic* Church fixed on 25th December to coincide with the winter solstice. Some *Orthodox* Churches keep to the pre-*Gregorian* calendar date of 6th or 7th January celebrating the birth of Jesus. For the other Churches, the 6th January is the twelfth night of Christmas, which closes the *Christmas* season with the festival of *Epiphany*.

Epiphany (6th January)

The word *Epiphany* is Greek meaning "manifestation". In the *Orthodox* Churches, this refers to the manifestation of Jesus at his *baptism* as the *Son of God*. In the Western

Churches *Epiphany* celebrates the adoration of Jesus by the *Magi* or *Wise Men*, and thus his being revealed to the *Gentiles* (non-Jews). It is sometimes referred to as the *Twelfth Night* as it is twelve days after *Christmas*.

Shrove Tuesday (February/March)

This is a popular folk festival marking the day before the start of *Lent*, and has a number of traditional and popular cultural customs attached to it. The name comes from the Middle English word *shriven* which referred to the practice of making confession before the beginning of *Lent*. The popular custom of making pancakes arose from the need to use up eggs before *Lent*, a period of fasting.

Ash Wednesday (February/March)

This is the first day of *Lent* and is so called because in some churches the priest marks the forehead of believers with ash as a sign of our mortality and of penitence before God. In the *Roman Catholic* Church and in *Anglican* churches of *Catholic* tradition, it is a day of fasting and abstinence.

Lent (February-March/April)

This is a period of forty days, not counting Sundays, between *Ash Wednesday* and the Saturday before *Easter*. It is a preparation for *Easter*. Its roots can be found in the *Gospel* stories of Jesus being tempted for forty days in the wilderness prior to the commencement of his public ministry. In the *Orthodox* tradition it is known as the *Great Fast* and starts on the Monday (known as *Clean Monday*) before the first Sunday of *Lent* rather than on the Wednesday as in the Western Churches. In all traditions it is a season of penitence and preparation in which many Christians abstain from some foods and/or luxuries.

The Annunciation to the Blessed Virgin Mary (25th March)

This celebrates the announcement by the Angel Gabriel to Mary that she is to give birth to a son to be called Jesus, and her assent to this. It is celebrated nine months prior to *Christmas* Day.

Mothering Sunday (March)

This is the fourth Sunday in *Lent* and is widely known as *Mother's Day*. Though it may have begun with the idea of Mother Church or of Jerusalem as the "mother of us all", it has become a more popular occasion upon which to recognise and thank mothers for all that they do.

Passion Sunday (March)

This is the fifth Sunday in *Lent* when Christians begin to concentrate their thoughts on the significance of the *Passion* (or suffering) of Jesus, in preparation for recalling the events of *Holy Week*.

Palm Sunday (March/April)

This is the first day of *Holy Week*. On this day Christians are often given pieces of palm leaf in the form of a cross to recall the *Gospel* accounts of how Jesus was greeted by crowds waving palm leaves as he entered into Jerusalem a few days before his crucifixion.

Holy Week (March/April)

The last week of *Lent*, which is dedicated to remembering the suffering and death of Jesus.

Maundy Thursday (March/April)

The Thursday in *Holy Week* which commemorates the day on which, at his *Last Supper* with his *disciples*, Jesus instituted the *Holy Communion*. It was also the occasion of Jesus' command to his disciples to wash one another's feet as a sign of mutual humility and service. A foot washing ceremony is held on this day in some churches. It is also the day on which Jesus gave his *disciples* the commandment to love one another, and prayed for their unity. The name *Maundy Thursday* comes from the Latin of the beginning of the *Gospel of John* chapter 13 verse 34, where Jesus is recorded as giving the *disciples* a new commandment (*Mandatum novum*). In churches in the *Catholic* tradition the altars are generally stripped bare at the end of this day.

Good Friday (March/April)

The Friday of *Holy Week* which commemorates the *crucifixion* of Jesus is generally an austere and solemn day, but is perhaps called "Good" because Christians believe salvation to be effected through the *crucifixion*. The symbolism of the *cross* of Jesus lies behind the traditional practice of eating buns marked with a cross on this day. In the *Roman Catholic* Church and in *Anglican* churches of *Catholic* tradition, it is a day of fasting and abstinence. In many churches a service with meditations upon Jesus's words from the cross is held between noon and three o'clock in the afternoon.

Holy Saturday (March/April)

This is a day of prayerful waiting and preparation for *Easter*. In the *Roman Catholic* and *Orthodox* traditions and among *Anglo-Catholic Anglicans*, a special night service takes place (the *Easter Vigil*) as the main celebration of *Easter*. This involves the biblical story of creation, the solemn proclamation of the *resurrection* of Jesus, the lighting of the *Paschal* candle and the renewal of *baptismal* vows.

Easter (March/April)

Easter commemorates the *resurrection* of Jesus. It is the central Christian festival and is full of joy. It was traditionally the main time for *baptism*. In the Western Christian tradition it is celebrated on the first Sunday following the first full moon after the vernal equinox. The date therefore varies within the solar calendar adopted by western countries. The *Orthodox* calculate *Easter* in a different way and their celebration of the season also continues, in total, for fifty days until *Pentecost*, and therefore also includes *Ascension Day*. The name *Easter* derives from the old English *eostre* which was the name for a pre-Christian Spring festival. The giving of *Easter* eggs, symbolising new life, appears to be a survival of an ancient fertility custom.

Ascension Day (May/June)
This is celebrated on the fortieth day after *Easter* and commemorates the last earthly appearance of the Risen Christ to his first *disciples* which is recorded in the scriptures. His *ascension* marks his transcending of all earthly limitations and the celebration of his kingly rule. It is always celebrated on a Thursday.

Pentecost (May/June)
The name derives from the Greek *pentecoste*, meaning fiftieth day and it is celebrated on the seventh Sunday after *Easter. Pentecost* (or the *Feast of Weeks*) is a Jewish harvest festival which has been given a different meaning by the Church. For Christians, it marks the outpouring of the Holy Spirit upon the followers of Jesus, and the commencement of the Church's *mission* to spread the message about Jesus throughout the world. It is sometimes known as *Whitsun* (*White Sunday*), from the custom of converts presenting themselves on this day for *baptism* dressed in white clothes.

Trinity Sunday (June)
This is celebrated in the West on the Sunday following *Pentecost*. The *Orthodox* Churches celebrate *All Saints* on this day. *Trinity Sunday* is devoted to contemplation of the mystery of God, which Christians see as an indivisible unity and yet revealed in the inter-related communion of God the Father, Son and Holy Spirit.

Corpus Christi (Thursday following Trinity Sunday, therefore usually in June)
This is particularly a *Roman Catholic* festival and celebrates belief in the presence of Jesus in the *Eucharist* in a more joyful way than is appropriate on *Maundy Thursday*. The festival is also observed by some *Anglicans* as a thanksgiving for the institution of the *Holy Communion* or *Eucharist*.

Transfiguration (6th August)
This recalls the scriptural acount of the shining of Jesus' face and clothes on the so-called Mount of *Transfiguration*, when his heavenly glory is believed to have been revealed to his *disciples*.

Assumption of the Blessed Virgin Mary (15th August)
Roman Catholics and *Orthodox* (who call it the Dormition - the falling asleep of the Mother of God) celebrate the belief that Mary, body and soul, was assumed, or taken up into heaven.

St. Michael and All Angels (29th September)
This day celebrates the *Archangel* Michael, the adversary of Satan. Sometimes known as *Michaelmas*, this is a season of the Western Church's year in which the ordination of *priests* and *deacons* may take place, though many ordinations also occur on *Trinity Sunday* and, in the *Anglican* tradition, at *Petertide* (at the end of June).

Harvest Festival (September/October)
Although it is not an official part of any Church year, the observance of a *harvest* festival has become a regular event in many Churches. It celebrates the bounty of God in creation. Such festivals became common from the Middle Ages onwards and were revived in the nineteenth century. Displays of foodstuffs are often made in church and these are then distributed to the needy after the festival is over.

All Saints Day (1st November)
Since the names of every saint cannot be known, this festival commemorates all the *saints*. It emphasises the so-called *Communion of Saints* - the unity in Jesus of all believers, past, present and future.

CHRISTIAN ORGANISATIONS

In the UK there are numerous Christian Churches belonging to the principal Christian traditions described earlier. In what follows, attention is focused on these Church bodies as such (often described as *ecclesiastical* bodies - from the Greek word *ecclesia* meaning Church). There are, in addition, very many Christian organisations with particular foci for their work, some of which are Church-sponsored, others of which are voluntary associations of Christians, such as the Christian Ecology Group or the Christian Disabled Fellowship. The current directory does not attempt to give extensive details of this large sector of organisations, full details of which can be found in the *UK Christian Handbook*.

The principal characteristics of the Churches in the UK reflect the wider, global Christian traditions of which they are a part. By reason of history and contemporary circumstances they are, however, to be found in different proportions within the UK and its various nations than is the case internationally.

Also arising from the history of the UK, it has been more common to distinguish between the established Churches, the *Roman Catholic* Church and the *Free Churches* than the more common global categorisations of *Roman Catholic, Protestant, Orthodox* and *Pentecostal*. The principal *Protestant* Churches in the UK include the Methodist Church, the United Reformed Church and Baptist churches which are also among the *Free Churches*.

The variations in the pattern of Churches in the UK are closely related to the diverse but connected national histories of these islands. In particular, the contemporary patterns of Christian organisation reflect the various national outworkings of the events of the *Reformation* as outlined below. As a religious movement which had political dimensions, the *Reformation* affected different parts of these islands in different ways.

England and Wales

In England and Wales the *Reformation* led to the formation of what is now called the Church of England through the 1534 *Act of Supremacy* of King Henry VIII, who initially styled himself *Head of the Church*. This title was later modified under Queen Elizabeth I to *Supreme Governor*. Thus the Church in England and Wales became independent of the jurisdiction of Rome, but closely identified with the monarchy.

In the period which followed in England, Christians who maintained allegiance to the *Bishop of Rome* (*Roman Catholics*) were persecuted under King Edward VI (1549-53). Under the *Catholic* Queen Mary (1553-58), *Protestants* were persecuted. Under Queen Elizabeth I, the position was again reversed.

The English Church preserved many of the characteristics of *Catholic* Christianity, but also embraced certain *Protestant* features, such as a stress on the availability of the Christian scriptures to be read and studied in the everyday language of ordinary believers rather than in Latin. Latin was accessible only to *priests*, scholars and others who had received a formal education and, in any case, had not been the original language of the scriptures. During the sixteenth and early seventeenth centuries the *Bible* and the *Book of Common Prayer* (containing prescribed orders of worship and the doctrine of the Church of England) were translated into Welsh and were quickly accepted into common use among Christians in Wales.

By the end of the sixteenth century, *Congregationalists* (whose origins lay in the conviction that the Church consists of committed believers and who argued that therefore spiritual authority resides in the local congregation rather than in supra-local Church structures) were emerging, followed during the seventeenth century by *Baptists* and *Quakers*.

In Wales, the substantial majority of the Churches which were formed as a result of these developments worshipped and conducted their congregational and individual Christian life in the Welsh language. Today in Wales, the Union of Welsh Independents, the majority of congregations in the Baptist Union of Wales and the Presbyterian Church of Wales, and all churches within the Cymru District of the Methodist Church, continue to conduct their worship and congregational life in Welsh, as do some *Anglican* churches.

After the period of political and religious upheaval which followed the English civil war and the restoration of the monarchy, the 1662 *Act of Uniformity* led to over one thousand clergy being ejected from their *parishes* in England due to their refusal to be bound by its provisions which made the *Book of Common Prayer* compulsory. This strengthened the *Independent* and *Congregationalist* movements.

Scotland

In Scotland, *Calvinism* had the greatest impact. In 1560 the Church of Scotland was reformed along *Calvinist* principles, with a *Presbyterian* form of Church government based upon a collective of local church leadership of both *clergy* and non-clerical *elders*. Known as the *presbytery* (from the Greek *presbuteros* meaning *elder*), it is not to be confused with the residence of a *Roman Catholic parish priest*, usually also known as a *presbytery*.

Following the union of the crowns of England and Scotland, unsuccessful attempts were made to impose an *Episcopalian* (from the Greek *episcope*, meaning oversight) model of church government upon Scotland, centred upon *bishops* operating at the regional level. Those who supported the *Episcopalian* model formed the minority Scottish Episcopal Church. The dominant *Presbyterian* form of Christianity became the Church of Scotland which is the established Church in Scotland. *Presbyterianism* came to Ireland from Scotland and is now the largest *Protestant* Christian tradition in Northern Ireland.

Anglican Churches

There are four autonomous *Anglican* Churches in these islands which correspond to its main nations. The Church of England, the Scottish Episcopal Church, the Church in Wales, and the Church of Ireland (which operates in both Northern Ireland and the Republic of Ireland.) According to the *UK Christian Handbook 1996/97* there are 26,200,000 *Anglicans* in the UK. In England and Wales there are 16, 496 *Anglican* places of worship recorded with the General Register Office.

At the regional level, the Churches of the *Anglican* tradition are organised into *Provinces*

and *dioceses*. At the local level, they are organised into *parishes* (the neighbourhood area) and *deaneries* (groupings of *parishes*). In England, Church of England *parishes* are legal entities and taken together cover the whole country.

The Church of England is the established Church in England. Its special constitutional position in the UK state is reflected by twenty-six of its senior *bishops* having reserved places in the House of Lords. The Church of England has two *Provinces* (of Canterbury and York) and forty-three *dioceses*. Although an *episcopal* Church (led by *bishops*), the Church of England is governed by a *General Synod* which includes three categories of *diocesan* representatives: laity, clergy and *bishops*, with similar *synods* operating at *diocesan* and *deanery* levels.

The *Anglican* Churches in Scotland, Wales and Ireland are not established Churches. The Scottish Episcopal Church has seven *dioceses*. It is the smallest of the *Anglican* Churches in these islands and numerically it is concentrated in Perthshire and in the north and east of Scotland. The Church of Ireland has two *Provinces* (Dublin and Armagh). The Province of Dublin is almost entirely in the Irish Republic whilst Armagh is mostly in Northern Ireland. The disestablishment of the Church of England in Wales led, in 1920, to the formation of the Church in Wales which has six *dioceses* and is a bi-lingual Church.

Roman Catholic Church

Although there is a continuity in the English *Roman Catholic* tradition with Christianity before King Henry VIII's repudiation of *Papal* authority, the Roman Catholic Church's contemporary strength in England and Wales is mainly due to the nineteenth and early twentieth century immigration of *Roman Catholics* from Ireland. According to the *UK Christian Handbook 1996/97* there are 5,700,000 *Roman Catholics* in the UK, and in England and Wales there are 3,701 places of

Roman Catholic worship, certified as such with the Registrar General.

In Scotland in 1560 there was an attempt to suppress Roman Catholic Christianity and Papal authority by law. However, the Catholic tradition survived in the south-west and in the highlands and islands of the north-west of Scotland. Immigration from Ireland also increased the Catholic population, which is concentrated around Glasgow.

In Ireland as a whole the Roman Catholic Church is by far the largest Christian tradition. It is also numerically the largest single Church in Northern Ireland even though Catholics make up only approximately forty per cent of Northern Ireland's total population.

In these islands the Roman Catholic Church has three national Bishops' Conferences: the Bishops' Conference for England and Wales, another for Scotland, and another for Ireland. However, Roman Catholic life is focused upon parish and diocesan, rather than national level.

Orthodox Churches

In the UK the Orthodox Churches as such are a relatively recent presence apart from a number of individuals who settled in the UK from the seventeenth century onwards. Larger numbers resulted from the arrival of significant emigré groups of Russians after the Russian revolution, and the post Second World War migrations of Greeks, Serbs and other ethnic groups which have a traditionally close relationship with Orthodox Christianity. The Orthodox Churches in the UK are, in fact, still related to these older national and ethnic Orthodox Churches. The Greek Orthodox Church is numerically the largest, principally due to immigration from Cyprus.

The UK Christian Handbook 1996/97 gives a figure of 500,000 Orthodox Christians in the UK. The Registrar General's lists of places of worship for England and Wales does not keep a running total for a separate category of Orthodox churches.

There are now also a growing number of Churches of the Oriental Orthodox tradition including the Armenian, Coptic, Ethiopian, Indian and Syrian Orthodox, and there is a Council of Oriental Orthodox Churches which seeks to group these Churches together co-operatively. Because the Orthodox in general are not numerically strong and their members are geographically scattered, there is usually only one diocese for each Church, covering the whole of the UK.

Protestant Churches

Reformed Churches

The largest non-Anglican Protestant tradition in the British Isles is the Reformed tradition, within which Presbyterianism is the biggest strand. The word Presbyterian comes from the Greek word presbuteros, meaning elder and it refers to the local leadership of a Christian community. Presbyterianism is so called because of its emphasis on the local and collective leadership of such elders. The UK Christian Handbook 1996/97 gives a figure of 2,600,000 Presbyterians in the UK, and the Registrar General's list of places of worship gives 1,756 certified places of worship for the United Reformed Church in England and Wales.

The main Reformed Churches of the UK are the Church of Scotland, the Presbyterian Church in Ireland, the Presbyterian Church of Wales and the United Reformed Church (which also includes the Churches of Christ and Congregational traditions, having been formed initially in 1972 through the uniting of the Presbyterian Church of England and the Congregational Church, formerly the Congregational Union).

Also active in Scotland are a number of smaller Presbyterian bodies - the Free Church of Scotland, the Free Presbyterian Church of Scotland, the Reformed Presbyterian Church of Scotland and the United Free Church of Scotland. There are also a number of smaller Presbyterian bodies in Ireland. These include the Reformed Presbyterian Church of Ireland, the

Evangelical Presbyterian Church, the Non-Subscribing Presbyterian Church of Ireland, and the Free Presbyterian Church of Ulster.

Methodism

The *UK Christian Handbook 1996/97* gives a figure of 1,300,000 *Methodists* in the UK. There are 7,627 Methodist places of worship recorded in the Registrar General's list of certified places of worship. *Methodism* is the second most numerous *Protestant* tradition in the UK and is in the *Free Church* stream of Christianity. Its origins go back to the *Evangelical Revival* of the eighteenth century and specifically to the religious movement led by John Wesley, aided by his brother, the hymn writer Charles Wesley.

The Methodist Church of Great Britain covering England, Scotland and Wales is the largest *Methodist* body. Smaller *Methodist* bodies are the Methodist Church in Ireland, the Free Methodist Church, the Wesleyan Reform Union, and the Independent Methodist Connexion. *Methodist* numerical strength is concentrated in England, especially in the South West, and the northern counties.

The word *Methodist* was used to describe the systematic and methodical approaches to Christian conduct and training that were adopted by its founders, John and Charles Wesley within their Society, which began as a fellowship within the Church of England. *Methodism* is organised on the basis of local *congregations* grouped together into what are known as *circuits*, each with a *Superintendent Minister*. These circuits are then part of wider regional bodies known as *Districts*.

Each *District* is overseen by a *Chairman*, who is a senior ordained *minister*, and all are governed by a national *Conference*, which annually appoints a senior ordained *minister* as *President* of the Methodist Conference and a senior lay person as *Vice-President*. *Methodists* are noted for their emphasis upon pastoral care by lay people; for the large proportion of worship services led by lay *Local Preachers*; for the use of hymns to express their faith, and for

emphasising that the Christian *Gospel* is for all people.

Baptist movement

The *Baptist* movement emerged at the beginning of the sixteenth century. Today *Baptists* are organised into four main *Unions* of churches with some overlap of membership: these are the Baptist Union of Great Britain (the largest), the Baptist Union of Scotland, the Baptist Union of Wales, and the Baptist Union of Ireland. There are, however, also smaller groups of *Seventh Day* and *Strict Baptists*. The largest number of *Baptists* are to be found in the counties to the north of London and around the Bristol Channel, as well as to some extent in the rest of south-east England.

The *UK Christian Handbook 1996/97* gives a figure of 600,000 *Baptists* in the UK, and in England and Wales the Registrar General lists 3,333 certified *Baptist* places of worship. The word *Baptist* is used because of this tradition's practice of reserving *baptism* as a rite of Christian initiation for those who have confessed personal Christian faith rather than administering it to infants. Other than in exceptional circumstances (such as on medical grounds), *baptism* is administered in *Baptist congregations* by complete immersion in water.

The individual *congregation* is the basic unit of Baptist Church life. *Congregations* are grouped together into *Districts* which often operate at the level of large towns, small cities or counties. At the regional level there are *Associations*, which sometimes cover a number of counties. Regional level leadership is provided by *Area Superintendents*. *These are* senior ordained *ministers* who operate in what are called *Areas*, which generally incorporate a number of *Associations*. Each *Union* has a governing *Council* and holds an annual *Assembly*.

Congregationalism

Congregationalism goes back to the early *Puritan Separatists* from the Elizabethan Church. It grew with the imposition of the *Book of Common Prayer* in 1662, following the Restoration of the

Monarchy following the Commonwealth and the Protectorate. In Ireland, the Congregational Union of Ireland is the main representative of this *Congregational* tradition.

Congregationalists accounted for seventy per cent of the membership of the United Reformed Church at its formation in 1972. The United Reformed Church, which has *congregations* in England, Wales and Scotland, and combines elements of both *Congregational* and *Presbyterian* patterns of Church government as well as those of the *Churches of Christ*. Local *congregations* are grouped into *Districts*, and *Districts* into twelve *Provinces*, each with a *Provincial Moderator.*

The *UK Christian Handbook 1996/97* does not give a separate community figure for Christians in the *Congregationalist* tradition in the UK. It does, however, give a combined membership figure of 69,976 for *Congregationalist* Churches in the UK, and the Registrar General's list for England and Wales gives 1,379 certified *Congregationalist* places of worship.

Continuing *Congregational* groups which did not join the United Reformed Church include the Union of Welsh Independents, the Scottish Congregational Church, the Congregational Federation (in England) and the Evangelical Fellowship of Congregational Churches. In addition, there are a number of totally unaffiliated *Congregational* congregations which, at the time of the formation of the United Reformed Church, stated that they would not join any other body, with their structures being similar to those of the *Baptists.*

Salvation Army

The Salvation Army was founded by William Booth who, in the 19th century, tried to respond to both the social and the spiritual needs of the industrial working class. The *UK Christian Handbook 1996/97* does not give a separate community figure for *Salvationists* in the UK but it does give a combined figure of 58,962 for officers, soldiers and adherents in the UK and the Registrar General's list for England and Wales gives 945 certified Salvation Army places of worship.

Its members can be recognised by their distinctive uniforms and its officers have military-style ranks. It is well known for its social service projects among the poor and homeless. The Salvation Army is organised into local *corps*, which are then grouped into regional level *Divisions.* It does not administer the sacraments of *baptism* or the *eucharist* but is firmly within the *Evangelical* Christian tradition.

Lutheran

Compared with continental Europe, the *Lutheran* Christian tradition is very small in the UK. The *UK Christian Handbook 1996/97* does not give a separate community figure for Christians in the *Lutheran* tradition in the UK, although it gives a figure of 14,025 members in the UK. The Registrar General's list for England and Wales does not keep separate cumulative totals of certified *Lutheran* places of worship. Most *Lutheran* congregations in the UK have a significant proportion of members who are of German or Scandanavian descent.

Moravian

The *Moravian* tradition, which traces its origins to 1457 in what is now the Czech Republic, has a small presence in the UK and Ireland. The *UK Christian Handbook 1996/97* does not give a separate community figure for Christians in the *Moravian* tradition in the UK, although it does give a formal church membership figure of 4,103. The Registrar General's list for England and Wales does not keep separate cumulative totals of *Moravian* places of worship.

The Moravian Church is *Free Church* and *Evangelical* in orientation while having an *episcopal* form of Church Government. Local Churches are grouped into *Districts* and *Districts* which together form the British Moravian Church Province. The *Unity (International) Synod* meets every seven years.

Brethren

The *Brethren* movement was formed in the nineteenth century with Plymouth as an important geographical centre. The *UK Christian Handbook 1996/97* does not give a separate community figure for Brethren in the UK, but gives a membership estimate of 80,397 in the UK and the Registrar General's list for England and Wales gives 952 certified *Brethren* places of worship.

The popular name of "Plymouth Brethren" is derived from the movement's place of origin, although its members have never accepted this designation, preferring the terminology of Christian Brethren. There are also other *Brethren* groups, such as those known as the Exclusive Brethren and the Churches of God in the British Isles and Overseas. Churches of the *Brethren* tradition are local, independent *congregations* following what they understand to be the pattern of Christianity found in the *New Testament*.

Pentecostal Churches

Pentecostal Churches include the Assemblies of God, the Elim Pentecostal Church, the Apostolic Church and a significant number of black-majority Churches, many of which have roots in Caribbean, North American and indigenous African forms of Christianity. The *UK Christian Handbook 1996/97* gives a figure of 400,000 *Pentecostalists* in the UK. The Registrar General's list of certified places of worship in England and Wales does not keep a separate running total of churches under the category of *Pentecostalist*.

Black-Majority Churches

The black-majority Churches are a fast-growing and increasingly significant section of the Christian community in the UK. These Churches are very diverse in terms of their doctrines, practices and forms of Church organisation. They range from *Pentecostal* and *Holiness* Churches, through to those of *Sabbatarian* and other traditions.

Some of these Churches, such as the New Testament Church of God or the Church of God of Prophecy, are becoming numerically significant. Others are quite local and consist of only one or two *congregations*, although they quite often co-operate with other larger groups within the framework of co-ordinating organisations such as the International Ministerial Council of Great Britain and the Council of African and Afro-Caribbean Churches.

House Churches

Over the past quarter of a century, a number of independent *House Churches* have been established under local leaderships which have gradually built patterns of wider networking and association. These Churches have developed new forms of worship which have often proved attractive to young people. The *UK Christian Handbook 1996/7* gives approximately 300,000 Christians involved in the movement.

Quakers and Unitarians

The Religious Society of Friends was founded out of the sixteenth century life and work of George Fox. Today, alongside a recognisably *Christian Quaker* tradition, a *Universalist Quaker* tradition has also emerged. *Quakers* do not use creeds, have no ordained ministers, embrace pacifism and have a distinctive style of worship rooted in shared silence and decision-making which aims at consensus. The *UK Christian Handbook 1996/97* does not give separate community or active membership figures for the Society of Friends.

Unitarian Churches had their origins in the seventeenth century. In the nineteenth and twentieth centuries there has been a strong influence from the North American Unitarian Universalist Church. The *UK Christian Handbook 1996/97* does not give a separate community figure for *Unitarians* in the UK, although it does give a figure of 8,000 members. The Registrar General's list gives 180 certified *Unitarian* places of worship.

Ecumenical Structures

The Council of Churches for Britain and Ireland (CCBI) was founded in 1990 as a result of a so-called *Inter-Church Process* which was known as "Not Strangers But Pilgrims" and it replaced the former British Council of Churches. Amongst its thirty members are some of the largest Churches, including the Roman Catholic Church as well as a number of smaller Churches.

It relates to a number of *ecumenical* networks and organisations in Britain and Ireland and, as in the case of the other similar bodies operating at the levels of the four individual nations, it is known as an *ecumenical instrument*. The CCBI works largely through a series of *Networks*, *Agencies* and *Commissions* (see the Christian organisational listings).

The national *ecumenical instruments* are Churches Together in England (CTE), Action of Churches Together in Scotland (ACTS), Churches Together in Wales (CYTUN), the Irish Council of Churches (ICC) and Irish Inter-Church Meeting (IICM). The Free Church Federal Council performs an important function by co-ordinating representation of the numerically smaller *Free Church* denominations on many of the *Networks*, *Agencies* and *Commissions* of the CCBI and the CTE.

At a local level, many individual *congregations* and *parishes* co-operate in what are known as local *Councils of Churches* or local *Churches Together* groups (of which there are approximately 55 in England) or in what were originally called *Local Ecumenical Projects* and are now known as *Local Ecumenical Partnerships* (LEPs), of which there are approximately 800 in England. Member Churches of Churches Together in England are also working closely together in fifty so-called *Intermediate Bodies*. These operate at a level approximating to a county and are serviced by a full or part-time *ecumenical* officer.

Other Interdenominational Networks

In addition to the Churches involved in these structures, there are also networks which link together other national bodies and local congregations which understand their commitment to *Evangelical* Christian tradition as requiring them not to be directly involved in these formal *ecumenical* structures. There is, for example, a Fellowship of Independent Evangelical Churches (FIEC) which operates throughout the UK and there is also the Evangelical Alliance which links both Churches and other Christian bodies which assent to its basis of faith and belief.

Personnel

Local Leadership
Unordained members of the Church are generally known as the *laity* (from the Greek word *laos*, meaning people). In some *Protestant* Churches the *laity* can, in principle at least, conduct all the ceremonies, rites and functions of the Church, even if in practice these are usually carried out by designated leaders.

Ordained leadership
The names and functions of the designated religious leadership of various Christian Churches vary according to their tradition. Nevertheless, broad categories of personnel can be discerned among *ordained* (set apart and recognised) leaders of the *Roman Catholic*, *Orthodox* and *Protestant* Churches.

Among some of the Churches which have a shorter history in the UK, and which have geographical origins in Africa and the Caribbean, an even wider variety of titles and functions can be found. For example, among a number of the African Churches there is a specific office of *prophet* or *prophetess* and another of *apostle*. Other Christian groups within the *House Church* and *Restorationist* movements recognise leaders who have wider than local ministries and special gifts of ministry as *apostles* (a word which other Christians generally reserve for the first *disciples* of Jesus who are believed to have had a uniquely special role within the Christian community).

In the *Roman Catholic*, *Anglican* and *Orthodox* traditions, *ordained* leadership at the local level is provided by religious leaders and functionaries who are known as *priests*. In the Western *Roman Catholic* tradition *priests* are not allowed to marry, although some married former *Anglican priests* have recently been *ordained*, or conditionally *ordained*, as *Roman Catholic priests*. In the *Anglican* and *Orthodox* tradition *priests* may be married. In these traditions, presiding at the *Eucharist* is reserved for *priests*.

Priests are also authorised to *baptise* and to preach. In these traditions, *priests* are seen both as representing the people to God and also as representing Christ to the *congregation*, as the focal points through whom God cares for the Christian community. This is especially believed to be the case in the *Eucharist*.

In the *Anglican* tradition authorised lay people, known as *Readers*, can preach. There is also an *ordained* order of ministry known as *deacons* or the *diaconate* (from the Greek word - *diakonos*, meaning servant). This is technically an order in its own right, although *priests*-to-be are first of all ordained *deacon* as a stage on the way to full *ordination* to the *priesthood*. The *diaconate* exists in other Christian traditions, too, sometimes as a permanent order of ministry.

Protestant Churches generally have a more functional view of their local *ordained* leadership. In the *Protestant* Churches *ordained* local leaders are known as *ministers* (Baptist, Methodist, United Reformed Church, Church of Scotland as well as other Reformed Churches) or as pastors (*Christian Brethren*, many branches of the *Pentecostal* movement, and some *Baptist churches*).

In the *Roman Catholic* and *Orthodox* traditions the *priesthood* is not open to women. Women are now able to be ordained as *priests* in the Churches of the *Anglican* tradition in England, Ireland, Scotland and Wales. For many years there have been divided convictions on this issue even though there have been been women *priests* in other parts of the worldwide *Anglican* tradition. Tensions still remain within the Churches which have *ordained* women as *priests*. In the *Protestant* Churches women are generally able to serve as local *ministers* and some have also assumed responsibilities in regional and national leadership.

Pastoral Care
In all Churches, local *clergy* have a role in the *pastoral* care of the *congregation* as well as in preaching and administering the sacraments. In the understanding of the established Church of England, the *priest's* duty of *pastoral care* extends to everyone within the geographical area of the *parish*, regardless of whether or not they are *Anglican* or even Christian. A similar duty applies to ministers of the established Church of Scotland. In many Churches designated lay Christians also share in the *pastoral* ministry of the Church.

Regional, National and International Leadership
In the *Orthodox*, *Roman Catholic* and *Anglican* traditions the focus of unity of the Church's leadership is vested in the *bishop*. *Bishops* are senior *clergy* who are responsible for the geographical and ecclesiastical areas known as *dioceses*. *Roman Catholic* bishops and *priests* do not marry. *Anglican* bishops may be married, but whilst *Orthodox* priests may marry before ordination as *priests*, the office of *bishop* in the *Orthodox* Churches is open only to *monks* and therefore only to *priests* who are not married or who have become widowers.

In the *Protestant* Churches regional leaders are known by a wide variety of titles such as *Provincial Moderator* (United Reformed Church) *Area Superintendent* (*Baptists*), and *District Chairman* (*Methodist*). The Church of England has two *Archbishops*, namely, the *Archbishop of Canterbury* and the *Archbishop of York*. The *Archbishop of Canterbury* is the Church of England's senior *bishop* and is also recognised as having a special seniority in the worldwide *Anglican* communion.

In the *Protestant* Churches national leaders usually have very functional titles such as *General Secretary* (Baptist Union of Great Britain), *Moderator* of the *General Assembly* (Church of Scotland) or *President of the Conference* (Methodist Church). These indicate the different kinds of roles in each of the Churches. In general, *General Secretaryships* are stipendiary posts which are held for several years, whilst the offices of *Moderators of Assembly* and those of *Presidents* tend to be honorary officers, appointed annually (with the exception of the *Moderator* of the Free Church Federal Council who is appointed on a four yearly basis).

In the *Orthodox* Churches, senior *Archbishops* are known by the title of *Patriarch* and they may have responsibilities which extend across national boundaries. In the Roman Catholic Church in some parts of the world there are also *Patriarchs*. A group of senior *bishops* and *Archbishops* from all over the world are members of the College of *Cardinals*. *Cardinals* under eighty years of age at the time of an election choose the *Pope* (meaning *Father*) who is installed as *Bishop of Rome* and is recognised as the chief *pastor* of the Roman Catholic Church throughout the world. He is often referred to by *Roman Catholics* as the *Holy Father*.

Among *Protestant* Churches, the international leadership, like the national leadership, has a variety of more functional titles. In keeping with the military imagery used by the Salvation Army, the leader of the Salvation Army worldwide is known as *General*. The World Alliance of Reformed Churches, the Lutheran World Federation and the Baptist World Alliance all have *General Secretaries*. Each of these bodies has a mainly co-ordinating and consultative role in contrast to the more integrated and hierarchical structure of the Salvation Army.

FURTHER READING

Attwater, D, *A Dictionary of Mary*, P J Kennedy, Longmans, 1957.

Ballard, P and Jones, D (eds), *This Land and People: Y Wlad a'r Bobl Hyn: A Symposium on Christian and Welsh National Identity*, Collegiate Centre of Theology, University College, Cardiff (revised edition) 1980.

Barraclough, G (ed), *The Christian World*, Abrams, London, 1981.

Barrett, D, *The World Christian Encyclopaedia: A Comparative Study of Churches and Religions in the Modern World, AD1900-2000*, Oxford University Press, Oxford, 1982.

Bettenson, H, *Documents of the Christian Church*, Oxford University Press, London, 1975.

Bisset, P, *The Kirk and Her Scotland*, Handsel Press, Edinburgh, 1986.

Bowden, J, *Dictionary of Christian Theology*, SCM Press, London, 1983.

Brierley, P, *Christianity by Numbers, No1*, Christian Research Association, London, 1989 (updated 1994).

Brierley, P, *Irish Christian Handbook, 1995-96*, Christian Research Association, London, 1994.

Brierley, P, *UK Christian Handbook 1996/97*, Christian Research Association, London, 1996.

Brierley, P & Macdonald, F, *Prospects for Scotland 2000*, Christian Research Association, London, 1995.

Catholic Bishops' Conference of England and Wales, *What Are We to Teach?*, Catholic Education Service, London, 1994.

Catholic Church, *Catechism of the Catholic Church*, Geoffrey Chapman, London, 1994.

Chadwick, O, *The History of Christianity*, Weidenfeld & Nicolson, London, 1995.

Childs, J F, and Macquarrie, J (eds), *A New Dictionary of Christian Ethics*, SCM, London, (2nd edition) 1987.

Coggins, R J, and Houlden, J L, *A Dictionary of Biblical Interpretation*, SCM, London, 1990.

Cross, F L, and Livingstone, E A (eds), *Oxford Dictionary of the Christian Church*, Oxford University Press, London, (3rd revised edition) 1997.

Davies, J G, *A New Dictionary of Liturgy and Worship*, SCM, London, 1986.

Dickens, A G, *The English Reformation*, Collins, London, 1967.

Dupre, L and Saliers, D E (eds), *Christian Spirituality: Reformation and Modern*, SCM, London, 1989.

Edwards, D L, *Christian England*, Collins, London, 1985.

Gerloff, R, *A Plea for British Black Theologies: The Black Church Movement in Britain in its Transatlantic Cultural and Theological Interaction, Parts I and II*, Peter Lang, Frankfurt am Main, Germany, 1992.

Hastings, A, *A History of English Christianity, 1920-1985*, Collins, London, 1986.

Keeley, R (ed), *The Lion Handbook of Christian Belief*, Lion Publishing, Tring, 1982.

Latourette, K, *A History of Christianity, (2 volumes)*, Harper and Row, London, 1975.

Lossky, N; Bonino, M; Pobee, J; Stransky, T; Wainwright G; and Webb, P, *Dictionary of the Ecumenical Movement*, World Council of Churches, Geneva, 1991.

Marthaler, B, *The Creed*, Twenty-Third Publications, 1993 (revised edition).

McAdoo, H R, *Anglican Heritage*, Canterbury Press, Norwich, 1991.

McBrien, R P, *Catholicism*, Chapman, 1980.

McGinn, B and Meyendorff, J (eds), *Christian Spirituality: Origins to the Twelfth Century*, SCM, London, 1986.

McKenzie, P, *The Christians: Their Practices and Beliefs*, SPCK, London, 1988.

McManners, J (ed), *The Oxford Illustrated History of Christianity*, Oxford University Press, Oxford, 1990.

Nunn, Roger, *This Growing Unity: A Handbook on Ecumenical Development in the Counties, Large Cities and New Towns of England*, Churches Together in England (Publications), London, 1995.

Raitt, J (ed), *Christian Spirituality: High Middle Ages and Reformation*, SCM, London, 1987.

Smart, N, *The Phenomenon of Christianity*, Collins, London, 1979.

Strange, R, *The Catholic Faith*, Oxford University Press, 1985.

Wakefield, G, *A Dictionary of Christian Spirituality*, SCM, London, 1983.

Walker, A, *Restoring the Kingdom: The Radical Christianity of the House Church Movement*, Hodder and Stoughton, London, 1988.

Ware, Kallistos, *The Orthodox Way*, Mowbray, London, 1987.

Welch, Elizabeth and Winfield, Flora, *Travelling Together: A Handbook on Local Ecumenical Partnerships*, Churches Together in England (Publications), London, 1995.

CHRISTIAN UNITED KINGDOM ORGANISATIONS

There is an enormous range of other Christian organisations of varied kinds including the Christian Ecology Group, the Christian Socialist Movement and many others. Details of many of these organisations can be found in the *UK Christian Handbook.*

The format of the Christian listings varies from the directory's normal layout. Because of the large number of Christian places of worship and local organisations and since the structures of the Churches are very developed, information is given only on UK, national and regional levels of organisation.

Churches which operate at the level of one country alone (eg the Church of England) are listed in the "Christian National and Regional Listings" section under the county concerned rather than in this section. The "affiliations" field is not normally used in this chapter and the "traditions" field is also not normally used where the tradition in question is already clearly indicated in the organisation's title.

UNITED KINGDOM ECUMENICAL INSTRUMENTS

Council of Churches for Britain and Ireland
Inter-Church House, 35–41 Lower Marsh, London, SE1 7RL
Tel: 0171-620-4444 Tel: 01727-852921 (h)
Fax: 0171-928-0010
Contact: Revd John P Reardon
Position: General Secretary
Activities: Umbrella, visits, youth, women, books, inter-faith
Languages: Welsh, Greek, Serbian
CCBI works closely with the national ecumenical bodies.

Member Bodies:
Baptist Union of Great Britain
Cherubim and Seraphim Council of Churches
Church in Wales
Church of England
Church of Ireland
Church of Scotland
Congregational Federation
Council of African and African-Caribbean
    Churches UK
Council of Oriental Orthodox Churches
Free Church Federal Council
Greek Orthodox Church
Independent Methodist Churches
International Ministerial Council of Great Britain
Joint Council for Anglo-Caribbean Churches
Lutheran Council of Great Britain
Methodist Church
Methodist Church in Ireland
Moravian Church
New Testament Assembly
Presbyterian Church of Wales
Religious Society of Friends
Roman Catholic Church in England and Wales
Roman Catholic Church in Scotland
Russian Orthodox Church
Salvation Army
Scottish Congregational Church
Scottish Episcopal Church
Serbian Orthodox Church
Undeb Yr Annibynwyr Cymraeg (Union of Welsh
    Independents)
United Free Church of Scotland
United Reformed Church
Wesleyan Holiness Church

Bodies in Association:
Action by Christians Against Torture
Afro-West Indian United Council of Churches
Association of Centres of Adult Theological
  Education
Association of Interchurch Families in Britain and
  Ireland
Centre for Black and White Christian Partnership
Christian Education Movement
Christianity and the Future of Europe
Church Action on Poverty
Churches' Council for Health and Healing
Churches' East West European Relations Network
Ecumenical Committee for Corporate
  Responsibility
Feed the Minds
Fellowship of Prayer for Unity
Fellowship of St Alban and St Sergius
Iona Community
Irish School of Ecumenics
Living Stones
National Association of Christian Communities
  and Networks
National Christian Education Council
New Assembly of Churches
William Temple Foundation
Women's Inter Church Consultative Committee
Young Men's Christian Association
Young Women's Christian Association

Observers:
Irish Episcopal Conference

Commissions:
Churches' Commission for Inter-Faith Relations
Churches' Commission for Racial Justice
Churches' Commission on Mission

Agencies:
Christian Aid
Christians Abroad
Catholic Fund for Overseas Development
Churches' Commission on Overseas Students
One World Week
Scottish Catholic International Aid Fund

Formal Networks:
Aids Monitoring Group
Churches' Advisory Group for Local Broadcasting
Churches' Community Work Alliance
Churches' Human Rights Forum
Churches' Joint Education Policy Committee
Churches' Peace Forum

Churches' Stewardship Network
Consultative Group on Ministry Among Children
Environmental Issues Network
International Affairs Liaison Group
Justice, Peace and the Integrity of Creation Group
Social Responsibility Consultation

UNITED KINGDOM GROUPINGS OF CHURCHES

Afro-West Indian United Council of Churches
New Testament Church of God, Arcadian
Gardens, High Road, Wood Green, London, N22
Tel: 0181-888-9427
Contact: Revd Eric Brown
Position: General Secretary
Affiliations: Inter Faith Network for the UK

Member Bodies include:
Bibleway Church of our Lord Jesus Christ
  Worldwide
Community Church of God
Melchisedek Spiritual Baptist Church
New Testament Assembly
New Testament Church of God
Pentecostal Revival Fellowship
Redemption Church of God
Shiloh United Church of Christ Apostolic
  Worldwide
United Church of God
Wesleyan Holiness Church

Cherubim & Seraphim Council of Churches UK
The Prayer House, 175 Earlham Grove, Forest
Gate, London, E7 9AP
Tel: 0181-534-5101 **Tel:** 0181-671-0144 (h)
Fax: 0181-534-0378
Contact: Most Revd J A Odufona
Position: Chairman
Activities: Worship, resource, inter-faith
Traditions: African Independent
Other Languages: Yoruba (Nigerian)
The Council was founded in 1976 to embrace all
Cherubim and Seraphim Churches in the UK and
to promote inter-relationships among all Christian
Churches in the UK and all over the world.

Council of African & African-Caribbean Churches (UK)
31 Norton House, Sidney Road, Stockwell,
London, SW9 0UJ (h)

Tel: 0171-274-5589 (h)
Contact: Most Revd Father Oluwole Aremu Abiola
Position: Chairman
Activities: Umbrella
Traditions: African Independent, Pentecostal
Other Languages: Yoruba, Twi, French, Patua
Affiliations: Inter Faith Network for the UK
The Council is a medium through which African and Afro-Caribbean Churches may work with a joint effort to perform those services which Churches cannot conveniently provide themselves, especially in the training of ministers and officers.

Member Bodies Include:
Aladura International Church
Celestial Church of Christ
Cherubim and Seraphim Church (Imole)
Cherubim and Seraphim Church Movement
Cherubim and Seraphim Society St Stephen's
     Church
Christ Apostolic Church
Christ the King Pentecostal Church
Christ the Resurrection Church
Church of Salvation
Church of the Lord Aladura
Church of the Lord Brotherhood
Crystal El-Shaddai Church of Christ
Divine Prayer Society, 1944
ESO New Temple Cherubim and Seraphim
     Church
Eternal Glory Church
Eternal Order of Cherubim and Seraphim
Eternal Order of the Morning Star
Holy Emmanuel Church of Christ
Holy Mount Zion Revival Church
Holy Order of Cherubim and Seraphim Church
Imimsi Oluwa Cherubim and Seraphim Church
Iraw Ogo Jeusu
Kimbanguist Church
Love Divine Church of Christ
Melchisedec Spiritual Baptist Church
Musama Disco Christo Church
Newborn Apostolic Church
Pentecostal Revival Church of Christ
Redeemed Church of Christ Cherubim and
     Seraphim
St James Cherubim and Seraphim Redemption
     Church
St Francis Spiritual Baptist Church
St John the Divine Spiritual Baptist Church
United Prayerist of Christ Church

Council of Oriental Orthodox Churches UK
34 Chertsey Road, Church Square, Shepperton, Middlesex, TW17 9LF
Tel: 01932-232913   **Tel:** 0181-368-8447
Fax: 0181-368-8447
Contact: Aziz M A Nour
Position: Secretary
Activities: Resource, media, umbrella, visits youth, elderly, women, newsletters, books, inter-faith
Other Languages: Arabic, Armenian, Coptic, Amharic
This ecumenical body co-ordinates the ecumenical and interfaith activities in the UK and Ireland of the Orthodox Churches which are in full communion with each other. Each Church has a supreme head who usually resides outside the UK.

Member Bodies:
Armenian Apostolic Church
Coptic Orthodox Church
Eritrean Orthodox Church
Ethiopian Orthodox Church
Syrian Orthodox Church
Syro Indian Church

Evangelical Alliance UK
Whitefield House, 186 Kennington Park Road, London, SE11 4BT
Tel: 0171-207-2100   **Fax:** 0171-207-2150
EMail: enquiry@eauk.org
Contact: Revd Joel Edwards
Position: UK Director
Activities: Umbrella, newsletters
Represents Evangelical views on social, political and moral issues. Has 50,000 individuals; 3,000 local churches and 700 groups in membership. There are Local Evangelical Fellowships grouping a number of local churches and ministries in the following areas:

Local Evangelical Fellowships:
Bath
Beckenham
Brent
Brentwood
Brighton and Hove
Bristol
Bromley
Hackney
Hull
Inverness
Ipswich
King's Lynn

Leyton
Manchester (Network)
Merseyside EA Trust (MEAT)
Mid-Cotswolds EA (MCEA)
Paisley
Peterborough (PACE)
Portsmouth
South East Essex (SEELEF)
South Wessex EA (SWEA)
Southampton
Taunton
Teeside
Thamesdown
Tiverton
Torbay
Tower Hamlets
Wolverhampton

Free Church Federal Council
27 Tavistock Square, London, WC1H 9HH
Tel: 0171-387-8413 **Fax:** 0171-383-0150
Contact: Revd Geoffrey H Roper
Position: General Secretary
Activities: Umbrella, women, newsletters
Other Languages: Welsh
Co-ordinates and represents nineteen constituent denominations and includes a Women's Council, an education committee and a Health Care Chaplaincy Board. The Moderator of the Council is the public representative of the Free Churches at national level.

Members:
Afro-West Indian United Council of Churches
Assemblies of God
Baptist Union of Great Britain
Baptist Union of Wales
Congregational Federation
Council of African and Afro-Caribbean Churches UK
Countess of Huntingdon's Connexion
Fellowship of Churches of Christ
Free Church of England
Independent Methodist Churches
Methodist Church
Moravian ChurchNew Testament Church of God
Old Baptist Union
Presbyterian Church of Wales
Salvation Army
Union of Welsh Independents
United Reformed Church in the United Kingdom
Wesleyan Reform Union

International Ministerial Council of Great Britain
55 Tudor Walk, Watford, Hertfordshire, WD2 4NY
Tel: 01923-239266 **Fax:** 01923-239266
Contact: Revd S M Douglas
Position: General Secretary
Activities: Umbrella, books, inter-faith
Traditions: Ecumenical
Other Languages: African, Asian, German, Portuguese
The only Christian body which accepts membership of all faiths that confess God whether in oneness or trinity, we form relationships with countries whose government is other than Christian.

Members based in the UK:
Amazing Grace International Worship Centre
Beneficial Veracious Christ Church
Bethel Church of Christ (Apostolic)
Bethel Church of Jesus Christ
Born Again Evangelistic Ministry
Bread of Life Ministries
British Enabling Committee for the Pentecostal Association of Ghana
Calvary Believers Church International
Calvary Healing Temple
Christ Believers Fellowship
Christ Foundation Bible Church
Christ is Alive Ministries
Christian Care Fellowship
Christian Faith Foundation Ministries
Christians in Action (Africa) Ministries
Church of the Lord Jesus Christ Apostolic
Church of the Lord, The
Christ Life Mission Church
Christ Resurrection Souls Revival Ministry
Community of Christ in London
Divine Healing Church of Christ (Pentecostal)
Divine Prayer Society, 1944
Evangelical Mission of Europe
Foundation of Life Ministries
Greater Grace Bible Fellowship
God's Vision Ministry
Harvestime Evangelical Ministries International
Holy Moses Pentecostal Church
International Worship Centre
Jehovah El-Shaddai Ministries
Jesus Christ Healing Ministries
Jesus Christ of Nazareth International Church
Jesus is Lord Outreach Ministries International
Jesus Miracles Ministries

Jordan River Pentecostal Church
Latter Rain Gospel Ministries International
Living Springs International Church
Living Tower Ministries International
Living Word Church
New Life International Ministries
Park Lane Methodist Church
Pentecostal Association of Ghana
Pentecostal Flames Ministry International
Pentecostal Revival Church of Christ
Power Pentecostal Church (Christ Message
    Ministry)
Quex Road Methodist Church
Restoration Christian Outreach Ministries
Resurrection Power Evangelistic Ministries
Rhema Ministries International
Shiloh United Church of Christ
Shiloh United Church of Christ Apostolic
    Worldwide
Tehillah Prophetic Ministries
Torchbearers Worldwide Ministry
Universal Prayer Group Ministries
Walworth Methodist Church
Word of Life Bible College
Worldwide Gospel Outreach Ministry
Zamar International Ministries

Joint Council for Anglo-Caribbean Churches
141 Railton Road, Brixton, London, SE24 0LT
Tel: 0171-733-2812
Contact: Revd Esme Beswick
Position: General Secretary
Activities: Youth, inter-faith
Traditions: Pentecostal

Member Bodies include:
Bible Truth Church of God
Church of God Assembly
Church of God Independent
Church of God Pentecostal
Firstborn Church of the Living God
Humble Heart Church
Mount Hermon Church of God Assembly
Mount Refuge Firstborn Church
New Testament Assembly
Union Reformed Church
Universal Group of Apostles
Zion Pentecostal Church of God

New Assembly of Churches
15 Oldridge Road, Balham, Wandsworth,
London, SW12 8PL
Tel: 0181-673-0595 **Fax:** 0181-675-8768

Contact: Revd Carmel E Jones
Position: Chief Executive Officer
Activities: Umbrella, youth, elderly, women,
inter-faith
Traditions: Pentecostal

Member Bodies include:
African Methodist Zion Church
All Nations Christian Fellowship
Assemblies of the First Born
Calvary Church of God in Christ
Church of God Worldwide Mission Faith Chapel
International Fellowship for Christ
New Life Assembly
New Testament Assembly
New Testament Church of God
Seventh Day Adventists
Shiloh United Church of Christ Apostolic

CHURCHES OPERATING AT A UNITED KINGDOM OR GREAT BRITAIN LEVEL

Aladura International Church (UK & Overseas)
31 Norton House, Sidney Road, Stockwell,
London, SW9 0UJ (h)
Tel: 0171-274-5589 (h)
Contact: Most Revd Father Oluwole Aremu
Abiola
Position: General Superintendent
Traditions: African Independent
Other Languages: Yoruba, Twi, Patua, French
Its aim is to give professionally trained people the
opportunity to minister to those around them on
completion of their studies, using their spare time to
preach, teach and propagate the Gospel.

Apostolic Church, The
PO Box 389, 24/27 St Helens Road, Swansea,
West Glamorgan, SA1 1ZH
Tel: 01792-473992 **Fax:** 01792-474087
Contact: Mark Davies
Position: Administrative Secretary
Activities: Newsletters, books
Traditions: Pentecostal

Armenian Apostolic Oriental Orthodox Church
St Peter's Church, Cranley Gardens, London,
SW7 3BB
Tel: 0171-937-0152
Contact: Rt Revd Archbishop Y Gizirian
Position: Primate

Assemblies of God in Great Britain & Ireland
16 Bridgford Road, West Bridgford, Nottingham,
Nottinghamshire, NG2 6AF
Tel: 0115-981-1188 **Fax:** 0115-981-3377
Contact: Basil D Varnam
Position: Administrator
Traditions: Pentecostal
An organisation of more than 650 autonomous
churches in the British Isles.

Assyrian Church of the East
89 Leighton Road, London, W13 9DR
Tel: 0181-579-7259
Contact: Revd Yonan Yowel Yonan
Position: Archdeacon
Traditions: Orthodox

Baptist Union of Great Britain
Baptist House, P O Box 44, 129 Broadway,
Didcot, Oxfordshire, 0X11 8RT
Tel: 01235-512077
EMail: 100442.1750@compuserve.com
Contact: Revd David Coffey
Position: General Secretary
Activities: Resource, umbrella, youth, elderly,
women, newsletters, books
Traditions: Free Church

Bulgarian Orthodox Church
188 Queen's Gate, London, SW7 5ML (h)
Tel: 0171-5844607 (h)
Contact: Revd Simeon Iliev
Activities: Worship
Other Languages: Bulgarian

Byelorussian Autocephalic Orthodox Church
Holy Mother of God of Zyrovicy Church,
Chapel Road, Rainsborough, Prestwich,
Manchester, Greater Manchester, M22 4JW
Tel: 0161-740-8230
Contact: Very Revd Father John Ababurko
Position: Administrator

Coptic Orthodox Church
Allen Street, London, W8 6UX
Tel: 0171-937-5782 **Tel:** 0171-385-1991 (h)
Fax: 0171-385-6832
Contact: Revd Fr Antonious T Shenouda
Position: Priest in Charge
Activities: Worship
Other Languages: Arabic, Coptic

Countess of Huntingdon's Connexion
69 Jubilee Road, Middleton, Manchester, Greater
Manchester, M24 2LT (h)
Tel: 0161-643-4108 (h)
Contact: Marjorie Jacques Crossley
Position: Secretary
Activities: Youth, elderly, newsletters
Traditions: Free Church
Affiliations: Free Church Federal Council

Eritrean Orthodox Church (St Michael)
11 Anfield Close, Weir Road, London, SW12
0NT
Tel: 0171-627-8296 (h) **Fax:** 0181-675-5115
Contact: Father Yohannes Sebhatu
Position: Chair
Activities: Youth, inter-faith
Other Languages: Tigrigna, Tigre, Billen

Ethiopian Orthodox Church
253b Ladbroke Grove, London, W10 6HF
Tel: 0181-960-3848
Contact: Very Revd Aragawi W Gabriel
Position: Head Priest

Fellowship of Churches of Christ
25 Robert Avenue, Erdington, Birmingham,
West Midlands, B23 5RD (h)
Tel: 0121-373-7942 (h)
Contact: Mrs Hazel Wilson
Position: Fellowship Secretary
Activities: Umbrella
Traditions: Free Church

*General Assembly of Unitarian & Free Christian
Churches*
Essex Hall, 1-6 Essex Street, London, WC2R
3HY
Tel: 0171-240-2384 **Fax:** 0171-240-3089
EMail: ga@unitarian.org.uk
Contact: Matthew Smith
Position: Information Officer
Activities: Resource, umbrella, youth, women,
newsletters, books, inter-faith
Other Languages: Welsh
Seeks to unite in fellowship those bodies which
uphold religious freedom for their members
unconstrained by creeds. The General Assembly is
the national co-ordinating body for Unitarian
congregations in Britain.

**Greek Orthodox Archdiocese of Thyateira &
Great Britain**
Thyateira House, 5 Craven Hill, London,
W2 3EN
Tel: 0171-723-4787 **Fax:** 0171-224-9301
Contact: His Eminence Archbishop Gregorios
of Thyateira and Great Britain
Position: Head of the Greek Orthodox
Archdiocese
Affiliations: Churches Together in England
Other Languages: Greek

Greek-Orthodox Patriarchate of Antioch
St Georges Antiochan Cathedral Church,
1a Redhill Street, London, NW1 4BG
Tel: 0171-383-0403 **Tel:** 0181-879-3046 (h)
Fax: 0171-383-0403
Contact: Father Samir Gholam
Position: Priest
Activities: Worship, resource, visits, youth,
women, inter-faith
Other Languages: Arabic
Antiochan Greek-Orthodox Christians in
England are under the jurisdiction of a patriarchal
vicar bishop for western Europe residing in Paris.
More recently, nine parishes have been set up in a
deanery under the same jurisdiction.

Lutheran Council of Great Britain
8 Collingham Gardens, London, SW5 0HU
Tel: 0171-373-1141
Contact: Very Revd Robert J Patkai
Position: Chairman

Methodist Church
25 Marylebone Road, London, NW1 5JR
Tel: 0171-486-5502 **Fax:** 0171-224-1510
Contact: Revd Brian E Beck
Position: Secretary of Conference
Traditions: Free Church
The Methodist Church claims and cherishes its
place in the Holy Catholic Church. It is
committed to the ecumenical movement and is
involved in many local ecumenical partnerships
and in joint worship, witness, action and mission
with other Churches.

Moravian Church in Great Britain & Ireland
Moravian Church House, 5 Muswell Hill,
London, N10 3TJ
Tel: 0181-883-3409 **Fax:** 0181-442-0112
Contact: Revd W John Hamilton McOwat

Position: Provincial Elder
Activities: Worship, resource, media, umbrella,
visits youth, elderly, women, newsletters, books,
inter-faith
Traditions: Free Church

New Testament Assembly
70 Vicarage Road, London, E10 5EA
Tel: 0181-539-2755
Contact: Revd Io Smith
Position: General Secretary
Traditions: Pentecostal

New Testament Church of God
Main House, Overstone Park, Overstone,
Northamptonshire, NN6 0AD
Tel: 01604-643311 **Fax:** 01604-790254
Contact: National Overseer
Activities: Umbrella, youth, elderly, women,
inter-faith
Traditions: Pentecostal
This organisation has a Theological College based
at 11-13 Oughton Road, Highgate, Birmingham
12 and its Principal is Revd C L Ryan, Tel: 0121-
446-6859.

Old Baptist Union Inc
79 Ainslie Wood Road, Chingford, London,
E4 9BX (h)
Tel: 0181-529-0783 **Fax:** 0181-529-0783
Contact: Mrs Aileen Thody
Position: General Secretary
Activities: Newsletter
Traditions: Free Church, Evangelical Baptist

Pioneer
PO Box 97c, Esher, Surrey, KT10 9LP
Tel: 01932-789681 **Fax:** 01932-789691
Contact: Gerald Coates
Position: Director/Leader
Activities: Worship, resource, media, umbrella,
visits, youth, elderly, women, newsletters, books,
inter-faith
Traditions: Free Church
Pioneer consists of a network of charismatic
Evangelical churches. It has several training
programmes and helped initiate the largest AIDS
initiative ACET (Aids Care Education Training)
and the prayer initiative March for Jesus.

Religious Society of Friends (Quakers)
Friends House, Euston Road, London, NW1 2BJ

Tel: 0171-387-3601   **Fax:** 0171-388-1977
Contact: Harvey Gillman
Position: Outreach Secretary
Activities: Worship, youth, newsletters, books, inter-faith
Other Languages: Welsh
Quakers spring out of the Christian tradition but their belief of God in everyone makes them open to other traditions as well. They meet together for worship in silence. They are also noted for their concern for peace and social justice.

Roman Catholic Church in England & Wales
Catholic Communications Centre, 39 Eccleston Square, Victoria, London, SW1V 1BX
Tel: 0171-233-8196   **Fax:** 0171-933-7497
EMail: 101454.103@compuserve.com
Contact: Dr Jim McDonnell
Position: Director
Activities: Media

Romanian Orthodox Church in London
186 Fleet Street, London, EC4A 2EA
Tel: 0171-242-6027   **Tel:** 0171-735-9515 (h)
Contact: Revd S P Pufulete
Position: Priest in Charge
Activities: Worship, visits, inter-faith
Other Languages: Romanian
Has parishes in Leeds and Birmingham.

Russian Orthodox Church
Cathedral of the Dormition & All Saints, 67 Ennismore Gardens, Knightsbridge, London, SW7 1NH
Tel: 01234-354374 (h)   **Fax:** 0171-584-9864
Contact: Gillian Crowe
Position: Secretary
Activities: Worship, visits, youth, newsletters, books, inter-faith
Other Languages: Russian

St James Mar Thoma Church UK
St Katherine Cree Church, 86 Leadenhall Street, London, EC3 9DH
Tel: 0181-471-2446 (h)
Contact: Revd Abey T Mammen
Position: Vicar
Activities: Worship, newsletters
Traditions: Eastern Reformed Independent
Other Languages: Malayalam, Hindi
Contact can also be made c/o Mar Thoma Centre, 22 Altmore Avenue, London, E6 2BY.

Salvation Army, The
101 Queen Victoria Street, London, EC4P 4EP
Tel: 0171-236-5222   **Fax:** 0171-236-6272
Contact: Captain William Cochrane
Position: External Relations Officer
Activities: Resource, youth, elderly, women, newsletters, books, inter-faith
Traditions: Free Church
Founded by William Booth in 1865 and operating through a network of local corps, the Army's objectives are the advancement of Christian religion and education, the relief of poverty and the provision of charitable work beneficial to society as a whole.

Serbian Orthodox Church
131 Cob Lane, Bournville, Birmingham, West Midlands, B30 1QE
Tel: 0121-458-5273   **Fax:** 0121-458-4986
Contact: Father Zebic

Seventh Day Adventist Church
British Isles Headquarters, Stanborough Park, Garstan, Watford, Hertfordshire, WD2 6JP
Tel: 01923-672251   **Fax:** 01923-893217
EMail: 74532.505@compuserve.com
Contact: John Surridge
Position: Communications Director
Activities: Youth, elderly, women, books, inter-faith
Traditions: Free Church
Other Languages: Spanish
The main purpose is to communicate the Christian Gospel. Specialised departments cater for many activities including youth, education, family life, health and temperence, international, national humanitarian aid and religious liberty.

Syrian Orthodox Church
"Antaccia", 77 Exeter Road, London, N14 5JU (h)
Tel: 0181-654-7531   **Tel:** 0181-368-8447
Fax: 0181-368-8447
Contact: Aziz M A Nour
Position: Secretary
Activities: Worship, resource, visits, youth, elderly, women, newsletters, books, inter-faith
Other Languages: Syriac, Arabic, Malayalam, Turkish
The Syrian Orthodox Church of Antioch is the first Gentile Church which was founded by Barnabas, Peter and Paul at Antioch, where the disciples were

first called Christian. Worship takes place at St Marks Church, Allen Street, Kensington, London.

Syrian Orthodox Church's Council (UK)
Antaccia, 77 Exeter Road, London, N14 5JU
Tel: 0181-368-8447 **Tel:** 01932-232-913 (h)
Fax: 0181-368-8447
Contact: Aziz M A Nour
Position: Secretary
Activities: Resource, media, umbrella, visits, youth, elderly, women, newsletters, books, inter-faith
Other Languages: Syriac, Arabic, Malayalam, Turkish
The Council endevours to promote knowledge of the Syriac language, Syriac studies, the use of ancient liturgies and Oriental Orthodoxy. We are active in the field of inter-faith and are represented on the Churches' Commission for Inter-Faith Relations.

Ukrainian Autocephalous Orthodox Church
1a Newton Avenue, Acton, London, W3 8AJ
Tel: 0181-992-4689 **Tel:** 01274-574483
Fax: 01706-521634
EMail: bohdan.mat@zen.co.uk
Contact: Very Revd Protopresbyter Mychajlo Hutorny
Position: Chairman of the Diocesan Council
Languages: Ukrainian

United Reformed Church in the United Kingdom
86 Tavistock Place, London, WC1H 9RT
Tel: 0171-916-2020 **Fax:** 0171-916-2021
Contact: Revd Anthony G Burnham
Position: General Secretary
Activities: Worship, resource, newsletters, books, inter-faith

Wesleyan Holiness Church
Holyhead Road, Birmingham, West Midlands, B21 0LA
Tel: 0121-523-7849
Contact: Revd Kecious Gray
Position: Superintendent

Wesleyan Reform Union of Churches
Church House, 123 Queen Street, Sheffield, South Yorkshire, S1 2DU
Tel: 0114-272-1938 **Fax:** 0114-272-1965
Contact: Revd E W Downing

Position: General Secretary
Traditions: Free Church

BODIES CONNECTED WITH UNITED KINGDOM ECUMENICAL INSTRUMENTS

ACATE (Association of Centres of Adult Theological Education)
The Old Deanery, Wells, Somerset, BA4 4HD
Tel: 01749-670777 **Fax:** 01749-674240
Contact: Helen Stanton
Position: Honorary Secretary
Activities: Umbrella, newsletters, books
ACATE links over 200 centres which provide theological education among adults. These include seminaries, theological colleges, courses, lay training institutions and departments, and higher education departments of Theology.

Action by Christians Against Torture
Quex Road Methodist Church, Kilburn, London, NW6 4PR
Tel: 0171-372-7347 **Tel:** 01752-843417 (h)
Fax: 01727-843417
Contact: Lois Stamelis
Position: Director
Activities: Resource, newsletters, inter-faith

Association of Interchurch Families
Inter-Church House, 35-41 Lower Marsh, London, SE1 7RL
Tel: 0171-620-4444 **Fax:** 0171-928-0010
Contact: Dr Ruth Reardon
Position: Secretary
Activities: Resource, newsletters
Other Languages: French
The Association of Interchurch Families offers an information service and a network of support for mixed (inter-denominational) marriages and interchurch families, and a voice for such families in the Churches.

Bible Society
Stonehill Green, Westlea, Swindon, Wiltshire, SN5 7DG
Tel: 01793-418100 **Fax:** 01793-418118
EMail: corpcomfbs.org.uk
Activities: Resource, books
The Bible Society aims to communicate the credibility and relevance of the Bible message through campaigning programmes at home and

overseas, in order to see the Bible 'work', changing attitudes and society.

CAFOD (Catholic Fund for Overseas Development)
Romero Close, Stockwell Road, London, SW9 9TY
Tel: 0171-733-7900 **Fax:** 0171-274-9630
Activities: Resource, youth, newsletters, books
CAFOD is one of the UK's major relief and development agencies. It funds over 1,000 development projects and emergencies in 75 countries, helping people regardless of race, religion or politics.

Canon Law Society of Great Britain & Ireland
The Good Shepherd Centre, 511 Ormeau Road, Belfast, County Antrim, BT7 3GS
Tel: 01232-491990 **Fax:** 01232-491440
Contact: The Reverend Eugene D O'Hagan
Position: Executive Secretary
Activities: Resource, newsletters, books
Traditions: Roman Catholic
Other Languages: Italian, Spanish
The society's aim is to promote the understanding of Canon Law (Catholic Church Law).

Catholic Education Service
39 Ecleston Square, London, SW1V 1BX
Tel: 0171-828-7604 **Fax:** 0171-233-9802
Contact: Mrs M M Smart
Position: Director
Activities: Resource, umbrella, newsletters, books, inter-faith
Other Languages: French

Centre for Black & White Christian Partnership
Selly Oak Colleges, Birmingham, West Midlands, B29 6LQ
Tel: 0121-472-7952 **Fax:** 0121-472-8852
Contact: Bishop Joseph Aldred
Position: Director
Activities: Resource
Bridge-building between black and white churches.

CEWERN (Churches' East-West European Relations Network)
81 Thorney Leys, Witney, Oxfordshire, OX8 7AY
Tel: 01993-771778
Contact: Dr Philip Walters
Position: General Secretary
Activities: Resource, umbrella, newsletters, inter-faith

With 100 individual members and 30 corporate members, CEWERN is the organisation by means of which member churches of CCBI keep each other informed about their East-West work. CEWERN holds regular briefing meetings for its members.

Christian Aid
P O Box 100, London, SE1 7RT
Tel: 0171-620-4444 **Fax:** 0171-620-0719
EMail: caid@gn.apc.org
Contact: Revd Michael H Taylor
Position: Director
Activities: Resource, media, newsletters, inter-faith
Christian Aid is sponsored by 40 churches in Britain and Ireland, supporting work in 60 countries worldwide to strengthen poor communities. In Europe it campaigns about the structural causes of global poverty.

Christian Education Movement
Royal Buildings, Victoria Street, Derby, Derbyshire, DE1 1GW
Tel: 01332-296655 **Fax:** 01332-343253
Contact: Dr Stephen Orchard
Position: Director
Activities: Resource, umbrella, visits, newsletters, books, inter-faith
CEM is committed to supporting and developing Religious Education and Collective Worship in schools and professionally representing the needs of all teachers of Religious Education.

Christianity & the Future of Europe
Westcott House, Jesus Lane, Cambridge, Cambridgeshire, CB5 8BN

Christians Abroad
1 Stockwell Green, London, SW9 9HP
Tel: 0171-737-7811 **Fax:** 0171-737-3237
EMail: csouth@cabroad.u-net.com
Contact: Colin South
Position: General Secretary
Christians Abroad's 'World Service Enquiry' activity provides information and guidance to people of any faith or none wanting to work overseas in development or mission. `World Service Projects' recruits Christian people to work overseas in development.

Church Action On Poverty
Central Buildings, Oldham Street, Manchester,
Greater Manchester, M1 1JT
Tel: 0161-236-9321 **Fax:** 0161-237-5359
Contact: Niall Cooper
Position: National Co-ordinator
Activities: Resource, newsletters
Campaigns to raise awareness especially within the
churches about poverty in the UK. Our recent
initiative, Local People National Voice, aims to
ensure that those with direct experience of
poverty are heard more clearly at national level.

Church & Peace (Britain & Ireland)
c/o 4 The Square, Clun, Shropshire, SY7 8JA (h)
Tel: 01588-640398 (h) **Fax:** 01588-640107
Contact: Stephen Tunnicliffe
Position: Steering Committee Member
Activities: Umbrella, newsletters, inter-faith
Church and Peace was founded by the historic
peace churches - Quakers, Mennonites and the
Church of the Brethren; its stance is pacifist and
ecumenical. It is pan-European in its scope.

Churches' Advisory Council for Local Broadcasting (CACLB)
PO Box 124, Westcliff-on-Sea, Essex, SS0 0QU
Tel: 01702-348369 **Fax:** 01702-348369
Contact: Jeff Bonser
Position: General Secretary
Activities: Resource, media, umbrella,
newsletters
The Churches' organisation to develop, encourage
and promote Christian involvement in local or
regional broadcasting. It organises annual awards, a
local broadcasting conference, and a network of
over 400 Christians in local broadcasting.

Churches' Commission for Inter-Faith Relations
Church House, Great Smith Street, London,
SW1P 3NZ
Tel: 0171-222-9011 **Fax:** 0171-799-2717
Contact: Revd Canon Dr Christopher Lamb
Position: Secretary
Activities: Umbrella, inter-faith
Other Languages: Welsh
CCIFR is the main agency of the British
Churches in their relationship with other faith
communities.

Churches' Commission on Mission
Inter-Church House, 35-41 Lower Marsh,
Waterloo, London, SE1 7RL
Tel: 0171-620-4444 (h)
EMail: donx@cix.compulink.co.uk
Contact: Revd Donald W Elliott
Position: Commission Secretary
Activities: Umbrella, newsletters

Churches' Commission for Racial Justice
Inter Church House, 35-41 Lower Marsh,
Waterloo,London, SE1 7RL
Tel: 0171-620-4444 **Fax:** 0171-928-0010
Contact: Revd David Haslam
Position: Associate Secretary
Activities: Umbrella, newsletters

Churches' Commission on Overseas Students
1 Stockwell Green, London, SW9 9HP
Tel: 0171-737-1101 **Fax:** 0171-737-3237
Contact: Gillian Court
Position: Executive Secretary
Activities: Resource, umbrella, inter-faith

Churches' Committee for Hospital Chaplaincy
c/o Free Church Federal Council, 27 Tavistock
Square, London, WC1H 9HH
Tel: 0171-387-8413 **Fax:** 0171-383-0150
Contact: Revd Christine M Pocock
Position: Secretary
Activities: Umbrella
The Committee brings together representatives of
the Health Care Chaplaincy Board (Free Church),
Hospital Chaplaincies Council (Cof E) and of
Roman Catholic Chaplaincies. We also have
observers from Wales, Scotland and Ireland and the
College of Health Care Chaplains.

Churches' Community Work Alliance
39 Sandygate, Wath-upon-Dearne, Rotherham,
South Yorkshire, S63 7LW (h)
Tel: 01709-873254 (h) **Fax:** 01709-873254
Contact: Revd Brian J Ruddock
Position: Resource Officer
Activities: Umbrella, newsletters, inter-faith

Churches' Council for Health & Healing
St Marylebone Parish Church, Marlebone Road,
London, NW1 5LT

Churches' Human Rights Forum
57a Anson Road, London, N7 0AR (h)
Tel: 0171-609-5560 (h)

EMail: jarmans@gn.apc.org
Contact: Dr Peter Jarman
Position: Secretary
Activities: Inter-faith
Other Languages: German, French
The Forum is concerned with an overview of the commitment of the Churches and with the implementation of those international human rights conventions to which the UK government is a signatory. The Forum does not normally act on single issues of human rights.

Churches' Joint Education Policy Committee
c/o Free Church Federal Council, 27 Tavistock Square, London, WC1H 9HH
Tel: 0171-387-8413 **Fax:** 0171-383-0150
Contact: Miss Gillian Wood
Position: Secretary
Activities: Umbrella, inter-faith
The Committee is a Co-ordinating group of CTE and co-ordinates the views and interests of the Churches within and beyond the ecumenical bodies of Churches in England and Wales. Its main activity is representing public education to the Government and others.

Churches' Stewardship Network
The Diocesan Office, Auckland Castle, Bishop Auckland, County Durham, DL14 7QJ
Tel: 01938-604823

Committee for International Justice & Peace
39 Eccleston Square, London, SW1V 1PD
Tel: 0171-834-5138 **Fax:** 0171-630-5166
Contact: Robert Beresford
Position: Secretary
Activities: Resource
The Committee is an advisory body for the Catholic Bishops' Conference of England and Wales on international development, social justice, peace issues, and human rights.

Conference of Religious in England & Wales (CMRS)
114 Mount Street, London, W1Y 6DQ
Tel: 0171-493-1817 **Fax:** 0171-409-2321
Contact: Sister Gabriel Robin CSA
Position: General Secretary
Activities: Umbrella, newsletters
Traditions: Roman Catholic
Other Languages: French, Italian, German

Voluntary association of Provincial Superiors in England and Wales. It is one of the four consultative bodies of the Catholic Bishops' Conference for England and Wales and liaises with other national conferences of religious and lay associations.

Consultative Group on Ministry Among Children
St Colms, 18/23 Inverleith Terrace, Edinburgh, Lothian, EH3 5NS
Tel: 0131-332-0343 **Fax:** 0131-315-2161
Contact: Miss Ionwen Roberts
Position: Secretary
Activities: Resource
Exists to bring together all those with a national responsibility to work with children in the denominations and Christian agencies which are in sympathy with the aims and objectives of the Council of Churches for Britain and Ireland.

Environmental Issues Network
National Agricultural Centre, Stoneleigh Park, Warwick, Warwickshire, CV8 2LZ
Tel: 01203-696969 **Fax:** 01203-414808
Contact: David Manning
Position: Secretary
The Environmental Issues Network meets twice yearly and has representatives from all the main Christian Churches. It is a "clearing house" for environmental concerns and projects arising nationally, internationally or denominationally.

Feed the Minds
Robertson House, Leas Road, Guildford, Surrey, GU1 4QW
Tel: 01483-577877 **Fax:** 01483-301387
Contact: Dr Alwyn Marriage
Position: Director
Activities: Newsletters, books
We provide financial support to Christian organisations in Africa, Asia, Eastern Europe and Latin America, to help with publication or distribution of literature.

Fellowship of Prayer for Unity
29 Ramley Road, Pennington, Lymington, Hampshire, SO41 8LH (h)
Tel: 01590-672646 (h)
Contact: Revd Paul Renyard
Position: Chaplain
Activities: Newsletters
Prays and works locally for unity (retreats, quiet days, group meetings).

Fellowship of Reconciliation, England

The Eirene Centre, Old School House, Clopton, Kettering, Northamptonshire, NN14 3DZ
Tel: 01832-720257 **Fax:** 01832-720557
EMail: fellowship@gn.apc.org
Contact: Robert Drost
Position: Warden
Activities: Youth, newsletters, books
FOR, England is a religious society rooted in the Christian pacifist tradition which seeks to promote spiritual development, witness and service as a means of reconciling all people with God and with each other.

Fellowship of St Alban & St Sergius

1 Canterbury Road, Oxford, Oxfordshire, OX2 6LU
Tel: 01865-552991 **Fax:** 01685-316700
Contact: General Secretary
Activities: Newsletters, books, inter-faith
Traditions: Orthodox, Western Christian
Other Languages: French, Russian, Greek
The charity gives grants of money to applicants who require help in financing work that promotes understanding between the Eastern Orthodox Church and the Churches of the West.

Focolare Movement

62 Kings Avenue, London, SW4 8BH
Tel: 0181-671-8355 **Tel:** 0181-671-8355
Fax: 0181-674-1606
Contact: Celia Blackden
Position: Interfaith Contact
Activities: Visitors, youth, elderly, women, newsletters, books, inter-faith
Traditions: Roman Catholic
Languages: Italian
Focolare is an international movement for unity. Its founder, Chiara Lubicj, was recently awarded the 1996 UNESCO Prize for Peace Education. UK centres are in Glasgow, Edinburgh, Leeds, Liverpool, Welwyn Garden City and London.

Iona Community

Pearce Institute, 840 Govan Road, Glasgow, Strathclyde, G51 3UU
Tel: 0141-445-4561 **Tel:** 0141-339-4421 (h)
Fax: 0141-445-4295
Contact: Revd Norman Shanks
Position: Leader
Activities: Worship, visits, youth, newsletters, books, inter-faith

Through the work of its islands centres (on Iona and Mull), its mainland work and the commitment of its members to the renewal of the Church, social change and action for justice and peace, the Iona Community seeks "new ways to touch the hearts of all" that are relevant to today's world.

Keston Institute

4 Park Town, Oxford, Oxfordshire, OX2 6SH
Tel: 01865-311022
Fax: 01865-311280
EMail: keston.institute@keston.org
Contact: Dr Philip Walters
Position: Head of Research
Activities: Resource, visits, newsletters, books, inter-faith
For 25 years Keston Institute has been producing accurate and objective information on the life of religious believers of all demoninations in communist and formerly communist countries. It publishes a regular journal and a news service.

Living Stones

St Mary's University College, Waldergrave Road, Strawberry Hill, Twickenam, Middlesex, TW1 4SX
Tel: 0181-240-4198 **Fax:** 0181-240-4255
Contact: Revd Dr Michael Prior
Position: Chair
Activities: Resource, newsletters, inter-faith
Living Stones is an ecumenical trust which promotes contacts between Christians in Britain and those in the Holy Land and neighbouring countries.

National Association of Christian Communities & Networks (NACCAN)

Woodbrooke, 1046 Bristol Road, Selly Oak, Birmingham, West Midlands, B29 6LJ
Tel: 0121-472-8079 **Fax:** 0121-472-5173
Contact: Sylvia Barnes
Position: Volunteer Office Co-ordinator
The Association organises regional meetings and an annual assembly, and produces a magazine.

National Christian Education Council

1020 Bristol Road, Selly Oak, Birmingham, West Midlands, B29 6LB
Tel: 0121-472-4242 **Tel:** 01452-538164 (h)
Fax: 0121-472-7575
Contact: Bernard B Morgan
Position: Marketing Coordinator

Activities: Resource, youth, newsletters, books
Other Languages: German, French

One World Week
PO Box 100, London, SE1 7RT
Tel: 0171-620-4444 **Fax:** 0171-620-0719
EMail: oneworldweek@gn.apc.org
Contact: Sue Errington
Position: Staff
Activities: Resource, youth, elderly, women, newsletters, inter-faith
OWW aims to celebrate, reflect, act and break out of our normal boxes! OWW shares the vision of Peace with Justice for the whole of creation. The Week is offered to all by the Churches as a sign of hope, a point of sharing in celebration and struggle.

William Temple Foundation
Manchester Business School, Manchester, Greater Manchester, M15 6PB
Tel: 0161-275-6534 **Fax:** 0161-272-8663
EMail: ccq-wen@mcrl.poptel.org.uk
Contact: Revd Malcolm Brown
Position: Executive Secretary
Activities: Resource, newsletters, books
A research and training body examining the links between Christian theology, economics and urban communities. It works in Britain and Europe.

Women's Inter-Church Council
c/o 27 Tavistock Square, London, WC1H 9HH
Tel: 0171-387-8413 **Fax:** 0171-383-0150
Contact: Pauline Butcher
Position: Secretary
Activities: Umbrella
WICC brings together women representatives from Christian denominations and women's organisations to plan work together and to share concerns, ideas and resources.

Young Men's Christian Association
640 Forest Road, Walthamstow, London, E17 3DZ
Tel: 0181-520-5599 **Fax:** 0181-509-3190
Contact: Andy Winter
Position: Operation Director
Activities: Resource, media, umbrella, visits, youth, elderly, women, newsletters, books, inter-faith
YMCA England is part of the worldwide Christian movement of YMCAs. Its central purpose is to support local YMCAs and help form new YMCAs.

Young Women's Christian Association
YWCA Headquarters, Clarendon House, 52 Cornmarket Street, Oxford, Oxfordshire, OX1 3EJ
Tel: 01865-726110 **Fax:** 01865-204805
Contact: Ms Gill Tishler
Position: Chief Executive
Activities: Resource, youth, women, inter-faith
Other Languages: Welsh
The YWCA works alongside women and young people, regardless of race or religion. It provides secure, affordable accommodation, runs women's centres, family workshops and youth clubs, and develops educational materials for use in schools.

CHRISTIAN NATIONAL AND REGIONAL ORGANISATIONS

In this section entries are included on regional rather than local levels of organisation in the UK. Some regional bodies have entries appearing in more than one region because they operate across the regional boundaries used in this directory. Each of the regional bodies listed here is able to supply detailed local information concerning places of worship and other organisations within their membership.

Churches which operate at the level of one country alone (eg the Church of England) are listed in this section of the chapter rather than in the section on "Christian United Kingdom Organisations".

The "affiliations" field is not normally used in this section, except to note any regional ecumenical instrument to which the regional body is affiliated. The "traditions" field is also not normally used where the tradition in question is already clearly indicated in the organisation's title.

ENGLAND

ENGLISH ECUMENICAL INSTRUMENT

Churches Together in England
Inter-Church House, 35-41 Lower Marsh, London, SE1 7RL
Tel: 0171-620-4444 **Fax:** 0171-928-5771
Contact: Revd Canon Martin Reardon (Revd Bill Snelson from 1.10.97)
Position: General Secretary
Activities: Umbrella, newsletters, books
A formal visible sign of the Churches' commitment "in search of the unity for which Christ prayed", enabling the Churches to proclaim the Gospel together by common witness and service.

Churches Together in England North & Midlands Office
Crookes Valley Methodist Church, Sheffield, South Yorkshire, S6 3FQ
Tel: 0114-268-2151 **Fax:** 0114-266-8731
Contact: Mrs Jenny Carpenter

Churches Together in England South Office
Room S17, Baptist House, 129 Broadway, Didcot, Oxfordshire, OX11 8XD

Tel: 0123-551-1622 **Fax:** 0123-581-1537
Contact: Revd. Roger Nunn

CHURCHES OPERATING AT AN ENGLISH LEVEL

Church of England General Synod
Church House, Great Smith Street, London, SW1P 3NZ
Tel: 0171-222-9011 **Fax:** 0171-233-2660
Position: Director of Communications
The General Synod sets the rules and regulations of the Church of England, covering many areas of Church life. The Synod is also responsible for relations with other Churches and at its meetings debates issues of concern to the Church and society.

Church of Scotland England Presbytery
St Columba's Presbytery, Pont Street, London, SW1X 0BD
Tel: 0171-584-2321
Contact: Revd W A Cairns
Position: Presbytery Clerk

Congregational Federation
4 Castle Gate, Nottingham, Nottinghamshire, NG1 7AS
Tel: 0115-941-3801 **Fax:** 0115-948-0902
Contact: Graham Adams
Position: General Secretary
Activities: Worship, newsletters
Traditions: Free Church

Free Church of England
45 Broughton Road, Wallasey, Wirral, Merseyside, LL44 4DT
Tel: 0151-638-2564 (h) **Fax:** 0151-638-2564
Contact: William James Lawler
Position: General Secretary
Traditions: Free Church, Episcopal

CHURCH REGIONAL BODIES

NORTH EAST

REGIONAL ECUMENICAL INSTRUMENTS

Durham Church Relations Group
Gateshead Rectory, 91 Old Durham Road, Gateshead, Tyne and Wear, NE8 4BS (h)

Tel: 0191-477-3990 (h)
Contact: Keith Huxley
Position: Secretary
Activities: Umbrella
Traditions: Ecumenical
Affiliations: Churches Together in England

Newcastle Church Relations Group
Bishop's House, 29 Moor Road South, Gosforth, Newcastle upon Tyne, Tyne and Wear, NE3 1PA
Tel: 0191-285220 **Tel:** 0191-2852220
Contact: Kenneth Edward Gill
Position: Secretary
Activities: Umbrella
Traditions: Ecumenical
Affiliations: Churches Together in England

ASSEMBLIES OF GOD REGIONS

Assemblies of God in Great Britain & Ireland North East Regional Council
6 Arncliffe Gardens, Hartlepool, County Durham, TS26 9JG

BAPTIST UNION AREAS

Baptist Union of Great Britain North Eastern Area
65 Manor Drive North, Acomb, North Yorkshire, YO2 5RY
Tel: 01904-780133 (h)
Contact: Revd Iain Collins
Position: General Superintendent

CHURCH OF ENGLAND DIOCESES

Church of England Diocese of Durham
Diocesan Office, Auckland Castle, Bishop Auckland, County Durham, DL14 7QJ
Tel: 01388-604515 **Fax:** 01388-603695
Contact: Mr William Hurworth
Position: Diocesan Secretary

Church of England Diocese of Newcastle
Church House, Grainger Park Road, Newcastle upon Tyne, Tyne and Wear, NE4 8SX
Tel: 0191-273-0120 **Fax:** 0191-256-5900
Contact: John Michael Craster
Position: Diocesan Secretary
Activities: Resource, newsletters, inter-faith

CONGREGATIONAL FEDERATION AREAS

Congregational Federation North East Area
63 Vicarage Gardens, Scunthorpe, Lincolnshire,
DN15 7BB
Tel: 01724-876149
Contact: Wayne Hawkins
Position: Chair
Activities: Worship, youth, elderly, newsletters,
inter-faith
Traditions: Free Church

METHODIST CHURCH DISTRICTS

Methodist Church Darlington District
2 Edinburgh Drive, Darlington, County Durham,
DL3 8AW
Tel: 01325-468119
Contact: Revd Graham Carter
Position: Chairman of District
Traditions: Free Church

Methodist Church Newcastle upon Tyne District
2 Pilton Road, Westerhope, Newcastle upon Tyne,
Tyne and Wear, NE5 4PP (h)
Tel: 0191-286-9655 (h)
Contact: Revd J W Wesley Blakey
Position: Synod Secretary
Traditions: Free Church

ROMAN CATHOLIC DIOCESES

Roman Catholic Diocese of Hexham & Newcastle
Bishops House, East Denton Hall, 800 West Road,
Newcastle upon Tyne, Tyne and Wear, NE5 2BJ
Tel: 0191-228-0003   **Fax:** 0191-274-0432
Contact: Secretary

SALVATION ARMY DIVISIONS

Salvation Army Northern Division
2 Hutton Terrace, Jesmond, Newcastle upon Tyne,
Tyne and Wear, NE2 1QT
Tel: 0191-281-4202   **Fax:** 0191-281-5130
Contact: Major Kenneth Monk
Position: Divisional Director
Traditions: Free Church
Affiliations: Durham Church Relations Group;
Newcastle Church Relations Group

SEVENTH DAY ADVENTIST CONFERENCES

Seventh Day Adventist Church North England Conference
22 Zulla Road, Mapperley Park, Nottingham,
Nottinghamshire, NG3 5DB
Tel: 0115-960-6312   **Tel:** 01476-578224 (h)
Fax: 0115-969-1476
EMail: 74532.452@compuserve.comm
Contact: Eric C Lowe
Position: Executive Secretary
Activities: Youth, women

UNITARIAN AND FREE CHRISTIANS

Northern Unitarian Association
2 Burn Valley Road, Hartlepool, County Durham,
TS26 9BS (h)
Tel: 01429-235632 (h)
Contact: Peter Whitham
Position: Secretary
Activities: Umbrella
Traditions: Free Church

UNITED REFORMED CHURCH PROVINCES

United Reformed Church Northern Province
Room 1, First Floor, 65 Westgate Road, Newcastle
upon Tyne, Tyne and Wear, NE1 1SG
Tel: 0191-232-1168   **Fax:** 0191-232-1811
EMail: npoffice@cix.compulink.co.uk
Contact: Revd David Jenkins
Position: Moderator
Activities: Umbrella, newsletters, books
Affiliations: The Churches Regional Commission
in the North East

YORKSHIRE

REGIONAL ECUMENICAL INSTRUMENTS

West Yorkshire Ecumenical Council & Sponsoring Body
32 Merton Road, Bradford, West Yorkshire,
BD7 1RE
Tel: 01274-732567   **Fax:** 01724-395324
Contact: Revd Bill Snelson
Position: Ecumenical Officer
Activities: Umbrella, newsletters

KEY (Kingston-upon-Hull & East Yorkshire)
Churches Together
The Vicarage, Skirlaugh, Hull, East Riding of
Yorkshire, HU11 5HE (h)
Tel: 01964-562259 (h)   **Fax:** 01964-563383
Contact: Revd David William Perry
Position: Ecumenical Officer
Activities: Umbrella

South Teeside Ecumenical Forum
60 West Green, Stokesley, Middlesbrough, TS9 5BD
Contact: Revd Gordon Bates
Position: Convenor
Activities: Umbrella, newsletters

Ecumenical Forum
62 Palace Road, Ripon, North Yorkshire,
HG4 1HA
Tel: 01765-604342
Contact: Venerable Kenneth Good
Position: Convenor
Activities: Umbrella, newsletters

Churches Together in South Yorkshire
Crookes Valley Methodist Church, Crookesmoor
Road, Sheffield, South Yorkshire, S6 3FQ
Tel: 0114-266-6156   **Fax:** 0114-266-8131
Contact: Colin Brady
Position: Ecumenical Development Officer
Activities: Umbrella, newsletters

Churches Together in the Vale of York
The Manor, Moss End Farm, Hawkhills,
Easingwold, York, North Yorkshire, Y06 3ES
Tel: 01347-838593
Contact: Mrs Jean Abbey
Position: Secretary
Activities: Umbrella, newsletters

North Yorkshire Moors Ecumenical Forum
13 Lawnway, Stockton Lane, York, North Yorkshire,
YO3 0JD
Tel: 01904-424739 Fax: 01904-424739
Contact: Revd Stuart Burgess
Position: Covenor
Activities: Umbrella, newsletters

ASSEMBLIES OF GOD REGIONS

Assemblies of God, East Pennine Region
16 Richard Road, Rotherham, South Yorkshire,
S60 2QR
Tel: 01709-517871 (h)   **Fax:** 01709-517871

Contact: Bernard James Sword
Position: Regional Administrator
Traditions: Pentecostal

BAPTIST UNION OF GREAT BRITAIN AREAS

Baptist Union of Great Britain North Eastern Area
65 Manor Drive North, Acomb, North Yorkshire,
Y02 SRY
Tel: 01904-780133 (h)
Contact: Revd Iain Collins
Position: General Superintendent

CHURCH OF ENGLAND DIOCESES

Church of England Diocese of Bradford
Diocesan Office, Cathedral Hall, Stott Hill,
Bradford, West Yorkshire, BD9 5QJ
Tel: 01274-725958 **Fax:** 01274-726343
Contact: Malcolm K Halliday
Position: Diocesan Secretary

Church of England Diocese of Ripon
St Martin's Vicarage, 2a St Martin's View,
Potternewton, Leeds, West Yorkshire, LS7 3LB (h)
Tel: 0113-262-4271 (h)   **Fax:** 0113-249-1129
Contact: Jim Siller
Position: Diocesan Race Relations Officer
Activities: Worship, resource

Church of England Diocese of Sheffield
Diocesan Church House, 95-99 Effingham Street,
Rotherham, South Yorkshire, S65 1BL
Tel: 01709-511116 **Fax:** 01709-512550
Contact: Mr Charles Anthony Beck
Position: Diocesan Secretary
Activities: Resource
Affiliations: Churches Together in South Yorkshire

Church of England Diocese of Wakefield
Church House, 1 South Parade, Wakefield, West
Yorkshire, WF1 1LP
Tel: 01924-371802 **Tel:** 01924-254624 (h)
Fax: 019024-364834
Contact: John Clark
Position: Diocesan Secretary
Activities: Resource, umbrella

Church of England Diocese of York
Church House, Ogleforth, York, North Yorkshire,
YO1 2JE

Tel: 01904-611696 **Fax:** 01904-620375
Contact: Keith Dodgson
Position: Diocesan Secretary

CONGREGATIONAL FEDERATION AREAS

Congregational Federation North East Area
63 Vicarage Gardens, Scunthorpe, Lincolnshire,
DN15 7BB
Tel: 01724-876149
Contact: Wayne Hawkins
Position: Chair
Activities: Worship, youth, elderly, newsletters,
inter-faith

METHODIST CHURCH DISTRICTS

Methodist Church Leeds District (including Wakefield, Harrogate & Dewsbury)
4 Mardale Road, Dewsbury, West Yorkshire,
WF12 7NR (h)
Tel: 01924-461788 (h) **Fax:** 01924-453894
Contact: Revd John Anthony Santry
Position: Synod Secretary
Activities: Umbrella
Traditions: Free Church
Affiliations: West Yorkshire Ecumenical Council

Methodist Church West Yorkshire District
10 Knowler Hill, Liversedge, West Yorkshire,
WF15 6PH
Tel: 01924-402219
Contact: Revd J Harry Scott
Position: Synod Secretary
Affiliations: West Yorkshire Ecumenical Council

Methodist Church Lincoln & Grimsby District
193 Ashby Road, Old Brumby, Scunthorpe,
Lincolnshire, DN16 2AQ
Tel: 01724-843053
Contact: Revd John D Robinson
Position: Synod Secretary
Affiliations: Churches Together in Lincolnshire

Methodist Church Sheffield District
Victoria Hall Methodist Church, Norfolk Street,
South Yorkshire, Sheffield, S1 2JB
Tel: 0114-281-2733 **Tel:** 0114-279-7596 (h)
Fax: 0114-281-2734
EMail: 100450.3312@compuserve.com
Contact: Revd David Halstead
Position: Chairman

Activities: Umbrella
Traditions: Free Church
Affiliations: Churches Together in South Yorkshire

Methodist Church York & Hull District
13 Lawnway, York, North Yorkshire, Y03 0JD
Tel: 01904-424739 **Fax:** 01904-424739
Contact: Revd Stuart J Burgess
Position: Chairman of the District
Activities: Resource, newsletters, inter-faith
Affiliations: KEY Churches Together; Churches
Together in the Vale of York

MORAVIAN CHURCH DISTRICTS

Moravian Church Yorkshire District Conference
The Moravian Manse, 177 Quarry Road,
Gromersal, Cleckheaton, West Yorkshire,
BD19 4JB (h)
Tel: 01274-874374 (h)
Contact: Robert James Hopcroft
Position: Chairman
Activities: Worship, newsletters
Traditions: Free Church
Affiliations: West Yorkshire Ecumenical Council

NEW TESTAMENT CHURCH OF GOD DISTRICTS

New Testament Church of God District
Jonson Street, Sheffield, South Yorkshire, S3 8GL (h)
Tel: 0114-273-9565 **Tel:** 0114-247-0459 (h)
Fax: 0114-272-5722
Contact: Bishop Benjamin Grey
Position: Minister
Activities: Worship, resource, youth, elderly,
women
Traditions: Pentecostal
Affiliations: Churches Together in South Yorkshire

ROMAN CATHOLIC DIOCESES

Roman Catholic Diocese of Leeds
St Mary's Presbytery, East Parade, Bradford, West
Yorkshire, BD1 5EE (h)
Tel: 01274-721430 (h) **Fax:** 01274-721430
Contact: Mgr William James Steele
Position: Episcopal Vicar
Activities: Worship, inter-faith
Affiliations: West Yorkshire Ecumenical Council

Roman Catholic Diocese of Middlesbrough
Bishops House, 16 Cambridge Road,
Middlesbrough, North Yorkshire, TS5 5NN
Tel: 01642-818253
Contact: Rt Revd John Crowley
Position: Bishop

Roman Catholic Diocese of Hallam
St Wilfred's Presbytery, St Ronan's Road, Sheffield,
South Yorkshire, S7 1DX
Tel: 0114-255-0827
Contact: Mgr William Kilgannon
Position: Administrator
Affiliations: Churches Together in South
Yorkshire; Churches Together in Derbyshire

SALVATION ARMY DIVISIONS

Salvation Army Yorkshire Division
1 Cadman Court, Hanley Road, Morley, Leeds,
West Yorkshire, LS27 0RX
Tel: 0113-281-0100   **Fax:** 0113-281-0111
EMail: 106236.272@compuserve.com
Contact: Paul Hendy
Position: Public Relations
Activities: Worship, visits, youth, elderly, women,
newsletters, books, inter-faith
Traditions: Free Church

SEVENTH DAY ADVENTIST CONFERENCES

Seventh Day Adventist Church North England Conference
22 Zulla Road, Mapperley Park, Nottingham,
Nottinghamshire, NG3 5DB
Tel: 0115-960-6312   **Tel:** 01476-578224 (h)
Fax: 0115-696-1476
EMail: 74532.452@compuserve.com
Contact: Eric C Lowe
Position: Executive Secretary
Activities: Youth, women
Traditions: Free Church

UNITARIAN AND FREE CHRISTIANS

Sheffield & District Association of Unitarian & Free Christian Churches Inc
Upper Chapel, Norfolk Street, Sheffield, South
Yorkshire, S1 2JD
Tel: 0114-276-7114   **Tel:** 0114-233-1218 (h)
Contact: Revd Geoffrey R Usher

Position: Secretary
Activities: Worship, visits, youth, elderly, women,
inter-faith

Yorkshire Union of Unitarian & Free Christian Churches
132 Welbeck Street, Hull, East Riding of Yorkshire,
HU5 3SG (h)
Tel: 01482-491097 (h)
Contact: David Arthur
Position: Honorary Secretary
Activities: Worship, umbrella, inter-faith

UNITED REFORMED CHURCH PROVINCES

United Reformed Church Yorkshire Province
43 Hunslet Lane, Leeds, West Yorkshire, LS10 1JW
Tel: 0113-245-1267   **Fax:** 0113-234-1145
Contact: Moderator
Activities: Umbrella, newsletters
Traditions: Free Church
Affiliations: West Yorkshire Ecumenical Council

OTHER BODIES

Hull & District Evangelical Alliance
Good News Bookshop, 66-67 Wright Street, Hull,
East Riding of Yorkshire, HU2 8JD
Tel: 01482-328135   **Tel:** 01482-802186 (h)
Contact: M G Morfin
Position: Secretary
Activities: Umbrella

NORTH WEST

REGIONAL ECUMENICAL INSTRUMENTS

Churches Together in Cumbria
Church House, West Walls, Carlisle, Cumbria,
CA3 8UE
Tel: 01228-22573   **Tel:** 01524-271657 (h)
Fax: 01228-48769
Contact: Anne Kerr
Position: Ecumenical Officer
Activities: Resource, umbrella, newsletters

Churches Together in Man
The Manse, 11 Bayr Grianwagh, Castletown,
Isle of Man, IM9 1HN
Tel: 01624-822541   **Fax:** 01624-822541
EMail: ia1085@advsys.co.ik

Contact: Revd Stephen Frederick Caddy
Position: Secretary

Churches Together in Cheshire
5 Abbey Green, Chester, Cheshire, CH1 2JH
Tel: 01244-347500
Contact: Canon Michael Rees
Position: Ecumenical Officer

Churches Together in Lancashire
45 Alder Drive, Hoghton, Preston, Lancashire,
PR5 0AE (h)
Tel: 01254-852860 (h)
Contact: Revd Donald A Parsons
Position: Ecumenical Officer
Activities: Umbrella, newsletters

Merseyside & Region Churches Ecumenical Assembly
Friends Meeting House, 65 Paradise Street,
Liverpool, Merseyside, L1 3BP
Tel: 0151-709-0125 **Tel:** 0151-722-1100 (h)
Fax: 0151-707-1968
Contact: Rev Fr Anthony E Hodgetts
Position: Ecumenical Officer
Activities: Umbrella, newsletters, inter-faith
Affiliations: Churches Together North West

Greater Manchester Churches Together
St Peter's House, Precinct Centre, Oxford Road,
Manchester, Greater Manchester, M13 9GH
Tel: 0161-273-5508 **Fax:** 0161-272-7172
Contact: Sister Maureen Farrell
Position: Ecumenical Officer
Activities: Umbrella, newsletters,
inter-faith

ASSEMBLIES OF GOD REGIONS

Assemblies of God in Great Britain & Ireland NorthWest Regional Council
377 Hollinwood Avenue, New Moston,
Manchester, Greater Manchester, M10 0JQ

Assemblies of God, North Wales & Cheshire Region
142 Elmwood Road, Barnton, Northwich,
Cheshire, CW8 4NN (h)
Tel: 01606-76426 (h)
Contact: David Hunter Gill
Position: Administrator
Traditions: Pentecostal

BAPTIST UNION AREAS

Lancashire & Cheshire Association of Baptist Churches
Latchford Baptist Church, Loushers Lane,
Warrington, Cheshire, WA4 2RP
Tel: 01925-633929 **Fax:** 01925-418796
Contact: Revd Christopher D Haig
Position: General Secretary
Activities: Newsletters
Traditions: Free Church

CHURCH OF ENGLAND DIOCESES

Church of England Diocese of Blackburn
St Mark's Vicarage, Buncer Lane, Witton,
Blackburn, Lancashire, BB2 6SY (h)
Tel: 01254-676615 (h)
Contact: Revd Colin Albin
Position: Bishop's Adviser
Activities: Inter-faith
Affiliations: Churches Together in Lancashire

Church of England Diocese of Carlisle
Church House, West Walls, Carlisle, Cumbria,
CA3 8UE
Tel: 01228-22573 **Fax:** 01228-48769
Contact: Revd Colin Hill
Position: Diocesan Secretary
Affiliations: Churches Together in Cumbria

Church of England Diocese of Chester
Diocesan House, Raymond Street, Chester,
Cheshire, CH1 4PN
Tel: 01244-379222 **Fax:** 01244-383835
Contact: Stephen P Marriott
Position: Diocesan Secretary
Affiliations: Churches Together in Cheshire

Church of England Diocese of Sodor & Man
24 Athol Street, Douglas, Isle of Man
Tel: 01624-675367
Contact: Worshipful P W S Farrant
Position: Vicar General

Church of England Diocese of Liverpool
Church House, Hanover Street, Liverpool,
Merseyside, L1 3DW
Tel: 0151-709-9722 **Fax:** 0151-709-2885
Contact: Mr K W Cawdron
Position: Diocesan Secretary
Affiliations: Merseyside and Region Churches
Ecumenical Assembly

Church of England Diocese of Manchester
1st Floor, Diocesan Church House, 90 Deansgate,
Manchester, Greater Manchester, M3 2GH
Tel: 0161-833-9521 **Fax:** 0161-833-2751
Contact: Mrs J A Park
Position: Diocesan Secretary
Affiliations: Churches Together in Greater
Manchester

CONGREGATIONAL FEDERATION AREAS

Congregational Federation North West Area
13 Springhead Avenue, Springhead, Oldham,
Lancashire, 0L4 5SP (h)
Tel: 0161-624-8778 (h)
Contact: Revd Donald G Openshaw
Position: Area Secretary
Activities: Umbrella, newsletters
Traditions: Free Church

FREE CHURCH OF ENGLAND DIOCESES

The Free Church of England Northern Diocese
10 Hest Bank Road, Morecombe, Lancashire,
LA4 6HJ

METHODIST DISTRICTS

Methodist Church Cumbria District
Glen Millans, Millans Park, Ambleside, Cumbria,
LA22 9AG
Tel: 01539-433232 (h)
Contact: Revd R Barker
Position: Synod Secretary
Activities: Umbrella
Traditions: Free Church
Affiliations: Churches Together in Cumbria

Methodist Church Bolton & Rochdale District
5 Hill Side, Heaton, Bolton, Lancashire,
BL1 5DT (h)
Tel: 01204-843302 (h) **Fax:** 01204-843302
Contact: Revd David B Reddish
Position: Chairman of District
Traditions: Free Church
Affiliations: Churches Together in Greater
Manchester; Churches Together in Lancashire

Methodist Church Isle of Man District
12 Ballamillaghyn, Mount Rule, Braddan, Douglas,
Isle of Man
Tel: 01624-851975
Contact: Revd Maurice B Johnson
Position: Secretary
Traditions: Free Church
Affiliations: Churches Together in Man

Methodist Church Manchester & Stockport District
10 Dene Brow, Haughton Green, Denton,
Manchester, Greater Manchester, M34 7PX (h)
Tel: 0161-320-6224 (h)
Contact: Revd Alec M Roberts
Position: Synod Secretary
Activities: Worship, youth, elderly, women
Traditions: Free Church
Affiliations: Churches Together in Greater
Manchester

Methodist Church North Lancashire District
28 Lower Greenfield, Ingol, Preston, Lancashire,
PR2 3ZT (h)
Tel: 01772-733496 (h) **Fax:** 01772-733496
Contact: G Michael Wearing
Position: Chairman of District
Traditions: Free Church
Affiliations: Churches Together in Lancashire

Methodist Church Liverpool District
2 Ash Street, Southport, Merseyside, PR8 6JH (h)
Tel: 01704-500285 **Tel:** 01704-540130 (h)
Fax: 01704-540130
Contact: Revd Neil A Stubbens
Position: Synod Secretary
Activities: Umbrella
Traditions: Free Church
Affiliations: Merseyside and Region Churches
Ecumenical Assembly

ROMAN CATHOLIC DIOCESES

Roman Catholic Diocese of Shrewsbury
Curial Offices, 2 Park Road South, Birkenhead,
Merseyside, L43 4UX
Tel: 0151-652-9855 **Fax:** 0151-653-5172
Contact: Revd Peter C Montgomery
Position: Bishop's Secretary
Activities: Worship, resource, umbrella, youth,
elderly, women, newsletters, inter-faith
Affiliations: Churches Together in Cheshire and
Shropshire

Roman Catholic Diocese of Lancaster
Bishop's House, Cannon Hill, Lancaster, Lancashire,
LA1 5NG
Tel: 01524-32231 (h) **Fax:** 01524-849296
Contact: Bishop's Secretary
Activities: Worship, umbrella, youth, elderly,
women, newsletters, inter-faith
Affiliations: Churches Together in Cumbria;
Churches Together in Lancashire

Roman Catholic Archdiocese of Liverpool
Curial Offices, 152 Brownlow Hill, Liverpool,
Merseyside, L3 5RQ
Tel: 0151-709-4801 **Fax:** 0151-708-5167
Contact: Archbishop Patrick Kelly
Position: Archbishop
Activities: Resource, media, umbrella, youth,
elderly, women, newsletters, books, inter-faith
Other Languages: Italian
Affiliations: Merseyside and Region Churches
Ecumenical Assembly

Roman Catholic Diocese of Salford
Cathedral House, 250 Chapel Street, Salford,
Greater Manchester, M3 5LL
Tel: 0161-834-9052
Contact: Diocesan Curia

SALVATION ARMY DIVISIONS

Salvation Army North Western Division
401 Prescot Road, Liverpool, Merseyside, L13 3BT
Tel: 0151-220-4210
Contact: Major Howard Grottick
Position: Divisional Commander
Affiliations: Merseyside and Region Ecumenical
Council; Churches Together in Cheshire

Salvation Army Central North Division
80 Eccles New Road, Salford, Greater Manchester,
M5 2RU
Tel: 0161-743-3900 **Fax:** 0161-743-3911
Contact: Major Keith Howarth
Position: Divisional Commander
Affiliations: Churches Together in Lancashire,
Cheshire and Manchester

SEVENTH DAY ADVENTIST CONFERENCES

Seventh Day Adventist North England Conference
22 Zulla Road, Mapperley Park, Nottingham,
Nottinghamshire, NG3 5DB
Tel: 0115-960-6312 **Tel:** 01476-578224 (h)
Fax: 0115-969-1476
EMail: 74532.452@compuserve.com
Contact: Eric C Lowe
Position: Executive Secretary
Activities: Youth, women
Traditions: Free Church

UNITARIANS AND FREE CHRISTIANS

North & East Lancashire Unitarian Mission
754 Blackburn Road, Astley Bridge, Bolton,
Lancashire, BL1 7JW (h)
Tel: 01204-303257 (h)
Contact: Revd Tony McNeile
Position: Secretary
Activities: Resource, umbrella, youth, elderly,
women, newsletters, inter-faith

East Cheshire Union of Unitarian & Free Christain Churches
156 Yew Tree Lane, Dunkinfield, Cheshire,
SK16 5DU

Merseyside & District Missionary Association (Unitarian)
23 Cheltenham Avenue, Sefton Park, Liverpool,
Merseyside, L17 2AR (h)
Tel: 0151-735-0538 (h) **Fax:** 0151-735-0538
Contact: Revd Jeffrey L Gould
Position: Secretary
Activities: Worship, umbrella, visits, youth, elderly,
women, newsletters, books, inter-faith
Affiliations: Merseyside and Region Churches
Ecumenical Assembly

Manchester District Association of Unitarian & Free Christian Churches (Incorporated)
Cross Street Chapel, Cavendish House, 30 Pall
Mall, Manchester, Greater Manchester, M2 1JY
Tel: 0161-833-1176 **Fax:** 0161-928-1687
Contact: Geoffrey Head
Position: General Secretary
Activities: Umbrella, newsletters, inter-faith
Affiliations: Greater Manchester Churches
Together

UNITED REFORMED CHURCH PROVINCES

United Reformed Church Mersey Province
The Annexe, 63 Alton Road, Birkenhead,
Merseyside, L43 1UZ
Tel: 0151-653-7096 **Fax:** 0151-653-7096
Contact: Revd Graham Cook
Position: Moderator
Activities: Resource, youth, elderly, women,
newsletters, inter-faith
Affiliations: Merseyside and Region Churches
Ecumenical Assembly

United Reformed Church North Western Province
Provincial Office, Franklin Street, Patricroft, Eccles,
Manchester, Greater Manchester, M30 0QZ
Tel: 0161-789-5583 **Tel:** 0161-445-9608 (h)
Fax: 0161-707-9117
Contact: Revd C Keith Forecast
Position: Moderator
Activities: Umbrella, youth, elderly, women,
newsletters
Traditions: Reformed
Affiliations: Churches Together in Lancashire;
Greater Manchester and Cumbria

OTHER BODIES

Network
c/o Nazerene Theological College, Dene Road,
Didsbury, Manchester, Greater Manchester,
M20 2GU
Tel: 0161-445-5738 **Fax:** 0161-448-2075
Contact: The Chair
Position: Chair
Activities: Umbrella, newsletters
Traditions: Interdenominational
Other Languages: Chinese, Nigerian
Affiliations: Evangelical Alliance

EAST MIDLANDS

REGIONAL ECUMENICAL INSTRUMENTS

Northamptonshire Ecumenical Council
4 The Slade, Daventry, Northamptonshire,
NN11 4HH
Tel: 01327-705803
Contact: Mrs Christine Nelson

Position: Secretary
Activities: Umbrella

Churches Together in Derbyshire
64 Wyndale Drive, Kirk Hallam, Ilkeston,
Derbyshire, DE7 4JG (h)
Tel: 0115-932-9402 (h)
Contact: Mr Colin Garley
Position: Honorary Secretary
Activities: Umbrella, newsletters

Churches Together in Leicestershire
Church House, 3/5 St Martins East, Leicester,
Leicestershire, LE1 5FX
Tel: 0116-262-7445 **Fax:** 0116-253-2889
Contact: Mr Jonathan Patrick Cryer
Position: Secretary
Activities: Umbrella, newsletters, inter-faith

Churches Together in Nottinghamshire
35 Aylesham Avenue, Woodthorpe View, Arnold,
Nottingham, Nottinghamshire, NG5 6PP (h)
Tel: 0115-926-9090 (h)
Contact: Alan J W Langton
Position: Secretary
Activities: Umbrella

Churches Together in All Lincolnshire
11 Rowan Drive, Silk Willoughby, Sleaford,
Lincolnshire, NG34 8PQ (h)
Tel: 01529-303207 (h)
Contact: Revd Brian Levick
Position: Ecumenical Officer
Activities: Umbrella

ASSEMBLIES OF GOD REGIONAL COUNCILS

East Midlands Region, Assemblies of God in GB & Ireland
Emmanuel Christian Centre, Sherwood Avenue,
Newark, Nottinghamshire, NG24 1QF
Tel: 01636-74965 **Fax:** 01636-74965
Contact: Pastor Kenneth Aubrey Morgan
Position: Chair
Traditions: Pentecostal

BAPTIST UNION AREAS

Baptist Union of Great Britain East Midland Area
9 Wilshere Close, Kirby Muxloe, Leicester,
Leicestershire, LE9 2DN (h)

Tel: 0116-238-7012 (h) **Fax:** 0116-238-7012
EMail: 100620.67@compuserve.com
Contact: Revd Peter Grange
Position: General Superintendent
Activities: Umbrella
Traditions: Free Church

Baptist Union of Great Britain Central Area

6 Sunridge Close, Newport Pagnell,
Buckinghamshire, MK16 0LT (h)
Tel: 01908-616093 (h) **Fax:** 01908-616093
Contact: Revd Roy A Freestone
Position: General Superintendent
Traditions: Free Church

CHURCH OF ENGLAND DIOCESES

Church of England Diocese of Derby

Derby Church House, Full Street, Derby,
Derbyshire, DE1 3DR
Tel: 01332-382233 **Fax:** 01332-292969
Contact: Mr Robert John Carey
Position: Diocesan Secretary
Affiliations: Churches Together in Derbyshire

Church of England Diocese of Leicester

Church House, 3/5 St Martins East, Leicester,
Leicestershire, LE1 5FX
Tel: 0116-2627445 **Fax:** 0116-2532889
EMail: chouse@leicester.anglican.org
Contact: Jonathan Patrick Cryer
Position: Secretary
Activities: Resource, newsletters, inter-faith
Affiliations: Churches Together in Leicestershire

Church of England Diocese of Lincoln

Church House, The Old Palace, Lincoln,
Lincolnshire, LN2 1PU
Tel: 01522-529541 **Fax:** 01522-512717
Contact: Phil Hamlyn Williams
Position: Diocesan Secretary
Activities: Resource, visits, youth, newsletters
Affiliations: Churches Together in All Lincolnshire

Church of England Diocese of Peterborough

The Palace, Peterborough, Cambridgeshire,
PE1 1YB
Tel: 01733-64448 Fax: 01733-55271
Contact: Mr Philip M Haines
Position: Diocesan Secretary
Affiliations: Greater Peterborough Ecumenical
Council; Northamptonshire Ecumenical Council

Church of England Diocese of Southwell

Dunham House, 8 Westgate, Southwell,
Nottinghamshire, NG25 0JL
Tel: 01636-814331 **Fax:** 01636-815084
Contact: Brian Richard Edward Noake
Position: Diocesan Secretary
Activities: Newsletters, inter-faith
Affiliations: Churches Together in
Nottinghamshire

CONGREGATIONAL FEDERATION AREAS

Congregational Federation East Midlands Area

11 Hillberry Close, Narborough, Leicester,
Leicestershire, LE9 5EW (h)
Tel: 0116-2864742 (h)
Contact: Doreen Willson
Position: Secretary
Traditions: Free Church
Affiliations: Churches Together in Leicestershire

Congregational Federation North East Area

63 Vicarage Gardens, Scunthorpe, Lincolnshire,
DN15 7BB
Tel: 01724-876149
Contact: Wayne Hawkins
Position: Chair
Activities: Worship, youth, elderly, newsletters,
inter-faith
Traditions: Free Church

METHODIST DISTRICTS

Methodist Church Oxford & Leicester District

9 Laverstock Road, Wigston, Leicester,
Leicestershire, LE18 2RJ (h)
Tel: 0116-257-1069 (h)
Contact: Martin T Smithd
Position: Synod Secretary
Activities: Umbrella
Traditions: Free Church
Affiliations: Churches Together in Leicestershire

Methodist Church Nottingham & Derby District

12 Cheviot Avenue, Codnor Park, Ironville,
Nottingham, Nottinghamshire, NG16 5QQ (h)
Tel: 01773-603902 (h)
Contact: Ms Averil George
Position: Synod Secretary
Activities: Umbrella, youth, elderly, women
Traditions: Free Church

Affiliations: Churches Together in Derbyshire; Churches Togther in Nottinghamshire

Methodist Church Lincoln & Grimsby District
193 Ashby Road, Scunthorpe, Lincolnshire, DN16 2AQ (h)
Tel: 01274-843053 (h)
Contact: Revd John Robinson
Position: Synod Secretary
Traditions: Free Church
Affiliations: Churches Together in All Lincolnshire

MORAVIAN CHURCH DISTRICTS

Moravian Church Eastern District Conference
Hillside, 29 The Settlement, Ockbrook, Derby, Derbyshire, DE72 3RJ
Tel: 01332-6745932
Contact: Revd Michael Rea
Position: Chairman
Traditions: Free Church
Affiliations: Churches Together in Derbyshire

NEW TESTAMENT CHURCH OF GOD DISTRICT

New Testament Church of God Derby District
59 Harrow Drive, Burton-on-Trent, Staffordshire, DE14 3AY (h)
Tel: 01332-726031 **Tel:** 01283-541395 (h)
Contact: Keith N Channer
Position: District Overseer
Activities: Worship, visits, youth, elderly, women
Traditions: Pentecostal

ROMAN CATHOLIC DIOCESES

Roman Catholic Diocese of Northampton
Bishops House, Marriott Street, Northampton, Northamptonshire, NN2 6AW
Tel: 01604-715635 **Fax:** 01604-792186
EMail: mod1@cableol.co.uk
Contact: Revd Mark O'Donnell
Position: Bishop's Chaplain
Affiliations: Northamptonshire Ecumenical Council

Roman Catholic Diocese of Nottingham
27 Cavendish Road East, The Park, Nottingham, Nottinghamshire NG7 1BB (h)
Tel: 0115-947-4786 (h) **Fax:** 0115-947-5235
Contact: Revd Father Edward Jarosz

Position: Bishop's Secretary
Affiliations: Churches Together in Derbyshire; Churches Together in Nottinghamshire; Churches Together in Leicestershire; Churches Together in All Lincolnshire

SALVATION ARMY DIVISIONS

Salvation Army East Midlands
Paisely Grove, Nottingham, Nottinghamshire, NG9
Tel: 0115-929-5365 **Fax:** 0115-942-5796
Contact: Lieutenant Colonel Alex Morris
Position: Divisional Commander
Traditions: Free Church

SEVENTH DAY ADVENTIST CONFERENCES

Seventh Day Adventist Church North England Conference
2 Zulla Road, Mapperley Park, Nottingham, Nottinghamshire, NG3 5DB
Tel: 0115-960-6312 **Tel:** 01476-578224 (h)
Fax: 0115-969-1476
EMail: 74532.452@compuserve.com
Contact: Eric C Lowe
Position: Executive Secretary
Activities: Youth, women
Traditions: Free Church

UNITED REFORMED CHURCH PROVINCES

United Reformed Church East Midlands Province
Sherwood United Reformed Church, 1 Edwards Lane, Sherwood, Nottingham, Nottinghamshire, NG5 3AA
Tel: 0115-960-9241 **Fax:** 0115-960-9202
Contact: Revd A Christopher White
Position: Synod Clerk
Activities: Resource, umbrella, newsletters, books
Affiliations: Churches Together in Derbyshire; Churches Together in Nottinghamshire; Churches Together in Leicestershire; Churches Together in All Lincolnshire; Northamptonshire Ecumenical Council; Greater Peterborough Ecumenical Council

UNITARIAN AND FREE CHRISTIAN

North Midland Presbyterian & Unitarian Association Inc.
Unitarian Chapel, 3 Plumptre Street, Nottingham, Nottinghamshire, NG1 1JL
Tel: 0115-989-2198 (h)
Contact: Michael Adcock
Position: Secretary
Activities: Umbrella, inter-faith

WEST MIDLANDS

REGIONAL ECUMENICAL INSTRUMENTS

Birmingham Churches Together
Carrs Lane Church Centre, Birmingham, West Midlands, B4 7SX
Tel: 0121-643-6603
Contact: Revd Mark Fisher
Position: General Secretary
Activities: Newsletters
Affiliations: West Midlands Region Churches Forum

West Midlands Region Churches' Forum
Carrs Lane Church Centre, Birmingham, West Midlands, B4 7SX
Tel: 0121-643-6603
Contact: Revd Mark Fisher
Position: General Secretary
Activities: Umbrella

Dudley & Worcestershire Ecumenical Council
The Rectory, Clifton-on-Teme, Hereford and Worcester, WR6 6DJ (h)
Tel: 01886-812483 (h)
Contact: Revd Clifford Owen
Position: Secretary
Activities: Umbrella
Affiliations: West Midlands Churches' Forum

Churches Together in Herefordshire
Malvern View, Garway Hill, Orcop, Hereford, Hereford and Worcester, HR2 8EZ (h)
Tel: 01981-580495 (h)　**Fax:** 01981-580495 (h)
Contact: Anne Double
Position: County Ecumenical Officer
Activities: Umbrella, newsletters

Staffordshire Plus Ecumenical Council
66 Heritage Court, Lichfield, Staffordshire, WS14 9ST (h)
Tel: 01543-417179 (h)　**Fax:** 01543-417179
Contact: Donald Brockbank
Position: Ecumenical Officer
Activities: Umbrella, newsletters

Churches Together in Shropshire
Fern Villa, Four Crosses, Llanymynech, Powys, SY22 6PR (h)
Tel: 01691-831374 (h)
Contact: Gerard Cliffe
Position: Ecumenical Secretary
Activities: Umbrella, newsletters, inter-faith

Coventry & Warwickshire Ecumenical Council
31 Tiverton Drive, Horeston Grange, Nuneaton, Warwickshire, CV11 6YJ (h)
Tel: 01203-352551 (h)
Contact: David Rowland
Position: Ecumenical Officer
Activities: Umbrella, newsletters

Telford Christian Council
Meeting Point House, Southwater Square, Town Centre, Telford, Shropshire, TF3 4HS
Tel: 01952-291904　**Fax:** 01952-290617
Contact: Revd David Lavender
Position: Ecumenical Chaplain
Activities: Worship, resource, umbrella, visits, youth, newsletters

BAPTIST UNIONS AREAS

Baptist Union of Great Britain West Midland Area
Unit 8, 137 Newhall Street, Birmingham, West Midlands, B3 1SF
Tel: 0121-212-4842　**Fax:** 0121-212-4512
Contact: Revd Brian Nicholls
Position: Gen Superintendent
Activities: Umbrella, visits, newsletters
Traditions: Free Church
Affiliations: West Midlands Region Churches Forum

CHURCH OF ENGLAND DIOCESES

Church of England Diocese of Birmingham
175 Harborne Park Road, Harborne, Birmingham, West Midlands, B17 0BH

Tel: 0121-427-5141 **Fax:** 0121-428-1114
Contact: Sue Primmer
Position: Diocesan Communications Officer
Affiliations: Birmingham Churches Together

Church of England Diocese of Coventry
Church House, Palmerston Road, Coventry, West
Midlands, CV5 6FJ
Tel: 01203-674328 **Fax:** 01203-674328
Contact: Ms Isobel Chapman
Position: Diocesan Secretary
Affiliations: Coventry and Warwickshire
Ecumenical Council

Church of England Diocese of Hereford
Diocesan Office, The Palace, Hereford, Hereford
and Worcester, HR4 9BL
Tel: 01432-353863 **Fax:** 01432-352952
Contact: S Green
Position: Diocesan Secretary
Affiliations: Churches Together in Herefordshire;
Churches Together in Shropshire

Church of England Diocese of Lichfield
St Mary's House, The Close, Lichfield, Staffordshire,
WS13 7LD
Tel: 01543-414551 **Fax:** 01543-205935
Contact: D R Taylor
Position: Diocesan Secretary
Affiliations: Staffordshire Plus Ecumenical
Council; Churches Together in Shropshire

Church of England Diocese of Worcester
The Old Palace, Deansway, Worcester, Hereford and
Worcester, WR1 2JE
Tel: 01905-20537 **Tel:** 01299-250214 (h)
Fax: 01905-612302
Contact: Rt Revd Peter Selby
Position: Bishop of Worcester
Activities: Resource, umbrella, newsletters
Affiliations: Dudley and Worcestershire
Ecumenical Council

CONGREGATIONAL FEDERATION AREAS

Congregational Federation North West Midlands Area
Sawrey Lodge, Cotton Lane, Cheadle, Stoke-on-
Trent, ST10
Tel: 01473-247043 **Tel:** 01538-702587
Contact: Malcolm Hayden
Position: Secretary

Congregational Federation South West Midlands Area
4 Jolyffe Court, Clopton Road, Stratford-upon-
Avon, Warwickshire, CV37 6SW
Tel: 01789-294908 (h)
Contact: Pastor Ron Clarke
Position: Secretary

METHODIST CHURCH DISTRICTS

Methodist Church Birmingham District
36 Amesbury Road, Moseley, Birmingham, West
Midlands, B13 8LE
Tel: 0121-449-0131 (h) **Fax:** 0121-449-0131 (h)
Contact: Revd Christina Le Moignan
Position: Chair of District
Activities: Worship, resource, youth, elderly,
women, inter-faith
Traditions: Free Church
Affiliations: Birmingham Churches Together;
Coventry and Warwickshire Ecumenical Council;
Dudley and Worcestershire Ecumenical Council;
Churches Together in Herefordshire

Methodist Church Chester & Stoke District
9 Fairview Avenue, Alsager, Stoke-on-Trent,
Staffordshire, ST7 2NW (h)
Tel: 01270-882243 (h)
Contact: Revd Andrew L Gunstone
Position: Synod Secretary
Activities: Worship, umbrella, youth, elderly,
women, newsletters
Traditions: Free Church
Affiliations: Churches Together in Cheshire;
Staffordshire Plus Ecumenical Council

Methodist Church Wolverhampton & Shrewsbury District
Trinity Manse, Hustons Hill, Codsall,
Wolverhampton, West Midlands, WV8 2ER
Tel: 01902-842256
Contact: Revd Derrick R Lander
Position: Secretary
Affiliations: Churches Together in Shropshire;
Dudley and Worcestershire Ecumenical Council;
Staffordshire Plus Ecumenical Council; Telford
Christian Council

MORAVIAN DISTRICTS

Moravian Church Eastern District Conference
The Manse, Keys Lane, Prior Marston, Rugby,
Warwickshire, CV23 8SA

Tel: 01327-261375
Contact: Revd Michael Rea
Position: Chairman

NEW TESTAMENT CHURCH OF GOD

New Testament Church of God Coventry District
8 The Rowans, Off Silverbirch Avenue, Bedworth, Warwickshire, CV12 0ND
Tel: 01203-687502 **Tel:** 01203-313970 (h)

New Testament Church of God Birmingham District
244 Lozells Road, Lozells, Birmingham, West Midlands, B19 1NP
Tel: 0121-554-1358 **Tel:** 0121-554-7752 (h)
Contact: Sydney Uriah Thompson
Position: Minister
Activities: Visits youth, elderly, women
Traditions: Pentecostal

ROMAN CATHOLIC DIOCESES

Roman Catholic Diocese of Shrewsbury
Curial Offices, 2 Park Road South, Birkenhead, Merseyside, L43 4UX
Tel: 0151-652-9855 **Tel:** 0151-648-0623
Fax: 0151-653-5172
Contact: Revd Michael Gannon
Position: Bishop's Secretary
Activities: Worship, resource, umbrella, youth, women, elderly, newsletters, inter-faith
Affiliations: Churches Together in Cheshire; Churches Together in Shropshire; Telford Christian Council

Roman Catholic Archdiocese of Birmingham
Cathedral House, St Chad's Queensway, Birmingham, West Midlands, B4 6EU
Tel: 0121-236-5535 **Fax:** 0121-233-9266
Contact: Revd T Farrell FCJ
Position: Treasurer
Activities: Worship, resource, umbrella, visits, youth, elderly, women, newsletters, books, inter-faith
Other Languages: Vietnamese, Italian, Polish
Affiliations: Birmingham Council of Christian Churches; Staffordshire Plus Ecumenical Council; Coventry and Warwickshire Ecumenical Council; Dudley and Worcestershire Ecumenical Council

SALVATION ARMY DIVISIONS

Salvation Army West Midlands Division
24 St Chad's Queensway, Birmingham, West Midlands, B4 6HH
Tel: 0121-212-7800
Contact: Lt Col Ronald Smith
Position: Divisional Commander
Traditions: Free Church
Affiliations: Birmingham Churches Together

SEVENTH DAY ADVENTIST CONFERENCES

Seventh Day Adventist North England Conference
22 Zulla Road, Mapperley Park, Nottingham, Nottinghamshire, NG3 5DB
Tel: 0115-960-6312 **Tel:** 01476-578224 (h)
Fax: 0115-969-1476
EMail: 74532.452.@compuserve.comm
Contact: Eric C Lowe
Position: Executive Secretary
Activities: Youth, women
Traditions: Free Church

UNITARIAN AND FREE CHRISTIAN

Midland Union of Unitarian & Free Christian Churches
139 Deans Way, Kingsholm, Gloucester, Gloucestershire, GL7 2QB
Tel: 01452-307261
Contact: Mr James Absalom
Position: Secretary
Activities: Newsletters
Affiliations: Observer at Birmingham Council of Christian Churches

UNITED REFORMED CHURCH PROVINCES

United Reformed Church West Midlands Province
Digbeth-in-the-Field URC, Moat Lane, Yardley, Birmingham, West Midlands, B92 8NT
Tel: 0121-783-1177 **Tel:** 0121-427-4582
Fax: 0121-786-1329
Contact: Mr Simon Rowntree, JP
Position: Administrative Officer
Traditions: Free Church

OTHER BODIES

Wolverhampton Evangelical Fellowship
51 Lennox Gardens, Wolverhampton, West
Midlands, WV3

EAST ANGLIA

REGIONAL ECUMENICAL INSTRUMENTS

Suffolk Churches Together
Bishop's House, 4 Park Road, Ipswich, Suffolk,
IP1 3ST
Tel: 01473-252829 **Fax:** 01743-323552
Contact: Colin R Bevington
Position: Ecumenical Officer
Activities: Umbrella

Norfolk Churches Together
Marsham Rectory, Norwich, Norfolk, NR10 5PP
(h)
Tel: 01263-733249 (h)
Contact: Revd Robin Hewetson
Position: Secretary
Activities: Umbrella

Greater Peterborough Ecumenical Council
61 Hall Lane, Werrington, Peterborough,
Cambridgeshire, PE4 6RA (h)
Tel: 01733-51915 **Tel:** 01733-32145 (h)
Contact: Mr Frank Smith
Position: Secretary
Activities: Umbrella

BAPTIST UNION AREAS

Baptist Union of Great Britain Eastern Area
c/o Baptist House, P O Box 44, 129 Broadway,
Didcot, Oxfordshire, 0X11 8RT
Tel: 01235-512077

CHURCH OF ENGLAND DIOCESES

Church of England Diocese of Ely
Diocesan Office, Bishop Woodford House, Barton
Road, Ely, Cambridgeshire, CB7 4DX
Tel: 01353-663579 **Fax:** 01353-666148
EMail: office@ely.anglican.org
Contact: Dr Matthew Lavis
Position: Diocesan Secretary
Activities: Worship, resource, media, umbrella, visits

youth, elderly, women, newsletters, books, inter-
faith
Affiliations: Churches Together in
Cambridgeshire; Greater Peterborough Ecumenical
Council

Church of England Diocese of St Edmundsbury & Ipswich
Diocesan House, 13 Tower Street, Ipswich, Suffolk,
IP1 3BG
Tel: 01473-211028 **Fax:** 01473-232407
Activities: Resource, media, youth, elderly,
women, newsletters
Affiliations: Churches Together in Suffolk

Church of England Diocese of Norwich
Diocesan Office, 109 Dereham Road, Easton,
Norwich, Norfolk, NR9 5ES
Tel: 01603-880853 **Fax:** 01603-881083
Contact: David Adeney
Position: Diocesan Secretary
Activities: Resource, umbrella, newsletters, inter-
faith
Affiliations: Norfolk Churches Together

Church of England Diocese of Peterborough
The Palace, Peterborough, Cambridgeshire,
PE1 1YB
Tel: 01733-64448 **Fax:** 01733-555271
Contact: Mr Kenneth H Hope-Jones
Position: Diocesan Secretary
Affiliations: Greater Peterborough Ecumenical
Council

CONGREGATIONAL FEDERATION AREAS

Congregational Federation Eastern Area
34 Clarence Road, Ipswich, Suffolk, IP3
Tel: 01394-274345
Contact: John Gale
Position: Secretary
Activities: Umbrella
Traditions: Free Church

Congregational Federation Norfolk Area
Marinka, 6 Flowerpot Lane, Long Stratton,
Norwich, Norfolk, NR15 2TS (h)
Tel: 01508-530511 (h)
Contact: Len Willis
Position: Secretary
Activities: Umbrella, visits, youth, newsletters
inter-faith

Traditions: Free Church
Affiliations: Norfolk Churches Together

METHODIST CHURCH DISTRICTS

Methodist Church in Oxford & Leicester District
9 Laverstock Road, Wigston, Leicester,
Leicestershire, LE18 2RJ (h)
Tel: 0116-257-1069 (h)
Contact: Revd Martin T Smithson
Position: Synod Secretary
Activities: Umbrella
Traditions: Free Church
Affiliations: Greater Peterborough Ecumenical
Council

Methodist Church East Anglia District
26 Wentworth Green, Norwich, Norfolk,
NR4 6AE
Tel: 01603-52257
Contact: Malcolm Braddy
Position: District Chairman
Traditions: Free Church

ROMAN CATHOLIC DIOCESES

Roman Catholic Diocese of East Anglia
The White House, 21 Upgate, Poringland,
Norwich, Norfolk, NR14 7SH
Tel: 01508-492202 **Fax:** 01508-495358
Contact: Rt Revd Peter D Smith
Position: Bishop
Activities: Worship, resource, youth, elderly,
women, newsletters, inter-faith
Affiliations: Norfolk and Suffolk Churches
Together; Cambridgeshire Ecumenical Council;
Greater Peterborough Ecumenical Council

SALVATION ARMY DIVISIONS

Salvation Army Anglia Division
Dencora Way, Carrow Road, Norwich, Norfolk,
NR1 1DL
Contact: Major Robert Street
Position: Divisional Commander
Traditions: Free Church, Holiness
Affiliations: Norfolk Churches Together/Suffolk
Churches Together; Cambridgeshire Ecumenical
Council

UNITED REFORMED CHURCH PROVINCES

United Reformed Church Eastern Province
The United Reformed Church, Duxford Road,
Whittlesford, Cambridge, Cambridgeshire, CB2
4ND
Tel: 01223-830770 **Fax:** 01223-830771
EMail: urc7@aol.com
Contact: Ms Ann Barton
Position: Provincial Secretary
Activities: Resource, newsletters
Affiliations: Cambridgeshire Ecumenical Council

UNITARIAN AND FREE CHRISTIAN CHURCHES DISTRICT

Eastern Union of Unitarian & Free Christian Churches
Tithe Farm, North Walsham Road, Happisburgh,
Norwich, Norfolk, NR12 0QS (h)
Tel: 01692-651467 (h)
Contact: Rodney Stuart Voegeli
Position: Secretary
Activities: Umbrella, newsletters, inter-faith

OTHER BODIES

King's Lynn Evangelical Fellowship
11 Gloucester Road, Gaywood, King's Lynn,
Norfolk, PE30 4AB
Tel: 01553-772036 (h)
Contact: Mr Mike Brown
Position: Secretary
Activities: Umbrella

Peterborough Alliance of Christian Evangelicals (PACE)
5 Elm Close, Market Deeping, Peterborough,
Cambridgeshire, PE6 8JN
Tel: 01778-347011 (h)
Contact: Revd Graham Timson
Position: Chairman

GREATER LONDON

REGIONAL ECUMENICAL INSTRUMENTS

Barking Area Church Leaders' Group
349 Westbourne Grove, Westcliff-on-Sea, Essex,
SS0 0PU (h)
Tel: 01702-342327 (h) **Fax:** 01702-342327

Contact: Revd D C Hardiman
Position: Ecumenical Officer
Activities: Umbrella, newsletters
Affiliations: Essex Churches Consultative Council; Churches Together in England

Churches Together in North London
St Paul's Vicarage, Hammers Lane, Mill Hill, London, NE7 4EA (h) **Tel:** 0181-959-1856 (h)
Contact: Revd Martin Kettle
Position: Convenor
Activities: Umbrella

Churches Together in North West London
80 Leamington Crescent, South Harrow, Middlesex, HA2 9HQ
Tel: 0181-422-7015 **Fax:** 0181-422-7015
Contact: Mr Bill Boyd
Position: Convenor
Activities: Umbrella

Churches Together in South London
Sisters of St Andrew, St Peter's House, 308 Kennington Lane, London, SE11 (h)
Tel: 0171-587-0087
Contact: Sister Liz Grant
Position: Ecumenical Officer
Activities: Umbrella

Churches Together in West London
St Andrew's Manse, 2 King's Avenue, Ealing, London, W5 2SH (h)
Tel: 0181-998-7405 (h)
Contact: Revd Mary Frost
Position: Link Person
Activities: Umbrella

East London Church Leaders Group
East End Mission, 585 Commercial Road, London, E1 0HJ
Tel: 0171-790-3366
Contact: Revd Pauline Barnett
Position: Secretary
Activities: Umbrella

Essex Churches Consultative Council
349 Westbourne Grove, Westcliff-on-Sea, Essex, SS0 0PU (h)
Tel: 01702-342327 (h) **Fax:** 01702-342327
Contact: Revd David C Hardiman
Position: Ecumenical Officer
Activities: Umbrella, newsletters

London Churches' Group
The City Temple, Holborn Viaduct, London, EC1A 2DE
Tel: 0171-353-8354 **Fax:** 0171-353-8354
Contact: Executive Officer
Activities: Umbrella (pan-London)

ASSEMBLIES OF GOD REGIONS

Assemblies of God in Great Britain & Ireland London & South East Regional Council
18 Christchurch Square, Hackney, London, E9 7HU

BAPTIST UNION AREAS

Baptist Union of Great Britain Metropolitan Area
25 Springwell Road, Streatham, London, SW16 2QU (h)
Tel: 0181-769-6519 (h) **Fax:** 0181-769-6519
Contact: Revd Douglas McBain
Position: Gen Superintendent
Traditions: Free Church

CHURCH OF ENGLAND DIOCESES

Church of England Diocese of London
London Diocesan House, 36 Causton Street, London, SW1P 4AU
Tel: 0171-932-1100 **Fax:** 0171-932-1113

Church of England Diocese of Southwark
Trinity House, 4 Chapel Court, Borough High Street, London, SE1 1HW
Tel: 0171-403-8686 **Fax:** 0171-403-4770
EMail: trinity@dswark.org.uk
Contact: Mr Martin C Cawte
Position: Diocesan Secretary

METHODIST CHURCH DISTRICTS

Methodist Church London North East District
2 South Road, Bishop's Stortford, Hertfordshire, CM23 3JH
Tel: 01279-654475
Contact: Revd Michael Hayman
Position: Synod Secretary
Traditions: Free Church
Affiliations: Essex Consultative Council; Barking Area Church Leaders' Group; East London Church Leaders' Group; Churches Together in North London

Methodist Church London North West District
6 Woodcock Hill, Kenton, Middlesex, HA3 0JG (h)
Tel: 0181-907-8755 (h)
Contact: Revd Geoff Cornell
Position: Synod Secretary
Traditions: Free Church
Affiliations: Churches Together in Bedfordshire;
Churches Together in Hertfordshire;
Buckinghamshire Ecumenical Council; Churches
Together in North West London

Methodist Church London South East District
87 Lower Queens Road, Ashford, Kent,
TN24 8HD
Tel: 01233-621216
Contact: Revd Jeremy Dare
Position: Synod Secretary
Activities: Worship youth, elderly, women,
newsletters
Traditions: Free Church
Affiliations: Churches Together in Kent; Churches
Together in South London

Methodist Church London South West District
76 Coombe Lane West, Kingston-upon-Thames,
KT2 7DA
Tel: 0181-949-3340 **Fax:** 0181-949-3340
Contact: Revd Martin Broadbent
Position: Chairman
Traditions: Free Church
Affiliations: Churches Together in South London;
Churches Together in Surrey

MORAVIAN CHURCH DISTRICTS

Moravian Church Eastern District Conference
Hillside, 29 The Settlement, Ockbrook, Derby,
Derbyshire, DE72 3RJ
Tel: 01332-6745932
Contact: Revd Michael Rea
Position: Chairman
Traditions: Free Church

ROMAN CATHOLIC DIOCESES

Roman Catholic Archdiocese of Southwark
Archbishop's House, 150 St Georges Road,
London, SE1 6HX (h)
Tel: 0171-928-2495 (h)   **Fax:** 0171-928-7833
Contact: Revd Richard Moth
Position: Vice-Chancellor
Affiliations: Churches Together in South London

Roman Catholic Archdiocese of Westminster
Archbishops House, Ambrosden Avenue, London,
SW1P 1QJ
Tel: 0171-834-7452
Contact: The Vicar General
Affiliations: Churches Together in North West
London

SALVATION ARMY DIVISIONS

Salvation Army Central South Division
1st Floor Frays Court, 71 Cowley Road, Uxbridge,
Middlesex, UB8 2AE
Tel: 01895-208800 **Fax:** 01895-208811
Contact: Lt Col Raymond Houghton
Position: Divisional Commander

Salvation Army London Central Division
9 Salisbury Road, Barnet, Hertfordshire, EN5 4JW
Tel: 0181-447-1422 **Fax:** 0181-449-4097
Contact: Lt Col Hugh Rea
Position: Divisional Commander
Activities: Worship, youth, elderly, women
Traditions: Free Church

Salvation Army London North East Division
423 Forest Road, Walthamstow, London, E17 4PY
Tel: 0181-520-2244 **Tel:** 0181-520-3755
Contact: Lt Col David Phillips
Position: Divisional Commander
Activities: Worship, visits, youth, elderly, women,
newsletters, books, inter-faith
Traditions: Free Church
Affiliations: Essex Council of Churches

Salvation Army London South East Division
3 West Court, Armstrong Road, Maidstone, Kent,
ME15 6QR
Tel: 01622-775000
Contact: Lieutenant Colonel Keith Burridge
Position: Divisional Commander
Traditions: Free Church
Affiliations: Churches Together in Kent; Churches
Together in Surrey; Churches Together in South
London

SEVENTH DAY ADVENTIST REGIONAL CONFERENCES

Seventh Day Adventist Church South England Conference
25 St John's Road, Watford, Herfordshire,
WD1 1PY

Tel: 01923-232728 **Tel:** 01923-893511 (h)
Fax: 01923-250582 **EMail:**
74532.1047@compuserve.com
Contact: Dr Jonathan Gallagher
Position: Executive Secretary
Activities: Resource, umbrella, visits, youth, elderly, women, newsletters, inter-faith
Traditions: Independent

UNITED REFORMED CHURCH PROVINCES

United Reformed Church Southern Province
Synod Office, East Croydon United Reformed Church, Addiscombe Grove, Croydon, Surrey, CR0 5LP
Tel: 0181-688-3730 **Fax:** 0181-688-2698
Contact: Mrs Christine P Meekison, DCS
Position: Synod Clerk

United Reformed Church Thames North Province
The City Temple, Holborn Viaduct, London, EC1A 2DE
Tel: 0171-583-8701 **Fax:** 0171-353-1558
Contact: Revd Janet Sowerbutts
Position: Provincial Moderator

OTHER BODIES

Brent Evangelical Fellowship
PO Box 326, Wembley, Middlesex, HA9 6HL

Leyton Evangelical Fellowship
St Mary's Vicarage, 4 Vicarage Road, Leyton, London, E10 5EA (h)
Tel: 0181 539 7882 (h)
Contact: Revd David Ainge
Position: Chair
Activities: Umbrella

SOUTH EAST

REGIONAL ECUMENICAL INSTRUMENTS

Churches Together in Buckinghamshire
124 Bath Road, Banbury, Oxfordshire, OX16 0TR (h)
Tel: 01295-268201 (h)
Contact: Canon Derek Palmer
Position: Secretary
Activities: Umbrella, newsletters

Bedfordshire Ecumenical Committee
Flat 1, 43 Benslow Lane, Hitchin, Hertfordshire, SG4 9RE (h)
Tel: 01462-452784 (h)
Contact: Mrs Jenny Nicholson
Position: Secretary
Activities: Umbrella, newsletters

Churches Together in Hertfordshire
Flat 1, 43 Benslow Lane, Hitchin, Hertfordshire, SG4 9RE (h)
Tel: 01462-452784 (h)
Contact: Mrs Jenny Nicholson
Position: Secretary
Activities: Umbrella, newsletters

Sussex Churches
14 Ledgers Meadow, Cuckfield, West Sussex, RH17 5EB
Tel: 0144-4456588
Contact: Revd Terry Stratford
Position: Ecumenical Officer
Activities: Umbrella

Oxfordshire Ecumenical Council
"Sea Fever", 188 Elmer Road, Middleton-on-Sea, P022 6JA
Tel: 01243-586344
Contact: Norman LeFort
Position: County Ecumenical Officer and Executive Secretary
Activities: Resource, media, umbrella, newsletters
Other Languages: German, French, Greek, Russian

Churches Together in Kent
St Lawrence Vicarage, Stone Street, Seal, Sevenoaks, Kent, TN15 0LQ
Tel: 01732-761766
Contact: Revd Dr Michael Cooke
Position: Ecumenical Officer
Activities: Umbrella

Milton Keynes Christian Council
c/o Church of Christ the Cornerstone, 300 Saxon Gate West, Central Milton Keynes, Milton Keynes, Buckinghamshire, MK9 2ES
Tel: 01908-230655 **Tel:** 01908-265053 (h)
Fax: 01908-200216
Contact: Revd Murdoch MacKenzie
Position: Ecumenical Moderator
Activities: Umbrella

Churches Together in Hampshire & the Islands
6 West Road, Woolston, Southampton, Hampshire,
SO19 9AJ (h)
Tel: 01703-446948 (h)
Contact: Carol Cunio
Position: Ecumenical Officer
Activities: Worship, media, umbrella, newsletters

Churches Together in Surrey
The Parish Centre, Station Approach, Stonleigh,
Epsom, Surrey, KT19 0QZ
Tel: 0181-394-0536 **Fax:** 0171-394-0536
Contact: Ms Rosemary Underwood
Position: Ecumenical Co-ordinator
Activities: Umbrella, newsletters

Essex Churches Consultative Council
349 Westbourne Grove, Westcliff-on-Sea, Essex,
SS0 0PU (h)
Tel: 01702-342327 (h) **Fax:** 01702-342327
Contact: Revd David C Hardiman
Position: Ecumenical Officer
Activities: Umbrella, newsletters

ASSEMBLIES OF GOD REGIONAL COUNCILS

Assemblies of God in Great Britain & Ireland Eastern Regional Council
61 Southend Road, Wickford, Essex, S11 8BA

BAPTIST UNION AREAS

Baptist Union of Great Britain Eastern Area
35 Chaucer Way, Lexden, Colchester, Essex,
CO3 4HE
Tel: 01206-570673 (h)
Contact: Revd D Harper
Position: General Superintendent
Traditions: Free Church
Affiliations: Norfolk and Suffolk Churches
Together; Essex Churches' Council

Baptist Union of Great Britain Southern Area
70 Westwood Road, Newbury, Berkshire,
RG14 7TL (h)
Tel: 01635-31464 (h)
Contact: Revd Geoffrey Reynolds
Position: General Superintendent
Traditions: Free Church
Affiliations: Churches Together in Oxfordshire,
Berkshire, Hampshire & Islands

Baptist Union of Great Britain Central Area
6 Sunridge Close, Newport Pagnell,
Buckinghamshire, MK16 0LT (h)
Tel: 01908-616093 (h) **Fax:** 01908-616093
Contact: Revd Roy A Freestone
Position: General Superintendent
Traditions: Free Church
Affiliations: Milton Keynes Christian Council;
Churches Together in Buckinghamshire; Churches
Together in Bedfordshire; Churches Together in
Hertfordshire

Baptist Union of Great Britain South Eastern Area
41 Newlands Road, Tunbridge Wells, Kent,
TN4 9AS
Tel: 01892-530033
Contact: Revd Peter Tongeman
Position: General Superintendent
Traditions: Free Church
Affiliations: Churches Together in Kent; Sussex
Churches; Surrey Churches Together

CHURCH OF ENGLAND DIOCESES

Church of England Diocese of Canterbury
Diocesan House, Lady Wootton's Green,
Canterbury, Kent, CT1 1NQ
Tel: 01227-459401 **Fax:** 01227-450964
Contact: Mr David S Kemp
Position: Diocesan Secretary
Affiliations: Churches Together in Kent

Church of England Diocese of Chelmsford
53 New Street, Chelmsford, Essex, CM1 1AT
Tel: 01245-266731 **Fax:** 012445-492786
Contact: Mr David R Phillips
Position: Diocesan Secretary
Affiliations: Barking Area Church Leaders' Group;
Essex Churches Consultative Council

Church of England Diocese of Guildford
Diocesan House, Quarry Street, Guildford, Surrey,
GU1 3XG
Tel: 01483-571826 **Fax:** 01483-567896
Contact: Diocesan Secretary
Affiliations: Churches Together in Surrey

Church of England Diocese of Chichester
Diocesan Church House, 211 New Church Road,
Hove, East Sussex, BN3 4ED
Tel: 01273-421021 **Tel:** 01273-202497 (h)

Fax: 01273-421041
Contact: Jonathan Martin Robin Prichard
Position: Diocesan Secretary
Activities: Resource, umbrella, visits, youth, newsletters, books
Affiliations: Sussex Churches

Church of England Diocese of Southwark
Trinity House, 4 Chapel Court, Borough High Street, London, SE1 1HW
Tel: 0171-403-8686 **Fax:** 0171-403-4770
EMail: trinity@dswark.org.uk
Contact: Mr Martin C Cawte
Position: Diocesan Secretary

Church of England Diocese of Oxford
Diocesan Church House, Oxford, Oxfordshire, OX2 0NB
Tel: 01865-244566 **Fax:** 01865-790470
Contact: Mr T C Landsbert
Position: Diocesan Secretary
Affiliations: Churches Together in Berkshire; Churches Together in Buckinghamshire; Milton Keynes Christian Council

Church of England Diocese of Portsmouth
Cathedral House, St Thomas's Street, Portsmouth, Hampshire, P01 2HA
Tel: 01705-825731 **Fax:** 01705-752967
Contact: Michael Frank Jordan
Position: Diocesan Secretary
Affiliations: Churches Together in Hampshire and the Islands

Church of England Diocese of Rochester
Diocesan Office, St Nicholas Church, Boley Hill, Rochester, Kent, ME1 1SL
Tel: 01634-830333 **Fax:** 01634-829463
Contact: Mr Peter G H Law
Position: Diocesan Secretary
Affiliations: Churches Together in Kent

Church of England Diocese of St Albans
41 Holywell Hill, St Albans, Hertfordshire, AL1 1HE
Tel: 01727-854532 **Fax:** 01727-844469
Contact: Mr L M Nicholls
Position: Diocesan Secretary
Affiliations: Churches Together in Hertfordshire and Bedfordshire

Church of England Diocese of Winchester
Church House, 9 The Close, Winchester, Hampshire, SO23 9LS
Tel: 01962-844644 **Fax:** 01962-841815
Email: 100517.721@compuserve.com
Contact: Mr Ray Anderton
Position: Diocesan Secretary
Activities: Resource, media, youth, elderly, women
Affiliations: Churches Together in Hampshire and the Islands

CONGREGATIONAL FEDERATION AREAS

Congregational Federation South East Area
17 Overbrook, West Horsley, Leatherhead, Surrey, KT24 6BH
Tel: 01483-282541 (h)

Congregational Federation Central Southern Area
41 Warrenside, South Harting, Petersfield, Hampshire, GU31

METHODIST DISTRICTS

Methodist Church London North East District
2 South Road, Bishop's Stortford, Hertfordshire, CM23 3JH
Tel: 01279-654475
Contact: Revd Michael Hayman
Position: Synod Secretary
Traditions: Free Church
Affiliations: Essex Consultative Concil; Barking Area Church Leaders' Group; East London Church Leaders' Group; Churches Together in North London

Methodist Church Oxford & Leicester District
11 Woodham's Drive, Brackley, Northamptonshire, NN13 6NB
Tel: 01280-705601
Contact: Revd Dr Martin Wellings
Position: Synod Secretary
Traditions: Free Church
Affiliations: Churches Together in Oxfordshire; Churches Together in Leicestershire; Churches Together in Northamptonshire

Methodist Church London South East District
8 Elgin Road, Croydon, Surrey, CR0 6XA
Tel: 0181-654-2845 (h)

Contact: Roger Cresswell
Position: Synod Secretary
Traditions: Free Church
Affiliations: Churches Together in Kent; Churches Together in South London

Methodist Church London North West District
6 Woodcock Hill, Kenton, Middlesex, HA3 0JG (h)
Tel: 0181-907-8755
Contact: Revd Geoff Cornell
Position: Secretary
Traditions: Free Church

Methodist Church London South West District
76 Coombe Lane West, Kingston-upon-Thames,
KT2 7DA
Tel: 0181-949-3340 **Fax:** 0181-949-3340
Contact: Revd Marin Broadbent
Position: Chairman
Traditions: Free Church
Affiliations: Churches Together in Surrey; Sussex Churches

Methodist Church Channel Islands District
West Lea, Route des Quennevais, St Brelade, Jersey
Tel: 01534-43933
Contact: Revd Colin Hough
Position: Chairman
Traditions: Free Church
Affiliations: Churches Together in Hampshire and the Islands

MORAVIAN CHURCH DISTRICTS

Moravian Church Eastern District Conference
Hillside, 29 The Settlement, Ockbrook, Derby,
Derbyshire, DE72 3RJ
Tel: 01332-6745932
Contact: Revd Michael Rea
Position: Chairman
Traditions: Free Church

ROMAN CATHOLIC DIOCESES

Roman Catholic Diocese of Brentwood
Cathedral House, Ingrave Road, Brentwood, Essex,
CM15 8AT
Tel: 01277-214821 **Fax:** 01277-214060
Contact: Very Revd Gordon Read
Position: Chancellor
Affiliations: Essex Churches Consultative Council

Roman Catholic Diocese of Arundel & Brighton
Bishop's House, Upper Drive, Hove, East Sussex,
BN3 6NE
Tel: 01273-506387 **Tel:** 01273-563017 (h)
Fax: 01273-501527
Internet: http://www.roehampton.ac.uk
Contact: Revd Mgr Canon J Hull
Position: Vicar General
Activities: Worship, resource, newsletters, inter-faith
Other Languages: Italian, Polish, French
Affiliations: Churches Together in Surrey and Sussex

Roman Catholic Archdiocese of Westminster
Archbishops House, Ambrosden Avenue, London,
SW1P 1QJ
Tel: 0171-834-7452
Contact: Vicar General
Affiliations: Churches Together in Hertfordshire

Roman Catholic Diocese of Portsmouth
Bishop's House, Edinburgh Road, Portsmouth,
Hampshire, PO1 3HG
Contact: Rt Revd Crispian Hollis
Position: Bishop
Affiliations: Churches Together in Hampshire and the Islands; Churches Together in Berkshire

SALVATION ARMY DISTRICTS

Salvation Army Southern Division
111a Lodge Road, Southampton, Hampshire,
S014 6RE
Tel: 01703-333348 **Fax:** 01703-330027
Contact: Lt Col John Pearce-Haydon
Position: Divisional Commander
Activities: Worship, resource, visits, youth, elderly, women, newsletters, books, inter-faith
Traditions: Free Church
Affiliations: Churches Together in Hampshire and the Islands; Churches Together in Dorset; Churches Together in Wiltshire

Salvation Army Central South Division
1st Floor Frays Court, 71 Cowley Road, Uxbridge,
Middlesex, UB8 2AE
Tel: 01895-208800 **Fax:** 01895-208811
Contact: Lt Col Raymond Houghton
Position: Divisional Commander

SEVENTH DAY ADVENTISTS
CONFERENCES

Seventh Day Adventist Church South England Conference
25 St Johns Road, Watford, Hertfordshire, WD1 1PY
Tel: 01923-232728 **Tel:** 01923-893511 (h)
Fax: 01923-250582
EMail: 74532.1047@compuserve.com
Contact: Dr Jonathan Gallagher
Position: Executive Secretary
Activities: Worship, youth, women, newsletters, inter-faith
Traditions: Independent
Other Languages: Spanish, Portugese

UNITARIAN AND FREE CHRISTIANS

General Assembly of Unitarian & Free Christian Churches
Southern Unitarian Association, 35 Brookfield Road, Fratton, Portrsmouth, Hampshire, PO1 5HZ (h)
Tel: 01705-736686 (h)
Contact: Daisy Roxburgh-Gunter
Position: Secretary
Activities: Worship, umbrella, newsletters, inter-faith

UNITED REFORMED CHURCH
PROVINCES

United Reformed Church Southern Province
Synod Office, East Croydon United Reformed Church, Addiscombe Grove, Croydon, Surrey, CR0 5LP
Tel: 0181-688-3730
Contact: Mrs Christine Meekison
Position: Synod Clerk

United Reformed Church Wessex Province
King's Road, Chandler's Ford, Eastleigh, Hampshire, SO53 2EY
Tel: 01703-266548
Contact: Revd Derek M Wales
Position: Provincial Moderator
Traditions: Free Church

United Reformed Church Thames North Province
4 Duncan Court, Green Lanes, Winchmore Hill, London, N21 3RL **Tel:** 0181-360-1773

Contact: Revd G W Satchell
Position: Synod Clerk

United Reformed Church Eastern Province
The United Reformed Church, Stowmarket, Suffolk, IP14 1AD
Tel: 01449-615130
Contact: Mr William McVey
Position: Synod Clerk

OTHER BODIES

Beckenham & Penge Evangelical Fellowship
76 Village Way, Beckenham, Kent, BR3 3NR (h)
Tel: 0181-289-3572 (h)
Contact: Andrew A Cooke
Position: Chair
Activities: Umbrella, newsletters

Brighton & Hove Evangelical Fellowship
118 Nevill Avenue, Hove, East Sussex, BN3 7ND

South East Essex Evangelical Fellowship
14 Elsenham Court, Tendring Avenue, Rayleigh, Essex, SS6 9SB

Southampton Evangelical Fellowship
Central Hall, St Mary Street, Southampton, Hampshire, SO14 1NF

Portsmouth Evangelical Fellowship
63 Burnside, Waterlooville, Hampshire, PO7 7GG

Bromley Evangelical Fellowship
81 Kingsway, Coney Hall, West Wickham, Kent, BR4 9JE

SOUTH WEST

REGIONAL ECUMENICAL INSTRUMENTS

Greater Bristol Ecumenical Council
St Nicholas House, Lawford's Gate, Bristol, Greater Bristol, BS5 0RE
Tel: 0117-954-2133 **Tel:** 0117-962-2519 (h)
Contact: Mr Brian J H Blancharde
Position: Executive Secretary
Activities: Resource, umbrella, newsletters

Somerset Churches Together
56 Grange Road, Saltford, Bristol, Greater Bristol, BS18 3AG

Tel: 01225-873609 **Fax:** 01225-874110
Contact: Venerable Bob Evens
Position: Chairman
Activities: Umbrella, newsletters

Churches Together in Dorset
22 D'Urberville Close, Dorchester, Dorset,
DT1 2JT (h)
Tel: 01305-264416 (h)
Contact: Valerie Potter
Position: Ecumenical Officer
Activities: Umbrella, newsletters

Gloucestershire Churches Together
151 Tuffley Road, Gloucester, Gloucestershire,
GL1 5NP
Tel: 0145-2301347 **Tel:** 0122-5336003 (h)
Contact: Revd David Calvert
Position: Ecumenical Officer
Activities: Worship, youth, elderly, newsletters

Wiltshire Churches Together
16 Sherwood Avenue, Melksham, Wiltshire,
SN12 7HJ
Contact: Anne Doyle
Position: Ecumenical Officer
Activities: Umbrella, visits, newsletters, inter-faith

Christians Together in Devon
Grenville House, Whites Lane, Torrington, Devon,
EX38 8DS
Tel: 01865-62509
Contact: Revd John Bradley
Position: Ecumenical Officer
Activities: Umbrella, newsletters

Churches Together in Cornwall
138 Bodmin Road, Truro, Cornwall, TR1 1RB (h)
Tel: 01872-273154 (h)
Contact: Revd Gerald Matthison Burt
Position: County Ecumenical Secretary
Activities: Umbrella, newsletters

ASSEMBLIES OF GOD REGIONS

Assemblies of God, West Country Regional Council
102 Cowick Lane, Exeter, Devon, EX2 (h)
Tel: 01392-210146 **Tel:** 01392-438766 (h)
Fax: 01392-210146
Contact: Norman Wilfred Wreford
Position: Chair
Traditions: Pentecostal

BAPTIST UNION AREAS

Baptist Union of Great Britain Western Area
15 Fenshurst Gardens, Bristol, Greater Bristol,
BS18 9AU
Tel: 01275-394101
Contact: Revd Roger Hayden
Position: General Superintendent
Traditions: Free Church
Affiliations: Greater Bristol Ecumenical Council;
Gloucestershire Churches Together; Somerset
Churches Together

Baptist Union of Great Britain South Western Area
10 Lymeborne Avenue, Exeter, Devon,
EX1 3AU (h)
Tel: 01392-221736 (h) **Fax:** 01392-221736
Contact: R Gwynne Edwards
Position: General Superintendent
Traditions: Free Church
Affiliations: Churches Together in Dorset;
Somerset Churches Together; Christians Together in
Devon; Churches Together in Cornwall

CHURCH OF ENGLAND DIOCESES

Church of England Diocese of Bristol
Diocesan Church House, 23 Great George Street,
Bristol, Greater Bristol, BS1
Tel: 0117-921-4411 **Fax:** 0117-925-0460
Contact: Mrs Lesley Farrall
Position: Diocesan Secretary
Activities: Resource
Affiliations: Greater Bristol Ecumenical Council;
Wiltshire Churches Together

Church of England Diocese of Exeter
Diocesan House, Palace Gate, Exeter, Devon,
EX1 1HX
Tel: 01392-272686 **Fax:** 01392-499594
Contact: Diocesan Secretary
Traditions: Anglican
Affiliations: Churches Together in Devon

Church of England Diocese of Gloucester
Church House, College Green, Gloucester,
Gloucestershire, GL1 2LY
Tel: 01452-410022 **Fax:** 01452-308324
Contact: Mrs Hilary Penney
Position: Executive Officer
Activities: Resource, umbrella
Affiliations: Gloucestershire Churches Together

Church of England Diocese of Salisbury
Church House, Crane Street, Salisbury, Wiltshire,
SP1 2QB
Tel: 01722-411922 **Fax:** 01722-411990
Contact: Revd Karen Curnock
Position: Diocesan Secretary
Affiliations: Churches Together in Dorset;
Wiltshire Churches Together

Church of England Diocese of Truro
Diocesan House, Truro, Cornwall, TR1 3DU
Tel: 01872-74351 **Fax:** 01872-74351
Contact: Mr C B Gorton
Position: Diocesan Secretary
Affiliations: Churches Together in Cornwall

Church of England Diocese of Bath & Wells
Diocesan Office, Old Deanery, Wells, Somerset,
BA5 2UG
Tel: 01749-670777 **Fax:** 01749-674240
Contact: Mr N Denison
Position: Diocesan Secretary
Affiliations: Somerset Churches Together

*CONGREGATIONAL FEDERATION
AREAS*

Congregational Federation South West Area
85 Bowden Park Road, Crownhill, Plymouth,
Devon, PL6 5NQ (h)
Contact: Mrs Greta White
Position: Assistant Secretary
Activities: Umbrella
Traditions: Free Church

METHODIST CHURCH DISTRICTS

Methodist Church Plymouth & Exeter District
Fairlawn, 133 New Road, Brixham, Devon,
TQ5 8DB
Fax: 01803-854431 (h)
Contact: Revd Peter B Williamson
Position: Synod Secretary
Activities: Umbrella, inter-faith
Traditions: Free Church
Affiliations: Churches Together in Devon;
Somerset Churches Together

Methodist Church Bristol District
80 Leckhampton Road, Cheltenham,
Gloucestershire, GL53 0BN
Tel: 01242-524889
Contact: Revd Ian Suttie

Position: Synod Secretary
Traditions: Free Church
Affiliations: Greater Bristol Ecumenical Council;
Gloucestershire Churches Together; Somerset
Churches Together; Wiltshire Churches Together

Methodist Church Cornwall District
Wesley Manse, 15 Pednandrea, St Just, Penzance,
Cornwall, TR19 7UA (h)
Tel: 01736-788506 (h)
Contact: Revd Howard Curnow
Position: Synod Secretary
Traditions: Methodist
Affiliations: Churches Together in Cornwall

MORAVIAN DISTRICTS

The Moravian Church Western District
Glengariff, Weston Lane, Bath, Somerset,
BA1 4AA (h)
Tel: 01225-421026 (h)
Contact: Paul Gubi
Position: Chair
Activities: Worship

ROMAN CATHOLIC DIOCESES

Roman Catholic Diocese of Clifton
St Anthony's Presbytery, Satchfield Crescent,
Henbury, Bristol, Greater Bristol, BS10 7BE
Tel: 01272-502509
Contact: Mgr Canon W Mitchell
Position: Vicar General
Affiliations: Greater Bristol Ecumenical Council;
Gloucestershire Churches Together; Somerset
Churches Together; Wiltshire Churches Together

Roman Catholic Diocese of Plymouth
Bishop's House, 31 Wyndham St West, Plymouth,
Devon PL1 5RZ
Tel: 01752-224414

SALVATION ARMY DISTRICTS

Salvation Army South Western Division
Marlborough Court, Manaton Close, Matford
Business Park, Exeter, Devon, EX2 8PF
Tel: 01392-822100 **Fax:** 01392-822111
Contact: Lt Col Clifford E Hurcum
Position: Divisional Commander
Activities: Youth, elderly, women, newsletters,
books, inter-faith
Traditions: Free Church

UNITED REFORMED CHURCH PROVINCES

United Reformed Church South Western Province
The Manse, Norton Fitzwarren, Taunton, Somerset, TA2 6RU
Tel: 01823-275470 **Fax:** 01823-275470
Contact: Revd S Lloyd Langston
Position: Synod Clerk
Affiliations: Greater Bristol Ecumenical Council; Somerset Churches Together; Christians Together in Devon; Churches Together in Cornwall

SEVENTH DAY ADVENTIST CONFERENCES

Seventh Day Adventist Church South England Conference
25 St John's Road, Watford, Hertfordshire, WD1 1PY
Tel: 01923-232728 **Tel:** 01923-893511 (h)
Fax: 01923-250582
Contact: Dr Jonathan Gallagher
Position: Executive Secretary
Activities: Resource, umbrella, visits youth, elderly, women, newsletters, inter-faith

UNITARIANS AND FREE CHRISTIANS

Western Union of Unitarian & Free Christian Churches
2a Cotham Road, Cotham, Bristol, Greater Bristol, BS6 6DR

OTHER BODIES

South Wessex Evangelical Alliance
Delta House, 56 Westover Road, Bournemouth, Dorset, BH1 2BS

Mid Cotswolds Evangelical Alliance
127 Ashlands Road, Cheltenham, Gloucestershire, GL51 0DJ

Swindon Christian Fellowship
PO Box 336, Swindon, Wiltshire, SN2 1TD
Tel: 01793-525585
Contact: Mr Nigel Marsh
Position: Church leader
Activities: Youth
Traditions: New Church or House Church
Affiliations: Pioneer

Taunton Evangelical Fellowship
Canon Street Pentecostal Church, Canon Street, Taunton, Somerset

Torbay Evangelical Fellowship
Ellacumbe Vicarage, 1a Lower Ellacombe Church Road, Torquay, Devon, TQ1 1JH (h)
Tel: 01803-293441 (h)
Contact: Revd Roy William Taylor
Position: Chair
Activities: Resource, media, umbrella, youth

IRELAND

IRISH ECUMENICAL INSTRUMENTS

Irish Council of Churches
Inter-Church Centre, 48 Elmwood Avenue, Belfast, County Antrim, BT9 6AZ
Tel: 01232-663145 **Fax:** 01232-381737
Contact: Dr David Stevens
Position: General Secretary
Activities: Umbrella, books

Member Bodies:
Church of Ireland
Greek Orthodox Church in Britain and Ireland
Irish District of the Moravian Church
Lutheran Church in Ireland
Methodist Church in Ireland
Non-Subscribing Presbyterian Church of Ireland
Presbyterian Church in Ireland
Religious Society of Friends
Salvation Army

Irish Inter-Church Meeting
Inter Church Centre, 48 Elmwood Avenue, Belfast, County Antrim, BT9 6AL
Tel: 01232-663145 **Fax:** 01232-381737
Contact: Dr. David Stephens
Umbrella body for member Churches of the Irish Council of Churches and the Catholic Church in Ireland.

CHURCHES OPERATING AT AN IRISH LEVEL

Assemblies of God in Great Britain & Ireland, Ireland Regional Council
5 Glenburn Park, Ballymena, County Antrim, BT43 6HG

Baptist Union of Ireland
117 Lisburn Road, Belfast, County Antrim,
BT9 7AF
Tel: 01232-663108 **Tel:** 01846-622291 (h)
Fax: 01232-663616
EMail: BUofI@aol.com
Contact: Pastor William Colville
Position: Union Secretary
Activities: Resource, youth, elderly, women,
newsletters, books
Other Languages: Irish
We are an association of 108 independent local
Baptist churches which co-operate together in the
field of mission, education, welfare, men and women
and youth.

Catholic Bishops' Conference (Ireland)
Iona, 65 Newry Road, Dundalk, County Louth,
Republic of Ireland
Tel: 00-3534238087 **Fax:** 00-3534233575
Contact: Revd Dr Hugh G Connolly
Position: Executive Secretary
Other Languages: Irish

Church of Ireland
Church of Ireland House, Church Avenue,
Rathmines, Dublin 6, Republic of Ireland
Tel: 01-4978422 **Fax:** 01-4978821
Contact: Mr David Meredith
Position: Assistant Secretary
Activities: Umbrella, newsletters, books, inter-faith
Traditions: Anglican
Other Languages: Irish

Congregational Union of Ireland
38 Edgecumbe Gardens, Belfast, County Antrim,
BT4 2EH
Tel: 01232-653140
Contact: Revd Malcolm Coles
Position: Secretary

Lutheran Church in Ireland
Lutherhaus, 24 Adelaide Road, Dublin 2, Republic
of Ireland
Tel: 0035316766548
Contact: Church Leader
Activities: Worship, visits, youth, elderly, women,
newsletters, inter-faith
Other Languages: German, Swedish, Finnish,
Swahili
Established in Dublin in 1697, there are about 1000
Lutherans living in Ireland (North and South).

Congregations in Dublin (St Finian's), Belfast,
Castle-pollard, Cork, Galway, Killarney, Limerick,
Sligo and Wexford.

Methodist Church in Ireland
1 Fountainville Avenue, Belfast, County Antrim,
BT9 6AN
Tel: 01232-324554 **Fax:** 01232-239467
Contact: Edmund T I Mawhinney
Position: Secretary
Activities: Youth, women, newsletters

Moravian Church (Irish District)
Moravian Avenue, 153 Finaghy Road South, Upper
Malone, Belfast, County Antrim, BT10 0DG (h)
Tel: 01232-619755 (h)
Contact: Leonard Broadbent
Position: Chair
Activities: Worship
Traditions: Free Church

Non-Subscribing Presbyterian Church of Ireland
"Drumcorran", 102 Carrickfergus Road, Larne,
County Antrim, BT40 3JT (h)
Tel: 01574-272600 (h)
Contact: Revd Dr John W Nelson
Position: Clerk of the Synod
Activities: Worship, visits, youth, elderly, women,
newsletters, books, inter-faith
This denomination represents the liberal wing of
the Irish Presbyterian spectrum.

Presbyterian Church in Ireland
Church House, Fisherwick Place, Belfast, County
Antrim, BT1 6DW
Tel: 01232-322284 **Tel:** 01846-665586 (h)
Fax: 01232-236609
Contact: Revd Samuel Hutchinson
Position: Clerk of Assembly
Activities: Worship, resource, media, umbrella,
visits, youth, elderly, women, newsletters, books,
inter-faith
Although the headquarters are in Belfast, Northern
Ireland, it is an all-Ireland Church operating in the
Irish Republic as well.

Religious Society of Friends in Ireland
Swanbrooke House, Bloomfield Avenue, Dublin 4
Tel: 01-6683684 **Fax:** 01-6677693
Contact: Valerie O'Brien
Position: Recording Clerk

Seventh Day Adventist Church, Ireland
9 Newry Road, Banbridge, County Down, BT32
3HF
Tel: 018206-26361   **Tel:** 018206-26191 (h)
Fax: 018206-26361
EMail: 102555.2156@compuserve.com
Contact: Alan David Hodges
Position: President
Activities: Worship, visits, youth, elderly,
newsletters, books

CHURCH REGIONAL BODIES

BAPTIST ASSOCIATIONS

Northern Association of Irish Baptist Churches
65 Taylorstown Road, Toomebridge, County
Antrim, BT41 3RW (h)
Tel: 01-648-50386 (h)   **Fax:** 01-648-50386
Contact: Pastor Gerald Rogers
Position: Secretary
Activities: Newsletters
Traditions: Free Church

CHURCH OF IRELAND DIOCESES

Church of Ireland Diocese of Armagh
Church House, 46 Abbey Street, County Armagh,
BT61 7DZ
Tel: 01861-522858
Contact: J R McConnell
Position: Diocesan Secretary

*Church of Ireland Diocese of Down & Dromore &
Diocese of Connor*
Diocesan Office, Church of Ireland House, 61-67
Donegall Street, Belfast, County Antrim, BT1 2QH
Tel: 01223-322268
Contact: T N Wilson
Position: Diocesan Secretary
Traditions: Anglican

Church of Ireland Diocese of Clogher
The Deanery, 10 Augher Road, Clogher, County
Tyrone, BT76 0AD (h)
Tel: 016625-48235 (h)   **Fax:** 016625-48235
Contact: Very Revd Thomas R Moore
Position: Dean of Clogher
Activities: Worship, resource, umbrella, visits,
newsletters
Traditions: Anglican
Other Languages: French

Church of Ireland Diocese of Derry & Raphoe
Diocesan Office, London Street, County
Londonderry, BT48 6RQ
Tel: 0180504262440
Contact: A McConnell
Position: Diocesan Secretary
Traditions: Anglican

METHODIST CHURCH DISTRICTS

Methodist Church in Ireland Portadown District
3 Old Rectory Park, Lurgan Road, Banbridge,
County Down, BT32 4QA
Traditions: Free Church

Methodist Church in Ireland Down District
2 Lyndhurst Avenue, Bangor, County Down, N.
Ireland
Traditions: Free Church

Methodist Chuch in Ireland Belfast District
8 Richhill Crescent, Belfast, County Antrim,
BT5 6HF
Traditions: Free Church

Methodist Church In Ireland North East District
2 Balmoral Avenue, Whitehead, Carrickfergus,
County Antrim, BT38 9QA (h)
Tel: 01960-373327 (h)
Contact: Revd M Elizabeth Hewitt
Position: Secretary of Synod
Activities: Worship, youth, elderly, women
Traditions: Free Church

Methodist Church in Ireland Londonderry District
48 Upper Stabane Road, Castlederg, County
Tyrone, BT81 7BE

NON-SUBSCRIBING PRESBYTERIAN CHURCH IN IRELAND PRESBYTERIES

*Non Subscibing Presbyterian Church of Ireland
Presbytery of Bangor*
15 Windmill Hill, Comber, County Down,
BT23 5EQ

*Non-Subscribing Presbyterian Church of Ireland,
Presbytery of Antrim*
Drumcorran, 102 Carrickfergus Road, Larne,
County Antrim, BT40 3JX (h)
Tel: 01574-272600 (h)
Contact: Revd Dr John Wallace Nelson
Position: Presbytery Clerk
Traditions: Presbyterian

PRESBYTERIAN CHURCH IN IRELAND

Presbyterian Church in Ireland Ballymena Presbytery
166 Cullybackery Road, Ballymena, County Antrim, BT43 5DQ

Presbyterian Church in Ireland Ards Presbytery
3 Second Avenue, Baylands, Bangor, County Down, BT20 5JZ (h)
Tel: 01247-450141 (h)
Contact: Revd Dr Donald J Watts
Position: Presbytery Clerk
Activities: Umbrella, youth

Presbyterian Church in Ireland East Belfast Presbytery
234 Lower Braniel Road, Belfast, County Antrim, BT5 7NJ (h)
Contact: John McVeigh
Position: Clerk

Presbyterian Church in Ireland Belfast North Presbytery
11 Waterloo Gardens, Belfast, County Antrim, BT15 4EX

Presbyterian Church in Ireland Belfast South Presbytery
The Manse, 3 Shrewsbury Gardens, Balmoral Avenue, Belfast, County Antrim, BT9 6PJ (h)
Tel: 01232-667247 (h)
Contact: Revd R Trevor Anderson
Position: Prebytery Clerk

Presbyterian Church in Ireland Route Presbytery
The Manse, Bushmills, County Antrim, BT57 8XJ

Presbyterian Church in Ireland Coleraine Presbytery
8 Ballywatt Road, Coleraine, County Londonderry, BT52 2LT (h)
Tel: 012657 31310 (h)
Contact: Revd William Ivan Hunter
Position: Presbytery Clerk
Activities: Umbrella

Presbyterian Church in Ireland Foyle Presbytery
48 Scoggy Road, Limmavady, County Londonderry, BT49 0NB

Presbyterian Church in Ireland Derry & Strabane Presbytery
19 Clearwater, Caw, Londonderry, County Londonderry, BT47 1BE

Contact: Revd Dr Joseph Fell
Position: Clerk

Presbyterian Church in Ireland Tyrone Presbytery
c/o Minister's Walk, Moneymore, Magherafelt, County Londonderry, BT45 7QE (h)
Tel: 016487-48012 (h)   **Fax:** 016587-48012
Contact: James B McCormick
Position: Presbytery Clerk

Presbyterian Church in Ireland Iveagh Presbytery
19 Shimna Road, Newcastle, County Down, BT33 0AT

Presbyterian Church in Ireland Down Presbytery
35 Manse Road, Ballygowan, Newtonards, County Down, BT23 6HE
Tel: 01238-528962 (h)
Contact: Revd James Harper
Position: Clerk of Presbytery
Activities: Umbrella

ROMAN CATHOLIC DIOCESES

Roman Catholic Archdiocese of Armagh
Ara Coeli, Armagh City, County Armagh, BT61 7QY
Tel: 01861-522045   **Fax:** 01861-526182
Contact: Archbiship Seán Brady
Position: Archbishop of Armagh and Primate of All-Ireland

Roman Catholic Diocese of Down & Connor
"Lisbreen", 73 Somerton Road, Belfast, County Antrim, BT15 4DE
Contact: Most Revd Patrick Walsh
Position: Bishop

Roman Catholic Diocese of Kilmore
The Presbytery, Cavan, County Cavan, Republic of Ireland

Roman Catholic Diocese of Derry
Derry Diocese Office, Bishop's House, St Eugene's Cathedral, Derry, County Londonderry, BT48 9AP
Tel: 01504-262302   **Fax:** 01504-371960
Contact: The Most Revd Seamus Hegarty
Position: Bishop of Derry
Other Languages: Irish, French, Italian, German

Roman Catholic Diocese of Dublin
Archbishop's House, Dublin 9, Republic of Ireland
Tel: 00-3531-837-3732   **Fax:** 00-3531-836-9796

Contact: Most Revd Desmond Connell
Position: Archbishop & Primate
Activities: Worship, resource, media, umbrella, youth, elderly, newsletters, inter-faith
Other Languages: Irish

Roman Catholic Diocese of Clogher
Tigh an Easpaig, Monaghan, Republic of Ireland
Tel: 047-81019 (h) **Fax:** 047-84773
Contact: Most Revd Joseph Duffy
Position: Bishop
Other Languages: Irish, French

Roman Catholic Diocese of Dromore
St Colman's College, Newry, County Down, BT35 6PN

Roman Catholic Archdiocese of Cashell & Emly
Archbishop's House, Thurles, County Tipperary, Republic of Ireland
Tel: 01504-21512
Contact: Most Revd Dermot Clifford
Position: Archbishop

Roman Catholic Archdiocese of Tuam
Archbishop's House, Tuam, County Galway, Republic of Ireland
Tel: 0035309324166
Contact: Most Revd Jospeh Cassidy

SALVATION ARMY DIVISIONS

Salvation Army Northern Ireland Division
12 Station Mews, Sydenham, Belfast, County Antrim, BT4 1TL
Tel: 01232-675000 **Tel:** 01233-419269 (h)
Fax: 01232-675011
Contact: Major Geoff Blurton
Position: Divisional Commander
Activities: Youth, elderly, women, newsletters, books
Traditions: Free Church

OTHER IRISH BODIES

Evangelical Alliance
3 Fitzwilliam Street, Belfast, County Antrim, BT9 6AW

Irish FOR
224 Lisburn Road, Belfast, County Antrim, BT9 6GE

National Council of YMCAs of Ireland Limited
St Georges Building, 37/41 High Street, Belfast, County Antrim, BT1 2AB
Tel: 01232-327757 **Fax:** 01232-438809
EMail: bev@ymca-ire.dnet.co.uk
Contact: Beverley Cuthbert
Position: Administration/Finance Manager
Activities: Umbrella, youth, women
Traditions: Cross-denominational

Irish School of Ecumenics
Bea House, Milltown Park, Dublin 6, Republic of Ireland
Tel: 0035312601144 **Fax:** 0035312601158
Contact: Geraldine Smyth
Position: Director
Activities: Resource, visits, women, newsletters, inter-faith
Traditions: Ecumenical
Other Languages: German, French

SCOTLAND

SCOTTISH ECUMENICAL INSTRUMENT

Action of Churches Together in Scotland
Scottish Churches House, Dunblane, Central, FK15 0AJ
Tel: 01786-823588 **Tel:** 01786-823147 (h)
Fax: 01786-825844
Contact: Revd Maxwell Craig
Position: General Secretary
Activities: Worship, umbrella, visits, youth, women, newsletters, books, inter-faith
ACTS is nine Scottish Churches uniting in commitment to work together in the cause of Christ's Kingdom. Its activities include commitment to justice and peace.

Members Churches:
Church of Scotland
Congregational Union of Scotland
Methodist Church
Religious Society of Friends
Roman Catholic Church in Scotland
Salvation Army
Scottish Episcopal Church
United Free Church
United Reformed Church

CHURCHES OPERATING AT A SCOTTISH LEVEL

Church of Scotland
121 George Street, Edinburgh, Lothian, EH2 4YN
Tel: 0131-225-5722 **Fax:** 0131-220-3899
EMail: kirkeculink@gn.apc.org
Contact: Revd Dr Finlay MacDonald
Position: Principal Clerk
Activities: Resource, youth, elderly, women, newsletters, books, inter-faith
Traditions: Presbyterian
The Church of Scotland is recognised by the State as a national church, free to order its own government, worship and discipline. The highest court for decision making affecting the whole Church is the General Assembly.

Congregation Federation in Scotland
3 Goldie Place, Stevenston, Strathclyde, KA21 3DO

Methodist Church in Scotland
Central Hall, West Toll Cross, Edinburgh, Lothian, EH3 9BP
Tel: 0131-229-7937   Fax: 0131-447-6359
Contact: David Cooper
Position: Synod Secretary
Activities: Worship, youth, women, newsletters, inter-faith
Traditions: Free Church
The Methodist Church in Scotland is a District of the Methodist Church in Great Britain.

Roman Catholic Church in Scotland
Bishops' Conference of Scotland, 64 Aitken Street, Airdrie, Strathclyde, ML6 6LT
Tel: 01236-764061 **Tel:** 0414-882-7493 (h)
Fax: 01236-762489
Contact: Revd Mgr Henry Docherty
Position: General Secretary
Activities: Worship, resource, media, umbrella, youth, elderly, women, newsletters, inter-faith
Other Languages: Gaelic

Scottish Congregational Church
P O Box 189, Glasgow, Strathclyde, G1 2BX
Tel: 0141-332-7667 **Fax:** 0141-332-8463
EMail: 100520,2150@compuserve.com
Contact: Revd John Arthur
Position: General Secretary
Activities: Newsletters
Traditions: Free Church

Scottish Episcopal Church
General Synod Office, 21 Grosvenor Crescent, Edinburgh, Lothian, EH12 5EE
Tel: 0131-225-6357 **Tel:** 0131-669-7115 (h)
Fax: 0131-346-7247
EMail: scotepis@ecunet.org
Contact: John F Stuart
Position: Communications
Activities: Worship, visits newsletters, books, inter-faith
Traditions: Anglican
Other Languages: Gaelic

Scottish Regional Council of Assemblies of God in Great Britain & Ireland Incorporated
"Beracah", 109 Burnhead Road, Larbert, Central, FK5 4RJ (h)
Tel: 01324-558531 (h) **Fax:** 01324-558531
Contact: Michael George Rollo
Position: Administrator
Activities: Umbrella, youth, women
Traditions: Pentecostal

Scottish Unitarian Association
18 Woodend Place, Aberdeen, Grampian, AB15 6AL (h)
Tel: 01224-317450 (h)
Contact: William S Stephen
Position: Honorary Secretary
Activities: Resource, media, umbrella, visits, youth, elderly, women newsletters, books, inter-faith

Seventh Day Adventist Church, Scotland
5 Ochilview Gardens, Crieff, Tayside, PH7 3EJ
Tel: 01764-653090 (h) **Fax:** 01764-653090
Contact: A R Rodd
Position: President
Activities: Worship, resource, visits, youth, elderly, women, newsletters, books, inter-faith
Other Languages: Spanish

United Free Church of Scotland
11 Newton Close, Glasgow, Strathclyde, G3 7PR
Fax: 0141-332-3435 **Fax:** 0141-332-3435
Contact: Revd John Fulton
Position: General Secretary
Activities: Visits, youth, women, newsletters
Tradition: Presbyterian
A small Presbyterian denomination of 63,000 members in 70 congregations served by 45 ministers and pastors.

CHURCH REGIONAL BODIES

CHURCH OF SCOTLAND PRESBYTERIES

Church of Scotland Aberdeen Presbytery
c/o Mastrick Church, Greenfern Road, Aberdeen, Grampian, AB16 6TR
Tel: 01224-690494 **Fax:** 01224-690494
Contact: Revd Andrew McDouglas
Position: Presbytery Clerk
Activities: Resource, umbrella
Traditions: Presbyterian

Church of Scotland Kincardine & Deeside Presbytery
The Manse, Aboyne, Grampian, AB34 4YN
Tel: 01339-881233
Position: Presbytery Clerk

Church of Scotland South Argyll Presbytery
Tigh-Na-Coille, Ardrishaig, Highlands and Islands, PA30 8EP (h)
Tel: 01546-603454 (h) **Fax:** 01546-603454
Contact: Michael Arthur John Gossip
Position: Presbytery Clerk
Activities: Umbrella
Traditions: Presbyterian

Church of Scotland Lorn & Mull Presbytery
Appin, Argyll, Highland, PA38 4DD
Tel: 01631-73206
Contact: Revd Walter M Ritchie
Position: Presbytery Clerk

Church of Scotland West Lothian Presbytery
St John's Manse, Mid Street, Bathgate, Lothian, EH48 1QD (h)
Tel: 01506-653146 (h)
Contact: Revd Duncan Shaw
Position: Presbytery Clerk
Activities: Worship
Traditions: Presbyterian

Church of Scotland Duns Presbytery
The Manse, Swinton, Duns, Borders, TD11 3JJ
Tel: 01890-860228
Contact: Revd Alan Cartwright
Position: Presbytery Clerk
Traditions: Presbyterian

Church of Scotland Lanark Presbytery
c/o Kirkton Manse, Station Road, Carluke, South Strathclyde, ML8 5AA (h)

Tel: 01555-771262 (h) **Fax:** 01555-771262
EMail: IainDC@aol.com
Contact: Revd Iain D Cunningham
Position: Presbytery Clerk
Traditions: Presbyterian

Church of Scotland Ayr Presbytery
30 Garden Street, Dalrymple, Strathclyde, KA6 6DG
Tel: 01292-289220
Contact: Revd C L Johnston
Position: Presbytery Clerk
Traditions: Presbyterian

Church of Scotland Stirling Presbytery
13 Harvieston Road, Dollar, Central, FK14 7HG
Tel: 01259-442609
Contact: Revd George McCutcheon
Position: Presbytery Clerk
Traditions: Presbyterian

Church of Scotland Dumfries & Kirkcudbright Presbytery
11 Laurieknowe, Dumfries, Dumfries and Galloway, DG2 7AH (h)
Tel: 01387-252929 (h) **Fax:** 01387-252929
Contact: Revd Gordon M A Savage
Position: Presbytery Clerk
Traditions: Presbyterian

Church of Scotland Dundee Presbytery
Presbytery Office, Nicoll's Lane, Dundee, Tayside, DD2 3HG
Tel: 01382-611415
Contact: James A Roy
Position: Presbytery Clerk
Activities: Umbrella
Traditions: Presbyterian

Church of Scotland Dunfermline Presbytery
Townhill Manse, Dunfermline, Lothian, KY12 0EZ
Tel: 01383-723835
Contact: Revd William Farquhar
Position: Presbytery Clerk
Traditions: Presbyterian

Church of Scotland Edinburgh Presbytery
10 Palmerston Place, Edinburgh, Lothian, EH12 5AA
Tel: 0131-225-9137
Contact: Revd W Peter Graham
Position: Presbytery Clerk
Activities: Umbrella
Traditions: Presbyterian

Church of Scotland Moray Presbytery
1 Seaview Farm Paddock, Burghead, Elgin,
Grampian, IV30 2XY (h)
Tel: 01384-830890 (h)
Contact: Revd John T Stuart
Position: Presbytery Clerk
Traditions: Presbyterian

Church of Scotland Falkirk Presbytery
30 Russell Street, Falkirk, Central, FK2 7HS (h)
Tel: 01324-624461 (h)
Contact: Duncan Elliott McClements
Position: Presbytery Clerk
Activities: Resource, umbrella
Traditions: Presbyterian

Church of Scotland Orkney Presbytery
Finstown Manse, Finstown, Orkney, KW17 2EG
Tel: 01856-761328 **Fax:** 01856-761328
EMail: tghorkney@aol.com
Contact: Revd Trevor G Hunt
Position: Presbytery Clerk
Traditions: Presbyterian

Church of Scotland Angus Presbytery
Presbytery Office, St Margaret's Church, West High
Street, Forfar, DD8 1BJ
Tel: 01307-464224 **Fax:** 01307-465587
Contact: Revd R J Ramsey
Position: Presbytery Clerk
Traditions: Presbyterian

Church of Scotland Lochaber Presbytery
McIntosh Manse, 26 Riverside Park, Lochyside,
Fort William, Highlands and Islands, PH33 7NY (h)
Tel: 01397-702054 (h)
Contact: Revd Alan Ramsay
Position: Presbytery Clerk
Traditions: Presbyterian

Church of Scotland Melrose & Peebles Presbytery
St Aidan's Manse, High Road, Galashiels, Borders,
TD1 2BD (h)
Tel: 01896-752420
Contact: Revd Jack M Brown
Position: Presbytery Clerk
Traditions: Presbyterian
Activities: Umbrella
Traditions: Presbyterian

Church of Scotland Dumbarton Presbytery
14 Birch Road, Killearn, Glasgow, Strathclyde,
G63 9SQ

Contact: Revd David P Munro
Position: Presbytery Clerk
Traditions: Presbyterian

Church of Scotland Glasgow Presbytery
260 Bath Street, Glasgow, Strathclyde, G2 4JP
Tel: 0141-332-6606 **Tel:** 01236-763012 (h)
Fax: 0141-332-6606
Contact: Revd Alex Cunningham
Position: Presbytery Clerk
Activities: Worship, resource, media, youth, elderly,
women, newsletters, inter-faith
Traditions: Presbyterian
Other Languages: Gaelic, German, South Korean

Church of Scotland Greenock Presbytery
105 Newark Street, Greenock, Strathclyde,
PA16 7TW (h)
Tel: 01475-639602 (h)
Contact: Revd David Mill
Position: Presbytery Clerk
Activities: Inter-faith
Traditions: Presbyterian

Church of Scotland Annandale & Eskdale Presbytery
The Manse, Gretna Green, Dumfries and Galloway,
DG16 5DU
Tel: 01461-338313
Contact: Rev C Bryan Haston
Position: Presbytery Clerk
Traditions: Presbyterian

Church of Scotland Uist Presbytery
The Manse, Griminish, Isle of Benbecula,
Highlands and Islands, HS7 5QA (h)
Tel: 01870-602180 (h)
Contact: Adrian Varwell
Position: Presbytery Clerk
Activities: Resource, umbrella
Traditions: Presbyterian
Other Languages: Gaelic

Church of Scotland Hamilton Presbytery
Presbytery Office, 18 Haddow Street, Hamilton,
Strathclyde, ML3 7HX
Tel: 01698-286837
Contact: Revd James H Wilson
Position: Presbytery Clerk
Traditions: Presbyterian

Church of Scotland Jedburgh Presbytery
Teviot Manse, Buccleuch Road, Hawick, Borders,
TD9 0EL (h)

Tel: 01450-372150 (h)
Contact: Neil R Combe
Position: Presybtery Clerk
Activities: Umbrella, youth, elderly, women
Traditions: Presbyterian

Church of Scotland Ross Presbytery
Kilmuir and Logie Easter Manse, Delny,
Invergordon, Highlands and Islands, IV18 0NW
Tel: 01862-842280
Contact: Revd Roderick M Mackinnon
Position: Presbytery Clerk
Traditions: Presbyterian

Church of Scotland Ardrossan Presbytery
St Columba's Manse, Kilbirnie, Strathclyde,
KA25 7JU (h)
Tel: 01505-683342 (h) **Fax:** 01505-684024
EMail: pres@davbros.demon.co.uk
Contact: Revd David Broster
Position: Presbytery Clerk
Activities: Youth, elderly, women
Traditions: Presbyterian

Church of Scotland Irvine & Kilmarnock Presbytery
51 Portland Road, Kilmarnock, Strathclyde,
KA1 2EQ
Contact: Revd Coline G F Brockie
Position: Presbytery Clerk
Activities: Worship, resource, youth, elderly,
women, newsletters, inter-faith
Traditions: Presbyterian

Church of Scotland Paisley Presbytery
6 Southfield Avenue, Paisley, Strathclyde, PA2 8BY
Tel: 0141-884-3600
Contact: Revd David Kay
Position: Presbytery Clerk
Traditions: Presbyterian

Church of Scotland Sutherland Presbytery
The Manse, Lairg, Highlands and Islands, IV27 4EH
Tel: 01549-402373
Contact: Revd J L Goskirk
Position: Presbytery Clerk
Traditions: Presbyterian

Church of Scotland Abernethy Presbytery
The Manse, Nethy Bridge, Grampian,
PH25 3DG (h)
Tel: 01479-821280 (h)
Contact: Revd James A I MacEwan

Position: Presbytery Clerk
Traditions: Presbyterian

Church of Scotland Lothian Presbytery
Auchindinny House, Penicuik, Lothian, EH26 8PE
Tel: 01968-675338
Contact: John D McCulloch
Position: Presbytery Clerk
Traditions: Presbyterian

Church of Scotland Perth Presbytery
The Manse, Glencarse, Perth, Tayside, PH2 7NF
Tel: 01738-860816 **Fax:** 01738-860837
Contact: Revd Michael J Ward
Position: Presbytery Clerk
Traditions: Presbyterian

Church of Scotland Buchan Presbytery
The Manse, Hatton, Peterhead, Grampian,
AB42 0QQ (h)
Tel: 01779-841229 (h) **Fax:** 01779-841822
Contact: Revd Rodger Neilson
Position: Presbytery Clerk
Traditions: Presbyterian

Church of Scotland Dunoon Presbytery
12 Crichton Road, Rothesay, Isle of Bute,
Highlands and Islands, PA20 9JR (h)
Tel: 01700-502797 (h) **Fax:** 01700-502797
Contact: Revd Ronald Samuel
Position: Presbytery Clerk
Activities: Umbrella
Traditions: Presbyterian

Church of Scotland St Andrews Presbytery
34 Claybraes, St Andrews, Fife, KY16 8RS (h)
Tel: 01334-473606 (h)
Contact: Revd John W Patterson
Position: Presbytery Clerk
Traditions: Presbyterian

Church of Scotland Lewis Presbytery
Martin's Memorial Manse, Matheson Road,
Stornoway, Highlands and Islands, PA87 2LR
Tel: 01851-702206
Contact: Revd T S Sinclair
Position: Presbytery Clerk
Traditions: Presbyterian

Church of Scotland Wigtown & Stranraer Presbytery
High Kirk Manse, Leswalt High Road, Stranraer,
Dumfries and Galloway, DG9 0AA
Tel: 01776-3268

Contact: Revd D W Dutton
Position: Presbytery Clerk
Traditions: Presbyterian

Church of Scotland Lochcarron & Skye Presbytery

The Manse, Lochcarron, Strathcarron, Highlands and Islands, IV54 8YD (h)
Tel: 01520-722278 (h) **Fax:** 01520-722674
Contact: Revd Allan I MacArthur
Position: Presbytery Clerk
Activities: Worship
Traditions: Presbyterian
Other Languages: Gaelic

Church of Scotland Caithness Presbytery

The Manse, Watten By Wick, Highlands and Islands, KW1 5YN
Tel: 01955-621220 (h)
Contact: Michael Graeme Mappin
Position: Presbytery Clerk
Traditions: Presbyterian

Church of Scotland Gordon Presbytery

The Manse, Skene, Westhill, Grampian, AB32 6LX (h)
Tel: 01224-743277 (h) **Fax:** 01224-743277
Contact: Rev Iain Urquhart Thomson
Position: Presbytery Clerk
Activities: Worship
Traditions: Presbyterian

FREE CHURCH OF SCOTLAND SYNODS

Free Church of Scotland Southern Synod

Free Church Offices, The Mound, Edinburgh, Lothian, EH1 2LS
Tel: 0131-226-5286 **Tel:** 0131-441-4281 (h)
Fax: 0131-220-0597
Contact: Revd Professor John L Mackay
Position: Assembly Clerk
Activities: Worship, youth, elderly, women, newsletters, books
Traditions: Free Church, Presbyterian

Free Church of Scotland Western Synod

Free Church Manse, Isle of Lewis, Highlands and Islands, PA86 9AG
Tel: 01851-73208
Contact: Revd Donald MacDonald
Position: Clerk
Traditions: Free Church, Presbyterian

Free Church of Scotland Northern Synod

Free Church Manse, Scotsburn Road, Tain, Highlands and Islands, IV19 1PR (h)
Tel: 01862-892156 (h)
Contact: Innes M MacRae
Position: Clerk
Traditions: Free Church, Presbyterian

METHODIST DISTRICTS

Methodist Church in Scotland Edinburgh District

Methodsit Central Hall, West Toll Cross, Edinburgh, Lothian, EH3 9BT
Tel: 0131-229-7937 **Fax:** 0131-447-6359
Contact: Revd David Cooper
Traditions: Free Church

Methodist Church in Scotland Shetland District

Burnside, Houl Road, Scalloway, Shetland, Highlands and Islands, ZE1 0UA
Tel: 01595-880204 (h) **Fax:** 01595-880204
Contact: Leslie Hann
Position: Secretary of Synod
Activities: Worship, youth, women
Traditions: Free Church

ROMAN CATHOLIC DIOCESES

Roman Catholic Diocese of Aberdeen

Bishop's House, 3 Queen's Cross, Aberdeen, Grampian, AB15 4XU
Tel: 01224-319154 **Fax:** 01224-325570
Contact: Rt Rev Mario Joseph Conti
Position: Bishop

Roman Catholic Diocese of Galloway

Candida Casa, 8 Corsehill Road, Ayr, Strathclyde, KA7 2ST (h)
Tel: 01292-266750 (h) **Fax:** 01292-266750
Contact: Rt Revd Maurice Taylor
Position: Bishop
Activities: Worship, newsletters

Roman Catholic Diocese of Dunkeld

Diocesan Centre, 24–28 Lawside Road, Dundee, Tayside, DD3 6XY

Roman Catholic Archdiocese of Glasgow

Curial Offices, 196 Clyde Street, Glasgow, Strathclyde, G1 4JY
Tel: 0141-226-5898 **Fax:** 0141-225-2600
EMail: Glasgow_Archdiocese@compuserve.com

Contact: The Chancellor
Activities: Resource, media, youth, newsletters, inter-faith

Roman Catholic Diocese of Motherwell
Diocesan Centre, Coursington Road, Motherwell, Strathclyde, ML1 1PW
Tel: 01698-269114 **Tel:** 01698-811637 (h)
Fax: 01698-275630
Contact: Revd Thomas M Gault
Position: Chancellor
Activities: Resource, newsletters

Roman Catholic Diocese of Argyll & the Isles
Bishop's House, Esplanade, Oban, Highlands and Islands, PA34 5AB
Tel: 01631-62010
Contact: Bishop

Roman Catholic Diocese of Paisley
Cathedral House, 8 East Buchanan Street, Paisley, Strathclyde, PA1 1HS
Tel: 0141-889-3601 **Fax:** 0141-848-6136
Contact: Revd Chancellor
Position: Chancellor

Roman Catholic Archdiocese of St Andrews & Edinburgh
Diocesan Offices, Gillis Centre, 113 Whitehouse Loan, Edinburgh, Lothian, EH9 1BB
Tel: 0131-452-8244 **Fax:** 0131-452-9153
Contact: Archdiocesan Secretary
Activities: Worship, resource, media, umbrella, visits, youth, elderly, women, newsletters, inter-faith

SALVATION ARMY

Salvation Army North Scotland Division
Deer Road, Woodside, Aberdeen, Grampian, AB24 2BL
Tel: 01224-497000 **Fax:** 01224-497011
Contact: Major David Hinton
Position: Divisional Commander
Activities: Worship, visits, youth, elderly, women, newsletters, books
Traditions: Holiness

Salvation Army East Scotland Division
5 East Adam Street, Edinburgh, Lothian, EH8 9TF
Tel: 0131-662-3300
Contact: Major John Hunt

Position: Divisional Commander
Traditions: Holiness

Salvation Army West Scotland Division
4 Buchanan Court, Cumbernauld Road, Stepps, Glasgow, Strathclyde, G33 6HZ
Tel: 0141-779-5000
Contact: Lt Col William Main
Position: Divisional Commander
Activities: Worship, youth, elderly, women, newsletters
Traditions: Holiness

SCOTTISH CONGREGATIONAL CHURCH AREAS

Scottish Congregational Church Northern Area Council
20 Forvie Circle, Bridge of Don, Aberdeen, Grampian, AB2 8RF
Traditions: Free Church

Scottish Congregational Church Mid-Scotland Area Council
2 Cherry Bank Walk, Airdrie, Strathclyde, ML6 0HZ
Traditions: Free Church

Scottish Congregational Church Solway Area Council
15 Preston Park, Annan, Dumfries and Galloway, DG12 5HS
Tel: 01461-205197
EMail: k.forbes@ukonline.co.uk
Contact: Revd Kenneth McArthur Forbes
Position: Secretary
Traditions: Free Church

Scottish Congregational Church Edinburgh & Borders Area Council
53 Echline Terrace, South Queensferry, Edinburgh, Lothian, EH30 9XH
Contact: Miss Kate Durham
Position: Secretary
Traditions: Free Church

Scottish Congregational Church West Scotland Area Council
Greenock, Strathclyde, PA16 8QT
Traditions: Free Church

SCOTTISH EPISCOPAL CHURCH

Scottish Episcopal Church Diocese of Aberdeen & Orkney
Diocesan Centre, 39 King's Crescent, Aberdeen,
Grampian, AB24 3HP
Tel: 01224-636653 **Fax:** 01224-636186
Contact: Rt Revd Bruce Cameron
Position: Bishop
Traditions: Anglican

Scottish Episcopal Church Diocese of Brechin
c/o Cathedral Office, 1 High Street, Dundee,
Tayside, DD1 1TD
Tel: 01382-224486 **Tel:** 01382-669883 (h)
Contact: Revd Gordon J H Pont
Position: Diocesan Secretary
Traditions: Anglican

Scottish Episcopal Church Diocese of Glasgow & Galloway
Diocesan Office, 2 St Vincent Place, Glasgow,
Strathclyde, G1 2DH
Tel: 0141-221-5720 **Fax:** 0141-221-7014
Contact: The Diocesan Secretary
Activities: Resource, newsletters, inter-faith
Traditions: Anglican

Scottish Episcopal Church Diocese of Edinburgh
Diocesan Centre, 21a Grosvenor Crescent,
Edinburgh, Lothian, EH12 5EL
Tel: 0131-538-7033 **Fax:** 0131-538-7088
Contact: Elizabeth A Brady
Position: Diocesan Secretary
Traditions: Anglican

Scottish Episcopal Church Diocese of Moray, Ross & Caithness
11 Kenneth Street, Inverness, Highlands and Islands,
IV3 5HR
Tel: 01463-226255 **Tel:** 01463-231059 (h)
Fax: 01463-226255
Contact: Rt Revd Gregor Macgregor
Position: Bishop
Activities: Resource, youth, elderly, women,
newsletters, inter-faith
Traditions: Anglican
Other Languages: Gaelic

Scottish Episcopal Church Diocese of Argyll & the Isles
The Pines, Ardconnel Road, Oban, Argyll,
Highlands and Islands, PA34 5DR (h)

Tel: 01631-566912 **Fax:** 01631-566912
Contact: Douglas Cameron
Position: Bishop
Traditions: Anglican

Scottish Episcopal Church Diocese of St Andrews, Dunkeld & Dunblane
Bishop's House, Fairmount Road, Perth, Tayside,
PH2 7AP
Tel: 0738-21500 **Fax:** 0738-441326
Contact: Mrs D Bruce-Gardyne
Position: Diocesan Secretary

OTHER SCOTTISH BODIES

Churches' Agency for Inter-Faith Relations in Scotland (CAIRS)
326 West Princes Street, Glasgow, Strathclyde,
G4 9HA
Tel: 0141-339-8174
EMail: ismyth@stac.ac.uk
Contact: Sister Isabel Smyth
Position: Secretary
Activities: Umbrella, inter-faith
Traditions: Ecumenical
CAIRS exists to promote good interfaith relations in
Scotland and to encourage dialogue and the
dissemination of information about the different
faiths in Scotland. It is an agency of Action of
Churches Together in Scotland.

Evangelical Alliance Scotland
Challenge House, 29 Canal Street, Glasgow,
Strathclyde, G4 0AD
Tel: 0141-322-8700 **Fax:** 0141-322-8704
Contact: Revd David J B Anderson
Position: General Secretary
Activities: Resource, media, umbrella, newsletters,
books

Fellowship of Reconciliation Scotland
The Manse, Kirkton of Airlie, Kirriemuir Angus,
Tayside, DD8 5NL
Tel: 01575-530245 (h)
Contact: Robert J Ramsey
Position: Chair
Activities: Resource, visits, newsletters, inter-faith
Traditions: All Christian Denominations
Organises seminars; courses; conferences. Produces
quarterly newsletter.

SCIAF (Scottish Catholic International Aid Fund)
5 Oswald Street, Glasgow, Strathclyde, G1 4QR
Tel: 0141-221-4447 **Fax:** 0141-221-2373
EMail: sciaf.scotland@geo2.poptel.org.uk
Contact: Paul Chitnis
Position: Executive Director
Activities: Resource, newsletters, books, inter-faith
Traditions: Roman Catholic
Other Languages: Spanish
SCIAF is the official overseas agency of the Catholic
Church in Scotland. It supports aid and development
projects in Asia, Latin America and Africa regardless
of race, creed or politics and runs a development
education programme at home.

WALES

WELSH ECUMENICAL INSTRUMENTS

CYTÛN: Churches Together in Wales (Eglwysi Ynghyd Yng Nghymru)
11 St Helen's Road, Swansea, West Glamorgan,
SA1 4AL
Tel: 01792-460876 **Fax:** 01792-469391
Contact: Revd Noel A Davies
Position: General Secretary
Activities: Umbrella, visits, newsletter, books
Activites: Umbrella, newsletter, books
Languages: Welsh

Full Members include:

Churches and Denominations with Headquarters in Wales:
Eglwys Bresbyteraidd Cymru (Presbyterian Church
of Wales)
Eglwys Yng Nghymru (Church in Wales)
Undeb Bedyddwyr Cymru (Baptist Union of
Wales)
Undeb Yr Annibynwyr Cymraeg (Union of Welsh
Independents)

Churches and Denominations with Headquarters in England:
Byddin Yr Iachawdwriaeth (Salvation Army)
Cymdeithas Grefyddol Y Cyfeillion (Religious
Society of Friends)
Eglwys Ddiwygiedig Unedig (United Reformed
Church)
Eglwysi Cyfamodol Undeb Bedyddwyr Prydain
(Baptist Union of Great Britain Covenanted
Churches)

Eglwys Fethodistaidd (Methodist Church)
Eglwys Gatholig Rufeinig (Roman Catholic
Church)
Y Gynghrair Gynulleidfaol (Congregational
Federation)

Observers:
Eglwys Adfentaidd Y Seithfed Dydd (Seventh Day
Adventist Church)
Eglwys Liwtheraidd (Lutheran Church)
Yr Eglwys Uniongred (Orthodox Church)

ENFYS - Covenanted Churches in Wales (Eglwysi Cyfamodol Yng Nghymru)
2 Woodland Place, Penarth, South Glamorgan,
CF64 2EX
Tel: 01222-705278 **Tel:** 01222-515884 (h)
Fax: 01222-712413
EMail: 106074.133@compuserve.com.uk
Contact: Revd Gethin Abraham-Williams
Position: General Secretary
Activities: Umbrella, newsletters, books
Other Languages: Welsh
ENFYS, founded in 1975, is a multi-lateral
conversation between episcopal and non-episcopal
churches committed to visible unity.

Bodies covenanted together are:
Eglwys Bresbyteraidd Cymru (Presbyterian Church
of Wales)
Eglwys Ddiwygiedig Unedig (United Reformed
Church)
Eglwys Fethodistaidd (Methodist Church)
Eglwys Yng Nghymru (Church in Wales)
Yr Eglwysi Bedyddiedig Cyfamodol yng Nghymru
(Covenanted Baptist Churches)

Free Church Council for Wales (Cyngor Eglwysi Rhyddion Cymru)
Ilston House, 94 Mansel Street, Swansea, West
Glamorgan, SA1 5TZ
Tel: 01792-655468 **Fax:** 01792-469489
Contact: Revd Peter Dewi Richards
Position: Secretary
Activities: Resource, umbrella
Other Languages: Welsh

Member Bodies:
Byddin Yr Iachawdwriaeth (Salvation Army)
Eglyws Bresbyterraid Cymru (Presbyterian
Church of Wales)
Eglwys Fethodistaidd (Methodist Church)
Undeb Bedyddwr Cymru (Baptist Union of Wales)

Undeb Bedyddwr Prydain (Baptist Union of Great Britain)

Undeb Yr Annibynwyr Cymraeg (Union of Welsh Independents)

Y Cyngraiu Gynwlleidfaol (Congregational Federation)

Yr Eglwys Unedig Ddiwygiedig (United Reformed Church)

CHURCHES OPERATING AT A WELSH LEVEL

Assemblies of God in Great Britain & Ireland South Wales Regional Council
56 Tynewyedd, Nant-Y-Bwch, Tredegar, Gwent, NP2 3SG
Traditions: Pentecostal

Baptist Union of Great Britain South Wales Area
19 Melrose Close, St Mellons, Cardiff, South Glamorgan, CF3 9SW (h)
Tel: 01222-795919 (h) **Fax:** 01222-795919
Contact: Peter D Manson
Position: General Superintendent
Activities: Umbrella
Traditions: Free Church

Baptist Union of Wales (Undeb Bedyddwr Cymru)
Ilston House, 94 Mansel Street, Swansea, West Glamorgan, SA1 5TZ
Tel: 01792-655468 **Fax:** 01792-469489
Contact: Revd Peter Dewi Richards
Position: Chief Executive
Activities: Worship, umbrella, youth, women, newsletters
Traditions: Free Church
Other Languages: Welsh

Church in Wales (Eglwys Yng Nghymru)
39 Cathedral Road, Cardiff, South Glamorgan, CF1 9XL
Tel: 01222-231638 **Fax:** 01222-387835
Contact: Mr J W D McIntyre
Position: Secretary General
Activities: Worship, media, umbrella, visits, youth, books, inter-faith
Traditions: Anglican
Other Languages: Welsh
The Church in Wales was disestablished and partially disendowed by the Welsh Church Acts of 1914 and 1919, which came fully into force on 1 April 1920.

On that date the new Province of Wales was created with six dioceses and fourteen archdeaconries.

Congregational Federation in Wales (Gynghrair Gynulleidfaol)
Crosslyn, Spittal, Haverfordwest, Dyfed, SA62 5QT (h)
Tel: 01437-741260 (h) **Fax:** 01437-741260
Contact: Revd Christopher Gillham
Position: Secretary
Activities: Newsletters

Covenanted Baptist Churches in Wales (Yr Eglwysi Bedyddiedig Cyfamodol yng Nghymru)
3 Edith Road, Diras, Powys (h)
Tel: 01222-514630 (h)
Contact: Revd J M Garland
Position: Chairman
Traditions: Free Church

General Assembly of Unitarian & Free Christian Churches South East Wales Society
10 Tan y Lan Terrace, Morriston, Swansea, West Glamorgan, SA6 7DU
Tel: 01792-794542
Contact: Revd E W Phillips
Position: Secretary

Lutheran Church Wales (Yr Eglwys Liwtheraidd)
32 Heol-y-Felin, Rhiwbina, Cardiff, South Glamorgan, CF4 6NT (h)
Tel: 01222-616481 (h)
Contact: Revd H Volker
Position: Minister
Activities: Elderly, women, newsletters, inter-faith
Other Languages: German

Methodist Church
Heulfryn, Barmouth Road, Dolgellau, Gwynedd, LL40 2VT (h)
Tel: 01341-422524 (h) **Fax:** 01341-422524
Contact: Patrick Slattery
Position: Secretary
Activities: Worship
Traditions: Free Church
Other Languages: Welsh

Orthodox Church in Wales, The (Yr Eglwys Uniongred yng Nghymru)
11 Manod Road, Blaenau Ffestiniog, Gwynedd, LL41 4DE
Tel: 01766-831272 (h)
Contact: The Very Revd Father Deiniol

Position: Administrator
Activities: Worship, resource, visits
Other Languages: Welsh, Greek, Old Church Slavonic
Promotion of knowledge and veneration of the early Saints of Wales is an important part of the work of our Church, enabling people to discover their Welsh Christian roots, and making the Orthodox faith and worship accessible in this part of Wales.

Presbyterian Church of Wales (Eglwys Bresbyteraidd Cymru)

53 Richmond Road, Cardiff, South Glamorgan, CF2 3UP
Tel: 01222-494913 **Fax:** 01222-464293
Contact: Dafydd Henry Owen
Position: General Secretary
Other Languages: Welsh

Roman Catholic Church in England & Wales

39 Eccleston Square, London, SW1V 1BX
Tel: 0171-828-8709 **Fax:** 0171-931-7678
EMail: cathmedia@easynet.co.uk
Contact: Rt Revd Mgr P Carroll
Position: General Secretary
Activities: Media, newsletters

Seventh Day Adventists Church (Welsh Mission)

Glan Yr Afon, 10 Heol Y Wen, Caerphilly, Mid Glamorgan, CF3 3EY
Tel: 01222-882097
EMail: 100527.3046@compuserve.com
Contact: John Charles Surridge
Position: Communications Director
Activities: Worship, resource, visits, youth, elderly, women, newsletters, books, inter-faith
Traditions: Evangelical
Other Languages: Spanish, Ghanian

Union of Welsh Independents (Undeb yr Annibynwyr Cymraeg)

Y John Penry, 11 St Helen's Road, Swansea, West Glamorgan, SA1 4AL
Tel: 01792-650647 **Fax:** 01792-650647
Contact: Revd Derwyn Morris Jones
Position: General Secretary
Traditions: Ecumenical
Languages: Welsh
The Union is a voluntary association of Welsh Congregational Churches in England and Wales, plus personal members.

United Reformed Church Wales Province

United Reformed Church, Minster Road, Cardiff, South Glamorgan, CF2 5AS
Tel: 01222-499938
Contact: Mr John Rhys
Position: Synod Clerk
Traditions: Free Church, Reformed

CHURCH REGIONAL BODIES

BAPTIST UNION OF WALES ASSOCIATIONS

Baptist Union of Wales Anglesey Association

Dolydd, Cemaes, Anglesey, Gwynedd, LL67 0DS (h)
Tel: 01407-710450 (h)
Contact: Rev Emlyn John
Traditions: Free Church

Baptist Union of Wales Brecon Association

The Sycamores, Ffostyll Road, Talgarth, Brecon, Powys, LD3 0DW (h)
Tel: 01874-711061 (h)
Contact: Terence J Matthews
Traditions: Free Church

Baptist Union of Wales Carmarthenshire & Cardiganshire Baptist Association

Minyrhos, Efailwen, Clunderwen, Dyfed, SA66 7UZ
Contact: Revd Tecwyn R Ifan
Traditions: Free Church

Baptist Union of Wales DFM

Efrydfa, Glynceiriog, Llangollen, Clwyd, LL20 (h)
Tel: 01691-718200 (h)
Contact: Miss Jones
Traditions: Free Church

Baptist Union of Wales East Glamorgan Association

17 Ivor Terrace, Dowlais, Mid Glamorgan, CF4 3SW (h)
Tel: 01685-377896 (h)
Contact: Revd Eifion Wynne
Traditions: Free Church

Baptist Union of Wales Pembrokeshire Association (Welsh Wing)

Morawel, 78 Heol Fawr, Abergwaun, Fishguard, Dyfed, SA65 9AU (h)
Tel: 01348-872190 (h)

Contact: David Carl Williams
Position: Secretary
Traditions: Free Church
Other Languages: Welsh

Baptist Union of Wales Radnor & Montgomery Association

Arosfa, Hillfield, Llanidloes, Powys, SY18 6ET (h)
Tel: 01686-412452 (h)
Contact: Meredith Powell
Traditions: Free Church

Baptist Union of Wales Gwent Association

12 Park Place, Risca, Newport, Gwent, NP1 6AS (h)
Tel: 01633-601764 (h)
Contact: Revd Ian Murdoch-Smith
Position: Secretary
Traditions: Free Church

Baptist Union of Wales Arfon Association

Brynmor, Penygroes, Gwynedd, LL54 6PN (h)
Tel: 01286-881159 (h)
Contact: John Treharne
Traditions: Free Church

Baptist Union of Wales West Glamorgan Association

Hafan, 10 Wern View, Pontrhydyfen, Port Talbot, West Glamorgan, SA12 9TN (h)
Tel: 01639-896291 (h)
Contact: Eric Williams
Traditions: Free Church

CHURCH IN WALES DIOCESES

Church in Wales Diocese of Bangor

Diocesan Office, Cathedral Close, Bangor, Gwynedd, LL57 1RL
Tel: 01248-354999
Contact: Philip Davies
Position: Diocesan Secretary
Activities: Newsletters
Traditions: Anglican

Church in Wales Diocese of Swansea & Brecon

Swansea and Brecon Diocesan Centre, Cathedral Close, Brecon, Powys, LD3 9DP
Tel: 01874-623716
Contact: David Hugh Thomas
Position: Diocesan Secretary
Activities: Visits, youth, elderly, women, newsletters
Traditions: Anglican
Other Languages: Welsh

Church in Wales Diocese of Llandaff

Board for Social Responsibility, Heol Fair, Llandaff, Cardiff, South Glamorgan, CF5 2EE
Tel: 01222-578899 **Tel:** 01685-722375 (h)
Fax: 01222-576198
Contact: Gareth Foster
Position: Executive Officer
Activities: Youth, elderly, women, newsletters, books, inter-faith
Traditions: Anglican
Other Languages: Welsh, Dutch

Church in Wales Diocese of St Davids

Diocesan Office, Abergwili, Carmarthen, Dyfed, SA31 2JG
Tel: 01267-236145
Contact: Mr D Vincent Lloyd
Position: Diocesan Secretary
Traditions: Anglican

Church in Wales Diocese of Monmouth

64 Caerau Road, Newport, Gwent, NP9 4HJ
Tel: 01633-267490 **Tel:** 01873-854223 (h)
Fax: 01633-265586
Contact: Richard John Tarran
Position: Secretary
Traditions: Anglican
Other Languages: Welsh

Church in Wales Diocese of St Asaph

Diocesan Office, High Street, St Asaph, Clwyd, LL17 0RD
Tel: 01745-582245 **Fax:** 01745-583566
Contact: Christopher Seaton
Position: Secretary
Traditions: Anglican
Other Languages: Welsh

METHODIST CHURCH DISTRICTS

Methodist Church South Wales District

12 Llwyn-y-Grant Road, Cardiff, South Glamorgan, CF3 7ET (h)
Tel: 01222-486751 (h)
Contact: Revd William R Morrey
Position: Chairman
Traditions: Free Church
Other Languages: Welsh

Methodist Church North Wales District

Abbey View, Pant Lane, Gresford, Wrexham, Clwyd, LL12 8HB (h)
Tel: 01978-852883 (h) **Fax:** 01978-852883

Contact: Revd Donald H Ryan
Position: District Chairman
Traditions: Free Church

ROMAN CATHOLIC DIOCESES

Roman Catholic Archdiocese of Cardiff
Archbishop's House, 41-43 Cathedral Road,
Cardiff, South Glamorgan, CF1 9HD
Tel: 01222-220411 **Fax:** 01222-345950
Contact: Archbishop's Secretary
Activities: Worship, resource, media, umbrella,
newsletters, inter-faith
Other Languages: Welsh

Roman Catholic Diocese of Menevia
Curial Office, 115 Walter Road, Swansea, West
Glamorgan, SA1 5RE
Tel: 01792-644017
Contact: Monsignor Clyde Hughes Johnson
Position: Chancellor
Activities: Worship, resource, women, newsletters,
inter-faith
Other Languages: Welsh

Roman Catholic Diocese of Wrexham
Bishops House, Sontley Road, Wrexham, Clwyd,
LL13 7EW
Tel: 01978-262726 (h) **Fax:** 01978-354257
Contact: Bishop Edwin Regan
Position: Bishop
Activities: Umbrella
Other Languages: Welsh

SALVATION ARMY DIVISIONS

Salvation Army South & Mid Wales Division
38 Cathedral Road, Cardiff, South Glamorgan,
CF1 9SU
Tel: 01222-341399 **Fax:** 01222-641800
Contact: Major David A Jones
Position: Divisional Commander
Activities: Worship, resource, media, visits, youth,
elderly, women, newsletters, books
Traditions: Free Church, Holiness
Other Languages: Welsh

Salvation Army North Wales Division
Divisional HQ, 401 Prescott Road, Liverpool, L13
Contact: Major A Bennett

UNITARIAN AND FREE CHRISTIANS

South Wales Unitarian Association
2 Morfa Gwyn House, Newquay, SA45 9SB (h)
Tel: 01545-560995 (h) **Fax:** 01545-560940
EMail: celticwaves@enterprise.net
Contact: Alun-Wyn Dafis
Position: Secretary
Activities: Resource, umbrella, newsletters, books
Other Languages: Welsh

OTHER WELSH BODIES

CAFOD Wales
St Mary's Parish Centre, Union Street, Carmarthen,
Dyfed, SA31 3DE
Tel: 01267-221549 **Tel:** 01222-702411 (h)
Fax: 01267-221549
Contact: Elfed Jones
Position: National Organiser
Activities: Resource, visits, youth, newsletters
Traditions: Roman Catholic
Other Languages: Welsh

Christians Against Torture
16 Melbourne Road, Llanishen, Cardiff, South
Glamorgan, CF4 5NH (h)
Tel: 01222-757339 (h) **Fax:** 01222-743503
EMail: wontner@cf.ac.uk
Internet: http://www.cf.ac.uk/uwcm/pr/
cat/about.html
Contact: Mrs Karen L Wontner
Position: Comm Co-ordinator
Activities: Resource, newsletters
Other Languages: Welsh
A Welsh ecumenical Christian organisation affiliated
to Amnesty International encouraging Christian
concern for human rights issues, especially torture.
Practical involvement through bi-lingual (English/
Welsh) newsletters and other material.

Cymdeithas Y Cymod Yng Nghymru (Fellowship of Reconciliation in Wales)
Ty Hen Gapel John Hughes, Pontrobert, Meifod,
Maldwyn, Powys, SY22 6JA (h)
Tel: 01938-500631 (h) **Fax:** 01938-500631
Contact: Nia Rhosier
Position: General Secretary
Activities: Resource, visits, newsletters, books
Traditions: Ecumenical
Other Languages: Welsh

Our branch of the I.F.O.R. operates through a network of regional cells throughout Wales with an annual council and occasional conference for all members to meet.

Evangelical Alliance
20 Heol Fawr, High Street, Caerdydd, South Glamorgan, CF1 2BZ
Tel: 01222-229822 **Fax:** 01222-229741
Contact: Arfon Jones
Position: General Secretary
Activities: Umbrella, newsletters
Other Languages: Welsh

KEY TO TERMS USED IN CHRISTIAN ORGANISATION TITLES

Note: This is not a complete glossary of significant Christian terms. It is a guide to the meaning and/or background of some of the words used in the titles of Christian organisations listed in this directory. More information on the italicised words can be tracked down either elsewhere in the key and/or in the section on "Introducing the Christian Community" by using the directory's "Significant Word Index".

Adventist: From the Latin for "coming" and related to both the first coming of Jesus in Palestine and also to the traditional Christian hope of his *Second Coming* in glory at the end of all things. The *Adventist* Churches have a strong belief in this hope. Many are also *Seventh Day* Churches which means that they continue to observe Saturday as their day of rest and worship in continuity with the *Shabbat* of the Jewish people.

Agency: One of the possible categories under which a body or organisations may be affiliated to a UK or national *ecumenical instrument*. It is applicable to bodies such as Christian Aid which are not ecclesiastical organisations in the sense of being Churches themselves, but which are agencies of the Churches working together on specific issues.

Alliance: The word "alliance" appears in the title of the Evangelical Alliance and expresses the nature of the organisation as a coming together of a variety of different Churches, organisations and individuals.

Apostolic: From the Greek word *apostolos* meaning "one who is sent", the word was first applied to the first twelve disciples of Jesus and then to a wider group of leaders in the early Christian Church. The word *apostolic* is often used to emphasise the continuity of Christian tradition which is consistent with the teaching of the leaders of the early Church. In this sense, the word applies to the self-understanding of Churches such as the Roman Catholic Church. However, many groups or Churches which use the word in their title are signalling a self-understanding which is concerned with an attempt to get back to what they perceive as the original pattern of early Church life prior to what they believe are alien doctrinal and organisational accretions arising from Greek philosophy and Roman social structures. Some of these groups or Churches baptise in the name of Jesus only and are not *Trinitarian* in theology.

Archdiocese: In the Roman Catholic Church a *diocese* (see below) of which the senior *bishop* is an *Archbishop*.

Area: The Baptist Union of Great Britain uses this word to describe the geographical region for which there is an *Area Superintendent* who has pastoral care of the Churches and ministers within this area. An *Area* is usually composed of a number of *Associations* which cover one or more counties. *Associations* are made up of *Districts* which are, in turn, composed of individual local *congregations*. Baptist *Areas* are not decision-making bodies. The word is also used of those United Areas of the Methodist and United Reformed Churches which simultaneously have the status of a *circuit* in the Methodist Church and a *district* in the United Reformed Church.

Assembly: The name for a national gathering of representatives which is used by a number of Churches such as the Baptist Union of Great Britain and the United Reformed Church. It is also part of the title of some Churches and, as such, indicates that these Churches have a strong local Church polity in which the national level of representation is seen as an expression of the primarily local character of the Church.

Association: The name of a regional level grouping of *congregations* in both the *Baptist* and *Congregational* traditions, often covering a number of counties and composed of local *Districts*. Also used of voluntary groupings of individual Christians as, for example, in the Association of Inter Church Families.

Autocephalic: From the Greek *autokephalos* literally meaning "himself the head". Many Churches in the *Orthodox* tradition have their own national synods whilst remaining in communion with the Patriarch of Constantinople.

Baptist: The name of a Christian movement which is present in the UK in a number of organisational forms, the largest of which is the Baptist Union of Great Britain. The name derives from the the the word *baptism* which describes the act of Christian initiation which *Baptists* believe is appropriate for those who can exercise faith and commitment in their own right rather than it being exercised on their behalf by parents and godparents. *Baptists* characteristically have a local level of Church government focused on individual *congregations*.

Catholic: From the Greek *katholicos* and meaning "universal" or "general". It is often used to signify membership of the Church in all places and times and some individual Churches use it to underline their self-understanding of being in continuity with this universal Christian community. It is used in this sense, for example, by the Roman Catholic Church.

Chaplaincy: Is the name given to a form of authorised and recognised Christian presence in a variety of social institutions such as universities, hospitals and the armed forces.

Cherubim: The name of the highest order of angels in Christian angelology often grouped together with *seraphim* (see below). It is part of the name of the *Cherubim and Seraphim* Christian movement which originated in West Africa.

Christ: From the Greek *Christos,* meaning "anointed one" which, in turn, comes from the Hebrew *Mashiah*. When used of Jesus this title underlines that he is believed by Christians to be the promised one of Jewish expectation and therefore in the line of the Jewish king David, but exercising a spiritual Kingship in inaugurating the *Kingdom of God*.

Christian: Originally a nickname applied in Antioch to the early followers of Jesus confessed as the *Christ*. The earliest Christian self-description appears to have been "followers of the Way". However, as often occurs, names given by outsiders are appropriated by those to whom they are applied.

Church: From the Greek *kuriakos* meaning "belonging to the Lord (*kurios*)" and related to the Scots *kirk*. It is now used for the collective body of Christian believers. Sometimes it refers to these believers in the universal sense of the Church in all times and places. In other instances, it refers only to Christians in one local geographical place and time. Often it refers to a particular ecclesiastical and organisational form of Christianity as in, for example, the Methodist Church. It is also often used with a small "c" to describe the building in which Christians worship.

Churches Together: Part of the title adopted by a number of what are known as *ecumenical instruments* operating at national, regional and local levels of Church life. It is followed by a particular geographical referent as in Churches Together in England or Churches Together in Derbyshire. The title expresses a vision or stage of Christian unity in which the integrity of each individual Christian tradition and denomination is recognised whilst also affirming their oneness in fundamental Christian belief and common action.

Commission: The collective name of a formal body of people appointed by their Churches to serve the *ecumenical instruments* of the Council of Churches for Britain and Ireland in relation to a particular aspect of Christian life or work which the Churches have prioritised as an area for co-operative work, such as the Churches' Commission for Inter-Faith Relations.

Conference: The name given to the national governing body of the Methodist Church and also the regional bodies of the Seventh Day Adventist Church.

Congregational: The name of a Christian tradition which emphasises the independence of the local church or *congregation*. Most *congregations* within this tradition in England joined the United Reformed Church although some continue as part of the Congregational Federation.

Connexion: The name given to the national form of organisation in a number of Christian traditions including the *Countess of Huntingdon* Churches and some *Methodist* traditions.

Council: Usually the name of a formal gathering of Church representatives. Historically, the word is used of the *Councils* of the early undivided Church which defined orthodox doctrine and practice. It is now used to describe organisations formed in order to assist different Churches to work together at various geographical levels. For example, the Council of African and Afro-Caribbean Churches and many local Councils of Churches.

Countess of Huntingdon: Selina, Countess of Huntingdon (1707-1791) was the founder, in 1790, of this grouping of local churches in the tradition of *Calvinistic Methodism* known as the Countess of Huntingdon's Connexion.

Covenanted: The idea of a *covenant* comes from the Jewish concept of a *brith* which is a legal term expresssing the mutual obligations of the parties involved. The Covenanted Churches in Wales have therefore *covenanted* together in the sense of moving beyond loose co-operation into a more formalised mutual responsibility and recognition with the aim of visible unity.

Diocese: From the Greek *diokesis*, it is the name of the regional level of Church organisation in Churches with *episcopalian* traditions such as the *Anglican* Churches and the *Roman Catholic* Church. A *diocese* is presided over by a *bishop*.

District: The name of the regional level of organisation in the Methodist Church and the New Testament Church of God and of more localised groupings of *congregations* within the various Baptist

Unions in the UK and in the United Reformed Church.

Division: The name of a regional level of organisation in the Salvation Army.

Ecumenical: From the Greek *oikoumene* meaning "the whole inhabited earth". More often it has come to describe the relations between the various Christian Churches, traditions and denominations in their attempts to give expression to Christian unity.

Episcopal: From the Greek *episcope* meaning "oversight". It is a word which describes the form of Church government adopted by Churches with *bishops*.

Evangelical: From the Greek *euangelion* meaning "good news". It is a word of eighteenth century origin and is usually used of Christians in many different Churches and traditions to emphasise continuity with what is understood to be historic Christianity, a central place for the *Bible* as the inspired and authoritative Word of God, and the necessity of a personal experience of faith and conversion to Jesus.

Federation: The name of the national form of organisation of the continuing *Congregational* tradition in England and Wales (in Scotland it is called a *Union*, see below). It expresses the particular vision of the *Congregational* tradition where the emphasis is on the local *congregation*.

Free Church: The *Free Churches* are those Churches in England and Wales which historically sought to separate religion from the State and include traditions such as *Baptist*, *Methodist* and *Congregational*. The Free Church of Scotland indicates by its name that it is not a part of the established Church of Scotland.

Friends: The Religious Society of Friends is the preferred name of those who are often more popularly known as the *Quakers*.

Holiness: The *Holiness* tradition of Christianity is historically rooted in a belief in the possibility of a "*second blessing*" following conversion understood as a *baptism* in the Holy Spirit leading to holiness of life rather than to an emphasis on spiritual gifts as in the *Pentecostal* tradition.

Inter-Church: Was the name given to the process of seeking new expressions of Christian unity which was begun in the 1980s under the title of the *Inter-Church Process*. A number of bodies which had their origins in this vision of Christian unity still have the word within their titles.

Lutheran: The name of the Christian tradition originating in the work of the German Protestant reformer Martin Luther.

Methodist: The name of the tradition which finds its origin in the work of George Whitfield and of the brothers, John and Charles, Wesley. It began within the Church of England with groups of believers sharing a common discipline, but eventually became a distinctive Christian tradition with its own forms of Church organisation.

Ministry: Originates with the Greek word *diakonia* meaning "service". It can apply to particular forms of Christian work undertaken by any Christians, lay or ordained, but in a number of Churches it specifically applies in a special sense to those who have become *ordained ministers* of those Churches.

Ministerial: That which pertains to *ministry* (see above), particularly in the sense of *ordained* service.

Orthodox: Describes the tradition of Christianity found in what was originally the Eastern Roman Empire rather than that which grew up in Western Europe focused on the primacy of the *Bishop of Rome*. Among the *Orthodox* are the *Oriental Orthodox* which include the *Coptic*, *Armenian* and other Churches.

Pentecostal: From the Greek *pentecoste* meaning "fiftieth day". It is the name of the Christian festival commemorating the descent of the Holy Spirit upon the first disciples fifty days after the *resurrection* of Jesus. It is used of those Churches which have sought to recover the role of the Holy Spirit in the life and experience of the Christian believer, including the exercise of gifts of prophecy, healing, and speaking in tongues.

Presbyterian: From the Greek word *presbuteros* meaning "elder", it is indicative of a form of Church government in which *ordained ministers* and *elders* from local *congregations* form Church structures at the level of the *presbytery* (local), the *synod* (regional) and the *General Assembly* (national).

Protestant: From the *Protestatio* (Latin for "protest") made by a minority of reformers against the *Catholic* majority in the Diet of Speyer in 1529 CE. It now applies as a general description of those Churches which appeal to the Christian scriptures rather than to Church *Tradition* as the primary source of authority in the Church.

Province: In *Episcopal* (see above) Churches it is a geographical unit made up of a number of *dioceses* and originally arose because such areas were coincidental with the Provinces of the Roman Empire. It is also used by the United Reformed Church for its regional level of Church organisation.

Reformed: The name of the Christian tradition which takes its inspiration from the theological work of Swiss *Protestant* (see above) leader John Calvin. It appears in the title of the United Reformed Church.

Roman Catholic: The name of the numerically largest Christian Church of which the head is the *Bishop of Rome*, known as the *Pope*, meaning "father".

Salvation Army: The name of the movement founded by William Booth in order to bring the Christian message to the industrial working class in the late nineteenth century. Its members have military-style uniforms and its structures and titles reflect military terminology. *Salvation* is the word used by Christians to describe liberation from sin and self-centredness and the establishment of wholeness.

Seraphim: The name of an order of *angels* in Christian angelology often grouped together with *cherubim* (see above). It is part of the name of the *Cherubim and Seraphim* Christian movement which originated in West Africa.

Seventh Day: Appears in the title of those Christians who observe Saturday as the day of worship and rest believing that the beginning of the Christian era did not abrogate the commandment given to the Jewish people to observe the *Sabbath* Day and keep it holy. *Seventh Day* Christians also generally do not celebrate *Christmas* as a Christian festival.

Synod: The name of a regional form of Church government in a number of Churches, including those within the *Presbyterian* traditions of Christianity, for example, the Church of Scotland. It is also used at the regional level with respect to the Methodist *Synods* and in the *Anglican* tradition at the local *Deanery Synod*), regional (*Diocesan Synod*) and national (*General Synod*) levels.

Theology: The name given to what was traditionally viewed as the science of the knowledge of God, from the Greek words *theos* meaning God and *logos* meaning word and used, in a number of fields, with reference to rational thought.

Theological: That which pertains to *theology* (see above).

Union: Part of the organisational title of the Baptist Union of Great Britain. It emphasises the local nature of the tradition, in which the supra-local body is a union of the primary unit of organisation and life, the *congregation*.

Unitarian: The name of the Christian tradition which does not accept the traditional doctrinal formulations of *Trinitarian* theology. The Church has a strong belief in religious tolerance and in the religious role of human reason.

Wesleyan: The brothers John and Charles Wesley were founders of what was originally a movement within the Church of England but which eventually became a separate Christian tradition.

INTRODUCING THE HINDU COMMUNITY

HINDUS IN THE UNITED KINGDOM

Migration

Small numbers of Hindus have visited and worked in the United Kingdom for centuries and the number of students and professionals increased greatly from the late nineteenth century onwards. However, it was not until the 1950s and 1960s that significant numbers of Hindus settled here. Some came to Britain directly from India. With the development of Africanisation policies in the newly independent African states, others came from the countries to which their foreparents had previously migrated, such as Kenya, Tanzania, Uganda, Zambia, and Malawi. Between 1965 and 1972 some of these came as economic migrants and others, especially those from Uganda, came seeking refuge from persecution.

Hindu migrants also came from Fiji, and from Trinidad and other Caribbean islands. Hindus are now settled in most large towns and cities in the UK. The largest Hindu communities are in Greater London (especially in Wembley and Harrow), Birmingham, Coventry and Leicester. This directory records around 161 Hindu places of worship in the UK.

There are approximately 806,099,000 Hindus in the world. Estimates of the size of the Hindu community in the UK vary considerably not least because of differences in defining who is included in the term "Hindu". An estimate of 400,000–555,000 is suggested by this directory although some Hindus would see the community as larger because they would include as expressions of the *Sanatana Dharma* (see below) Buddhists, Jains and Sikhs (which this directory covers in separate chapters), and some would also perhaps wish to include the members of a range of more recent groupings which are, to various degrees, influenced or shaped by Hindu perspectives.

Ethnic Composition

Between fifty-five and seventy per cent of Hindus in the UK are thought to be Gujarati (including those from the Northern Kutch region) and between fifteen and twenty per cent Punjabi, with the remainder having their ancestral origins in other parts of India such as Uttar Pradesh, West Bengal, and the Southern states, as well as in other countries such as Sri Lanka. Even where a family has lived for generations in another part of India, or outside India, its members often maintain links with their ancestral region and often speak their ancestral language among themselves. Thus the Hindu community is constituted of many ethnic groups, each of which was originally often based in a particular geographical region of India.

Languages

Hindus in the UK, in addition to English, speak one or more other languages. The most common are Gujarati, Hindi, Punjabi, Bengali and Tamil. They mostly use the ancient language Sanskrit in their worship, and the majority of the sacred texts are in this language. Most of the Indian words and names used below are Sanskrit. However, Sanskrit words are adapted in form and pronunciation to the different regional languages, and this accounts for some variations in the transliteration of such words: e.g. Siva or Shiv; Rama or Ram.

ORIGINS AND DEVELOPMENT OF THE HINDU TRADITION

Origins

The term "Hindu" is related to the Sanskrit word *Sindhu* which is the name of the river which in English is called the Indus. In Iranian languages such as Persian, this river was called "Hindu", and the name "Hindu" was applied also to the country adjoining the river, and to its people. The name "Hindusthan" was also applied to the whole of North India, and sometimes to the whole of India. These names were made current in India by Persian-speaking people from Afghanistan.

Some Hindus refer to the origin of the terms "Hindu" and "Hindusthan" as being found in the scripture known as the *Brihaspati Agam*. The term "Hinduism" became current in English during the nineteenth century. The Hindu way of life is referred to as *Dharma* or sometimes as the *Sanatana Dharma* (eternal way of life), and many Hindus prefer this description to the word "Hinduism".

Sanatana Dharma is a tradition which is believed by many Hindus to go beyond time and space. It has no precisely traceable beginning, nor a single founder or teacher. Modern historians, including many who are themselves Hindus, point to some formative periods in Indian religious history. The Indus Valley civilization flourished in north-west India in the third and second millennia BCE, but is known only from archaeological finds.

Other Hindus do not accept this view of the ancient history of India and believe that key events such as the birth of Krishna and the Battle of Kurukshetra (see section on the *Mahabharata*, below) can be dated to a period around 3100BCE by utilising interpretations of astrological data in the *Vedas*. What many identify as the Vedic period (1500–500BCE) has left a large body of literature. The time of the Buddha (c.450BCE) was also a period of great social and political change.

Since then, the tradition has undergone further transformations (see section below on "Traditions in Hinduism") and developed into richly diverse ways of life and thought. Some of the famous figures in this development who are given prominence by many Hindus are: Shankara (seventh century CE), Ramanuja (eleventh century CE), Madhva (eleventh to twelfth century CE), Nimbarka (twelfth century CE), Chaitanya (fifteenth to sixteenth century CE), Vallabha (fifteenth to sixteenth century CE) and Sahajananda (eighteenth to nineteenth century CE).

Some Hindus reject the notion of an historical development of the tradition since it conflicts with the idea of degenerative time (see *Yuga* below), according to which past ages were more glorious and closer to the eternal truth than this one. However, many Hindus see Hinduism as evolving and as coming to fresh understandings throughout time in ways that do not conflict with the idea of an eternal *dharma*.

Variety

Because of its ancient origins and its visions of truth, the Hindu traditions embrace a very wide range of belief and practices, with regional, linguistic, and doctrinal variations. Within the Hindu traditions' various schools of thought, a whole range of philosophical positions, religious practices and devotional foci are accepted.

The Hindu traditions are often described as more a way of life than a religion based upon commonality of belief. However, within this diversity there are a number of beliefs and practices which are more commonly accepted, and the diverse systems of thought have themselves been tested, codified and accepted throughout the centuries. Perhaps the greatest degree of commonality concerns acceptance of the authority of the *Vedas* (see below).

SOURCES OF HINDU BELIEFS AND PRACTICES

Hindus hold a number of texts to be sacred and at the root of their beliefs and practices. Many of them are in Sanskrit, and fall into two broad categories: *shruti* (that which is heard) and *smriti* (that which is remembered).

The four *Vedas* (see below) are *shruti*. Some Hindus believe that *smriti* such as the *Puranas* and the *Ramayana* are less authoritative than the *shruti*, although others stress that *smriti* texts are extensions of the truths hidden in the *shruti*, made accessible through story and simple language. For example, many *Vaishnavas* (see below) consider the *shruti* and

the *smriti* to be on the same level, and call the *Bhagavata Purana* (or *Shrimad Bhagavatam*) the "fifth *Veda*". The *Mahabharata* also is often considered to be the "fifth *Veda*."

Sacred texts are treated with great respect. They are often wrapped in silk or cotton cloth and devout Hindus will avoid placing them on the floor and touching them with feet or with dirty hands. Prayers are often recited before reading from such texts.

Shruti

Oral Tradition
For Hindus, sacred texts are essentially spoken rather than written. This is why the *Vedas*, the most ancient sacred texts, are referred to as *shruti* (that which is heard). Some Hindus believe that the original revelations were given in *Dev Vak* (the language of God) and that Sanskrit later emerged from this, modifying and adapting the original language of revelation in order to make it understandable to human beings. Some Hindus believe that there are some revelations which have, until now, been kept as unwritten secrets which are only orally passed on to those qualified to receive them.

The Four Vedas

The *Vedas* (meaning "knowledge") are believed to be eternal. Tradition says that there was originally one *Veda*, but it was divided into four at the beginning of the third age of the world (see *Yuga* below), and learnt by the four *rishis* (sages) Paila, Jaimini, Vaishampayana and Sumantu. They are then said to have been passed on by word of mouth by the people of that age who possessed remarkable memories until the beginning of the *Kali-Yuga* (3102 BCE, see below), the present age of degeneration. After that it became necessary to commit the teachings to writing in the form of the four books in which they are known today.

The four *Vedas* are: the *Rig Veda*, which contains *mantras* (verses) spoken in worship; the *Sama Veda*, containing sung *mantras* with their tunes; the *Yajur Veda*, containing further *mantras*, and instructions for the actions (*karma*) used in worship; and the *Atharva Veda*, containing *mantras* for particular purposes such as cure of diseases. There are altogether over 20,000 *mantras* in the *Vedas*, including *mantras* which some believe deal in ways ahead of their times with matters of physics, astronomy and mathematics.

According to some traditions, there are also five main *Upavedas* (sub-branches of the *Vedas*). The *Upavedas* are: *Ayurveda*, which is related to the *Rig Veda*, and is concerned with medical knowledge; the *Gandharvaveda*, which is related to the *Sama Veda*, and is concerned with expertise in music, dance and drama; the *Dhanurveda*, which is related to the *Yajur Veda*, and is concerned with military science; the *Arthaveda*, which is related to the *Artharva Veda*, and is concerned with the practice of government; and the *Shilpaveda*, which deals with architecture.

Each of the four *Vedas* consists of four parts: the *Samhitas*, the *Brahmanas*, the *Aranyakas* and the *Upanishads*. The *Samhitas* contain *mantras* for recitation; the *Brahmanas* are concerned with ritual and sacrifice, the purpose of which is material prosperity on earth and joy in heaven after death; the *Aranyakas* reflect on the cosmic role of *Vedic* rituals; and the *Upanishads* contain more philosophical and meditative material and discuss the knowledge through which one is liberated from ignorance and finds self-realisation.

Smriti

The *smriti* consist of six categories: *Itihasa, Purana, Grihya Sutra, Vedanga, Dharma Shastra* and *Prasthana Vakya*. The *Itihasas* (histories) consist of the two epics: the *Ramayana* (written by Valmiki) and the *Mahabharata*, which includes the *Bhagavad Gita*. The *Ramayana* and *Mahabharata* are believed by some Hindus to be historical, whilst others see them in more symbolic terms. They contain accounts of the *Lilas* (pastimes) of the divine manifested in human form, as Rama and Krishna.

Some Hindus believe that it is Vishnu who was manifested in this way, whilst others see the manifestations as those of Krishna in his divine form (for further information on Rama, Krishna and Vishnu see section below on "Key Hindu Beliefs"). The *Ramayana* and the *Mahabharata* illustrate Hindu conceptions of divinity, of human nature and of *dharma* (see below). They deal with the morality which can guide personal life and protect the social order. Both epics illustrate and inspire perseverance and detachment in dealing with adverse circumstances.

Ramayana

The *Ramayana* is set in ancient India and tells the story of how King Rama fought against the forces of evil headed by Ravana. For many Hindus, Rama and his wife Sita are the epitome of right action and righteousness. Rama acts as the dutiful son, obeying his father's every wish, whilst Sita is seen as the perfect wife. Rama Rajya, the reign of Rama as King of ancient Bharat (India), is considered an ideal example of social and political leadership.

Mahabharata

The *Mahabharata* is also set in ancient India. It contains the *Bhagavad Gita* or the *Song of the Blessed Lord* which is a discourse between Krishna and his devotee Prince Arjuna. The *Mahabharata* tells a story which culminates in the battle of Kurukshetra, which marks the beginning of the present degenerate age, the *Kali Yuga*.

Immediately before the war, Prince Arjuna, who is called upon to fight, is perplexed at a situation in which he might have to kill his relatives in the enemy's army. Responding to Arjuna's questions, Krishna (who is in human form as Arjuna's charioteer) speaks to Arjuna and teaches him that the essence of *dharma* is to discharge all duties without selfishness or attachment to their rewards and in dedication to the divine.

The *Bhagavad Gita* is one of the most important scriptures for many Hindus throughout the world because of its teachings about *dharma* and about the different ways of reaching the divine, including through right action. Through the characters of the *Mahabharata*, a code of conduct and a social and ethical philosophy of human relations and problems are presented.

Puranas

The *Puranas* contain stories about the deities Brahma, Vishnu and Shiva and stories about the great sages of Hindu tradition, together with expositions of Hindu theology and religious practice. Whilst some Hindus see these as historical, many understand them as colourful mythology and interpret them in symbolic terms. There are traditionally eighteen principal *Puranas*, the most widely used of which is the *Bhagavata Purana*, which tells of the activities of Vishnu and some of the famous stories about Krishna.

Other Texts

The *Grihya Sutras* are instructions for domestic rituals, including a special emphasis upon the fire sacrifice and the rites of passage through life.

There are six *Vedangas* (literally limbs of the *Vedas*). These are: *Shiksa*, dealing with phonetics; *Vyakarana*, dealing with Sanskrit grammar; *Nirukti*, dealing with Sanskrit etymology; *Chandas*, dealing with the rules of metre; *Jyotisha*, dealing with astrology and astronomy; and *Kalpa*, setting out regulations for ritual.

The *Dharma Shastras* (law books), the most famous of which is the *Manusmriti* (see also below under Gender Roles) or *Laws of Manu* (the ancestor of humankind), contain codes of conduct.

The *Prasthana-vakyas* is a generic title for a wide range of literature, much of which is often specific to particular traditions within the Hindu community. The most significant of these are the *Vedanta-Sutras* which summarise the key aspects of *Vedic* philosophy and the *Tantras*, which are esoteric texts related to Shiva or to Shakti (the Goddess).

KEY HINDU BELIEFS

One and Many

Some non-Hindus have perceived Hindu belief as polytheistic because of its multiplicity of forms and representations of the divine and of *devas* and *devis* (see below - often inadequately rendered into English as gods and goddesses), which the *Vedas* number symbolically at 330 million.

The Hindu traditions allow the use of a variety of symbols, names, terms and images which enable people to discover the divine in ways which are appropriate to them. Within the Hindu *dharma* there are both *monotheists* (believers in one God, and for whom there is a clear distinction between God and the world) as well as *monists* who argue that it is not contradictory to believe that the divine is simultaneously both one and many.

Most Hindus in the UK adhere either to a philosophy of *Advaita*, a form of *monism*, or to a philosophy of *Dvaita,* which is *monotheistic* (For both *Advaita* and *Dvaita* see section below on "Traditions in Hinduism"). Both schools accept the existence of the One Supreme. This is understood either impersonally as the all-pervading Brahman (the *Advaita* position) or as a Supreme Person (the *Dvaita* position). The divine is often represented in a threefold form as *trimurti*. This consists of Brahma with his consort, Saraswati; Vishnu with his consort, Lakshmi; and Shiva with his consort, Parvati (also known by many other names, eg Durga or Shakti).

Simultaneously with accepting the One Supreme in either understanding outlined above, the Hindu traditions also refer to many other beings. Among the best known of these *devas* and *devis* are: Indra (god of rain), Surya (sun god), Chandra (moon god), Ganesha (remover of obstacles), Yama (god of death), Sarasvati (goddess of learning), Lakshmi (goddess of wealth), Hanuman, the ardent devotee of Rama (who is believed to have assumed the monkey-form to fulfil the prophecy of Nandi whom Ravana called "monkey-face") and Murugan (with Ganesha, one of the two sons of Shiva and Parvati). Some Hindus see these as manifestations of different powers and functions of the divine, whilst others accept them as distinctly existing beings.

The Hindu tradition recognises a female principle as a form, and in some cases as the highest form, of the divine. The universal energy of existence is referred to as Shakti, the consort of Shiva, who is considered as the personification of the material energy or Mother Nature. She has various forms, some gentle and nurturing and others fierce and terrible. These go by different names such as Devi, Ambaji, Parvati, Durga and Kali. She is often referred to simply as *Mataji*, meaning respected mother.

Atman

Atman is understood to be the spirit which is present in all life and not just human life. It is the energy which activates the body and fills it with consciousness and is distinct from the material body, which consists of *prakriti* (inert matter). *Prakriti* is understood to be composed of three *gunas* (qualities) namely: *sattva* (goodness), *rajas* (passion) and *tamas* (ignorance). These affect the make-up of each individual human being according to the proportions in which they are found. The *atman* is eternal, but is repeatedly embodied, so that it goes through a cycle of birth and death. At death the *atman* is believed to leave the body and, in accordance with the law of *karma* (see below), its actions in one life are believed to determine the nature and circumstances of its future lives.

Moksha

Hindus understand the ultimate goal of all living beings to be the transcendence of *samsara* (the cycle of birth and death). This is known as *moksha* (liberation). The goal of Hindu practice is to realise union between *atman* and Brahman. In the *Advaita* perspective this is understood as the *atman* recognising its identity with Brahman, the Supreme Spirit. In the *Dvaita* view (also see below), union is understood as serving God eternally and the union is a qualitative rather than a quantitative one. In either case it is believed that it can take many lives to reach this goal.

Dharma

The concept of *dharma* is central to the Hindu traditions. It has no exact English equivalent, although it is often loosely translated as "religion", "law", "duty" or "righteousness". Its linguistic root is the Sanskrit *dhr* meaning "to sustain" or "hold together". Its meaning is therefore approximately "that which sustains", "that which upholds" or "the intrinsic property of something". Thus, for example, the *dharma* of water is its wetness. Following one's *dharma* is essential to achieving *moksha*.

Karma

For Hindus, *karma* is the universal principle of actions and their consequences. While one is free to act, all actions have their inevitable consequences - good, bad or mixed, depending upon the nature of the act and the intention behind its performance. Because of the relationship between actions and consequences, the results shape one's destiny, whether in the present or in a future life. Whilst one remains ignorant of the principle of *karma*, it leads to *janma* (birth), resulting in *dukkha* (unsatisfactoriness). Hindu teaching advises that, in order to be released from *karma*, every action should be carried out from a holy sense of duty and dedication, shunning attachment to its results.

Maya

Maya (sometimes explained as meaning "that which is not") is the state of illusion which comes about through ignorance of the *Sanatana Dharma* (the eternal truth). Many Hindus speak more of "ignorance" and "knowledge" than of "evil" and "good". The illusion of *maya* and our dependence upon the world of appearances decreases as our knowledge increases.

Yuga

A very common belief is that there has been a gradual spiritual degradation of civilisation in the current age, which is itself part of a cycle of four ages, called *Yugas*. This present age is known as the *Kali Yuga* (*Kali* in this context is not to be confused with the name of the goddess Kali) or "dark age". It is believed to have begun with the departure of Krishna after the destruction of the *Mahabharata* war, in 3102BCE. At the end of the *Kali Yuga* it is believed that the divine will appear in human form in order to eradicate all evil from the world and clear the way for the return of the next cycle of four ages, beginning with the perfect age.

TRADITIONS IN HINDUISM

The Six Darshanas

Classically, there are six *Darshanas* (systems of Hindu philosophy). These are the *Purva Mimamsa* (also called *Mimamsa* for short), *Nyaya*, *Vaisheshika*, *Samkhya*, *Yoga* and *Vedanta* (otherwise known as the *Uttara Mimamsa*).

They are each concerned with different aspects of knowledge: *Mimamsa* is concerned with action and with responsibility; *Nyaya* with logic; *Vaisesika* with the analysis of matter in terms of its atomic structure; *Samkhya* with the analysis of matter in terms of its functioning; *Yoga* with training of the mind and body; and *Vedanta* with knowledge of ultimate reality.

The six different systems developed at different points in time and exist side by side in the Hindu tradition, resulting in a variety of philosophies ranging from *atheistic* to *theistic* and from *monistic* to *dualistic*. Despite their differences, in most of these systems the common theme is that the goal of human existence is liberation of the *atman* from the cycle of birth and death.

There is also a commitment to the idea that the spiritual life consists of four principal paths: *karma yoga* (way of action), *jnana yoga* (way of knowledge), *raja yoga* (way of self-control) and *bhakti yoga* (way of devotion). The systems do not exclude one another; for instance, a person who follows the *Vedanta* as the way to liberation may also use *Purva Mimamsa* as a guide to ritual practice, *Nyaya* as a system for conducting arguments, and *Yoga* as a means of self-discipline.

Vedanta: Dvaita and Advaita

Many Hindus today subscribe to the *Vedanta* system in one form or another, which seeks to understand the teaching of the *Upanishads*. *Vedanta* literally means "the ultimate purpose of the *Vedas*" or "the conclusion of all knowledge". It is concerned with three ultimate entities: God, the *atman* (spirit) and *prakriti* (matter). Within *Vedanta* there are different views of the relation between these three. However, there are two main tendencies – the *dvaita* (*dualist*) and the *advaita* (*monist*).

Dvaita

The term *dvaita* refers to personalist *monotheism*, in which the nature of God is that of an unlimited supreme personality. In this tendency, the *atman* and *prakriti* are seen as eternally distinct from God, and the *atman* depends upon God for its liberation. *Dvaitins* believe some deities to be *avataras* (manifestations and descents) of God. Besides these, it is also believed that there are numerous *devas* and *devis*, each of whom has specific functions within the material sphere.

Advaita

The *Advaita* or *monist* tendency insists that the *atman* and *prakriti* have no existence of their own, but depend for their existence on God, often called Brahman. Brahman is not a personal name, since God has no name or gender and is seen more in terms of permeative energy than of personality. The *atman* which is the eternal spirit in each conscious being is a manifestation of Brahman. Most humans are seen as being unaware of this identity, and think that they exist as separate beings. *Moksha* (salvation) is reached when this limited outlook is overcome and identity with Brahman is realised.

Brahman is believed to have been manifested in a variety of different times and places and personified in many different forms. Because of this, *Advaitins* believe that union with Brahman can be attained through the worship of any deity which is chosen as one's personal object of devotion.

In the *Advaita* view, Brahman can be seen as the underlying principle behind the universe from which is manifested the trinity of creative force (personified as Brahma), preservative force (personified as Vishnu) and dissolving force (personified as Shiva). Everything in the universe is seen as being part of an eternal cycle in which it is created, maintained for some time, and then destroyed.

Dvaita and *Advaita*, as summarised above, represent two poles of thought within the *Vedanta*. Between these poles can be found a range of subtly varied schools of thought associated with famous Hindu teachers and philosophers. These include the following:

Advaita Vedanta

Non-dualist Vedanta, a philosophy that was propounded by Shankara (7th-8th century CE), in which it is believed that the *atman* or *jiva* (living entity) is identical with God and this has simply to be realised. Only the divine is absolutely real, and everything else is *maya* (illusion or provisional), being real only in a relative and limited sense.

Vishishta-Advaita

A qualified *non-dualism* propounded by Ramanuja (c.1017-1137CE), which holds that there is a difference between God, the living entities, and *prakriti* (nature). Nevertheless, the *atman* and *prakriti* are God, in rather the same way as a person's body is that person: it is God who permeates them and gives them purpose and meaning. Ramanuja identified God as Vishnu.

Navya Vishishta-Advaita

A qualified *non-dualism*, propounded by Sahajananda (c.1781-1830CE). Five eternal realities are distinguished: *jivas* (living entities that are infinite in number); *Ishwara* or the Lord (cosmic self-ominiscience); *maya* (matter in both manifested and unmanifested forms); *Akshar Brahman* (supreme divine abode of God); and *Parabrahman* (Supreme Godhead).

Shuddha-Dvaita

A pure *dualism* propounded by Madhva (c.1239-1319CE), also known as Swaminarayan (see section on Spiritual Movements below), in which God (seen as Vishnu), the living entities and the material world (*prakriti*) are eternally distinct. Madhva maintained even more strongly than Ramanuja the distinctness of these three, and particularly the distinction between the individual soul and God.

Dvaita-Advaita

A philosophy of oneness and difference propounded by Nimbarka (13th or 14th century CE), a worshipper of Krishna.

Shuddha-Advaita

A purified *monism* taught by Vishnuswami and his successor Vallabha (c.1479-1531BCE) (see "Spiritual Movements" below), who rejected the doctrine of *maya*.

Achintya-Bhedha-Abheda

A doctrine of inconceivable simultaneous oneness and difference, propounded by Chaitanya (c.1486-1534CE) and by his successors, including Bhaktivedanta Swami Prabhupada (1896-1977) (see "Spiritual Movements" below). It holds that God (identified as Krishna), the living entities and *prakriti* are both one and different at the same time, in a way that cannot be conceived by the human mind.

Shaiva Siddhanta

The system of the worshippers of Shiva, codified in the 12th-14th centuries CE. This system teaches that there are innumerable living entities, trapped in the world of rebirth, but enabled to escape from it by the grace of Shiva.

Sampradaya

The above are the doctrines of some of the many *sampradayas* (traditions) which can be encountered within the Hindu community in the UK. Each *sampradaya* has its set of doctrines and its form of worship, usually directed to a particular personal form of God, flourishing in a particular region of India and passed down through a succession of *gurus*. *Gurus* are spiritual leaders who are seen by their followers as providing great insight and guidance in spiritual matters. (See further "Spiritual Movements" below.)

Not all Hindus are members of *sampradayas*. However, many Hindus worship a particular form of God, called their *ishta-devata* (choicest deity). On the basis of the form of God which they chiefly worship, they can be classed as *Vaishnavas*, *Shaivas* and *Shaktas*.

Vaishnavas, Shaivas and Shaktas

The term *Vaishnava* is applied to worshippers of Vishnu who understand the Divine and its relationship with humanity in the *Dvaita* way, seeing Vishnu as the supreme divine personal reality and also to those who see Krishna as the divine personal reality. Many British Hindus belong to one or another of the *Vaishnava sampradayas*.

Shaivas are worshippers of Shiva, and *Shaktas* are worshippers of Shakti or the Goddess (also known by other names including Durga and Parvati) and sometimes seen as the consort of Shiva. Some see Shiva and Shakti as alternative and complementary manifestations of *Brahman*, understood as supra-personal in the *Advaita* manner.

HINDU LIFE

The Four Aims

The traditional Hindu view of human life is characterised by the four *purusharthas* (aims for

human existence). These are: *dharma* (religious life) as a foundation for everything else; *artha* (economic development) as a necessity for life; *kama* (sense gratification) in order to keep a healthy body and mind, but the desire for which should also be controlled through regulation; and *moksha* (liberation, salvation) from the cycle of birth and death.

Most Hindus consider liberation to be the ultimate goal, but among *Vaishnavas* some would say that *bhakti* (devotion to the divine) is a fifth and final goal and that *prema* (love of God) and selfless devotion is higher than liberation (which for the devotees comes by means of the grace of God and not just by personal efforts).

Values

There are a number of core ideals and values which are shared by most Hindus, although in practice they are subject to different interpretations which result in varying degrees of observance. These ideals and values include: respect for parents and elders; reverence for teachers; regard for guests; a general adoption of vegetarianism; *ahimsa* (non-violence); tolerance of all races and religions; controlled relations between the sexes in which marriage is considered sacred and divorce, and pre-marital or extra-marital sexual relationships are strongly discouraged; sacredness of the cow whose milk sustains human life; and an appreciation of the equality of all living beings and the sanctity of life.

Hindus seek to promote the *Sanatana Dharma* among all people although, in general, they do not engage in activity aimed at converting non-Hindus to Hindu practice. Nevertheless, individuals are generally welcome to embrace the Hindu way.

Varnashrama Dharma

An understanding of one's personal and social role within the cosmic order of things is at the centre of Hindu life. Understanding *sva-dharma* (literally, "one's own *dharma*") in its relationship to *varna* (social position, or class) and *ashrama* (meaning "stage in life" or "spiritual order") is crucial. *Dharma*, understood as a whole, is the morality by which righteousness and religious codes and duties are protected.

The mutual obligations involved in this system are symbolised for many by the ceremony of *Rakshabandhan*, which involves the tying of a thread (*rakhi*) by sisters around the wrist of their brothers, by students around the wrist of their teachers, and by people in general around the wrist of their leaders. This symbolises the vow to protect *dharma* and promote unity within society.

Various *dharmas* correspond with particular *varnas* and *ashramas* (see below) of which, in each case, there are believed to be four. As already noted (see *dharma* above), *dharma* can mean "intrinsic property", which is different for different things. Similarly, there are different *dharmas* for different people. Among the factors that differentiate people are the four *varnas* and four *ashramas* described below.

The Four Varnas

In the Hindu ideal, everyone belongs to one of four *varnas*, traditionally and ideally perceived as having complementary, separate and distinct social roles. These are defined in a well-known *Vedic* hymn, the *Purusha Sukta* (*Rig-Veda*, book 10, hymn 90), in which the whole of society is seen as one person and the *varnas* as interdependent parts of the one social body. A person's *varna* traditionally indicates his or her status and responsibility, and thus the kind of duty which he or she must execute to transmigrate into a higher existence.

According to some interpretations of the scriptures, the system of the four *varnas* is not wholly applicable in this age (*Kali Yuga*). Some Hindus say that it was only after the *Vedic* period that this social system became rigidly hereditary, whereas others maintain that it was always so. According to the *Bhagavad Gita* an individual's *varna* should be understood according to the person's qualities and the tendency towards a particular kind of work. The traditional *varnas* consist of:

Brahmins
Intelligentsia and priests who are characterised by austerity, knowledge, self-control, honesty and cleanliness and who seek to promote these more widely.

Kshatriyas
Administrators and military characterised by power, courage and leadership whose purpose in life is to establish peace and prosperity.

Vaishyas
Agriculturalists and merchants whose work is in producing and trading, being responsible for the generation and distribution of material wealth.

Sudras
Workers who provide labour and service.

The four-fold differentiation of *varnas* is no longer rigidly followed in the contemporary Hindu community, but it reflects the broad outlines of a division of labour and responsibilities which are found in many historical and contemporary societies.

Jati

The ideal division of society into four *varnas* is an important concept in *dharma*. But in practice a person tends to identify himself or herself with an hereditary group called a *jati* that is associated with one of the *varnas*. These groups are often referred to in English as *castes* or *sub-castes*. This should not be taken as implying any inherent differences between groups.

While the system of four *varnas* is known throughout India, the pattern of *jatis* varies from region to region. In each region there are dozens of *jatis*, many of them unknown even by name in other regions, and in India as a whole there are thousands.

Many *jatis* are traditionally linked to particular occupations, although their members do not necessarily practise them. *Jati* remains a significant social, cultural and economic factor for many aspects of internal community life in the UK; for instance, many Hindus marry within their *jati*. Examples of *jatis* include the following: *Patidars* (traditionally, traders), *Mochis* (traditionally, shoemakers), *Lohanas* (traditionally, traders), *Anavil Brahmins* (traditionally, agriculturalists), *Khattris* and *Aroras* (both traditionally traders), *Balmikis* (traditionally, manual workers), *Ravidasis* (traditionally, shoemakers), *Rarhi Brahmins* (traditionally, priests) and *Baidyas* (traditionally, physicians).

Certain *jatis*, generally associated with what are viewed as polluting occupations, have historically been identified as "outcastes" and "untouchables", and have often suffered social discrimination as a result. The official term used in India to describe this group of people is the "scheduled castes", and following independence, the Indian Government granted a special status to this group with the intention of achieving social equity.

Many of the present leaders of this group now prefer the self-designation of *Dalit* (oppressed). The majority contemporary Hindu position is that untouchability has no sanction within the Hindu *dharma*. The Hindu leader *Mahatma* (Great Soul) Gandhi called such people *Harijans* (children of God).

Gender Roles

The Hindu tradition has advocated equality of worth between women and men but with differentiation of social roles. These are set out in the *Manusmriti* (the *Law of Manu*), where a woman's role is defined primarily as that of an educator of children and housekeeper, with a man's role being one of overall authority coupled with financial responsibility for the family. Views as to how far the *Manusmriti* applies in the circumstances of contemporary society vary within different sections of the Hindu community and, in the UK, specific gender roles vary from family to family. In spiritual terms, many Hindu women point to the strength and dignity which they derive from the Hindu tradition's representation of the divine in female as well as male forms.

Ashramas

The *ashramas* are the four stages which have traditionally and ideally been followed in the course of one's life. In this ideal sequence one first becomes a *brahmacharin* (student) living a celibate life of study under a *guru*.

Next, one becomes a *grihastha* or *grihini* (householder). In this stage, marriage, family and the bringing up and educating of children, together with hospitality for guests and care for the elderly and disabled, are the main focus of responsibility.

The third stage is that of a *vanaprastha* (hermit who has retired to the forest). This stage can only be entered after the completion of social obligations through the marriage of all one's daughters and preferably also of one's sons, and the handing over to them of all business affairs. This *ashrama* is traditionally a time in which there are increasing periods of withdrawal from society in order to enable more concentration on the spiritual dimension of life.

The fourth and final stage which may be undertaken is that of the *sannyasin*, who has renounced all earthly ties and looks to the whole world as a family rather than to an immediate biologically-related unit. When a husband becomes a *sannyasin*, the husband and wife part, with the husband going to live in an *ashram* and the wife coming under the care of her sons. This stage is followed only very rarely in conventional society.

Traditionally, *brahmins* go through all four *ashramas*, *kshatriyas* never directly take *sannyasa*, and *vaishyas* do not take vanaprastha or sannyasa, with *sudras* only accepting the householder *ashrama*. Some early Hindu texts allow for the possibility of becoming a *sannyasi* soon after completing the *brahmacharin* stage. Whilst the *ashrama* system has not been fully operative since medieval times, a sequence of study followed by familial responsibilities and finally withdrawal from the world remains a powerful ideal for many Hindus, including those in the UK, since these stages are seen as based on a natural progression through life.

Guru-Disciple Relationship

For many Hindus, the *Guru Shishya Sambandh* (*Guru*-disciple relationship) is of great importance. *Gurus* are revered as those who have attained a spiritual perfection and as embodiments of the divine. The guidance and grace of a *guru* is therefore often seen as being essential for those those aspire to liberation.

Vegetarianism

Within the Hindu tradition there is a variety of views on the permissibility of a range of foods and drinks. However, whilst Hindus recognise that every living organism depends upon others for food, many Hindus are vegetarians and even those who eat meat normally abstain from beef. Hindu vegetarianism arises from a belief in the principle of *ahimsa* (non-harming) and thus generally precludes the eating of meat, fish or eggs. Sometimes onions and garlic are also not eaten.

However, as well as the principle of *ahimsa*, there is also a positive conviction concerning the effect of food upon human development, especially for those who practise spiritual disciplines. Milk, yoghurt, butter, ghee (clarified butter) and fruits are usually acceptable because no killing has taken place and they are considered to be foods which promote *sattva* (purity and harmony). When preparing their own food, many Hindus offer their food to a deity before eating it, and keep aside a portion for animals.

Products which have been cooked in, or contain, by-products from slaughtered animals would not be acceptable to strict Hindu vegetarians. For example, neither conventional ice cream (which may contain animal fats) nor cheese which contains rennet (extracted from the pancreas of the cow), nor chips which have been cooked in animal fats, would be acceptable. Hindus may also refrain from intoxicating drinks such as alcohol, and in some cases from tea and coffee too.

Fasting

Many Hindus (and especially women) observe fasts or *vrats* (vows) as devotion to a deity and on behalf of the well-being of themselves and their family. These vows entail the avoidance of certain foods at certain times, such as on particular days of the week, of the lunar month, and of the year.

HINDU WORSHIP

The practice of domestic worship is widespread. In their own homes, most Hindus have a shrine or small area for worship (*ghar mandir*, "house temple") containing pictures and/or *murtis* (see below) of favourite deities and the women of the household have an important role in the religious devotions centred on these shrines. In addition to private worship some fairly large gatherings for worship may also take place in private homes. *Havan* (the rite of the sacred fire) may also be performed at home on important occasions.

However, many Hindus also attend a place of worship to associate with saintly persons from whom they can learn about spiritual topics. In a land in which Hindus are in a minority, worship at the *mandir* (see below) also fulfils an important social function, providing an opportunity to engage in community and cultural activities and consolidate faith together.

Mandirs

At present *mandirs* (temples) in the UK are generally converted public or religious buildings and private houses, with only a few purpose-built buildings. One such is the recently completed Shri Swaminarayan Mandir in Neasden, North West London. This is the first ever traditional mandir carved in white marble stone to be built in Europe and was opened in August 1995.

Within individual *mandirs*, one may see different *murtis* (sacred images or figures that represent deities) and pictures of holy people. This variety can reflect the range of *sampradayas* within the community that use the temple. *Mandirs* are more likely than in India to cater for a variety of *sampradayas*. This may be partly because of the minority position of Hindus in the UK and the financial constraints within which they must operate, but it is also made possible by the inclusive approach of the Hindu traditions with respect to the commonalities shared by different deities. As well as the hall for worship, *mandirs* may also have other facilities on their premises, such as social, cultural, educational, and administrative rooms.

Murtis

Inside the *mandir*, there is usually a main hall with a shrine where the *murtis* of the *mandir* are installed. There may also be other side shrines. For those who are outsiders to the Hindu tradition, it is sometimes difficult to gain an accurate understanding of the nature of *murtis*. They are more than purely symbolic representations of deities and yet Hindus do not believe that the reality of a deity is limited to a particular *murti* in a particular place. *Murtis* are specifically dedicated and they are venerated as deities, being dressed in the finest fabrics and decorated with ornaments, jewellery and garlands of flowers. This is in order to foster a mood of *seva* (sacrifice and selfless service) by centring people's devotion on the deity.

The *murtis* are usually made of marble, but can also be made of other kinds of stone, wood or metal. For the believer, the presence of a particular deity is manifested by *murtis* with specific characteristics. For example, Ganesha is represented by an elephant-headed *murti* with four arms; Krishna is represented as a cowherd seen standing with one leg crossing the other at the ankles, playing a flute, and accompanied by his favourite devotee, a *gopi* (cowherd girl) *Radha*.

Deities are often accompanied by *murtis* of their *vahana* (a vehicle, the animal or bird on which they ride). For example, Shiva rides on the bull, Nandi. Brightly coloured and sweet-smelling flowers are laid before the murtis or hung over them as garlands. The *murtis* may be housed in a *garbha-griha* (inner sanctum), which only the priest is permitted to enter.

Other Features and Activities

In the main hall there may also be one or more *vyasasanas*. These are decorated thrones on which *swamis* (religious teachers) sit when they deliver discourses to religious gatherings. In a *mandir* it is also likely that there will be incense to purify the air and create a spiritual atmosphere; the *AUM* (or *OM*) symbol to symbolise the primaeval sound representing God in the simplest form; and the *swastika*. This is not to be confused with the swastika of Nazism. The original Hindu form of this symbol is a sign of auspiciousness. Hindus feel a sense of outrage at the Nazi co-option and distortion of such a sacred symbol, and also at the use of *OM* on some hallucinogenic drugs.

One might also find a conch shell, the sound of which assists concentration on worship; a *trishul*, which is the trident weapon of Shiva and represents God, the soul and the ignorance through which the soul is held in bondage; a coconut, which is believed to represent the three-eyed Shiva and is symbolic of life by being hard on the outside but sweet on the inside; images of the *lotus*, which is an ancient symbol of the cosmos, of wisdom and of humanity; and a *kalasha*, which is a pot representing the human body. The mouth of a *kalasha* is considered as Vishnu; its base as Brahma; and its middle as Shiva. The water within it stands for purity and love of the divine.

Corporate devotional activities include *bhajan* and *kirtan* (singing songs and *mantras*); *pravachan* (sermon); *havan* (the sacred fire ceremony); and the *arti* ceremony (see below). Private devotions, in the temple and at home, include *japa* (*mantra* meditation), prayer, *puja* (worship of the *murti*) and the study of sacred texts.

When visiting a *mandir*, it is customary for Hindus to take some kind of offering for the deity, such as food, money or flowers, *haldi* (turmeric) and *kumkum* (red powder). Anyone entering a *mandir* for any purpose must remove their shoes. A bell may be hung for worshippers to ring on entering, to invite the presence of the gods and to ward off evil spirits. The worshipper then comes face to face with the *murti*. This is called taking *darshan* (sight) of the deity, which is understood as a blissful experience.

The worshipper offers respect to the deity/deities by folding hands or by bowing down, and may then offer prayers and a gift, or respectfully sip a few drops of *charnamrita* (holy water used to bathe the deity). The worship of the *murti* with offering of gifts is called *puja*. More formal *puja* is performed by the temple priest.

In the *arti* ceremony, performed several times a day, the priest offers articles of worship to the deity including lighted ghee lamps, incense, water for bathing, small napkins for drying, flowers and peacock and yak-tail fans, during which worshippers play musical instruments, sing *bhajans*, and clap their hands in rhythm.

Almost all Hindu temples welcome people from all religions to visit them and, if they wish, to take part in the worship. Prior to *arti*, food is offered to the deity and is blessed for later distribution. Food that has been offered to a deity is said to be sanctified and is known as *prasad* or *prasadam*.

HINDU CALENDAR AND FESTIVALS

Calendar

The Hindu year is based on the waxing and waning of the moon. Since it consists normally of twelve lunar months, it is ten days shorter than it is in the *Gregorian* calendar year. Approximately once every three years an extra month is added to bring the lunar year in phase with the solar year. Hindu years carry a name instead of the numbers of the Gregorian calendar. For example, 1996-97 was Dhatu; 1997-98 is Ishvara, and 1998-99 will be Bahudaanya.

Hindu seasons and festival dates do not remain the same each year within the framework of the *Gregorian* calendar, except for a few which are timed by the sun and not the moon. The Hindu calendar is set out in *panchang* (almanacs) which provide information on the dates of festivals and other rituals to be followed by various Hindu groups.

Festivals

There are many Hindu festivals, but the following are some of the principal ones. The approximate time of their occurrence indicated below refers to the *Gregorian* calendar in common use in the UK:

Shivaratri or Mahashivaratri
(February/March)
Worship dedicated to Lord Shiva. Devotees spend the night at the temple chanting and singing. Milk is poured continuously, as an offering, on to the *linga*, the symbolic form of Lord Shiva. Among some families, there is also a tradition of fasting.

Holi (February/March)
This festival of colours is associated with many stories of Vishnu and his devotees, and with that of the half-man, half-lion incarnation, Narasimha or Narasingha, and Prahlada, a devotee of Krishna. In India, traditionally, liquid dyes, coloured powders and water are liberally sprinkled on the participants as fun. In the UK the inclement climate, and the fact that it could easily be misunderstood by the wider society, can curtail this traditional practice, but many British Hindus enjoy the bonfire which is another traditional feature of *Holi*.

Yugadi or Gudi Parva (March-April)
For many Hindus, this festival marks the beginning of the New Year. *Puja*, feasting and greetings are common. A special mixture of

neem leaves and jaggery is eaten to symbolise acceptance of both bitter and happy things in life.

Rama Navami/Hari Jayanti (March/April)

Celebrates the birth of Lord Rama as an avatar at Ayodhya in India. Devotees fast, and the Ramayana, the story of Rama and Sita, is read aloud in temples. Devotees of Lord Swaminaryan also celebrate his birth on this day by fasting, prayers, *bhajans* and discourses about his life.

Janmashtami (August/September)

Marks the birth of Lord Krishna who is believed to have appeared in human form in the fourth century BCE, or in traditional chronology five thousand years ago shortly before the *Kali Yuga*, in the district of Mathura, India, in order to deliver the pious, destroy miscreants and establish the principles of the *Sanatana Dharma*. Devotees perform *puja* and sing *bhajans*.

Navaratri (September/October)

Navaratri means "nine nights". It is celebrated with dancing and is held in honour of Lakshmi, Durga and Sarasvati, as well as other goddesses worshipped in this season. It ends with *Dussehra* or *Vijayadashami*, the tenth day, a time of celebration of the victory of good over evil.

Diwali or Deepawali (October/November)

According to some Hindu groups, this festival marks the beginning of a new Hindu year. It is concerned with the celebration of the victory of light over darkness and knowledge over ignorance. The festival is also a time when Hindus worship the Goddess Lakshmi (Goddess of prosperity) and is known as the "festival of lights" because of the lighting everywhere of *dipas* or *divas* (small oil lamps). These are lit to illuminate Lakshmi's way to the home and to celebrate the return of Rama and Sita to Rama's kingdom of Ayodhya after fourteen years of exile.

Annakuta or Nutan Varsh (October/November)

This is the day after *Divali*. Large quantities of sweets and other food stuffs are brought to the temple to be offered to the deities in celebration of a story from Krishna's childhood concerned with Mount Govardhan.

Pilgrimages

Pilgrimages also form an important part of Hindu religious observance. Visits to holy places in India may be undertaken with special intentions in mind, such as cure of disease or blessing for the family.

In the *Advaita* Hindu tradition, the most holy of all places of pilgrimage is Varanasi (also known as Benares or Kashi). This is situated on the sacred River Ganga (Ganges) and is especially sacred to those Hindus who venerate Shiva and Rama. Pilgrims who have visited the River Ganga often bring home bottles of water from the river to place in their family shrines. Dying people may request to sip Ganges water and also to have their ashes spread in the river.

In the *Vaishnava* Hindu tradition, Vrindavan and Nathdwar are of special importance because of their connections with Krishna. Ayodhya, Badrinath, Kedaranath, Mathura, Tirupathi and Vaishnodevi, Kashmir, Dwarka are other important places of pilgrimage. There are also some more recently evolved centres of pilgrimage such as Akshardham, in Gandhinagar, Gujarat, a memorial to Lord Swaminarayan.

HINDU ORGANISATIONS

The first Hindu organisations in the UK were set up in the late 1950s. Since then a number of different kinds of organisation have developed, many of which serve multiple functions, including lobbying and campaigning groups, youth activities, language classes, women's groups, trust funds, education and propagation of Hindu culture, in addition to more specifically religious activities. Some of the local and national groupings are part of international organisations mainly based in India.

Jati (Community) Associations

Although *jatis* (see above) may be historically associated in India with particular occupations, in the UK they do not generally correlate with one's social, economic or occupational status. *Jati* groups do, however, remain a significant social, cultural and economic factor for many aspects of internal Hindu community life in the UK.

Different patterns of settlement have influenced patterns of organisational development and therefore *jati* groups are concentrated in particular localities in the UK. For example, there has been a concentration of *Mochis* in Leeds, and of *Lohanas* in Leicester and North London.

Jati associations exist at both national and local levels. They have functions ranging from social networking through to voluntary welfare support and provision. Local organisations may be affiliated to a national organisation. As one example, the Gujarati Federation of Anavil Samaj is an organisation representing members of the Anavil *jati* and has local branches in various parts of the country.

National *jati* organisations are much more characteristic of Gujarati Hindus than Punjabi Hindus and they co-ordinate joint events between local groups and provide a networking function across the country. National *jati* organisations often produce annual directories of members of the local *jati* groups affiliated to them, although these are not readily available to the general public.

Jati associations are sometimes recognisable from the *jati* name in their title, for example, the National Association of Patidar Samaj (Patidar), the Shri Kutch Leva Patel Samaj (members of the Leva Patel jati from the Kutch region of the state of Gujarat), or Brahma Samaj (Brahmin). The Brahma Samaj is a Gujarati Brahmin association and should not be confused with the Brahmo Samaj,

which is a religious society founded in Calcutta in 1828.

Spiritual Movements

Another form of organisation, often with a regional base in India, is the *sampradaya* or spiritual tradition (see above). A number of *sampradayas*, some relatively modern, have a strong presence in the UK.

Swaminaryans

Swaminarayan Hindus in the UK are predominantly of Gujarati origin and follow teachers in the line of Sahajananda Swami (1781-1830), also called Swaminarayan, who is believed to have been an incarnation of the Supreme Lord. *Swaminarayanis* combine traditional Hindu practices with specific customs of their own, including the strict separation of men and women in the temple.

There are various *Swaminarayan* groupings in the UK, reflecting different views concerning the proper line of succession to Sahajananda Swami. The largest in the UK is the Akshar Purushottam Sanstha (the Swaminarayan Hindu Mission) which looks to the leadership of Pramukh Swami and whose main UK centre is in Neasden, London. Another is the group which looks for leadership to Acharya Tejendraprasad Pande and whose main UK centre is in Willesden Lane, London.

Pushtimargis

Other devotional groups include the *Pushtimarg* or *Vallabha sampradaya* (founded in the sixteenth century). Its members, who are largely Lohana by *jati*, follow the teachings of Vallabha (c.1479-1531 CE) and worship Krishna, particularly in the form of Srinathji and as the infant Krishna.

Krishna Consciousness

There is also the International Society for Krishna Consciousness (ISKCON) whose devotees follow the teachings propounded by A C Bhaktivedanta Swami Prabhupada (1896-1977) in the Chaitanya Vaishnava tradition which flourishes in Bengal. The first ISKCON temple in the UK was opened in 1969 in central London. Later, George Harrison (one of the Beatles) donated Bhaktivedanta Manor in Hertfordshire where, every year, a festival involving thousands of Hindus from all over the UK has been held to celebrate *Krishna-Janmashtami*. The long-running planning dispute which threatened this temple with closure for public worship was settled in 1996.

Arya Samajis

Members of the Arya Samaj follow the teachings of Swami Dayananda Saraswati (1824-1883CE) who rejected the concept of *jati* and the worship of *murtis*. Hindus in the Arya Samaj, who are mainly Punjabis, stress belief in, and the purity of, the *Vedas* and reject those parts of post-*Vedic* Hindu teachings which they believe do not conform to the *Vedic* revelation, including parts of the *Puranas* and *Tantras*.

Ramakrishna Mission

The Ramakrishna Mission was founded by the Bengali Swami Vivekananda (1863-1902CE) in the name of his master Ramakrishna (1836-1886). It teaches *Advaita Vedanta*, and is headed by a highly disciplined and organised body of *sannyasins*.

Hindu-Related Groups

There are also many Hindu-related movements and groups which practise the disciplines of *yoga*. Some of these focus purely on the more physical exercises of *Hatha Yoga* whilst others seek to present a complete religious approach through *Raja Yoga*. Some of these *Yoga* groups are connected with the wider Hindu community, whilst others have recruitment and management from a cross section of the wider community. These include the Divine Life Society, the Transcendental Meditation movement and others.

Educational Organisations

The Swaminarayan Hindu Mission in London has started an independent Hindu school where, in addition to the National Curriculum, students are taught about moral and ethical values and Hindu religion, culture and music. There are also many supplementary schools which teach Indian languages and Hindu religion and culture out of school hours.

Regional/Linguistic Groups

Some groups are organised on the basis of a specific shared regional or linguistic background. Punjabis or Gujaratis or Bengalis have often joined together to form associations. Such groups can sometimes be recognised by the inclusion of regional names in their organisational titles, as in for example, the Preston Gujarat Hindu Society.

Representative Groups

There is no single national representative organisation of Hindus in the UK, although the Hindu Council of the UK, founded in November 1994, aspires to a comprehensive role as an umbrella organisation for the various national groupings. Among these groupings are the National Council of Hindu Temples, which has played a significant role in the formation of the Hindu Council of the UK. There is also the UK branch of the international organisation, the Vishwa Hindu Parishad (The World Council of Hindus) which has local branches throughout the UK.

A number of local and regional areas have seen the development of representative groups such as the Hindu Council (Brent), the Hindu Council of Birmingham, the Leicester Gujarat Hindu Association, the Hindu Council of the North, the Hindu Council of Nottingham, and the Hindu Resource Centre (Croydon).

Personnel

A Hindu priest is often referred to as *pandit*, *swami*, or *maharaj*. A priest whose function is to perform *puja* in a temple is called a *pujari*. One who performs life-cycle rituals for families in their homes is called a *purohit*.

Traditionally, these roles have been restricted to those of the *Brahmin varna*. However (as explained in the section on *varna* above), the term *Brahmin* can be understood in a qualitative sense, so that anyone who is knowledgeable and shows *Brahmin*-like qualities can be a priest.

Priests are usually male, but can also be female. In some other temples wives of priests act as *pujari* when their husbands are away. Priests may be resident in the *mandir*, and may be appointed and paid by the congregation. Their role is to conduct religious ceremonies and to care for the holy shrines.

The *mandir* is usually governed by a managing committee including the offices of temple president and a secretary. Many *pandits* are from India, staying only for a temporary period before returning home. As such, they will not necessarily speak English. Therefore when wishing to visit a *mandir* it may be preferable to contact the secretary or president of the *mandir*.

Swamis or *gurus* are religious teachers, and they are venerated by Hindus because they are learned in the scriptures, know the methods of worship and have renounced all worldly attachments. Some have authority in relation to particular *sampradayas*, but they also receive respect from non-members.

FURTHER READING

Ballard, R (ed), *Desh Pardesh: The South Asian Presence in Britain*, C. Hurst and Co, London, 1994.

Barot, R, "Caste and Sect in the Swaminarayan Movement", in Burghart, R (ed), *Hinduism in Great Britain*, Tavistock Publications, London, 1987.

Bharatiya Vidya Bhavan, *Hindu Dharma: The Universal Way of Life*, Bharatiya Vidya Bhavan, London, nd.

Bowen, D G (ed), *Hinduism in England*, Faculty of Contemporary Studies, Bradford College, Bradford, 1986.

Brockington, J L, *The Sacred Thread: Hinduism in Its Continuity and Diversity*, Edinburgh University Press, Edinburgh, 1981.

Burghart, R (ed), *Hinduism in Great Britain: The Perpetuation of Religion in an Alien Cultural Milieu*, Tavistock, London, 1987.

Carey, S, "The Hare Krishna movement and Hindus in Britain", in *New Community*, Volume X, Spring 1983, pp. 477–486.

Carey, S, "The Indianisation of the Hare Krishna movement in Britain", in Burghart, R (ed), *Hinduism in Great Britain*, Tavistock, London, 1987.

Chandrashekharendra Sarasvati Swami, His Holiness, *Hindu Dharma: The Universal Way of Life*, Bharatiya Vidya Bhavan, Bombay, 1995.

Dwyer, R, "Caste, Religion and Sect in Gujarat: Followers of Vallabhacharya and Swaminarayan" in Ballard, R (ed), *Desh Pardesh: The South Asian Presence in Britain*, C. Hurst and Co, London, 1994, pp. 165-190.

Firth, S, "Changing Patterns in Hindu Death Rituals in Britain", in Killingley, D; Menski, W; and Firth, S, *Hindu Ritual and Society*, S.Y. Killingley, Newcastle upon Tyne, 1991.

Flood, G, *An Introduction to Hinduism*, Cambridge University Press, Cambridge, 1996.

Henley, A, *Caring for Hindus and Their Families: Religious Aspects of Care*, National Extension College, Cambridge, 1983.

Jackson, R, "Holi in North India and in an English city: some adaptations and anomalies", in *New Community*, Volume V, 1976, pp. 203-209.

Jackson R, and Killingley, D, *Approaches to Hinduism*, John Murray, London, 1988.

Jackson R, and Killingley, D, *Moral Issues in the Hindu Tradition*, Trentham Books, Stoke-on-Trent, 1991.

Jackson, R and Nesbitt, E, *Listening to Hindus*, Unwin Hyman, London, 1990.

Jackson, R and Nesbitt, E, *Hindu Children in Britain*, Trentham Books, Stoke-on-Trent, 1993.

Kanitkar, H and Cole, O, *Teach Yourself Hinduism*, Hodder, 1995.

Killingley, D (ed), *A Handbook of Hinduism for Teachers*, Grevatt & Grevatt, Newcastle upon Tyne, 1984.

Killingley, D; Menski, D; and Firth, S, *Hindu Ritual and Society*, S Y Killingley, Newcastle-upon-Tyne, 1991.

King, U, *A Report on Hinduism in Britain*, Community Religions Project Research Papers, No 2, University of Leeds Department of Theology and Religious Studies, Leeds, 1984.

Knott, K, *Hinduism in Leeds: A Study of Religious Practice in the Indian Hindu Community and in Hindu-Related Groups*, Community Religions Project Monograph, University of Leeds, 1986 (reprinted, 1994).

Knott, K, *My Sweet Lord: The Hare Krishna Movement*, Aquarian Press, Wellingborough, 1986.

Knott, K, "Hindu Communities in Britain", in Badham, P (ed), *Religion, State and Society in Modern Britain*, Edwin Mellen Press, Lampeter, 1989, pp. 243-257.

Knott, K, "The Gujarati Mochis in Leeds: From Leather Stockings to Surgical Boots and Beyond", in Ballard, R (ed), *Desh Pardesh: The South Asian Presence in Britain*, C. Hurst and Co, London, 1994, pp. 213-230.

Law, J, *The Religious Beliefs and Practices of Hindus in Derby*, Community Religions Project Papers (new series), University of Leeds, Leeds, 1991.

Lipner, J, *Hindus: Their Religious Beliefs and Practices*, Routledge, London, 1994.

Michaelson, M, "The relevance of caste among East African Gujaratis in Britain", in *New Community*, Volume VII, pp. 350-360.

National Council of Hindu Temples, *Hinduism*, National Council of Hindu Temples, 1983.

Nesbitt, E, *My Dad's Hindu, My Mum's Side Are Sikhs: Studies in Religious Identity*, Arts, Culture and Education Research Papers, National Foundation for Arts Education, University of Warwick, Coventry, 1991.

Nesbitt, E, "Gender and religious traditions: the role learning of British Hindu children", in *Gender and Education*, Volume V, No. 1, 1993, pp. 81-91.

Nye, Malory, "Temple congregations and communities: Hindu constructions in Edinburgh", in *New Community*, Volume XXIX, 1993, pp. 201-215.

Nye, Malory, *A Place for Our Gods: The Construction of a Hindu Temple Community in Edinburgh*, Curzon Press, 1995.

Pandey, Rajbali, *Hindu Samskaras*, Motilal Banarsidass, Delhi, 1993.

Pocock, D, "Preservation of the religious life: Hindu immigrants in England", in *Contributions to Indian Sociology*, ns. Volume X, 1976, pp. 341-165.

Prabhupada, A.C. Bhaktivedanta Swami, *Bhagavad-Gita As It Is*, Bhaktivedanta Book Trust, London, 1986.

Radhakrishnan, S, *Indian Religions*, Vision Books, Delhi, 1983.

Stutley, M, *Hinduism: The Eternal Law*, Crucible, Wellingborough, 1985.

Stutley, M & J, *A Dictionary of Hinduism*, Routledge and Kegan Paul, London, 1987.

Subramaniyaswami, Satguru Sivaya, *Dancing with Siva: Hinduism's Contemporary Catechism*, Himalayan Academy Publications, Hawaii, 1993.

Thomas, T, "Hindu Dharma in Dispersion", in Parsons, G (ed), *The Growth of Religious Diversity: Britain from 1945, Volume I: Traditions*, Routledge, 1993, pp. 173-204.

Vertovec, S (ed), *Aspects of the South Asian Diaspora*, Oxford University Press, Delhi, 1991.

Vertovec, S, "Community and congregation in London Hindu Temples: divergent trends", in

New Community, Volume XVIII, 1992, pp. 251–264.

Vertovec, S, "Caught in an Ethnic Quandary: Indo-Carribean Hindus in London", in Ballard, R (ed), *Desh Pardesh: The South Asian Presence in Britain*, C. Hurst and Co, London, 1994, pp. 272-290.

Vishwa Hindu Parishad, *Explaining Hindu Dharma: A Guide for Teachers*, Chansitor Publications, 1996.

Warrier, Shrikala, "Gujarati Prajapatis in London: Family Roles and Sociability Networks", in Ballard, R (ed), *Desh Pardesh: The South Asian Presence in Britain*, C. Hurst and Co, London, 1994, pp. 191-212.

Williams, M, "The Vaisnava Religion, with Special Reference to the Shikshapatri of the modern sect called Svami-Narayana", in *The Journal of the Royal Asiatic Society*, Volume XIV, pp. 289-316.

Williams, R B, *A New Face of Hinduism: The Swaminarayan Religion*, Cambridge University Press, Cambridge, 1984.

Zaehner, R C (ed), *Hindu Scriptures*, J M Dent and Sons, London, 1986.

HINDU UNITED KINGDOM ORGANISATIONS

The organisations listed in this section include both head offices of organisations with branches throughout the country and organisations which aspire to serve the Hindu community on a UK-wide basis.

Arya Pratinidhi Sabha (UK)
Flat B, 3 Chapel Road, Hounslow, Middlesex, TW3 1XT
Tel: 0181-569-6403
Contact: Professor S N Bharadwaj
Position: President
Affiliations: Inter Faith Network for the UK
Aims to propagate the Vedic religion in the UK; to devise means and measures for its propagation; and to establish and maintain libraries and centres of learning for the Vedic Dharma (religion).

Basava International Foundation
59 Kingsfield Avenue, North Harrow, Middlesex, HA2 69Q (h)
Tel: Mr Sharma Mahadevaiah
Position: Executive Chairman
Activities: Resource, media, visits, youth, elderly, women, inter-faith
Traditions: Sharma, Multi-Traditional, Yoga
Other Languages: Kannada

Bharatiya Vidya Bhavan
4a Castletown Road, West Kensington, London, W14 9HQ
Tel: 0171-381-4608 **Tel:** 0171-381-3086 (h)
Fax: 0171-381-8758
Contact: Dr H V S Shastry
Position: Academic Director
Activities: Resource, visits youth, elderly, women, newsletters, books, inter-faith
Traditions: Multi-Traditional
Other Languages: Gujarati, Hindi, Tamil, Bengali
Affiliations: Bharatiya Vidya Bhavan, India; Inter Faith Network for the UK
Promotes Indian art and culture as an integral part of the culture of the UK. The Bhavan holds classes, concerts and workshops on Indian classical music, dance and drama.

Brahmrishi Mission Yoga & Meditation
Cultural Centre, Heston, Middlesex, TW5 0RT
Tel: 0181-571-3879 (h) **Fax:** 0181-571-3879
Contact: Surami Vishva Bharti
Position: Religious Preacher
Activities: Worship, resource, visits, youth, elderly, women, newsletters, books, inter-faith
Traditions: Sanatanist, Vaishnava
Other Languages: Hindi, Punjabi, Sanskrit, Dutch
An international organisation working for humanity and preaching the scientific Sanatanan Dharma through discourses and books. Teaches Hindi,

Punjabi to children and teaches Yoga and meditation free of charge.

Confederation of Indian Organisations
5 Westminster Bridge Road, London SE1 7XW
Tel: 0171-928-9889   **Fax:** 0171-620-4025
Contact: Tazeem Ahmed
Position: Acting Director
Activities: Umbrella, visits, newsletters, books, inter-faith
Other Languages: Hindi, Gujrati, Urdu, Bengali
Aims to provide services to strengthen and support voluntary organisations so they may have sustainable structures allowing them to deliver effective services and attract and manage resources.

Federation of Anavil Samajes
Hollybank Post Office, 306 Haunch Lane, Kings Heath, Birmingham, West Midlands, B13 0QS
Tel: 0121-444-2045 (h)
Contact: Mr Baldev Naik
Position: President

Federation of Brahmin Associations of Europe
125 Warwick Road, London, N11 2SR
Tel: 0181-368-4881
Contact: Mr Dakshesh Gor
Position: Secretary

Federation of Patidar Associations
Patidar House, 22 London Road, Wembley, Middlesex, HA9 7EX
Tel: 0181-795-1648 **Fax:** 0181-795-1648
Contact: Ramesh Patel
Position: Honorary Secretary
Activities: Youth, elderly, women
Traditions: Sanatanist
Social Groups: Patidar
Other Languages: Gujarati

Hindu College London
50 Morland Avenue, Croydon, Surrey, CR0 6EA (h)
Tel: 0181-656-1835 (h)
Contact: Dr J C Sharma
Position: Principal
Activities: Resource, youth, books
Traditions: Non-Sectarian (Vedic)
Movements: Arya Samaj
Other Languages: Hindi, Punjabi, Sanskrit

Hindu Council of the UK
c/o 150 Penn Road, Wolverhampton, West Midlands, WV3 0EN
Tel: 01902-334331 (h) **Fax:** 01902-605318
Contact: Mr Om Parkash Sharma
Position: President
The Council was founded in 1994 and links a wide range of Hindu organisations.

Hindu Cultural Trust Centre
55 Manor Avenue, Hounslow, Middlesex, TW4 7JN (h)
Tel: 0181-230-0571
Contact: Gian Chand Gaur
Position: General Secretary
Activities: Worship, resource, umbrella, visits, youth, elderly, women, newsletters, books, inter-faith
Traditions: Sanatanist
Movements: Vedic, Cultural or Sanatanic
Other Languages: Hindi, Punjabi, Gujarati

Hindu Marathon
15 Higher Downs, Fairweather Green, Bradford, West Yorkshire, BD08 0Na (h)
Tel: 01274-577395 **Fax:** 01274-521211
Contact: Rajnikant B Parmar
Position: National Secretary
Activities: Youth
Traditions: Multi-Traditional
Movements: Hindutva
Social Groups: All Social Groups
Other Languages: Hindi, Gujarati, Punjabi
Affiliations: Vishwa Hindu Parishad-West Yorkshire; Hindu Swayamsevak Sangh (UK)
Organises annual half marathon and fun runs. The event is open to all.

Hindu Resource Centre
10 De Montfort Road, London, SW16 1LZ
Tel: 0181-675-6717 **Fax:** 0181-6756717
Contact: Mrs Saraswati Dave
Position: Chair
Activities: Resource, media, umbrella, youth, elderly, women, inter-faith
Traditions: Multi-Traditional
Other Languages: Gujarati, Panjabi, Hindi, Tamil
Affiliations: Vishwa Hindu Parishad
An umbrella organisation providing services to the cross-section of the community including counselling and advice on all matters to various age groups. Also acts as a pressure group.

Hindu Swayamsevak Sangh (UK)
Keshav Pratishthan, 46–48 Loughborough Road,
Leicester, Leicestershire, LE4 5LD
Tel: 0116-266-5665 **Fax:** 0116-261-1931
Contact: Mr Pravin V Ruparelia
Position: General Secretary
Activities: Youth
Traditions: Cultural Organisation
Movements: Hindutva
Other Languages: Hindi, Gujarati, Punjabi,
Marathi
The organisation's objective is to provide and
propagate Hindu thoughts, ideals and values of life,
and to promote unity among Hindus and
harmonious relations with other faiths. Working
mainly with Hindu youth it has branches all over
the country.

International Society for Krishna Consciousness
Dharam Marg, Hilfield Lane, Aldenham, Watford,
Hertfordshire, WD2 8EZ
Tel: 01923-857244 **Tel:** 01923-856269 (h)
Fax: 01923-852896
EMail: Bimal.Krishna@yoga.dircom.co.uk
Contact: Bimal Krishna Das
Position: Public Relations
Activities: Worship, resource, visits, youth, elderly,
women, newsletters, books, inter-faith
Traditions: Vaishnava
Movements: Chaitanya
Other Languages: Gujarati, Hindi
Affiliations: National Council of Hindu Temples;
Hindu Council of the UK
A centre of living Hindu spirituality which promotes
Vedic culture, especially through the Gaudiya
Vaishnava teachings of Chaitanya Maha Prabhu in
the fifteenth century. Also a Vedic college for
theological training.

ISKCON Communications
2 St James' Road, Watford, Hertfordshire, WD1 8EA
Tel: 01923-249144 **Fax:** 01923-238677
EMail: bhagavat@moose.co.uk
Contact: Bhagavat Dharma
Position: Communication Manager
Activities: Media
Traditions: Vaishnava
Movements: Chaitanya
Other Languages: Gujarati, Hindi, Bengali
Affiliations: National Council of Hindu Temples;
ISKCON Communications is the registered office

of the charity and deals with financial and
membership matters. It aims to facilitate
communications between the movement and
interested groups such as the media, educationalists
and other religious faiths.

ISKCON Educational Services
Dharam Marg, Hilfield Lane, Aldenham, Watford,
Hertfordshire, WD2 8EZ
Tel: 01923-859578 **Fax:** 01923-852896
EMail: rasamandala@yoga.dircon.co.uk
Contact: Rasamandala Das
Position: Director
Activities: Worship, resource, visits, books
Traditions: Vaishnava
Movements: Chaitanya
Other Languages: Gujarati, Hindi
Affiliations: The International Society for Krishna
Consciousness
Information, artefacts and other resources covering
all aspects of Hinduism. Guest speakers, dance and
drama available for schools, colleges, INSET etc. Free
correspondence service. All enquiries welcome.

Iyengar Yoga Institute
223a Randolph Avenue, London, W9 1NL
Tel: 0171-624-3080 **Fax:** 0171-624-3080
Contact: Gerry Chambers
Position: Chairperson
Activities: Resource
Traditions: Yoga
Movements: Iyengar Yoga

Jignyasu Satsang Seva Trust
12 Sidmouth Road, Willesden Green, London,
NW2 5JX (h)
Tel: 0181-459-4466 (h) **Fax:** 0181-459-4000
Contact: Secretary
Activities: Worship, youth, elderly, women, inter-
faith
Traditions: Sanatanist
Other Languages: Hindi, Gujarati, Sindhi,
Punjabi

Lohana Community of the UK
580 North Circular Road, London, NW2 7PY
Tel: 0181-450-1967 **Fax:** 0181-208-1266
Contact: Dhiraj Kataria

National Association of Patidar Samaj
102 Junction Road, Archway, London, N19 5QY
Tel: 0171-263-6269
Contact: Mahendrabhai Patel

Position: Co-ordinator
Activities: Worship, visits, youth, elderly, women
Traditions: Multi-Traditional
Movements: Sanatan
Social Groups: Patidar
Other Languages: Gujarati, Hindi, Punjabi
Affiliations: National Council of Hindu Temples
Hindu community centre and temple with an advisory service for immigration, unemployment, family concerns and education. There are language classes for adults in English and Gujarati. Religious services and marriage registration. Hall hire and library.

National Council of Hindu Temples
c/o Shree Sanatan Mandir, Weymouth Street, off Catherine Street, Leicester, Leicesershire, LE4 6FP
Tel: 0116-266-1402 **Tel:** 01923-856269 (h)
Fax: 01923-856269
Contact: Mr Vipin Kumar Aery
Position: Secretary
Activities: Umbrella, youth, elderly, women, newsletters, books, inter-faith
Traditions: Sanatanist
Other Languages: Gujarati, Hindi
Affiliations: Inter Faith Network for the UK; Hindu Council of the UK
Membership is open to Hindu Temples and similar organisations. The Council aims to promote the Hindu religion; maintain uniformity among Hindu Temples; provide advice and information for local and public authorities and government departments.

National Council of Vanik Associations
1 Elmcroft Gardens, London, NW9 9QP
Tel: 0181-206-1396 (h)
Contact: Mr R D Shah
Position: General Secretary

National Hindu Students Forum (UK)
46-48 Loughborough Road, Leicester, Leicestershire, LE4 5LD
Fax: 0116-261-1931
EMail: kanaiya@msn.com
Contact: Janhavi Ambekar
Position: Chairperson
Activities: Resource, umbrella, youth, newsletters, books, inter-faith
Traditions: Multi-Traditional
Other Languages: Hindi, Sanskrit
Largest Hindu student body in Europe. We work towards the better understanding of Hindu Dharma,

and to provide a platform for Hindu youth to express their views.

Navnat Vanik Association of the UK
36 Masons Avenue, Wealdstone, Harrow, Middlesex, HA3 5AR
Tel: 01923-893421 **Tel:** 0181-861-5825
Fax: 0181-935-9565
Contact: Mr Subash K Bakhai
Position: President
Activities: Worship
Promotes understanding of the Jain and Hindu religions. Its principles are non-violence, human and animal welfare and the preservation of nature.

Patanjali Centre for Classical Yoga
The Cot (Kutiya), Marley Lane, Battle, East Sussex, TN33 0RE
Tel: 01424-870538 (h) **Fax:** 01424-870538
Contact: Sri Indar Nath
Position: Founder Director
Activities: Youth, elderly, women, newsletters, books, inter-faith
Traditions: Yoga
Movements: Vedanta/Yoga

Shree Mirzapur Association (UK)
37 Prout Grove, Neasden, London, NW10 1PU (h)
Tel: 0181-452-1394 (h) **Fax:** 0181-208-1968
Contact: Mr Veljibhai Hirani
Position: Secretary
Activities: Resource, youth, elderly, women
Movements: Swaminaryan
Social Groups: Leva Patel
Other Languages: Gujarati
Affiliations: Hindu Council (Brent)

Shri Madhavashram & Gandhi Bapu Memorial Trust
Gandhi Centre, 213A Deansbrook Road, Edgware, Middlesex, HA8 9BU
Tel: 0181-906-0716 **Tel:** 0181-933-2223 (h)
Fax: 0181-963-1334
Contact: Mr Jivanjibhai Patel
Position: President
Activities: Visits, youth, elderly, women, newsletters, inter-faith
Traditions: Multi-Traditional
Other Languages: Gujarati, Hindi
The centre works for the propagation and spread of the principles and ideals of Mahatma Gandhi. It caters for the establishment of a society free from

exploitation and holds talks, lectures, seminars and arranges exhibitions. It has a well stocked library.

Shri Vallabh Nidhi UK
c/o Alberton Baptist Church, Ealing Road, Wembley, Middlesex, HA0 4LT
Tel: 0181-795-1391 **Tel:** 0181-903-9195 (h)
Fax: 0181-795-1391
Contact: Nalinikarit T Pandia
Position: Honorary General Secretary
Activities: Resource, umbrella, youth, elderly, newsletters, inter-faith
Traditions: Sanatanist
Movements: Pushtimargi, Sanatani
Other Languages: Gujarati, Hindi
Affiliations: National Council of Hindu Temples

Sivananda Yoga Vedanta Centre
51 Felsham Road, Putney, London, SW151AZ
Tel: 0171-780-0160 **Fax:** 0181-780-0128
EMail: siva@dial.pipex.com
Contact: Swami Saradananda
Position: Director
Activities: Worship, umbrella, visits, youth, elderly, women, newsletters, books, inter-faith
Traditions: Yoga, Vedanta
Movements: Swami Sivananda
Affiliations: Sivananda Yoga Vedanta Centres Headquarters, Quebec, Canada
The Centre offers Yoga classes, meditation and chanting classes; also organises fasting weekends, retreats, and a wide range of workshops. Courses from beginners to advanced levels. All welcome.

Sri Aurobindo Yoga & Information Society
35 Circular Road, Withington, Manchester, Greater Manchester, M20 3LB (h)
Tel: 0161-445-9196 (h) **Fax:** 0161-448-1072
Contact: Mr Mahendra Bhatt
Position: General Secretary
Activities: Youth, elderly, women, newsletters, inter-faith
Traditions: Yoga
Other Languages: Gujarati, Hindi
Affiliations: Hindu Council of the North

Swaminarayan Hindu Mission
Shri Swaminarayan Manor, 105-119 Brentfield Road, Neasden, London, NW10 8JP
Tel: 0181-965-2651 **Tel:** 0181-445-6903 (h)
Fax: 0181-965-6313
Contact: Dr R B Shah

Position: Co-ordinator
Affiliations: Inter Faith Network for the UK

Vanik Association of the United Kingdom
5 Beechdene, Tadworth, Surrey, KT20 5EA (h)
Tel: 01737-813977 (h)
Contact: Mrs Mradula S Shah
Position: General Secretary

Vedanta Movement
13 Elsenham Street, Southfields, London, SW18 5UN
Tel: 0181-874-6100 (h)
Contact: Mrs Iris Rafferty
Position: General secretary
Activities: Umbrella, newsletters, books, inter-faith
Traditions: Tantra, Yoga
Movements: Chaitanya, Rama Krishna Order
Affiliations: Rama Krishna Order

Vishwa Hindu Parishad (UK)
48 Wharfedale Gardens, Thornton Heath, Surrey
Tel: 0181-684-9716 (h) **Fax:** 0181-684-9716 (h)
Contact: Mr Kishor Ruparelia
Position: General Secretary
Activities: Worship, resource, umbrella, media, visits, youth, elderly, women, newsletters, books
Traditions: Multi-traditional
Other Languages: Hindi, Gujarati
Affiliations: Vishwa Hindu Parishad, India and Europe; Inter Faith Network for the UK
Provides religious, social, educational and welfare services to all communities; runs centres for the elderly, women and youth. Its office bearers play an active part in governmental organisations and agencies and strive for equal opportunity for all.

HINDU REGIONAL AND LOCAL ORGANISATIONS AND MANDIRS

A variety of forms of Hindu local organisations are listed in this directory. These include *mandirs*, many of which are in buildings adapted from other, original, uses and only a few of which are purpose-built. *Caste* groups and other organisations often meet either in hired premises or in the homes of their members.

ENGLAND

NORTH EAST
City, Town or Local Bodies

Hindu Mahila Samaj
4 Mistletoe Road, Jesmond, Newcastle upon Tyne, Tyne and Wear, NE2 2DX

Hindu Temple
172 West Road, Newcastle upon Tyne, Tyne and Wear, NE4 9QB
Tel: 0191-273-3364 **Tel:** 0191-243-2238 (h)
Contact: Sahm Lal Vedhara
Position: President
Activities: Worship, resource, youth, elderly, women, inter-faith
Traditions: Multi-Traditional
Other Languages: Hindi, Gujarati, Bengali

ISKCON Newcastle
304 Westgate Road, Newcastle upon Tyne, Tyne and Wear, NE4 5QU
Tel: 0191-272-1911
Contact: Bhakti Rasa Das
Position: Temple President
Activities: Worship, resource, visits, youth, books, inter-faith
Traditions: Vaishnava
Movements: Chaitanya
Affiliations: National Council of Hindu Temples

Istree Samaj
10 Eastlands, High Heaton, Newcastle upon Tyne, Tyne and Wear, NE7 7YE (h)
Tel: 0191-281-1509 (h)
Contact: Mrs Ravi Chowdhry
Position: Sectretary
Activities: Elderly women, inter-faith
Traditions: Sanatanist
Movements: Arya Samaj
Other Languages: Hindi, Punjabi

YORKSHIRE
Regional or County Bodies

Hindu Education Council (Yorkshire)
52 Rugby Place, Bradford, West Yorkshire, BD7 2DF
Tel: 01274-577395 **Tel:** 01422-361381 (h)
Contact: Joniah Parthasarathi

Position: Secretary
Activities: Resource, umbrella, inter-faith
Traditions: Multi-Traditional, Vedanta
Movements: Vedanta
Social Groups: Hindu, Vedanta
Other Languages: Hindi, Gujarati
Affiliations: Vishwa Hindu Parishad (Yorkshire);
Vishwa Hindu Parishad (UK); World Council Of
Hindus

Leuva Patidar Samaj Yorkshire

Legramms Hill Lane, off Legramms Lane, Lidget
Green, Bradford, West Yorkshire, BD7 2BA
Tel: 01274-521185 **Tel:** 01274-651366 (h)
Contact: Mr Mukesh Patel
Position: Public Relations
Activities: Worship, resource, visits, youth, elderly,
women
Traditions: Vaishnava
Movements: Arya Samaj
Social Groups: Leuva Patidar
Other Languages: Gujarati, Hindi
Affiliations: National Council of Hindu Temples

City, Town or Local Bodies

Bharat Social Club

502 Great Horton Road, Bradford, West Yorkshire,
BD7 3HR

Bharata Mandal

14 Sawrey Place, Bradford, West Yorkshire, BD7

Dharmic Vidhi

c/o 52 Rugby Place, Lidget Green, Bradford, West
Yorkshire, BD7 2DF

Hindu Cultural Society of Bradford

321 Leeds Road, Bradford, West Yorkshire,
BD3 9LS
Tel: 01274-725923 **Tel:** 01274-543145
Fax: 01274-395603
Contact: Manojkumar Narottam Joshi
Position: Honorary Secretary
Activities: Worship, resource, visits, youth, elderly,
women, inter-faith
Traditions: Multi-Traditional
Other Languages: Punjabi, Hindi, Gujarati,
Urdu/Bengali
Affiliations: Hindu Council of the North;
National Council of Hindu Temples; Vishwa Hindu
Parishad

Hindu Economic Development Forum

3 Beech Road, Bradford, West Yorkshire, BD6 1EB

Hindu Education Council (Yorkshire)

52 Rugby Place, Bradford, West Yorkshire,
BD7 2DF
Tel: 01274-577395 **Tel:** 01422-361381 (h)
Contact: Joniah Parthasarathi
Position: Secretary
Activities: Resource, umbrella, inter-faith
Traditions: Multi-Traditional, Vedanta
Movements: Vedanta
Social Groups: Hindu, Vedanta
Other Languages: Hindi, Gujarati
Affiliations: Vishwa Hindu Parishad (Yorkshire);
Vishwa Hindu Parishad (UK); World Council Of
Hindus

Hindu Swayamsevak Sangh

52 Rugby Place, Bradford, West Yorkshire,
BD7 2DF
Tel: 01274-577395 **Fax:** 01274-521211
Contact: Bhupendra Mistry
Position: Assistant Secretary
Other Languages: Hindi, Gujarati, Punjabi
Affiliations: Vishwa Hindu Parishad (Yorkshire);
Vishwa Hindu Parishad (UK); Vishwa Hindu
Parishad, international

Kshatriya Sudharak Mandal

138 Legrams Lane, Bradford, West Yorkshire,
BD7 3AG

Leuva Patidar Samaj Yorkshire

Legramms Hill Lane, off Legramms Lane, Lidget
Green, Bradford, West Yorkshire, BD7 2BA
Tel: 01274-521185 **Tel:** 01274-651366 (h)
Contact: Mr Mukesh Patel
Position: Public Relations
Activities: Worship, resource, visits, youth, elderly,
women
Traditions: Vaishnava
Movements: Arya Samaj
Social Groups: Leuva Patidar
Other Languages: Gujarati, Hindi
Affiliations: National Council of Hindu Temples

Shree Prajapati Association & Hindu Temple

Thornton Lane, off Little Horton Lane, Bradford,
West Yorkshire, BD5 9DN
Tel: 01274-578115 **Tel:** 01274-677490 (h)
Contact: Mr Vasanti L Lad

Position: Secretary
Activities: Worship, resource, visits, youth, elderly, women, newsletters, inter-faith
Traditions: Sanatanist
Movements: All Hindu Sanatan
Social Groups: Prajapati
Other Languages: Gujarati, Hindi
Affiliations: Hindu Council of the North; The National Council of Hindu Temples

Sri Jalaram Shakti Mandal
148 Arncliffe Terrace, Bradford, West Yorkshire, BD7 3AG (h)
Tel: 01274-572337 (h)
Contact: Mr Kunverji Jivanji Mistry
Position: Secretary
Activities: Worship, visits
Traditions: Multi-Traditional
Other Languages: Gujarati
Affiliations: Hindu Cultural Society Community Centre

Sujaav
c/o 17 Sunningdale, Bradford, West Yorkshire, BD8 0LX

Vidhya Varg
c/o 52 Rugby Place, Lidget Green, Bradford, West Yorkshire, BD7 2DF

Hindu Community
4 Holyrood Road, Town Moor, Doncaster, South Yorkshire, DN2 5HR

Punjabi Hindu Society
50 Bawtry Road, Bessacarr, Doncaster, South Yorkshire, DN4 7BQ
Tel: 01302-535126 (h)
Contact: Mr B Ram

Sanatan Dharam Society
2 Holyrood Road, Town Moor, Doncaster, South Yorkshire, DN2 5HB
Tel: 01302-363732
Contact: Mr R A Gugg

Shree Sita Ram Temple
20 Zetland Street, Huddersfield, West Yorkshire, HD1 2RA
Tel: 01484-431515 (h)
Contact: Raizada Sanjeev Bali
Position: Vice-President

Hindu Charitable Trust
6 Moor Allerton Gardens, Leeds, West Yorkshire, L17

Hindu Garba Group
8 Wells House Gardens, Leeds, West Yorkshire, LS8

Hindu Samaj
68 Manor Drive, Leeds, West Yorkshire, LS6

Sanatan Temple & Community Centre
281 Chapeltown Road, Leeds, West Yorkshire, LS7 3JT
Tel: 0113-262-2358
Contact: Mr Om Prakash Sharma

Shree Hindu Mandir
36 Alexandra Road, Leeds, West Yorkshire, LS6 1RF
Tel: 0113-261-2342
Contact: Mr Shah
Position: President
Affiliations: Hindu Council of the North

Shree Ram Krishna Bhajan Mandal
26 Warmsley Road, Leeds, West Yorkshire, LS6
Tel: 0113-275-3327

Swaminarayan Hindu Mission
23 Eddison Walk, Adel, Leeds, West Yorkshire, LS16 8DA (h)
Contact: Dr Vijay R Pancholi
Position: Chair

Hindu Cultural Society of Cleveland
54 Westbourn Grove, North Ormesby, Middlesbrough, North Yorkshire
Tel: 01642-218428 **Tel:** 01642-825965 (h)
Contact: Dr V M Dave
Position: Vice Chairman
Activities: Worship, visits, youth, elderly, women, newsletters, inter-faith
Traditions: Multi-Traditional
Movements: Arya Samaj
Other Languages: Hindi, Punjabi, Gujarati, Bengali
Affiliations: National Council of Hindu Temples

Hindu Samaj (Sheffield District)
20-25 Richmond Street, Pitsmoor, Sheffield, South Yorkshire, S3 9EA
Tel: 0114-273-3021 **Tel:** 0114-230-5227 (h)
Fax: 0114-230-8016
Contact: Dr Dhavendra Kumar

Position: Chairperson
Activities: Worship, resource, media, visits, youth, elderly, women, newsletters, inter-faith
Traditions: Multi-Traditional
Movements: All movements
Other Languages: Hindi, Gujrati, Punjabi
Affiliations: Hindu Council of the North; National Council of Hindu Temples

Sheffield Durga Puja Committee
Sheffield, South Yorkshire, c/o 19 Kirkdale, Worksop, Nottinghamshire, S81 0HA
Contact: Dr B N Patel

Sri Chaitanya Saraswat Math
66b Owler Lane, Sheffield, South Yorkshire, S10 8GA

NORTH WEST
Regional or County Bodies

Hindu Council of the North
348 Denton Lane, Chadderton, Oldham, Lancashire, 0L9 8QE (h)
Tel: 01772-253901
Contact: Mr Ratilal Chhagan Chohan
Position: General Secretary
Activities: Worship, resource, media, umbrella, visits, youth, elderly women, inter-faith
Traditions: Sanatanist, Shaiva
Movements: Arya Samaj
Other Languages: Gujarati, Hindi
Affiliations: Hindu Council of UK; National Council of Hindu Temples

City, Town or Local Bodies

Shree Bhartiya Mandal
103 Union Road, Ashton-under-Lyne, Lancashire, OL6 8JN
Tel: 0161-330-2085
Contact: Mr Mistry
Position: Honorary Secretary
Affiliations: Hindu Council of the North

Shree Jalaram Bhajan Mandal
58 Kenyon Street, Ashton-under-Lyne, Lancashire
Contact: Mr V Kara

Shree Prajapati Association UK
5 Holden Street, Ashton-under-Lyne, Lancashire
Contact: Mr Kanti Mistry

Swaminarayan Hindu Mission
29 Russell Street, Ashton-under-Lyne, Lancashire
Tel: 0161-330-5196
Contact: Vinubhai D Patel
Position: President

Blackburn Hindu Centre
c/o 11 The Dene, Beardwood, Blackburn, Lancashire, BB2 7QS (h)
Tel: 01254-678183 (h) **Tel:** 01254-676796
Contact: Mr Ashok Chudasama
Position: Honorary General Secretary
Activities: Resource, youth, elderly, women, inter-faith
Traditions: Sanatanist
Other Languages: Gujarati, Hindi
Affiliations: Hindu Council of the North

Blackburn Lohana Union
4 Durham Close, Blackburn, Lancashire
Contact: Mr N Lakhani

Hindu Elderly Persons Association
23 Columbia Way, Blackburn, Lancashire
Tel: 01254-64130
Contact: Mr A Dayal

Shree Jansari Gnati Mandal
c/o 33 Maple Street, Blackburn, Lancashire, BB1 6LP (h)
Tel: 01254-677988 (h)
Contact: Mr Shantilal Vadher
Position: Honorary Secretary
Activities: Resource, youth, elderly, women, inter-faith
Traditions: Sanatanist
Social Groups: Jansari
Other Languages: Gujarati
Affiliations: Jansari Organisations UK

Vishwa Hindu Parishad, Blackburn
168 St Aidanes Avenue, Blackburn, Lancashire, BB2 4AY
Contact: Thakorbhai B Patel

Mandhata Hitradak Mandal (Bolton)
Krishna Temple, 10 Beverley Road, Bolton, Lancashire, BL1 4DT
Contact: Mr G R Patel
Position: President
Affiliations: Hindu Council of the North

Shree Krishna Mandir
10 Beverley Road, Bolton, Lancashire, BL1 4DT
Tel: 01204-386893

Shree Kutch Leva Patel Society
50 Church Street, Bolton, Lancashire

Shree Kutch Satsang Swaminarayan Temple
11 Adelaide Street, Bolton, Lancashire, BL3 3NT
Tel: 01204-652604 **Fax:** 01204-652604
Contact: Secretary
Activities: Worship, resource, visits, youth
Traditions: Sanatanist
Movements: Swaminaryan
Languages: Gujarati
Affiliations: Shree Swaminaryan Temple, Bhuj-Kutch, India

Shree Kutchhi Leva Patel Society
13 Jauncey Street, Bolton, Lancashire

Shree Sorathia Prajapati Community UK
39 Hawthorne Road, Bolton, Lancashire, BL3 5RF
Tel: 01204-655111
Contact: Mr M M Singadia

Shree Swaminarayan Sidhant Sajivan Mandal
164 Deane Road, Bolton, Lancashire, BL3 5DL
Tel: 01204-533558 **Tel:** 0161-280-3508
Contact: Mr Kanji V Naran
Position: Trustee
Activities: Worship, umbrella
Traditions: Swaminaryan
Movements: Swaminaryan
Social Groups: Kutch
Other Languages: Gujrati

Vishwa Hindu Parishad (UK) Bolton
1 Thomas Holden Street, Bolton, Lancashire,
BL1 2QG
Tel: 01204-527492 **Tel:** 01204-658230 (h)
Contact: Mr Jagdish Ranpura
Position: Secretary
Activities: Worship, umbrella, visits, youth, elderly,
women, newsletters, books, inter-faith
Traditions: Sanatanist
Movements: All Sampradaya
Other Languages: Gujarati, Hindi
Affiliations: Vishwa Hindu Parishad in India

Hindu Religious Gandhi Hall
21 Troutebeck Road, Gatley, Cheshire, SK8 4RP

Lohana Association Manchester
48-50 Market Street, Hyde, Cheshire, SK14 1AH
Contact: Mr S Robheru
Position: Secretary
Affiliations: Hindu Council of the North

Hindu Society - Lancaster & Morecambe
10 Langton Close, Halton Road, Lancaster,
Lancashire, LA1 2TJ (h)
Tel: 01524-849705 (h)
Contact: Praful Upadhyay
Position: Chair
Activities: Media, inter-faith
Traditions: Multi-Traditional
Other Languages: Gujarati, Punjabi, Bengali,
Hindi

Hare Krishna Centre (ISKCON)
114a Bold Street, Liverpool, Merseyside, L1 4HY
Tel: 0151-708-9400 **Tel:** 0151-727-7191 (h)
EMail: arjuna@atma.u-net.com
Contact: Arjunanatha dasa
Position: Secretary
Activities: Worship, visits, newsletters, books, inter-faith
Traditions: Vaishnava
Movements: Chaitanya
Other Languages: French, Mauritian
Affiliations: International Society for Krishna
Consciousness

Hindu Cultural Organisation
253 Edge Lane, Liverpool, Merseyside, L7 5NA
Tel: 0151-263-7965 **Tel:** 0151-526-0370
Contact: Bal Krishan Aggarwal
Position: Secretary
Activities: Worship, visits, youth, elderly, women,
newsletters, inter-faith
Traditions: Multi-Traditional
Movements: Arya Samaj, Sanatan
Languages: Hindi, Punjabi, Gujerati, Bengali
Affiliations: National Council of Hindu Temples;
Vishwa Hindu Parishad (UK)

Brahma Samaj Manchester
Manchester, Greater Manchester, c/o 26 Prestbury
Road, Wilmslow, Cheshire, SK9 2LL (h)
Tel: 01625-531156 (h) **Fax:** 01625-548200
Contact: Mrs Ramaben M Oza
Position: President
Activities: Resource, media, youth, elderly,
women, newsletters, inter-faith

Traditions: Sanatanist
Movements: Swaminaryan
Other Languages: Gujarati
Affiliations: Hindu Council of the North;
National Council of Hindu Temples; Federation of
Brahmin Associations of Europe

Gita Bhavan (Centre)
231 Withington Road, Wilbraham Road, Whalley
Range, Manchester, Greater Manchester, M16 8LU

Gita Bhavan Care Group
534 Kings Road, Stretford, Manchester, Greater
Manchester

Bharatiya Vidya Bhavan (Manchester) Ltd
Unit 5 West Point Enterprise Park, Clarence
Avenue, Manchester, Greater Manchester, M17 1QS
Tel: 01204-699311
Contact: Dr K R Korlipara
Activities: Resource
Traditions: Multi-Traditional
Other Languages: Hindi, Gujrati, Kannada

Hindu Swayamsevak Sangh
Karam House, 79 Lever Street, Manchester, Greater
Manchester, M1 1FL
Tel: 0161-236-8621 **Fax:** 0161-228-0056
Contact: Mr T L Gupta
Position: Public Relations

Indian Association Manchester
Gandhi Hall, Brunswick Road, Manchester, Greater
Manchester, M20 9QB
Tel: 0161-445-1134 **Tel:** 01625-531156 (h)
Fax: 01625-548200
Contact: Mrs R M Oza
Position: President
Activities: Resource, media, visits, youth, elderly,
women, newsletters
Traditions: Sanatanist
Other Languages: Gujarati, Hindi

Indian Women's Organisation
Indian Association Women's Group, Gandhi Hall,
Brunswick Road, Manchester, Greater Manchester,
M20 9QB
Tel: 0161-445-1134 **Tel:** 01625-531156 (h)
Fax: 01625-548200
Contact: Mrs Ramaben M Oza
Position: Chairman

Activities: Resource, media, youth, elderly,
women, inter-faith
Traditions: Sanatanist, Vaishnava
Movements: Swaminaryan
Other Languages: English, Gujarati, Hindi
Affiliations: International Women's Organisation

ISKCON Manchester
Hare Krishna Centre, 20 Mayfield Road, Whalley
Range, Manchester, Greater Manchester, M16 8FT
Tel: 0161-860-6117 **Fax:** 0161-860-6117
EMail: krishna.dharma@yoga.nildram.co.uk
Contact: Krishna Dharma
Position: Director
Activities: Worship, resource, visits, books, inter-
faith
Traditions: Vaishnava
Movements: Chaitanya
Affiliations: National Council for Hindu Temples

Vishwa Hindu Parishad
Karam House, 79 Lever Street, Manchester, Greater
Manchester, M1 1FL
Tel: 0161-236-8621 **Fax:** 0161-228-0056
Contact: Mr Tarsem Lal Gupta
Position: Treasurer
Activities: Resource, umbrella, youth, elderly,
newsletters, books, inter-faith
Traditions: Multi-Traditional
Movements: All Sampradayas
Other Languages: Hindi, Gujarati, Punjabi,
Kannada
Affiliations: Vishwa Hindu Parishad (UK), Vishwa
Hindu Parishad, India

North West Gujarati Samaj
60 Grenham Avenue, Hulme, Manchester, Greater
Manchester, M15 4HD

Hindu Society Lancaster & Morecombe
20 Ashbourne Grove, Westgate, Morecombe,
Lancashire, LA3 3NH

Hindu Council of the North (UK)
348 Denton Lane, Chadderton, Oldham,
Lancashire, OL9 8QE (h)
Tel: 01772-253901
Contact: Mr Ratilal Chhagan Chohan
Position: General Secretary
Activities: Worship, resource, media, umbrella,
visits, youth, elderly women, inter-faith

Traditions: Vedantism
Movements: Arya Samaj
Other Languages: Gujarati, Hindi
Affiliations: Hindu Council of UK; National Council of Hindu Temples

India Culture & Social Centre
Couldhurst Community Centre, Rochdale Road, Oldham, Lancashire
Tel: 0161-682-5189
Contact: Mr Kanu Patel
Position: President
Affiliations: Hindu Council of the North

Indian Association
57-59 Fern Street, Oldham, Lancashire, OL8 1SH
Tel: 0161-633-0043 **Fax:** 0161-633-0043
Contact: Mr Bharatbhai Sisodia
Position: Executive Member
Activities: Worship, resource, visits, youth, elderly, women, newsletters, inter-faith
Traditions: Sanatanist
Movements: Arya Samaj
Other Languages: Gujarati, Hindi
Affiliations: North West Hindu Council; National Council of Hindu Temples

Shree Swaminarayan Temple
270 Lee Street, Oldham, Lancashire, Lancashire, OL8 1BG
Contact: Secretary
Activities: Worship, youth, elderly, women
Traditions: Vaishnava
Movements: Swaminaryan
Social Groups: Leva Patel
Other Languages: Gujarati

Andhra Social & Community Organisation
28 St Mary's Street, Preston, Lancashire, PR1 5LN
Tel: 01772-793924
Contact: Mr K V Babu

Gujarat Hindu Society
South Meadow Lane, off Fishergate Hill, Preston, Lancashire, PR1 8JN
Tel: 01772-253901
Fax: 01772-882221 **Contact:** D H Nayee
Position: Secretary
Activities: Worship, resource, visits, youth, elderly, women, newsletters, books, inter-faith
Traditions: Sanatanist
Social Groups: Multi-cultural

Other Languages: Gujarati, Hindi
Affiliations: Hindu Council of the North; National Council of Hindu Temples; National Congress of Gujarati Organisations

Shree Prajapati Association
105 Lowndes Street, Preston, Lancashire, PR1 7XU

Swaminarayan Hindu Mission
8a Avenham Place, Preston, Lancashire, PR1 3SX
Tel: 01772-562252
Contact: Mr Gandhi

Lord Rama Krishna Temple
7 Haydock Street, Warrington, Cheshire, WA2 70M
Tel: 01925-5720420 **Tel:** 01925-724672 (h)
Contact: Mr R Kumar
Position: Chairperson
Activities: Worship

EAST MIDLANDS
Regional or County Bodies

Leicestershire Brahma Samaj
15 Belgrave Road, Leicester, Leicestershire, LE4 6AR
Tel: 0116-262-4359 **Tel:** 0116-288-9069 (h)
Contact: Mohanlal Meghji Bhogaita
Position: President
Activities: Worship, visits, youth, elderly, women, inter-faith
Traditions: Shaiva
Social Groups: Brahmin
Other Languages: Gujarati, Hindi
Affiliations: Hindu Council of Leicestershire; National Council of Hindu Temples; Vishwa Hindu Parishad

Hindu Council of Nottinghamshire
PO Box 74, Long Eaton, Nottingham, Nottinghamshire, N610 3EZ
Tel: 0115 9730353 **Fax:** 0115 9730353
Contact: Mr Nitin J M Lakhani
Position: Secretary
Activities: Resource, media, umbrella
Traditions: Multi-Traditional
Languages: Hindi

City, Town or Local Bodies

Geeta Bhawan Hindu Temple
312 Normanton Road, Derby, Derbyshire,
DE23 6W
Tel: 01332-380407 **Tel:** 01332-735908 (h)
Contact: Raj Bali
Position: President
Activities: Worship, resource, visits, youth, elderly,
women, inter-faith
Traditions: Sanatanist
Other Languages: Hindi, Gujarati, Punjabi
Affiliations: National Council of Hindu Temples

Hindu Welfare Association
c/o Geeta Bhawan Temple, 312 Normanton Road,
Derby, Derbyshire, DE3 6WE
Tel: 01332-380407
Contact: Swayam Parkash Joshi

Hindu Womens Association
143 Clarence Road, Derby, Derbyshire, DE3 6LS
Tel: 01332-49114
Contact: Mrs Sudesh Chabba

Lohana Community
28 Mostyn Avenue, Littleover, Derby, Derbyshire,
DE3 6HW (h)
Tel: 01332-380407 **Tel:** 01332-771285 (h)
Contact: Mr Mansukh Modi
Position: Chair
Activities: Worship, resource, youth, women
Traditions: Vaishnava
Movements: Pushtimargi, Swaminarayan
Other Languages: Gujarati
Affiliations: Geeta Bhawan, Normanton Road,
Derby

Asian Sports Club & Cultural Centre
29 Coral Street, Leicester, Leicestershire, LE4 5BF
Tel: 0116-266-9207 (h)
Contact: Maganbhai P Patel
Position: President
Activities: Resource, youth, inter-faith
Traditions: Sanatanist
Social Groups: Patel
Other Languages: Gujarati, Hindi
Affiliations: Leicester Hindu Festival Council

Audich Gadhia Brahmasamaj
62 Lockerbie Avenue, Leicester, Leicestershire,
LE4 7NJ

Tel: 0116-266-0612
Contact: Mr Indubhai Vyas
Position: Honorary Secretary
Affiliations: Leicester Gujarat Hindu Association

Bajarang Bali Bhajan Mandal
16 Brambling Road, Leicester, Leicestershire
Tel: 0116-251-9041

Beaumont Leys Hindu Community
The Community Centre, Marwood Road,
Leicester, Leicestershire

Charotar Patidar Samaj (Leicester)
20 Southchurch Gate, Entrance on Bay Street,
Leicester, Leicestershire, LE1
Tel: 0116-251-4465 **Tel:** 0116-268-0101 (h)
Contact: Mr Ashwin C Patel
Position: Secretary
Activities: Resource, visits, youth, women,
newsletters
Traditions: Vaishnava
Other Languages: Gujarati
Affiliations: Gujarat Hindu Association

Charotaria Leuva Patidar Samaj
29 Shipley Road, Leicester, Leicestershire
Tel: 0116-268-1821
Contact: Mr Nagarbhai Patel
Position: Honorary Secretary
Affiliations: Leicester Gujarat Hindu Association

Fiji Sanatan Dharam Ramayan Mandli
77 Strathmore Avenue, Rushey Mead, Leicester,
Leicestershire, LE4 7HE (h)
Tel: 0116-266-6649 (h)
Contact: Mr James Sanker
Position: Secretary

Friends of Vrindavan
Environment City, Town Hall, Leicester,
Leicestershire, LE1 6BF
Tel: 0116-255-4244
Contact: Ranchor Prime

Gujarati Arya Association
10 Burnaby Avenue, Leicester, Leicestershire,
LE5 3QX
Contact: Mr Chimanbhai Champanaria
Position: Honorary Secretary
Affiliations: Leicester Gujarat Hindu Association

Gujarati Valand Gnati Mandal
30 Kensington Street, Leicester, Leicestershire,
LE4 5GL
Tel: 0116-253-0422
Contact: Arun Nayer
Position: Honorary Secretary
Affiliations: Leicester Gujarat Hindu Association

Haveli Shreeji Dwar
58 Loughborough Road, Leicester, Leicestershire,
LE4 5LD
Tel: 0116-268-2425 **Fax:** 0116-268-2425
Contact: Mr Giriraj Prasad Goswami
Position: Priest
Activities: Worship, inter-faith
Traditions: Vaishnava
Movements: Pushtimargi
Social Groups: Anavil, Lohana, Patidar
Other Languages: Hindi

Hindu Festival Council
51 Loughborough Road, Leicester, Leicestershire,
LE4 5LJ
Tel: 0116-266-8266 **Fax:** 0116-261-3066
Contact: Bharatbhai D Patel
Position: General secretary
Activities: Umbrella, youth, elderly, women, inter-faith
Traditions: Multi-Traditional
Other Languages: Hindi, Gujarati

Hindu Religious & Cultural Society
Geeta Bhavan, 70 Clarendon Road, Knighton,
Leicester, Leicestershire, LE2 3AD
Tel: 0116-270-7756 **Tel:** 0116-235-0667 (h)
Contact: Mahesh Chander Prasher
Position: Secretary
Activities: Worship, youth, elderly
Traditions: Sanatanist
Other Languages: Hindi, Panjabi
Affiliations: Council of Hindu Organisations,
Leicester; National Council of Hindu Temples

Hindu Sahitya Kendra
46/48 Loughborough Road, Leicester,
Leicestershire, LE4 5LD
Tel: 0116-611303 **Fax:** 0116-611931
Contact: Liladhar Raithatha
Position: Shop Manager
Activities: Resource, books
Traditions: Sanatanist
Other Languages: Gujarati, Hindi, Punjabi

Affiliations: Vishwa Hindu Parishad UK, Leicester;
Vishwa Hindu Parishad UK

Hindu Sevika Samiti
12 The Circle, Leicester, Leicestershire

Hindu Swayamsevak Sangh
5 Wylam Close, Leicester, Leicestershire

Hindu Temple & Community Association
75 Prospect Hill, Leicester, Leicestershire
Tel: 0116-262-2221
Contact: Mr Rashmikant Joshi
Position: Honorary Secretary
Affiliations: Leicester Gujarat Hindu Association

Hindu Temple (Sanatan Mandir)
7 Shakerdale Road, Leicester, Leicestershire

Indian Cultural Society
47 Tavistock Drive, Leicester, Leicestershire
Tel: 0166-273-0357
Contact: Dr H D Vyas
Position: Honorary Secretary
Affiliations: Leicester Gujarat Hindu Association

Indian Education Society
10 Woodbridge Road, Leicester, Leicestershire
Tel: 0116-268-1071
Contact: Mr Jayantilal Mistry
Position: Honorary Secretary
Affiliations: Leicester Gujarati Hindu Association

ISKCON Leicester
21 Thoresby Street, North Evington, Leicester,
Leicestershire, LE5 4GU
Tel: 0116-276-2587 **Tel:** 0116-236-7723
Fax: 0116-236-7723
EMail: gauranga.sundara@com.bbt.se
Contact: Gauranga Sundara Das
Position: President
Activities: Worship, resource, media, visits, youth,
elderly, women, newsletters, books, inter-faith
Traditions: Vaishnava
Movements: Chaitanya
Other Languages: Gujerati, Hindi
Affiliations: International Society for Krishna
Consciousness, national; International Society for
Krishna Consciousness, International.

Jalaram Satsang Mandal
254 Hinckley Road, Leicester, Leicestershire
Tel: 0116-285-8560

Contact: Mrs Indiraben Thobhani
Position: Honorary Secretary
Affiliations: Leicester Gujarat Hindu Association

Leicester Sangit Kala Kendra
c/o Mr. Patel, 27 Bradbourne Street, Leicester,
Leicestershire

Leicester Gujarat Hindu Association
51 Loughborough Road, Leicester, Leicestershire,
LE4 5LJ
Tel: 0116-266-8266 **Fax:** 0116-261-3066
Contact: Mr Dipak Joshi
Position: Secretary
Activities: Resource, media, umbrella, youth,
elderly, newsletters
Traditions: Sanatanist
Other Languages: Gujarati

Leicestershire Brahma Samaj
15 Belgrave Road, Leicester, Leicestershire,
LE4 6AR
Tel: 0116-262-4359 **Tel:** 0116-288-9069 (h)
Contact: Mohanlal Meghji Bhogaita
Position: President
Activities: Worship, visits, youth, elderly, women,
inter-faith
Traditions: Shaiva
Social Groups: Brahmin
Other Languages: Gujarati, Hindi
Affiliations: Hindu Council of Leicestershire;
National Council of Hindu Temples; Vishwa Hindu
Parishad

Leuva Patidar Samaj (SD)
3 Saltcoates Avenue, Leicester, Leicestershire,
LE4 7NP
Tel: 0116-268-2625
Contact: Mr Ratilal Patel
Position: Secretary
Affiliations: Leicester Gujarat Hindu Association

Lohana Mahila Mandal
3 Dorset Street, Leicester, Leicestershire, LE4 6BG

Lohana Youth League
Lohana Centre, Hildyard Road, Belgrave, Leicester,
Leicestershire, LE4 5GG
Tel: 0116-266-4643 **Tel:** 0116-276-9042 (h)
Contact: Mr Piyush Kotecha
Position: Secretary
Activities: Worship, resource, visits, youth, elderly,
women, newsletters, inter-faith

Traditions: Multi-Traditional
Social Groups: Lohana
Other Languages: Gujarati, Hindi
Affiliations: Gujarat Hindu Association Leicester;
Lohana Community of the UK

Maher Community Association
15 Ravenbridge Drive, St Margaret's Way, Leicester,
Leicestershire, LE4 0BJ
Tel: 0116-242-5360 **Fax:** 0116-251-0769
Contact: Mr Jaimale Odedra
Position: Secretary
Activities: Worship, resource, youth, elderly,
women, newsletters, inter-faith
Traditions: Multi-Traditional
Other Languages: Gujarati, Hindi
Affiliations: Leicester Hindu Festival Council;
Gujarat Hindu Association and Maher Community
Association (UK)

Mandhata Samaj Sahayak Mandal
1 Hartington Road, Leicester, Leicestershire,
LE2 0GP
Tel: 0116-262-3648
Contact: Maganbhai P Patel
Position: President
Activities: Worship, resource, visits, youth, elderly,
women
Traditions: Sanatanist
Social Groups: Patel
Other Languages: Gujarati, Hindi
Affiliations: Leicester Hindu Festival Council;
Mandhata UK Samaj

National Council of Vanik Associations
77 Ethel Road, Leicester, Leicestershire, LE5 5ND

Navnat Social Service Group
Flat 21, Azad House, 2 Taurus Close, Leicester,
Leicestershire, LE2 0UZ (h)
Tel: 0116-262-1769 (h)
Contact: Zaverchand Chhajrisha
Position: Chair
Activities: Visits, youth, elderly, inter-faith
Traditions: Sanatanist
Movements: Vanik
Other Languages: Gujarati
Affiliations: Leicester Hindu Festival Council;
National Council of Vanik Associations; Leicester
Gujarat Hindu Association

Pancholi Samaj
38 Gipsy Road, Leicester, Leicestershire, LE4
Tel: 0116-276-864

Parajiya Pattni Association
46 Patton Street, Leicester, Leicestershire

Rajput Bhoi Gnati Samaj Association
51 Woodgreen Walk, Leicester, Leicestershire

Rajput Gnati Mandal
87 Buller Road, Leicester, Leicestershire

Rajput Sangathan Samaj
61 Lancashire Street, Leicester, Leicestershire,
LE4 7PF
Tel: 0116-261-0793
Contact: Mr Jayantilal Rajput
Position: Honorary Secretary
Affiliations: Leicester Gujarat Hindu Association

Rana Samaj
85 Coral Street, Leicester, Leicestershire, LE4 5BG
Tel: 016-266-1165
Contact: Mr Bharatbhai Rana
Position: Honorary Secretary
Affiliations: Leicester Gujarat Hindu Association

R K Yuvak Mandal
61 Osbourne Road, Leicester, Leicestershire

Samanvay-Parivar
14 Goodwood Road, Leicester, Leicestershire

Sarvodaya Arya Samaj
13 Rowsley Avenue, Leicester, Leicestershire

Sarvodaya Mahila Mandal
c/o Janta Store, Belgrave Road, Leicester,
Leicestershire,

Sewa Samaj
7 Parkville Street, Leicester, Leicestershire

Shree Anavil Samaj
59 Acorn Street, Leicester, Leicestershire
Tel: 0116-266-4890
Contact: Honorary Secretary
Affiliations: Leicester Gujarat Hindu Association

Shree Bardai Brahman Samaj UK
38 Stanley Drive, Leicester, Leicestershire, LE5 1EA
Tel: 0116-271-6545
Contact: Mr Harishbhai Joshi

Position: Honorary Secretary
Affiliations: Leicester Gujarat Hindu Association

Shree Darji Gnati Mandal (SD) Leicester
21 Sawley Street, Leicester, Leicestershire, LE5 5JR
Contact: Mr Navin Topiwala
Position: Committee Member
Activities: Youth, elderly, women, inter-faith
Traditions: Multi-Traditional
Social Groups: Surti Darji
Other Languages: Gujarati

Shree Girnara Soni Samaj
176 Glenfield Road, Leicester, Leicestershire

Shree Gurjar Kshatriya Gnati Mandal
3 Agar Street, Leicester, Leicestershire,
LE4 6NE (h)
Tel: 0116-238-6228 (h)
Contact: Mr Prabhulal Jivanlal Manani
Position: Honorary Secretary
Activities: Youth, elderly, women, newsletters,
inter-faith
Traditions: Sanatanist
Movements: Swaminaryan, Ramanandi
Other Languages: Gujarati
Affiliations: Leicester Hindu Festival Council;
Gujarat Hindu Association

Shree Hindu Temple
47 Cromford Street, Leicester, Leicestershire,
LE2 0FW

Shree Hindu Temple & Community Centre
34 St Barnabas Road, Leicester, Leicestershire,
LE5 4BD
Tel: 0116-246-4590
Contact: Mr Govindbhai Rambhai Patel
Position: Secretary
Activities: Worship, resource, visits, youth, elderly,
women, newsletters, inter-faith
Traditions: Sanatanist
Movements: Sanatan Dharma
Other Languages: Gujarati, Hindi
Affiliations: Leicester Hindu Festival Council;
Gujarat Hindu Association; National Council of
Hindu Temples; Confederation of Indian
Organisations

Shree Jalaram Prathna Mandal
85 Narborough Road, Leicester, Leicestershire,
LE3 0LF

Tel: 0116-254-0117 **Tel:** 0116-289-9711 (h)
Fax: 0116-254-7488
Contact: Thakersi Vithaldas Morjaria
Position: President
Activities: Worship, resource, visits, youth, women, inter-faith
Traditions: Sanatanist
Movements: Sanatan Dharma
Other Languages: Gujarati, Hindi, Punjabi
Affiliations: Leicestershire Hindu Council; National Council of Hindu Temples

Shree Jansari Gnati Mandal
42 Silverstone Drive, Rushey Mead, Leicester, Leicestershire, LE4 7RR (h)
Tel: 0116-268-2257 (h)
Contact: Mr Dipakhai Vadher
Position: Honorary Secretary
Activities: Resource, umbrella, visits, elderly, women, newsletters, inter-faith
Traditions: Sanatanist
Movements: Arya Samaj
Other Languages: Gujarati
Affiliations: Leicester Gujarat Hindu Association; Hindu Council

Shree Jansari Gnati Mandal Gayatri Nivas
21 Brixham Drive, Wigston, Leicester, Leicestershire

Shree Jansari Gnati Mandal Leicester
109 Burfield Street, Leicester, Leicestershire, LE4 6AQ (h)
Contact: Mr Makesh K Chauhan
Position: Secretary
Activities: Youth, elderly, women, newsletters
Tradition: Sanatanist
Movements: Anya Sanaj
Social Group: Jansaris
Other languages: Gujarati, Hindi
Affiliations: Gujarat Hindi Association; Jansari Organisation UK

Shree Jignashu Satsang Mandal
Mahatma Gandhi House, Block 10, First Floor, Leicester, Leicestershire, LE4 6BH
Contact: Mr Bhimjibhai Kotecha
Affiliations: Leicester Gujarat Hindu Association

Shree Limbachia Gnati Mandal
14 Buller Road, Leicester, Leicestershire
Tel: 0116-268-089
Contact: Mr M M Nai

Position: Secretary
Affiliations: Leicester Gujarat Hindu Association

Shree Lohana Mahajan
Hilyard Road, off Ross Walk, Leicester, Leicestershire, LE4 5GG
Tel: 0116-266-4642 **Tel:** 0116-266-4643
Contact: Parful Thakrar
Position: Secretary
Activities: Worship, religious
Traditions: Gujrati
Social Groups: Lohana
Other Languages: Gujarati

Shree Maisonia Gnati Mandal
46 Woodgate Walk, Leicester, Leicestershire

Shree Mandata Samaj Sahayak Mandal
Melbourne Rd/Hartington Rd, Leicester, Leicestershire
Tel: 0116-262-3648
Contact: Mr M R Patel
Position: Secretary
Affiliations: Leicester Gujarat Hindu Association

Shree Matiyiya Patidar Samaj
3 Colebrooke Close, Leicester, Leicestershire, LE5 5NG
Contact: Mr Ramanlal Patel
Position: Honorary Secretary
Affiliations: Leicester Gujarat Hindu Association

Shree Navrang Society
15 Rushford Drive, Leicester, Leicestershire, LE4 7UF
Tel: 0116-276-7816
Contact: Mr Girishbhai Maher
Position: Honorary Secretary

Shree Pancholi Samaj
38-40 Gipsy Lane, Leicester, Leicestershire, LE4 6QH
Tel: 0116-266-5738
Contact: Mr Mahendrabhai Pancholi
Position: Honorary Secretary
Affiliations: Leicester Gujarat Hindu Association

Shree Prajapati Association
Shree Prajapati Community Centre, Ulverscroft Road, Leicester, Leicestershire, LE4 6BY
Tel: 0116-262-8560 **Tel:** 0116-270-5409 (h)
Contact: Mr Jay Mistry

Position: Secretary
Activities: Worship, resource, visits, youth, elderly, women, newsletters, inter-faith
Traditions: Sanatanist
Other Languages: Gujarati, Hindi

Shree Prajapati Youth
59 Fairfield Street, Leicester, Leicestershire

Shree Radhakrupa Satsang Mandal
36 Abney Street, Leicester, Leicestershire, LE5 5AA
Tel: 0116-254-7343
Contact: Mrs Kamuben N Joshi
Affiliations: Leicester Gujarat Hindu Association

Shree Rajput Bhoiraj Gnati
2 Jubilee Drive, Leicester, Leicestershire, LE3 9LJ
Tel: 0116-287-7827
Contact: Mr Kantilal Daudia
Affiliations: Leicester Gujarat Hindu Association

Shree Rajput Sangham Samaj
66 Ivydale Road, Thurmaston, Leicester, Leicestershire

Shree Ram Mandir
Hildyard Road, Off Ross Walk, Leicester, Leicestershire, LE4 5GG
Tel: 0116-266-4643 **Tel:** 0116-271-4372 (h)
Contact: Praful Thakrar
Position: Secretary
Activities: Worship, umbrella, visits, youth, elderly, newsletters
Traditions: Sanatanist
Movements: Sanatan
Social Groups: Lohana
Other Languages: Gujarati, Hindi
Affiliations: Shree Lohana Mahajan

Shree Sanatan Mandir
Weymouth Street, off Catherine Street, Leicester, Leicestershire, LE4 6FP
Tel: 0116-266-1402 **Tel:** 0116-276-1356 (h)
Contact: Mr Dullabhbhai B Patel
Position: President
Activities: Worship, resource, visits, youth, elderly, women, newsletters, books, inter-faith
Traditions: Sanatanist
Movements: Sanatan Dharma
Other Languages: Gujarati, Hindi, Sanskrit
Affiliations: Hindu Council of Leicestershire; Gujarat Hindu Association, Leicester; National

Council of Hindu Temples (UK); Hindu Council of UK; Vishwa Hindu Parishad

Shree Sanatan Mandir Community Centre
Belper Street, Leicester, Leicestershire, LE4 6ED

Shree Sarvodaya Samaj
20 Ingersby Drive, Leicester, Leicestershire, LE5 6HA
Tel: 0116-241-3639
Contact: Mr Kantilal Solanki
Position: Honorary Secretary
Affiliations: Leicester Gujarat Hindu Association

Shree Satsang Mandal
53 Moira Street, Leicester, Leicestershire, LE4 6LB
Tel: 0116-224-1268 (h)
Contact: Mrs P J Patel
Position: Honorary Secretary
Activities: Worship, visits, elderly
Traditions: Sanatanist
Movements: All sampradaya
Other Languages: Gujarati, Hindi
Affiliations: National Council of Hindu Temples

Shree Shakti Mandir
Moira Street, Leicester, Leicestershire, LE4 6NH
Tel: 0116-266-4138
Contact: K V Purohit
Position: Chairperson
Affiliations: Leicester Gujarat Hindu Association

Shree Sitaram Seva Trust (UK)
54 Woodville Road, off Glenfield Road, Leicester, Leicestershire, LE9 6DU
Tel: 0116-255-7177   **Tel:** 0116-266-7393
Contact: Ratilad G Vegad
Position: Honorary Secretary
Affiliations: Leicester Gujarat Hindu Association

Shree Sorathia Prajapati Community
75 Moores Road, Leicester, Leicestershire, LE4
Contact: Mr Harish Kukadia
Position: Secretary
Activities: Resource, youth, elderly, women, newsletters
Traditions: Multi-Traditional
Other Languages: Gujarati
Affiliations: Hindu Council of Leicestershire

Shree Swaminarayan Satsang Mandal
32 Rendell Road, Leicester, Leicestershire, LE4 5LE
Tel: 0116-266-7021

Shree Swaminarayan Temple
139/141 Loughborough Road, Leicester,
Leicestershire, LE4 5LQ

Shree UK Luhar Gnati Mandal
32 Evington Drive, Leicester, Leicestershire,
LE5 5PB (h)
Tel: 0116-273-0305 (h)
Contact: Mr Ramesh Purshottam Sidpara
Position: Secretary
Activities: Resource, youth, elderly, women, inter-faith
Traditions: Multi-Traditional
Other Languages: Gujarati
Affiliations: Leicester Hindu Festival Council;
Gujarat Hindu Association; Vishwa Hindu Parishad

Shree UK R K Seva Samaj
9 Osmaston Road, Leicester, Leicestershire

Shree Wanza Community
Pasture Lane, off Sanvey Gate, Leicester,
Leicestershire, LE1 4EY
Contact: Mr Prabhudas Shikotra
Position: Secretary
Activities: Worship, youth, elderly, women,
newsletter
Traditions: Vaishnava
Social Groups: Wanza Community
Other Languages: Gujarati
Affiliations: Hindu Council of Leicestershire;
Gujarat Hindu Association; Vishwa Hindu Parishad

Shree Yamuna Mandal
56 Burfield Street, Leicester, Leicestershire,
LE4 6AN
Tel: 0116-268-0282
Contact: Miss C S Parmar
Position: Committee member

Shri Ji Dwar
152 Belgrave Road, Leicester, Leicestershire
Tel: 0116-266-1805
Contact: Mr Chandhubhai Mattani
Position: Honorary Secretary
Affiliations: Leicester Gujarat Hindu Association
Other Languages: Gujarati, Hindi

Shrimali Soni Samaj (Leicester)
41 Peebles Way, Leicester, Leicestershire

Swaminarayan Hindu Mission
3 St James Street, Off Humberstone Gate, Leicester,
Leicestershire, LE1 3SU
Tel: 0116-262-3791
Contact: President
Activities: Worship
Affiliations: Leicester Gujarat Hindu Association

Swaminarayan Youth Mission
3 St James Street, Off Lee Circle, Leicester,
Leicestershire

Vanik Samaj (Leicester)
60 Belgrave Road, Leicester, Leicestershire, LE4
Tel: 0116-262-2662
Contact: Vanmali Gordhandas
Position: President

Vasenev Satsang Mandal
44 Paton Street, Leicester, Leicestershire

Vishwa Hindu Parishad (Leicester Branch)
46-48 Loughborough Road, Leicester,
Leicestershire, LE4 5LD
Tel: 0116-266-5665   **Fax:** 0116-261-1931
Contact: Harish Raj
Position: Secretary
Activities: Resource, umbrella, youth, elderly,
women, visits
Affiliations: Vishwa Hindu Parishad, UK

West End Diwali Festival
Manor Neighbourhood Centre, Leicester,
Leicestershire

Charotar Patidar Samaj
50 Ratcliff Road, Loughborough, Leicestershire

Charotar Patidar Samaj
30 Garendon Road, Loughborough, Leicestershire,
LE11 0QD

Geeta Bhawan
Lemyngton Street, Loughborough, Leicestershire,
LE11 1UH
Tel: 01509-233570
Contact: Dr Sri Ram Chhabra
Position: Honorary Secretary
Activities: Worship, visits, youth, elderly, women,
inter-faith
Traditions: Sanatanist
Other Languages: Punjabi, Hindi
Affiliations: National Council of Hindu Temples

Limbachia Hittechu Mandal
4a Boyer Street, Loughborough, Leicestershire
Tel: 01509-239897
Contact: Mr Nareshbhai Valand
Position: Honorary Secretary
Affiliations: Leicester Gujarat Hindu Association

Shree Prajapati Samaj
66 Cartwright Street, Loughborough, Leicestershire

Shree Prajapati Samaj
40 Baxtergate, Loughborough, Leicestershire

Shri Prajapati Samaj
25 Ratcliffe Road, Loughborough, Leicestershire

Shree Ram Krishna Centre
Alfred Street, Loughborough, Leicestershire,
LE11 1NG
Tel: 01509-237396
Contact: Secretary

Melton Asian Community
4 Field Close, Melton Mowbray, Leicestershire,
LE13 1DS
Tel: 01664-63746
Contact: Mr Chetan Bharti
Position: Honorary Secretary
Affiliations: Leicester Gujarat Hindu Association

Hindu Swayam Sevak Sangh
1 East Leys Court, Moulton, Northampton,
Northamptonshire, NN3 1TX

Vishwa Hindu Parishad
10 South Paddock Court, Lings, Northampton,
Northamptonshire, NN3 8LH
Tel: 01604-404869
Contact: Chhotubhai Vasanji Mistry
Position: Chair
Activities: Resource, media, umbrella, visits, youth,
elderly, women, books
Traditions: Multi-Traditional
Other Languages: Gujarati, Hindi
Affiliations: Vishwa Hindu Parishad, national;
Vishwa Hindu Parishad, international

Brahma Samaj Nottingham
30 Northdown Road, Lenton Boulevard,
Nottingham, Nottinghamshire

Brahma Samaj Nottingham
4 Haynes Close, Nottingham, Nottinghamshire,
NG11 8SN

Brahmin Welfare Association
c/o Bosworth Primary School, Ainsworth Drive,
The Meadows, Nottingham, Nottinghamshire

Brahmin Welfare Association
79 Stamford Road, West Bridgeford, Nottingham,
Nottinghamshire, NG2 6GG

**Derby & Notts Gujarati Lohana Community
Association**
71 Wellington Street, Long Eaton, Nottingham,
Nottinghamshire

Derbyshire & Notts Lohana Community
2 Angrave Close, St Anns, Nottingham,
Nottinghamshire, NG3 3NF

Gujarat Samaj
15 Maun Avenue, Bobbersmill, Nottingham,
Nottinghamshire

Gujarat Samaj Association
28 Nuthall Road, Nottingham, Nottinghamshire

Gujarat Samaj Elderly Luncheon Club
213 Bramcote Lane, Wollaton, Nottingham,
Nottinghamshire

Gujarat Samaj Nottingham
1 Rodney Road, West Bridgeford, Nottingham,
Nottinghamshire

Gujarat Samaj Nottingham
16 Derby Grove, Nottingham, Nottinghamshire

Hindu Association
8 Musters Road, West Bridgeford, Nottingham,
Nottinghamshire

Hindu Centre
22 Claremont Avenue, Bramcote, Nottingham,
Nottinghamshire

Hindu Council of Nottinghamshire
PO Box 74, Long Eaton, Nottingham,
Nottinghamshire, N610 3EZ
Tel: 0115 9730353 **Fax:** 0115 9730353
Contact: Mr Nitin J M Lakhani
Position: Secretary
Activities: Resource, media, umbrella
Traditions: Multi-Traditional
Other Languages: Hindi

Hindu Temple & Cultural Centre
215 Carlton Road, Nottingham, Nottinghamshire,
NG3 2FX
Tel: 0115-911-3384 **Tel:** 0115-913-1426 (h)
Contact: Mrs K S Mohindra
Position: Secretary
Activities: Worship, resource, visits, youth, elderly,
women, newsletters
Traditions: Multi-Traditional
Movements: Arya Samaj, Sanatan Dharam
Other Languages: Hindi, Punjabi, Gujarati

Hindu Youth Group
Radford Youth & Community Centre, Lenton
Boulevard, Radford, Nottingham, Nottinghamshire,
NG7 2BY
Tel: 0115- 923-1595 (h) Tel: 0115-979-2171
Contact: Sudheer Kumar Gupta
Position: Hon Secretary
Activities: Youth, women
Traditions: Multi-Traditional
Other Languages: Hindi
Affiliations: Hindu Swayamsevak Sangh UK

ISKCON Nottingham
313 Wollaton Road, Nottingham, Nottinghamshire,
NG8 1FS
Tel: 0115-928-1371 (h)
Contact: Paul Oliver
Position: President

Swaminarayan Hindu Mission
8 Howseman Gardens, Nottingham,
Nottinghamshire, NG2 2HX
Tel: 0115-986-5848
Contact: Diyeshbhai Rughani

Vishwa Hindu Parishad (UK)
21 Kenneth Road, Redhill, Nottingham,
Nottinghamshire, NG5 8HY
Tel: 0115-955-9251 (h)
Contact: D V Dhanda
Position: Chairman
Activities: Inter-faith
Traditions: Multi-Traditional
Movements: All movements
Other Languages: Hindi, Gujarati, Punjabi

Hindu Association
39 York Road, Wellingborough, Northamptonshire

Nav-Kala Association
18 Cannon Street, Wellingborough,
Northamptonshire, NN8 4DN

Pravasi Day Centre (Asian Group)
c/o Victoria Centre, Palk Road, Wellingborough,
Northamptonshire, NN8 1HT
Tel: 01933-442955
Contact: Niraj Jani
Position: Development Officer
Activities: Elderly, women, inter-faith
Other Languages: Gujarati, Hindi

Swaminarayan Hindu Mission
16-20 Mill Road, Wellingborough,
Northamptonshire, NN8 1PE
Tel: 01933-315961 (h)
Contact: Mukeshbhai Pabari

Wellingborough District Hindu Association
133 Highfield Road, Wellingborough,
Northamptonshire, NN8 1PL
Tel: 01933-4407132
Contact: Mrs Roopa Master-Coles
Position: Community Development Officer
Activities: Worship, resource, visits, youth, elderly,
women, newsletters
Traditions: Multi-Traditional
Other Languages: Gujarati
Affiliations: National Council of Hindu Temples

WEST MIDLANDS
Regional or County Bodies

Arya Samaj (Vedic Mission) West Midlands
Vedic Cultural and Social Centre, 188 Inkerman
Street (Off Erskine Street), Nechells, Birmingham,
West Midlands, B7 4SA
Fax: 0121-707-0225
Contact: Krishan Chupra
Position: President
Activities: Worship, youth, elderly, newsletters,
inter-faith
Traditions: Vedic
Movements: Arya Samaj
Other Languages: Hindi
Affiliations: Arya Pratinidhi Sabha

City, Town or Local Bodies

Arya Samaj (Vedic Mission) West Midlands

Vedic Cultural And Social Centre, 188 Inkerman
street (Off Erskine Street), Nechells, Birmingham,
West Midlands, B7 4SA
Fax: 0121-707-0225
Contact: Krishan Chupra
Position: President
Activities: Worship, youth, elderly, newsletters,
inter-faith
Traditions: Vedic
Movements: Arya Samaj
Other Languages: Hindi
Affiliations: Arya Pratinidhi Sabha

Birmingham Pragati Mandal

107 Dearman Road, Birmingham, West Midlands,
B11

Bochasanwasi Shri Akshar Purushottamni Sansatha, The Swaminarayan Hindu Mission

Satsang Bhavan, 23-43 Ivor Road, Sparkhill,
Birmingham, West Midlands, B11 4NR
Tel: 0121-772-3086 **Tel:** 0121-772-5320
Contact: Madhubhai Joshee

Geeta Bhavan

99 Grove Lane, Handsworth, Birmingham, West
Midlands, B21 9HF

Hindu Bengali Association

2 Wingfield Road, Great Barr, Birmingham, West
Midlands, B42 1QD

Hindu Council of Birmingham

c/o Shree Geeta Bhavan Mandir, 107-115
Heathfield Road, Birmingham, West Midlands,
B19 1YL
Tel: 0121-554-4120
Activities: Umbrella

Hindu Mission (UK)

13 Leyton Road, Birmingham, West Midlands

Hindu Sevika Samita

18 Adria Road, Sparkhill, Birmingham, West
Midlands, B11 4JN

Hindu Swayamsevak Sangh

22 Pipson Road, Birmingham, West Midlands
Tel: 0121-773-2214
Contact: Mr Ramesh Shah

Indian Cultural Centre

360 Soho Road, Birmingham, West Midlands, B21

ISKCON Birmingham

84 Stanmore Road, Edgbaston, Birmingham, West
Midlands, B16 9BT
Tel: 0121-420-4999
Contact: Janarda das
Position: President
Activities: Worship
Traditions: Vaishnava
Movements: Chaitanya
Affiliations: Hindu Council of Birmingham;
National Council of Hindu Temples

Kalyan Ashram Trust Aid Committee

17 Victoria Road, Birmingham, West Midlands, B23

Mabarun Hindu Cultural Association

132 Alexander Road, Acocks Green,
Birmingham, West Midlands, B27 6HB
Contact: P K Deb

Shree Gita Bhavan & Charitable Trust

107-115 Heathfield Road, Handsworth,
Birmingham, West Midlands, B19 1HE
Tel: 0121-554-4120 **Tel:** 0121-525-1960 (h)
Contact: Mr Jagdish Chander Gupta
Position: General Secretary
Activities: Worship, resource, visits, youth, elderly,
newsletters, books
Traditions: Sanatanist
Other Languages: Hindi, Punjabi, Gujarati,
Andhra
Affiliations: Birmingham City Hindu Council;
National Council of Hindu Temples

Shree Hindu Community Centre

56 Grantham Road, Sparkbrook, Birmingham, West
Midlands, B11 1LX

Shree Hindu Community Centre & Temple

541a Warwick Road, Tysley, Birmingham, West
Midlands, B11 2JP
Tel: 0121-707-3154 **Tel:** 0121-772-4277 (h)
Contact: P A Amin
Position: President
Activities: Worship

Shree Jansari Gnati Mandal

5 Glover Close, Hall Green, Birmingham, West
Midlands, B28 0JG

Shree Krishna Mandir
10 Sampson Road, Sparkbrook, Birmingham, West
Midlands, B11 1JL
Tel: 0121-771-4478 **Tel:** 0121-745-4102 (h)
Contact: Veni Chauhan
Position: Secretary
Activities: Worship, visits, youth
Social Groups: Hindu Mochi Samaj
Other Languages: Gujarati, Hindi
Affiliations: National Council of Hindu Temples

**Shree Laxmi Narayan Mandir & Shree Hindu
Community Centre**
541a Warwick Road, Tyseley, Birmingham, West
Midlands, B11 2JP
Tel: 0121-707-3154 **Tel:** 0121-705-3024
Fax: 0121-764-4214
Activities: Worship, resource, umbrella, visits,
youth, elderly, women, newsletters, inter-faith
Traditions: Multi-Traditional
Other Languages: Gujarati, Hindu, Bengali,
Punjabi
Affiliations: Hindu Council of Birmingham;
National Council of Hindu Temples

Shree Limbachia Vanand Gnati
2 Ashfield Gardens, Kings Heath, Birmingham, West
Midlands, B14

Shree Lohana Association
121 Grove Road, Kingsheath, Birmingham, West
Midlands, B14 6SX (h)
Tel: 0121-443-1354 (h) **Fax:** 0121-326-6185
Contact: Mr Shanti Gordhandas Kotecha
Position: President
Activities: Youth, elderly women, newsletters,
inter-faith
Traditions: Sanatanist, Multi-Traditional
Other Languages: Gujarati, Hindi
Affiliations: Lohana Community of the UK

Shree Pajapati Association (Birmingham)
249 Warwick Road, Tyseley, Birmingham, West
Midlands, B11
Contact: Mr Hasmukhbhai Mistry
Position: Secretary
Activities: Resource, youth, elderly, women,
newsletters, inter-faith
Traditions: Multi-traditional
Social Group: Prajapatis
Other Languages: Gujrati, Hindi
Affiliations: Hindu Council, Midlands

Shree Ram Mandir
8 Walford Road, Sparkbrook, Birmingham, West
Midlands, B12 1NR
Tel: 0121-773-5735
Contact: Dhirubhai Rajgor
Position: Priest
Activities: Worship, resource, youth, elderly,
women, newsletters, inter-faith
Traditions: Multi-Traditional
Social Groups: Soathia Prajapati
Other Languages: Gujarati, Hindi, Punjabi
Affiliations: Hindu Council of Birmingham; Shree
Sorathia Prajapati Community (UK)

Shree Sorathia Prajapati (UK)
8 Walford Road, Sparkbrook, Birmingham, West
Midlands, B11 1NR
Tel: 0121-773-5735 **Tel:** 0121-783-4699 (h)
Contact: Dr N M Gohil
Position: Honorary Secretary
Activities: Worship, visits, youth, women,
newsletters
Traditions: Multi-Traditional
Social Groups: Prajapati
Other Languages: Gujarati
Affiliations: Hindu Council of Birmingham

Shri Venkateswara Bahaji Temple
119 New Road, Rubery, Birmingham, West
Midlands, B45 9JR
Tel: 0121-457-7597 **Fax:** 0121-457-7770
Contact: Mrs S A Gurney
Position: Office Coordinator
Activities: Resource, youth, newsletters, inter-faith
Traditions: Sanatanist
Other Languages: Telegu, Tamil, Kanada,
Maharashtra
Affiliations: Hindu Council of Birmingham;
National Council of Hindu Temples

Shree Vishwakarma Association
29 Arley Road, Solihull, Birmingham, West
Midlands, B91 1NJ

**Vishwa Hindu Parishad (UK) (Birmingham
Branch)**
208 Mansel Road, Small Heath, Birmingham, West
Midlands, B10 9NL (h)
Tel: 0121-773-1985 (h)
Contact: Mr M T Parmar
Position: Chairperson
Activities: Youth, elderly, women

Traditions: Sanatanist, Yoga
Movements: Arya Samaj
Other Languages: Hindi, Gujarati

Bawa Balak Nath Ji Mandir
Proffit Avenue, Coventry, West Midlands, CV6 7EQ
Tel: 01203-686590

Coventry Hindu Society
43 Sullivan Road, Coventry, West Midlands

Hindu Mandir
91 Bersford Avenue, Coventry, West Midlands

Hindu Sevika Samiti (Ladies Group)
75 Knoll Drive, Coventry, West Midlands, CV3 5PJ

Hindu Swayamsevak Sangh
75 Knoll Drive, Coventry, West Midlands, CV3 5PJ
Contact: I D Gandhi
Position: Public Relations
Activities: Youth
Traditions: Multi-Traditional
Other Languages: Hindi, Gujarati
Affiliations: Vishwa Hindu Parishad

Hindu Temple Society
274 Stoney Stanton Road, Coventry, West
Midlands, CV6 5GX
Tel: 01203-685898 **Tel:** 01203-220346 (h)
Contact: P K Bhakri
Position: President
Activities: Worship, visits, youth, elderly, women
Traditions: Multi-Traditional
Movements: Arya Samaj
Other Languages: Hindi, Punjabi, Urdu
Affiliations: National Council of Hindu Temples,
Hindu Council of UK

Institute of Indian Culture & Studies
16 Knoll Drive, Styvechale, Coventry, West
Midlands
Tel: 01203-314266

Leuva Patidar Youth Samaj
63 Grangemouth Road, Coventry, West Midlands,
CV6 3EZ

Lohana Community of Coventry
15 Priors Harnall, Coventry, West Midlands,
CV1 5FE

Lohana Mahajan Mandal
32 David Road, Coventry, West Midlands

Sanatan Dharam Hindu Society
56 Mason Road, Foleshill, Coventry, West Midlands,
CV6 7FJ
Tel: 01203-685125
Contact: Ramesh Kumar Murria
Position: President
Activities: Worship, visits, women
Traditions: Sanatanist
Movements: Sanatan Dharm
Other Languages: Hindi, Punjabi

Sat Sang Janki Mandli
c/o Hindu Temple Society, 274 Stoney Stanton
Road, Foleshill, Coventry, West Midlands,
CV2 4GX
Tel: 01203 685898 **Tel:** 01203 220346 (h)
Contact: Mrs Sudarshan Bhakri
Position: Secretary
Activities: Worship, visits, elderly, women
Traditions: Multi-Traditional
Movements: Arya Samaj, ISKCON
Other Languages: Punjabi, Hindi, English, Urdu
Affiliations: National Council Of Hindu Temples,
Hindu Council (UK)

Shree Gujarati Hindu Satsang Mandal & Shree Krishna Mandir
Harnall Lane West, Nr Halfords, Coventry, West
Midlands, CV1 4FB
Tel: 01203-256981
Contact: B G Garala
Position: Secretary

Shree Hindu Satsang Mandir (Shree Khrishna Temple)
92a Stoney Stanton Road, Coventry, West
Midlands, CV1 4FL

Shree Kadwa Patidar Samaj UK
10 Cannon Close, Coventry, West Midlands

Shree Limbachia Gnati Hittechhu Samaj
11 Alton Close, Wood End, Coventry, West
Midlands, CV2 1TT

Shree Radha Krishna Cultural Centre (ISKCON)
Kingfield Road, Coventry, West Midlands
Tel: 01203-555420 (h)
Contact: Haridas
Activities: Worship

Shree Shakti Bhajan Mandal
6 Talland Avenue, Coventry, West Midlands, CV6
7NX (h)
Tel: 01203-685368 (h)
Contact: Mr Kanti M Patel
Position: Secretary
Activities: Visits, youth, elderly, women, inter-faith
Traditions: Multi-Traditional
Movements: Sanatan Dharma
Social Groups: Koli-Patel
Other Languages: Gujarati, Hindi
Affiliations: Shree Krishna Temple-Coventry

Shree Sorathia Prajaptisam
20 Brinklow Road, Coventry, West Midlands,
CV3 2HY
Contact: Mr H K Pakhamia

Sorathia Prajapati Samaj
7 Grantham Street, Coventry, West Midlands,
CV2 4FP

Vedic Mission
58 Branstree Drive, Holbrooks, Coventry, West
Midlands

Shree Hindu Samaj Mandir
18 Salisbury Street, Off Walsall Road, Darlaston,
West Midlands, WS10 8BQ
Tel: 0121-526-2344
Contact: Mr D Patel
Position: Co-ordinator

Krishna Temple & Gujarati Hindu Centre
Hope Street, Off Churchfield Street, Dudley, West
Midlands, DY2
Tel: 01384-253253
Contact: Mr R D Patel
Position: Secretary

Hindu Religious Association & Temple
10b High Street, Leamington Spa, Warwickshire,
CV31 1LW
Tel: 01926-452247
Contact: Yash Paul Tara
Position: Chair
Activities: Worship, visits, inter-faith
Traditions: Multi-Traditional
Other Languages: Punjabi, Hindi
Affiliations: National Council of Hindu Temples

Shri Hindu Gujarati Samaj
40 Alderbrooke Drive, Nuneaton, Warwickshire,
CV11 6PL (h)
Tel: 01203-344940
Contact: Mahendra Soni
Position: Secretary
Activities: Worship, resource, umbrella, visits, youth,
elderly, women, newsletters, inter-faith
Traditions: Sanatanist
Movements: Arya Samaj
Social Groups: Patidar
Other Languages: Gujarati, Hindi
Affiliations: National Council Of Hindu Temples

Bharat Sevak Samaj Rugby
Hindu Swayam Sevak Sangh, 4 Kimberley Road,
Rugby, Warwickshire, CV21 3EZ (h)
Tel: 01788-565105
Contact: Vasant Mistry
Position: Vice President
Activities: Worship, visits, youth, elderly, women
Traditions: Sanatanist
Other Languages: Gujarati, Hindi, Punjabi
Affiliations: Kalyan Prathna Mandir; Hindu
Swayam Sevak Sangh; Vishva Hindu Parishad

Shree Kalyam Mandal
4 Kimberley Road, Rugby, Warwickshire,
CV21 2SU
Tel: 01788-565105 **Tel:** 01788-573515 (h)
Contact: Mr Ambaram Mistry
Position: Chair
Activities: Worship, visits
Traditions: Sanatanist
Movements: Sanatan
Other Languages: Gujarati, Hindi
Affiliations: National Council of Hindu Temples

Shree Prajanati Samaj (UK)
73 King Road, Rugby, West Midlands

Hindu Cultural Society, Staffordshire
Trent Centre, 645 Leek Road, Hanley, Stoke-on-
Trent, Staffordshire, ST1 3NF
Tel: 01782-205332 **Fax:** 01782-210841
Contact: Nalinbhai Patel
Position: Coordinator
Activities: Resource, visits, elderly, women,
newsletters
Traditions: Multi-Traditional
Movements: Multi
Other Languages: Hindi, Gujarati, Marathi,
Punjabi

Stoke Gujarati Samaj
Stoke, Staffordshire
Tel: 01538-399599 (h)
Contact: Prakash Samani
Position: Secretary
Activities: Youth, elderly, women
Traditions: Multi-Traditional
Other Languages: Gujarati, Hindi

Mahan Sabha
10 Church Way, Stirchley, Telford, Shropshire
Contact: Mr B Marjaria

Hindu Samaj Mandir
48 Cook Street, Daraston, Walsall, West Midlands

Mandir Baba Balak Nath (Temple)
96a Cladmore Road, Walsall, West Midlands,
WS1 3PD
Tel: 01922 21177 **Tel:** 0860 528 245 (h)
Fax: 01922 21177
Contact: Jaspal Singh Bhatti
Position: Priest
Activities: Worship
Traditions: Sanatanist, Shaiva
Movements: Baba Balak Nath
Other Languages: Punjabi, Hindi, English

Shree Hindu Mandir
139 Darlaston Road, Walsall, West Midlands, WS1
4JL
Tel: 01922-647428
Contact: Mr Patel

Shree Hindu Mandir Walsall Youth Society
40 Victor Street, Caldmore, Walsall, West Midlands,
WS1 4HZ

Shree Ram Mandir
Ford Street, Pleck, Walsall, West Midlands,
W52 9BU
Tel: 01922-724024

Hindu Religious Association
70 Beauchamp Road, Warwick, Warwickshire

Hindu Samaj Mandas Temple
18 Salisbury Street, Wednesbury, West Midlands
Tel: 0121-526-2344

Shree Krishna Mandir
81 Old Meeting Street, West Bromwich, West
Midlands, B70 9SZ

Tel: 0121-553-5375 **Tel:** 01958-437003 (h)
Contact: Chandhu Patel
Position: President
Activities: Worship, visits, youth, elderly, women,
newsletters, inter-faith
Traditions: Multi-Traditional, Vaishnava
Social Groups: Mandhata
Other Languages: Gujarati, Hindi, Punjabi

Gujarati Centre
Mander Street, Wolverhampton, West Midlands

Hindu Association
54 Villiers Avenue, Bilston, Wolverhampton, West
Midlands, WV14 6QY
Tel: 01902-45277
Contact: Ms M Patel

Hindu Cultural Society
34 Stubbington Close, Mosley Road, Whitmore
Reans, Wolverhampton, West Midlands

Hindu Sabha
54 Goldthorn Crescent, Penn, Wolverhampton,
West Midlands, WV4 5TX (h)
Tel: 01902-330735 (h)
Contact: Tirath Ram Bhardwaj
Position: President
Activities: Resource, inter-faith
Traditions: Shaiva
Movements: Sanatan Dharam
Other Languages: Hindi, Punjabi, Gujarati, Urdu
Affiliations: Race Relation Wolverhampton;
National Council of Hindu Temples

*Leuva Patidar Samaj (Bilston, Wolverhampton,
Willenhall)*
4 Fenmere Close, Goldthorn Park, Wolverhampton,
West Midlands, WV4 5EN (h)
Contact: Mr Hasmukh Patel
Position: Chair
Activities: Youth, elderly, women
Traditions: Shaiva
Movements: Arya Samaj
Social Groups: Leuva Partidar Samaj
Other Languages: Gujarati, Hindi
Affiliations: Leuva Patidar Samaj UK

Shri Krishan Mandir
123 Penn Road, Wolverhampton, West Midlands,
WV3 0DR
Tel: 01902-772416 **Tel:** 01902-340324 (h)

Contact: Darshanlal Chadha
Position: President
Activities: Worship, resource, visits, youth, elderly, women, inter-faith
Traditions: Sanatanist
Other Languages: Hindi, Gujarati, Punjabi
Affiliations: National Council of Hindu Temples

Sri Ram Krishna Temple
39 Wellington Road, Wolverhampton, West Midlands

EAST ANGLIA
City, Town or Local Bodies

Indian Cultural Association Cambridge
70 Bishops Road, Trumpington, Cambridge, Cambridgeshire, CB2 2NH (h)
Tel: 01223 564 477
Contact: R Kotecha
Position: Treasurer
Activities: Resource, youth, elderly, women
Traditions: Sanatanist
Social Groups: Hindu
Other Languages: Gujarati
Affiliations: National Council Of Hindu Temples

Ipswich Hindu Samaj
72 Belmont Road, Pinewood, Ipswich, Suffolk, IP2 9XT (h)
Tel: 01473-685608 (h)
Contact: Dr Sushil Kumar Soni
Activities: Worship, resource, inter-faith
Traditions: Sanatanist, Multi-Tradition
Movements: Arya Samaj
Social Groups: Sanatani, Arya Samaj
Other Languages: Hindi, Punjabi

Bharat Hindu Samaj
6 New England Complex, Rock Road, Peterborough, Cambridgeshire, PE1 3BU
Tel: 01773-347188 **Fax:** 01773-570793
Contact: Mansukh Ladwa
Position: Chair
Activities: Worship, visits, youth, elderly, women, inter-faith
Traditions: Sanatanist
Other Languages: Gujarati, Hindi, Tamil, Bengali
Affiliations: National Council of Hindu Temples

GREATER LONDON
Regional and Area Bodies

Aryasamaj London
69a Argyle Road, West Ealing, London, W13 0LY
Tel: 0181-991-1732 **Tel:** 0181-569-6403
Fax: 0181-991-1732
Contact: Professor S N Bharadwaj
Position: President
Activities: Worship, visits, youth, elderly, newsletters, inter-faith
Traditions: Vedic, Arya Samaj (Hindu)
Movements: Arya Samaj
Social Groups: Vedic dharma/tradition
Other Languages: Hindi, Punjabi, Sanskrit
Affiliations: Arya Pratinidhi Sabha (UK); Sarvadeshik Arya Partinidhi Sabha, New Delhi, India

Brahmin Society - North London
17 Argyll Road, Edgware, Middlesex, HA8 5HB
Tel: 0181-951-3840 (h)
Contact: Mr Kamlesh Rajyaguru
Position: Secretary
Affiliations: Hindu Council (Brent)

Hindu Centre London
39 Grafton Terrace, off Malden Road, London, NW5 4JA
Tel: 0171-485-8200
Contact: Deva Savara
Position: President
Activities: Worship, resource, visits, youth, women, newsletters, books, inter-faith
Traditions: Multi-traditional
Other Languages: Hindi, Punjabi, Gujrati

Leuva Patidar Samaj of London
109 Gosport Road, Walthamstow, London, E17 7LX (h)
Tel: 0181-520-0268 (h)
Contact: Mr Bhikhubhai P Patel
Position: Secretary
Activities: Resource, youth, newsletters
Traditions: Vaishnava
Social Groups: Leuva Patidar
Other Languages: Gujarati
Affiliations: Hindu Council (Brent), Leuva Patidor Samaj (SNB) UK

Lohana Community North London
50 Argyle Road, North Harrow, Middlesex,
HA2 7AJ
Contact: Mr Jamnadas Raithatha
Position: Secretary
Affiliations: Hindu Council (Brent)

Lohana Community (South London)
70 Heathfield Vale, Selsden, Surrey, CR2 8AS
Tel: 0181-651-4170 (h)
Contact: Narendra Chotai
Position: Secretary

Maharashtra Mandal London
30 Penney Close, Dartford, Kent, DA1 2NE

South East Hindu Association
103 Donaldson Road, London, SE18

Vanza Society of North London
95 Northumberland Avenue, Harrow, Middlesex,
HA2 7RA
Tel: 0181-866-7264
Contact: Mr Kishor Davdra
Position: Secretary
Affiliations: Hindu Council (Brent)

Borough and Local Bodies

BARKING AND DAGENHAM

Jan Kshatriya Sevak Mandal (UK)
32 Mount Pleasant Road, Chigwell, Essex,
IG7 5ER
Contact: B N D Vadher
Position: Secretary
Affiliations: Hindu Council (Brent)

BARNET

Asian Indian Society
23 Woodstock Road, Golders Green, London,
NW11

Brahmin Centre North London
10 Holders Hill Drive, London, NW4 1NL
Tel: 0181-203-3053
Contact: Mr T H Vyas

Hindu Cultural Society
321 Coney Hatch Lane, Friern Barnet, London,
N11

Hindu Cultural Society
86 Chanctonbury Way, London, N12 7AB

Karamsad Samaj
70 Great North Way, Hendon, London, NW4 1HS

Sattavis Gam Patidar Samaj
52 Dersingham Road, Cricklewood, London,
NW2 1SL
Tel: 0181-452-3561 (h)
Contact: Mr Ashokumar Patel
Position: Secretary
Affiliations: Hindu Council (Brent)

Shree Aden Depala Mitra Mandal (UK)
67a Church Lane, East Finchley, London, N2 8DR
Tel: 0181-446-5057
Contact: Madhusudan C Jogam
Position: Secretary, Executive Committee
Activities: Worship, visits, youth, elderly, women
Traditions: Sanatanist
Other Languages: Gujarati

Shree Kadwa Patidar Samaj UK
117 Devonshire Road, London, NW7 1EA

Shree Vishwakarma Association of UK
56 Ridge Hill, Golders Green, London, NW11 8PS

Swaminarayan Sidhant Sajeevan Mandal
3 Neeld Crescent, London, NW4

Swami Narayan Temple
Finchley Road, Golders Green, London, NW11
Tel: 0181-458-5356
EMail: uccamva@ucl.ac.uk
Contact: M Varsani
Position: Secretary
Activities: Worship, resource, elderly
Movements: Swaminaryan
Other Languages: Gujarati, Hindi

Vishwakarma Association
50a Brookhill Road, East Barnet, Hertfordshire,
EN4 8SL
Tel: 0181-447-0049
Contact: Mr Rajni Bakrania
Position: Secretary
Affiliations: Hindu Council (Brent)

BRENT

Anand Overseas Brotherhood
4 Winchester Avenue, Kingsbury, London, NW9 9SY

Contact: Mr Ramesh Patel
Position: Secretary
Affiliations: Hindu Council (Brent)

Bavis Gam Patidar Samaj UK
950 Harrow Road, Sudbury, Middlesex, HA0 2PY
Tel: 0181-904-4936 (h)
Contact: Ms Shobhaben Patel
Position: Secretary
Affiliations: Hindu Council (Brent)

Chovis Gam Patidar Samaj
36 Mayfields, Wembley, Middlesex

Dharmaj Samaj
35 Landsdowne Grove, London, NW10 4RG

Hindu Council (Brent)
7 The Leadings, Wembley Park, Middlesex,
HA9 9DT
Tel: 0181-961-5444 **Tel:** 0181-908-0192 (h)
Fax: 0181-961-6811
Contact: Mr Venilal Vaghela
Position: Secretary General

Hindu Young Persons & Professionals
Dennis Jackson Centre, London Road, Wembley,
Middlesex
Tel: 0181-903-2965
Contact: Dr Subash Patel
Activities: Worship, resource, visits, youth, elderly,
women
Traditions: Multi-Traditional
Other Languages: Gujarati, Tamil, Bangoli, Hindi

Jignyasu Satsang Seva Trust
12 Sidmouth Road, Willesden Green, London,
NW2 5JX (h)
Tel: 0181-459-4466 **Fax:** 0181-459-4000
Contact: Shree Rambapa
Activities: Worship, religious, youth, elderly, inter-
faith
Traditions: Sanatanist
Other Languages: Hindi, Gujarati, Sindhi,
Punjabi

Kadwa Patidar Samaj UK
c/o 8 Mayfields, Wembley Park, Wembley,
Middlesex, HA9 9PS (h)
Tel: 0181-909-2711
Contact: Mr Suryakant A Patel
Position: Secretary

Activities: Youth, elderly, women, newsletters,
inter-faith
Traditions: Multi-Traditional
Social Groups: Kadwa Patidar
Other Languages: Gujarati, Hindi
Affiliations: Hindu Council (Brent); Patidar
Association

Kshatriya Association UK
2a Villiers Road, London, NW2 5PH
Contact: Mr Anil Mohanlal
Position: Secretary
Affiliations: Hindu Council (Brent)

Lohana Community Centre North London
28 North Way, Kingsbury, London, NW9 0RG

London Sevashram Sangha
19 Bassingham Road, Wembley, Middlesex

Maharashtra Mandal (London)
306 Dollis Hill Lane, London, NW2 6HH
Tel: 0181-450-5009

Maharashtra Mandal (London)
9 Talbot Court, Blackbird Hill, London, NW9

Mandhata Youth & Community Association
84 Swinderby Road, Wembley, Middlesex,
HA0 4SG
Tel: 0181-903-4312
Contact: Mr Bharat Patel
Position: Secretary
Affiliations: Hindu Council (Brent)

Matiya Patidar Samaj
122 East Lane, North Wembley, Middlesex,
HA0 3NL
Tel: 0181-904-2380 (h)
Contact: Mr Bipik Uka
Position: Secretary
Affiliations: Hindu Council (Brent)

**Navnat Vanik Association of the United
Kingdom**
43 Burgess Avenue, London, NW9 8TX
Tel: 0181-205-0856 (h)
Contact: Mr Bhupendra J Shah
Position: General Secretary
Affiliations: Hindu Council (Brent)

North London Lohana Community
130 Harrowdene Road, North Wembley, Middlesex

Palana Europe Society
47 Glendale Gardens, Wembley, Middlesex,
HA9 8PR
Tel: 0181-904-5760 (h)
Contact: Mr Amritlal Patel
Position: Secretary
Affiliations: Hindu Council (Brent)

Panch Gam Union
PO Box 430, Wembley, Middx

Parajiya Pattni Association
3 Adamas Close, Kingsbury, London, NW9
Tel: 0181-205-2675 (h)
Contact: Mr Kishore Pattni
Position: Secretary
Affiliations: Hindu Council (Brent)

Sanatan Seva Mandal
21 Dean Court, Wembley, Middlesex, HA0 3PU (h)
Tel: 0181-904-1759 (h) **Fax:** 0171-371-1902
Contact: Chhotalal Damji Pattni
Position: Chairperson
Traditions: Sanatanist
Other Languages: Gujarati, Hindi
Affiliations: Hindu Council (Brent); Sanatan Seva
Mandal – Dwarka India

Sarvajanik Pragati Mandal
50 Clayton Avenue, Wembley, Middlesex, HA0 4TL
Affiliations: Hindu Council (Brent)

Saurashtra Leva Patel
20 Christchurch Green, Wembley, Middlesex
Tel: 0181-903-7968 (h)
Contact: Mr Kantilal Patel
Position: President
Affiliations: Hindu Council (Brent)

SEVAK
Clifton Lodge, 12 Pasture Road, North Wembley,
Middlesex, NA0 3JD
Tel: 0181-908-0402 (h)
Contact: Mrs Kundan Gill
Position: Secretary
Affiliations: Hindu Council (Brent)

Shakti Mandir
28 Talbot Road, Wembley, Middlesex

Shavika Satsang Mandal
12 Audrey Gardens, Wembley, Middlesex
Contact: Mrs V Dharani

Shishukunj
98 Chaplin Road, London, NW2 5PR
Tel: 0181-459-1545
Contact: Mr Ashokbhai Shah
Position: President
Affiliations: Hindu Council (Brent)

Shree Bavis Gam Patidar Samaj
40 Alliance Close, off Milford Garden, Wembley,
Middlesex, HA0 2NG (h)
Tel: 0181-902-2669 (h)
Contact: Mr Rajesh B Patel
Position: Secretary
Activities: Umbrella, women
Traditions: Multi-Traditional
Movements: Swaminaryan
Other Languages: Gujarati, Hindi
Affiliations: Hindu Council (Brent); Federation of
Patidar Organisations

Shree Cutch Leva Patel Community (UK)
43 Chaplin Road, London, NW2

Shree Kadwa Patidar Samaj (UK)
55 Crummock Gardens, London, NW9 0DE

Shree Satavis Gam Patidar Samaj (Europe)
11 Woodford Place, Wembley, Middlesex, HA9 8TE

Shri Swaminarayan Temple
220-222 Willesden Lane, Brent, London,
NW2 5RG
Tel: 0181-459-4506
Contact: Mr K D Patel
Position: Secretary
Activities: Worship, resource
Traditions: Sanatanist
Movements: Swaminarayan
Other Languages: Gujarati, Hindi
Affiliations: Shree Swaminarayan Temple – Bhuj

Sojitra Samaj
36 Byron Avenue, London, NW9

Vallabhnidhi UK
80 Ealing Road, Wembley, Middlesex, HA0 4TH
Tel: 0181-903-9195
Contact: Mr Nalinikant Pandya
Position: Secretary
Affiliations: Hindu Council (Brent)

Vishwa Hindu Parishad Wembley
93 Swinderby Road, Middlesex, HA0 4SE (h)

Tel: 0181-903-2466 (h)
Contact: Vinod Wadher
Position: Secretary
Traditions: Sanatanist
Movements: Sanatan
Other Languages: Hindi, Gujarati
Affiliations: Hindu Council (Brent)

Wanza Samaj UK
7 The Leadings, Wembley Park, Middlesex,
HA9 9DT
Tel: 0181-908-0192 (h)
Contact: Mr Venilal Vaghela
Position: Secretary
Affiliations: Hindu Council (Brent)

Willesden Asian Centre
9 Victoria Mansion, Grange Road, London,
NW10 2RG
Contact: Mr Girish Mehta
Position: President
Affiliations: Hindu Council (Brent)

CAMDEN

Hindu Centre London
39 Grafton Terrace, off Malden Road, London,
NW5 4JA
Tel: 0171-485-8200 **Tel:** 0181-200-0931
Contact: Deva S Samaroo
Position: President
Activities: Worship, resource, youth, elderly,
women, newsletter, books, inter-faith
Traditions: Multi-Traditional
Movements: Arya Samaj
Other Languages: Hindi, Punjabi, Gujerati

Krishna Centre
4 Carlingford Road, London, NW3
Contact: Secretary

CROYDON

Arya Samaj Croydon
50 Morland Avenue, Croydon, Surrey, CRO 6EA
(h)
Tel: 0181-656-1835 (h)
Contact: Dr J C Sharma
Position: President
Activities: Worship, visits, inter-faith
Traditions: Vedic Dharma
Movements: Arya Samaj

Other Languages: Hindi, Punjabi, Urdu, Sanskrit
Affiliations: Arya Pratinidhi Sabha (UK); Arya
Sarvdeshik Sabha (Delhi) India

Bharatiya Sanskar Kendra
33 Goldwell Road, Thornton Heath, Croydon,
Surrey, CR4 6HZ
Tel: 0181-681-1125
Contact: Mr Nitin Mehta

Global Sanskritik Cultural Society
24 Limes Road, Croydon, Surrey, CR0 2HE
Tel: 0181-684-7298 **Fax:** 0181-239-1606
Contact: Jagan Nath Kharbanda
Position: Chair
Activities: Resource, youth, elderly, women,
newsletters, books, inter-faith
Traditions: Yoga, Vedic
Movements: Arya Samaj, Swaminarayan
Other Languages: Hindi, Urdu, Panjabi, Sanskrit
Affiliations: Croydon Ethnic Forum; National
Hindu Council; Hindu College, Bhaivir Singh
Sadan, New Delhi, India

Hindu Sevikha Samiti (UK)
34 Croham Park, South Croydon, Surrey
Tel: 0181-681-1083
Contact: Miss Shilpa Chheda
Position: Secretary
Activities: Resource, visits, youth, women
Traditions: Multi-traditional
Other Languages: Hindi, Panjabi, Gujarati

Hindu Swayamsevak Sangh
58 Greenwood Road, Mitcham, Croydon, Surrey,
CR4 1PE
Tel: 0181-764-2805
Contact: Mr R A Shah

*Lohana Community South Croydon (Youth
Wing)*
6 Butler Hill, Wallington, South Croydon, Surrey,
CR2

Lohana Community (South London)
70 Heathfield Vale, Selsdon, Surrey, CR2 8AS
Tel: 0181-651-4170 (h)
Contact: Narendra Chotai
Position: Secretary

Lohana Union
21 Weybridge Road, Thornton Heath, Surrey

National Association of Patidar Samaj
31 Bishop's Park Road, Norbury, London,
SW16 5TX

Shree Radha Krishna Cultural Centre (ISKCON)
42 Enmore Road, South Norwood, London,
SE25 5NG
Tel: 0181-402-1814 **Tel:** 0181-764-7765 (h)
Contact: Satya Navayana das
Position: President
Activities: Worship, resource, visits, youth, elderly,
women, newsletters, books, inter-faith
Traditions: Vaishnava
Movements: Chaitanya
Other Languages: Gujarati, Hindi
Affiliations: International Society for Krishna
Consciousness

Surrey Gujarati Hindu Society
33 Galpins Road, Thornton Heath, Surrey
Tel: 0181-674-8902 (h)
Contact: Rajni Patez
Position: Secretary

Surrey Hindu Brotherhood
107 Broughton Road, Thornton Heath, Surrey

Swaminarayan Hindu Mission
9 Gonville Road, Thornton Heath, Croydon,
Surrey, CR4 6DF
Contact: Sumanbhai Patel

UK Valam Brahmin Association
68 Lucern Road, Thornton Heath, Surrey, CR4
Contact: Mr B P Vyas
Position: President
Affiliations: Hindu Council (Brent)

Vishwa Hindu Parishad
14 Southbrook Road, Norbury, London, SW16
Tel: 0181-675-6717 **Fax:** 0181-240-7411
Fax: 0181-673-5556
Contact: Mr Ramesh Jhalla
Position: Honorary Secretary
Activities: Worship, resource, umbrella, youth,
elderly, women, newsletters, books, inter-faith
Traditions: Multi-traditional
Other Languages: Hindi, Gujarati, Panjabi, Tamil

EALING

Arya Pratinidhi Sabha (UK)
69a Argyle Road, West Ealing, London, W13

Aryasamaj London
69a Argyle Road, West Ealing, London, W13 0LY
Tel: 0181-991-1732 **Tel:** 0181-569-6403
Fax: 0181-991-1732
Contact: Professor S N Bharadwaj
Position: President
Activities: Worship, visits, youth, elderly,
newsletters, inter-faith
Traditions: Vedic, Arya Samaj (Hindu)
Movements: Arya Samaj
Social Groups: Vedic dharma/tradition
Other Languages: Hindi, Punjabi, Sanskrit
Affiliations: Arya Pratinidhi Sabha
(UK);Sarvadeshik Arya Partinidhi Sabha, New
Delhi, India

Bhatia Association UK
60/62 Endsleigh Road, Southall, Middlesex,
UB2 5QN
Contact: President
Affiliations: Hindu Council (Brent)

Chovis Gam Patidar Samaj UK
69 Lancaster Road, Northolt, Middlesex, UB5 4TD
Tel: 0181-423-1986 (h)
Contact: Mr Indravadan Patel
Position: Secretary
Affiliations: Hindu Council (Brent)

Durga Ma Vidyalya
17 Elmfield Road, Southall, Middlesex
Tel: 0181-574-0016

Hindu Cultural Society Southall
82 Saxon Road, Ealing, Southall, Middlesex,
UB1 1QJ (h)
Tel: 0181-574-6079 (h)
Contact: Methta Baldev Mohan
Position: General Secretary
Activities: Youth, elderly, inter-faith
Traditions: Vedic
Movements: Arya Samaj
Other Languages: Hindi, Punjabi, Sanskrit

Middlesex Eckankar Satsang Society
124 Elthorne Avenue, Hanwell, Middlesex, W7
Contact: Mr and Mrs Grewal

Panch Gam Union (POSON UK)
17 Manor Avenue, Northolt, Middlesex, UB5 5BZ
Contact: Mr C C Patel
Position: President
Affiliations: Hindu Council (Brent)

Shree Baba Balaknathji Temple
51 Orchard Road, Southall, Middlesex

Shree Ram Mandir
22 King Street, Southall, Middlesex, UB2
Tel: 0181-574-5376
Contact: Mrs S Whig
Position: Trustee/co-ordinator

Shree Sanatan Dharma Mandal
84 Northcote Avenue, Southall, Middlesex

Shree Sanatan Dharma Mandal
125 Cranleigh Gardens, Southall, Middlesex

Shree Sorathia Prajapati Youth Mandal (Southall)
162 Hambrough Road, Southall, Middlesex

Shree Sorthia Prajapati Community (Southall)
14 Hartington Road, Southall, Middlesex,
UB2 5AU

Shri Krishan Sewa Ashram
15 Elmfield Road, Southall, Middlesex
Tel: 0181-571-6931

Vishwa Hindu Kendra
2 Lady Margaret Road, Southall, Middlesex,
UB1 2RA
Tel: 0181-574-3870 **Tel:** (h)
Contact: Mr Ram Prakash Verma
Position: General Secretary
Activities: Worship, resource, visits, youth
Traditions: Sanatanist
Other Languages: Hindi, Punjabi, Gujarati

Kalaniketan
31 Horsenden Crescent, Greenford, Middlesex,
UB6
Tel: 0181-422-7647 (h)
Contact: Mr Mansukh Unadkat
Position: Secretary
Affiliations: Hindu Council (Brent)

United Sports Club
77 Bilton Road, Perivale, Greenford, Middlesex,
UB6 7BB

Tel: 0181-998-4609 (h)
Contact: Mrs Taraben Patel
Position: Secretary
Affiliations: Hindu Council (Brent)

ENFIELD

Bhadran Bandhu Samaj (UK)
2 Connaught Gardens, London, N13

Krishna Yoga Mandir
c/o 61 Churchbury Road, Enfield, Middlesex,
EN1 3HP (h)
Tel: 0181-363-9187 (h)
Contact: Pandit Keshava C Krishnatreya
Position: Founder Trustee
Activities: Worship, resource, elderly, inter-faith
Traditions: Multi-Traditional
Movements: Krinvanto, Sanaatanaaryam
Other Languages: Hindi, Sanskrit

GREENWICH

Greenwich Gujarati Samaj
78a Sandy Hill Road, Woolwich, London,
SE18 7AZ

Greenwich Hindu Temple (Mandir)
Greenwich Hindu Temple, 63-67 Bannockburn
Road, London, SE18 1ET
Tel: 0181-854-4566
Contact: Mrs Vidya Misra
Position: Scretary
Activities: Worship, resource, visits, youth, elderly,
women, newsletters, inter-faith
Traditions: Sanatanist
Movements: Sanatan
Other Languages: Hindi, Punjabi, Gujarati,
Bengali

Hindu Mandir
51 Crescent Road, Plumstead, London, SE18
Tel: 0181-855-1148

Hindu Swayamsevak Sangh
Woolwich Branch, 27 Vicarage Park, Plumstead,
London, SE18
Tel: 0181-854-4143

Rama Sri Krishna
76 Herbert Road, Plumstead, London, SE18

Shree Kutch Satsang Swaminarayan Temple

St Margaret's Grove, Plumstead, London, SE18 7RL
Tel: 0181-855-0823 **Tel:** 0181-317-1309 (h)
Contact: Dr Ravji Dhanji Pindoria
Position: Chair
Activities: Worship, resource, visits, youth, elderly,
women, newsletters, books, inter-faith
Traditions: Sanatanist
Movements: Swaminaryan
Social Groups: Kutchi-Gujarati
Other Languages: Gujarati, Hindi, Kutchi
Affiliations: Shree Swaminarayan Temple Bhut
Kutch India

South East Hindu Association Hindu Temple

5 Anglesea Avenue, London, SE18 6EH
Tel: 0181-854-4906 **Tel:** 0181-310-6482 (h)
Contact: R P Gupta
Position: Secretary
Traditions: Multi-Traditional
Movements: Sanatan Dharam Hindu Temple
Other Languages: Hindi, Gujarati, Punjabi

HACKNEY

Hackney Gujarati Samaj

22 Lynmouth Road, London, N2 6XL

Hackney Hindu Council

498 Kingsland Road, London, E4

HAMMERSMITH AND FULHAM

London Sevashram Sangha

99a Devonport Road, Shepherds Bush, London,
W12 8PB
Tel: 0181-723-4257 **Fax:** 0181-726-4257
Contact: Swami Nirliptananda
Position: Secretary
Activities: Worship, resource, visits, youth,
newsletters, books, inter-faith
Traditions: Multi-Traditional
Movements: Bharat Sevashram Sangha
Other Languages: Hindi, Bengali, Gujarati
Affiliations: Bharat Sevashram Sangha

Mohyal Community Association (UK) London

84b Telephone Place, London, SW6 1TL
Tel: 0171-385-8592 (h)
Contact: Mr S L Mehta
Position: Secretary
Activities: Youth, elderly, women, newsletters

Traditions: Non-religious organisation
Social Groups: Mohyal Brahmin
Other Languages: Hindi, Punjabi
Affiliations: General Moyhal Sabha Registered

Shree Akshar Purushottam Youth Organisation

143 Askew Road, London, W12

HARINGEY

Brittania Hindu (Shiva) Temple Trust

Highgate Hill Murugan Temple, 200a Archway
Road, Highgate, London, N6 5BA
Tel: 0181-348-9835 **Tel:** 0181-998-1703 (h)
Fax: 0181-348-9835
Contact: Kanthiah Ranganathan
Position: Chairperson
Activities: Worship, resource, visits, youth, elderly,
women, inter-faith
Traditions: Shaiva
Movements: Veda Agama
Social Groups: Tamil
Other Languages: Tamil, Hindi, Gujarati
Affiliations: National Council of Hindu Temples

HARROW

Brahmin Society - North London

17 Argyll Road, Edgware, Middlesex, HA8 5HB
Tel: 0181-951-3840 (h)
Contact: Mr Kamlesh Rajyaguru
Position: Secretary
Affiliations: Hindu Council (Brent)

Cutch Social & Cultural Society

26 St Paul's Avenue, Kenton, Harrow, Middlesex,
HA3 9PS
Tel: 0181-204-6488 (h)
Contact: Mr Jethalal Savani
Position: Secretary
Affiliations: Hindu Council (Brent)

Harrow Lohana Education Group

287a Kenton Lane, Harrow, Middlesex, HA3 8RR
(h)

Hindu Cultural Society

15 Village Way, Pinner, Middlesex, HA5 5AB
Tel: 0181-248-5277 (h)
Contact: Sudershan Kumar Bedi
Position: Secretary
Activities: Worship, resource, youth, elderly,
women, newsletters, inter-faith

Traditions: Multi-Traditional
Movements: Arya Samaj
Other Languages: Hindi, Punjabi, Urdu

Hindu Cultural Society (Youth Wing)
219 The Mall, Harrow, Middlesex, HA3 9TX

Hindu Swayamsewak Sangh
31 Devonshire Road, Harrow, Middlesex, HA1 4LS
Tel: 0181-863-1042
Contact: Mr Jayantibhai Patel
Position: Secretary
Affiliations: Hindu Council (Brent)

Kadwa Patidar Samaj (UK)
41 The Ridgeway, Kenton, Harrow, HA0 0lN

Kenton Satsang Mandal
15 Kenton Lane, Kenton, HA3 8UH

Kingsbury Asian Elders Group
305 Byron Road, Wealdstone, Harrow, Middlesex, HA3 7TE
Tel: 0181-427-2594 **Tel:** 0181-863-3847 (h)
Contact: Mr Dhirubhai Lavingia
Position: Secretary
Affiliations: Hindu Council (Brent)

Kutch Leva Patel Community
58 Lamorna Grove, Stanmore, Middlesex
Tel: 0181-951-3405 (h)
Contact: Mr Virjibhai Varsani
Position: Secretary
Affiliations: Hindu Council (Brent)

Kutch Madhapar Karyalaya UK
31 Ruskin Gardens, Kenton, Harrow, Middlesex, HA3 9PX
Contact: Mr Harilal Murji Halai
Position: Chairman
Affiliations: Hindu Council (Brent)

Lohana Community North London
50 Argyle Road, North Harrow, Middlesex, HA2 7AJ
Contact: Mr Jamnadas Raithatha
Position: Secretary
Affiliations: Hindu Council (Brent)

Maharashtra Mandal (London)
59 Preston Hill, Harrow, Middlesex

Malawi Hindu Association
67 Orchard Grove, Edgware, Middlesex, HA8 5BN

Tel: 0181-952-4685 (h)
EMail: 100600, 1245@compuserve.com
Contact: Mr K N Thakrar
Position: Chairman
Activities: Resource, youth, elderly, women, newsletter
Traditions: Sanatanist
Languages: Gujrati, Hindi
Affiliations: Hindu Council (Brent); Brent Indian Association; National Congress of Gujrati Organisations

Milip Mandal
21 Kynaston Wood, Harrow, Middlesex

Navnat Vanik Mandal
10 Radley Gardens, Kenton, Harrow, Middlesex

Prajapati Association
30 Morley Crescent West, Stanmore, Middlesex, HA7 2LW
Tel: 0181-907-5086
Contact: Mr Jayantilal Mistry
Position: Secretary
Affiliations: Hindu Council (Brent)

Pushtimargiya Vaishnav - Mahila Samaj
Charnwood, 147 Uxbridge Road, Harrow, Middlesex, HA3 6DG
Tel: 0181-954-2142 (h)
Contact: Madhuben Somani
Position: Secretary
Affiliations: Hindu Council (Brent)

Rajput Seva Samaj
3 Darcy Gardens, Kenton, Harrow, Middlesex
Contact: Rasik Vaghel
Position: President
Affiliations: Hindu Council (Brent)

Ram Nivas - Gujrat Vaishnav Mandal
26 Greenhill Way, Harrow, Middlesex

Shree Sakhi Mandal
101 Coles Crescent, South Harrow, HA2 0TR

Shree Sattar Gam Patidar Samaj (UK)
10 Newquay Crescent, Rayners Lane, Harrow, HA2 9LQ

Shri Vallabh Nidhi (UK)
59 Kingsfield Avenue, North Harrow, Middlesex, HA2 6AQ (h)
Tel: 0181-863-6384 (h)

Contact: Dev S Mahadevaiah
Position: Chairman
Activities: Worship, resource, visits, youth, elderly, women, inter-faith
Traditions: Sanatanist, Sanatan Hindu Dharma
Other Languages: Gujarati, Hindi, Bengali, Tamil
Affiliations: Brent Indian Association; National Council of Hindu Temples; Vishwa Hindu Parishad

Shree Visgam Patel Samaj UK

12 Pinner Park Gardens, Harrow, Middlesex, HA2 6LQ (h)
Tel: 0181-795-1648 **Tel:** 0181-863-7828 (h)
Contact: Ramesh F Patel
Position: President
Activities: Umbrella
Traditions: Sanatanist
Movements: Arya Samaj
Social Groups: Patidar
Other Languages: Gujarati, Hindi
Affiliations: Patidar House, Wembley - Federation of Patidar Samaj

Swaminarayan Temple

3 Vaughan Road, Harrow, Middlesex
Tel: 0181-422-3337

Vanza Society of North London

95 Northumberland Avenue, Harrow, Middlesex, HA2 7RA
Tel: 0181-866-7264
Contact: Mr Kishor Davdra
Position: Secretary
Affiliations: Hindu Council (Brent)

Young Lohana Association

106 Emsleigh Avenue, Harrow, Middlesex, HA3 8JA
Contact: Mr Sunil Radia
Position: Secretary
Affiliations: Hindu Council (Brent)

HAVERING

Hare Krishna Centre (ISKCON Romford)

24 Alexandra Road, South Hornchurch, Essex, RM13 7AA
Tel: 01708-553147
Contact: Jayadeva Das

HILLINGDON

Hindu Society

37 Stowe Crescent, Ruislip, Middlesex, HA4 7SR
Tel: 01895-676939 (h)
Contact: Dr Bholanath Bhargava
Position: Chair
Activities: Resource, media, umbrella, visits, youth, elderly, women, newsletters
Traditions: Multi-Traditional
Movements: Multi-Movement
Other Languages: Hindi, Gujarati, Punjabi, Bengali

Shree Gurjar Kshatriya Gnati Mandal (London)

50 Spencer Avenue, Hayes, Middlesex, UB4 0QY

Shree Limbachia Gnati Mandal

3 Strone Way, Yeading, Hayes, Middlesex, UB4 9RU
Contact: Mr Mahendra Solankee
Position: Secretary
Affiliations: Hindu Council (Brent)

HOUNSLOW

Hindu Cultural Society

30 Heathdale Avenue, Hounslow West, Middlesex, TW4 7HD
Tel: 0181-570-1552 (h)
Contact: S R Rattana

Hindu Swayamsevak Sangh, Vikram Shakha

5 Rosemary Avenue, Hounslow, Middlesex, TW4 7DE
Contact: Mr H Makwana

Sarvodaya Sangh

213 Wellington Road South, Hounslow, Middlesex, TW4 5HA (h)
Tel: 0181-230-3691 (h)
Contact: Mr Damjibhai Limbachia
Position: Secretary
Activities: Resource, youth
Traditions: Sanatanist
Movements: Sarvodaya
Other Languages: Gujarati, Hindi
Affiliations: Hindu Council (Brent)

Shree Lohana Youth Mandal (Southall)

116 St Stephen's Road, Hounslow, Middlesex

Shree Sorathia Prajapati Community
80 Berkeley Avenue, Hounslow, Middlesex,
TW4 6LA
Contact: Mr N G Pankhania
Position: Honorary Secretary

Shree Sorathia Prajapati Youth Community
12 Laburnam Road, Hounslow, Middlesex
Tel: 0181-577-0986

Vedic Mission
15 Spring Grove Crescent, Hounslow, Middlesex

Vedic Mission (Arya Samaj) London
14 Penderel Road, Hounslow, Middlesex

Vishwa Hindu Parishad (UK)
26 Osterley Avenue, Isleworth, Middlesex,
TW7 4QF

Vishwa Hindu Parishad/Sanatana International (UK)
53 Manor Avenue, Hounslow, Middlesex,
TW4 7JN
Tel: 0181-572-2784 (h)
Contact: Mr Gian Gaur
Position: Secretary

Visva Adhyatmik Sanathan
48 Sutton Lane, Hounslow, Middlesex, TW3 3BD
Tel: 0181-572-9227
Contact: Balraj Kumar Sidher
Position: Secretary
Activities: Worship, youth, elderly, women, books, inter-faith
Traditions: Multi-Traditional
Other Languages: Hindi, Gujarati, Punjabi, German

West London Hindu Temple Trust
15 Waye Avenue, Cranford, Hounslow, Middlesex

ISLINGTON

Islington Hindu Association
83b Hartham Road, Islington, London, N7 7BP

Sanatan Hindu Mandir
102 Junction Road, Archway, London, N19 5GY
Tel: 0171-263-6269
Contact: Mahendrabhai Patel
Position: Secretary
Activities: Worship, visits, youth, elderly, women
Traditions: Multi-Traditional

Movements: Sanatan
Social Groups: Patidar
Other Languages: Gujarati, Hindi, Punjabi
Affiliations: National Council of Hindu Temples

KENSINGTON AND CHELSEA

Shanti Sadan
29 Chepstow Villas, Notting Hill Gate, London,
W11 3DR
Tel: 0171-727-7846
Fax: 0171-792-9817
Contact: Anthony Collins
Position: Secretary
Activities: Resource newsletters, books
Traditions: Yoga of Self-Knowledge

KINGSTON-UPON-THAMES

Hindu Bai Bhawan
45 Church Meadow, Long Ditton, Surbiton,
KT6 5EP

Sarvoday Hindu Association
c/o 243 Raeburn Ave, Kingston-upon-Thames,
Surrey, KT5 3DF
Tel: 0181-390-3646
Contact: Mr H Desai

LAMBETH

Anavil Association (UK)
44 Kestrel Avenue, London, SE24 0EB

Caribbean Hindu Society
16 Ostade Road, Brixton Hill, Lambeth, London,
SW2 2BB
Tel: 0181-674-0755 **Tel:** 0181-690-3646 (h)
Fax: 0181-674-0755
Contact: Mr Y N Singh
Position: Co-ordinator
Activities: Worship, resource, youth, elderly, newsletters
Traditions: Sanatanist
Other Languages: Hindi

Hindu Mission
1 Hepworth Road, London, SW16

MERTON

Audichya Gadhia Brahma Samaj Society
42 Parkside Gardens, London, SW19 5ET

Audichya Gadia Brahma Samaj Society (London)
85 Toynbee Road, Wimbledon, London, SW20 8SJ

Hindu Association of Great Britain
8 Ashen Grove, London, SW19

Hindu Association of Great Britain
76 Grand Drive, Raynes Park, London, SW20

National Association of Patidar Samaj
22 Avenue Road, London, SW16 4HL

Shree Ganapathy Temple
125-133 Effra Road, Wimbledon, London, SW19 8PU
Tel: 0181-542-4141   **Tel:** 0181-946-1140 (h)
Fax: 0181-542-0029
Contact: Sinnathurai Ratna Singham
Position: Chief Co-ordinator
Activities: Worship, resource, youth, elderly, women
Traditions: Shaiva
Other Languages: Tamil, Hindi, French, Singhalese
Affiliations: National Council of Hindu Temples

NEWHAM

Aarti Society
37 Dunbar Road, Forest Gate, London, E7 9HH
Tel: 0181-472-2718
Contact: Mrs R J Patel

Balak Mahan Vidhyala
102 Osborne Road, Forest Gate, London, E7 0PL
Tel: 0181-519-0619
Contact: Mr B S Gahir

East London & Essex Brahma Samaj
Upton Centre, Off Bishops Avenue, Claude Road, Plaistow, London, E13 0PU

Gujarat Welfare Association
141 Plashet Road, London, E13 0RA

Gujarati Ladies Club
127 Plashet Road, London, E6 (h)
Tel: 0181-54-0939 (h)
Contact: Mrs Shanta Gujjar
Position: President
Activities: Worship, resource, umbrella, visits, elderly, women

Traditions: Shaiva
Movements: Pushtimargi
Social Groups: All Hindus
Other Languages: Gujarati, Hindi
Affiliations: Gujarat Welfare Association

Hindu Centre
5 Cedars Road, Stratford, London, E15 4NE
Tel: 0181-534-8879
Contact: Mr Lal Aggarwal
Position: Secretary
Activities: Worship, visits, youth, elderly
Traditions: Sanatanist
Movements: Sanatan Dharam
Other Languages: Hindi, Gujarati, Punjabi, Urdu

Hindu Swayamsevak Sangh (Newham)
20 Sprowston Road, Forest Gate, London, E7 8HZ
Tel: 0181-471-4647 (h)
Contact: Mr H Bhudia

Jai Amba Mata Mandal
Upton Centre, Claude Road, Plaistow, London, E13 0PU

Lakshmi Narayana Trust
272 High Street North, Manor Park, London, E12 6SA
Tel: 0181-552-5082   **Tel:** 0181-502-6163 (h)
Contact: Dr P Alagrajah
Position: Chairperson
Traditions: Vaishnava
Other Languages: Tamil, Malayalam, Telugu

Lohana Community East London
110 Howards Road, Plaistow, London, E13 8AY
Contact: Mr Swesh Tejwaha

London Sri Murugan Temple
78 Church Road, Manor Park, London, E12 6AF
Tel: 0181-478-8433
Contact: Mr Sampathkumer

Mahalakshmi Temple
272 High Street North, Manor Park, London, E12 6SA
Tel: 0181-552-5082   **Tel:** 0181-502-6163 (h)
Contact: Dr P A Alagrajah
Position: Chairperson
Activities: Worship
Traditions: Vaishnava
Other Languages: Tamil, Malayalam, Telugu

Shree Kutch Leva Patel Community UK (Newham)
35 Heigham Road, London, E6 2JL
Tel: 0181-471-4760
Contact: Mrs V Patel
Position: Secretary

Shree Kutch Satsang Swaminarayan Temple
22-24 Shaftesbury Road, Forest Gate, London, E7 8PD
Contact: Mr Shamji K Vekaria
Position: President
Activities: Worship, visits, youth, elderly, women
Movements: Swaminaryan
Other Languages: Gujarati, Hindi

Shree Narayana Guru Mission of the UK
16 Barking Road, London, E6 3BP
Tel: 0181-471-0720 **Tel:** 0181-550-1821 (h)
Contact: Mr Subash Sadasivan
Position: General Secretary
Activities: Visits, inter-faith
Traditions: Atmopadesa Sadakam
Other Languages: Malayalam

Shree Swaminarayan Hindu Mission UK (Newham)
1a Lucas Avenue, Plaistow, London, E13 0QP
Tel: 0181-472-3795 (h)
Contact: Mr S C Amin
Position: Secretary

Swaminarayan Hindu Mission, East London
Upton Centre, Claude Road, London, E13 (h)
Tel: 0181-552-8646 (h)
Contact: Shivaprasad C Trivedi
Position: Secretary
Activities: Worship, youth, elderly, women, inter-faith
Traditions: Sanatanist
Movements: Swaminaryan
Other Languages: Gujarati, Hindi
Affiliations: Swaminarayan Hindu Mission, Neasden

Upton Community Centre
Upton Park, London, E13 0PU
Tel: 0181-552-8647
Contact: Mr Hamant

Vishwa Hindu Parishad (Newham Branch)
518 Green Street, Plaistow, London, E13 9DA
Contact: Mr D P Sharma

REDBRIDGE

Brentwood Hindu Cultural Association
72 Billet Road, Chadwell Heath, Romford, Essex

Hindu Swayamsevak Sangh (UK)
95 Coventry Road, Ilford, Essex, IG1 4QT

London Brahma Samaj
3 Glenovern Lodge, Lansdowne Road, South Woodford, London, E18

London Hindu Sangham
398 Thorold Road, Ilford, Essex, IG1 4HF

National Association of Patidar Samaj (E London)
53 Green Lane, Ilford, Essex

Vishwa Hindu Parishad
Ilford Hindu Centre, 43 Cleveland Road, Ilford, Essex, 141 1EE
Tel: 0181-553-5471 **Tel:** 0181-598-8611 (h)
Fax: 0181-518-5499
Contact: Mr Raj Kumar Chanan
Position: Chair
Activities: Worship, resource, media, visits, youth, elderly, women, newsletters, inter-faith
Traditions: Sanatanist
Other Languages: Hindi, Punjabi, Gujarati
Affiliations: Vishwa Hindu Parishad

SOUTHWARK

Southwark Hindu Centre
24 Mayard Road, Benhill Road, London, SE5 8AF

Southwark Hindu Cultural Community Group
42 Southwark Street, London, SE1 1U

SUTTON

Surrey Satsang Samiti
1 Newlyn House, Benhill Wood Road, Sutton, Surrey, SM1 HHE
Tel: 0181-643-0388
Contact: Jyoti Bhoyrul

Sutton Subrang
131 Church Hill Road, Cheam, Surrey, SM3 8LJ

TOWER HAMLETS

Tower Hamlets Sanatan Association
37 Noble Court, Cable Street, London, E1 8HS
Tel: 0171-481-9707 **Tel:** 0181-5502846 (h)
Contact: Mr P K R Chowdhury
Position: General Secretary

WALTHAM FOREST

Bavis Gam Patidar Samaj UK
76 Leslie Road, Leytonstone, London, E11 4HG

Hindu Cultural Association
129 New Road, Chingford, London, E4 9EZ

Leuva Patidar Samaj of London
109 Gosport Road, Walthamstow, London,
E17 7LX (h)
Tel: 0181-520-0268 (h)
Contact: Mr Bhikubhai P Patel
Position: Secretary
Activities: Resource, youth, newsletters
Traditions: Vaishnava
Movements: Arya Samaj
Social Groups: Leuva Patidar
Other Languages: Gujarati
Affiliations: Hindu Council (Brent), Leuva Patidar
Samaj (SNB) UK

Shree Vallabh Nidhi UK
159/161 Whipps Cross Road, Leytonstone,
London, Waltham Forest, E11 1NP
Tel: 0181-989-2034
Contact: Rameshchandra Gordhambhai
Position: Secretary/Treasurer
Activities: Visits
Traditions: Sanatanist
Movements: Pushtimargi
Other Languages: Gujarati, Hindi

Shri Narthi Sanatan Hindu Mandir
159-161 Whipps Cross Road, Leytonstone,
London, E11

WANDSWORTH

Brahma Samaj (Society) South London
131 Tranmere Road, Earslfield, London,
SW18 3QP
Tel: 0181-947-4709 (h)
Contact: L D Bhatt
Position: President

Gujarat Samaj
35 Manville Road, London, SW17

Gujarati Brahma Samaj
294 Franciscan Road, London, SW17
Tel: 0181-672-1918
Contact: Mr J Thaker

Hindu Society
673 Garrett Lane, London, SW17 0PB
Tel: 0181-944-0251
Contact: Rajendra Singh
Position: Secretary
Activities: Worship, resource, youth, elderly,
women, newsletters, inter-faith
Traditions: Sanatanist
Other Languages: Hindi, Punjabi

Lohana Community Association of Wandsworth
c/o 94 Croydon Road, Beckenham, Kent

Radha-Krishna Temple
33 Balham High Road, London, SW12
Tel: 0181-673-6437
Contact: Secretary

Rajput Dhobi Youth
127 Hebdon Road, London, SW17 7NL
Contact: Mr Umesh Solanki
Position: Secretary
Affiliations: Hindu Council (Brent)

Satyananda Yoga Centre
70 Thurleigh Road, London, SW12 8UD
Tel: 0181-673-4869 **Fax:** 0181-675-4080
Contact: Swami Pragyamurti Saraswati
Position: Director
Activities: Meditation, resource, umbrella, youth,
elderly, women, newsletters, inter-faith
Traditions: Yoga
Movements: Bihar School of Yoga and Swami
Satyananda Saraswati
Affiliations: Bihar School of Yoga, India

Virsad Union of UK
273 Balham High Road, London, SW17 7BD

Wandsworth Asian Community Centre
57-59 Trinity Road, Tooting Bec, London,
SW17 7SD
Tel: 0181-871-7774
Contact: Centre Manager
Activities: Youth, elderly, women

Traditions: Multi-Traditional
Other Languages: Gujarati, Urdu, Punjabi

WESTMINSTER, CITY OF

Navkala
21 Hanway Place, London, W1

Radha Krishna Temple
10 Soho Street, London, W1V 5DA
Tel: 0171-437-3662 **Tel:** 0171-380-0749 (h)
Fax: 0171-439-1127
EMail: bhagavat@moose.co.uk
Contact: Ranchor Prime
Position: Secretary
Activities: Worship, visits, inter-faith
Traditions: Vaishnava
Movements: Chaitanya
Affiliations: National Council of Hindu Temples;
International Society for Krishna Consciousness

SOUTH EAST
City, Town or Local Bodies

Basildon Hindu Association
69 Wickham Place, Basildon, Essex
Contact: Mr Amalani
Position: President

Maha Lakshmi Satsang
60 Allen Road, Beckenham, Kent, BR3 4NP (h)
Tel: 0181-650-3728 (h)
Contact: Ramesh Charan
Position: Secretary
Activities: Resource, youth, elderly, women,
newsletters, books, inter-faith
Traditions: Sanatanist
Other Languages: Hindi

Gujarati Mitra Mandal Bedford
11 Ullswater Close, Kempston, Bedford,
Bedfordshire, MK42 8JX (h)
Tel: 0181-854911 (h) **Fax:** 01234-3000
EMail: 6-Shah4@ti.com
Contact: Navinchandra Shah
Position: Member
Activities: Resource, media, umbrella, visits, youth,
elderly, women, newsletters, inter-faith
Traditions: Multi-Traditional
Other Languages: Gujarati, Hindi, French
Affiliations: Gujarati Sahitya Academy-Wembley

Hindu Centre
78 Shakespeare Road, Bedford, MK40 2DN

Hindu Society of Bedford
105 Wentworth Drive, Bedford, Bedfordshire
Contact: Dr Khiani

Punjabi Hindu Society, Bedford
20 Hawk Drive, Bedford, Bedfordshire, MK41 7JE
(h)
Contact: Jai Shankar Joshi
Position: Secretary
Activities: Visits, youth, elderly, women, inter-faith
Traditions: Multi-Traditional
Other Languages: Gujarati, Hindi, Punjabi
Affiliations: Bedford Race Equality Council

Hindu Community
21 Woodlane Road, Brighton, East Sussex,
BN3 6HB

Hindu Union
136 Phyllis Avenue, Peacehaven, Brighton, East
Sussex, BN10 7FN

Hindu Women's Group
259 Preston Drove, Brighton, East Sussex,
BN1 7FN

North Harrow Satsang Mandal
Shri Kunj, 121 Chiltern Avenue, Bushey,
Hertfordshire, WD2 3QE (h)
Tel: 0181-950-1172 (h)
Contact: Mrs Manorama Ghelani
Position: Main Organiser
Activities: Elderly
Traditions: Vaishnava
Movements: Pushtimargi
Other Languages: Gujarati
Affiliations: Hindu Council

Geeta Ashram
Greenacres, Heathbourne Road, Bushey Heath,
Hertfordshire, WD2 1PB

Medway Hindu Centre
71 Ernest Road, Chatham, Kent, ME4 5PT (h)
Tel: 01634-402843 (h)
Contact: Mr Ramanbhai B Patel
Position: President
Activities: Resource, visits, youth, elderly, women,
inter-faith
Traditions: Sanatanist

Movements: Vedic Culture
Social Groups: Gujarat Samaj, Patidar, Lohana, All Artisan Castes
Other Languages: Gujarati, Hindi, Punjabi, Swahili
Affiliations: National Congress of Gujarati Organisations

Gurjar Hindu Union
29 Livingstone Road, Tilgate, Crawley, West Sussex, RH10 5NS (h)
Tel: 01293-548151 (h) **Fax:** 01293-530105
Contact: Mr Umesh Nayee
Position: Honorary Secretary
Activities: Worship, resource, visits, youth, elderly, women, newsletters, inter-faith
Traditions: Sanatanist
Other Languages: Gujarati
Affiliations: National Council of Hindu Temples

Swaminarayan Hindu Mission
17 Mendip Walk, West Green, Crawley, West Sussex, RH11 7JZ
Tel: 01293-526825
Contact: Dhirajbhai K Patel

Medway Hindu Sabha
361 Canterbury Street, Gillingham, Kent, ME7 5XS
Tel: 01642-575645
Contact: Mr S L Gupta
Position: Honorary Secretary

Hindu Association Hastings
Hastings, East Sussex c/o 4 Collington Mansions, Collington Avenue, Bexhill-on-Sea, East Sussex, TN39 3PU (h)
Tel: 01424-220232 (h) **Fax:** 01424-220232
Contact: Mrs Jayshree S Patel
Position: President
Activities: Resource, youth, women, newsletters
Traditions: Multi-Traditional
Social Groups: All Hindus
Other Languages: Gujarati

Hindu Women's Group
Mrs R Patel, 68 Westbourne Gardens, Hove, East Sussex, BN3 5PQ (h)
Contact: Mrs Rama Patel
Position: Treasurer
Activities: Umbrella, youth, elderly, women
Traditions: Sanatanist, Multi-Tradition

Movements: Sanatanist
Other Languages: Gujarati, Hindi

Hove Hindu Community
59 Addison Road, Hove, East Sussex, BN3 1TQ

Bardai Brahmin Samaj London
79 Buttermere Place, Leavesden, Hertfordshire, WD2 7DW
Tel: 01923-670911 (h)
Contact: Mr Bipin Thanki
Position: Secretary
Affiliations: Hindu Council (Brent)

Southend & District Hindu Association
10 Stonehill Close, Leigh-on-Sea, Essex, SS9 4AZ
Tel: 01702-348944, Ext: 6408,
Tel: 01702-524851 (h)
Contact: Mr M D Solanki

Athia Samaj
120 Benson Close, Luton, Bedfordshire, LU3 3QR
Contact: Mr Dhirajlal Makan
Position: Secretary
Affiliations: Hindu Council (Brent)

Geeta Ashram, Geeta Nivas
147 Old Bedford Road, Luton, Bedfordshire, LU2 7EF (h)
Tel: 01582-421990 **Fax:** 01582-421990
Contact: Mr Vinod B Tailor
Activities: Worship, youth, women, books, inter-faith
Traditions: Vaishnava
Other Languages: Hindi
Affiliations: International Federation of Geeta Ashrams New Delhi India

Luton Bharatiya Association
78 Stanton Road, Luton, Bedfordshire, LU4 0BJ

Satsang Mandal
56 Leyhill Drive, Luton, Bedfordshire

Shree Mandhata Mandal
44 Grasmere Road, Luton, Bedfordshire

Shree Sanatan Seva Samaj
Hindu Mandir/Hindu Centre, Hereford Road, Lewsey Farm, Luton, Bedfordshire, LU4 0PS
Tel: 01582-663414 **Tel:** 01582-27704 (h)
Contact: Madhusudan Mohanlal Gandhi
Position: Chair

Activities: Worship, resource, visits, youth, elderly, women, newsletters, inter-faith
Traditions: Sanatanist, Multi-Traditional
Other Languages: Gujarati, Hindi
Affiliations: National Council of Hindu Temples; National Congress of Gujarati Organisations

Milton Keynes Hindu Association
8 Sandywell Drive, Downhead Park, Milton Keynes, Buckinghamshire, MK15 9AJ (h)
Tel: 01908-674421 (h)
Contact: Mr Ashok Patel
Position: Secretary
Other Languages: Gujarati, Hindi

Berkshire Mandir
c/o St Bartholomew Church, 72 London Road, Reading, Berkshire, RG1 5AS
Tel: 01734-751291
Contact: Mr R Mall

Gujrat Samaj
8 Willowside, Woodley, Reading, Berkshire, RG5 4HJ (h)
Tel: 0118-969-7722 (h)
Contact: Mr T K Desai
Position: General Secretary
Activities: Resource, elderly, women, inter-faith
Traditions: Sanatanist, Multi-Traditional
Other Languages: Gujarati, Hindi

Reading Hindu Temple
343 Wokingham Road, Reading, Berkshire, RG6 2EB
Tel: 01734-750356
Contact: Secretary

Essex Hindu Society
72 Billet Road, Romford, Essex, RM6 5PP
Tel: 0181-599-7106
Contact: Shri V Chuttoo
Position: President

Hindu Community Service
37 Stowe Crescent, Ruislip, HA4 7SR

Hindu Cultural Society of Slough
Hindu Temple, Keele Drive, Chalvey, Slough, Berkshire, SL1 2XU
Tel: 01753-790135 **Tel:** 01753-673663 (h)
Contact: Vinay Kumar Anand
Position: President

Activities: Worship, visits, youth, elderly, women, inter-faith
Traditions: Sanatanist
Movements: Sanatan
Other Languages: Hindi, Gujarati, Punjabi
Affiliations: National Council of Hindu Temples

Sarvodaya Bhajan Mandal
34 Wellesley Road, Slough, Berkshire

Saurashtra Leva Patel Samaj
87 Kendal Drive, Slough, Berkshire

Serena Memorial Hall
Burlington Road, Slough, Berkshire

Hampshire Hindu Welfare Association
7 Bassett Court, Southampton, Hampshire

Lohana Mahajan
37 Water Lane, Totton, Southampton, Hampshire

Vedic Society Hindu Temple
75-195 Radcliffe Road, Northam, Southampton, Hampshire, SO14 0PS
Tel: 01703-632275
Contact: Secretary
Activities: Worship, youth, elderly, women, newsletters, inter-faith
Traditions: Sanatanist
Other Languages: Hindi, Punjabi, Gujarati
Affiliations: National Council of Hindu Temples

Vishwa Hindu Parishad
6 Bassett Crescent West, Bassett, Southampton, Hampshire, SO16 7DZ (h)
Tel: 01703 790770
Contact: Mr Mahesh Sareen
Position: Honorary Secretary
Activities: Resource, umbrella, youth, elderly, women, inter-faith
Traditions: Sanatanist
Movements: Arya Samaj
Other Languages: Hindi, English
Affiliations: Vedic Society of Southampton; Vishwa Hindu Parishad UK

Swaminarayan Hindu Mission
9 Gonville Road, Thorton Heath, Surrey, CR7 6DE

Savodhay Hindu Association
104 Largewood Avenue, Tolworth, Surrey

Shree Prajapati Association UK
28 Colne Way, Watford, Hertfordshire,
WD2 4NA (h)
Contact: Jayantilal Mistry
Position: Treasurer
Activities: Youth, elderly, women, newsletters,
inter-faith
Traditions: Sanatanist
Movements: Arya Samaj
Social Groups: Surti
Other Languages: Gujarati, Hindi
Affiliations: Hindu Council (Brent); Vishwa
Hindu Parishad

Vedic Centre of Understanding
63 Jubilee Road, Watford, Hertfordshire

Watford Hindu Group
32 Orchard Drive, Watford, Hertfordshire,
WD1 3DY (h)
Tel: 01923-229090 (h)
EMail: JOSHI@NCA.BBC.CO.UK.
Contact: Yogesh Joshi
Position: Secretary
Activities: Resource, youth, elderly, women, inter-faith
Traditions: Sanatanist
Other Languages: Gujarati, Hindi, Punjabi

Greenwich Gujarati Samaj
46 Lulworth Road, Welling, Kent

Swaminarayan Hindu Mission
CIPRICE, Fanton Chase, Wickford, Essex,
SS11 8QX
Tel: 01268-765188
Contact: Bipinbhai Desai

National Association of Patidar Samaj
77 Brockenhurst Avenue, Worcester Park, Surrey,
KT4 7RH

SOUTH WEST
City, Town or Local Bodies

Hindu Temple
163b Church Road, Redfield, Bristol, Greater
Bristol, BS5 9LA
Tel: 0117-935-1007
Contact: Batook Pandya
Position: Chairperson
Activities: Worship, resource, visits, youth, elderly,
women, newsletters, inter-faith

Traditions: Sanatan Dharma
Other Languages: Gujarati, Hindi, Punjabi
Affiliations: National Council of Hindu Temples

ISKCON Bristol
Bristol, Greater Bristol, c/o New Jagannath Puri,
Alberta Cottage, Bristol Road, Wraxall, Somerset,
BS19 1BN
Tel: 01275-853788 (h)
Contact: Minaketanarama dasa
Position: President
Activities: Worship, resource, visits, youth,
newsletters, books, inter-faith
Traditions: Vaishnava
Movements: Chaitanya
Other Languages: Hindi, Gujarati

Hindu Community Centre
64 Swindon Road, Cheltenham, Gloucestershire,
GL50 4AY
Tel: 01242-584250
Contact: President

Indian Association (Cheltenham)
Hindu Community Centre, 64 Swindon Road,
Cheltenham, Gloucestershire, GL50 4AY
Tel: 01242-584250
Contact: Secretary
Activities: Worship, resource, visits, youth, elderly,
women, inter-faith
Traditions: Sanatanist, Shaiva
Other Languages: Gujarati, Hindi
Affiliations: National Council of Hindu Temples

Gloucester Hindu Centre
15 Cherston Court, Barnwood, Gloucester,
Gloucestershire, GL4 7LE
Tel: 01452-653314
Contact: Mr Lallu Patel
Position: Chair

Hindu Centre
81 London Road, Gloucester, Gloucestershire,
GL1 3HH

Shree Kadwa Patidar Samaj (UK)
148 West Way, Broadstone, Poole, Dorset,
BH18 9LN

Hindu Samaj
33 Okebourne Park, Liden, Swindon, Wiltshire,
SN3 6AH (h)
Tel: 01793-722447 (h)

Contact: Mr Prakash Naranbhai Patel
Position: Secretary
Activities: Resource, visits, youth, elderly, women
Traditions: Multi-Traditional
Other Languages: Gujarati, Hindi, Punjabi

Shree Lohana Mahajan
12 Thackeray Close, Liden, Swindon, Wiltshire

NORTHERN IRELAND

City, Town or Local Bodies

Hindu Mandir
Clifton Street, Carlisle Circus, Belfast, County
Antrim

*International Society for Krishna Consciousness
(ISKCON)*
Brooklands, 140 Upper Dunmurray Lane, Belfast,
County Antrim, BT17 0HE
Tel: 01232-620530
Contact: Padma-malini devi dasi
Position: Temple President
Activities: Worship, visits, women, newsletters,
books, inter-faith
Traditions: Vaishnava
Movements: Chaitanya
Affiliations: National Council of Hindu Temples

Radha Krishna Temple
49 Malone Road, Belfast, County Antrim,
BT9 6RY

Hare Krishna Monastery
Isle of Inisrath, Upper Loch Erne, nr Linaskea,
County Fermanagh, BT92 2GN
Tel: 013657-21512
Contact: Mr Tim Peter McEvitt
Position: Secretary
Activities: Worship, visits, books
Traditions: Vaishnava
Movements: Chaitanya
Other Languages: Hindi, Bengali, Russian
Affiliations: National Council of Hindu Temples

SCOTLAND

National or Regional Bodies

Gujarati Association of Scotland
189 Harvie Avenue, Newton Mearns, Glasgow,
Strathclyde, G77 6LT (h)

Tel: 0141-639-6946 (h)
Contact: Mr Anant Gandhi
Position: Treasurer
Activities: Youth, newsletters
Traditions: Multi-Traditional
Movements: Multi-Movements
Other Languages: Gujarati

ISKCON (Scotland)
Karuna Bhavan, Bankhouse Road, Lesmahagow,
Strathclyde, ML11 0ES
Tel: 01555-894790 **Fax:** 01555-894526
Contact: Prabhupada Vani Das
Position: Vice President
Activities: Worship, resource, newsletters, books
Traditions: Vaishnava
Movements: Chaitanya
Affiliations: National Council of Hindu Temples,
ISKCON (UK); International Society for Krishna
Consciousness

City, Town or Local Bodies

Tayside Hindu Cultural & Community Centre
10 Taylors Lane, Dundee, Tayside, DD2 1AQ
Tel: 01382-669652 **Tel:** 01382-779328 (h)
Contact: Dr A Munishankar
Position: Chairman
Activities: Worship, visits
Other Languages: Tamil, Telegu, Punjabi,
Gujarathi, Hindi, Kannada

Hindu Temple & Community Centre
St Andrew Place, Leith, Edinburgh, Lothian,
EH6 7ED
Tel: 0131-663-4689 (h)
Contact: Dinesh Joshi
Position: Secretary
Activities: Worship, visits, youth, elderly,
newsletters, inter-faith
Traditions: Sanatanist
Other Languages: Punjabi, Gujarati, Bengali

Greenhills Hindu Mandir Sabha
40 Alder Place, Greenhills, Glasgow, Strathclyde, G7

Gujarati Association of Scotland
189 Harvie Avenue, Newton Mearns, Glasgow,
Strathclyde, G77 6LT (h)
Tel: 0141-639-6946 (h)
Contact: Mr Anant Gandhi
Position: Treasurer

Activities: Youth, newsletters
Traditions: Multi-Traditional
Movements: Multi-Movements
Other Languages: Gujarati

Hindu Mandir

1 La Belle Place, Glasgow, Strathclyde, G3 7LH
Tel: 0141-332-0482 **Tel:** 0141-956-1058 (h)
Fax: 0141-420-1764
Contact: Balraj Kishan Marwaha
Position: President
Activities: Worship, resource, visits, youth, elderly, women, newsletters, inter-faith
Traditions: Sanatanist
Other Languages: Hindi, Punjabi, Bengali, Gujarati

ISKCON (Scotland)

Karuna Bhavan, Bankhouse Road, Lesmahagow, Strathclyde, ML11 0ES
Tel: 01555-894790 **Fax:** 01555-894526
Contact: Prabhupada Vani Das
Position: Vice President
Activities: Worship, resource, newsletters, books
Traditions: Vaishnava
Movements: Chaitanya
Affiliations: National Council of Hindu Temples, ISKCON (UK); International Society for Krishna Consciousness

WALES

Regional or County Bodies

Gwent Hindu Community

7 Gaudi Walk, Rogerstone, Newport, Gwent (h)
Tel: 01633-893141 (h)
Contact: Mr D O Trevedi

City, Town or Local Bodies

ISKCON Cardiff

18 Greenfield Place, Caerphilly, Mid Glamorgan
Tel: 01222-831579
Contact: Tarakanath
Position: President

Gujarati Hindu Association

32 Canton Street, Canton, Cardiff, South Glamorgan

Sanatan Dharma Mandal & Hindu Community Centre

22 The Parade, Roath, Cardiff, South Glamorgan, CF2 3AB
Tel: 01222 455564 **Tel:** 01222-228760 (h)
Contact: Mr Hemant G Patel
Position: Plc Relation Officer
Activities: Worship, visits, youth, elderly
Traditions: Sanatanist
Social Groups: Gujarati
Other Languages: Gujarati

Shree Kutchi Leva Patel Samaj

Mardy Street, Grangetown, Cardiff, South Glamorgan
Tel: 01222-372032
Contact: Mr Vishram Varsani
Position: Trustee

Shree Swaminarayan Temple

4 Merches Place, Riverside, Cardiff, South Glamorgan, CF1 7QU
Tel: 01222-371128
Contact: Naran B Patel
Position: President
Activities: Worship
Traditions: Vaishnava
Movements: Swaminaryan
Other Languages: Gujarati, Hindi

Gwent Hindu Community

7 Gaudi Walk, Rogerstone, Newport, Gwent (h)
Tel: 01633-893141 (h)
Contact: Mr D O Trevedi

Hindu Cultural Association

4 Uplands, Ystrad Rhondda, Pentre, Mid Glamorgan, CF41 7PG
Contact: Dr Kailash Bihari
Tel: 01443-430497
Position: Founder and Chief Co-ordinator
Activities: Resource, unmbrella, visits, youth, elderly, women, newsletters
Traditions: Multi-Traditional
Other Languages: Hindi

KEY TO TERMS USED IN HINDU ORGANISATION TITLES

Note: This is not a complete glossary of significant Hindu terms. It is a guide to the meaning and/or background of some of the words used in the titles of Hindu organisations listed in this directory. More information on the italicised words can be tracked down elsewhere in the key and/or in the section on "Introducing the Hindu Community" by using the directory's "Significant Word Index".

Aarti: A variant Romanisation of *arti* (see below).

Aden: Aden in the Arabian Peninsula had a Gujarati Hindu community and its use in an organisation's title indicates this historical connection.

Adhyatmik: Meaning "spiritual" or "philosophical".

Akshar: Meaning "imperishable", "immortal" or "indestructible". A name of God within the *Swaminarayan* Hindu movement.

Amba: Another name for Durga, the mother goddess.

Anand: Meaning "delight", "pleasure" or "bliss", but also a family name.

Anavil: The name of a Gujarati *caste*.

Andhra: Andhra Pradesh is the name of one of the states of India. The term is sometimes used in the title of Telugu-speaking Hindu organisations.

Anoopam: Hindi for "matchless" or "unique".

Arjuna: Sanskrit literally meaning "white". It is the name of the third of the five Pandava princes in the Hindu epic, the *Mahabharata*. He is called "white" because of the purity of his actions. Krishna acted as his charioteer on the battlefield of Kurukshetra and spoke the *Bhagavad Gita* to him on the first day of the battle in which he was originally unwilling to fight. Arjuna is seen among Hindus as an exemplary type of the spiritual seeker.

Arti: Literally meaning "greetings", it refers to worship entailing the clockwise circling of light in front of the deity and the offering of prayer.

Ashram: A Sanskrit word denoting a place of spiritual retreat, renewal and meditation. It can be anywhere that spiritual seekers gather and might be a home, a hermitage, a monastery or another kind of building.

Athia: The name of a Gujarati community.

Audich: The name of a Gujarati *caste*.

Aurobindo: Part of the name of Sri Aurobindo Ghose (or Ghosh), 1872-1950, a Hindu teacher who developed a system of what came to be called "integral *yoga* " which aimed to bring together the "ascent" of humanity to divinity with the "descent" of the divine into the material world. From 1920 onwards, he linked up with Mira Alfassa who later founded Auroville, in Pondicherry, India, where

Aurobindo devotees live and where she is known simply as "the Mother".

Arya: Sanskrit for "Aryan". The Arya Samaj, founded by Swami Dayanand Saraswati, promotes a return to what it understands to have been the *Vedic* practice of worship without deities.

Baba: A Hindi term of affectionate respect, used for elders and for some spiritual leaders.

Bajarang: Hindi for "healthy". Bajarangbali is a title of Hanuman, the monkey-headed god, servant of Rama.

Balaji: An affectionate name for Venkateswara (see below).

Balak: Hindi for "child" or "boy".

Balaknathji: The name of a spiritual leader from the medieval period believed by his followers to be immortal and depicted as a semi-naked blue-skinned youth. He is worshipped by devotees and because of his emphasis on celibacy, females are prohibited from entering the sanctuary of his temples.

Bali: Meaning "strong".

Bandhu: Hindi for "friend" or "brother".

Bapu: A term of respect for the elderly meaning "father" and used, for example, of Gandhi.

Bardai: A variant Romanisation of *vardai* meaning "rewarder".

Bari: Hindi for "widow".

Bavis: Gujarati for "twenty-two".

Bawa: A variant Romanisation of *baba* (see above).

Bengali: Pertaining to the region of Bengal in the North East of the subcontinent. Part of this region is the Indian state of West Bengal and the other part is Bangladesh.

Bhadran: The name of a town in Gujarat state, India.

Bhagvad: Sanskrit word for "Lord" and found in the *Bhagvad Gita* (literally "Song of the Lord") a frequently referred to Hindu scripture.

Bhagwad: A variant Romanisation of *Bhagvad* (see above).

Bhagwan: Hindi for "God".

Bhai: Hindi for "brother".

Bhajan: Hindi for "devotional song".

Bhakti: Sanskrit/Hindi for "devotion". It is used to refer to those Hindu traditions which focus upon personal devotion to, and love of, God understood in terms of a supreme Personality. *Bhakti-Marga* is the Hindu path which entails devotion to a personal God.

Bharat: A Sanskrit and Hindi word for a king and saint in the *Bhagavata Purana* and also for his descendent Bharata, otherwise known as Arjuna (see above). India was originally named Bharatavarsha after him. Bharat is the Hindi name for India.

Bharata: A variant Romanisation of Bharat (see above).

Bharatiya: The Sanskrit and Hindi word for "Indian" - that which pertains to India.

Bhartiya: A variant Romanisation of Bharatiya (see above).

Bhavan: The Sanskrit and Hindi for "house".

Bhawan: A variant Romanisation of *bhavan* (see above).

Bochasanwasi: Meaning "located in Bochasan", a town in Gujarat, India, where the first temple of the the Akshar Purushottam Sanstha *Swaminrayan* grouping was built. It is also a part of the name of the one of the *Swaminarayan* groupings.

Bodali: The name of a tribe.

Brahma: Sanskrit referring to the divine as creator of the universe. Brahma is one of the Hindu *trimurti* of Brahma, Vishnu and Shiva. Brahma Samaj denotes Gujarati *Brahmin* (see below) *caste* organisations.

Brahman: The Sanskrit word for the eternal Absolute.

Brahmarishi: The title of a *Brahmana* who has performed great austerities to attain mystic powers and insight.

Brahmbhatt: A *Brahmin* surname.

Brahmin: The priestly grouping among the four traditional *varna* of Hinduism.

Chaitanya: A Hindu mystic and devotee of Krishna, viewed by many *Vaishnavas* as an incarnation of Radha and Krishna.

Charotar: An area of Gujarat state in India.

Charotaria: That which pertains to *Charotar* (see above).

Chouis: Gujarati for "twenty-four".

Chovis: Variant Romanisation of *chouis* (see above).

Cutch: A part of the Indian state of Gujarat.

Darji: The name of an occupational *caste* associated with tailoring.

Dashashram: "*Dash*" is the Sanskrit/Hindi for "ten" and *dashashram* is the "ten *ashrams*".

Deevya: Meaning "transcendental".

Depala: A surname.

Dev: An honorific title meaning "god", "master" or "lord" and often appearing as a part of male names.

Dham: A holy or sacred place.

Dharam: Hindi for "righteousness" and "religion" (see *dharma* below).

Dharma: The Sanskrit word literally meaning "intrinsic function", "holding" or "carrying" or that which sustains and determines the basic structures of existence, ethics, order and religion. Hindus call their religion the *Sanatana-Dharma*, the "eternal religion".

Dhamarj: The name of an Indian town.

Dharmic: Related to *dharma* (see above).

Dhobi: A *caste* traditionally involved in clothes washing.

Dhyanyoga: *Dhyana* is Sanskrit for "meditation" and "absorption" and used together with the word *yoga* it refers to one of the first three stages of Patanjali's classical system of *yoga* as a path by which *samadhi* can be attained.

Diwali: The Hindu festival of lights.

Durga: Sanskrit meaning "hard to reach". It is one of the oldest and most widely used names for the Divine mother, the consort of Shiva. Durga appears as the destroyer of ignorance. It also means "prison" and Durga's role is also to keep conditioned souls in the material world.

Dwar: Meaning "gate".

Eckankar: Variant Romanisation of *Ekonkar*, meaning "there is only one God", and which is a name for God in the Sikh tradition.

Gadhia: Variant Romanisation of *gadia* (see below).

Gadia: The name of a community.

Gam: Hindi for "village". Some groups of *Patidar* families are named after groups of villages, for example, Chouis Gam, meaning "the twenty-four villages".

Ganapathy: Sanskrit variant name for Ganesha (or Ganesh), son of Shiva and Parvati. He is seen as a god of wisdom and as the remover of obstacles and bringer of success. He is celebrated in the *Ganesh-Purana* and is depicted as an elephant-headed god.

Ganati: Variant Romanisation of *gnati* (see below).

Gandhi: A Gujarati surname of a trading community and the name of Mohandas Karamchand Gandhi (1869-1948), known as the *Mahatma* (Sanskrit for "great soul"). Gandhi played a leading role in the Indian independence movement basing his actions upon the principles of *satyagraha* (Sanskrit literally meaning "holding fast to truth") and *ahimsa* (Sanskrit for "non-injury").

Garba: A Gujarati folk dance involving circular music and performed by women during festivals, especially *Navratri*.

Gayatri: The *Gayatri mantra* is one of the most sacred of the verses of the *Rigveda*. *Gayatri* is also the name of the demi-goddess who presides over the *mantra*.

Geeta: Sanskrit/Hindi for "song". When used alone it usually refers to the *Bhagavad Gita* ("Song of the Lord"), although there are other *Geetas* or *Gitas* like the *Ganesha-Gita*.

Girnara: Traditionally a goldsmiths' grouping from the foothills of Mount Girnar in India.

Gita: A variant Romanisation of *Geeta* (see above).

Gnati: Gujarati for "*caste*".

Guja: The name of a town in Gujarat (see below).

Gujarat: An Indian state on the west coast of India in which approximately seventy per cent of Britain's Hindus have ancestral origins.

Gujarati: Adjective referring to Gujarat (see above), especially used as a way of describing the mother tongue and ethnicity of people whose family roots are in Gujarat.

Gujerati: A variant Romanisation of Gujarati (see above).

Gujrat: A variant Romanisation of Gujarat (see above).

Guru: Sanskrit or Hindi for "teacher". It is especially used of a spiritual teacher or Master, although Hinduism traditionally recognises that one has different *gurus* in the four stages of life. One's first *gurus* are one's parents, then one's intellectual teachers, then one's spiritual Master, but also there is the god whom one worships who is one's ultimate *guru.* One's relationship with a *guru* should be characterised by trust in their wisdom.

Hare: The vocative form of Hara, another name for Radha (see below), the divine consort of Krishna and embodiment of *bhakti* (loving devotion). The word appears in the phrase "Hare Krishna Movement" sometimes used as a popular way of referring to the International Society for Krishna Consciousness.

Haveli: Hindi and Gujarati for a "large house".

Hindi: The name of the official language of India and the mother tongue of many Hindus from the north of India. It is transcribed in the Devanagar script.

Hitechu: Barbar *caste.*

Hittechhu: Variant Romanisation of *Hitechu* (see above).

Hitradak: Related to the Sanskrit *hita-radhaka,* meaning "promoting welfare".

Istree: Variant Romanisation of *stree,* the Hindi for "woman". It is often used in the title of women's organisations.

Iyengar: A title used by some South Indian *brahmins.* Iyengar Yoga is the form of *yoga* taught by B K S Iyengar.

Jagriti: Hindi for "awake".

Jai: Hindi for "victory to...", "all glory to..." or "long live....".

Jalaram: Appears in the name of Jalaram Bapa, a saintly trader in Virpur and devotee of Ram, especially revered by Gujarati Hindus.

Jan: Hindi meaning "people".

Janki: Another name for Sita (see below), the wife of Rama (see below).

Jansari: The name of a community.

Jatiya: The name of a community.

Ji: A suffix used in conjunction with a name, denoting respect.

Jignashu: Variant Romanisation of jignyasu (see below).

Jignyasu: Sanskrit, meaning "seeker of knowledge".

Kadwa: A Gujarati *caste* name for a section of the *Patidars* (see below).

Kala: Sanskrit for "art".

Kalaniketan: A place for performing arts.

Kali: Sanskrit meaning literally "the black one". Pronounced as K*aa*li and not to be confused with *Kali Yuga.* It is the name of the Divine Mother, the consort of Shiva. Kali particularly has devotees in West Bengal.

Kalyan: Hindi for "welfare".

Karamsad: The name of a town in Gujarat, India.

Karyalaya: Sanskrit, meaning "place of administration", in other words, an "office".

Kendra: Sanskrit for "centre", often used today of a place where Hindus meet.

Keshavashram: Keshav relates to Krishna. For *ashram* see above.

Kisumu: A town in Kenya from which many Hindus came who migrated to Britain from East Africa.

Kripalu: Meaning "merciful".

Krishan: A variant Romanisation of Krishna (see below).

Krishna: Sanskrit meaning literally "dark blue" and also "all attractive". It is the name of the Hindu deity who features in the *Bhagavad Gita* as the instructor of Arjuna (see above). In some Hindu traditions Krishna is seen as an *avatar* of Vishnu and in others, as the Supreme Deity Himself.

Krishnamurti: The name of a twentieth century philosopher.

Kshatriya: Sanskrit word for the second *varna* of Indian society. Often translated into English as "warrior", its duty was to protect the community. It is a term used by contemporary *caste* organisations within this community.

Kutch: A variant Romanisation of Cutch (see above) referring to an area of the Indian state of Gujarat.

Kutchi: An adjective referring to that which pertains to what originates in Kutch (see above), for example, their culture or mother tongue.

Kutchhi: A variant Romanisation of *kutchi* (see above).

Lakshmi: The name of the consort of Vishnu, she is the goddess of fortune and prosperity. Although no temple is dedicated to her name alone, she is the object of much devotion among Hindus.

Laxmi: A variant Romanisation of Lakshmi (see above.)

Leuva: A variant Romanisation of Leva (seebelow).

Leva: The name of a traditionally artisan *caste* associated with the *Patidars* and the *Patels*, many of whom follow the *Swaminarayan* (see below) movement.

Limbachaya: The name of a traditional "barber" occupational grouping.

Limbachia: A variant Romanisation of *Limbachaya* (see above).

Lohana: The name of a Gujarati *caste* traditionally associated with trading.

Luhar: The name of a *caste* traditionally associated with "blacksmithing".

Ma: Hindi for "mother", used of the leader of Auroville, founded on the basis of the teachings of Sri Aurobindo (see above). Also used as a title for any goddess.

Madhapar: A town in Kutch, India.

Madhavashram: Meaning "*ashram* of Madhava", being one of the great 13th century figures of *Vaishnavism*.

Mahajan: The name of a *caste* based organisation which also means "great person".

Mahan: Sanskrit/Hindi for "great".

Maharashtra: The name of a state in India.

Mahatma: A title applied to Gandhi and other saints, meaning "great soul".

Maher: A *caste* from Maharashtra.

Mahila: Hindi for "woman".

Mandal: Hindi for "circle", often used as a way of describing a Hindu group or organisation.

Mandata: Variant romanisation of *Mandhata* (see below).

Mandhata: A Gujarati *caste* name.

Mandir: Hindi for "temple".

Mandli: Hindi for "group" or "society", often used of Hindu organisations.

Mata: Sanskrit, meaning "mother".

Math: A monastery of centre of learning.

Matyia: The name of the Gujarati *caste* of Patels.

Matyiya: Variant Romanisation of *Matyia* (see above).

Milip: Meaning "union" or "meeting".

Mirzapur: The name of a town on the River Ganges, near Varanasi, India.

Mitra: Hindi for "friend", and also the name of the sun god and ruler of the day associated in the *Vedas* with Varuna, the ruler of the night.

Mohyal: The name of a small clan.

Moksha: Sanskrit describing liberation from *samsara* and rebirth, seen by some Hindus as being the highest goal of life.

Muktananda: The name of a *swami* who lived 1908-1983. He followed *siddha-yoga*, the *yoga* of powers, and taught the identity of one's true Self with the Absolute Consciousness.

Murti: Sanskrit for the deities used in Hindu worship.

Murugan: The name of the son of Shiva (see below), brother of Ganesh. He is particularly worshipped by Hindus from Tamil Nadu in India and Tamil Hindus from Sri Lanka.

Nadiad: The name of a town in Gujarat.

Nagrik: Hindi for "municipal" or "citizen".

Nar: Sanskrit for "man".

Narayan: Sanskrit for "God", used of Vishnu.

Narayana: Variant Romanisation of Narayan (see above).

Nath: Hindi for "Lord". It is often found as part of a name, for example, Balaknath.

Nathji: See above for *Nath*. The suffix *ji* (see above)

denotes respect. It is also the name of a deity of Krishna in Rajasthan, India.

Nav: Hindi for "new".

Navnat: Gujarati surname.

Navrang: Meaning "nine colours". At the *Holi* festival, Hindus throw coloured powders at one another for fun.

Nidhi: Sanskrit for "foundation", used of a "Trust".

Nivas: Hindi/Sanskrit for "place of abode" or "residence".

Oshwal: The name of a Gujarati *caste* group.

Palana: The name of a town in Gujarat.

Panch: Meaning "five".

Pancholi: A Gujarati surname and community.

Pandurang: The name of a Hindu saint.

Paramahansa: A spiritual title forming part of the name of Ramakrishna Paramahansa, a Bengali saint.

Parishad: Sanskrit/Hindi for "organisation", as for example, in Vishwa Hindu Parishad.

Parivar: Hindi for "family".

Patel: Name used by several Gujarati *caste* groups. It is often equivalent to *Patidar* (see below).

Patidar: The name of a Gujarati *caste* traditionally associated with agriculture.

Pattni: A Gujarati goldsmiths' *caste*.

Pij: The name of a town.

Pragati: Hindi for "progress".

Prajapati: Sanskrit for "Lord of creatures" or "Progenitor of creatures". It is used in the *Vedas* to refer to Indra and also other deities. The *Laws of Manu* refer to Prajapati as being *Brahman* in the role of the one who creates and sustains the universe. It is also a title used by a Gujarati *caste* traditionally associated with carpentry, members of which have names such as Mistry.

Prajnayama: *Prajna* is Sanskrit for "consciousness" and *ayama* means "control".

Prathna: Meaning "prayer".

Pratinidhi: Hindi for "representative". Used, for example, in the organisational name Arya Pratinidhi Sabha, meaning "Hindu Representative Council" (see below for *sabha*).

Pravasi: Hindi for "traveller".

Punjabi: An adjective referring to that which pertains to the Punjab, a state in contemporary India. It is used of the mother tongue and culture of the people originating from this area which originally included land that is now part of the country of Pakistan. Also found written as Panjabi.

Purnima: Hindi for "full moon".

Purshottami: Pertaining to the *Swaminaryan* grouping below.

Purushottam: Sanskrit for "Supreme God". Akshar Purushottam Sanstha is the name of one sector of the *Swaminarayan* movement.

Pushtimargiya: Pertaining to the *Pushtimarga sampradaya*, a tradition of devotion to Krishna founded by Vallabh and followed by many Gujaratis.

Radha: The name of the eternal consort of Krishna (see above). Radha and Krishna are central in *Gaudiya* Bengali *Vaishnava* devotion where Radha is seen as the personification of Krishna's spiritual energy and the supreme form of devotion.

Radhakrupa: Sanskrit, meaning "grace of Radha".

Rajput: Is the name of a *kshatriya* caste associated with the military.

Ram: Ram (or Rama) is the name of an *avatara* of Vishnu, appearing at the beginning of the *Treta Yuga* (the Hindu name for the second of the four ages, the current one being *Kali Yuga*). Rama is the hero of the *Ramayana* epic, the substantial authorship of which is attributed to the sage Valmiki. He and his wife Sita (see below) are viewed as the ideal of husband and wife.

Rama: Alternative form of the name Ram (see above).

Ramakrishna: The name of a Bengali spiritual leader (1836-1886) worshipped by many as an *avatara* and who taught that all religions lead to the realisation of God. One of his famous disciples was Swami Vivekananda. The Ramakrishna Mission is now a monastic order in the *Shankara* tradition of Hinduism, combining service to God with service to human beings in social activities for the sick, the homeless and other disadvantaged people. *Vedanta* Centres are founded by the Mission when monks visit at the invitation of local people.

Ramayan: Alternative version of the name *Ramayana* (see below).

Ramayana: Sanskrit for "the life story of Rama", the oldest epic in Sanskrit which is attributed to Valmiki. It consists of twenty-four thousand couplets arranged in seven *kanda* (or "chapters"). It tells the story of Rama (see above) and Sita (see below), including Sita's abduction by Ravana, the battle with demons, the return to Ayodhya, and their ascent into the spiritual realm.

Rana: A Rajputi *caste*, meaning "brave" or "fighter".

Sabha: Hindi for "assembly", "conference" or "council".

Sadan: Hindi for "house".

Sahaja: Sanskrit for "natural". Truth is seen as being natural, whilst ignorance arises from the workings of the mind.

Sahayak: Meaning "helper" or "volunteer".

Sahetiya: Variant Romanisation of *sahitya* (see below).

Sahit: Panjabi for "literature".

Sahitya: Sanskrit, meaning "literature".

Sajeevan: Hindi for "alive".

Samaj: Sanskrit/Hindi for "society", as for example, in the organisation title Arya Samaj.

Samanvay: Sanskrit, meaning "inter-relation", "connection", "co-ordination" or "synthesis".

Samiti: Hindi for "committee".

Sanatan: Sanskrit or Hindi meaning "imperishable" or "eternal". Hindus call their religion *Sanatana Dharma* ("the eternal religion") to characterise their belief in its revealed and universal nature.

Sanatana: Variant Romanisation of *Sanatan* (see above).

Sanathan: Variant Romanisation of *Sanatan* (see above).

Sandesh: Hindi for "message".

Sangam: Hindi for "confluence" or "joint".

Sangathan: Hindi for "union" or "jointly".

Sangh: Variant Romanisation of *sangha* (see below).

Sangha: Sanskrit or Hindi for a "crowd" or "group".

Usually used in the Hindu context of a group of seekers who gather around a *guru* (see above) for teaching and spiritual enlightenment.

Sangit: Hindi for "music".

Sanskar: Refers to a "purificatory process", such as a life-cycle ritual.

Sanskritik: Sanskrit for "perfect" and "cultured". The language of Sanskrit is not a contemporary conversational language, but it is the sacred language of Hinduism in which all its major texts are composed. It has its own alphabet called Devanagari, from *deva* (meaning "god") and *nagari* (meaning "city"). Sanskrit is therefore thought of as the language that is spoken in the cities of the demi-gods.

Sanstha: Sanskrit for "appearance" or "form", used in the name of one of the section of the *Swaminarayan* movement.

Sansthan: Hindi for "institution".

Sant: Hindi and Panjabi, used of a charismatic religious leader.

Saraswat: Consort of Vishnu and goddess of the arts and scholarship.

Sardar: Panjabi for "chief", often used as equivalent of the title "mister".

Sarvajanik: Sanskrit for "universal", with *sara* meaning "all" and *janik* meaning "people".

Sarvoday: Hindi for "uplift of all". It was a term promoted by *Mahatma* Gandhi.

Sarvodaya: Variant Romanisation of *Sarvoday* (see above).

Sat: Sanskrit for "truth".

Satavis: Gujarati for "twenty-seven".

Satsang: From the Sanskrit *sat* (see above) meaning "truth" and *sang*, meaning "company" or "group". It is used in Hindi and Punjabi to describe a devotional group.

Sattavis: Variant Romanisation of *satavis* (see above).

Seva: Hindi for "service". It can include reference to purely devotional service or to humanitarian service.

Sevak: Hindi for a male "volunteer" or "servant".

Sevashram: An *ashram* (see above) devoted to service.

Sevika: Hindi for a female "volunteer" or "servant".

Sewa: Variant Romanisation of *seva* (see above).

Shakha: Sanskrit meaning "branch". It is used to describe a school of the *Vedas* which were originally transmitted orally and had a variety of *shakhas* or "schools" associated with each line of oral transmission.

Shakti: Sanskrit and Hindi for "power", "force" or "energy". It is the name for primal energy, venerated under different personal names in India - for example, Kali and Durga - as the consort of Shiva. Shakti is of particular importance in the *Tantra* path of Hinduism.

Shanti: Sanskrit for "peace".

Shavika: Variant Romanisation of *sevika* (see above).

Shikha: Hindi for "hair" and, more specifically, the tuft of hair at the back of the head worn by *Vaishnavas.*

Shishukunj: Meaning "children's group", from the Sanskrit *shishu,* meaning "children" and *kunja,* literally meaning "forest".

Shiva: Sanskrit literally meaning "the kind, friendly one", Shiva is the name of the third of the Hindu *trimurti* of Brahma, Vishnu and Shiva. Shiva is seen as the destroyer of ignorance. His symbol is a *linga* and he is often portrayed together with his wife Shakti whose symbol is a *yoni,* representations of the male and female sexual organs respectively.

Shree: Sanskrit for "eminent one". An honorific title of respect used in front of the names of gods, saints, or teachers. Shree Nathji refers to a black representation of Krishna (see above), especially worshipped by the *Pushtimargis.*

Shri: Variant Romanisation of *Shree* (see above).

Shyam: Sanskrit for "dark" - an epithet for Krishna (see above).

Siddha: Sanskrit for "perfect" or "complete". In the *Puranas,* a *siddha* is a being of great power.

Siddhant: Sanskrit and Hindi, meaning theological or philosophical "principle".

Sita: Sita appears in the epic the *Ramayana* together with her husband Rama (see above). Sita and Rama are viewed as the ideal of husband and wife.

Sitaram: Sita and Rama as a couple.

Sojitra: The name of a town.

Soni: The name of a Gujarati and Panjabi *caste* traditionally associated with goldsmithing.

Sorathia: A variant form of Sawshta, an ancient name for Gujarat.

Sorthia: Variant Romanisation of *sorathia* (see above).

Sri: Variant Romanisation of *shree* (see above).

Subhag: Hindi for "beautiful".

Sudharak: Sanskrit and Hindi name for "reformer".

Sujaav: Variant Romanisation of Sujthaav, meaning "advice".

Swami: Sanskrit for "sir" or "lord". In general, it appears as an honorific title before the name of a teacher or holy person, especially those who are *sunnyasis* or renunciants.

Swaminarayan: Literally meaning "Supreme Lord", it is the name of a Hindu movement followed by a significant number of Gujarati Hindus.

Swayamsevak: Hindi for "self-service" or "self-help". It is part of the title of the Swayamsevak Sangh, a twentieth century organisation of Hindu activists, which stresses self-discipline.

Tamil: The name of a people, language and culture originating in the South Indian state of Tamil Nadu.

Tantra: Sanskrit for "context" or "continuum". It describes the magical strand of Hinduism which focuses on the divine as Shakti (see above). There are two *Tantric* (see below) paths - the *Amachara* (left hand path) and the *Dakshinachara* (right hand path). The former is a dangerous path of freedom from normal conventions which can only be undertaken under close supervision. The latter is a path of self-discipline. In both the emphasis is on the feminine aspects of the divine and followers are guided by *Tantric* texts.

Tantric: That which pertains to the *Tantra* (see above).

Uttersanda: The name of a town in India..

Valam: The name of a town in India.

Vallabh: A variant of the name Vallabcharya, who is especially venerated by *Pushtimargis.*

Vanand: A Gujarati *caste* name.

Vanik: Gujarati surname for a trading or merchant *caste*.

Vanza: The name of an occupational grouping traditionally related to tailoring.

Vasenev: Related to *Vaishnav* (worshippers of Vishnu).

Vedanta: From the Sanskrit *veda*, meaning "knowledge" and *anta*, meaning "end". Hence *Vedanta* means the "conclusion of the *Vedas*", which are seen as eternal. Their quintessence is known as the *Uphanishads* which focus especially on the relationship between *atman* and *Brahman*. The *Vedanta* has several main branches.

Vedic: That which pertains to the *Vedas* (see above).

Venkateswara: A name of Vishnu. Venkata is a mountain in Ahdra Pradesh, in India, which is sacred to Krishna. *Ishwara* means "Lord".

Vidhi: Sanskrit for "rule", "system" or "ritual".

Vidhya: Variant Romanisation of *vidya* (see above).

Vidhyala: Variant Romanisation of *vidyala* (see below).

Vidya: Sanskrit, meaning "knowledge". *Apara vidya* is intellectually acquired knowledge, whilst *paravidya* is spiritual knowledge.

Vidyala: Sanskrit for "school", from the Sanskrit *vidya* (see above).

Vikram: The name of a Hindu king and an era of time.

Virsad: A *caste* name.

Visgam: Meaning "twenty villages".

Vishva: Sanskrit for "universal". Used in the title of the organisation Vishwa Hindu Parishad, meaning Universal Hindu Organisation, a twentieth century activist organisation.

Vishwa: Variant Romanisation of Vishva (see above).

Vishwakarma: Sanskrit for "all creating". In the *Rig Veda*, the activity of creation is celebrated in two hymns in which the world is described as being made from primordial matter. It is the name of the divine as architect, and in the *Puranas* Vishwakarma is seen as the inventor of the sciences and of mechanics. He is a patron deity of a number of originally artisan castes who use his name in the title of their organisations.

Visva: Variant Romanisation of *Vishwa* (see above).

Vrindavan: A holy village in India, particularly associated with Krishna.

Wanza: Variant Romanisation of *vanza* (see above).

Yamuna: The Sanskrit for the North Indian river also known as the Jumna or Jumnu, which is a tributary of the River Ganges. *Pushtimargis* and *Vaishnavas* worship Yamuna along with Shree Nathj (or Shrinathji) and Valabhacharya.

Yoga: Sanskrit meaning "joining". In a religious context it is used to describe the pathways used for seeking union with the divine including *karma yoga* (path of selfless action), *bhakti yoga* (path of devotion), *raja yoga* (royal yoga), *kundalini yoga* (tantric yoga), *jnanana* yoga (abstract knowledge). There is also *hatha yoga* which consists of the physical exercises that help the aspirant to other forms of *yoga*.

Yogashram: See *yoga* and *ashram* above.

Yuvak: Hindi meaning "youth".

INTRODUCING THE JAIN COMMUNITY

JAINS IN THE UNITED KINGDOM

Migration

Most Jains now living in the United Kingdom can trace their historical and ethnic origins back to the Gujarat and Rajasthan areas of India. Some migrated directly from India in the 1950s; others came in the 1960s and 1970s from the East African countries in which they or their forebears had previously settled, such as Kenya, Uganda and Tanzania.

Distribution

There are approximately 5-8 million Jains worldwide and some 25,000-30,000 in the UK. Many live in and around the Greater London area and in Leicester. Jain communities are also found in Coventry, Luton, Manchester, Northampton and Wellingborough. Jains have long been engaged in business and finance. In the UK, they are well-represented in the professions of acountancy, medicine and pharmacy.

Jain places of worship are not recorded as a separate category in the running totals of certified places of worship in England and Wales kept by the Registrar General. There are four Jain places of worship recorded in this directory, three in the Greater London area and one in Leicester, namely, the Oshwal Centre in Potters Bar, the Oshwal Association in Croydon, the Mahavir Foundation in Kenton, and the Jain Temple in Leicester.

ORIGINS AND DEVELOPMENT OF JAINISM

The Tirthankaras

The precise origins of Jainism cannot be traced, but it began in India. The term *Jain* means a follower of the *Jinas* (Spiritual Victors), a line of human teachers who are believed to have existed from time immemorial and to have attained *kevalajnana* (infinite knowledge) and perfect purity through their own spiritual efforts. The *Jinas* are also known as *Tirthankaras*, literally meaning *Ford-Makers*, those who help others to cross over the floods of *samsara* (the cycle of birth and death). Jains believe that in the present cosmic cycle there have been twenty-four *Tirthankaras* who have taught others the tenets of Jainism.

Mahavira

The twenty-fourth *Tirthankara*, Vardhamana, usually called *Mahavira* (the Great Hero), is traditionally said to have been born in 599 BCE into a *kshatriya* (noble) family in the area of what is now Bihar, in India, although some modern scholars have suggested a rather later date. When he was thirty years old, with the permission of his family he left home on a spiritual quest. Jains affirm that after twelve years he attained *kevalajnana* (omniscience). Shortly after this, eleven learned men came to the place where *Mahavira* was in order to challenge him, but when he answered their doubts they became the *Ganadharas* (leaders) of the fourfold order of monks and nuns, laymen and laywomen which he founded.

During the next thirty years, it is thought that his followers within this order grew to about 14,000 *sadhus* (male ascetics) and 36,000 *sadhvis* (female ascetics), with also approximately 500,000 *shravakas* (lay men) and *shravikas* (lay women) associated with the order. At the age of seventy-two, *Mahavira* died and attained *moksha* or *nirvana*, the state of perfection beyond the cycle of birth and death.

Jainism in India

At first, Jainism flourished throughout the Ganges valley area of India. After the fall of the Mauryan dynasty of Emperor Ashoka (c200 BCE) many Jains, together with their mendicant leaders, migrated west to the city of Mathura on the Yamuna River, with others migrating further west to Rajasthan and Gujarat, and south to Maharashtra and Karnataka, where Jainism rapidly grew in popularity.

SOURCES OF JAIN BELIEFS AND PRACTICES

Scriptures

Jain scriptures are known as the *Shruta*, *Agamas* or *Siddhanta* (doctrine) which comprise the canonical literature containing the teachings of *Mahavira* and other *Tirthankaras*. This literature consists of some sixty texts and is divided into three main groups of writings. These three groups are the *Purvas* (Older Texts); the *Angas* (Limbs); and the *Angabahyas* (Subsidiary Canon). A majority of these texts are written in Ardhamagadhi, an ancient language of Maghadha.

Purvas

The *Purvas* are believed to constitute the teachings of the former *Tirthankaras* as handed down in oral tradition. Jains in the *Shvetambara* tradition (see below under Traditions) believe that all this material was lost. Jains in the *Digambara* tradition (see below) claim that some of the material from these oral teachings is the basis for their early treatise, *Shat Khanda-Agama* (the Scripture in Six Parts).

Angas
The *Angas* consist of twelve books including such major texts as the *Acharanga Sutra*, which is the oldest, and the *Bhagavati Sutra*, which is the largest. Based on the teachings of *Mahavira*, they were compiled by the *Ganadharas* and contain materials about doctrinal matters, rules of discipline for monks and nuns, Jain cosmology, ecclesiastical law, and narratives for the instruction of the laity. *Digambaras* have traditionally maintained that these texts are no longer extant in their original form.

Angabahya
The *Angabahya* (Subsidiary Canon) texts were composed in a later period by mendicant authors. They mainly elucidate the material found in the *Angas*. The most well-known and popular of these is the *Kalpa Sutra* of the Shvetambaras, which contains the biographies of *Mahavira* and other *Tirthankaras*.

Other Texts

In addition to the *canon* itself, there are extensive Sanskrit commentaries and independent treatises written in both prose and verse forms. The *Tattvartha Sutra*, written in the second century BCE by Acharya Umasvati, belongs to this group of texts. This text, together with its several commentaries was the first significant Jain text written in Sanskrit and is viewed by contemporary Jains as being a fundamental text which provides the basis for Jain education. Its content summarises the key aspects of the whole of Jain teaching, including ethics, metaphysics, epistomology and cosmology.

KEY JAIN BELIEFS

Ahimsa

The cardinal principle of Jainism is *ahimsa*, generally translated as non-violence, although it goes far beyond that to encompass the avoidance of all physical or even mental harm to any living being, including the tiniest. Although they recognise that a completely harmless life is humanly impossible, Jains strive to the best of their ability to obey the precept of *ahimsa*.

Reality in Jain Perspective

Jainism is a religion without a belief in a creator god. According to its scriptures, there is *akasha* (infinite space) within which there is a finite area called *loka* (the universe). Within this universe there are an infinite number of *jiva* or *atmas* (sentient beings). There are also *pudgalas* (non-sentient material atoms) endowed with the qualities of palpability, such as softness/hardness, lightness/heaviness, as well as of taste, smell and colour.

In addition to matter and space, other *ajiva* (non-sentient existents) include the principles of *dharma* (motion), *adharma* (rest) and *kala* (time). These *dravyas* (existents) are all, like the universe itself, viewed as being uncreated, beginningless and eternal. It is only their appearances and surface attributes which are in a state of change, and these appearances and attributes are known as *paryayas* (modifications).

The attribution of two apparently opposite characteristics to the same entity (for example, eternal substance and changing modes) reflects the distinctive Jain view of *anekantavada* (the multi-faceted nature of reality). According to this principle, Jains believe that all aspects of reality must be taken into account for a complete and true understanding of its nature. The study of the totality of these aspects, when considered in the context of *dravya* (existents), *kshetra* (place), *kala* (time) and *bhava* (condition), produces *naya* (a correct view of reality).

The idea of *syadvada* (qualified assertion) further underlines the Jain approach of *anekantavada* and is illustrated by the use of the term *syat* (literally, "in some specific sense only") which is employed in Jain discourses on reality as describing only one aspect of the totality.

Sentient Beings

Consciousness is understood as that which distinguishes *jiva* or *atmas* (sentient beings or souls) from all other existents, including material atoms. During the state of embodiment, this consciousness manifests through the senses and the mind, resulting in what is understood by sentient beings as knowledge of objects. The ability to know is understood as varying almost infinitely from one being to another. However, Jains broadly categorise all forms of sentient life in a hierarchy based upon the number of senses they possess.

The lowest forms of life are believed to have only the sense of touch through which they experience pleasure and pain. These forms of life include, for example, algae and plants. Next are those beings with two, three and four senses, for example, insects. Higher than these are animals with five senses and a mind which exhibits some developed means of rational thinking. The most highly developed are seen as being the "hell beings", the "heavenly beings" and humans.

In Jain cosmology, the heavens and hells are temporary abodes and are located, respectively, in the upper and lower parts of the universe. Human beings and animals that have five senses occupy the smallest area of the universe between the heavens and the hells. It should be noted, however, that in Jain thought human beings are distinguished from all other forms of life because of their capacity for a high degree of spiritual progress. Jains believe that it is only from the human state that *moksha* (release from the cycle of birth and death) is possible.

Karma

The variety of life-forms, like life itself, is seen as having no beginning. There is no original form of life from which the others have evolved. Jains believe that, in its transmigration from one body to another, it is likely that one soul will have gone through a wide variety of life-forms. Such variety in embodiment and levels of consciousness is explained by means of the doctrine of *karma*.

The doctrine of *karma* maintains that the kind of body a soul may inhabit in its next life is determined primarily by the activities it undertakes in the present life. Unwholesome volitions, accompanied by attachment and aversion, necessarily produce evil acts such as hurting and lying, whilst wholesome volitions, accompanied by equanimity and friendliness, generate acts of charity and kindness. The strength of the volition of the soul at the time of a given action is considered to be the most significant factor in shaping future lives and perpetuating the cycle of birth and death.

In Jain understanding, all volitional acts attract a certain amount of a very subtle form of matter. This is drawn to the soul and binds with the already existing layer of *karmic* matter in a process known as *bandha* (bondage). An analogy used for this is of dust settling on a wet mirror. Just as a mirror's capacity to reflect perfectly is obstructed by accumulated dust, so the soul's capacity for *jnana* (knowledge) and *sukha* (the experience of happiness) is understood as being affected by varieties of *karmic* matter.

Jains categorise this *karmic* matter into eight main varieties according to their effects on the soul. The first two are those that obscure the qualities of knowledge and perception. The next two are the *karmas* that obstruct the practice of right conduct and limit the energy required for that conduct. The remaining four *karmas* affect body structure, longevity of the body, social environment and, most importantly, the feeling of happiness and unhappiness which is experienced in proportion to one's past good and evil acts. As understood by Jains, the doctrine of *karma*, far from being pessimistic as is sometimes alleged, is a spur to endeavour: the individual soul is seen as responsible for its own spiritual progress.

Jain Path to Moksha

The beginningless bondage of the soul to *karmic* matter and the soul's ensuing embodiment is, however, not seen as being necessarily endless. Jains affirm that a soul can terminate this bondage by gaining *samyak-darshana* (true faith in the nature of reality as taught by the *Jinas*), by *samyak-jnana* (knowing thoroughly the distinction between the soul and *karmic* matter), and by *samyak-caritra* (following proper conduct as exemplified in the lives of the *Jinas*).

Right faith, right knowledge and right conduct are known collectively as *The Three Jewels* of Jainism. Together they constitute the Jain path to *moksha*. Right conduct involves refraining from evil actions, speech and thoughts which prevent the influx of new *karmic* matter. This is a graduated development, the initial stages of which are viewed as being applicable to lay people and the advanced stages as being applicable to mendicants.

Through renunciation and the constant endeavour to follow their life-long vows (see below), a mendicant *monk* or *nun* effectively blocks the influx of all new *karmas* that will mature and, in the course of time, produce new births for the soul. The mendicant engages in *tapas* (austerities), mainly in the form of fasting and *dhyana* (sustained meditation), which are believed to bring about *nirjara* (exhaustion) of the mass of *karma* that has accumulated from the past.

It is believed that if one follows such a holy life over a long period of time, indeed over very many lifetimes, a soul may attain total emancipation from all destructive *karmic* matter and thus be freed from rebirth forever. Such a person is, at this stage, called an *arhat* (worthy of worship) or a *kevalin* (one who has attained omniscience), being a soul that has attained freedom from all residual *karmic* matter. At the end of life, such a soul rises instantaneously to the summit of the universe where, motionless, it abides forever in its omniscient glory and is called a *Siddha* (Perfected Being), being now free from all *karmic* matter.

TRADITIONS IN JAINISM

There are two main monastic groupings within Jainism, the *Shvetambara* and the *Digambara*. These terms are also used derivatively to describe their lay followers. The majority of Jains worldwide, and in the UK, are *Shvetambara*. The two groups, which emerged in the third and fifth centuries CE, differ in some of their beliefs and practices.

Shvetambara

The *Shvetambara* (white-robed) *monks* and *nuns* wear three pieces of white clothing and carry a set of begging bowls and a *rajoharana* (small woollen whisk-broom) used to avoid harm to insects. They travel on foot, do not stay in one place for more than four days except during the monsoon, and do not keep money or material possessions other than a walking stick and a blanket.

It is estimated that there are over 2,500 *Shvetambara monks* and 5,000 *Shvetambara nuns* living in India today. A group of the *Shvetambara*, known as the *Sthanakvasis*, and a sub-group of the latter called *Terapanthis*, additionally wear a *muhpatti* (piece of cloth) over the mouth to avoid harming minute living beings in the air they breathe.

Mendicant leaders of the *Terapanthi* community have introduced a practice of new renunciants spending a few years in training to teach the Jain religion. These young novices, called *samanas* (male novices) and *samanis* (female novices) are, prior to their full initiation as mendicants, permitted to use transport in order to visit Jain communities in India and overseas. In recent years they have been very active in educational work.

Digambara

The *Digambara* (sky-clad) *monks* renounce all forms of property including clothes and begging bowls. They are allowed to carry only a peacock-feather whisk-broom and a gourd for washing water. *Digambara nuns* are clothed in a white sari. In all other matters the nuns obey the same regulations as monks, including eating and drinking only once a day in the home of a Jain lay person.

Due to the severity of their mendicant rules there are probably no more than a few hundred *Digambara monks* and *nuns* living in India today. Because of the restrictions on travel for these ascetics, the day-to-day leadership of the *Digambara* community in India and abroad rests upon lay scholars and advanced laymen.

JAIN LIFE

Anuvratas

A lay person who undertakes to refrain from all forms of intentional violence expresses this by assuming the *anuvratas* (five life-long minor vows).

As has been explained, the vow of *ahimsa* (not harming) is the cardinal principle of Jainism. It includes not hurting sentient beings, and is therefore expressed in a strictly vegetarian diet. Jain scriptures permit the consumption of dairy products such as milk, curds and ghee (clarified butter), but prohibit the eating of meat, eggs and honey (the latter because of the harm to bees which gathering honey involves).

They also prohibit the consumption of certain vegetables that grow underground and produce numerous sprouts, such as potatoes, or fruits with many seeds such as figs, as well as fermented products such as alcohol.

Some lay people, as well as all mendicants, observe the restriction of not eating after sunset or before sunrise, an ancient practice which was designed to avoid unintentional harm to insects that appear after dark.

The principle of *ahimsa* also underlies the remaining vows of *satya* (truthfulness), *asteya* (not stealing), *brahmacharya* (refraining from sexual activity outside of marriage) and *aparigraha* (placing limits on one's possessions). Employment is also restricted to occupations where there is only a minimal likelihood of harm to human or animal life.

Mahavratas

Jains consider that the true path of emancipation does not begin until one renounces the household altogether in order to lead the celibate life of a *sadhu* (male mendicant) or *sadhvi* (female mendicant) by taking the *mahavratas* (the great vows). The vows taken by a mendicant are the same as those taken by a lay person, but are much more restrictive.

For example, for mendicants, the vow of *ahimsa* includes not harming even the most minute of one-sense beings. The vow of *brahmacharya* means complete celibacy and *aparigraha* means renouncing all possessions except the few items deemed necessary to support a mendicant life.

A mendicant, therefore, subsists on the voluntary support of the lay people. Giving food and providing necessities to mendicants are considered to be the most meritorious acts. The initiation (*diksha*) of a new monk or nun is accompanied by much ceremony and rejoicing. The mendicants are treated with great respect and play an important part in the religious instruction of the laity.

JAIN WORSHIP

Personal Puja

Jains may offer *puja* (worship) at their home shrines three times a day, before dawn, at sunset and, at night, by chanting *mantras* (litanies). The most important of these *mantras* is the *Pancanamaskara-mantra* saying, "I pay homage to the *Arhats* (the living omniscient beings), *Siddhas* (the perfected beings), *Acharyas* (the Jain mendicant leaders), *Upadhyayas* (Jain mendicant teachers) and the *Sadhus* (all other Jain ascetics)". The second important ritual is *pratikramana*, a confession of transgressions against one's religious vows committed knowingly or unknowingly.

Mandirs

In areas of the country where there is no temple, Jains meet in homes and halls. In addition to worshipping in their home shrines, many Jains also worship at *Shvetambara* or *Digambara mandirs* (temples). These *mandirs* contain images of one or more *Tirthankaras* depicted in meditation, either standing or seated in the lotus posture. Devotion to the *Jinas* represented by these images inspires Jains to engage in meritorious activities.

Before coming into a place of worship Jains purify themselves with a bath. Shoes and all leather objects are left outside. At the entrance to the *mandir*, a worshipper puts sandalwood paste-mark on his or her brow to signify their intention to live a life according to the teachings of *Jiva*. Using rice grains, a *swastika* design (not to be confused with the Nazi *swastika*) is made on a low table indicating a desire to be liberated from the four destinies of the world cycle. To the chant of *mantras*, worshippers bathe the images of the *Tirthankaras*, offer flowers and incense, and wave *arati* (lamps) in front of them.

While all *Digamabaras* and the majority of the *Shvetambaras* worship in temples, the *Shvetambara* groups called the *Sthanakvasis* and the *Terapanthis* do not participate in these temple rituals. Instead, they emphasise *bhava puja* (mental worship) and perform their religious rites in *upashraya* (meditation halls).

In India, *Shvetambaras* and *Digambaras* worship in separate temples, but in Leicester there is a purpose-built Jain *mandir* which provides places of worship for all Jains. Within this *mandir*, in addition to the main *Shvetambara* shrine, there is a also a *Digambara* shrine and a *Sthanakvasi upashraya* for *pratikramana* (the ritual of confession), as well as a meditation room dedicated to Shrimad Rajachandra (1868–1901), a great spiritual leader and counsellor to Mahatma Gandhi on religious matters. The *mandir* also contains a museum which displays the history, philosophy, architecture and way of life of the Jains. The Oshwal Centre in North London has a temple located in a separate building from its community hall.

JAIN CALENDAR AND FESTIVALS

Jain Calendar

Jains date the era of *Mahavira*, known as the *Vira-nirvana-samvat*, from the year of his death in 527 BCE. However, except for special events in Jain history, they have traditionally used the *Vikramasamvat* calendar which is also used among Hindus. Both calendars are lunar.

Jain festivals

The following are the most significant Jain festivals:

Mahavira Jayanti   (March/April)
Marks the anniversary of the birth of *Mahavira*.

Akshaya-tiritiya (April/May)
Means "Immortal Third" and celebrates the first time that alms were given to Jina Rishabha, the first *Tirthankara* of this cosmic cycle.

Shruta-pancami (May/June)
Or *Guru-pancami*, meaning "Teacher's Fifth", is celebrated by the *Digambaras* on the fifth (*pancami*) day of May/June. Among *Shvetambaras* this day is known as *Jnana-pancami* (Knowledge-Fifth) and is observed in October/November. It commemorates the day on which the Jain scriptures were first written down. At this time, copies of the scriptures are displayed in Jain *mandirs*.

Paryushana-parva (August/September)
A period of eight to ten days which marks the most important religious period during the four months of the rainy season in India. At this time, Jain *monks* and *nuns* find a fixed place of residence instead of moving from place to place as they do at other times of the year. During this time, lay people often observe special vows of eating only one meal or of fasting from sunrise to sunrise. Among *Shvetambaras*, the portion of the sacred *Kalpa Sutra* which contains the life of *Mahavira* is recited.

The *Digambaras* call this season *Dasha-lakshana-parva*, meaning "the Period of Cultivating the Ten Virtues", namely forgiveness, humility, honesty, purity, truthfulness, self-restraint, asceticism, study, detachment, and celibacy. During the festival, each day is devoted to a discourse on one of these virtues. The final day is the holiest in the year and is marked by the celebration of *Samvatsari-pratikramana*. This is an annual ceremony of confession in which all Jains participate, requesting forgiveness from relatives and friends for offences of thought, word or deed by uttering the words *micchami dukkadam* (meaning "may my transgressions be forgiven").

Vira-Nirvana (November)
This coincides with the Indian festival of *Diwali*, when Jains mark the death and *nirvana* of *Mahavira*.

Karttika-purnima (December)
Is the day on which the rainy season retreat for *monks* and *nuns* comes to an end, and they resume their travels on foot. This marks the end of the Jain religious year.

JAIN ORGANISATIONS

Jain Organisations

There are both national and local Jain organisations in the UK and they are known by such common Indian terms as *mandal* (the Hindi word literally meaning "circle"), *samaj* (the Hindi word meaning "society") and *sangh* (the Hindi word for "group" or "gathering"). Local groups may be open to general Jain membership or may be specific to certain social groupings, popularly known as *castes*, such as the Oshwal and Navnat who were originally Indian trading communities.

There are also interest groups which deal with issues of particular concern to Jains including, for example, the Young Indian Vegetarians. Some may be more specific in their membership as with the National Association of Vanik Associations. The Jain Academy and the Institute of Jainology are two organisations which are concerned with the promotion of Jainism and Jain principles at both national and international levels.

Personnel

As explained earlier, the Jain community is composed of four groups of people: *sadhus* (male ascetics or monks), *sadhvis* (female ascetics or nuns), *shravakas* (lay men) and *shravikas* (lay women). *Sadhus* and *sadhvis* dedicate themselves exclusively to the pursuit of *moksha*. They renounce their family and all their possessions and take the *mahavratas* (Five Great Vows) at an initiation ceremony known as *diksha*. Jainism has no priesthood, although at the *mandirs* there are sometimes designated lay men (*pujaris*) who perform the religious rituals.

FURTHER READING

Acharya Bhuvanbhanusoorishwarji, *Handbook of Jainology*, Sri Vishvakalyan Prakashan Trust, Mehsana, 1987.

Banerjee, S R, *Chhotelal Jain's Jaina Bibliography* (2 volumes), Vir Sewa Mandir, New Delhi, 1982.

Banks, Marcus, *Organising Jainism in India and England*, Clarendon Press, Oxford, 1992.

Bhargava, D, *Jain Ethics*, Motilal Banarsidass, Delhi, 1968.

Bhattacharya, B C, *The Jaina Iconography*, Motilal Banarsidass, Delhi, (2nd edition), 1974.

Bhattacharyya, N, *Jain Philosophy: Historical Outline*, Munshiram Manohalal, New Delhi, 1976.

Dundas, P, *The Jains*, Routledge, London, 1992.

Ghosh, A, *Jain Art and Architecture* (3 volumes), Bharatiya Jnanapith, New Delhi, 1974–1975.

Jain, J P, *Religion and Culture of the Jains*, Bharatiya Jnanpith, New Delhi, 1975.

Jain, M U K, *Jain Sects and Schools*, Concept Publishing, Delhi, 1975.

Jain Samaj Europe, *Mahavira Darshan and Rituals: Special Issue of The Jain*, April 1992.

Jaini, P S, *The Jaina Path of Purification*, University of California Press, Berkeley, 1979.

Jaini, P S, *Gender and Salvation: Jaina Debates on the Spiritual Liberation of Women*, University of California Press, Berkeley, California, 1991.

Johnson, W J, *Harmless Souls: Karmic Bondage and Religious Change in Early Jainism*, Motilal Banarsidass, Delhi, 1985.

Kapashi, V, *In Search of the Ultimate*, V K Publications, Harrow, 1984.

Laidlow, J, *Riches and Renunciation: Religion, Economy and Society among the Jains*, Clarendon Press, Oxford, 1995.

Marett, P, *Jainism Explained*, Jain Samaj Europe Publications, Leicester, 1985.

Nahar, P C, and Ghosh, J C, *Encyclopedia of Jainism*, Sri Satguru Publications, Delhi, 1986.

Sangave, V S, *Jaina Community: A Social Survey* (2nd edition), Popular Prakashan, Bombay, 1980.

Satyaprakash (ed), *Jainism: A Select Bibliography*, Indian Documentation Service, Gurgaon, 1984.

Shah, N K, *The World of the Conquerors* (2 Volumes), Sussex Academic Press, 1997.

Sogani, K C, *Ethical Doctrines in Jainism*, Jaina Samskrita Samrakshaka Sangha, Sholapur, 1967.

Umasvati/Umasvami, *Tattvartha Sutra: That Which Is*, translated by Nathmal Tatia, The Institute of Jainology, International Sacred Literature Trust Series, Harper Collins, London, 1994.

JAIN UNITED KINGDOM ORGANISATIONS

The organisations listed in this section include head offices of organisations with branches throughout the United Kingdom and organisations which aspire to serve the Jain community at a UK-wide level.

Federation of Jain Organisations in UK

11 Lindsay Drive, Kenton, Harrow, Middlesex, HA3 0TA
Tel: 0181-204-2871 (h) **Fax:** 0181-933-2353
Contact: Mr Vinod Kapashi
Position: Co-ordinator
Activities: Umbrella
Traditions: Multi-Traditional
Languages: Gujarati, Hindi

Institute of Jainology

Unit 18, Silicon Business Centre,
26-28 Wandsworth Road, Greenford, Middlesex, UB6 7JZ
Tel: 0181-997-2300 **Fax:** 0181-997-4964
Contact: Mr Nemu Chandaria
Position: Co-ordinator
Activities: Resource, umbrella, youth, elderly, women, newsletters, books, inter-faith
Traditions: Multi-Traditional
Other Languages: Gujarati, Hindi
Affiliations: Oshwal Association of the UK; Navnat Vanik Association of the UK; Bhagwan Mahavir Memorial Samiti, India; Federation of Jain Associations in North America; Inter Faith Network for the UK
Founded in 1983 at the World Jain Conference held in London. It aims to promote greater understanding of the Jain faith and to render Jain philosophy and teachings more accessible to all by developing, translating and publishing Jain texts.

Jain Academy

20 St James Close, London, NW11 9QX
Tel: 0181-455-5573 (h)
Contact: Dr Natubhai Shah
Position: Chair
Activities: Resource
Traditions: Multi-Traditional
Other Languages: Gujarati, Hindi
The Jain Academy aims to promote the study of Jainism and Jain values. It has established undergraduate and postgraduate studies at De Montfort University, Leicester and the Jain Educational and Research Centre at Bombay University.

Jain Samaj Europe

Jain Centre, 32 Oxford Street, Leicester, Leicestershire, LE1 5XU
Tel: 0116-254-3091

Contact: Dr Natubhai Shah
Position: Trustee
Activities: Resource, media, umbrella, visits youth, elderly, women, newsletters, books, inter-faith
Traditions: Multi-Traditional
Other Languages: Gujarati
Affiliations: Inter Faith Network for the UK

Jain Vishwa Bharati

148 Hendon Way, London, NW2 2NE (h)
Tel: 0181-458-5653 (h) **Fax:** 0181-458-0120
Contact: Mr Mangi Lal Baid
Position: President
Activities: Visits, youth, elderly, women
Traditions: Svetambara
Movements: Terapanthi
Other Languages: Hindi, Gujarati, Marwari, Urdu
Affiliations: Jain Vishwa Bharati Institute, Rajasthan, India
We organise visits of two or more *samanis* (Jain nuns) from India every year around Paryushan Parve for four to five weeks educational discourses on the Jain Agams and for training in practice of Prekshya Dhyan.

National Council of Vanik Organisations (UK)

1 Elm Croft Gardens, London, NW9 9QP
Tel: 0181-206-1396 (h)
Contact: D R Shah
Position: General Secretary

Navnat Vanik Association of the UK

36 Masons Avenue, Wealdstone, Harrow, Middlesex, HA3 5AR
Tel: 01923-893421 **Tel:** 0181-861-5825
Fax: 0181-935-9565
Contact: Mr Subash K Bakhai
Position: President
Activities: Worship
Promotes understanding of the Jain and Hindu religions. Its principles are non-violence, human and animal welfare and the preservation of nature.

Oshwal Association of the UK

Oshwal Centre, Coopers Lane Road, Northaw, Potters Bar, Hertfordshire, EN6 4DG
Tel: 01707-643838 **Fax:** 01707-644562
Activities: Worship, youth, elderly, women, newsletters, inter-faith

Traditions: Svetambara
Social Groups: Halari Oshwal
Other Languages: Gujarati
The largest Jain organisation in the UK.

Shree Digamber Jain Association

72b Royston Park Road, Hatch End, Middlesex, HA5 4AF
Tel: 0181-428-3005 (h) **Fax:** 0181-961-9449
Contact: Laxmichand Shah
Position: Chairman
Activities: Worship, visits youth, elderly, women
Traditions: Digambara
Social Groups: Vanik, Oshwal
Other Languages: Gujarati
Affiliations: Oshwal Association of the UK; Navnat Vanik Association; Shree Digamber Jain Swadhiyay Mandir Trust, Songadhi, Gujarat, India

Young Indian Vegetarians

226 London Road, West Croydon, Surrey, CR0 2TF
Tel: 0181-686-6931 **Fax:** 0181-681-7143
EMail: ahimsa@ahimsa.demon.co.uk
Contact: Nitin Mehta
Position: President
Activities: Resource, youth, newsletters, books, inter-faith
Traditions: Multi-Traditional
Other Languages: Gujarati, Hindi
Believes vegetarianism transcends all other "isms" and hopes that all will extend a hand of compassion towards animals who are at our mercy.

JAIN REGIONAL AND LOCAL ORGANISATIONS AND TEMPLES

There are a variety of forms of regional and local Jain organisations that are reflected in this directory. There are only three temples, but there are also a number of organisations which operate from premises that are either owned or hired, whilst other groups are run from and/or meet in the homes of members.

In the Greater London area, quite a number of the listed Jain organisations work at a geographical level beyond the local or even Borough boundaries. These are therefore listed in both the Regional and or Area sections of Greater London and also under the Boroughs in which they are based.

ENGLAND

YORKSHIRE
Regional or County Bodies

Yorkshire Jain Foundation
The Beeches, 14 Ancaster Road, West Park, Leeds, West Yorkshire, LS16 5HH (h)
Tel: 0113-2751483 (h) **Fax:** 0113-2751483
EMail: k.v.mardia@leeds.ac.uk
Contact: Professor Kanti V Mardia
Position: President
Activities: Resource, books, inter-faith
Traditions: Multi-Traditional
Other Languages: Hindi, Gujarati
Affiliations: Jain Academy

NORTH WEST
City, Town or Local Bodies

Jain Samaj Manchester
4 The Spinney, Cheadle, Cheshire, SK8 1JA (h)
Contact: Babubhai Kapadia
Position: President
Activities: Visits, youth, elderly, women, newsletters
Traditions: Multi-Traditional
Other Languages: Gujarati, Hindi
Affiliations: National Council of Vanik Associations

EAST MIDLANDS
City, Town or Local Bodies

Jain Centre
32 Oxford Street, Leicester, Leicestershire, LE1 5XU
Tel: 0116-254-3091 **Tel:** 0116-270-2773 (h)
Contact: Dr Ramesh Mehta
Position: President
Activities: Worship, visits, inter-faith
Traditions: Multi-Traditional
Other Languages: Gujarati, Hindi
Affiliations: National Council of Vanik Organisations; Jain Academy

Oshwal Association of the UK - Leicester
20 Woodgreen Walk, Leicester, Leicestershire, LE4 7UN (h)

Tel: 0116-760820 (h)
Contact: Mr N A Zakharia
Position: Secretary

Oshwal Association of the UK - Northamptonshire
12 Stonehill Court, The Arbours, Northampton, Northamptonshire, NN3 3RA
Contact: Mr Anil Shah
Position: Chairman

WEST MIDLANDS
City, Town or Local Bodies

International Mahavir Jain Mission
322 Hampstead Road, Handsworth Wood, Birmingham, West Midlands, B20 2RA
Contact: Mr. Roshan Lal Jain
Position: President
Activities: Worship, visits
Traditions: Multi-Traditional
Languages: Punjabi, Hindi, Gujarati

Jain Ashram
322 Hampstead Road, Birmingham, West Midlands, B20 2RA

Jain Sangh Birmingham
53 Sunningdale Close, Birmingham, West Midlands, B20 1LH (h)
Contact: Mr Vinodrai Mehta
Position: Secretary
Social Groups: Oshwal, Vanik
Other Languages: Gujarati, Hindi

Vanik Samaj - Coventry
1 Courtleet Road, Coventry, CV3 5GS
Tel: 01203-413033
Contact: Mr Kishore Shah
Position: Secretary

GREATER LONDON
Regional and Area Bodies

Jain Samaj Europe - London Branch
2 Mount Road, London, NW4 3PU
Tel: 0181-202-0469
Contact: Mr K C Jain
Position: Chairperson

Jain Social Group - London
12 Westchester Drive, Hendon, London, NW4 1RD (h)
Tel: 0181-203-1601 (h)
Contact: Rajni J Shah
Position: General Secretary
Languages: Gujarati, Hindi

Jain Social Group - South London
Hill Side, Bishops Walk, Croydon, Surrey, CR0 5BA (h)
Tel: 0181-655-1499 **Tel:** 0181-681-0886 (h)
Contact: Mr Bharat Vora
Position: President

Oshwal Association of the UK
1 Campbell Road, off London Road, Croydon, Surrey, CR0 2SQ
Tel: 0181-683-0258 **Tel:** 0181-764-8363 (h)
Contact: Miss Damyanti Shah
Position: Area Secretary
Activities: Worship, resource, umbrella, visits, youth, elderly, women, newsletters
Traditions: Svetambara
Movements: Oshwal
Other Languages: Gujarati

Oshwal Association of the UK - East London & Essex
18 Carlisle Gardens, Ilford, Essex, IG1 3SN (h)
Tel: 0181-518-6658 **Tel:** 09585-34567
Fax: 01707-644562
Contact: Mr Chandulal Shah
Position: Secretary
Traditions: Svetambara
Social Groups: Oshwal
Other Languages: Gujarati
Affiliations: Institute of Jainology; World Oshwal Federation

Oshwal Association of the UK - North London
18 Avondale Road, London, N3 2ES (h)
Tel: 0181-346-5015 (h)
Contact: Mr Laxmichand Shah
Position: Chairman

Oshwal Association of the UK - North West London
213 Kenton Lane, Kenton, Harrow, Hertfordshire, HA3 8TL (h)
Tel: 0181-907-9258 (h)
Contact: Mr Ashok Shah
Position: Chairman

Oshwal Association of the UK - West Area
28 Elmsworth Avenue, Hounslow, Middlesex,
TW3 4DY (h)
Tel: 0181-737-7746
Contact: Kiran Shah
Position: Chairperson
Traditions: Svetambara
Social Groups: Oshwal
Other Languages: Gujarati

Shree Jain Sangh - East London & Essex
744a Eastern Avenue, Ilford, Essex, IG2 7HU (h)
Tel: 0181-518-4545 (h) **Fax:** 0181-554-0054
Contact: Harshad Kothari
Position: Secretary
Activities: Youth, elderly, women
Traditions: Multi-Traditional
Social Groups: Vanik
Languages: Gujarati
Affiliations: National Council of Vanik
Organisations

Borough and Local Bodies

BARNET

Bhakti Mandal
14 Camrose Avenue, Edgware, Middlesex,
HA8 6EG (h)
Tel: 0181-952-6193 (h)
Contact: Miss Parfula Shah
Position: Secretary
Activities: Youth, elderly, inter-faith
Other Languages: Gujarati, Hindi
Affiliations: Brent Indian Association; Oshwal
Association of the UK

Jain Samaj Europe - London Branch
2 Mount Road, London, NW4 3PU
Tel: 0181-202-0469
Contact: Mr K C Jain
Position: Chairperson

Jain Social Group - London
12 Westchester Drive, London, NW4 1RD (h)
Tel: 0181-203-1601 (h)
Contact: Rajni J Shah
Position: General Secretary
Activities: Umbrella
Social Groups: Vanik
Languages: Gujarati

Oshwal Association of the UK - North London
18 Avondale Road, London, N3 2ES (h)
Tel: 0181-346-5015 (h)
Contact: Mr Laxmichand Shah
Position: Chairman

Veerayatan UK
Garnett House, 4 Percy Road, Finchley, London,
N12 8DQ
Tel: 0181-445-6625 **Fax:** 0181-445-0482
Contact: Mr Mahendra Mehta
Position: Chairman
Activities: Resource, youth, newsletters
Traditions: Multi-Traditional
Languages: Gujarati, Hindi

Young Jains
6 Delamere Gardens, Mill Hill, London,
NW7 3EB (h)
Contact: Mrs Dina Shah
Position: President
Activities: Youth, newsletters
Traditions: Multi-Traditional
Other Languages: Gujarati

Shree Navyug Jain Pragati Mandal UK
31 Wentworth Hill, Barnhill Estate, Wembley,
Middlesex, HA9 9SF (h)
Tel: 0181-904-5690 (h) **Fax:** 0181-904-0091
Contact: Mr Ramesh K Shah
Position: President
Traditions: Svetambara
Other Languages: Gujarati

CROYDON

Jain Social Group - South London
Hill Side, Bishops Walk, Croydon, Surrey,
CR0 5BA (h)
Tel: 0181-655-1499 **Tel:** 0181-681-0886 (h)
Contact: Mr Bharat Vora
Position: President

Oshwal Association of the UK (South London)
Corner of London Road and Campbell Road,
37 Florida Road, Croydon, Surrey, CR0 2SQ
Tel: 0181-683-0258
Contact: Miss Damyanti Shah
Position: Secretary
Activities: Worship, resource, umbrella, visits,
youth, elderly, women, newsletters
Traditions: Svetambara

Movements: Oshwal
Other Languages: Gujarati

ENFIELD

Oshwal Association of the UK - North East London
81 Evesham Road, London, N11 2RR (h)
Tel: 0181-361-9728 (h)
Contact: Mr Narendra Shah
Position: Chairman

HARROW

Mahavir Foundation Ltd
11 Lindsay Drive, Kenton, Harrow, Middlesex, HA3 0TA (h)
Tel: 0181-204-2871 (h)   **Fax:** 0181-933-2353
Contact: Vinod Kapashi
Position: President
Activities: Worship, visits, elderly, books, inter-faith
Traditions: Multi-Traditional
Other Languages: Gujarati, Hindi

Oshwal Association of the United Kingdom
23 Sudbury Court Road, Harrow, Middlesex

Oshwal Association of the United Kingdom - North West London
213 Kenton Lane, Kenton, Harrow, Hertfordshire, HA3 8TL (h)
Tel: 0181-907-9258 (h)
Contact: Mr Ashok Shah
Position: Chairman

HOUNSLOW

Jain Association of the United Kingdom
73 Chatsworth Crescent, Hounslow, Middlesex, TW3 2PF (h)
Contact: Mr Vinay Kumar Jain
Position: General Secretary
Activities: Youth, elderly, women, inter-faith
Traditions: Multi-Traditional
Other Languages: Hindi, Punjabi, Urdu

Oshwal Association of the UK - West Area
28 Elmsworth Avenue, Hounslow, Middlesex, TW3 4DY (h)
Tel: 0181-737-7746
Contact: Kiran Shah
Position: Chairperson
Traditions: Svetambara

Social Groups: Oshwal
Other Languages: Gujarati

REDBRIDGE

Digambar Jain Visa Mewada Association of the UK
86 Princes Avenue, Woodford Green, Essex, IG8 0LP
Tel: 0181-550-0660 (h)
Contact: Mr Dilip R Shah
Position: President

Oshwal Association of the UK - East London & Essex
18 Carlisle Gardens, Ilford, Essex, IG1 3SN (h)
Tel: 01707-643838 **Fax:** 01707-644562
Contact: Mr Chandulal Shah
Position: Secretary
Traditions: Svetambara
Social Groups: Oshwal
Other Languages: Gujarati
Affiliations: Institute of Jainology; World Oshwal Federation

Shree Jain Sangh - East London & Essex
744a Eastern Avenue, Ilford, Essex, IG2 7HU (h)
Tel: 0181-518-4545 (h) **Fax:** 0181-554-0054
Contact: Harshad Kothari
Position: Secretary
Activities: Youth, elderly, women
Traditions: Multi-Traditional
Social Groups: Vanik
Languages: Gujarati
Affiliations: National Council of Vanik Organisations

WANDSWORTH

Vanik Association of the UK
71 Pretoria Road, London, SW16
Contact: Mr Mradula Shah

SOUTH EAST
City, Town or Local Bodies

Vanik Samaj of the United Kingdom
92 Osbourne Road, Brighton, West Sussex, BN1 6LU (h)
Tel: 01273-555053 (h)
Contact: Mr B C Mehta
Position: Secretary

Oshwal Association of the UK - Luton
51 Marlborough Road, Luton, Bedfordshire,
LU3 1FF (h)
Tel: 01582-450304 (h)
Contact: Mr Chandrakant P Shah
Position: Chairman

Jain Meditation Centre UK
68 Chervil, Beanhill, Milton Keynes,
Buckinghamshire, MK6 4LG (h)
Tel: 01908-240150 (h)
Contact: Shantilal Kothari
Position: Convenor
Traditions: Multi-Traditional
Other Languages: Gujarati
Affiliations: Jain International Meditation Centre,
New York, USA

Aden Vanik Association of the UK
9 Cedar Drive, Watford, Hertfordshire, WD2 6RR
(h)
Tel: 01923-893421 (h)
Contact: Mr Subash Bakhai
Position: President

KEY TO TERMS IN JAIN ORGANISATION TITLES

Note: This is not a complete glossary of significant Jain terms. It is a guide to the meaning and/or background of some of the words used in the titles of Jain organisations listed in this directory. More information on the italicised words can be tracked down elsewhere in the key and/or in the section on "Introducing the Jain Community" by using the Directory's "Significant Word Index".

Aden: Aden in the Arabian peninsula had a Jain community and its usage in an organisation's title indicates this historical connection.

Ahimsa: Means "non-harming" in relation to any living being, whether through deed or thought or word. It is connected with a positive reverence for life.

Ashram: A word of Sanskrit origin meaning a "hermitage", although in the modern Jain context it usually means a place of spiritual rest and retreat and/or a school where religious instruction is offered.

Bhakti: Hindi for "devotion".

Digambar: Variant Romanisation of *Digambara*, the name of a Jain sect, the monks of which renounce all possessions, including clothes.

Mahavir: The title of the twenty-fourth *Tirthankara* of the Jain religion (599-527BCE).

Mahila mandir: Meaning "women's centre".

Mandal: Hindi for "circle" or "group".

Mewada: Meaning "group" or "community".

Navnat: Literally means "nine *castes*" and refers to a merchant *caste* from Gujarat, India.

Navyug: Meaning "new era".

Oshwal: The name of a Jain merchant *caste* in Western India.

Pragati: "Progress".

Samaj: Gujarati or Hindi for "society", often used of organisations or associations.

Sangh: Hindi for a "group" or "union", often used of organisations.

Shree: Sanskrit for "eminent one". An honorific title of respect.

Vanik: A merchant *caste*.

Visa Oshwal: A section or sub-group of the *Oshwal* community.

Vishwa Bharati: Meaning an "institute of advanced learning".

INTRODUCING THE JEWISH COMMUNITY

JEWS IN THE UNITED KINGDOM

There are approximately 14,180,000 Jews worldwide. The Jewish population of the United Kingdom is estimated at around 300,000. Jews have been present here for many centuries, with a community initially settling following the Norman conquest. They were expelled by Edward I in 1290. Following the English Civil War, Menasseh ben Israel of Amsterdam successfully campaigned for their readmission.

Sephardi and Ashkenazi

The Jewish community in the UK is composed of both *Sephardi* and *Ashkenazi* Jews. *Sephardi* is the name given to Jews who came originally from Spain and Portugal. *Sephardi* Jews have the longest continuous communal history here, having been present in an organised form since the mid-seventeenth century.

However, the majority of Jews in the UK today are descendants of two waves of immigration by *Ashkenazi* Jews. *Ashkenazi* is the name given to the Jews of Central and East European origins. *Ashkenazi* Jews migrated to England for economic reasons or fled from persecution in the Russian Empire between 1881-1914, and from 1933 onwards during the Nazi persecution in Germany and other European countries. Since 1956 small numbers of Jewish immigrants have arrived from Arab and East European countries.

Geographical Spread

The densest concentrations of the British Jewish community are in the Greater London area and the largest provincial Jewish populations are found in Manchester, Leeds and Glasgow. There are also other sizeable Jewish communities in Birmingham, Bournemouth, Brighton, Liverpool and Southend. 70 per cent of the Jewish community are affiliated to a *synagogue*. Of these, about 60.7 per cent belong to *Orthodox* (see below) *synagogues* and 27.3 per cent to the *Progressive* sector (see below) of Reform and Liberal *synagogues* and 1.5 per cent to *Masorti synagogues*. The Registrar General's list of certified places of worship records 361 Jewish places of worship in England and Wales and this directory includes details of 327 *synagogues* in the UK of which 303 are in England and Wales.

Languages

In the UK Jewish community English is used as the normal language for day-to-day communication, but Hebrew and Yiddish are also used. Ladino was the lingua franca of *Sephardi* Jews of Spanish origin and is based on Castilian Spanish. Judaeo-Arabic is spoken among some Jews originally from Arabic lands.

Hebrew is the language of the Bible, of prayer, and of modern Israel. It is the universal language which binds together all Jews in the *Diaspora*. It is the main language of worship and many children learn it in *Cheder* (synagogue-based religious instruction) or in Jewish day schools.

Yiddish is a Jewish language of Eastern European origin which was originally a Judaeo-German dialect with a number of Slavic and Hebrew words. Yiddish is used conversationally among a number of the *Haredim* (see "Traditions" below). However, the majority of Jews cannot conduct conversations in Yiddish and in modern Jewish circles it is generally spoken only amongst the older generation of *Ashkenazi* Jews. More recently, though, there has been a concern to prevent the language dying out and organisations have been set up to propagate Yiddish language and literature.

ORIGINS AND DEVELOPMENT OF JUDAISM

Patriarchs

The origins of Judaism are set out in the *Tenakh* or Hebrew Bible. It is believed that God entered into a *Brit* (a *covenant* forming a permanent relationship) with the Jewish community, first through Abraham and then through Moses at Sinai. Where an idea of "chosenness" appears within Judaism, it is a

reference to the belief that the Jews have been "chosen" for a particular task and to live within a *covenantal* relationship with God and its implications for living. Jews believe that this *covenantal* relationship gives them no advantage above others, but rather an extra responsibility to live in accordance with God's laws and to contribute to the world's moral order.

Abraham is traditionally considered to be the first of three *avot* (forefathers) of the kinship group who are seen as ancestors of the Jewish people. When Abraham died, the leadership of this growing community was passed on to his son Isaac who, in turn, passed it on to his son Jacob. The name *Israel* (meaning "one who struggles with God"), which was given to Jacob, is also used to describe the Jewish people as a whole.

Moses and the Israelites

Judaism centres on faith in one God and the belief that God made fundamental revelations to the Jewish people through Moses at Mount Sinai around 1300 BCE, after Moses had led them out of enslavement to the Pharaohs in Egypt. Following the death of Moses, Joshua became leader and led the conquest of the land of Canaan which the Israelites believed had been promised to them by God. After the conquest the land was divided into twelve areas for the twelve tribes of Israel descended from the sons and grandsons of Jacob (Reuben, Simeon, Judah, Issachar, Zebulun, Benjamin, Dan, Naphtali, Gad, Asher, Ephraim, and Menasseh). The terms Jew and Judaism derive from the name Judah, one of the twelve sons of Jacob.

Kingdoms and Exile

In 1030 BCE Saul was appointed to be King. He was later succeeded by King David, to be followed by King Solomon who erected the great temple in Jerusalem. In time, two kingdoms developed, the Southern Kingdom of Judah with Jerusalem as its capital and the Northern Kingdom of Israel. Both Kingdoms were eventually defeated and occupied by invading armies. In 586 BCE the Temple was destroyed during the Babylonian invasion and many Jews were exiled to Babylon. Eventually, some of the Jews returned to Jerusalem and rebuilt the Temple but it was again destroyed by the Romans in 70 CE, leading to a further *diaspora*, or dispersion, of the Jewish people throughout the Roman Empire.

A new *Torah* centre was set up at Yavneh, near Jerusalem, and the foundations were laid for a *rabbinic* form of Judaism, not dependent upon the continuation of the Temple rituals. The classical texts of *rabbinic* Judaism, such as the *Mishnah* (see below), were originally produced in first and second century Galilee. These were then taken up in the Jewish academies of Babylonia (contemporary Iraq) and Palestine where, by the sixth century, the *Talmud* (see below) was completed.

Rabbinic law, commentary and Biblical interpretation have been enriched in every generation. From philosophy to mysticism and religious poetry, a rich and diverse cultural tradition has been created and its development still continues in the contemporary world.

Diaspora, Holocaust and Israel

Today there are Jewish communities in many countries. Following the Holocaust of European Jewry in which six million Jews were systematically killed by the Nazis and those who collaborated with them, the modern State of Israel was founded in 1948. Jewish communities outside of Israel are collectively known as the *Diaspora*, and UK Jews are thus one of the many *Diaspora* communities.

SOURCES OF JEWISH BELIEFS AND PRACTICES

Tenakh

Judaism is derived from the Jewish scriptures as interpreted by the *rabbis* (teachers) past and present. These scriptures, traditionally referred to by Christians as the *Old Testament*, are known among Jews as the *Tenakh*. This is an acronym

of the names of the initials of its three constituent sections: *Torah*, *Nevi'im* and *Ketuvim*.

The *Torah* (teaching) is referred to within the community as the *Humash* (from the Hebrew word meaning five) because it consists of the five books of Moses (*Genesis*, *Exodus*, *Leviticus*, *Numbers* and *Deuteronomy*) which contain what are believed to be God's revelation to Moses on Mount Sinai. It includes 613 commandments dealing with questions of ethics, spirituality, diet, ritual and all other aspects of communal and social life.

The *Nevi'im* (plural of *navi* meaning prophet) consist of the books of the prophets such as *Isaiah*, *Jeremiah*, *Ezekiel* and the twelve minor prophets, together with the related historical books of *Joshua*, *Judges*, *Samuel* and *Kings* covering the period up to the Babylonian exile.

The *Ketuvim* (writings) include such texts as the books of *Ruth* and *Esther*, as well as the *Psalms* and the *Song of Songs* which are major sources of Jewish liturgy and spiritual expression.

Talmud

The *Tenakh* is complemented by the *Talmud* (from the Hebrew root meaning "to study") which was compiled by *rabbinic* scholars in the centuries following the destruction of the second Temple by the Romans in 70CE. *Orthodox* Jews believe that it includes material that was revealed at Sinai at the same time as the *Torah*, but which was then transmitted by oral tradition down the generations.

The *Talmud* has two components: the *Mishnah* (meaning learning or study) and the *Gemara* (from the Aramaic meaning "learning"). The *Mishnah* is primarily a summary of religious and civil law. It is divided into six *sedarim* (orders), each of which contains a varying number of volumes or tractates: *zera'im* (seeds), which contains materials on prayers and agricultural laws; *mo'ed* (festivals), which deals with matters related to the *Shabbat* or *Sabbath* (see below) and festivals; *nashim* (women), which includes laws on marriage and divorce; *nezikin* (damages), which contains civil and criminal law; *kodashim* (holy things), which includes laws of sacrifice and Temple ritual; and *tohorot* (purification), which contains laws relating to personal and religious purity.

The *Gemara* is a commentary on, and discussion of, the *Mishnah*. It comprises analysis, debate and clarification of legal source material. The text is an edited record of the argumentation and discussions of the scholars, retaining the thrust and parry of the *rabbinic* colleges. The *Gemara* also contains a wide range of narrative material, including historical anecdote, allegory, prayer, religious discussion and ethical guidance.

The non-legal material in the *Talmud* is known as the *Aggadah* (an Aramaic word derived from the Hebrew word for narrative). The legal material is known as *Halakhah* (see below), from a Hebrew root meaning "to go". *Halakhah* is the practice or "way" of the tradition.

Midrash

Another important literary genre of Jewish religious tradition is *Midrash*. The *Midrash* consists of *rabbinic* interpretation of the *Bible* and includes moral teachings, legends and parables from a variety of great *rabbis*. The earliest texts date perhaps from 400-500 CE, but they reflect generations of literary development. The latest collections are from 1100-1200 CE and major anthologies were made between 1200-1500 CE.

Halakhah

The life of the Jewish community is focused around the interpretation and practice of the *Halakhah* (Jewish law). The wealth of texts used as a basis for legal decisions include Moses Maimonides' twelfth century *Code* and the sixteenth century *Shulhan Arukh* of Joseph Caro together with numerous commentaries from all periods including the present. A *Beth Din* is a court of law that rules according to *Halakhah*. Members of the Jewish community approach it for rulings on issues in personal and social life such as divorce and conversion to Judaism.

KEY JEWISH BELIEFS

Shema

The *Shema* (hear) is a daily prayer composed of three passages in the *Torah*. It contains the basic affirmation of the Jewish faith. Its first line is a clear injunction to absolute monotheism, stating that the Lord is one God (Deuteronomy 6 v3). The one God created the world, extending justice, compassion and love to all women and men. Whilst God's ways can be known, He is also awe-inspiring in His transcendence and His ultimate essence lies beyond human cognition. God is seen as both King and Father, worshipped in awe, yet close to His people in intimacy and devotion.

Torah and Mitzvot

The *Torah* is the revelation of God's will that includes the *mitzvot* (commandments) which encompass every aspect of life. The *mitzvot* enable men and women to sanctify their daily lives and bring holiness into the world. Jews emphasise the obligations of love and reverence for God who created heaven and earth. Study of the *Torah* is a passionate and sacred task that is central in the religious life. Prayer is of great significance and the weekly *Shabbat* and festivals are set aside for celebration and devotion. *Torah*, prayer, the weekly *Shabbat* and festivals infuse the mundane with the transcendent and the eternal.

Humanity

The world is understood to be a creation of God and must be treated accordingly. Humanity is made in the Divine image and love of one's neighbour is the great principle of social life and the founding inspiration of the Jewish community. Justice and compassion are Divine attributes that Jewish people are obliged to realise in all aspects of their lives. Sin and spiritual estrangement are profound and ever-present and the *High Holy Days* of the Jewish year are devoted to penitence and prayer, but also to charity and forgiveness, since the compassion of God can restore broken relationships.

Kingdom of God

Jews have traditionally looked towards the establishment of God's *kingdom* on earth. Also, traditionally, this has been connected with a belief in a *Mashiach* (Anointed One), or *Messiah*. There are different Jewish understandings of the concept of *Mashiach*. In the original sense of "anointed one", the term covers Jewish kings such as David and Solomon.

The traditional belief is that a special person will reveal himself and the Jewish community will be gathered from its exile around the world and re-establish itself in the ancient land; the Temple will be rebuilt and never again be destroyed; and the *Kingdom of God* will be established on earth for everyone and the dead will be resurrected. Some understand this in a physical sense, whilst others think it refers to the spiritual continuity of the soul. Another perspective, often found among *Progressive* Jews, is that there will be no individual *Mashiach* but rather a new *Messianic* era without war and conflict.

Eretz Yisrael, Zionism and Attitudes Towards Israel

For the Jewish people as a whole, the land of Israel is of great importance. For centuries, Israel has been viewed by the Jewish people as the eternal homeland promised by God at the beginning of history. After centuries of exile, the foundation of the modern state of Israel has created a focus of Jewish life which is both religious and ethnic in its aspirations.

Jews everywhere tend to feel a common destiny with the Jews of Israel as well as with the *diaspora* throughout the world. When key events occur in Israel, Jews in the UK share in either the joy or the pain of these events. For the great majority of Jewish people, with the exception of some *Haredim* (or *Ultra-Orthodox* see below), the modern state of Israel is an integral part of their identity. It is seen as being of such paramount importance to the Jewish people that attempts to deny its right to exist are seen as veiled anti-semitism and there are few issues around which Jews unite as much as the defence and survival of Israel.

The term *Zionism* comes from Zion, another biblical name for Jerusalem and, by extension, for Israel. The concept of *Zionism* is found in both a religious and political sense. As a political movement, *Zionism* is understood within the Jewish community as a liberation movement of the Jewish people which is intended to end the centuries of exile and to secure a Jewish homeland in Palestine. This movement was officially begun at the end of the nineteenth century by Theodor Herzl who founded the World Zionist Organisation which is now based in Israel.

Some *Haredim* (mainly in Israel itself) oppose political *Zionism* on the basis of denying that a secular state can have religious significance. By contrast, religious *Zionists* see redemptive significance in the development of the State of Israel and view the ingathering of the Jewish exiles as a manifestation of Divine providence.

TRADITIONS IN JUDAISM

There are a number of different Jewish traditions present in the UK. Many Jews have moved between traditions. Some people brought up in *Orthodox* communities join *Progressive synagogues* in later life and vice versa.

Orthodox

The *Orthodox* Jewish community accords the *Bible* and its *rabbinical* interpretations full authority in determining law, life and religious practice. It believes both the *Torah* and the oral law contained in the *Talmud* to have been revealed by God and to contain God's unchanging words. *Orthodoxy* understands itself as representing the mainstream of Judaism in historical continuity with the Jewish inheritance.

Hasidic

Within the orbit of *Orthodoxy* is the *Hasidic* movement. The word *Hasidic* comes from *Hasid*, which literally means "pious". *Hasidic* groups originated in the *shtetls* (villages) of Central and Eastern Europe during the eighteenth and nineteenth centuries. They followed the teachings of Israel ben Eliezer also known as the Baal Shem Tov who lived in the seventeenth century in Poland, and took a mystical approach to Judaism. Today the term *Hasidic* generally refers to those *Orthodox* whose theology is influenced more by mystic spirituality than by an intellectual orientation.

Haredim

The *Haredim* (often popularly referred to by people outside this group as the *Ultra-Orthodox*), include many *Hasidic* Jews, although not all *Haredim* are *Hasidic*. The distinction between *Haredim*, whether *Hasidic* or not, and the more mainstream *Orthodox* is that the *Haredim* seek to exclude modern culture from their lives and tend to reproduce in minute detail the cultural ways of previous generations.

Some groupings are influenced by the body of Jewish mystical philosophy known as the *Kabbalah* which consists of teachings that were transmitted within select circles of disciples. The most important *Kabbalistic* text is the *Zohar*, which is a commentary on the *Humash* and was composed in thirteenth century Spain.

Progressive

Progressive (which includes both *Liberal* and *Reform* Jews, see section on "Jewish Organisations" below) Jews believe that the *Torah* was inspired by God, but written down by humans according to God's will. Thus they see it as open to challenge and revision and subject to the need of reinterpretation. Revelation is viewed as progressive because God's will is seen to be constantly unfolding. *Progressive* Jews make a distinction between those parts of Judaism that have eternal significance and absolute value, for example, the *Shabbat* and the pursuit of justice, and those seen as temporary and relative, such as gender distinctions in Jewish law.

The *Reform* movement began in the early nineteenth century as an attempt to create a Judaism consistent with the modern world. The *Liberal* movement was first established in Germany and the USA as an offshoot of the *Reform* movement. Its adherents considered sincerity of heart to be paramount in Judaism and believed that rituals should be relatively unimportant. They therefore reformed the *synagogue* services and belief and practice in the light of modern knowledge and circumstances. In modern times, there has been a return to many of the traditional rituals.

Masorti (Conservative)

Established at the beginning of the twentieth century, what is known as *Masorti* in the UK and as *Conservative* Judaism in the United States, is sometimes characterised as half-way between *Orthodox* Judaism and *Progressive* Judaism. *Masorti* Jews wish to maintain a commitment to the *Halakhah* whilst taking an historically contextual approach to its application. So, for example, the *Shabbat* liturgy may be very similar to that used in *Orthodox* congregations, but men and women may sit together in the synagogue during services. *Masorti* Jews attempt to comply with as much of the *Torah* as is practicable in modern society, but they may accept the inevitability, for example, of driving to *synagogue* on the *Sabbath* now that members may live further away.

JEWISH LIFE

In *Orthodox*, *Masorti* and *Reform* Judaism a Jew is traditionally understood to be any person born of a Jewish mother or a person who has converted to the Jewish faith. In *Liberal* Judaism and *Reform* Judaism in the United States, having a Jewish father may also be considered to qualify a child for membership of the community if the child has had a Jewish upbringing.

Circumcision

A number of ceremonies mark transitional points in Jewish life. As a sign of God's *covenant* with Abraham, Abraham was required to *circumcise* himself and his two sons (Isaac and Ishmael). Because of this, Jewish law asserts that a male Jew should normally be *circumcised* on the eighth day of his life. This requirement is known as *Brit Milah* and is carried out by a trained *Mohel* (circumciser) usually in the home with family and friends present. There is no equivalent requirement for girls, although in some communities a baby-naming ceremony for babies of either gender takes place and they may be blessed in the *synagogue*.

Barmitzvah and Batmitzvah

Before the age of thirteen, male Jews are not expected to carry responsibility for *mitzvot* (the commandments), but at thirteen years old they take up a new position within the community. The ceremony which marks this is called *Barmitzvah* (son of commandment) and it involves the young man reading in Hebrew from the weekly portion of the *Torah* scroll, usually during the Saturday morning service in the *synagogue*. After the service the family of the boy who has become *Barmitzvah* may provide *Kiddush* (see below under "Jewish Worship") for the congregation, presents are given to the boy, and some families may have a party for family and friends.

In *Progressive* Judaism there is also a *Batmitzvah* (daughter of commandment ceremony) for thirteen year old females which is in the same form as the *Barmitzvah* ceremony. In some *Orthodox* circles girls celebrate a *Batmitzvah* at the age of twelve, the traditional coming of age for females, whereas others may participate in a communal *Bat Hayil* ceremony. This ceremony often takes place on a Sunday and involves the recitation of *Psalms* and special readings. In *Progressive* Judaism there is also a ceremony called *Kabbalat Torah*, which takes place at the age of sixteen and marks the culmination of the young person's religious education.

Shabbat

The *Shabbat* (or *Sabbath*) is central to the rhythm of Jewish individual, family and communal life. It is observed as a day of worship, rest and peace. Saturday, the day on which it is observed, is believed to correspond to the seventh day of the creation on which God rested from creating the earth.

Shabbat begins about half an hour before sunset on the Friday evening and ends at nightfall on the Saturday night because it states in the scriptural *Book of Genesis* refers to "evening and morning", implying that a day is deemed to begin on its preceding night. The times therefore vary from week to week, starting later in summer and earlier in winter. Exact times are available in the Jewish press. *Shabbat* is concluded with *Havdalah*, a ceremony of separation marking the transition from the *Shabbat* to the working week, which is performed at home after the last *Shabbat* services.

During *Shabbat* it is forbidden for Jews to engage in any activities which are considered as work. This general rule has been variously interpreted by different Jewish traditions. For example, *Orthodox* Jews may not drive their cars on *Shabbat* as this entails making a spark in the engine. This is seen as synonymous with starting a fire which, in turn, is considered to be work. *Progressive* Jews, however, do not deem this as work and therefore do drive. The general exception to these *Shabbat* rules, as in other areas of Jewish life, is where there is danger to life, in which case the laws of the *Shabbat* are set aside and precedence is given to saving lives.

Kashrut

Judaism has a series of important food regulations known as *kashrut* (meaning "fitness"). Animals, birds and fish might be either *kosher* (permitted) or *treif* (forbidden). *Treif* is a Yiddish word, derived from the Hebrew *terephah*, which refers to an animal torn by a wild beast.

Acceptable animals for consumption are all those with split hooves which chew the cud, such as sheep, cows and deer. Pigs, rabbits and horses are unacceptable, as are birds of prey. Other birds are acceptable provided that there is a tradition that the bird is *kosher*. For example, chicken is acceptable but hawk is not. Eggs are considered *kosher* if they are from *kosher* fowl.

Only fish which have both fins and scales are acceptable. So, for example, cod is acceptable but prawns are not.

Provided that they are clear of all insects, fruit and vegetables are all acceptable and are also considered *parve*, which means that they are neither milk nor meat products and can be eaten with both (see below). Food which contains, or has been cooked in, products from non-acceptable animals would be unacceptable. Thus, for example, chips cooked in non-*kosher* animal fat are not acceptable.

For meat to be *kosher* it must have been humanely slaughtered by a *shochet* (a qualified slaughterer) working under the supervision of the *Beth Din*. *Shechitah* (which is slaughter according to Jewish law) involves the draining of blood from the animal by slitting its throat.

Once killed, the meat from the animal must then be *kashered*. This involves the meat being soaked and salted or, in certain cases such as liver, broiled, in order to remove excess blood. The prohibition against consuming blood comes from the view that blood represents life. So, for example, eggs with blood spots may also not be eaten.

Jewish law prohibits the mixing of milk foods with meat foods. This derives from biblical prohibitions against boiling a kid in its mother's milk. Separate sets of kitchen utensils are used for the two types of food and a time lapse is observed between eating one type of food and the other. Glass (although not pyrex) can be used for both types of food. Fish may be served with milk but then it would not be eaten at the same meal as meat. The extent to which Jewish people are observant of these food laws varies from person to person. If intending to provide food for Jewish guests it is wise to check first about any requirements.

Israel

The majority of Jews identify with Israel and many become involved with its life in several ways. For many Jews, their identity revolves much more around Israel than around the *synagogue* and other "religious" matters. The means of identification and involvement include: taking regular holidays there; taking an interest in Israeli news, politics and culture; becoming involved in and/or giving money to Israeli charities; eating Israeli food, and so on.

Many Jews view Israel as their "spiritual homeland". It is a common practice amongst Jewish teenagers to participate in an Israel experience "gap year" following their final examinations in order to learn Hebrew. These tours are often a key factor in developing a Jewish identity.

Women

Women, and especially mothers, are seen as having a key role in Jewish life because of their roles in the family which is at the centre of the practice of Judaism and, in particular, of many of its festivals and celebrations. In *Progressive* Judaism the gender role distinctions specified in Jewish law are no longer recognised as binding. They are, however, still upheld in *Orthodox* Judaism. For example, when a marriage breaks down, in the *Orthodox* and *Reform* traditions a woman may not remarry in her *synagogue* until she has been given a *get* (religious divorce) by her husband and a man normally cannot remarry until a woman has accepted a bill of divorce from him.

Halachically, a woman is believed to become ritually unclean by the process of menstruation. According to *Halachah*, before marriage, after menstruation, and after childbirth, women should visit a *mikveh*. Married women in the *Orthodox* tradition observe this tradition, but many *Progressive* Jews view the practice of visiting the *mikveh* as an option rather than as obligatory.

In *Progressive* Judaism both women and men can form a *minyan* (see section on "Jewish Worship"), carry the *Torah*, and become *rabbis*. In the *Orthodox* sector women do not to take on these roles, but many *Orthodox synagogues* employ women as teachers and elect women to positions of *synagogal* and organisational management.

JEWISH WORSHIP

Traditionally, during worship all males and married women should cover their heads as a sign of respect when addressing God. Some Jews keep their heads covered at all times in recognition of the continual presence of God. The traditional means for doing this is, for Jewish men, the small cap known as a *kippah* (in Hebrew) or a *yarmulkah* (in Yiddish). Among the *Orthodox*, many married women cover their heads at all times with a *sheitel* (wig). In principle, any form of headcovering is acceptable for either sex.

Shabbat Worship

Shabbat is the key occasion for Jewish communal worship. The most regular and well attended forms of communal worship on *Shabbat* are *Kabbalat Shabbat* (the first *Shabbat* service at dusk on Friday evening) and *Maariv* (the evening service said every day including Friday night), as well as *Shaharit* and *Musaf* on Saturday morning. In *Progressive synagogues* the Saturday morning service usually lasts one to two hours and in *Orthodox synagogues* between two and three hours.

In the *Orthodox* community the entire service, except the *rabbi's* sermon and the prayer for the Royal Family, is conducted in Hebrew. *Progressive* Jewish congregations often say other prayers in English, although the extent of English usage varies from congregation to congregation. In *Progressive synagogues*, the service may be accompanied by musical instruments. In *Orthodox synagogues* there is no instrumental accompaniment but there may be unaccompanied singing by a male choir.

During the *Shabbat* morning service a portion of the *Torah* is read. The *Torah* is divided into the weekly *Sidrah* or *Parashah* (fifty-four weekly portions) to be read each consecutive Saturday in the *synagogue*. In an *Orthodox synagogue* a minimum of seven men are called to the reading of the *Torah*. Following this reading, the *Haftarah* (an excerpt from the *Nevi'im* which has some connection with the *Torah* portion) is read.

In many congregations, either regularly every week or occasionally, *Kiddush* is recited after the service in an adjoining room or hall. This is the prayer proclaiming the holiness of the *Shabbat* and festivals and on those days it is recited before meals over a cup of wine. The congregation usually stays for biscuits, cake and a chat.

Other Communal Worship

Three daily prayers are stipulated. These are *Shaharit* (morning service), *Minhah* (afternoon prayers) and *Maariv* (evening prayers). In the *Orthodox* community formal communal prayers can only be said when a *minyan* (group of ten or more Jewish males) has been convened. Communal worship can take place anywhere. An example of this is where collective prayers are said at the home of a bereaved person during the seven days of mourning immediately after a death. This is known as *sitting Shivah*. It is not necessary for a *rabbi* to officiate at communal prayers and any person familiar with them may lead them.

The *Siddur* (prayer book - derived from the Hebrew word meaning "order") contains prayers for communal services, for private prayer, for special occasions and for travellers. The various Jewish traditions have different authorised *Prayer Books* for use in their synagogues. Prayers are mainly in Hebrew with the English translation given in prayer books on the opposite page. As with all Hebrew texts, prayer books open from right to left, since Hebrew is written from right to left. There are special prayer books for the *Pilgrim Festivals* and for the *High Holy Days*, known as *Mahzorim* (from the Hebrew word meaning cycle).

Special services for children are held in many larger *synagogues* to encourage them to be able to take an active role in the service when they are older. Above all, *Shabbat* is a family-orientated time with special meals and time for the whole family.

Synagogue

The principal place of Jewish communal worship is the *synagogue*, which *Ashkenazi* Jews usually refer to by the Yiddish word *shul*. Due to the *Orthodox* rule of walking to the synagogue on *Shabbat* and at festivals, *Orthodox synagogue* buildings have moved from inner city areas, where Jews first settled, to the suburbs of towns and cities where the main Jewish communities are now established.

The *synagogue* is a building where worship takes place, but it is also a central place of administration, cultural and social activities and education programmes. *Synagogues* are self-financing and may have a *Heder* (room) which is a school for Jewish education where children can gain religious knowledge and learn Hebrew. The *synagogue* might also offer adult Jewish education. In the larger *synagogues* services are held most mornings and evenings.

In *Orthodox synagogues* men and women are separated for reasons of propriety and women usually sit in a gallery above the section where the men conduct the service. Sometimes, where there is no gallery, the women are seated behind the men with a short curtain or partition separating the two. In some very small house *synagogues*, women and men worship in different rooms.

Inside the *synagogue*, a range of symbols and objects may be seen. The *Magen David* (Shield of David) is a six pointed star which is a Jewish symbol of no particular religious significance. The *Menorah* is an seven-branched candlestick of a type dating back to the Temple in Jerusalem prior to its destruction by the Romans.

The *Bimah* is a raised platform, usually in the centre of the *synagogue*, from which the *Torah* is read. Most *synagogues* also have a pulpit from which the sermon is preached. A *Chazzan* (see section on "Personnel") leads congregational prayer. The *Aron Ha-Kodesh* (Holy Ark) is an alcove or cupboard with wooden or ornate door panels and it contains the *Torah* scrolls. In Western countries it is usually on the East wall of the *synagogue* which is the direction of Jerusalem. It has an embroidered curtain across it, known as a *Parochet*. A *Ner Tamid* (everlasting light) is a lamp hung in front of the *Aron Kodesh*, reminding the congregation of the eternal presence of God.

The *Sefer Torah* is a hand-written scroll of the *Torah*. It is read four times a week, on Monday and Thursday mornings, Saturday mornings and Saturday afternoons. It is also read on other distinctive days such as the holy days. The *Torah* scroll is kept inside a velvet cover and is usually decorated with metal breastplates and adornments. It has an honoured place in Jewish worship, especially at the festival of *Simhat Torah* (see below). The sanctity of the *Sefer Torah* is underlined by the use of a *Yad* which is a long pointer in the shape of a hand used by the reader so that the place may be kept without touching the parchment.

A *mezuzah* (literally meaning door post) is a parchment scroll containing two sections of scripture (Deuteronomy 6 v. 4-9 and Deuteronomy 11 v. 13-21) which constitute the first paragraphs of the *Shema*, placed in a small, hollow box. These may be found on the doors of *synagogue* buildings and are also found on the doorposts of most Jewish homes. They are placed slanting in the top third of the right hand doorpost of every room except the toilet and the bathroom and they signify the sanctity of home and communal life.

Clothing and Prayer

Tephilin (phylacteries) are worn on the forehead and left arm by male *Orthodox* Jews over thirteen years old. They consist of two strap-on leather boxes which enclose parchment sections of the scriptures, the wearing of which is believed by the *Orthodox* to be in accordance with scriptural commandment. *Tephilin* are worn for morning prayers, but not for *Shabbat* or festival prayers.

Tallitot (the singular being *tallit* or *tallis*) are traditional prayer shawls, often with black or blue stripes. *Tzitzit* are the fringes which are attached to the four corners. Traditional style prayer shawls are usually made of wool.

Some *Orthodox* Jewish men may wear the fringes, known as *Arba Kanfot* (meaning "four corners"), at all times on a vest under their clothes. In *Progressive* Jewish communities women are often encouraged to wear a prayer shawl if they take a leading role in corporate worship, but they are not obliged to do so.

JEWISH CALENDAR AND FESTIVALS

Calendar

According to the Jewish calendar, which counts from what is traditionally believed to have been the year of the world's creation, the Common Era year 1997 is the Jewish year 5757. The relevant year appears on Jewish legal documents such as marriage certificates, on Jewish periodicals and on grave stones.

Jews use a combined lunar and solar calendar, where each month is equivalent to twenty-nine or thirty days, and a year is usually three hundred and fifty-four days. In a nineteen solar year cycle an extra month is inserted into years three, six, eight, eleven, fourteen, seventeen and nineteen.

Festivals

Because months are based on the moon, no fixed date for Jewish festivals can be given in the *Gregorian* calendar. With regard to the festivals mentioned below, the period of duration given is that followed by *Orthodox* Jews. *Progressive* Jews may celebrate the main festivals for a day less. The reason for this is that prior to mathematical calculation of the new moon, festivals were originally given an extra day in order to ensure their observance on the correct date, since a new moon could fall on one of two days. *Progressive* Jews believe that now the new moon can accurately be calculated the addition of an extra day is no longer needed and this has always been the practice in the State of Israel, except in the case of *Rosh Hashanah* (see below) which is observed for two days.

Jewish festivals always begin in the evening and are grouped into three types. These are: the *Yamim Noraim* (Days of Awe); the *Shalosh Regalim* (Hebrew literally meaning "three foot festivals") which are the three festivals that have an agricultural and historical significance and in which it was traditional for every Jew to go to Jerusalem; and the *minor festivals*.

The Yamim Noraim

Rosh Hashanah (September/October)
Rosh Hashanah is the Jewish New Year. It involves two days of judgement and penitence. The *Shofar* (ram's horn) is blown in the *synagogue* to remind people of their sins and to call them to spiritual awareness. It begins the Jewish year and the ten days of repentance which culminate in *Yom Kippur*. *Rosh Hashanah* and *Yom Kippur* are days during which no work may be done.

Yom Kippur (Day of Atonement)
A twenty-five hour fast devoted to prayer and worship, recollecting the sins of the past year and seeking forgiveness for them from one another and from God.

The Shalosh Regalim

Sukkot (September/October)
This is the festival of *Tabernacles* which commemorates the wandering of the children of Israel between Egypt and Canaan and God's protection during this period. There is a practice of building *sukkot* (temporary huts) onto the sides of houses or in gardens. This practice is intended to recall how the Jewish ancestors lived in the wilderness. Normally, the UK climate prevents Jews living in the *sukkot* for the entirety of the festival, but Jewish families may have their meals in them. *Sukkot* can often be seen on the sides of *synagogue* and Jewish communal buildings.

The festival has a harvest connection which is acknowledged by taking four types of plant which are carried in procession around the synagogue: a *lulav* (palm branch), an *etrog* (citron), two *aravot* (willow branches) and three *hadassim* (myrtle branches). In the *Diaspora*, *Sukkot* is a nine day period with the first two and last two days as festival days. The final day is *Simchat Torah*.

Simchat Torah (The Rejoicing of the Torah)
Celebrates the completion and recommencement of the annual cycle of readings from the *Torah* in the *synagogue*.

Pesach (March/April)

Pesach (often known in the English language as *Passover*) occurs at a time when the first fruits of barley would have been offered as sacrifice in the Temple when the barley harvest was gathered. It is an eight day period of which the first two and last two days are celebrated as festivals. It commemorates the Exodus from Egypt and God's redemption of the Hebrew people.

As a reminder that the Hebrews had no time to wait for bread to rise before they had to leave Egypt, no *hametz* (leavened products) are consumed at this time. Such foods must be removed from the home, either by eating them beforehand or by giving them away. Prior to the festival the house is scrupulously cleaned in order to remove any crumbs of *hametz*. *Matzah* (unleavened bread) is consumed during the festival period. A spare set of kitchen utensils is usually used for the duration of the festival.

The home ceremony centres around the *seder* meal which, in the *Diaspora*, takes place on the first two nights of the festival. The order of service surrounding this meal is found in the *Haggadah* (*Seder* service book) which utilises verses from the *Torah* and from *Midrashic* commentaries in order to tell the story of the *Exodus*. The *seder* is an important family occasion, in which all present, including young children, are encouraged to participate.

Shavuot (Pentecost) (May/June)

This festival commemorates the Israelites' reception of the *Torah* at Mount Sinai and their pledging of allegiance to God. On the night before the festival many Jews stay awake all night studying the *Torah* in preparation for the anniversary of the revelation on the next day. The *Book of Ruth* is read during *Shavuot*. This festival lasts for two days and is the harvest festival of Mediterannean first fruits such as olives, dates, grapes, and figs. Traditionally, dairy foods are eaten on *Shavuot*.

Minor festivals and additional fast days

There are other festivals which form a part of Jewish life but which are without restrictions on work:

Hanukah (December)

This festival commemorates the rededication of the Second Temple in Jerusalem by the Maccabees in 168 BCE after it had been desecrated by the Hellenists. *Rabbinic* legend recounts that only one jar of oil with the *High Priest's* seal on it was found which was fit for use to light the Temple *menorah* (seven-branched candlestick), but by a miracle the little jar lasted for eight whole days.

Hanukah lasts for eight days, and for each day one more candle on the *Hanukiah* (a nine-branched candelabrum) is lit at home and in the *synagogue*. It has a lamp for each of the eight days with an additional serving light. Sometimes large *Hanukiyyot* are erected outside the *synagogue* and in city squares. Some families give gifts to children at this time.

Purim (February/March)

Is the day which commemorates the story found in the *Book of Esther* about the saving of the Jews of the Persian empire from the evil government minister Haman. On this day children dress up and the *synagogue* services include the reading of the *Book of Esther*, with the worshippers booing and hissing whenever Haman's name is mentioned. Presents are given to friends as well as gifts to the poor. It is a time marked by fancy dress parties and general merry-making.

Yom Hashoa (April/May)

Holocaust Remembrance Day, marked by the lighting of candles and by communal services or meetings.

Yom Ha'atzma'ut (May)

Israeli Independence day is celebrated by a service in many *synagogues*.

Tishah Be-Av (July/August)

This day commemorates the destruction of the First Temple in 586BCE and the Second Temple in 70CE as well as other calamities affecting the Jewish people. It is widely observed as a fast day.

There are also a number of other fasts which are observed by Jews to varying degrees. For example, the day before *Purim* is the *Fast of Esther*.

JEWISH ORGANISATIONS

General Organisations

The main national representative organisation for British Jews is the Board of Deputies of British Jews which was founded in 1760. Every *synagogue* and national communal organisation is entitled to send delegates to the Board. It deals with secular matters affecting the status and rights of British Jews and has a number of Committees which deal with a range of issues (for example, Defence and Group Relations, Education, Israel and Foreign Affairs). It also has a Community Research Unit and a Central Enquiry Desk.

There are several other national representative organisations which are more specific in nature, such as the League of Jewish Women and the Anglo-Jewish Association. Local *Jewish Representative Councils* are found in areas of sizeable Jewish population and include both religious and community organisations. In terms of specifically religious organisations, there are national *synagogue* groupings which have local synagogues affiliated to them, for example, the United Synagogue, the Reform Synagogues of Great Britain and the Union of Liberal and Progressive Synagogues.

There are other national religious organisations of a more specific nature, for example the Initiation Society which trains and authorises people to circumcise in the *Orthodox* tradition, and the National Council of Shechita Boards which deals with issues concerning *shechita*. In addition there are many local religious organisations including local *shechita* boards and *kosher* meals-on-wheels services.

There is a range of national and local organisations which are particular to the Jewish community but do not as such serve a religious function. These include various welfare organisations such as Jewish Care and the Jewish Marriage Guidance Council. There are political organisations and also *Zionist* cultural groups and charitable refugee support groups.

There are several communal educational organisations and *Yeshivot* (plural of *Yeshiva*, a place of advanced Jewish learning, primarily concerned with *Talmudic* study). Whilst *Yeshivot* offer ordination to those studying within them who wish to serve in the *Rabbinate*, there are also academic Colleges which specifically serve this need. In *Orthodox* Judaism there is Jews' College in London and, in *Progressive* Judaism, the Leo Baeck College. In addition, there are many local and national organisations promoting Jewish education and culture in general, including historical societies, musical groups, youth groups and Holocaust remembrance organisations.

There is a whole range of multi-national Jewish organisations. For example, there is a Conference of European Rabbis to which all *Orthodox rabbis* are entitled to belong. The Reform Synagogues of Great Britain and the Union of Liberal and Progressive Synagogues are constituent members of the World Union of Progressive Judaism which aims to foster the growth and practice of *Progressive* Judaism. Further details of all Jewish organisations can be found in *The Jewish Year Book*, an annual publication.

Orthodox Organisations

There are a number of organised groupings of *Orthodox synagogues*, the largest of which is The United Synagogue, established in 1870. The spiritual leader of many *Orthodox Ashkenazi* Jews is the *Chief Rabbi* who is appointed by the Chief Rabbinate Council consisting of representatives of the Orthodox United Synagogue. Other *Orthodox* groupings are the smaller Federation of Synagogues and the Union of Hebrew Congregation Synagogues and there are also Spanish and Portuguese Sephardi congregations. The oldest *Orthodox synagogue* still in use in the UK is the Bevis Marks Sephardi *synagogue* in London, which was built in 1701.

The best known *Hasidic* group in Britain is part of a world movement known as *Lubavitch*. The *Lubavitch* feel a particular obligation to persuade Jewish people to become religiously observant and to prevent the assimilation of Jews into secular culture. *Hasidic* Jews are concentrated in London and Greater Manchester with smaller numbers in other places where there are large Jewish communities.

Reform and Liberal Organisations

There are two *Progressive* Jewish traditions in the UK: *Reform* Judaism and *Liberal* Judaism.

Reform Judaism is the larger of the two traditions and originally the *Liberal* movement was more radically different from the *Orthodox* community than was Reform Judaism. Now, however, the initial distinction between *Liberal* and *Reform* Judaism has diminished and the communities have, to a significant degree, converged in their practice. *Rabbis* for both communities are given the same training at Leo Baeck College in London. Most UK *Progressive* Jews live in London, the South of England, Manchester and Leeds.

The *Reform* movement has its own *Beth Din* (established in 1948), cemeteries, day school and a major cultural centre in North London and is organised nationally in the Reform Synagogues of Great Britain. The first *Reform synagogue* in the UK was the West London Synagogue opened in 1840.

The *Liberal* movement began in the UK in 1902 with the foundation of the Jewish Religious Union. The first *Liberal* Jewish congregation was set up in 1910 in London and was called the Liberal Jewish Synagogue. Since 1944 the name of the *Liberal* movement's national representative organisation has been the Union of Liberal and Progressive Synagogues.

Masorti

The *Masorti* congregations are affiliated to the Assembly of Masorti Synagogues which was founded in 1985.

Independent Synagogues

In addition to the formal groupings, there are a number of independent synagogues of both *Orthodox* and *Progressive* traditions.

Personnel

The *rabbi's* role within the Jewish community is to teach and to preach, to take on pastoral duties and to advise on Jewish law. All *rabbis* in the *Orthodox* sector are male whilst the *Progressive* sector has both male and female *rabbis*. *Rabbis* are often, but not always, salaried by the congregation. A *synagogue* minister can sometimes be referred to as *Reverend* which often implies that the minister does not have *rabbinic* ordination. *Hasidic* groupings are led by *Rebbes*. The *Rebbe* is a charismatic spiritual leader. The office of *Rebbe* is hereditary, often, but not always, being passed down to the eldest son.

A *Hazzan/Cantor* is a singer who leads the synagogue services and, in *Orthodox* synagogues, is male. Progressive *synagogues* tend not to have *Hazzanim* (plural of *Hazzan*), preferring to have a choir to assist the *rabbi* during services. A *sofer* (scribe) is a person who writes *Torah* scrolls, *tephillin*, and *mezuzot* by hand, using a quill pen on parchments.

A *dayan* is a judge in Jewish law who serves on the *Beth Din* and administers Jewish law in the cases brought before it. In an *Orthodox Beth Din*, *dayanim* are permanent salaried members, whilst in the *Reform Beth Din*, *rabbis* serve in rotation as *dayanim*. The *Hevra Kaddisha* (holy brotherhood) is a Jewish burial society responsible for washing and shrouding Jewish corpses and for looking after the needs of the bereaved.

Many *synagogues* have a committee structure. Some medium sized *synagogues* have part-time Secretaries and some large synagogues have full time Secretaries or Executive Directors who can be approached as a first point of contact with the community.

FURTHER READING

Alexander, P S (ed), *Textual Sources for the Study of Judaism*, Manchester University Press, Manchester, 1987.

Cohn-Sherbok, D, *The Jewish Heritage*, Blackwell, Oxford, 1988.

Cohn-Sherbok, D, "Judaism in Modern Britain: A New Orientation", in Badham, P (ed), *Religion, State and Society in Modern Britain*, Edwin Mellen Press, Lampeter, 1989, pp 209-224.

Close, B E, *Judaism*, Hodder and Stoughton, London, 1991.

Cooper, H and Morrison, P, *A Sense of Belonging: Dilemmas of British Jewish Identity*, Weidenfeld and Nicolson, London, 1991.

de Lange, N, *Judaism*, Oxford University Press, Oxford, 1987.

Englander, D, "Integrated But Insecure: A Portrait of Anglo-Jewry at the Close of the Twentieth Century" in Parsons, G (ed), *The Growth of Religious Diversity: Britain from 1945, Volume 1, Traditions*, Routledge, London, pp. 95-132.

Friesel, E, *Atlas of Modern Jewish History*, Oxford University Press, Oxford, 1990.

Gilbert, M, *Jewish History Atlas*, Weidenfeld and Nicholson, London, 1969.

Gilbert, M, *Holocaust Atlas*, Board of Deputies of British Jews, London, 1978.

Glatzer, N N (ed), *The Judaic Tradition*, Behrman, New York, 1969.

Goldberg, D and Rayner, J, *The Jewish People*, Viking Penguin, 1989.

Goodkin, J and Citran, J, *Women in the Jewish Community: Review and Recommendations*, Women in the Community, London, 1994.

Gubbay, L and Levy A, *Ages of Man: A Plain Guide to Traditional Jewish Custom, Practice and Belief in Modern Times*, DLT, London 1985.

Kushner, T (ed), *The Jewish Heritage in British History: Englishness and Jewishness*, Frank Cass and Company, London, 1992.

Lawton, C, *The Jewish People: Some Questions Answered*, Board of Deputies of British Jews (Central Jewish Lecture and Information Centre), London, 1983.

Massil, S W (ed), *The Jewish Year Book*, Vallentine Mitchell, London, 1997.

Neusner, J, *Between Time and Eternity: The Essentials of Judaism*, Dickenson Publishing Company, Califorrnia, 1975.

Pearl, C and Brookes, R S, *A Guide to Jewish Knowledge*, Jewish Chronicle Publications. London, 1965.

Pilkington, C , *Teach Yourself Judaism*, Hodder, 1995.

Reform Synagogues of Great Britain, *Faith and Practice: A Guide to Reform Judaism*, Reform Synagogues of Great Britain, London, 1991.

Sacks, J, *The Persistence of Faith*, Weidenfeld and Nicholson, London, 1991.

Schmool, M and Cohen, F, *British Synagogue Membership in 1990*, Board of Deputies of British Jews (Community Research Unit), London, 1991.

Schmool, M and Miller, S, *Women in the Jewish Community: Survey Report, Women in the Community*, London, 1994.

Seltzer, R M, *Jewish People, Jewish Thought*, Collier Macmillan, London, 1980.

Turner, R, *Jewish Living*, Jewish Chronicle Publications, London, 1982.

Union of Liberal and Progressive Synagogues, *Affirmations of Liberal Judaism*, London, 1992.

Unterman, A, *The Wisdom of the Jewish Mystics*, Sheldon Press, London, 1976.

Waterman, S and Kosmin, B, *British Jewry in the Eighties*, Board of Deputies of British Jews (Community Research Unit), London, 1986.

Williams, B, *The Making of Manchester Jewry: 1740-1875*, Manchester University Press, Manchester, 1976.

JEWISH UNITED KINGDOM ORGANISATIONS

The Jewish community has an extensive range of organisations operating at a United Kingdom level. This directory has prioritised the inclusion of those with a specifically religious focus or basis, although a number of more broadly communal organisations are also included. There are, however, a wider number of communal groups and bodies, contact details of which can be obtained from the annual publication, *The Jewish Year Book*.

Agency for Jewish Education
735 High Road, North Finchley, London, N12 0US
Tel: 0181-343-6266 **Fax:** 0181-343-6298
EMail: aje@brijnet.org
Contact: Simon Goulden
Position: Chief Executive
Activities: Resource, umbrella, visits, youth, newsletters, books
Traditions: Orthodox
Other Languages: Hebrew, French, Yiddish
Affiliations: United Synagogue
The Agency for Jewish Education is commited to serve the community by providing a quality professional response to its present and future needs. Its services are available to all.

Agudas Harabbanim (Association of Rabbis of Great Britian)
273 Green Lanes, London, N4 2EX
Tel: 0181-802-1544

Agudath Hashochtim V'Hashomrim of Great Britain (Cattle Section)
33 Elm Park Avenue, London, N15 6AR
Contact: S B Spitzer
Position: Honorary Secretary

Agudath Hashochtim V'Hashomrim of Great Britain (Poultry Section)
25 Rostrevor Avenue, London, N15 6LA
Contact: S Leaman
Position: Honorary Secretary

Anglo-Jewish Association
Commonwealth House, 1/19 New Oxford Street, London, WC1A 1NF
Tel: 0171-404-2111 **Fax:** 0171-404-2611
Contact: Esther Salasnik
Position: Secretary
Traditions: Cross-community
Offering grants and loans to Jewish students at UK Universities.

Assembly of Masorti Synagogues
1097 Finchley Road, London, NW11 0PU
Tel: 0181-201-8772 **Fax:** 0181-201-8917
EMail: masorti.uk@ort.org
Contact: H Freedman
Position: Director
Activities: Resource, umbrella, newsletters, books
Traditions: Masorti
Masorti Judaism is traditional, halachically

observant Judaism that considers the tools of modern critical scholarship and an awareness of historical development to be essential components of Jewish understanding.

Association of Adath Yisrael Synagogues
40 Queen Elizabeth's Walk, London, N16 0HH
Tel: 0181-802-6262

Association of Jewish Communal Professionals
17 Arden Road, London, N3 3AB
Tel: 0181-346-3121
Contact: Honorary Secretary

Association of Jewish Ex-Servicemen & Women
Ajex House, East Bank, London, N16 5RT
Tel: 0181-800-2844 **Fax:** 0181-880-1117
Contact: Mr Harry A Farbey
Position: General Secretary

Association of Jewish Friendship Clubs
26 Enford Street, London, WC1 2DD
Tel: 0171-724-8100 **Fax:** 0171-706-1710

Association of Jewish Refugees in GB
1 Hampstead Gate, 1a Frognal, London, NW3 6AL
Contact: Ernest David
Position: Director
Activities: Elderly, newsletters
Traditions: Cross-community
Other Languages: German
Day centre, meals on wheels, financial assistance, welfare advice, sheltered housing.

Association of Jewish Sixth Formers
Hillel House, 1-2 Endsleigh Street, London, WC1H 0DS
Tel: 0171-387-3384 **Fax:** 0171-387-3392
EMail: aj6.hq@ort.org
Contact: Ms Juliet Baum
Position: National Fieldworker
Activities: Resource, youth, newsletters, books
Traditions: Cross-community
Affiliations: Association of Jewish Youth; Board of Deputies of British Jews; Zionist Youth Council
A peer-led organisation for all Jewish 5th and 6th formers, with information on Jewish life at Universities and running a national conference to discuss topical issues as well as tours to Israel and Europe.

Association of Jewish Teachers
Education Department, 5th Floor, Commonwealth House, 1-19 New Oxford Street, London, WC1A 1NF
Tel: 0171-543-5402 **Tel:** 0181-903-6736 (h)
Fax: 0171-543-0010
Contact: Marilyn Nathan
Position: Chair
Activities: Newsletters
Affiliations: Board of Deputies of British Jews
AJT is a professional educational association for Jewish teachers. Most, but not all, of our members work in non-Jewish schools.

Association of Jewish Women's Organisations in UK
4th Floor, 24-32 Stephenson Way, London, NW1 2JW
Tel: 0171-387-7688
Fax: 0171-387-2110
Contact: Mrs Joy Conway
Position: Chair
Activities: Umbrella, women, inter-faith
Traditions: Cross-community

Association of Ministers (Chazanim) of Great Britain
9 Marlborough Mansions, Hampstead, London, NW6 1JP
Tel: 0171-431-0575 (h)
Contact: Revd Stanley Ivan Brickman
Position: Chairman
Activities: Worship, visits, youth, elderly, inter-faith
Traditions: Orthodox
Affiliations: United Synagogue

Association of Orthodox Jewish Professionals of GB
53 Wentworth Road, London, NW11 0RT

Association of Reform & Liberal Mohalim
Sternberg Centre for Judaism, 80 East End Road, London, N3 2SY
Tel: 0181-349-4731 **Fax:** 0181-343-0901
Contact: Mrs Sylvia Morris
Position: Secretary
Traditions: Liberal/Reform
Affiliations: Reform Synagogues of Great Britain; Union of Liberal and Progressive Synagogues
The Association lays down required standards of religious and medical practice for its members

(currently 14 nationwide) and has produced an explanatory leaflet which is available from the office.

Association of United Synagogue Women
735 High Road, Finchley, London, N12 0US
Tel: 0181-343-8989 **Fax:** 0181-343-6262
Contact: Josephine Wayne
Position: Liaison
Activities: Worship, resource, umbrella, elderly, women
Traditions: Orthodox
Affiliations: United Synagogue

Association for Jewish Youth
Norwood House, Harmony Way, Hendon, London, NW4 2BZ
Tel: 0181-203-3030 **Fax:** 0181-202-3030
Contact: Mr Eric Finestone
Position: Head of AJY
Activities: Resource, umbrella, newsletters
Traditions: Cross-Community

Bachad Fellowship (Friends of Bnei Akiva)
2 Hallswelle Road, London, NW11 0DT
Tel: 0181-458-9370 **Fax:** 0181-209-0107
Contact: Arieh Handler
Position: Chairman

Balfour Diamond Jubilee Trust
26 Emford Street, London, W1H 2DD
Tel: 0171-258-0008 **Fax:** 0171-258-0344
EMail: admin@bdjt.win-uk.net

B'nai B'rith Hillel Foundation
Hillel House, 1–2 Endsleigh Street, London, WC1H 0DS
Tel: 0171-388-0801 **Fax:** 0171-383-0390
Activities: Inter-faith

B'nai B'rith Youth Organisation
Hillel House, 1/2 Endsleigh Street, London, WC1H 0DS
Tel: 0171-387-3115 **Tel:** 01378-305115 (h)
Fax: 0171-387-8014
EMail: bbyo@ort.org
Contact: Craig Levison
Position: Youth Co-ordinator
Activities: Resource, visits, youth
Traditions: Cross-community
Affiliations: Zionist Youth Council; B'nai B'rith Youth Organisation International

Board of Deputies of British Jews
Commonwealth House, 1-19 New Oxford Street, London, WC1A 1NF
Tel: 0171-543-5400 **Fax:** 0171-543-0010
EMail: bod@ort.org
Contact: Neville Nagler
Position: Director General
Activities: Resource, media, umbrella, women, newsletters, books, inter-faith
Traditions: Cross-community
Other Languages: Hebrew
Affiliations: World Jewish Congress; European Jewish Congress: Inter Faith Network for the UK
The Board of Deputies is the elected body of British Jewry. The Board exists in order to represent, defend and unite the British Jewish community. It is composed of elected representatives from approximately 200 synagogues throughout the UK and about fifty other communal organisations.

Campaign for the Protection of Shechita
66 Townshend Court, Townshend Road, Regents Park, London, NW8 6LE
Tel: 0171-722-8523

Central Council for Jewish Community Services
17 Highfield Road, Golders Green, London, NW11 9LSNK,
Tel: 0181-458-1035 **Fax:** 0181-731-7462
Contact: Daphne Band
Position: Administrative Director
Activities: Umbrella, newsletters
Traditions: Cross-community
Affiliations: European Council of Jewish Communities
The Central Council for Jewish Community Services is an "umbrella" for over 60 Jewish community service organisations. It provides a forum for meeting and discussion and organises conferences and seminars.

Centre for Jewish Education
Sternberg Centre for Judaism, 80 East End Road, Finchley, London, N3 2SY
Tel: 0181-343-4303 **Fax:** 0181-349-0694
Contact: Suzanne Zetuni Ophir
Position: Programme Administrator
Activities: Resource, media, umbrella, visits, newsletters, books, inter-faith
Traditions: Reform, Liberal, Masorti
Other Languages: Hebrew

Affiliations: Reform Synagogues of Great Britain; Union of Liberal and Progressive Synagogues

College for Higher Rabbinical Studies Tiferes Sholom
37 Craven Walk, London, N16 6BS
Tel: 0181-800-3868 **Fax:** 0181-809-2610
Contact: A Y Landau
Position: Administrator
Activities: Worship, resource
Traditions: Charedi
Other Languages: Yiddish, Hebrew, French
Affiliations: Union of Orthodox Hebrew Congregations

Committee for the Welfare of Iranian Jews in GB
17 Arden Road, London, N3 3AB
Tel: 0181-346-3121

Commonwealth Jewish Council & Trust
BCM Box 6871, London, WC1N 3XX
Tel: 0171-222-2120 **Fax:** 0171-222-1781
EMail: ipcaa@diron.co.uk
Contact: Maureen Gold
Position: Administrative Director
Activities: Resource, umbrella, newsletters
Traditions: Cross-community
Other Languages: Hebrew, French
Affiliations: Commonwealth Institute; World Jewish Congress

Council of Reform & Liberal Rabbis
Manor House, 80 East End Road, London, N3 2SY
Tel: 0181-349-4731 **Fax:** 0181-343-0901
Contact: Chairman

Federation of Synagogues
65 Watford Way, Hendon, London, NW4 3AQ
Contact: Gerald Kushner
Position: Head Administrator
Activities: Worship, resource, umbrella, newsletters
Traditions: Orthodox
Other Languages: Yiddish, Ivrit
Affiliations: Conference of European Rabbis
The Federation operates Synagogues, Beth Din (Court of Jewish Law), Kashrut Authority, Educational Establishments, Ritualarium and Jewish Cemeteries.

Friends of Sephardi & Other Jewish Refugees
New House, 67-68 Hatton Gardens, London, EC1N 8JY
Tel: 0171-242-4556 **Fax:** 0171-242-2418
Contact: Sidney L Shipton
Position: Honorary Secretary

Guild of Jewish Journalists
103 Highfield Avenue, London, NW11 9TU
Tel: 0181-455-9425
Contact: John Lewis
Position: Honorary Secretary

Holocaust Educational Trust
BCM Box 7892, London, WC1N 3XX
Tel: 0171-222-6822 **Fax:** 0171-233-0161
EMail: ipcaa@dircon.co.uk
Contact: Hon Greville Janner QC MP
Position: Chairman
Activities: Resource, media, newsletter, books
Langauges: Hebrew, Arabic, German, French

Initiation Society
47 The Ridgeway, London, NW11 8QP
Tel: 0181-455-2008
Contact: Dr M Sifman
Position: Medical Officer

Institute of Community Relations
101 Dunsmure Road, London, N16 5HT
Tel: 0181-800-8612
Contact: Rabbi Henri Brand
Position: Director
Activities: Resource
Traditions: Charedi
Other Languages: French, Hebrew, Yiddish
The Institute of Community Relations is about race and not about religion. However, the Synagogue Francaise de Londres, 101 Dunsmure Road, Stamford Hill, London, N16 5HT, Tel: 0181-800-8612 is a religious organisation.

Institute of Jewish Policy Research
79 Wimpole Street, London, W1M 7DD
Tel: 0171-935-8266 **Fax:** 0171-935-3252
Contact: Antony Lerman
Position: Director
An independent think-tank which informs and influences policy, opinion and design-making on issues affecting Jewish life worldwide by conducting and commissioning research, developing and disseminating policy proposals and promoting public debate.

Institute of Jewish Studies

University College, Gower Street, London,
WC1E 6BT
Tel: 0171-380-7171 **Fax:** 0171-209-1026
Activities: Resource
Traditions: Liberal
Established in 1954 to promote the academic study
of all branches of Jewish civilisation. Its activities
include public lectures, seminars, research projects
and international conferences. Inclusion in the
mailing list and admission to programmes is free.

International Jewish Vegetarian Society

Bet Teva, 853-855 Finchley Road, Golders Green,
London, NW11 8LX
Tel: 0181-455-0692 **Fax:** 0181-455-0692
Contact: Shirley Labelda
Position: Secretary
Activities: Youth, elderly, newsletters, books
Traditions: Orthodox
The Jewish Vegetarian Society is an international
movement and membership is open to everyone.
There are two types of membership, practising
vegetarians and non-vegetarians who are
sympathetic to our cause.

Jewish Aids Trust

HIV Education Unit, Colindale Hospital,
Colindale Avenue, London, NW9 5HG
Tel: 0181-200-0369 **Fax:** 0181-905-9250
Contact: Rosalind Collin
Position: Director
Activities: Resource, youth, women, books, inter-
faith
Traditions: Cross-community
The Jewish Aids Trust provides face-to-face
counselling and telephone helpline for people
affected by HIV; financial support for people with
Aids; and educational programmes for the entire
community.

Jewish Association for the Mentally Ill

707 High Road, Finchley, London, N12 0BT
Tel: 0181-343-111 **Fax:** 0181-343-3355
Position: Administrator
Activities: Resource, newsletters
Traditions: Cross-community
JAMI positively helps the mentally ill providing a
day centre with activities for those in the 18-45 age
group.

Jewish Blind & Physically Handicapped Society

118 Seymour Place, London, W1H 5DJ
Tel: 0181-883-1000 **Fax:** 0181-444-6729
EMail: jbphs@jaysoft.compulink.co.uk
Contact: Jason J Ozin
Position: Campaign Director
Activities: Visits
Traditions: Cross-community
Provides caring, sheltered housing for the Jewish
blind, partially sighted or disabled persons or
families with a disabled member.

Jewish Book Council

98 Belsize Lane, Belsize Park, London, NW3 5BB
Tel: 0171-453-5008 **Tel:** 0171-722-7925 (h)
Fax: 0171-435-5220
Contact: Marion Cohen
Position: Chair
Activities: Resource
Traditions: Cross-community
Other Languages: Hebrew
The main focus is the setting up and organisation of
Jewish Book Week - the largest Jewish Book Fair in
Europe. Alongside the book fair we organise a series
of literary events featuring local, national and
international figures plus a schools programme.

Jewish Care

Stuart Young House, 221 Golders Green Road,
London, NW11 9DQ
Tel: 0181-458-3282 **Fax:** 0181-731-8307
EMail: info@jcare.org
Contact: Paul Summerfield
Position: Communications
Activities: Elderly
Traditions: Cross-community
Offers services for visually impaired people and
people with mental health problems and their
families. It also meets the needs of Holocaust
survivors and their families.

Jewish Committee for H M Forces

25-26 Enford Street, London, W1H 2DD
Tel: 0171-724-7778 **Fax:** 0171-706-1710
Contact: Revd Michael Weisman
Position: Senior Chaplain
Activities: Resource, inter-faith
Traditions: Cross-community
Other Languages: French, German, Hebrew

Jewish Council for Racial Equality

33 Seymour Place, London, W1N 6AT

Tel: 0181-455-0896 **Fax:** 0181-455-0896
Contact: Dr Edie Friedman
Position: Director
Activities: Resource, newsletters, books, inter-faith
Traditions: Cross-community
The Jewish Council for Racial Equality was set up to encourage the Jewish community to play a more active role in combatting racism and developing Britain's multi-racial society.

Jewish Crisis Helpline (Miyad)
23 Ravenshurst Avenue, Hendon, London, NW4 4EE
Tel: 0181-203-6311 **Fax:** 0181-203-8727
Contact: Mr Jeffery Blumenfeld
Position: Director
Traditions: Cross-community
Other Languages: Hebrew
Affiliations: Jewish Marriage Council
The lines (0181-203-6211 and 0345-581999) are open Sunday to Thursday 12 noon to midnight, Friday 12 noon till 1 hour before sunset and on Saturdays we open 1 hour after sunset till midnight.

Jewish Deaf Association
90 Cazenove Road, Julius Newman House, London, N16 6AB
Tel: 0181-806-6147 **Fax:** 0181-806-2251
Contact: Mrs Pat Goldring
Position: Executive Director
Activities: Resource, visits youth, elderly, newsletters
Traditions: Orthodox, cross-community
Other Languages: Sign Language
Affiliations: United Synagogue
Our Honorary Chaplain, Revd Michael Plaskow, is available to liaise, instruct and give advice on spiritual and pastoral matters (moving to new address in early Autumn 1997).

Jewish Education Bureau
8 Westcombe Avenue, Leeds, West Yorkshire, LS8 2BS
Tel: 0113-293-3523 **Fax:** 0113-293-3533
Contact: Rabbi Douglas S Charing
Position: Director
Activities: Resource, visits, inter-faith
Traditions: Cross-community
Although a Jewish organisation, the Jewish Education Bureau promotes the study of Judaism as part of multi-faith Religious Education in county schools and colleges.

Jewish Educational Development Trust
Jews College, 44 Albert Road, London, NW4 2SJ
Tel: 0181-203-6427 **Fax:** 0181-203-6420
Contact: Ronald Metzger

Jewish Guide Advisory Council
115 Francklyn Gardens, Edgware, Middlesex, HA8 8SB
Tel: 0181-958-6440 (h)
Contact: Mrs N Mitchell
Position: Chair

Jewish Lads & Girls Brigade
Camperdown, 3 Beechcroft Road, London, E18 1LA
EMail: jlgb@ort.org
Contact: Richard S Weber
Position: Secretary
Activities: Youth
Traditions: Orthodox - Central Ashkenazi
The JLGB is the longest established Jewish youth movement in the UK. It provides activities through uniformed groups throughout the UK and, through the Outreach-Kiruv project in Jewish state schools, clubs and other movements.

Jewish Lesbian & Gay Helpline
BM Jewish Helpline, London, WC1N 3XX
Tel: 0171-706-3123
Contact: David Marks
Position: Secretary
Activities: Resource
Traditions: Liberal, Reform
Affiliations: Central Council for Jewish Community Services; World Congress of Jewish Gay and Lesbian Organisations
We provide information, support and counselling to Jewish lesbians and gay men, their families and friends.

Jewish Marriage Council
23 Ravenhurst Avenue, Hendon, London, NW4 4EE
Tel: 0181-203-6311 **Fax:** 0181-203-8727
Contact: Mr Jeffery Blumenfeld
Position: Director
Activities: Visits
Traditions: Cross-community
Other Languages: Hebrew
We offer counselling for marital, personal or relationship problems to both individuals and couples. Groups are run for those undergoing

change in their lives: ie divorce support and pre-marriage, and we also help those who have problems with Jewish divorce.

Jewish Memorial Council

25-26 Enford Street, London, W1H 2DD
Tel: 0171-724-7778 **Fax:** 0171-706-1710
Contact: Mr Y Zaltzman
Position: General Manager
Activities: Worship, resource, youth, books, inter-faith
Traditions: All Traditions
Other Languages: Hebrew, Yiddish
Rev Malcolm Weisman is Religious Adviser to the Small Communities both in the British Isles and the Commonwealth.

Jewish Museum - Camden Town

Raymond Burton House, 129-131 Albert Street, London, NW1 7NB
Tel: 0171-284-1997 **Fax:** 0171-267-9008
Contact: Rickie Burman
Position: Director
Activities: Resource, visits, youth, elderly, women, newsletters, books, inter-faith
Traditions: Cross-community
Other Languages: French
The museum has permanent displays and collections on Jewish history and religion in Britain and one of the world's finest collections of Jewish ceremonial art. Changing exhibitions, cultural events and educational programmes on Judaism and Jewish history.

Jewish Museum - Finchley

80 East End Road, Finchley, London, N3 2SY
Tel: 0181-349-1143 **Fax:** 0181-343-2162
Contact: Rickie Burman
Position: Director
Activities: Resource, visits, youth, elderly, women, newsletters, books, inter-faith
Traditions: Cross-community
Other Languages: German
The Museum has displays and collections relating to the roots and history of London's Jewish community. Its resources include an extensive photographic archive and offers travelling exhibitions, walking tours of Jewish London and educational programmes.

Jewish Refugees Committee, World Jewish Relief

Drayton House, 30 Gordon Road, London, WC1H 0AN

Tel: 0171-387-4747 **Fax:** 0171-383-4810
EMail: wjr@ort.org
Contact: Luisa Biasiolo
Position: Director
Other Languages: Russian, German, French, Italian
The Jewish Refugees Committee assists Jewish refugees and asylum seekers in the UK. We are part of a registered charity.

Jewish Scout Advisory Council (JSAC)

9 Graham Lodge, Graham Road, Hendon Central, London, NW4 3DG
Tel: 0181-202-8613 (h)
Contact: Mr Peter Russell
Position: Honorary Secretary
Activities: Umbrella, youth
Traditions: Cross-community
Affiliations: Association of Jewish Youth
JSAC is an umbrella organisation to which Jewish Scout groups in England and Wales are affiliated. Activities are arranged in which groups take part. Affiliated to the Scout Association.

Jewish Woman's Network

41 Dorset Drive, Edgware, Middlesex, HA8 7NT

Jewish Womens' Aid

BM JWAI, London, WC1
Tel: 0171-486-0860
Contact: Judith Usiskin
Position: Chair
Activities: Resource, media, women
Traditions: Cross-community
Other Languages: Hebrew, French, Yiddish, Spanish
Affiliations: Central Council, Association of Jewish Womens Organisations
Refuge for 8 Jewish women and their children in Barnet and a helpline for women on Freephone 591203 are available. The organisation will supply speakers on domestic violence to community groups for puposes of education, publicity and fundraising.

Jews' College, London

Schaller House, Albert Road, Hendon, London, NW4 2SJ
Tel: 0181-203-6427 **Fax:** 0181-203-6420
Contact: Deborah Stanhill
Position: Administrator
Other Languages: Hebrew
Affiliations: University of London

Educates the future teachers and leaders of the Jewish Community through its BA, MA and PhD courses in Jewish Studies, and its rabbinical ordination and training programmes. It houses one of the most extensive Judaica libraries in Europe.

League of Jewish Women

24-32 Stephenson Way, London, NW1 2JW
Tel: 0171-387-7688 **Fax:** 0171-387-2110
Contact: Corinne Van Colle
Position: President
Activities: Youth, elderly, women
Traditions: Cross-community
Affiliations: Association of Jewish Women's Organisations; International Council of Jewish Women
A non-fundraising voluntary welfare organisation with 70 groups throughout Great Britain. Its members care for all communities irrespective of race, religion, creed, colour, able or disabled. The organisation will also give opinion on social issues.

Leo Baeck College

The Manor House, 80 East End Road, London, N3 2SY
Tel: 0181-349-4525 **Fax:** 0181-343-2558
EMail: Leo-Baeck-College@mailbox.ulcc.ac.u
Contact: John Olbrich
Position: Registrar
Activities: Resource
Traditions: Reform, Liberal

Link Psychotherapy Centre

110 Cholmley Gardens, Fortune Green Road, London, NW6 1UP
Tel: 0181-349-0111
Contact: Eduardo Pitchon
Position: Chair

London Beth Din

735 High Road, London, WC1H 9HP
Tel: 0181-343-6270 **Fax:** 0181-343-6257
Contact: Mrs Fraybin Gottlieb
Position: Assistant Registrar
Traditions: Orthodox
Other Languages: Hebrew, Yiddish, French
Affiliations: United Synagogue
The London Beth Din is divided into three divisions; Family, which supervises divorces, adoptions and conversions; Judicial, which resolves legal disputes; and Kashrut, which supervises most of London's restaurants, bakers, caterers and issues food certificates.

Lubavitch Foundation

107-115 Stamford Hill, London, N16 5RP
Tel: 0181-800-0022
Contact: Rabbi N Sudak
Position: Principal

Manor House Centre for Psychodynamic Counselling

Sternberg Centre for Judaism, 80 East End Road, London, N3 2SY
Tel: 0181-349-4525

National Council of Shechita Boards

PO Box 579, Adastra House, 401/405 Nether Street, London, N3 1YR
Tel: 0181-349-9160 **Fax:** 0181-346-2209

Noam (Masorti Youth)

97 Leeside Crescent, London, NW11 OJL
Tel: 0181-201-8773 **Fax:** 0181-458-4027
EMail: noam@ort.org
Contact: Ben Whine
Position: Director
Activities: Youth, newsletters, inter-faith
Traditions: Masorti
Affiliations: Assembly of Masorti Synagogues; Zionist Youth Council

Office of the Chief Rabbi

735 High Road, North Finchley, London, WC1N 9HN
Tel: 0181-343-6301 **Fax:** 0181-343-6310
Contact: Mrs Syma Weinberg
Activities: Resource, umbrella, books, inter-faith
Traditions: Orthodox
Other Languages: Hebrew, French
Affiliations: United Synagogue; European Council of Rabbis

Operation Judaism

95 Willows Road, Birmingham, B12 9QF
Tel: 0121-440-6673
Contact: Rabbi Shmuel Arkush
Position: Director
Activities: Resource, media, books
Traditions: Cross-community

Rabbinical Commission for the Licensing of Shochetim

Office of the Chief Rabbi, 735 High Road, North Finchley, London, N12 0US
Tel: 0181-343-6301 **Fax:** 0181-343-6310
Contact: Revd Alan Greenbat

Position: Secretary
Activities: Umbrella
Traditions: Orthodox
Other Languages: Hebrew, Yiddish, French

Rabbinical Council of the Provinces
151 Shadwell Lane, Leeds, West Yorkshire,
LS17 8DW
Tel: 0113-237-0852 **Fax:** 0113-237-0851
EMail: 101344.3636@compuserve.com
Contact: Rabbi Ian S Goodhardt
Position: Honorary Secretary
Activities: Media
Traditions: Orthodox
The Rabbinical Council of the Provinces is the
forum and representative body of Orthodox Rabbis
in the UK outside London.

Rabbinical Council of the United Synagogue
98 Anthony Road, Borehamwood, Hertfordshire,
WD6 4NB
Tel: 0181-207-3759 (h) **Fax:** 0181-207-0568
Contact: Rabbi A Plancey
Position: Chairperson

Reform Synagogues of Great Britain
The Sternberg Centre for Judaism, 80 East End
Road, Finchley, London, N3 2SY
Tel: 0181-349-4731 **Tel:** 0181-346-2288
Fax: 0181-343-0901
Contact: Mrs N Landau
Position: Administrative Director
Activities: Worship, resource, media, umbrella,
visits, youth, newsletters, books, inter-faith
Traditions: Reform
Other Languages: Hebrew, German
The Reform Movement seeks, through a
partnership between its synagogues and the
Movement infrastructure (volunteers and staff, lay
leaders and rabbis) to articulate, teach and live out
the faith and values of Reform Judaism.

Reform Synagogues of Great Britain Youth & Students Division
The Sternberg Centre, 80 East End Road,
Finchley, London, N3 2SY
Tel: 0181-349-4731 **Fax:** 0181-343-4972
EMail: rsy.rsgb@ort.org
Contact: Sara-Joy Leviten
Position: Director
Activities: Resource, youth
Traditions: Reform

Other Languages: Hebrew
Affiliations: World Union for Progressive Judaism
Reform Judaism is an informed and questioning,
compassionate and egalitarian expression of a
unique faith and culture, rooted in the tradition of
Torah yet in dialogue with modernity.

RSGB/ULPS Social Action
c/o Reform Synagogues of GB, The Sternberg
Centre for Judaism, 80 East End Road, London,
N3 2SY
Tel: 0181-349-4731 **Fax:** 0181-343-0901
Contact: Vicky Joseph and Steve Miller
Position: Co-ordinators
Activities: Resource, inter-faith
Traditions: Reform/Liberal
Affiliations: Reform Synagogues of Great
Britain; Union of Liberal and Progressive
Synagogues
Social Action is a joint initiative of the Reform and
Liberal Synagogues that offers a practical Jewish
response to current events and issues of social and
ethical concern.

Society for Jewish Study
15 Sunny Hill Court, Sunningfields Crescent,
London, NW4 4RB
Tel: 0181-203-1352
Contact: Alex Minn
Position: Secretary

Spiro Institute for the Study of Jewish History, Culture & Language
The Old House, c/o Kings College, Kidderpore
Avenue, London, NW3 7ST
Tel: 0171-431-0345 **Fax:** 0171-431-0361
EMail: spiro@booshie.demon.co.uk
Contact: Ms Diana Midgen
Position: Administrative Director
Activities: Resource, newsletters
Traditions: Cross-community
Other Languages: Hebrew, Yiddish
Founded in 1978, Spiro is an educational body
which aims to bring a knowledge and understanding
of Jewish history, culture and language to Jews and
non-Jews through courses, cultural events and tours.

Sternberg Centre for Judaism
The Manor House, 80 East End Road, London,
N3 2SY
Tel: 0181-346-2288
A national centre for the promotion of Jewish

religious, educational, cultural and intellectual matters by means of a range of bodies located in the Centre, which also houses an Interfaith Dialogue Centre and Library.

Student & Academic Campaign for Jews of the former Soviet Union
16 Western Park, London, N8 9TJ
Tel: 0181-348-6957 (h)
Contact: Adam Rose
Position: Chairperson

Synagogue Française
101 Dunsmure Road, London, N16 5HT
Tel: 0181-800-8612
Contact: Rabbi Henri Brand
Position: Grand Rabbin
Activities: Worship
Traditions: Charedi
Other Languages: French, Hebrew, Yiddish
The French Synagogue is the organisation for French-speaking Jews in the UK.

Synagogue Secretaries' Association
Edgware Synagogue, Edgware Way, Edgware, Middlesex, NW8 8YE
Contact: L Ford
Position: Chair

Tay Sachs & Allied Diseases Association
17 Sydney Road, Barkingside, Ilford, Essex, IG6 2ED
Tel: 0181-550-8989

Traditional Alternatives
3 First Avenue, London, NW4 2RL
Tel: 0181-203-9044

Tzedek (Jewish Action for a Just World)
61 Pine Road, Cricklewood, London, NW2 6SB
Tel: 0181-452-5146
Contact: Steven Derby
Activities: Resource, newsletters
Traditions: Cross-community
Tzedek provides direct support to sustainable self-help projects in the developing world regardless of race or religion. It also aims to educate as to the causes and effects of poverty and the Jewish obligation to respond.

Union of Jewish Students
Hillel House, 1-2 Endsleigh Street, London, WC1H 0DS

Tel: 0171-387-4644 **Fax:** 0171-383-0390

Union of Liberal & Progressive Synagogues
The Montagu Centre, 21 Maple Street, London, W1P 6DS
Tel: 0171-580-1663 **Fax:** 0171-436-4184
Contact: Michael Burman
Position: Administrative Director
Activities: Worship, resource, media, umbrella, visits, youth, elderly women, newsletters, books, inter-faith
Traditions: Liberal
Other Languages: Hebrew, French
Affiliations: World Union of Progressive Judaism
Also houses the European Headquarters of the World Union of Progressive Judaism and the West Central Liberal Synagogue. The Evening Institute of the Union of Liberal and Progressive Synagogues also takes place on these premises.

Union of Maccabi Associations
Gildesgame House, 73a Compayne Gardens, West Hampstead, London, NW6 3RS
Tel: 0171-328-0382 **Fax:** 0171-328-9118
Contact: Henry Minkoff
Position: Chair
Activities: Resource, umbrella, youth, newsletters, inter-faith
Traditions: Cross-community
Languages: Hebrew
Affiliations: Maccabi World Union

Union of Orthodox Hebrew Congregations
140 Stamford Hill, London, N16 6QT
Tel: 0181-802-6226 **Fax:** 0181-809-7092
Contact: A Klein
Position: Administrator
Activities: Resource, umbrella, newsletters
Traditions: Charedi
Other Languages: Yiddish, Hebrew
Established in 1926 as a congregational association for Orthodox Jews of primarily Central and Eastern European origin, including many of the Hasidic Congregations.

United Synagogue
735 High Road, London, N12 0US
Tel: 0181-343-8989 **Fax:** 0181-343-6262
Contact: Jonathan M Lew
Position: Chief Executive

JEWISH REGIONAL AND LOCAL ORGANISATIONS AND SYNAGOGUES

A variety of forms of local Jewish organisations are listed in this directory. These include synagogues; welfare bodies; representative bodies; student societies and houses; *yeshivot*; and other educational institutions with the general exception of schools.

ENGLAND

NORTH EAST
Regional or County Bodies

Representative Council of North East Jewry
39 Kenton Road, Gosforth, Newcastle upon Tyne, Tyne and Wear, NE3 4NH (h)
Tel: 01429-264101 **Tel:** 01429-284-4647 (h)
Contact: Martin Levinson
Position: Honorary Secretary
Activities: Umbrella, newsletters
Traditions: Cross-community

City, Town or Local Bodies

Darlington Hebrew Congregation
Bloomfield Road, Darlington, County Durham
Contact: John Starr
Position: Secretary
Activities: Worship, visits, women, inter-faith
Traditions: Reform
Affiliations: Newcastle Reform Synagogues; Reform Synagogues of Great Britain; World Union for Progressive Judaism

Beth Midrash Lemoroth
50 Bewick Road, Gateshead, Tyne and Wear, NE8
Tel: 0191-477-2620

Gateshead Hebrew Congregation
180 Bewick Road, Gateshead, Tyne and Wear, NE8
Tel: 0191-477-0111 **Tel:** 0191-477-3871 (h)
Contact: M Guttentag
Position: Senior Warden

Gateshead Jewish Family Service
7 Oxford Terrace, Bensham, Gateshead, Tyne and Wear, NE8 1RQ (h)
Tel: 0191-477-5677 **Fax:** 0191-477-2241
Contact: Mrs R Hirsch
Position: Scheme Manager
Traditions: Charedi

Institute of Higher Rabbinical Studies
22 Claremont Place, Gateshead, Tyne and Wear, NE8 1TL

Sunderland Talmudical College & Yeshiva
Prince Consort Road, Gateshead, Tyne and Wear, NE3 4DS

Tel: 0191-490-0195
Contact: Rabbi S Zahn
Position: Principal

Yeshiva Lezeirim
36-38 Gladstone Terrace, Gateshead, Tyne and
Wear, NE8 4EF
Tel: 0191-477-1317
Contact: Rabbi Jaffe
Position: Principal

Jewish Students' Society
Hillel House, 1 St George's Terrace, Jesmond,
Newcastle upon Tyne, Tyne and Wear, NE2
Tel: 0191-281-2106

Jewish Welfare Society
Lionel Jacobson House, Graham Park Road,
Gosforth, Newcastle upon Tyne, Tyne and Wear,
NE3 4BH
Tel: 0191-284-0959
Contact: Mrs P Ashton
Position: Secretary

Newcastle Jewish Housing Association Ltd
c/o Lionel Jacobson, 40 Graham Park Road,
Gosforth, Newcastle upon Tyne, Tyne and Wear,
NE3 4BH

Newcastle Reform Synagogue
The Croft, off Kenton Road, Gosforth, Newcastle
upon Tyne, Tyne and Wear, NE3 4RF
Tel: 0191-284-8621
Contact: Rabbi Moshe Yehudai
Position: Rabbi

Representative Council of North East Jewry
24 Adeline Gardens, Gosforth, Newcastle upon
Tyne, Tyne and Wear, NE3 4JQ (h)
Tel: 0191-285-1253 (h)
Contact: Clive Van Der Velde
Position: Honorary Secretary
Activities: Umbrella, newsletters
Traditions: Cross-community

United Hebrew Congregation
Graham Park Road, Gosforth, Newcastle upon
Tyne, Tyne and Wear, NE3 4BH
Tel: 0191-284-0959 **Fax:** 0191-284-0959
Contact: Mrs P Ashton
Position: Secretary
Activities: Worship, resource, visits, youth, elderly,
women, inter-faith

Traditions: Orthodox
Affiliations: Representative Council of North
East Jewry; Chief Rabbinate

Sunderland Hebrew Congregation
Ryhope Road, Sunderland, Tyne and Wear,
SR2 7EQ
Tel: 0191-565-8093
Contact: Secretary

Whitley Bay Hebrew Congregation
2 Oxford Street, Whitley Bay, Tyne and Wear,
NG26 3TB
Tel: 01632-2521367 (h)
Contact: M A Sonn
Position: Honorary Secretary

YORKSHIRE
City, Town or Local Bodies

B'nai B'rith
26 Thorndale Rise, Poplars Farm, Kings Road,
Bradford, West Yorkshire, BD2 1NU (h)
Tel: 01274-390783 (h)
Contact: Anne Fabian
Position: Representative
Activities: Resource, media, umbrella, elderly,
women, newsletters, books, inter-faith
Traditions: Orthodox, Reform
Other Languages: German, Hebrew
Affiliations: North Regional Council
Manchester & Leeds; B'nai B'rith HQ London;
B'nai B'rith Washington DC, USA

Bradford Hebrew Congregation
The Synagogue, Spring Hurst Road, Shipley,
Bradford, West Yorkshire, BD18 3DN
Contact: Albert Waxman
Position: President
Activities: Worship, umbrella, women
Traditions: Orthodox
Other Languages: German

Bradford Jewish Benevolent Society
Bradford, West Yorkshire, c/o Buckstone Court,
Cliffe Drive, Rawdon, West Yorkshire, LS19 6LL
Tel: 01274-504468
Contact: M Levi
Position: Treasurer

Bradford Synagogue (Reform)
Bowland Street, Bradford, West Yorkshire,
BD2 1NV
Tel: 01274-390783 (h)
Contact: Anne Fabian
Position: Religion Teacher
Activities: Religious, resource, media, visits,
youth, elderly, women, newsletters, inter-faith
Traditions: Reform
Other Languages: German
Affiliations: Leeds Reform Synagogue; Reform
Movement; Reform Movement B'nai B'rith

Sir Moses Montefiore Synagogue
Holme Hill, Heneage Road, Grimsby, East Riding
of Yorkshire, DN32 9DZ
Tel: 01472-351404 (h)
Contact: Bernard Greenberg
Position: Secretary
Activities: Worship
Traditions: Orthodox
Affiliations: United Synagogue

Harrogate Hebrew Congregation
St Mary's Walk, Harrogate, North Yorkshire
Contact: Sandy Royston
Position: President
Activities: Worship
Traditions: Orthodox
Affiliations: Leeds Jewish Representative Council

Hull Hebrew Congregation
277 Beverley Road, Kirk Ella, Hull, East Riding of
Yorkshire, HU10 7AQ (h)
Tel: 01482-653398 (h)
Contact: Edward Pearlman
Position: Honorary Secretary
Activities: Worship, visits, youth, elderly, women,
newsletters, inter-faith
Traditions: Orthodox
Affiliations: Hull Jewish Representative Council

Hull Jewish Representative Council
4 Drydales, Kirkella, Hull, East Riding of
Yorkshire, HU10 7JU
Tel: 01482-658902
Contact: B Donn
Position: Honorary Secretary

Hull University Jewish Students Society
c/o Hillel House, 18 Auckland Avenue, Hull, East
Riding of Yorkshire
Tel: 01482-48196

Contact: Lindsey Rose
Position: Chair

Neve Shalom - Hull Reform Synagogue
Great Gutter Lane West, Willerby, Hull, East
Riding of Yorkshire, HU10 6DP
Tel: 01482-658312 **Tel:** 01482-665375
Contact: Mrs G M Barker
Position: Honorary Secretary
Activities: Worship, resource, visits, newsletters,
inter-faith
Traditions: Reform
Affiliations: Hull Jewish Representative Council;
Reform Synagogues of Great Britain; World
Union of Progressive Judaism

Beth Hamedrash Hagadol Synagogue
399 Street Lane, Leeds, West Yorkshire, LS17 6HQ
Tel: 0113-269-2181 **Tel:** 0113-269-6375 (h)
Fax: 0113-237-0113
EMail: yaakovshem@globalnet.co.uk
Contact: Myrna Wilson
Position: Executive Officer
Activities: Worship, resource, visits, youth, elderly,
women, newsletters, books, inter-faith
Traditions: Orthodox
Affiliations: Leeds Jewish Representative
Council; London Rabbinate Council

Chassidishe Synagogue
Flat 8 Sandhill Lawns, Sandhill Lane, Leeds, West
Yorkshire, LS17 6TT (h)
Contact: Mr Maurice Kent
Position: President
Activities: Worship
Traditions: Chassidic
Affiliations: Leeds Jewish Representative Council

Etz Chaim Synagogue
411 Harrogate Road, Leeds, West Yorkshire,
LS17 7TT

Jewish Day Centre
26 Queenshill Avenue, Leeds, West Yorkshire, LS17
Tel: 0113-269-2018
Contact: Jackie King
Position: Organiser

Jewish Students' Association
c/o Hillel House, 2 Springfield Mount, Leeds,
West Yorkshire, LS2
Tel: 0113-243-3211

Leeds Jewish Education Board (Talmud Torah)
2 Sand Hill Lane, Leeds, West Yorkshire, LS17 6AQ
Tel: 0113-268-3390
Contact: Mrs Elana Fligg
Position: Secretary

Leeds Jewish Representative Council
151 Shadwell Lane, Leeds, West Yorkshire,
LS17 8DW
Tel: 0113-269-7520 **Fax:** 0113-237-0851
Contact: Barry Abis
Position: Executive Officer
Activities: Umbrella, newsletters
Traditions: Orthodox

Leeds Jewish Welfare Board
311 Stonegate Road, Moortown, Leeds, West
Yorkshire, LS17 6AZ
Tel: 0113-268-4211 **Fax:** 0113-266-4754
Contact: Pippa Landey
Position: Director Social Care
Activities: Youth, elderly, women
Traditions: Cross-community
Affiliations: Leeds Jewish Representative Council

Leeds Kashrut Authority
151 Shadwell Lane, Leeds, West Yorkshire,
LS17 8DW
Tel: 0113-269-7520 **Fax:** 0113-237-0851
Contact: Mr Barry Abis
Position: Administrator
Affiliations: Leeds Jewish Representative
Council; London Council of Shechita Boards

Makor-Jewish Resource Centre
411 Harrogate Road, Leeds, West Yorkshire,
LS17 7TT
Tel: 0113-268-0899 **Fax:** 0113-266-8419

New Central Vilna Synagogue
7a Stainburn Parade, Leeds, West Yorkshire,
LS17 8AN

Queenshill Synagogue
26 Queenshill Drive, Moortown, Leeds, West
Yorkshire, LS17 6BE (h)
Tel: 0113-268-7364 (h)
Contact: Mrs Louise N Diamond
Position: Honorary Secretary
Activities: Elderly
Traditions: Orthodox
Affiliations: Leeds Jewish Representative
Council; United Synagogue

Shomrei Hadass Congregation
368 Harrogate Road, Leeds, West Yorkshire,
LS17 6QB

Sinai Synagogue
Roman Avenue, Roundhay, Leeds, West Yorkshire,
LS8 2AN
Tel: 0113-266-5256 **Fax:** 0113-266-1539
EMail: 100253.3060@compuserve.com
Contact: Rabbi Ian Morris
Position: Rabbi
Activities: Worship, resource, visits, youth, elderly,
newsletters, inter-faith
Traditions: Reform
Other Languages: Hebrew
Affiliations: Leeds Jewish Representative
Council; Reform Synagogues of Great Britain;
World Union of Progressive Judaism

United Hebrew Congregation Shadwell Lane Synagogue
151 Shadwell Lane, Leeds, West Yorkshire,
LS17 8DW
Tel: 0113-269-6141
Contact: Mrs A P Silver
Position: Administrator

Middlesbrough Synagogue
Park Road South, Middlesbrough, North Yorkshire
Tel: 01642-819034
Contact: Lionel Simons
Position: Honorary Secretary

Jewish Centre Charitable Trust
Psalter House, Psalter Lane, Sheffield, South
Yorkshire, S11
Tel: 0114-255-2296

Jewish Welfare Organisation
275 Dobcroft Road, Sheffield, South Yorkshire,
S11 9LG
Tel: 0114-236-6800
Contact: M Ballin
Position: Honorary Secretary

Representative Council of Sheffield & District Jews
105 Bents Road, Sheffield, South Yorkshire,
S11 9RH
Tel: 0114-236-0970 **Fax:** 0114-236-0970
Contact: Mr Tony Kay
Position: Honorary Secretary
Activities: Umbrella

Traditions: Cross-community
Affiliations: Northern Representative Councils'
Forum

Sheffield & District Reform Jewish Congregation
PO Box 675, Sheffield, South Yorkshire, S11 8SP
EMail: j.kinderlerer@sheffield.ac.uk
Contact: Dr Julian Kinderlerer
Position: Chair
Activities: Worship, visits, newsletters
Traditions: Reform
Affiliations: Sheffield Jewish Representative
Council; Reform Synagogues of Great Britain

United Hebrew Congregation
Wilson Road, Sheffield, South Yorkshire, S11 8RN
Tel: 0114-236-2217 (h)
Contact: Mrs M Shaw
Position: Honorary Secretary

Synagogue
Top Storey of Bowman's Buildings, Aldwark, York,
North Yorkshire

NORTH WEST
Regional and County Bodies

Merseyside Jewish Representative Council
Shifrin House, 433 Smithdown Road, Liverpool,
Merseyside, L15 3JL
Tel: 0151-733-2292 **Fax:** 0151-734-0212
Contact: Mrs Susan Lander
Position: President
Activities: Umbrella

Merseyside Jewish Welfare Council
Shifrin House, 433 Smithdown Road, Liverpool,
Merseyside, L15 3JL
Tel: 0151-733-2292 **Fax:** 0151-734-0212
Contact: Marilyn Fetcher
Position: Chief Executive
Activities: Elderly
Traditions: Cross-community
Affiliations: Merseyside Jewish Representative
Council; Central Council for Jewish Community
Services

Jewish Representative Council of Greater Manchester & Region
Jewish Cultural Centre, Bury Old Road,
Manchester, Greater Manchester, M8 6FY
Tel: 0161-720-8721 **Fax:** 0161-720-8721

Contact: Mr I Fromson
Position: President
Activities: Umbrella, inter-faith

Jewish Social Services (Greater Manchester)
12 Holland Road, Crumpsall, Manchester, Greater
Manchester, M8 4NP
Tel: 0161-795-0024 **Tel:** 0161-733-1529 (h)
Fax: 0161-795-3688
Contact: Ivan Lewis
Position: Chief Executive
Activities: Elderly, newsletters
Traditions: Cross-community
Affiliations: Jewish Representative Council of
Greater Manchester; Central Council for Jewish
Community Services

League of Jewish Women - North West Region
7 Sunningdale Avenue, Whitefield, Manchester,
Greater Manchester, M45 7GW (h)
Tel: 0161-766-3587 (h)
Contact: Mrs Rosalind Levene
Position: Chair
Activities: Elderly, women
Traditions: Cross-community
Affiliations: League of Jewish Women

City, Town or Local Bodies

Blackburn Hebrew Congregation
Blackburn, Lancashire, c/o Orchard Road,
St Annes-on-Sea, Lancashire, FY8 1RT
Tel: 01253-728245
Contact: Rabbi R Fisher

Blackpool Reform Synagogue
40 Raikes Parade, Blackpool, Lancashire, FY1 4EX
Tel: 01253-23687
Contact: B Raven
Position: Honorary Secretary

Blackpool United Hebrew Congregation
The Synagogue, Leamington Road, Blackpool,
Lancashire, FY3 9DX
Tel: 01253-28164 **Tel:** 01253-392382 (h)
Contact: Revd David Braunold
Position: Rabbi
Activities: Worship, resource, media, visits, youth,
inter-faith
Traditions: Orthodox
Other Languages: Hebrew
Affiliations: Manchester Jewish Representative
Council

Bury Hebrew Congregation
Sunnybank Road, Bury, Lancashire

Yeshurun Hebrew Congregation
Coniston Road, Gatley, Cheadle, Cheshire,
SK8 4AP
Tel: 0161-428-8242 **Fax:** 0161-491-5265
Contact: Alan Unterman
Position: Minister
Activities: Worship
Traditions: Orthodox
Other Languages: Hebrew, Yiddish
Affiliations: Manchester Synagogue Council

Chester Jewish Community
5 Nield Court, Chester, Cheshire, CH2 1DN

Hale & District Hebrew Congregation
Shay Lane, Hale Barns, Cheshire, WA15 8PA
Tel: 0161-980-8846

Allerton Hebrew Congregation
Corner Booker Avenue, Mather Avenue, Allerton,
Liverpool, Merseyside, L18 9TB
Tel: 0151-427-6848
Contact: Ronald L Hyman
Position: Administrator
Activities: Worship
Traditions: Orthodox

Childwall Hebrew Congregation
Synagogue Chambers, Childwall, Liverpool,
Merseyside, L15 6XL
Tel: 0151-722-2079
Contact: Mrs Angela Reuben
Position: Administrator
Activities: Worship
Traditions: Orthodox
Other Languages: Hebrew
Affiliations: Merseyside Jewish Representative
Council

Community Centre
Dunbabin Road, Liverpool, Merseyside, L15 6XL
Tel: 0151-722-5825

Greenbank Drive Synagogue
Greenbank Chambers, Greenbank Drive,
Liverpool, Merseyside, L17 1AF
Tel: 0151-733-1417
Contact: Revd Chait

Hillel House
25 Arundel Drive, Liverpool, Merseyside,
L17 3BX
Tel: 0151-733-2819

Jewish Women's Aid Society
Shifrin House, 433 Smithdown Road, Liverpool,
Merseyside, L15 3JL
Contact: Mrs J Shoham
Position: President
Activities: Elderly
Affiliations: Liverpool Jewish Welfare Council

Liverpool Jewish Resource Centre
Harold House, Dunbabin Road, Liverpool,
Merseyside, L15 6XL
Tel: 0151-722-3514
Contact: Hilary Cohen
Position: Administrator
Activities: Resource, visits, inter-faith
Traditions: Orthodox
Affiliations: Merseyside Jewish Representative
Council; Jewish Resource Centres, UK

Liverpool Jewish Youth & Community Centre
Harold House, Dunbabin Road, Liverpool,
Merseyside, L15 6XL
Tel: 0151-475-5671 **Fax:** 0151-475-2212
EMail: harold.house@ort.org
Contact: Esmond Sidney Rosen
Position: Director
Activities: Resource, umbrella, visits, youth,
elderly, women
Traditions: Cross-community
Other Languages: Ivrit, Yiddish
Affiliations: Merseyside Jewish Representative
Council; Maccabi; Association of Jewish Youth;
World Confederation of JCC's

Liverpool Old Hebrew Congregation
Synagogue Chambers, Princes Road, Liverpool,
Merseyside, L8 1TG
Tel: 0151-709-3431 **Tel:** 0151-733-3587 (h)
Contact: Revd Stanley Cohen
Position: Minister
Activities: Worship
Traditions: Orthodox
Other Languages: Hebrew
Affiliations: Merseyside Jewish Representative
Council; United Synagogue

Liverpool Progressive Synagogue
28 Church Road North, Liverpool, Merseyside,
L15 6TF

Tel: 0151-733-5871 (h)
Contact: Mrs N Golduck
Position: Honorary Secretary

Merseyside Amalgamated Talmud Torah
King David Primary School, Beauclair Drive,
Liverpool, Merseyside, L15
Contact: Mrs E Wolfson
Position: Chair

Merseyside Jewish Representative Council
Shifrin House, 433 Smithdown Road, Liverpool,
Merseyside, L15 3JL
Tel: 0151-733-2292 **Fax:** 0151-734-0212
Contact: Mrs Susan Lander
Position: President
Activities: Umbrella

Merseyside Jewish Welfare Council
Shifrin House, 433 Smithdown Road, Liverpool,
Merseyside, L15 3JL
Tel: 0151-733-2292 **Fax:** 0151-734-0212
Contact: Marilyn Fetcher
Position: Chief Executive
Activities: Elderly
Traditions: Cross-community
Affiliations: Merseyside Jewish Representative
Council; Central Council for Jewish Community
Services

Synagogue
2 Dovedale Road, Liverpool, Merseyside

Ullet Road Synagogue
101 Ullet Road, Liverpool, Merseyside, L17
Contact: Arnold Cooklin
Position: Honorary Secretary

University Jewish Students' Society
c/o Students Union, Bedford Street, Liverpool,
Merseyside, L7

Beth Hamedrash Daesek Eliezer
74 King's Road, Prestwich, Manchester, Greater
Manchester

Cheetham Hebrew Congregation
453 Cheetham Hill Road, Manchester, Greater
Manchester, M8 7PA
Tel: 0161-740-7788

Cheshire Reform Congregation
Menorah Synagogue, 198 Altrincham Road,
Manchester, Greater Manchester, M22 4RZ

Tel: 0161-428-7746
Contact: Rabbi Dr Michael Hilton
Position: Rabbi
Activities: Worship, visits, youth, elderly,
newsletters, inter-faith
Traditions: Reform
Affiliations: Reform Synagogues of Great Britain

Damesek Eliezer Synagogue
74 Kings Road, Prestwich, Manchester, Greater
Manchester
Tel: 0161-740-2486
Contact: Rabbi S Goldberg

Higher Crumpsall & Higher Broughton Hebrew Congregation
Bury Old Road, Manchester, Greater Manchester,
M8 6EX
Tel: 0161-740-1210

Higher Prestwich Hebrew Congregation
Highbury House, 445 Bury Old Road,
Manchester, Greater Manchester, M25 1PP
Tel: 0161-713-4800
Contact: Malcolm Bower
Position: President
Activities: Worship
Traditions: Orthodox
Other Languages: Hebrew
Affiliations: Manchester Jewish Representative
Council

Hillel House
Greenheys Lane, Manchester, Greater Manchester,
M15 6LR
Tel: 0161-226-1061

Hillock Hebrew Congregation
13 Mersey Close, Hillock Estate, Whitefield,
Manchester, Greater Manchester, M45 8LB (h)
Tel: 0161-766-1162 (h)
Contact: Richard Elliott Walker
Position: Honorary Secretary
Activities: Worship
Traditions: Orthodox
Affiliations: Manchester Jewish Representative
Council; Manchester District Council of
Synagogues

Hulme Hebrew Congregation
Hillel House, Greenheys Lane, Manchester,
Greater Manchester, M15 6LR

Jewish Cultural Centre
Jubilee School, Bury Old Road, Manchester,
Greater Manchester, M7 4QY
Tel: 0161-795-4000 **Fax:** 0161-792-6222
Contact: Rabbi C Farro
Position: Director
Activities: Worship, resource, visits, youth, elderly,
women
Traditions: Lubavitch
Other Languages: Ivrit, Yiddish

Jewish Programmes Material Project (JPMP)
142 Bury Old Road, Manchester, Greater
Manchester, M8 6HD
Tel: 0161-795-7050 **Fax:** 0161-740-7407
Contact: Doreen Gerson
Position: Director

**Jewish Representative Council of Greater
Manchester & Region**
Jewish Cultural Centre, Bury Old Road,
Manchester, Greater Manchester, M8 6FY
Tel: 0161-720-8721 **Fax:** 0161-720-8721
Contact: Mr I Fromson
Position: President
Activities: Umbrella, inter-faith

Jewish Social Services (Greater Manchester)
12 Holland Road, Crumpsall, Manchester, Greater
Manchester, M8 4NP
Tel: 0161-795-0024 **Tel:** 0161-733-1529 (h)
Fax: 0161-795-3688
Contact: Ivan Lewis
Position: Chief Executive
Activities: Elderly, newsletters
Traditions: Cross-community
Affiliations: Jewish Representative Council of
Greater Manchester; Central Council for Jewish
Community Services

League of Jewish Women - North West Region
7 Sunningdale Avenue, Whitefield, Manchester,
Greater Manchester, M45 7GW (h)
Tel: 0161-766-3587 (h)
Contact: Mrs Rosalind Levene
Position: Chair
Activities: Elderly, women
Traditions: Cross-community
Affiliations: League of Jewish Women; National
Council of Women; International Council of
Women

Manchester Jewish Blind Society
85 Middleton Road, Manchester, Greater
Manchester, M8 4JY
Tel: 0161-740-0111 **Fax:** 0161-721-4273
Contact: Michael Galley
Position: Chief Executive
Activities: Elderly, newsletters
Traditions: Cross-community
Affiliations: Manchester Jewish Representative
Council; Central Council for Jewish Community
Services

Manchester Jewish Homes For Aged
c/o Heathlands Drive, Prestwich, Manchester,
Greater Manchester
Contact: Voluntary Service Co-ordinator

**Manchester Jewish Marriage Council
(Manchester)**
Levi House, Bury Old Road, Manchester, Greater
Manchester, M8 6FX
Tel: 0161-740-5764
Traditions: Cross-Community
Affiliations: Jewish Marriage Council, London

Manchester Jews' Benevolent Society
Levi House, Bury Old Road, Manchester, Greater
Manchester, M7 4QX
Tel: 0161-740-4089
Contact: Harold Weisberg
Position: President
Activities: Elderly
Traditions: Cross-community
Affiliations: Manchester Jewish Representative
Council

Manchester Reform Synagogue
Jackson's Row, Manchester, Greater Manchester,
M2 5NH
Tel: 0161-834-0415 **Fax:** 0161-834-0415
Contact: Norman Joel Franks
Position: General Secretary
Activities: Worship, resource, visits, youth, elderly,
women, newsletters, inter-faith
Traditions: Reform
Affiliations: Reform Synagogues of Great Britain

Morris Feinmann Home Trust
178 Palatine Road, Didsbury, Manchester, Greater
Manchester, M20 2YW
Tel: 0161-445-3533 **Fax:** 0161-448-1755
Contact: Miss Christine Barlow

Position: Matron/Manager
Traditions: Cross-community
Other Languages: German
Affiliations: Manchester Jewish Representative Council

Outreach Community & Residential Services
24a Bury New Road, Manchester, Greater Manchester, M25 8LD
Tel: 0161-798-0180
Contact: P Sutton
Position: Director

Prestwich Beth Hamedrash Synagogue
74 Kings Road, Manchester, Greater Manchester, M25 8HU
Tel: 0161-740-2486 (h)
Contact: Rabbi S Goldberg
Position: Minister

Prestwich Hebrew Congregation
The Shrubbery, Bury New Road, Prestwich, Manchester, Greater Manchester, M25

Sha'are Sedek Synagogue
Old Lansdowne Road, West Didsbury, Manchester, Greater Manchester, M20 8NZ
Tel: 0161-445-5731
Contact: Mrs D Stewart
Position: Secretary

Sha'arei Shalom North Manchester Reform Synagogue
Elms Street, Whitefield, Manchester, Greater Manchester, M45 8GQ
Contact: Mrs Simone Cohen
Position: Membership Officer
Activities: Worship, resource, resource, visits, youth, elderly, newsletters, inter-faith
Traditions: Reform
Affiliations: Manchester Jewish Representative Council; Reform Synagogues of Great Britain

Shechita Board
435 Cheetham Hill Road, Manchester, Greater Manchester, M8 7PF
Tel: 0161-740-9711
Contact: Y Brodie
Position: Administrator

South Manchester Synagogue
Wilbraham Road, Manchester, Greater Manchester, M14 6JS

Tel: 0161-224-1366   **Fax:** 0161-225-8033
Contact: S L Rydz
Position: Administrator

United Synagogue
Meade Hill Road, Manchester, Greater Manchester, M8 4LP
Tel: 0161-740-9586   **Tel:** 0161-795-0078 (h)
Contact: Mr Sidney Huller
Position: President
Activities: Worship, visits
Traditions: Orthodox
Affiliations: Manchester Jewish Representative Council; United Synagogues

University of Manchester Jewish Society
c/o Student Union, Oxford Road, Manchester, Greater Manchester, M13 9PL
Tel: 0161-232-9958
EMail: jsoc@compsoc.man.ac.uk
Contact: Emma Blasebalk
Position: Chairperson
Activities: Youth, resource
Traditions: Cross-community
Other Languages: Hebrew
Affiliations: Union of Jewish Students of Great Britain and Ireland

Whitefield Hebrew Congregation
Park Lane, Whitefield, Manchester, Greater Manchester, M25 7PB
Tel: 0161-766-3732

Preston Synagogue
Preston, c/o 31 Avondale Road, Southport, Merseyside, PR9 0NH
Tel: 01704-538276 (h)
Contact: Dr C E Nelson
Position: Honorary Secretary

St Annes Hebrew Congregation
The Synagogue, Orchard Road, St Annes-on-Sea, Lancashire, FY8 1PJ
Tel: 01253-721831   **Tel:** 01253-723920 (h)
Contact: Peter Davidson
Position: President
Activities: Worship, resource, visits, youth, women
Traditions: Orthodox
Affiliations: Manchester Jewish Representative Council

Sale & District Hebrew Congregation
14 Hesketh Road, Sale, Cheshire, M33 5AA
Tel: 0161-973-2172 **Tel:** 0161-962-1882 (h)
Contact: Mrs Iris Gould
Position: Honorary Secretary
Activities: Worship, resource, visits, youth,
women, newsletters, inter-faith
Traditions: Orthodox - Central Ashkenazi
Other Languages: Hebrew
Affiliations: Manchester Jewish Representative
Council

Academy for Rabbinical Research (Kolel)
134 Leicester Road, Salford, Greater Manchester,
M7 0LU
Tel: 0161-740-1960
Contact: Revd J Freedman
Position: Secretary

Adass Yeshurun Synagogue
Cheltenham Crescent, Salford, Greater
Manchester, M7 0FE
Tel: 0161-740-4548
Contact: S Gluckstadt
Position: Honorary Secretary

Adath Israel Synagogue
Upper Park Street, Salford, Greater Manchester,
M7 0HL
Tel: 0161-740-3905 (h)
Contact: Revd S Simon
Position: Secretary

Great & New (Stenecourt) Synagogue
Singleton Road, Holden Road, Salford, Greater
Manchester, M7 0NL
Tel: 0161-792-8399
Contact: E Levene
Position: Secretary

Kahal Chassidim Synagogue (Lubavitch)
72 Singleton Road, Salford, Greater Manchester,
M7 0LU
Tel: 0161-740-3632
Contact: S Topperman
Position: Secretary

Lubavitch Foundation
62 Singleton Road, Salford, Greater Manchester,
M7 0LU
Tel: 0161-720-9514 **Fax:** 0161-740-9514
Contact: Rabbi Levi Wineberg
Position: Youth Director

Activities: Worship, resource, youth, elderly,
women
Traditions: Charedi
Other Languages: Yiddish, Hebrew
Affiliations: Lubavitch England

Lubavitch Yeshiva
72 Singleton Road, Salford, Greater Manchester,
M7 0LU
Tel: 0161-740-9264
Contact: Rabbi A Cohen
Position: Dean

**Manchester Central Board for Hebrew
Education & Talmud Torah**
Emanuel Raffles House, Salford, Greater
Manchester, M7 0DA
Tel: 0161-708-9200
Contact: Mr S Pine
Position: Chairperson

**Manchester Congregation of Spanish &
Portuguese Jews**
10 Rutland Drive, Salford, Greater Manchester,
M7 4WJ
Tel: 0161-792-7406
Contact: David Salem
Position: Chair
Activities: Worship, resource
Traditions: Sephardi
Other Languages: Spanish
Affiliations: Manchester Jewish Representative
Council

Manchester Council of Synagogues (Orthodox)
c/o The Synagogue, Leicester Road, Salford,
Greater Manchester, M7 4EP
Tel: 0161-740-4830
Contact: M Green
Position: Secretary

Nefusot Yehudah Synagogue
Emanuel Raffles House, 2 Upper Park Road,
Salford, Greater Manchester, M7 0HL
Tel: 0161-795-4567
Contact: Dr D J Marshall
Position: Honorary Secretary

North Salford Synagogue
2 Vine Street, Kersal, Salford, Greater Manchester,
M7 0NX
Tel: 0161-740-7958
Contact: Rabbi L W Rabinowitz

Reshet Torah Education Network
4 Hanover Gardens, Broughton Park, Salford,
Greater Manchester, M7 4FQ
Tel: 0161-740-5735 **Fax:** 0161-795-4295
Contact: Rabbi S M Kupetz
Position: Executive Director
Activities: Resource, books
Traditions: Charedi
Other Languages: Yiddish, Hebrew

Talmud Torah Chinuch N'orim
11 Wellington Street East, Salford, Greater
Manchester, M7 9AU
Tel: 0161-792-4522
Contact: B Waldman
Position: Chair

Telzer & Kovner Synagogue
Ground Floor, 134 Leicester Road, Salford,
Greater Manchester

Zeive Agudath Israel Synagogue
Ground Floor, 35a Northumberland Street,
Broughton, Salford, Greater Manchester

Jewish Convalescent & Aged Home
81 Albert Road, Southport, Merseyside, PR9 9LN
Tel: 01704-531975
Contact: Teviot Freeman
Position: Religious Adviser
Activities: Worship, resource, visits, elderly,
newsletters
Traditions: Orthodox
Other Languages: Hebrew

Southport Jewish Representative Council
7 Grange Road, Southport, Merseyside, PR9 9AB
Tel: 01704-532367 **Fax:** 01704-542075
Contact: Gillian L Mayer
Position: Honorary Secretary

Southport New Synagogue
Portland Street, Southport, Merseyside, PR8 1LR
Tel: 01704-535950 **Fax:** 01704-535950
Contact: Mrs Eileen Lippa
Position: Administrator
Activities: Worship, inter-faith
Traditions: Reform
Affiliations: Southport Jewish Representative
Council; Reform Synagogues of Great Britain

Wirral Jewish Community
1 The Knapp, Dawstone Road, Heswall, Wirral,
Merseyside, L60 0GX

EAST MIDLANDS
City, Town or Local Bodies

Jewish Communal Centre
Highfield Street, Leicester, Leicestershire

Jewish Students Society
c/o Students Union, Leicester University,
Leicester, Leicestershire

Leicester Hebrew Congregation
Synagogue, Highfield Street, Leicester,
Leicestershire
Tel: 0116-254-0477 **Tel:** 0116-270-0997 (h)
Contact: Geoffrey J Louis
Position: Honorary Secretary
Activities: Worship, umbrella, visits, newsletters,
inter-faith
Traditions: Orthodox
Affiliations: The United Synagogue

Leicester Progressive Jewish Congregation
24 Avenue Road, Stoneygate, Leicester,
Leicestershire, LE2 3EA
Tel: 0116-244-8968 **Tel:** 0116-271-5584 (h)
Fax: 0116-271-5584
Contact: Lily & Jeffrey Kaufman
Position: Honorary Secretaries
Activities: Worship, resource, visits, youth, elderly,
women, newsletters, inter-faith
Traditions: Liberal
Affiliations: Union of Liberal and Progressive
Synagogues

Northampton Hebrew Congregation
The Synagogue, Overstone Road, Northampton,
Northamptonshire, NN1 3JW
Tel: 01604-33345
Contact: Mr Alex Moss
Position: Honorary Secretary
Activities: Worship, visits, elderly, women,
newsletters
Traditions: Orthodox
Affiliations: United Synagogue

Nottingham Hebrew Congregation
Shakespeare Villas, Nottingham, Nottinghamshire,
NG1 4FQ
Tel: 0115-947-2004
Contact: Secretary
Activities: Worship, visits, youth, elderly,
newsletters, inter-faith
Traditions: Orthodox
Other Languages: Hebrew, Ivrit
Affiliations: Nottingham Jewish Representative
Council; United Synagogue

Nottingham Jewish Welfare Board
35 Arnot Hill Road, Nottingham,
Nottinghamshire, NG5 6LN
Tel: 0115-926-0245
Contact: Dr M Caplan
Position: Chair

Nottingham Jewish Women's Benevolent Society
c/o Nottingham Hebrew Congregation,
Shakespeare Villas, Nottingham, Nottinghamshire,
NG1 4FQ
Tel: 0115-947-6663 (h)
Contact: Gillian Gordon
Position: Chair
Activities: Elderly, women
Traditions: Orthodox, Liberal/Reform/Cross-
community
Affiliations: Nottingham Representative Council

Nottingham Progressive Jewish Congregation
Nottingham Progressive Synagogue, Lloyd Street,
off Mansfield Road, Sherwood, Nottingham,
Nottinghamshire, NG5 4BP
Tel: 0115-962-4761 **Tel:** 0115-928-1613
Contact: Lynne Chapman
Position: Secretary
Activities: Worship, resource, visits, elderly,
newsletters, inter-faith
Traditions: Liberal
Other Languages: Hebrew
Affiliations: Nottingham Representative
Council; Union of Liberal and Progressive
Synagogues; World Union of Progressive Judaism
(Europe)

Nottingham Trent University Jewish Societry
c/o Nottingham Trent University, Nottingham,
Nottinghamshire, NG1 4BU
Tel: 0115-979-2624
Contact: Abigail Gold

Position: Chair
Activities: Youth
Traditions: Cross-community
Affiliations: Union of Jewish Students

Nottingham University Jewish Society
c/o Nottingham University, University Park,
Nottingham, Nottinghamshire, NG7 2RD
Contact: President
Activities: Youth, newsletters
Traditions: Orthodox, Liberal/Reform/Masorti
Other Languages: Hebrew
Affiliations: Nottingham Jewish Representative
Council; Union of Jewish Students

WEST MIDLANDS
Regional or County Bodies

Lubavitch in the Midlands
Birmingham Lubavitch Centre, 95 Willows Road,
Birmingham, West Midlands, B12 9QF
Tel: 0121-440-6673
Contact: Rabbi Shmuel Arkush
Position: Director
Activities: Resource, youth, elderly, women
Traditions: Cross-community
Affiliations: Lubavitch UK; Lubavitch
International

**Representative Council of Birmingham &
Midlands Jewry**
Singershill, Blucher Street, Birmingham, West
Midlands, B1 1QL
Tel: 0121-643-2688 **Tel:** 0121-440-4142 (h)
Fax: 0121-643-2688
Contact: Mr Leonard Jacobs
Position: Honorary Secretary
Activities: Umbrella
Traditions: Cross-community

City, Town or Local Bodies

Birmingham Central Synagougue
133 Pershore Road, Edgbaston, Birmingham, West
Midlands, B5 7PA
Tel: 0121-440-4044 **Tel:** 0121-440-4142 (h)
Fax: 0121-440-4044
Contact: Mr Leonard Jacobs
Position: President
Activities: Worship
Traditions: Orthodox

Birmingham Hebrew Congregation
Singers Hill, Ellis Street, City Centre,
Birmingham, West Midlands, B1 1HL
Tel: 0121-643-0884 **Tel:** 0121-449-2398 (h)
Fax: 0121-643-5950
Contact: Mr Bernard Gingold
Position: Administrator
Activities: Worship, resource, visits, inter-faith
Traditions: Orthodox - Central Ashkenazi
Affiliations: Birmingham Jewish Representative
Council; London Beth Din

Birmingham Jewish Welfare Board
1 Rake Way, Off Tennant Street, Edgbaston,
Birmingham, West Midlands, B15 1EG
Tel: 0121-643-2835 **Tel:** 0121-704-4049 (h)
Fax: 0121-643-5291
Contact: Irving Myers
Position: Chief Executive
Activities: Elderly
Traditions: Cross-community
Affiliations: Birmingham and Midlands Jewish
Representative Council; Central Council Jewish
Community Services; Regional Jewish Welfare
Federation

Birmingham Jewish Youth Trust
The Youth Centre, 19 Sandhurst Road, Moseley,
Birmingham, West Midlands, B13 8EU
Tel: 0121-442-4459
EMail: birmingham.jyt@ort.org
Contact: Chris Jennings
Position: Community Youth Worker
Activities: Resource, youth, newsletters
Traditions: Cross-community
Other Languages: Hebrew
Affiliations: Representative Council of
Birmingham and Midland Jewry; Association for
Jewish Youth

Birmingham Progressive Synagogue
4 Sheepcote Street, (off Broad Street),
Birmingham, West Midlands, B16 8AA
Tel: 0121-643-5640
Contact: Mrs Rosa Plotnek
Position: Administrator
Activities: Worship, visits, youth, elderly,
newsletters, inter-faith
Traditions: Liberal
Affiliations: Birmingham Jewish Representative
Council; Union of Liberal and Progressive
Synagogues; World Union of Progressive Judaism

Hillel House
26 Somerset Road, Edgbaston, Birmingham, West
Midlands, B15 2QD
Tel: 0121-454-5684 **Tel:** 0121-455-8116

Lubavitch in the Midlands
Birmingham Lubavitch Centre, 95 Willows Road,
Birmingham, West Midlands, B12 9QF
Tel: 0121-440-6673
Contact: Rabbi Shmuel Arkush
Position: Director
Activities: Resource, youth, elderly, women
Traditions: Cross-community
Affiliations: Lubavitch UK; Lubavitch
International; Representative Council of
Birmingham & Midlands Jewry

Representative Council of Birmingham & Midlands Jewry
Singers Hill, Blucher Street, Birmingham, West
Midlands, B1 1QL
Tel: 0121-643-2688 **Fax:** 0121-643-2688
EMail: rjacobs@iicmids.u-net.com
Contact: Mrs Ruth Jacobs
Position: Administrator
Activities: Umbrella
Traditions: Cross-community

Synagogue
Blucher Street, Singer's Hill, Birmingham, West
Midlands

Union of Jewish Students in Birmingham
c/o Hillel House, 26 Somerset Road, Edgbaston,
Birmingham, West Midlands, B15 2QD
Tel: 0121-454-5684
Contact: Mr Neil Bredski
Position: Vice-Chair
Activities: Resource, umbrella, youth, newsletters
Other Languages: Hebrew, French, Spanish
Affiliations: Midlands Region of the Union of
Jewish Students; Union of Jewish Students

Coventry Jewish Reform Community
24 Nightingale Lane, Canley Gardens, Coventry,
West Midlands, CV5 6AY (h)
Tel: 01203-672027 (h)
Contact: Dr Martin Been
Position: Chair
Activities: Worship, resource, youth, newsletters
Traditions: Reform
Other Languages: Hebrew
Affiliations: Reform Synagogues of Great Britain

Coventry Synagogue
Barras Lane, Coventry, West Midlands, CV1 3BU
Tel: 01203-220168
Contact: L R Benjamin
Position: Honorary Secretary

Leamington & District Progressive Jewish Group
Leamington Spa, Warwickshire, c/o Birmingham
Progressive Synagogue, 4 Sheepcote Street,
Birmingham, West Midlands, B16 8AA
Traditions: Liberal
Affiliations: Union of Liberal and Progressive
Synagogues; World Union of Progressive Judaism

Stoke-on-Trent Hebrew Congregation
Stoke-on-Trent, Staffordshire, c/o 27 The Avenue,
Basford, Newcastle under Lyme, Staffordshire, ST5
0ND (h)
Tel: 01782-616417 (h)
Contact: Harold Sydney Morris
Position: President
Activities: Worship, resource, visits, inter-faith
Traditions: Orthodox
Affiliations: Manchester Jewish Representative
Council; United Synagogue

Solihull & District Hebrew Congregation
3 Monastery Drive, Solihull, West Midlands, B91
1DW
Tel: 0121-707-5199 **Fax:** 0121-706-8736
Contact: Rabbi Yehuda Pink
Position: Minister
Activities: Worship
Traditions: Orthodox

Wolverhampton Hebrew Congregation
Fryer Street corner, Longc Street, Wolverhampton,
West Midlands, WV1 1HT
Tel: 01902-752474
Contact: Harvey Cronheim
Position: Honorary Secretary
Activities: Worship, visits, inter-faith
Traditions: Orthodox - Central Ashkenazi
Affiliations: Birmingham Representative
Council; Jewish Council for Small Communities

EAST ANGLIA
City, Town or Local Bodies

Beth Shalom Reform Synagogue
86 Union Lane, Cambridge, Cambridgeshire,
CB4 1QB

Tel: 01223-67175
Contact: Jonathan Harris

Cambridge Traditional Jewish Congregation
3 Thompsons Lane, Cambridge, Cambridgeshire,
CR5 8AU
Tel: 01223-354783
Contact: Sharon Blaukopf
Position: Chairperson
Activities: Worship, resource
Traditions: Orthodox

Cambridge University Jewish Society
c/o The Synagogue, 3 Thompson's Lane,
Cambridge, Cambridgeshire, CB5 8AQ
Tel: 01223-354783
Contact: President

Cambridge University Progressive Jewish Group
1 Merton Street, Cambridge, Cambridgeshire
Tel: 01223-64793
Contact: Rabbi Dr N R M de Lange
Position: Chaplain

Jewish Ladies' Society
3a Earlham Road, Norwich, Norfolk, NR2 3RA
Contact: Mrs E Griffiths
Position: Secretary

Norwich Hebrew Congregation
Norwich Synagogue, 3a Earlham Road, Norwich,
Norfolk, NR2 3RA
Tel: 01603-623948 **Tel:** 01603-417810 (h)
Contact: Mr Jack Griffiths
Position: Honorary Secretary
Activities: Worship, visitors, youth, women,
newsletters, inter-faith

Peterborough Hebrew Congregation
142 Cobden Avenue, Peterborough,
Cambridgeshire, PE1 11L
Tel: 01733-571282
Contact: C Cunn
Position: Chairperson

Peterborough Liberal Jewish Community
25 Sycamore Avenue, Dogsthorpe, Peterborough,
Cambridgeshire, PE1 4JW (h)
Contact: Mrs Julie H Vart
Position: Secretary
Activities: Umbrella, visits, newsletters, inter-faith
Traditions: Liberal
Other Languages: German, French, Spanish

Affiliations: Union of Liberal and Progressive Synagogues

GREATER LONDON
Regional or Area Bodies

London Board for Shechita
PO Box 579, Adastra House, 401-405 Nether Street, London, N3 1YR
Tel: 0181-349-9160

Borough or Local Bodies

BARNET

Beth Abraham Synagogue
46 The Ridgeway, London, NW11
Contact: Rabbi C Schmahl

Beth Hamedrash D'Chasidey
98 Bridge Lane, London, NW11

Beth Hamedrash Divrei Chaim
71 Bridge Lane, London, NW11
Tel: 0181-458-1161
Contact: Rabbi Chaim A Z Halpern

Beth Hamedrash Hendon
3 The Approach, London, NW4 2HU
Tel: 0181-202-5499
Contact: Rabbi D Halpern

Beth Shmuel Synagogue
171 Golders Green Road, London, NW11
Tel: 0181-458-7511
Contact: Rabbi E Halpern

Beth Yisachar Dov Beth Hamedrash
2/4 Highfield Avenue, London, NW11
Contact: Rabbi G Hager

Edgware Adath Yisroel Synagogue
261 Hale Lane, Edgware, Middlesex, HA8 8NX
Tel: 0181-905-4813 (h)   **Fax:** 0181-958-8121
EMail: Rabbi@eayc.demon.co.uk
Contact: Rabbi Z Lieberman
Position: Minister
Activities: Worship, youth, elderly, women, newsletters
Traditions: Traditional Orthodox
Other Languages: Hebrew, Yidish

Edgware & District Reform Synagogue
118 Stonegrove, Edgware, Middlesex, HA8 8AB
Tel: 0181-958-9782   **Fax:** 0181-905-4710
Contact: Mrs J Altman
Position: Administrator
Activities: Worship, visits, youth, elderly, newsletters, inter-faith
Traditions: Reform
Affiliations: The Reform Movement

Edgware Masorti Synagogue
Stream Lane, Edgware, Middlesex, HA8 7AY
Tel: 0181-905-4096   **Fax:** 0181-905-4096
EMail: chaim.weiner@ort.org
Contact: Harold Segal
Position: Co-Chair
Activities: Worship, resource, visits, youth, women, newsletters, books, inter-faith
Traditions: Masorti
Other Languages: Hebrew
Affiliations: Association of Masorti Synagogues; World Council of Synagogues

Edgware United Synagogue
Edgware Way, Edgware, Middlesex, HA8 8JT
Tel: 0181-958-7508

Finchley Central Synagogue
Redbourne Avenue, London, N3 2BS

Finchley Progressive Synagogue
54a Hutton Grove, Finchley, London, N12 8DR
Tel: 0181-446-4063   **Fax:** 0181-446-4063
Contact: Joan Shopper
Position: Administrator
Activities: Worship, visits, youth, elderly, newsletters, inter-faith
Traditions: Liberal
Other Languages: German, French, Hebrew
Affiliations: Union of Liberal and Progressive Synagogues; World Union of Progressive Judaism

Finchley Reform Synagogue
Fallow Court Avenue, Finchley, London, N12 0BE
Tel: 0181-446-3244
Contact: Rabbi Jeffrey Newman

Finchley Road Synagogue
4 Helenslea Avenue, London, NW11
Tel: 0181-455-4305
Contact: Rabbi S Rubin

Finchley Synagogue
Kinloss Gardens, Finchley, London, N3 3DU
Tel: 0181-346-8551 **Fax:** 0181-343-1180
Contact: Beryl Fireman
Position: Administrator
Activities: Worship, resource, visits, youth, elderly,
women, newsletters
Traditions: Orthodox
Other Languages: Ivrit
Affiliations: United Synagogue

Garden Suburb Beth Hamedrash
Jacob and Alexander Gordon House, 5 The
Bishops Avenue, London, N2
Tel: 0181-458-3765
Contact: Rabbi C Wilschanski

Golders Green Synagogue
41 Dunstan Road, London, NW11 8AE
Tel: 0181-455-2460 **Tel:** 0181-455-2891
Contact: Mrs Stella Alexander
Position: Administrator
Activities: Worship, resource, visitors, youth,
elderly, women, newsletters
Traditions: Orthodox - Central Ashkenazi

Ha-Makon
The Manor House, 80 East End Road,
London, N3
Tel: 0181-904-2802 (h)
Contact: Robin
Position: Co-ordinator

Hampstead Garden Suburb (United) Synagogue
Norrice Lea, Hampstead Garden Suburb, London,
N2 0RE
Tel: 0181-455-8126 **Fax:** 0181-201-9247
Contact: Mrs M S Wolff
Position: Administrator
Activities: Worship, youth, elderly, women
Traditions: Orthodox
Other Languages: Hebrew
Affiliations: United Synagogue

Hendon Adath Yisroel Synagogue
11 Brent Street, London, NW4 2EU
Tel: 0181-202-9183
Contact: N Hammond
Position: Secretary

Hendon Reform Synagogue
Danescroft Avenue, Hendon, London, NW4 2NA

Tel: 0181-203-4168
Contact: Mrs Marianne Djora
Position: Secretary
Activities: Worship, visits, youth, elderly, women,
newsletters, inter-faith
Traditions: Reform
Affiliations: The Reform Synagogues of Great
Britain; World Union of Progressive Judaism

Hendon Synagogue
Raleigh Close, Wykeham Road, Hendon, London,
NW4
Tel: 0181-202-6924 **Fax:** 0181-202-1720
EMail: peryyburns@aol.com
Contact: Jonathan Benson
Position: Executive Secretary
Activities: Worship, visits, youth, elderly, women,
newsletters, inter-faith
Traditions: Orthodox
Other Languages: Hebrew, French, German
Affiliations: United Synagogue

Jewish Bereavement Counselling Service
PO Box 6748, London, N3 3BX
Tel: 0181-349-0839 **Fax:** 0181-349-0839
Contact: June Epstein
Position: Co-ordinator
Activities: Resource
Traditions: Cross-community
Affiliations: Visitation Committee; Central
Council of Jewish Social Services

Kingsley Way Beth Hamedrash
3-5 Kingsley Way, London, N2

London Board for Shechita
PO Box 579, Adastra House, 401-405 Nether
Street, London, N3 1YR
Tel: 0181-349-9160

New Whetstone Masorti Synagogue
Oxford & St Georges Henriques House,
120 Oakleigh Road, London, N20

Manor House Society
Sternberg Centre for Judaism, 80 East End Road,
London, N3 2SY
Tel: 0181-346-2288 **Fax:** 0181-349-0694
Contact: Pam Lewis
Position: Administrator

Machzikei Hadath Synagogue
Highfields Road, London, NW11
Tel: 0181-204-1887 (h)
Contact: R Shaw
Position: Honorary Secretary

Mill Hill Synagogue
Station Road, London, NW7

Na'amat UK
132 Anson Road, London, NW2

New North London Synagogue
The Manor House, 80 East Road, Finchley,
London, N3 2SY
Tel: 0181-346-8560
Contact: Barbara Anders
Position: Administrator
Activities: Worship, resource, youth, elderly,
newsletters
Traditions: Masorti
Affiliations: Assembly of Masorti Synagogues

North Hendon Adath Yisroel Synagogue
31 Holders Hill Crescent, Hendon, London,
NW4 1NE
Tel: 0181-203-0797 (h)
Contact: A H Ehreich
Position: Secretary
Activities: Worship, newsletters
Traditions: Charedi
Other Languages: Hebrew, Yiddish
Affiliations: Union of Orthodox Hebrew
Congregations

North Western Reform Synagogue
Alyth Gardens, Finchley Road, London,
NW11 7EN
Tel: 0181-455-6763 **Tel:** 0181-458-2469 (h)
Contact: Rabbi Charles Emanuel
Position: Rabbi
Activities: Worship, visits, youth, elderly,
newsletters, inter-faith
Traditions: Reform
Other Languages: Hebrew
Affiliations: Reform Synagogues of Great
Britain; Beit Daniel Reform Community, Tel Aviv,
Israel & Rostov-on-Don, former Soviet Union

Ohel David Synagogue
Lincoln Institute, Broadwalk Lane, Golders Green
Road, London, NW11

Tel: 0181-806-8109
Contact: D Elias
Position: Honorary Secretary

**Oxford & St George's Jewish Youth &
Community Centre**
Henriques House, 120 Oakleigh Road North,
Whetstone, London, N20 9EZ
Tel: 0181-446-3101 **Fax:** 0181-446-4971
Contact: John Wosner
Position: Director of Centre
Activities: Worship, resource, youth, elderly
Traditions: Cross-community
Affiliations: Association of Jewish Youth

Sinai Synagogue
54 Woodstock Avenue, London, NW11 9RJ
Tel: 0181-455-6876 (h)
Contact: C Cohen
Position: Secretary

Spec Jewish Youth & Community Centre
87 Brookside South, East Barnet, Hertfordshire,
EN4 8LL
Tel: 0181-368-5117
Contact: Liz Gordon
Position: Centre Director
Activities: Youth
Traditions: United
Affiliations: Association for Jewish Youth; United
Synagogue

Woodside Park Synagogue
Woodside Park Road, Finchley, London,
N12 8RZ
Tel: 0181-445-4236 **Fax:** 0181-445-4236
Contact: Deanna Bruce
Position: Administrator
Activities: Worship, youth, newsletters
Traditions: Orthodox
Affiliations: United Synagogue

Yakar Educational Foundation
2 Egerton Gardens, London, NW4 4BA
Tel: 0181-202-5551 **Fax:** 0181-202-9653
Contact: Phillipa Claydon

BARKING AND DAGENHAM

Barking & Becontree United Synagogue
200 Becontree Avenue, Becontree, Essex
Tel: 0181-590-2737

BRENT

Cricklewood United Synagogue
131 Walm Lane, Cricklewood, London,
NW2 3AU
Tel: 0181-452-1739
Contact: Revd G Glawsiusz
Position: Minister
Activities: Worship, inter-faith
Traditions: Orthodox
Affiliations: United Synagogue

Dollis Hill United Synagogue
Parkside, Dollis Hill Lane, London, NW2 6RJ
Tel: 0181-542-7172
Contact: Warren Land
Position: Administrator

Etz Chaim Yeshiva
83-85 Bridge Lane, London, NW11

Kingsbury United Synagogue
Kingsbury Green, London, NW9 8XR
Tel: 0181-204-8089
Contact: Mrs M Lazarus
Position: Administrator

Ohel Israel (Skoler) Synagogue
11 Brent Street, London, NW4

Wembley Synagogue
Forty Avenue, Wembley, Middlesex, HA9 8JW
Tel: 0181-904-6565 **Fax:** 0181-908-2740
EMail: 100346.260@compuserve.com
Contact: Mrs Rita Garfield
Position: Administrator
Activities: Worship, visits, youth, elderly, women, newsletters
Traditions: Orthodox
Other Languages: Hebrew, Yiddish, German
Affiliations: United Synagogue

Willesden & Brondesbury United Synagogue
143-145 Brondesbury Park, London, NW2 5JL
Tel: 0181-459-1083
Contact: Mrs J Questle
Position: Administrator

CAMDEN

Belsize Square Synagogue
51 Belsize Square, London, NW3 4HX
Tel: 0171-794-3949 **Fax:** 0171-431-4559

Contact: Judith Berman
Position: Secretary
Activities: Worship, resource, visits, youth, elderly, newsletters, books, inter-faith
Traditions: Independent-Progressive
Other Languages: German
Affiliations: World Union of Progressive Judaism

Hampstead Adath Yisroel Congregation
10a Cranfield Gardens, London, NW6

Hampstead Reform Jewish Community
37a Broadhurst Gardens, London, NW6
Tel: 0171-794-8488 (h) **Fax:** 0171-794-8488
Contact: Mr Michael Teper
Position: Chairperson
Activities: Worship, newsletters, inter-faith
Traditions: Reform
Affiliations: Reform Movement; World Union of Progressive Judaism

Hampstead Synagogue
1 Dennington Park Road, West Hampstead,
London, NW6 1AX
Tel: 0171-435-1518 **Fax:** 0181-431-8369
Contact: Mr I Nadel
Position: Administrator
Activities: Worship, visits, elderly, newsletters, inter-faith
Traditions: Orthodox – Central Ashkenazi
Other Languages: Hebrew, Yiddish
Affiliations: United Synagogue

Sanz Klausner's Synagogue
31 Broadhurst Gardens, London, NW3

South Hampstead Synagogue
20/22 Eton Villas, Eton Road, London, NW3 4SP
Tel: 0171-722-1807

West Central Liberal Synagogue
The Montagu Centre, 21 Maple Street, Camden,
London, W1P 6DS
Tel: 0171-636-7627
Contact: Henry J Berman
Position: Honorary Secretary
Activities: Worship, visits, newsletters, inter-faith
Traditions: Liberal
Affiliations: Union of Liberal and Progressive Synagogues

CITY OF LONDON

Bevis Marks Synagogue
Bevis Marks, London, EC3
Tel: 0171-626-1274 **Fax:** 0171-283-8825
Contact: Henry Valier
Position: Shamas
Activities: Worship, visits, youth
Traditions: Sephardi
Other Languages: French, Spanish
Affiliations: Spanish and Portugese Jews
Congregation

CROYDON

Croydon & District Synagogue
The Almonds, Shirley Oaks, Croydon, Surrey

EALING

Ealing Liberal Synagogue
Lynton Avenue, Drayton Green, West Ealing,
London, W13 OEB
Tel: 0181-997-0528 **Fax:** 0181-997-0528
Contact: Mr Arnold Aarons
Position: Administrator
Activities: Worship, visits, newsletters, inter-faith
Traditions: Liberal
Other Languages: German
Affiliations: Union of Liberal and Progressive
Synagogues

Ealing Synagogue
15 Grange Road, Ealing, London, W5 5QN
Tel: 0181-579-4894
Contact: Mrs S Hayman
Position: Administrator
Activities: Worship, visits, youth, elderly, women,
newsletters, books, inter-faith
Traditions: Orthodox
Affiliations: United Synagogue

Greenford Synagogue
39-45 Oldfield Lane, Greenford, Middlesex,
UB6 9LB
Tel: 0181-578-2256 **Tel:** 0181-421-6366 (h)
Contact: Ronald Hyams
Position: Honorary Secretary
Activities: Worship
Traditions: Orthodox
Other Languages: Yiddish, Russian
Affiliations: Federation of Synagogues

ENFIELD

Cockfosters & North Southgate Synagogue
Old Farm Avenue, Southgate, London, N14 5QR

Enfield & Winchmore Hill United Synagogue
53 Wellington Road, Bushill Park, Enfield,
Middlesex, EN1 2PG
Tel: 0181-363-2697 **Tel:** 0181-367-2569 (h)
Contact: S Leon
Position: Honorary Secretary

Palmer's Green & Southgate United Synagogue
Brownlow Road, New Southgate, London,
N11 2BN
Tel: 0181-881-0037
Contact: Mr Martin M Lewis
Position: Administrator
Activities: Worship, visits, youth, elderly, women,
newsletters
Traditions: Orthodox
Affiliations: United Synagogue

Southgate & District Reform Synagogue
45 High Street, Southgate, London, N14 6LD
Tel: 0181-882-6828 **Fax:** 0181-882-7539
Contact: Mrs C Z Elf
Position: Administrator
Activities: Worship, women, newsletters
Traditions: Reform
Other Languages: Hebrew, Yiddish
Affiliations: Reform Synagogues of Great
Britain; World Union for Progressive Judaism

Southgate Progressive Synagogue
75 Chase Road, London, N14 4QY
Tel: 0181-886-0977 **Fax:** 0181-882-5394
Contact: Rabbi Stephen Howard

GREENWICH

Woolwich & District Synagogue
81 Marlborough Lane, London, SE7
Tel: 0181-856-0845
Contact: J M Gaus
Position: Secretary

HACKNEY

Aden Jews' Congregation
Clapton Common, London, E5
Tel: 0181-806-1320

Contact: M A Solomon
Position: Honorary Secretary

Ahavat Israel Synagogue D'Chasidey Viznitz
89 Stanford Hill, London, N16
Tel: 0181-800-9359
Contact: Rabbi F Schneelbalg

Beth Chodosh Synagogue
51 Queen Elizabeth's Walk, London, N16
Tel: 0181-800-6754

Beth Hamedrash Beis Nadvorna
43-45 Darenth Road, London, N16 6ES
Tel: 0181-806-2030
Contact: Rabbi Mordechai Leifer
Position: Rabbi
Activities: Worship, elderly
Traditions: Orthodox, Charedi
Other Languages: Yiddish, Hebrew
Affiliations: Union of Orthodox Hebrew Congregations

Beth Hamedrash D'Chasidey Gur
2 Lampard Grove, London, N16
Tel: 0181-806-4333

Beth Hamedrash D'Chasidey Ryzin
33 Paget Road, London, N16
Tel: 0181-800-7979

Beth Hamedrash D'Chasidey Sanz Klausenburg
42 Craven Walk, London, N16

Beth Hamedrash D'Chasidey Square
22 Dunsmure Road, London, N16
Tel: 0181-800-8448

Beth Hamedrash D'Chassidey Belz
96 Clapton Common, London, E5
Tel: 0181-800-3741
Contact: Dayan J D Babad

Beth Hamedrash of the Agudah Youth Movement
69 Lordship Road, London, N16
Tel: 0181-800-8873
Contact: M J Kamionka

Beth Hamedrash Torah Chaim Liege
145 Upper Clapton Road, London, E5
Contact: Rabbi Y Meisels

Beth Hamedrash Torah Etz Chayim
69 Lordship Road, London, N16
Tel: 0181-800-7726
Contact: Rabbi Z Feldman

Beth Hamedrash (Trisker) Synagogue
146 Osbaldeston Road, London, N16
Tel: 0181-806-3551

Beth Hamedrash Yetiv Lev D'Satmar
86 Cazenove Road, London, N16
Tel: 0181-800-2633
Contact: Rabbi C Wosner

Beth Sholom Synagogue
27 St Kilda's Road, London, N16
Tel: 0181-809-6224
Contact: Rabbi M Deutsch

Buckhurst Hill Reform Synagogue
c/o The Manor House, 80 East End Road,
London, N3 2SY

Central Mikvaot Body
40 Queen Elizabeths Walk, London, N16 0HH

Clapton Federation Synagogue
47 Lea Bridge Road, London, E5
Tel: 0181-806-4369 **Tel:** 0181-806-7565 (h)
Contact: K Franklin
Position: Secretary

Commercial Road Talmud Torah Synagogue
153 Stamford Hill, London, N16 5LG
Tel: 0181-800-1618117

Hackney United Synagogue
Brenthouse Road, Mare Street, London, E9 6AG
Tel: 0181-985-4600
Contact: Mrs B Heumann
Position: Administrator

Hatzola Trust
The Knoll, Fountayne Road, Hackney, London,
N16
Tel: 0181-806-9497 (h)
Contact: Rabbi Eli Kerncraut
Position: Trustee
Traditions: Orthodox - Central Ashkenazi
Other Languages: Yiddish, Hebrew

Jacob Benjamin Elias Synagogue
140 Stamford Hill, London, N16

Tel: 0181-806-8109 (h)
Contact: D Elias
Position: Honorary Secretary

Kehal Chasidim Synagogue
Queen Elizabeth Walk, London, N16 0HJ
Tel: 0181-802-6226
Contact: Mr A Barnett
Position: Honorary Secretary

Kehillath Chasidim Synagogue
85 Cazenove Road, London, N16

Lubavitch Synagogue
107-115 Stamford Hill, London, N16
Tel: 0181-800-0022
Position: Rabbi N Sudak

Mesifta Synagogue
82-84 Cazenove Road, London, N16

New Synagogue
Egerton Road, London, N16 6UD
Tel: 0181-800-6003

North London Chevrat Bikur Cholim
35 Paget Road, Stamford Hill, London, N16 5ND
(h)
Tel: 0181-802-5032 (h)
Contact: Mrs Caroline Joseph
Position: Honorary Organiser
Traditions: Charedi
Other Languages: Yiddish, Hebrew

North London Progressive Synagogue
100 Amhurst Park, London, N16 5AR
Tel: 0181-800-8931 **Fax:** 0181-800-0416
Contact: Rabbi Marcia Plumb
Position: Rabbi
Activities: Worship, visits, youth, elderly, women,
newsletters, inter-faith
Traditions: Liberal
Affiliations: Union of Liberal and Progressive
Synagogues; World Union for Progressive Judaism

Springfield Synagogue
202 Upper Clapton Road, London, E5 9DH
Tel: 01702-340762 (h)
Contact: L Blackman
Position: Honorary Secretary

Stamford Hill Beth Hamedrash
50 Clapton Common, London, E5

Tel: 0181-802-4017 (h)
Contact: M Chontow
Position: Secretary

Stanislowa Beth Hamedrash
93 Lordship Park, London, N16
Tel: 0181-800-2040
Contact: Rabbi M Asckenasi

Walford Road Synagogue
99 Walford Road, London, N16 8EF
Tel: 0171-249-5604 (h)
Contact: S Raymond
Position: Secretary
Activities: Worship, visits
Traditions: Orthodox, Cross-community
Other Languages: Hebrew, French, Arabic

West Hackney Synagogue
233a Amhurst Road, London, E8
Tel: 0181-254-2128 (h)
Contact: C Pollock
Position: President

Yavneh Synagogue
25 Ainsworth Road, London, E9
Tel: 0181-530-5816 (h)
Contact: R I Jacobs
Position: Secretary

Yeshiva Horomoh Beth Hamedrash
100 Fairholt Road, London, N16 5HH
Tel: 0181-809-3904 **Tel:** 0181-800-2194 (h)
Contact: Rabbi E Schlesinger

Yeshuath Chaim Synagogue
45 Heathland Road, London, N16
Tel: 0181-800-2332
Contact: I Kohn
Position: Honorary Secretary

Yesodey Hatorah Synagogue
2/4 Amhurst Park, London, N16

HAMMERSMITH AND FULHAM

**Hammersmith & West Kensington United
Synagogue**
71 Brook Green, Hammersmith, London, W6 7BE
Tel: 0171-602-1405
Contact: Mr S Williams
Position: Administrator
Activities: Worship

Traditions: Orthodox - Central Ashkenazi
Affiliations: United Synagogue

HARINGEY

Finsbury Park United Synagogue
220 Green Lanes, London, N4 2NT
Tel: 0181-800-3526
Contact: H Mather
Position: Administrator

Highgate United Synagogue
Grimshaw Close, 57 North Road, Highgate,
London, N6 4BJ
Tel: 0181-340-7655
Contact: Mr Ben Soller
Position: Secretary

Muswell Hill United Synagogue
31 Tetherdown, London, N10 1ND
Tel: 0181-833-5925
Contact: H Hankin
Position: Administrator

South Tottenham Synagogue
111 Crowland Road, London, N15 6UL
Tel: 0181-880-2731
Contact: R Danan
Position: Administrator

HARROW

Belmont United Synagogue
101 Vernon Drive, Stanmore, Middlesex,
HA7 2BW
Tel: 0181-863-9783
Contact: Mrs C Fletcher
Position: Administrator

Brady-Maccabi Youth & Community Centre
4 Manor Park Crescent, Edgware, Middlesex,
HA8 7NL
Tel: 0181-952-2948

Harrow & Wembley Progressive Synagogue
326 Preston Road, Harrow, Middlesex, HA3 0QH
Tel: 0181-904-8581
Contact: Mrs Sandra Rose
Position: Secretary
Activities: Worship, visits, youth, elderly, women,
newsletters, inter-faith
Traditions: Liberal
Affiliations: Union of Liberal and Progressive
Synagogues

Harrow Jewish Day Centre
26 Adelaide Close, Stanmore, Middlesex,
HA7 3EN

Kenton Synagogue
Shaftesbury Avenue, Kenton, Harrow, Middlesex,
HA3 0RD
Tel: 0181-907-5959
Contact: A Primhak
Position: Secretary
Activities: Worship, resource, youth, elderly,
women, newsletters
Traditions: Orthodox
Affiliations: United Synagogue

Middlesex New Synagogue
39 Bessborough Road, Harrow, Middlesex,
HA1 3BS
Tel: 0181-864-0133 **Fax:** 0181-864-0133
Contact: Rabbi Simon J Franses
Position: Minister
Activities: Worship, resource, visits, youth, elderly,
women, newsletters, inter-faith
Traditions: Reform
Other Languages: Hebrew, German
Affiliations: Reform Synagogues of Great
Britain; World Union of Progressive Judaism

Neveh Shalom Community, David Ishag Synagogue
352-4 Preston Road, Harrow, Middlesex,
HA3 0QL
Tel: 0181-904-3009
Contact: C Benson
Position: Honorary Secretary

Pinner Synagogue
1 Cecil Park, Pinner, Middlesex, HA5 5HJ
Tel: 0181-868-7204
Contact: Mrs Christine Lipman
Position: Administrator
Activities: Worship, visits, youth, elderly,
newsletters, inter-faith
Traditions: Orthodox
Affiliations: United Synagogue

Ravenswood Foundation/Norwood Child Care
80-82 The Broadway, Stanmore, Middlesex,
HA7 4HB
Tel: 0181-954-4555 **Fax:** 0181-420-6800
Contact: Vivienne Lewis

Position: Fundraising & PR
Traditions: Cross-community

Stanmore & Canons Park United Synagogue
London Road, Stanmore, Middlesex, HA7 4NS
Tel: 0181-954-2210 **Fax:** 0181-954-4369
EMail: 101773.733@compuserve.com
Contact: Mrs B S Dresner
Position: Administrator
Activities: Worship, resource, youth, elderly,
women, newsletter
Traditions: Orthodox - Central Ashkenazi
Affiliations: United Synagogue

HAVERING

Elm Park (Affiliated) Synagogue
64 Herbert Road, Emmerson Park, Hornchurch,
Essex, RM11 3LL (h)
Tel: 01708-442079 **Tel:** 01708-449305 (h)
Contact: Mrs Sonia Gaynor
Position: Secretary
Activities: Worship, elderly, women
Traditions: Orthodox
Affiliations: United Synagogue

Harold Hill & District Affiliated Synagogue
Trowbridge Road, Harold Hill, Essex
Tel: 01402-348904 (h)
Contact: Honorary Secretary

Romford & District Affiliated Synagogue
25 Eastern Road, Romford, Essex
Tel: 01708-746190
Contact: J R Rose
Position: Administrator

HILLINGDON

Middlesex New Synagogue Community
44 Kingsend, Ruislip, Middlesex, HA4 7DA

Northwood & Pinner Liberal Synagogue
Oaklands Gate, Northwood, Middlesex, HA6 3AA
Tel: 01923-822592 **Fax:** 01923-824454
Contact: Rabbi Andrew Goldstein
Position: Minister
Activities: Worship, resource, visits, youth, elderly,
newsletters, inter-faith
Traditions: Liberal
Affiliations: Union of Liberal and Progessive
Synagogues

Ruislip & District Affiliated Synagogue
Sheney Avenue, Ruislip Manor, Middlesex,
HA4 6BP
Tel: 01895-622059
Contact: A Barnett
Position: Administrator

HOUNSLOW

Hounslow & Heathrow Synagogue
100 Staines Road, Hounslow, Middlesex
Tel: 0181-572-2100 **Tel:** 0181-894-4020 (h)
Contact: Louis Gilbert
Position: Honorary Treasurer
Activities: Worship
Traditions: Orthodox
Other Languages: Hebrew
Affiliations: United Synagogue

KENSINGTON AND CHELSEA

Beit Klal Yisrael
North Kensington Reform Synagogue,
PO Box 1828, London, W10 5RT
Tel: 0181-960-5750
Contact: Chair
Activities: Worship, resource, visits, youth,
women, newsletters, inter-faith
Traditions: Reform
Other Languages: Hebrew
Affiliations: Reform Synagogues of Great
Britain; World Congress of Jewish Gay and
Lesbian Organisations

Notting Hill Synagogue
206 Kensington Park Road, London, W11 1NR
Tel: 0181-952-4654 (h)
Contact: H Lamb
Position: Secretary

Sephardi Centre
2 Ashworth Road, Maida Vale, London, W9 1JY
Tel: 0171-266-3682 **Fax:** 0171-266-3682
Contact: Mrs Michelle Shemtob
Position: Assistant Director
Activities: Resource, visits, youth, women,
newsletters
Traditions: Sephardi, Cross-community
Other Languages: Hebrew Arabic
Affiliations: Spanish & Portugese Jews
Congregation

Sephardi Woman's Association
5 Vale Close, London, W9 1RR

Spanish & Portuguese Jews' Congregation
Lauderdale Road Synagogue, 2 Ashworth Road,
Maida Vale, London, W9 1JY
Tel: 0171-289-2573 **Fax:** 0171-289-2709
Contact: Mr Howard Miller
Position: Chief Administrator
Activities: Worship, resource, youth, elderly,
women, newsletters, books
Traditions: Sephardi
Other Languages: Hebrew, Spanish, French

Spanish & Portugese Synagogue
8 St James Gardens, Holland Park, London,
W11 4RB
Tel: 0171-603-7961 **Fax:** 0171-603-9471
Contact: Mrs Z Fineburgh
Position: Secretary
Activities: Worship, resource, newsletters, books,
inter-faith
Traditions: Sephardi
Other Languages: Spanish, Ladino
Affiliations: Sephardi Synagogues

KINGSTON-UPON-THAMES

Kingston & Surbiton District Synagogue
33-35 Uxbridge Road, Kingston-upon-Thames,
Surrey, KT1 2LL
Tel: 0181-546-9370 **Tel:** 0181-399-8689 (h)
Contact: Rabbi Stanley Coten
Activities: Worship, resource, umbrella, visits,
youth, elderly, women, newsletters, inter-faith
Traditions: Orthodox
Other Languages: Hebrew
Affiliations: United Synagogue

LAMBETH

South London Liberal Synagogue
Prentis Road, Streatham, London, SW16 1QB
Tel: 0181-769-4787
Contact: Derek Aarons
Position: Chairperson
Activities: Worship, resource, visits, youth, elderly,
women, newsletters, inter-faith
Traditions: Liberal
Affiliations: Union of Liberal and Progressive
Synagogues; World Union of Progressive Judaism

South London United Synagogue
45 Leigham Court Road, London, SW16 2NF
Tel: 0171-677-0234
Contact: Mrs A Gabay
Position: Administrator

MERTON

Wimbledon & District Reform Synagogue
44-46 Worple Road, Wimbledon, London,
SW19 4EJ
Tel: 0181-946-4836 **Fax:** 0181-944-7790
Contact: Mrs Flory Solomon
Position: Administrator
Activities: Worship, newsletters, inter-faith
Traditions: Reform
Affiliations: Reform Synagogues of Great Britain

NEWHAM

Forest Gate Federated Synagogue
52 Claremont Road, London, E7

West Ham & Upton Park Synagogue
93-95 Earlham Grove, Forest Gate, London,
E7 9AR
Tel: 0181-522-1917
Contact: Mrs E Benjamin
Position: Secretary
Activities: Worship
Traditions: Orthodox
Affiliations: United Synagogue

Woodford & District Liberal Jewish Synagogue
Marlborough Road, South Woodford, London,
E18 1AR

REDBRIDGE

Barkingside Progressive Synagogue
129 Perryman's Farm Road, Ilford, Essex,
IG2 7LX
Tel: 0181-554-9682
Contact: Mr Barry Lautman
Position: Secretary
Activities: Worship, resource, visits, youth, elderly,
newsletters
Traditions: Liberal
Affiliations: World Union of Progressive Judaism

Chabad Lubavitch Centre
372 Cranbrook Road, Ilford, Essex, IG2 6HW

Tel: 0181-554-1624 **Fax:** 0181-518-2126
Contact: Rabbi A M Sufrin
Position: Director
Activities: Worship, resource, umbrella, visits,
youth, women, newsletters
Traditions: Orthodox
Other Languages: Yiddish, Hebrew, French
Affiliations: Lubavitch Foundation UK; United
Synagogue; World Headquarters Lubavitch
Movement

Clayhall United Synagogue

Sinclair House, Woodford Bridge Road,
Redbridge, Essex
Contact: Mrs Fishman
Position: Secretary

Eastern Jewry Community

Newbury Park Station, Newbury Park, Essex, IG2
Tel: 0181-806-8109 (h)
Contact: D Elias
Position: Honorary Secretary

Ilford Congregation (Ohel David)

Newbury Park Station, Ilford, Essex
Tel: 0181-806-8109 (h)
Contact: D Elias
Position: Honorary Secretary

Ilford Federation Synagogue

14/16 Coventry Road, Ilford, Essex, IG1 4QR
Tel: 0181-554-5289
Contact: Mrs P Hacker
Position: Secretary

Ilford Synagogue

22 Beehive Lane, Ilford, Essex, IG1 3RT
Tel: 0181-554-5969
Contact: Hazel Michaels
Position: Administrator
Activities: Worship, visits, elderly, newsletters
Traditions: Orthodox
Other Languages: Hebrew
Affiliations: United Synagogue

New Essex Masorti Synagogue

Prince Regent Hotel, Woodford Bridge Road,
Woodford Bridge, Essex

Newbury Park Synagogue

23 Wessex Close, Suffolk Road, Ilford, Essex,
IG3 8JU

Tel: 0181-597-0958
Contact: Mrs Elizabeth Benjamin
Position: Secretary
Activities: Worship, resource, visits, elderly,
women, newsletters
Traditions: Orthodox
Affiliations: North East London Region
Orthodox Synagogues; United Synagogue

Ohel Jacob Beth Hamedrash

1st Floor, 478 Cranbrook Road, Ilford, Essex
Contact: D Grant
Position: Honorary Secretary

Redbridge Jewish Youth & Community Centre

Sinclair House, Woodford Bridge Road, Ilford,
Essex, IG4 5LN
Tel: 0181-551-0017 **Fax:** 0181-551-9027
Contact: Mr Neil Taylor
Position: Operations Manager
Activities: Worship, resource, umbrella, visits,
youth, elderly, women, newsletters, inter-faith
Traditions: Cross-community
Other Languages: Hebrew, Yiddish
Affiliations: Jewish Care

Sukkat Shalom Reform Synagogue

(Formerly Buckhurst Hill Reform Synagogue)
1 Victory Road, Hermon Hill, Wanstead, London,
E11 1HL
Tel: 0181-530-3345 **Tel:** 0181-508-2414
Contact: Mr Cecil Dalton
Position: Honorary Secretary
Activities: Worship
Traditions: Reform
Other Languages: Ivrit
Affiliations: Eastern Communities Associated
Progressive Synagogues; Reform Synagogues of
Great Britain; World Union of Progressive Judaism

Wanstead & Woodford United Synagogue

20 Churchfields, South Woodford, London,
E18 2QZ
Tel: 0181-504-1990
Contact: Mrs S Braude
Position: Administrator

Woodford Progressive Synagogue

Marlborough Road, South Woodford, London,
E18 1AR
Tel: 0181-989-7619
Contact: Rabbi Mark Goldsmith

Position: Rabbi
Activities: Worship, visits, youth, elderly, newsletters
Traditions: Liberal
Affiliations: Eastern Counties Association of Progressive Synagogues; Union of Liberal and Progressive Synagogues; World Union of Progressive Judaism

SUTTON

Sutton & District Synagogue
14 Cedar Road, Sutton, Surrey, SM2 5AA
Tel: 0181-642-5419 **Tel:** 0181-642-9285 (h)
Contact: Mrs Trudy Raphael
Position: Administrator
Activities: Worship, resource, visits, elderly, newsletters
Traditions: Orthodox - Central Ashkenazi
Affiliations: United Synagogue

TOWER HAMLETS

Commercial Road Great Synagogue
262 Commercial Road, London, E1

Congregation of Jacob
351-353 Commercial Road, London, E1
Contact: A Segal
Position: Secretary

East London Central Synagogue
30-40 Nelson Street, London, E1 2DE
Tel: 0171-790-9809 **Tel:** 0181-202-7571 (h)
Contact: A Berniger
Position: Secretary

Ezras Chaim Synagogue
2 Heneage Street, London, E1

Fieldgate Street Great Synagogue
41 Fieldgate Street, Whitechapel, London, E1 1JU
Tel: 0171-247-2644
Contact: Mrs D Jacobson
Position: Secretary
Activities: Worship
Traditions: Orthodox
Affiliations: Federation of Synagogues

Food For The Jewish Poor
17-19 Brune Street, Spitalfields, London, E1 7HJ

Nelson Street Sephardic Synagogue
Nelson Street, London, E1

Sandy's Row Synagogue
Sandy's Row, Middlesex Street, London, E1 7HW
Tel: 0171-253-8311
Contact: A Wilder
Position: Secretary

Settlement Synagogue
2-8 Beaumont Grove, Stepney, London, E1 4NQ
Tel: 0181-599-0956
Contact: Rabbi Rigal
Position: Rabbi
Activities: Worship, resource, visits, elderly, inter-faith
Traditions: Liberal/Reform
Other Languages: Yiddish, Hebrew, French, German
Affiliations: Reform Synagogues of Great Britain; World Union of Progressive Judaism

Stepney B'nai B'rith Clubs & Settlement
Beaumont Hall, 2/8 Beaumont Grove, London, E1 4NQ
Tel: 0171-790-6441
Contact: Nicholas Collins
Position: Director

Teesdale Street Synagogue
68-70 Teesdale Street, London, E2

United Workman's Synagogue
21-22a Cheshire Street, Bethnal Green, London, E2

WALTHAM FOREST

Highams Park & Chingford United Synagogue
Marlborough Road, Highams Park, London, E4 9AZ
Tel: 0181-527-0937 (h)
Contact: Mrs S R Benjamin
Position: Secretary

Leytonstone & Wanstead Synagogue
2 Fillebrook Road, London, E11
Tel: 0181-924-7505 (h)
Contact: Mr S Pizer
Position: Secretary
Activities: Worship
Traditions: Orthodox - Central Ashkenazi

Waltham Forest Hebrew Congregation
140 Boundary Road, London, E17 8LA
Tel: 0181-509-0075
Contact: D Magnus
Position: Secretary

WANDSWORTH

New Wimbledon & Putney District Synagogue
The Clubroom, Toland Square, Eastwood Estate,
Roehampton Lane, London, SW15
Tel: 0181-788-0176 (h)
Contact: J Leigh
Position: Honorary Secretary

WESTMINSTER, CITY OF

Central Synagogue
Great Portland Street, 36 Hallam Street, London,
W1N 6NN
Contact: Mrs C Jowell
Position: Secretary/Administrator

Evening Institute for the Study of Judaism
Union of Liberal and Progressive Synagogues, The
Montagu Centre, 109 Whitfield Street, London,
W1P 5RP
Tel: 0171-580-1663

Liberal Jewish Synagogue
28 St Johns Wood Road, St Johns Wood, London,
NW8 7HA
Tel: 0171-286-5181 **Fax:** 0171-266-3591
EMail: 101335.1350@compuserve.com
Contact: David Rigal
Position: Organising Secretary
Activities: Worship, resource, visits, youth, elderly,
newsletters, inter-faith
Traditions: Liberal
Other Languages: Hebrew
Affiliations: Union of Liberal and Progressive
Synagogues; World Union of Progressive Judaism

London Jewish Medical Society
The Medical Society of London, 11 Chandos
Street, London, W1M 0EB
Contact: Dr J Schwartz
Position: Honorary Secretary
Activities: Resource
Traditions: Cross-community

New London Synagogue
33 Abbey Road, London, NW8 0AT
Tel: 0171-328-1026

New West End Synagogue
St Petersburgh Place, London, W2 4JT
Tel: 0171-229-2631 **Fax:** 0171-229-2355
Contact: Mrs S Hayman
Position: Administrator
Activities: Worship, visits, youth, elderly,
newsletters
Traditions: Orthodox - Central Ashkenazi
Affiliations: United Synagogue

St John's Wood Synagogue
37/41 Grove End Road, St Johns Wood, London,
NW8 9NG
Tel: 0171-286-3838 **Fax:** 0171-266-2123
Activities: Worship, visits, youth, elderly, women,
newsletters
Traditions: Orthodox
Affiliations: United Synagogue

West End Great Synagogue
21 Dean Street, London, W1V 6NE

West London Synagogue of British Jews
33 Seymour Place, London, W1
Tel: 0171-723-4404 **Fax:** 0171-224-8258
Contact: Maurice Ross
Position: Executive Director
Activities: Worship, resource, visits, youth, elderly,
women, newsletters, inter-faith
Traditions: Reform
Other Languages: Hebrew
Affiliations: Reform Synagogues of Great Britain;
World Union of Progressive Judaism

Western Charitable Foundation
32 Great Cumberland Place, London, W1H 7DJ
Tel: 0171-723-7246
Contact: Sidney Jaque
Position: Chair

Western Marble Arch United Synagogue
32 Great Cumberland Place, London, W1H 7DJ
Tel: 0171-723-7246
Contact: Martin Frey
Position: Administrator

Western Synagogue
37 Brendon Street, London, W1

Westminster Synagogue
Rutland Gardens, Knightsbridge, London,
SW7 1BX
Tel: 0171-584-3953
Contact: Mrs M R Henriques
Position: Secretary
Traditions: Reform

SOUTH EAST
City, Town or Local Bodies

Basildon Hebrew Congregation
3 Furlongs, Basildon, Essex
Tel: 01268-524947
Contact: M M Kochmann
Position: Chair

Bognor Regis Hebrew Congregation
Elm Lodge, Sylvan Way, Bognor Regis, West Sussex
Tel: 01243-823006 (h)
Contact: J S Jacobs
Position: Honorary Secretary

Borehamwood & Elstree Synagogue
PO Box 47, Croxdale Road, Borehamwood,
Hertfordshire, WD6 4QF
Tel: 0181-386-5227 **Fax:** 0181-386-3303
Contact: Barry Winterman**Position:**
Administrator
Activities: Worship, visits, youth, elderly,
newsletters
Traditions: Orthodox
Affiliations: United Synagogue

Bromley & District Reform Synagogue
28 Highland Road, Bromley, Kent, BR1 4AD
Tel: 0181-460-5460 **Fax:** 0181-460-5460
Contact: Rabbi Sylvia Rothschild
Position: Rabbi
Activities: Worship, visits, youth, elderly,
newsletters, inter-faih
Traditions: Reform
Other Languages: Hebrew, Dutch, French,
German
Affiliations: Reform Synagogues of Great
Britain; Pro-Zion; Zionist Federation; World
Union of Progressive Judaism

Bushey & District United Synagogue
177-189 Sparrows Herne, Bushey, Hertfordshire,
WD2 1AJ

Tel: 0181-950-7340 **Fax:** 0181-421-8267
Contact: Rabbi Z M Salasnik
Position: Rabbi
Activities: Worship, resource, visits, youth, elderly,
women, newsletters
Traditions: Orthodox
Other Languages: Yiddish, Hebrew, French
Affiliations: United Synagogue

Chelmsford Jewish Community
17 Taffrail Gardens, South Woodham Ferrers,
Chelmsford, Essex, CM3 5WH
Contact: S Keller
Position: Publicity Officer

Chigwell & Hainault Synagogue
Limes Farm Estate, Limes Avenue, Chigwell, Essex,
IG7 5NT
Tel: 0181-500-2451 **Fax:** 0181-500-1991
Contact: Rabbi E E Sufrin
Position: Minister
Activities: Worship, visits, youth, elderly,
newsletters
Traditions: Orthodox
Other Languages: Hebrew, Yiddish
Affiliations: United Synagogue

Colchester & District Jewish Community
The Synagogue, Fennings Chase, Priory Street,
Colchester, Essex, CO1 2QB
Tel: 01206-45992 **Tel:** 01206-575266 (h)
Contact: Sidney Moss
Position: Membership Secretary
Activities: Worship, resource, visits, youth, elderly,
women, inter-faith
Traditions: Orthodox
Other Languages: Ivrit
Affiliations: United Synagogue

Essex University Jewish & Israeli Society
c/o Students union, Wivenhoe Park, Colchester,
Essex, CO4 3SQ
Tel: 01206-863211 **Fax:** 01206-870915
Activities: Youth, newsletters, inter-faith
Traditions: Cross-community
Other Languages: Ivrit
Affiliations: Eastern Region Jewish Students;
Union of Jewish Students; International Union of
Jewish Students

Crawley Progressive Jewish Congregation
44 Brighton Road, Crawley, RH10 6AT
Tel: 01293-34294

Contact: Mrs L Bloom
Position: Honorary Secretary

East Grinstead & District Jewish Community

7 Jefferies Way, Crowborough, East Sussex,
TN6 2UH
Tel: 01892-653949
Contact: E Godfrey
Position: Warden

Eastbourne Hebrew Congregation

22 Susans Road, Eastbourne, East Sussex,
BN21 3HA
Tel: 01435-866928 (h) **Fax:** 01435-865783
Contact: Margaret Mindell
Position: Honorary Secretary
Activities: Worship
Traditions: Orthodox
Other Languages: Hebrew, Yiddish
Affiliations: Brighton Representative Council

Hertsmere Progressive Synagogue

High Street, Elstree, Hertfordshire, WD6 3BY
Tel: 0181-953-8889 **Tel:** 0181-950-3268 (h)
Fax: 0181-386-9462
Contact: Valerie Dickson
Position: Honorary Secretary
Activities: Worship, visits, youth, elderly, women,
newsletters, inter-faith
Traditions: Liberal
Affiliations: Union of Liberal and Progressive
Synagogues

Harlow Jewish Community

Harberts Road, Hare Street, Harlow, Essex
Tel: 01378-424668 (h)
Contact: Mrs C Petars
Position: Honorary Secretary

Potters Bar United Synagogue

Meadowcroft, Great North Road, Bell Bar,
Hatfield, Hertfordshire, AL9 6DB
Tel: 01707-56202 (h)
Contact: Rev G Burns
Position: Minister

Hemel Hempstead United Synagogue

Lady Sarah Cohen Community Centre, Midland
Road, Hemel Hempstead, Hertfordshire, HD1 1RP
Tel: 01923-32007
Contact: H Nathan
Position: Honorary Secretary

Brighton & Hove Hebrew Congregation

The Synagogue, 31 New Church Road, Hove,
East Sussex, BN3 4AD
Tel: 01273-888855 **Fax:** 01273-888810
Contact: Mrs Sorrel Bourne
Position: Administrator
Activities: Worship, visits, youth, elderly,
newsletters
Traditions: Orthodox
Other Languages: Hebrew, French, Yiddish
Affiliations: Brighton and Hove Representative
Council

Brighton & Hove Independent Talmud Torah

31 New Church Road, Hove, East Sussex,
BN3 4AD
Tel: 01273-776170
Contact: Administrator

Brighton & Hove Jewish Centre

Ralli Hall, 81 Denmark Villas, Hove, East Sussex,
BN3 3TH
Tel: 01273-202254
Contact: Norina Duke
Position: Administrator
Activities: Youth, elderly, inter-faith
Traditions: Cross-community
Other Languages: Ivrit, Yiddish
Affiliations: Brighton and Hove Jewish
Representative Council; Maccabi Union of Great
Britain and Northern Ireland; B'nai Brith Youth
Organisation

Brighton & Hove Jewish Representative Council

PO Box 2178, Hove, East Sussex, BN3 3SZ
Tel: 01273-747722 **Fax:** 01273-746622
Contact: Mrs. Samuels
Position: Honorary Secretary
Activities: Umbrella, inter-faith
Traditions: Cross-community

Brighton & Hove Progessive Synagogue

6 Lansdowne Road, Hove, East Sussex, BN3 1FF
Tel: 01273-737223 **Fax:** 01273-737223
Contact: Peter B Vos
Position: Chairman
Activities: Worship, resource, youth, elderly,
newsletters, inter-faith
Traditions: Liberal
Affiliations: Union of Liberal and Progressive
Synagogues; World Union of Progressive Judaism

Hove Hebrew Congregation
Holland Road, Hove, East Sussex
Tel: 01273-732035
Contact: Sol Farrell
Position: Secretary

Jewish Community Centre
Denmark Villas, Hove, East Sussex, BN3 3TH
Tel: 01273-202254
Contact: Roger Abrahams
Position: Chairman

Jewish Welfare Board
2 Modena Road, Hove, East Sussex
Tel: 01273-722523
Contact: Mrs J Markham
Position: Honorary Secretary

Lubavitch Foundation
15 The Upper Drive, Hove, East Sussex
Tel: 01273-21919
Contact: Rabbi P Efune
Position: Director

Sussex Jewish Continuity
PO Box 2178, Hove, East Sussex, BN3 3SZ
Tel: 01273-747722 **Fax:** 01273-746622
Contact: Doris Levinson
Position: Community Co-Ordinator
Activities: Resource

Torah Academy
31 New Church Road, Hove, East Sussex
Tel: 01273-28675
Contact: Rabbi P Efune
Position: Rabbi

Kingston Liberal Synagogue
Rushett Road, Long Ditton, Surrey, KT10 9BE
Tel: 0181-398-7400 **Fax:** 0181-398-4252
Contact: Danny Rich
Position: Rabbi
Activities: Worship, resource, visits, youth, elderly, newsletters, inter-faith
Traditions: Liberal
Affiliations: Union of Liberal and Progressive Synagogues; World Union of Progressive Judaism

Maidenhead Synagogue
9 Boyn Hill Avenue, Maidenhead, Berkshire, SL6 4ET
Tel: 01628-73012
Contact: Rabbi Dr Jonathan Romain

Position: Minister
Activities: Worship, resource, visits, youth, elderly, women, newsletters, inter-faith
Traditions: Reform
Affiliations: Reform Synagogues of Great Britain

Chatham Memorial Synagogue
Sutton Place, Sutton Road, Maidstone, Kent, ME15 9DU (h)
Tel: 01622-753040 (h)
Contact: Dr C Harris
Position: Honorary Secretary
Activities: Worship, visits, elderly, women, inter-faith
Traditions: Orthodox
Other Languages: Hebrew, French, German

Margate Hebrew Congregartion
Margate Synagogue, Albion Road, Cliftonville, Margate, Kent, CT9 2HP
Tel: 01843-293082 **Tel:** 01843-228550
Contact: Mr Denis Coberman
Position: Honorary President
Activities: Worship, resource, visitors, books
Traditions: Orthodox - Central Ashkenazi
Languages: Hebrew
Affiliations: United Synagogue

Milton Keynes & District Reform Synagogue
74 Cornhill, Two Mile Ash, Milton Keynes, Buckinghamshire, MK8 8JR (h)
Tel: 01908-569661 (h)
Contact: Stanley Cohen
Position: Chair
Activities: Worship, visits, youth, newsletters, inter-faith
Traditions: Reform
Other Languages: Ivrit
Affiliations: Reform Synagogues of Great Britain

South Bucks Jewish Community
The Friends Meeting House, Whielden Street, Old Amersham, Buckinghamshire
Contact: David Sacker
Position: Chairman
Activities: Worship, resource, visits, youth, elderly, women, newsletters, books, inter-faith
Traditions: Liberal
Affiliations: Union of Liberal and Progressive Synagogues

Oxford Jewish Congregation
The Synagogue, 21 Richmond Road, Oxford,
Oxfordshire, OX1 2JL
Tel: 01865-53042 **Tel:** 01865-725129 (h)
Contact: Kayla Sue Tomlinson
Position: Honorary Secretary
Activities: Worship, resource, visits, youth, elderly,
newsletters
Traditions: Orthodox (Progressive and Liberal
Services held, too).

Oxford Progressive Synagogue
2a Northmoor Road, Oxford, Oxfordshire
Tel: 01865-512802 (h)
Contact: Mr Michael Cross

Oxford University L'Chaim Society
Albion House, Littlegate Street, Albion Place,
St Ebbes, Oxford, Oxfordshire, OX1 1QZ
Tel: 01865-794462 **Tel:** 0171-722-2455 (h)
Fax: 01865-794622
EMail: l'chaim@atlas.co.uk
Contact: Rabbi Shmuel Boteach
Position: Director
Activities: Worship, resource, youth, women,
newsletters, books
Traditions: Orthodox, Chassidic
Other Languages: Hebrew, Yiddish

Radlett & Bushey Reform Synagogue
118 Watling Street, Radlett, Hertfordshire,
WD7 7AA
Tel: 01923-856110 **Fax:** 01923-856110
Contact: Karen Young
Position: Honorary Secretary
Activities: Worship, resource, visits, youth, elderly,
newsletters, inter-faith
Traditions: Reform
Affiliations: Reform Synagogues of Great
Britain; World Union of Progressive Judaism

Sir Moses Montefiore Synagogue
Honeysuckle Road, Ramsgate, Kent

Thanet & District Reform Synagogue
239a Margate Road, Ramsgate, Kent, CT12 6TE
Tel: 01843-851164 **Tel:** 01304-853385 (h)
Contact: Esther Solomon
Position: Chairman
Activities: Worship, visits, newsletters, inter-faith
Traditions: Reform
Affiliations: Reform Synagogues of Great Britain

Reading Hebrew Congregation
46 Margaret Close, Reading, Berkshire, RG2 8PU

Reading Synagogue
Goldsmid Road, Reading, Berkshire, RG1 7YB
Tel: 01734-571018
Contact: Louise Creme
Position: Honorary Secretary
Activities: Worship, visits, youth, newsletters,
inter-faith
Traditions: Orthodox

University Jewish Society
c/o Reading Hillel, 82 Basingstoke Road,
Reading, Berkshire, RG2 0EL (h)
Tel: 01739-613367
EMail: leurosen@reaging.ac.uk
Contact: Richard Sassoon
Position: Hillel House Warden
Activities: Resource, youth
Traditions: Cross-community
Other Languages: Ivrit
Affiliations: Union of Jewish Students

Hebrew Congregation
Oswald Road, St Albans, Hertfordshire
Tel: 01727-825295 (h)
Contact: H Turner
Position: Honorary Secretary

Jersey Jewish Congregation
Route Des Genets, St Brelade, Jersey, JE3 8FY
Tel: 01534-44946 **Tel:** 01534-43384 (h)
Fax: 01534-499533
Contact: David B Regal
Position: President
Activities: Worship, visits
Traditions: Orthodox

Hastings & District Jewish Society
6 Gilbert Road, St Leonards on Sea, TN38 0RH
(h)
Tel: 01424-436551 (h)
Contact: Mrs Ilse Julie Eton
Position: Honorary Secretary
Activities: Women, inter-faith
Traditions: Reform
Affiliations: Brighton and Hove Jewish
Representative Council

Southampton Synagogue
Mordaunt Road, Inner Avenue, Southampton,
Hampshire, SO3 0GP

Tel: 01703-220129
Contact: C D Freeman
Position: Honorary Secretary
Activities: Worship, visits, inter-faith
Traditions: Orthodox
Affiliations: Bournemouth Representative Council

Southend-on-Sea & District Jewish Representative Council

8 Earls Hall Avenue, Southend-on-Sea, Essex,
S22 6PD
Tel: 01702-343114 (h)
Contact: D G Harris
Position: Chairperson

Staines & District United Synagogue

Westbrook Road, South Street, Staines, Middlesex,
TW18 4PR
Tel: 01784-254604 (h)
Contact: Phyllis Fellman
Position: Honorary Secretary
Activities: Worship, visits, women, newsletters,
inter-faith
Traditions: Orthodox
Affiliations: United Synagogue

East Grinstead Jewish Community

5 Sandown Road, Tunbridge Wells, Kent,
TN2 4RW

Watford United Synagogue

16 Nascot Road, Watford, Hertfordshire,
WD1 3RE
Tel: 01923-232168
Contact: Mrs C Silverman
Position: Secretary

Welwyn Garden City United Synagogue

Barn Close, Handside Lane, Welwyn Garden City,
Hertfordshire, AL8 6ST
Tel: 01582-762869 (h)
Contact: Mr Stanley Hirshfield
Position: Honorary Secretary
Activities: Worship, resource, visitors, newsletters
Affiliations: United Synagogue

Colman Levene Talmud Torah (Orthodox)

Synagogue Office, Finchley Road, Westcliff-on-
Sea, Essex, SS0 8AD
Tel: 01702-344900
Contact: Principal

Jewish Lads & Girls Brigade

1 Hall Park Avenue, Westcliff-on-Sea, Essex
Contact: Mrs R Linton
Position: Secretary

Kashrut & Shechita Board

c/o Synagogue Office, Finchley Road, Westcliff-
on-Sea, Essex, SS0 8AD
Tel: 01702-344900
Contact: David Gordon
Position: Warden

Kosher Meals on Wheels Service

93 The Ridgeway, Westcliff-on-Sea, Essex
Tel: 01702-74230
Contact: Mrs H Davies
Position: Honorary Secretary

Southend & District Reform Synagogue

851 London Road, Westcliff-on-Sea, Essex,
SS0 9SZ
Tel: 01702-75809
Contact: Mr N Klass
Position: Chairman
Activities: Worship, visits, women, newsletters,
inter-faith
Traditions: Reform
Affiliations: Reform Synagogues of Great Britain

Southend & Westcliff Hebrew Congregation

Synagogue Office, Finchley Road, Westcliff-on-
Sea, Essex, SS20 8AD
Tel: 01702-344900
Contact: Minister

Southend & Westcliff Hebrew Education Board

Synagogue Office, Finchley Road, Westcliff-on-
Sea, Essex, SS0 8AD
Tel: 01702-344900
Contact: Mr. Alan Gershlick
Position: Chair

Southend Jewish Youth Centre (SJYC)

38 Ceylon Road, Westcliff-on-Sea, Essex,
SS0 7HP
Tel: 01702-346545 **Tel:** 01702-76205
Contact: David Jay
Position: Secretary
Activities: Visits, youth
Traditions: Orthodox - Central Ashkenazi
Affiliations: Southend and Westcliff Hebrew
Congregation; Maccabi Union; Association of
Jewish Youth

Talmud Torah (Reform)
851 London Road, Westcliff-on-Sea, Essex
Tel: 01702-75809 (h)
Contact: Mrs Woods
Position: Principal

Youth Centre (Orthodox)
38 Ceylon Road, Westcliff-on-Sea, Essex
Tel: 01702-346545
Contact: D Jay
Position: Secretary

North West Surrey Synagogue
Horvath Close, Rosslyn Park, Weybridge, Surrey,
KT13 9QZ
Tel: 01932-855400 **Fax:** 01932-855400
Position: Minister
Activities: Worship, resource, visits, youth, elderly,
newsletters, books, inter-faith
Traditions: Reform
Other Languages: Hebrew, German, French,
Yiddish
Affiliations: Reform Synagogues of Great
Britain; Progressive Zionist Organisation; World
Union of Progressive Judaism

South Hampshire Reform Jewish Community
PO Box 179, Winchester, Hampshire, SO21 2SP
Tel: 01703-619776 **Tel:** 01703-641632 (h)
Contact: Ms Irit Shillor
Position: Chairperson
Traditions: Reform
Other Languages: Hebrew
Affiliations: Reform Synagogues of Great Britain

SOUTH WEST
City, Town or Local Bodies

Bournemouth District Jewish Representative Council
59 Fitzharris Avenue, Bournemouth, Dorset,
BH9 1BY
Tel: 01202-523550 (h)
Contact: Mrs T Lurie
Position: Secretary

Bournemouth Hebrew Congregation
Wootton Gardens, Bournemouth, Dorset,
BH1 1PW
Tel: 01202-557433
Contact: Mrs R Bloom
Position: Secretary

Bournemouth Reform Synagogue
PO Box 8550, Bournemouth, Dorset, BH1 3PN
Tel: 01202-557736
Contact: The Administrator
Activities: Worship, resource, umbrella, visits,
youth, elderly, women, newsletters, inter-faith
Traditions: Reform
Affiliations: Bournemouth Jewish Representative
Council; Reform Synagogues of Great Britain

Jewish Association for Cultural Studies
2 Southwood Avenue, Bournemouth, Dorset,
BH6 3QA
Tel: 01202-417416
Contact: Mr E Williams

Jewish Care
Braemar Royal, Grand Avenue, Southbourne,
Bournemouth, Dorset
Tel: 01202-423246

Lubavitch Centre
Chabad House, 8 Gordon Road, Boscombe,
Bournemouth, Dorset
Tel: 01202-36615

Bristol & West Progressive Congregation
43/45 Bannerman Road, Easton, Bristol, Greater
Bristol,
BS5 0RR
Tel: 0117-954-1937 **Tel:** 0117-973-8633 (h)
Contact: Isobel Wagen
Position: Honorary Secretary
Activities: Worship, visits, youth, elderly,
newsletters, inter-faith
Traditions: Liberal
Affiliations: Bristol Jewish Liaison Committee;
Union of Liberal and Progressive Synagogues;
World Union of Progressive Judaism

Bristol Hebrew Congregation
9 Park Row, Bristol, Greater Bristol, BS1 5LP
Tel: 0117-925-5160 (h) **Fax:** 0117-925-5160
EMail: hillel.simon@bristol.ac.uk
Contact: Rabbi Hillel Simon
Position: Rabbi
Activities: Worship, resource, visits, elderly,
newsletters
Traditions: Orthodox
Other Languages: Hebrew, Yiddish
Affiliations: Office of the Chief Rabbi

Bristol Hillel
8 Alma Vale, Bristol, Greater Bristol, BS8
Tel: 0117-973-7177

Bristol Jewish Liaison Committee
14 Tennyson Road, Horfield, Bristol, Greater
Bristol, BS7 8SB (h)
Tel: 0117-942-4837 (h)
Contact: Bernard Barnett
Position: Chair
Activities: Worship, resource, visits, youth, elderly,
newsletters, inter-faith
Traditions: Orthodox, Liberal
Affiliations: Union of Liberal and Progressive
Synagogues; United Synagogue

Bristol University Jewish Society
45 Oakfield Road, Clifton, Bristol, Greater Bristol,
BS8 2BA (h)
Tel: 0117-946-6589
Contact: Miss Amy Lindemann
Position: Chairperson
Activities: Youth, newsletters, inter-faith
Traditions: Pluralistic
Affiliations: Western Region of Union of Jewish
Students; National Union of Jewish Students

Synagogue
St James Square, Cheltenham, Gloucestershire

Exeter Hebrew Congregation Synagogue
Synagogue Place, Mary Arches Street, Exeter,
Devon, EX4 3BA
Tel: 01392-251529
Position: President
Activities: Worship, resource, visits, youth,
newsletters, inter-faith
Traditions: Orthodox
Other Languages: French, Hebrew, German

Plymouth Hebrew Congregation
Synagogue Chambers, Catherine Street,
Plymouth, Devon, PL1 2AD
Tel: 01752-664995
Contact: Dr Peter Lee
Position: Honorary Secretary
Affiliations: United Synagogue

Bournemouth University Jewish Society
Bournemouth University, Wallisdown Road,
Poole, Dorset, BH12 5BB
Tel: 01202-524111

Torquay & Paignton Synagogue
Abbey Road, Torquay, Devon

Torquay Synagogue
Son Bou, 7 Broadstone Park Road, Livermead,
Torquay, Devon, TQ2 6TY
Tel: 01803-607197 (h)
Contact: E Freed

NORTHERN IRELAND

City, Town or Local Bodies

Jewish Community Centre
49 Somerton Road, Belfast, County Antrim, BT15
Tel: 01232-777974

Jewish Ladies Guild
45 Glandore Avenue, Belfast, County Antrim
Tel: 01232-777795
Contact: Mrs B Danker
Position: President

SCOTLAND

Scottish National Bodies

Jewish Blind Society (Scotland)
May Terrace, Giffnock, Glasgow, Strathclyde,
G46 6LD
Tel: 0141-638-0066
Contact: Mrs Carole Blake
Position: Secretary
Traditions: Orthodox
Affiliations: Glasgow Jewish Representative
Council

Jewish Care Scotland
May Terrace, Giffnock, Glasgow, Strachclyde,
G46 6LD
Tel: 0141-620-1800 **Fax:** 0141-620-1088
Contact: Mrs Ethne Woldman
Position: Chief Executive
Activities: Visits, elderly
Traditions: Cross-Community
Affiliations: Glasgow Jewish Representative
Council

Scottish Council of Synagogues
28 Field Road, Busby, Glasgow, Strathclyde,
G76 8SE
Tel: 0141-644-3611 **Fax:** 0141-644-4430

Contact: Bernard Mann
Position: Secretary
Activities: Umbrella
Traditions: Orthodox

Scottish Jewish Archives Committee
Garnethill Synagogue, 125-127 Hill Street,
Glasgow, Strathclyde, G3 6UB
Tel: 0141-649-4526 (h)
Contact: Harvey L Kaplan
Position: Director

City, Town and Local Bodies

Aberdeen Hebrew Congregation
74 Dee Street, Aberdeen, Grampian, AB1 2DS
Tel: 01224-582135
Contact: Ms Sandra Shrago
Position: Honorary Secretary

Dundee University Jewish Society
c/o Synagogue, 9 St Mary Place, Dundee, Tayside

Edinburgh Hebrew Congregation
4 Salisbury Road, Edinburgh, Lothian, EH9
Tel: 0131-667-3144
Contact: Dr Nathan A Oppenheim
Position: President
Activities: Worship, umbrella, visits, youth, elderly,
women, newsletters, inter-faith
Traditions: Orthodox – Central Ashkenazi
Other Languages: Hebrew
Affiliations: Scottish Standing Jewish
Conference; Office of the Chief Rabbi

Edinburgh University Jewish Society
c/o Societies' Centre, 48 The Pleasance,
Edinburgh, Lothian, EH8
Tel: 0131-667-3144
EMail: jewish.society@ed.ac.uk
Contact: Miss Juliet Cohen
Position: Chairperson
Activities: Youth
Traditions: Cross-Community
Other Languages: French, Hebrew
Affiliations: Northern Region of Union of
Jewish Students; Union of Jewish Students of
Great Britain and Ireland; World Union of Jewish
Students

Board of Jewish Education
28 Calderwood Road, Newlands, Glasgow,
Strathclyde, G43 2RU

Tel: 0141-637-5654 **Fax:** 0141-637-4446
Contact: Mrs Dianna Wolfson
Position: Head Teacher
Activities: Religious, resource
Traditions: Orthodox
Other Languages: Hebrew
Affiliations: Glasgow Jewish Representative
Council

Garnethill Hebrew Congregation
129 Hill Street, Glasgow, Strathclyde, G3 6UG
Tel: 0141-332-4151 **Tel:** 0141-339-4837 (h)
Contact: Rhoda Livingston
Position: Secretary
Activities: Worship, resource, visits, newsletters,
inter-faith
Traditions: Orthodox
Affiliations: Scottish Representative Council;
United Synagogue

Glasgow Jewish Representative Council
222 Fenwick Road, Giffnock, Glasgow,
Strathclyde, G46 6UE
Tel: 0141-620-1700 **Fax:** 0141-638-2100
EMail: glasgow@ort.org
Contact: Ephraim Borowski
Position: Honorary Secretary
Activities: Umbrella, inter-faith
Traditions: Cross-community
Affiliations: European Council of Jewish
Communities

Glasgow Jewish Resource Centre
222 Fenwick Road, Giffnock, Glasgow,
Strathclyde, G46 6UE
Tel: 0141-620-2194 **Fax:** 0141-638-2100
Contact: Dorothy Zolkwer
Position: Director
Activities: Resource, visits, youth
Traditions: Cross-community
Affiliations: Jewish Programmes and Material
Project; Youth & Hechalutz Department of the
World Zionist Organisation

Glasgow New Synagogue
147 Ayr Road, Newton Mearns, Glasgow,
Strathclyde, G77 6RE
Tel: 0141-639-4083 **Tel:** 0141-637-2955 (h)
Contact: Pete Tobias
Position: Minister/Rabbi
Activities: Worship, resource, visits, youth,
women, newsletters, inter-faith

Traditions: Reform
Affiliations: Glasgow Jewish Representative
Council; Reform Movement (RSGB)

Giffnock & Newlands Synagogue
Maryville Avenue, Giffnock, Glasgow, Strathclyde
Tel: 0141-638-6600

Jewish Blind Society (Scotland)
49 Coplaw Street, Glasgow, Strathclyde, G42 7JE
Tel: 0141-423-2288
Contact: Mrs Carole Blake
Position: Secretary
Traditions: Orthodox
Affiliations: Glasgow Jewish Representative
Council

Jewish Care Scotland
May Terrace, Giffnock, Glasgow, Strathclyde, G46 6LD
Tel: 0141-620-1800 **Fax:** 0141-620-1088
Contact: Mrs Ethne Woldman
Position: Chief Executive
Activities: Visits, elderly
Traditions: Cross-Community
Affiliations: Glasgow Jewish Representative
Council

Jewish Hospital & Sick Visiting Association
49 Coplaw Street, Glasgow, Strathclyde, G42
Tel: 0141-423-8916

Langside Hebrew Congregation
125 Niddrie Road, Glasgow, Strathclyde
Tel: 0141-423-4062

Lubavitch Foundation of Scotland
8 Orchard Drive, Giffnock, Glasgow, Strathclyde,
G46 7NR
Tel: 0141-638-6116 **Fax:** 0141-638-6478
Contact: Rabii Chaim Jacobs
Position: Scottish Regional Director
Activities: Resource, youth, elderly, women,
newsletters
Traditions: Charedi, Chassidic
Other Languages: Hebrew, Yiddish
Affiliations: Glasgow Jewish Representative
Council; Lubavitch UK; World Lubavitch
Movement

Netherlee & Clarkston Hebrew Congregation
Clarkston Road, Clarkston, Glasgow, Strathclyde,
G76
Tel: 0141-637-8206 **Tel:** 0141-639-7194 (h)

Contact: Mrs Pamela Livingston
Position: Secretary
Activities: Worship
Traditions: Orthodox - Central Ashkenazi
Affiliations: Glasgow Jewish Representative
Council

Newton Mearns Synagogue
14 Larchfield Court, Newton Mearns, Glasgow,
Strathclyde, G77 5BH
Tel: 0141-445-2231
Contact: Kenny Davidson

Queen's Park Hebrew Congregation
Falloch Road, Glasgow, Strathclyde, G42 9QX
Tel: 0141-632-1743
Contact: Geraldine Fox
Position: Secretary
Activities: Worship, visits
Traditions: Orthodox
Affiliations: Glasgow Jewish Representative
Council

Scottish Council of Synagogues
28 Field Road, Busby, Glasgow, Strathclyde,
G76 8SE
Tel: 0141-644-3611 **Fax:** 0141-644-4430
Contact: Bernard Mann
Position: Secretary
Activities: Umbrella
Traditions: Orthodox

Scottish Jewish Archives Committee
Garnethill Synagogue, 125-127 Hill Street,
Glasgow, Strathclyde, G3 6UB
Tel: 0141-649-4526 (h)
Contact: Harvey L Kaplan
Position: Director

Yeshiva
Giffnock Synagogue, Maryville Avenue, Glasgow,
Strathclyde
Tel: 0141-638-2030
Contact: I Jesner
Position: Chair

WALES

City, Town or Local Bodies

Cathedral Road Synagogue
Cathedral Road, Cardiff, South Glamorgan

Hillel House
17 Howard Gardens, Cardiff, South Glamorgan
Tel: 01222-481227

Union of Jewish Students
c/o Hillel House, 17 Howard Gardens, Cardiff,
South Glamorgan
Tel: 01222-841227

Swansea Hebrew Congregation
17 Mayals Green, Mayals, Swansea, West
Glamorgan, SA3 5JR
Tel: 01792-401205
Contact: H M Sherman
Position: Chair

KEY TO TERMS USED IN JEWISH ORGANISATION TITLES

Note: This is not a complete glossary of significant Jewish terms. It is a guide to the meaning and/or background of some of the words used in the titles of Jewish organisations listed in the directory. More information on the italicised words can be tracked down elsewhere in the key and/or in "Introducing the Jewish Community", by using the directory's "Significant Word Index".

Abraham: The name of the first of the *avot* (forefathers) of the Hebrew people.

Adass: A construct of the Hebrew word *edah*, *adath* is the Hebrew for "congregation" or "community of…".

Adath: A variant Romanisation of *adass* (see above).

Aden: A port in the Gulf State of South Yemen in which there was a significant Jewish community until the establishment of the State of Israel and the end of the British Protectorate in Aden.

Agudah: Hebrew, meaning "union" or "association", a group bound by a common purpose.

Agudas: *Ashkenazi* pronunciation of a construct of the Hebrew word *agudah*, it means "union of…" or "association of…".

Ahavat: A construct form of the Hebrew word *ahavah*, meaning "love".

Akiva: The name of a major Jewish *rabbi* and martyr (c. 50-135CE).

Ari: The name of a major sixteenth century mystic and *Kabbalist* (from *Kabbalah*).

Bachad: Hebrew acronym for *Beit Chalutzim Dat'im*, meaning "covenant of religious pioneers" (in relation to settlement in, and development of, the land of Israel).

Baeck: The surname of Leo Baeck, a twentieth century German *Liberal rabbinic* leader, after whom a *Progressive* College for the training of *rabbis* and the study of Judaism is now named.

Beis: *Ashkenazi* pronunciation of a construct of the Hebrew word *bayit*, it means "house of", in other words, "home".

Belz: The name of a Ukrainian town near Lvov with a Jewish settlement from the beginning of the sixteenth century CE onwards. It was the spiritual centre of the Belzer *Chasidim* before the Holocaust. The *Chasidim* are known by the name of their town of origin.

Benjamin: A personal name.

Bernhard Baron: Surname of Bernhard Baron, an industrialist in the USA and the UK (c. 1850-1929 CE) who was a philanthropist, especially with regard to Jewish causes including endowment of the Jewish Settlement that bears his name.

Beth: *Sephardi* pronunciation of the Hebrew for "house", often used of a "group" or "gathering of people".

Bevis Marks: Bevis Marks is the name of the London location of a major *Sephardi* synagogue. The name itself has no Jewish connection.

Bikur: Hebrew, meaning "visit". *Chevat Bikur Chohim* means "society for visiting the sick".

Binah: Hebrew, meaning "understanding".

Birkath: Hebrew, meaning "blessing of...".

B'nei: Hebrew, meaning "sons of..." or "children of...". Used in the name of the major Jewish organisation Bnei B'rith (see below), which has branches throughout the world and was founded in the USA in 1843CE.

Brady: Brady Street in the East End of London was the address of the original club for working boys which later amalgamated with Maccabi, the world union of Jewish athletic organisations.

B'rith: Hebrew, meaning "covenant". Hence, B'nei B'rith means "children of the covenant".

Chabad: Hebrew acronym for *Chochma, Binah, Da'at*, meaning "widsom", "understanding" and "knowledge", which is the motto of the *Lubavitch* movement.

Chai: Hebrew for "living".

Chaim: Hebrew, meaning "life" or "health".

Chasidim: Plural of the Hebrew word *chasid*, it is the collective name of those Jewish groups which emphasise the mystical tradition in Judaism and are part of a broad movement initiated in the eighteenth century CE by Baal Shem Tov.

Chasidische: Yiddish, meaning "pertaining to *Chasidim*" (see above).

Chavurah: Hebrew, meaning "fellowship".

Chayim: Variant Romanisation of *chaim* (see above).

Chazanim: Hebrew, meaning "cantors", the plural of the Hebrew word *chazan* meaning "cantor".

Chevrat: Hebrew construct of *chevrah*, meaning "society".

Chinuch: Hebrew, meaning "education".

Chodosh: *Ashkenazi* pronunciation of the Hebrew word for "new".

Cholim: Hebrew plural for the "sick".

Colman: A personal name.

D'Chasidey: Variant Romanisation of *D'Chasside* (see below).

D'Chasside: Meaning "of the *Chasidim* of...".

D'Chassidey: Variant Romanisation of *D'Chasside* (see above).

D'Satmar: Meaning "of Satmar", a town in North West Romania, from which the *Chasidim* of Satmar originate.

Damesek: Hebrew for Damascus, the capital of contemporary Syria.

David: Biblical name of the major Jewish king and psalmist.

Din: Meaning "law", found in the name of *Beth Din*, a *rabbinical* court.

Divrei: Hebrew construct, meaning "words of...".

Dor: Hebrew, meaning "generation".

Dov: A Hebrew personal name.

Dvar: Hebrew, meaning "word of...".

Elias: A surname.

Eliezer: The name of a Biblical servant of the Patriarch Abraham, as in the *Book of Genesis*, chapter 15 verse 2.

Emet: Hebrew, meaning "truth".

Etz: Hebrew, meaning "tree".

Ezras: *Ashkenazi* pronunciation of the construct form *ezrah*, which means "help".

Falashas: A term sometimes used to describe Ethiopian Jews.

Feinmann: A surname.

Gur: Polish *Chasidic* centre of the Gerer *Chasidim* before the Holocaust.

Hadass: *Ashkenzi* pronunciation of *hadath*, meaning "the faith".

Hadath: Hebrew word meaning "the faith", with *ha* being the definite article.

Hagadol: Hebrew, meaning "the great", with *ha* being the definite article.

Hamakom: Hebrew literally meaning "the place", with *ha* being the definite article. Often used as a name for the Divine.

Hamedrash: Hebrew meaning "the learning" or "the study", with *ha* being the definite article. Hence *Beth Hamedrash* is literally a "house of study," (see *beth*) in other words a *synagogue*/study centre.

Harabbanim: Hebrew, meaning "the *rabbis*", with *ha* as the definite article.

Haramah: Hebrew, meaning "the high", "the exalted", or "advanced", with *ha* as the definite article.

Hashochtim: Hebrew, meaning "the slaughterers", with *ha* as the definite article and used of those who slaughter animals according to the *shechita* regulations.

Hatorah: Hebrew for "the *Torah*", with *ha* as the definite article. *Torah* literally means "teaching" and refers to the five books of Moses believed to have been revealed at Mount Sinai as well as their accompanying oral interpretation and tradition.

Hatzola: Hebrew for "rescue" or "deliverance". An emergency ambulance service goes by this name.

Hebrew: Original language of the *Torah* and of modern Israel. It is also used in *Orthodox synagogue* services and in parts of *Progressive synagogue* services.

Hechalutz: Hebrew meaning "the pioneer". It is used of those who developed the land of Israel in the pre-1948 period.

Hillel: The name of a major *rabbinic* leader of *Pharisaic* Judaism in the first century BCE, often used in the names of centres for Jewish students.

Holocaust: The name given to the systematic genocide of Jewish people in Europe during the Second World War.

Horomah: *Ashkenazi* pronounciation of *haromah* (see above).

Ishag: A surname, which is a form of Yishai or Jesse.

Ishah: Hebrew, meaning "woman".

Ishmael: The name of the Biblical half-brother of Isaac, who are both the sons of Abraham.

Jacob: Jacob is the third Biblical patriarch, the son of Isaac, and the father of the twelve tribes of Israel.

Kahal: Hebrew, meaning "congregation".

Kashrus: *Ashkenazi* pronunciation of the Hebrew word for "dietary laws".

Kashrut: *Sephardi* pronunciation of the word *kashrus*, (see above).

Kehillath: A construct of the Hebrew word *kehillah* meaning "community", *kehillath* means "community of ...".

Klal: A construct of the Hebrew word *kollel* (see below).

Kolel: Variant Romanisation of *kollel* (see below).

Kollel: Hebrew, meaning "congregation of..."

Kosher: Hebrew, meaning "fit" or "suitable". The word which describes food and its preparation which conforms with Jewish dietary laws.

Kowner: *Yiddish* adjective meaning "from the city of Kovno", in Lithuania.

L'Chaim: Hebrew for "to life".

Lemoroth: Meaning "for women teachers".

Lev: Hebrew literally meaning "heart", often used as a name.

Levene: Surname derived from Levi, the name of one of the sons of the Biblical Jacob and the name of one of the twelve tribes.

Lezeirim: Meaning "for young men".

Liberal: A Jewish grouping originating in nineteenth century Germany which believed that the tradition had to be adapted to the demands of modern culture.

Liege: The name of the town in Belgium from which the community in question originated.

Lubavitch: The name of a Lithuanian *Chasidic* centre which was the origin of the contemporary *Lubavitch* group in Judaism.

Maccabi: The name of the second century BCE Jewish leader Judah ha-Maccabi who defeated the Hellenist Syrians. Now used in the name of Jewish sports and athletic groups derived from his name.

Machzikei: Hebrew for "strengtheners" or "upholders of", used in Machzikei Hadas meaning "Upholders of the Faith".

Makom: Hebrew, meaning "place". The term can also refer to the Almighty.

Makor: Hebrew for "source".

Masorti: Hebrew for "traditional" and used in the name of the contemporary Jewish group who combine traditional practice with an acceptance of modern scholarly analysis of the Biblical texts. It is the British equivalent of the American *Conservative* Judaism tradition.

Mesifta: Aramaic for "place of study" equivalent to the Hebrew term *yeshiva*.

Midrash: The name given to a body of rabbinic interpretation of the *Torah*.

Mikavaot: Hebrew plural for *mikveh* (ritual baths).

Miyad: Hebrew, meaning "immediately".

Mohalim: Variant Romanisation of *Mohelim* (see above).

Mohelim: The plural of the Hebrew word *mohel*, it describes those who perform *milah* which is circumcision.

Moses Montefiore: The name of a famous leader of Anglo-Jewry in the nineteenth century.

Na'amat: From the Hebrew, *na'am*, meaning "lovely" or "pleasant".

Nadvorna: The name of an *Chasidic* centre in Galicia.

Nefusot: Hebrew for "scattered ones".

Neve: Hebrew for "meadow".

Neveh: Variant Romanisation of *neve* (see above).

Noam: Hebrew, literally meaning "pleasant".

Noar: Hebrew, for "youth".

Noraim: Variant Romanisation of *N'orim* (see below).

N'orim: Plural of the Hebrew word *nora* which means awe-inspiring and is used of the *High Holy Days* of Judaism, as in the Hebrew *Yamian Noraim*.

Nusach: Hebrew word for liturgical text or "chant". Jews from different areas or sects have different *nuschaot*. These range from different tunes for chanting, through different words in common prayers, to different prayers and orders of service.

Ohel: Hebrew, literally meaning "tent" or "tent of...".

Orthodox: The name of the majority Jewish tradition in the UK, the major organised form of which is the United Synagogue led by the *Chief Rabbi*.

Progressive: The collective name covering both *Liberal* and *Reform* Judaism and which is used to describe the attempt, beginning in the nineteenth century, to adapt the tradition in keeping with modern "progressive" developments.

Rabbi: Hebrew for "my master", applied to religious teachers.

Rabbinate: The name of a representative body of *rabbis*, or "teachers".

Rabbinical: The name of a body of *rabbis* (see above).

Rabbinics: The study of the teaching of the *rabbis* (see above).

Rashey: A construct plural of the Hebrew singular rosh, *rashey* means "heads of ...".

Reform: The name of one of the *Progressive* traditions of Judaism organised in the UK as the Reform Synagogues of Great Britain.

Representative Council: The name given to the body operating at a local level in a number of cities with significant Jewish populations, on which all communal bodies may be represented.

Reshet: Hebrew for "network".

Ryzin: A Ukrainian *Chasidic* centre.

Sabbath: The Jewish day of rest, celebration, renewal, devotion to the *Torah* and family, observed from Friday sunset to Saturday sunset and during which time no work is done except in the case of alleviating suffering or other similar emergencies.

Sanz-Klausenberg: Eastern European towns which were centres of pre-Second World War *Chasidim*. Sanz is in Galicia and Klausenberg is in Romania.

Sanz-Klausner: Pertaining to Sanz-Klausenberg (see above).

Schmuel: Hebrew for Samuel, also spelt Shmuel.

Sedek: Hebrew for "righteousness". A variant Romanisation, which is often found, is *zedek* (see also *tzedek*, below).

Sephardi: *Sepharad* is the Hebrew word for Spain. *Sephardi* is the word for Jews of Spanish, and later also of Oriental, origin.

Sha'arei: Hebrew literally meaning "gates of...".

Shalom: *Sephardi* pronunciation of the Hebrew word for "peace", often used in a greeting.

Shechita: The slaughtering of animals for consumption in accordance with Jewish law.

Shem: The name of one of the sons of Noah from whom the Semitic peoples are believed to be descended and from which the English words "semite" and "semitic" are derived.

Shochetim: The plural word for "religious slaughterers".

Sholom: An alternative *Ashkenazi* pronunciation of *shalom* (see above).

Shomrei: Hebrew literally meaning "guardians of…".

Sinai: The mountain upon which it is believed that the *Torah* was revealed to Moses.

Skoler: The name of a group of *Chasidim* originating in Skolai, Galicia.

Spanish and Portuguese: The name of *synagogues* set up by and for those people and their descendents who were expelled from the Iberian peninsula in the 15th century CE.

Spiro: Robin Spiro is the name of the man who founded the Spiro Institute, an adult Jewish educational institute.

Stanislowa: The name of an *Chasidic* group which originated in Stanislaw, Russia.

Sternberg: The surname of Sir Sigmund Sternberg who endowed the Sternberg Centre named after him.

Sukkat: Hebrew construct meaning "tabernacle of….", from *sukka* meaning "tabernacle".

Synagogue: The name for a Jewish place of worship.

Talmud: A very important collection of law, narrative, history, allegories and moral, philosophical and religious discussion.

Talmudical: Meaning "concerned with the *Talmud*" (see above).

Tay Sachs: The name of a rare hereditary disease found in *Ashkenazi* Jewry. An organisation is dedicated to supporting sufferers from the disease.

Telzer: Yiddish adjective for "from the town of Telz", for the town in Lithuania from which the community originated.

Tiferes: *Ashkenazi* pronunciation of the Hebrew word meaning "beauty" or "splendour".

Torah: Hebrew word meaning "instruction". Technically, it refers to the part of the Jewish *Bible* comprising the first five books of Moses. Colloquially, it includes all Jewish learning.

Trisker: The name of *Chasidim* originating in Trisk in the Ukraine.

Tzedek: Variant Romanisation of *sedek* (see above).

United Synagogue: The name of the major modern *Orthodox synagogue* grouping in the UK, the leader of which is the *Chief Rabbi*.

V'Hashomrim: Hebrew literally meaning "and the guardians". The *shomer* ensures that dietary laws are observed in restaurants and similar establishments.

Vilna: Now called Vilnius, the capital of Lithuania which, before the Second World War was a major centre of Jewish learning.

Vishnitz-Monsey: Vishnitz is the name of the town of origin in Hungary of a group of *Chasidim*. Monsey is an American branch of the group based in Monsey, New Jersey.

Viznitz: Variant Romanisation of Vishnitz (see above).

Yakar: Hebrew literally meaning "precious".

Yavneh: A major centre of *rabbinic* learning after the destruction of the *Temple* by the Romans. It is in central Israel.

Yehudah: The Hebrew word for "Judah", a *Biblical* name of one of the sons of Jacob from whom the kings are believed to have been descended. Later, it was also the name of a kingdom in Southern *Eretz Yisrael* and an area of *Eretz Yisrael*. It is also the word from which the English word "Jew" is derived.

Yeshuath: Hebrew, meaning "salvation".

Yerushalayim: Hebrew for the city of "Jerusalem" in Israel.

Yeshiva: A centre for *Talmudic* (from *Talmud*) study.

Yeshuath: Hebrew literally meaning "salvation of…".

Yeshurun: A Biblical synonym for Israel.

Yesodey: Hebrew for "foundations of…".

Yetiv: Aramaic word for "settled" or "tranquil".

Yisachar: The Hebrew of the Biblical name Issachar.

Yisrael: The Hebrew word for "Israel". This was an alternative name for Jacob, earned after the story of his struggle with an angel. Hence, "children of Israel" and "*Eretz Yisrael*", name of the modern State of Israel.

Yisroel: Variant Romanisation of *Yisrael* meaning Israel.

INTRODUCING THE MUSLIM COMMUNITY

MUSLIMS IN THE UNITED KINGDOM

Migration and Patterns of Settlement

There has been a significant Muslim presence in the United Kingdom since the early nineteenth century when Muslim seamen and traders from the Middle East and the Indian subcontinent began to settle around major ports. For example, Yemeni Muslims settled in South Shields and established a Muslim community there and similar communities grew up around the ports of Liverpool and Cardiff. Some of the seamen later moved inland after failing to secure employment in the ports or on the ships and the pattern of settlement thus widened. After the First World War there was further settlement by Muslims who had been demobilised from military service in the British army.

The size of the community increased significantly with the arrival in the 1950s and 1960s of workers from the Indo-Pakistani subcontinent who had been recruited for, or were seeking employment in, the mills and factories due to a shortage of workers in the aftermath of the Second World War. As a direct result of the implementation of Africanisation policies in the newly independent African states, the early 1970's saw the arrival from Kenya and Uganda of a large number of Muslims of Asian ethnic origins. Recently, some Muslim refugees have arrived from countries such as Somalia and Bosnia.

The global Muslim population is around 1,154,302,000. In the UK, based on recent extrapolations from the 1991 Census, it is estimated there are between 1,000,000–1,500,00 Muslims, although some community representatives suggest a significantly higher figure. The largest communities are found in the West Midlands, West Yorkshire, Lancashire, Greater London and in Scotland's central belt, but Muslim communities are also found in most major towns and cities. The first *mosques* in the UK were established in Liverpool and Woking around the end of the nineteenth century. In England and Wales the Registrar General lists 562 *mosques* which are certified as places of worship and this directory includes records of 660 *mosques* in the UK of which 635 are in England and Wales.

Ethnic Backgrounds and Languages

Approximately two thirds of the Muslims in the UK have ancestral origins in the Indo-Pakistani subcontinent, coming to Britain either directly or via earlier migrations to East Africa and the Caribbean. The remaining one third have their ethnic and national origins in a variety of other countries and regions, such as Cyprus, Malaysia, Iran and the Middle East. There are also indigenous Britons who have embraced Islam.

Because the ethnic background of the UK Muslim community is quite diverse, a number of different languages are spoken in addition to English. Arabic, Bengali, Farsi, Gujarati, Hausa, Malay, Punjabi, Pushto, Turkish, and Urdu are among the most commonly used of these. Among Muslims, a reading knowledge of Arabic is considered very important since this is the language of the *Qur'an* (see below).

ORIGINS AND DEVELOPMENT OF ISLAM

Revelation

According to Muslim belief, the last Prophet of Islam was the Prophet Muhammad (570-632CE), who was born in the Arabian city of Makka and, from the age of forty, received a series of revelations from God (in Arabic, *Allah*).

The revelations are believed to have come to Muhammad through the Angel Jibreel (Gabriel) over a period of twenty-three years. It is stressed by Muslims that Muhammad did not bring a new faith. As the "seal of the prophets" he is understood to complete the succession of prophets, renewing and completing the teachings of Abraham, Moses and Jesus who are seen as being among the greatest of the prophets.

Muslims believe that essentially the same message, guiding people to the right path, was communicated by God through all the prophets. Because people kept disobeying and corrupting the code of guidance which the prophets preached, other prophets were sent to restate the original message. Muslims therefore affirm the *Torah* brought by Moses and the *Gospel* or *Injil* of Jesus, although it is believed by Muslims that these have been corrupted from their original purity. Muhammad is thus seen as the last of the prophets, correcting error and calling people back to Islam or submission to God's ways.

Prophet Muhammad and the 'Ummah

All those who believed in Muhammad as the last of the prophets and in the revelation to him which forms the *Qur'an*, were welcomed into the 'Ummah (world Muslim community) irrespective of their place of origin, language or colour of skin. With this newly established Muslim community, in 622CE Muhammad migrated from Makka to Madina, five hundred kilometres away. This migration is known as the *Hijra*. The formative significance of this event in Islamic history can be seen from the fact that the Muslim dating system begins from the *Hijra* and that therefore, in English, dates in the Muslim calendar are expressed as "AH" (after *Hijra*).

Caliphate and Imamate

Following the death of the Prophet Muhammad, the *Caliphate* (from *khalifa* meaning viceroy) was established to provide leadership for the Muslim community. Among *Sunni* Muslims (see below) Abu Bakr, 'Umar, 'Uthman and 'Ali are recognised as the first four *Caliphs* and are often called *al-khulafa ar-rashidun* (the rightly guided *Caliphs*) because their exemplary lives are viewed as role models for the community.

However, after the death of Muhammad there was a serious dispute within the Muslim community concerning the location of authority, and this led to the development of the distinctive *Sunni* and *Shi'a* traditions of Islam (see below), with a different line of authority emerging within the *Shi'a* tradition. The word *Sunni* comes from "one who adheres to the sunna", the *sunna* (see below) being one of the four sources of Islamic law which relates to the actions and sayings of the Prophet Muhammad. The name *Shi'ite* comes from *shiat 'Ali* (the follower of 'Ali).

The *Shi'a* advocated the appointment of 'Ali ibn Abi Talib as successor to the Prophet instead of Abu Bakr. After 'Umar's death following his appointment by Abu Bakr, 'Ali the son-in-law of the Prophet Muhammad was offered the *Caliphate* on certain conditions, but an arbiter awarded the function to 'Uthman. Following 'Uthman's assassination 'Ali was elected as the Fourth *Caliph*, but was himself assassinated. Following a series of disputes and a civil war, his son Hasan was elected *Caliph* but gave up the office for the sake of reconciliation.

Upon Hasan's death his brother Husayn led a revolt to re-establish the legitimacy of the *Caliphate* against those who violated the reconciliation agreement of his brother. Husayn was betrayed and killed at Karbala in confrontation with the armies of the *Caliph* Yazid. This event became the foundation of the developing themes of suffering and persecution to be found in the Shi'a tradition of Islam and Husayn is seen as an inspiration to all who suffer and struggle against injustice. Reverence for 'Ali and his successors led to the development of the *Shi'a* idea of the *Imamate* in which descendants of Ali have a special sanctity and role in the spiritual leadership of the community.

In *Sunni* Islam, the idea of the *Caliphate* continued under a succession of Muslim dynasties, beginning with the Umayyad dynasty (661-750CE), centred upon the geographical region known today as Syria. Following the Abbasid dynasty centred upon Baghdad, rival Caliphates were established with Cordoba in Spain being ruled by a second Umayyad dynasty from 929CE and Cairo becoming the capital of the Fatimid dynasty from 969CE. The concept of the *Caliphate* survived into modern times with the Ottoman Empire.

Development and Diversity

From its origins in Arabia, Islam spread towards the Indian sub-continent after 750CE, and also into Africa and Europe. In Europe the history of Islam is at its longest in the Balkans, Sicily and Spain. In Spain, after its initial establishment by military force in the early eighth century, Islamic culture spread through the land influencing many aspects of life and thought, developing peacefully alongside Christian and Jewish culture, until the Muslims were finally expelled by the Christian monarchs of the early sixteenth century.

During the Moghul empire (1516-1707CE) Islam made deep inroads into India, from where it spread to Malaysia, Indonesia and the Philippines. The partition of the Indian sub-continent in 1947, following the end of British colonial rule, resulted in the creation of the Muslim majority state of Pakistan. Following a civil war, in 1971 the eastern part of Pakistan became the independent country of Bangladesh.

SOURCES OF MUSLIM BELIEFS AND PRACTICES

Qur'an

The *Qur'an* is the fundamental source of guidance for Muslims. They regard it as the pre-eminent "sign" or "miracle" of God and as the final and ultimate source of guidance which is for all places and all times. It can be applied in each age in the way most suitable to the conditions of that age and is a guide to ethics, human relationships, social justice, political principles, law, trade and commerce.

The text of the *Qur'an* is divided into *surahs* (or chapters) which are of varying lengths and are not in chronological order but are believed to be in this order under divine instruction. The opening surah, called the *Fatiha*, is a key prayer of Muslims and a summary of Islamic belief which must be read in Arabic during the observance of every *salat* (Muslim obligatory daily prayers - see below).

Because the *surahs* of the *Qur'an* are viewed as the actual words of God, the learning and recitation of the *Qur'an* is a central duty and joy for believers. The language in which the *Qur'an* was revealed was Arabic, and an understanding of this is therefore seen as essential for penetrating its true meaning. It is thus considered preferable to read it in its original Arabic version although translations (or more strictly, in Islamic understanding, interpretations) are available in English and many other languages.

Shari'ah

The framework within which Muslim life has evolved is the *Shari'ah* (law). The sources of *Shari'ah* are the *Qur'an*, the *Sunna, Ijma, Ijtihad* and *Qiyas*.

The *Sunna* is the example of the Prophet and his way of life which acts as a model for Muslims to emulate. The *Hadith* are the traditions which contain accounts of the words and actions of Muhammad and his companions and they have been gathered into generally recognised collections of material.

Ijma is the practice of reaching consensus of approval for particular aspects of *Shari'ah*. Where Islamic legislation is unclear about a situation, experts who are knowledgeable about the holy texts propose clarifications which must gain their consensus agreement for it to become an accepted principle.

Ijtihad (*Sunni* term) or *'aql* (*Shi'a* term) is the concept of independent reasoning or intelligence. Rational discussion and debate is very much at the heart of Islam. One form of reasoning which is often employed is that of *Qiyas* (or analogy). In the use of *Qiyas*, analogies are drawn between situations in the *Qur'an, Sunna* and *Hadith* and contemporary circumstances in order to determine the application of the *Shari'ah* to novel situations.

However, among *Sunni* Muslims many have argued that, following the development of classical Islamic jurisprudence, the "gates of *ijtihad*" became closed in the tenth century CE.

Schools

Among the *Sunni* Muslims there are four recognised *madhahib* or *madhhabs* (schools of law) whose scholars have the task of discerning the way of applying the *Shari'ah* in various contexts. These are named after their founders: the *Hanafi*, the *Hanbali*, the *Maliki* and the *Shafi'i* schools. They are all recognised as having developed out of the *usul al-fiqh* (principles of Islamic jurisprudence), and each school therefore recognises the other as being truly Muslim.

Different schools have come to predominate in various areas of the world. The *Hanafi* school is predominant in India and most parts of the former Ottoman Empire, the *Maliki* school in West Africa and the Arab West, and the *Shafi'i* in Indonesia, Malaysia and the Philippines. The *Shafi'i* is also important in Egypt where the first two schools can also be found. The *Hanbali* school is found in Saudi Arabia and Qatar. Muslims in Britain with ethnic or ancestral backgrounds in these various areas of the world might therefore be expected to follow the relevant predominant school. The *Shi'a* tradition of Islam also has a number of schools, the most widespread of which is the *Ja'fari* school of the *Twelvers* (see below).

KEY MUSLIM BELIEFS

The Seven Key Beliefs and Five Pillars of Islam

Islam rests upon seven basic beliefs. It affirms the oneness of God, the books revealed by God, belief in the prophets, the angels, the Day of Judgement, life after death and that all power belongs to God. The essentials of Muslim practice are summarised in the *Five Pillars of Islam*. The five pillars are:

Shahadah

The declaration of faith which states that there is no god except God and Muhammad is his messenger.

Salat

Ritual prayer carried out five times a day (see section on worship).

Zakat

A welfare due which should consist of two and a half per cent of a Muslim's total annual savings and income in order to help the service of the needy. An additional charity is due at the end of *Sawm* (fasting) during the month of *Ramadan*, and this is known as *Sadaqa al-Fitr*.

Ramadan

A month of fasting and spiritual discipline (for details see section on "Muslim Calendar and Festivals").

Hajj

Pilgrimage to Makka which involves visiting the *Ka'bah* (the House of God), believed to have been built around four thousand years ago by Abraham, and performing certain prescribed rituals in and around Makka. For those who can afford it, the *Hajj* is a requirement at least once in a lifetime.

Monotheism

Islam is strictly monotheistic. God, Allah, is believed to be one and unique and is spoken of in masculine terms although the Divine Reality is affirmed as being beyond the limitations of human gender. He is merciful and powerful, omniscient and omnipresent. He is in control of events in history and of the Day of Judgement. He created the universe and sustains it and has prescribed Islam (submission to God) as the correct way of life for the people he has created. It is also believed that, although humans have a choice as to whether they follow this way or not, all will eventually return to God to whom they will be accountable for their deeds in this world.

Goal and Purpose of Human Life

The purpose of human life is to exercise *khilafa* (authority and trust) to manage the world in a responsible way and to live in accordance with God's creative will. Human beings are called back to a life in submission to God's will as expressed in the revelations of *Torah*, *Injil* (*Gospel* of Jesus), of all the other prophets of God and, finally, through the revelation of the *Qur'an*. How each person individually responds to the will and revelation of God is believed to determine their eternal destiny. Muslims expect the coming of a descendant of the Prophet before the end of time, in order to establish justice on the earth. Belief in the *Day of Judgement*, when an individual's actions will be placed on the scales of good and evil, acts as a powerful reinforcement for the personal responsibility of each human being.

TRADITIONS IN ISLAM

There are two principal traditions within Islam - *Sunni* and *Shi'ia*. There is also an aspect of Islam known as *Sufism* (see below) which either *Sunni* or *Shi'a* Muslims might embrace.

Sunni

Ninety per cent of the world's Muslims are *Sunni*. They recognise the first four "rightly guided" *Caliphs* and understand the *Qur'an*, *Sunna*, *Ijma* and *Qiyas* to be the four sources of the law. Within the *Sunni* branch of Islam there are a range of movements and groupings which have particular emphases or concerns. They are not, however, as organisationally clear-cut as, for example, Christian denominations and there may well be cross-membership of the various tendencies. In the UK, the majority of these groupings are of South Asian origin and are organised in a variety of *Sunni* Muslim traditions:

Barelwis

Barelwi is the term commonly used to denote a devotional style of Islam found among some groups of Muslims with origins in the Indian subcontinent. It holds in high esteem the teachings of Maulana Ahmad Raza Khan (1856-1921) of Bareilly, Uttar Pradesh, in India who was a member of the *Qadiri Sufi* order and a great *Mufti* (Jurist) of the *Hanafi* school of interpretation.

Barelwis celebrate the *milad* (birthday) of the Prophet Muhammad as a major festival, giving a particularly high respect to the person of the Prophet Muhammad as a model and inspiration for Muslim life but also affirming that he had access to knowledge of "the unseen". A key concept of *Barelwi* thought is that the Divine Light which existed from the beginning of time can be seen in Muhammad.

They look to *sayyids* (descendents of the Prophet) and to *pirs* (spiritual guides) for spiritual authority, teaching, guidance and intercession with God and they defend the Islamic legitimacy of popular devotional practice at the shrines of *pirs*.

Deobandis

The *Deobandi* movement was founded in India by Maulana Muhammad Qasim. It is named after a *daral 'ulum* (training college) for Indian Muslim religious scholars founded in 1867 in the Indian town of Deoband. Established in the context of British colonial power in India its scholars were concerned to defend a clear Islamic identity against the influence of non-Islamic ideas.

Its curriculum, and that of the many colleges which came to be modelled upon it, promotes an interpretation of Islam in which the emphasis is on textual scholarship, with pre-eminence given to study of the *Qur'an*, *Hadith* and *Shari'ah* (interpreted through the *Hanafi* school). Although its scholars were, like the *Barelwi* movement, within the *Sufi* tradtion, the *Deobandi* movement emphasised the role of spiritual guides as exemplars, not accepting the legitimacy of any intercessory role for *pirs*.

Tablighi Jamaat

Tablighi Jamaat was founded in India in 1927 by Maulana Muhammad Ilyas (1885-1944), a *Sufi* and a student of Deoband. The movement is broadly within the *Deobandi* tradition and is usually non-political. It attempts to encourage other Muslims to practise the ritual aspects of Islam on a more fervent and regular basis and its committed members travel widely to spread its message.

Ahl-i-Hadith

Ahl-i-Hadith is a movement whose followers accept only the teachings of the *Qur'an* itself and the earliest teachings in the *Hadith*. It rejects any regulations which are not from these sources. This movement is sometimes known as *ghayr muqallidun* (not attached to any school of thought).

Jamaat-i-Islami

Jamaat-i-Islami operates as a religious movement in India and Sri Lanka, but as a religio-political party in Pakistan and Bangladesh. It was founded in India in 1941 by Sayyid Abul A' la Mawdudi (1903-1979). It favours a return to the following of traditional Muslim doctrine in the face of the secular influences of Western civilisation and, more specifically, is committed to seeing Islamic ideology enshrined in an Islamic state.

Shi'a

About ten per cent of Muslims worldwide are *Shi'a*, an Arabic word which literally means follower or associate. The *Shi'a* believe that Muhammad instituted from within his family (the descendants of Ali and Fatima, the Prophet's youngest daughter) a succession of individual *Imams* (spiritual leaders) to guide the community. The *Shi'a* concept of the *Imam* should not be confused with the general use of the term by Muslims to describe their local prayer leaders (see section on personnel).

In common with other Muslims, *Shi'as* believe that the process of revelation was completed with the coming of Muhammad, but they differ from other Muslims in believing that *Imams* or *Hujjah* (Proofs of God) are specially selected by God and have the authority to interpret the *Qur'an* and to provide guidance to believers.

Shi'as observe more festivals than *Sunnis* (see section on festivals). In addition, they value pilgrimages to the shrines of their Imams and saints - in particular those of Imam Ali (in Najaf) and Imam Husayn (in Karbala) in Southern Iraq.

Twelvers and Seveners

All *Shi'a* Muslims agree that Ali was the first Imam, but thereafter there are differences of view concerning the succession. A minority are known as the *Seveners*, whilst the majority are known as the *Twelvers* (or *'Ithna Asherites*). The *Twelvers* believe in a series of twelve Imams, the last of whom, Muhammad Al-Muntazar, was last seen in 873CE and is believed to have been the *Mahdi* (Guided One). He is believed to be still alive but is now hidden and waiting for God's command to reappear.

Ismailis are a *Shi'a* Muslim group who accept the leadership of the first six *Imams*, but thereafter claim the primacy of the elder son of the sixth *Imam*, Ismail and therefore are known as *Seveners*. Among the *Ismailis* are the *Nizaris* who are also known as the *Agha Khanis*. They believe in the *Aga Khan* as their living *Imam* and expect that he will, in turn, choose a member of his family to succeed him. The *Nizari* and the *Musta'lian Ismailis* disagreed over two opposing claimants to the *Imamate*. The *Bohras* are a group which emerged out of the *Musta'lian Ismailis*.

Tasawwuf

Tasawwuf (*Sufism*) is the name for the mystical strand of Islam which can be found in both the *Sunni* and *Shi'a* traditions of Islam. The word is thought to derive from the Arabic *suf* (wool) which characterised the simple clothing worn by early ascetics. *Sufism* traces its origins back through *silsilahs* (lines of spiritual initiation) and is led by spiritual authorities known as *shaykhs* or *pirs* who advise the initiates of the *Sufi* Orders in their quest for an intimately spiritual relationship with God.

Sufism involves a commitment to the practical and readily accessible aspects of Islam based on the *Shari'ah*, but also emphasises the inner or esoteric aspects of Islam. As aids to their spiritual development, the members of *Sufi* Orders may engage in various practices such as meditation, chanting the names of God, or ritual dancing. There are many worldwide *Sufi* Orders including, for example, the *Naqshbandi*, the *Qadiri*, the *Chishti* and the *Suhrawardi*.

MUSLIM LIFE

Becoming a Muslim

In order to become a Muslim a person must accept and declare that there is "no god except God" and that "Muhammad is his messenger" (*Shi'a* Muslims adding "and Ali is the seal on the will of the Prophet"). This declaration of faith is known as the *Shahada*.

Shari'ah

The basic Muslim beliefs are put into practice by means of the way of life given by God, revealed through the Prophet Muhammad, and known as the *Shari'ah* (pathway). The *Shari'ah* is not only concerned with prayer and ritual matters but also governs and regulates conduct of all kinds, for example attitudes to economics, family life, and the behaviour of rulers, thus codifying Islamic values as they apply to the whole of life.

Jihad

Jihad, the striving to protect, promote and live by the message of the *Qur'an* through words and actions, is central to Islam. It involves *da'wah*, which is the task of spreading the message of Islam through invitation issued by means of words and deeds; creating satisfactory social conditions for Islam to be practised freely; increasing the self-discipline of people who are already Muslims so that they become better Muslims; and, in limited circumstances, defending Islam by force of arms if necessary. This last aspect is only one dimension of *jihad* although outside the Muslim community *jihad* is often mistakenly assumed to mean only this. *Jihad* does not include imposing Islam by force on non-Muslims because the *Qur'an* forbids compulsion in matters of religion.

Halal

The term *halal* simply means permitted, and refers to a wide range of things which are allowed to Muslims. In popular usage in the UK however, it is often identified with food laws which are also an important part of Muslim values and ethics. The *Qur'an* does not allow consumption of the meat of pigs and carnivorous animals. This includes pork products and foods which contain the by-products of pigs or carnivorous animals. They are *haram* (unlawful). Other meats are also haram unless the animal has been ritually slaughtered. Ritual slaughter involves prayers during slaughter, and a method of butchery which allows the blood to flow from the animal's body. Fish is permitted.

When *halal* meat is not available for consumption by Muslims, *kosher* meat (slaughtered according to the Jewish shechita method) is permissible for *Sunni* Muslims (although not for *Shi'a 'Ithna Asherites*) or a vegetarian meal will suffice. Foods which contain the by-products of non-*halal* meat are also considered unlawful, for example cheese which contains an animal product such as rennet. Also unlawful for Muslims is any food or drink perceived by Muslims to have been offered to an idol or to a false god. Alcohol of any kind is also prohibited under Islamic law and any drinks or foods which contain alcohol in any amount are unacceptable.

Gender and Family

According to Muslim understanding the *Shari'ah* confers equal dignity on both women and men. Men and women generally have the same religious duties, and in most cases the same legal rights, as in the possibility of owning property in their own right. However, women are not obliged to participate in congregational prayers. There are also gender differentiations of rights and responsibilities with regard to social and legal roles, some of which are believed by many Muslims to have been divinely revealed in the *Qur'an*.

In Islam, marriage and procreation are viewed very positively and celibacy is discouraged. Traditionally, the role of a man is believed to involve financial support of his wife and family (irrespective of his wife's wealth), and the protection of female family members including wife, daughters and, if his father is deceased, his mother as well.

Muslims believe that it is a duty to marry, and the ideal family structure is based on monogamy which is the normal practice among Muslims in the UK. However, under the terms of the *Shari'ah*, polygamy (although not polyandry) is considered lawful in certain circumstances. These include infertility of the first wife, or permanent physical or mental infirmity of the first wife.

Under Islamic law a man may take up to four wives at any one time, although the regulations regarding such marriages are such that polygamy is often a practical impossibility. These regulations include that a man must have the means to provide for each wife and that he must treat each wife absolutely equally, in both financial and social terms. The contracting of a polygamous marriage is not allowed in law in this country, but recognition can be accorded to polygamous marriages that have been contracted in overseas countries where this is permitted.

Modesty is an important concept in Islam. For men, modest dress should cover, at a minimum, the area from the navel to the knees. For women, it involves covering the full body and this is interpreted variously. Traditionally, in most Islamic societies this has involved the wearing of a *hijab* or veil of varying kinds. In some Islamic societies, including a number from which people have come to the UK, there may be an expectation that women will cover their faces from the sight of men other than their husbands and family members and avoid the company of such men by remaining primarily within the home and in female company. This practice is referred to as *purdah*. In mixed contexts it can take the form of the two sexes sitting separately.

MUSLIM WORSHIP

Salat

The main form of *'ibadah* (worship) is that of *salat* (Arabic for the five times a day obligatory prayers) or *namaz* (Urdu). The exact times at which prayer takes place vary throughout the year. Prayer time-tables are published with details of the times, and can often be found on display in *mosques*.

Generally speaking, prayer takes place at around the following periods of the day: *Fajr* (dawn), *Zuhr* (midday), *Asr* (late afternoon), *Maghrib* (after sunset), and *Isha* (late evening). Prayers are obligatory from puberty onwards, except for women who are menstruating or in the post-natal period. People who are not fully conscious are also exempted from prayers.

Friday is the day for congregational prayers. Most male Muslims attend the *mosque* for this *Salat al-Jum'ah* which is mandatory for them. *Wudu* (ablutions or ritual washing) must take place prior to all prayers. This includes washing hands, face, hair, mouth, nose, arms (up to the elbows), and the feet (up to the ankles).

During prayer, worshippers face Makka, the *qiblah* (direction) of which is marked by the *mihrab*, a small niche in the wall of the *mosque*. In the UK, this direction is towards the south-east.

A Muslim can pray in any clean place and use a prayer mat if he or she cannot reasonably attend a *mosque*. Muslim employees, school children and students should have the opportunity to conduct their obligatory prayers while at work or in school or college.

Mosques

The English word *mosque* comes from the Arabic word *masjid*, meaning a place of prostration. Within the Muslim community *mosques* are known by a number of terms, the most common being *masjid*. *Jami* is often used among South Asian Muslims to refer to a "central *mosque*".

The first *mosques* in the UK were established and financed by the personal efforts of individuals living in the area. For example, the first *mosque* in Birmingham was established in 1941 by two Yemeni Muslims who were concerned to make arrangements for Muslim prayers, burial rites, and religious education for children.

At present many *mosques* are buildings which were formerly private residences, or even rooms in houses which are still used as private residences. Others are in public buildings which had former uses, for example as warehouses or, occasionally, as Christian churches. Recently, however, a number of purpose built *mosques* have been constructed.

No images, paintings or decorations which represent living beings are to be found inside *mosques*. In some *mosques*, however, Arabic calligraphy may be observed on the walls and perhaps some geometrical patterns. There are no seats in a *mosque* but the floor is carpeted. Music is not played although in some *mosques* there may be congregational chanting. There is a *minbar* (pulpit or raised steps) to one side of the *mihrab* from which the *imam* delivers sermons on Fridays and at festival times. There may also be a symbol of the crescent moon and star which has come to be associated with Islam.

Although every *mosque* is, in principle, open to all Muslims, their management committees may in practice reflect specific Muslim tendencies or national or regional groupings. As a result, particular dominant languages are used for instruction and general communication, although the language of the prayers themselves is always Arabic. *Mosques* of different types do, however, sometimes join together to form councils of *mosques*, such as the Bradford Council of Mosques.

Mosques provide a number of services like the channelling of *Zakat* to the poor; providing imams to visit Muslims who are sick in hospital or who are inmates in prison; offering educational facilities (see below) and instruction in the Urdu and Arabic languages. In addition to this, many *mosques* are now registered for the solemnisation of marriages, and some *mosques* have installed morgues ensuring that Muslims can perform Islamic burial rites for their fellow Muslims.

Attendance at the *mosque* is not obligatory for Muslim women and, in practice, many *mosques* do not cater for their attendance. Where provision is made for women to pray at the same time as men they usually sit separately, for example in a room upstairs which is also considered as part of the *mosque*, although in some *mosques* women worship behind the men on the same floor. In some cases women are discouraged from worshipping in *mosques* and are only expected to attend for cultural events and special occasions.

MUSLIM CALENDAR AND FESTIVALS

Calendar

The Muslim calendar is a lunar one, with each year composed of twelve months and each month of twenty-nine or thirty days. As such, the Muslim year is eleven days shorter than a solar year. This means that festival dates move through the solar year and cannot be conclusively dated a long way in advance since they depend upon the sighting of the new moon for the start of a new month.

Al Hijrah

The first day of the Muslim year is the anniversary of the *Hijra* with which the Muslim calendar begins. This marks the Prophet Muhammad's original migration from Makka to Madina which led to the creation of the Muslim community. The year 1997CE is therefore, according to the Muslim calendar, the year 1417/1418AH.

'Ashurah

Is a *Shi'a* commemoration marking the martyrdom of Imam Husayn, the grandson of the Prophet Muhammad. This is the tenth day of the month of *Muharram* in the Islamic calendar. It is the occasion for "passion plays" and ritual mourning through which *Shi'as*, and some *Sunni* Muslims with Indian sub-continental origins, express their identity with the suffering of the Husayn's martyrdom.

Milad al-Nabi

Is a celebration of the birthday of the Prophet on the twelfth day of *Rabi 'al-Awwal*, the third month of the Muslim calendar. It is particularly important among *Barelwis* in view of their special veneration of the Prophet.

Lailat al-Baraat

Takes place fifteen days before *Ramadan* and celebrates the popular belief that on this night the fate of humankind is ordained for the next year.

Ramadan

Ramadan is the name of the ninth month (which is either twenty-nine or thirty days long) of the lunar year. During this time Muslims should abstain, from before dawn to sunset, from eating, drinking and sexual intercourse. These daylight abstentions are deemed by Muslims to reflect devotion to God as the person abstains for God alone. Fasting is also seen as increasing self-discipline and patience, decreasing selfishness and lending a sense of solidarity between Muslims and equality before God.

There are, however, some categories of people who can be exempt from the requirements of fasting. These include children who are below the age of puberty and people who are mentally unfit. They do not have to fast nor do they have to compensate in any way for missing the fast. People travelling long distances may temporarily break the fast but should make up for this by fasting at another time for each day they have missed. People whose health would be severely affected by fasting may fast in compensation at another point in the year for an equivalent length of time.

Those who will not recover from the risk of ill health or are very old may offer a poor Muslim a meal or the financial equivalent for each day of fasting missed. Menstruating women, pregnant women, and women who are breast feeding, are also not bound to fast. They must make up for each day they do not fast by fasting at another point in the year.

Lailat al-Qadr (Night of Power)

Occurs as one of the odd nights of fasting in the last third of the month of *Ramadan*. The *Shi'as* regard it as the twenty third night and the *Sunnis* generally as the twenty seventh night of fasting in *Ramadan*. It marks the day when it is believed that the *Qur'an* began its descent to earth and was first revealed to the Prophet Muhammad.

Eid al-Fitr

This a festival marking the breaking of the *Ramadan* fast which occurs on the first day of the following month, *Shawwal*. It is one of the major festivals in the Muslim calendar. Between one and two days leave from work is usually taken to participate in this festival. Presents are given and charitable donations are encouraged. The festival emphasises unity and togetherness. An atmosphere of celebration is promoted, with gatherings held at *mosques* that often overflow outside.

Eid al-Adha

This is the *Festival of Sacrifice* which is a three day festival that marks the end of the *Hajj* to Makka and occurs on the tenth day of the *Dhu'l Hijjah* month. It celebrates the supreme example of sacrifice and submission exhibited by the Prophets Abraham and his son Ishmael.

It is celebrated not just in Mecca but throughout the Muslim world. In Muslim countries all Muslim families who can afford to do so sacrifice an animal as Abraham is believed to have done in substitution for his son, Ishmael. A third of this meat is then distributed to the poor, with the rest being shared amongst relatives to mark the festival. In the UK this slaughter is usually carried out centrally on behalf of the community rather than by individuals.

MUSLIM ORGANISATIONS

The composition of the Muslim community in the UK is varied and can be considered from a number of different perspectives including groupings with an ethnic/national component and movements within the two main traditions within Islam, the *Sunni* and the *Shi'a*. Individual Muslims might identify themselves with one or more of these groupings at the same time. The *Barelwis*, *Deobandis* and *Tablighi Jamaat* are numerically the strongest of the Muslim movements in the UK and there is some overlap between them. The general background to the various Muslim movements has already been described in the earlier section on "Traditions in Islam".

Barelwis

This tendency is particularly numerous amongst communities with rural origins. Two national organisations linked to the *Barelwi* movement are the Jamaat Ahl-e-Sunnat and the World Islamic Mission.

Deobandi

In the UK, the *Deobandi* movement is found in many areas, but it is at its strongest in Lancashire, West Yorkshire and the Midlands. Two organisations with links to this movement are the Jamiat-e-Ulama of Britain and Dar-ul-Uloom seminary in Bury.

Tablighi Jamaat

The *Tablighi Jamaat* movement in the UK is centred in Dewsbury but is also very active elsewhere in West Yorkshire, Lancashire and the Midlands. Its organisations can also be found elsewhere in Britain. The movement is closely related to the *Deobandi* movement.

Ahl-e-Hadith

Within the UK this movement is mainly concentrated in Birmingham and London.

Jamaat-i-Islami

There are several organisations which have a relationship to the idealist, thinker and founder of *Jamaat-i-Islami*, Abul A'la Mawdudi (1903-1979). Such organisations include the UK Islamic Mission, which has several branches throughout the UK. The movement was originally found mainly amongst migrants from Pakistan. After the emergence of Bangladesh, Bengali Muslims established their own *Dawat-ul-Islam* movement in 1976. Later, the Islamic Forum of Europe was also formed by young Bangladeshis to serve the intellectual needs of Bangladeshi youth throughout Europe.

Sufi Orders

Sufi Orders have branches in most UK towns and cities with a substantial Muslim presence. There are also a number of *Sufi* centres associated with specific Orders. These Orders are generally *Sunni* rather than *Shi'a*. There are also a number of western *Sufi* organisations.

Other National and Regional Organisations

Several organisations with an international membership have a presence in the UK, such as the Muslim World League, which was established in Makka in 1962 and has an office, library and prayer hall in London.

There are a number of federations and councils of Islamic organisations at both regional and national levels. Regionally, these include the Bradford Council of Mosques and the Lancashire Council of Mosques. Nationally, they include the Imams and Mosques Council and the Union of Muslim Organisations (established in 1970). These have some overlap in terms of membership, but no single organisation has yet established itself as a generally accepted and authoritative national council.

In addition to the general organisations, which are related to particular movements within Islam, there are also a number of Muslim organisations which campaign on specific major concerns for the Muslim community. For example, the UK Action Committee on Islamic Affairs, formed in 1988 in the wake of the controversy over Salman Rushdie's book *The Satanic Verses*, has a particular interest in the law, having campaigned for the withdrawal of the book and for the introduction of legal provision to protect against religious discrimination; The Islamic Society of Britain was formed in 1990 with the aim of projecting Islam's image in the UK not as an "immigrant religion", but as a global tradition developing appropriate national traditions, priorities and policies to meet the challenges facing Islam and Muslims.

Political Organisations

In recent years some Muslims in the UK have begun to form explicitly political organisations. One example of this is the Islamic Party of Britain which was launched in July 1989, mainly by a group of indigenous followers of Islam. Their declared aim is to work for a better future for Islam in the UK and for a radical change to the economic injustice to be found in British society. Another example is the Muslim Parliament which was established in 1991, aspiring to represent Muslim opinion within British social and political life. Its founder, Dr. Kalim Siddiqi, died in 1996.

Educational Organisations

There is a range of educational bodies which operate on a national level and serve a variety of functions. For example, the Muslim College in London, which trains imams; the Islamic Foundation in Leicester, an educational, research and training organisation founded in 1973 which produces literature and runs courses on Muslim belief and practice for non-Muslim professionals working in a multi-cultural context; the Muslim Community Studies Institute in Leicester, which carries out research and produces publications on Muslim life in both Muslim societies and Western societies; the Muslim Education Co-ordinating Council UK in London, which monitors and advises on the teaching of Muslim children in local education authority schools; the Muslim Educational Trust, which caters for the educational needs of Muslim children; the Islamic Academy in Cambridge, an educational research organisation; and the Muslim Education Forum, which brings together a number of these bodies in an informal network designed to co-ordinate their activities.

Madrassahs are *Qur'anic* schools which are local in nature and are usually attached to a *mosque* and many Muslim children attend them in the evening after day school. Both boys and girls attend such lessons where they read and learn sections of the *Qur'an* which in turn necessitates the learning of Arabic. They also learn the rituals and practices of Islam. There are also a few private Muslim day schools which provide a full time educational service for Muslim children. Many Muslim organisations wish to see the establishment of Muslim schools with voluntary aided or grant maintained status. At the time of writing, however, none have been granted this by the Department for Education and Employment.

Dawah
Dawah literally means invitation – the invitation to people to embrace Islam. There are a number of organised *dawah* initiatives which aim to spread the message of Islam throughout the UK. Some are local independent organisations. Others are affiliates of national organisations such as the UK Islamic Mission, which has branches and affiliated *mosques* nationwide. Some missionary groups aim to spread the word of Islam to non-Muslims, whilst most focus on drawing back Muslims who have drifted away from their faith.

Youth
Muslim youth organisations include local independent groups of Muslims and local groups affiliated to national organisations such as Young Muslims UK and the Federation of Student Islamic Societies (FOSIS), both of which organise workshops and "camps" for Muslim youth. In recent times radical Islamic groups such as Hizb-ut-Tahrir have been active in many institutions of higher education.

Community Groups
Local Muslim community groups are usually attached to the *mosque* and are also normally loosely related to particular Muslim movements, or are composed of a group with the same ethnic origins and languages, such as the various Pakistan Muslim Welfare Associations. They have a welfare and cultural role and may be eclectic with sub-groups for certain sectors of the community, for example youth groups and women's groups.

Personnel

Individual *mosques* are usually controlled by *mosque* committees which generally include a president and secretary. Committee membership elections are normally held annually. The *mosque* committee co-ordinates funding for the *mosque* and connected Muslim organisations and is also responsible for appointing an *imam*.

The *imam* is the leader of the prayers. *Imam* is an Arabic word meaning "the one who stands in front". In principle, this can be any Muslim who is well versed in the *Qur'an* and the liturgy for prayer. There is no hierarchy of ordained clergy although the *imam* may act as a spokesperson for the community.

Although *imams* are now being trained in the UK, frequently they will have arrived in adulthood from an area of the world where the majority of the members of a *mosque* community have their ethnic origins, and may therefore only have a poor command of the English language. In these circumstances, the chairperson or secretary of the *mosque* Committee might more usually represent the community to the outside world.

Fuqaha are experts in Islamic law. *Pirs* or *shaykhs* are spiritual guides from the *Sufi* orders. *Ulama* is a term denoting religious scholars in general.

FURTHER READING

Abdalati, H, *Islam in Focus*, American Trust Publications, Indianapolis, 1975.

Abdul-Fadl, M, *Introducing Islam from Within*, Islamic Foundation, Leicester, 1991.

Ahmad, K, *Family Life in Islam*, Islamic Foundation, Leicester, 1981.

Ahsan, M and Kidwai, A (eds), *Sacrilege Versus Civility: Muslim Perspectives on The Satanic Verses Affair*, Islamic Foundation, Leicester, 1993 (revised and enlarged edition).

Ahsan, M, "Islam and Muslims in Britain", in Mutalib, H and Hashmi, T (eds), *Islam, Muslims and the Modern State*, Macmillan, Basingstoke, 1994, pp. 339-361.

Andrews, A, "Sociological Analysis of Jamaat-i-Islami in the United Kingdom", in Barot, R (ed), *Religion and Ethnicity: Ethnic Minorities and Social Change in the Metropolis*, Kok Pharos, Kampen, The Netherlands, 1993, pp. 68-79.

Anwar, M, *Muslims in Britain: 1991 Census and Other Statistical Sources*, Centre for the Study of Islam and Christian-Muslim Relations, Selly Oak Colleges, Birmingham, 1993.

Anwar, M, *Young Muslims in Britain: Attitudes, Educational Needs and Policy Implications*, Islamic Foundation, Leicester, 1994.

Awan, B A, "Islam", in Tiptaft, N, *Religion in Birmingham*, Norman Tiptaft Ltd, Warley, 1972.

Badawi, Z, *Islam in Britain*, Ta-Ha Publishers Ltd, London, 1981.

Barton, S W, *The Bengali Muslims of Bradford*, Community Religions Project, University of Leeds, Leeds, 1986.

Coulson, N J, *A History of Islamic Law*, Edinburgh University Press, Edinburgh, 1964.

Daftari, F, *The Ismailis: Their History and Doctrine*, Cambridge University Press, Cambridge, 1990.

Darsh, S M, *Muslims in Europe*, Ta-Ha Publishers, London, 1987.

Greaves, R, *Sectarian Influences within Islam in Britain: with Reference to the Concepts of Ummah and Community*, Community Religions Project Monograph Series, Department of Theology and Religious Studies, University of Leeds, Leeds, 1996.

Glassé, C, *The Concise Encyclopaedia of Islam*, Stacey International, London, (2nd edition), 1991.

Henley, A, *Caring for Muslims and their Families: Religious Aspects of Care*, National Extension College, Cambridge, 1982.

Islamic Foundation, *Islam: The Essentials*, Islamic Foundation, Leicester, 1974.

Joly, D, "Making a place for Islam in British Society: Muslims in Birmingham", in Gerholm, T and Lithman, Y F (eds), *The New Islamic Presence in Western Europe*, Mansell, London, 1990, pp. 32-52.

Joly, D and Nielsen, J S, *Muslims in Britain: An Annotated Bibliography, 1960-1984*, Centre for Research in Ethnic Relations, University of Warwick, Warwick, 1985.

Lemu, A and Heeren, F, *Women in Islam*, Islamic Foundation, Leicester, 1978.

Lewis, P, *Islamic Britain: Religion, Politics and Identity Among British Muslims*, I B Tauris, London, 1994.

Lewis, P, *The Function, Education and Influence of the Ulama in Bradford's Muslim Communities*, Community Religions Project Monograph

Series, Department of Theology and Religious Studies, University of Leeds, Leeds, 1996.

Lings, M, *What is Sufism?*, Unwin Paperbacks, London, 1975.

McDermott, M Y and Ahsan, M M, *The Muslim Guide: For Teachers, Employers, Community Workers and Social Administrators in Britain*, Islamic Foundation, Leicester, 1992 (revised edition).

Mawdudi, A, *Towards Understanding Islam*, Islamic Foundation, Leicester, 1981.

Nadwi, S A H A, *Muslims in the West: Message and Mission*, Islamic Foundation, Leicester, 1983.

Nasr, S H, *Ideals and Realities of Islam*, George Allen and Unwin, London, 1966.

Nasr, S H, *Living Sufism*, Unwin Paperbacks, London, 1980.

Nielsen, J S, *A Survey of British Local Authority Response to Muslim Needs*, Research Papers on Muslims in Europe No 30/31, June/September, 1986.

Nielsen, J S, "Muslims in Britain: searching for an identity", in *New Community*, Volume XIII, No 3, Spring 1987, pp 384-394.

Nielsen, J S, *Muslims in Western Europe*, Edinburgh University Press, Edinburgh, 1995 (2nd edition).

Padwick, C, *Muslim Devotions*, SPCK, London, 1961.

Peach, C, "The Muslim population of Great Britain", in *Ethnic and Racial Studies*, Volume XIII, No 3, 1990, pp. 415-419.

Rahman, F, *Islam*, University of Chicago Press, Chicago (2nd edition), 1979.

Rahman, T, *A Code of Muslim Personal Law*, Volumes I & II, Islamic Publishers, Karachi, 1978 and 1980.

Raza, M S, *Islam in Britain: Past Present and Future*, Volcano Press Ltd, Leicester, (2nd edition) 1992.

Rex, J, "The Urban Sociology of Religion and Islam in Birmingham", in Gerholm, T and Lithman, Y G, *The New Islamic Presence in Western Europe*, Mansell, London, 1990, pp 206-218.

Robinson, F, *Varieties of South Asian Islam*, Research Paper No.8, Centre for Research in Ethnic Relations, University of Warwick, Coventry, 1988.

Schimmel, A, *Islamic Names*, Edinburgh University Press, Edinburgh, 1989.

Shaykh Haeri, F, *The Elements of Sufism*, Element Books, Dorset, 1990.

Trimingham, J S, *The Sufi Orders in Islam*, Oxford University Press, Oxford, 1971.

UK Action Committee on Islamic Affairs, *Need for Reform: Muslims and the Law in Multi-Faith Britain*, UK Action Committee on Islamic Affairs, London, 1993.

Vertovec, S, *Annotated Bibliography of Academic Publications Regarding Islam and Muslims in the United Kingdom, 1985-1992*, Centre for Research in Ethnic Relations, University of Warwick, Coventry, 1993.

Wahab, I, *Muslims in Britain: Profile of a Community*, The Runnymede Trust, London, 1989.

Wolffe, J, "Fragmented Universaility: Islam and Muslims", in Parsons, G (ed), *The Growth of Religious Diversity: Britain from 1945, Volume 1: Traditions*, Routledge, London, 1993, pp. 133-172.

Yawar, T, *Caring About Faith: Muslim Children and Young Persons in Care*, Islamic Foundation, Leicester, 1992.

MUSLIM UNITED KINGDOM ORGANISATIONS

The organisations listed in this section include both head offices of organisations with branches throughout the country and organisations which aspire to serve the Muslim community on a UK-wide level.

Ahlul-Bayt Tours Association
24 Cassiobury Park Avenue, Watford, Hertfordshire, WD1 7LB (h)
Tel: 01923-240905 (h)   **Fax:** 01923-240905
Contact: Mrs Ragaa Ali
Position: President
Activities: Resource, youth, elderly, women, inter-faith
Traditions: Sunni
Other Languages: Arabic
The association encourages Muslims and non Muslims to visit Islamic places of cultural heritage in Egypt, Cairo and Saudi Arabia, especially Mosques; to create and raise awareness of these holy places in a cultural educational sense.

Al-Furqan Charity Trust
1 Wynne Road, London, SW9 0BB
Tel: 0171-737-7266   **Fax:** 0171-737-7267
Contact: A Siddiqui
Position: Secretary
Activities: Visits, women, newsletters
Traditions: Sunni
Other Languages: English, Urdu, Arabic, French

Al-Furqan Islamic Heritage Foundation
Eagle House, High Street, Wimbledon, London, SW19 5EF
Tel: 0181-944-1233   **Fax:** 0181-944-1633
Contact: Dr H Sharifi
Position: Secretary General
Activities: Resource, books
Other Languages: Arabic, Persian, French, German
A research institute for the preservation of the Islamic heritage in the form of Islamic manuscripts.

Al-Hoda Limited
76-78 Charing Cross Road, London, WC2H 0BB
Tel: 0171-240-8381   **Fax:** 0171-497-0180
Contact: The Manager
Position: Manager
Activities: Books
Other Languages: Persian/Arabic, Urdu/Swahili, Kachi, Gujarati
We are publishers, booksellers and distributors.

Al-Hurau Schools Trust
Midland House, 71 Hob Moor Road, Small Heath, Birmingham, West Midlands, B10 9AZ
Tel: 0121-766-5454   **Fax:** 0121-766-8556
Contact: Mohammad Abdul Karim Saqib

Position: Chairman
Activities: Worship, resource, youth, elderly, newsletters, books
Traditions: Sunni
Other Languages: Urdu, Punjabi, Bengali, Arabic
Established Islamic School. Aims to provide Islamic knowledge and subjects of the National Curriculum for boys and girls in a segregated Islamic environment.

Al Khoei Foundation
Stone Hall, Chevening Road, London, NW6 6TN
Tel: 0171-372-4049 **Fax:** 0171-372-0694
Contact: Yousif Al-Khoei
Position: Director
Activities: Worship, resource, media, visits, youth, elderly, women, newsletters, books, inter-faith
Traditions: Ithna Asheri
Other Languages: Arabic, Persian, Urdu, Punjabi

Al-Muhajiroun
PO Box 349, Edmonton, London, N9 7RR
Tel: 0181-884-0074 **Tel:** 0956-920006
Fax: 0181-8034-541
Internet: http://www.almuhajiroun.org
Contact: Sheik Omar Bakri Muhammad
Position: The Leader
Activities: Worship, resource, media, umbrella, visits, youth, women, newsletters, books
Traditions: Sunni
Movements: All
Other Languages: Urdu, Arabic, French, Turkish
Affiliations: The Islamic World League; London School of Shari'ah; The name means "the voice, the eyes and the ears of the Muslims".

Al Muntada Al Islami Trust
7 Bridges Place, off Parson's Green Lane, Fulham, London, SW6 4HW
Tel: 0171-736-9060 **Fax:** 0171-736-9060
Contact: Baraq Albayaty
Position: Administrator
Activities: Worship, resource, visits, youth, newsletters, books
Traditions: Sunni
Other Languages: English, Arabic

Al-Muttaqiin
62 West Avenue, Wallington, Surrey, SM6 8PH
Tel: 0181-686-1637
Fax: 0181-686-1637
Contact: Shafi Chowdhury

Position: Chairman
Activities: Worship, resource, youth, inter-faith
Traditions: Sunni
Movements: Al-Muttaqiin
Other Languages: Bangla, Arabic
Affiliations: Muslim Council of Britain; UK Action Committee on Islamic Affairs
Al-Muttaqiin (Allah-Conscious Careful Ones Keeping Safe from the Shaitan) is also engaged in refugee and school activities and in prison visits, as well as English/Arabic Qur'an lessons.

Albanian Islamic Centre & Society
PO Box 2383, 233 Seven Sisters Road, London, W8 6WQ
Tel: 01956-379526 **Fax:** 0171-263-7318
Contact: Mr Zymer Salihi
Position: Chair
Activities: Worship, resource, books, inter-faith
Other Languages: Albanian, Arabic
Affiliations: UK Action Committee on Islamic Affairs

All Muslim Funeral Society
127 Kingsway, Luton, Bedfordshire, LU1 1TS
Tel: 01582-451853 **Tel:** 01582-451853 (h)
Contact: Mr Abdul Shakur
Position: General Secretary
Other Languages: Punjabi, Urdu
The Society assists in the cost of funeral expenses for deceased members and their families.

AMANA
P O Box 2842, London, W6 9ZH
Tel: 0181-748-2424
Contact: Umar Hegedus & Khadijah Knight
Activities: Resource
AMANA exists to promote an understanding of Islam and its followers. It adddresses both Muslims and non-Muslims providing well-grounded advice and information. It offers resources for training to schools, colleges, social service departments and employers.

Anjumen-e-Jamali (Dawoodi Bohra Jumaat)
47 Elizabeth Street, Little Horton, Bradford, West Yorkshire, BD5 0SD
Tel: 01274-482970 **Tel:** 01274-441433 (h)
Fax: 01274-482972
Contact: Mr Husaini A Master
Position: Honorary Treasurer
Activities: Worship, resource

Traditions: Other Shi'a
Movements: Fatemi
Other Languages: Gujarati, Arabic
Affiliations: Anjuman-E-Jamali; Dawat-E-Hadiyah; Anjuman-E-Burhani (London); Al Vazaratus Saifiyah (Bombay)

Association of Muslim Researchers
P O Box 8715, London, SE23 3ZB
Tel: 0181-699-1887 **Fax:** 0181-699-1887
Email: amr@amrnet.demon.co.uk
Contact: Miss S Sheriff
Position: Development Officer
Activities: Resource, newsletters, books
Other Languages: Arabic, Urdu, Farsi, Turkish
Generation, dissemination and application of knowledge, networking. Societies: Economic, Education, History of Islam, Humanities and Information Technology.

Association of Muslim Schools of UK & Eire (AMS)
88 Sparkenhoe Street, Leicester, Leicestershire, LE2 02A
Tel: 0116-251-9519 **Fax:** 0116-251-9519
Contact: Ibrahim Hewitt
Position: Development Officer
Activities: Resource, umbrella, newsletters
Affiliations: Muslim Council of Britain
Umbrella body for Britain's full-time Muslim schools - offers in-service training for teachers, curriculum development and management advice.

Association of Muslim Youth & Community Workers
81 Melbourne Road, Spinney Hill North, Highfields, Leicester, Leicestershire, LE2 0GW (h)
Tel: 0116-251-5296 **Tel:** 0116-251-5296 (h)
Contact: Mr Shamsuddeen Hassan
Position: Chair
Activities: Worship, resource, media, youth, elderly, women, newsletters, inter-faith
Traditions: Sunni
Other Languages: Gujarati, Urdu, Arabic, Bengali
Affiliations: Federation of Muslim Organisations, Leicester; Union of Muslim Organisations (UK and Eire)
A cohort of Muslim professionals and volunteers which is a training and education organisation. It responds to requests for Islamic input to school assemblies, seminars, conferences etc; trains Muslim school governors; supports Muslim voluntary groups.

Association for British Muslims
47 Davis Road, London, W3 7SE (h)
Tel: 0181-723-8976 (h) **Fax:** 0181-723-8976
Email: dro@dalhelve.demon.co.uk
Contact: Daoud Rosser-Owen
Position: Amir (President)
Activities: Resource, media, visits, youth, women, newsletters, inter-faith
Traditions: Sunni, Other Shi'a
Movements: All types of Islam
Other Languages: French, Arabic, Malay, Urdu/Turkish/ Bosnian
Affiliations: Union of Muslim Organisations of UK and Eire
The senior Muslim organisation in the British Isles, established in 1889 to help converts to Islam. A social and not a political body working for all British Muslims, not exclusivist or racist it aims to keep in touch with foreign Muslim organisations.

British Muslim Association
58 Parkway, West Wimbledon, London, SW20 9HF
Tel: 0181-542-8507 **Fax:** 0181-542-8508
Contact: Mr I Rahman
Position: Welfare Officer
Activities: Resource
Traditions: Sunni
Movements: All Muslims
Other Languages: Urdu, Hindi, Punjabi, Bangladeshi
Affiliations: British Muslim Association (Pakistan)
It is a volunteer based organisation set up to assist members of the community in their time of need eg financial hardship, domestic violence, educational problems etc.

British Muslim Council
22 Lynmouth Road, London, N16 6XL
Tel: 0181-806-2892 **Tel:** 0181-806-2898 (h)
Fax: 0181-806-2898
Contact: Shuja Shaikh
Position: Chair
Activities: Worship, umbrella, youth, elderly, women, newsletters, inter-faith
Other Languages: Urdu, Turkish, Bengali
The British Muslim Council is an umbrella organisation of a number of Muslim Councils in the Greater London area. It hopes to set up similar Muslim Councils in other parts of the UK. It is not an exclusively religious group.

British Muslim League of Overseas
30 Vaughton Street, Highgate, Birmingham, West Midlands, B12 0SS (h)
Tel: 0121-440-1444 (h) **Fax:** 0121-440-1444
Contact: Akbar Khan
Position: Chair
Other Languages: Urdu

Central Jamiat Ulama UK
183 St Georges Road, Bolton, Lancashire, BL1 2PG
Tel: 01204-406862 **Tel:** 01204-361759 (h)
Fax: 01204-361759
Contact: Mohmmed Musa Qasmi
Position: Secretary General
Activities: Worship, resource, visits, women, newsletters, inter-faith
Traditions: Sunni
Other Languages: Urdu, Gujrati, Punjabi
Affiliations: UK Action Committee on Islamic Affairs; The Muslim World League

Central Moonsighting Committee of Great Britain
98 Ferham Road, Rotherham, South Yorkshire
Contact: Mufti Muhammas Aslam, S61 1BN
Tel: 01709-563677

Council of European Jamaats
4 Burton Street, Peterborough, Cambridgeshire, PE2 5HD
Tel: 01733-340261
Contact: Abdul Hirji
Position: Secretary
Links Shi'a Khoja 'Ithna Asheri mosques across Europe.

Council of Representatives of UK Muslims
48 Wilberforce Road, London, N4 2SR

Council for the Preservation of the Holy Places of Islam
34 Francis Road, Leyton, London, E10 6PW

Dar al-Hekma Trust
45 Chalton Street, London, NW1 1HY
Tel: 0171-383-2058 **Fax:** 0171-383-3601
Contact: Mohamed Ali
Position: Clerk/Organiser
Activities: Worship, visits, youth, women, inter-faith
Traditions: Ithna Asheri
Other Languages: Arabic

Dar al-Islam Foundation
61 Anson Road, Cricklewood, London, NW2 3UY
Tel: 0181-452-3220 **Fax:** 0181-208-4354
Contact: Mr F Sherif
Position: Voluntary Admin
Activities: Visits, youth, women, inter-faith
Traditions: Ithna Asheri
Other Languages: Arabic

Dar-ul-Ehsan Publications
252 Almondbury Bank, Almondbury, Huddersfield, West Yorkshire, HD5 8EL
Tel: 01484-309852 (h)
Contact: Dr Muhammad Iqbal
Position: Secretary/Treasurer
Activities: Books
Traditions: Sunni
Aims to promote better understanding of Muslims and Islam by all, especially non-Muslims, through publications on all aspects of Islam, particularly the spiritual dimensions of the Faith.

Dawatul Islam Youth Group
52 Fieldgate Street, London, E1 1DL
Tel: 0171-247-3832 **Fax:** 0171-247-0689
Activities: Youth

Edhi International Foundation UK
7 Shakespeare Road, Finchley Central, London, Middlesex, N3 1XE
Tel: 0181-346-9232 **Fax:** 0181-349-0296
Contact: Haroon A Dada
Position: Chairman
Activities: Charity
Other Languages: Urdu, Gujrati, Punjabi

European Islamic Mission
22 Roberts Road, Balby, Doncaster, South Yorkshire, DN4 0JW
Tel: 1302-819470 (h)
Contact: Muhammed Shafi Chaudhary
Position: Chairman
Activities: Worship, resource, visits, youth, elderly, newsletters, books, inter-faith
Traditions: Sunni
Other Languages: English, Urdu, Arabic

Federation of Islamic Organisations in Europe
PO Box MAR005, Markfield, Leicestershire, LE67 9RY
Tel: 01530-245919 **Tel:** 0385-770662
Fax: 01530-245913

Contact: Mr Ahmad K Al-Rawi
Position: President
Activities: Umbrella
Other Languages: Arabic, French
Traditions: Sunni

Federation of Students Islamic Societies of the UK & Eire (FOSIS)
38 Mapesbury Road, London, NW2 4JD
Tel: 0181-452-4493 **Fax:** 0181-208-4161
Email: Fosis@Fosis.demon.co.uk
Internet: http://www.fosis.demon.co.uk
Contact: President
Activities: Resource, umbrella, visits, youth, women, newsletters, books, inter-faith
Traditions: Sunni
FOSIS aims to: unite student Islamic societies on Islamic principles; encourage formation of new Islamic societies and support existing ones; protect and promote the interests of Muslim students; develop Muslim students; invite other students to Islam.

Guyana United Sad'r Islamic Anjuman
8 Hazledean Road, Craven Road, London, NW10 8QU
Tel: 0181-961-3814 **Fax:** 0181-961-3814
Contact: Haji Abdool Hafiz Rahaman
Position: Vice President
A branch of an organisation in Georgetown, Guyana, which represents Muslims, founded in 1936. Its aim is to spread Islam in Guyana, where approximately ten per cent of the population are Muslim.

Hijaz College
Watling Street, Nuneaton, Warwickshire, CV11 6BE
Tel: 01203-641333 **Tel:** 01203-444504
Fax: 01203-353345
Contact: Hazrat Moulana Noor Siddiqi
Position: Vice Principal
Activities: Worship, resource, umbrella, visits, youth, elderly, women, books, inter-faith
Traditions: Sunni
Movements: Barelwi, Tassawuf
Other Languages: Urdu, Arabic, Punjabi, Dutch
The College aims to become a centre of excellence that offers Muslims the opportunity to acquire higher education within the spiritual and intellectual framework of Islam.

Hizbul Ulama UK
7 Troy Street, Blackburn, Lancashire, BB1 6NY
Tel: 01254-6633177

Hizbut-Tahrir
PO Box 3894, Edmonton, London, N9 0ET

Idara Isha'at al Islam
15 Stratton Road, Gloucester, Gloucestershire, GL1 4HD
Tel: 01452-540544
Contact: Ebraheem Yoosuf Bawa
Position: Founder
Activities: Newsletters, books
Traditions: Sunni
Movements: Deobandi
Other Languages: Urdu, Gujarati, Burmese
Idara was established by Haji E Y Bawa, a renowned author of Islamic religious books, whose five daughters amd two sons, now ministers, memorised the Qur'an. He has written Islamic books in English and his "Al-Islam" (in Urdu) is popular throughout the world.

Imams & Mosques Council
20-22 Creffield Road, London, Greater London, W5 3RP
Tel: 0181-992-6636 **Fax:** 0181-993-3946
Contact: Moulana Mohamad Shahid Raza
Position: Executive Director
Activities: Umbrella, inter-faith
Other Languages: Urdu, Arabic
Affiliations: Inter Faith Network for the UK
The Council offers in-service training to the Imams to enhance their ability to work as religious leaders in the UK; operates a private pension scheme for Imams, contributing on a pound for pound basis. It is an organisation of affiliated mosques.

Indian Muslim Federation (UK)
Trinity Close, Leytonstone, London, E11 4RP
Tel: 0181-558-6399 **Tel:** 0181-556-1992 (h)
Fax: 0181-539-4192
Contact: R Anwar Sharif
Position: Director
Activities: Youth, elderly, women, inter-faith
Traditions: Sunni
Other Languages: Urdu, Punjabi, Hindi, Bengali
Affiliations: Leytonstone Islamic Association; Union of Muslim Organisations of UK and Eire; UK Action Committee on Islamic Affairs; The Muslim World League
Strives to promote educational, social, cultural, economical, political and religious activities and equality of opportunities for the Muslims in India.

Institute of Islamic Banking and Insurance
ICIS House, 144-146 Kings Cross Road, London,
WC1X 9DH
Tel: 0171-833-8275 **Fax:** 0171-278-4797
Email: icisibi.demon.co.uk
Contact: Ghazanfar Adil
Position: Director General.
Activities: Resource, newsletters, books
Aims and objectives: Promotion of Islamic financial
system through banking and insurance through
conference seminars, lectures and publications.
Education of prospective personnel in Islamic
banking and insurance and developing Islamic
financial instruments.

Institute of Islamic Studies
34 Kinver Croft, High Gate, Birmingham, West
Midlands, B12 9HE
Tel: 0121-446-6428 **Fax:** 0121-446-6426
Contact: Dr Khalid Alai
Position: Secretary
Activities: Books, inter-faith
Traditions: Sunni
Other Languages: Urdu, Punjabi, Arabic
Affiliations: UK Action Committee on Islamic
Affairs; Educational Forum

Institute of Ismaili Studies
14-15 Great James Street, London, WC1N 3DP

Institute of Muslim Minority Affairs
46 Goodge Street, London, W1P 1FJ
Tel: 0171-636-6740 **Fax:** 0171-255-1473
Contact: Hamid Ismail
Position: Resident Director
The primary purpose of the Institute is to encourage,
support and pursue research in, and to extend the
study and knowledge of, the conditions of life of
Muslim minority communities wherever they reside.

International College of Islamic Sciences
253 Kilburn Lane, London, W10 4BQ
Tel: 0181-960-6823 **Tel:** 0181-459-6379 (h)
Fax: 0181-860-1597
Email: islamcol.demon.co.uk
Contact: Dr Seyed Ehsan Shahrestani
Position: Public Relations
Activities: Resource, visits, newsletters, books,
inter-faith
Traditions: Ithna Asheri

Other Languages: Arabic, Farsi
Affiliations: World Ahl ul Bayt Islamic League

IQRA Trust
24 Culross Street, London, W1Y 3HE
Tel: 0171-491-1572 **Fax:** 0171-493-7899
Email: INFOQRA Trust.mhs.compuserve.com
Activities: Resource, books, inter-faith
Traditions: Sunni
Other Languages: Arabic
IQRA Trust supplies clear, readable and accurate
information about Islam and the Muslim way of life.
It aims to improve understanding of Islam in Britain.

Islamia Schools Trust
129 Salusbury Road, Brondesbury, London, Greater
London, NW6 6RG
Tel: 0171-372-2171 **Tel:** 0171-404-2556 (h)
Fax: 0171-372-0655
Contact: Muhammad Zamir
Position: Administrator
Activities: Worship, resource, visits, youth, elderly,
women, newsletters, books, inter-faith
Traditions: Sunni
Other Languages: Arabic, Urdu, Bengali
Affiliations: Association of Muslim Schools
Islamia Schools Trust runs two schools in North
London. Islamia primary school admits both boys
and girls. The secondary school is for the girls only
and has topped the league table for the second year
in succession among Brent schools.

Islamic Academy, The
23 Metcalfe Road, Cambridge, Cambridgeshire,
CB4 2DB
Tel: 01223-350976 **Tel:** 01223-321061 (h)
Fax: 01223-350976
Contact: Dr Shaikh Abdul Mabud
Position: Deputy Director General
Other Languages: Arabic, Bengali, Urdu
The Academy aims to: provide Muslim scholars
around the world with a central forum for the
exchange of ideas; formulate Islamic concepts for
teaching different subjects; revise and redesign
curricula; publish and distribute textbooks; educate
teachers.

Islamic Book Club (UK)
Chashtiah Bookcentre, 49 Milkstone Road,
Rochdale, Lancashire, OL11 1EB
Tel: 01706-50487 **Fax:** 01706-350140

Contact: Mr Jamil Chishti
Position: Manager
The bookshop offers free catalogues, translations of the Qu'ran and Children's books with first orders. The book centre houses a large selection of Islamic literature in English, audio and video cassettes and Islamic artefacts and gifts.

Islamic Centre England
140 Maida Vale, W9 1QB
Tel: 0171-258-0526 **Tel:** 0181-952-0998 (h)
Fax: 0171-723-9629
Email: icel@ic-el.org
Internet: http://www.ic-el.org
Contact: Hyder Shirazi
Position: Secretary
Traditions: Shi'a 'Ithna Asheri
Languages: Arabic, Farsi, Urdu, French
Answering questions on Islamic affairs via the Internet, Fax, telephone etc. Homepage in three languages showing prayer times and *Adhan*. Supplies books in Arabic, Persian, English, Urdu, French, Turkish and German.

Islamic College London
16 Settles Street, London, E1 1JP
Tel: 0171-377-1595 **Fax:** 0171-377-1595
Contact: Abu Syed
Position: Principal
Activities: Worship, resource
Traditions: Sunni
Other Languages: Bengali
Affiliations: Dawatul Islam UK and Eire; Association of Muslim Schools

Islamic Council of Europe
16 Grosvenor Crescent, London, Greater London, SW1X 7EP
Tel: 0171-235-9832 **Fax:** 0171-823-1590
Contact: Mr Saleem Azzam
Position: Secretary General
Activities: Umbrella, books, inter-faith
Affiliations: UK Action Committee on Islamic Affairs; Muslim Council of Britain; Observer at Organisation of Islamic Conference

Islamic Council on Palestine
46 Goodge Street, London, W1P 1FJ

Islamic Cultural Centre & the London Central Mosque Trust Ltd
146 Park Road, London, NW8 7RG

Tel: 0171-724-3363 **Fax:** 0171-724-0493
Contact: Bashir Ebrahim-Khan
Position: Officer
Activities: Worship, resource, media, umbrella, visits, youth, elderly, women, newsletters, books, inter-faith
Traditions: Sunni
Other Languages: Arabic, French, Urdu, Bengali
Affiliations: Inter Faith Network for the UK

Islamic Education Board
Dar Al Tableegh, Jackets Lane, Harefield, Middlesex, UB9 6PZ
Tel: 01923-823606 **Fax:** 01923-823132
EMail: ieb@tableegh.org.uk
Contact: Muhsin Jaffer
Position: Chairman
Activities: Resource, umbrella, visits, books, inter-faith
Traditions: 'Ithna Asheri
Affiliations: World Federation of Khoja Shia Ithna-Asheri Muslim Communities
Languages: Gujarati, Urdu

Islamic Educational Welfare Association
25 Evershot Road, London, N4 3DG
Tel: 0171-272-7031
Contact: Abdul Aleem Siddiqui
It aims to: promote the Islamic faith and impart religious knowledge of Islam to Muslims and non-Muslims in the UK; promote unity and good will among Muslims living in the UK; provide moral and practical support to Muslims.

Islamic Forum Europe
169 Mile End Road, London, E1 4AQ
Tel: 0171-4239766 **Tel:** 0171-739-0556 (h)
Fax: 0171-7027254
Contact: Habibur Rahman
Position: Secretary General
Activities: Resource, youth, women, newsletters, inter-faith
Other Languages: Bengali, Urdu, Somalian
Centre for research, education and publication and runs regular training courses for non-Mulsim professionals.

Islamic Foundation
Ratby Lane, Leicester, Leicestershire, LE67 9RN
Tel: 01530-244944 **Fax:** 01530-244946
Email: islamicf@islamf.demon.co.
Contact: Mr Mohammad Sadiq

Position: Administrative Officer
Activities: Worship, resource, visits, youth, women, newsletters, books, inter-faith
Traditions: Sunni
Other Languages: Arabic, Urdu

Islamic Foundation for Ecology & Environmental Sciences
PO Box 5051, Birmingham, West Midlands, B20 3RZ
Tel: 0121-523-4264 **Fax:** 0121-523-4264
Contact: Fazlun Khalid
Position: Director
Activities: Resource, umbrella, books, inter-faith
IFEES is an Islam focussed environmental organisation, networked internationally and collaborating with non-governmental organisations, universities and grass roots organisations world wide to produce books and resource materials.

Islamic Information Centre (London)
99 Uxbridge Road, Shepherd's Bush, London, W12 8NL
Tel: 0181-749-3877
Contact: Ghafoor Hussain
Position: Secretary
Activities: Worship, resource, visits, youth, inter-faith
Traditions: Sunni
Other Languages: Urdu, Hindi, Punjabi, Arabic

Islamic Men & Women's Association
52 Oulton Terrace, Bradford, West Yorkshire, BD7 1QF (h)
Tel: 01274-411799 (h)
Contact: Mubarik Iqbal
Position: Chairperson
Other Languages: Urdu, Punjabi
This organisation is set up to unite Muslims and work for the welfare of the community. It forbids personal attack and welcomes Muslims from all sects and from all countries.

Islamic Museum In London
c/o 44 Crofton Road, Camberwell, London, SE5 8NB (h)
Tel: 0171-701-3670 **Fax:** 0171-701-3670
Contact: Dr H Alsaigh
Position: Secretary General
Activities: Resource
Traditions: Multi-Traditional
The Islamic Museum aims to provide a major forum for information on all aspects of the culture that is Islam, together with its social, geographical, political and religious importance.

Islamic Prayer Group (IPG)
PO Box 4268, London, SE11 4BD
Tel: 0956-964258 **Tel:** 0181-251-2041 (h)
Fax: 0171-582-6295
Contact: Maroof Abedye
Position: Secretary General
Activities: Visits, youth, inter-faith
Traditions: Sunni
Other Languages: Yoruba

Islamic Propagation Centre International Ltd
481 Coventry Road, Small Heath, Birmingham, West Midlands, B10 0JS
Tel: 0121-773-0137 **Fax:** 0121-766-8577
EMail: ipci@globalnet.co.uk
Contact: Shamshad Mohammad Khan
Position: Chairman
Activities: Charity
Other Languages: Urdu, Arabic
Devoted to supplying information and literature on Islam. The Group works to gain new members of the faith and engages in *daw'ah*, in other words, presenting and preaching the message of Islam.

Islamic Relief World-wide (National Office)
151b Park Road, London, NW8 7HT
Tel: 0171-722-0039 **Fax:** 0171-722-3228
Email: 100667.130@compuserve.com
Contact: Mr Fadi Itani
Position: UK Manager
Activities: Youth, newsletters
Other Languages: Arabic, Urdu, French
Affiliations: The International Islamic Council For Relief
National office of Islamic Relief: an international relief and development organisation working for the long term development of the world's poorest nations. Our aim is to alleviate suffering wherever it occurs and whoever its victims.

Islamic Relief World-wide (International Office)
19 Rea Street South, Digbeth, Birmingham, West Midlands, B5 6LB
Tel: 0121-605-5555 **Fax:** 0121-622-5003
Email: 100667.130@compuserve.com
Contact: Dr Hany El Banna
Position: Managing Director
Activities: Charity
Other Languages: Arabic, French, Dutch, German

International office of Islamic Relief which aims to alleviate poverty by providing humanitarian aid during emergencies and promoting sustainable and appropriate development through working with local communities and partners overseas.

Islamic Research Academy (IRAP)

PO Box 15002, Dunblane, Central, FK15 0ZA
Tel: 01786-822238 (h) **Fax:** 01786-824370
Contact: Dr Abd al-Fattah El-Awaisi
Position: Secretary General
Activities: Resource, newsletters, books, inter-faith
Other Languages: Arabic
The object of the Academy's establishment is to advance Islamic education and research with special reference to the promotion of studies and research into Islamic Jerusalem.

Islamic Research Institute of GB

34 Warren Street, Savile Town, Dewsbury, West Yorkshire, WF12 9LX
Tel: 01924-464523 **Tel:** 01924-464523 (h)
Fax: 01924-464523
Contact: Moulana Yakub Ismail Qasimi
Position: President
Activities: Resource, umbrella, elderly, books
Traditions: Sunni
Movements: Deobandi, Tabilghi Jamaat
Other Languages: Arabic, Urdu, Gutarati
Affiliations: Islamic Fiqh Acedemy, Jeddah; Islamic Fiquh Academy, India; International Islamic Calendar Programme, Malaysia

Islamic Rights Movement

P O Box 139, Leicester, Leicestershire, LE2 2YH
Tel: 0116-706714 **Fax:** 0116-706714
Contact: Mr A Hussain
Position: Chairperson
Activities: Resource, inter-faith
The Islamic Rights Movement takes an interfaith approach to human rights. It believes all religions must unite to exert pressure on governments and raise the social consciousness of the people to safeguard human life, freedom of thought and from torture.

Islamic Sharia Council of UK & Eire

34 Francis Road, London, E10 6PW
Tel: 0181-558-0581 **Fax:** 0181-881-3984
Contact: Dr Suhaib Hasfan
Position: General Secretary
Activities: Charity
Tradition: Sunni

Other Languages: Urdu, Arabic
Semi-legal court, established in 1980 to cater for families in dispute in order to effect reconciliation and, failing this, to dissolve the marriage Islamically. It also deals with issues related to access to minors and inheritance.

Islamic Society of Britain

Markfield Conference Centre, Ratby Lane, Markfield, Leicestershire, LE67 9RN
Tel: 01902-711892 **Tel:** 0468-835184 (h)
Fax: 01902-711892
Email: dilwarslamf.demon.co.uk
Contact: Mr Zahid Parvez
Position: President
Activities: Resource, umbrella, visits, youth, elderly, women, newsletters, books, inter-faith
Other Languages: Urdu, Punjabi, Bengali

Islamic Society for the Promotion of Religious Tolerance in the UK

121 Harley Street, London, W1N 1DH
Tel: 0171-935-3330 Tel: 0171-722-6568
Contact: Dr H El-Essawy
Position: Chairman
Activities: Resource, media, visits, youth, elderly, women, inter-faith
Traditions: Sunni
Languages: Arabic, French, Italian
The Society is dedicated to the promotion of tolerance through promoting of understanding.

Islamic Texts Society

22a Brooklands Avenue, Cambridge, Cambridgeshire, CB2 2DQ
Tel: 01223-314387 **Fax:** 01223-324342
EMail: faazame@its.org.uk
Contact: Miss Fatima Azzam
Position: Secretary of the Trust
Activities: Books
Other Languages: Arabic, Urdu

Islamic Vision Ltd

481 Coventry Road, Birmingham, West Midlands, B10 0JS
Tel: 0121-773-0137 **Fax:** 0121-766-8577
Contact: Shamshad Mohammad Khan
Position: Director
Activities: Resource, books
Publishers, producers of videos and audio titles on Islam and comparative religions. Distributors of books, pre-recorded videos, audio cassettes and CD-ROMS etc.

Ismaili Centre
1 Cromwell Gardens, London, SW7 2SL
Tel: 0171-581-2071
Contact: Mr Shafik Sachedina
Traditions: Ismaili

Jama't Ahl-e-Sunnat UK (Association of Sunni Muslims, UK)
106 Leslie Road, Nottingham, Nottinghamshire, NG7 6PR
Tel: 01602-790956
Contact: Maulana Syed Zahid Hussain
Position: President
Movements: Barelvi
An organisation of imams and Ulama of the Sunni Muslim tradition, representing the Barelvi movement. It mainly acts to liaise between mosques and Sufi organisations within the Barelvi circle and organises national conferences on issues affecting Muslims.

Jambah Islambah
Cattshill, Mark Cross, Crowborough, East Sussex, TN6 3NJ
Tel: 01892-853051
Contact: Ab.Rashid Salloo
Position: Secretary
Activities: Resource, visits, youth
Traditions: Sunni
Other Languages: Urdu, Gujrati, Bengali, Arabic
Affiliations: U.M.O

Jamiat-e-Ulama of Britain
6 Victoria Crescent, Birkdale Road, Dewsbury, West Yorkshire, WF13 4HJ
Tel: 01924-451857
Contact: Maulana Abdul Rashid Rabbani
Position: General Secretary
Movements: Deobandi
Affiliations: Inter Faith Network for the UK
A national organisation of Muslim scholars, with links to the Deobandi movement. It conducts educational activities, provides advice to Muslims on Islamic observance and plays a role in building up relationships with other communities.

Kafel Fund International
6 Oakhurst Grove, East Dulwich, London, SE22 9AQ
Tel: 0181-693-9253 **Tel:** 0370-302-822 (h)
Fax: 0181-299-2308
EMail: Htnbetkf@netcomuk.co.uk
Contact: Hawk Savas

Position: Trustee
Activities: Worship, inter-faith
Traditions: Sunni
Other Languages: Turkish, Urdu, Bengali, Arabic
Affiliations: Indirect Affiliation to Saudi Groups

Khaniqahi-Nimatullahi
41 Chepstow Place, Bayswater, London, W2 4TS
Tel: 0171-229-0769 **Fax:** 0171-229-0769
Contact: Dr Alireza Nurbakhsh
Activities: Worship, newsletters, books
Movements: Sufism
Other Languages: French, Persian, German, Italian

Kokani Muslim World Foundation
28 West Avenue Road, London, E17 9SE
Tel: 0181-521-0907 (h)
Contact: Abdulla Mukadam
Position: Secretary
Activities: Resource, newsletters
Traditions: Sunni
Other Languages: English, Urdu

League of British Muslims UK
Ilford Muslim Community Centre, Eton Road, Ilford, Essex, IG1 2UE
Tel: 0181-514-0706 **Tel:** 0181-599-5125 (h)
Contact: Mr B A Chawdhry
Position: Chairman
Activities: Worship, resource, umbrella, visits, youth, elderly, women, newsletters, inter-faith
Traditions: Sunni
Other Languages: Urdu, Punjabi, Bensali, Gujarati
Affiliations: The Muslim World League; UK Action Committee on Islamic Affairs

Malaysian Islamic Study Group - UK & Eire
90 St Thomas Road, Finsbury Park, London, N4 2WQ
Tel: 0181-345-2318

Markazi Jamiat Ahl-e-Hadith (UK)
20 Green Lane, Small Heath, Birmingham, West Midlands, B9 5DB
Tel: 0121-773-0019 **Fax:** 0121-766-8779
Contact: Shouiab Ahmed Mirpuri
Position: General Secretary
Activities: Worship, resource, visits, youth, elderly, women, newsletters, books, inter-faith
Movements: Ahl-e-Hadith

Other Languages: Urdu, Mirpuri, Punajbi, Arabic
Affiliations: Ittehad-ul-Ulema (UK); Muslim
Unity of Britain; Muslim Council of Britain;
Muslim World League
Over 35 Branches in the UK. Headquarters in this
country of Jamiat Ahl-e-Hadith.

Medina Islamic Mission
35 Martindale Road, Hounslow West, Middlesex,
TW4 7EW
Tel: 0181-577-0647
Contact: Khawaja Mahmood Ahmed
Position: President
Activities: Resource
Traditions: Sunni
Other Languages: Urdu, Arabic, Punjabi

Memon Association UK
3 Weir Road, Balham, London, SW12 8UW
Tel: 0181-743-3233 (h) **Fax:** 0181-743-3233
Contact: Mr A A Yousuf
Position: Honorary General Sec
Works towards the advancement of Islam and the
education of Muslim children in accordance with
the tenets of the Sunni school of thought. It aims to
give financial assistance to members of the Muslim
community, and others, who are poor and needy.

Message of Islam Movement
14 Lea Road, Sparkhill, Birmingham, West
Midlands, B11 3LU
Tel: 0121-771-3680

Minaret House
9 Leslie Park Road, Croydon, Surrey, CR0 6TN
Tel: 0181-681-2972 **Tel:** 0181-654-8801 (h)
Fax: 0181-667-1280
Contact: Riadh El-Droubie
Position: Director
Activities: Resource, media, umbrella, newsletters,
books, inter-faith
Other Languages: Arabic, German

Mountain of Light Productions Limited
PO Box 7404, London, N7 8JQ
Tel: 0171-700-7586 **Fax:** 0171-700-0425
Email: mul@yigroup.demon.co.uk
Contact: Tayyeb Shah
Position: Projects Manager
Activities: Resource
Traditions: Sunni
Other Languages: Urdu, Punjabi, French,
German

Mountain of Light produces Islamic visuals, audio
and books for educational purposes.

Movement for Islamic Resurgence
11 Turpin House, Battersea Park Road, London,
SW11 5HR
Tel: 0171-627-0426 (h)

Muhammadi Trust
17 Beverley Way, West Wimbledon, Surbiton, Surrey,
SW20 0AW
Tel: 0181-336-1018 **Fax:** 0181-336-1017
Email: 10074.1553@compuserve.com**Contact:**
Mr Syed Shabbar
Position: Managing Trustee
Activities: Resource, umbrella, visits, youth, books,
inter-faith
Traditions: Ithna Asheri
Other Languages: Urdu, Arabic, Farsi
Affiliations: Majlis Muhammadi
The parent body of Muhammadi Trust publishes
Islamic books, and translates them from Arabic into
English by University Professors in the UK and
USA.

Muslim Advisory & Community Welfare Council
317 Markhouse Road, Walthamstow, London,
E17 8EE
Tel: 0181-925-9050
Contact: M Salah-Ud-Din
Position: Secretary
Activities: Resource, media, youth, elderly, inter-
faith
Traditions: Sunni
Other Languages: Urdu, Panjabi
The object of this organisation is to promote social
welfare, advise and render charitable services for the
benefit of the Muslim Community and to improve
unity amonst the Muslims and also to promote and
to encourage fellowship through religion.

Muslim Aid
PO Box 3, London, N7 8LR
Tel: 0171-609-4425 **Fax:** 0171-609-4943
Email: mail@muslim aid.org.uk
Contact: Mr Mahmood Hassan
Position: Director
Activities: Newsletters
Other Languages: Urdu, Punjabi, Arabic, French
Muslim Aid is a charitable relief and development
agency which works to alleviate the poverty and
suffering amongst some of the world's poorest
communities.

Muslim Association of Nigeria (UK)
365 Old Kent Road, London, SE1 5JH
Tel: 0171-231-0100 **Tel:** 0171-249-9256 (h)
Contact: Alhaji Tajudeen A Salami
Position: Chief Imam
Activities: Worship
Traditions: Sunni
Other Languages: Yoruba, Hausa, Arabic
Affiliations: Nigerian Muslims Organisations; Union of Muslim Organisations (UK); Muslim World League; Saudi Arabia World Assembly of Muslim Youth

Muslim College
20-22 Creffield Road, London, W5 3RP
Tel: 0181-992-6636 **Fax:** 0181-993-3946
Contact: Dr M A Zaki Badawi
Position: Principal
Activities: Resource, visits, women
Other Languages: Arabic
The College offers: a 3 year post-graduate Diploma course in Islamic Studies for the training of those who wish to work as an imam in the West; courses in modern Arabic; short training courses in Islam and Muslim culture for other faith communities.

Muslim Community Studies Institute
P O Box 139, Leicester, Leicestershire, LE2 2YH
Tel: 0116-706714 **Fax:** 0116-706714
Contact: Asaf Hussain
Activities: Resource, youth, women, books, inter-faith
A research and consultancy organisation which also publishes; mobilises Muslim youth and women for active participation in community affairs; and raises the consciousness of Muslims by educating them in Islamic Human Rights.

Muslim Education Consultative Committee
93 Court Road, Balsall Heath, Birmingham, West Midlands, B12 9LQ
Tel: 0121-440-3500 **Tel:** 0121-440-8218
Fax: 0121-440-8144
Contact: Dr S Qureshi
Position: Treasurer
Activities: Resource, women
Languages: Arabic, Punjabi, Urdu, Mirpuri

Muslim Education Forum
93 Court Road, Birmingham, West Midlands, B12 9LQ
Tel: 0121-440-3500 **Tel:** 0121-440-8218

Fax: 0121-440-8144
Contact: Akram Khan Cheema

Muslim Educational Co-ordinating Council (UK)
7 Paul Gardens, East Croydon, Surrey, CR0 5QL
Tel: 0181-681-6087
Contact: Mr Nazar-e Mustafa
Position: Chair
Activities: Resource
Other Languages: Arabic, Bengali, Urdu
Affiliations: The Islamic Cultural Centre; Muslim College
Helps refugees to go through exams in various fields; helps students to re-sit exams to improve grades; helps students in research work; asks examination boards to use a roll number and centre number rather than names on examination papers.

Muslim Educational Trust
130 Stroud Green Road, London, N4 3RZ
Tel: 0171-272-8502 **Fax:** 0171-281-3457
Contact: Mr Ghulam Sarwar
Position: Director
Activities: Resource, books
Traditions: Sunni
Other Languages: Urdu, Bengali, Punjabi
The Muslim Educational Trust advises on the educational needs of British Muslim children, and on educational issues in general.

Muslim Food Board
37 Hazlewood Road, Leicester, Leicestershire, LE5 5HR
Tel: 9116-273-8228 **Fax:** 0116-273-8228
Contact: Mr Yusuf Aboobakar
Position: Secretary
Activities: Resource, newsletters
Other Languages: Urdu
Provide consultancy on the preparation of food products according to the dietary laws of Islam; research into available food products; authentication and issue of Halal certification for food products; and information on food products suitable for Muslims.

Muslim Hands
205 Radford Road, Hyson Green, Nottingham, Nottinghamshire, NG7 5GT
Tel: 0115-970-4490 **Tel:** 070 500 786 92
Fax: 0115-979-2183
EMail: amjad.shah@dial.pipex.com
Contact: Ajad Shah
Position: Office Manager

Activities: Inter-faith
Other Languages: Urdu, Punjabi, Arabic
Traditions: Sunni
A UK-based charity with the aim of providing for those in need around the world by monetary and used clothes collections from around the country. Assistance is offered in monetary contributions, medical, food or clothing supplies and in long-term schemes.

Muslim Information Centre: Showroom and Muslim Bookshop
233 Seven Sisters Road, London, N4 2DA
Tel: 0171-272-5170 **Fax:** 0171-272-3214
Contact: Mohammed Tameem
Position: Manager
Activities: Books
Traditions: Sunni
Other Languages: Arabic, Urdu, Somali

Muslim Information Service
233 Seven Sisters Road, London, Greater London, N4 2DA
Tel: 0171-272-5170 **Fax:** 0171-272-3214
Contact: Mohammed Tamime
Position: Managing Director
Activities: Resource, books, inter-faith
Traditions: Sunni
Other Languages: Arabic
Affiliations: Muslim Solidarity Committee; UK Action Committee on Islamic Affairs

Muslim Institute for Research & Planning
109 Fulham Palace Road, London, W6 8JA
Tel: 0181-563-1995 **Fax:** 0181-563-1993
Email: 106313.3711@compuserve.com
Contact: Dr Maqsood Ali Siddiqi
Position: Administrator
Activities: Resource, media, youth, elderly, women, newsletters, books
Traditions: Sunni
Other Languages: Urdu, Punjabi, Arabic, Farsi
Affiliations: The Muslim Parliament; The Muslim Institute Trust
Undertakes research on Islam; organises seminars and conferences, lectures, Arabic language courses; study of the life of the Prophet; issues in the Islamic movement.

Muslim Ladies Hostel (FOSIS)
Staverton Lodge, 122 Brondesbury Park, Willesden Green, London, NW2 5JR (h)
Tel: 0181-459-0834

Email: ladies hostel.@fosis.demon.co.uk
Contact: Miss A Jaweed
Position: General Secretary
Activities: Resource, youth, newsletters, books
Other Languages: Urdu, Arabic
Student services provided.

Muslim Law (Shariah) Council
20-22 Creffield Road, London, W5 3RP
Tel: 0181-992-6636 **Fax:** 0181-993-3946
Contact: Moulana Mohammad Shahid Raza
Position: Executive Secretary
Other Languages: Urdu, Arabic
Operates an information desk on Islam; provides services to the Muslims concerned with questions of marriage, divorce, inheritance etc; gives Islamic legal opinion on questions put to it; offers expert information on Islamic law to non-Muslims.

Muslim Parliament of Great Britain
109 Fulham Palace Road, London, W6 8JA
Tel: 0181-563-1995 **Tel:** 081-561-1994
Fax: 0181-563-1993
Contact: Dr Muhammad Ghayasuddin Siddiqui
Position: Leader
Activities: Media, youth, women, newsletters
Other Languages: Urdu/Punjabi, French, Farsi, Arabic
Affiliations: Bait Al-Mal Al-Islami; Halal Food Authority; Halal Food Consumers Association; Human Rights Committee

Muslim Scholars Movement of Europe
40 Albion Road, Wellgate, Rotherham, South Yorkshire, S60 2NF
Tel: 01709-560038
Contact: Abdul Kabir
Activities: Worship, resource, media, umbrella, visits, youth, elderly, women, newsletters, inter-faith
Other Languages: English, Urdu, Punjabi, Arabic

Muslim Teachers Association
146 Park Road, London, NW8 7RG
Tel: 0171-724-3363 **Fax:** 0181-933-1618
Contact: Mr S Syed
Position: General Secretary
Activities: Resource, youth, inter-faith
Traditions: Sunni
Other Languages: Urdu

Muslim Ummah Solidarity Movement
64 Somerville Road, Small Heath, Birmingham, West Midlands, B10 9EL

Tel: 0121-328-8466 **Tel:** 0121-328-8466 (h)
Contact: Malik Fazal Hussain
Position: General Secretary
Activities: Media, umbrella, books, inter-faith
Traditions: Sunni
Other Languages: Urdu, Arabic
Affiliations: Urdu forum (UK) Birmingham;
Jamiate Nizame Islam; Pakistan Community Centre;
Pakistan Workers Association

Muslim Welfare House

233 Seven Sisters Road, Finsbury Park, London,
N4 2DA
Tel: 0171-263-3071 **Fax:** 0171-281-2680
Contact: Y Ballali
Position: Director
Activities: Worship, resource, media, umbrella,
visits, youth, women, books, inter-faith
Traditions: Sunni
Movements: Ahl-e-Hadith
Other Languages: Arabic

Muslim Women's Helpline

Unit 3, GEC Estate, East Lane, Wembley, Middlesex,
HA9 7PX
Tel: 0181-908-3205 **Fax:** 0181-291-2005
Activities: Women
Contact: Miss Sarah Sheriff
Position: Secretary
Activities: Newsletter
Other Languages: Urdu, Punjabi, Arabic
An independent organisation that provides a
confidential counselling service. Our methods are
founded upon the Islamic model of the self and based
on the teachings of the Qu'ran and the propetic
traditions.

Muslim World League

46 Goodge Street, London, W1P 1FJ
Tel: 0171-636-7568 **Tel:** 0181-220-8700 (h)
Fax: 0171-637-5034
Contact: Mr Ghulamur Rahman
Position: Deputy Director
Activities: Worship, resource, visits, newsletters
Traditions: Sunni
Movements: Ahl-e-Hadith
Other Languages: Arabic, Urdu, Bengali, Hindi
Affiliations: Muslim World League, Makkah, Saudi
Arabia

Naqshbandi Haqqani Trust

St. Mary's Priory, 277 St Anne's Road, Tottenham,
London, N15 5RG

Tel: 0181-771-7330 **Fax:** 0181-771-4704
Contact: Shahid Khan
Position: Member, managment
Activities: Worship, visits, youth, women, books,
inter-faith
Traditions: Sunni
Movements: Tassawuf
Other Languages: Turkish, Urdu, Arabic
Affiliations: Naqshbandi Sufi Order
The name Naqshbandi means "he who works to
make a design" ie, the person who imprints the name
of God on his or her heart. We encourage
participation of young people and women and
welcome people who are not of the Muslim faith for
discussions.

National Muslim Education Council of UK

109 Campden Hill Road, London, W8 7TL
Tel: 0171-221-6608 **Fax:** 0171-792-2130
Contact: Dr S A Pasha
Position: Secretary
Activities: Resource, youth, books
Other Languages: Urdu, Arabic, Bengali, Gujarati
Affiliations: Union of Muslim Organisations of
UK and Eire; Organisation of Islamic Conference
As an organ of the Union of Muslim Organisations,
the National Muslim Education Council of the UK
has the status of being the representative body for the
educational needs of the Muslim community.

Organisation of British Muslims

7 Penner Close, Wimbledon, London, SW19 6QA
Tel: 0181-944-5859 (h) **Fax:** 0181-944-5697
Contact: Abdul Latif Bahalim
Position: National Secretary
Activities: Resource, umbrella
Traditions: Sunni, Ismaili/Ithna Asheri/ Shi'a
Other Languages: Urdu, Punjabi, Arabic, Persian
Affiliations: Organisation of European Muslims;
Organisation of World Muslims
OBM seeks proper representation of the largest
minority of the British Muslims in the British and
European Parliaments. The British and European
Muslims can contribute towards better understanding
and better relations between UK/EU and 52 Muslim
Countries.

Popda Muslim Welfare Association

40 Milton Street, Walsall, West Midlands (h)
Contact: Ali Adam Mohammed
Position: Secretary
Activities: Resource

Traditions: Sunni
Movements: Deobandi
Other Languages: Gujarati

Qur'anic Society
26 Newill Close, West Bowling, Bradford, West
Yorkshire, BD5 8QY
Contact: Saifullah Taj (ESQ)
Position: Secretary
Activities: Youth
Traditions: Sunni
The objective of the organisation is to promote a
better understanding/practice of the Qur'anic
message. "Do, they not ponder the Qur'an or are
there locks on their hearts?" Qur'an(47:24)

Raza Academy
138 Nothgate Road, Edgeley, Stockport, Cheshire,
SK3 9NL (h)
Tel: 0161-477-1595 **Tel:** 0161-291-1390
Contact: M I Kashmiri
Activities: Resource, newsletters, books
Traditions: Sunni
Movements: Barelwi, Tassawuf
Other Languages: Urdu, Punjabi
Affiliations: Jamiat Tabligh ul Islam, Bradford;
World Islamic Mission

S I Education Society
133 Rowan Road, London, SW16 5HU
Tel: 0181-241-0222 **Fax:** 0181-241-2214
Contact: Moulana Syed Shamim-us Sibtan Rizvi
Position: Managing Trustee
Activities: Worship, resource, media, visits, youth,
elderly, women, books
Traditions: Muslim Shi'a, 'Ithna Asheri
Other Languages: Urdu, Gujarati, Punjabi
Has an Islamic bookshop; Islamic library; weekly
religious gathering; marriage bureau; monthly
magazines "The Minister" (English). "Al-Moballigh"
(Urdu) and audio magazine "The Voice" (English);
recorded religious messages (English) (0181-241-
2212) and for religious guidance (0956-129188).

Seerah Foundation
78 Gillespie Road, London, N5 1LN
Tel: 0171-359-8257
Contact: Yasmin Hassan
Position: Secretary
Activities: Books
Traditions: Sunni
Other Languages: Urdu

Shariat Council & Darul IFTA & Europe
98 Ferham Road, Rotherham, South Yorkshire,
S61 1AW (h)
Tel: 01709-563677 **Fax:** 01709-563677
Contact: Mohammed Aslam
Activities: Resource, inter-faith
Movements: Deobandi
Other Languages: Urdu, Arabic, Punjabi, Pashto

Somali Islamic Circle Organisation
16 Settles Street, London, E1
Tel: 0171-471-0394 (h)

South Indian Muslim Association (UK)
123 Burgess Road, East Ham, London, E6 2BL
Tel: 0181-952-2105 (h) **Fax:** 0181-962-2105
Contact: Mr A K Salim

Sri Lanka Islamic Association/Sri Lanka Islamic Cultural Home (UK)
7 Broadway Buildings, Boston Road, Hanwell,
London, W7 3TT
Tel: 0181-840-3270 **Tel:** 0181-952-2105 (h)
Fax: 0181-952-2105
Contact: A.Azahim Mohamed
Position: Chairman
Activities: Resource, visits, youth, women,
newsletters, inter-faith
Traditions: Sunni (Sunath Jamath)
Other Languages: Sinhalese, Arabic, Tamil
Affiliations: Union of Muslim Organisations UK
& Eire; Muslim Communities Development
Project; Muslim World League
The organisation has children's Quran classes at the
weekends and classes for adults on Saturdays. It holds
youth activities on Fridays and plays cricket during
the Summer months. It also celebrates the Muslim
festival of Eid and has a library service.

Sri Lanka Islamic UK Association
62 Rose Glen, Colindale, Kingsbury, London,
NW9 LJS
Tel: 0181-952-2105 (h) **Fax:** 0181-962-2105
Contact: A Azahim Mohamed
Position: General Secretary
The organisation was formed in 1973 to get Sri
Lankan Muslims together. Today its membership
covers over five hundred families and it is the only
representative body for Sri Lankan Muslims in the
UK.

Sri Lanka Muslim Refugee Assistance (UK)
60 Cumberland Road, Harwell, London, W7 2EB
Tel: 0181-840-5819   **Fax:** 0181-959-5180
Contact: Mr Nuski Mohammed
Position: President
Activities: Charity
Other Languages: Tamil

Sufi Movement UK
Arama, Hawthorn Road, Highfield, Southampton,
Hampshire, SO17 1PX (h)
Tel: 01703-558357 (h)
Contact: Virya Best
Position: Murshida
Activities: Resource, newsletters, inter-faith
Affiliations: Sufi Movement, The Hague, Holland
The Sufi Movement was established by Hazrat Inayat
Khan (1882-1927).

Ta Ha Publishers Ltd
1 Wynne Road, London, SW9 0BB
Tel: 0171-737-7266   **Fax:** 0171-737-7267
Contact: Afsar Siddiqui
Position: Director
Activities: Books
Traditions: Sunni
Other Languages: Urdu, Arabic
Affiliations: Islamic Publishers Association
We have published over 175 titles for both adults and
children. Our publications are of high quality but at
very low prices. Catalogue and price list can be
obtained on request.

Ujala Trust
Badar Nazish, 63 Windermere Avenue, Wembley,
Middlesex, HA9 8QU (h)
Tel: 0181-904-1489 (h)
Contact: Mrs Badar Nazish
Position: Chairperson
Activities: Resource, youth, women
Traditions: Sunni
Other Languages: Urdu

UK Action Committee on Islamic Affairs
146 Park Road, London, NW8 7RG
Tel: 0181-974-2780   **Fax:** 0181-974-2781
Contact: Iqbal Sacranie
Position: Joint Convenor
Activities: Umbrella, inter-faith
Other Languages: Urdu, Arabic, Bengali, Gujurati
Affiliations: Inter Faith Network for the UK
UKACIA was formed in October 1988. It is an
umbrella body representing Muslim organisations
and mosques throughout the country. Activities have
particularly been on issues relating to the community
and law in Britain, especially religious discrimination.

UK Islamic Education Waqf (UKIEW)
2 Digswell Street, London, N7 8JX
Tel: 0171-607-8839   **Fax:** 0171-700-0320
Contact: Zafar Shahid
Position: Executive Secretary
Activities: Resource
Traditions: Sunni
Other Languages: Urdu, Punjabi, Arabic
The UKIEW is committed to raise funds for Muslim
Independent Schools in the UK. UKIEW is the only
recognised Trust fund established to finance Muslim
schools, full and part-time.

UK Islamic Mission
202 North Gower Street, London, NW1 2LY
Tel: 0171-387-2157   **Fax:** 0171-383-0867
Contact: Maulana Syed Sherif Ahmed
Position: President
Activities: Umbrella, inter-faith
A charitable organisation which aims to help the
Muslim community in the UK to project its cultural
identity and to promote and encourage mutual
appreciation and friendly relations between Muslims
and non-Muslims, as well as unity among Muslims.

Union of Muslim Families (UK)
46 Goodge Street, London, W1P 1FJ
Tel: 0171-637-1971
Contact: Mr Naz Usmani
Position: Assistant Secretary
Activities: Resource, media, umbrella, visits, youth,
elderly
Traditions: Sunni

**Union of Muslim Organisations of UK & Eire
(UMO)**
109 Camden Hill Road, London, W8 7TL
Tel: 0171-221-6608   **Fax:** 0171-792-2130
Contact: Dr Sayid Aziz Pasha
Position: General Secretary
Activities: Umbrella, youth, inter-faith
Other Languages: Urdu, Arabic, Bengali, Gujerati
Affiliations: World Muslim League
The Union of Muslim Organisations is the
democratically-elected national representative body
of British Muslims.

WAQF Al-Birr Educational Trust
2 Digswell Street, London, N7 8JX
Tel: 0171-700-7565 **Fax:** 0171-700-0425
Contact: Raheez Daud
Position: Head of Finance
Activities: Resource
Other Languages: Urdu, Arabic

World Ahl Ul-Bayt (AS) Islamic League (UK)
17a Phillimore Gardens, London, NW10 3LL
Tel: 0181-459-8475 **Tel:** 0181-459-6051 (h)
Fax: 0181-451-7059
EMail: S.M.Musawi.wabil@wabil.demon.co.uk
Contact: His Holiness Sayyed Mohammed Musawi
Position: Secretary General
Activities: Resource, umbrella, youth, women, newsletter, books, inter-faith
Other Languages: Arabic, Persian
Worldwide organisation with afilliates of *Shi'a* oranisations and carrying out welfare activities for the upliftment of the poor, financially, educattionally and morally
Traditions: Sh'a 'Ithna Asheri
Open to Shi'a personalities well-known for their interest and endeavour in Islamic affairs. It aims to co-ordinate activities of Shi'a organisations throughout the world and to create better understanding between Shi'as and other Muslims and non-Muslims.

World Assembly of Muslim Youth (WAMY) Western Europe Office
46 Goodge Street, London, W1P 1FJ
Tel: 0171-636-7010 **Fax:** 0171-636-7080
Contact: Mr Hussain Al Mehdar
Position: Officer-in-Charge
Activities: Resource, umbrella, visits, youth, elderly, women, newsletters, books, inter-faith
Traditions: Sunni
Other Languages: Arabic
Affiliations: Muslim Council of Britain; World Assembly of Muslim Youth Headquarters, Riyadh, Saudi Arabia
WAMY is an independent, international Islamic working to improve the Islamic awareness among Muslim youth and introducing Islam to people of other faiths. Founded in 1972 in Riyadh, Saudi Arabia.

World Federation of Khoja Shia Ithna-Asheri Muslim Communities
Islamic Centre, Wood Lane, Stanmore, Middlesex, HA7 4LQ
Tel: 0181-954-9881 **Fax:** 0181-954-9034
Email: worldfed@dircon.co.uk
Internet: http://www.dircon/ worldfed.
Contact: Muhsin Dharansi
Position: Office Manager
Activities: Worship, resource, umbrella, visits, books, inter-faith
Traditions: Shi'aI 'Ithna Asheri
Other Languages: Gujarati

World Islamic Mission (UK)
4th Floor, 53-56 Great Sutton Street, London, EC1V 0DF, Tel: 0171-608-3799
Tel: 0171-608-3799 **Fax:** 0171-608-3792
Contact: Mr S G Syedaiu
Position: Senior Vice Presiden
Activities: Youth, women, books, inter-faith
Traditions: Sunni
Other Languages: Urdu, Arabic
Affiliations: Imams and Mosques Council UK; World Islamic Mission International; Inter Faith Network for the UK

World Islamic Propagation Establishment (UK)
409 Northolt Road, South Harrow, Middlesex, HA2 8JQ
Tel: 0181-422-3916 **Fax:** 0181-426-8999
EMail: wipecrc@home.virtual.pc.com
Contact: Mr Shahid Akmal
Position: Chair
Activities: Resource, youth, inter-faith
Traditions: Sunni
Other Languages: Urdu, Punjabi, Gujarati, Swahili
We specialise in comparative religions, especially Christianity and Islam. We are the official London distributors of literature, video and audio products by Sheikh Ahmed Deedat (S.Africa), Dr Khalid Al-Mansour (USA) and Dr. Zakir Naik (India)

World Muslim Commission (World MC)
36 Rivermead Road, Rose Hill, Oxford, Oxfordshire, OX4 4UE
Tel: 01865-747660 **Tel:** 01865-747660 (h)
Fax: 01865-747660
Contact: Lt.Ustad Shah Ali Ahmed
Position: Director General
Traditions: Sunni

Movements: Deobandi, Tablighi Jamaat
Other Languages: Arabic, Bangladeshi
Affiliations: Bangladesh Muslim-Sunni
Commission; Islamic Volunteers Organisation;
Tablighi Jamaat; Green Empire of the World MC
The World MC is the new world empire to enforce
submission to the rule of 'Command of I.Law' as our
basic aim is to return the strict application of the
'Command of I.Law' to every aspect of life, under
the 'green seal' of World MC.

World of Islam Festival Trust
33 Thurloe Place, London, SW13 9QZ
Tel: 0171-581-3522 **Fax:** 0171-584-1977
Contact: Alistair Duncan
Position: Director
Activities: Resource, books, inter-faith
The Trust helps towards understanding and
apppreciating the contribution of Islamic culture and
civilisation to the Family Of Nations.

Young Muslim Organisation UK - Central Office
54 Fieldgate Street, London, E1 1ES
Tel: 0171-247-7918 **Fax:** 0171-375-3844
Email: YMO-UK.demon.co.uk
Contact: Abdullah Folik
Position: Central President
Activities: Resource, visits, youth, newsletters,
inter-faith
Traditions: Sunni
Other Languages: English, Bengali, Arabic
Affiliations: East London Mosque; Islamic Forum
Europe; UK Action Committee on Islamic Affairs
YMO UK caters mainly for the young in providing
for their moral, spiritual and recreational needs. The
organisation also plays a significant role in the
community in tackling issues such as drugs, racism
and violence.

Youth Adventure & Training
P O Box 70, Gloucester, Gloucestershire, GL1 4AH
Tel: 0468-296410 **Tel:** 0468-296410 (h)
Contact: Mohammed Dhalech
Position: Co-ordinator
Activities: Resource, media, umbrella, youth,
women, inter-faith
Traditions: Sunni
Other Languages: Urdu, Turkish, Arabic, French
The organisation empowers Muslims in the UK and
Europe through the use of information technology,
media and adventure. It runs training courses,
activities and outdoor education courses for
Muslims. It facilitates youth exchanges and
development training.

Zahra Trust UK
PO Box 1021, London, W2 4JQ
Contact: Mrs Aliya Haeri
Position: Representative
Activities: Resource, books
Movements: Tassawuf
Other Languages: Arabic, Urdu

MUSLIM REGIONAL AND LOCAL ORGANISATIONS AND MOSQUES

A variety of forms of Muslim local organisation are listed in this directory. These include *mosques*, schools, welfare bodies and student societies. In some cases there are separate entries at the same address where a welfare association owns a *mosque* but receives a separate entry because its objectives and activities are wider than the *mosque* activities alone, or where a number of organisations with a particular sectional remit, such as women's or youth work, are based at the same address and are sometimes different parts of the same organisation.

ENGLAND

NORTH EAST
City, Town or Local Bodies

Mosque
4 Moyorswall Close, Durham City, County Durham
Tel: 01386-7972

Mosque
25-26 North Lodge Terrace, Darlington, Durham City, County Durham

Muslim Welfare Association Hartlepool
94 Milton Road, Hartlepool, County Durham, TS26 8DS
Contact: Mr Karem Elahi

Heaton Mosque
1 Rothbury Terrace, Heaton, Newcastle upon Tyne, Tyne and Wear, NE6 5XH
Tel: 0191-265-4083
Contact: Secretary

Islamic Society
King George VI Building, University of Newcastle upon Tyne, Kings Walk off Thomas Street, Newcastle upon Tyne, Tyne and Wear, NE1 7RU
Tel: 0191-232-6889 **Tel:** 0191-232-3055 (h)
Email: irwanprasetyo@newcastle.ac.uk
Contact: Irwan Prasetyo
Position: Secretary
Activities: Worship, resource, visits, youth, women
Other Languages: Arabic, Malay, Turkish
Affiliations: Muslim Welfare House; Federation of Students Islamic Society

Muslim Cultural Promotional
c/o 4 Abbots Way, Westlands, Newcastle upon Tyne, Tyne and Wear

Muslim Welfare House
6 North Terrace, Spital Tongues, Newcastle upon Tyne, Tyne and Wear, NE2 4AD
Tel: 0191-232-3055
Contact: Mahmoud El-Kurdi
Position: Secretary
Activities: Worship
Traditions: Sunni
Other Languages: Arabic, Bengali, Urdu
Affiliations: Muslim Welfare House, London

Muslim Womens Association of Newcastle
20 Cavendish Place, Newcastle upon Tyne, Tyne
and Wear
Contact: Mrs Christine Ahmed

Newcastle Mosque & Islamic Centre
Malvern Street, off Elswick Road, Newcastle upon
Tyne, Tyne and Wear, NE4 6SU
Tel: 0191-226-0562
Contact: Zafar Jung Khan
Position: President
Activities: Worship, resource, youth, inter-faith
Traditions: Sunni
Movements: Barelwi
Other Languages: Punjabi, Urdu

Pakistan Muslim Association
Malvern Street, Newcastle upon Tyne, Tyne and
Wear, NE4 6SU
Tel: 0191-226-0562
Contact: Mr Z J Khan
Position: Chairperson

UWAIS Foundation
113/115 Fenham Hall Drive, Fenham, Newcastle
Upon Tyne, Tyne and Wear, NE4 9XB
Tel: 0191-274-7540 **Tel:** 0191-273-1608 (h)
Contact: Mr Mohammed Mushtaq Ahmed
Position: Chair/Trustee
Activities: Resource, youth, women
Other Languages: Urdu, Punjabi, Arabic

Alazhar Mosque
Laygate Lane, South Shields, Tyne and Wear
Tel: 0191-545-0738

**South Tyneside Bangladesh Muslim Cultural
Association & Mosque**
3-5 Baring Street, off Ocean Road, South Shields,
Tyne and Wear
Tel: 0191-454-2501 (h)
Contact: Syed F Hussain
Position: Chairperson

Jamiat e Jundullah
39 Hartington Road, Stockton-on-Tees, County
Durham, TS18 1HD
Tel: 01642-679943
Contact: Mr M Hussain
Position: Secretary

Mosque
9 Kenley Gardens, Stockton-on-Tees, County
Durham, TS20 1QF

Stockton Mosque
10 Shaftsbury Street, Stockton-on-Tees, County
Durham
Contact: Mr M Iqbal

Thornaby Muslim Association
69 Oxford Road, Stockton-on-Tees, County
Durham
Contact: Mr H Farooq

Sunderland Mosque
73-77 Chester Road, Sunderland, Tyne and Wear
Tel: 0191-565-8708
Contact: Imam Syed Imamudih

Thornaby Muslim Association
127/129 Westbury street, Thornaby-on-Tees,
County Durham, TS17 6NF
Contact: Mohammed Anwar
Position: Secretary
Activities: Worship, resource
Traditions: Sunni
Other Languages: Punjab, Urdu

Mosque
11 East Parade, Whitley Bay, Tyne and Wear

YORKSHIRE
City, Town or Local Bodies

Mosque
22 Roberts Road, Balby, South Yorkshire

Anjuman-Zinatul Islam
78 Taylor Street, Batley, West Yorkshire, WF17 5BA
Tel: 01924-472216

Anwar-ul-Islam
90 Dark Lane, Clark Green, Batley, West Yorkshire

Bridge Street Madressah
1a Bridge Street, Batley, West Yorkshire, WF17 5NU
Contact: Mr E Bham

Dabhel-Simlak Muslim Welfare Society
20 Purlwell Crescent, Batley, West Yorkshire,
WF1 7PA

Indian Muslim Welfare Society
28 Trunk Road, Batley, West Yorkshire, WF17 5BA
Tel: 01924-500555 **Fax:** 01924-500556
Contact: Masa Kazi
Position: Administration Officer

Islamic Cultural & Welfare Association
Henry Street, Batley Carr, Batley, West Yorkshire,
WF17 6JT
Tel: 01924-463275 **Tel:** 01924-453531 (h)
Fax: 01924-463275
Contact: Ismail Ebrahim Dajz
Position: President
Activities: Worship, resource, visits, youth, elderly,
women
Traditions: Sunni
Movements: Deobandi, Tablighi Jamaat
Other Languages: Gujarati, Urdu
Affiliations: Indian Muslim Welfare Society

Jama Masjid Mosque
1 Whitaker Street, Batley, West Yorkshire
Tel: 01924-472215

Jummah Masjid
2-4 West Street, Batley, West Yorkshire

Masjid & Madrassa Noor ul Islam
Snowden Street, Batley, West Yorkshire, WF17 7RS
Contact: Secretary/Chairman
Activities: Worship, resource, visits, youth, elderly
Traditions: Sunni
Movements: Tablighi Jamaat
Other Languages: Gujarati, Urdu, Arabic, Punjabi

Masjid Anwar Islam
90 Dark Lane, Batley, West Yorkshire

Masjid-e-Zinatul Islam
Taylor Street, Batley, West Yorkshire

Mosque
206 Bradford Road, Batley Carr, Batley, West
Yorkshire

Mount Pleasant Islamic Trust
Purlwell Lane, Batley, West Yorkshire, WF17 7NQ
Tel: 01924-472378 **Tel:** 01924-520568 (h)
Fax: 01924-420786
Contact: Ismail Y Lunat
Position: Secretary
Activities: Worship, resource, visits, youth, elderly,
women, books, inter-faith

Traditions: Sunni
Movements: Deobandi
Other Languages: Gujarati, Urdu, Arabic
Affiliations: Indian Muslim Welfare Society;
Union of Muslim Organisations; Central
Moonsighting Committee of GB; World Muslim
League

Muslim Burial Committee
29 Purlwell Hall Road, Batley, West Yorkshire,
WF17

Muslim Community Council
26 Cedar Grove, Batley, West Yorkshire, WF17 6BQ

Muslim Elderly & Disabled Organisation
18 Woodsome Estate, Batley, West Yorkshire,
WF17 7EB
Tel: 01924-503640
Contact: Ahmed Patel
Position: Chair
Activities: Visits, youth, elderly, women
Traditions: Sunni
Other Languages: Gujarati, Urdu

Muslim Funeral Society
112 Halifax Old Road, Fartown, Huddersfield, West
Yorkshire, HD2 2RW
Tel: 01484-309850 (h)
Contact: Mr Habib Ullah
Position: Treasurer
Traditions: Sunni
Languages: Urdu

Muslim Girls' High School
111 Warwick Road, Batley, West Yorkshire,
WF17 6AJ

North Kirklees Muslim Womens Group & Asian Womens Association
c/o Warwick Road School, Batley, West Yorkshire

Pakistan Funeral Society
19 Lower North Street, Mount Pleasant, Batley,
West Yorkshire, WF17 7PH

Pakistan Muslim Welfare Association
1 Whitaker Street, Batley, West Yorkshire

Soothill Muslim Society
14 Lady Ann Road, Soothill, Batley, West Yorkshire,
WE17 6PG

Soothill Muslim Welfare Society
4/6 West Street, Soothill, Batley, West Yorkshire,
WF17 5ST

Abu Bakar Mosque
479 Leeds Road, Bradford, West Yorkshire,
BD3 9LD
Tel: 01274-668643 **Tel:** 01274-667804 (h)
Contact: Amanullah Khan
Position: President
Activities: Worship
Traditions: Sunni
Movements: Deobandi
Other Languages: Urdu, Pashto, Punjabi
Affiliations: Council of Mosques Bradford

Al-Falah Islamic Youth Mission
Al-Falah Building, Richmond Road, Bradford, West
Yorkshire, BD7 1DR
Tel: 01274-724998 **Fax:** 01274-742736
Contact: Mohammed Iqbal
Position: Manager

Anjuman-e-Haideria
47/48 Southfield Square, Bradford, West Yorkshire,
BD8 7SL
Tel: 0973-749898
Contact: Syed Shamsher Kazmi
Position: General Secretary
Activities: Worship, resource, youth, women, inter-faith
Traditions: 'Ithna Asheri
Other Languages: Punjabi, Urdu
Affiliations: Council of Mosques

Azad Kashmir Muslim Association
11 Farcliffe Place, Bradford, West Yorkshire,
BD8 8QD (h)
Tel: 01274-498677 (h)
Contact: Mohammed Amin Qureshi
Position: Chairman
Activities: Resource, umbrella, visits, youth, elderly,
inter-faith
Traditions: Sunni
Other Languages: Urdu, Punjabi, Persian

Bait ul Aman Jamia Mosque & Madrassah
6 Maudsley Street, Bradford, West Yorkshire,
BD3 9JT

Blenheim Mosque
Bundria Court, off: Church Street, Bradford, West
Yorkshire, BD8 7PD

Bradford Council of Mosques
6 Claremont, Bradford, West Yorkshire, BD7 1BG
Tel: 01274-732479
Contact: Sher Azam
Position: President

Bradford Eid Committee
5 Hallfield Road, Bradford, West Yorkshire,
BD1 3RP
Tel: 01274-308291 **Fax:** 01274-305865
Contact: Mohammad Abbas
Position: Treasurer
Activities: Resource, inter-faith
Traditions: Sunni
Other Languages: Urdu, Punjabi

Bradford Khalifa Muslim Society
32 Bertram Road, Bradford, West Yorkshire,
BD8 7LN
Contact: Abdul Hamid Ismail
Position: Chairperson

Bradford Muslim Sunnatwal Society
8 Fairfield Road, Toller Lane, Bradford, West
Yorkshire, BD8 8QQ

Bradford Muslim Welfare Association
58-62 St Margret's Road, Bradford, West Yorkshire,
BD7 3AE

Council for Mosques, Elderly Centre
378-380 Great Horton Road, Bradford, West
Yorkshire, BD7 3HS
Tel: 01274-521792
Contact: Mohammed Saleem Khan
Position: Centre Co-ordinator
Activities: Elderly, women
Other Languages: English, Urdu, Punjabi, Pashto

Dar-al-Argam
16 Neal Street, Bradford, West Yorkshire, BD7

Dawatul Islam
14 Nesfield Street, Bradford, West Yorkshire,
BD3 0AN

East African Muslim Association (Bradford)
17 Daleside Walk, Bradford, West Yorkshire,
BD5 8PP
Tel: 01274-400206
Contact: Mr K A Hafeez
Position: Secretary
Activities: Charity

Traditions: Sunni
Other Languages: Urdu, Punjabi, Kiswahili, Gujrati

Feversham College
Feversham Street, Off Leeds Road, Bradford, West Yorkshire, BD3 9QL
Tel: 01274-743428 **Fax:** 01274-729890
Contact: Mohammed Ibrahim
Position: Chairperson
Activities: Resource, visits, inter-faith
Traditions: Sunni
Other Languages: Urdu, Punjabi, Pushto/Bengali, Arabic
Affiliations: Muslim Association of Bradford; Muslim Education Forum; Muslim Teachers Association

Frinzhall Islamic Association
167 Bradford Road, Shipley, Bradford, West Yorkshire, BD18 3TP

Ghosia Community Association
39 Haslingden Drive, Bradford, West Yorkshire, BD9 5HT
Tel: 01274-480706 **Tel:** 01274-480706 (h)
Contact: Mr Mohammed Bashir
Position: Chairman
Activities: Inter-faith
Traditions: Sunni
Movements: Barelwi
Other Languages: Punjabi, Urdu, English

Girlington Islamic Trust
350 Girlington Road, Bradford, West Yorkshire, BD8 9PA

Girlington Muslim Welfare Association
182a Durham Road, Girlington, Bradford, West Yorkshire, BD8
Tel: 01274-544358
Contact: Ghulam Rasul
Position: Chair
Activities: Worship, resource, youth, elderly, women
Traditions: Sunni
Movements: Deobandi, Tablighi Jamaat
Other Languages: Urdu, Pushto, Gujarati, Punjabi
Affiliations: Bradford Council of Mosques

Hanifa Mosque
Carlisle Road, Bradford, West Yorkshire, BD8

Hussainia Islamic Mission
All Saints Road, Bradford, West Yorkshire, BD7 3AY
Tel: 01274-724506 **Tel:** 01274-522716 (h)
Contact: Mureed Hussain Buraishi
Activities: Worship, youth
Traditions: 'Ithna Asheri
Other Languages: Urdu, Panjabi, Persian, Arabic
Affiliations: Bradford Council for Mosques

Islamic Centre Darul Islam Masjid & Madressa
10 Hanover Square, Bradford, West Yorkshire, BD1 3BY

Islamic Circle
c/o 31 Duckworth Grove, Bradford, West Yorkshire, BD9 5HQ

Islamic Cultural & Educational Association
c/o 25 Leeds Old Road, Bradford, West Yorkshire, BD3 8JX (h)
Contact: Abdul Ghaffar Khan
Position: General Secretary
Activities: Worship, resource, visits, youth
Traditions: Sunni
Movements: Barelwi
Other Languages: Punjabi, Urdu

Islamic Cultural Centre
9 Ashgrove, Great Horton Road, Bradford, West Yorkshire

Islamic Cultural Centre
44 March Street, Bradford, West Yorkshire, BD9 9PB

Islamic Cultural Eductaional Centre
190 Toller Lane, Heaton, Bradford, West Yorkshire, BD9 5JB

Islamic Educational Institute
9 Ambler Street, off Carlisle Road, Bradford, West Yorkshire, BD8
Tel: 01274-487549

Islamic Girls Group
c/o Pakistan Community Centre, White Abbey Road, Bradford, West Yorkshire, BD8 8EJ

Islamic Madressah
45 Woodview, Bradford, West Yorkshire, BD8 7AJ

Islamic Men & Women's Association
52 Oulton Terrace, Bradford, West Yorkshire, BD7 1QF
Tel: 01274-411799

Islamic Missionary College
28 Shearbridge Road, Bradford, West Yorkshire, BD7 3AF
Tel: 01274-305654 **Tel:** 01274-501743
Contact: Mohammed Yousaf
Position: President
Activities: Worship, resource, visits
Traditions: Sunni
Movements: Barelwi
Other Languages: Punjabi, Urdu

Islamic Relief Worldwide
314 Leeds Road, Bradford, West Yorkshire, BD3 9QX
Tel: 01274-733375 **Fax:** 01274-733375
Contact: Gulfraz Ahmed
Position: Manager
Activities: Resource, visits
Other Languages: Urdu, Punjabi

Jamia Islamic Mosque
Cross Lane, Great Horton Road, Bradford, West Yorkshire

Jamia Masjid & Muslim Association of Bradford
30 Howard Street, Bradford, West Yorkshire, BD5 0BP
Tel: 01274-724819
Contact: President Afsar Khan

Jamia Masjid Hanfia
Ambler Street, Bradford, West Yorkshire, BD8 8AW

Jamia Mosque & Islamic Centre
Manningham Lane, Bradford, West Yorkshire, BD1 3ET

Jamiyat Tabligh-ul-Islam
68-69 Southfield Square, Manningham, Bradford, West Yorkshire, BD8 7SN
Tel: 01274-729087 **Tel:** 01724-823044 (h)
Contact: Mr Liaqat Hussain
Position: Trustee
Activities: Worship, umbrella, visits, youth, interfaith
Traditions: Sunni
Movements: Barelwi
Other Languages: Punjabi, Urdu
Affiliations: Bradford Council of Mosques

Jamiyat Tabligh ul-Islam
1-3 Burnett Place, Marsh Field, Bradford, West Yorkshire, BD5 9LX

Tel: 01274-729087 **Tel:** 01274-823044 (h)
Contact: Mr L Hussain
Position: Trustee

Jamiyat Tabligh-ul-Islam
Fairbank Road, Bradford, West Yorkshire

Jamiyat Tabligh-ul-Islam
54 Airville Road, Bradford, West Yorkshire
Tel: 01274-729087 **Tel:** 01274-823044 (h)
Contact: Mr L Hussain
Position: Trustee

Jamiyat Tabligh-ul-Islam
Hilton Road, Bradford, West Yorkshire
Tel: 01274-729087 **Tel:** 01274-823044 (h)
Contact: Mr L Hussain
Position: Trustee

Jamiyat Tabligh-ul-Islam
23 Cleveland Road, Heaton, Bradford, West Yorkshire, B9 4PB (h)
Tel: 01274-548232 **Tel:** 01274-496096 (h)
Fax: 01274-496096
Contact: Mr Khadim Hussain
Position: President
Activities: Worship
Traditions: Sunni
Movements: Barelwi
Other Languages: Arabic, Urdu

Jamiyat Tabligh-ul-Islam
Roxy Buildings, Barkerend Road, Bradford, West Yorkshire, BD3 9AP
Tel: 01274-729087 **Tel:** 01274-823044 (h)
Contact: Mr L Hussain
Position: Trustee

Jamiyat Tabligh-ul-Islam
2 Browning Street, Bradford, West Yorkshire, BD3 9DX
Tel: 01274-729087 **Tel:** 01274-823044 (h)
Contact: Mr L Hussain
Position: Trustee

Jamiyat Tabligh-ul-Islam
87-89 Ryan Street, Bradford, West Yorkshire, BD5 7AP
Tel: 01274-729087 **Tel:** 01274-823044 (h)
Contact: Mr L Hussain
Position: Trustee

Jamiyat Tabligh-ul-Islam
564a Thornton Road, Bradford, West Yorkshire,
BD8 9NF
Tel: 01274-729087 **Tel:** 01274-823044 (h)
Contact: Mr L Hussain
Position: Trustee

Jamiyat Tabligh-ul-Islam
St Lukes Church Hall, Victor Street, Bradford,
West Yorkshire, BD9

Jamiyat Tabligh-ul-Islam
Victor Street, Bradford, West Yorkshire, BD9

Jamiyat Tabligh-ul-Islam
13 Jesmond Avenue, Bradford, West Yorkshire,
BD9 5DP
Tel: 01274-729087 **Tel:** 01274-823044 (h)
Contact: Mr L Hussain
Position: Trustee

Jamiyat Tablighul Islam
21 Aberdeen Place, Bradford, West Yorkshire, BD7

Jamiyat Tablighul Islam
89/91 White Abbey Road, Bradford, West Yorkshire,
BD8 8DR

Jamiyat Tabligh-ul-Islam Mosque
133 Toller Lane, Bradford, West Yorkshire, BD8
Tel: 01274-729087 **Tel:** 01274-823044 (h)
Contact: Mr Mohammad Ashraf
Position: Secretary
Activities: Worship, resource, visits, inter-faith
Traditions: Sunni
Movements: Barelwi, Tassawuf
Languages: Punjabi, Urdu
Affiliations: Bradford Council for Mosques

Madinatul Uloom
14 Nesfield Street, Manningham Lane, Bradford,
West Yorkshire, BD1 3ET

Madrasa
84 Beamsley Road, Frizinghall, Bradford, West
Yorkshire, BD9

Madrasa-al-Islamia
163 Amberley Street, Bradford, West Yorkshire,
BD3 8QS

Madrassah & Mosque Tarteel-ul-Quran
42 Woodview Terrace, Manningham, Bradford, West
Yorkshire, BD9 7AJ

Tel: 01274-775723 **Tel:** 01274-405975 (h)
Contact: Maulana Zafar Iqbal Ahmed
Position: Imam
Activities: Worship, resource, youth, inter-faith
Traditions: Sunni
Movements: Deobandi, Tablighi Jamaat/Hanafi
Other Languages: Punjabi, heinko, Pushto, Urdu
Affiliations: Council of Mosques, Bradford;
International Khatme Nubuwwat Movement

Madrassah Hizab-ul Ahnaf Barelvi
9 Ambler Street, Bradford, West Yorkshire,
BD8 8AW

Madressa Islam Talimuddin Blenheim Mosque
off Church Street, Bradford, West Yorkshire,
BD8 7PD
Tel: 01274-542027 **Tel:** 01274-493732 (h)
Contact: Mohamed Cassam Bham
Position: Secretary

Millat-e-Islamia Cultural Centre
Ivanhoe Road, off: Great Horton Road, Bradford,
West Yorkshire, BD7 3HY

Mirpur Welfare Society
23 Duckworth Terrace, Bradford, West Yorkshire,
BD9 5HJ

Mosque
5 Thorncliffe Square, Bradford, West Yorkshire,
BD8

Mosque
Brown Steet, Bradford, West Yorkshire, BD3

Mosque
18 Southfield Square, off Lumb Lane, Bradford,
West Yorkshire, BD8 7SL

Mosque
68 Stanacre Place, Bradford, West Yorkshire,
BD3
Tel: 274-638648

Mosque
75 Ryan Street, West Bowling, Bradford, West
Yorkshire, BD8

Mosque
17 Marlborough Road, Bradford, West Yorkshire,
BD8

Mosque
9 Stephens Terrace, Bradford, West Yorkshire, BD8

Mosque & Bradford Muslim Welfare Society
62 St Margarets Road, Bradford, West Yorkshire,
BD7 3AE
Tel: 01274-575919
Contact: A H Pandor
Position: Secretary

Mosque & Tawakkulia Islamic Society
48 Cornwall Road, Bradford, West Yorkshire,
BD1 7JN
Tel: 01274-734563

Mosque (Jamiyat-ahl-e-Hadith)
5 Camden Terrace, Bradford, West Yorkshire,
BD8 7HX
Tel: 01274-728993

Mosque / Madresa Islamiya Talimud Din
Blenham Road, off Church Street, Bradford,
West Yorkshire, B8
Tel: 01274-542027

Mosque Nusrati Islam Mosque
94/98 Preston Street, Bradford, West Yorkshire,
BD7 1JE
Tel: 01274-724488

Muslim Association for the Bradford Elderly Day Centre
24 Howard Street, Bradford, West Yorkshire,
BD5 0BP

Muslim Association of Bradford
32 Howard Street, Bradford, West Yorkshire,
BD5 0BP
Tel: 01274-724819
Contact: Mr Nawaz Khan
Position: Secretary
Activities: Worship, resource, elderly
Other Languages: Urdu
Affiliations: Bradford Council for Mosques

Muslim Cultural Association
37 Heath Road, Bradford, West Yorkshire,
BD3 0PR

Muslim Girls Community School
Ryan Street, Manchester Road, Bradford, West
Yorkshire, BD5 7DQ

Muslim Health Clinic
145 Portland Road, Hove, Bradford, West Yorkshire,
BN3 5QJ

Muslim Information Centre
16 Neal Street, Bradford, West Yorkshire, BD5 0BX

Muslim Parent's Association
12 Masham Place, Bradford, West Yorkshire,
BD9 5DL

Muslim Youth Movement
68-69 Southfield Square, Bradford, West Yorkshire,
BD8 7SL

Noor-e-Islam
62 Margret's Road, Bradford, West Yorkshire,
BD7 3AE

Nusrat-ul-Islam-Mosque
94-98 Preston Street, Bradford, West Yorkshire,
BD7 1JE

Shahjalal Islamic Society
149a Little Horton Lane, Bradford, West Yorkshire,
BD5 0HS
Tel: 01275-304092
Contact: Mr Konuhar Ali
Position: Devlopment Worker
Activities: Worship, resource, visits, youth, elderly,
women
Traditions: Sunni
Other Languages: Bengali, Urdu
Affiliations: Bradford Council for Mosques;
Muslim World League

Sufat-ul-Islam
154 Sunbridge Road, Bradford, West Yorkshire,
BD1 2HF

Sultan Bahu Educational Trust
466 Great Horton Road, Bradford, West Yorkshire,
BD7 3HS (h)
Tel: 01274-410156
Contact: M Aslam Baig
Position: Convenor
Activities: Worship, resource, youth, elderly,
women
Traditions: Sunni
Other Languages: Punjabi, Urdu
Affiliations: Council for Mosques

Surti Khalifa Sunatwal Society & Mosque
27 Ventnor Street, off Leeds Road, Bradford, West
Yorkshire, BD3 9JZ

Surti Muslim Khalifa Society
32 Bertram Road, Khalifa House, Manningham,
Bradford, West Yorkshire, BD8 7LN
Contact: Gulamhussein M Mussa
Position: Chairman
Activities: Worship, resource, visits, youth, elderly,
women, inter-faith
Traditions: Sunni
Movements: Deobandi
Other Languages: Gujarati, Urdu
Affiliations: Bradford Council of Mosques; The
Foundation of UK Khalifa Societies; UK Council
of Mosques; Muslim World League

Tabligh-ul-Islam
84 Beamsley Road, Shipley, Bradford, West
Yorkshire

Tawakkulia Islamic Society
48 Cornwall Road, Bradford, West Yorkshire,
BD8 7JN
Tel: 01274-542584 (h)
Contact: A M Tarafder
Position: President
Activities: Worship, resource
Traditions: Sunni
Movements: All Movements
Other Languages: Bangla

UK Islamic Mission
3 Byron Street, Bradford, West Yorkshire, BD3 0AD
Tel: 01274-306299

UK Islamic Mission
17 Marlborough Road, Bradford, West Yorkshire,
BD8 7LS

West Bowling Islamic Society
133 Newton Street, West Bowling, Bradford, West
Yorkshire, BD5 7BJ

World Islamic Mission
28 Shearbridge Road, Bradford, West Yorkshire,
BD7 1NX
Tel: 01274-729087

Young Muslims
162 Dirkhall Road, Bradford, West Yorkshire,
BD7 1QR

Central Ahl-e-Sunnat Jamat
31 Sackville Street, Ravensthorpe, Dewsbury,
West Yorkshire, WE13 3BX

Dewsbury Muslim Association
25 South Street, Savile Town, Dewsbury, West
Yorkshire, WF12 9NB (h)
Tel: 01924-454178 (h)
Contact: Mr Mohamed Musa Patel
Activities: Worship
Other Languages: Gujarati, Urdu

Gulzar-e-Madina Mosque
3 High Street, West Town, Dewsbury, West Yorkshire
Tel: 01924-430338
Contact: Mr M Bashir

Ilaahi Masjid & Madressa
2 Hope Street, Dewsbury, West Yorkshire,
WF13 2BT (h)
Tel: 01924-460761 (h)
Contact: Mr Ahmed Akudi
Position: Chairman
Activities: Worship, resource, visits, youth,
Traditions: Sunni
Movements: Tablighi Jamaat
Other Languages: Gujarati, Urdu
Affiliations: Indian Muslim Welfare Society

Insitute of Islamic Education
South Street, Dewsbury, West Yorkshire, WF12 9NG

Islamic Book Centre
70 Alexandra Terrace, Halifax Road, Dewsbury,
West Yorkshire, WF13 4HD
Tel: Tel: 01924-452042 (h)
Contact: Mr Kassim Pandor
Traditions: Sunni
Movements: Deobandi
Other Languages: Urdu, Gujarati, English

Jamia Tulumul Islam
South Street, Savile Town, Dewsbury, West
Yorkshire, WF12 9NP

**Madni Jamia Masjid & Pakistan Muslim
Association**
North Gate, Dewsbury, West Yorkshire
Tel: 01924-467760
Contact: Maulana Manzoor Hussain
Activities: Worship, resource
Other Languages: Urdu, Panjabi
Traditions: Sunni

Movements: Deobandi
Affiliations: Education Centre; Jamiat-e-Ulana, Britain

Madressa Muslim Association
Pilgrim Drive, Dewsbury, West Yorkshire
Tel: 01924-430612

Makki Madani Masjid
33 Kertland Street, Saville Town, Dewsbury, West Yorkshire, WF12 9PU
Tel: 01924-458388 **Tel:** 01924-453125 (h)
Contact: Safdar Ali
Position: Secretary
Activities: Worship, resource, visits, inter-faith
Traditions: Sunni
Movements: Barelwi, Tassawuf
Other Languages: Urdu, Punjabi
Affiliations: Jamaat-e-Ahl-e-Summat

Markaz Ahl-e-Jamat
106 Clarkson Street, Ravensthorpe, Dewsbury, West Yorkshire

Markazi Jamia Masjid Anwar-e-Madina
Crawshaw Street, Ravensthorpe, Dewsbury, West Yorkshire, WF13 3ER
Tel: 01924-459554 **Tel:** 01924-455872 (h)
Contact: Abdul Qayum Khan
Position: Imam
Activities: Worship, resource
Traditions: Sunni
Movements: Barelwi
Other Languages: Urdu, Punjabi

Markazi Mosque & Mosque Committee
South Street, Savile Town, Dewsbury, West Yorkshire

Masjid-e-Umar & Madressa-e-Talimuddin
North View, Savile Town, Dewsbury, West Yorkshire, WF12 9LF
Tel: 01924-464686 (h)
Contact: Mr Muhammad Dedat
Position: Joint Secretary
Activities: Worship, resource, inter-faith
Traditions: Sunni
Movements: Tablighi Jamaat
Languages: Urdu, Gujrati

Masjid Ghausia
13 Warren Street, Dewsbury, West Yorkshire

Mosque
North Road, Ravensthorpe, Dewsbury, West Yorkshire
Tel: 01924-461089

Mosque
Halifax Road, Dewsbury, West Yorkshire

Mosque
7-11 Savile Grove, Savile Town, Dewsbury, West Yorkshire

Mosque
Huddersfield Road, Raventhorpe, Dewsbury, West Yorkshire

Mosque
206 Bradford Road, Dewsbury, West Yorkshire, WF13 2HD

Mosque
Jeremy Lane, Heckmondwike, Dewsbury, West Yorkshire
Tel: 01924-402602

Mosque
1 Stoney Bank Street, Scout Hill, Dewsbury, West Yorkshire, WF13 3RJ
Tel: 01924-451085
Contact: Mr Mohammad Razaq
Position: Secretary

Mosque & Madresa-e-Taumuddin
10-11 Thornleigh, Savile Town, Dewsbury, West Yorkshire

Muslim Jamat
5-9 Savile Grove, Savile Town, Dewsbury, West Yorkshire, WF12 9PN

Muslim Welfare Society
3 Birkdale Road, Dewsbury, West Yorkshire, WF13 4HG

Muslim Welfare Society, Madrassa & Mosque
24–26 Hope Street, Dewsbury, West Yorkshire, WF13 2BT

Muslims Girls High School
3-4 Thornie Bank, Savile Town, Dewsbury, West Yorkshire, WF12 9PN

Pakistani Mosque Committee
5 Falcon Road, Savile Town, Dewsbury, West Yorkshire

Zakaria Mosque/Savile Town Muslim Jamaat
2 Chapel Street, Savile Town, Dewsbury, West Yorkshire, WF12 9NQ
Contact: Mr Yusuf Adam Patel

Doncaster Mosque Trust
Bentinck Close, St James Street, Hyde Park, Doncaster, South Yorkshire, DN1 3ST
Tel: 01302-368336 **Tel:** 01302-326356 (h)
Contact: M M Mufti
Position: Secretary
Activities: Worship, resource, visits
Traditions: Sunni
Movements: Deobandi
Other Languages: Arabic, Urdu, Punjabi

Doncaster Pakistani Cultural Centre & Mosque
12 Thoresby Avenue, Belle Vue, Doncaster, South Yorkshire, DN4 5BJ

Pakistani Cultural Centre & Mosque
8 St Helens Road, Belle Vue, Doncaster, South Yorkshire, DN4 5EH
Contact: Ali Asghar
Position: Assistant Secretary
Activities: Worship, resource, visits
Traditions: Sunni
Other Languages: Urdu, Arabic

Anjuman Islah-ul-Muslemeen
18 Rothwell Road, Halifax, West Yorkshire
Tel: 01422-380934
Contact: Dr Rahmat A Chaudhry

Bain-ul-Aqwami Anjuman Tabligh-ul-Islam
Vincent Street, Hopwood Lane, Halifax, West Yorkshire, HX1 4EN
Tel: 01422-342366
Contact: Mohammad Tariq
Position: Chief Organiser
Activities: Worship, resource, youth, elderly, women
Traditions: Sunni
Movements: Barelwi
Other Languages: Urdu, Punjabi

British Muslim Association
Victoria House, 86 Hopwood Lane, Halifax, West Yorkshire, HX1 4EJ
Tel: 01442-362276 **Tel:** 01422-344732 (h)
Contact: Mohammed Rahoof
Position: Chair
Activities: Worship, resource, umbrella, youth, elderly, women, inter-faith
Traditions: Sunni
Movements: Jamati-i-Islami
Other Languages: Urdu, Punjabi, Arabic
Affiliations: Calderdale Racial Equality Council; Calderdale Council of Mosques

Calderdale Islamic Youth/Dawat-e-Islami
372 Queens Road, Halifax, West Yorkshire, HX1 4PH (h)
Tel: 01422 344 732 (h)
Contact: Mohammed Rauf
Position: Chairman
Activities: Youth, inter-faith
Traditions: Sunni
Movements: Jamati-i-Islami
Other Languages: Urdu, Punjabi
Affiliations: Dawat-e-Islami-Karachi Pakistan

Central Mosque & Islamic Centre
3 Alfred Street, Halifax, West Yorkshire
Contact: Haji Mohammed Rafiq

Elland Mosque Association
26/34 Elizabeth Street, Elland, Halifax, West Yorkshire, HX5 0JH
Tel: 01422-378808 **Tel:** 01422-375297 (h)
Fax: 01422-517985
Contact: Fazal-ur-Rehman Tariq
Position: Chairperson
Activities: Worship, visits, inter-faith
Other Languages: Urdu, Arabic

Halifax Islamic Society
30 Parkinson Lane, Halifax, West Yorkshire, HX1 3XL

Islamic Cultural Association
14 Milton Terrace, Halifax, West Yorkshire
Contact: Mr A H Shah

Islamic Welfare Society
9 Crossley Gardens, Halifax, West Yorkshire

Islamic Youth (Peace) Movement of Calderdale
164a Gibbert Street, Halifax, West Yorkshire

Jamiat Ahl-e-Hadith Mosque
124 Hanson Lane, Halifax, West Yorkshire

Madni Jamia Mosque
Gibbet Street, Halifax, West Yorkshire
Contact: Secretary

Madni Jamia Mosque
15 Newstead Terrace, Halifax, West Yorkshire

Mahfil-e-Ahl Sukhan
30 Hyde Park Road, Kings Cross, Halifax, West
Yorkshire

Markazi Jamia Masjid
49 Rhodes Street, Halifax, West Yorkshire
Tel: 01422-330041

Mehfil-e-Ahl-Sukhan
27 Mayfield Avenue, Halifax, West Yorkshire
Tel: 01422-346511
Contact: Mr Haji M Rafique

Minhaj-ul-Qur'an Movement
164a Gibbet Street, Halifax, West Yorkshire, HX1

Mosque
10 Franklin Road, Halifax, West Yorkshire

Mosque & Bangladeshi Muslim Association
117 Gibbet Street, Halifax, West Yorkshire
Tel: 01422-55218
Contact: Mr Siddat Ali

Muslim Youth Sports Club
4 Dean Street, Elland, Halifax, West Yorkshire
Contact: Mr Mohammed Aslam

Young Muslims
14 Mile Cross Place, Halifax, West Yorkshire,
HX1 4HW

**Heckmondwike Mosque & Pakistan Muslim
Welfare Society**
Community Centre, Jeremy Lane, Heckmondwike,
West Yorkshire, WF16 9HN
Contact: Mr M B Jee
Position: General Secretary

Anjuman Ghausi Razvia
129 Halifax Road, Birkby, Huddersfield, West
Yorkshire

Anjuman Islamia Razvia
15 Percy Street, Fartown, Huddersfield, West
Yorkshire, HD2 2SB
Contact: Mr M Riaz

Anjuman Rai
39 Birkby Lodge Road, Birkby, Huddersfield, West
Yorkshire
Contact: Mr Nisar-Ul-Haq

Bilal Mosque
245 Yewhill Road, Huddersfield, West Yorkshire

Birkby/Fartown Jamia Mosque
27 Yew Street, Huddersfield, West Yorkshire
Contact: Mr S Mohammed

British Muslim Solidarity in Huddersfield
155 Halifax Old Road, Huddersfield, West
Yorkshire

Ghosia Mosque
18 St Steven Road, Lockwood, Huddersfield, West
Yorkshire

**Huddersfield Council of Islamic Affairs
Charitable Trust (HCIACT)**
c/o Muslim Community Centre, Clare Hill, off
Cambridge Road, Huddersfield, West Yorkshire,
HD1 5BU
Tel: 01484-515311 **Tel:** 01422-375297 (h)
Fax: 01484-517985
Contact: Fazul-ur-Rehman Tariq
Position: Secretary General
Activities: Umbrella, visits, youth, elderly, women,
inter-faith
Other Languages: Urdu, Punjabi

Huddersfield Muslim Burial Council
2 New Street, Huddersfield, West Yorkshire,
HD1 2AR
Tel: 01484-515311 **Tel:** 01422-375297 (h)
Fax: 01484-517985
Contact: Fazul-ur-Rehman Tariq
Position: Chairman
Other Languages: Urdu

Huddersfield Muslim Welfare Association
9 Moorbottom Road, Thorton Lodge,
Huddersfield, West Yorkshire, HD1 3JT

Islamic Cultural Centre
16a Springdale Avenue, Huddersfield, West Yorshire,
HD5 8EL

Islamic Socialist Movement
155 Halifax Old Road, Birkby, Huddersfield, West Yorkshire
Contact: Secretary

Jamia Masjid
32 Upper George Street, Huddersfield, HD1 4AW

Jamiat Ahl-e-Hadith
45 Marley Lane, Milnbridge, Huddersfield, West Yorkshire, HD3 4NZ (h)
Tel: 01484-460894 (h)   **Fax:** 01484-460894
EMail: alison.haneef@virgin.net
Contact: Brother Mohammed Hanif Asad
Position: Chair
Activities: Worship, resource, youth, women, inter-faith

Khatm-e-Nabuwat Committee
10c Thorton Lodge Road, Huddersfield, West Yorkshire

Madani Jamia Masjid Association
73 Victoria Road, Lockwood, Huddersfield, West Yorkshire
Contact: Mr Abdul Aziz

Madni Masjid
Bland Street, Lockwood, Huddersfield, West Yorskhire
Tel: 01484-4224444

Madressa Ghar-e-Hira
10b Thornton Lodge Road, Huddersfield, West Yorkshire

Jame Mosque Riza & Islamic Centre
129 Old Halifax Road, Birkby, Huddersfield, West Yorkshire, HD2 2RN
Tel: 01484-540449   **Tel:** 01484-309754
Contact: Mr Hajji Sardar Mohammad
Position: Secretary
Activities: Worship, resource, visits, youth, elderly, women
Traditions: Sunni
Movements: Barelwi
Other Languages: Urdu, Arabic, Punjabi

Majlis Ansarullah Huddersfield
72 St Johns Road, Birkby, Huddersfield, West Yorkshire, HD1 5EY
Contact: Mr M M A Mehmood

Masjid Anwarul Madina
Clara Street, Fartown, Huddersfield, West Yorkshire, HD2 6JX
Tel: 01484-421236   **Tel:** 01484-451965 (h)
Contact: Mr Rana Allah Dad Khan
Position: Chairman
Activities: Worship, resource, media, visits, youth, elderly
Traditions: Sunni
Movements: Barelwi
Other Languages: Urdu, Arabic, Punjabi

Masjid-e-Noor
Crosland Road, Thornton Lodge, Huddersfield, West Yorkshire, HD1 3JS

Masjid Noor
15 Thornton Lodge Road, Crosland Moor, Huddersfield, West Yorkshire

Masjid Omar
32 Blacker Road, Birkby, Huddersfield, West Yorkshire
Tel: 01484-541634

Mosque
Victoria Road, Lockwood, Huddersfield, West Yorkshire

Mosque
1 Cobcroft Road, Fartown, Huddersfield, West Yorkshire

Mosque Omar
4 Arnold Street, Birkby, Huddersfield, West Yorkshire
Contact: Mr Ali Mushtaq

Muslim Community Centre
Clare Hill, Off Cambridge Road, Huddersfield, West Yorkshire, HD1 5BU

Muslim Funeral Association
45 Morley Lane, Milnsbridge, Huddersfield, West Yorkshire
Contact: Mr M Asad

Muslim Funeral Society
181 Manchester Road, Thornton Lodge, Huddersfield, West Yorkshire, HD1 3TE
Tel: 01484-548298
Contact: Mr K Uddin
Position: President

Traditions: Sunni
Movements: Ahl-e-Hadith
Other Languages: Punjabi, Urdu
Affiliations: Jamiat Ahl-e-Hadith, Birmingham

Muslim Welfare Association
1 Lynndale Avenue, Birkby, Huddersfield, West Yorkshire
Contact: Mr Fazal Rahaman

Shah Jalal Mosque
85 Fenton Street, Lockwood, Huddersfield, West Yorkshire

Hull Mosque & Islamic Centre
Berkeley Street, Hull, East Riding of Yorkshire, HU3 1PR
Tel: 01482-24833
Contact: Dr Ayyub

Islamic Society Hull University
Union Building, Cottingham Road, Hull, East Riding of Yorkshire, HU6 7RX
Contact: H G Mustafa
Position: Chair
Activities: Worship, visits
Traditions: Sunni
Other Languages: Malesian, Arabic, Urdu
Affiliations: Federation of Students Islamic Societies

Mosque
153 Boulevard, Hull, East Riding of Yorkshire, HU3 3EJ
Tel: 01482-24833

Pearson Park Mosque & Islamic Centre
20 Pearson Park, Hull, East Riding of Yorkshire, HU5 2TD

UK Islamic Mission
Berkeley Street, Hull, East Riding of Yorkshire, HU3 1PR

Al-Amin Talimul Islamic Society
33 Victoria Road, Keighley, West Yorkshire, BD21 1HD
Tel: 01535-607 620 (h)
Contact: Afruj Ali Ruf
Position: Secretary
Activities: Worship, resource, inter-faith
Traditions: Sunni,
Other Languages: Bengali, Urdu

Bangladesh Islamic Association
20 Clarendon Street, Keighley, West Yorkshire
Contact: Mr Toymus Ali

Bangledeshi Islamic Organisation
Sefton Place, Keighley, West Yorkshire

Jamia Mosque & Muslim Association
75 Emily Street, Keighley, West Yorkshire, BD21 3EG
Tel: 01535-607039
Contact: Alhaj Zafar Iqbal
Position: General Secretary
Activities: Worship, umbrella, visits, youth, elderly, women, newsletters, books, inter-faith
Traditions: Sunni,
Other Languages: Punjabi, Urdu, Arabic,
Affiliations: Bradford Council of Mosques, Imams and Mosques Council

Keighley Muslim Community Centre
47 Emily Street, Keighley, West Yorkshire, BD21 3EG

Madrasa
10-12 Belgrave Road, Keighley, West Yorkshire
Contact: M Iqbal

Madrassa Alenath
2 East Avenue, Keighley, West Yorkshire
Contact: Faiz Alam

Madrassa Ghosia
55 Ashleigh Street, Keighley, West Yorkshire

Mosque
70 Marlborough Road, Keighley, West Yorkshire

Pakistan Muslim Association
c/o The Mosque, 45 Asa Leigh Road, Keighley, West Yorkshire

Sangat Day Centre
Keighley Muslim Community Centre, 47 Emily Street, Keighley, West Yorkshire, BD21 3EG

Shahjalal Mosque & Bangladesh Islamic Organisation
Temple Row, Keighley, West Yorkshire, BD21 2AH
Tel: 01535-603444
Contact: Mr Mohammed Tahir

Almadina Jamia Mosque
33 Brundell Grove, Leeds, West Yorkshire, LS6 1HR
Tel: 0113-275-8615

Ahlul Bayt Islamic Centre
35 Hanover Square, Leeds, West Yorkshire, LS3 1BQ
Tel: 0113-244-3419 **Tel:** 0113-2949-253 (h)
Fax: 0113-244-3419
Contact: Dr Mohammad Jarad Gohari
Position: Director
Activities: Worship, resource, media, visits, youth, elderly, women, inter-faith
Traditions: Ithna Asheri
Other Languages: Arabic, Persian

Bangladesh Islamic Society
27 Ellers Road, Leeds, West Yorkshire, LS8 4JH

Bangladesh National Association
21 Leopold Street, Chapeltown, Leeds, West Yorkshire, LS7 4DA
Tel: 0113-266-2034
Contact: Mr M Rahman
Position: Chairman
Activities: Worship, inter-faith

Leeds Girls Academy
Tel: 0113-237-4543 **Tel:** 0113-237-4543
Contact: Mrs Nighat Afza Mirza
Position: Head Teacher
Activities: Resource
Other Languages: Urdu, Punjabi
Traditions: Sunni

Leeds Grand Mosque
2 Hyde Park Road, Leeds, West Yorkshire, LS6 1PY
Tel: 0113-225127 **Fax:** Tel: 0113-225127
Contact: Mr Ghassan Khalil
Position: Imam
Activities: Resource, youth, women
Traditions: Sunni
Other Languages: Arabic

Leeds Islamic Centre
44-48 Spencer Place, Leeds, West Yorkshire, LS7 4BR
Tel: 0113-262-1300 **Tel:** 0113-246-8640 (h)
Contact: Mr Muhammad Khan Chaudhary
Position: Secretary
Activities: Worship, resource, media, umbrella, visits, youth, elderly, women, newsletters, inter-faith
Traditions: Sunni
Movements: Deobandi
Other Languages: Urdu, Panjabi, Bangla
Affiliations: Yorkshire Council of Mosques; Union of Muslim Organisations; Muslim World League

Jinaah Mosque
118 Street Lane, Leeds, West Yorkshire, L8

Kashmir Muslim Community Centre & Mosque
1 Hardy Street, Beeston, Leeds, West Yorkshire, LS11 6BJ
Tel: **Tel:** 0113-277-4591 (h)
Contact: Mohammed Kaman Bhatti
Position: Chairman
Activities: Worship, inter-faith
Traditions: Sunni,
Other Languages: Punjabi, Urdu

Khoja Sh'ia Ithna Asheri Mosque
Muslim Community of Metropolitan Leeds, 168 Beeston Road, Leeds, West Yorkshire, LS11 8BD
Tel: 0113-265-9073
Contact: Noorali Bhamamni
Position: Honorary Secretary

Leeds Muslim Council
31-33 Brudenell Grove, Leeds, West Yorkshire, LS6 1HR
Tel: 0113-275-2535

Masjid-e-Bilal & Muslim Community Centre
Harehills Place, Harehills Road, Leeds, West Yorkshire, LS14 3DZ
Tel: 0113-248-0711
Contact: Ghulam Hussain
Position: Secretary

Masjid-e-Shah Jalal
27 Ellers Road, off Markham Avenue, Leeds, West Yorkshire, LS8 4JH
Tel: 0113-248-1860

Masjid-e-Umar & Muslim Association
29 Stratford Street, off Dewsbury Road, Leeds, West Yorkshire, LS11 6JG
Tel: 0113-270-9536

Mosque
off: Brookyn Terrace, Leeds, West Yorkshire, L12

Mosque
29 Stretford Street, Leeds, West Yorkshire, LS11

Mosque
45 St Martin's Gardens, Leeds, West Yorkshire, LS7 3LD

Mosque
145 Spencer Place, Leeds, West Yorkshire, LS7 4DU
Tel: 0113-262-1989

Mosque
1 Brundell Road, Leeds, West Yorkshire, LS6

Mosque & Muslim Welfare Centre
2 Nancroft Terrace, Armley, Leeds, West Yorkshire,
LS12 2DQ

Muslim Association of Leeds 11
278 Dewsbury Road, Leeds, West Yorkshire,
LS11 6JT

Muslim Centre
Conway Road, Leeds, West Yorkshire,

Muslim Commonwealth
18 Winston Mount, Leeds, West Yorkshire, L8

Muslim Community & Education Centre
69 Woodsley Road, Leeds, West Yorkshire, LS3 1DU

Muslim Cultural Society
71 Elford Grove, Leeds, West Yorkshire, L8

Muslim Women's Counselling Service
6 Baldovan Place, Leeds, West Yorkshire, LS8

Omar Welfare House
5 St Johns Terrace, Leeds, West Yorkshire, LS3 1DY
Tel: 0113-245-1306
Fax: 0113-234-2472
Contact: Dr Kadhem Al-Rawi
Position: Manager

Pakistan Muslim Association
137 Gipton Wood Road, Leeds, West Yorkshire, LS8

Shahjalal Mosque
27 Ellers Road, Leeds, West Yorkshire, LS8 4JH

Bazme Urdu Adab Cleveland
44 Wellesley Road, Middlesbrough, North Yorkshire

Islamic Cultural Association
3 South Terrace, South Bank, Middlesbrough,
North Yorkshire, TS6
Tel: 01642-458259
Contact: Mr Rashid-Abdul Rehman
Position: Chairman
Activities: Worship, resource, visits
Traditions: Sunni
Movements: Ahl-e-Hadith

Other Languages: Urdu, Arabic
Affiliations: Cleveland Mosques

Langbaurgh Islamic & Quranic Cultural Association
52 Middlesbrough Road, South Bank,
Middlesbrough, North Yorkshire, TS6 6LZ
Tel: 01642-45704 **Tel:** 01642-457048 (h)
Contact: A Rohman
Position: Secretary
Activities: Worship, resource
Traditions: Sunni
Other Languages: Bengali, Arabic
Affiliations: East London Mosque Committee

Mosque
51 Abingdon Road, Middlesbrough, North
Yorkshire

Madrassa-Zia-ul-Qur'an
Bow Street, Middlesbrough, North Yorkshire
Tel: 01642-230408
Contact: Mr M A Khan
Position: Secretary

Masjide-e Jamia Al Madina
133a Waterloo Road, Middlesbrough, North
Yorkshire, TS1 3JB
Tel: 01642-245855 **Tel:** 01642-818617 (h)
Contact: M A Durrani
Position: General Secretary

Muslim Federation, Cleveland
9 Park Road North, Middlesbrough, North
Yorkshire, TS1 3LF
Tel: 01642-248498 **Fax:** 01642-253610
Contact: Mr Ali Luft
Position: Chair
Activities: Worship, resource, visits, youth, women
Traditions: Sunni
Other Languages: Arabic, Urdu, Somali, French

Jamiah Mosque & Community Centre
114a College Road, Rotherham, South Yorskhire,
S60 1JF
Tel: 01709-563631
Contact: Mr K M Shabbir

Jamiat-ahl-e-Hadith
Moorgate Street, Rotherham, South Yorkshire,
S60 2EY
Tel: 01709-369715, **Tel:** 01709-360594 (h)
Contact: Nazir Ahmed
Position: Secretary

Activities: Worship, resource, visits, youth, elderly, women, inter-faith
Traditions: Sunni
Movements: Ahl-e-Hadith
Other Languages: Urdu, Arabic, Punjabi
Affiliations: Jamiat Ahl-e-Hadith UK Birmingham

Mosque
Chapel Walk, Rotherham, South Yorkshire, S60 1EP
Tel: 01709-560038
Contact: Abdul Kabir
Position: Imam
Activities: Worship, resource, visits, youth, elderly, women, newsletters, inter-faith
Movements: Deobandi, Tablighi Jamaat
Other Languages: Urdu, Punjabi, Gujarati,
Affiliations: United Muslim Organisation

Mosque
46 Milton Road, Eastwood, Rotherham, South Yorkshire

Muslim Community Centre & Mosque
20 Mile Oak Road, Rotherham, South Yorkshire
Contact: Mr M Sardar

Pakistan Muslim Welfare Association
8 North Road, East Dene, Rotherham, South Yorkshire

Rotherham Mosque Trust
12 Davis Street, Rotherham, South Yorkshire, S60 1JX
Contact: Mr Afzal

Taleem ul Haq
Chapel Walk Mosque, Rotherham, South Yorkshire, S60 1EP
Tel: 01709-560038   **Tel:** 01709-835675 (h)
Contact: Abdul Kabir
Position: Imam
Activities: Worship, resource, media, youth, elderly, women, books, inter-faith
Movements: Deobandi, Tablighi Jamaat
Other Languages: Punjabi, Urdu, English, Arabic
Affiliations: Bradford Council of Mosques; The Dawa Academy, Leicester; Muslim Scholars Movement of Europe

Allahi Mosque & Islamic Cultural Centre
14 Wilfred Road, Sheffield, South Yorkshire, S9 3ES

Anjuman-e-Haideria
140 Steade Road, Sheffield, South Yorkshire, S7 1DU
Tel: 0114-258-8459   **Tel:** 0370-768882 (h)
Fax: 0114-236-3882
Contact: Nasir Hussain Sherazi
Position: Secretary
Activities: Worship, youth, elderly, women
Traditions: Ithna Asheri
Movements: Jafferia
Other Languages: Urdu, Persian, Punjabi
Affiliations: Sheffield Racial Equality Council; Islamic Centre, London; Majlis Ullema Shia Europe, Harrow; World Ahl-ul-Bayt Islamic League, London

Arabic Mosque
275 Staniforth Road, Sheffield, South Yorkshire, S9
Tel: 0114-244-6179

Association of Muslim Scholars of Islamics in Britain
Jamiat-e Ulama of Britain, 54 Sheldon Road, Nether Edge, Sheffield, South Yorkshire, S7 1GW
Tel: 0114-255-0318 (h)
Contact: Mr M Ismail
Position: Secretary

Bangladesh Allya Mosque & Islamic Centre
16-18 Swarcliffe Road, Sheffield, South Yorkshire, S9 3FA
Contact: Chairperson

British Muslim Association
53 Barncliffe Road, Sheffield, South Yorkshire, S10 4DG
Contact: Mr M Rashid

Council for Islamic Affairs
71 Broad Oaks, Sheffield, South Yorkshire, S9

Council of Mosques & Islamic Organisations in Sheffield
226 Darnell Road, Sheffield, South Yorkshire, S9
Contact: Mr C M Walayat
Position: Secretary

Dar ul Aloom Siddiqia Mosque
24 Burngreave Road, Sheffield, South Yorkshire, S3 9DD
Tel: 0114-270-1034
Contact: Chairperson

Elahi Mosque & Islamic Cultural Centre
305 Staniforth Road, Darnall, Sheffield, South Yorkshire
Tel: 0114-243-1270

Ghousia Mosque
Owler Lane, Sheffield, South Yorkshire, S4
Tel: 0114-238-7966
Contact: Chairperson

Haqqani House Sufi Centre
Former Christian Science Church Buildings, Vincent Road, Nether Edge, Sheffield, South Yorkshire, S7 1DE
Tel: 0114-2589-408 (h)
Contact: Noah Nazir
Position: Trustee
Activities: Worship, visits, youth, women, newsletters, inter-faith
Traditions: Sunni,
Movements: Tassawuf,
Other Languages: Urdu, Arabic, Turkish, Spanish

Islamic Cultural Centre
36 St Lawrence Road, Sheffield, South Yorkshire, S9
Contact: Mr Munshi
Position: Chairperson

Islamic Society
Sheffield University, Pond Street, Sheffield, South Yorkshire, S1 2BD

Ittehad Committee
8 Brair Road, Sheffield, South Yorkshire, S4
Contact: Mr S Khan

Jaime Masjid Trust
13 Industry Road, Sheffield, South Yorkshire, S6
Tel: 0114-244-7686

Jamia Islamia Mosque
42 Earl Marshal Road, Sheffield, South Yorkshire, S4
Tel: 0114-243-2475

Jamia Masjid Hanifa
372 Sheffield Road, Tinsley, Sheffield, South Yorkshire, S9
Tel: 0114-244-3824

Jamia Mosque Committee
214 Darnall Road, Darnall, Sheffield, South Yorkshire, S9 5AF

Contact: Mr M Siddique
Position: President

Jamiat Islah-ul-Muslimeem
c/o Makki Mosque, Plantation Road, Sheffield, South Yorkshire, S8 9TH
Tel: 0114-258-2348, **Tel:** 0114-281-8744 (h)
Contact: Barkat Ali
Position: Secretary
Activities: Worship, resource, visits, youth, elderly, women, inter-faith
Traditions: Sunni
Movements: Deobandi
Other Languages: Punjabi, Urdu

Jamiyate Tablige Islam
Bodmin Street, Sheffield, South Yorkshire, S9 3TA
Tel: 0114-244-5618
Contact: Mr Hafiz M Rafique

Madina Mosque
24 Wolsely Road, Sheffield, South Yorkshire, S8 0ZU

Madni Islamic Community Association & Mosque
22 Wincoba Lane, Sheffield, South Yorkshire, S4 8AA
Tel: 0114-244-2998
Contact: Mr Q M Siddique

Makki Masjid
Plantation Road, off Albert Road, Sheffield, South Yorkshire, S8 9IJ
Tel: 0114-258-2348
Contact: Maulana Obaid-ur-Rehman
Position: Chair
Activities: Worship, visits, youth, inter-faith
Traditions: Sunni,
Movements: Deobandi, Tablighi Jammaat
Other Languages: Urdu

Markazi Mosque Trust
13 Industry Road, Sheffield, South Yorkshire, S9 5SP
Tel: 0114-244-1500
Contact: Haji Mohammed Siddique
Position: Chair/Secretary
Activities: Worship, resource, umbrella, visits, youth, elderly, women
Other Languages: Arabic, Urdu

Mosque Al Khair
21-23 Rothay Road, Brightside, Sheffield, South
Yorkshire, S4 8BD

Mosque/Bangledesh Islamic Centre
16-18 Swarcliffe Road, Sheffield, South Yorkshire,
S9 3FA

Muslim Butchers Association
c/o Raza Brothers, 102 Attercliffe Common,
Sheffield, South Yorkshire, S9

Muslim Parents Association
244 Staniforth Road, Sheffield, South Yorkshire, S9

Muslim Welfare House Sheffield
10-12 Severn Road, Sheffield, South Yorkshire,
S10 2SU
Tel: 0114-267-1969 **Fax:** 0114-267-1969
Contact: Abdul Razak Bougara
Position: Chairperson

Noor-al-Hadi
275 Staniforth Road, Sheffield, South Yorkshire,
S9 3FP

Pakistan Chhachhi Association
29 Firth Park, Firvale, Sheffield, South Yorkshire,
S5 6WL
Tel: 0114-244-4457 (h)
Contact: Mohammad Ilyas
Position: Chairperson

Pakistan Muslim Welfare Association
Darnall Star Works, Darnall, Sheffield, South
Yorkshire, S9 5AF
Contact: Mr M Rafique
Position: Chairperson

Quba Culra Mosque
120 Worksop Road, Attercliffe, Sheffield, South
Yorkshire, S9
Tel: 0114-244-0235

**Sheffield Allyah Jame Mosque & Islamic Cultural
Centre**
Roundall Street, Darnall, Sheffield, South Yorkshire,
S9 3LE
Tel: 0114-2618162
Contact: Sheikh Zubairahmod Hamidi
Position: First Imam
Traditions: Sunni
Other Languages: Bengali, Urdu
Affiliations: Imams and Mosques Council; Muslim
World League

Sheffield Islamic Centre & Madina Mosque
24-32 Wolseley Road, Sheffield, South Yorkshire,
S8 0ZU
Tel: 0114-258-5021   **Tel:** 0114-255-0391 (h)
Contact: Mr M Nazir
Position: Secretary

**Sheffield, Rotherham & District Council of
Muslims**
1 Derriman Glen, Silverdale Road, Sheffield, South
Yorkshire, S11 9LQ
Tel: 0114-236-0465
Contact: Dr A K Admani

Sufi Islamic Centre
Haqqani House Sufi Centre, Vincent Road, Nether
Edge, Sheffield, South Yorkshire, S7 1DE
Tel: 0114-258-9408 (h)
Contact: Noah Nazir
Position: Trustee
Activities: Worship, resource, visits, youth, elderly,
women, newsletters, inter-faith
Traditions: Sunni
Movements: Ahle Sunnatwat Jamaat
Other Languages: Urdu, Arabic, Spanish, Italian

Tinsley Islamic Cultural Centre
372 Sheffield Road, Tinsley, Sheffield, South
Yorkshire, S9 1RQ
Tel: 0114-261-8648
Contact: Mr Mohammed Riaz
Position: Secretary
Activities: Worship, resource, umbrella, visits,
youth, elderly, women, inter-faith
Other Languages: Urdu, Punjabi, Arabic
Affiliations: Sheffield Council of Mosques

University of Sheffield Islamic Circle
c/o International Office, Students Union, Sheffield
University, Sheffield, South Yorkshire, S10 2TG
Tel: 0114-275-8247 (h)
Email: islam.circle@sheffield.ac.uk
Contact: Omer Hasem El-Hamdoon
Position: Chair
Activities: Worship, visits, youth, women,
newsletters, inter-faith
Traditions: Sunni,
Other Languages: Malay, Arabic, Urdu, Turkish
Affiliations: FOSIS, IIFSO

UK Islamic Mission, Sheffield Branch
525 Abbeydale Road, Sheffield, South Yorkshire,
S7 1FU

Tel: 0114-250-8695 (h)
Contact: Qari Abdul Hamid
Position: President
Activities: Resource, visits, youth, elderly, women, inter-faith
Traditions: Sunni
Movements: Jamati-i-Islami
Other Languages: Punjabi, Urdu
Affiliations: UK Islamic Mission, Jamaat-I-Islami (Pakistan)

Young Muslims Sheffield Girls Group
10 Severn Road, Sheffield, South Yorkshire, S10 2SU

Young Muslims UK, Sheffield
20 Exeter Place, Hanover, Sheffield, South Yorkshire, S3 7TS
Tel: 0114-275-8247 (h)
Email: o.h.el-hamdoon@sheffield.ac.uk
Contact: Omer Hasem El-Hamdoon
Position: Chair
Activities: Resource, youth, women, inter-faith
Other Languages: Arabic, Urdu, Bengali
Affiliations: Young Muslims UK; Islamic Society of Britain

Jame Masjid & Islamic Centre
18 Greenfield Street, Skipton, North Yorkshire, BD23 1SJ

Jamiat Ahl-e-Hadith
25 Midland Street, Skipton, North Yorkshire, BD23 1SE
Tel: 01758-790374
Contact: Mr Sana Ullah
Position: Imam
Activities: Worship, resource, inter-faith
Traditions: Sunni
Movements: Ahl-e-Hadith
Other Languages: Urdu
Affiliations: Jamiat Ahl-e-Hadith UK, Muslim World League

Agbrigg Muslim Association
26 St Catherine Street, Wakefield, West Yorkshire, WF1 5BW
Tel: 01924-256635
Contact: Rashid Ahmed Mughal
Position: President
Activities: Worship, resource, visits, youth, elderly, women

Traditions: Sunni
Movements: Deobandi, Tablighi Jamaat
Other Languages: Urdu, Arabic

Duke of York Street Mosque Committee
241 Doncaster Road, Wakefield, West Yorkshire, WF1 5DA
Contact: Mr M Bashir

Jamia Sawfia Mosque
Park Hill Lane, Eastmoor, Wakefield, West Yorkshire, SF1 4NJ

Madressa Arabia Islamia
18 Marsland Place, Wakefield, West Yorkshire, WF1 4NU
Tel: 01924-215053 **Tel:** 01924-379468 (h)
Contact: Mr Islam Ali Shah
Position: Trustee
Activities: Worship, resource, youth, elderly, women, books, inter-faith
Traditions: Sunni,
Movements: Deobandi, Tablighi Jamaat
Other Languages: Urdu, Arabic, Punjabi
Affiliations: Markazi Masjid, Dewsbury

Markazi Jamia Mosque
12 Grange Street, Wakefield, West Yorkshire, SF2 8TF
Tel: 01924-71469

Mosque
26 Katherine Street, off Agrbrigg Road, Wakefield, West Yorkshire
Tel: 01924-71469

Mosque
3 Marsland Street, Wakefield, West Yorskshire

Wakefield Muslim Society
3 Benjamin Street, Wakefield, West Yorkshire
Contact: Mr M Younas

Mosque
62 Heslington Road, York, North Yorkshire
Tel: 01904-31098

UK Islamic Mission
Bull Lane, Bull Compound, York, North Yorkshire
Contact: H Mohamud Buccus
Position: President
Activities: Worship, umbrella, visits, inter-faith
Traditions: Sunni

Movements: Ahl-e-Hadith
Other Languages: Arabic, Urdu, French
Affiliations: UK Islamic Mission

York Mosque (UK Islamic Mission)
Bull Lane, Hull Road, York, North Yorkshire
Contact: Mr S Khan

York Muslim Association
76 Fourth Avenue, York, North Yorkshire, YO3 0UA
Tel: 01904-413081   **Tel:** 01904-426261 (h)
Contact: Aziz Suleman Karbani
Position: Secretary
Activities: Worship, resource, inter-faith
Other Languages: Urdu, Bangali, Katchi, Gujarati

York University Islamic Society
c/o Students Union, York, North Yorkshire,
Y01 5DD

NORTH WEST
Regional and County Bodies

Lancashire Council of Mosques
Bangor Street Community Centre, Norwich Street,
Blackburn, Lancashire, BB1 6NZ
Tel: 01254-692289   **Fax:** 01254-692289
Contact: Abdul Hamid Qureshi
Position: Director
Activities: Umbrella, visits, youth, elderly, women
Other Languages: Urdu, Gujarati, Bengali, Pushto
Affiliations: Muslim Council of Britain

City, Town or Local Bodies

Accrington Masjid Committee
62 Nelson Street, Accrington, Lancashire,
BB5 2HQ

Gousia Razvia Jamia Mosque & Islamic Centre
Higher Antley Street, Accrington, Lancashire,
BB5 0QH
Tel: 01254-389972
Contact: Mr M Iqbal

Itehad Muslimen
18 Richmond Hill Street, Accrington, Lancashire,
BB5 0SP

Itehad-ul-Muslimeen
160 Blackburn Road, Accrington, Lancashire,
BB5 0SP

Madressah Talim-ul-Islam
50 Fountain Street, Accrington, Lancashire,
BB5 0QP
Tel: 01254-231533
Contact: Mr M S Bhatti
Position: Chairperson

Muslim Youth Movement
6 Richmond Hill Street, Accrington, Lancashire,
BB5 1RH

Naemia Academy
134 Richmond Hill Street, Accrington, Lancashire,
BB5 0PZ

Pakistan/Kashmir Death Committee
48 Portland Street, Accrington, Lancashire, BB5
1RH
Contact: c/o Mr K Hussain

Raza Jamia Mosque
Grimshaw Street, Accrington, Lancashire, BB5 0AZ
Tel: 01254-393454
Contact: Mr Haji F Ellahi
Position: Chairman

Raza Jamia Mosque & Islamic Centre
229 Blackburn Road, Accrington, Lancashire,
BB5 0AL
Tel: 01254-393454
Contact: Mr Haji F Ellahi
Position: Chairman

United Muslim Mothers Association
12 Charter Street, Accrington, Lancashire, BB5 0SG

Dar-ul-Uloom Qadiria Jilania
95 Burling Street, Ashton-under-Lyne, Lancashire,
OL6 6HJ
Tel: 0161-308-3510
Contact: Mohammed Zafar Iqbal Qazi
Position: Secretary
Activities: Worship, resource, elderly, inter-faith
Traditions: Sunni
Movements: Barelwi
Other Languages: Urdu, Punjabi, Arabic, Persian
Affiliations: Jamat Hal Sunit UK

International Muslim Movement
26/28 Albion Street, Ashton-under-Lyne,
Lancashire, OL6 6HQ

Jamia Masjid
Newton Street, Penny Meadow, Ashton-under-Lyne, Lancashire, OL6 6EJ
Tel: 0161-330-0617
Contact: Mr M Azhar
Position: Trustee
Activities: Worship
Traditions: Sunni
Movements: Deobandi
Other Languages: Urdu

Madrassa Arbia Taleemul Qur'an & Mosque
Richmond Hill, Katherine Street, Ashton-under-Lyne, Lancashire, OL7 0AL
Tel: 0161-330-9837

Muslim Welfare Society
St Mary's School, Newton Lane, Ashton-under-Lyne, Lancashire, OL6 6EJ

Tameside Muslim Welfare Association Mosque
225 Stamford Street, Ashton-under-Lyne, Lancashire

Tameside Muslim Welfare Society
230 Oldham Road, Ashton-under-Lyne, Lancashire
Contact: Mr Zikar-Ur-Rehman

Blackburn Council of Mosques
108-110 Audley Range, Blackburn, Lancashire, BB1 1TF
Tel: 01254-676989
Contact: Mr Nizam Makda
Position: Chairman

Hanfi-Sunni Circle & Mosque
48 Altom Stret, Blackburn, Lancashire, BB1 7NE
Tel: 01254-52608

Hanfi Sunni Jamia Masjid & Hanfi Sunni Muslim Association
33a Randall Street, Blackburn, Lancashire, BB1 7LG
Tel: 01254-52170
Contact: Malik Khadam Hussain

Hanfia Muslim Raza Mosque
40 Balaclava Street, Blackburn, Lancashire

Hazrat Sulton Bahan Trust, Blackburn, UK
300 Whalley Range, Blackburn, Lancashire
BB1 6NL
Tel: 01254-673395

Contact: Mr Khaliq Hussain
Activities: Resource
Tradition: Sunni
Movements: Barelwi Tassawuf
Other Languages: Punjabi, Urdu
Affiliations: Lancashire Council of Mosques

Islamic Academy UK
c/o 2 Blackburn Street, Blackburn, Lancashire

Islamic Centre & Mosque
2 Kendal Street, Blackburn, Lancashire

Islamic Cultural Centre & Jamee Mosque
Cumberland Street, Blackburn, Lancashire, BB1 1JP
Tel: 01254-583345 (h)
Contact: Moulana Ahmed Suleman Sidat JP
Position: Chairman
Activities: Worship, resource, visits, youth, elderly, women
Traditions: Sunni
Other Languages: Gujarati, Urdu
Affiliations: Blackburn Council of Mosques; Lancashire Council of Mosques; UK Action Committee on Islamic Affairs; Muslim World League

Islamic Education Centre
44 Devonport Road, Blackburn, Lancashire, BB2 1HW
Contact: Mr Mohammed Sabir

Islamic Jihad of Europe
14 Corwen Close, Blackburn, Lancashire, BB1 8HZ

Islamic Lending & Reference Library
55 Whalley New Road, Blackburn, Lancashire, BB1 6JY
Tel: 01254-681558

Islamic Religious Centre & Mosque
209 Preston New Road, Blackburn, Lancashire, BB2 6BN
Tel: 01254-2607319
Contact: Yakood Fancy
Position: President

Islamic Welfare Association
25 Logwood Street, Blackburn, Lancashire, BB1 9TU
Contact: Mr Mohammed Hussain
Position: Secretary
Traditions: Ithna Asheri

Jame Masjid-e-Noor
71 Saunders Road, off Preston New Road,
Blackburn, Lancashire, BB2 6LS
Tel: 01254-698609
Contact: Raja Muhammad Sharif Qazi
Position: President

Jamia Ghosia Mosque
98-99 Chester Street, Blackburn, Lancashire,
BB1 1DR
Tel: 01254-51080
Contact: M Aslam

Jamiah Mosque
Merry Street, off: Audley Range, Blackburn,
Lancashire, BB1

Kokni Muslim Association
Newton Street, Blackburn, Lancashire, BB1 1NE

Lancashire Association of Muslims
c/o Comet Cash and Carry Company, Empire
Building, Blackburn, Lancashire
Contact: Mr A Patel

Lancashire Council of Mosques
Bangor Street Community Centre, Norwich Street,
Blackburn, Lancashire, BB1 6NZ
Tel: 01254-692289   **Fax:** 01254-692289
Contact: Abdul Hamid Qureshi
Position: Director
Activities: Umbrella, visits, youth, elderly, women
Other Languages: Urdu, Gujarati, Bengali, Pushto
Affiliations: Muslim Council of Britain

Madina Mosque
19-23 Oak Street, Blackburn, Lancashire

Madni Mosque
19 Lancaster Place, Blackburn, Lancashire,
BB2 6GT
Tel: 01254-676618
Contact: Mr M A Sharif

Madressa e Talimul-Islam
86 Stansfield Street, Blackburn, Lancashire, BB2
2NG
Contact: Abdul Aziz Mulla

Madressa Islamia
Segar Street, Great Harwood, Blackburn, Lancashire
Contact: M Anwar
Position: Trustee/Chairman
Activities: Worship, resource, visits

Trditions: Sunni
Movements: Tablighi Jamaat
Other Languages: Punjabi, Urdu
Affiliations: Lancashire Council of Mosques

Madressa Talim-ul-Islam
Bangor Street Community Centre, Blackburn,
Lancashire, BB1 6NZ

Madressa-e-Raza
Chorlton Street, Blackburn, Lancashire, BB1 6NF
Contact: Mr Mohammed Patel

Masjid-e-Aneesul Islam
Troy Street, off Whalley Range, Blackburn,
Lancashire, BB1 6NY
Tel: 01254-583245
Contact: Mr A Patel

Masjid-e-Hidayah
50 Millham Street, Blackburn, Lancashire,
BB1 6EU
Contact: Imam Patel
Position: Imam

**Masjid-e-Noor-ul-Islam & Islamic Education
Society**
108-110 Audley Road, Blackburn, Lancashire,
BB1 1TF
Tel: 01254-676989
Contact: Mr M Patel
Position: Vice President

Masjid-e-Rizwan
Newton Street, Blackburn, Lancashire, BB1 1NE
Tel: 01254-263707
Contact: Mr B Mullah

Masjid-e-Sajedeen & Madressa-e-Islamiah
Plane Tree Road, Little Harwood, Blackburn,
Lancashire, BB1 5PA
Contact: Mr Ibrahim Hassan Chopdat
Position: General Secretary
Activities: Worship, resource, visits
Traditions: Sunni (Imam Hanafi)
Movements: Tablighi Jamaat (Madressa Deoband)
Other Languages: Arabic, Gujarati, Urdu
Affiliations: Blackburn Council of Mosques;
Lancashire Council of Mosques; Muslim World
League; UK Action Committee on Islamic Affairs

Masjide Tauheedul Islam Mosque
31 Bicknell Street, Blackburn, Lancashire, BB1 7EY
Tel: 01254-54021   **Tel:** 01254-662442 (h)

Contact: Hanif Soofi
Position: President
Activities: Worship, resource, visits
Traditions: Sunni
Movements: Deobandi, Tablighi Jamaat
Other Languages: Urdu, Gujarati, Arabic
Affiliations: Lancashire Council of Mosques;
Union of Muslim Organisations of UK & Eire

Masjidul-Momineen & Kokni Muslim Welfare Society
Ash Street, Little Harwood, Blackburn, Lancashire,
BB1 6LX
Contact: Secretary

Mosque
19-21 Oak Street, Blackburn, Lancashire

Mosque
40 Lambeth Street, Blackburn, Lancashire

Muslim Community Centre
Opposite Balaclava Hotel, 69 Victoria Cross,
Blackburn, Lancashire, BB1 6DN

Muslim Welfare Institute
35 Wellington Street, St John's, Blackburn,
Lancashire, BB1 8AF
Contact: Manlana Mohammed Hanif Dudhwalia
Position: Secretary
Activities: Youth, newsletters
Other Languages: Urdu, Gujarati, Punjabi, Kokan

Naqshbandia Aslamiyya Spiritual Centre
112 Pringle Street, Blackburn, Lancashire, BB1 1SA
Tel: 01254-52480 **Tel:** 0958-609096 (h)
Contact: Sufi Mohammad Asghar
Activities: Worship, youth
Traditions: Sunni
Movements: Tassawuf
Other Languages: Urdu, Punjabi
Affiliations: Lancashire Council of Mosques; Imams
and Mosques Council; Naqshbandia Aslamiyya
Spiritual Trust

Religious Advice Centre
c/o Brookhouse Youth & Community Centre,
Bangor Street, Blackburn, Lancashire, BB1 6NZ
Tel: 01254-691551
Contact: Mr Imtiaz Hussain
Position: Preacher
Activities: Worship, resource, visits, youth, elderly,
women, newsletters, books, inter-faith

Traditions: Sunni, Spirituality Healing
Movements: All
Other Languages: Urdu, Punjabi, Gujarati, Arabic

Shi`a Islamic Centre (Mosque)
143 Preston New Road, Blackburn, Lancashire,
BB2 6BJ
Tel: 01254-265592 (h)
Contact: Nazir Hussain
Position: Secretary
Activities: Worship, resource, visits, youth, elderly,
women, inter-faith
Traditions: Ithna Asheri
Other Languages: Urdu, Punjabi, Gujarati
Affiliations: Lancashire Council of Mosques;
Majlis Ulama-e-Europe, Harrow; World Federation
of Khoja Ithna Asheri Jamaat, Stanmore

Surti Sunni Vohra Association
4 Norwich Street, Blackburn, Lancashire

UK Islamic Mission
Jame Masjid-e-Noor, 71 Saunders Road,
Blackburn, Lancashire, BB2 6LS
Tel: 01254-698609
Contact: Raja Muhammad Sharif Qazi
Position: President

Unity
P. O. Box 22, Blackburn, Lancashire, BB1 1RW

Islamic Community Centre & Mosque Bina Mahal
100 Rigby Road, Blackpool, Lancashire

Al Jamiah al Islamiyah Darul Uloom Lancashire, UK
Hospital Road (Former Blair Hospital), Bromley
Cross, Bolton, Lancashire, BL7 9PY
Tel: 01204-301550 **Fax:** 01204-598509
Contact: Quari Yakub Nanji
Position: Principal
Activities: Worship, resource, visits
Traditions: Sunni
Movements: Deobandi, Tablighi Jamaat
Other Languages: Gujarati, Urdu, Bengali, Arabic
Affiliations: UK Action Committee on Islamic
Affairs; Muslim Council of Britain; Muslim World
League

Al Rahman Masjid & Daubhill Muslim Society
2-14 Randal Street, Daubhill, Bolton, Lancashire,
BL3 4AQ

Tel: 01204-660177
Contact: Rashid Ahmed Nadat
Position: Secretary
Activities: Worship, resource, visits
Traditions: Sunni
Movements: Deobandi
Other Languages: Gujrati, Urdu

Anjuman Womens Group
c/o The Community Centre, High Street, Bolton,
Lancashire
Contact: Ms C Forrest

Ashrafia Mosque
Cannon Street North, Bolton, Lancashire,
BL3 5DN
Tel: 01204-384713
Contact: Mr Gulam Hussain Mohamed Kotwal
Position: Secretary
Activities: Worship
Traditions: Sunni
Movements: Deobandi
Languages: Gujarati, Urdu, Bengali, Arabic

Bolton Central Islamic Society
Taiyabah Mosque & Community Centre
31a Draycott Street, Bolton, Lancashire, BL1 8HD
Tel: 01204-335997
Contact: Mr A Aziz
Position: Spokesperson
Activities: Worship, resource, umbrella, visits,
youth, newsletters, books, inter-faith
Traditions: Sunni
Movements: Deobandi, Tablighi Jamaat
Other Languages: Gujarati, Arabic, Urdu
Affiliations: Lancashire Council of Mosques

Bolton Muslim Childrens Association
318 Crescent Road, Great Lever, Bolton, BL3 2LZ
(h)
Tel: 01204-523845 (h)
Contact: Abdul Khalique
Position: President
Activities: Resource, youth, inter-faith
Traditions: Sunni
Movements: Ahle Sunnah wal Jamaat
Other Languages: Urdu, Punjabi, Gujarati
Affiliations: Makka Mosque Community
&Cultural Centre

Bolton Muslim Community Association
392 Derby Street, Bolton, Lancashire, BL3 6LS

Bolton Muslim Welfare Trust
High Street, Bolton, Lancashire, BL3 6TA
Tel: 01204-361103 **Fax:** 01204-361103
Contact: Yakub M Patel
Position: Secretary
Activities: Resource, visits, youth, elderly, women,
books, inter-faith
Traditions: Sunni
Other Languages: Gujarati, Urdu
Affiliations: Association of Muslim Schools UK

Bolton Somali Muslims
48 Langdon Close, Bolton, Lancashire, BL1 2QN
Contact: c/o Mrs J Ibrahim

Bolton Surti Sunni Vohra Muslim Association
c/o 98 High Street, Bolton, Lancashire, BL3 6SZ
Tel: 01204-426489
Contact: Mr K Motala
Position: Manager

Canning Street Mosque
Canning Street, Bolton, Lancashire

Farnworth Cultural Centre
118 Market Street, Farnworth, Bolton, Lancashire
Tel: 01204-793793
Contact: Mr Iftkhar Khan

Great Lever Muslim Society
35 Sheringham Place, Daubhill, Bolton,
BL3 5EX (h)
Tel: 01204-385780 (h)
Contact: Mr Haroon Ibrahim
Position: Coordinator
Activities: Worship, resource
Traditions: Sunni
Movements: Deobandi
Other Languages: Gujarati, Urdu, Hindi

Kamboli Muslim Welfare Association
101 Mancroft Avenue, Bolton, Lancashire

Macca Mosque Muslim Community Centre
Grecian Crescent, Bolton Crescent, Bolton,
Lancashire, BL3 6QU
Tel: 01204-524200
Contact: Muhammad Zahoor
Position: General Secretary
Activities: Worship, resource, visits, youth
Traditions: Sunni
Other Languages: Urdu

Makki Mosque
352 Halliwell Road, Bolton, Lancashire, BL1 8AP

Makki Mosque & Islamic Cultural Centre
Eskrick Street, Bolton, Lancashire

Masjeed-e-Ghosia
81 Auburn Street, Bolton, Lancashire, BL3 6TQ
Contact: Yunus Chashmawala
Position: Secretary
Activities: Worship, resource
Traditions: Sunni
Movements: Hanfi
Other Languages: Gujarati, Urdu

Masjid-e-Noor-ul-Islam
Prospect Street, off Halliwell Road, Halliwell,
Bolton, Lancashire, BL1 3QH
Tel: 01204-535738
Contact: Shafiq Patel
Position: Secretary
Activities: Worship, resource, visits, youth, elderly,
women, inter-faith
Traditions: Sunni
Movements: Barelwi
Other Languages: Gujarati, Urdu
Affiliations: Bolton Council of Mosques,
Lancashire Council of Mosques; World Islamic
Mission

Mosque
Dean Road, Bolton, Lancashire

Mosque
64 Lawrence Street, Farnworth, Bolton, Lancashire

Muslim Youth & Community Centre
Astley Street, Bolton, Lancashire, BL1 8EH

Rehman Mosque
6 Broadhurst Court, Bolton, Lancashire, BL3 6JB
Contact: Y A Patel

Sugra Mosque
24 Egerton Street, Farnworth, Bolton, Lancashire,
B14 7LE

Zakaria Mosque
20 Peace Street, Bolton, Lancashire, BL3 5LJ
Tel: 01204-435002
Contact: Mr Ayoob Limbada

Ithaas ul-Muslimih
5 Bird Street, Brierfield, Lancashire

Jamiah Sultania Mosque
3-7 Bridge Street, Brierfield, Lancashire, BB9 5PE
Tel: 01254-692764

**Anjaman-e-Muhibban-e-Ahel-e-Bait Hussainia
Mosque**
37 Grey Street, Burnley, Lancashire, BB10 1BA
Contact: Imam

Burnley Council of Mosques
3 Elm Street, Burnley, Lancashire, BB10 1AJ
Tel: 01282-412107
Contact: Mr Mohamed Shareef Quadri
Position: Secretary

Burnley Funeral Committee
81 Gordon Street, Burnley, Lancashire
Contact: Mr A Khan

Central Jamia Masjid-e-Farooq-i-Acam
North Street, Burnley, Lancashire, BB10 1LU

Darul Uloom
141 Leyland Road, Burnley, Lancashire, BB11 3DN
Tel: 01282-412082 (h)
Contact: Abdul Aziz
Position: Secretary
Activities: Resource, youth
Traditions: Sunni
Movements: Barelwi
Other Languages: Urdu
Affiliations: Lancashire Council of Mosques

Ghausiah Mosque
66-68 Colne Road, Burnley, Lancashire

Hussania Young Muslims Asccociation
36 Grey Street, Burnley, Lancashire, BB10 1BA

Islamic Centre
38 Brougham Street, Burnley, Lancashire,
BB12 0AS
Contact: Mr G N Chaudhry

Ithaad
51 Fairfield Drive, Burnley, Lancashire, BB10 2PU

Itifaq
135 Grey Street, Burnley, Lancashire

Jamia Masjid Abu-Baker
56 Brougham Street, Burnley, Lancashire,
BB12 0AT
Tel: 01282-422358 **Tel:** 01282-423089 (h)

Fax: 01282-701062
Contact: Mohammad Bashir
Position: President
Activities: Worship, resource, umbrella, visits, youth, elderly, women, inter-faith
Traditions: Sunni
Movements: Barelwi, Deobandi/Jamati-i-Islami
Other Languages: Arabic, Urdu, Bengali
Affiliations: Lancashire Council of Mosques

Jamia Masjid-e-Farooq-e-Azam
North St (off Colne Rd), Duke Bar, Burnley, Lancashire, BB10 1LU
Tel: 01282-22321
Contact: Mr Izat Khan

Mosque
54 Hebrew Road, Burnley, Lancashire, BB10 1NQ

Shah Jalal Mosque & Madrassa
112-114 Burns Street, Burnley, Lancashire, BB12 0AJ
Tel: 01282-456497 (h)
Contact: Councillor Mozaquir Ali
Position: President
Activities: Worship, resource, visits, youth, elderly, women
Traditions: Sunni
Movements: Ahl-e-Hadith
Other Languages: Bangladeshi, Urdu
Affiliations: Lancashire Council of Mosques

UK Islamic Mission
54 Hebrew Road, Burnley, Lancashire BB10 1NQ

Urdu Society Mosque
18 March Street, Burnley, Lancashire BB12 0BT
Contact: Mr Nasar Ullah Khan

Young Muslims (UK)
Burnley Branch, Burnley, Lancashire, BB10 1NQ

Darul Uloom Muslim Training College
Holcombe Hall, Holcombe Brook, Ramsbottom, Bury, Lancashire, BL8 4NG
Tel: 01706-825160
Contact: Mufti Shabbir

Imamia Islamic Mission
104 Rochdale Road, Bury, Lancashire, BL9 7B
Tel: 01173-491434   **Tel:** 0161-280-8901
Fax: 0161-280-8901
Contact: Mr Qulab Hussain Shah

Position: Secretary
Activities: Worship, visitors, youth, women, inter-faith
Traditions: 'Ithna Asheri'
Other Languages: Urdu, Punjabi

Islamic Centre
Church Street, Bury, Lancashire, BL9 6AZ
Tel: 0161-764-7306
Contact: Mr Liaqat Ali
Position: Trustee

Islamic Cultural Association
108 Walmersley Road, Bury, Lancashire, BL9 6DX
Tel: 0161-764-7306
Contact: Mr Qudrat Ali
Position: Chair
Activities: Youth, elderly, women, inter-faith
Traditions: Sunni
Other Languages: Urdu, Punjabi

Jinnah Youth
65 Shepard Street, Bury, Lancashire

Khizra Mosque
85 Warmersley Road, Bury, Lancashire, BL9 5AN
Tel: 0161-764-1638   **Fax:** 0161-763-6884
Contact: Moulana Muhammad Bilal
Position: Imam
Activities: Worship
Traditions: Sunni
Movements: Deobandi, Tablighi Jammaat
Other Languages: Urdu, Punjabi, Pushto

Mosque
32 Heywood Street, Bury, Lancashire
Tel: 0161-764-0491

Mosque & Dar-ul-Uloom
Holcombe Hill, Holcombe, Bury, Lancashire, BL8 4NG
Tel: 01706-826106

Noor Islam
48 Bridgefield Street, Bury, Lancashire

Noor-ul-Islam Mosque
2/4 Yarwood Street, Bury, Lancashire, BL9 7AU
Tel: 0161-705-2891   **Tel:** 0161-797-1932 (h)
Contact: Muzamil Khan
Position: President
Activities: Worship, visits, youth, inter-faith
Traditions: Sunni

Movements: Barelwi, Tassawuf
Other Languages: Punjabi, Urdu, Arabic

Prestwich Muslim Parents Association
20 Harman Avenue, Prestwich, Bury, Lancashire

Mosque
85 Walmersley Road, Bury, Lancashire

Mosque
King Street, Botcher Gate, Near City Centre,
Carlisle, Cumbria

Chester Islamic Society
8 Westlorne Street, Chester, Cheshire, CH1 4AF

Shah-Jalal Mosque
45 Egerton Street, Chester, Cheshire, CH1 3NP
Tel: 01244-316356 **Tel:** 01244-313424 (h)
Contact: Al Haj Mohammad Mubarak Ali
Position: Trustee
Activities: Worship, visits
Traditions: Sunni
Movements: Ahl-e-Hadith
Other Languages: Bengali, Hindi

Chorley Muslim Welfare Society
142 Lyons Lane, Chorley, Lancashire, PR6 0PJ
Tel: 01257-268644
Contact: Mohammed Sajid
Position: Secretary
Activities: Worship, resource, youth
Traditions: Sunni
Movements: Deobandi, Tablighi Jamaat
Other Languages: Urdu, Gujarati, Bengali
Affiliations: Racial Equality Council, Preston;
Lancashire Council of Mosques

Madina Mosque
3 Chapel Street, Colne, Lancashire, BB8 5AH

Madina Masjid
910 Knotts Lane, Colne, Lancashire

Shajalal Mosque
286 Walthall Street, Crewe, Cheshire

Mosque
21-23 Victoria Street, Darwen, Lancashire, BB1 5JJ
Tel: 01254-692488 (h)
Contact: Mahmood Dalvi
Position: Secretary
Activities: Worship, resource, inter-faith
Traditions: Sunni

Movements: Tablighi Jamaat
Other Languages: Urdu, Punjabi, Hindi, Gujarati
Affiliations: Lancashire Council of Mosques;
Muslim World League

Mosque
64 Lawrence Road, Farnworth, Lancashire

Great Harwood Mosque & Mosque Committee
1 Park Street, Great Harwood, Lancashire, BB6 7BP
Contact: Mr M Ashraf
Position: Secretary

Mosque
24 Edmond Street, off Princess Street, Great
Harwood, Lancashire

Bait-ul-Mukarram Mosque
Union Street, Haslingden, Lancashire, BB4 5QD

Masjid-e-Bilal
2-4 Beaconsfield Street, Haslingden, Lancashire,
BB4 5TD
Tel: 01706-218830 (h)
Contact: Muhammad Rahman
Position: Secretary
Activities: Worship
Traditions: Sunni
Movements: Deobandi, Tablighi Jamaat
Other Languages: Urdu, Pushto, Punjabi, Hindi
Affiliations: Lancashire Council of Mosques

Masjid-e-Bilal & Islamic Centre
127 Blackburn Road, Haslingden, Lancashire,
BB4 5HN
Tel: 01706-25335
Contact: Mr Said-ul-Rahman

Muslim Welfare Association
30 Sandown Road, Haslingden, Lancashire,
BB4 6PL

Rawtenstall Islamic Centre
154 Manchester Road, Haslingden, Lancashire

Jamee Mosque
21 Jackson Street, Hyde, Cheshire, SK14 1BX
Tel: 0161-366-1551
Contact: The Chairman
Activities: Worship, resource
Traditions: Sunni
Movements: Ahle-Sunnah Wal Jamaat
Other Languages: Bengali, Urdu, Arabic

Mosque
28 St Thomas Street, Hyde, Cheshire

Lancaster Islamic Society
Fenton Street, Lancaster, Lancashire, LA1 1LA
Tel: 01524-64131
Contact: The President
Activities: Worship, visits
Traditions: Sunni
Movements: Deobandi, Tablighi Jamaat
Other Languages: Urdu, Arabic, Gujarati
Affiliations: Lancashire Council of Mosques;
Markaji Masjid Dewsbury; Darool Uloom Deoband

Lancaster Islamic Society Mosque
1/2 Hawerden Cottages, Off Hinde Street,
Lancaster, Lancashire, LA1 9DJ
Tel: 01524-64131
Contact: Mr I Patel
Position: Secretary

Masjide Tauheedul Islam
29 Bicknell Street, Lancaster, Lancashire
Tel: 01254-54318

Muslim Welfare Society & Raza Mosque
71 Blade Street, Lancaster, Lancashire, LA1 1TS
Tel: 01524-32087
Contact: Mr I Sulliman
Position: Secretary

Al-Rahma Mosque & Liverpool Muslim Society
29-31 Hathersley Street, Liverpool, Merseyside,
L8 2TJ (h)
Tel: 0151-709-2560 **Tel:** 0151-709-7504 (h)
Contact: Mr Mohammad Al-Khateeb
Position: Imam
Activities: Worship, resource, visits, youth, elderly,
women, inter-faith
Other Languages: Arabic, Urdu, Somali
Traditions: Sunni

Islamic Society of Britain (Liverpool Branch)
119 Queen's Drive, Mossley Hill, Liverpool,
Merseyside, L18 1JL
Tel: 0151-733-2940 (h)
Contact: Dr A Z Khan
Position: President
Activities: Worship, youth, women, newsletters,
inter-faith
Traditions: Sunni
Other Languages: Urdu, Turkish, Arabic,
Malaysian
Affiliations: UK Islamic Mission UK; World

Islamic Movement

Liverpool University Islamic Society
Islamic Prayer Room, Old Students Union,
Brownlow Hill, Liverpool, Merseyside

UK Islamic Mission (Liverpool Branch)
119 Queens Drive, Mossley Hill, Liverpool,
Merseyside, L18 1JL
Tel: 0151-733-2940 (h)
Contact: Dr A Z Khan
Position: President
Activities: Worship, visits, youth, women,
newsletters, inter-faith
Traditions: Sunni
Movements: Jamati-i-Islami
Other Languages: Urdu, Punjabi, Pushtu, Arabic
Affiliations: UK Islamic Mission; World Islamic
Movement

Anjuman-e-Hamidiyah
10 Tollgate Close, Longsight, Manchester, Greater
Manchester, M13 0LG

Anjuman-e-Taraqqi-e-Urdu
6 Birkdale Road, Manchester, Greater Manchester,
M8
Contact: Mrs Rizui

Bohra Mosque
2-4 Slade Lane, Longsight, Manchester, Greater
Manchester

College of Islamic Studies
3 Woodlands Road, Cheetham Hill, Manchester,
Greater Manchester, M8
Tel: 0161-773-5257 **Tel:** 0161-740-3696 (h)
Contact: Qamaruzzaman Azmi

**Dar-ul-Uloom Islamia Education & Cultural
Society**
1 Hawkhurst Road, Longsight, Manchester, Greater
Manchester, M13 0SJ
Tel: 0161-256-2812
Contact: Zahir Ahmed
Position: Trustee
Activities: Worship, resource
Other Languages: Urdu
Affiliations: Manchester Council of Mosques

**Dar-Ul-Aman North West Muslim Housing
Association Limited**
Mazda House, 40 Raby Street, Greater Manchester,
M16 7EB

Didsbury Mosque & Islamic Centre
271 Burton Road, Off Barlow Moor Road, West
Didsbury, Greater Manchester, M20 2WA
Tel: 0161-434-2254 **Tel:** 0161-491-2943
Contact: Mohammed Saeed Al-Badinjiki
Position: Chair
Activities: Worship, visits, youth, elderly, women,
newsletters, inter-faith
Traditions: Sunni
Other Languages: Arabic

Eccles & Salford Islamic Society
5 Liverpool Road, Eccles, Manchester, Greater
Manchester, M30 0WB
Activities: Worship

Hidayah Mosque
2 Seymour Place, off Humphrey Road, Old
Trafford, Manchester, Greater Manchester, M16
Position: Maulana Abdulhai Pat

Hiduyutal Muslim Society
83 Humphrey Road, Old Trafford, Manchester,
Greater Manchester, M16

Hijaz Islamic Foundation
62 Richmond Avenue, Sedgley Park, Prestwich,
Manchester, Greater Manchester, M25
Tel: 0161-773-5257
Contact: Naqar Azmi

Hijra Mosque
63 Humphrey Road, Manchester, Greater
Manchester, M16

Hijra School
28 Hall Lane, Manchester, Greater Manchester,
M23 8AQ
Contact: c/o Dr A M Mangood

Ibad-ul-Rahman Trust
3 Woodlands Road, Manchester, Greater
Manchester, M8 7LF
Tel: 0161-740-3696 **Tel:** 0161-643-5499 (h)
Contact: Dr Bashir Ahmad
Position: Trustee

Islamic Academy of Manchester
19 Chorlton Terrace, Brunswick, Manchester,
Greater Manchester, M13 9TD
Tel: 0161-273-1145
Contact: Maulana Hafiz Muhammad Iqbal
Rangooni

Position: Imam
Activities: Worship, resource, visits, youth, elderly,
women, newsletters, books, inter-faith
Traditions: Sunni
Movements: Deobandi
Languages: Punjabi, Urdu, Arabic, Gujrati
Affiliations: Deoband, India

Islamic Centre
271 Burton Road, West Didsbury, Manchester,
Greater Manchester, M20 8WA

Islamic Centre
48 Bridgefield Street, Radcliffe, Manchester, Greater
Manchester, M26

Islamic Society
Manchester University, Oxford Road, Manchester,
Greater Manchester, M13 9PL

Islamic Welfare Circle
c/o 127 Manley Road, Whalley Range,
Manchester, Greater Manchester

Islamic Welfare Circle
c/o 28 Hanley Avenue, Stretford, Manchester,
Greater Manchester
Position: Mr A Ghandi Choudhury

Islamic Welfare Circle
c/o 29 Northleigh Road, Firstwood, Manchester,
Greater Manchester
Contact: Mr Azmat Ullah

Islamic Welfare Circle
403 Barlow Moor Road, Chorlton, Manchester,
Greater Manchester, M21

Islamic Youth Movement
66 Woodlands Road, Cheetham, Manchester,
Greater Manchester, M8 7NF
Tel: 0161-740-1665 **Tel:** 0161-740-0577 (h)
Contact: Mr Salam
Position: Chair

Itehad-ul-Muslimeen
92 Duncan Road, Manchester, Greater Manchester,
M13 0GU

**Jamia Mosque & Ibadur Rahman Cultural
Society**
3 Woodlands Road, off Cheetham Hill Road,
Cheetham, Manchester, Greater Manchester,
M8 7LF

Tel: 0161-740-3696 **Tel:** 161-643-5499 (h)
Contact: Dr Bashir Ahmad
Position: Trustee

Jamiat Ahle Hadith
125 Beresford Road, Manchester, Greater
Manchester, M13 0TA

Ladies Islamic Circle
271 Burton Road, Manchester, Greater Manchester,
M20

Lajna Ama-U-Lah
4 Greenhays Lane, Hulme, Manchester, Greater
Manchester

Madina Masjid & Islamic Centre
2 Barlow Road, off Stockport Road, Manchester,
Greater Manchester, M19 3DJ
Tel: 0161-224-5143 **Tel:** 0161-224-4974
Contact: Habib ur Rahman
Position: Imam
Activities: Worship, resource, visits, youth, elderly,
inter-faith
Traditions: Sunni
Movements: Deobandi, Jamati-i-Islami
Other Languages: Urdu, Panjabi, Bengali
Affiliations: Muslim Educational Trust, London;
UK Action Committee on Islamic Affairs; Muslim
World League

Manchester Central Mosque & Islamic Cultural Centre
20 Upper Park Road, Manchester, Greater
Manchester, M14 5RU
Tel: 0161-224-4119
Contact: Shabbir Ahmed
Position: Committee Member
Activities: Worship, visits
Traditions: Sunni
Other Languages: Urdu, Punjabi
Affiliations: Greater Manchester Council of
Mosques; Ahl-e-Sunnat

Manchester Council of Mosques
c/o North Manchester Mosque, 3 Woodland Road,
Manchester, M8 7LF
Tel: 0161-643-5499 (h)
Contact: Dr Bashir Ahmed
Position: Chairman

Manchester Islamic High School For Girls
55 High Lane, Chorlton, Manchester, Greater
Manchester, M21 9FA
Tel: 0161-881-2127 **Fax:** 0161-861-0534
Contact: Mrs Mona Mohamed
Position: Acting Headteacher
Activities: Resource
Traditions: Sunni
Movements: Ahl-e-Hadith
Other Languages: Urdu, Arabic, Bengali

Manchester Muslim Educational Council
PO Box 28, Eccles, Manchester, Greater
Manchester, M30 9AB

Manchester Muslim Welfare Association
180 Brook Lane, Levenshulme, Manchester, Greater
Manchester, M19
Tel: 0161-225-5960

Masjid-cum-Khanquah Imdadiah
Blackburn Street, Old Trafford, Manchester, Greater
Manchester, M16
Tel: 0161-226-9883 **Fax:** 0161-227-9011
Contact: Hafiz Muhammad Iqbal Rangooni
Position: Trustees
Activities: Worship, resource, visits, youth, elderly,
newsletters, books, inter-faith
Traditions: Sunni
Movements: Deobandi
Other Languages: Urdu, Gujarati, Hindi/Punjabi,
Burmese

Masjid-e-Imdadiah
c/o 52 Milner Street, Blackburn Street, Manchester,
Greater Manchester, M16 7GG

Masjid-e-Noor
38 Carlton Street, Old Trafford, Manchester, Greater
Manchester, 16
Tel: 0161-226-3163 (h)
Contact: Abu Chunara
Position: Chairman
Activities: Worship, resource
Traditions: Sunni
Movements: Deobandi
Other Languages: Gujrati, Urdu

Mosque
229 Clarendon Road, Whalley Range, Manchester,
Greater Manchester

Mosque
25 Bellot Street, Manchester, Greater Manchester,
M8 7PQ

Mosque
Barlowmoor Road, Off: Burton Road, Manchester,
Greater Manchester, M20

Mosque
94 Bignoe Street, Manchester, Greater Manchester,
M8 7SE

Mosque & Darul Uloom
81 Stamford Road, Longsight, Manchester, Greater
Manchester, M13 O5W
Tel: 0161-256-2812

Muslim Advice Centre (UK Islamic Mission)
443 Cheetham Hill Road, Cheetham Hill,
Manchester, Greater Manchester, M8 0PF
Tel: 0161-740-3351 **Tel:** 0161-740-1665 (h)
Contact: M. Abdus Salam
Position: Chairman
Activities: Worship, resource, media, umbrella,
visits, elderly, women, inter-faith
Traditions: Sunni
Movements: Deobandi, Jamati-i-Islami
Other Languages: Urdu, Arabic
Affiliations: UK Islamic Mission; The Muslim
World League

Muslim Association of Manchester
78 Dickenson Road, Rusholme, Manchester,
Greater Manchester, M14 5HF

Muslim Educational Society
c/o 272 Dickenson Road, Manchester, Greater
Manchester, M13 0YL

Muslim Parents Association
13 Hazel Avenue, Whalley Range, Manchester,
Greater Manchester, Lancashire, M16 8DY
Tel: 0161-860-7869 **Tel:** 0161-860-7869 (h)
Fax: 0161-860-7869
Contact: Napir Ahmed
Position: Co ordinator
Activities: Youth, elderly, women, inter-faith
Traditions: Sunni
Other Languages: Punjabi, Urdu, English, Arabic

Affiliations: Manchester Council of Mosques;
Union Of Muslim Organisations

Muslim Parliament of Britain (Northern Office)
458a Cheetham Fill Road, Manchester, Greater
Manchester, M8 9JW
Tel: 0161-720-9959 **Fax:** 0161-720-9959

Muslim Society & Community Advisory Service
76 Moss Park Road, Stretford, Manchester, Greater
Manchester

Muslim Welfare Association
180 Brown Lane, Levensholme, Manchester, Greater
Manchester, M19

Muslim Welfare House
272 Dickenson Road, Manchester, Greater
Manchester, M13 3DJ

Muslim Womens Co-op Association
c/o College Road, Manchester, Greater
Manchester, M16

Muslim Youth Foundation
Clydesdale House, 27 Turner Street, Manchester,
Greater Manchester, M4 1DY
Tel: 0161-832-5352 **Fax:** 0161-839-2104
Contact: Mr Ali Akbar
Position: Secretary

Muslim Youth Movement of Malaysia
63 Humphrey Road, Old Trafford, Manchester,
Greater Manchester, M16 9DE

Noor-Ul-Quran
83 Hamilton Road, Longsight, Manchester, Greater
Manchester, M13 0PD
Tel: 0161-224-0774
Contact: Mr Shahzada
Position: Chairman
Activities: Resource, media, umbrella, visits, youth,
elderly, women
Traditions: Sunni
Other Languages: Urdu, Arabic, Bengali

North Manchester Central Mosque
3 Woodlands Road, Cheetham Hill Road,
Manchester, Greater Manchester, M8 7LF
Tel: 0161-773-5257 **Tel:** 0161-740-3696 (h)
Contact: Dr Amanat Ali

Old Trafford Muslim Society
38 Carlton Street, Old Trafford, Manchester, Greater
Manchester

Salford Mosque
4 Harris Avenue, Davyhulme, Manchester, Greater
Manchester, M31
Tel: 0161-748-9261

Shah Jalal Mosque & Islamic Society
1a Eileen Grove, Off Platt Lane, Rusholme,
Manchester, Greater Manchester, M14 5WE
Tel: 0161-224-2165
Contact: The Chair
Activities: Worship
Traditions: Sunni
Other Languages: Bengali

Somali Women's Group
13 Horace Barnes Close, 31 Barne Hill Street, Moss
Side, Rusholme, Manchester, Greater Manchester,
M14 4LJ (h)
Tel: 0161-226-4038 (h)
Contact: Zenab Barud
Position: Secretary
Activities: Youth, elderly, women
Traditions: Sunni
Other Languages: Somali, Arabic

Sunni Muslim Association
20 Bridesoak Street, Cheetham, Manchester,
Greater Manchester, M8 7PN

Sunni Muslim Association
c/o 27 Greenstead Drive, Cheetham, Manchester,
Greater Manchester, M8

UK Islamic Mission
26 Denison Road, Victoria Park, Manchester,
Greater Manchester

UK Muslim Women Association
83 Denison Road, Rusholme, Manchester

UMIST Islamic Society
UMIST, PO Box 88, Manchester, Greater
Manchester, M60 1QD
Tel: 0161-236-3311
Email: L.M.Bourghli@stud.umist.ac.uk
Contact: Laurence Bourghli
Position: Chair
Activities: Worship, resource, women, inter-faith
Traditions: Sunni

Other Languages: Malaysian, Arabic, Urdu
Affiliations: Coordination Council of Islamic
Societies of Manchester; FOSIS North Federation
of Students Islamic Societies "FOSIS"

Young Muslim Organisation
c/o 81 Stamford Hill, Longsight, Manchester,
Greater Manchester, M13 05W

Young Muslim Sports Club
258 Barlow Moor Road, Chorlton-Cum Hardy,
Manchester, Greater Manchester, M21 8HA
Contact: Mr Aman Khan

Zakariyya Mosque & Madrassa
22-24 Clarendon Road, Whalley Range,
Manchester, Greater Manchester, M16 8LD
Tel: 0161-881-9860

Mossley Community Mosque
81 Egmont Street, Mossley, Lancashire
Tel: 01457-55507
Contact: Shazidur Rahman

Alim-o-Adab Society
8 Giles Street, Nelson, Lancashire

Anjuman-e-Adab (Nelson)
49 Vernon Street, Nelson, Lancashire

Anjuman-e-Urdu Adab
50 Brunswick Street, Nelson, Lancashire

Anjuman-e-Urdu-Adab
100 Hibson Road, Nelson, Lancashire

Anjuman Islahul Muslimin
7 Parrock Street, Nelson, Lancashire
Tel: 01282-696987
Contact: Rana Farooq Alam Khan

Anjuman Urdu Adab
8 Fountain Street, Nelson, Lancashire

Ghousia Jamia Mosque
Every Street, Nelson, Lancashire, BB9 7HG
Tel: 01282-694471
Contact: Mr Khan

Ilm-o-Adab Mission
155 Every Street, Nelson, Lancashire, BB9 7HG

Ilm-o-Adab Mission
13 Giles Street, Nelson, Lancashire, BB9 9UD

Tel: 01282-603296
Contact: Mr A Salimee

Islamic Mission UK
Islamic Centre, 4 Forest Street, Nelson, Lancashire, BB9 7NB

Ithaad Advice Centre
7 Cross Street, Nelson, Lancashire, BB9 7EN
Tel: 01282-694700 **Tel:** 01282-604016 (h)
Contact: Abdul Hazif Malik
Position: General Secretary
Activities: Youth, elderly, women, inter-faith
Traditions: Sunni
Movements: Jamati-i-Islami
Other Languages: Urdu, Punjabi

Ithaad ul Muslimin
27 Hartington Street, Brierfield, Nelson, Lancashire

Jamiat Ahl-e-Hadith
Mohammadi Masjid, Netherfield Road, Nelson, Lancashire
Tel: 01282-698229 **Tel:** 01282-705357 (h)
Contact: Mohammad Aslam
Position: President
Activities: Worship, resource, visits
Traditions: Sunni
Movements: Ahl-e-Hadith
Other Languages: Punjabi, Urdu, Arabic
Affiliations: Jamiat Ahl-e-Hadith

Jamia Ahle Sultania
49 Commercial Street, Brierfield, Nelson, Lancashire, BB9 5SG

Jamia Masjid Ghousian
Clayton Street, Nelson, Lancashire
Tel: 01282-61976
Contact: Sufi M Nosherwan

Jamnia Masjid Sultana
7 Bridge Street, Brierfield, Nelson, Lancashire
Tel: 01282-692764 **Tel:** 01282-698705 (h)
Contact: Raja Jemroze Khan
Position: President

Lahore Welfare Association
60 Hibson Road Nelson, Nelson, Lancashire, BB9 9AB (h)
Tel: 01282-690074 (h)
Contact: Mohamed Afzaal Chaudry
Position: President

Activities: Resource, youth, women
Traditions: Sunni
Movements: Barelwi
Other Languages: English, Urdu, Punjabi, Mir-Puri

Madina Masjid
45 Newport Street, Nelson, Lancashire

Markazi Bazami Ghosia & Mehria
26 Barkerhouse Road, Nelson, Lancashire
Contact: Iftikhar H Shah

Muslim Parents Association Madressa
68 Beaufort Street, Nelson, Lancashire, BB9

Pakistan Muslim League
54 Lomeshaye Road, Nelson, Lancashire

Pakistan Muslim League
19 Albert Street, Nelson, Lancashire

Pendle Council of Mosques
41 Forest Street, Nelson, Lancashire, BB9 7NB
Tel: 01282-694471
Contact: Mr Syed Akhtar Shah
Position: Chair

UK Islamic Mission (Nelson Branch)
4-6 Forest Street, Nelson, Lancashire, BB9 7NB
Tel: 01282-694471
Contact: Mr Ishtiaq Mohammed
Position: Secretary
Activities: Worship, resource, visits, women
Traditions: Sunni
Movements: Ahl-e-Hadith, Deobandi/ Jamati-i-Islami
Other Languages: Urdu, Punjabi, Arabic
Affiliations: Lancashire Council of Mosques; UK Islamic Mission; The Muslim World League

Asian Muslim Association
16 Brompton Street, Oldham, Lancashire

Asian Muslim Welfare Association
196 Waterloo Street, Glodwick, Oldham, Lancashire, OL4 1ES
Contact: Shamim Akhtar Khan

British Pakistan Muslim Welfare Association
11 Brompton Street, Glodwick, Oldham, Lancashire, OL14 1AB
Contact: Nadir Hussein

Coldhurst Mosque Committee
8 Rederse Street, Oldham, Lancashire, OL1 2EH
Contact: Mr Miah

Glodwick Bangladesh Mosque Committee & Jallalabad
Mosque, 52 Orme Street, Oldham, Lancashire, OL41RZ
Tel: 0161-6260132　**Tel:** 0161-6244565 (h)
Contact: Abdul Rahman
Position: Chairperson

Hussainia Islamic Mission
41 Kersley Street, Oldham, Lancashire, OL4 1DN
Tel: 0161-627-2155 (h)
Contact: Agha Hadi Ali Khan
Position: Priest
Activities: Worship, umbrella, youth, women, inter-faith
Traditions: Shi`a `Ithna Asheri
Other Languages: Urdu, Punjabi, Arabic

Islamic Centre
Stenfield Street, Couldhurst, Oldham, Lancashire

Jamia Islamic Ghausia
112 Oxford Street, Werneth, Oldham, Lancashire

Jamia Mosque
Derby Street, Werneth, Oldham, Lancashire

Jamia Mosque
116 Manchester Road, Werneth, Oldham, Lancashire, OL9 7AX
Tel: 0161-624-5448
Contact: Azam Khan
Position: President
Activities: Worship
Traditions: Sunni
Movements: Deobandi
Other Languages: Pushto, Punjabi, Urdu

Jamiat Ahl-e-Hadith
46 St Thomas Street, North Oldham, Lancashire

Jamiat Ahl-e-Hadith
23 Villiers Drive, Oldham, Lancashire, OL8 1DY
Contact: M I Bhatti

Jamiat Ahl-e-Hadith Mosque
11 Ross Street, Werneth, Oldham, Lancashire, OL8 1UA
Tel: 0161-620-8548 **Tel:** 01973-890976 (h)

Contact: Maulana Shariqur Rehman
Position: Imam
Activities: Worship, resource, visits, youth, women, books
Traditions: Sunni
Movements: Ahl-e-Hadith
Other Languages: Urdu, Arabic
Affiliations: Markzi Jamiat Ahl-e-Hadith UK

Jamiat Tabligh-ul-Islam
397 Park Road, Glodwick, Oldham, Lancashire, OL4 1SF
Contact: Mohammed Iqbal

Madina Mosque & Islamic Centre
29 Stanfield Centre, Oldham, Lancashire, OL1 2HA

Madrassar Taleem ul Quran
201 Lees Road, Oldham, Lancashire, OL14 1NW
Tel: 0161-678-0593
Contact: Iftikhar Ahmed Naweed
Position: Secretary

Middleton Road Mosque
101 Mars Street, Oldham, Lancashire, OL9 6QF

Minhaj-ul-Qur'an Movement UK
288 Manchester Street, Oldham, Lancashire, OL9 6HB
Tel: 0161-624-1425

Mosque
92 Napier Street East, Oldham, Lancashire

Muslim Workers Association
114 Bolton Street, Oldham, Lancashire, OL8 4BB

Nagina Mosque & Urdu School
74 Werneth Hall Road, Coppice, Oldham, Lancashire, OL8 1QZ
Tel: 0161-626-5194
Contact: Bashir Bhatti
Position: Vice President

Nusrat-ul-Islam
Pitt Street, Glodwick, Oldham, Lancashire
Tel: 0161-284-6053　**Tel:** 0161-284-3394 (h)
Contact: Mohammed Tufail
Position: President
Activities: Worship, resource, media, visits, youth, elderly, women, inter-faith
Traditions: Sunni
Movements: Deobandi, Tablighi Jamaat

Other Languages: Urdu, Punjabi, Pushtu, Bangla
Affiliations: Muslim World League

Nusrat-ul-Islam Mosque & Urdu School
266 Waterloo Street, Glodwick, Oldham,
Lancashire, OL4 1ER
Contact: M Rafique

Oldham Mosque & Islamic Centre
156-158 Middleton Road, Oldham, Lancashire,
OL9 6BG
Contact: Mr Arju Miah
Position: President
Activities: Worship, resource, visits
Traditions: Sunni
Movements: Barelwi
Other Languages: Bangladeshi

Oldham Muslim Housing Association Ltd
121 Union Street, Oldham, Lancashire, OL4 1TE

Oldham Muslim Housing Association Ltd
28 Gartside Street, Oldham, Lancashire, OL4 1BX

Pakistan Cultural Association
8-10 Worcester Street, Werneth, Oldham, Lancashire

Tabligh-ul-Islam Mosque
87 Greengate Street, Oldham, Lancashire

UK Islamic Mission
44 Manchester Road, Werneth, Oldham,
Lancashire, OL9 7AP
Tel: 0161-284-5913 **Tel:** 0161-284-0846 (h)
Contact: Mr Feroz Din
Position: President
Activities: Worship, resource, visits, youth, women,
inter-faith
Traditions: Sunni
Movements: Jamati-i-Islami
Other Languages: Urdu, Punjabi, Pushtu
Affiliations: Imams and Mosques Council; UK
Action Committee on Islamic Affairs

Werneth Mosque & Urdu School
48 Hereford Street, Oldham, Lancashire, OL9 7RQ
Tel: 0161-652-8018
Contact: Mr M Khan

Co-op Mosque
32 Holmbrook Road, Deepdale, Preston, Lancashire

Gujarat Sunni Muslim Community Centre
15 Eldon Street, Preston, Lancashire, PR1 7YD
Contact: G H Mulla
Position: Honorary General Sec

Gujarati Sunni Muslim Society - Masjid-e-Noor
Noor Street, Preston, Lancashire, PR1 1QS
Tel: 01772-881786
Contact: Secretary

Madrassa-e-Noorul-Islam
Noor Hall, Noor Street, Preston, Lancashire
Tel: 01772-827531
Contact: Hajji Ibrahim

Masjid-e-Aqsa Preston Hanfi Sunni Muslim Society
95-99 Fishwick Parade, Preston, Lancashire,
PR1 4XR
Tel: 01772-490965 **Tel:** 01772-462588 (h)
Contact: Haji Sandal Hussain
Position: General Secretary
Activities: Worship, resource
Traditions: Sunni
Movements: Barelwi
Other Languages: Urdu, Gujarati, Punjabi
Affiliations: Lancashire Council of Mosques;
Imams and Mosques Council; Muslim World
League

Masjid-e-Falah
135/137 Kent Street, Preston, Lancashire, PR1 1PE

Masjeed-e-Quba
17 Lex Street, Preston, Lancashire, PR1 4XL
Tel: 01772-701970
Contact: Bashir Ahmed
Position: Secretary

Masjid-e-Raza
103-105 St Paul's Road, Preston, Lancashire
Tel: 01772-203578 **Tel:** 01772-827785 (h)
Contact: Ghulam A Kausar

Medina Mosque
26-28 Fishwick Parade, Preston, Lancashire,
PR1 4XQ
Tel: 01772-788847
Contact: Musa Roked
Position: Secretary

Mosque
8 Portland Street, Preston, Lancashire

Muslim Girls Secondary School
Unit 1, 36 Deepdale Mill Street, Preston,
Lancashire, PR1 6QL

Preston & West Lancashire Council of Mosques
4 Varley Street, Preston, Lancashire
Tel: 01772-8844962
Contact: Mr Ibrahim Kabir
Position: Chair

Preston Muslim Cultural Centre
21 Fishergate Hill, Preston, Lancashire, PR1 8JB
Tel: 01772-824357
Contact: Sikander Vorajee
Position: Secretary
Activities: Worship, resource
Traditions: Sunni
Movements: Tablighi Jamaat
Other Languages: Gujarati, Urdu
Affiliations: Lancashire Council of Mosques

Preston Muslim Forum
17 Holmrook Road, Preston, Lancashire, PR1 6SR

Preston Muslim Society
18 Clarendon Street, Preston, Lancashire, PR1 3YN
Tel: 01772-257127
Contact: The Secretary
Activities: Worship
Other Languages: Gujarati, Urdu

Quwwatul Islam Mosque & Preston Muslim Society
Peel Hall Street, Deepdale, Preston, Lancashire
Tel: 01772-54578
Contact: Secretary

Bolton Bangladesh Association
8 Bury/Bolton Road, Radcliffe, Lancashire, M26 0LD
Contact: Dr F R Bhuiyan

Masjed Noor & Islamic Education Centre
72 Eton Hill Road, Radcliffe, Lancashire, M26 2XT
Tel: 0161-724-5465 (h)
Contact: M Muneer
Position: Chairman
Activities: Worship, resource, youth, inter-faith
Traditions: Sunni
Other Languages: Urdu, Punjabi, Pushtoo
Affiliations: Lancashire Council of Mosques; Racial Equality Council Bury

Pakistan Islamic Centre
18 Peter Street, Rawtenstall, Lancashire, BB4 7NR
Tel: 01706-216603
Contact: Mohammed Safdar
Position: Chairperson

Rossendale Council of Mosques
2 Peter Street, Rawtenstall, Lancashire, BB4 7NR

Shah Jalal Mosque & Cultural Centre
13a Longholme Road, Rawtenstall, Lancashire, BB4 7NJ
Tel: 01706-219151 **Tel:** 01706-210285 (h)
Contact: Muhammed Abu Asad Choudhury
Position: General Secretary
Activities: Worship
Traditions: Sunni
Movements: Ahlay Sunnath Al-Jamaat
Other Languages: Bangladeshi

Al-Amin Religious Teaching Centre
40 Corbet Street, Rochdale, Lancashire, OL16 2EX
Tel: 01706-359317 (h)
Contact: Mr Abdul Barik
Position: Religious Secretary
Activities: Worship, resource, visits
Traditions: Sunni
Movements: Barelwi
Other Languages: Bengali, Urdu, Arabic

Al-Quba Islamic Centre
Copenhagen Street, Rochdale, Lancashire, OL16

Anjumane Ahle Sunnat Wal Jamaat
2 South Street, Rochdale, Lancashire
Tel: 01706-45095

Bilal Mosque
Bulwer Street, Rochdale, Lancashire, OL16

Dar-ul-Uloom Jamia Chashtiah Monir Ul-Islam
Multi Purpose Community and Worship Centre, 49/53a Milkstone Road, Rochdale, Lancashire, OL11 1EB
Tel: 01706-50487
Contact: Hafiz Abdul Haq Chishti
Position: General Secretary
Activities: Worship, visits, youth, elderly, women, inter-faith
Traditions: Sunni
Affiliations: Rochdale Council Of Mosques; Imam & Mosques Council London; Jama'at Ahle Sunnat; World Islamic Mission

Golden Mosque
Lower Sheriff Street, Rochdale, Lancashire,
OL12 6TG
Tel: 01706-48681
Contact: Mr Ghauri
Position: President

Idara Talimul Islam
43 William Street, Rochdale, Lancashire,
OL11 1HW
Tel: 01706-45135 **Fax:** 01706-42517
Contact: Mr Muhammed Anwar
Position: Chairperson

Idarul Munawar Islamic Teaching Centre
94 Durham Street, off Oldham Road, Deeplish,
Rochdale, Lancashire, OL11 1UZ
Tel: 01706-41206 (h)
Contact: Mr Shafiq
Position: President
Activities: Worship, resource, youth, newsletters
Traditions: Sunni
Movements: Barelwi
Other Languages: Urdu, Pippuri, Punjabi
Affiliations: Ahle Sunnat Wal Jamaat; Sunni Youth
Movement; Darbar-e-Alia Shamkol Sharif

Islamic-Asna-e-Ashria
c/o 51 Pilling Street, Rochdale, Lancashire

Islamic Cultural Centre & Golden Mosque
Cornfield Steps, Off: Lower Sherriff Street,
Rochdale, Lancashire

Islamic Studies Centre
2 South Street, Rochdale, Lancashire, OL16

Islamic Youth Movement
25 Hare Street, Rochdale, Lancashire

Jalalia Jame Mosque
66 Trafalgar Street, Rochdale, Lancashire, OL1 6JL
Tel: 01706-46822
Contact: Moulana Mohammed L Faroque
Position: Chair
Activities: Worship
Traditions: Sunni
Other Languages: Bangladeshi, Bengali

Jamia Masjid Al-Furqhan
17 Philip Street, off Deeplish Road, Rochdale,
Lancashire
Tel: 01706-523370 **Tel:** 01706-33487 (h)

Contact: Mr Riaz ul-Haq
Position: President
Traditions: Sunni
Movements: Ahl-e-Hadith
Languages: Urdu, Punjabi
Affiliations: Markazi Jamiat Ahle-Hadith,
Birmingham

Madrassa Islamia Urdu Centre
58 Morley Street, Rochdale, Lancashire, OL16 4AL
Tel: 01706-343551 **Tel:** 01706-351008 (h)
Contact: M Ismail Misbahi
Position: Head
Activities: Worship, resource, visits, youth, women,
newsletters, inter-faith
Traditions: Sunni
Movements: Barelwi
Other Languages: Urdu, Hindi, Arabic, Persian

Madina Islamic Cultural Studies Centre
35 Whitworth Road, Rochdale, Lancashire,
OL12 0RA
Contact: Mohammed Ayub
Position: Religious Teacher
Activities: Youth
Traditions: Sunni
Other Languages: Urdu

Muslim Brothers Association
c/o 59 King Street East, Rochdale, Lancashire

Muslim Community of Wardleworth
12 Trafalgar Street, Rochdale, Lancashire

Neelie Mosque & Islamic Centre
25-27 Hare Street, Deeplish, Rochdale, Lancashire,
0L11 1JL
Tel: 01706-48094 **Tel:** 01706-59307 (h)
Contact: Mohammed Sharif Baleem
Position: Chairman
Activities: Worship, visits, youth, elderly, women
Traditions: Sunni
Other Languages: Urdu, Punjabi

Roch Aid
P. O. Box 786, Rochdale, Lancashire, OL12 6QE

Rochdale Muslim Society
47 Norford Way, Bamford, Rochdale, Lancashire,
OL11 5QS
Tel: 01706-526036 (h)
Contact: Dr A Rauf
Traditions: Sunni

Other Languages: Urdu, Punjabi

UK Islamic Mission

25 Hare Street, Deeplish, Rochdale, Lancashire,
OL11 1JL
Tel: 01706-48094 **Tel:** 01706-344167 (h)
Contact: Zamir Ahmed
Position: President
Activities: Resource, visits, youth, elderly, women,
inter-faith
Traditions: Sunni
Other Languages: Urdu, Punjabi
Affiliations: UK Islamic Mission

Mosque

5 Gardener Street, Salford, Greater Manchester, M6
Tel: 0161-748-9261

Muslim Welfare Association

17 Oakdale Avenue, Salford, Greater Manchester,
M6 8EE

Salford University Islamic & Cultural Association

15 Murray Street, Salford, Greater Manchester,
M7 9DX

Muslim Welfare & Educational Organisation

69 Fox Street, Edgeley, Stockport, Cheshire,
SK3 9EL
Tel: 0161-282-7059 (h)
Contact: The Chair
Activities: Resource, youth, women
Traditions: Sunni
Movements: Hanfi

Muslim Society & Masjid-e-Hamza

Eagle Street Mosque, Eagle Street, Todmorden,
Lancashire, OL14 5HQ
Tel: 01706-816310
Contact: Mubarak Ali
Position: Imam
Activities: Worship
Traditions: Sunni
Movements: Tablighi Jamaat
Other Languages: Urdu, Punjabi, Bengali

Jamait-ul-Muslemeen

9 Arpley Street, Warrington, Cheshire
Contact: Mr N Mohammed

Islamic Cultural Centre & Mosque

Poolstock, Clifton Street, Worsley Menses, Wigan,
Lancashire, WN3 5HN

Tel: 01942-495038 **Tel:** 01942-700724 (h)
Contact: A Nasir
Position: Secretary
Activities: Worship, visits, youth, elderly
Traditions: Sunni
Movements: Ahl-e-Hadith
Other Languages: Urdu, Arabic

EAST MIDLANDS
Regional and County Bodies

*Federation of Muslim Organisations in
Leicestershire*

11 Breedon Street, Spinney Hill North, Highfields,
Leicester, Leicestershire, LE2 0FG
Tel: 0116-262-3518 **Tel:** 0116-251-8688 (h)
Contact: Mr Ebrahim Bayat
Position: Chairman
Activities: Media, umbrella, visits, youth, elderly,
women, inter-faith
Traditions: All
Other Languages: Gujarati, Kutchi, Urdu, Arabic
Affiliations: Union of Muslim Organisations UK

City, Town or Local Bodies

Chesterfield Muslim Students

5 Shirland Street, Chesterfield, Derbyshire

Derby Jamia Mosque

6 Rose Hill Street, Derby, Derbyshire, DE3 8EX
Tel: 01332-344838
Contact: Ajmal Rehmat
Position: Treasurer
Activities: Worship, resource, visits, inter-faith
Traditions: Sunni
Movements: Barelwi
Other Languages: Urdu, Punjabi
Affiliations: Council of Sunni Mosques

Islamic Centre Derby

The Central Mosque, Sacheveral Street, Derby,
Derbyshire, DE1 2JR
Tel: 01332-292021
Contact: Rafaqat Ali Mba
Position: Treasurer
Activities: Worship, resource, media, visits, youth,
elderly
Traditions: Sunni
Other Languages: Urdu, Punjabi, Arabic

Jamia Hanfia-Taleem-ul-Islam
26 Western Road, Derby, Derbyshire, DE23 6SE
Tel: 01332-204187 **Tel:** 01332-737153
Contact: Abdullah Abdusshakur
Activities: Worship, resource, youth, elderly,
women
Traditions: Sunni
Other Languages: Urdu, Bangali, Arabic, Serbo-
Croat

Jamiat-Ahl-e-Hadith
7a Hastings Street, Normanton, Derby, Derbyshire,
DE3 6QQ
Tel: 01332-766237
Contact: Mr Abdul Rauf
Position: Public Relations
Activities: Worship, resource, youth, elderly,
women
Movements: Ahl-e-Hadith
Other Languages: Urdu, Punjabi
Affiliations: Muslim World League

Mosque
25 Dexter Street, Derby, Derbyshire, DE3

Mosque
54 Dairyhouse Road, Derby, Derbyshire, DE3 8HL

Muslim Culture Association
54 Becher Street, Derby, Derbyshire, DE3 8NN
Tel: 01332-367439
Contact: Mr R T Khan

Muslim Womens & Girls Group
c/o Madeley Centre, Madeley Street, Derby,
Derbyshire

Muslim Women Organisation
11 Peartree Crescent, Peartree, Derby, Derbyshire,
DE3 8RN
Tel: 01332-730552 **Tel:** 0115-958-7900 (h)
Contact: Ms Nina Akhter
Position: Chair
Activities: Women, inter-faith
Traditions: Sunni
Other Languages: Urdu, Punjabi, Mirpuri

Pakistan Muslim Welfare Association
9 Madeley Street, Derby, Derbyshire, DE3 8EX
Tel: 01332-365845

Young Muslims Derby
c/o Madeley Centre, Rosehill Street, Derby,
Derbyshire, DE3 8EX

Tel: 01332-47509
Contact: Shokat Ali

Islamic Association of South Humberside
204 Stanley Street, Grimsby, Lincolnshire,
DN32 7LH
Tel: 01472-362600 **Tel:** 01472-340698 (h)
Contact: Soab Mohamed Nawab
Position: Imaam
Activities: Worship, visits, women
Traditions: Sunni
Movements: Tablighi Jamaat
Other Languages: Arabic, Urdu, Bengali

Hinckley Muslim Association
1 Manor Close, Burbage, Hinckley, Leicestershire,
LE10 2NL
Tel: 01455-611480 (h)
Contact: Mr Manzoor E Moghal
Position: President
Activities: Resource
Traditions: Sunni
Movements: Ahl-e-Sunna
Other Languages: Urdu, Punjabi, Bengali
Affiliations: Federation of Muslim Organisations
Leicester

Al Hilal Muslim Youth Association
c/o Highfields Youth Community Centre, 96
Melbourne Road, Leicester, Leicestershire,
LE2 5BE
Tel: 0116-254-0903 (h)
Contact: Khalid Rashid
Position: Chairman
Activities: Umbrella, youth
Traditions: Sunni
Other Languages: Gujarati, Urdu, Punjabi
Affiliations: Federation of Muslim Organisations;
Union of Muslim Organisations

All Jammu & Kashmir Muslim Conference
4 Crowns Hill Rise, Leicester, Leicestershire,
LE5 3DG
Tel: 0116-235-8511

Anjuman-e-Saifee
3-5 Wellington Street, Leicester, Leicestershire,
LE1 6HH
Tel: 0116-247-0446
Contact: S H Jaffer A Kapasi
Position: Treasurer

Association of Muslim Youth
81 Melbourne Road, Spinley Hill North, Leicester, Leicestershire, LE2 0GW

Association of Sunni Muslim Youth
116 Mere Road, Leicester, Leicestershire, LE5 3HR

Association of Sunni Muslims
39 Farringdon Street, Leicester, Leicestershire, LE5 0EB

Bangledesh Association
23 Melbourne Road, Leicester, Leicestershire

Belgrave Muslim Education Welfare Association
38 Glendon Street, Leicester, Leicestershire, LE4 6JR
Tel: 0116-268-0943 (h)
Contact: Mr Abdul Jamal
Position: Secretary
Activities: Resource
Traditions: Sunni
Other Languages: Gujarati, Urdu
Affiliations: Federation of Muslim Organisations in Leicestershire

British Pakistan & Muslim Welfare Association
Jinnah Advice Centre, 6 Beeby Road, Leicester, Leicestershire, LE5 3LE
Tel: 0116-274-1022

Darul Uloom Leicester
119 Loughborough Road, Leicester, Leicestershire, LE4 5LN
Tel: 0116-266-8922 **Tel:** 0116-266-4390
Fax: 0116-266-8922
Contact: Mr I A Patel
Position: Principal
Activities: Resource, youth
Traditions: Sunni
Movements: Deobandi
Other Languages: Urdu, Arabic

Dar-us-Salam Mosque
55-57 Upper Tichbourne Street, Leicester, Leicestershire, LE2 1GL
Tel: 0116-254-3887 **Tel:** 0116-276-4448 (h)
Fax: 0116-254-5050
Contact: Nizam Chowdhury
Position: General Secretary
Activities: Worship, resource, visits, elderly, inter-faith

Traditions: Sunni
Other Languages: Bengali

Dawoodi Bohra Jamaat
3-5 Wellington Street, Leicester, Leicestershire, LE1 6HH
Tel: 0116-266-4668

Dawoodi Bohra Welfare Society
1b Royal Road, Leicester, Leicestershire, LE4 5DP (h)
Tel: 0116-266-0866 (h)
Contact: Mr Mohsin Sulemanji
Position: Secretary
Activities: Worship
Traditions: Dawoodi Bohra
Other Languages: Gujarati
Affiliations: Dawoodi Bohra Welfare Society GB; Federation of Muslim Organisations, Leicester

De Montfort University Islamic Society
Students Union, 4 Newark Close, Leicester, Leicestershire, LE2 7BJ
Tel: 0116-255-5576

Evington Muslim Association
9 Kedlestone Road, Leicester, Leicestershire, LE5 5HX
Tel: 0116-273-5529

Federation of Muslim Organisations in Leicestershire
11 Breedon Street, Spinney Hill North, Highfields, Leicester, Leicestershire, LE2 0FG
Tel: 0116-262-3518 **Tel:** 0116-251-8688 (h)
Contact: Mr Ebrahim Bayat
Position: Chairman
Activities: Media, umbrella, visits, youth, elderly, women, inter-faith
Traditions: All
Other Languages: Gujarati, Kutchi, Urdu, Arabic
Affiliations: Union of Muslim Organisations UK

Gujarati Muslim Association
54 Frederick Road, Leicester, Leicestershire, LE5 5HE
Tel: 0116-251-0219

Hera Islamic Centre
8a Chapel Lane, Knighton, Leicester, Leicestershire

His Highness Prince Aga Khan Shia Imami Ismaili Jamat (Khana)
2 Westcotes Drive, Leicester, Leicestershire, LE3 0QR
Tel: 0116-254-6006 **Tel:** 0116-266-0620 (h)
Contact: A F Sayani

Inter Islamic Association
79 Melbourne Road, Leicester, Leicestershire

Islamic Centre
55 Barclay Street, Leicester, Leicestershire

Islamic Centre
2a Sutherland Street, Leicester, Leicestershire, LE2 1DS
Tel: 0116-254-7124 **Fax:** 0116-254-7124
Contact: Mr Khalid Chugtai
Position: Secretary
Activities: Worship, resource, visits, youth, elderly, women, newsletters, books, inter-faith
Traditions: Sunni
Movements: Barelwi, Tassawuf
Other Languages: Urdu, Gujarati, Punjabi, Bengali
Affiliations: Federation of Leicester Mosques; Imams and Mosques Council; Union of Muslim Organisations; World Islamic Mission

Islamic Education Trust
3-11 Keythorpe Street, Leicester, Leicestershire, LE2 0AL
Tel: 0116-251-1833 **Tel:** 0116-262-0071 (h)
Contact: Enayat K Pathan
Position: General Secretary
Activities: Worship, resource, visits, youth, inter-faith
Traditions: Sunni
Movements: Deobandi
Other Languages: Urdu, Gujrati
Affiliations: Federation Of Muslim Organisations

Islamic Educational Publications
PO BOX 139, Leicester, Leicestershire, LE2 2YH

Jame Masjid (King Faisal Mosque)
Atkinson Street, off Asfordby Street, Leicester, Leicestershire, LE5 3QK
Tel: 0116-262-1963 **Tel:** 0116-246-0300 (h)
Contact: Mr I Omarji
Position: Secretary

Jame Mosque
48 Ashfordby Street, Leicester, Leicestershire, LE5 3QJ

Kashmiri Muslim Women's Association
11 Overton Road, Leicester, Leicestershire, LE5 0JB

Kokni Muslim Jamat
157 Beatrice Road, Leicester, Leicestershire

Kokni Muslim Youth Club
43 Milverton Avenue, Leicester, Leicestershire, LE4 0HY

Leicester Central Mosque
Conduit Street, Leicester, Leicestershire, LE2 0JN
Tel: 0116-254-4459 **Tel:** 0116-273-8338 (h)
Fax: 0116-254-4459
Contact: Mr M H Khan
Position: Chairman
Activites: Worship, resources, youth, women, inter-faith
Traditions: Sunni
Movements: Barelwi
Other Languages: Urdu

Leicester Islamic Academy
320 London Road, Leicester, Leicestershire, LE2 2PJ
Tel: 0116-2705343 **Fax:** 0116-2448503
Activities: Resource, youth
Traditions: Sunni
Affiliations: Association of Muslim Schools

Leicester Islamic Centre
147 East Park Avenue, Leicester, Leicestershire, LE5 5AZ

Leicester Madressa Talim-u-Deen
Spinney Hill Primary School, Leicester, Leicestershire, LE2 0SE
Tel: 0116-262-6502 (h)
Contact: Sheikh Ahmed Makda
Position: Head Teacher
Activities: Resource, visitors, youth
Traditions: Sunni
Movements: Ahle Sunnah Wal Jammat
Other Languages: Urdu, Arabic, Gujerati
Affiliations: Federation of Muslim Associations

Leicester Mosque Trust
55-57 Upper Tichbourne Street, Leicester, Leicestershire, LE2 1DR

Tel: 0116-254-3887 **Tel:** 0116-276-4448 (h)
Fax: 0116-254-5050
Contact: Nizam Chowdhury
Position: Secretary
Activities: Worship, resource, visits, youth, elderly, inter-faith
Traditions: Sunni
Other Languages: Bengali, Urdu, Hindi

Leicester Muslim Association
28 Melbourne Road, Leicester, Leicestershire

Leicestershire Muslim Kokni Association
17 Gillbank Drive, Leicester, Leicestershire, LE6 0NH
Tel: 0116-239-4471

Loughborough Islamic Centre
257 Forest Road, Leicester, Leicestershire, LE11 3HT

Madressa-e-Anjuman-e-Ghousai Asrafia
3-5 Evington Street, Leicester, Leicestershire
Tel: 0116-254-6544 (h)
Contact: Aziz Thadha**Position:** Chairman

Masjid al Bukhari & Muslim Education Centre
159-161 Loughborough Road, Leicester, Leicestershire, LE4 5LR
Tel: 0116-266-5506 **Tel:** 0116-266-5472 (h)
Contact: Gulam Omarji Makadam
Position: Chairperson

Masjid-e-Noor & Leicester Muslim Society
146-152 Berners Street, Leicester, Leicestershire, LE2 0FU

Masjid Tabuk & Evington Muslim Centre
59 Stoughton Drive North, Leicester, Leicestershire, LE5 5UD
Tel: 0116-273-5529 **Tel:** 0116-273-7183 (h)
Fax: 0116-246-1611
Contact: Mohamed Seedat
Position: Secretary

Mosque
146 Welford Road, Leicester, Leicestershire

Muslim Aid
84 Romway Road, Leicester, Leicestershire

Muslim Aid
216 Evington Road, Leicester, Leicestershire, LE2 1HN

Muslim Aid Leicester
104 Nedham Street, Leicester, Leicestershire, LE2 0HB

Muslim Association
28 Melbourne Road, Leicester, Leicestershire

Muslim Education Centre
159 Loughborough Road, Leicester, Leicestershire, LE4 5LQ
Tel: 0116-266-5506

Muslim Khatri Association
95 Rowsley Avenue, Leicester, Leicestershire, LE5 5JP

Muslim Khatri Society
77 Peebles Way, Leicester, Leicestershire

Muslim Khoja Ithna-Asheri Community
127 Loughborough Road, Leicester, Leicestershire, LE4 5LQ
Tel: 0116-268-2828 **Tel:** 0116-266-4584 (h)
Fax: 0116-268-2828
Contact: Mr Muslim Kassamali Rajani
Position: President
Activities: Worship, resource, visits, youth, elderly, women, newsletters, inter-faith
Traditions: Khuja Sh'ia 'Ithna Asheri
Other Languages: Urdu, Gujarati, Kutch, Swahili
Affiliations: Federation of Muslim Organisations in Leicestershire; World Federation of Khoja Shi'a `Ithna-Asheri Muslim Communities

Muslim Ladies' Association
1 Fairstone Hill, 172 Evington Lane, Oadby, Leicester, Leicestershire, LE2 5RL (h)
Tel: 0116-271-8499 (h)
Contact: Dr Atia Sheikh
Position: Secretary
Activities: Resource, youth, women
Traditions: Sunni
Other Languages: Urdu, Punjabi

Muslim Luharwadha Jamat Leicester
Flat 5 Canterbury House, 63a Melton Road, Leicester, Leicestershire, LE4 6PN
Tel: 0116-2854052 **Tel:** 0116-2613051 (h)
Contact: Kassim Rahemtulla Lohar
Position: Chairman
Activities: Youth, elderly, women
Traditions: Sunni
Movements: Barelwi

Other Languages: Kutchee, Gujarati, Kishwahili, Urdu

Muslim Newsletter
185a Evington Road, Leicester, Leicestershire

Muslim Society
85 Berners Street, Leicester, Leicestershire

Muslim Welfare House
176 Welford Road, Leicester, Leicestershire, LE2 4RH

Muslim Welfare Trust
c/o 24 Wilson Street, Leicester, Leicestershire, LE2 0BB
Tel: 0116-251-7948

Muslim Youth Education Council
28 Bakewell Street, Leicester, Leicestershire, LE2 1GN

Muslims Girls School
27 Hazelwood Road, Leicester, Leicestershire

Muslims Girls School
115 Mere Road, Leicester, Leicestershire

Muslims Girls School
112 Osamaston Road, Leicester, Leicestershire

Pakistan Association Muslim Community
Muslim Community Centre, Old Boys School, Melbourne Road, Leicester, Leicestershire, LE2 0GU
Tel: 0116-225670
Contact: Mr R T Khan
Position: Chairperson

Sunni Muslim Jamat
14 Lanbourne Street, Leicester, Leicestershire, LE2 6HL
Tel: 0116-288-4508 (h)
Contact: Mr H S Majothi
Position: Chairperson

Surati Muslim Khalifa Society
127 Mere Road, Highfield, Leicester, Leicestershire, LE5 5GQ
Tel: 0116-251-1120 **Tel:** 0116-262-5919 (h)
Contact: Mr Mustafa Fakir Karim
Position: President
Activities: Resource, visits, youth, elderly, women, newsletters, inter-faith

Traditions: Sunni
Movements: Ahl-e-Hadith, Deobandi
Other Languages: Gujarati, Urdu, Arabic
Affiliations: Federation of Muslim Organisations in Leicestershire; Federation of G M Khalifa Societies of UK

UK Islamic Mission Leicester
41 Gwendolen Road, Leicester, Leicestershire, LE5 5FL
Contact: Mr Sadiq Khokhar
Position: Secretary
Activities: Resource, women, books, inter-faith
Other Languages: Urdu
Affiliations: UK Action Committee on Islamic Affairs

Young Muslim Association
31 Lambourne Road, Leicester, Leicestershire

Lincoln Islamic Association
Orchard Street, Lincoln, Lincolnshire, LN1 1XX
Tel: 0116-242-5943 (h)
Contact: Farouq Mullah
Position: Secretary
Activities: Worship, youth
Traditions: Sunni
Other Languages: Urdu, Arabic, Bengali

Loughborough Mosque
81-83 King Street, Loughborough, Leicestershire

Loughborough Students Union Islamic Society
Loughborough Students Union, Loughborough University, Loughborough, Leicestershire, LE11 3TU
Email: s.miah@lboro.ac.uk
Contact: Mr S Miah
Position: President
Activities: Worship, resource, visits, youth, newsletters
Other Languages: English, Malay, Arabic
Affiliations: FOSIS

Mosque & Islamic Cultural Association
85 King Street, Loughborough, Leicestershire, LE11 1SB
Tel: 01509-214500
Contact: Imam
Activities: Charity
Traditions: Sunni
Other Languages: Bengali

Young Muslims Loughborough
79 Empress Road, Loughborough, Leicestershire, LE11 1RH
Tel: 01509-212942 (h) **Fax:** 01509-210912
Contact: Mahboob-ur-Rashid Chowdhury
Position: President

International Council for Islamic Information
Markfield Day Centre, Ratby Lane, Markfield, Leicestershire, LE6 RN

Al Jamat-ul-Muslimin of Bangladesh
8 St George's Street, off Regent Square, Northampton, Northamptonshire, NN1 2TR
Tel: 01604-24930
Contact: Chairperson or Secretary
Activities: Worship, resource, youth, elderly, women
Traditions: Sunni
Movements: Ahl-e-Hadith, Tablighi Jamaat
Other Languages: Bengali

Institute of Islamic Studies
Norpak House, Harold Street, Northampton, Northamptonshire

Islamic Pakistani Community Centre
98a Colwyn Road, Northampton, Northamptonshire, NN1 3PX
Tel: 01604-21125 **Tel:** 01604-585505 (h)
Contact: Mr Riaz Bhatti

Islamic Union
c/o Norpak House, Harold Street, Northampton, Northamptonshire

Mosque
43 Argyle Street, Northampton, Northamptonshire
Tel: 01604-57230

Voice of Islam
89 Cloutsham Street, Northampton, Northamptonshire, NN1 3LL

Anjum Ithad-U-Muslimeen
38 Mayo Road, Sherwood Rise, Nottingham, Nottinghamshire

Islamic Centre
3 Curzon Street, St. Ann's Road, Nottingham, Nottinghamshire, NG3 6DG
Tel: 0115-959-0001
Contact: Mr R Azam
Position: Chairman

Islamic Education Centre
39 Bridlington Street, Hyson Green, Nottingham, Nottinghamshire, NG7 5LX
Tel: 0115-929106
Contact: Mr Abdul Ghafar

Islamic Society
13 Maples Street, Hyson Green, Nottingham, Nottinghamshire, NG7 6AF

Islamic Youth Movement
69 Wiverton Road, Forest Fields, Nottingham, Nottinghamshire, NG7 6NU

Jamiah Fatimia
c/o 18 Austen Avenue, Forest Fields, Nottingham, Nottinghamshire, N67 6PE
Tel: 0115-978-6006 **Tel:** 0115-924-4004 (h)
Contact: A H Bhatti
Position: Secretary
Activities: Worship, resource, inter-faith
Traditions: Sunni
Movements: Barelwi
Other Languages: Urdu

Jinnah Society
63 Trent Road, Sneinton, Nottingham, Nottinghamshire, NG2 4FB

Lenton Muslim Centre
56 Rothsay Avenue, Lenton, Nottingham, Nottinghamshire, NG7 1PY
Tel: 0115-947-0484
Contact: Mr Nazan Khan

Madni Masjid & Muslims Education Centre
289 Gladstone Street, Forest Fields, Nottingham, Nottinghamshire, NG7 6HX
Tel: 0115-962-3344 **Fax:** 0115-985-8997
Contact: Information Officer
Activities: Worship, resource, visits, youth, elderly, women, inter-faith
Other Languages: Urdu, Punjabi, Arabic

Madrassa-e-Islamia
58 Thurgarten Street, Sneinton, Nottingham, Nottinghamshire, NG2 4AG
Tel: 0115-911-7601 **Tel:** 0115-911-1917 (h)
Contact: Aurangzeb Khan
Position: Chair
Activities: Worship, resource, youth, elderly, women
Traditions: Sunni

Movements: Barelwi
Other Languages: Urdu,Punjabi

Meadows Muslim Action Group
Meadows Muslim Centre, Collygate Road,
Meadows, Nottingham, Nottinghamshire, NG2 2EJ
Tel: 0115-952-7133 **Tel:** 0115-952-8860 (h)
Contact: Mohammed M Ishaq Kashmiri
Position: Secretary
Activities: Worship, resource, visits, youth, elderly,
women, inter-faith
Other Languages: Kashmiri, Mirpuri, Punjabi,
Urdu

Mosque Islamic Centre
Curzon Street, St Annswell Road, Nottingham,
Nottinghamshire

Muslim Action Committee
15 Holgate Road, The Meadows, Nottingham,
Nottinghamshire, NG2 2EB

Muslim Association
10 Radford Road, Hyson Green, Nottingham,
Nottinghamshire, NG7 5FS

Muslim Liaison Committee
c/o Unit 4, 6 Ebury Road, Sherwood Rise,
Nottingham, Nottinghamshire

Muslim Welfare House
215 Derby Road, Nottingham, Nottinghamshire,
NG7 1QJ
Tel: 0115-941-2462

Muslim Women Organisation
165a Ilkeston Road, The Lodge, Lenton,
Nottingham, Nottinghamshire, NG7 3HF
Contact: Mrs Ubaida Moin
Position: Chair
Activities: Charity
Traditions: Sunni
Other Languages: Urdu, Punjabi

Muslim Youth Cultural Society
3 Cranmer Grove, Cranmer Street, Nottingham,
Nottinghamshire, NG3 4HE
Tel: 0115-970325 **Tel:** 0115-952-5177 (h)
Contact: M Yasin

Njum-e-Ezzi (Dawoodi Bohra Jamaat)
20 Cheadle Close, Bilborough, Nottingham,
Nottinghamshire, NG5 1BL

Nottingham University Islamic Society
Students Union, Nottingham, Nottinghamshire,
NG7 2RD

Pakistan Community Centre
163 Woodborough Road, Nottingham,
Nottinghamshire
Tel: 0115-958-2973
Position: Mr Masood

Pakistan Muslim Association
10 Radford Road, Hyson Green, Nottingham,
Nottinghamshire

Sneinton Muslim Centre
5 Kingsley Road, Sneinton, Nottingham,
Nottinghamshire, NG2 4AR

Mosque
165 Woodborough Road, Nottingham,
Nottinghamshire

Mosque
13 Enna Avenue, Sneiton, Nottingham,
Nottinghamshire, NG2 4NA

Mosque
65 Belper Avenue, Carlton, Nottingham,
Nottinghamshire, NG4 3SE

Young Muslim Society
6 Erskin Road, Sherwood Rise, Nottingham,
Nottinghamshire

Bangladesh United Muslim Society
56 Fox Street, Scunthorpe, Lincolnshire
Contact: Mr A Noor

Bangledesh United Muslim Society
15 Parkinson Avenue, Scunthorpe, Lincolnshire

Bangladesh United Muslim Society
62 Frances Street, Scunthorpe, Lincolnshire

Bangladeshi Mosque
29 Gilliatt Street, Scunthorpe, Lincolnshire

Madrassa Mosque
105 Cliff Gardens, Scunthorpe, Lincolnshire,
DN15 7BJ

Madrassa Taleem ul Quran Mosque
44 Percival Street, Scunthorpe, Lincolnshire,
DN15 6JD
Tel: 01724-852491

Mosque
107 West Street, Scunthorpe, Lincolnshire,
DN15 6EQ
Tel: 01724-842772

Scunthorpe Mosque Committee
107 West Street, Scunthorpe, Lincolnshire,
DN15 6EQ
Tel: 01724-842772
Contact: Syed Abdul Rouf
Position: Chairman
Activities: Worship
Traditions: Sunni
Movements: Ahl-e-Hadith, Barelwi
Other Languages: Bengali, Urdu

United Muslim Mosque
125 West Street, Scunthorpe, Lincolnshire

Islah-ul-Muslimin Mosque & Community Centre
Winstanley Road, Wellingborough,
Northamptonshire, NN8 1EL
Tel: 01933-384306 **Tel:** 01933-381054 (h)
Contact: Ashraf Ullah Khan
Position: Chairman
Activities: Worship, visits, youth, elderly, women
Traditions: Sunni
Movements: Ahl-e-Hadith
Other Languages: Urdu, Bengali, Punjabi, Pushto

Islamic Union
5 Gosolar Queensway, Wellingborough,
Northamptonshire

WEST MIDLANDS
Regional and County Bodies

Confederation of Sunni Mosques Midlands
107 Golden Hillock Road, Small Heath,
Birmingham, West Midlands, B10 0DP
Tel: 0121-622-1369
Contact: Raja M Saleem Akhtar
Position: Chairman

Town, City and Local Bodies

Ahl-e-Sunnat-wal-Jamaat
108 Reginald Road, Saltley, Birmingham, West
Midlands, B8 1LU

Al-Hijrah Mosque
59 Hob Moor Road, Small Heath, Birmingham,
West Midlands, B10 9AZ
Tel: 0121-766-5454 **Fax:** 0121-766-8556
Contact: M A K Saqib
Position: President
Activities: Worship, resource, visits
Traditions: Sunni
Other Languages: Urdu, Arabic, Punjabi, Bengali

Al Hijra School
Midland House, 71 Hobmoor Road, Small Heath,
Birmingham, West Midlands, B10 9AZ

All-Muslim Welfare Association
91 Soho Road, Birmingham, West Midlands,
B21 9SP

All Zamindar Sabha
43 Castleford Road, Sparkhill, Birmingham, West
Midlands, B11 3SW

Amina Association
18 Fulham Road, Sparkhill, Birmingham, West
Midlands
Tel: 0121-240-7850
Contact: Hamid Lea
Position: Secretary
Activities: Resource, visits, youth, women, books,
inter-faith
Traditions: Sunni
Movements: Tassawuf (Sufi)
Other Languages: Urdu, Arabic, Bengali, Punjabi

Amir-e-Millat Mosque & Community Centre
144 Stoney Lane, Spark Hill, Birmingham, West
Midlands, B11
Tel: 0121-449-6001

Anjuman Arian
321 Northfield Road, Harborne, Birmingham, West
Midlands, B17 0TS
Contact: Mr M S Mian

Anjumane Islam
23 Arden Road, Aston, Birmingham, West
Midlands, B6 6AP

Anjuman-e-Naqeebul Islam Mosque
82 Washwood Heath Road, Satley, Birmingham,
West Midlands, B8 1RD
Tel: 0121-328-4930

Anjuman-e Tabligh-ul-Islam
6 Wyecliffe Road, Handsworth, Birmingham, West
Midlands, B20 3TB
Tel: 0121-523-7529
Contact: Mr Masam Khan
Position: Secretary
Activities: Worship
Other Languages: Urdu, Hindi, Punjabi
Traditions: Sunni
Movements: Deobandi, Tablighi Jamaat

Anjuman-e-Taraqqi-Urdu
55 Langley, Olton, Birmingham, West Midlands

Anjuman-Faiz-ul-Quran
188 Somerville Road, Small Heath, Birmingham,
West Midlands, B10 9HB
Tel: 0121-771-2931 **Tel:** 0121-771-2931 (h)
Fax: 0121-773-7417
Contact: Mohammed Tahir Azad
Position: President
Activities: Worship, resource, youth, elderly,
women
Traditions: Sunni
Movements: Tassawuf
Other Languages: Urdu, Punjabi, Mirpuri,
Pashtow
Affiliations: Confederation Of Sunni Mosques
Midlands; Pakistan Forum, Birmingham

Anjuman Khuddam-ud-Din
11-15 Woodstock Road, Moseley, Birmingham,
West Midlands, B13 9BB

Anjuman Mohy-ul Islam Siddiquia
12-18 Victoria Road, Aston, Birmingham, West
Midlands, B6 5HA

Anjuman Noor-ul-Islam & Mosque
33 Yewtree Road, Witton, Birmingham, West
Midlands, B6 6RT
Tel: 0121-328-1297

Anjuman-e-al-Islam
60a Stratford Road, Sparkbrook, Birmingham, West
Midlands, B11 1AN
Tel: Mr Azad Choudhury
Position: Chair
Other Languages: Bengali, Urdu, Hindi
Traditions: Sunni
Movements: Tablighi Jamaat

Anjuman-i-Tareej
64 Somerville Road, Small Heath, Birmingham,
West Midlands, B10 9EL

Anwar-ul-Madina
726 Washwood Heath Road, Ward End,
Birmingham, West Midlands, B8

Association of Muslim Youth
31 Farm Road, Birmingham, West Midlands, B11

Aston University Islamic Society
Students Union, Gosta Green, Birmingham, West
Midlands, B4 7ET

Bangledesh Islamic & Social Organisation
526-528 Moseley Road, Balsall Heath,
Birmingham, West Midlands, B12 9AE

Bangladesh Islamic Centre
64 Osborn Road, Sparkbrook, Birmingham, West
Midlands, B11 1RS

Bangladesh Islamic Centre
8 Mayfield Road, Lozells, Birmingham, West
Midlands, B19

Bangladesh Islamic Centre & Mosque
296 Burbury Street, Lozells, Birmingham, West
Midlands, B19

**Bangledesh Islamic Projects & Consultative
Council**
19/21 Alum Rock Road, Saltley, Birmingham, West
Midlands, B8 1LL

Bangladesh Welfare Association & Mosque
19-21 Alum Rock Road, Saltley, Birmingham, West
Midlands, B8 1LL
Tel: 0121-328-4746
Contact: Mr A Rahman
Position: Vice President

Birmingham Anjumane Islam Mosque Trust
Saddam Hussein Mosque, 2 Trinity Road,
Birchfield, Birmingham, West Midlands, B6 6AG
Tel: 0121-554-9157 **Tel:** 0121-686-2707 (h)
Fax: 0121-240-4786
Contact: Hazratmian Kazi
Position: Chairman
Activities: Worship, visits, youth, elderly, women,
inter-faith
Traditions: Sunni
Movements: Ahl-e-Hadith, Deobandi

Other Languages: Urdu
Affiliations: Council of Mosques; Union of
Muslim Organisation UK & Ireland; The Muslim
World League UK; The Muslim World League
Saudi Arabia

Birmingham Dawatul Islam
523-527 Coventry Road, Small Heath,
Birmingham, West Midlands, B20 1SB
Tel: 0121-772-8408 Fax: 0121-773-4340

Birmingham Islamic Centre (BIC) & Jami Mosque
521/527 Coventry Road, Small Heath,
Birmingham, West Midlands, B10 0LL
Tel: 0121-772-6408 Fax: 0121-773-4340
Contact: Dr Maulana Abdur Rahim
Position: Director
Activities: Worship, resource, umbrella, visits,
youth, elderly, women, books, inter-faith
Traditions: Sunni
Other Languages: Bangla, Urdu, Pushto, Arabic
Affiliations: UK Action Committee on Islamic
Affairs; The Muslim World League

Birmingham Islamic Society
125 Wake Green Road, Edgbaston, Birmingham,
West Midlands, West Midlands

Birmingham Islamic Society
63 Moor Green Lane, Mosely, Birmingham, West
Midlands, B13 8NE
Contact: Dr Ethisham

Birmingham University Islamic Society
Guild of Students, University of Birmingham,
Edgbaston, Birmingham, West Midlands, B15
Contact: The President
Activities: Worship, resource, youth, newsletters,
inter-faith
Other Languages: Arabic, Malay, Urdu
Affiliations: Federation of Students of Islamic
Societies; West Midlands, Federation of Students of
Islamic Societies; International Federation of
Student Organisations

British Association of Muslims
2 St Annes Close, Handsworth Wood, Birmingham,
West Midlands, B20 1SB

Central Mosque Birmingham
180 Belgrave Middleway, Highgate, Birmingham,
West Midlands, B12 0XS

Tel: 0121-440-5355 Fax: 0121-446-4410
Contact: Dost Mohammad Khan
Position: General Secretary
Activities: Worship, resource, visits, youth,
newsletters, inter-faith
Traditions: Ahle Sunnah wa Jamaat
Other Languages: Urdu, Punjabi, Arabic, Bengali

Chashma-e-Rahmat Mosque
Oldbury Road, Smethwick, Birmingham, West
Midlands, B66
Tel: 0121-552-8729
Contact: Hafiz Mohammed Miyas
Position: Iman

Confederation of Sunni Mosques Midlands
107 Golden Hillock Road, Small Heath,
Birmingham, West Midlands, B10 0DP
Tel: 0121-622-1369
Contact: Raja M Saleem Akhtar
Position: Chairman

Council of Birmingham Mosques
15 Woodstock Road, Birmingham, West Midlands,
B13 9BB
Tel: 0121-429-1193

Dar-ul-Alume
69 Nelson Road, Aston, Birmingham, West
Midlands, B6 6HQ

Dar-ul-Uloom Islamia
107-113 Golden Hillock Road, Small Heath,
Birmingham, West Midlands, B10 0DP
Tel: 0121-771-4533 Fax: 0121-753-0778
Contact: Mohammed Nasir Anwer
Position: Manager
Activities: Worship, resource, umbrella, visits,
youth, elderly, women, inter-faith
Traditions: Sunni
Movements: Barelwi
Other Languages: Mirpuri, Urdu, Punjabi
Affiliations: Confederation of Sunni Mosques

Darul Uloom Islamic High School
521 Coventry Road, Small Heath, Birmingham,
West Midlands, B10 0LL
Tel: 0121-772-6408 Tel: 0121-773-7706
Fax: 0121-773-4340

Dawatul Islam
171 Makmesbury Road, Birmingham, West
Midlands, B10

Dawatul Islam Womens Group
81 Umberside Road, Selly Oak, Birmingham, West
Midlands, B29 7SB

East African Muslim Association
55 Showell Green Lane, Sparkhill, Birmingham,
West Midlands, B11
Tel: 0121-771-4511
Contact: Wali Din

Erdington Muslims Social & Welfare Association
219 Slade Road, Erdington, Birmingham, West
Midlands (h)
Tel: 0121-350-3910 (h)
Contact: M.Y. Farid
Position: Chairman
Activities: Resource
Traditions: Sunni
Movements: Barelwi
Other Languages: Urdu, Punjabi

Faiz-ul-Quran Madrassa
298 Dudley Road, Winson Green, Birmingham,
West Midlands, B18 4EL

Federation of Muslim Organisations (UK)
30 Townley Gardens, Aston, Birmingham, West
Midlands, B6

**Federation of Student Islamic Societies &
Community Centre**
237 Albert Road, Aston, Birmingham, West
Midlands, B6 5LX

Ghamkol
126 Durham Road, Sparkhill, Birmingham, West
Midlands, B11 4LQ

**Ghausia Mosque Trust And Islamic Community
Centre**
232 Slade Road, Erdington, Birmingham, West
Midlands, B23 7RH
Tel: 0836-607608 **Tel:** 0121-326-0847 (h)
Fax: 0121-326-0847
Contact: Khalid Mahmood
Position: President
Activities: Worship, resource, visits, youth
Traditions: Sunni
Movements: Barelwi
Other Languages: Urdu, Punjabi
Affiliations: Confederation of Sunni Mosques,
Midlands

Halal Food Board
517 Moseley Road, Birmingham, West Midlands,
B12 9BX

Handsworth Islamic Centre
27 Putney Road, Handsworth, Birmingham, West
Midlands, B20 3PY (h)
Tel: 0121-551-9012 (h)
Contact: Quari A Wafi
Position: Chairperson
Activities: Worship, resource, umbrella, youth,
elderly, women, newsletters, inter-faith
Traditions: Sunni
Movements: Jamati-i-Islami; Tablighi Jamaat
Other Languages: Urdu, Punjabi, Pushto, Gujarati
Affiliations: UK Islamic Mission

Handsworth Mosque & Islamic Centre
23 Booth Street, Handsworth, Birmingham, West
Midlands, B21 0NX
Contact: H.Fazlur Rahman
Position: Secretary
Activities: Worship
Traditions: Sunni
Other Languages: Bengali

Haroonia Islamic Centre
74 College Road, Alum Rock, Birmingham, West
Midlands

Hazarat Sultan Bahu Trust
17 Ombersley Road, Balsall Heath, Birmingham,
West Midlands, B12 8UT
Tel: 0121-440-4096 **Fax:** 0121-440-6841
Contact: Muhammad Amin Qadri
Position: Finance Director
Activities: Worship, resource, visits, youth, elderly,
women, books, inter-faith
Traditions: Sunni
Movements: Barelwi, Tassawuf
Other Languages: Arabic, Urdu

Idara Maarif-e-Islam
3 Woodview Drive, Edgbaston, Birmingham, West
Midlands, B15 2JF
Tel: 01210440-4124 **Tel:** 0121-771-0868 (h)
Contact: Mr Sakhawat Hussain Shah
Position: President
Activities: Worship, resource, youth, elderly,
women, newsletters, inter-faith
Traditions: Ithna Asheri
Other Languages: Urdu, Punjabi

Institute of Islamic Studies
34 Kinver Croft, High Gate, Birmingham, West
Midlands, B12 9HE
Tel: 0121-446-6428 **Fax:** 0121-446-6426
Contact: Dr Khalid Alavi
Position: Secretary
Activities: Books, inter-faith
Traditions: Sunni
Other Languages: Urdu, Punjabi, Arabic
Affiliations: UK Action Committee on Islamic
Affairs; Educational Forum

Iqbal Academy (UK)
5 Woodbourne Road, Edgbaston, Birmingham,
West Midlands, B15 3QJ

Islamia Alouia Zawiya
294 Edward Road, Edgbaston, Birmingham, West
Midlands, B12

Islamia Ibadat Khan Association
62 Osbourne Road, Sparkhill, Birmingham, West
Midlands, B11

Islamic Book Service
527 Coventry Road, Small Heath, Birmingham,
West Midlands, B10 0LL
Tel: 0121-773-7706 **Fax:** 0121-773-4340

Islamic Centre
30 Anderton Road, Birmingham, West Midlands,
B1

Islamic Centre
238 Charles Road, Small Heath, Birmingham, West
Midlands, B10 9AY (h)
Tel: 0121-772-6578 (h) **Fax:** 0121-753-3623
Contact: Mr Qari Mohammed Sultan
Position: Imam
Activities: Worship, resource
Traditions: Sunni
Movements: Ahl-e-Hadith
Other Languages: Urdu, Arabic, Pushto, Punjabi

Islamic Centre
122 Bordesley Green, Birmingham, West Midlands,
B9 4TS

Islamic College
14 Lea Road, Greet, Birmingham, West Midlands,
B11 3LU
Tel: 0121-771-3680

Islamic Cultural Centre
6 Bevington Road, Aston, Birmingham, West
Midlands, B6

Islamic Cultural Centre
25 Park Street, Aston, Birmingham, West Midlands,
B6 5SH

Islamic Cultural Study Centre
262 Washwood Heath Road, Birmingham, West
Midlands, B8 1RJ
Tel: 0121-326-0966 **Tel:** 0121-311-0014 (h)
Contact: Sheikh Mahmood H Rashid
Position: Chairman
Activities: Worship, resource, youth, elderly,
newsletters, books, inter-faith
Traditions: Sunni
Movements: Tassawuf
Other Languages: Urdu, Qur'anic Arabic
Affiliations: Sunni Council; Council of Mosques;
Muslim World League

Islamic Education & Cultural Centre
14 Linwood Road, Handsworth, Birmingham, West
Midlands, B21
Tel: 0121-515-2110 **Tel:** 0121-551-9956 (h)
Contact: Haji Md.Abdul Jalil
Position: Secretary
Activities: Worship, visits
Traditions: Sunni
Movements: Jamati-i-Islami
Other Languages: Bengali, Urdu, Pushto

Islamic Education Centre
232 Witton Road, Aston, Birmingham, West
Midlands, B6 6LB
Tel: 0121-523-4265 (h)
Contact: Mr A Sabur Choudhury
Position: Chairperson
Activities: Worship
Traditions: Sunni
Movements: Tablighi Jamaat
Other Languages: Bengali, Urdu, Punjabi

Islamic Educational & Cultural Centre, Islamic School
129 Normandy Road, Perry Barr, Birmingham,
West Midlands, B20
Tel: 0121-327-4204 **Tel:** 0121-328-0837 (h)
Contact: Moulana Bostan Kadri
Position: President
Activities: Worship, resource, visits, youth, elderly,
women, books

Traditions: Sunni
Movements: Barelwi
Other Languages: Urdu, Arabic
Affiliations: UK Action Committee on Islamic Affairs; Confederation of Sunni Mosques, Midlands

Islamic Library & Central Hanafiyah Mosque
28 Tennyson Road, Small Heath, Birmingham, West Midlands, B10 0HA
Tel: 0121-773-6094
Contact: Adil al-Farooqi
Position: Imam

Islamic Moroccan Association
5 St Benedicts Road, Small Heath, Birmingham, West Midlands, B10 9DP
Tel: 0121-772-4391
Contact: Hamid Mohammed

Islamic Resource Centre
93 Court Road, Balsall Heath, Birmingham, West Midlands, B12 9LQ
Tel: 0121-440-3500 **Tel:** 0121-440-8218
Fax: 0121-440-8144
Contact: Safdar Butt
Position: Director
Activities: Resource, youth, women
Other Languages: Urdu, Arabic, Punjabi, Mirpuri

Islamic Society
3 Blackthorne Close, Solihull, Birmingham, West Midlands

Islamic Teaching & Community Centre
141 Nechells Park Road, Nechells, Birmingham, West Midlands, B7 5PH
Contact: Mr M Bashir

Jalalabad Association
12 Pugh Road, Aston, Birmingham, West Midlands, B6 5LL
Position: M A Islam

Jalalabad Bangladesh Islamic & Language Centre
267 Malmesbury Road, Small Heath, Birmingham, West Midlands, B10 0JE

Jalalabad Mosque & Madrassa
76 Etting Road, Aston, Birmingham, West Midlands, B6 6ET

Jalalabad Mosque & Islamic Centre
24-26 Dartmouth Road, Selly Oak, Birmingham, West Midlands, B29 6EA
Tel: 0121-471-1556
Contact: Hira Miah
Position: Secretary

Jamait Ulma-e-Islam
34 Farndon Road, Alum Rock, Birmingham, West Midlands, B8 3HS

Jamatia Islamic Centre
179-181 Woodland Road, Sparkhill, Birmingham, West Midlands, B11 4ER
Tel: 0121-778-6612 **Tel:** 0121-778-3195 (h)
Contact: Ashfaq Ahmed
Position: Secretary
Activities: Worship, resource, visits, youth, elderly, women, inter-faith
Traditions: Sunni
Movements: Barelwi
Other Languages: Urdu, Punjabi, Bengali, Arabic
Affiliations: Confederation of Sunni Mosques; Pakistan Forum

Jamia Islamia (Naqshbandia)
1 Willow Crescent, Cannon Hill, Birmingham, West Midlands

Jamia Mosque
2 Trinity Road, Birmingham, West Midlands, B6

Jamia Mosque & Community Centre
62 Wills Street, Lozells, Birmingham, West Midlands, B19
Tel: 0121-523-0810
Contact: Mr Mohammed Siddique Baig
Position: Secretary
Activities: Worship, resource, visits
Traditions: Sunni
Other Languages: Mirpuri, Punjabi, Urdu
Affiliations: Sunni Confederation of Mosques

Jamia Mosque Hanza Islamic Centre
88 Church Road, Moseley, Birmingham, B13 9AE
Tel: 0121-449-1193 **Tel:** 0121-449-4385
Contact: M David
Position: Secretary
Activities: Worship, elderly
Traditions: Sunni
Movements: Deobandi, Tabligh Jamaat

Other Languages: Urdu, Punjabi, Handko
Affiliations: Birmingham Council of Mosques

Jamia Naqshbandia Newabia
108 Bordesley Green Road, Birmingham, West Midlands, B9

Jamiat ahl-e- Hadith
53 George Arthur Road, Birmingham, West Midlands, B8

Jamiat ahl-e Hadith
188 Kenelm Road, Small Heath, Birmingham, West Midlands, B12

Jamiat-e-Ulama Britain
98 Walford Wall, Sparkbrook, Birmingham, West Midlands, B11 1QA

Jamiat-ul-Muslimin
28 Tennyson Road, Small Heath, Birmingham, West Midlands, B10 9AR
Tel: 0121-773-6094

Jamiate Nizame Islam
64 Somerville Road, Small Heath, Birmingham, West Midlands, B10 9EL
Tel: 0121-328-8466 (h)
Contact: Malik Fazal Hussain
Position: Nazim
Activities: Worship, youth, newsletters
Traditions: Sunni
Other Languages: Urdu, Arabic
Affiliations: Pakistan Community Centre; Urdu Forum (UK), Birmingham

Kashif-ul-Uloom Mosque
2 Blake Lane, Birmingham, West Midlands, B9
Tel: 0121-771-3247

Khoja Shia Ithna'sheri Muslim Community of Birmingham
17 Clifton Road, Balsall Heath, Birmingham, West Midlands, B12 8SX
Tel: 0121-446-6437   **Fax:** 0121-446-6437
Contact: Mr Mohamed Bharwani
Position: President
Activities: Worship, resource, visits, youth, elderly, women, newsletters
Traditions: Shi`a `Ithna Asheri
Other Languages: Gujarati, Urdu, Arabic
Affiliations: Council of European Jamaats; World Federation of Khoja Shi`a `Ithna-Asheri Muslim Communities

King's Heath Mosque
113 Station Road, Birmingham, West Midlands
Tel: 0121-444-5428

Kokni Muslim Association
14 Arden Road, Aston, Birmingham, West Midlands, B6 5AP

Lozells Islamic Centre
258 Burbury Street, Lozells, Birmingham, West Midlands, B19

Madina Masjid
Corner of Adderley Road and Ash Road, Saltley, Birmingham, West Midlands, B8
Tel: 0121-327-1123

Madni Masjid
68 Wright Road, Saltley, Birmingham, West Midlands, B8 1NS
Contact: M Qasim

Madrasa Talimul Qur'an
159 Krywicks Lane, Sparkbrook, Birmingham, West Midlands, B12 9SS
Tel: 0121-440-6721
Contact: Haji Mir Afzal Khan
Position: Chair
Activities: Worship, resource, visits, youth, elderly
Traditions: Sunni
Other Languages: Urdu, Arabic, Pushtu

Madrasah-e-Hifzul Quran
527 Coventry Road, Small Heath, Birmingham, West Midlands, B10 0LL

Madrasah Muhy-ul-Islam
153 Albert Road, Aston, Birmingham, West Midlands

Madrassa Islamia
221 Alexander Road, Acocks Green, Birmingham, West Midlands, B27 6EH
Tel: 0121-628-2179 (h)
Contact: Abdil Malik
Position: General Secretary
Activities: Worship, resource, umbrella, youth, women
Traditions: Sunni
Movements: Barelwi
Other Languages: Urdu, English
Affiliations: Sunni Confederation

Madrassa Islamia Taleem-ul-Quran
59 Kyrwicks Lane, Sparkbrook, Birmingham, West
Midlands

Madrassa Jila-ul-Quloob
253 Bordesley Green, Birmingham, West Midlands,
B9 5EX

Madrassa Naim-ul-Qur'an
37 Whitehall Road, Small Heath, Birmingham, West
Midlands, B10

Madrassa Zia Medina
2 Tarry Road, Alum Rock, Birmingham, West
Midlands, B8

Madressa Binat
44 Mayfield Road, Birmingham, West Midlands,
B13

Madressa Islamia Talimuddin Society
113 Station Road, King's Heath, Birmingham, West
Midlands
Tel: 0121-444-8988   **Tel:** 0121-444-1425 (h)
Contact: Abdus Samad Esakjee
Position: Chairperson

Maroof-e-Islam
183 Grove Lane, Handsworth, Birmingham, West
Midlands, B20 2HD

Masjid Adam & Madrasah Salfia
53 George Arthur Road, Saltley, Birmingham, West
Midlands, B8 1LN
Tel: 0121-327-5168

Masjid & Madrassah Faiz-ul-Qur'an
298 Dudley Road, Edgbaston, Birmingham, West
Midlands, B18 4HL
Tel: 0121-455-6581   **Tel:** 0956-976366 (h)
Contact: Mr Mohammed Altaf
Position: Trustee
Activities: Worship, visits, youth, elderly
Movements: Ahl-e-Sunnat Jamaat
Other Languages: Urdu, Punjabi

Masjid-e-Noor
158 Frederick Road, Aston, Birmingham, West
Midlands, B6 6DG
Tel: 0121-328-0156

Masjid-e Noor
36 Prestbury Road, Aston, Birmingham, West
Midlands, B6 6EP

Masjid-e-Noor
8 Towell Road, Kingstanding, Birmingham, West
Midlands, B44 8EA

Medina Mosque
17 Park Avenue, Hockley, Birmingham, West
Midlands, B18 5ND
Tel: 0121-554-6717

Maulana Nisar Dawah Trust
33 Dolobran Road, Sparkbrook, Birmingham, West
Midlands, B11 1HL
Tel: 0121-766-6147   **Fax:** 0121-773-4340
Contact: M Noor
Position: Secretary
Activities: Resource, media, visits, youth, elderly,
women, newsletters, inter-faith
Traditions: Sunni
Movements: Jamati-i-Islami
Other Languages: Urdu, Arabic
Affiliations: Jami Mosque, 521 Coventry Road,
Birmingham; Sharia Council

Mehr-ul-Millat Mosque
21 Shakespeare Street, Sparkhill, Birmingham, West
Midlands, B11
Tel: 0121-773-5966

Minhajul Qur'an
180 Ladypool Road, Birmingham, West
Midlands, B12 8JS

Moroccan Islamic Association
5 St Benedicts Road, Small Heath, Birmingham,
West Midlands, B10 9DP

Mosque
109 Frederick Road, Aston, Birmingham, West
Midlands

Mosque
Dawlish Road, Bournbrook, Birmingham, West
Midlands

Mosque
126 Suffolk Street, Queensway, Birmingham, West
Midlands, B1

Mosque
22 Hugh Road, Small Heath, Birmingham, West
Midlands, B10

Mosque
40 Oakfield Road, Mosely, Birmingham, West
Midlands, B12

Mosque
8 Manfield Road, Lozells, Birmingham, West Midlands, B19

Mosque
Stafford Road, Handsworth, Birmingham, West Midlands, B21

Mosque
15 Ministead Road, Erdington, Birmingham, West Midlands, B24 8PS
Tel: 0121-328-4627

Mosque
58 Trinity Road, Aston, Birmingham, West Midlands, B6

Mosque
44 Fentham Road, Aston, Birmingham, West Midlands, B6
Tel: 0121-523-9963

Mosque
239 Alum Rock Road, Alum Rock, Birmingham, West Midlands, B8

Mosque
49 Couchman Road, Alum Rock, Birmingham, West Midlands, B8

Mosque
2 Black Lane, Bordesley Green, Birmingham, West Midlands, B9 5QY

Mosque
330 Witton Road, Aston, Birmingham, West Midlands

Mosque
314–318 Long Lane, Halesowen, Birmingham, West Midlands

Mosque
22 Hugh Road, Small Heath, Birmingham, West Midlands, B10

Mosque
38 Warwick Road, Sparkhill, Birmingham, West Midlands, B11 4QR

Mosque
158 Handsworth New Road, Winson Green, Birmingham, West Midlands, B18

Mosque
11a Haseley Road, Handsworth, Birmingham, West Midlands, B21 0QU

Mosque
50 Chantry Road, Handsworth, Birmingham, West Midlands, B21 9JB

Mosque
218-220 Washwood Heath Road, Saltley, Birmingham, West Midlands, B8

Mosque & Anjuman Khuddamuddin
11-15 Woodstock Road, Mosely, Birmingham, West Midlands, B13 9BB
Tel: 0121-449-1193

Mosque Gamkol Sharif
38 Warwick Road, Sparkhill, Birmingham, West Midlands, B11

Mosque Ghausia & Community Centre
237 Albert Road, Aston, Birmingham, West Midlands, B6 5LX
Tel: 0121-327-1123
Contact: Mr M Azim
Position: President

Mosque Jamia & UK Islamic Mission
401-403 Alum Rock Road, Alum Rock, Birmingham, West Midlands, B8 3DT

Muath Welfare Trust
The Bordesley Centre, Statford Road, Camp Hill, Birmingham, West Midlands, B11 1AR
Tel: 0121-753-0297   **Fax:** 0121-766-6853
Contact: Muhammad Al Masyabi
Position: Director
Activities: Worship, resource, visits, youth, elderly, women, newsletters, inter-faith
Traditions: Sunni
Other Languages: Arabic, Urdu

Muhul Islam Saddiqia Mosque
12 Victoria Road, Aston, Birmingham, West Midlands, B6

Muslim Education Trust
55 Portland Road, Edgbaston, Birmingham, West Midlands, B16 9HS
Tel: 0121-454-0671
Contact: Dr Am Rajput

Muslim Family Support Service
180 Belgrave Middleway, Birmingham, West
Midlands, B12 0XS

Muslim Foundation
122 Stamford Road, Handsworth, Birmingham,
West Midlands, B20 3PS
Tel: 0121-523-2772 (h)
Contact: Haider Zaman
Position: Chair
Activities: Worship, resource, youth, women
Traditions: Sunni
Movements: Tablighi Jamaat
Other Languages: Urdu, Arabic

Muslim Liaison Committee
Central Jamia Mosque, 180 Belgrave Road,
Birmingham, West Midlands, B12 0XS
Tel: 0121-440-5355
Contact: Mr M Y Qamar

Muslim Prayer House
594 Coventry Road, Small Heath, Birmingham,
West Midlands, B10

Muslim Prayer House
66 Fentham Road, Aston, Birmingham, B6

Muslim Prayer House & Community Centre
1 Willows Crescent, Balsall Heath, Birmingham,
West Midlands, B12 9NN
Tel: 0121-440-3502
Contact: Mr Abdul Rahman

Muslim Student House
517-519 Moseley Road, Moseley, Birmingham,
West Midlands, B12 9BX
Tel: 0121-440-3589
Contact: Mr Y Ballali
Position: Chair
Activities: Worship, resource, visits, youth, women,
inter-faith
Traditions: Sunni,
Other Languages: Arabic

Muslim Welfare & Community Centre
61 Algernon Road, Edgbaston, Birmingham, West
Midlands, B16 0HX
Contact: Mr M Dad

Muslim Welfare Association
98 Walford Road, Sparkbrook, Birmingham, West
Midlands, B11 1QA

Tel: 0121-772-2396
Contact: Qari Tassawar Ul-Haq
Position: Chairperson

Muslim Welfare Society & Parents Association
35 Selly Park Road, Selly Park, Birmingham, West
Midlands, B29 7PH
Tel: 0121-472-0949 (h)
Contact: Haji M Rafique
Position: Chairperson
Activities: Resource
Traditions: Sunni
Other Languages: Urdu, Punjabi
Affiliations: Council of Birmingham Mosques and
Pakistan Welfare Society

Muslim Women's Centre
52 Mackenzie Road, Mosely, Birmingham, West
Midlands, B11 4EL

Muslims Women's Group
6 Johnston Close, Hodge Hill, Small Heath,
Birmingham, West Midlands, B8 2RF

Naqshbandi Order
175 Warren Road, Washwood Heath, Birmingham,
West Midlands, B8 2YD
Tel: 0121-328-3478 (h)

New Muslim Organisation
41 Malthouse Lane, Birmingham, West Midlands,
B8 1SR

Noor-ul-Uloom Mosque
85 St Oswald Road, Small Heath, Birmingham,
West Midlands, B10 9RB
Tel: 0121-773-7036
Position: M Sadiq

Organisation of Muslim Women
Masjid Adam, 53 George Arthur Road, Saltley,
Birmingham, West Midlands, B8 1LN
Tel: 0121-327-5168

Paigham-e-Islam Trust
423 Stratford Road, Sparkhill, Birmingham, West
Midlands, B11 4LB
Tel: 0121-773-8301 **Fax:** 0121-773-1735
Contact: Mr Abdul Malik Chaudhry
Position: Secretary
Activities: Worship, resource, visits, youth, elderly,
women, books
Traditions: Sunni

Other Languages: Urdu, Punjabi, Pushto
Affiliations: UK Islamic Mission

Pakistan Community Muslim Care Association
111 Hurstcroft Road, Lea Village, Birmingham,
West Midlands, B33 9RA

Pakistan Muslim League U.K.
32 Malmesbury Road, Small Heath, Birmingham,
West Midlands, B10 0JQ
Tel: 0121-772-4253 **Fax:** 0121-766-8588
Contact: Dr S A Khan
Position: Chairman
Activities: Resource, media, youth, elderly, inter-faith
Traditions: Sunni
Other Languages: Urdu, Punjabi, Pashto, English

Pakistan Muslim Organisation
120 Malmesbury Road, Small Heath, Birmingham,
West Midlands, B10 0JH
Tel: 0121-772-3740 (h)
Contact: Mr Faisal Haseen
Position: Chairman
Activities: Visits, youth, elderly, women, inter-faith
Traditions: Sunni
Movements: Ahl-e-Hadith
Other Languages: Urdu
Affiliations: Pakistani Forum; Edhi Foundation

Pan-Islamic Society
59 Wilson Road, Handsworth, Birmingham, West
Midlands

Qur'anic Foundation
472 Moseley Road, Balsall Heath, Birmingham,
West Midlands, B12 9AM

Quwat-ul-Islam Mosque
97 Florence Road, Smethwick, Birmingham, West
Midlands
Contact: A E Qureshi
Position: Chairperson

Raza Mosque & Islamic Educational Cultural Centre
9 Serpentine Road, Witton, Birmingham, West
Midlands, B6 6SB
Tel: 0121-327-4204 **Tel:** 0121-328-0837 (h)
Contact: Maulana Bostan Qadri
Position: President
Activities: Worship, resource, youth

Traditions: Sunni
Movements: Barelwi
Other Languages: Urdu, Punjabi, Pakistani
Affiliations: Confederation of Sunni Mosques,
Midlands; UK Action Committee on Islamic Affairs

Selly Park Muslim Welfare Society
1014 Pershore Road, Selly Park, Birmingham, West
Midlands, B29 7PX
Contact: Mr S A Malik

Shah Jalal Bengali School & Islamic Centre & Mosque
61 Poplar Road, Sparkhill, Birmingham, West
Midlands, B11 1UH
Tel: 0121-772-1933 **Tel:** 0121-771-4326 (h)
Contact: Dewan Abdulla Harum Choudhury
Position: President
Activities: Worship, youth, elderly, inter-faith
Traditions: Sunni
Movements: Ahl-e-Hadith; Barelwi/Deobandi/
Tablighi
Other Languages: Bengali, Urdu, English
Affiliations: Birmingham Jami Masjid & Islamic
Centre; Darul Uloom Islamic School & College

Small Heath Mosque
6 Johnson Close, Small Heath, Birmingham, West
Midlands, B8 2RF
Tel: 0121-784-3930
Contact: Mr Ghani

South African Muslim Association
265 Golden Hillock Road, Small Heath,
Birmingham, West Midlands, B10

Sparkbrook Islamic Centre
179-187 Anderton Road, Sparkbrook, Birmingham,
West Midlands, B11 1ND
Tel: 0121-773-8651
Contact: Mohammad Afzal
Position: Centre Manager
Activities: Worship, resource, visits, youth, elderly,
women, newsletters, books, inter-faith
Traditions: Sunni
Movements: Jamati-i-Islami
Other Languages: Punjabi, Urdu, Bengali, Arabic
Affiliations: UK Islamic Mission

Sufi Centre (Naqshbandi Order)
38 Warwick Road, Birmingham, West Midlands,
B11 4QR

Tel: 0121-772-8120
Contact: Sufi Abdullah Khan

UK Islamic Mission
26 Kinniths Way, Halesowen, Blackheath,
Birmingham, West Midlands

UK Islamic Mission
7 Witton Road, Aston, Birmingham, West Midlands,
B6

United Muslim Social Centre
141 Lozells Road, Lozells, Birmingham, West
Midlands

**Washwood Heath Muslim Centre & Madrassah
Qasim Ul-Uloom**
790 Washwood Heath Road, Washwood Heath,
Birmingham, West Midlands, B8 2JG
Tel: 0121-327-7434
Contact: Qari Tassawar Ul-Haq
Position: Director

Witton Islamic Centre
311-313 Witton Road, Witton, Birmingham, West
Midlands, B6

World Council of Muslim Youth
47 Wellington Road, Edgbaston, Birmingham, West
Midlands, B15 2EP

Young Muslim Organisation
523 Coventry Road, Small Heath, Birmingham,
West Midlands, B10 0LL
Tel: 0121-772-6408
Contact: Dr Abdur-Rahim
Position: President

Young Muslims (UK)
194 St Saviour's Road, Saltley, Birmingham, West
Midlands, B8 1HA (h)
Contact: Shakila Begim
Position: Secretary

Young Muslims UK (Sisters Section)
83 Gladstone Road, Sparkbrook, Birmingham, West
Midlands, B11 1LN

Zawiya Islamic Centre
126 Pershore Road, Edgbaston, Birmingham, West
Midlands, B5 7NY
Tel: 0121-440-1347
Contact: Councillor S Abdi

Zawiya Mosque
294 Edward Road, Edgbaston, Birmingham, West
Midlands, B5 7PH
Tel: 0121-440-5746
Contact: Sheikh Mohamed Kassam
Position: Sheikh Kassam

Zia-ul-Qur'an Mosque
218-220 St Saviours Road, Alum Rock,
Birmingham, West Midlands, B8
Tel: 0121-328-1584

Burton Muslim Mosque
66 Waterloo Street, Burton-on-Trent, Staffordshire

Burton Muslim Welfare Association
89 South Broadway Street, Burton-on-Trent,
Staffordshire

Central Mosque
47 South Uxbridge Street, Burton-on-Trent,
Staffordshire

Mosque
134 Princess Street, Burton-upon-Trent,
Staffordshire
Contact: Afzal Quarashi

Mosque
7-10 York Street, Burton-upon-Trent, Staffordshire,
DE14 2XL
Tel: 01283-536040 (h) **Tel:** 01283-512026 (h)
Contact: Mohammed Sadiq
Position: Chairperson
Activities: Worship, resource, umbrella, visits,
women, inter-faith
Movements: Ahl-e-Hadith
Other Languages: Urdu, Punjabi
Affiliations: Jamia-al-Hadith; Muslim World
League

Mosque Committee
173 Uxbridge Street, Burton-upon-Trent,
Staffordshire
Tel: 01283-551163
Contact: Mr Rafaqat Hussain
Position: Chairman

Muslim Community Education Centre
12/13 Albert Street, Burton-on-Trent, Staffordshire,
DE14 2NL (h)
Tel: 01283-536040 (h)
Contact: Mr Mohammed Sadiq

Position: Chairman
Activities: Worship, resource, visits, youth, elderly, inter-faith
Movements: Ahl-e-Hadith
Other Languages: Urdu, Punjabi, Arabic
Affiliations: Muslim World League

Anjuman-e-Gujerati Mosque
283-287 Stoney Stanton Road, Coventry, West Midlands, CV1 2FR
Tel: 01203-622774
Contact: President

Coventry Muslim Community Association Ltd
Coventry Muslim Resource Centre, Red Lane, Foleshill, Coventry, West Midlands, CV6 5EE
Tel: 01203-637933　**Fax:** 01203-638234
EMail: abdul.muslimctr@pop3.hiway.co.uk
Contact: Mr. Ghulam Choudhary
Position: Centre Manager
Activities: Resource, visits, youth, elderly, women, inter-faith
Traditions: Sunni
Other Languages: Urdu, Gujarati, Punjabi, Bangla

Federation of Muslim Organisations
146 Eagle Street, Coventry, West Midlands, CV1 4GQ

Hazrat Dewan-e-Hazoori Centre
130 Station Street West, Foleshill, Coventry, West Midlands, CV6 5JJ
Tel: 01203-581219　**Tel:** 01203-581449 (h)
Fax: 01203-581667
Contact: Mohammed Iqbal Khan
Position: President
Activities: Worship, resource
Traditions: Sunni
Other Languages: Punjabi, Urdu

Hillfields Mosque & Muslim Association
1-3 Berry Street, Hillfields, Coventry, West Midlands, CV1 5JT
Tel: 01203-251184
Contact: Mr Shabbir Ahmed Abbasali
Position: Honorary General Secretary
Activities: Worship, resource
Traditions: Sunni
Movements: Deobandi, Tablighi Jamaat
Other Languages: Gujarati, Urdu, Bengali

Iqbal Academy
17 Holmesdale Road, Coventry, West Midlands

Islamic Brotherhood
57 Leicester Causeway, Foleshill, Coventry, West Midlands, CV1 4HL
Contact: Mr M Ayoub

Islamic Centre
18 Belgrave Road, Coventry, West Midlands, CV2 5AY

Islamic Education & Cultural Society
59 Highland Road, Earlsdon, Coventry, West Midlands, CV5 6GQ

Islamic Society
c/o Students Union, Coventry University, Priory Road, Coventry, West Midlands

Jamia Mosque
Eagle Street, Foleshill, Coventry, West Midlands, CV1 4GY
Tel: 01203-22169　**Tel:** 01203-419514 (h)
Contact: Mr M Ali
Position: Secretary

Khalifa Islamic Society
15 Brooklyn Road, Coventry, West Midlands, CV1 4JW

Masjid-e-Zeenat-ul-Islam
283-287 Stoney Stanton Road, Coventry, West Midlands, CV1 4FR

Muslim Community Centre Association
59 Kingsway, Coventry, West Midlands, CV1 4JW

Muslim Girls & Young Womens Association
4th Floor, Spire House, New Union Street, Coventry, West Midlands

Muslim Womens Group
Eagle Street, Play Centre, Coventry, West Midlands

Tazeem-e-Banatul Islam
148 West Morland Road, Wyken, Coventry, West Midlands, CV2 5BU (h)
Tel: 01203-621055 (h)
Contact: Mrs Haminda Shah
Position: Chairperson
Activities: Visits, youth, women
Traditions: Sunni

Movements: Barelwi
Other Languages: Urdu, Punjabi, English, Gujarati

World Islamic Mission
85 Northfield Road, Coventry, West Midlands

Zeenut-ul-Islam Mosque
Cambridge Street, Coventry, West Midlands
Contact: Mr Y Badat

Brierley Hill Muslim Welfare Association
55 William Street, Brierley Hill, Dudley, West Midlands, DY5 3XH

Dudley Mosque
Birmingham Street, Castle Hill, Dudley, West Midlands
Tel: 01384-253951 **Tel:** 01384-233081 (h)
Contact: Mr M Hanif
Position: General Secretary

Jamia Masjid & Islamic School Ahl-e-Hadith
29 Queen's Cross, Dudley, West Midlands, DY1 1QU
Tel: 01384-258479 **Tel:** 01384-861608 (h)
Contact: Mr M Shabir
Position: Secretary
Activities: Worship, visits, elderly, women
Movements: Ahl-e-Hadith
Other Languages: Urdu

Lye Islamic & Welfare Association
92 Brook Street, Dudley, West Midlands

Muslim Community House
39 Claughton Road, Dudley, West Midlands, DY2 7EA
Tel: 01384-233081
Contact: Mr G H Choudhary
Position: Chairperson

Muslim Youth Association
16 North Street, Dudley, West Midlands

Mosque
20 Bourne Street, Dudley, West Midlands

Mosque
20 Burridge Street, Dudley, West Midlands

Rizvia Mosque
60 Talbot Street, Brierley Hill, Dudley, West Midlands, DY5 3DT (h)
Tel: 01394-75616 (h)

Contact: Mohammed Amin
Position: Secretary General
Activities: Worship, resource, visits, youth
Traditions: Sunni
Movements: Barelwi
Other Languages: Urdu, Punjabi

Bengali Muslim Mosque & Community Centre
149/150 New John Street, Halesowen, Nr Birmingham, West Midlands, B62 8HT
Contact: Mr Hiron Miah
Position: Chair

Blackheath Jamia Mosque Trust
21 Vicarage Road, Halesowen, West Midlands, B62 8HU
Tel: 0121-561-2768 (h)
Contact: Mr Abdul Razzaq
Position: General Secretary
Activities: Worship, visits, youth, elderly
Traditions: Sunni
Movements: Barelwi
Other Languages: Urdu, Arabic

Blackheath Islamic & Community Centre / UK Islamic Mission
314-318 Long Lane, Halesowen, Nr Birmingham, West Midlands, B26 9LQ
Tel: 0121-559-7314

Mosque
314-318 Long Lane, Halesowen, West Midlands

United Muslim Committee
14 Victoria Road, Halesowen, West Midlands, B26

Young Muslims Welfare Association
116 New John Street, Halesowen, West Midlands

Madinatul Uloom-al-Islamiya
Summerfield, Nr Kidderminster, DY10 4BH

Mosque
2 Radford Avenue, Kidderminster, Worcestershire

Mosque
48 Radford Avenue, Kidderminster, Worcestershire

Muslim Community Association
10-12 New Street, Leamington Spa, Warwickshire, CV31 1HP
Tel: 01926-429100
Contact: Chand Mubarak
Position: Secretary
Activities: Worship, resource, visits, youth, elderly,

women, inter-faith
Traditions: Sunni
Other Languages: Urdu, Punjabi

Muslim Culture & Promotional Group
4 Abbots Way, Newcastle-under-Lyme, Staffordshire,
ST5 2ET
Tel: 01782-615978   **Fax:** 01782-615978
Contact: Farhat Y Khan
Position: Secretary
Traditions: Sunni
Other Languages: Urdu, Punjabi

Muslim Community
152 Edward Street, Nuneaton, Warwickshire,
CV11 5RA
Tel: 01203-327882

Nuneaton Muslim Society
The Mosque, Frank Street, Nuneaton,
Warwickshire, CV11 5RB
Tel: 01203-382372
Contact: Mr Awanzieb Ghunra
Position: Secretary
Activities: Worship, resource, umbrella, visits,
youth, inter-faith
Other Languages: Urdu, Gujarati
Traditions: Sunni
Movement: Deobandi, Jamati-i-Islami, Tablighi
Janaat
Affiliations: Union of Muslim Organisations

Council for British Muslims
84 Sillins Avenue, Redditch, Worcestershire

Al-Qu'ran Trust
Mount Pleasant, Southcrest, Redditch,
Worcestershire, B97 4GH
Tel: 01527-403187   **Tel:** 01527-597020 (h)
Contact: Sufi Abdul Wahid
Position: General Secretary
Activities: Worship, resource, visits, youth, elderly,
women, inter-faith
Traditions: Sunni
Movements: Deobandi
Other Languages: Urdu, Punjabi, Bengali

Mosque
28 Easemore Street, Redditch, Worcestershire,
B98 8HA
Tel: 01527-63834
Contact: Mohammed Akram

Blackheath Bangladesh Association
34 Beeches Road, Rowley Regis, West Midlands,
B65 0BT
Contact: Mr Hiron Miah

Rugby Mosque
Grosvenor Hall, 88 Grosvenor Road, Rugby,
Warwickshire
Tel: 01788-543680

Bangladesh Islamic Centre
67 Dartmouth Street, West Bromwich, Sandwell,
West Midlands, B70 8BZ
Tel: 0121-553-5598
Contact: Mr A Jalil
Position: Secretary

Bangladeshi Eshat-ul-Islam in UK
99 Edward Street, West Bromwich, Sandwell, West
Midlands, B70 8NT
Tel: 0121-553-4567   **Tel:** 0121-558-7581 (h)
Contact: Mr M Younus

Islamic Centre of West Bromwich
19a Victoria Street, West Bromwich, Sandwell, West
Midlands, B70 8ET
Tel: 0121-525-1742 (h)
Contact: Mr Haji Mohammad Khalid

Muslim Welfare Association
64 Beeches Road, West Bromwich, Sandwell, West
Midlands, B70 6HH
Tel: 0121-553-7950
Contact: Mr Mohammed Malik
Position: Chairman
Activities: Resource, youth, elderly, inter-faith
Traditions: Sunni
Movements: Barelwi
Other Languages: Urdu

Staffordshire University Islamic Society
Students Union, Beaconside, Stafford, Staffordshire,
ST18 0AD

Cobridge Muslim Community Centre
4 Kirby Street, Cobridge, Stoke-on-Trent,
Staffordshire
Contact: K Iqbal

Federation of Mosques
53 Mulgrave Street, Hanley, Stoke-on-Trent,
Staffordshire, ST1 5EP
Tel: 01782-46765

Contact: Mr Raja
Position: Director

Ghausia Mosque (Trust)
191 Waterloo Road, Cobridge, Stoke-on-Trent,
Staffordshire, ST1 3BS
Contact: Mr Ghulam Ghause Mirza
Position: Chair
Activities: Worship, resource
Traditions: Sunni
Movements: Barelwi
Other Languages: Urdu, Punjabi
Affiliations: Minhaj-ul-Quran

Gilani Noor Mosque
2 Chaplin Road, Longton, Stoke-on-Trent,
Staffordshire, ST3 4QS
Tel: 01782-335606
Contact: K Hussain

Islamic Cultural Centre
16 York Street, Hanley, Stoke-on-Trent,
Staffordshire, ST1 5EH
Tel: 01782-268122 **Tel:** 01782-265801 (h)
Contact: Abdul Matin
Position: Secretary
Activities: Worship
Traditions: Sunni
Movements: Ahl-e-Hadith
Other Languages: Bangali, Urdu
Affiliations: Federation of Mosques, Stoke-on-
Trent

Islamic Cultural Education
13 Havelock Place, Shelton, Stoke-on-Trent,
Staffordshire, ST1 4PS

Madina Mosque
273 Waterloo Road, Cobridge, Stoke-on-Trent,
Staffordshire
Tel: 017882-261429 **Tel:** 01782-267329 (h)
Contact: Mr Dean Merchant
Position: Chairperson

Muslim Defence Council
21 Furnace Road, Longton, Stoke-on-Trent,
Staffordshire
Tel: 01782-341076
Contact: Mr Habib Ullah Siddiqi

Muslim Funeral Society
5 Chatham Street, Shelton, Stoke-on-Trent,
Staffordshire, ST1 4NY

Tel: 01782-269661
Contact: Mr M Akram

Muslim Youth Association
17 Rushton Road, Stoke-on-Trent, Staffordshire
Contact: Mr Mohammed Farooq

Naqshabandia Mosque
18 Dyke Road, Hanley, Stoke-on-Trent,
Staffordshire
Tel: 01782-287432
Contact: Mr A Akbar

Stoke-on Trent Muslim Welfare & Community Association
Bedford Road, Shelton, Stoke-on-Trent,
Staffordshire, ST1 4PJ
Contact: Mr Rana Muhammad Tufail
Position: Trustee
Activities: Resource
Traditions: Sunni, Hanafi
Movements: Barelwi
Other Languages: Urdu, Punjabi

Tabligh-ul-Islam Mosque
31 Upper Belgrave Road, Normacot, Longton,
Stoke-on-Trent, Statffordshire, ST3 4RA

Talim-ul-Qur'an & Mosque
1 Ashford Street, Shelton, Stoke-on-Trent,
Staffordshire
Tel: 01782-8478731 (h)
Contact: Mr Nashir Din
Position: Chairperson and Trustee
Activities: Worship, resource, youth, women
Traditions: Sunni
Movements: Deobandi
Other Languages: Urdu, Punjabi

Tunstall Mosque
2a Keele Street, Tunstall, Stoke-on-Trent,
Staffordshire
Tel: 01782-813617 **Tel:** 01782-827677 (h)
Contact: Mr B Ali

Ghausia Jamia Mosque & Welfare Association
7 Cross Walks Road, Lye, Stourbridge, West
Midlands (h)
Tel: 01384-893110
Contact: Mahboob Hussain
Position: Treasurer
Activities: Worship, visits, youth, elderly
Traditions: Sunni

Movements: Sunat Al Jamat
Other Languages: Urdu, Punjabi

Jamia Ghausia Mosque & Welfare Association
2a High Street, Lye, Stourbridge, West Midlands,
DY9 8AU
Contact: Mr M Akram
Position: President
Activities: Worship
Traditions: Sunni
Movements: Barelwi
Other Languages: Urdu, Punjabi

Lye Islamic & Welfare Association
13c Vale Street, Amblecote, Stourbridge, West
Midlands

Mosque
Valley Road, Lye, Stourbridge, West Midlands

Medina Mosque
7 Park Avenue, Hockley, Tamworth, Warwickshire,
B18 5ND

Mosque
44 Regent Street, Wellington, Telford, Shropshire

Muslim Mosque Trust
119 Crescent Road, Hadley, Telford, Shropshire
Contact: c/o Mr Abdul Kaliq

Pakistan Welfare Association & Mosque
47-49 Mill Bank, Wellington, Telford, Shropshire
Tel: 01952-55389

Telford Central Mosque
41 Tan Bank, Wellington, Telford, Shropshire, TF1
1HJ
Tel: 01952-242933
Activities: Worship, visits
Traditions: Sunni
Movements: Deobandi, Tablighi Jamaat
Other Languages: Punjabi, Urdu, Arabic

Al-Islah Community Trust
93 Park Lane East, Tipton, West Midlands, DY4
8RD
Tel: 0121-557-9174 **Tel:** 0121-557-9174 (h)
Fax: 0121-557-6789
Contact: Ahmadul Haque
Position: President
Activities: Worship, resource, visits, youth, elderly,
women, inter-faith

Traditions: Sunni
Movements: Tassawuf
Other Languages: Bengali, Urdu
Affiliations: Muslim World Aid

Kanz-ul-Iman Muslim Welfare Association
8 Peel Street, Tipton, West Midlands, DY4 8RG
Tel: 0121-557-6556
Contact: Mr M Arif

Mosque & Tipton Muslim Trust Association
17 Wellington Road, Tipton, West Midlands,
DY4 8RS
Tel: 0121-530-1511 **Tel:** 0121-530-3898 (h)
Contact: Hurmuz Ali
Position: Chairman
Activities: Worship, resource
Traditions: Sunni
Movements: Ahl-e-Sunnat
Other Languages: Bengla
Affiliations: Sandwell Confederation of
Bangladeshi Muslim Organisations

Tipton & Tividale Muslim Welfare Association
10 Gate Street, Tipton, West Midlands, DY4 7SP
Tel: 0121-520-5832
Contact: Abdul Qayyum
Position: Chair
Activities: Worship, resource, youth, elderly,
women
Traditions: Sunni
Other Languages: Urdu, Arabic
Affiliations: Confederation of Sunni Mosques

Muslim Welfare Association
26 Tividale Road, Tividale, West Midlands

Anjuman-e-Gosia Mosque
68 Selbourne, Chuckery, Walsall, West Midlands

Anjuman-e-Ishat
37 Hilary Street, Walsall, West Midlands

Anjuman-i-Ishaat e Islam
102-104 Wednesbury Road, Walsall, West Midlands

Anjuman Isha'at Islam
110 Prince Street, Walsall, West Midlands
Contact: A Hussain

Bangladesh Islamic Cultural Association
9 Mount Street, Walsall, West Midlands
Contact: Jayfar Ali

Bangladesh Mosque (Bangladesh Islamic Cultural Association)
74 Wednesbury Road, Walsall, West Midlands, WS1 3RR
Tel: 01922-20051 **Tel:** 01922-641073 (h)
Contact: Mr Kaisor Ali
Position: Secretary

Bangledesh Islamic Cultural Association
5 Small Street, Walsall, West Midlands

Central Mosque
41 Selborne Street, Walsall, West Midlands

Ghausia Qasmia Trust
28 Little London, Walsall, West Midlands
Contact: M Yasin

Ghosia Qasmia Mosque & Darul Uloom
34–35 Mount Street, Walsall, West Midlands
Tel: 01922-34862

Islamic Cultural Society
49 Cecil Street, Walsall, West Midlands

Islamic Society of Britain (Walsall Branch)
52a Milton Street, Walsall, West Midlands, WS1 4JS
Tel: 01922-21659 (h) **Fax:** 01922-32338
Contact: Mr Sohaib Siddiq
Position: President(Ameer)

Jame Ghosia
14 Selbourne Street, Chuckery, Walsall, West Midlands
Tel: 01922-31586

Jamia Mosque
Green Lane, Birchill, Walsall, West Midlands

Madrassah Talim Uddin
42 Lime Street, Walsall, West Midlands

Madrassah Talim Uddin
39 Kinnerley Street, Walsall, West Midlands

Markazi Jamia Masjed Raza Committee
56 Florence Street, Walsall, West Midlands
Contact: A K Qadri

Markazi Jamia Masjid Mosque
41 Selbourne Street, Walsall, West Midlands, WS1 3RR

Masjid-al-Farouq
Milton Street, Palfrey, Walsall, West Midlands, WS1 4JS

Tel: 01922-645786 **Tel:** 01922-37526 (h)
Contact: Dr Habibkhan Pathan
Position: Secretary
Activities: Worship, resource, umbrella, visits, youth, elderly, inter-faith
Traditions: Sunni
Movements: Deobandi, Tablighi Jamaat
Other Languages: Urdu, Gujarati, Bengali, Punjabi
Affiliations: Federation of Indian Muslim Organisations; Union of Muslim Organisations (UK & Eire); Indian Muslim Federation(UK); Muslim World League

Mosque & Butts Muslim Community
22 Cannon Street, Butts, Walsall, West Midlands, WS2 8AY
Contact: Hasan Mohammed Salloo
Position: Secretary
Activities: Worship, resource
Traditions: Sunni
Movements: Deobandi, Tablighi Jamaat
Other Languages: Urdu, Punjabi

Mosque & Islamic Centre
4 Rutter Street, Caldmore, Walsall, West Midlands, WS1 4HN
Tel: 01922-20982
Contact: Saeed Ur Rahman
Position: Imam

Mosque & Islamic Cultural Society
156 Wednesbury Road, Walsall, West Midlands
Tel: 01922-20618

Mosque & Madresa Talimuddin
38 Florence Street, Walsall, West Midlands
Tel: 01922-20982

Orthodox Islamic Mission
524 Pleck Street, Walsall, West Midlands

Pakistan Muslim Welfare Association
62 Dalkeith Street, Birchill, Walsall, West Midlands, WS2 8QB
Tel: 01922-640787

Palfrey Gujerati Muslim Association
127 Lord Street, Palfrey, Walsall, West Midlands, WS1 4DR

Popda Muslim Welfare Association
c/o 40 Milton Street, Palfrey, Walsall, West
Midlands, WS1 4JS

Shah Jalal Mosque
32-33 Mount Street, Walsall, West Midlands
Tel: 01922-647624
Contact: Mr H Rahman
Position: Chairperson

UK Islamic Mission & Islamic Youth Movement
25 Corporation Street, Walsall, West Midlands,
WS1 4HW

UK Islamic Mission Walsall Branch
4 Rutter Street, Walsall, West Midlands
Tel: 01922-20982

Union of Muslim Organisations, Walsall
37 Moorside Gardens, Walsall, West Midlands,
WS2 8SY
Tel: 01922-442861 **Tel:** 01922-22486 (h)
Fax: 01922-644946
Contact: Khawaja-Mohammed Aslam
Position: Chairman
Activities: Resource, umbrella, inter-faith
Traditions: Sunni
Movements: Barelwi
Other Languages: Urdu

Young Muslims Walsall
4 Rutter Street, Walsall, West Midlands, WS1 4HN

Bangladesh Islamic Association
10-11 Lewisham Road, Smethwick, Warley, West
Midlands, B66 2BP
Tel: 0121-558-8204 **Fax:** 0121-558-8204
Contact: Mr Musleh Uddin
Position: Centre Manager
Activities: Worship, resource, visits, youth, women
Traditions: Sunni
Other Languages: Bengali

Islamic Centre & Library
273 Montague Road, Smethwick, Warley, West
Midlands, B66 4PS
Tel: 0121-565-3782
Contact: Mr Fazlur Rehman
Position: Organiser

Jame Masjid Quba
43 Highgate Street, Old Hill, Cradley Heath,
Warley, West Midlands, B64 5RY

Tel: 01384-566203 **Tel:** 01384-456055 (h)
Contact: Ataur Rahman
Position: Chair
Activities: Worship, resource, youth
Traditions: Sunni
Movements: Ahl-e-Hadith
Other Languages: Bengali, Urdu, Arabic, Punjabi

Mosque
89 Edgeware Road, Smethwick, Warley, West
Midlands, B66 4LF

Mosque Muslim Association
43 High Gate Street, Old Hill, Cradley Heath,
Warley, West Midlands

Muslim Association
43 Plant Street, Cradley Heath, Warley, West
Midlands

Muslim Mother Tongue Association
18 Holly Lane, Smethwick, Warley, West Midlands,
B66 1QN
Tel: 0121-558-6982
Contact: Mr Allah Dad

Oldbury Mosque & Muslim Welfare Association
Formerly Oldbury Labour Club, Oldbury Road,
Smethwick, Warley, West Midlands, B66 1HN
Tel: 0121-565-2666 **Tel:** 0121-565-5062 (h)
Contact: Mr M Hanif
Position: General Secretary

Pakistani Muslim Islamic Community Centre
205 Cheshire Road, Smethwick, Warley, West
Midlands
Tel: 0121-555-6047
Contact: Mr Mohammed Saeed

Rowley Regis Muslim Welfare Association
99 Beeches Road, Rowley Regis, Warley, West
Midlands
Tel: 0121-559-7954
Contact: Mr Umar Faruq

Sandwell Central Mosque Trust & Ittehad-ul-Muslemeen Sandwell
49 Barker Street, Oldbury, Warley, West Midlands
Tel: 0121-552-6775 **Tel:** 0121-552-8679 (h)
Contact: Mr S J Shah

Sandwell Muslims Organisation
First Floor, 52 Birmingham Street, Oldbury, Warley,
West Midlands, B69 4DZ

Tel: 0121-544-7864 **Fax:** 0121-544-2425
Contact: Mr Javed Iqbal
Position: Community Services
Activities: Resource, umbrella, visits, youth, women
Traditions: Sunni
Other Languages: Mirpuri, Urdu, Punjabi

Sandwell Pakistan Muslim Welfare Association
46 Grange Road, Cradley Heath, Warley, West Midlands
Tel: 0121-561-4250
Contact: Mr R G Khan

Sandwell Pakistan Muslim Womens Association
1 Rectory Gardens, Vicarage Street, Oldbury, Warley, West Midlands
Tel: 0121-552-6775
Contact: Mrs Z Durrani

Smethwick Bangladeshi Muslim Welfare Association
253 Halfords Lane, Smethwick, Warley, West Midlands, B66 1BD
Contact: Mr Asad Uddin
Position: Secretary
Activities: Worship, resource, visits, youth, elderly
Traditions: Sunni
Other Languages: Bengali

Smethwick Pakistani Muslims Association
1-7 Corbett Street, Smethwick, Warley, West Midlands, B66 3PY
Tel: 0121-555-6047
Contact: Mr Mohammed Azad
Position: Chairperson

Young Muslim Organisation (Smethwick)
2 Kimberley Road, Smethwick, Warley, West Midlands, B66 2DA
Contact: Abdul Hannan
Position: Chairman
Activities: Resource, youth, inter-faith
Traditions: Sunni
Other Languages: Bengali
Affiliations: Bangladesh Islamic Association

Anwar-ul-Qur'an Mosque & Muslim Community Centre
153 Walsall Road, Darlaston, Wednesbury, West Midlands, WS10 8BD

Bangladesh Islamic Society
48 Cook Street, Darlaston, Wednesbury, West Midlands, WS10 9RH
Tel: 0121-526-6790 (h)
Contact: Bashir Ahmed
Position: Trustee
Activities: Worship, youth
Traditions: Sunni
Movements: Jamati-i-Islami
Other Languages: Bengali
Affiliations: Union of Muslim Organisations

Bangladesh Muslim Association
93 Vicarage Road, Wednesbury, West Midlands
Tel: 0121-556-0491 **Tel:** 0121-502-2137 (h)
Contact: Mr Gous Ahmed

Muslim Education & Cultural Trust
51 Cobden Street, Darlaston, Wednesbury, West Midlands, WS10
Contact: Maulana Azim Uddin
Position: Imam
Activities: Worship, resource, youth
Traditions: Sunni
Movements: Ahl-e-Hadith
Other Languages: Bangladeshi, Urdu

Muslim Welfare Association
59B Walsall Road, Darlaston, Wednesbury, WS10 9JS

Muslim Welfare Society
Masjid-e-Umar, Bills Street, Darlaston, Wednesbury, West Midlands, WS10 8BB
Tel: 0121-526-6596
Contact: Mahmood Ebrahim Patel
Position: Honorary Secretary
Activities: Worship, resource, visits, youth, women
Traditions: Sunni
Movements: Deobandi
Other Languages: Gujarati, Urdu
Affiliations: Union of Muslim Organisations

Wednesbury Bangladesh Muslim Welfare Association
9 Brunswick Park Road, Wednesbury, West Midlands, WS10 9HL
Tel: 0121-500-5441 (h)
Contact: Mr Arju Miah
Position: Chairman
Activities: Worship, youth, elderly
Traditions: Sunni

Other Languages: Bengali
Affiliations: Confederation of Bangladeshi Muslim Organisations, Sandwell

Ad-Dharam Brotherhood Wolverhampton UK
71 Park Street South, Wolverhampton, West Midlands, WV2 3JG (h)
Tel: 01902-345271 **Tel:** 01902-871909 (h)
Contact: Mr Janak Raj
Position: General Secretary
Activities: Youth, elderly, women, newsletters, booksYes
Other Languages: Punjabi, English, Hindi, German
Affiliations: All India Ad-Dharam, India

Anjuman-e-Arian
42 Austin Street, Whitmore Reans, Wolverhampton, West Midlands

Bilal Jamia Masjid
283 Newhampton Road West, Whitmore Reans, Wolverhampton, West Midlands, WV1 0RS
Tel: 01902-752190 **Tel:** 01902-20717 (h)
Contact: Hajee Altaf-Hussain Chaudhury
Position: Chairperson
Activities: Worship, visits, youth, elderly, women, inter-faith
Traditions: Sunni
Movements: Barelwi
Other Languages: Urdu
Affiliations: Sunni Muslim Organisation, West Midlands

East African Muslim Association
14 Albert Road, Tettenham, Wolverhampton, West Midlands

Islamic Cultural Centre
202 Newhampton Road East, Whitmore Reans, Wolverhampton, West Midlands

Islamic Society of Britain
19 Albert Road, Wolverhampton, West Midlands, WV6 0AD
Contact: Zaheed Parvez
Position: President

Muslim Doctors & Dentists Association
136 Linden Lea, Wolverhampton, West Midlands, WV3 8BE

Muslim Senior Citizens' Association
202 Newhampton Road East, Whitmore Reans, Wolverhampton, West Midlands

Pakistan Muslim Welfare Association
197 Waterloo Road, Wolverhampton, West Midlands, WV1 4RA
Tel: 01902-312232 **Fax:** 01902-312232
Contact: Mr Qudrat Ullah
Position: Secretary
Activities: Visits, youth, elderly, women
Traditions: Sunni
Movements: Deobandi, Tablighi Jamaat
Other Languages: Urdu, Punjabi

Penfield Mosque & Madresa
84 Lime Street, Wolverhampton, West Midlands

Sahara Centre
18 Leicester Street, Wolverhampton, West Midlands, WV6 0PR
Tel: 01902-560039 **Fax:** 01902-833695
Email: raabita@demon.co.uk
Contact: Mr M U Quazi
Position: Secretary
Activities: Resource, youth, newsletters
Traditions: Sunni
Other Languages: Urdu, Punjabi

UK Islamic Mission
213 Newhampton Road East, Whitmore Reans, Wolverhampton, West Midlands, WV1 4BB
Tel: 01902-711304 **Tel:** 01902-25553 (h)
Contact: Mohammed Shahin Aktar
Position: Vice Chairman
Activities: Worship, resource, visits, youth, elderly, women, newsletters, inter-faith
Traditions: Sunni
Movements: Jamati-i-Islami
Other Languages: Urdu, Arabic
Affiliations: Wolverhampton Council of Mosques; UK Islamic Mission; Muslim World League

United Muslim Welfare Association
3 Lea Road, Pennfields, Wolverhampton, West Midlands

Wolverhampton Mosque Trust
197 Waterloo Road, Wolverhampton, West Midlands, WV1 4RA
Tel: 01902-312232 **Tel:** 01902-343107 (h)
Fax: 01902-312232

Contact: Shah Ali
Position: Vice Chairman
Activities: Worship, resource, visits, youth, elderly, inter-faith
Traditions: Sunni
Movements: Deobandi, Tablighi Jamaat
Other Languages: Urdu, Bangali, Punjabi

Wolverhampton Muslim Trust
Glebe House, Dunstall Road, Wolverhampton, West Midlands, WV6 0NR
Tel: 01902-24360
Contact: Mr M Baig

Young Muslims Wolverhampton
213 Newhampton Road East, Wolverhampton, West Midlands

Al Medina Muslim Association
20 Middle Street, Worcester, Hereford and Worcester
Tel: 01905-29532
Contact: A Sattar

Mosque & Muslim Community Centre
Tallow Hill, Worcester, Hereford and Worcester

Mosque & Muslim Welfare Association
52 Shrub Hill Road, Worcester, Hereford and Worcester, WR4 9EE
Tel: 01905-396044
Contact: Mohammed Riaz
Position: Secretary

EAST ANGLIA
City, Town or Local Bodies

Cambridge Muslim Welfare Society & Abu Bakar Siddiq Mosque
Mawson Road, off Mill Hill, Cambridge, Cambridgeshire, CB1 2BZ
Tel: 01223-350134 **Tel:** 01223-425910 (h)
Contact: Wanis Mohammed Al-Ashgar
Position: Community Member
Activities: Worship, resource, visits, youth, elderly, women, inter-faith
Traditions: Sunni
Other Languages: Bengali, Urdu, Arabic, Turkish
Affiliations: London Central Mosque

Mosque
175 Chesterton Road, Cambridge, Cambridgeshire
Tel: 01223-50134

Mosque
17 Hills Road, Cambridge, Cambridgeshire
Tel: 01223-54605

Muslim Welfare Society
18 Wolsey Way, Cherry Hinton, Cambridge, Cambridgeshire

Ipswich Bangledesh Mosque & Community Centre
Bond Street, Ipswich, Suffolk, IP4 1JE

Ipswich Bangladesh Muslim Community
73 Richmond Road, Ipswich, Suffolk, IP1 4DL

Jamiat Ilhya Minhaj al-Sunnah
P O Box 24, Ipswich, Suffolk, LP3 8EN (h)
Fax: 01473-251578
EMail: ahmed@rang.demon.co.uk

Council of Muslim Women
107 Newmarket Road, Flat 4, Norwich, Norfolk
Tel: 01603-485390

Islamic Society
University of East Anglia, Student Union, Norwich, Norfolk, NR4 7TJ

Norwich City College Islamic Society
Welfare Dept, Ipswich Road, Norwich, Norfolk, NR1 3PU

Norwich Ihsan Mosque
Chapelfield East, Norwich, Norfolk
Tel: 01603-23337
Contact: A Abdullah

Norwich Muslim Community
c/o 11 The Laithes, Norwich, Norfolk
Tel: 01603-615008

World Organisation of Islamic Dawa
3 Christchurch Road, Norwich, Norfolk, NR3 4KJ

Ismaili Community
65 Eyrescroft, Bretton, Peterborough, Cambridgeshire

Mosque
406 Gladstone Street, Peterborough, Cambridgeshire

Pakistan British Social Association
104 Gladstone Street, Peterborough, Cambridgeshire, PE1 2BL

Tel: 01773-64325
Contact: Mr G Y Kayai
Position: President

Shi'a Ithna Asheri Mosque

2 Burton Street, Peterborough, Cambridgeshire,
PE2 5HD
Tel: 01773-68592
Contact: Mahmood Huda
Activities: Worship, resource, visits, inter-faith
Other Languages: Urdu, Gujarati
Affiliations: World Federation of Sh`ia `Ithna
Asheri Muslim Communities

Sunni Mosque

60 Cromwell Road, Peterborough, Cambridgeshire,
PE1 2EB

UK Islamic Mission Peterborough

311 Cromwell Road, Peterborough,
Cambridgeshire, PE1 2HP
Tel: 01733-54425   **Tel:** 01733-705351 (h)
Fax: 01733-54425
Contact: Muzaffar Hussain
Position: Secretary
Activities: Worship, resource, visits, youth, women
Traditions: Sunni
Movements: Jamati-i-Islami
Other Languages: Punjabi, Urdu
Affiliations: UK Islamic Mission

GREATER LONDON
London-Wide or Area Bodies

Council of Mosques for North East London

c/o 711 High Road, Leyton, London, E10 6RA

Essex Islamic Trust

(See entry on page 559 which should be located
here).

Islamic Association of North London

36 Long Lane, Finchley, London, N3 2PU
Tel: 0181-346-9730   **Tel:** 0181-368-1064
Contact: Mr Saeed ul Haq Qazi
Position: Honorary Secretary
Activities: Worship, resource, visits, youth, women
Traditions: Sunni
Movements: Ahl-e-Hadith, Deobandi, Tablighi
Jamaat
Other Languages: Urdu, Bengali, Gujrati, Arabic
Affiliations: Muslim Council of Britain

Khoja Shia Ithna-Asheri Muslim Community of London

Islamic Centre, Wood Lane, Stanmore, Middlesex,
HA7 4LQ
Tel: 0181-954-6247   **Tel:** 0181-429-1349 (h)
Fax: 0181-954-8028
Contact: Fadhl Tharoo
Position: Honorary Secretary
Activities: Worship, resource, umbrella, visits,
youth, elderly, women, newsletters, books, inter-
faith
Traditions: Shi`a `Ithna Asheri
Other Languages: Urdu, Arabic, Gujarati,
Kutchi/Swahili
Affiliations: World Federation of Khoja Shi`a
Ithna-Asheri Muslim Communities

Muslim Directory

65a Grosvenor Road, London, W7 1HR
Tel: 0181-840-0020   **Fax:** 0181-840-8819
EMail: musdir@enterprise.net
Activities: Books
Other Languages: Urdu, Punjabi, Swahili, Arabic

South London Islamic Centre

8 Mitcham Lane, Streatham, London, SW16 6NN
Tel: 0181-677-0588   **Tel:** 0181-769-5723 (h)
Contact: Mohammed Aslam Ijaz
Position: Hon Gen Secretary
Activities: Worship, resource, visits, youth, elderly,
women, inter-faith
Traditions: Sunni
Other Languages: Urdu Gujerati, Bengali, Arabic,
Bosnian Somali
Affiliations: Council of Mosques, South London
and Surrey; Union of Muslim Organisation of UK
and Eire; World Assembly of Muslim Youth, Saudi
Arabia

South London Muslim Association

76 Elmwood Road, West Croydon, Surrey, CR0 2SJ
Contact: Mr M I Mohamed

Borough and Local Bodies

BARKING AND DAGENHAM

Barking Muslims Association

2 Victoria Road, Barking, Essex, IG11 8PY
Tel: 0181-478-8526   **Tel:** 0181-591-0930 (h)
Contact: Mr Mohammad Ayub Mirza
Position: Secretary

Activities: Worship, resource, umbrella, visits, youth, elderly, women, inter-faith
Traditions: Sunni
Other Languages: Urdu, Punjabi, Bengali, Pushto

Barking Muslim Social & Cultural Society
7 Triangle, Tanner Street, Barking, Essex, IG11

Barking Muslim Social & Cultural Society
1 Monteagle Avenue, Barking, 1G11 8RA

League of British Muslims
32 Somerby Road, Barking, Essex

Majlis-e-Iqbal Islamic Education Society
33 Salisbury Avenue, Barking, Essex, IG11 9XQ

Muslim Association Barking & Dagenham
43 Cecil Avenue, Barking, IG11 9TD

Muslim Parents Association -Barking & Dagenham
5 Wilmington Gardens, Barking, Essex

Pakistan Muslim Association
43 Cecil Avenue, Barking, IG11 9TD

World Islamic Mission (Greater London Branch)
70 The Lintons, Barking, Essex, IG11 8NX
Tel: 0181-591-1710
Contact: Mufti Younas Kashmiri
Position: President

BARNET

Golders Green Muslim Committee
17 Courtleigh Gardens, London, NW11
Contact: Dr Mohammed

Hendon Islamic Association
32 Bertram Road, London, NW4

Hendon Islamic Centre
Brent View Road, West Hendon, London, NW9 7EL
Tel: 0181-202-3236
Contact: Mr S M Kadri
Position: Secretary
Activities: Worship, visits, youth, women
Traditions: Sunni
Movements: Deobandi, Tablighi Jamaat
Languages: Urdu
Affiliations: Union of Muslim Organisations; UK Ruiyate Hilal Committee; Muslim World League

Islamic Association of North London
36 Long Lane, Finchley, London, N3 2PU
Tel: 0181-346-9730 **Tel:** 0181-368-1064
Contact: Mr Saeed ul Haq Qazi
Position: Honorary Secretary
Activities: Worship, resource, visits, youth, women
Traditions: Sunni
Movements: Ahl-e-Hadith, Deobandi, Tablighi Jamaat
Other Languages: Urdu, Bengali, Gujrati, Arabic
Affiliations: Muslim Council of Britain

Khawateen
40 Church Crescent, Whetstone, London, Greater London, N20 (h)
Tel: 0181-368-2120
Contact: Mrs Shahida Parveen Rehman
Position: President
Activities: Youth, elderly, women, inter-faith
Other Languages: Urdu, Punjabi

Kokni Muslim Cultural & Youth Organisation UK
83 Sheaveshill Court, Collindale, London, NW9 6LT
Activities: Youth

Kokani Muslims (Golders Green)
127 Hamilton Road, London, NW11 9EG
Contact: Mr S A Kadri
Position: General Secretary

Memon Jamaat
15 Woodside Avenue, London, N12

Mosque & Islamic Centre
Brent View Road, West Hendon, London, NW9
Tel: 0181-202-3236
Contact: Sayed M Kadizi
Position: Secretary
Activities: Worship, resource, visits, youth, elderly, women
Traditions: Sunni
Other Languages: English, Arabic, Urdu
Affiliations: Union of Muslim Organisation

Muslim Educational & Literary Sevices
61 Alexandra Road, Hendon, London, NW4 2BX
Tel: 0181-202-1799 **Fax:** 0181-201-5924
Contact: Mr Abdulwahid Hamid
Position: Director
Activities: Resource, books

Muslim Students Society
Hendon College of FE, Silkstream Road, Edgware, Middlesex

UK Islamic Mission
14 Harcourt Avenue, Edgware, Middlesex, HA8 8XN
Tel: 0181-958-4697
Contact: Naseem Haider Mir
Position: Secretary
Activities: Worship, resource
Traditions: Sunni
Movements: Jamati-i-Islami
Other Languages: Urdu, Punjabi

BRENT

An-Nisa Society
Bestways Complex, Rear Entrance, Abbey Road, Park Royal, London, NW10 7BW
Tel: 0181-838-0311 **Fax:** 0181-838-0311
Contact: Ms Khalida Khan
Position: Co-ordinator
Activities: Resource, youth, elderly, women, newsletters
Other Languages: Urdu, Arabic, Somali

Brent Islamic Circle
16 Brampton Road, Kingsbury, London, NW9 9BU

Brent Islamic Forum
PO Box 408, Wembley, Middlesex, HA0 4DE
Tel: 0181-838-0191 **Fax:** 0181-838-0191
Contact: Dr Iftikhar Saraf
Position: Chair
Activities: Umbrella
Other Languages: Urdu, Arabic, Somali

Central Mosque of Brent
Station Parade, Willesden Green, London, NW2
Tel: 0181-452-4103 **Tel:** 0181-451-0009 (h)
Contact: Raja Mohammad Riaz
Position: Chairman
Activities: Worship
Traditions: Sunni
Movements: Barelwi
Other Languages: Arabic, Urdu, Punjabi, English

Federation of Muslim Organisations UK
44 Linden Avenue, Wembley, Middlesex

Ghana Muslim Union
15 Exton Crescent, Stonebridge, London, NW10

Islamic Centre, Edgware
42 Beverley Drive, Edgware, Middlesex
Tel: 0181-204-2006
Traditions: Sunni
Other Languages: Urdu, Punjabi, Pushto, Gujrati
Affiliations: Union of Muslim Organisations

Islamia Girls School
184 Walm Lane, London, NW2

Islamic Centre Edgware
63 North Way, London, NW9 0RA
Tel: 0181-204-2461

Islamic Centre of Brent
c/o Jajji Abdul, 26a Chichele Road, London, NW2 3DA

Islamic Cultural House
107 Anson Road, London, NW2

Islamic Guidance Society
24a District Road, Sudbury, Wembley, Middlesex, HA0 2LD
Tel: 0181-902-6215
Contact: Maulana M A Ovaisi
Position: Director

Islamic Welfare Association Mosque
106 Harrowdene Road, Wembley, Middlesex
Tel: 0181-904-2260

Kokni Muslim Cultural & Youth Organisation
277a High Road, London, NW10 2JY

Memon Jammat
270 Kilburn High Road, London, NW6

Mosque & Islamic Centre of Brent
33a Howard Road, London, NW2 6DS
Activities: Worship
Tel: 0181-450-1986 **Fax:** 0181-452-7403
Contact: Hafiz Bashir Ahmed

Muslim Welfare Association
224a Ealing Road, Wembley, HA0 4QL

Orphan Relief Fund
PO Box 2916, Church Lane, Kingsbury, London, NW9 8EF

Sri Lanka Islamic UK Association
62 Rose Glen, Collindale, London, NW9 1JS

Stonebridge Islamic Group
27 Donavan Court, Exton Crescent, London, NW10

Sudbury Muslim Community Centre
24A District Road, Sudbury, Wembley, Middlesex, HA0 2LD

Wembley Mosque & Islamic Centre
5 Stanley Avenue, near Alperton Station, Wembley, Middlesex, HA0 4JA
Tel: 0181-9023258 **Tel:** 0181-9001808 (h)
Contact: Sultan Ahmed Hakim
Position: Secretary
Activities: Worship, visits, youth, elderly, inter-faith
Traditions: Sunni
Other Languages: Arabic, French, Gujrati, Urdu

BROMLEY

Bromley Muslim Council
11 High Street, London, SE20 7HJ
Tel: 0181-659-0640 (h)
Contact: Mr Khalid Sharif-Knight (Lord of Camster)
Position: Chair
Activities: Umbrella, inter-faith
Traditions: Sunni
Other Languages: English, Urdu, Punjabi
Affiliations: British Muslim Council

CAMDEN

Al-Sadiq & Al-Zahra High Schools
Chevening Road, London, NW6 5TN

Dar al-Ifta
46 Goodge Street, London, W1P 1FJ
Tel: 0171-636-2080

Families Relief
B M Box 7289, London, WC1N 3XX

Indian Muslims Relief Committee
P O Box 415, London, NW1 2LD
Tel: 0171-338-3678

Institute of Arabic & Islamic Culture
PO Box 408, London, WC1H 0XP

International Centre for Islamic Studies
144-146 Kings Cross Road, London, WC1X 9DH

Islamic Arts Centre
ICIS House, 144-146 Kings Cross Road, London, WC1X 9DH

Islamic Book Centre
120 Drummond Street, London, NW1 2HL
Tel: 0171-388-0710

Islamic Cultural Centre & the London Central Mosque Trust Ltd
146 Park Road, London, NW8 7RG
Tel: 0171-724-3363 **Fax:** 0171-724-0493
Contact: Bashir Ebrahim-Khan
Position: Officer
Activities: Worship, resource, media, umbrella, visits, youth, elderly, women, newsletters, books, inter-faith
Traditions: Sunni
Other Languages: Arabic, French, Urdu, Bengali
Affiliations: Inter Faith Network for the UK

Islamic Dawah Centre
31b Woodsome Road, London, NW5 7HT

Islamic Society
School of Oriental and African Studies, 7 Malet Street, London, WC1

Shah Jalal Masjid-e-Noor
204a North Gower Street, Euston, London, NW1
Tel: 0181-387-8346
Activities: Worship

University College, London, Islamic Society
University College, London, Union Building, 25 Gordon Street, London, WC1 0AH

CROYDON

Croydon Mosque & Islamic Centre
525 London Road, Thornton Heath, Croydon, Surrey, CR7 6AR
Tel: 0181-684-8200
Contact: Imran Khan
Position: Caretaker
Activities: Worship, resource, visits, youth, elderly, women, inter-faith
Traditions: Sunni
Other Languages: Urdu, Punjabi, Bengali, Arabic
Affiliations: South London Mosques

Muslim Association of Croydon
7 Stuart Road, Thornton Heath, Croydon, Surrey,
CR7 8RA
Tel: 0181-683-3699 (h)
Contact: Mr M H Rahman
Position: Secretary

Muslim Womens' Association of Croydon
44 Whitehall Road, Thornton Heath, Croydon,
Surrey

Muslim Womens' Association of Croydon
61a Windmill Road, West Croydon, Surrey
Contact: Mrs N Sami
Activities: Women

Muslim Youth Association
95 Beluah Road, Thorton Heath, Croydon, Surrey,
CR4 8JG

South Indian Muslim Welfare Association
72 Eldon House, Thornton Road, Thornton Heath,
Croydon, Surrey CR7, 6BA
Tel: 0181-684-3862 **Tel:** 0181-853-4376 (h)
Fax: 0181-665-1334
Contact: M Osmon
Position: Chair
Activities: Resource, media, youth, elderly, women
Traditions: Sunni
Other Languages: English, Tamil, Malayalam,
Urdu
Affiliations: Union of Muslim Organisations

South London Muslim Association
76 Elmwood Road, West Croydon, Surrey, CR0 2SJ
Contact: Mr M I Mohamed

Sunni Razvi Society
11 Carew Road, Thornton Heath, Croydon, CR4
7RF

Tehrik-i-Nizam-i-Qur'an & Sunnah
395 Sydenham Road, West Croydon, Surrey, CR0
2EH (h)
Tel: 0181-2391279
Contact: Mr H I Faryad
Position: Director
Activities: Inter-faith
Traditions: Sunni
Other Languages: Urdu, Punjabi, Hindi

Uganda Society for Islamic Propagation
290 Brighton Road, South Croydon, Croydon,
CR2 6AG

Young Muslim Association
95 Beulah Road, Thornton Heath, Croydon,
Surrey, CR4 8JG
Tel: 0181-653-0957
Contact: Mr J A Sharif (Jnr)

EALING

Abubakr Mosque
30 Villiers Road, Southall, Middlesex, UB1 3BS

Acton Mosque
40 Churchfield Road, London, W3
Activities: Worship

Anjuman-e-Burhani
Mohamedi–Park Masjid Complex, Rowdell Road,
Northolt, Middlesex, UB5 6AG
Tel: 0171-229-6404 **Tel:** 0181-969-1060
Fax: 0171-221-2691
Contact: Sheikh Walijee Hassanali
Activities: Worship
Traditions: Shi`a Imami Ismalia Talybi Dawoodi
Bohra
Movements: Dawoodi Bohras
Languages: Gujarati, Hindi, Urdu, Arabic

Anjuman-e-Nau
108 Hill Rise, Greenford, Middlesex

Arabic & Islamic Cultural Society
15a Grange Park, London, W5 3PL

Central Jamia Masjid
Montague Waye, Southall, Middlesex, UB2 5NZ
Tel: 0181-813-9218 **Fax:** 0181-813-9219
Contact: Mohammad Bashir
Position: Chairman
Activities: Worship, visits, women
Traditions: Sunni
Movements: Tablighi Jamaat
Other Languages: Urdu, Punjabi, Somali, Arabic

Ealing Muslim Welfare Association
4 Eccleston Road, West Ealing, London, W13 0RL
Tel: 0181-573-2369 **Tel:** 0181-566-5417 (h)
Contact: Abdul Hadi
Position: Secretary
Activities: Worship, resource
Traditions: Sunni
Movements: Barelwi
Other Languages: Urdu, Sohali

Islamic School Greenford
61 Daryngton Drive, Greenford, Middlesex, UB6 8BH

Jamia Masjid
Brownlow House, Browlow Road, West Ealing, London, W13 0SQ
Tel: 0181-840-4140 **Tel:** 0181-579-2185
Contact: Syed Mohammed Ali
Position: Secretary
Activities: Worship, resource, umbrella, visits, youth, elderly, women, inter-faith
Traditions: Sunni
Movements: Jamati-i-Islami
Other Languages: Urdu, Gujarati, Punjabi, Pushto
Affiliations: UK Islamic Mission

Larden Hall Mosque
Larden Road, Acton, London, W3
Activities: Worship

Mosque
121 Oaklands Road, Hanwell, London, W7
Tel: 0181-579-2185
Activities: Worship

Mosque
223 Oldham Terrace, Acton, London, W3

Mosque
1 Madley Road, Ealing, London, W5 2LA

Mosque
103 Townsend Road, Southall, Middlesex
Tel: 0181-574-6014

Muslim Association & UK Islamic Mission
21 Costons Avenue, Greenford, Middlesex

Muslim Directory
65a Grosvenor Road, London, W7 1HR
Tel: 0181-840-0020 **Fax:** 0181-840-8819
EMail: musdir@enterprise.net
Activities: Books
Other Languages: Urdu, Punjabi, Swaheli, Arabic

Muslim Women's Association
c/o Central Jamia Masjid, Montague Waye, Southall, Middlesex
Tel: 0181-574-5380
Contact: Mrs N Haq

UK Islamic Mission
23 Elthorne Park Road, Harwell, London, W7

UK Islamic Mission
74 Western Road, Southall, Middlesex

West London Islamic Centre
120 North Road, Southall, Middlesex, UB1 2JR
Tel: 0181-574-8037
Contact: Mr A Vora
Position: General Secretary

Young Muslim Association
120 North Road, Southall, Middlesex

ENFIELD

Edmonton Islamic Centre
198 Upper Fore Street, London, N18 2JD
Tel: 0181-807-5151 **Tel:** 0181-807-9578 (h)
Contact: Wasil Yar Khan
Position: Chairman
Activities: Worship, resource, visits, youth, elderly, women, inter-faith
Traditions: Sunni
Movements: Practice of Qur'an/Hadith
Other Languages: Urdu, Punjabi, Bengali, Arabic/Turkish
Affiliations: Union of Muslim Organisations, UK & Ireland

Enfield Mosque
228 High Street, Ponders End, Enfield, Middlesex

Mosque
146 Nags Head Road, Enfield, Middlesex

North London Muslim Welfare Association
51 Northfield Road, Enfield, EN3 4BP

GREENWICH

Asian Youth & Social Club
6 Tuam Road, Plumstead Common, London, SE18 2QU
Tel: 0181-855-8877 (h) **Fax:** 0181-855-8877
Contact: Saeed Ahmad
Position: Chairman
Activities: Resource, visits, youth, elderly, inter-faith
Traditions: Sunni
Other Languages: Urdu, Panjabi, Hindi, Gujerati

Charlton Mosque
30 Ransome Road, Charlton, London, SE7 8SR
Tel: 0181-858-4479 **Tel:** 0181-858-0209 (h)
Contact: Mr Asghar Hamid
Position: Chair
Activities: Worship

Greenwich Islamic Association
82 Admaston Road, Plumstead, London, SE18

Greenwich Islamic Centre
Woolwich Mosque, 131 Plumstead Road, London,
SE18 7DU
Tel: 0181-855-0786
Contact: Abdul Hamid Ismail
Position: Director
Activities: Worship, resource, visits, youth, elderly,
women, inter-faith
Other Languages: Urdu, Bengali, Somali, Gujarati
Affiliations: Central London Mosque; Muslim
World League

Muslim Association (Greenwich)
6 Tuam Road, London, SW18 2QU

Muslim Project
115-123 Powis Street, Woolwich, London, SE18

Muslim Womens Association
c/o Greenwich Muslim Project, 115-123 Powis
Street, London, SE18 6JL

Muslim Youth Association in the UK
49 Chearsley Street, Deacon Way, London, SE7
1SW

**South East Muslim Cultural & Educational
Society**
41 Westhorne Avenue, Eltham, London, SE9

University of Greenwich Islamic Society
Student's Union, Thomas Street, Woolwich,
London, SE18

HACKNEY

**Aziziye Mosque & UK Turkish Islamic
Association**
117-119 Stoke Newington Road, London, N16
Tel: 0171-254-0046
Contact: Ahmet Ali
Position: Secretary

Dalston Mosque
160 Dalston Lane, London, E8
Tel: 0181-254-3266

Hackney Muslim Council
14 Warneford Street, London, E9 7NG

Hackney Muslim Social & Cultural Society
45 Chatsworth Road, London, E5 0LH

Hackney Muslim Women's Council
101 Clapton Common, London, E5 9AB
Tel: 0181-809-0993
Contact: Amna Khan
Position: Co-ordinator
Activities: Resource, youth, elderly, women
Traditions: Sunni
Other Languages: Urdu, Punjabi, Gujarati
Affiliations: Regents Park Mosque; The Muslim
World League

Hayabah Girls School
88 Filey Avenue, Stamford Hill, London, N16 6JJ

London Islamic Turkish Association
16 Green Lanes, London, N16 9ND
Tel: 0181-249-5417 (h)

Madina Mosque Trust
2a Lea Bridge Road, Clapton, London, E5 9QD
Tel: 0181-985-8204
Contact: Yusuf Hajat
Position: Trustee
Activities: Worship, resource, visits, youth
Traditions: Sunni
Other Languages: Gujarati, Urdu, Hindi
Affiliations: Imams and Mosque Council (East
London); Union of Muslim Organisations; Jamiat-
ul-Ulama UK; Muslim World League

Medina Mosque
16 Mildenhall Road, London, E5 9QP
Tel: 0181-985-8204

Muridin al Haq
98 Greenwood Road, London, E8 1NE

Mosque
4 Linthorpe Road, London, N16

Muslim Cultural Society
48 Stoke Newington Church, London, N16 0NB

North London Mosque
70-72 Cazenove Road, Stamford Hill, London, N16
Tel: 0181-806-6540

North London Muslim Housing
62 Cazenove Road, Stamford Hill, London, N16 6AA

Stamford Hill Mosque
82 Foreberg Road, London, N16

Tayyibah Girls School
88 Filey Avenue, Stamford Hill, London, N16 6JJ
Tel: 0181-880-0085 **Fax:** 0171-249-1767
Contact: Mr Mohamed Saeed Alibhai Dana
Position: Trustee
Activities: Resource
Traditions: Sunni
Movements: Deobandi, Tablighi Jamaat
Other Languages: Gujarati, Urdu, Bengali, Turkish
Affiliations: Association of Muslim Schools UK

Turkish Mosque
9-15 Shacklewell Lane, London, E8

UK Islamic Trust
9-15 Shacklewell Lane, London, E8
Tel: 0181-254-0431

UK Turkish Islamic Cultural Centre Trust
Suleymaniye Mosque, 212-216 Kingsland Road, London, E2 8AX
Tel: 0171-613-2223 **Fax:** 0171-613-3303
Contact: Mehmet Bolukbasi
Position: President
Activities: Worship, resource, visits, youth, elderly, women, books, inter-faith
Traditions: Sunni
Movements: Ahl-e-Hadith
Other Languages: Turkish, Arabic

Union of Muslims in Hackney
14 Warneford Street, London, E9 7NG
Tel: 0181-985-3258

Upper Clapton Muslim Welfare & Womans Ass.
66 Detmold Road, London, E5 9NJ

UK Turkish Islamic Cultural Centre Trust Suleymaniye Mosque
212-216 Kingsland Road, London, E2 8AX
Tel: 0171-613-2223 **Fax:** 0171-613-3303

Contact: Mehmet Bolukbasi
Position: President
Activities: Worship, resource, visits, youth, elderly, women, books, inter-faith
Traditions: Sunni
Movements: Ahl-e-Hadith
Other Languages: Turkish, Arabic

UK Turkish Islamic Cultural Centre Trust & Validesultan Mosque
1a Clissold Road, London, Greater London, N16 9EX
Tel: 0171-241-5425 **Tel:** 0850-983121 (h)
Fax: 0181-518-2861
Contact: Mehmet Bolukbasi
Position: President
Activities: Worship, resource, umbrella, visits, youth, elderly, inter-faith
Traditions: Sunni
Movements: Ahl-e-Hadith, Jamati-i-Islami
Other Languages: Turkish, Arabic

UK Turkish Islamic Trust Mosque & Cultural Centre & Funeral Services
60 Green Lanes, Hackney, London, N16 9NH
Tel: 0171-254-5337 **Tel:** 0836-338766 (h)
Fax: 0171-923-2554
Contact: Nr Ramadan Houssein Guney
Position: Chair
Activities: Worship, resource, youth, elderly, women
Traditions: Sunni
Other Languages: Turkish, Arabic, Urdu

HAMMERSMITH AND FULHAM

Anjuman-e-Burhani
354 Lillie Road, Fulham, London, SW6 6DD

Bait al-Mal al-Islami
109 Fulham Palace Road, London, W6 8JA

Burhani Community Centre
354 Lillie Road, London, SW6
Tel: 0171-229-6404 (h)
Contact: Dr Idris Zainuddin
Position: Chairperson

Hammersmith Imamwada
30-32 Southerton Road, London, W6

Holy Party
62 St Stephen's Avenue, Shepherd's Bush, London, W12 TD

Tel: 0181-743-9699
Contact: Mr S B Khawaja

Kanoon Tawhid Islamic Centre
30-32 Southerton road, Hammersmith, London, W6
Tel: 0181-746-3158 **Fax:** 0181-746-3158
Contact: H Khoshkoo
Position: Director
Activities: Worship, resources
Traditions: Shi`a `Ithna Asheri
Other Languages: Farsi (Iranian)
Affiliations: Al-Tawhid Charity

Mosque
112 Goldolphin Road, London, W12
Tel: 0181-740-0463
Activities: Worship

Mosque
69 Tunis Road, London, W12
Activities: Worship

Muslim Womens Association
66 Rosebury Road, London, SW6 2NG (h)
Tel: 0171-731-5455 (h)
Contact: Mrs Mussarrat Aftab
Position: Chair
Activities: Resource, visits, youth, elderly, women, inter-faith
Traditions: Sunni, Other Shi`a
Other Languages: Urdu, Punjabi, Turkish, Bengali/Hindi

Shepherd's Bush Mosque & Muslim Centre
302 Uxbridge Road, Shepherd's Bush, London, W12 7LJ
Tel: 0181-740-0463 **Fax:** 0181-742-9070
Contact: Dr Ahmed Adam Badaj
Position: President
Activities: Worship, resource, visits, youth
Traditions: Sunni
Other Languages: Urdu, Bengali, Arabic

Somali Islamic Centre
1 Keithgrove Road, Shepherds Bush, London, W12

HARINGEY

Al-Qur'an Society
101 Belmont Road, Tottenham, London, N17 6AT
Tel: 0181-889-6662 **Fax:** 0181-881-3984
Contact: Dr Suhaib Hasan

Position: Chairperson
Activities: Resource, books
Traditions: Sunni
Other Languages: Urdu, Arabic

Al Laggani Centre
227 St Anns Road, London, N15 5RJ

Bangladesh Muslim Organisation
90 Sydney Road, London, N8

Haringey Muslim Council
54 Alexandra Road, London, N8 0PP

Hornsey Mosque & Islamic Centre
385-389 Hampden Road, Hornsey, London, N8

Islamic Community Centre
115 Clyde Road, London, N15 4JS

Islamic Medical Association
c/o 233 Seven Sisters Road, London, N4 2DA

Islamic Missionary Guild International of the Caribbean & S. America
150a Gladstone Avenue, London, N22 6LG

Islamic Video & Audio Services
10 Hampden Road, London, N8 0HT

Islamic Youth Trust
20 Cranley Gardens, Muswell Hill, London, N10 3AP

London Islamic Cultural Society
389-395 Wightman Road, Hornsey, London, N8
Tel: 0181-348-0353 **Tel:** 0181-372-3023 (h)
Contact: Mr Abdool Alli
Position: President
Activities: Worship, resource, visits, youth, elderly, women, newsletters, inter-faith
Traditions: Sunni
Other Languages: Bengali, Urdu, Turkish

Muslim Cultural Society of UK
55 Park Ridings, London, N8

Muslim Cultural Society of Enfield
203 Lordship Lane, Tottenham, London, N17 6XF

United Islamic Association
9 Willoughby Road, London, N8

World Forum of Indian Muslims
9 Alfoxton Avenue, London, N15

Young Muslim Organisation UK
Haringey Branch, 115 Clyde Road, London, N15 4JS

HARROW

Harrow Central Mosque
36-38 Station Road, Harrow, Middlesex, HA1 2SQ
Tel: 0181-861-2071
Contact: Fazal Rahman
Position: Secretary
Activities: Worship, resource, visits, youth, elderly, women, inter-faith
Traditions: Sunni
Other Languages: Urdu, Punjabi, Bengali, Arabic
Affiliations: Union of Muslim Organisations; Islamic Cultural Centre, London

Harrow Muslim Education Society
417 Pinner Road, Harrow, Middlesex
Tel: 0181-427-1481

Harrow Muslims Collective
60 Rosslyn Crescent, Harrow, Middlesex, HA2 7NW

Indian Muslim Federation
70 Turner Road, Edgware, Middlesex

Islamic & Culural Society of Harrow
1 Church Drive, North Harrow, Middlesex, HA2 7NW

Khoja Shi'a 'Ithna-Asheri Muslim Community of London
Islamic Centre, Wood Lane, Stanmore, Middlesex, HA7 4LQ
Tel: 0181-954-6247 **Tel:** 0181-429-1349 (h)
Fax: 0181-954-8028
Contact: Fadhl Tharoo
Position: Honorary Secretary
Activities: Worship, resource, umbrella, visits, youth, elderly, women, newsletters, books, inter-faith
Traditions: Shi`a `Ithna Asheri
Other Languages: Urdu, Arabic, Gujarati, Kutchi/Swahili
Affiliations: World Federation of Khoja Shi`a Ithna-Asheri Muslim Communities

Kokni Muslim Culture & Youth Organisaton UK
98 The Chase, Edgware, Middlesex

Taleem Bookshop
79 Hindes Road, Harrow, Middlesex, HA1 1SQ

HILLINGDON

Essex Islamic Trust
67 Essex Road, Romford, Essex, RM7 8BB
Tel: 01708-705293 (h)
Contact: Kamal Ahmed Siddiqui
Position: President
Activities: Worship, resource, visits, youth, elderly, women, newsletters, inter-faith
Traditions: Sunni, Other Shi'a
Other Languages: English, Urdu, Hindu, Arabic
Affiliations: Union of Muslim Organisations
(This entry should be located at page 550 under London-Wide or Area Bodies).

HOUNSLOW

Anjuman-e-Khwateen
28 Lansdowne Road, Hounslow, Middlesex, TW3 1LQ
Tel: 0181-570-1394
Position: c/o Mrs Ahsan Shah

Hounslow Jamia Masjid & Islamic Centre
235 Staines Road, Hounslow, Middlesex, TW3 3JN
Tel: 0181-570-0938 **Tel:** 0181-893-4594 (h)
Contact: Mr Abdul Kayum Qureshi
Position: General Secretary
Activities: Worship, resource, visits, youth, elderly, women
Traditions: Sunni
Other Languages: Urdu, Arabic, Somali, Hindi
Affiliations: Council of Mosques UK & Eire; Union of Muslim Organisations

Hussaini Islamic Mission
19 Thornbury Road, Isleworth, Middlesex
Tel: 0181-570-3438 **Fax:** 0181-570-3438
Contact: Hojjatol Islam S M S Razavi
Position: Resident Alim

Islamic Society
University of Brunel, Uxbridge, Middlesex, UB8 3PH

Isleworth Muslim Women's Association
1 Witham Road, Isleworth, Middlesex, TW7 4AJ
Tel: 0181-560-6702 (h)
Contact: Naseem Yousef

Position: Organiser
Activities: Resource, visits, youth, elderly, women, inter-faith
Traditions: Sunni
Other Languages: Urdu, Hindi, Punjabi, Gujrati
Affiliations: Pakistan Welfare Assocation; Muslim World League

Madina Islamic Mission & Islamic Centre
35 Martindale Road, Hounslow West, Middlesex, TW4 7EW

Muslim Women's Association
157 Kingsley Road, Hounslow, Middlesex, TW3

Sri Lanka Islamic (UK) Association
24 Vine Place, Hounslow, Middlesex

UK Islamic Mission (Unit)
7 Marnellway, Hounslow, Middlesex

Young Muslim Association
122 Kingsley Road, Hounslow, Middlesex, TW3 4AD

ISLINGTON

Bazmi-i-Tafreeh
25 Evershot Road, London, N4 3DG
Tel: 0171-272-7031
Contact: Abdul Aleem Siddiqui

Holborn Islamic & Welfare Centre
1a Rosebery Avenue, 4th Floor, London, EC1 4RT

Islamic Computer Centre
73 St Thomas's Road, London, N4 2QJ

Islington Muslim Association
71 Caledonian Road, Islington, London, N1

Islington Muslim Association
38 Northdown Street, London, N1
Tel: 0171-837-1771

Kings Cross Mosque & Islamic Centre
62 Paddington House, Rodney Street, London, N1

Malaysian Islamic Study Group
90 St Thomas's Road, Finsbury Park, London, N4 2WQ

Medical Aid for Palestinians
33a Islington Park Street, London, N1 1QB

Mosque
251 Pentonville Road, Kings Cross, London, N1
Tel: 0171-278-0877

Mosque
11 Woodfall Road, London, N4

Muslim Welfare Centre
13 Leconfield Road, London, N5 2RX

Muslim Welfare Centre
13-15 St Thomas's Road, Finsbury Park, London, N4 2QH

Seerah Foundation
78 Gillespie Road, London, N5 1LN
Tel: 0171-359-8257
Contact: S W Hassan
Position: Director
Activities: Resource, books
Languages: Urdu

Union of Muslim Families UK
55 Balfour Road, Islington, London, N5 2HD (h)
Tel: 0171-226-0934 (h)
Contact: M.W. Khan
Position: Chair
Activities: Resource, visits, youth
Traditions: Sunni
Movements: Ahl-e-Hadith
Other Languages: Urdu, Bengali, Arabic, French
Affiliations: The Muslim World League

KENSINGTON AND CHELSEA

Ahl-ul-Bayt Foundation
31 Draycott Place, Chelsea, London, SW3

Islamic Museum
37 Queen's Gate, London, SW7 5HR

Islamic Universal Association
20 Penzance Place, Holland Park Avenue, London, W1 4PG
Tel: 0171-602-5273 **Fax:** 0171-603-0525
Contact: Mr Alemi
Position: Chairman
Activities: Worship, resource, media, umbrella, visits, youth, inter-faith
Traditions: Sh`ia `Ithna Asheri
Other Languages: Farsi, Arabic

Kensington Mosque
170 Old Brompton Road, London, SW5 OBD
Tel: 0171-373-0238
Contact: Chairperson
Activities: Worship

Mosque
33 St Lukes Mews, Kensal, London, W10

Mosque
3-5 Palace Gate, Kensington, London, W8
Activities: Worship

Muslim Cultural Heritage Centre Administration Office
2-4 Malton Road, London, W10 5UP
Tel: 0181-964-1496 **Tel:** 0181-960-0403
EMail: tclrc@rbk.gov.uk
Contact: Abdulkarim Khalil
Position: Acting Director
Activities: Worship, resource, youth, vistors, elderly, women, inter-faith
Other Languages: Arabic, Urdu, Bengali, Somali

World Sufi Council
114 Highlever Road, London, W10 6PL

KINGSTON-UPON-THAMES

Islamic Dawah Centre
60 Albert Road, New Malden, Surrey, KT3 6BS

Islamic Society Kingston College
Kingston Hall Road, Kingston-upon-Thames, Surrey, KT1 2AQ

Kingston Mosque & Muslim Association
55/55a East Road, Kingston-upon-Thames, Surrey, KT2 6EJ
Tel: 0181-549-5315
Contact: Mohammed Anwar Malik
Position: Secretary
Activities: Worship, resource, visits, youth, women, inter-faith
Traditions: Sunni
Movements: Sunni Jamati
Other Languages: Arabic, Urdu, Bengali

Kingston Muslim Womens Welfare & Cultural Association
38 Gainsborough Road, New Malden, Surrey, KT3 5NU
Tel: 0181-715-2227 (h) Fax: 0181-942-7678

Contact: Hamida Syed
Position: Secretary
Activities: Resource, youth, women, inter-faith
Traditions: Sunni
Other Languages: Urdu, Punjabi
Affiliations: Community Youth and Leisure Services Kingston

LAMBETH

Afro Caribbean Islamic Cultural Mission
70 Fitzgerald House, Stockwell Park Road, London, SW9

Ahl-ul-Bayt Islamic Centre
11-13 Edgeley Road, London, SW4 6EH
Tel: 0181-627-2230

Al Furquan Charity Trust
1 Wynne Road, London, SW9 0BB

Al Hilal Masjid
24 Brailsford Road, Tulse Hill, London, SW2 2TB
Tel: 0181-674-2825
Contact: A Devon
Position: Secretary
Activities: Worship, resource, elderly, books
Traditions: Sunni, 'Ithna Asheri
Other Languages: English, Urdu, Arabic
Affiliations: London Islamic Cultural Centre; Muslim World League

Ansarullah Community
70 Fitzgerald House, Stockwell Park Road, London, SW9 0UQ

Ash-Shahada Housing Association
1a Gresham Road, Brixton, London, SW9 7PH

Brixton Mosque & Islamic Cultural Centre
1 Gresham Road, London, SW9 7PH
Tel: 0171-326-4098 **Fax:** 0171-326-4098
Contact: Abdul Haqq Baker
Position: Chairman/Ameer
Activities: Worship, resource, umbrella, visits, youth, women, newsletters, books
Traditions: Sunni
Movements: Salafee
Other Languages: Arabic, French, Somali
Affiliations: South London Council of Mosques

Islamic Community Centre
64 Cottage Grove, London, SW9 9NQ

Islamic Education & Training Centre
147 Fentiman Road, London, SW8 1JZ

Islamic Information Bureau
26 Estreham Road, London, SW16 5PQ
Tel: 0171-733-7970 (h)
Contact: Rizwan Ali-bhai

Khatme Nubuwwat Centre
35 Stockwell Green, Stockwell, London, SW9 9HZ
Tel: 0171-737-8199
Contact: M B Patel
Position: Secretary
Activities: Worship

Ksisli Jamaat Hyderi Islamic Centre
26 Estreham Road, Streatham, London, SW16 5PQ
Tel: 0181-788-5554
Contact: Secretary
Activities: Worship

Lambeth Islamic Cultural Centre
30 Belfields Road, Brixton, London, SW9
Tel: 0181-683-0907 (h)
Contact: Mohammed Abdul Basith
Position: Secretary
Activities: Worship
Traditions: Sunni
Other Languages: Urdu

Mosque
25 Bellfield Road, Brixton, London, SW9
Activities: Worship

South London Islamic Centre
8 Mitcham Lane, Streatham, London, SW16 6NN
Tel: 0181-677-0588 **Tel:** 0181-769-5723 (h)
Contact: Mohammed Aslam Ijaz
Position: Hon Gen Secretary
Activities: Worship, resource, visits, youth, elderly, women, inter-faith
Traditions: Sunni
Other Languages: Urdu Gujerati, Bengali, Arabic
Affiliations: Council of Mosques, South London and Surrey; Union of Muslim Organisation of UK and Eire; World Assembly of Muslim Youth, Saudi Arabia

South Indian Muslim Association
8 Mitcham Lane, London, SW16 6NN

UK Islamic Mission

72 Holmdene Avenue, London, SE24 9LE

World Islamic Forum
35 Stockwell Green, London, SW9 9HZ

LEWISHAM

Lewisham & Kent Islamic Centre
283 Brownhill Road, Catford, London, SE6 1AE
Tel: 0181-698-4316 **Tel:** 0181-467-2764 (h)
Contact: Dr Sabiha Saleem
Position: Executive Committee Member
Activities: Worship, visits, youth, women, inter-faith
Traditions: Sunni
Other Languages: Urdu, Punjabi, Bengali, Arabic
Affiliations: South London Mosques; Union of Muslim Organisation

MERTON

Al-Furqan Islamic Heritage Foundation
Eagle House, High Street, Wimbledon, London, SW19 5EF

Al-Medina Trust
161 South Park Road, London, SW19

Darul Amaan Islamic Centre
54 High Street, Merton, London, SW19 1DH
Tel: 0181-543-5687

Education & Welfare Charitable Fund
59 Home Park Road, London, SW19 2JF

Muhammadi Trust
17 Beverley Way, West Wimbledon, SW20 0AW

Muslim Women's Association
63 Coombe Lane, London, SW20 0BD
Tel: 0181-946-1052
Contact: Mrs Khanum Hassan
Position: President
Activities: Women

Wimbledon Mosque
262-270 Dunsford Road, Wimbledon Park, London, SW19 8DS
Tel: 0181-946-3350
Contact: Mr M A Hamid
Position: Chairperson
Activities: Worship

UK Islamic Mission
2 Firtree Avenue, Mitcham, Surrey

UK Muslim Association
19 Dryden Road, Wimbledon, London, SW19

United Muslims Association
91 Framfield Road, Mitcham, Surrey

NEWHAM

Alliance of Newham Muslim Associations
159 Plashet Road, Upton Park, London, E13 0QZ
Tel: 0181-470-5233
Position: Mr M Farhat

Anjuman-e-Islamia (Newham) & Mosque
266-268 High St North, Manor Park, London,
E12 6SB
Tel: 0181-472-5663
Contact: Chairman

Azeemia Foundation (UK)
Azeemia House, 92b Hampton Road, Forest Gate,
London, E7 0NU
Tel: 0181-555-4577
Contact: Mrs A Azeemi

Bangladesh Shomity
52 Upton Park Road, Forest Gate, London,
E7 8LD
Tel: 0181-471-0800
Contact: Mr M Ali

Bilal Mosque & Islamic Centre
6 Dickens Road, East Ham, London, E6 3BY

British Muslim Association
56 Harold Road, Plaistow, London, E13 0SQ
Tel: 0181-471-2107
Contact: Mr M A Siddiqi

Canning Town Islamic Centre
5 Market Place, Ordinance Road, London, E16
Tel: 0181-474-3674
Contact: Mr M Y Iqbal
Position: Secretary

Canning Town Mosque & Welfare Association
Muslim Community Centre, 269 Barking Road,
Canning Town, London, E13 8EQ
Tel: 0181-472-5096 (h)
Contact: Mr S Ali
Position: Secretary

Darul-Uloom London
11-13 St George's Road, Forest Gate, London,
E7 8HT

Forest Gate Mosque
451 Romford Road, Forest Gate, London, E7 8AB

Imamia Mission
519 Romford Road, Forest Gate, London, E7 8AD
Tel: 0181-472-3588
Contact: Mr Ali Naqui

Islamic Association East Ham Muslim Cultural Centre
Madina Masjid, 225 High Street North, East Ham,
London, E6 1JG (h)
Tel: 0181-472-3069 **Tel:** 0181-470-6769 (h)
Contact: Abdul Rahman Sheikh
Position: President
Activities: Worship, resource
Traditions: Sunni
Movements: Deobandi
Other Languages: Urdu, Gujarati, Bengali

Islamic Centre
72 Selwyn Road, Upton Park, London, E13 0PY
Tel: 0181-472-2745
Contact: Mr Naeem Khan

Islamic Centre (Upton Park)
175-177 Plashet Grove, Upton Park, London,
E6 1BX
Tel: 0181-472-2957 (h)
Contact: Mr V A Patel

Islamic Voluntary Service (Newham)
205 Harold Road, Plaistow, London, E13 0SE
Tel: 0181-470-3674
Contact: Mr M Rafiq

Manor Park Islamic Cultural Centre & Shajalal Mosque
722-726 Romford Road, Manor Park, London,
E12 6BT
Tel: 0181-514-7772 **Tel:** 0181-553-5826
Contact: Mr Mahmud Khan
Position: General Secretary
Activities: Worship, visits
Traditions: Sunni
Movements: Ahl-e-Hadith
Other Languages: Bengali, Urdu
Affiliations: Muslim World League

Markaz-ud-Dawat-Wal Irshad Muslim Community Centre
177-179 Plashet Grove, East Ham, London

Masjid-e-Bilal & East London Islamic Centre
295 Barking Road, East Ham, London, E6 1LB
Tel: 0181-471-9355
Contact: Mr Afzal

Masjid-e-Falah
510 Barking Road, Plaistow, London, E13 8QE

Medina Mosque & Muslim Cultural Centre
225 High Street North, London, E6 1JG
Tel: 0181-472-3069
Contact: Mr L Hussain
Position: Secretary

Mosque
197 Milton Avenue, East Ham, London, E6 1BN

Muslim Welfare Association Plaistow
40 Newham Way, Canning Town, London, E16 4ED
Tel: 0171-474-4936

Muslim Women's Welfare Association
83 Stopford Road, Plaistow, London, E13 0NA
Tel: 0181-471-7648
Contact: Ms S Sarwar

Newham Muslim Citizens Association
81 Katherine Road, East Ham, London, 1EW
Tel: 0181-4703360 (h) **Fax:** 0181-472-4651
Contact: Mahmood Ahmad
Position: Chair Person
Activities: Resource, visits, youth, women, inter-faith
Other Languages: Urdu, English, Punjabi
Affiliations: Tlu-e-Islam, International

Newham Muslim Council
72 Boleyn Road, Forest Gate, London, E7 9QE
Tel: 0181-472-1615
Contact: Mr Z Ali

Newham Muslim Womens Association
423 Romford Road, Forest Gate, London, E7 8AB
Tel: 0181-555-3784
Contact: Mrs Modi

Newham North Islamic Association Mosque & Community Centre
88 Green Street, London, E7 8JG

Tel: 0181-472-6887 **Tel:** 0181-471-3677 (h)
Contact: Mr Shahan H Hussain
Position: General Secretary

Quwwat-ul-Islam Mosque & Islam Society
62-66 Upton Lane, London, E7 9LN
Tel: 0181-472-1072 **Tel:** 0181-534-4248 (h)
Contact: Maulana Osman Adam

South Indian Muslim Association (UK)
123 Burgess Road, East Ham, London, E6 2BL

UK Islamic Mission
108 Katherine Road, London, E6

World Islamic Mission (East London Branch)
28 Essex Road, Manor Park, London, E12 6RE
Tel: 0181-552-9050
Contact: Mr G Haider
Position: General Secretary

REDBRIDGE

British Muslim Association
222 Ley Street, Ilford, Essex, IG1 4BP
Tel: 0181-220-8462
Contact: Mr M A Shah Siddiqi
Position: Secretary
Activities: Resource
Other Languages: Urdu

Idara Minhaj ul Quran
19 St. Thomas Gardens, Ilford, Essex, IG1 2PQ
Tel: 0181-553-0498 (h)

Ilford Islamic Centre & Mosque
52-56 Albert Road, Ilford, Essex, IG1 1HW
Tel: 0181-478-3115

Ilford Muslim Society
112 Balfour Road, Ilford, Essex, IG1 4JE
Tel: 0181-478-0347 **Tel:** 0181-220-8968 (h)
Contact: Mr Yusuf Umerji Patel
Position: Secretary
Activities: Worship, resource, visits, inter-faith
Traditions: Sunni
Movements: Deobandi, Tablighi Jamaat
Other Languages: Gujarati, Hindi, Urdu

Ilford Muslim Welfare Association
1 Kingswood Road, Ilford, Essex

Islamic Dawah Centre
PO B0x 262, Ilford, Essex, 4SU

Mosque
119 St Albans Road, Seven Kings, Ilford, Essex

Mosque
17 Cambridge Road, Ilford, Essex

Muslim Defence Council UK
17 Natal Road, Ilford, Essesx
Tel: 0181-514-4436
Contact: Mr Raja Adalat Khan
Position: General Secretary

Pakistan Muslim Association of Barking & Ilford
75 Mayfair Avenue, Ilford, Essex

Redbridge & Chigwell Muslim Association
36 Woodford Avenue, Gants Hill, Ilford, Essex,
IG2 6XQ
Tel: 0181-551-6189　**Tel:** 0181-551-0570 (h)
Fax: 0181-551-9819
Contact: Ali Muhammad Qureshi
Position: Chair
Activities: Visits, youth, women, inter-faith
Traditions: Sunni
Movements: Unity of Muslims
Other Languages: Arabic, Bengali, Urdu, Sindhi
Affiliations: Union of Muslim Organisations UK
and Eire; The Council of Mosques and Muslim
Organisations (UK); The Muslim World League

Seven Kings Muslim Educational Trust
703 High Road, Seven Kings, Ilford, Essex
Tel: 0181-599-6865

RICHMOND-UPON-THAMES

International Institute of Islamic Thought
P. O. Box 126, Richmond, Surrey, TW9 2UD

SOUTHWARK

Baitul Aziz Masjid & Madrassa
1 Dickens Square, off Harper Road, London,
SE1 4JL
Tel: 0171-378-7764　**Tel:** 0171-274-4985

Dulwich Islamic Centre
23 North Cross Road, London, SE22 9ET
Tel: 0181-693-8682 (h)
Contact: Hussain Malik
Position: Chairman
Activities: Worship, resource, youth, elderly,
women
Traditions: Sunni

Other Languages: Urdu, Bengali, Arabic
Affiliations: South London Mosques

Muslim Association of Nigeria (UK)
M.A.N.'s Building, 365 Old Kent Road, London,
SE1 5JH
Tel: 0171-231-0100　**Tel:** 0956-962195 (h)
Fax: 0171-237-0009
Contact: Mr Adewusi
Position: President
Activities: Worship, resource, media, umbrella,
visits, youth, elderly, women, newsletters
Movements: Ahl-e-Hadith, Quarian
Other Languages: Nigerian Languages, Arabic

Muslim Brotherhood
21 Andrews Walk, John Ruskin Street, London,
SE17 3JQ

Muslim Education & Cultural Society
411 Westhorne Avenue, London, SE12

Muslim League
19 Trafalgar Avenue, London, SE15

Noorul Islam Turkish Mosque
99 Cobourg Road, Off Old Kent Road, Peckham,
London, SE5
Tel: 0171-703-0985
Activities: Worship

Peckham Mosque
1 Peckham High Street, London, SE15
Tel: 0171-703-5995
Activities: Worship

South Bank University Islamic Society
Students's Union, Rotary Street, London, SE1

Southwark Muslim Women's Association
Bellenden Old School, Bellenden Road, London,
SE15
Tel: 0171-732-8053　**Tel:** 0171-277-7320 (h)
Fax: 0171-732-3310
Contact: Zafar Iqbal
Position: Centre Co-ordinator
Activities: Resource, visits, youth, elderly, women
Traditions: Sunni, Ismaili
Other Languages: Urdu, Bangali, Turkish, Patwa

Zara Muslims Womens Group
c/o Thomas Calton Centre, Alpha Street, London,
SE15 4NX

SUTTON

Bangladesh Welfare Association
32 Mollison Drive, Wallington, Sutton, Surrey,
SM6 9BY
Contact: Mrs H J Kabir
Activities: Youth, women

British Islamic Academy
40 Park Lane, Wallington, Sutton, Surrey, SM6 0TN
Tel: 0181-715-3093
Contact: Dr Mohammad Abdul Mannan
Position: President
Activities: Resource, youth, women
Traditions: Sunni
Other Languages: Bengali, Urdu

Muslim Cultural & Welfare Association of Sutton
Wentworth Hall, 80 Ruskin Road, Carshalton,
Surrey, SM5 3DH
Tel: 0181-647-9041 **Tel:** 0181-647-9041 (h)
Contact: Lal Hussain
Position: Secretary
Activities: Worship, resource, media, visits, youth,
elderly, women, newsletters, inter-faith
Traditions: Sunni
Movements: Ahl-e-Hadith
Other Languages: English, Urdu, Bengali
Affiliations: Union of Muslim Organisations

Sutton Islamic Centre
62 Oakhill Road, Sutton, Surrey
Contact: Misdiq Zaida

TOWER HAMLETS

Assembly of Muslim Youth
14 Stanborough House, Empson Street, London,
E3 3LY (h)
Tel: 0171-987-7321 (h)
Contact: Hafiz Abdullah Mohammad
Position: Chief Organiser
Activities: Resource, youth, books, inter-faith
Traditions: Sunni,
Other Languages: Bengali

Dawatul Islam Coventry Cross Mosque & Islamic Centre
6 Broxbourne House, Devas Street, London,
E3 3LS
Tel: 0171-515-6714

Dockland Dar ul Amanat Mosque & Islamic Centre
23 Farnworth House, Manchester Road, London,
E14 3HY
Tel: 0171-537-2705 **Tel:** 0171-537-2705 (h)
Contact: MD Shoeb Ahammad
Position: Chair
Activities: Worship
Traditions: Sunni
Other Languages: Bengali, Urdu, Arabic

East London Mosque
82/92 Whitechapel Road, London, E1 1JE
Tel: 0171-247-1357 **Fax:** 0171-377-9879
Contact: M A R Khan
Position: Caretaker
Activities: Worship, resource, visits, youth, elderly,
women, inter-faith
Traditions: Sunni
Other Languages: Bengali, Urdu,
Nigerian/Somalian, Arabic

East London Mosque Bookshop
92 Whitechapel Road, London, E1

Esha'atul Islam Mosque
16 Ford Square, London, E1 2HS
Tel: 0171-790-3966 **Tel:** 0171-265-1890 (h)
Contact: Maulana Shamsul Haque
Position: Imam
Activities: Worship, resource, youth, elderly,
women, inter-faith
Traditions: Sunni
Other Languages: Bengali, Urdu, Arabic
Affiliations: Council of Mosques; Muslim World
League

Holburn Islamic & Welfare Centre
4th Floor, 1a Centre, London, E1 4RT
Tel: 0171-278-3393, Ext: 127
Contact: Fazlul Karim Chowdhury
Position: Chairperson

Islamic Book Services
52 Fieldgate Street, London, E1 1DL

Islamic College
16 Settles Street, London, E1 1JP

Islamic Community Centre
Limborough House, Thomas Road, London,
E14 7AW

Jamia Masjid
59 Brick Lane, Aldgate East, London, E1
Tel: 0171-247-3507 **Tel:** 0171-247-6052 (h)

Madrasa-e-Darul Kerat
46/48 Cannon Street, London, E1 0BH

Markazi Mosque
9-11 Christian Street, off Commercial Road,
London, E1 1SE
Tel: 0171-481-1294 **Tel:** 0171-488-4820 (h)

Mosque
141 Leman Street, London, E1

Mosque
10 Brick Lane, London, E1 0AS

Mosque
Hale Street (cabin), Poplar, London, E14

Mosque
Limborough House, Wallwood Street, London, E14

Mosque
Devon Street, 3 Broxburne House, London, E3
Tel: 0171-987-2133

Mosque
39 Fournier Street, Spitalfields, London, E1

Shair-e-Rabbani Islamic Centre
33 Granby Street, London, E2 6DR

Shoreditch Mosjid Trust
53-55 Red Church Street, Tower Hamlets, London,
E2 7DP
Tel: 0171-739-5530 (h)
Contact: Lukman Ali
Position: Secretary
Activities: Worship
Traditions: Sunni
Movements: Jamati-i-Islami, Tablighi Jamaat and
Tassawuf
Other Languages: Bengali (Sylhati Dialect),
Urdu, Hindi

Somali Islamic Circle
84 Whitechapel Road, London, E1

Somali Islamic Circle Organisation
16 Settles Street, London, E1 1JP

Stepney Shahjalal Mosque
Duckett Street, Shandy Park, London, E1
Contact: Mr Mohammad Shahid Ali
Position: General Secretary
Activities: Worship
Traditions: Sunni
Languages: Bengali

Tower Hamlets Islamic Service
28 Tunis House, Harford Street, London, E1 4RP

Young Muslim Organisation
39 Fashion Street, Bethnel Green, London, E1

**Young Muslim Organisation (UK) Shadwell
Branch**
22 Tunis House, Hartford Road, London, E1

WALTHAM FOREST

Al-Tawhid Mosque & Madrasah Ahl-e-Hadith
80 High Road, Leyton, London, E15
Tel: 0181-519-6655 **Tel:** 0181-471-1894
Contact: Mohammed Idrees Sethi
Position: Secretary
Activities: Worship, resource, youth, women
Traditions: Sunni
Movements: Ahl-e-Hadith
Other Languages: Urdu, Punjabi, Arabic
Affiliations: Walthamstow Islamic Sharia Council;
Al Qur'an Society; World League League; Call to
Islam

Council of Mosques for North East London
c/o 711 High Road, Leyton, London, E10 6RA

International Muslim Movement
12 East Avenue, St Mary Road, London, E17
Tel: 5204121

Islamic Educational Centre
39 Beaconsfield Road, Leyton, London, E10

Jamait Ahl-e-Hadith
58 Wallwood Road, Leytonstone, London, E11
1AZ

Leyton Muslim Cultural Society
715 High Road, London, E10 5AB
Tel: 0181-539-0769
Contact: Yusuf Hansa
Position: Chair
Activities: Worship, resource, youth, elderly,
women, newsletters, inter-faith

Traditions: Sunni
Other Languages: Creole or Patois, French, Urdu
Affiliations: Noor ul Islam; Council of Mosques for North East London

Leytonstone Mosque & Islamic Association
Dacre Road, London, E11 3AG
Tel: 0181-539-7251

Masjide Aqsa & Waltham Forest Muslim Welfare Society
79 Queens Road, Walthamstow, London, E17
Tel: 0181-520-2658
Contact: Mr Z A R Oomerjee
Position: Secretary

Mauritian Islamic Welfare Association (MIWA)
715 High Road, Leyton, London, E10 5AB
Tel: 0181-539-0769
Contact: Mr Aslam Hansa
Position: Chair
Activities: Youth, elderly, women, newsletters
Traditions: Sunni
Other Languages: Patois, Urdu
Affiliations: Noor ul Islam

Muslim Community Development Project
31 Second Avenue, Walthamstow, London, E17 9QH

Muslim Ladies & Families Circle
108 Capworth Street, Leyton, London, N10 7HE

Muslim Welfare Society
79 Queens Road, Walthamstow, London, E17

Mosque
134a Ashville Road, Leyton, London, E11 4DU
Tel: 0181-558-5601
Contact: Maulana Sharif Pathan
Position: Imam
Activities: Worship
Traditions: Sunni
Movements: Deobandi, Tablighi Jamaat
Other Languages: Urdu, Gujarati, Arabic, French

Mosque
14 Leonard Road, Chingford, London, E4

Muslim Ladies Circle
187b Francis Road, Leyton, London, E10 6NQ

Muslim Parents Association
c/o 13c Hoe Street, London, E17

Muslim Women's Welfare Association
School Annexe, Bickley Road, London, E10 7HL
Tel: 0181-539-7478
Contact: Mrs Meher Khan
Position: Co-ordinator

Noor-ul-Islam
711 High Road, Leyton, London, E10 5RA
Tel: 0181-923-7860
Contact: Mr Yusuf Hansa
Position: Chairman
Activities: Worship, visits, youth, elderly, women, inter-faith
Traditions: Sunni
Other Languages: English, French, Urdu, Arabic
Affiliations: Council of Mosques for North East London

Wall Mosque
1 Higham Hill Road, Walthamstow, London, E17 6EA

Waltham Forest Islamic Association & Leabridge Road Mosque
439-451 Lea Bridge Road, Leyton, London, E10 7EA
Tel: 0181-539-4282 **Tel:** 0181-558-3117
Fax: 0181-558-3117
Contact: Haji Mohammed Ramzan
Position: President
Activities: Worship, resource, visits, youth, elderly, inter-faith
Traditions: Sunni
Movements: Barelwi
Other Languages: Urdu, Punjabi, Bengali, Gujrati

Waltham Forest Muslim Welfare Society
79 Queen's Road, Walthamstow, London, E17 2JB

Waltham Forest Pakistan Muslim Welfare Association
6 Exeter Road, London, E17

World Islamic Council
PO Box 1736, London, E10 6NF

WANDSWORTH

Al-Medina Trust
85A Upper Tooting Road, London, SW17 7TW

Balham Mosque
47a Balham High Road, London, SW12 9AW
Tel: 0181-675-7912 **Fax:** 0181-675-7912
Contact: Mr Iqbal M Khalfey
Position: Secretary
Activities: Worship, resource, visits, youth, elderly, women, inter-faith
Traditions: Sunni
Other Languages: Urdu, Gujarati, Punjabi, Arabic
Affiliations: Council of Mosques in South London and Surrey

Battersea Mosque
75 Falcon Road, Battersea, London, SW11 2PF
Activities: Worship

Caribbean Islamic Cultural Society
c/o Gatton Road Mosque, 8 Gatton Road, Tooting, London, SW17
Tel: 0181-769-2795 (h)
Contact: Mozamil Ouhla
Position: Coordinator
Activities: Worship, visits, youth, elderly, women, inter-faith

H H Aga Khan Ismailli Mosque
113 Blegborough Road, Streatham, London, SW16

Idara-e-Jaaferiya Mosque
18a Church Lane, Tooting, London, SW17 9PP
Tel: 0181-672-5373 **Tel:** 0181-682-0233
Contact: Hujattul Islam Maulana Raza Haider
Position: Resident Alim
Activities: Worship, resources, youth, women, newsletters
Traditions: Shi`a `Ithna Asheri
Movements: Ahl-e-Bayt, Koran
Other Languages: Urdu, Arabic, Punjabi, Persian

Islamic Cultural & Education Centre/Islamic Youth Group
73/75 Falcon Road, Battersea, London, SW11 2PG
Tel: 0171-228-4267
Contact: Taswar Hussain
Position: Senior Youth Worker
Activities: Worship, resource, visits, youth, women, inter-faith
Traditions: Sunni
Other Languages: Urdu, Bengali, Arabic, Somali
Affiliations: Union of Muslim Organisation

Islamic Education & Training Centre
30 Rowfant Road, London, SW17 7AS
Tel: 0181-675-0404

Islamic Education Centre
51 Gassiot Road, London, SW17
Contact: Mrs Sultanat Khan

Memon Jamaat
37 Wonter Road, Tooting, London, SW17
Contact: Mr I Sacranie

Mosque
49 Lower Richmond Road, Putney, London, SW15
Tel: 0181-788-5554
Activities: Worship

Movement for Islamic Resurgence
11 Turpin House, Battersea Park Road, London, SW11 5HR

Muslim Sisters Jamaat
107 Graveney Road, Tooting Broadway, London, SW17 0EJ

Muslim Women Welfare
18 Trinity Road, Tooting, London, SW17 7RE
Contact: Co-ordinator
Activities: Women

Muslim Womens Group
72 Upper Tooting Road, London, SW17
Tel: 0181-767-4894
Contact: Mrs Siddiqui
Activities: Women

Muslim Youth Centre
64 Foulser Road, Tooting, London, SW17
Tel: 0181-767-4894
Contact: Waseem Siddiqui
Activities: Youth

Muslim Youth Organisation
72 Upper Tooting Road, Tooting, London, SW17
Tel: 0181-767-4894

Tooting Islamic Centre
145 Upper Tooting Road, London, SW17 7TJ
Tel: 0171-326-4098 **Fax:** 0171-326-4098
Contact: Abdul Haqq Baker
Position: Chairman/Ameer
Activities: Worship, resource, umbrella, visits, youth, women, newsletters, books-
Traditions: Sunni
Movements: Salafee
Other Languages: Arabic, French, Somali
Affiliations: South London Council of Mosques

WESTMINSTER, CITY OF

Ahl-ul-Bait Foundation
3 Dorset Square, London, NW1 6PY

Alhani Books Ltd
102 Crawford Street, London, W1H 1AN

Al-Kashkool Bookshop
56 Knightsbridge, London, SW1 7NJ

Al Majid Bookshop
18-24 Westbourne Grove, London, W2 5RH

Al Noor Bookshop
54 Park Road, London, NW1 4SH

As Saqi Bookshop
26 Westbourne Grove, London, W2 5RH
Fax: 0171-229-7492
EMail: Alsaqibooks@compuserve.com
Activities: Books
Other Languages: Arabic, French

Dar al-Dawa
32 Hereford Road, Bayswater, London, W2 4AJ

Darul Muslimat
3 Dunraven Street, London, W1Y 3FG
Tel: 0171-499-4741

Imperial College Islamic Society
Imperial College, Prince Consort Street, London,
Greater London, SW7 2BB
Email: j.sheikh@ic.ac.uk
Contact: Junaid Sheikh
Position: Committee Member
Activities: Worship, youth, women, newsletters
Traditions: Sunni
Other Languages: Urdu, Malay, Bengali

Islamic Centre (Central London) West End Mosque
10 Berwick Street, London, Greater London, W1
Tel: 0171-437-8840
Contact: Muhitul Islam
Position: Trustee
Activities: Worship, resource, youth
Traditions: Sunni
Other Languages: Bengali, Urdu, Hindi, Arabic

Islamic Information Services Ltd
Trafalgar House, 11 Waterloo Place, London, SW1Y 4AS

Islamic Society
University of Central London, Students Union, London, W1

Islamic Society
London School of Economics, Houghton Lane, London, WC2A 2AE

Jama Mosque
15 Chesham Place, Knightsbridge, London, SW1
Activities: Worship

Kings College Islamic Society
Students Union, The Strand, London, WC2

Madina House
146 Gloucester Place, London, NW1 6DT
Tel: 0171-262-5314
Contact: Mrs N Ali
Position: Officer in charge

Mosque
35-46 Norfolk Square, Paddington, London, NW1
Activities: Worship

Mosque
Pakistan Embassy, 35 Lowndes Square, Knightsbridge, London, SW1
Tel: 0181-235-2044
Activities: Worship

Mosque
71 Westbourne Road, Bayswater, London, W2
Tel: 0171-727-0729
Activities: Worship

Muslim Book Society
18 Eccleston Square, London, SW1

Muslim Womens Association
146 Park Road, London, NW8
Activities: Women

Nigerian Student Islamic Society
12 Somers Crescent, London, W2

Ramadan Bookshop
104 Queensway, London, W2

School of Islamic Sufism
3 Henrietta Street, London, WC2E 8LU

SOUTH EAST
Regional or County Bodies

Hertfordshire Muslim Education Council
70 Mount Pleasant Lane, Bricketwood, St. Albans,
Hertfordshire, AL2 3XB (h)
Tel: 01932-673820 (h)
Contact: Khalil ur Rehman Moghul
Position: Chairman
Activities: Resource, umbrella, youth, inter-faith
Traditions: Sunni
Other Languages: Urdu, Punjabi, Bengali

Sussex Muslim Society
8 Caburn Road, Hove, Sussex, East Sussex,
BN3 6EF
Tel: 01273-722438 (h) **Fax:** 01273-279438
Contact: Imam Dr Abdul Jalil Sajid JP
Position: Director
Activities: Resource, umbrella, youth, women,
newsletters, books, inter-faith
Traditions: All Traditions
Other Languages: Arabic, Urdu, Punjabi, Bengali
Affiliations: The Sussex Muslim Society; The
Muslim Council of Britain; Union of Muslim
Organisations; The Muslim World League

City, Town or Local Bodies

Islamic Students Association
c/o MCR, Wye College, Wye, Ashford, Kent,
TN25 5AH

Mosque
33 Buckingham Road, Aylesbury, Buckinghamshire
Tel: 01296-33794

Mosque Committee
4 Fleet Street, Aylesbury, Buckinghamshire

Banbury Madni Mosque
Merton Street, Banbury, Oxfordshire
Tel: 01295-256662 **Tel:** 01295-267432
Contact: Mr Gul Bahar
Position: Chair
Activities: Worship, resource, umbrella, visitors,
youth, elderly, women, inter-faith
Traditions: Sunni
Other Languages: Urdu, Punjabi, Arabic

Basildon Muslim Association
36 Gordons, Pitsea, Basildon, Essex, SS13 3DZ

Tel: 01268-554234 (h)
Contact: Mr Sarfraz Sarwar
Position: Secretary
Activities: Worship
Traditions: Sunni
Other Languages: Urdu, Punjabi, Swahali, Arabic
Affiliations: Mosques Council of UK; Muslim
World League

Islamic Society of Basingstoke
32 Tweedsmuir Close, Basingstoke, Hampshire,
RG22 5DR (h)
Tel: 01256-816758 (h)
Contact: Mukhtar Hamid Siddiqui
Position: Chairman
Activities: Youth, elderly, women
Traditions: Sunni
Other Languages: Urdu, Bengali, Franch, Turkish,
Gujarati and Arabic

Bangladesh Islamic Mission
65 Commercial Road, Bedford, Bedfordshire
Tel: 01234-219472 **Tel:** 01234-308373 (h)
Contact: Mr A S Choudhury
Position: President
Activities: Worship, youth
Movements: Tablighi Jamaat
Other Languages: Bengali

Jamah Masjid Gulshane Baghdad
97 Ford End Road, Queens Park, Bedford,
MK40 4LA

Mosque
92 Ford End Road, Bedford

Mosque
2 The Avenue, Bedford, Bedfordshire

Mosque
10/12 Iddesleigh Road, Bedford, Bedfordshire,
MK40 4JU
Tel: 01234-350395
Contact: Cllr M S Khan
Position: Chair

Mosque & Community Centre
1-7 Westbourne Road, Bedford, Bedfordshire

Mosque & Cultural Centre
34 Alexandra Road, Bedford, Bedfordshire
Tel: 01234-47032

Pakistan Mosque Committee
97 Ford End Road, Queens Park, Bedford,
Bedfordshire, MK40 4JU
Tel: 01234-351770 **Tel:** 01234-350392 (h)
Contact: Muhammad Siddip Khan
Position: Chair Person
Activities: Worship, resource, visits, youth, elderly,
women, inter-faith
Traditions: Sunni
Other Languages: Urdu, Punjabi, Bengali

East Sussex Islamic Association
41 Jameson Road, Bexhill, East Sussex
Contact: Mr Elzayat

**Brighton Islamic Centre, Mosque, & Muslim
Community Centre**
150 Dyke Road, Brighton, East Sussex, BN1 5PA
Tel: 01273-505247 **Tel:** 01273-722438 (h)
Fax: 01273-729438
Contact: Abduljalil Sajid
Position: Director
Activities: Worship, resource, media, youth,
women, newsletters, books, inter-faith
Other Languages: Arabic, Urdu, Bengali, Punjabi
Affiliations: Sussex Muslim Society; British
Muslim Council; Union of Muslim Organisations;
Imams and Mosques Council; Muslim World
League

Gujerati Muslim Community Al-Madina
21c Bedford Place, Brighton, East Sussex

Mosque
9 Charlotte Street, Brighton, East Sussex
Activities: Worship

Mosque
21a Bedford Place, off Western Road, Brighton,
East Sussex, BN1 2AA
Contact: Imam Hanif
Position: Imam
Activities: Worship

Students Islamic Society & Mosque
c/o Students Union, University of Sussex, Falmer,
Brighton, East Sussex, BN1 9QF
Tel: 01273-606755
Contact: Secretary
Activities: Worship

Sudanese Muslim Association
109 Epper Lewes Road, Brighton, East Sussex

Islamic Welfare Association
9 Hartford Rise, Camberley, Surrey, GU14 4HT

Canterbury Islamic Centre
PO Box 98, Canterbury, Kent, CT2 2XB

Islamic Society
c/o Students Union, University of Kent,
Canterbury, Kent, CT2 7NZ

Wessex Shi'a 'Ithna Asheri Jamat
42 Beechwood Close, Chandlers Ford, Hampshire,
S05 1DB
Tel: 01705-550142 **Tel:** 01329-662319 (h)
Contact: Jaffer Dharamsi
Traditions: Ithna Asheri

Kent Muslim Welfare Association
46a Salisbury Road, Chatham, Kent

Chelmsford Mosque Committee
18 Burns Crescent, Chelmsford, Essex, CM2 0TS

Mosque
6 Baddow Road, Chelmsford, Essex

Muslim Shia Ithna Asheri Jamaat of Essex
32 Ockelford Avenue, Chelmsford, Essex,
CM1 2AP
Tel: 01245-250059

Anjuman ul Muslameen Limited
163 Bellenden Road, Chesham, Buckinghamshire,
HP5 2NN
Contact: Zafar Ali Raja
Position: Chairman
Activities: Worship, resource
Traditions: Sunni
Other Languages: Punjabi, Urdu
Affiliations: Chesham Mosque

Mosque
59 Waterside, Chesham, Buckinghamshire

Colchester Islamic Cultural Association
2 Priory Street, Colchester, Essex, CO1 2PY
Tel: 01206-794919 **Tel:** 0181-804-3855 (h)
Contact: Muhammad Ashar Miah
Position: Imam
Activities: Worship, resource, visits, youth, elderly
Traditions: Sunni
Other Languages: Bengali, Arabic, Urdu, Creole

Islamic Society
University of Essex, Wivenhoe Park, Colchester,
Essex, CO4 3SQ

Islamic Society
Lancaster Hall, Cranfield Institute of Technology,
Cranfield, MX43 0AL

Crawley Islamic Centre & Mosque
157 London Road, Langley Green, Crawley, West
Sussex
Tel: 01293-532889 (h)
Contact: Mr Mohammad Hussain
Position: General Secretary
Activities: Worship
Traditions: Sunni
Other Languages: Punjabi, Urdu

Jamiat ul Muslemeen
20 Aston Court, Broadfield, Crawley, West Sussex
Contact: Mr K Mahmood

Jamiat ul Muslemeen & Quwatul Islam Masjid
1 Strachey Court, Webb Close, Crawley, West
Sussex
Activities: Worship

Mosque
99 Fennell Crescent, Broadfield, Crawley, West
Sussex
Tel: 01293-26895
Activities: Worship

Mosque
20 Selsey Road, Crawley, West Sussex
Tel: 01293-512555

Pakistani Muslim Welfare Association
32 Beckett Lane, Langley Green, Crawley, West
Sussex
Tel: 01293-515341 **Tel:** 01293-517201 (h)
Contact: Mr M A Rajah

UK Islamic Mission
66 Kilnmead, Northgate, Crawley, West Sussex,
RH10 2BE

UK Islamic Mission
13 Thatcher Close, Southgate, Crawley, West Sussex,
RH10 6DZ

UK Islamic Mission
11 Ailsa Close, Broadfield, Crawley, West Sussex,
RH11 9DW

Ismaili Muslim Group
13 Keats House, Bexley Lane, Crayford, Kent
Traditions: Ismaili

Muslim Women's Association
38 Seamons Close, Dunstable, Bedfordshire,
LU6 3EQ
Tel: 01582-606672 (h)
Contact: Mrs Nasyer Sultana Jaffari JP
Position: Director
Activities: Resource, media, visits, youth, elderly,
women, inter-faith
Traditions: Sunni, `Ithna Asheri
Movements: Ahl-e-Hadith
Other Languages: Urdu, Bangali, Hindi, Gujarati
Affiliations: Anjumane-Haideria, Luton; Adare-e-
Jafria, London

Eastbourne Islamic Cultural Centre
Ashford Square, Eastbourne, East Sussex,
BN21 3TX
Tel: 01323-727866 **Fax:** 01323-727866
Contact: Taleb Durgahee
Position: Secretary
Activities: Worship, resource, visits, youth, elderly,
women
Traditions: Sunni
Other Languages: Arabic, Urdu, Bengali, French

Eastbourne Islamic Project
2 Barn Close, Stone Cross, Pevensey, Eastbourne,
East Sussex, BN24 5EN

Eastbourne Islamic Society
54 Seaside Road, Eastbourne, East Sussex

Eastbourne Mosque
(Top Floor Room) Al-Islam Resturant, 6 South
Street, Eastbourne, East Sussex

South-East Islamic Society
209 Kings Drive, Eastbourne, East Sussex,
BN21 2UJ
Tel: 01323-638755 (h) **Fax:** 01323-638755
Contact: Dr Taleb Dugahee
Position: Secretary
Activities: Worship, resource, visits, youth, elderly,
women, inter-faith
Traditions: Sunni

Movements: Tablighi Jamaat
Other Languages: French, Urdu, Bengali, Arabic

Hajra Sanuallah Trust
26 Burgfield, Epsom, Surrey, KT17 4ND

Wessex Shi'a 'Ithna Asheri Jamaat
Al Mahdi, Wickham Road, Fareham, Hampshire,
PO17 5BU
Tel: 01705-360835 (h)   **Tel:** 01705-360835 (h)
Fax: 01705-529766
EMail: bashirrahim@interalpha.co.uk
Contact: Mr Yashim Rahim
Position: Secretary
Activities: Worship, visits, youth, elderly, women,
inter-faith
Other Languages: Persian, Arabic, Kiswahili,
Gujarati
Affiliations: World Federation of Khoja Shi'a
'Ithna Asheri Muslim Communities

Islamic Society
Farnborough College of Technology, Farnborough,
Hampshire

Gillingham Mosque
114 Canterbury Street, Gillingham, Kent,
ME7 5UH
Tel: 01643-850878
Contact: Khilzar Hayat Khan-Lodhi
Position: Chairman
Activities: Worship, resource, visits, youth, elderly,
women, newsletters
Traditions: Sunni
Other Languages: Urdu, Arabic, Punjabi,
Kiswahili

Kent Muslim Welfare Association (KMWA)
114 Canterbury Street, Gillingham, Kent,
ME7 5UH
Tel: 01634-50878
Contact: Syed Ikram Ali
Position: Secretary General
Activities: Worship, youth, elderly, women
Traditions: Sunni

Gravesend & Dartford Muslim Association
14 Brandon Street, Gravesend, Kent, DA11 0PL
Tel: 01474-351336
Contact: Mr M E Aslam
Position: Joint Secretary

Islamic Society
University of Surrey, Guildford, Surrey, GU2 5XH

Religious Institution (Madarsa)
24 Oakfields, Guildford, Surrey, GU3 3AU
Tel: 01483-826788 **Tel:** 01483-34479 (h)
Contact: Dr and Mrs Al-Banday
Position: Managing Directors
Activities: Resource
Traditions: Sunni
Other Languages: Urdu, Arabic, Punjabi

Harlow & Essex Muslim Cultural Association
10 Rosemount, Harlow, Essex
Contact: Dr Hoda
Position: Chairperson

East Sussex Islamic Association (Hastings Mosque)
The Cedars, Pett Road, Pett, Hastings, East Sussex,
TN35 4HB (h)
Tel: 01424-426232 **Fax:** 01424-755560
Contact: Dr Tariq Yusuf Rajbee
Position: Secretary
Activities: Worship, visits, youth, women
Traditions: Sunni
Other Languages: Arabic, Bengali, French, Urdu

Islamic Information Trust
38 Ridge Avenue, Hastings, East Sussex, TN37 7IS

Islamic Society
University of Hertfordshire Students Union,
PO Box 109, College Lane, Hatfield, Hertfordshire,
AL10 9AB
Tel: 01707-268343
Contact: President

Islamic Education & Cultural Society
Hayes Civic Hall, 3 Pump Lane, Hayes, Middlesex,
UB3 3NB
Tel: 0181-561-4654
Contact: Obaid R Siddiqui
Position: Chairman
Activities: Worship, resource, visits, youth, elderly,
women, inter-faith
Traditions: Sunni
Other Languages: Urdu, Punjabi, Arabic,
Somalian

Young Muslim Association
357 Station Road, Hayes, Middlesex

Muslim Welfare Association
67 Seaton Road, Hemel Hempstead, Hertfordshire

Quwwatul Islam Markazi Jamia Mehria Mosque
Hill Crest, 150 St Albans Hill, Bennet End, Hemel
Hempstead, Hertfordshire, HP3 9NH
Tel: 01422-343785
Contact: Maulana Mohammad Abdul Latif
Position: Imam
Activities: Worship, resource, visits, youth, elderly
Traditions: Sunni
Movements: Barelwi
Other Languages: Urdu
Affiliations: Sunnat Wal Jamat UK

Ansar As-Sunnnah
251 Micklefield Road, Micklefield, High Wycombe,
Buckinghamshire, HP13 7HU (h)
Tel: 01494-537031
Contact: Hatim Suleiman
Position: Committee Member
Activities: Worship, resource, umbrella, youth,
women, newsletters, inter-faith
Traditions: Sunni
Other Languages: Urdu, Arabic, Punjabi

Mosque
1 Hillview Road, High Wycombe,
Buckinghamshire

Muslim Students Association
52 Oakridge Road, High Wycombe,
Buckinghamshire, HP11 2PL

UK Islamic Mission
8 Sussex Close, High Wycombe, Buckinghamshire

Wycombe Islamic Mission & Mosque Trust Ltd
34 Jubilee Road, High Wycombe,
Buckinghamshire, HP11 2PG
Tel: 01494-520807
Contact: Mr Mohammed Hanif
Position: Secretary
Activities: Worship, resource, inter-faith
Traditions: Sunni
Movements: Barelwi
Other Languages: Urdu, Punjabi, Arabic
Affiliations: Union of Muslim Organisations

Wycombe Muslim Education Concern
24 Sussex Close, High Wycombe, Buckinghamshire

Wycombe Muslim Youth Forum
34 Perth Road, High Wycombe, Buckinghamshire,
HP13 6XX
Tel: 0171-216-4648 (h)
Contact: Rafiq M Raja
Position: Chairman
Activities: Resources, youth
Traditions: Sunni
Other Languages: Urdu, Punjabi, Bengali

Hitchin Mosque & Islamic Centre
28 Florence Street, Hitchin, Hertfordshire, SG5
1QZ
Tel: 01462-626234 (h)
Contact: Haji Mohammed Moinul Islam
Position: President
Activities: Worship, resource, visits, youth, elderly
Traditions: Sunni
Movements: Deobandi
Other Languages: Bengali, Urdu

Brighton Islamic Centre
8 Caburn Road, Hove, East Sussex, BN3 6EF
Tel: 01273-505247 **Tel:** 01273-722438 (h)
Fax: 01273-279438
Contact: Dr Imam Abduljalil Sajid
Position: Director
Activities: Worship, youth, women, newsletters,
books, inter-faith
Other Languages: Arabic, Urdu, Bengali, Punjabi
Affiliations: Muslim Council of Britain; Union of
Muslim Organisations; Imams and Mosques
Council; World Muslim League

Brighton Islamic Mission
8 Caburn Road, Hove, East Sussex, BN3 6EF
Contact: Dr Imam Abduljalil Sajid
Position: Director/Imam
Activities: Worship, resource, media, visits, youth,
elderly, women, newsletters, books, inter-faith
Other Languages: Arabic, Urdu, Bengali, Punjabi
Affiliations: Sussex Muslim Society; British
Muslim Council; Union of Muslim Organisations;
Rabita (World Muslim League)

Indian Muslim Professionals Group
66 Nevil Avenue, Hove, East Sussex, BN3 7NA

Muslim Ladies Circle
Sussex Muslim Society, 8 Caburn Road, Hove, East
Sussex, BN3 6EF
Contact: Mrs Jamila Sajid

Position: Chair
Activities: Resource, women, books, inter-faith
Traditions: Sunni
Movements: Ahl-e-Hadith, Deobandi/Jamati-i-Islami
Other Languages: Urdu, Bengali, Arabic, Punjabi
Affiliations: The Sussex Muslim Society; Council of British Muslims; Union of Muslim Organisations; World Muslim League

Sussex Muslim Society
8 Caburn Road, Hove, Sussex, East Sussex, BN3 6EF
Tel: 01273-722438 (h)   **Fax:** 01273-279438
Contact: Imam Dr Abdul Jalil Sajid JP
Position: Director
Activities: Resource, umbrella, youth, women, newsletters, books, inter-faith
Traditions: All Traditions
Other Languages: Arabic, Urdu, Punjabi, Bengali
Affiliations: The Sussex Muslim Society; The Muslim Council of Britain; Union of Muslim Organisations; The Muslim World League

Young Muslims (Girls Section)
141 Montgomery Street, Hove, East Sussex, BN3 5FP

All Muslim Funeral Society
127 Kingsway, Luton, Bedfordshire, LU1 1TS
Contact: Mr Abdul Shakur
Position: General Secretary
Other Languages: Punjabi, Urdu

All Rahman School
44 Shirley Road, Luton, Bedfordshire

Anjuman-e-Haderiya
18 Brentwood Road, Luton, Bedfordshire

Bain-ul-Aqwami Anjuman Ashait-Ul-Islam
8 Vernon Road, Luton, Bedfordshire

Bury Park Masjid Mosque
25 Bury Park Road, Luton, Bedfordshire
Tel: 01582-25412

International Islamic Propagation Mission
62 Maidenhall Road, Luton, Bedfordshire

Islamic Cultural Centre
23 Westbourne Road, Luton, Bedfordshire, LU4 8JD

Tel: 01582-410704 (h)   **Fax:** 01582-410704
Contact: Abdul Aziz Qazi-
Position: Managing Trustee
Activities: Worship, resource, media, visits, youth, elderly, women, inter-faith
Traditions: Sunni
Movements: Barelwi
Other Languages: Punjabi, Urdu, Kashmiri
Affiliations: Markzi Jamat Ahle Sunnat (UK)

Lewsey Muslim Cultural Society
9 Sussex Close, Luton, Bedfordshire, LU4 0UE
Tel: 01582-608500
Contact: Abdul-Khaleq Vazifdar

Luton Islamic Society
100 Biscot Road, Luton, Bedfordshire

Luton Muslim Women's Association
207 Dunstable Road, Luton, Bedfordshire, LU1 1BG

Masjid-e-Noor
20 Cromwell Road, Luton, Bedfordshire
Tel: 01582-410379

Mosque (UK Islamic Mission)
128-130 Oak Road, Luton, Bedfordshire, LU4 8AD
Tel: 01582-27734

Muslim Association
41 Highfield Road, Luton, Bedfordshire

Muslims (UK) Asian Advisory Centre
198 Dunstable Road, Luton, Bedfordshire, LU4 8JJ

Obaid ul Rahman Islamic Society
123 Biscot Road, Luton, Bedfordshire, LU3 1AN
Tel: 01582-455092

Pakistan Muslim Association
131 Ashburnham Road, Luton, Bedfordshire, LU1 1JW
Tel: 01582-27713 (h)
Contact: Mr Abdul Rahim Malik
Position: President
Activities: Resource, media, youth, elderly, women, inter-faith
Traditions: Sunni
Other Languages: Urdu, Punjabi, Arabic

UK Islamic Mission
128-130 Oak Road, Luton, Bedfordshire

Young Muslims
368 Dunstable Road, Luton, Bedfordshire, LU4 8JT
Tel: 01582-753845 (h)
Contact: Rashid Nazar
Position: President
Activities: Resource, visits, youth, newsletters, inter-faith
Traditions: Sunni
Movements: Jamati-i-Islami
Other Languages: Urdu, Bengali
Affiliations: Medina Masjid, Luton

World Islamic Mission
156 Biscot Road, Luton, Bedfordshire
Tel: 01582-480881
Contact: Mohammed Iqbal

Zakariya Mosque & Madressa-r-Furqaniah
c/o 21a Drayton Road, Luton, Bedfordshire, LU4
Tel: 01582-608500
Contact: Abdul-Khaleq Vazifdar

Islamic Trust (Maidenhead)
The Mosque, Holmanleaze, Maidenhead, Berkshire, SL6 8AW
Tel: 01628-29423 **Tel:** 01628-24159 (h)
Contact: Abdor Rashid Malik
Position: Chair
Activities: Worship, resource, visits, elderly, inter-faith
Traditions: Sunni
Other Languages: Punjabi, Urdu, Arabic, Bangla/Turkish
Affiliations: Union of Muslim Organisation in UK and Eire; World Muslim League (Rabita-Al-Alam-Al-Islami-Makka); Saudi Arabia

Jamiat Ahl-e-Hadith
36 Grenfell Road, Maidenhead, Berkshire

Maidenhead Mosque
6 Halt Drive, off Ray Mill Road, Maidenhead, Berkshire, SL6 8S

Al-Miftah (Education)
PO Box 844, Oldbrook, Milton Keynes, Buckinghamshire, MK6 2YT
Tel: 01908-671756 **Fax:** 01908-694035
Contact: Mrs Tabinda Bleher
Position: Organiser

Activities: Resource, youth, women, inter-faith
Other Languages: Urdu, Arabic, Bengali

Bletchley Mosque
52 Duncombe Street, Bletchley, Milton Keynes, Buckinghamshire, MK2 2LY
Tel: 01908-74380

Jamia al-Karam
1a Bradwell Road, Milton Keynes, Bukinghamshire, MK13 0EJ
Tel: 01908-313804
Contact: Mr M I H Pirzada
Position: Managing Trustee

Mosque
52 Dunstable Street, Milton Keynes, Buckinghamshire
Tel: 01908-74380

UK Islamic Mission
60 Albert Road, New Malden, Surrey

Bangladeshi Islamic Education Centre & Mosque
57 Cowley Road, Oxford, Oxfordshire, OX4 1HR
Tel: 01865-793118
Contact: Mr L Rahman
Position: Assistant Secretary

Islamic Books
62 Kilburn Road, Oxford, Oxfordshire, OX4 3SH
Tel: 01865-777951
Contact: Sheikh Ahmad Bullock

Madina Mosque & Muslim Welfare House
2 Stanley Road, Cowley, Oxford, Oxfordshire, OX4 1QZ
Tel: 01865-243149 **Tel:** 01865-246811 (h)
Contact: Mr M A Khan
Position: Khadim
Activities: Worship, resource, visits, youth, elderly, women
Traditions: Sunni
Movements: Barelwi
Languages: Arabic, Urdu

Oxford Brookes University Islamic Society
7 Warnerford Road, Oxford, Oxfordshire, OX4 1LT
Tel: 01865-792250
Contact: Imran Abbasi

Oxford Centre for Islamic Studies
George Street, Oxford, Oxfordshire, OX1 2AR
Tel: 01865-278730 **Fax:** 01865-248942
EMail: islamic.studies@oxcis.ac.uk
Contact: Dr Basil Mustafa
Position: Assistant Registrar
Languages: Arabic, Urdu, French, Latin

Oxford Islamic Centre
62 Kilburn Road, Oxford, Oxfordshire, OX4 3FH

Oxford Mosque Society
10-11 Bath Street, St Clements, Oxford,
Oxfordshire, OX4 1AY
Tel: 01865-245547
Contact: Sabir Hussain
Position: Chairman
Traditions: Sunni
Other Languages: Punjabi, Urdu, Pashto

Oxford University Islamic Society
c/o Mohammed Haris Alan, Lincoln College,
Oxford, Oxfordshire, OX1 3DR
Contact: Mohammed Haris Ashar Alam
Position: President
Activities: Youth, women, newsletters
Other Languages: Urdu, Arabic, Punjabi,
Malaysian

Highbury Islamic Society
College of Technology, Dovercourt Road,
Portsmouth, Hampshire

Portsmouth Jamia Mosque & Islamic Centre
73-75 Marmion Road, Southsea, Portsmouth,
Hampshire, PO5 2AX
Tel: 01705-832541
Contact: Secretary
Activities: Worship, youth, women

Portsmouth Muslim Society
Portsmouth, Hampshire, c/o 90 Westbourne
Avenue, Emsworth, Hampshire

Anjuman Muhibban-e-Rasool
15 Bulmershe Road, Reading, Berkshire,
RG1 5RH
Tel: 01734-666796 (h)
Contact: Raja Mohammed Banaras
Position: Trustee
Activities: Worship, resource, visits, youth, elderly
Traditions: Sunni

Movements: Barelwi
Other Languages: Urdu, Punjabi

Islamic Society
26 Apple Close, Tilehurst, Reading, Berkshire,
RG3 6UR
Contact: Mr A Razzak

Jamia Khulafa-e-Rashidin & Haq Char-yar Islamic Centre
2a Valentia Road, Reading, Berkshire, RG30 1DL
Tel: 01734-566618 **Tel:** 01734-266587 (h)
Contact: Iman M A Qari
Position: Chair and Trustee
Activities: Worship, resource, media, visits, youth,
elderly, women
Traditions: Sunni
Movements: Deobandi, Tablighi Jamaat, Tassawuf
Other Languages: Urdu, English, Arabic, Panjabi,

Jamia Masjid
45 Chomley Road, Reading, Berkshire
Tel: 01734-67767
Contact: Mr A Q Khan
Position: President

Jamiat Ahl-e-Hadith (Reading Branch)
31 Cumberland Road, Reading, Berkshire,
RG1 3LB
Contact: Mr R A Mir
Position: Chair
Activities: Worship, resource, youth, elderly,
women
Traditions: Sunni
Movements: Ahl-e-Hadith
Other Languages: Urdu, Punjabi, Arabic
Affiliations: Jamiat Ahl-e-Hadith (HQ,
Birmingham)

Reading Islamic Centre
50/52 South Street, Reading, Berkshire, RG1 4QU
Tel: 01734-504756 **Tel:** 01734-267152 (h)
Contact: Altaf H Khan
Position: General Secretary
Activities: Worship, resource
Traditions: Sunni
Movements: Barelwi, Ahl-e-Sunnat-Wal-Jamat
Other Languages: Urdu, Punjabi, Bengali

UK Islamic Mission (Reading Branch)
4 Palmerstone Road, Earley, Reading, Berkshire,
RG6 1HL

Contact: Mr F Culasy
Position: General Secretary
Traditions: Sunni
Movements: Jamati-i-Islami
Other Languages: Urdu

World Islamic Organisation
7 Cholmeley Road, Reading, Berkshire

Islamic Centre Redhill
30 Earlswood Road, Redhill, Surrey, RH1 6HW
Tel: 01737-760251
Contact: Zulfiqar Khan Noon
Position: President
Activities: Worship, resource, visits, youth, elderly
Traditions: Sunni
Movements: Barelwi
Other Languages: Urdu, Punjabi, Bengali
Affiliations: Union of Muslims Organisations;
Minhaj-ul-Quran

Hertfordshire Muslim Education Council
70 Mount Pleasant Lane, Bricketwood, St. Albans,
Hertfordshire, AL2 3XB (h)
Tel: 01932-673820 (h)
Contact: Khalil ur Rehman Moghul
Position: Chairman
Activities: Resource, umbrella, youth, inter-faith
Traditions: Sunni
Other Languages: Urdu, Punjabi, Bengali

Islamic Centre
141 Hatfield Road, St Albans, Hertfordshire,
AL1 4JX
Tel: 01727-836272
Contact: Mr Akhtar Zaman
Position: Secretary
Traditions: Sunni
Other Languages: Urdu, French

Muslim Association
148 Hatfield Road, St Albans, Hertfordshire
Tel: 01727-30949

Muslim Welfare
21 Harlesden Road, St Albans, Hertfordshire

St Albans Muslim Association
12 Blandford Road, St Albans, Hertfordshire

UK Islamic Mission
100 Sopwell Lane, St Albans, Hertfordshire

**East Sussex Islamic Association & Masjid Al
Haque, Hastings Mosque**
Mercatoria, St Leonards-on-Sea, East Sussex,
TN38 0EB
Tel: 01424-462232
Contact: Secretary
Activities: Worship, youth, women

Islamic Information Centre
38 Little Ridge Avenue, St Leonards on Sea, East
Sussex, TN37 7LS
Tel: 01424-755355 **Tel:** 01424-812727 (h)
Fax: 01424-755560
Contact: Dr Tariq Yusuf Rajbee
Position: Chairman
Activities: Resource, inter-faith
Traditions: Sunni
Movements: Ahle-Sunnah wal Jamaa
Other Languages: Urdu, Hindi
Affiliations: Al Qur'an Society, London; Islamic
Propagation Centre International, Birmingham;
International Council of Islamic Information
(Leicester/Riyadh)

Islamic Education Committee
181 Goodman Park, Slough, Berkshire, SL2 5NR

Jamia Masjid & Islamic Centre
83 Stoke Poges Lane, Slough, Berkshire, SL1 3NY
Tel: 01753-522561
Contact: Muhammad Ikram
Position: Secretary
Activities: Worship, resource, visits
Traditions: Sunni
Other Languages: Urdu, Punjabi

Khalifa-e-Rashida Movement
45 Warrington Avenue, Slough, Berkshire

Slough Islamic Trust
78 Diamond Road, Slough, Berkshire, SL1 1RX
Tel: 01753-517372 **Tel:** 01753-531919 (h)
Contact: Khalid Masud
Position: Secretary
Activities: Worship, resource, visits, inter-faith
Traditions: Sunni
Movements: Barelwi
Other Languages: Punjabi, Urdu

Slough Mosque Committee
35 Ragstone Road, Slough, Berkshire

UK Islamic Mission
106 St Pauls Avenue, Slough, Berkshire, SL2 5ER

Islamic Cultural Association
15 Merton Road, Highfield, Southampton,
Hampshire
Contact: Mr B Rahman

Mosque
Grove Road, Southampton, Hampshire
Activities: Worship

Southampton Islamic Movement
15 Minestead Avenue, Harefield, Southampton,
Hampshire, SO18 5FU (h)
Tel: 01703-233544 **Tel:** 01703-323785 (h)
Fax: 01703-323785
Contact: Sumayya James
Position: Chairperson
Activities: Resource, visits, youth, women,
newsletters, inter-faith
Traditions: Sunni
Other Languages: Urdu, Arabic
Affiliations: Southampton Muslim Womens
Association

Southampton Medina Mosque Trust
Medina House, Rowlands Cut, Nr St Mary's Road,
Southampton, Hampshire, S014 0BH
Tel: 01703-231216
Contact: Mohammad Aslam
Position: Chair
Activities: Worship, resource, visits, youth, elderly,
women, inter-faith
Other Languages: Urdu, Punjabi

Southampton Mosque Trust
189 Northumberland Road, Southampton,
Hampshire, S014 0EP
Tel: 01703-635941 Tel: 01703-327259 (h)
Contact: Hamid Hamirani
Position: Secretary
Activities: Worship, visits, youth
Traditions: Sunni
Other Languages: Urdu, Punjabi, Bangladeshi,
Arabic

Southampton University Islamic Society
Students Union, Southampton, Hampshire,
SO9 5NH

UK Islamic Mission, Southampton
186 Priory Road, St Denys, Southampton,
Hampshire, S02 1HS
Tel: 01703-321485 **Tel:** 01703-584798 (h)
Contact: Wasim Darr

Position: President
Activities: Resource, media, visits, inter-faith
Traditions: Sunni
Movements: Jamati-i-Islami
Other Languages: Urdu, Punjabi
Affiliations: UK Islamic Mission

Islamic Trust
191-197 West Road, Westcliff-on-Sea, Southend-
on-Sea, Essex, SS0 9DH

Mosque
191 West Road, Westcliff-on-Sea, Southend-on-Sea,
Essex

Mosque
53-54 Milton Road, West Cliff, Southend-on-Sea,
Essex

Mosque
18 Gordon Road, Southend-on-Sea, Essex,
SS1 1NQ

Southend Mosque & Southend Islamic Trust
191 West Road, Westcliff-on-Sea, Southend-on-Sea,
Essex, SS0 9DH
Tel: 01702-347265

Southend Muslim Association
The Mosque, Westborough Road, Westcliff-on-Sea,
Southend-on-Sea, Essex

Southend Young Muslim Organisation
c/o Southend Islamic Trust, 191-197 West Road,
Westcliff-on-Sea, Southend-on-Sea, Essex

UK Islamic Mission
29 Highfield Gardens, Westcliff-on-Sea, Southend-
on-Sea, Essex

Jamia Mosque & Islamic Centre
73-75 Marmion Road, Southsea, Hampshire,
PO5 2AX

Mosque Islamic Cultual Centre
26 Walker Road, Stevenage, Hertfordshire
Tel: 01483-313103

Anjuman-e-Jaafariyah
74 Kensington Avenue, Watford, Herts, WD1 7RY
Tel: 01923-231257 **Tel:** 01923-237670 (h)
Contact: Sayyid Zulafkar Ali Shah
Position: Secretary
Activities: Worship, resource, youth

Traditions: Shi`a `Ithna Asheri
Other Languages: Urdu, Punjabi
Affiliations: World Federation of Khoj Shi'a 'Ithna
Asheri Muslim Communities

Crescent Youth Club
Multi-Racial Community Centre, Durban Road
West, Watford, Hertfordshire

Dar-ul-Ehsan
8 Bruce Grove, Watford, Hertfordshire, WD2 7LB

Mosque
273 Gladstone Road, Watford, Hertfordshire,
WD1 2QZ

Watford British Muslims
27 Park Gate Road, Watford, Hertfordshire,
WD2 4BS

Watford Islamic Association
c/o 8 Bruce Grove, Watford, Hertfordshire,
WD2 5AG

**Watford Mosque & Welfare Association For The
Muslim Community**
Watford Jamia Mosque, Cambridge Road, Watford,
Hertfordshire, WD1 8AJ
Tel: 01923-245367
Contact: Mohammed Aslam Khan
Position: Secretary/Chairman
Activities: Worship, resource, visits, youth, elderly,
women, inter-faith
Traditions: Sunni
Movements: Barelwi
Other Languages: Urdu, Bengali, Arabic

Watford Muslim Association
49 Kelmscott Cresent, Watford, Hertfordshire

Watford Muslim Association of Friendship
37 Margaret Close, Abbots Langley, Hertfordshire

Watford Muslim Community Project
15 Harwoods Road, Watford, Hertfordshire,
WD1 7RB
Tel: 01923-223466 **Fax:** 01923-228388
Contact: Maqsood Ahmed
Position: Project coordinator
Activities: Elderly
Other Languages: Urdu, Paharri, Punjabi
Affiliations: Watford Council; Citizens Advice
Bureau; Shelter; CPAG

Watford Muslim Womens Association
16a Cassiobury Park Avenue, Watford, Hertfordshire

Watford Muslim Youth Forum
Multi-Racial Community Centre, Durban Road
West, Watford, Hertfordshire

Watford Muslim Youth Forum
16 Princes Avenue, Watford, Hertfordshire

Watford School of Arabic & Islamic Studies
492 Wippendell Road, Watford, Hertfordshire,
WD1 7QJ
Tel: 01923-245670 **Fax:** 01923-213377
Contact: Dr A Ghany Saleh
Position: Founder and Director

Mosque
14 Wick Drive, Wickford, Essex

United Islamic Association (UK)
21 Mill House, Mill Lane, Woodford Green, Essex,
IGB 0UL

Islamic Society
21 Birdcroft Road, Welwyn Garden City,
Hertfordshire

Islamic Society of Welwyn Garden City
32 Marsden Green, Welwyn Garden City,
Hertfordshire, AL8 6YB

Muslim Youth Movement
7 Kerry Terrace, Walton Road, Woking, Surrey
Activities: Youth, elderly

Shahjahan Mosque
149 Oriental Road, Woking, Surrey, GU22 7BA
Tel: 01493-760679
Contact: Mr Nisar Ahmad Suleimani
Activities: Worship, resource, visits, youth, elderly
Traditions: Sunni
Movements: Ahl-e-Hadith
Other Languages: English, Urdu, Punjabi, Arabic
Britain's first mosque, established 1889.

Masjed Assalam
Ivy Arch Road, Worthing, West Sussex, BN14 8BX
Tel: 01903-215163
Contact: Imam Anis Chowdburry
Position: Imam
Activities: Worship, visitors, youth, elderly

Other Languages: Bengali, Urdu, Arabic
Traditions: Sunni

Muslim Society Worthing
157 Tarring Road, Worthing, West Sussex,
BN12 4JG

SOUTH WEST
City, Town or Local Bodies

Bath Islamic Centre & Mosque
8 Pierrepont Street, Bath, Somerset, BA1 1LA
Tel: 01225-460922
Contact: Derradji Boumrah
Position: Chairman
Activities: Worship, resource, visits, youth
Other Languages: Arabic, Malaysian

Bath University Islamic Society
Students Union, Bath University, Bath, Somerset,
BA2 8AY

Bournemouth Islamic Centre
4 St Stephen's Road, Bournemouth, Dorset,
BH2 6JJ
Tel: 01202-557072 **Fax:** 01202-298681
Contact: Mr Majid Yasin
Position: Director
Activities: Worship, resource, visits, youth, women,
inter-faith
Traditions: Sunni
Movements: Ahl-e-Hadith
Other Languages: Arabic, Turkish, Urdu

Sufi Order of the Christi
Sufi House, Barton Farm, Bradford-upon-Avon,
Wiltshire

Bristol & Avon Muslim Association Girls Group
c/o 10 The Old Co-op, 42 Chelsea Road, Eaton,
Bristol, Greater Bristol, BS5 6JH

Bristol & Avon Muslim Association
Unit 10, 42 Chelsea Road, Bristol, Greater Bristol,
BS5 6AF
Tel: 0117-955-2686 **Tel:** 0117-942-4963 (h)
Fax: 0117-955-2686
Contact: Nazim Ali
Position: Link Officer
Activities: Resource, visits, inter-faith
Traditions: Sunni
Movements: Barelwi
Other Languages: Urdu, Punjabi, Bengali, Gujarati

Affiliations: Bristol Council of Mosques; UK
Council of Mosques

Bristol Jamia Mosque
Green Street, Totterdown, Bristol, Greater Bristol,
BS3 4UB
Tel: 9770944
Contact: Asaf Khan
Position: Secretary
Traditions: Sunni
Other Languages: Urdu, Punjabi

Bristol University Islamic Society
c/o University Union, Queen's Road, Bristol,
Greater Bristol, BS8 1LN

Eaton Islamic Darsagah
2 Roman Road, Eaton, Bristol, Greater Bristol,
BS5 6DD
Tel: 0117-954-0127 (h)
Contact: Imam Ahmed Sarfraz
Position: Minister of religion
Activities: Worship, resource, visits, youth, inter-
faith
Traditions: Sunni
Movements: Ahl-e-Hadith
Other Languages: Urdu, Arabic, Punjabi
Affiliations: Bristol Council of Mosques; The
Muslim World League

Eaton Masjid
St Marks Road, Eaton, Bristol, Greater Bristol,
BS5 6JH
Tel: 0117-9510317 **Tel:** 0117-9522062 (h)
Contact: Khizar Hayat Malik
Position: Secretary
Activities: Worship, visits, inter-faith
Traditions: Sunni
Movements: Jamati-i-Islami
Other Languages: Urdu, Punjabi

Islami Darasagh Bristol
109 Lower Cheltenham Place, Montpelier, Bristol,
Greater Bristol, BS6 5LA
Tel: 01272-414301
Contact: Secretary

Islamic Society University of the West of England
Coldhabour Lane, Frenchay, Bristol, Greater Bristol

Mosque
56 Goodwind Street, Bristol, Greater Bristol, BS5
Activities: Worship

Taleem-ul-Islam Trust
28 Chelsea Park, Easton, Bristol, Greater Bristol,
BS5 6AG
Tel: 0117-9558155   **Tel:** 0117-9558155 (h)
Contact: Javed Yousuf
Position: Treasurer
Activities: Youth
Traditions: Sunni
Other Languages: Urdu, Arabic

Mosque & Muslim Association
416-418 High Street, Cheltenham, Gloucestershire,
GL50 3JA
Contact: Mohalleel Mohammed
Position: Secretary
Activities: Worship
Traditions: Sunni
Other Languages: Gujarati, Urdu, Arabic

Mosque & Islamic Centre
15 York Road, Exeter, Devon, EX4 6BA
Activities: Worship

New Mosque
5 Derby Road, Exeter, Devon

Islamic Trust Youth Section
18 Charles Street, Gloucester, Gloucestershire
Contact: Mr I Patel
Activities: Youth, elderly

Ismaili Muslim Group
87 Howard Street, Tredworth, Gloucester,
Gloucestershire
Contact: Mr T A Uka
Traditions: Ismaili

Jamia Mosque & Gloucester Islamic Trust
All Saints Road, Gloucester, Gloucestershire,
GL1 4EE
Tel: 01452-506870
Contact: Secretary
Activities: Worship, youth, elderly

Gloucester Muslim Welfare Association Ltd
Masjid-e-Noor, 44-46 Ryecroft Street, Gloucester,
Gloucestershire, GL1 4LY
Tel: 01452-416830
Contact: Mr Yakub Patel
Position: Honorary President
Activities: Worship, resource, visits, youth, elderly,
women, newsletters, inter-faith
Traditions: Sunni

Movements: Deobandi, Tablighi Jamaat
Other Languages: Gujarati, Urdu, Bengali
Affiliations: Union of Muslim Organisations;
Muslim World League

Mosque & Muslim Welfare Association
44-46 Ryecroft Street, Gloucester, Gloucestershire,
GL1 4LY
Tel: 01452-416830
Contact: Ismail Y Ginwalla
Position: Honorary Secretary
Activities: Worship, visits, newsletters, inter-faith
Traditions: Sunni
Other Languages: Gujarati, Urdu, Punjabi,
Bengali
Affiliations: Union of Muslim Organisations in
UK and Eire; Muslim World League

Al-Isra Islamic College
Heathland, Upper Welland Road, Malvern,
WR14 4HN

Khoja Shi'a Muslim Community of Gloucester
Wainsbridge, 69 Bristol Road, Quedgeley,
Gloucestershire, GL2 6NE
Tel: 01452-530337   **Tel:** 01452-539556
Fax: 01452-533888
Contact: Mr Gulam Musa
Position: Vice President
Traditions: Shi'a 'Ithna Asheri
Other Languages: Urdu, Gujarati

Islamic Benevolent Society
140 Manchester Road, Swindon, Wiltshire,
SN1 2AF

Mosque
133 Broad Street, Swindon, Wiltshire
Activities: Worship

Pakistan Muslim Association
2 Angler Road, Ramleaze, Swindon, Wiltshire,
SN5 9SX
Contact: Mohammad Salas Khan
Position: Representative
Activities: Resource, youth, elderly, women
Traditions: Sunni
Movements: Barelwi
Other Languages: Punjabi, Urdu
Affiliations: Sultan Baho Trust Birmingham;
Pakistan Embassy London

Swindon Ismaili Community
32 County Road, Swindon, Wiltshire, SN1 2EW
Contact: Mr A A Moledina
Activities: Worship
Traditions: Ismaili

Thamesdown Islamic Association
12 Don Close, Green Meadow, Swindon, Wiltshire,
SN2 3LS
Tel: 01793-523831   **Tel:** 01793-693569 (h)
Contact: Khan Ahmad Nawaz
Position: Secretary
Activities: Worship, resource, visits, youth, inter-faith
Traditions: Sunni
Other Languages: Urdu, Panjabi, Bangali
Affiliations: Union of Muslim Organisations;
Islamic Cultural Centre, London; Muslim World
League

Torbay Islamic Centre
130 Avenue Road, Torquay, TQ2 5LQ
Tel: 01803-211818

Trowbridge Islamic Association
PO Box 22, Trowbridge, Wiltshire, BA14

NORTHERN IRELAND

City, Town or Local Bodies

Belfast Islamic Centre
38 Wellington Park, Belfast, County Antrim,
BT9 6DN
Tel: 01232-664465
Contact: Dr Mamoun Mobayed
Position: President
Activities: Worship, visits, youth, women, inter-faith
Other Languages: Urdu, Arabic

Islamic Centre
4 Eglantine Avenue, Belfast, County Antrim, BT9

SCOTLAND

SCOTTISH NATIONAL BODIES

Islamic Council of Scotland
30 Clyde Place, Glasgow, Strathclyde, G5
Contact: Mr Bashir Mann

United Muslim Organisations of Scotland
26 Bank Street, Glasgow, Strathclyde, G12 8ND
Tel: 0141-339-5513   **Fax:** 0141-357-5554
Contact: Dr M.S.Kausar
Position: General Secretary
Activities: Resource, umbrella, inter-faith
Other Languages: Urdu, Punjabi, Bengali

City, town and local bodies

Mosque & Islamic Association of Aberdeen
164 Spital, Aberdeen, Grampian, AB2 3JD
Tel: 01224-493764 Tel: 01224-631493
Fax: 01224-403764
Contact: Mr Mohammad Nacef
Position: President of Mosque Committee
Activities: Resource, visits, youth, women,
newsletters, inter-faith
Traditions: Sunni
Other Languages: Urdu, Arabic, Malay

Muslim Students Association
c/o The Mosque, 164 Spital, Aberdeen, Grampian

Sarajia Islamic Studies And Community Centre
5 Whitburn Road, Bathgate, Lothian, EH48 1HE
Tel: 01506-635380+ **Tel:** 01506-631777 (h)
Fax: 01506-635305
Contact: Mohammad Ajmal Tariq
Position: Secretary
Activities: Worship, resource, media, visits, youth,
elderly, women, newsletters
Traditions: Sunni
Movements: Deobandi
Other Languages: Urdu, Punjabi
Affiliations: Jamiat Ittihad-Ul-Muslimin

Dundee Islamic Centre & Hilltown Mosque
114 Hilltown, Dundee, Tayside
Tel: 01382-228374 **Tel:** 01382-450151
Contact: Mohammed Saleem Mirza
Position: Chairman
Activities: Worship
Languages: Urdu, Punjabi
Traditions: Tablighi Jamaat

Islamic Association
18 Park Place, Dundee, Tayside, DD1 4HW
Tel: 01382-69950
Contact: c/o Mr I Jamal
Position: Secretary

Jamia Masjid Tajdare - Madina
96 Victoria Street, Dundee, Tayside, DD1 2NR
Tel: 01382-24817
Contact: Mohamad Sadiq
Position: Secretary

Victoria Road Mosque
2 Wellington Street, Dundee, Tayside

Dunfermline Mosque
56 Hospital Hill, Dunfermline, Lothian

Bazm-e-Urdu
16 Eildon Terrace, Edinburgh, Lothian, EH3 5LU

Heriot-Watt Islamic Society
Heriot-Watt University, Room 1.11, LBB,
Riccarton, Edinburgh, Lothian, EH14 4AS
Tel: 0131-451-3272 **Tel:** 01506-438386 (h)
Fax: 0131-449-5153
Email: h.ahmad@hw.ac.uk
Contact: Hamayun Ahmad
Position: Secretary
Activities: Worship
Traditions: Sunni
Other Languages: Urdu, Arabic

Idara Taleem-ul-Quran
8-10 Temple Park Crescent, Polwarth, Edinburgh,
Lothian, EH11 1HT (h)
Tel: 0131-229-3844 **Tel:** 0131-221-9923 (h)
Contact: Hafiz Abdul Hamid
Position: Director
Activities: Worship, resource, visits, youth, women,
inter-faith
Traditions: Sunni
Movements: Deobandi
Other Languages: Urdu, Punjabi, Bangali

Islam Teaching Centre
2 Lockharton Avenue, Edinburgh, Lothian,
EH14 1AZ

Islamic Centre Trust
5 Foxcourt Avenue, Edinburgh, Lothian

Livingston Mosque & Community Centre
1 Craig's Hill, East Road, Livingston, Edinburgh,
Lothian, EH5 5DD
Tel: 01506-31936
Contact: Mahmood Ali

Mosque & Islamic Centre
50 Potter Row, Edinburgh, Lothian, EH8 9BT
Tel: 0131-667-0140
Contact: Abdul Rahman Al Matrodi

Mosque & Islamic Community Centre
12 Roxburgh Street, Edinburgh, Lothian, EH8 9TA
Tel: 0131-556-1902 **Fax:** 0131-558-7211
EMail: khalid@endnet.co.uk
Contact: Hafiz Mohammad Abdul Karim
Position: Imam
Traditions: Sunni
Movements: Deobandi
Other Languages: Urdu, Punjabi, Arabic

Mosque Anwar-e-Madina & Community Centre
Zetland Hall, 11 Pilrig Street, Edinburgh, Lothian,
EH6
Tel: 0131-554-9904
Contact: Mr Abdul Ghafoor
Position: Imam

Pakistan Association
11 Pilrig Street, Edinburgh, Lothian, EH6
Tel: 0131-441-3443
Contact: Mr Jusuf Inayat

UK Islamic Mission
4 Gillespie Place, Edinburgh, Lothina, EH10

West Lothian Mosque & Community Centre
14 Gleneagles Way, Deans South, Livingstone,
Edinburgh, Lothian, EH54 8DP

Falkirk Islamic Centre
8 Burnhad Lane, Falkirk, Central, FK11
Tel: 01324-611018
Contact: Mr A Farooqi

Young Muslim Movement
18 Ashlea Drive, Giffnock, Strathclyde, G46 6BH

Al Furqhan Islamic School
27-31 Arlington Street, Glasgow, Strathclyde,
G3 6DT
Tel: 0141-333-9105
Contact: Mohammad Ishaq
Position: Chair
Activities: Resource, youth
Other Languages: Urdu

Al-Huda Islamic Centre
65 Albert Road, Glasgow, Strathclyde, G42
Tel: 0141-423-7003
Contact: Maulana Naqui
Position: Imam

Anjaman-Ehyae-Islam
275 Tantallon Road, Glasgow, Strathclyde, G41 3JW
Contact: Mr N S Naqshbandi

Dawat-ul-Islam Mosque
31 Oakfield Avenue, Glasgow, Strathclyde, G12 8LL
Tel: 0141-334-5559

Glasgow University Muslim Students Association
c/o SRC Glasgow University, University Avenue,
Glasgow, Strathclyde, G12 8QQ
Email: zak@src.gla.ac.uk
Contact: Zakariyya Abdel-Hady
Position: President
Activities: Resource, youth, women, newsletters,
inter-faith
Traditions: Sunni
Other Languages: Urdu, Arabic, Malay

Islamic Council of Scotland
30 Clyde Place, Glasgow, Strathclyde, G8

Islamic Defence Council
Flat 6, 8 Riverview Gardens, Glasgow, Strathclyde,
G5

Islamic Outreach
16 Queens Crescent, Glasgow, Strathclyde, G4 9BL

Islamic Society of Britain (Glasgow)
16 Queens Crescent, Woodlands, Charing Cross,
Glasgow, Strathclyde, G4 9BL
Tel: 013552-34608 **Tel:** 013552-34608 (h)
Fax: 013552-34608
Email: 100744.377@compuserve.com
Contact: Dr Salah Beltagui
Position: President
Activities: Resource, media, visits, youth, women,
newsletters, inter-faith
Traditions: Sunni
Other Languages: Urdu, Arabic, Punjabi, Bengali
Affiliations: Islamic Society of Britain (Scotland);
Islamic Society Of Britain

**Jamait Ittihad-ul-Muslimin, Glasgow Islamic
Centre & Central Mosque**
Mosque Avenue, Gorbals, Glasgow, Strathclyde,
G5 9TX
Tel: 0141-429-3132 **Tel:** 0141-420-3030
Fax: 0141-429-7171
Contact: Dr Abu Zar Mohammad Sayeed
Chowdhury
Position: Director
Activities: Worship, resource, visits, youth, elderly,
women
Traditions: Sunni
Movements: Deobandi
Other Languages: Urdu, Punjabi, Arabic

Kizra Central Mosque
138 Butter Biggins Road, Glasgow, Strathclyde,
G42 7AF (h)
Tel: 0141-422-1154 **Tel:** 0141-334-1895 (h)
Contact: Maulana Mohammad F Quadri
Activities: Worship, resource
Traditions: Sunni
Movements: Barelwi
Other Languages: Arabic, Urdu, Punjabi
Affiliations: World Islamic Mission

Langside Mosque & Madrassah
196 Langside Road, Glasgow, Strathclyde, G42

Madrasa Alarabia al-Islamia
490 Paisley Road West, Ibrox, Glasgow, Strathclyde,
G51 1PY
Tel: 0141-427-2152
Contact: Dr Mohammed Sarwar
Position: Trustee
Activities: Worship, resource
Traditions: Sunni
Movements: Deobandi
Other Languages: Urdu, Punjabi, Gujarati

Madrasa Taleem-ul-Islam
161 Nithsdale Road, Pollokshields, Glasgow,
Strathclyde, G41 2QS
Tel: 0141-424-0787 **Tel:** 0141-424-1638 (h)
Contact: Mr Mohammad Ashraf
Position: Secretary
Activities: Worship, resource, visits
Traditions: Sunni
Other Languages: Urdu, Arabic

Masjid al Furqan
19 Carrington Street, Glasgow, Strathclyde, G4 9AJ

Tel: 0141-332-2811 **Tel:** 0141-331-1119
Fax: 0141-332-2811

Masjid-e-Khizra
69 Albert Road, Glasgow, Strathclyde

Masjid Noor
79 Forth Street, Pollockshield, Glasgow, Strathclyde,
G41 2TA
Tel: 0141-429-3383 **Tel:** 0141-422-1586 (h)
Fax: 0141-429-3383
Contact: Khaliq-uz-Zaman Ansari
Position: Secretary
Activities: Worship, resource
Traditions: Sunni
Movements: Tablighi Jamaat
Other Languages: Urdu, Punjabi
Affiliations: Islamic Reform Centre; Anjuman-e-
Islahul Muslimeen of UK

Mosque
Langside, Glasgow, Strathclyde, G53

Mosque & Islamic Centre
27 Arlington Street, Charing Cross, Glasgow,
Strathclyde, G1 6DT

Muslim House
16 Queen Crescent, Glasgow, Strathclyde, G4 9BL
Tel: 0141-332-5223
Contact: Mr Hassain Hemsy
Position: President

Muslim Reform Centre for Scotland
79 Forth Street, Pollockshields, Glasgow, Strathclyde,
G41

Muslims Women's Welfare Society
37 Glasgow Street, Hillhead, Glasgow, Strathclyde,
G12 8JR

Pakistan Muslim League
168 Battlefield Road, Newton Mearns, Glasgow,
Strathclyde, G77

Pakistan Muslim Welfare Society
21 Maxwell Drive, Glasgow, Strathclyde, G41
Contact: Mr L Bhatti

Strathclyde University Muslim Students Association (SUMSA)
c/o The Union, 90 John Street, Glasgow,
Strathclyde, G1 1XQ

Tel: 0141-552-4400, Ext 4375
Email: zulkieflimansyah@strath.ac.uk
Contact: Ahmad Jais Alias
Position: President
Activities: Worship, resource, youth, women,
newsletters
Other Languages: Arabic, Urdu
Affiliations: Federation of Students Islamic
Societies

Tanzeem Tableeg-ul-Islam
219 Allison Street, Govanhill, Glasgow, Strathclyde,
G24

Tanzeem Tableeg-ul-Islam
16 Algie Street, Longside, Glasgow, Strathclyde, G41

UK Islamic Mission
19 Carrington Street, Glasgow, Strathclyde, G4 9AJ
Tel: 0141-331-1119 **Fax:** 0141-332-2811
Contact: M. Ishaq
Position: Imam
Activities: Worship, resource, visits, youth, women,
inter-faith
Traditions: Sunni
Movements: Jamati-i-Islami
Other Languages: Urdu, English, Arabic

UK Islamic Mission (Ladies Section)
19 Carrington Street, Glasgow, Strathclyde, G4 9AJ
Tel: 0141-331-1119 **Fax:** 0141-332-2316
Contact: Mrs Salma Shaika
Position: In Charge of Ladies
Activities: Worship, resource, media, umbrella,
visits, youth, elderly, women, inter-faith
Other Languages: Urdu, Punjabi
Affiliations: UK Islamic Mission Branch; Islamic
Society for Britain; Imams and Mosques Council

United Muslim Organisation, Strathclyde
26 Bank Street, Glasgow, Strathclyde, G12 8ND
Tel: 0141-339-5513
Contact: Dr M S Kauser

Young Muslims - Glasgow Branch
19 Carrington Street, Woodlands, Glasgow,
Strathclyde, G4 9AJ
Tel: 0141-332-2811 **Tel:** 0141-571-7870 (h)
Fax: 0141-332-2811
Email: sqna@enterprise.net
Contact: Mr Sajid S Quayum
Position: In Charge of Branch

Activities: Youth, women, inter-faith
Affiliations: Islamic Society of Britain(Glasgow Branch); Young Muslims UK; Islamic Society of Britain

World Islamic Mission

138 Butterbiggins Road, Glasgow, G42 7AF
Tel: 0141-422-1152   **Tel:** 0141-423-4332 (h)
Contact: Mohammad Farqhul Quadri
Activities: Worship, resource, media, youth, elderly, women, newsletters, books, inter-faith
Traditions: Sunni
Movements: Barelwi
Other Languages: Arabic, Urdu, Panjabi
Affiliations: World Islamic Mission

Young Muslims Movement

126 Forth Street, Pollokshields, Glasgow, Strathclyde

Masjid Holytown

2 Cleland Road, Carfin, Holytown, Strathclyde

Stirling University Islamic Society

c/o Stirling University Students Association, Robbins Building, Stirling, Central, FK9 4LA

WALES

City, Town or Local Bodies

University College of Wales Students Islamic Society

University College of Wales, Aberystwyth, Dyfed, SY23 2AX

Bangor Islamic Centre

61 High Street, Bangor, Gwynedd, LL57 1NR
Tel: 01248-354612
Contact: Mr Mirwaz Khan
Position: Chairman
Activities: Worship, resource, visits, youth, elderly, women, inter-faith
Traditions: Sunni
Other Languages: Arabic, Urdu, Bangladeshi, Turkish
Affiliations: Muslim Welfare House

Islamic Centre

27 Union Square, Upper Bangor, Gwynedd

Islamic Centre

Weston Hill, Barry, South Glamorgan

Madrassah Ta'leem al-Qur'ann Wal-Sunnah

3 Vere Street, Barry, South Glamorgan, CF63 2HX

Tel: 01446-722044   **Tel:** 01446-733133 (h)
Fax: 01446-733723
Contact: Mr S Sufyan
Position: Manager/Principal
Activities: Resource, visits, youth, elderly, women, books, inter-faith
Other Languages: Urdu, Arabic
Affiliations: Jamiyat Madaras Taleem ul-Quran Wal-Sunnah, Lahore, Pakistan

Muslim Welfare Association of the Vale of Glamorgan

Community Education, Cultural and Welfare Centre, Barry, South Glamorgan, CF63 4HX
Tel: 01446-745822   **Tel:** 01446-722044 (h)
Contact: S U Sufyan
Position: Secretary
Actitivies: Worship, resource, umbrella, youth, elderly, women, newsletters, in-faith
Traditions: Sunni
Movements: Tablighi Jamaat
Other Languages: Urdu, Gujraji, Bengla, Panjabi

Al-Manar Islamic & Cultural Centre

2 Glyn Rhondda Street, Cathays, Cardiff, South Glamorgan, CF2 4AN
Tel: 01222-226650   **Fax:** 01222-226650
Contact: Nacer Bedre
Position: General Secretary
Activities: Worship, resource, media, umbrella, visits, youth, elderly, women, newsletters, books, inter-faith
Traditions: Sunni
Other Languages: Arabic

Bangladesh Muslim Association

13 Miskin Street, Cardiff, South Glamorgan, CF2 4AQ

British Muslim Association

42 Louisa Place, Cardiff, South Glamorgan, CF1 6BY

Canton Mosque & Madresa Talimul Quran

61-63 Severn Road, off Cowbridge Road, Canton, Cardiff, South Glamorgan, CF1
Tel: 01222-397640
Contact: Mr Mohammed Is'haq
Position: Secretary
Activities: Worship, resource
Traditions: Sunni
Movements: Deobandi, Tablight Jamaat
Other Languages: Urdu, Bengali, Arabic

Affiliations: South Wales Council of Mosques; UK Council of Mosques

Dar Al-Manar
2 Glynrhondda Street, Cathys, Cardiff, South Glamorgan, CF2 4AN

Darul Islah Waddawah
13 Deburgh Street, Cardiff, South Glamorgan, CF1 8LB
Contact: Banuri Manzil

Darul Isra Muslim Community Centre
25 Wyeverne Road, Cathays, Cardiff, South Glamorgan, CF2 4BG

Islami Darasgah
68 Connaught Road, off Albany Road, Roath, Cardiff, South Glamorgan, CF2 3PX
Tel: 01222-488454
Contact: H N K Khattak
Position: Secretary

Islamic Centre
123 Sloper Road, Leckwith, Cardiff, South Glamorgan

Islamic Educational Trust
129 Channel View Road, Grangetown, Cardiff, South Glamorgan

Islamic Prostisan
19 Dulwich Gardens, Llandaff, Cardiff

Islamic School Trust
253 Penarth Road, Grangetown, Cardiff, South Glamorgan, CF1 7HS

Madina Mosque
163-167 Woodville Road, Cathays, Cardiff, South Glamorgan

Madrassa Taleemul Qur'an
61-63 Severn Road, Canton, Cardiff, South Glamorgan
Tel: 01222-259410
Contact: Mohammad Ibrahim K?
Position: Secretary
Tradition: Sunni
Movements: Deobandi, Tablighi Jamaat
Other Languages: Urdu

Masjid Noor
Butetown, Cardiff, South Glamorgan

Mosque
17 Peel Street, Cardiff, South Glamorgan

Mosque
1 Tydfil Place, Roath Park, Cardiff, South Glamorgan

Mosque
60 Beauchamp Street, Cardiff, South Glamorgan

Mosque (Islamic Shikka Prophieshtan)
37 Plantagenet Street, off Tudor Road, Cardiff, South Glamorgan, CF1 8RF
Tel: 01222-221309
Contact: Muktar Ali
Position: Secretary

Muslim Education & Family Welfare Society
249 Pennsylvania, Llanedeyrn, Cardiff, South Glamorgan, CF1 7LW
Tel: 01222-731848
Contact: M A Fardoqui
Position: Chair

New Mosque
Penarth Road, Grangetown, Cardiff, South Glamorgan

Shah Jalal Mosque & Islamic Cultural Centre
3, Crwys Road, Roath, Cardiff, South Glamorgan
Tel: 01222-480217
Contact: Mr Ana Miah
Position: Secretary
Activities: Worship, resource
Other Languages: Bengali, Urdu, Arabic

South Wales Islamic Centre
Alice Street, Butetown, Cardiff, South Glamorgan
Tel: 01222-460243
Contact: Sheikh Said Hassan Ismail
Position: Secretary
Activities: Worship, resource, visits
Traditions: Sunni
Movements: Shafai
Other Languages: Arabic

UK Islamic Mission
21 Glenroy Street, Roath, Cardiff, South Glamorgan

UK Islamic Mission
3 Crwys Road, Cathays, Cardiff, South Glamorgan, CF2 4NA

Ulmist Islamic Society
50 Plantagenet Street, Riverside, Cardiff, South Glamorgan

University of Cardiff Islamic Society
Students Union, 5 Riverside, Cardiff, South Glamorgan, CF1 7AC

Mosque
2 Albert Street, Haverfordwest, Dyfed
Tel: 01437-765791 (h)
Contact: Mr Islamadean
Position: Treasurer

UK Islamic Mission
Glynbedw, Cwmamm, Lampeter, Dyfed

Alexandra Road Mosque
20 Alexandra Road, Newport, Gwent
Tel: 01633-257781
Contact: Mr M Mahmoud

Al-Noor Mosque
23a Harrow Road, Newport, Gwent, NP9
Tel: 01633-244395 (h)
Contact: Mr A R Mujahid

Al-Rahman Mosque
26 Ruperra Street, Newport, Gwent
Tel: 01633-255150
Contact: Mrs F Nasser

Anjuman Raza-e-Mustafa
15 Methuen Road, Newport, NP9 0BN
Tel: 01633-665021 **Tel:** 01633-277166 (h)
Contact: Mr A R Mujahid
Position: Chair
Activities: Resource, youth, elderly, women
Traditions: Sunni
Movements: Barelwi
Other Languages: Urdu, Punjabi

East Newport Islamic Cultural Centre
12 Cedar Road, Mainsee, Newport, Gwent, NP9 0BA
Tel: 01633-212254 **Tel:** 01633-666142 (h)
Contact: Maulana Farid Khan
Position: Imam

Activities: Worship, youth, elderly
Other Languages: Bengali, Arabic, Urdu, Parsi
Affiliations: South Wales Council of Mosques; East London Mosque: Regents Park Mosque; Muslim World League

Hussaini Mission
Commercial Street, Newport, Gwent

Islamic Society for Gwent
63 Stow Hill, Newport, Gwent
Tel: 01633-259005
Contact: Mr Ramzan
Position: Secretary

Jamia Mosque
183-186 Commercial Road, Newport, Gwent, NP9 2PF
Tel: 01633-215420 **Tel:** 01633-244395 (h)
Contact: Mr A R Mujahid

Sunni Muslim Association
Eton Road, Newport, Gwent

Mosque & Islamic Community Centre
14 St Helens Road, Swansea, West Glamorgan, SA1 4AW
Tel: 01792-54532
Contact: Mr M Khan
Position: Imam

University of Swansea Islamic Society
Students Union, Singleton Park, Swansea, West Glamorgan, SA2 8PP

Muslim Association of Wrexham
c/o Dr F Jishi, 28 Mayflower Drive, Marford, Wrexham, Clwyd, LL12 8LD (h)
Email: farookh.jishi@msn.com
Contact: Dr F Jishi
Position: Secretary
Activities: Worship, resource, inter-faith
Other Languages: Arabic, Urdu

KEY TO TERMS USED IN MUSLIM ORGANISATION TITLES

Note: This is not a complete glossary of significant Muslim terms. It is a guide to the meaning of some of the words used in the titles of Muslim organisations listed in the directory. More information on the italicised words can be tracked down elsewhere in the key and/or in "Introducing the Muslim Community" by using the directory's "Significant Word Index".

Abad: Arabic meaning "eternity" in the sense of "without end".

Abd: Arabic meaning "slave" or servant" referring to a state of dependence upon God and conformity to God's will. It is a title applied to the Prophet Muhammad and is also an element of many Muslim names.

Abel: Pertaining to *Abu* (see below). Correctly written as *Abul-*, meaning "father of....".

Abu: Arabic for "father".

Abu-Bakr: The name of the first *Caliph* (632-634) following the death of Muhammad. He was known as *al-siddiq* or "the faithful". His daughter Aishah was a favourite wife of the Prophet and he is believed to be one of the two people who transmitted the *tasawwuf* (esoteric *Sufi*) doctrines from Muhammad.

Adab: Arabic for "correctness", "propriety" or "good manners", concerning which the *Hadith* (see below) have much to say.

Adam: The name of the first man who is also believed by Muslims to have been the first prophet and the viceregent of God on earth.

Aga Khan: The name and title of the *Imam* of the *Nizari* branch of the *Isma'ilis*. The title was first given in 1818 by the then Shah of Persia to Abul Hasan Ali Shah. In 1841 the *Aga Khan* fled Persia after a rebellion against the Shah and, via Afghanistan, went to India. The present *Aga Khan*, Karim, is the fourth to have the title. In the belief of his followers he is also the forty-ninth *Imam* (see below) in unbroken line of succession.

Ahl: Arabic for "people".

Ahla: Pertaining to *Ahl* (see above).

Ahlebait: Alternative Romanisation of *Ahl-ul-Bait* (see below).

Ahl-e-Hadith: A Muslim group which claims not to follow any *madhhab* or "school of law". It can also be found as *Ahl Al-Hadith*.

Ahl-ul-Bait: Arabic for "people of the House". A term used for descendants of the Prophet through his daughter Fatima and his cousin and son-in-law 'Ali. In some countries a register is maintained of the Prophet's descendants who now number many thousands.

Ahl-ul-Bayt: Variant Romanisation of *Ahl-ul-Bait* (see above).

Ahnaf: Plural of *Hanafi* (see below), referring to followers of Imam Abu Hanifa's school of jurisprudence.

Al: Arabic, meaning "the".

Al-Azhar: Meaning "the glorious". It is the name of the foremost centre of *Sunni* Muslim learning, founded in Egypt in 969CE. It is the oldest surviving university in the Muslim world.

Alim: Singular of *ulama*, meaning a learned person, including *imams*, *muftis*, *qazis* and *maulvis*. The name *al-Alim* (The Wise) is also one of the ninety-nine "Most Beautiful Names" of God.

Aliya: Meaning "higher".

Allah: The Arabic name of the Supreme and Almighty God whom Muslims worship and believe in. He is also known by ninety-nine other attributes known collectively as "The Most Beautiful Names", in Arabic, *'Asma 'al-Husna*.

Allahi: An African, in particular Nigerian, form of describing *Allah*.

Almadina: See Madina below.

Aloom: Variant Romanisation of *Uloom* (see below).

Alume: Variant Romanisation of *Uloom* (see below).

Aman: Arabic, depending on proununciation, meaning either "peace" or "safety" or "security", usually in the sense of what is achieved through belief.

Ameen: Used at the end of prayer and meaning "O God, accept our prayers". Pronounced *Aameen*.

Amin: Variant Romanisation of *ameen* (see above).

Amina: The name of Muhammad's mother.

Amir: Arabic meaning "ruler", "commander" or "chief". It is part of an honorific title applied to the *Caliphs*, namely, *Amir al-Mu'minin* meaning "Commander of the Faithful".

An: Variant Romanisation of the definite article *al* meaning "the".

Aneesul: Arabic, first half of a title meaning "close friends of...".

Anjamin: Variant Romanisation of *Anjuman* (see below).

Anjuman: Arabic meaning "society", "association" or "organisation".

Anjumen: Variant Romanisation of *Anjuman* (see above).

Anjumin: Variant Romanisation of *Anjuman* (see above).

Ansarullah: Arabic meaning "the helpers of Allah's cause", a common name for both Muslim individuals and associations.

Anwar: Plural of *noor* (see below) meaning "light". It is also one of the Names of God.

Anwarul: Arabic for "light of...".

Aqsa: Al-aqsa means literally "the farthest (mosque)" and is the name given by the *Qur'an* to the Temple Mount in Jerusalem.

Ar: Variant Romanisation of the Arabic definite article *al* meaning "the" (see above).

Arabia: The name of the Arabian peninsula. Arab means "nomad". Traditionally, north Arabians claim descent from a patriarch called 'Adnan, and from him, also descent through Ishmael, son of Abraham. The south Arabians claim descent from a patriarch called Qahtan. By 636CE the peninsula had become Muslim following the beginning of the revelation of the *Qur'an* in 612CE.

Arabiya: Variant Romanisation of Arabia (see above).

Arqam: The name of a *Companion* of the Prophet and an early convert to Islam who migrated to Madina because of persecution in Makka. He took part in the early struggles to establish Islam and lived to an old age. Before the conversion of 'Umar his house was one of the key meeting places for the early Muslim community and its site is now incorporated into that of the Grand Mosque in Makka.

Ashariyya: From *'Ithna Ashariyya* (see below), the *Twelvers* of *Shi'a* Islam, founded by Ab al-Hasan 'Ali ibn Isma'il.

Asheri: Variant Romanisation of *Ashariyya* (see above).

Ashia: Variant Romanisation of *Ashariyya* (see above).

Ashrafia: From Ashraf, the name of a *Sufi* of Persian origin whose full name was Syed Mohammed Ashraf (1289-1405CE). He was the ruler of Samnan until he became a *Sufi* and left his kingdom. He settled in Northern India at Kaccauchha where his tomb is.

Many Muslims in the UK have contacts with his spiritual descendants.

Ashriia: Variant Romanisation of *ashariyya* (see above).

Aslamiyya: Variant Romanisation of *assalam* (see below).

Asna: Variant Romanisation of *ithna* (see below).

Asrafia: Variant Romanisation of *ashrafia* (see above).

Assalam: Arabic meaning "of peace", as in *Dar Assalam*, meaning "house of peace" and relating to Paradise.

Azad: Meaning "free" or "independent".

Azam: Meaning "great".

Azeemia: A family group from Karachi following a spiritual leader called Azeemi.

Aziza: From *Aziz*, one of the Names of God, meaning "mighty" or "powerful". Another meaning of *aziz* (feminine, *aziza*) is "dear" or "beloved".

Aziziye: See *Aziza* above.

Bahu: Title of a *Sufi* poet from the Punjab, born in 1639CE.

Bait: Part of *Ahl-ul-Bait* (see above).

Baitulaman: Meaning "house of peace" or "house of safety", from *bait* meaning "house" and *aman* meaning "peace".

Bakar: Variant Romanisation of Bakr (see above).

Bakr: From Abu-Bakr, the name of the second *Caliph*.

Banatul: Arabic, meaning "daughters of…".

Barkat: Variant Romanisation of the Arabic *barakat* meaning "blessing".

Bayt: See *Ahl-ul-Bait* above.

Bazami: Meaning "circle" or "gathering".

Bazar: Meaning "market".

Bazme: Variant Romanisation of *bazami* (see above).

Bazmi: Variant Romanisation of *bazami* (see above).

Bilal: The name of the first *muezzin* or "caller to prayer", Bilal was a black slave from Abyssinia who was an early convert to Islam, ransomed and freed by Abu-Bakr after his master had persecuted him for his beliefs.

Bina: Meaning "foundation" or "structure".

Birr: Meaning "blessing", "gift", "goodness", "kindness", or "piety".

Bohra: A Muslim community originating from Gujarat in India. There are both *Sunni* and *Shi'a Bohra* groups in the UK.

Bukhari: The name of an important collection of 7,000 *Hadith* made by Abu 'Abdu'ilah Muhammad ibn Ismai'il ibn Abraham ibn al-Mughirrah al-Jufi al-Bukhari (810–870CE). He was born in Bukhara (in what is now modern Uzbekistan) and devoted his life to the collection and classification of *hadith*.

Burhani: Pertaining to Syed Burhanuddin, leader of the *Shi'a Bohra* group.

Chachhi: Variant Romanisation of Cutchi (see below).

Chashma: Meaning "fountain".

Chashtiah: Variant Romanisation of *Chistiyyah* (see below).

Chistiyyah: A *Sufi* order.

Cutchi: Applying to those who originate in the Cutch or (Kutch) area of Gujarat State in India.

Dabhel: The name of a city in Gujarat, India.

Dar: Arabic for "house".

Darasagh: Persian for *madrassah* (see below).

Darawi: The name of a *Sufi* renewer of Islam in Morocco, whose full name was Mulay-l'Arabi Darqawi (1737-1823CE). He left a strong influence among *Sufi* orders in Morocco.

Darqawi: A *Sufi* tradition following Mulay-l'Arabi Darqawi (1737-1823CE).

Darul: Arabic meaning "house of…" or "place of…", giving *Darul-Islam* meaning "house of peace".

Da'wah: Arabic for "to call", used in the context of calling people into the path of Allah and spreading the message of Islam.

Dawat: Alternative Romanisation of *da'wah* (see above). Used as part of the organisational name Dawatul Islam, meaning "the call of Islam".

Da'watul: Pertaining to *da'wah* (see above).

Dawatul: Pertaining to *da'wah* (see above).

Dawoodi: A branch of the *Bohra* (see above) community, originating in Western India. They are

Ismaili Shi'as who believe in Dawood, son of Qutb Shah as a true successor of Dawood, son of Adjab Shah (d. 1588CE). The head of this group generally resides in Bombay.

Deral: Variant Romanisation of *darul* (see above).

Dewan: Variant Romanisation of *diwan* (see below).

Dharam: Meaning "religion".

Din: Arabic for "religion" and its practice. A specific religion is often known as a *millah* meaning "way".

Diwan: A "court" of "hall of audience", often used for the base of a *Sufi* master.

Ehsan: Variant Romanisation of *ihsan* (see below).

Ehyae: Variant Romanisation of *ihya* (see below).

Eid: Meaning "festival". Part of the name of the two most important festivals of the Muslim calendar, *Eid-ul-Fitre* (festival of feast) and *Eid-ul-Adha* (festival of sacrifice).

Elahi: Arabic, meaning "of God", or "divine".

Eshat: Meaning "propagation", "circulation", "publicity" or "preaching".

Fahd: A male name.

Faisal: A male name.

Faiz: Meaning "bounty" or "grace".

Faizul: Pertaining to *faiz* (see above).

Falah: Arabic for the fulfillment of the aim of creation and the goal towards which a righteous life leads, other words "success" or "salvation".

Farooq: A male name meaning "one who distinguishes between right and wrong". It was also a title of Umar, the second *Caliph* of Islam.

Farouq: Variant Romanisation of Farooq (see above), now spelt Faruq.

Fatimia: Pertaining to the daughter of the Prophet, called Fatima.

Furkania: Pertaining to *furqan* (see below).

Furqan: Arabic literally meaning "divider" in the sense of a criterion distinguishing one thing from another. It is the name of *Surah* 25 in the *Qur'an* and is also used of the *Qur'an* itself in terms of distinguishing between truth and falsehood.

Gamkol: Variant Romanisation of Ghamkol (see below).

Ghamkol: A village in the Province of Sarhad in Pakistan, which is the centre of a *Sufi* tradition.

Ghar: Arabic for "cave". Ghar Hira is the name of the cave at the top of Mount Hira, to which the Prophet Muhammad used to retreat to meditate. The mountain is now called *Jabal an-Nur* (The Mountain of Light). It is pronounced as *Ghaar*.

Ghausia: Ghaus Al-Azam (the Great Helper) was a title given to Shaikh Abdul Qadir Jeelani (or Gilani) of Baghdad, a founder of the *Qadiria Sufi* Order. Many *mosques* and Muslim organisations in the UK and throughout the world adopt this name to show their respect for, and affiliation to, the *Shaikh*.

Ghousia: Variant Romanisation of *Ghausia* (see above).

Ghousian: That which pertains to *Ghausia* (see above)

Ghosia: Variant Romanisation of *Ghausia* (see above).

Gilani: Part of the name of Abdu'l-Qadir Gilani (1078-1166CE) who was a famous *Sufi* saint who founded the *Qadiri* school of *Sufism*.

Gosia: Variant Romanisation of *Ghausia* (see above).

Gosiah: Variant Romanisation of *Ghausia* (see above).

Gousia: Variant Romanisation of *Ghausia* (see above).

Gousiah: Variant Romanisation of *Ghausia* (see above).

Gujerat: The name of a state in north east India and of a city in the Province of Panjab, Pakistan. Also found as Gujarat.

Gujerati: That which pertains to Gujarat (see above).

Habibiyya: The name of a *Sufi* tradition, the word literally means "lover" or "friend".

Hadit: A variant Romanisation of *Hadith* (see below).

Hadith: Arabic literally meaning "speech" or "account", it refers to traditions which deals with the deeds, sayings and approval of others' actions by the Prophet Muhammad. There is a special kind of *hadith*: *hadith qudsi* (sacred *hadith*) in which Allah is believed to be speaking through the Prophet Muhammad. After the *Qur'an*, the *hadith* form the second fundamental basis of *Shar'iah*.

Haideria: The name of a *Sufi* tradition.

Haideriah: Variant Romanisation of *Haideria* (see above).

Halal: Arabic literally meaning "released" (from prohibition) which in Islamic law relates to all things permitted. It therefore also refers to the meat of animals which have been slaughtered according to Islamic practice. Its opposite is *haram* (meaning "prohibited").

Hanafia: Pertaining to *Hanfi* (see below).

Hanfi: One of the four orthodox *madhhab* (schools of jurisprudence) recognised among *Sunni* Muslims. It was founded by Abu Hanifah (d. 767CE) and is predominant in most countries of the former Turkish Empire and in India, as well as among Muslims in the UK originating in those countries.

Hanfia: Pertaining to *Hanafi* (see above).

Hanif: Arabic literally meaning "one who is inclined" and it is the name used in the *Qur'an* for those who did not join in the idolatry of pre-Islamic *Jahilijjah* (Age of Ignorance).

Hanifa: Pertaining to Imam Abu Hanifah.

Haq: Arabic for "reality" or "absolute". It is a centrally important name of Allah.

Haqq: Variant Romanisation of *haq* (see above).

Haqqani: Pertaining to *haq* (see above).

Haqque: Variant Romanisation of *haq* (see above).

Haroonia: The name of a *Sufi* based in Pakistan who has followers in the UK.

Hazarat: A title of dignity applied to a great person.

Hazoori: Literally meaning "presence", symbolically meaning "the reverent".

Hazrat: Variant Romanisation of *Hazarat* (see above).

Hefzul: Arabic for the memorisation of the *Qur'an*.

Hekma: Meaning "wisdom". Also found as *hikma*.

Heraa: Variant Romanisation of *Hira* (see below).

Hidaya: Varian Romanisation of *Hidayah* (see below).

Hidayah: Arabic literally meaning "guidance" and the name of one of the *Sunni* books of law in Arabic.

Hidayatul: Pertaining to *hidayah* (see above).

Hijra: Arabic for "migration", it refers to the 622 CE migration of Muhammad and his Makkan *Companions* (the *muhajirun* or emigrants) from persecution in Makka to Yathrib, later called *Madinat-an-Nabi* (City of the Prophet) or Madina. The Muslim calendar starts with this historical event.

Hilal: Arabic referring to the crescent of the moon, in other words, the new moon.

Hira: Ghar Hira is the name of the cave at the top of Mount Hira, to which the Prophet Muhammad used to retreat to meditate. The mountain is now called *Jabal an-Nur* (The Mountain of Light). It is a few miles from Makka and the opening of the cave faces Makka. It was on *Laylat al-Qadr* (The Night of Destiny), at the end of the month of *Ramadan*, that Muslims believe the prophet Muhammad started to receive the revelation of the *Qur'an*. The revelation of the entire *Qur'an* took almost 23 years to complete.

Hizaz: A province of Saudi Arabia.

Hizb: Meaning "party".

Hizbut: Pertaining to *hizb* (see above).

Hoda: Pertaining to *hidayah* (see above).

Huda: Arabic meaning "guidance".

Hurairah: Arabic meaning "kitten". It pertains to the surname of Abu Hurairah, a famous *Companion* of the Prophet Muhammed who gave him this title because of his intense love for a cat which he usually carried in his sleeve.

Hussain: The name of the second son of 'Ali and Fatima (the daughter of the Prophet) and hence the grandson of the Prophet. He was killed in 680 CE at a place called Karbala. Hussain's death was central to the development of the *Shi'a* tradition of Islam. It is commemorated in the *Shi'a Muharram* festival and re-enacted in *Ta'ziyah* (martyrdom plays) in the days preceding the 10th *Muharram*. The site of Hussain's tomb in Karbala, has been an important *Shi'a* place of pilgrimage.

Hussaini: That which pertains to Hussain (see above).

Hussainia: That which pertains to Hussain (see above).

Ibadah: Meaning "act of worship", from the Arabic *abada* meaning "to serve and *abd* meaning "slave".

Ibadat: Variant Romanisation of *ibadah* (see above).

Ibadur: Variant Romanisation of *ibadah* (see above).

Idara: Arabic meaning "organisation".

Idarul: Pertaining to *idara* (see above).

Idera: Variant Romanisation of *idara* (see above).

Ifta: A name for a religious or judicial opinion, also known as a *fatwa*.

Ihsan: Arabic literally meaning "to perform an action perfectly", it is used in the *Hadith* to describe sincere worship of God.

Ihya: Meaning "revival".

Il: Variant Romanisation of the Arabic definite article *al* (see above) meaning "the".

Ilaahi: Pertaining to Allah.

Ilm: Arabic, meaning "knowledge".

Imam: Literally means "model", "example" or "leader". In *Shi'a* Islam it refers to people with special authority who are successors of the family of Ali and his wife Fatima. The various *Shi'a* groupings disagree over the identification of the *Imam*. In *Twelver Shi'ism*, the *Imam* has absolute right to civil and political as well as spiritual authority. It also refers to the leader of *salat*, although it is sometimes used an as honorific title.

Imama: Arabic, literally meaning "the followers of the *Imam*", especially used by *Sh'ia* Muslims.

Imambarra: Arabic, meaning literally "place of the Imam", it is used to designate some *Shi'a* congregational halls.

Imami: Sometimes used as a description of *Shi'a* Muslims and also as an adjective describing their doctrines.

Imamia: The name given to the *Shi'a* Muslim followers of the *Jaffari* legal code and the *Twelve Imams*.

Imdadiah: Meaning "co-operative help" or "charitable organisation".

Injaman: Variant Romanisation of *anjuman* (see above).

Iqbal: Sir Muhammad Iqbal (1873–1938) was a philosopher, poet and President of the Muslim League in pre-independence India. He wrote extensively on Islam and modernity. His poetry helped in the revival of Islam in India and influenced the demand for the creation of Pakistan.

Iqra: Arabic meaning "read!", which relates to the command in the *Qur'an* to read.

Irshad: Arabic meaning "guidance".

Ishaat: Meaning "preaching" or "publication".

Isla: Variant Romanisation of *islah* (see below).

Islah: Arabic meaning "reform", indicating a movement for Islamic revival.

Islahul: Pertaining to *islah* (see above).

Islam: Islam literally means "surrender" and is the name of the religion followed by Muslims which is given in the *Qur'an* itself.

Islami: Meaning that known as Islamic which pertains to Islam and is, therefore, known as Islamic.

Islamia: Pertaining to Islam.

Islamiah: See *Islami* above.

Islamiyah: Pertaining to Islam.

Islamic: Pertaining to Islam.

Islamiya: That which pertains to Islam.

Ismaili: The name of a group who are often considered to be part of *Shi'a* Islam. *Isma'ilis* began as an offshoot of *Twelver Shi'a* Islam. Ismail was the eldest son of Ja'far, the sixth *Imam* of the *Shi'ites*. Followers of Ismail came to be called *sab'iyyah* (*Seveners*), and among these *Seveners* various ways developed of recognising the *Seventh Imam*.

Isnah: Variant Romanisation of *ithna* (see below).

Issha'at: Variant Romanisation of *ishaat* (see above).

Isshatul: Meaning "preaching of …".

Ithna: *Ithna 'Ashariyyah* means literally "*Twelvers*" from *ithna 'ashar*. It is part of the name of the *Shi'a* Muslim group which believes in a line of twelve *Imams*, with the Twelfth having been occulted in the nineteenth century and being expected to reappear as the *Mahdi*.

Itifaq: Variant Romanisation of *ittefaq*, meaning "unity".

Ittehad: Arabic meaning "unity" or "federation".

Ittihas: Variant Romanisation of *itihash*, meaning "history".

Jafferia: The name applied to the followers of the *Jafferia* legal code.

Jafferiya: Variant Romanisation of *Jafferia* (see above).

Jaime: Variant Romanisation of *Jamia* (see below).

Jalal: Meaning "grandeur" or "eminence", it is the name of a *Sufi* leader, Shah Jalal, whose tomb lies in Sylhet in Bangladesh. A number of Bangladeshi Muslim *mosques* and organisations in the UK are named after him.

Jalalabad: The name of a city in Northern India. Many Bangladeshi Muslims call Sylhet Jalalabad after the famous *Sufi* Saint, Shah Jalal.

Jallalabad: Variant Romanisation of *Jalalabad* (see above).

Jama'at: Arabic meaning "association" or "society".

Jamaat: Variant Romanisation of *Jama'at* (see above).

Jamali: A family name, meaning "my beauty".

Jama'nt: Variant Romanisation of *Jamaat* (see above).

Jamat: Variant Romanisation of *Jamaat* (see above.)

Jame: Variant Romanisation of *Jami* (see *Jamia* below).

Jamia: Arabic meaning literally "meeting place" and used for university or academic institutions and generally of *mosques*. The word *jami',* however, especially refers to a central *mosque* in a geographical area.

Jamiah: Variant Romanisation of *Jamia* (see above).

Jamiat: Variant Romanisation of *Jama'at* (see above).

Jamiyat: Meaning "organisation".

Jamiyate: Variant Romanisation of *Jama'at*, or *jamiyat* (see above).

Jammat: Variant Romanisation of *Jama'at* (see above).

Jammu: From Jammu Kashmir (see below).

Jamnia: Variant Romanisation of *Jamia* (see above).

Jehan: Persian meaning "world".

Jihad: Arabic meaning "struggle".

Jinnah: Muhammad Ali Jinnah (1876-1948), the name of the President of the Muslim League in the India of the British Raj and the founder and first Governor General of the state of Pakistan in 1948.

Judullah: Arabic meaning "the army of Allah".

Juma: The name for Friday, the day on which special congregational prayers are held in *mosques.*

Jumaat: Variant Romanisation of *jama'at* (see above).

Kafel: Variant Romanisation of *kafil,* meaning "security" or "guarantor".

Kair: Meaning "charitable".

Kallayan: Bengali, meaning "charitable".

Kamboli: The name of a small town in Gujarat, India.

Kanoon: Variant Romanisation of *Qanun,* meaning "law" or "constitution".

Kanz: Meaning a "treasure".

Karam: Meaning "generous" or "noble", it is the name of a spiritual and religious leader, *Pir* Karan Shah of Pakistan, whose followers can be found in the UK.

Karimia: Pertaining to *karam* (see above).

Kashif: Meaning "discover".

Kashkool: Meaning, literally, a "beggar's bowl".

Kashmir: The name of a geographical area of the north east of the Indo-Pakistan sub-continent, part of which is in Pakistan and is known by Muslims as Azad Kashmir (see *Azad* above) and part of which is in the state of India.

Kerat: Variant Romanisation of *Qira't,* it relates to the reading of the *Qur'an* according to the science of recitation.

Khalifa: Arabic for "successor" or "viceroy". Adam, as the first man, was given *khilafa* and the word is also used of the first four "*Rightly Guided*" Caliphs of the early Muslim community, namely Abbu Bakr, 'Umar, 'Uthman and 'Ali. It is both a spiritual and a civil function.

Khalifad: See *khalifa* above.

Khalifate: The name of the institution within *Sunni* Islam in which community authority was vested. The insitution eventually became de facto hereditary with rival claimants and was formerly abolished by Kemal Ataturk of Turkey in 1924.

Khan: A Turkish word for "prince" or "chief".

Khaniqahi: A name by which *Sufi* centres are sometimes known.

Khanquah: A variant Romanisation of *khaniqahi* (see above).

Khatme: Arabic meaning "conclusion" or "seal".

Khatri: An ethnic group from western India and East African Indians.

Khawateen: Persian, meaning "ladies".

Khizra: Variant Romanisation of *khazia*, meaning "green", often used in conjunction with the word *Gurbad* (tomb) since the colour of the Prophet's tomb is green.

Khoei: Ayatollah Abdul Qasim Al-Khoei came from the town of Khoei in Azerbaijan.

Khoja: Term applied to converts to *Shi'a* Islam from the Gujerat area of India. They are mostly *Ismailis*, but some also joined the *'Ithna Asheri* group and are numerically strong in the UK.

Khuddam: Arabic meaning "servants".

Khuddamuddin: Arabic meaning "servants of the faith".

Khuddamul: Pertaining to *khuddam* (see above).

Khuddum: Variant Romanisation of *khaddam* (see above).

Khwateen: Variant Romanisation of *khawateen* (see above).

Kizra: Variant Romanisation of *khizra* (see above).

Kokani: Variant Romanisation of *kokni* (see below).

Kokni: Refers to people originating in Kokan, a region of India near Bombay. Many UK Muslims have their origins there.

Kumba: Urdu, meaning "family".

Li: Arabic meaning "to" or "unto".

Luharwadha: An Indian social grouping originally associated with ironmongering.

Maarif: Arabic meaning "knowledge" or "insight".

Macca: Variant Romanisation of Makka (see below). Also found as Mecca.

Madani: Arabic, meaning "that which originates in Madina" (see below).

Madina: The name of the city one hundred and eighty miles to the north of Makka, to which Muhammad and his followers migrated in 622CE. It is the second most sacred city for Muslims and contains the tombs of Muhammad and the first two *Caliphs*. Also found as Medina (see below).

Madni: Variant Romanisation of *Madani* (see above).

Madrasa: Variant Romanisation of *Madrasah* (see below).

Madrasah: Variant Romanisation of *Madrassah* (see below).

Madrassah: Literally meaning a "place of study". Traditionally, it is used of a school of higher learning. It is now generally used in the UK to refer to *Qur'anic* schools for children.

Madressa: Variant Romanisation of *Madrassah* (see above).

Madressah: Variant Romanisation of *Madrassah* (see above).

Mahal: The name given to the seat of a *Sufi sheikh* as a centre of learning.

Mahfil: Meaning "place of assembly" or "congregation".

Majlis: Arabic meaning literally "sitting" or "assembly". It is often used of a parliament or other representative assembly. It is also used of a *Sufi* gathering for meditating and chanting God's name.

Majlusus: Variant Romanisation of *majlis* (see above).

Makka: The city in Saudi Arabia where the *Ka'bah* (God's House) is located. Muslim prayers are made in this direction and it is the place to which the *hajj* is made.

Makki: Meaning "Makka".

Manar: Arabic, literally meaning "lighthouse".

Markazi: Arabic meaning "central".

Maroof: Meaning "generally recognised". It is a common male name among Muslims.

Masjeed: Variant Romanisation of *masjid* (see below).

Masjid: Arabic meaning literally a "place of prostrations". It is used for *mosques* which are places of worship of One God. It can be either an enclosed or an open space which is clean and into which Muslims should enter only in a condition of ritual purity. There are a range of architectural designs, but the prototype of a mosque was built by the Prophet at Quba' in Madina.

Masjide: Pertaining to "*masjid*" (see above).

Medina: Also found as Madina (see above).

Mehfil: Variant Romanisation of *mahfil*.

Mehr: Meaning "kindness" or "affection", it is in the name of *Pir* Mehr Ali Shah of Golara in Pakistani Panjab. He was a *Sufi* leader of the *Chishtia* order and has a number of followers in the UK mainly among Muslims originating in Pakistan and Kashmir.

Mehria: Pertaining to the *Pir* Mehr Ali Shah (see above).

Memon: The name of an ethnic group mainly originating from Western India but also settled in Malawi and other parts of the world.

Miftah: Arabic, meaning "the key".

Milad: Arabic, meaning "birth", as in *Milad un-Nabi* (the birthday of the Prophet).

Millat: Meaning a specific religion as distinct from *din* which refers to all aspects of religion as a way of life. *Millat* was particularly used in the Ottoman period to refer to the different religious groups within their administration.

Minhaj: Variant Romanisation of *minaj* (see below).

Minajul: Arabic meaning "road of...".

Minaret: Derived from the Arabic *manarah* meaning "lighthouse", the word refers to the towers of many mosques from which *muezzin* (callers to prayer) make the *adhan* (call to prayer) five times a day.

Minaj: Arabic meaning "road".

Mohammedi: That which relates to Muhammad, the Prophet of Islam who, according to tradition, was born in 570CE and died in 632CE. His name means in Arabic "the praised one" or "he who is glorified". Traditionally, every mention of his name is followed by *sall-al-Lahu alayhi wa-sallam*, meaning "God bless him and give him peace".

Mohammedia: The *Tariqah-i-Muhammadiyya* is the way of the Prophet Muhammad.

Mohi: A "reviver" or "revivalist".

Mohiban: Variant Romanisation of *muhibban* (see below).

Mohibban: Variant Romanisation of *muhibban* (see below).

Momineen: Arabic, meaning "the believers".

Monir: Variant Romanisation of *munir* (see below).

Mosque: The English name given to a Muslim place of worship (in Arabic, *masjid*).

Muhajiroun: Arabic meaning "the migrants".

Muhibban: Meaning "friends".

Muhul: Variant Romanisation of *mohi'ul* (see *mohi* above).

Mukarram: Arabic for "revered" or "honoured".

Munawar: Variant Romanisation of *munir* (see below).

Munir: Meaning "radiant" or "luminous". Also, part of a male name.

Muntada: Meaning "a place of gathering".

Muntazar: Arabic meaning "the expected one", usually referring to "the *Hidden Imam*" of *Sh'ia* Muslim belief.

Muridin: Arabic meaning "disciples" and usually connected with a *Sufi sheikh*.

Muslamin: Variant Romanisation of the masculine *Muslimim* (see below).

Muslemeen: Variant Romanisation of *Muslimim* (see below).

Muslim: Arabic literally meaning "one who has surrendered to God", derived from the Arabic *salam* meaning "to surrender" and "to seek peace". The "s" in Muslim should be pronounced as in the English word "slim" and not as in "nose", as this latter pronunciation can sound like a word meaning "cruel" and could therefore be misunderstood and offensive.

Muslimat: Feminine plural of Muslim (see above).

Muslimeen: Variant Romanisation of *Muslimim* (see below).

Muslimin: Masculine plural of Muslim (see above).

Mustafa: Arabic meaning "the pure one", an alternative name by which Muhammad is known among Muslims.

Muttaqeen: Arabic meaning "careful ones" or "pious ones".

Nabawut: Arabic, meaning "prophethood".

Nabi: A prophet who prophesises within an existing revelation and does not bring a new revelation (such a prohet being a *rasul*).

Nagina: Meaning a "gem".

Naqeebul: Pertaining to *Naqeeb* which means "leader".

Naqshbandia: A *Sufi* order founded by Muhammad ibn Muhammad Baha ad-Din Naqshband (1317CE-1389CE) of Bukhara. The observance of silence is a characteristic of the order along with *dhikr* which is the invocation from the heart of the Divine Name.

Nau: Meaning "new".

Neelie: Meaning "blue colour".

Newabia: Pertaining to *nawab*, meaning "lord" or "governor".

Nimatullah: Meaning "gift of Allah", it is the name of a *Sufi* saint.

Nimatullahi: Pertaining to *Nimatullah* (see above).

Nisa: Arabic meaning "women".

Nizama: Variant Romanisation of *nizame* (see below).

Nizame: Arabic, meaning "order" or "system".

Nizami: Variant Romanisation of *nizama* (see above).

Noor: Arabic meaning "light". *Masjide-e-Noor* therefore means "mosque of light".

Noorull: Pertaining to *noor* (see above).

Nubuwwat: Variant Romanisation of *nabawut* (see above).

Nujum: Arabic, meaning "stars".

Nural: Variant Romanisation of *Noorull*.

Nusrat: Female name meaning "victory".

Nusrati: Pertaining to *nusrat* (see above).

Nusratul: Pertaining to *nusrat* (see above).

O: Arabic meaning "he", "she" or "it".

Omar: Omar, or 'Umar ibn al-Khattab (d644CE), was the second *Caliph* and one of the main figures of Islam. Before he became a Muslim he originally set out to kill the Prophet and to dispute with his sister and her husband who had become Muslims.

However, he let them recite to him verses from the *Qur'an* and this led to his conversion. Islam spread rapidly during his *Caliphate*.

Paigham: A Persian word for "message". *Paighambar* is the Persian word for "prophet", equivalent to both the Arabic *nabi* (see above) and *rasul* (see *rasool* below).

Pak: Meaning "pure". A part of the name of the state of Pakistan.

Pratisthan: Malaysian and Hindi word meaning "centre" or "department".

Qaafia: Meaning "rhyme".

Qadiria: A *Sufi Order*, known after Abdul Qadir Jilani.

Qamrul: Pertaining to *qamar*, meaning "moon".

Qasmia: A *Sufi* tradition of Pakistan. Sometimes attributed to the famous Indian scholar, Maulana Qasim Nanatwi.

Quawwatul: Pertaining to *quwwat* meaning "ability" or "power".

Quba: The name of a place three miles outside of Madina where the Prophet Muhammad stopped during the *hijra* from Makka to Madina. The first *mosque* which he built was at Quba and was later called *al-Taqwa* (The Mosque of Piety).

Qul: Arabic meaning "say!", an injunction.

Quloob: Plural of *qalb*, meaning "heart".

Qur'an: Arabic literally meaning "recitation". The *Qur'an* is the book at the centre of Islam and was revealed over a period of twenty-three years and recorded in the Arabic language.

Qusma: A *Sufi* tradition of Pakistan.

Rabbani: Pertaining to God – *rab* is an Arabic word for "lord" and is one of the names of God.

Rahimiyah: The name of a *Sufi* tradition.

Rahmah: Variant Romanisation of *rahman* (see below).

Rahman: *Ar-Rahman*, meaning "the Merciful One" is, after the name of Allah, one of the most important and commonly used of the Names of God.

Rahmat: Variant Romanisation of *rahman* (see above).

Rai: Name of a tribal group from the Indian subcontinent.

Rashida: Feminine Arabic form of *rashid* meaning "righteous" or "guided".

Rashool: Variant Romanisation of *rasool* (see below).

Rasool: Arabic meaning "messenger". Also found as *rasul*.

Raza: The surname of the founder of the *Barelwi* movement in Islam, Maulana Ahmed Raza Khan of Bareilly in India (1856-1921CE).

Razvi: Pertaining to Raza (see above).

Razvia: Pertaining to Raza (see above).

Rehman: Variant Romanisation of *rahman* (see above).

Risalah: The word describing the mission of a *rasul* or messenger.

Riza: Variant Romanisation of Raza (see above).

Rizvia: Pertaining to Raza (see above).

Rizwan: Meaning "delight" or "approval".

Sadiq: Arabic, meaning "the truthful", a title of Imam Ja'far al-Sadiq (699-765CE), founder of a *Shi'a* school of law.

Sad'r: Arabic, meaning "chief" or "head" of an organisation.

Sahaba: Arabic for "the *Companions* of the Prophet".

Saifee: Relates to the followers of Saifuddin, a spiritual leader of the *Bohra Shi'a* Muslims.

Sajadeen: Plural of *sajid*, meaning "people who prostrate in prayer".

Sajedeen: Variant Romanisation of *sajadeen* (see above).

Salam: Arabic, meaning "peace".

Sanaullah: Meaning "admirer of Allah", a common male name among Muslims.

Seerah: Or *Si'ra*. Arabic, meaning "character", "conduct" or "way of life", the term is especially used in relation to the Prophet Muhammad's biography and way of life.

Shafyiah: Orthodox *Sunni* school of jurisprudence named after its founder, Muhammad ibn Idris al-Shafi'l (767-820CE).

Shah: Meaning "king" or "prince". An honorific title for a leader.

Shahadah: The basic declaration of Islam, that "there is no God but Allah and that Muhammad is his Messenger".

Shair: Meaning "poet".

Shajalal: See "Jalal" above.

Shari'ah: From the Arabic root *shara'a* meaning "to prescribe". It refers to the Islamic way of life in the *Qur'an* and the *Sunnah* as interpreted, in *Sunni* Islam, by the four orthodox schools of the law.

Sharif: Meaning "noble".

Shi'a: From the Arabic word meaning "faction" or "party", its original use was in relation to the supporters of the *Caliphate* of Ali ibn Abi Talib. Today it refers to the tradition of Islam which is organised in three main groupings, the *'Ithna Ashariyyah* (*Twelvers*), the *Isma'ilis* (or *Seveners*) and the *Zaydis* (or *Fivers*) who are found in the Yemen.

Shomity: A Bengali word meaning "association".

Shoura: Variant Romanisation of *Shura*, meaning "consultation".

Siddiqia: Pertaining to Abu Bakr Siddiq (see Abu Bakr above).

Siraat: Variant Romanisation of *Seerah* (see above).

Sirajia: Meaning of "light".

Somity: Variant Romanisation of *shomity* (see above).

Sufat: Meaning "best friend".

Sufi: The name of the mystical tradition within Islam which emphasises its inner or esoteric aspects as well as its outer or exoteric forms.

Sughra: Feminine Arabic form of *saghir* meaning "small".

Sugra: Variant Romanisation of *sughra* (see above).

Sultana: A title for the wife of a Sultan, or a woman ruler.

Sultania: Pertaining to a *sultana* (see above).

Sunnat: The Arabic for "custom", referring to the spoken, approved, or acted example of the Prophet Muhammad which shows Muslims how to live.

Sunnatwal: Arabic meaning "*Sunnat* and…" (see above).

Sunnawatul: Variant Romanisation of *sunnatwal* (see above).

Sunni: From the Arabic word *sunnat* meaning "custom", it refers to the majority of the global Islamic community who recognise the four "*Rightly-Guided*" *Caliphs* and are organised in one of four orthodox schools of law.

Sukhan: Persian word meaning "talk".

Surati: Alternative Romanisation of *Surti* (see above).

Surti: Denotes origins in Surat in Gujarat, India.

Tableeg: Variant Romanisation of *tabligh* (see below).

Tablig: Variant Romanisation of *tabligh* (see below).

Tabligh: Arabic meaning "preaching" or "message"

Tablique: Variant Romanisation of *tabligh* (see above).

Tabliquel: Pertaining to *tabligh* (see above).

Tabuk: Name of a place where the prophet Muhammad led a military expedition and made a treaty with the Christian prince of Ailah.

Tafreeh: Meaning "entertainment" or "recreation".

Tahrir: Arabic, meaning "liberation".

Taiba: Variant Romanisation of *taiyabah* (see below).

Taijdare: Meaning "crown", a title used of the Prophet Muhammad in the Persian language.

Taiyabah: Meaning "well disposed" or "pleasant", the word often appears together with Madina (see above).

Taleem: Variant Romanisation of *ta'lim* (see below).

Taleemul: Arabic meaning "teaching of…"

Ta'lim: Arabic meaning "teaching".

Talimud: Variant Romanisation of *taleemul* (see above)

Talimuddin: Arabic meaning "teaching the religion".

Talimul: Variant Romanisation of *taleemul* (see above).

Taqwa: Arabic meaning "piety".

Taraqqi: Arabic meaning "development" or "promotion". It often refers specifically to various *Sufi* "ways" within Islam.

Tarteel: Reciting the Qur'an in a correct, clear and distinct way.

Tauheedul: Pertaining to *tawhid* (see below).

Tayabba: Variant Romanisation of *taiyabah* (see above).

Tawakkulia: The name of a *Sufi* tradition.

Tawakullia: Meaning "reliance".

Tawhid: The verbal noun in Arabic of *wahhada* meaning "to make one", referring to the Absoluteness and Oneness of God.

Tayba: Variant Romanisation of *taiyabah* (see above).

Tayyibah: Variant Romanisation of *taiyabah* (see above).

Tehrik: Meaning "movement".

Telemuddin: Variant Romanisation of *talimuddin* (see above).

Ujala: Arabic, meaning "daylight" or "bright".

Ul: Alternative Romanisation of the Arabic definite article *al* (see above) meaning "the".

Ulama: Plural of *'alim* meaning "learned" and referring to Muslim religious scholars who are competent to make judgements and lead the Muslim community. In the *Shi'a* tradition of Islam such competent people are called *Mullahs* or *Mujtahids*.

Ulami: Variant Romanisation of *ulama* (see above).

Ulma: Variant Romanisation of *ulama* (see above).

Uloom: Arabic plural of *Ilm*, meaning "knowledge" or "science", usually used in the sense of the religious sciences.

Umar: A variant Romanisation of the name of the *Caliph* Omar (see above).

Urdu: The national language of Pakistan.

Us: Variant Romanisation of the Arabic definite article *al-* (see above) meaning "the".

Usman: Variant Romanisation of 'Uthman ibn 'Affan (d.656CE), the name of the third *Caliph*.

Validesultan: Meaning "father of the sultan".

Vohra: Variant Romanisation of *Bohra* (see above).

Waqf: Meaning "endowment" or "trust".

Wal: Arabic meaning "and the…"

Zahra: Meaning "the resplendent", a title used of Fatimah, one of the daughters of the Prophet.

Zakaria: Part of the name of an Indian Muslim *hadith* scholar who loved and died in Madina, *Maulana* Zakariya. He is the author of "Tablighi Nisab" used by the Tablighi Jama'at.

Zakarryia: Variant Romanisation of Zakaria (see above).

Zaminder: Persian, meaning "farmer" or "landlord".

Zawiya: Variant romanisation of *zawiyah* (see below).

Zawiyah: Arabic meaning "corner". In North Africa it tends to refer to a small *mosque*, but it also often refers to a *Sufi* meeting place for prayer and invocation of God's name.

Zawiyya: Variant Romanisation of *zawiyah* (see above).

Zeenatul: Variant Romanisation of *zinatul* (see below).

Zinatul: Meaning "decoration of …".

Ziyaul: Pertaining to *zia* meaning "brightness" or "light".

INTRODUCING THE SIKH COMMUNITY

SIKHS IN THE UNITED KINGDOM

Beginnings in the UK

Over eighty per cent of the world's 20,159,000 Sikhs live in the Punjab, in the Indian subcontinent. The older Punjab Province was partitioned in 1947 with the end of British rule in the sub-continent, when West Punjab became part of Pakistan and East Punjab part of India. Most Sikhs living in the UK are of Punjabi ethnic origin.

A young Sikh prince called Dalip Singh, the son of Maharaja Ranjit Singh, was exiled to the UK and was one of the first Sikhs to reside here. He acquired the Elveden Estate in Norfolk and this place is now frequently visited by Sikhs marking their early connections with the UK. Although a number of Sikhs settled in the UK between the 1920s and the 1940s, the vast majority arrived in the 1950s and 1960s.

Many of these came directly to the UK from the Punjab, although a significant minority came from East Africa and other former British colonies to which members of their families had initially migrated. Many Sikhs served in the British Indian armies in the First and Second World Wars and a number of ex-servicemen migrated to Britain, particularly after the Second World War. A few Sikhs in the UK are converts, but conversion to the Sikh religion is not common because Sikhism is not an actively proselytising faith and accords respect to all other faiths.

The size of the Sikh community in the UK is estimated to be around 350,000-500,000. This makes it the largest Sikh community outside the Indian subcontinent. Sikhs reside in most large towns and cities in the UK and the most substantial communities are to be found in Birmingham, Bradford, Cardiff, Coventry, Glasgow, Leeds, Leicester, Greater London (especially in Southall) and Wolverhampton.

The first *gurdwara* in the UK was opened in Shepherd's Bush in 1911 at the initiative of Sant Teja Singh, and with funding from Maharaja Bhupinder Singh of Patiala. As the size of the

UK Sikh community grew, the number of *gurdwaras* increased. The Registrar General's list of certified places of worship gives 178 *gurdwaras* in England and Wales and this directory records 202 *gurdwaras* in the UK of which 190 are in England and Wales.

Community Languages

Most Sikhs in the UK speak Punjabi and English, with almost all *gurdwaras* running Punjabi classes. Gurmukhi is the script of the Sikh Scriptures, which is also used for writing the modern Punjabi language. Punjabi is held in great esteem and respect by Sikhs and the community has gone to great efforts to transmit it to second and third generation children. Some Sikhs who came to the UK from East Africa may also be orally fluent in Swahili. Punjabi speakers can communicate to some degree with Urdu and Hindi speakers as the three languages have some common vocabulary and grammar.

ORIGINS AND DEVELOPMENT OF SIKHISM

The Ten Gurus

Sikhs understand the Sikh *dharam* (the Sikh way of life), also known as *Gurmat* and *Khalsa Panth* (meaning "path of the pure ones", from *Khalsa* meaning "pure ones" and *panth* meaning "path" or "road") to be an original, revealed religion. It is based upon the teachings of the ten *Gurus* of Sikhism. The first *Guru* and founder of the faith, Guru Nanak Dev (1469-1539) was born in the Punjab at a place called Talwandi, renamed Nankana Sahib in his honour, which is now within the territory of the state of Pakistan.

Sikhs believe that Guru Nanak Dev was born in an enlightened state. Accounts of his early life illustrate that not only was he a precocious child, but that he also possessed divine charisma. When he was about thirty years old, he received the call to preach God's Word and over the next twenty-two years undertook four great journeys called *Udasis*. He is believed to have travelled extensively within and beyond the Indian subcontinent, as far as Assam in the east, Sri Lanka in the south, and the Middle East in the west, including Baghdad and the Muslim holy places of Makka and Madina.

He preached a message of universal love, peace and brotherhood and emphasised worship of the one God. He taught that the worship of God, in whatever tradition one practised it, should be sincere and honest and not clouded by hypocrisy or ritualism. He eventually settled at Kartarpur in the Punjab and founded a community who became known as *Sikhs* (meaning disciples, or learners).

Guru Nanak Dev was succeeded by nine other *Gurus*: Guru Angad Dev (1504-1552); Guru Amar Das (1479-1574); Guru Ram Das (1534-1581); Guru Arjan Dev (1563-1606); Guru Hargobind (1595-1644); Guru Har Rai (1631-1661); Guru Har Krishan (1656-1664); Guru Tegh Bahadur (1622-1675); and Guru Gobind Singh (1666-1708). Sikhs believe that the *Gurus* who conveyed God's word were all spiritually one.

In an Indian context, the word *guru* usually refers to a spiritual leader. But among the Sikhs, when applied to their ten *Gurus*, its significance is much greater. The Sikh *Gurus* are seen as the divine teachers and exemplars who conveyed God's Word. They are not, however, objects of worship since the Word they convey is itself the *Guru*.

After the line of the ten *Gurus*, Sikhism acknowledges no more human *Gurus*. The tenth *Guru*, Guru Gobind Singh, vested spiritual authority in the *Guru Granth Sahib* (the Sikh scripture) and temporal authority in the *Khalsa Panth*. Henceforth, the living *Guru*, the *Guru Granth Sahib*, was to be the eternal *Guru* embodying the Divine word. In 1699, Guru Gobind Singh instituted *Amrit Pahul* (see below) for both men and women, and in doing so completed the spiritual and temporal structure of the Sikh faith in the form of the *Khalsa Panth*. [See also the section on "the Namdhari Sikh Community" in the Chapter on "Some Other Religious Communities and Groups"].

History

Sikhism has distinctive religious beliefs and institutions together with its own language, literature, tradition and conventions. The early Sikh community faced considerable persecution in the Mughal Empire and later many Sikhs were martyred for their faith. However, the Sikh community in the Punjab eventually emerged as a temporal as well as spiritual community with its own military, economic and governmental structures. It was a sovereign nation under Maharaja Ranjit Singh (1799-1849) and remained so until the advent of the British Raj in the Punjab in 1849.

The Sikh *Gurus* founded several towns including Amritsar and its *Darbar Sahib* (commonly known among non-Sikhs as the *Golden Temple*) which was developed by Guru Arjan Dev who installed the *Guru Granth Sahib* at its centre. Guru Hargobind built the *Akal Takhat* (seat of the immortal) in front of the *Darbar Sahib*, declaring it to be the seat of temporal authority. The Sikh sovereign, Maharaja Ranjit Singh, spent lavishly on buildings within its precincts, donating gold and other precious gifts.

SOURCES OF SIKH BELIEFS AND PRACTICES

The Guru Granth Sahib

Sikhs believe that God has revealed himself continuously since before the advent of the ten *Gurus* and since their departure continues to do so by means of the scriptures. The *Guru Granth Sahib* is the most revered of the Sikh scriptures. This is the honorific title for those Sikh scriptures which, in academic usage, are often called *Adi Granth*. *Adi Granth* is also the name of an earlier version of the present scriptures, compiled by Guru Arjan Dev and installed by him at Amritsar in 1604. *Ad* or *adi* means "first", in importance, and *Granth* means volume.

This original manuscript version of the *Adi Granth* is often referred to as the *Kartarpuri Birh*

(*Birh* meaning version), after the place name of Kartarpur in the Punjab where it is kept. In this manuscript version there are 5551 *shabads* (hymns) set to 30 *rag* (musical compositions) laid out over 975 pages. The *Adi Granth* contains the teaching of the first five *Gurus* and the *Bhagat Bani*, which contains verses from Hindu and Muslim saints which were found to be compatible with Sikh teachings. These were included to underline that divine truth could be perceived by anyone from any nation, creed or caste.

In 1706, at Damdama Sahib, Guru Gobind Singh added Guru Tegh Bahadur's *shabads*. In 1708, Guru Gobind Singh bestowed the status of *Guru* upon this *Damdama Birh*. The current canonical version of the *Guru Granth Sahib* in its standard modern print version now contains 5817 *shabads* set to 31 *rags*, in 1430 pages.

Dasam Granth

The *Dasam Granth* contains numerous writings of Guru Gobind Singh, together with the work of some poets. It was compiled by Bhai Mani Singh, who was the *granthi* (reader of the *Granth*) of the *Darbar Sahib* and was completed in 1734. Both the *Guru Granth Sahib* and the *Dasam Granth* are written in the Gurmukhi script.

Rahit Nama

Rahit Nama (*Code of Discipline*) consists of a set of principles according to which a Sikh's way of life should be conducted. They cover spiritual, moral and social discipline, and are reputed to be based on the injunctions of Guru Gobind Singh and compiled by various Sikh theologians from the late seventeenth to the late nineteenth century. However, the *Gurbani* (teaching of the *Gurus* - see further below) provides the fundamental guidelines and takes precedence in interpreting and following the *Rahit Nama*.

Rahit Maryada

Rahit Maryada is the Sikh *Code of Conduct* which is published by the Shromani Gurdwara

Parbandhak Committee in Amritsar, established in 1920 in the wake of the Gurdwara Reform Movement. Amongst its responsibilities are the organisation and administration (in accordance with Sikh tenets) of a large number of *gurdwaras* in the Punjab, as well as hospitals and educational institutions. The *Code of Conduct* was first drawn up in 1936, but was formally approved and adopted with some amendments in 1945.

Works of Bhai Gurdas and Bhai Nandlal

Although they do not have the same status as the *Guru Granth Sahib* and the *Dasam Granth*, expositions by Bhai Gurdas and Bhai Nandlal are also highly regarded and are approved for reading and discourse in *gurdwaras*.

Bhai Gurdas (1551-1637CE) was a Sikh scholar and theologian of distinction to whom the fifth Guru, Arjan Dev, dictated the *Adi Granth* when it was first compiled. His own thirty-nine *vars* (theological and historical expositions in verse form) were held in very high esteem by the fifth *Guru* who declared that these writings would be a key to the proper understanding of the *Guru Granth Sahib*. Bhai Nandlal (1633-1713) was an eminent scholar and poet who worked in the Mughal Court of the Emperor Aurangzeb. He was a follower of Guru Gobind Singh and his writings, which were largely in the Persian language, were on Sikh philosophy.

KEY SIKH BELIEFS

Definitions

In the *Rahit Maryada* (see above) a Sikh is defined as one who believes in *Akal Purakh* (the one immortal God), the ten *Gurus*, the *Guru Granth Sahib* and the *Gurbani* (the teaching of the ten *Gurus* considered as a unity and incorporated in the *Guru Granth Sahib*). The *Gurbani* is also known as *Gurshabad* (or hymns of the *Guru*) and is believed by Sikhs to be divine guidance. A Sikh also believes in the *Amrit Pahul* (the Sikh form of initiation) of the tenth *Guru* and adheres to no other religion.

God

Sikhs are strictly monotheistic (believing in only one God). This one God is known among Sikhs by many names including Ram, Mohan, Gobind, Hari, Nirankar, and others. However, the two names traditionally used in worship, and especially in *Nam Japna* (the recitation of God's name), are *Satnam* (*sat* meaning "true" and *nam* meaning "name") and *Waheguru* (translated as "Wonderful Lord").

Sikhs believe that God is *nirgun* (transcendent) and also *sagun* (immanent) but that God never becomes incarnate. It is believed that God can be experienced but is beyond human comprehension. The *Mul Mantar*, with which every section of the *Guru Granth Sahib* begins, is a distillation of the fundamental belief of Sikhism that there is only one God: "There is but One God, the Eternal Truth, the Creator, without fear, without enmity, timeless, immanent, beyond birth and death, self-existent: by the grace of the *Guru*, made known."

Sikhs believe that creation evolved slowly as a result of the creative will of God, developing from lower to higher forms of life: that from air came water, from water came the lower forms of life, leading to plants, birds and animals and culminating in humans as the supreme form of created life on earth.

Goal of Life

Guru Nanak Dev taught that everything which exists or happens ultimately does so within God's will and that nothing exists or occurs outside of it. This concept of the divine order or will is known as *hukam*. The purpose of a human life is understood as being to seek its creator and to merge with God, thus breaking the cycle of birth and death. The highest form of life on this earth is the human.

Since human beings are conscious of their actions and the consequences of them a human life is therefore the time when the cycle of transmigration can potentially be broken The *karam* (actions and their consequences) of this life partly determine whether a person will achieve union with God. Failure to do so leads to the cycle of rebirth which may include lower forms of life than human. Liberation from rebirth is known as *mukti*.

Barriers to the liberation of the soul are believed to include *maya*, which is seen as an illusory, materialistic view of the world, producing ignorance of one's own true nature and destiny and of God's will. This results in *haumai* (self-centredness), giving rise to *kam* (lust), *karodh* (anger), *lobh* (greed), *moh* (worldly attachment/obsessions) and *hankar* (pride), all of which block union with God. One must therefore overcome these barriers, developing instead *santokh* (contentment), *dan* (charity), *daya* (kindness), *parsanta* (happiness) and *nimarta* (humility).

The path to union with God is seen as having five stages: *Dharam Khand* (the region of realising one's spiritual duty), *Gian Khand* (region of divine knowledge), *Saram Khand* (region of wisdom and effort), *Karam Khand* (region of divine grace) and *Sach Khand* (region of truth).

Khalsa Panth

Sikhs believe in the collective identity of the *Khalsa Panth* (see above) as a society of equals irrespective of their background. The first five people to be initiated in it are known as the *Panj Pyare* (the five beloved ones). These five, from a variety of caste-groups, volunteered from the crowd of around 80,000 Sikhs who had been summoned by Guru Gobind Singh to Anandpur Sahib on 30th March 1699 when the *Guru* asked who would offer sacrifice to the *Guru*.

Prior to their initiation, the *Panj Pyare* had the original names of Daya Ram, Dharam Das, Mohkam Chand, Himmat Rai, and Sahib Chand. They were all given the name Singh as a substitute for their original caste names, in order to signify that Sikhism recognises no castes. Guru Gobind Singh knelt before the *Panj Pyare* and requested them to give the *Amrit Pahul* to him thus emphasising the importance of the *Khalsa Panth*.

TRADITIONS IN SIKHISM

Sikhs do not acknowledge internal groupings on the basis of doctrinal schools. Organisations do, however, exist within the *Panth* to cater for various interests or to reflect particular aspects of Sikh life. An example is that of the Sewa Panthial, a group devoted to the service of humanity founded in memory of Bhai Kanhaya. He was a Sikh who cared for the wounded without any discrimination whether they were the "enemies" or Sikh soldiers, and was highly praised for this by Guru Gobind Singh. When, in reply to a question, he stated that he saw no distinction between friend and foe but saw the *Guru* residing in all, the *Guru* warmly embraced him.

There are also groups whose origins can be found in the revivalist movements which have developed throughout Sikh history. These have generally been founded by Sikh individuals who are often given the honorific titles of *Sant*, *Bhai* or *Baba* on the basis of their reputation for spiritual guidance and teaching. They are expounders of the *Gurbani* and may hold significant influence within particular *gurdwaras* or Sikh organisations.

SIKH LIFE

Nam Japna

Nam Japna involves meditating on God and his attributes, reading and contemplating *bani* (passages) from the *Guru Granth Sahib*. It is said by Sikhs to result in being *gurmukh* (God-filled and God-centred) as opposed to being *manmukh* (self-centred). *Nam Japna* can be an individual or a group activity. In congregational worship it can be facilitated by *kirtan*, the singing of hymns from the *Guru Granth Sahib*, accompanied by music played on drums, harmoniums and other instruments. Although prayers can be said either individually or as a family, *sadh sangat* (congregational worship) is very important to Sikhs since it is believed that being in the company of enlightened souls helps purify one's own soul.

Birth, Marriage and Death

A few weeks after the birth of a child, a naming ceremony may be held in the *gurdwara*. After a prayer from the family, the name of the child is taken from the first letter of the *vak*, which is a passage of the *Guru Granth Sahib* read after its random opening.

Sikh marriage is known as *Anand Karaj* (ceremony of bliss). It is not viewed simply as a social or civil contract, but is seen as a spiritual state since living in this world and discharging family duties are advocated as the Sikh way of life. The marriage service involves the recitation of four stanzas, called *Lavan*, from the *Guru Granth Sahib*, in the presence of the bride, the bridegroom and their relatives and friends. After the recitation of each *Lav*, the bride and bridegroom usually walk around the *Guru Granth Sahib*. The ceremony concludes with *Gurmat*, advice on the institution of marriage and its importance and then, as is usual with all Sikh ceremonies, with *ardas*, a collective prayer said in the presence of relatives and friends.

At death, Sikhs normally cremate the body. At the crematorium the *granthi* leads the mourners in the reading of *Kirtan Sohila* from the *Guru Granth Sahib*, and this is followed by a prayer. The family and friends then return to the gurdwara where relevant passages are read from the *Guru Granth Sahib* and, following *ardas*, *langar* is taken before all leave for home. The family may also have a *sehaj path* (a reading, with breaks, of the entire *Guru Granth Sahib* over several days) in memory of the departed soul as well as to console the immediate family and friends.

Ethics

Sikhs believe that God should always be remembered in the course of everyday life. Guru Nanak Dev taught that truth is above everything, but that truthful living is higher than truth. There are certain ethical principles which are intrinsic to Sikh belief and practice. Foremost amongst these are: *nam japna* (reciting the name), *kirat karna* (earning a living by honest and approved means) and *vand chhakna* (sharing with the needy). *Sewa* (service) to the community at large, or in helping to meet a particular need for the benefit of others, is also an essential part of Sikh life.

The concept of equality was of central importance to Guru Nanak Dev. He taught that all people are born with the opportunity to attain *mukti*, regardless of caste or creed and of whether they are rich or poor, male or female, high or low, educated or uneducated. What influences *mukti* is the *karam*, *maya* and *haumai* of individuals and the grace of the *Guru* in overcoming *haumai* and *maya*. The ten Sikh *Gurus* did not believe in any *caste* distinctions and taught that every person is equal before God.

Equality

The Sikh concept of equality embraces women as well as men in both secular and religious life and was enjoined in the teachings and practices of the Gurus. Women have played a significant role in Sikhism, for instance at the first *Amrit Pahul* ceremony in Anandpur in 1699 in which Guru Gobind Singh's wife added sugar to the water. Both women and men can be fully initiated into the Sikh religion and can act as a *granthi* (see section below) in a *gurdwara*. However, in practice social and cultural conventions may influence gender roles.

Amrit Pahul

Amrit Pahul is the Sikh name for initiation into the *Khalsa Panth*. *Amrit* (the nectar of everlasting life) refers to the sweetened water used in *Amrit Pahul*. When coupled with adherence to the ethical principles of Sikhism this initiation is seen as the way to spiritual development and hence to the realisation of God's grace. The ceremony is for women as well as men and takes place at an age when the person can understand its significance.

The ceremony can take place anywhere, providing that it is held in the presence of the *Guru Granth Sahib* and that five members of the *Khalsa Panth*, who have themselves taken *amrit* and for this purpose constitute the *Panj Pyare*,

are present to officiate. The ceremony follows the same practice as the original *amrit* ceremony carried out by Guru Gobind Singh.

Amrit is prepared by mixing sugar with water by stirring the ingredients with a *khanda* (double-edged sword) and reciting the *Jap Ji*, *Jap*, *Ten Swayas* and *Charipan* from the *Dasam Granth* and six stanzas from the *Anand*. The initiate is also inducted into the Sikh code of discipline, takes the vows of the *Khalsa* and is then offered *amrit* and has some of it sprinkled on the eyes and hair.

The taking of *amrit* is an expression of commitment as a Sikh and a Sikh who has taken *amrit* is known as an *Amritdhari* Sikh. Sikhs who have not yet taken *amrit* and who do not wear the long hair and other outward symbols of Sikhism are sometimes referred to as *Sahajdhari* (literally meaning "slow adopters") Sikhs. They include those who believe in Sikhism but have deferred the commitment involved in taking *amrit* and those who have lapsed and would need to take *amrit* again if they were to return to the status of an *Amritdhari*. The term *Keshdhari* is often used for those Sikhs who keep a beard, uncut hair and turban whether or not they have taken *amrit*.

Five Ks

Many Sikhs expect to be initiated at some stage in their life. Belonging to the *Khalsa* involves taking *amrit* and wearing the five articles of faith which distinguish individual men and women as members of the *Khalsa*, commonly known as "the five Ks" because the Punjabi word for each begins with the sound of "k". The "five Ks" are:

Kesh (uncut hair)
Kesh refers to the uncut hair which is required of Sikhs as one of the outwardly distinctive signs of Sikh identity. Men usually tie up and cover their hair with a *turban* and some women may also choose to wear a *turban*. *Turbans* may be of any colour and tied in a variety of styles. Usually the style and colour of a *turban* signify personal preference only. Only in certain cases do colours have particular meanings.

As well as the "five Ks", the *turban* is seen as an essential and complementary adjunct to maintain the sanctity of the *kesh* and is treated by Sikhs with utmost respect. Historically, it is also a symbol of identity linked with royalty and responsibility. *Kesh* applies not only to the hair on the head and face: *Khalsa* Sikhs are enjoined not to cut or remove hair from any part of the body.

Kangha
A small comb which should be worn in the hair. It is used to keep the hair clean and symbolises orderly spirituality.

Kara
A steel bracelet worn by Sikhs, which is understood as a reminder of the universality of God and a symbol of spiritual allegiance, of brotherhood and sisterhood, as well as being a reminder of the covenant with the *Guru* to do good.

Kachhahera (or kachchha or kachha)
A knee length garment, tailored in a special manner, and usually worn under other clothes. It symbolises modesty and moral restraint.

Kirpan
A ceremonial sword which is a reminder of the dignity and self-respect which Sikhs are called upon to uphold. It represents a readiness to fight in self-defence or in the protection of the weak and oppressed.

In short, the "five ks" have not only a moral and practical significance, but also a deep spiritual importance and the wearing of them is, for Sikhs, a sign of obedience to the will of God and of care for, and obedience to, the *Gurus* and their teachings.

Singh and Kaur

As instituted by Guru Gobind Singh, all Sikh men take the religious name *Singh* (meaning lion) and all Sikh women have *Kaur* (meaning princess) as their second name, for example, Paramjit Kaur (female), Mohinder Singh (male). This practice relates to Guru Gobind

Singh's abolition of the *caste* system which was reflected in the surnames used by people.

It must, however, be noted that the name *Singh* does not necessarily mean that a person is a Sikh, since this name was common in India before the rise of Sikhism. In addition, in the UK, some Sikh wives use their husband's name of *Singh* as a surname following *Kaur*.

Sikhs will also often have a third name which may be derived from a place or a *got* (patrilinear clan) name. Some Sikhs use this third name as a surname, whilst others use only *Singh* or *Kaur*.

Diet

Sikhs are enjoined to avoid tobacco, alcohol and other intoxicants. Meat is only permitted for consumption if it is *jhatka*, where the animal is killed with one stroke instantaneously. Those Sikhs who eat meat must not eat *halal* meat (meat from animals killed according to Muslim law). Many Sikhs are, however, vegetarians and meat is never served in the *langar* (see below) in *gurdwaras*.

Pilgrimage

Although pilgrimage is not a religious duty for Sikhs, places associated with the Sikh *Gurus* are treated as places of pilgrimage. Many Sikhs going to the Punjab will visit the *Darbar Sahib* and some may also visit other sites, particularly Anandpur Sahib. A visit to the birthplace of Guru Nanak Dev at Nankana Sahib in Pakistan usually takes place in October/November each year when several hundred Sikhs from the UK join their fellow Sikhs from the Punjab in India and from other countries.

SIKH WORSHIP

Gurdwara

The Sikh place of congregational worship is called the *gurdwara*, meaning "doorway of the Guru". The *gurdwara* is not only a place for formal worship, but it is also a centre for religious education. In the West, other activities also take place in *gurdwaras*, such as Punjabi classes, social activities such as youth clubs, women's groups, welfare provision and elderly day centres. In keeping with the Sikh tradition of service, *gurdwaras* often provide temporary accommodation for the needy.

A *gurdwara* is usually recognisable from the outside by the *Nishan Sahib* (from *Nisham* meaning "flag" whilst *Sahib* is an honorific title of respect). This is normally a triangular saffron flag on which is sewn the *khanda* (*Khalsa* emblem) made out of black cloth. The emblem consists of a symbolic two-edged sword surrounded by a circle outside of which are two further swords, which symbolise the temporal and spiritual powers of God.

Before entering the hall of worship, as a mark of respect, shoes must be removed and heads must be covered. Visitors should ensure that they are dressed modestly. No smoking or drinking of alcohol is permitted anywhere in a *gurdwara* and nor should tobacco or alcohol be taken into the *gurdwara*. On entering the foyer of the *gurdwara*, visitors may see pictures of Sikh martyrs and in the prayer hall itself there may be pictures of Guru Nanak Dev, of Guru Gobind Singh and of other *Gurus*.

On entering the prayer hall, Sikh worshippers kneel, touching the floor with their foreheads before the *Guru Granth Sahib*. This should not be mistaken for regarding the *Guru Granth Sahib* as an object of worship since this is prohibited within Sikhism but rather as the respect shown to the revealed word of God believed to be within the scripture. At this time a worshipper also usually make a voluntary offering of money or fruit, milk or sugar.

As a social tradition, men and women tend to sit separately on opposite sides of the prayer hall. Children often remain with their mothers. Worshippers sit on the carpeted floor, with their legs crossed as a mark of respect for the *Guru Granth Sahib*. In the prayer hall, the focal point is the *Guru Granth Sahib* which is placed upon a dais. The dais is a raised platform with a canopy above it. The *Guru Granth Sahib* is placed on cushions and covered by *rumalas* (expensive cloths).

A Sikh is called upon to rise early and after a bath or shower to meditate on one God. Prayers can be said individually, together with the family or with other Sikhs in a congregation. Some Sikh homes may have a separate room in which the *Guru Granth Sahib* is kept but *diwan* (congregational worship) in the *gurdwara* is regarded as particularly important.

Sadh Sangat

No single day of the week is holy for Sikhs. In the UK, for convenience, the *gurdwara* is usually visited for *sadh sangat* on a Saturday or Sunday. The *gurdwara* is usually open daily and some Sikhs visit it every morning and evening. *Diwan* usually lasts between two and four hours.

A typical Sikh religious service consists of *Gurbani kirtan* (hymn-singing), a discourse on the divine name, followed by *Ardas* (a final corporate prayer) and is concluded by *Karah Prashad* (see below) and the sharing of *langar* (see below). The *Ardas* ends with the invocation of God's blessing on everyone and not just on the followers of the faith. In the morning service *Asa di Var* is followed by *Anand Sahib* and a collective prayer by the congregation.

Most Sikhs also recite the *Japji Sahib*, a prayer composed by Guru Nanak Dev. More devout Sikhs also recite *Jaap* (the tenth Guru's composition) and *Shabad Hazare* followed by the evening *Rehras* and late evening *Kirtan Sohila*. In the evening service, *Rehras* is usually followed by *Kirtan* and at the end of the service *Kirtan Sohila* is recited when the *Guru Granth Sahib* is laid to rest, usually in a separate room.

Path

The *Path* is the liturgical reading of the *Guru Granth Sahib*. On special occasions it is read from cover to cover by relays of readers. This form of reading is known as *Akhand Path* (which means "continuous reading") totalling forty-eight hours. It occurs at most Sikh festivals, when the path begins in the morning two days prior to the festival and also at weddings. *Saptah Path* is a form of *path* which is not continuous and which takes seven days.

Sehaj Path also is not continuous and is without time limit for the completion of reading.

While reading the *Guru Granth Sahib* the reader or another person close by will wave over it a *chaur sahib* (a whisk made of white yaks' hair). This is not intended to serve as a fly whisk or a fan, but is waved as a sign of respect for the *Guru Granth Sahib*.

Karah Prashad and Langar

Worship ends with the distribution of *Karah Prashad*. This is a sweet food made from semolina or brown flour, sugar, clarified butter and water which is served to every person present. *Karah Prashad* is blessed during *Ardas* at the end of worship and is therefore considered to be sanctified food. Its free distribution to every person present symbolises the central Sikh belief in the equality and unity of humankind and the repudiation of caste distinctions.

Langar, a communal meal, is provided free of charge after the service to all who attend the *gurdwara*. So that vegetarians may eat it, the food provided, which has been blessed, will not contain meat, fish or eggs or their by-products. Both *Karah Prashad* and *Langar* symbolise universal fraternity and equality since it is intended that all should eat together regardless of their social position.

SIKH CALENDAR AND FESTIVALS

Calendar

Most dates for Sikh festivals are calculated according to the lunar calendar and may vary from the Gregorian calendar within a period of fifteen days. A few festivals, notably *Vaisakhi*, are calculated by the *Vikrami* (North India) solar calendar, which is why the date of *Vaisakhi* remains almost constant in the *Gregorian* calendar. Sikh calendars and some Sikh authors use a dating system based on the first day of Guru Nanak Dev's birth. This calendar is known as *Sammat Nanak Shahi*. 1997 is the *Nanak Shahi Sammat* 528. The approximate times of the occurrence of the festivals which are cited below refer to when they take place according to the *Gregorian* calendar.

Festivals

Gurpurbs

Festivals which are celebrated by means of *Akhand Path*, *Kirtan*, prayers, religious lectures, *Karah Prasad* and *langar*. Those which specifically commemorate the birth or death of a *Guru* are known as *Gurpurbs*. The four major *Gurpurbs* which are celebrated in the UK are, in calendar order:

Guru Nanak Dev's birthday (November)
The celebration lasts for three days.

Martyrdom of Guru Tegh Bahadur
(November or December)

Guru Gobind Singh's Birthday
(December or January)

Martyrdom of Guru Arjan Dev
(May or June)

Other Sikh festivals include:

Installation of the Guru Granth Sahib
This festival occurs in August-September. It celebrates the installation of the *Adi Granth* in Amritsar in 1604.

Vaisakhi (April)
This celebrates the day in 1699 when Guru Gobind Singh founded the order of the *Khalsa* by offering *amrit* to the *Panj Pyare*. This is nearly always celebrated on 13th April, but very occasionally on 14th April, due to the discrepancy between the *Vikrami* and *Gregorian* solar calendars. On this day Sikhs usually replace the cover of the *Nishan Sahib* (see under section on *gurdwara* above) which flies outside the *gurdwara* with a new one, usually in the context of a *nagar kirtan* (procession) carrying the *Guru Granth Sahib* through the streets after *diwan* in the *gurdwara*.

Diwali (Oct/Nov)
For Sikhs, *Diwali* primarily commemorates Guru Hargobind's return from imprisonment by the Mughal Emperor, Jehangir, in Gwalior fort, together with fifty-two Hindu kings for whose freedom the *Guru* had asked. It is thus a festival of deliverance, and is celebrated by the illumination of *gurdwaras*. (*Diwali* is also celebrated by Hindus, but for a different reason).

SIKH ORGANISATIONS

General Organisations

There are national, regional and local Sikh organisations. A new national grouping, the Network of Sikh Organisations, has recently been established to facilitate co-operation within the Sikh community of the UK and to address common issues more effectively. There are also various groups which operate nationally and may have local branches. A number of groups see themselves as specifically related to the political demand for an independent Sikh homeland of Khalistan.

Sikh organisations often serve several functions including the provision of youth and women's activities and education in addition to what are often understood to be more specifically religious functions. Other groups exist which serve the diverse needs of particular sections of the community, including literary, social, cultural or professional societies and associations, for example, the Sikh Cultural Society.

Social Groupings

Sikhism teaches that there are no distinctions between people and rejects the concept of caste (or *Zat*), which therefore has no religious significance for Sikhs. The terms which appear in the titles of some *gurdwaras*, such as *Ramgarhia* and *Bhatra*, are historically related to economic categories and are rooted in the history of the forebears of the families concerned. They do not necessarily define any contemporary economic or social status or who is allowed to attend a *gurdwara*, although they may in practice indicate the background of those who do actually attend.

Historically, *Bhatras* were itinerant traders. Many settled in British ports before the second World War and therefore some of the earliest *gurdwaras* were founded by *Bhatras*. They retain their own organisations in order to maintain their specific traditions and way of life.

Ramgarhias were originally a community of blacksmiths, bricklayers, carpenters, engineers and technicians. The name *Ramgarhia* derives from the name of Guru Ram Das and the fort called Ramgarh, constructed to defend the *Darbar Sahib* by the *misal* (confederation) who thus became known as *Ramgarhias*. The British encouraged groups of *Ramgarhias* to move to East Africa at the end of the nineteenth century to assist in the development of the transport network. As a result of the Africanisation policies of the newly independent East African states, many migrated from there to the UK or arrived as refugees.

Personnel

A Management Committee, which consists of honorary office bearers, president, secretary and treasurer, usually runs a *gurdwara*. The people who serve on such committees are usually elected by the congregation every two years or so. Committees usually run for two years and change on *Vaisakhi Day*. There are also a number of *gurdwaras* which are led by a *sant* (individual charismatic leader), for example, Guru Nanak Nishkam Sewak Jatha of the late Baba Puran Singh Karichowale in Birmingham.

Any adult male or female Sikh is permitted to perform religious ceremonies but many gurdwaras employ a *granthi*. A *granthi* is a professional reader of the *Guru Granth Sahib* and is usually also responsible for its care.

Although the word "priest" is sometimes used by people outside of Sikhism, Sikhism recognises no priesthood and all Sikhs are of equal status in religious terms. Sikh leaders may

therefore be called *Bhai* (brother) or *Bhen* (sister). A *giani* is a learned and devout person who has meditated upon the *Guru Granth Sahib* and interprets its meaning to the congregation. There is often a regular group of *ragis* (singers and musicians) to help with *diwan*.

Other waged personnel may include a caretaker and sometimes, in the larger *gurdwaras*, a community development worker.

FURTHER READING

Babraa, D Kaur, *Visiting a Sikh Temple*, Lutterworth Educational, Guildford, 1981.

Ballard, R, "Differentiation and Disjunction Among the Sikhs", in Ballard, R (ed), *Desh Pardesh: The South Asian Presence in Britain*, Hurst, London, 1994, pp. 88-116 .

Ballard, R and C, "The Sikhs: The Development of South Asian Settlements in Britain," in J L Watson (ed), *Between Two Cultures*, Basil Blackwell, Oxford, 1977.

Beetham, D, *Transport and Turbans: A Comparative Study in Local Politics*, Open University Press, Milton Keynes, 1970.

Bhachu, P, *Twice Migrants: East African Sikh Settlers in Britain*, Tavistock, London, 1985.

Cole, W O, *A Sikh Family in Britain*, Religious Education Press, Oxford, 1973.

Cole, W O, *The Guru in Sikhism*, Darton, Longman and Todd, London, 1982.

Cole, W O, "Sikhs in Britain", in Paul Badham (ed), *Religion, State and Society in Modern Britain*, Edwin Mellen Press, Lampeter, 1989, pp. 259-276.

Cole, W O, *Teach Yourself Sikhism*, Hodder, London, 1994.

Cole, W O and Sambhi, P Singh, *Sikhism*, Ward Lock International, London, 1973.

Cole, W O and Sambhi, P Singh, *A Popular Dictionary of Sikhism*, London, 1990. ˙

Cole, W O and Sambhi, P Singh, *The Sikhs: Their Religious Beliefs and Practices* (2nd edition), Sussex Academic Press, London, 1995.

deSouza, A, *The Sikhs in Britain*, Batsford, London, 1986.

Helweg, A W, *Sikhs in England: The Development of a Migrant Community*, Oxford University Press, Delhi, (2nd edition), 1986.

Henley, A, *Caring for Sikhs and Their Families: Religious Aspects of Care*, National Extension College, Cambridge, 1983.

James, A, *Sikh Children in Britain*, Oxford University Press, London, 1974.

Kalra, S S, *Daughters of Tradition: Adolescent Sikh Girls and their Accommodation to Life in British Society*, Diane Balbir Publications, Birmingham, 1990.

Kalsi, S Singh, *The Evolution of a Sikh Community in Britain*, Community Religions Project, University of Leeds, Leeds, 1992.

Kaur, Kanwaljit and Singh, Indarjit (trans), *Rehat Maryada: A Guide to the Sikh Way of Life*, Sikh Cultural Society, Edgware, 1971.

MacLeod, W H (ed), *Textual Sources for the Study of Sikhism*, Manchester University Press, Manchester, 1984.

McCormack, M Kaur, *Brief Outline of the Sikh Faith*, Sikh Cultural Society of Great Britain, Edgware, London, 1987.

McCormack, M Kaur, *An Introduction to Sikh Belief*, Sikh Cultural Society of Great Britain, Edgware, 1987.

Nesbitt, E, *Aspects of Sikh Tradition in Nottingham*, unpublished MPhil thesis, University of Nottingham, 1980.

Nesbitt, E, *The Religious Lives of Sikh Children in Coventry*, unpublished PhD thesis, University of Warwick, 1995.

Shackle, C, *The Sikhs*, Minority Rights Group, London, 2nd edition, 1986.

Singh, G, *The Sikh Festivals*, Sikh Cultural Society of Great Britain, Edgware, 1982.

Singh, K, *The Sikhs Today*, Orient Longman Ltd, Bombay, 1976.

Singh, Kirpal, *The Sikh Symbols*, Sikh Missionary Society, London, 1970.

Tatla, D Singh, "The Punjab Crisis and Sikh Mobilisation in Britain". in Barot, R (ed), *Religion and Ethnicity: Minorities and Social Change in the Metropolis*, Kok Pharos, Kampen, The Netherlands, 1993, pp. 96–109.

Tatla, D Singh, *The Politics of Homeland: A Study of Ethnic Linkages and Political Mobilisation Among Sikhs in Britain and North America*, unpublished PhD Thesis, University of Warwick, Coventry, 1993.

Tatla, D Singh and Nesbitt, E, *Sikhs in Britain: An Annotated Bibliography*, University of Warwick Centre for Research in Ethnic Relations, Coventry, (revised edition) 1993.

Thomas, T, *Sikhism: The Voice of the Guru*, Open University, Cardiff, 1978.

Thomas, T, "Old Allies, New Neighbours: SIkhs in Britain", in Parsons, G (ed) *The Growth of Religious Diversity: Britain from 1945, Volume I: Traditions*, Routledge, London, 1993, pp. 205–241.

Thomas, T and Ghuman, P, *A Survey of Social and Religious Attitudes Among Sikhs in Cardiff*, Open University, Cardiff, 1976.

Thompson, M, *Sikh Belief and Practice*, Edward Arnold, London, 1985.

SIKH UNITED KINGDOM ORGANISATIONS

The organisations listed in this section include both head offices of organisations with branches throughout the country and organisations which aspire to serve the Sikh community on a UK-wide basis.

Babbar Khalsa International
153 Winson Street, Winson Green, Birmingham, West Midlands, B18 4JW
Tel: 0121-454-2996 **Fax:** 0121-456-4097
Contact: Joga Singh
Position: General Secretary
Other Languages: Punjabi
Affiliations: Council of Sikh Gurdwaras, Birmingham

Bebe Nanki Charitable Trust
Bebe Nanki Gurdwara, 189 Rookery Road, Handsworth, Birmingham, West Midlands, B2
Tel: 0121-551-3489 **Tel:** 0121-551-2120 (h)
Contact: K S Ajimal
Position: General Secretary
Activities: Worship, resource, visits, elderly, women, inter-faith
Other Languages: Punjabi, Hindi
Affiliations: Council of Sikh Gurdwaras, Birmingham; Bebe Nanki Satsang Charitable Trust, Sultanpur Lodhi, Panjab, India
The trust organises two eye camps and two polio camps in Sultanpur Lodhi every year where a free service is provided. They also provide help in major disasters.

British Organisation of Sikh Students
PO Box 4350, Handsworth, Birmingham, West Midlands, B20 2FB
Tel: 01268-558686
EMail: 101731.3045@Compuserve.com.co.uk
Contact: Inderjit Singh
Position: Sevadaar
Activities: Resource, umbrella, youth, newsletters, inter-faith
Other Languages: Panjabi
BOSS provides information on Sikhism and support in setting up Sikh societies and youth groups in universities, colleges and Gurdwaras. BOSS also provides exhibitions, speakers and organises youth camps, youth programmes and sports tournaments.

British Sikh Education Council
10 Featherstone Road, Southall, Middlesex, UB2 5AA
Tel: 0181-574-1902
Contact: Dr Kanawaljit Kaur-Singh
Position: Chairperson
Languages: Panjabi
Affiliation: Sikh Missionary Society; Network of Sikh Organisations

Prepares literature on Sikhism, InService training for teachers, promotion of Sikh Studies; liaison with the DFEE, SCAA, OFSTED, Shap etc on teaching of Religious Education, Collective Worship and values in state schools. Affiliated to the RE Council for England and Wales.

British Sikh Youth Network

c/o The Sikh Centre, 15 Park Street, Foleshill, Coventry, West Midlands, CV6 5AT
Tel: 01203-257509 **Fax:** 01203-524680
EMail: cesak@frost.warwick.ac.uk
Contact: Jagdish Singh
Position: Central Coordinator
Activities: Resource, media, umbrella, visits, youth, women, newsletters, books, inter-faith
Other Languages: Punjabi
Affiliations: National Sikh Forum; Sikh Commonwealth

Dal Khalsa (UK)

PO Box 1427, Handsworth, Birmingham, West Midlands, B21 8BA

European Institute of Sikh Studies

116 Station Road, Harpenden, Hertfordshire, AL5 4RH (h)
Tel: 01582-766447 **Fax:** 01582-766447
Contact: Baljit Singh Bagga
Position: Secretary
Activities: Resource
Other Languages: Punjabi, Hindi

Guru Nanak Nishkam Sewak Jatha

18-20 Soho Road, Handsworth, Birmingham, West Midlands, B21 9BH
Tel: 0121-554-1125 **Fax:** 0121-554-4363
Contact: Bhai Mohinder Singh Ji
Position: Chairman
Activities: Worship, resource, visits youth, elderly, women, inter-faith
Other Languages: Punjabi
Affiliations: Council of Sikh Gurdwaras in Birmingham; Network of Sikh Organisations
A non-political, non-profit making religious charity funded by voluntary donations dedicated to selfless service of humanity and propagation of religious belief and spirituality. All members are unpaid volunteers.

Guru Nanak Sikh Museum

9 Holybones, Leicester, Leicestershire, LE1 4LJ

Tel: 0116-262-8606 **Fax:** 0116-262-8606
Contact: Sarbjit Singh
Position: Assistant Secretary
Activities: Visits, youth, inter-faith
Other Languages: Punjabi
Affiliations: Guru Nanak Gurdwara
First museum of its kind in 1992. Won Heritage Award in 1993, open to the public on Thursdays 1pm to 4pm, other times for educational and other group visits with appointments.

International Sikh Youth Federation

Gate 2 Unit 5b, Booth Street, Warley, Birmingham, West Midlands, B66 2PF
Tel: 0121-565-2550 **Fax:** 0121-565-2550
EMail: 106004.1160@compuserve.com
Contact: Sukhninder Singh
Position: Public Relations Officer
Activities: Resource, media, umbrella, visits, youth, elderly, women, books, inter-faith
Other Languages: Punjabi
Affiliations: All India Sikh Student Federation
Its purpose is to highlight human rights issues in the Punjab. It is working for an independent state there through democratic structures.

National Council for Panjabi Teaching

Centre for Bilingualism, Haringey Professional Development Centre, Downhills Park Road, London, N17 6AR
Tel: 0181-829-5015 **Fax:** 0181-365-8590
Contact: Mr Surinder Singh Attariwala
Position: Chair
Activities: Resource, youth, newsletter
Other Language: Punjabi
The Council is committed to the teaching and development of the Punjabi language in British schools as well as in classes run by voluntary community groups.

National Sikh Youth Forum

c/o Central Gurdwara Resource Centre, 62 Queensdale Road, London, W11 4SG
Tel: 0171-460-2020
EMail: khalsa@bigfoot.com
Internet: http://www.demon.co.uk/charities/sikh.
Contact: Bhupinder Singh
Position: National Coordinator
Activities: Resource, media, umbrella, visits, youth, newsletters, books, inter-faith
Other Languages: Punjabi
Affiliations: World Sikh Council (Akaal Takht)

An umbrella body which holds seminars three or four times a year. The Central Gurdwara Resource Centre publishes a monthly youth newsletter and sells books and CDRoms etc.

Network of Sikh Organisations UK
Alice Way, Hanworth Road, Hounslow, Middlesex, TW3 3VA (h)
Tel: 0181-577-2793   **Tel:** 0181-540-4148 (h)
Contact: Indarjit Singh OBE
Position: Director
Activities: Resource, media, umbrella, youth, elderly, women, newsletters, inter-faith
Other Languages: Punjabi
Affiliations: Inter Faith Network for the UK
The Network is a loose linking of Gurdwaras and others. It facilitates cooperation on issues of common concern, organises national celebrations of major Sikh festivals and generally advances the interests and image of the Sikh community.

New Approach Mission of Occidental Sikhism (NAMOS)
52 Beaconsfield Street, Forest Fields, Nottingham, Nottinghamshire, NG7 6FN
Tel: 0115-970-4088
Contact: Mr Biant Singh
Position: Volunteer worker

Panjabi Language Development Board
2 Saint Annes Close, Handsworth Wood, Birmingham, West Midlands, B20 1B5 (h)
Tel: 0121-551-5272 **Fax:** 021-551-5272
Contact: Surjit Singh Kalra
Position: Executive Director
Activities: Resource, youth, books, inter-faith
Other Languages: Punjabi, Urdu, Hindi
Affiliations: Punjab Group; National Council of Punjab Teachers; Publishers Get Together-India; Global Connections-California USA
Our main interest is to promote the Sikh religion and Punjabi language. We publish materials and provide lecturers.

Shiromani Akali Dal Head Office
15 Manor Way, Southall, Middlesex, UB2 5JJ (h)
Tel: 0181-571-2842 (h)
Contact: Sardar Bachittar Singh
Position: President
Activities: Worship, resource, youth, inter-faith
Other Languages: Punjabi

The organisation is religious and political and undertakes to give information on the Sikh religion. It fights against racist misunderstandings and for basic human rights. It engages in Religious Education and the singing of religious hymns.

Sikh Council for Interfaith Relations UK
43 Dorset Road, London, SW19 3EZ (h)
Tel: 0181-540-4148 (h)
Contact: Mr Indarjit Singh OBE
Position: General Secretary
Affiliations: Network of Sikh Organisations
Aims to develop and focus interest on interfaith dialogue in the Sikh community and to promote a greater understanding of Sikhism among non-Sikhs producing suitable literature and disseminating information on interfaith dialogue with meetings and seminars.

Sikh Divine Fellowship
132 Eastcote Avenue, Sudbury, Greenford, Middlesex, UB6 0NR
Tel: 0181-903-7143
Contact: Professor Harmindar Singh
Position: Secretary
Activities: Worship

Sikh Educational Advisory Services
57 Austhorpe Road, Leeds, West Yorkshire, LS15 8EQ
Tel: 0113-260-2484 **Tel:** 01973-286585
Contact: Roop Singh
Position: Head of Service
Activities: Resource, visits, youth, inter-faith
Other Languages: Punjabi
Affiliations: Akal Takhat – Amritsar
Specialises in stories from the Sikh world.

Sikh Educational & Cultural Association (UK)
Sat Nam Kutia, 18 Farncroft, Gravesend, Kent, DA11 7LT (h)
Tel: 01474-332356 (h)
Contact: Kartar Surinder Singh
Position: Chair & Consultant
Activities: Resource, umbrella, youth, newsletters
Other Languages: Punjabi
Affiliations: Network of Sikh Organisations UK
Established in 1972, the association is a privately run voluntary centre whose objective is to create an awareness of the Sikh philosophy among the faith communities and to promote the understanding and practices of Sikh principles.

Sikh Human Rights Group

PO Box 45, Southall, Middlesex, UB2 4SP
Tel: 0181-813-8614 **Tel:** 0181-572-8957 (h)
Fax: 0181-813-8614
EMail: shrq@online.rednet.co.uk
Contact: Jasdev Singh Rai
Position: Director
Activities: Newsletters, inter-faith
Other Languages: Punjabi
Human Rights organisation based on the humanitarian principles of Sikhism. It is concerned with maintaining human rights around the world, particularly in India, and producing documentation and specialist asylum reports.

Sikh Missionary Society (UK)

10 Featherstone Road, Southall, Middlesex, UB2 5AA
Tel: 0181-574-1902 **Fax:** 0181-574-1902
EMail: mssibs@surrey.ac.uk
Contact: Bahadur Singh
Position: Secretary
Activities: Resource, visits, youth
Other Languages: Punjabi
Affiliations: Network of Sikh Organisations UK; SGPC Amritsar, Punjab, India; Inter Faith Network for the UK

Sikh Religion & Cultural Heritage Forum

Derby, Derbyshire
Tel: 01332-768972
Contact: Dr Hardial Singh Dhillon
Position: Consultant
Other Languages: Punjabi
Affiliations: Guru Arjan Dev Gurdwara, Derby
To promote Sikh religion and cultural awareness and provide help and advice to schools, colleges, universities, employers, employees; to encourage use of Punjabi among yougsters and develop multicultural skills.

Sikh Religious Symbols Action Committee International

11 Apollo Way, Parry Bar, Birmingham, West Midlands, B20 3ND (h)
Tel: 0121-356-7070 (h)
Contact: Bhai Madan Singh
Position: Chief Convenor
Activities: Resource, umbrella, books, inter-faith
Other Languages: Punjabi, Hindi, Urdu
Affiliations: Council of Sikh Gurdwaras in Birmingham; Shromani Akali Dal; Network of Sikh

Organisations; Sikh Students Federation
To promote Sikhism, particularly to schools and colleges where religious education is taught; provide advice, information and support and promote good relations between different communities.

Sikh Welfare & Cultural Society

77 Bodnant Avenue, Leicester, Leicestershire

World Sikh Foundation (Incorporating the Sikh Cultural Society of Great Britain)

88 Mollison Way, Edgware, Middlesex, HA8 5QW (h)
Tel: 0181-952-1215 **Tel:** 0181-257-0359 (h)
Contact: Amar Singh Chhatwal
Position: General Secretary
Activities: Media, umbrella, newsletters, books, inter-faith
Distributes worldwide, free of charge, pamphlets in English on every aspect of the Sikh religion. Since 1960 it has also published in English the quarterly "Sikh Courier International", whose circulation is worldwide.

SIKH REGIONAL AND LOCAL ORGANISATIONS AND GURDWARAS

A variety of forms of Sikh regional and local organisations are listed in this directory. These include *gurdwaras*, associations and centres.

ENGLAND

NORTH EAST
City, Town or Local Bodies

Darlington Sikh Temple
Louisa Street, Darlington, County Durham, DL1 4ED
Tel: 01325-461252
Contact: Mr A Singh Diwan
Position: President

Gurdwara Sri Guru Singh Sabha
Tindal Close, Newcastle upon Tyne, Tyne and Wear, NE4 5SA
Tel: 0191-273-8011
Contact: Sohan Singh
Position: General Secretary
Activities: Worship, resource, visits, youth, elderly, women, inter-faith
Other Languages: Punjabi

Sikh Gurdwara
53-57 Crown Street, Newcastle upon Tyne, Tyne and Wear

Gurdwara Khalsa Mero Roop Hai Khas
West Way, South Shields, Tyne and Wear, NE33 4SR
EMail: gurpreet.singh@sunderland.ac.uk
Contact: Gurpreet Singh
Position: Trustee
Activities: Worship, resource, visitors, youth, books
Other Languages: Panjabi
Affiliations: Akhal Takht Sahib

South Shields Sikh Temple
2 Dean Terrace, South Shields, Tyne and Wear, NE33 5JY
Tel: 0191-323-4048

Guru Nanak Gurdwara & Sikh Community Centre
31 Allens Street, Stockton-on-Tees, County Durham

YORKSHIRE
Regional or County Bodies

Yorkshire Sikh Forum
130 Ashbourne Way, Kings Park, Bradford, West Yorkshire, BD2 1ER

Tel: 01724-735918 Tel: 01724-735928 (h)
Contact: Mr Harjap Singh Pooni
Position: Secretary
Other Languages: Punjabi, Hindi, Urdu

City, Town or Local Bodies

Bradford Sikh Parents Association

54 Leeds Old Road, Thornbury, Bradford, West
Yorkshire, BD3 8HU (h)
Tel: 01274-661914
Contact: Kuldip Singh
Position: Secretary
Activities: Youth, elderly, women, inter-faith
Other Languages: Punjabi

Gurdwara Amrit Parchar Dharmik Diwan

Peckover Street, Little Germany, Bradford, West
Yorkshire, BD1 5BD
Tel: 01274-724853 **Tel:** 01274-667625 (h)
Contact: Sardar Pritam Singh
Position: President
Activities: Worship, resource, media, umbrella,
visits, youth, elderly, women, inter-faith
Other Languages: Punjabi, Hindi, Urdu
Affiliations: The Council of Sikh Gurdwaras,
Bradford; Gurdwara Nirmal Kutya Johal Jalandhar,
Punjab, India

Gurdwara Guru Nanak Dev Ji

Prospect Hall, Wakefield Road, Bradford, West
Yorkshire, BD4 7DP
Tel: 01274-723557
Contact: Piara Singh Nijjar
Position: President
Activities: Worship, resource, visits, youth, elderly,
women, inter-faith
Other Languages: Punjabi
Affiliations: Federation of Bradford Sikh
Organisations

Gurdwara Singh Sabha Bradford

10 Grant Street, off: Garnett Street, Bradford, West
Yorkshire, BD3 9HF
Tel: 01274-738834 **Tel:** 01274-666487 (h)
Contact: Sardar Tarsem Singh
Position: Chair
Activities: Worship, resource, visits youth, elderly,
women, inter-faith
Other Languages: Punjabi

Guru Gobind Singh Sikh Temple

Malvern/Ventnor Street, Off Leeds Road, Bradford,
West Yorkshire, BD3 7DG
Tel: 01274-727928
Contact: Sarbant Singh Dosanjh
Position: Jathadar
Activities: Worship, resource, visits, inter-faith
Other Languages: Punjabi, Hindi

Guru Nanak Charitable Trust UK

18 Usher Street, Bradford, West Yorkshire, BD4 7DS
Contact: Mr M S Bussan
Position: Secretary

Guru Nanak United Sikh Temple

64 Avenue Road, West Bailing, Bradford, West
Yorkshire, BD5

Ramgarhia Gurdwara

720 Bolton Road, Bradford, West Yorkshire,
BD3 0ND
Tel: 01274-632761 **Tel:** 01274-544932 (h)
Contact: Sukhdev Singh
Position: Assistant Secretary
Activities: Worship, resource, visits, youth, women,
inter-faith
Other Languages: Punjabi (Gurmukhi)
Affiliations: Sikh Missionary Society; Ramgarhia
Council UK

Sikh Temple

20 Newburn Street, Bradford, West Yorkshire, BD7

Sikh Youth Federation

2 Fagley Road, Bradford, West Yorkshire, BD7 2HU

United Sikh Association

7 Sunnybank Lane, Thornbury, Bradford, West
Yorkshire, BD3 7DG

Yorkshire Sikh Forum

130 Ashbourne Way, Kings Park, Bradford, West
Yorkshire, BD2 1ER
Tel: 01724-735918 Tel: 01724-735928 (h)
Contact: Mr Harjap Singh Pooni
Position: Secretary
Languages: Punjabi, Hindi, Urdu

Gurdwara Sri Guru Teg Bhadar Sahib Ji

163 Bentley Road, Bentley, Doncaster, South
Yorkshire, DN5 9TB
Tel: 01302-390056 (h) **Fax:** 01302-390056
Contact: Nirmal Singh Duhre

Position: General Secretary
Activities: Worship, resource, youth
Other Languages: Punjabi, Hindi
Affiliations: Council of Sikh Gurdwaras,
Birmingham

Guru Kalgidhar Gurdwara
73 St James Street, Waterdale, Doncaster, South
Yorkshire
Tel: 01302–369003
Contact: Mr Mehal Singh
Position: Secretary

Sikh Temple
125b Carr House Road, Hyde Park, Doncaster,
South Yorkshire, DN1 2BD

Guru Nanak Sikh Sangat Sikh Temple
219 Keldergate, Deighton, Huddersfield, West
Yorkshire, HD2 1LF
Contact: Mr G Singh Gill

Huddersfield Sikh Temple Committee
12 Woodbine Road, Fartown, Huddersfield, West
Yorkshire

International Sikh Youth Federation
1 Haysfield Avenue, Oaks, Huddersfield, West
Yorkshire

International Sikh Youth Federation
195 Long Lane, Dalton, Huddersfield, West
Yorkshire

Kirklees Sikh Doctor's Association
90 Norwood Road, Birkby, Huddersfield, West
Yorkshire

Shri Guru Nanak Sangat
Guru Nanak Gurdwara, Prospect Street,
Springwood, Huddersfield, West Yorkshire, HD1
Tel: 01484-423773 **Tel:** 01422-882535 (h)
Fax: 01484-450650
Contact: Gian Singh Sahota
Position: General Secretary
Activities: Worship, resource, visits, youth, elderly,
women, inter-faith
Languages: Punjabi, Urdu
Affiliations: Network of Sikh Organisations UK;
Golden Temple Amritsar, Punjab, India

Shri Guru Singh Sabha
34 Hillhouse Lane, Fartown, Huddersfield, West
Yorkshire

Tel: 01484-542982
Contact: Sukhdev Singh Pasla
Position: Assistant Secretary
Activities: Worship, resource
Other Languages: Punjabi
Affiliations: Network of Sikh Organisations UK

Sikh Social Care
56 Imperial Road, Marsh, Huddersfield, West
Yorkshire, HD1 4PG
Contact: Mr Mohan Singh Sokha

Sikh Temple
8 Bankfield Road, Huddersfield, West Yorkshire

Sikh Youth Association
144 Black House Road, Huddersfield, West
Yorkshire

Gurdwara Kalgidhar Sahib, Bhatra Sangat
138 Chapletown Road, Leeds, West Yorkshire, LS7
Tel: 0113-262-5427
Contact: President

Guru Nanak Nishkam Sewak Jatha (UK- Leeds)
78 Ladypit Lane, Beeston, Leeds, West Yorkshire,
LS11 6DP
Tel: 0113-276-0261
Contact: Mr Sagoo
Position: Administrator
Activities: Worship

Guru Nanak Temple
62b Tong Road, Armley, Leeds, West Yorkshire,
LS12 1LZ
Tel: 0113-263-6525
Contact: Mr N Flora
Position: General Secretary

Leeds Association of Sikhs
1 Noorwood Mount, Pudsey, Leeds, West Yorkshire,
LS28 9HR

Ramgarhia Board Leeds
8/10 Chapeltown Road, Sheepscar, Leeds, West
Yorkshire, LS7 3AL
Tel: 0113-262-5427
Contact: Surinder Singh Sambhi
Position: Trustee
Activities: Worship, youth, elderly, women

Sikh Temple
93 Carr Manor Road, Leeds, West Yorkshire, L17

Sikh Temple
16 Sholebroke Place, Leeds, West Yorkshire, LS7

Sikh Women & Children's Association
3 Chatsworth Road, Pudsey, Leeds, West Yorkshire,
LS28 8JS

Sri Guru Nanak Sikh Temple
165 Town Street, Leeds, West Yorkshire, LS12 3JF
Tel: 01132-632697 **Tel:** 01132-319410 (h)
Fax: 01132-637053
Contact: Mr Gurmukh Singh Bahra
Position: Secretary
Activities: Charities
Languages: Punjabi

Gurdwara Bhatra Singh Sabha
23 Lorne Street, Middlesbrough, North Yorkshire,
TS1 5QY
Tel: 01642-250125 **Tel:** 01642-881431 (h)
Contact: Golab Singh
Position: Vice President
Activities: Worship, resource, visits
Other Languages: Punjabi
Affiliations: Bhatra Sikh Temple, Middlesbrough

Bhatra Sikh Temple
151 Southfield Street, Middlesbrough, North
Yorkshire

Sikh Temple
120 Bushywood Road, Dore, Sheffield, South
Yorkshire, S17 (h)
Contact: Mr C S Hayre

Sikh Temple
Ellesmere Road North, Sheffield, South Yorkshire,
S4
Tel: 0114-242-0108
Contact: Mr Kalsi
Position: President

NORTH WEST
City, Town or Local Bodies

Singh Sabha Gurdwara
8 Culshaw Street, Blackburn, Lancashire, BB2 6HD
Tel: 01254-581965
Contact: Amarjit Singh Thind
Position: President
Other Languages: Punjabi

Affiliations: Singh Sabha Gurdwara, Amritsar,
India

Gurdwara & Sikh Community Centre
Wellington Avenue, Liverpool, Merseyside, L15

Dashmesh Darbar Sikh Temple
98 Haywood Street, corner of Huxley Avenue,
Cheetham Hill, Manchester, Greater Manchester

Guru Nanak Dev Ji Gurdwara
15 Monton Street, Moss Side, Manchester, Greater
Manchester, M14 4LS
Tel: 0161-226-1131 **Tel:** 0161-226-3852 (h)
Contact: Manjeet Singh Rattan
Position: General Secretary
Activities: Worship, visits, youth, women, inter-
faith
Other Languages: Punjabi, Hindi, Urdu
Affiliations: Siri Harmandir Sahib, Amritsar, India

Gurdwara Dasmesh Sikh Temple
98 Heywood Street, Cheetham Hill, Manchester,
Greater Manchester, M8 0PD
Contact: Mr Atwar Singh Purtley
Position: Secretary
Activities: Worship, youth, elderly, women, inter-
faith
Other Languages: Punjabi

*Shiri Guru Gobind Singh Gurdwara Mission
Centre*
(Sangat Bhatra Sikh Temple), 61 Upper Chorlton
Road, Whalley Range, Manchester, Greater
Manchester, M16 7RQ
Tel: 0161-226-7233 **Tel:** 0161-226-1942 (h)
Contact: Mukhtiar Singh
Position: General Secretary
Activities: Worship
Other Languages: Punjabi

Sikh Association
12 Sherbourne Street, Manchester, Greater
Manchester, M3 1EJ
Tel: 0161-832-2241
Contact: Mr J S Kohli

Sikh Union of Manchester
31 Burford Road, Whalley Range, Manchester,
Greater Manchester, M16 8EW (h)
Tel: 0161-881-7067 (h)
Contact: Mr Ujjal D Singh
Position: Honorary Secretary

Activities: Resource, media, youth, newsletters, inter-faith
Other Languages: Punjabi

Guru Nanak Gurdwara
Bhatra Singh Sabha, 2 Clarendon Street, Preston, Lancashire, PR1 3YN
Tel: 01772-251008
Contact: Mr Hazur Singh
Position: General Treasurer
Activities: Worship

Guru Nanak Gurdwara, Cultural & Recreation Centre
2-10 Tunbridge Street, Preston, Lancashire, PR1 5YP
Tel: 01772-798395 **Tel:** 01772-793027 (h)
Contact: S Harbhajan Singh
Position: President
Activities: Worship, youth, elderly, women
Other Languages: Punjabi, Hindi

Preston Sikh Cultural Association
56 Conway Drive, Fulwood, Preston, Lancashire, PR2 3EP (h)
Contact: Mr Nirmal Singh
Position: Organiser
Activities: Resource, youth, inter-faith
Other Languages: Gurmukhi, Hindi, Urdu

Greater Manchester Sikh Community
246 Brooklands Road, Sale, Cheshire

Sikh Association & Gurdwara
12 Sherborne Street, Strangeways, Salford, Greater Manchester
Tel: 0161-832-2241
Contact: Kuldip Singh
Position: President

Guru Nanak Gurdwara
Dover Road, Latchford, Warrington, Cheshire
Tel: 01925-418208 **Tel:** 01925-634378 (h)
Contact: Mr Jarnail Singh Gill
Position: President
Activities: Worship, visits, youth, elderly, women
Other Languages: Punjabi

EAST MIDLANDS
Regional or County Bodies

Federation of Sikh Organisations, Leicestershire
106 East Park Road, Leicester, Leicestershire, LE5 4QH
Tel: 0116-276-0517 **Tel:** 01509-239179 (h)
Fax: 0116-276-9297
Contact: S Gurbinder Singh
Position: Secretary
Activities: Worship, resource, media, umbrella, visits youth, elderly, women, newsletters, books, inter-faith
Other Languages: Punjabi

Leicestershire Sikh Education Forum
45 Newhaven Road, Evington, Leicester, Leicestershire, LE5 6JH (h)
Tel: 0116-243-2374 (h)
Contact: Mr Kartar Singh Sandhu MBE
Position: Chairman
Activities: Resource, inter-faith
Other Languages: Punjabi, Hindi, Urdu

City, Town or Local Bodies

Guru Arjan Dev Gurdwara
Stanhope Street, Derby, Derbyshire, DE23 6QJ
Tel: 01332-776872 **Fax:** 01332-776872
Contact: Mr Jogindar Singh Johal
Position: President
Activities: Worship
Other Languages: Punjabi, Hindi

Guru Nanak Istri Sabha
158 Peartree Street, Derby, Derbyshire

Ramgarhia Sabha Sikh Temple
14 St James Road, Derby, Derbyshire, DE3 8QX
Tel: 01332-371811
Contact: Mr Mohan S Manku

Shromani Akal Dal
67 Goodale Street, Derby, Derbyshire

Shromani Akali Dal
75 Overdale Road, Derby, Derbyshire, DE3 6AU

Sikh Preaching Association
16 Scott Street, Derby, Derbyshire

Sri Guru Sabha
1 Wavil Close, Kettering, Northamptonshire

Sri Guru Singh Sabha
23-25 King Street, Kettering, Northamptonshire, NN16 8QP
Tel: 01536-511447 **Tel:** 01536-515540 (h)
Contact: Mr S S Garcha
Position: Honorary Secretary
Activities: Worship
Other Languages: Punjabi

British Sikh Society
230 Loughborough Road, Leicester, Leicestershire, LE4 5LG
Tel: 0116-266-1293 **Tel:** 0116-264-0519 (h)
Contact: Mr Sukhdev Singh Sangha
Position: Secretary
Activities: Religious, media, inter-faith
Other Languages: Punjabi
Affiliations: Leicester Sikh Centre

Federation of Sikh Organisations, Leicestershire
106 East Park Road, Leicester, Leicestershire, LE5 4QH
Tel: 0116-276-0517 **Tel:** 01509-239179 (h)
Fax: 0116-276-9297
Contact: S Gurbinder Singh
Position: Secretary
Activities: Worship, resource, media, umbrella, visits youth, elderly, women, newsletters, books, inter-faith
Other Languages: Punjabi

Guru Amardas Gurdwara
219 Clarendon Park Road, Leicester, Leicestershire, LE2 3AN
Tel: 0116-270-1705 **Tel:** 0116-287-0801 (h)
Contact: Mr Sewa Singh
Position: President
Activities: Worship, resource, visits, youth, elderly, women, inter-faith
Other Languages: Punjabi
Affiliations: Leicester Sikh Centre; Sharomani Prabhadank Committee, Amritsar, India

Guru Nanak Community Centre
9 Holybones, Leicester, Leicestershire, LE1 4LJ
Tel: 0116-262-8606 **Fax:** 0116-262-8606
Contact: S Singh
Position: General Secretary
Activities: Youth, elderly, women
Other Languages: Punjabi
Affiliations: Guru Nanak Gurdwara

Guru Nanak Gurdwara
9 Holy Bones, Leicester, Leicestershire, LE1 4LJ
Tel: 0116-262-8606 **Fax:** 0116-262-8606
Contact: Jagpal Singh
Position: General Secretary
Activities: Worship, resource, visits, inter-faith

Guru Nanak Gurdwara Library
9 Holybones, Leicester, Leicestershire, LE1 4LJ
Tel: 0116-251-7460 **Fax:** 0116-262-8606
Contact: Harjinder Singh
Position: Librarian
Activities: Resource
Other Languages: Punjabi
Affiliations: Guru Nanak Gurdwara

Guru Nanak Khalsa
45 Lanesborough Road, Leicester, Leicestershire

Guru Nanak Panjabi School
9 Holybones, Leicester, Leicestershire, LE1 4LJ
Tel: 0116-262-8606 **Fax:** 0116-262-8606
Contact: Mrs Virpal Kaur
Position: School Administrator
Activities: Resource, youth
Other Languages: Punjabi
Affiliations: Guru Nanak Gurdwara

Guru Tegh Bahadur Gurdwara
106 East Park Road, Leicester, Leicestershire
Tel: 0116-276-0517 **Tel:** 0116-267-3903
Contact: Sardar Gurdev Singh Johal
Position: General Secretary
Activities: Worship, resource, youth, elderly, inter-faith
Other Languages: Punjabi
Affiliations: Federation of Sikh Organisations, Leicestershire; International Sikh Youth Federation

Leicester Sikh Centre
219 Clarendon Park Road, Leicester, Leicestershire, LE2 3AN
Tel: 0116-270-1705 **Tel:** 0116-241-5340 (h)
Contact: Mrs Jagdev Kaur Gill
Position: Chairperson
Activities: Worship, resource, media, visits, youth, elderly, women, inter-faith
Other Languages: Punjabi, Hindi, Hindi

Leicestershire Sikh Education Forum
45 Newhaven Road, Evington, Leicester, Leicestershire, LE5 6JH (h)
Tel: 0116-243-2374 (h)

Contact: Mr Kartar Singh Sandhu MBE
Position: Chairman
Activities: Resource, inter-faith
Other Languages: Punjabi, Hindi, Urdu

Ramgarhia Board Gurdwara
51 Meynell Road, Leicester, Leicestershire,
LE5 3NE
Tel: 0116-276-0765
Contact: General Secretary

Ramgarhia Sikh Circle
3 Landscape Drive, Evington, Leicester,
Leicestershire, LE5 6GA (h)
Contact: Joga Singh Bhamrah
Position: Secretary
Activities: Youth, elderly, women
Other Languages: Punjabi, Hindi
Affiliations: Confederation of Indian
Organisations

Shromani Akali Dal (UK) Leicestershire
Leicester Sikh Centre, 219/227 Clarendon Park
Road, Leicester, Leicestershire, LE2 3AN
Tel: 0116-270-1705 **Tel:** 0116-276-7041 (h)
Contact: Mr Reshwel Singh
Position: Secretary
Activities: Worship, visits, youth, elderly, women
Other Languages: Punjabi
Affiliations: Network of Sikh Organisations UK

Sikh Culture, Welfare & Religious Society
10 Edward Avenue, Braunstone, Leicester,
Leicestershire, LE3 2PB
Tel: 0116-282-3544
Contact: Mr Sukhwant Singh Dhillon
Position: Secretary
Activities: Resource, youth, inter-faith
Other Languages: Punjabi, Hindi, Urdu
Affiliations: Organisation of Sikh Gurdwaras,
Leicestershire

Sikh Education Council
14 Brightside Road, Evington, Leicester,
Leicestershire, LE5 5LD
Tel: 0116-278-8835

Sikh Parents' Association
Leicester Sikh Centre, 219/227 Clarendon Park
Road, Leicester, Leicestershire, LE2 3AN
Tel: 0116-270-1705 **Tel:** 0116-276-7041 (h)
Contact: Reshwel Singh

Position: Chairman
Activities: Resource, visits
Other Languages: Punjabi, Hindi, Urdu
Affiliations: Guru Amardas Gurdwara, Leicester

Sikh Senior Citizen's Association
19 Staveley Road, Leicester, Leicestershire, LE5 5JU
Tel: 0116-273-0865

Sikh Welfare & Cultural Society
77 Bodnant Avenue, Leicester, Leicestershire

Sikh Youth Missionary Project (IYSP)
106 East Park Road, Leicester, Leicestershire,
LE5 4QB
Tel: 0116-266-1712 **Tel:** 0116-2734787 (h)
Contact: Mr Kashmir Singh
Activities: Resource, youth
Languages: Punjabi
Affiliations: Guru Tegh Bahadhur Gurdwara,
Leicester; International Sikh Youth Federation
(UK); International Sikh Youth Federation.

Young Men's Sikh Association
41 Dashwood Road, Leicester, Leicestershire

Young Sikh Womens Association
88 Evington Drive, Leicester, Leicestershire,
LE5 5PE

Sikh Temple (Gurdwara Sahib)
33/34 Clarence Street, Loughborough,
Leicestershire, LE11 1DY
Tel: 01509-232411
Contact: Mr Udham Singh
Position: President
Activities: Worship, resource, visits, youth, elderly,
women, inter-faith
Other Languages: Punjabi, Hindi, Urdu
Affiliations: Council of Sikh Gurdwaras in
Leicestershire

Ramgarhia Board Northampton
Sikh Gurdwara Community Centre, 2 Craven
Street, Northampton, Northamptonshire,
NN1 3EZ (h)
Tel: 01604-21135 (h)
Contact: Satbachan Singh Sehmi
Position: General Secretary
Activities: Worship, resource, visits
Other Languages: Punjabi

Sikh Temple
53 Queen's Park Parade, Northampton,
Northamptonshire

Sri Guru Singh Sabha
17-19 St George's Street, Off Regent Square,
Northampton, Northamptonshire, NN5 2TN
Tel: 01604-34641 **Tel:** 01604-846973 (h)
Contact: Mr Ranjeet Singh Grewal
Position: Secretary
Activities: Worship
Other Languages: Punjabi, Hindi

Bhatra Sikh Temple
36 Church Street, Nottingham, Nottinghamshire
Contact: Piara Singh
Position: General Secretary

Gurdwara Baba Budha Ji
24 Gladstone Street, Nottingham, Nottinghamshire
Tel: 0115-978-0530
Contact: Sarabjit Singh Landa
Position: Liaison Officer

Gurdwara Nottingham
17 Berridge Road, Nottingham, Nottinghamshire

Guru Nanak Darbar
4 Waterloo Road, Nottingham, Nottinghamshire

Guru Nanak Dev Ji Gurdwara
1 Noel Street, Hyson Green, Nottingham,
Nottinghamshire
Tel: 0115-970-0750
Contact: Prithipal Singh
Position: President

Guru Nanak Sat Sang Gurdwara
60/62 Forest Road West, Nottingham,
Nottinghamshire, NG7 4EP
Tel: 0115-978-1394
Contact: Malkiat Singh Matharu
Position: President
Activities: Worship

Sikh Community & Youth Services
27 Park Road, Lenton, Nottingham,
Nottinghamshire
Tel: 0115-950-7481 **Tel:** 01976-262636 (h)
Fax: 0115-950-7481
Contact: Janak Singh Sanghera
Position: Co-ordinator

Activities: Rsource, umbrella, youth, women,
newsletters, books
Other Languages: Punjabi, Hindi, Urdu

Sikh Temple
Bentinck Road, Hyson Green, Nottingham,
Nottinghamshire

Sikh Temple
16 Ebury Road, Sherwood Rise, Nottingham,
Nottinghamshire, NG5 1BB
Tel: 0115-962-2132
Contact: Mr G S Sanghera
Position: Secretary
Activities: Worship

Sikh Temple
26 Nottingham Road, Basford, Nottingham,
Nottinghamshire, NG7 7AE

Sikh Temple Singh Sabha
97 Burford Road, Forestfield, Nottingham,
Nottinghamshire

Sikh Youth International
193 Wollaton Road, Wollaton, Nottingham,
Notinghamshire, NG8 1FU

Singh Sabha
50 Lees Hill Street, Nottingham, Nottinghamshire

Young Lions
c/o 1 Noel Street, Hyson Green, Nottingham,
Nottinghamshire
Tel: 0115-970-0750
Contact: Jagtar Singh
Position: President

Guru Nanak Gurdwara
22 Dale Street, Crosby, Scunthorpe, Lincolnshire
Tel: 01724-861880 (h)
Contact: Daljit Singh
Position: General Secretary
Activities: Worship, resource, visits, youth, elderly,
women
Other Languages: Punjabi, Hindi

Guru Nanak Gurdwara
41 Normandy Road, Scunthorpe, Lincolnshire,
DN15 6AS
Tel: 01724-841361
Contact: Jaswant Singh Dhinsa
Position: General Secretary

Activities: Worship, visits, youth, women, inter-faith
Other Languages: Punjabi

Guru Nanak Sikh Temple
207/209 Frodingham Road, Scunthorpe, Lincolnshire

WEST MIDLANDS
City, Town or County Bodies

Akhand Kirtani Jatha Midlands
48 Mervyn Road, Birmingham, West Midlands, B21 8DE

Aston University Sikh Society
Aston University, Costa Green, Birmingham, West Midlands, B4 7ES
Activities: Youth, inter-faith
Other Languages: Punjabi

Bhatra Sikh Singh Sabha Temple
221 Mary Street, Balsall Heath, Birmingham, West Midlands

Birmingham University Sikh Society
The Student Guild, Edgbaston Park Road, Edgbaston, Birmingham, West Midlands, B15 2TT
Contact: Mr Dalbir Singh Nijjer
Position: President
Activities: Resource, youth
Other Languages: Punjabi
Affiliations: British Organisation of Sikh Students

Council of Sikh Gurdwaras in Birmingham
PO Box 2318, Hockley, Birmingham, West Midlands, B19 2EZ
Tel: 0121-523-4144 **Fax:** 0121-515-4080
Contact: Gurdial Singh Atwal
Position: Chairman
Activities: Resource, umbrella, youth, elderly, women, inter-faith
Other Languages: Punjabi

Gurdwara Guru Hargobind Sahib Ji
Unit 1 Dudley Road West, Tividale, Birmingham, West Midlands, B69 2PJ
Tel: 0121-522-4828 **Fax:** 0121-522-2300
Contact: Balwinder Singh
Position: Chair
Activities: Worship
Other Languages: Punjabi

Affiliations: Council of Sikh Gurdwaras, Sandwell

Gurdwara Guru Nanak Bhatra Singh Sabha
Community Centre, 248-150 Moseley Road, Balsall Heath, Birmingham, West Midlands, B12
Tel: 0121-440-2387
Contact: President

Gurdwara Nanaksar
Old Methodist Church, Waterloo Road, Smethwick, Birmingham, West Midlands, B66 4JS
Tel: 0121-558-9048 **Tel:** 0121-420-1034 (h)
Contact: Bahadar Singh
Position: Sevadar
Activities: Worship

Gurdwara Singh Sabha
Somerset Road, Handsworth Wood, Birmingham, West Midlands, B20
Tel: 0121-523-7201

Gurdwara Yaadgar Baba Deep Singh Ji Shaheed
4 Holyhead Road, Handsworth, Birmingham, West Midlands, B21 0LT

Guru Nanak Gurdwara
136 Showell Green Lane, Sparkhill, Birmingham, West Midlands, B11 4LS (h)
Tel: 0121-771-0092 **Tel:** 0121-449-6229 (h)
Contact: Mr Mohan Singh
Position: President
Activities: Worship, resource, visits, youth, elderly, women, inter-faith
Other Languages: Punjabi
Affiliations: Council of Sikh Gurdwaras in Birmingham; Network of Sikh Organisations, UK

Guru Nanak Gurdwara
28 Grewwolde Road, Sparkhill, Birmingham, West Midlands, B11 4DL

Guru Nanak Gurdwara
219 Mary Street, Balsall Heath, Birmingham, West Midlands, B12

Guru Nanak Khalsa School
145a Soho Road, Handsworth, Birmingham, West Midlands, B21 9ST
Tel: 0121-551-1579

Guru Ramdas Khalsa School
495 Moseley Road, Balsall Heath, Birmingham, West Midlands, B12 9BX

Guru Ramdas Singh Sabha Gurdwara
495 Moseley Road, Balsall Heath, Birmingham,
West Midlands, B12 9BX
Tel: 0121-440-3653
Contact: Ram Singh
Position: General Secretary
Activities: Worship

Guru Ram Das Temple
290 Balsall Heath Road, Birmingham, West
Midlands, B12

Guru Ramdas Training Centre
495 Moseley Road, Balsall Heath, Birmingham,
West Midlands, B12 9BX

International Sikh Youth Federation
130 Sandwell Road, Birmingham, West Midlands,
B21 8SP

Khalsa Welfare Trust
Khalsa House, 4 Holyhead Road, Handsworth,
Birmingham, West Midlands, B21 0LT
Tel: 0121-554-8034 **Tel:** 0121-554-1972 (h)
Contact: Mr Charan Singh Pancchi
Position: Chairman
Activities: Worship, resource, visits, youth, women,
inter-faith
Other Languages: Punjabi, Hindi, Urdu
Affiliations: Council of Sikh Gurdwaras in
Birmingham; Network of Sikh Organisations;
Shiormani Akali Dal

Mahanraja Jassa Singh Ramgarhia Hall
New Hall Hill, Birmingham, West Midlands, B1

Punjab Culture Centre
127 Petersfield Road, Hall Green, Birmingham,
West Midlands, B28 0BG (h)
Tel: 0121-624-7339 (h)
Contact: Mr Jagjit Singh Taunque
Position: Chair
Activities: Resource, media, visits, youth, elderly,
women, inter-faith
Other Languages: Punjabi, Urdu, Gujarati,
Bengali
Affiliations: Council of Sikh Gurdwaras

**Punjab Hawks Student Union & Community
Service**
c/o 623 Stratford Road, Sparkhill, Birmingham,
West Midlands, B11 4LS

Punjabi Community Centre
66 Gipsy Lane, Erdington, Birmingham, West
Midlands, B23 7SR
Tel: 0121-681-3625 (h)
Contact: Mr Narinder Jit Singh
Position: President
Other Languages: Punjabi
Affiliations: Council of Sikh Gurdwaras in
Birmingham

Punjabi Cultural Society
145a Soho Road, Handsworth, Birmingham, West
Midlands, B21 9ST
Tel: 0121-551-1579

Ramgarhia Circle
108 Gladwys Road, Bearwood, Birmingham, West
Midlands, B67 5AN
Tel: 0121-429-6823
Contact: Prem Singh Kalsi
Position: General Secretary

Ramgarhia Gurdwara
25-29 Waverley Road, Small Heath, Birmingham,
West Midlands, B10 0EG
Tel: 0121-771-0680 **Tel:** 0121-554-1394
Contact: Gian Singh Bhogal
Position: Treasurer
Activities: Worship, resource, visits, women
Other Languages: Punjabi, Hindi
Affiliations: Council of Sikh Gurdwaras in
Birmingham

Ramgarhia Sikh Temple
Graham Street, Birmingham, West Midlands,
B1 3LA
Tel: 0121-236-5435
Contact: Mr G S Matharu

Shaheed Udham Singh Welfare Centre
346 Soho Road, Handsworth, Birmingham, West
Midlands, B21 8EG
Contact: Mr K S Sanghera

Sharomani Akali Dal Welfare & Sikh Centre
Khalsa House, 535-537 Park Road, Hockley,
Birmingham, West Midlands, B18 5TE

Sikh Commonwealth
71b Holly Lane, Erdington, Birmingham, West
Midlands, B24 9JP

Sikh Community & Youth Centre
348 Soho Road, Handsworth, Birmingham, West
Midlands, B21 9QL
Tel: 0121-523-0147 **Fax:** 0121-515-4880
EMail: 1000447.1022@Compuserve.com
Contact: Sukhvinder Singh
Position: Project Coordinator
Activities: Resource, youth, elderly, women, inter-
faith
Other Languages: Punjabi

Sikh Community Centre South Birmingham
623 Stratford Road, Sparkhill, Birmingham, West
Midlands, B11 4LS

Sikh Ex-Serviceman Association
12 Hartington Road, Birmingham, West Midlands,
B19 9JP

Sikh Istri Diwan
495 Moseley Road, Balsall Heath, Birmingham,
West Midlands, B12 9BX

Sikh Liaison Committee
160 Forman Road, Sparkhill, Birmingham, West
Midlands, B11 3BD

Sikh Parents Association
629/631 Stratford Road, Sparkhill, Birmingham,
West Midlands
Tel: 0121-771-0092
Contact: Mr Samra
Position: General Secretary

Sikh Parents Association of North Birmingham
74 Grestone Avenue, Handsworth Wood,
Birmingham, West Midlands

Sikh Parents Association (South Birmingham)
86 Tetley Road, Sparkhill, Birmingham, West
Midlands, B11 3BT
Tel: 0121-777-6391
Contact: Surjit Singh Khatra

Sikh Sahit & Sabhyachar Kendra
145a Soho Road, Handsworth, Birmingham, West
Midlands, B21 9ST
Tel: 0121-551-1579

Sikh School of Martial Arts
106 Wilton Road, Sparkhill, Birmingham, West
Midlands, B11 3HX

Sikh Temple
22 Goldshill Road, Birmingham, West Midlands,
B21

Sikh Temple
Churchill Road, Handsworth, Birmingham, West
Midlands, B20

Sikh Turban Action Group
145 Soho Road, Handsworth, Birmingham, West
Midlands, B21 9BX

Sikh Welfare Association
358 Olton Road Boulevard West, Tyseley,
Birmingham, West Midlands, B11 3HJ

Sikh Welfare Mission
3 Hatfield Road, Lozells, Birmingham, West
Midlands

Sikh Workers Association
507 Stratford Road, Sparkhill, Birmingham, West
Midlands, B11 4LP

Sikh Youth Circle
47 Serpentine Road, Aston, Birmingham, West
Midlands, B6 6SB

Sikh Youth Service
Khalsa House, 4 Holyhead Road, Handsworth,
Birmingham, West Midlands, B21 0LT
Tel: 0121-554-8034
Contact: Balwinder Singh

Sikh Youth Service
303 Soho Road, Handsworth, Birmingham, West
Midlands, B21 9SA

Singh Sabha Bhatra Gurdwara
221 Mary Street, Balsall Heath, Birmingham, West
Midlands, B12 9RN
Tel: 0121-440-2358
Contact: Mr N Singh
Position: Secretary

Singh Sabha Gurdwara
Somerset Road, Handsworth, Birmingham, West
Midlands, B20

Sri Dashmesh Sikh Temple
305 Wheeler Street, Lozells, Birmingham, West
Midlands, B19 2EU
Tel: 0121-523-6059 **Tel:** 0956-695193

Contact: Sardar Kulbir Singh Chitti
Position: General Secretary
Activities: Worship, resource, visits, youth, elderly, women, inter-faith
Other Languages: Punjabi
Affiliations: Council of Sikh Gurdwaras; World Sikh Council (Europe Zone)

Young Akali Dal Sandwell
144 West Bromwich Street, Warley, Birmingham, West Midlands (h)
Tel: 0121-544-4939 (h)
Contact: Mr B Singh
Position: Secretary

Ajit Durbar
27 St. Paul's Road, Coventry, West Midlands, CV6 5DE

Ajit Durbar Gurdwara
12 Churchill Avenue, Foleshill, Coventry, West Midlands, CV6 5JL

Akhand Kirtani Jatha
40 Trentham Road, Coventry, West Midlands, CV1 5BD

Babbar Khalsa International Gurdwara Sri Guru Singh Sabha
47-49 Cross Road, Foleshill, Coventry, West Midlands, CV6 5JR

Dhuram Parchar Sabha
90 Darbar Avenue, Coventry, West Midlands, CV6 5LY

Gurdwara Ajit Darbar Coventry UK
Lockhurst Lane, Foleshill, Coventry, West Midlands
Tel: 01203-662448
Contact: Mr S S Singh

Gurdwara Ajit Darbar (RD)
71 Elmsdale Avenue, Foleshill, Coventry, West Midlands, CV6 6ET

Guru Nanak Parakash Temples Sports Committee
70 Halford Lane, Holbrooks, Coventry, West Midlands

Gurdwara Prabandhak Committee
49 Charterhouse Road, Coventry, West Midlands

Gurdwara Guru Hargobind Charitable Trust
Sikh Temple, 53 Heath Road, Coventry, West Midlands, CV2 4QB
Tel: 01203-450260
Contact: Councillor Jaswant Singh Birdi
Position: Secretary General
Activities: Worship

Gurdwara Shri Guru Singh Sabha
47-49 Coventry Road, Coventry, West Midlands, CV6 5GR
Tel: 01203-684802 **Fax:** 01203-684802
Contact: Karnail Singh Mandir
Position: Secretary
Activities: Worship, visits, youth, elderly, women, inter-faith
Other Languages: Punjabi
Affiliations: Council of Sikh Gurdwaras in Coventry; Akal Takhat Amritsar Panjab, India

Guru Nanak Sewak Jatha
128 De Montfort Way, Cannon Park, Coventry, West Midlands, CV4 7DT
Contact: Mr A S Dhesi

International Sikh Brotherhood
24 Benthnell Road, Coventry, West Midlands

International Sikh Youth Federation
17 King George's Avenue, Foleshill, Coventry, West Midlands, CV6 6FE
Contact: Mr G S Atwal

Istri Sabha Gurdwara Guru Hargobind Sahib Ji
53 Heath Road, Coventry, West Midlands, CV2 4QB

Nanak Parkash Gurdwara
71/81 Harnall Lane West, Foleshill, Coventry, West Midlands, CV2 2GJ
Tel: 01203-220960
Contact: Mr G S Chohan

Nanaksar Gurdwara Gursikh Temple
224-226 Foleshill Road, Coventry, West Midlands, CV1 4HW
Tel: 01203-220434 **Tel:** 01203-688609 (h)
Fax: 01203-633326
Contact: Bhagwant Singh Pandher
Position: General Secretary
Activities: Worship, resource, visits, women, inter-faith

Other Languages: Punjabi, Hindi, Urdu
Affiliations: Council of Sikh Gurdwaras in
Coventry; Nanaksar Gurdwara Gursikh Temple

Ramgarhia Board
7 Pensilva Way, Primrose Park Estate, Coventry, West
Midlands

Ramgarhia Girls' Group
Ramgarhia Community Centre, 1063 Foleshill
Road, Coventry, West Midlands, CV6 6ER

Ramgarhia Gurdwara & Family Centre
1103 Foleshill Road, Foleshill, Coventry, West
Midlands, CV6 6EP
Tel: 01203-663048
Contact: Arjan Singh Bamrah
Position: General Secretary
Activities: Worship, resource, visits
Other Languages: Punjabi
Affiliations: Council of Sikh Gurdwaras in
Coventry, Ramgarhia UK Council

Shiromani Akali Dal
15 Park Street, Coventry, West Midlands, CV6 5AT
(h)
Tel: 01203-684042 (h)
Contact: Mr Mohinder Pal Singh Dhillon
Position: General Secretary
Activities: Resource
Other Languages: Punjabi
Affiliations: Sharomani Akali Dal UK; Sharomani
Akali Dal, Amritsar, Punjab

Sikh Centre
Martyr Jarnail Singh House, 15 Park Street,
Foleshill, Coventry, West Midlands, CV6 5AT (h)
Tel: 01203-237509 **Fax:** 01203-524680
EMail: cesak@frost.warwick.ac.uk
Contact: Jagdish Singh
Position: Director
Activities: Resource, media, umbrella, visits, youth,
women, newsletters, books, inter-faith
Other Languages: Panjabi
Affiliations: National Sikh Youth Forum; Sikh
Commonwealth

Sikh Cultural Centre
35 Burnaby Road, Holbrooks, Coventry, West
Midlands, CV6 4BE

Sikh Cultural Society
305 Walsgrave Road, Coventry, West Midlands,
CV2 4BL
Fax: 01203-454523
Contact: Dr G S Judge
Position: Secretary

Sikh Cultural Society
28 Orchard Street, Coventry, West Midlands,
CV3 6HU

Sikh Mission
Khalsa House, 19 St Luke's Road, Holbrooks, West
Midlands, Coventry, CV6 4JA
Tel: 01203-661442
Contact: D S Kundra
Position: Organiser

Supreme Council of Sikhs
70-72 Humber Road, Coventry, West Midlands,
CV3 1BA
Contact: Mr T S Shokar

United Akali Dal
44 Wright Street, Coventry, West Midlands

Gurdwara Guru Teg Bahadur
7 Vicar Street, Dudley, West Midlands, DY2 8RQ
Tel: 01384-238936
Contact: Mr Ajit Singh
Position: President
Activities: Worship, visits, youth, elderly, women,
inter-faith
Other Languages: Punjabi

Guru Nanak Sikh Temple
Sikh Temple, 118 Wellington Road, Dudley, West
Midlands, DY1 1UB
Tel: 01384-253054
Contact: Gurcharan Singh Behi
Position: Secretary
Activities: Worship, resource, visits, youth, elderly,
newsletters
Other Languages: Punjabi, Hindi

Shiromani Akali Dal UK
12 Molyneux Road, Netherton, Dudley, West
Midlands, DY2 2DH (h)
Contact: Mr Ranjit Singh
Position: President
Other Languages: Punjabi

Sikh Parents Association
20 Ravensitch Walk, Brierley Hill, Near Dudley,
West Midlands, DY5 2BY
Contact: Mr A S Kang

Sri Guru Nanak Singh Sabha Gurdwara
26 Wellington Road, Dudley, West Midlands
Contact: Mr A S Bedi
Position: General Secretarya

Gurdwara Sahib Leamington & Warwick
96-102 New Street, Leamington Spa, Warwickshire,
CV31 1HL
Tel: 01926-424297
Position: General Secretary
Activities: Worship, visits
Langauges: Punjabi

Shiromani Akali Dal UK
19a Leam Street, Leamington Spa, Warwickshire

Shiromani Akali Dal UK
89 Willes Road, Leamington Spa, Warwickshire

Shiromani Akali Dal
2 Mollington Road, Whitnash, Leamington Spa,
Warwickshire

Sikh Community Centre
1 Mill Street, Leamington Spa, Warwickshire,
CV31 1ES
Contact: Chanan Singh Aujla
Position: Manager

Sikh Temple
1 New Street, Leamington Spa, Warwickshire

Sikh Temple
25 St Mary's Road, Leamington Spa, Warwickshire

Gurdwara
84 Bracebridge Street, Nuneaton, Warwickshire,
CV11 5PB
Contact: c/o Mr G Singh

Guru Nanak Gurdwara
59-61 Park Avenue, Nuneaton, Warwickshire,
CV11 4PQ
Tel: 01203-386524
Contact: Mr Jasbir Singh Sekhon
Position: General Secretary
Activities: Worship, resource, visits, youth, elderly,
women, inter-faith
Other Languages: Punjabi, Hindi, Urdu

Guru Nanak Gurdwara
4 Craven Road, Rugby, Warwickshire, CV21 3HY
Tel: 01788-543192
Contact: P S Atwal
Position: Secretary

Nanaksar Gurdwara
90 Tithe Barn Road, Stafford, Staffordshire
Tel: 01785-258590 **Tel:** 01785-247534
Contact: Kirat Singh Takhar
Position: President
Activities: Worship, visits, inter-faith
Other Languages: Punjabi

Guru Nanak Gurdwara
61 Liverpool Road, Stoke-on-Trent, Staffordshire,
ST4 1AQ
Tel: 01782-415670 **Tel:** 01782-713265 (h)
Contact: Kewal Singh Sangha
Position: General Secretary
Activities: Worship, resource, visits, youth, elderly,
women, inter-faith
Other Languages: Punjabi
Affiliations: Network of Sikh Organisations

Ramgarhia Sikh Temple
141 Wheldon Road, Fenton, Stoke-on-Trent,
Staffordshire, ST4 4JG
Tel: 01782-844940
Contact: Balvinder Singh Devgon
Position: Secretary
Activities: Worship
Other Languages: Punjabi

Sikh Cultural Association
92 Soames Crescent, Longton, Stoke-on-Trent,
Staffordshire
Contact: Mrs D Singh

Guru Nanak Sikh Temple
Hadley Park Road, Hadley, Telford, Shropshire
Tel: 01952-251734 **Tel:** 01952-617515 (h)
Contact: Mr Malhi
Position: General Secretary
Activities: Worship

Guru Nanak Sikh Temple
19a Church Parade, Oakengates, Telford, Shopshire,
TF2 6EX**Tel:** 01952-616442
Tel: 01952-677632 (h)
Contact: Mr Jagtar Singh Gill
Position: General Secretary

Activities: Worship, resource, umbrella, visits, youth
Other Languages: Punjabi

Guru Nanak Gurdwara
Walsall Road, Willenhall, Staffordshire, West
Midlands, WV13 2RD
Tel: 01902-605286
Contact: General Secretary
Activities: Worship, resource, visitors, elderly,
women, inter-faith
Other Languages: Punbaji

Gurdwara Nanaksar
4 Wellington Street, Walsall, West Midlands
Tel: 01922-641040

Gurdwara Nanak Sar Temple
Pleck Street, Walsall, West Midlands

Guru Nanak Education & Community Service Board
156 West Bromwich Street, Walsall, West Midlands
Contact: Tara Singh

Guru Nanak Sikh Organisation
212 Prince Street, Pleck, Walsall, West Midlands
Contact: Ranjit Singh Virk

Walsall Sikh Association
51 Bescot Road, Walsall, West Midlands, WS2 9AD
Tel: 01922-29401 (h)
Contact: Harminder Singh Khera
Position: General Secretary

Bhai Budha Dal Sandwell
64 Tiverton Road, Warley, West Midlands,
B67 3HX
Tel: 0121-565-0043
Contact: Mr Bakshish Singh
Position: Chairman

Desh Bhagat Committee
33 Birch Street, Warley, West Midlands
Contact: Mr B Singh

Gurdwara Amrit Parchar Dharmik Diwan
65 Birmingham Road, Oldbury, Warley, West
Midlands, B69 4EH
Tel: 0121-552-3778 **Tel:** 0121-358-4837 (h)
Contact: Gian Singh Riat
Position: Secretary
Activities: Worship
Other Languages: Punjabi

Gurdwara Nanaksar
Waterloo Road, Smethwick, Warley, West Midlands,
B66 4JS
Tel: 0121-565-3162
Contact: Gurdial Singh Samra
Position: President
Activities: Worship, resource, visits, youth, elderly,
women, inter-faith
Other Languages: Punjabi, Hindi, Urdu

Guru Nanak Gurdwara
128-130 High Street, Smethwick, Warley, West
Midlands, B66 3AP
Tel: 0121-555-5926
Contact: Daljit Singh Shergill
Position: President
Activities: Worship, resource, umbrella, visits,
youth, elderly, women, newsletters, books, inter-
faith
Other Languages: Punjabi, Hindi, Urdu
Affiliations: Sandwell Council of Sikh Gurdwaras;
Sikh Welfare Association; Khalsa Human Rights;
Shiromani Gurdwara Parbandakh Committee

Sandwell Sikh Community & Youth Forum
74 Dudley Road West, Tividale, Warley, West
Midlands, B69 2HR
Tel: 0121-520-6542 **Tel:** 0121-520-5933 (h)
Contact: Balwinder Singh Khalsa
Position: Chair
Activities: Resource, youth, elderly, women, inter-
faith
Other Languages: Punjabi

Guru Har Rai Gurdwara
126-128 High Street, West Bromwich, West
Midlands, B70 6JW
Tel: 0121-553-7219 **Tel:** 0121-553-3090 (h)
Contact: Mr G S Sidhu
Position: Secretary
Activities: Resource, media, umbrella, visits, youth,
elderly, women, newsletters, books, inter-faith
Other Languages: Punjabi
Affiliations: Sandwell Council of Sikh Gurdwaras

Guru Nanak Gurdwara
8 Edward Street, West Bromwich, West Midlands,
B70 8NP
Tel: 0121-553-1242
Contact: President

Shiromani Akali Dal/Sikh Community Support Association
49 Springfield Crescent, West Bromwich, West Midlands
Contact: Mr B Singh Rai

Smethwick Sikh Temple
Community Centre, 130 High Street, Smethwick, Birmingham, West Midlands, B66

Council of Sikh Gurdwaras in Wolverhampton
c/o Cannock Road Temple, 200-204 Cannock Road, Wolverhampton, West Midlands, WV10 0AL
Tel: 01902-450453 **Tel:** 01902-21142 (h)
Contact: Mr Gurmit Singh
Position: Treasurer
Activities: Umbrella

Guru Nanak Gurdwara
Vernon Street, Wolverhampton, West Midlands
Tel: 01902-26325

Guru Nanak Gurdwara
Arthur Street, Off Wellington Road, Bilston, Wolverhampton, West Midlands, WV1H 0DG
Tel: 01902-492383
Contact: Ranjodh Singh Karam
Position: General Secreetary
Activities: Worship, visits
Other Languages: Punjabi
Affiliations: Council of Sikh Gurdwaras in Wolverhampton

Guru Nanak Gurdwara
Well Lane, Wednesfield, Wolverhampton, West Midlands

Guru Nanak Gurdwara
53/54 Gordon Street, All Saints, Wolverhampton, West Midlands, WV2 1DB

Guru Nanak Gurdwara
205-6 Lea Road, Penfields, Wolverhampton, West Midlands, WV3 0LG
Tel: 01902-710289
Contact: Mr Pritam Singh
Position: Secretary

Guru Nanak Sikh Gurdwara
200-204 Cannock Road, Park Village, Wolverhampton, West Midlands, WV10 0AL
Tel: 01902-450453 **Tel:** 01902-21142
Contact: Mr Gurmit Singh

Position: General Secretary
Activities: Worship, resource, youth, women, inter-faith
Other Languages: Punjabi, Hindi
Affiliations: Council of Sikh Gurdwaras in Wolverhampton

Guru Nanak Sikh Temple
Sedgley Street, Off Dudley Road, Blackenhall, Wolverhampton, West Midlands, WV2 3AJ
Tel: 01902-459413 **Tel:** 01902-344504 (h)
Fax: 01902-458877
Contact: Narinder Singh Chohan
Position: Secretary
Activities: Worship, inter-faith
Other Languages: Punjabi

Nanaksar Thath Isher Darbar
Mander Street, Wolverhampton, West Midlands, WV3 OJZ
Tel: 01902-29379
Contact: Dr Sadhu Singh
Position: General Secretary

Ramgarhia Board & Temple
Westbury Street, Wolverhampton, West Midlands, WV1 1JD
Tel: 01902-26885
Contact: Mr Lyall
Position: Secretary

Ramgarhia Sabha
342-344 New Hampton Road East, Whitmore Reans, Wolverhampton, West Midlands, WV1 4AD
Tel: 01902-425156 **Tel:** 01902-339718 (h)
Contact: Mr Jagjit Singh Bahra
Position: Presdent
Activities: Worship, resource, visits, youth, elderly, women, inter-faith
Other Languages: Punjabi
Affiliations: Wolverhampton Gurdwara Council; Ramgarhia Council, UK; Ramgaria Educational Council, Phagwar, Punjab, India.

Sikh Association of Great Britain
17 Smestow Street, New Park Village, Wolverhampton, West Midlands, WV10 9AB
Tel: 01902-871246 (h)
Contact: Mr Balbir S Gill
Position: Chair
Activities: Elderly
Other Languages: Punjabi, Hindi

Sikh Temple
80 Hart Road, Wednesfield, Wolverhampton, West
Midlands

EAST ANGLIA
City, Town or Local Bodies

Cambridge Sikh Society
17 Woodcock Close, Impington, Cambridge,
Cambridgeshire, CB4 4LD (h)
Tel: 01223-232519 (h)
Contact: Mr Amrik Singh Sagoo
Position: Trustee
Activities: Worship, visits
Other Languages: Punjabi

Sangat Sikh Bhatra Temple
Great Yarmouth Road, Ipswich, Suffolk, IP1 2EN

Sikh Bhatra Temple
186 Cromwell Road, Peterborough,
Cambridgeshire, PE1 2EG
Tel: 01733-65133
Contact: Dr Singh
Position: President

GREATER LONDON
Borough and Local Bodies

BARKING AND DAGENHAM

Gurdwara Singh Sabha
100 North Street, Barking, Essex, IG11 8JD
Tel: 0181-594-3940
Contact: Jagdev Singh Purewal
Position: Secretary
Activities: Worship, visits, youth, elderly, women,
inter-faith
Other Languages: Punjabi
Affiliations: Network of Sikh Organisations, UK;
Sri Akal Takhat Sahib, Amritsar

Kshatrya Sabha London
233 Reede Road, Dagenham East, Dagenham,
Essex, RM10 8EL

Sharomani Akali Dal (UK)
16 Oval Road, South Dagenham, Essex,
RM10 9DR

Shiromani Akali Dal UK
100 North Street, Barking, Essex, IG1 8JD
Tel: 0181-594-3940
Contact: Inder Singh Jamu
Position: President
Other Languages: Punjabi

Shiromani Akal Dal UK
24 First Avenue, Dagenham, Essex

BEXLEY

Guru Nanak Durbait
31 Mitchel Close, Belvedere, Kent, DA17 6DR
Tel: 013224-32847 **Tel:** 0181-311-6940 (h)
Contact: Balbir Singh Khella
Position: Trustee
Activities: Worship, visits, youth, elderly
Other Languages: Punjabi, Hindi

CROYDON

Nanak Community Centre
St James Road, Croydon, Surrey, CR0 2BU
Tel: 0181-688-8155
Contact: C S Dhanjal
Position: Chairperson
Activities: Worship

EALING

Dasmesh Sat Sangh Sabha
6 Evelyn Grove, Southall, Middlesex
Tel: 0181-843-1961

**Guru Amardas Gurmat Society & Education
Centre**
1a Clifton Road, Southall, Middlesex, UB2 5QP
Tel: 0181-571-1335 **Tel:** 0181-570-1508 (h)
Fax: 0181-813-9681
Contact: Daljit Singh Saggu
Position: President
Activities: Worship, resource, youth, elderly,
women
Other Languages: Punjabi
Affiliations: Baba Jaswant Singh Trust

Guru Granth Gurdwara
45 Villiers Road, Southall, Middlesex
Tel: 0181-574-1828
Contact: Dr N S Manget
Activities: Worship

Ramgarhia Sabha Southall
53-57 Oswald Road, Southall, Middlesex, UB 1HN
Tel: 0181-571-4867
Contact: Jaspal Singh Bhambra
Position: General Secretary
Activities: Worship

Ramgarhia Welfare Darbar
31 Hart Grove, Ealing, London, W5

Sikh Literary Society
217 Western Road, Southall, Middlesex

Sri Guru Singh Sabha Gurdwara
2 Park Avenue, Southall, Middlesex, UB2 4NP
Tel: 0181-571-9687 **Fax:** 0181-893-5094
Contact: Harpal Singh Brar
Position: General Secretary

ENFIELD

Nanak Darbar North London
136 High Road, New Southgate, London,
N11 1PK
Tel: 0181-368-7104 **Tel:** 0181-292-9725 (h)
Contact: Mrs Balwant Kaur Rehal
Position: Honorary Secretary
Activities: Worship, resource, visits, youth, elderly,
women, newsletters, inter-faith
Other Languages: Punjabi
Affiliations: Network of Sikh Organisations, UK;
Akhal Takhat, Amritsar, Punjab, India

GREENWICH

Greenwich Sikh Association
1 Calderwood Street, Woolwich, London, SE18
Tel: 0181-854-4233 **Tel:** 0181-301-1078 (h)
Contact: S Mokha
Position: President
Activities: Worship, resource, visits, youth, elderly,
women, inter-faith
Other Languages: Punjabi, Hindi, Urdu

Ramgarhia Gurdwara
Masons Hill, Woolwich, London, SE18 6EJ
Tel: 0181-854-1786
Contact: Rup Singh Bhogal
Position: President
Activities: Worship, visits, youth, elderly, women
Other Languages: Punjabi, Hindi, Urdu
Affiliations: Ramgarhia Council UK

HACKNEY

Singh Sabha Gurdwara
68 Gloucester Drive, London, N4
Tel: 0181-800-7233

HAMMERSMITH AND FULHAM

Gurbani Cassette Centre
68c Iffley Road, London, W6
Tel: 0171-741-9310
Contact: Secretary

HARROW

Edgware Gurdwara (Waltham Drive)
28 Highlands, Edgware, Middlesex
Tel: 0181-952-5402

HILLINGDON

Guru Nanak Sikh College
Springfield Road, Hayes, Middlesex, UB4 0LT
Tel: 0181-573-6085 **Fax:** 0181-561-6772

HOUNSLOW

*Gurdwara Guru Nanak Nishkam Sewak Jatha
(UK)*
142 Martindale Road, Hounslow, Middlesex,
TW4 7HQ
Tel: 0181-570-4774
Contact: Mr Grewal
Position: Trustee

Gurdwara Sri Guru Singh Sabha
Alice Way, Hanworth Road, Hounslow, Middlesex,
TW3 3UA
Tel: 0181-577-2793
Contact: Jagjiwan Singh
Position: Secretary
Activities: Worship, resource, visits, youth, elderly,
women, inter-faith
Other Languages: Punjabi
Affiliations: Network of Sikh Organisations UK

Shiromani Akali Dal
29 Waye Avenue, Cranford, Hounslow, Middlesex,
TW5 9SD
Tel: 0181-897-9612

Sikh Art & Culture Centre
21 Montague Road, Hounslow, Middlesex,
TW31LG

Contact: Sardar Harcharan Singh Dhillon
Position: Honorary Secretary
Activities: Worship, resource, youth,women
Languages: Panjabi, Hindi

Sikh Study Centre (UK)
93 Waye Avenue, Hounslow, Middlesex

Sri Guru Singh Sabha
48 Way Avenue, Cranford, Hounslow, Middlesex

KENSINGTON AND CHELSEA

London Central Gurdwara (Khalsa Jatha)
62 Queensdale Road, Shepherds Bush, London, W11 4SG
Tel: 0171-603-2789
Contact: Madhan Singh Jolly
Position: Secretary
Activities: Worship
Affiliations: Network of Sikh Organisations, UK

KINGSTON-UPON-THAMES

Kingston Sikh Association
19 Douglas Rd, Kingston-upon-Thames, Surrey, KT6 7RZ
Contact: Mr Harcharan

NEWHAM

Dashmesh Darbar Gurdwara
97-101 Rosebery Avenue, Manor Park, London, E12 6PT
Tel: 0181-471-2204 **Fax:** 0181-470-7313
Contact: Mr Harjinder Singh
Position: President
Activities: Worship, visits, youth, elderly, women, inter-faith
Other Languages: Punjabi

Kshatrya Sabha London & Bhaghat Namdev Mission
2a Lucas Avenue, Upton Park, London, E13
Tel: 0181-548-1546 **Tel:** 0181-552-9601 (h)
Contact: Dr Mohinder Singh
Position: President
Activities: Worship, elderly, women
Other Languages: Punjabi, Urdu, Hindi
Affiliations: Community Belonging to Bhagat Namdev; Sikh Organisation of Gurdwaras; Kshatrya Sabha of Glasgow; Kshatrya Midland Societies

Ramgarhia Sikh Gurdwara
10-16 Neville Road, Forest Gate, London, E7 9SQ
Tel: 0181-472-3738 **Tel:** 0181-514-6588 (h)
Contact: Maghar Singh Hunjan
Position: Honorary General Secretary
Activities: Worship, resource, media, umbrella, visits, youth, elderly, women, newsletters, inter-faith
Other Languages: Punjabi
Affiliations: Ramgarhia Council of UK

REDBRIDGE

Guru Nanak Satsang Sabha (Karmsar) UK
37 Lexden Drive, Chadwell Heath, Romford, Essex, RM6 4TJ

Redbridge Punjabi Sabhiacharik Sabha
293-297 Ley Street, Ilford, Essex, IG1 4BN
Tel: 0181-478-4962
Contact: Mr Sansar Singh Narwal
Position: General Secretary
Activities: Youth, elderly, women
Other Languages: Punjabi, Hindi, Urdu

Sikh Study Forum
85 Inglehurst Gardens, Redbridge, Ilford, Essex, IG4 5HA
Tel: 0181-550-5778
Contact: RS Dhesi

SOUTHWARK

Gurdwara Baba Bhudha Sahib Ji
2 Shawbury Road, East Dulwich, London, SE22 9HD
Tel: 0181-693-1162 **Tel:** 0181-693-7776 (h)
Contact: S Akbal Singh Taak
Position: General Secretary
Activities: Resource, visits
Other Languages: Punjabi, Hindi

Sikh Temple
1 Thorncombe Road, Camberwell, London, SE5

TOWER HAMLETS

Gurdwara Sikh Sangat
1a Campbell Road, Bow, London, E3 4DS
Tel: 0181-980-2281

Gurdwara Singh Sangat
Harley Grove, London, E3 2AT
Tel: 0181-980-8861

WALTHAM FOREST

Gurdwara Sikh Sangat
71 Francis Road, Leyton, London, E10 6PL
Tel: 0181-556-4732 **Tel:** 0181-504-9129 (h)
Contact: Bibi Sukhvinderjit Kaur Deol
Position: President
Activities: Worship, umbrella, visits, youth, elderly, women, inter-faith
Other Languages: Punjabi

WANDSWORTH

Khalsa Centre
95 Upper Tooting Road, London, SW17 7TW
Tel: 0181-767-3196
Contact: Mr H S Arora
Position: Assistant Secretary

South London Sikh Gurdwara
142 Merton Road, London, SW18 5SK
Tel: 0181-870-7594

SOUTH EAST
City, Town or Local Bodies

Guru Nanak Gurdwara
207 Lower Brook Street, Basingstoke, Hampshire, RG21 1RR
Tel: 01256-473874

Sikh Temple
4 Kingshill Road, Basingstoke, Hampshire, RG21 3JE

Guru Nanak Gurdwara
72 Ford End Road, Queens Park, Bedford, Bedfordshire
Contact: Mr Lal Singh Gill

Ramgarhia Sikh Society
21 Willow Road, Bedford, Bedfordshire

Ramgarhia Sikh Society Gurdwara
33-39 Ampthill Street, Bedford, Bedfordshire, MK42 9BT
Tel: 01234-342969
Contact: Mr Satnam Singh Riyait
Position: Secretary
Activities: Worship

Ramgarhia Sikh Temple
69 Victoria Road, Bedford, Bedfordshire

Shri Guru Singh Sabha Gurudwara
46 Miles Road, Bedford, Bedfordshire

Sikh Community
80 The Row, Woodingdean, Brighton, East Sussex, BN 6LN

Guru Nanak Sikh Sabha Watford
c/o 406 Bushley Mill Lane, Bushey, Hertfordshire, WD2 2AD

Sikh Sangat Gurdwara
Sydney Road, Chatham, Kent, ME4 5BR
Tel: 01634-815934
Contact: Mr Avtar Singh
Position: Chair
Activities: Worship, visits
Other Languages: Punjabi
Affiliations: Bhat Sangat

Sikh Union
41 Dovedale Crescent, Southgate West, Crawley, West Sussex
Contact: Mr R S Bedi
Position: Secretary

Sri Guru Singh Sabha
27-29 Spencer Road, West Green, Crawley, West Sussex, RH11 7DE
Tel: 01293-530163 **Tel:** 01293-411793 (h)
Contact: Mr Manmohan Singh Majhail
Position: Trustee
Activities: Worship, visits
Other Languages: Punjabi, Urdu, Hindi, Malay & Swaheli
Affiliations: Sikh Missionary Society of Great Britain

Gurdwara Guru Hargobind Sahib
8-10 Highfield Road, Dartford, Kent, DA1 2JJ
Tel: 01322-222951 **Tel:** 01322-221021 (h)
Contact: Surjit Singh Kandola
Position: Secretary
Activities: Worship, visits youth, elderly, women
Other Languages: Punjabi

Sikh Youth International
20 Mount Pleasant Road, Dartford, Kent
Tel: 01322-279664

Kent Ramgarhia Darbar & Community Centre
63 Franklyn Road, Gillingham, Kent, ME7 4DJ
Tel: 01634–576618
Contact: Mr Mohinder Singh Paddam
Position: Founder Member

Sri Guru Nanak Gurdwara
Byron Road, Gillingham, Kent
Tel: 01634–850921
Contact: Mr S S Sandhu
Position: President

Guru Nanak Darbar Gurdwara
Clarence Place, Gravesend, Kent
Tel: 01474–534121
Contact: Mr B S Sodhi
Position: General Secretary

Guru Nanak Day Care & Community Centre
11 The Grove, Gravesend, Kent

Guru Nanak Sandesh Parchar Board
Gurparsaad Cottage, 20 Peacock Street, Gravesend,
Kent, DA12 1EF
Tel: 01474–361834 (h)
Contact: Mr Kabul Singh Sodhi
Position: Chair
Activities: Resource
Other Languages: Punjabi

International Sikh Youth Federation
21 Brook Street, Gravesend, Kent
Contact: Mr Narinderjit Singh Thandi

Jugnu Bhangra & Youth
40 Singlewell Road, Gravesend, Kent
Contact: Mr Shaminder Singh Bedi

Kshatriya Sabha
28 Pelham Road, Gravesend, Kent
Contact: Mr G Singh

Shiromani Akali Dal
49 Milton Road, Gravesend, Kent

Sikh Cultural Society
10 Darnley Street, Gravesend, Kent

Sikh Gurdwara Committee
23 Wellington Street, Gravesend, Kent

Sikh Gurdwara Committee
55 Pelham Road South, Gravesend, Kent

Sikh Temple
4 Milton Avenue, Gravesend, Kent, DA12 1QL
Tel: 01474–567418
Contact: G Singh
Position: Secretary
Activities: Resource, youth, books
Other Languages: Punjabi

Sikh Temple
6 Maidstone Road, Grays Thurrock, Essex
Tel: 01375–376086
Contact: Sukhdev Singh
Position: Secretary

Harlow Sikh Society
80 Greygoose Park, Harlow, Essex, CM19 4JL (h)
Tel: 01279–432177 (h)
Contact: Mr D S Bawa
Position: Chair

**Gurdwara Amrit Parchar Dharmik Diwan (Sikh
Temple)**
Brook Street, High Wycombe, Buckinghamshire,
HP11 2EQ
Tel: 01494–440153 **Tel:** 01494–532102
Contact: Mr Sarup Singh Seehra, MBE, JP
Position: President
Activities: Worship, visits, youth, elderly, women,
inter-faith
Other Languages: Punjabi (Gurmukhi)
Affiliations: Gurdwara Amrit Parchar Dharmik
Diwan, Bradford; Gurdwara Amrit Parchar
Dharmik Diwan, Oldbury

Sikh Association
17 Rye View, High Wycombe, Buckinghamshire,
HP13 6HL
Tel: 01494–446347
Contact: Mr Joginder Singh Bnasil
Position: President
Activities: Resource, visits, youth, elderly, women,
inter-faith
Other Languages: Punjabi, Hindi, Urdu
Affiliations: Amrit Parchar Dhai Mak Diwan;
Singh Sabha Gurdwara, Southall; Ramgarhia Sabha,
Slough

Sri Guru Singh Saba
64 Hughenden Road, High Wycombe,
Buckinghamshire

Guru Nanak Sikh Gudwara
37 Wilbury Way, Hitchin, Hertfordshire

Guru Singh Sabha Gurdwara
Radcliffe Road, Hitchin, Hertfordshire
Tel: 01462-432993
Contact: Mr Ajit Singh Sarai
Position: Secretary

Ramgarhia Gurdwara Society - Hitchin
Bearton Avenue, Hitchin, Hertfordshire
Contact: Mr G S Sahota
Position: General Secretary
Activities: Worship

Sikh Community
24 Church Road, Hove, East Sussex, BN3 2FN

Nanaksar Sar Thath Ishar Darbar
7 Gernon Walk, Letchworth, Hertfordshire,
SG6 3HW
Tel: 01462-684153 **Tel:** 01462-686477 (h)
Contact: Resham Singh Johal
Position: Trustee

Guru Nanak Gurdwara
12-16 Portland Street, Luton, Bedfordshire,
LU4 8XT
Tel: 01582-571629
Contact: Karnail Singh Rajasansi
Position: General Secretary
Activities: Worship, visits, youth, elderly, women
Other Languages: Punjabi, Hindi, Urdu

Sikh Missionary & Literary Society
392 Selbourne Road, Luton, Bedfordshire,
LU4 8NU
Contact: G S Lakra

Guru Nanak Satsang Sabha
31 Rutland Road, Maidenhead, Berkshire,
SL6 4HZ
Tel: 01628-23507 **Tel:** 01628-415605 (h)
Contact: Karnail Singh Pannu
Position: President
Activities: Worship, resource, visits, youth, elderly,
women, inter-faith
Other Languages: Punjabi
Affiliations: Berkshire & Thames Valley Sikh
Temples; Council of Sikh Gurdwaras, Birmingham;
Gurdwaras' Organisation, Amritsar, India

Ramgarhia Sabha
Kiln Farm House, Kiln Farm, Tilers Road, Milton
Keynes, Buckinghamshire
Contact: Gursarn S Panesar
Position: Secretary

Activities: Worship, youth, elderly, women
Other Languages: Punjabi

Guru Nanak Sar Gurdwara
5 Margate Road, Southsea, Portsmouth, Hampshire,
PO5 1EY
Tel: 01705-751942 **Tel:** 01705-824965 (h)
Contact: Kirpal Singh Digpal
Position: President
Activities: Worship, resource, umbrella, visits youth,
elderly, women, newsletters, books, inter-faith
Other Languages: Punjabi, Hindi, Urdu

Ramgahria Sabha
PO Box 107, Reading, Berkshire
Tel: 01734-750760 (h)
Contact: Baldev Singh Sian
Position: General Secretary
Activities: Worship, resource, youth, elderly,
women, newsletters, inter-faith
Other Languages: Punjabi, Hindi, Urdu, Swaheli
Affiliations: Ramgarhia Council UK; Ramgarhia
Federation - International

Sri Guru Singh Sabha Gurdwara
30a Cumberland Road, Reading, Berkshire,
RG1 3LB
Tel: 01189-623836
Position: General Secretary
Activities: Worship, resource, visits, youth
Other Languages: Punjabi

Gurdwara Sabha
Cossack Street, Rochester, Kent, ME1 2EF
Contact: Mr T S Sandhu

Medway Towns Gurudwara Sabha
39 Rose Street, Rochester, Kent

Guru Nanak Punjabi Library
16 Arthur Road, Slough, Berkshire

International Sikh Brotherhood
32 Burlington Road, Slough, Berkshire

Ramgarhia Gurdwara
Woodland Avenue, Slough, Berkshire
Tel: 01753-525458
Contact: Mr I S Ghataura
Position: Secretary

Ramgarhia Sabha
31 Chalvey Road East, Slough, Berkshire

Ramgarhia Sabha
26 King Edward Street, Slough, Berkshire

Sabha Ramgarhia Temple
Baylis Road, Woodland Avenue, Slough, Berkshire, SL1

Sri Guru Gobind Singh Marg Gurdwara
76 Montague Road, Slough, Berkshire
Tel: 01753-579906

Sri Guru Singh Sabha Gurdwara
Waxham Court, Sheehy Way, Slough, SL2 5SS
Tel: 01753-526828
Contact: Mr Tarbedi Singh Benipal
Position: General Secretary
Activities: Worship

Gurdwara Nanaksar
3 Peterborough Road, Bevois Valley, Southampton, Hampshire, SO14 6HY
Tel: 01703-226464
Contact: Harjar Singh
Position: General Secretary
Activities: Worship, visits, youth, women
Other Languages: Punjabi
Affiliations: Golden Temple, India

Gurdwara Singh Sabha
128-130 Northumberland Road, Southampton, S02 0ER

Gurdwara Tegh Bahadur Sahib
7 St Mark's Road, Newtown, Southampton, Hampshire, SO14 0FB
Tel: 01703-393440
Contact: General Secretary
Activities: Worship, visits, youth, elderly, women, inter-faith
Tel: 01703-226744
Contact: Mr Aqbal Singh
Position: Secretary
Activities: Worship

Sikh Community Council
Sikh Temple, 3 Peterborough Road, Southampton, SO2 0HY
Tel: 01703-336464

Singh Sabha Gurdwara
Onslow Road, Cranbury Avenue, Southampton, Hampshire

Tel: 01703-333016 **Tel:** 01703-396115 (h)
Contact: Daljit Singh Grewal
Position: Secretary
Activities: Worship, resource, visits, youth, women, inter-faith
Other Languages: Punjabi, Hindi

Sri Guru Sanagat Association
41 Derby Road, Southampton, Hampshire
Tel: 01703-226464

Sikh Temple
18 Granvile Road, Watford, Hertfordshire

Sikh Youth Association
Gurdwara Sri Guru Singh Sabha, 48 Kings Close, Watford, Hertfordshire, WD1 8UB
Tel: 01923-244050 **Tel:** 01923-241686 (h)
Contact: Mr Jagtar Singh Dhindsa
Position: Chair
Activities: Worship, resource, visits, young, women, inter-faith
Other Languages: Punjabi

Watford Sikh Association
48 Kings Close, Watford, Hertfordshire, WD1 8UB
Tel: 01923-244050 **Tel:** 01923-220843 (h)
Contact: Sohan Singh Ahluwalia
Position: General Secretary
Activities: Worship, resource, visits, youth, elderly, women, inter-faith
Other Languages: Punjabi

Watford Sikh Youth Organisation
c/o Watford REC, 16 Clarendon Road, Watford, Hertfordshire, WD1 1JY

SOUTH WEST

City, Town or Local Bodies

Bristol Singh Sabha
c/o 491 Stapleton Road, Bristol, Greater Bristol, BS5 6PQ
Contact: Mukhtyar Singh

Guru Nanak Prakash Singh Sabha Gurdwara
71-75 Fishponds Road, Eastville, Bristol, Greater Bristol, B5 6SF
Tel: 0117-951-1609 **Tel:** 0117-975-0885 (h)
Contact: Mr Satnam Singh

Position: Secretary
Activities: Worship, resource, media, visits, youth, inter-faith
Other Languages: Punjabi
Affiliations: Sikh Resource Centre, Bristol

Ramgharia Sikh Temple

81 Chelsea Road, Easton, Bristol, Greater Bristol, BS5
Tel: 0117-955-4929
Contact: Mr Balwant Singh
Position: President

Sangat Singh Sabha Gurdwara

11 Summerhill Road, St George, Bristol, Greater Bristol, BS5
Tel: 0117-955-9333
Contact: Baldev Singh Roudh
Position: General Secretary
Activities: Worship, youth
Other Languages: Punjabi
Affiliations: Sikh Organisations UK

Sikh Resource Centre

114 St Marks Road, Easton, Bristol, Greater Bristol, B55 6JD
Tel: 0177-9525023
Contact: Jatindar Kaur
Position: Coordinator
Activities: Resource, media, umbrella, visits, youth, elderly, women, inter-faith
Other Languages: Punjabi, Hindi, Urdu
Affiliations: The Sikh Missionary Society

Guru Arjan Niwas Sikh Temple

46 Clifton Street, Exeter, Devon

Sikh Temple

North Street, Swindon, Wiltshire, SN1 3JX
Contact: Mr B S Nandra

NORTHERN IRELAND

City, Town or Local Bodies

Sikh Gurdwara

Hinton House, 1 Clooney Park West, Londonderry, County Londonderry, BT47 7TB
Contact: Mr K S Panesar

SCOTLAND

City, Town or Local Bodies

Sikh Temple

10 Taylors Lane, Dundee, Angus

Sikh Temple Guru Nanak Gurdwara

Victoria Road, Dundee, Angus

Sri Guru Nanak Gurdwara

1 Nelson Street, Dundee, DD1 2PN
Tel: 01382-23383
Contact: Secretary

Sikh Temple

11 Acedemy Street, Edinburgh, Lothian, EH6

Sikh Temple

1 Mill Lane, Edinburgh, Lothian
Tel: 0131-553-7207
Contact: Jaswant Singh
Position: President

Sikh Temple

66 Ferry Road, Edinburgh, Lothian, EH6 4AH

Central Gurdwara Singh Sabha

138 Berkeley Street, Glasgow, Strathclyde, G3 7HY
Tel: 0141-221-6698
Contact: Mr Mohinder Singh Gill
Position: President
Activities: Worship, resource, media, visits youth, elderly, women, inter-faith
Other Languages: Punjabi, Hindi, Urdu

Gurdwara Guru Granth Sahib Sikh Sabha

163 Nithsdale Road, Glasgow, Strathclyde, G41
Tel: 0141-423-8288 **Tel:** 0141-810-4911 (h)
Contact: Daljeet Singh Dilber
Position: President
Activities: Worship, umbrella, visits, elderly, women, inter-faith
Other Languages: Punjabi
Affiliations: Glasgow Gurdwara Committee

Guru Nanak Sikh Temple (Ramgarhia Association)

19-27 Otago Street, Glasgow, Strathcylde, G12 8JJ
Tel: 0141-334-9125 **Tel:** 0141-772-8457 (h)
Contact: Sardara Singh Jandooi
Position: Secretary

Activities: Worship, resource, visits, youth
Other Languages: Punjabi

Shri Guru Tegh Bahadur Gurdwara Bhatra Sangat

32 St Andrew's Drive, Glasgow, Strathclyde, G41 5SG
Tel: 0141-427-2763
Contact: Granthi
Activities: Worship

Sikh Temple

128 McCulloch Street, Glasgow, Strathclyde, G1

WALES

City, Town or Local Bodies

Bhatra Sikh Centre

80-82 Ninian Park Road, Riverside, Cardiff, South Glamorgan, CF1 8JD

Dasmais Singh Saba Gurdwara Bhatrta

20 Pitman Street, Pontcanna, Cardiff, South Glamorgan

Gurdwara Nanak Darbar Sikh Association

18 Copper Street, Roath, Cardiff, South Glamorgan, CF2 1LH
Tel: 01222-450175
Contact: Mr Kaboul Singh
Position: Chair
Activities: Worship, visits
Languages: Punjabi

Sikh Gurdwara

212a Pearl Street, Roath, Cardiff, South Glamorgan, CF2 8JD

Sikh Gurdwara

16 Wentloog Road, Rumney, Cardiff, South Glamorgan, CF3

Sri Dasmais Singh Sabha Gurdwara Bhatra Sikh Centre

97-103 Tudor Street, Cardiff, South Glamorgan
Tel: 01222-224806
Contact: Waleiti Singh Balkar
Position: Secretary
Activities: Worship

KEY TO TERMS USED IN SIKH ORGANISATION TITLES

Note: This is not a complete glossary of significant Sikh terms. It is a guide to the meaning and/or background of some of the words used in the titles of Sikh organisations listed in this directory. More information on the italicised words can be tracked down either elsewhere in the key or, in the section on "Introducing the Sikh Community", by using the directory's "Significant Word Index".

Ajit: Punjabi for "invincible". The first name of Ajit Singh, a son of the tenth *Guru* and also the name of a *sant*.

Akali: Punjabi for "timeless" or "deathless". *Akal* refers to God. Found within the term Sharomani Akali Dal, the name of a Sikh political party ("the Principal Party of God"), *shiromani* meaning "principal" and *dal* a "party" or organisation.

Akhand: Punjabi for "uninterrupted" or "continuous". An *akhand path* is a continuous reading of the *Guru Granth Sahib* over forty-eight hours. The Akhand Kirtani Jatha is so called because of their practice of continuous singing of *kirtan* overnight.

Amardas: The third of the Sikh *Gurus*.

Amrit: Punjabi for "nectar". It is the name for the sweet water blessed and used in the formal ceremony for initiating Sikhs into the *khalsa panth*.

Anand: Punjabi for "bliss" or "joy". It is used in *anand karaj* to refer to the Sikh marriage rite.

Arjan: The first name of the Sikhs' fifth *Guru*, Guru Arjan Dev, who was Sikhism's first martyr.

Ashram: Word of Sanskrit origin, used in English to denote a place of solace and spiritual rest and retreat.

Baba: Punjabi term of endearment and respect especially for older men such as grandfathers. A title given to eminent male Sikhs.

Babbar: Punjabi term for "a big lion" which was applied to Babbar Khalsa, members of a revolutionary movement in the Indian subcontinent in the 1920s. It now appears in the Babbar Khalsa and other similar organisations of Sikhs which aim to create a sovereign Sikh state.

Bebe: Title for a respected older woman usually carrying the sense of "mother". Found in the name of Guru Nanak Dev Ji's sister, Bebe Nanaki, regarded as his first follower.

Bhagat: Punjabi for "devotee". In Sikh tradition it can refer to several persons belonging to the *bhagti* tradition, for example, Kabir, Farid, Namdev and others. It is also the name of the twentieth century Sikh freedom fighter killed by the British, named Bhagat Singh. *Desh bhagat* means "patriot".

Bhai: Punjabi for "brother". It is a title of respect for Sikh men, as in Bhai Gurdas. It is sometimes used of *granthis*.

Bhangra: Traditional Punjabi male folk dance, now also a hybrid form of South Asian youth dance music.

Bhatra: The name of a Sikh endogamous community characterised by certain customs and traditionally by occupation. *Bhatra* Sikhs mainly migrated to Britain before the Second World War and *gurdwaras* founded by them can be found especially in the seaports as well as in inland areas where they have settled in significant numbers.

Budha: Punjabi for "old man" or "man of wisdom". Part of the name of Baba Budha, a disciple of the first *Guru* whose life spanned those of the first six *Gurus*.

Changa: Punjabi for "good".

Dal: Punjabi and Hindi for "group" and used for "party" or "organisation", as in the Sikh political party Akali Dal.

Darbar: Punjabi for "court" or "hall" used in Ajit Darbar Gurdwara in Coventry and in Dashmesh Darbar (Court of the Tenth *Guru*). Sometimes found written as *durbar*.

Das: Punjabi for "ten" or for "servant". It is usually a part of a name, such as Guru Amar Das.

Dasmesh: Variant Romanisation of *Dashmesh* (see below).

Dashmesh: Meaning "tenth" and therefore the title of the tenth *Guru*, Guru Gobind Singh Ji.

Deep: The name of a Sikh martyr - Baba Deep Singh.

Degh: Literally a "large cooking pan", reflecting the Sikh emphasis on providing free hospitality.

Des: Variant Romanisation of *desh* (see below).

Desh: Punjabi for "country". Desh *bhagat* means "patriot."

Dev: Punjabi for "God" and often appearing as part of male names, as in Guru Nanak Dev Ji or Guru Arjan Dev Ji.

Dewan: Meaning "assembly" or "court". It is a term used for Sikh corporate worship (on the analogy of the Moghul Emperors' audience chamber). It can also be found in Roman script as *diwan* (see below).

Dharam: Punjabi for "religion". Used, for example, Dharam Parchar Sanstha means "institution for preaching the faith."

Dharmak: Punjabi for "religious" or "pertaining to *dharam*". Also appears in Roman script as *dharmik* (see below).

Dharmik: Variant Romanisation of *dharmak* (see above).

Diwan: Variant Romanisation of *dewan* (see above).

Durbar: Variant Romanisation of *darbar* (see above).

Ekta: Punjabi for "unity".

Fateh: Punjabi and Persian for "victory", as in "*waheguru ji ki fateh*", meaning "victory to God". Fateh Singh was also the name of one of Guru Gobind Singh's sons.

Gobind: A title for God and the first name of the tenth *Guru*, Guru Gobind Singh Ji, a variant Romanisation of which is sometimes found as Govind (see below).

Govind: A variant Romanisation of Gobind (see above).

Granth: Punjabi for "volume". It is used in the name of the Sikh scriptures, the *Adi Granth* or *Guru Granth Sahib*.

Gurbani: Punjabi for "*Guru's* utterance" or "*Guru's* speech" and refers to the hymns of the *Guru Granth Sahib*.

Gurdwara: Punjabi for "door of the *Guru*". It is used as the name for any building in which the *Guru Granth Sahib* is installed although most often it is popularly used of a visibly religious building or place of Sikh worship.

Gurmat: Punjabi for "*Guru's* teaching" or "*Guru's* philosophy". It is the Sikh word for Sikhism.

Gursikh: Punjabi for "*Guru's* Sikh", a respectful title for an *Amritdhari* Sikh.

Guru: Punjabi for "teacher". In Sikhism the title is reserved for the ten human *Gurus* and the *Guru Granth Sahib* as well as appearing in titles for the divine, such as *Waheguru* and *Satguru*.

Gurudwara: Variant Romanisation of *gurdwara*.

Hai: Punjabi for "is", as in the words of Guru Gobind Singh, "*khalsa mero rup hai khas*", meaning "the *khalsa* is my very form".

Har: Meaning "Lord", it is a part of the names of the seventh and eighth *Gurus*, Guru Har Rai and Guru Har Krishan.

Hargobind: Literally "Lord God", from Guru Har Gobind, the sixth *Guru*.

Ishar: A name, meaning "God", but is also a part of the name of Baba Ishar Singh, a follower of Baba Nanak Singh of Nanaksar.

Isher: Variant Romanisation of *Ishar* (see above).

Istri: Punjabi for "woman", found for example in Istri Sabha, meaning "women's group".

Jassa: The name of a famous eighteenth century Sikh military leader.

Jatha: Punjabi for "band" or "squad", used of contemporary Sikh organisations such as Akhand Kirtani Jatha.

Ji: Suffix denoting respect as in, for example, *Baba Ji*.

Kalgidar: Literally "with a plume in his turban", a title for the tenth *Guru*, Guru Gobind Singh Ji.

Kambaj: A social grouping.

Khalistan: Punjabi for "Land of the Pure". The name of the sovereign Sikh state for which some Sikhs are campaigning.

Khalsa: Meaning "pure" and "owing direct allegiance". The name for Sikhs as a collective group or nation.

Khas: Punjabi for "special" or "particular", as in Guru Gobind Singh Ji's *"khalsa mero rup hai khas"*, meaning "the *khalsa* is my very form".

Kirpal: Punjabi for "benevolent" and a name, as of Kirpal Singh, who is revered by his followers.

Kirtani: Variant Romanisation of *kirtini* (see below).

Kirtini: Punjabi for "those who do *kirtan*" meaning "those who sing Sikh hymns".

Kirtni: Variant Romanisation of Punjabi for "performing *kirtan*", meaning "singing Sikh hymns."

Kshatriya: The second, warrior, social grouping in the classical groupings of Indian society, it is the Sanskrit word for Khatri, an urban grouping of Punjabi society.

Kshatrya: Variant Romanisation of *Kshatriya* (see above).

Maha: Punjabi for "great".

Mahanaja: Variant Romanisation of *Maharaja*, meaning "great king".

Marg: Punjabi for "way" or "spiritual path".

Mera: Punjabi for "my", as in the words of Guru Gobind Singh, *"khalsa mero rup hai khas"*, meaning "the *khalsa* is my very form".

Miri: Persian word relating to political power.

Namdev: *Nam* means "name" and *Dev* (see above) means "God". The name of a Hindu saint whose writings are included in the *Guru Granth Sahib*.

Nanak: Name of the first *Sikh Guru*, Guru Nanak Dev.

Nanaki: Name of Guru Nanak Dev Ji's sister, Bebe Nanaki, regarded as his first follower.

Nanaksar: Punjabi literally meaning "place of Nanak". It is also a *gurdwara* in the Ludhiana District of the Punjab with a line of Sikh saints who have established a chain of *gurdwaras* in Britain and elsewhere and is therefore found in the title of some *gurdwaras* in Britain.

Nanki: Variant Romanisation of *Nanaki* (see above).

Nish: A Punjabi prefix meaning "without".

Nishkam: Punjabi for "without desire" appearing in the phrase *nishkam seva*, meaning "service with no desire for reward", in other words, distinterested service. There is, for example, the Nishkam Sevak Jatha meaning literally "the band of selfless followers" which was set up by Sant Puran Singh.

Niwas: Punjabi for "house".

Panjab: Comes from the Persian for "five" and "water", in other words, the "Land of the Five Rivers" (tributaries of the River Indus). Also found written as Punjab in a variant Romanisation. The Punjab is the name for a current state within India, the much larger area originally known as the Punjab having been divided between India and Pakistan in 1947 and the Indian state of Punjab having been further reduced in size since 1966.

Panth: A collective term for Sikh society as in *Khalsa Panth*.

Parbandhak: Punjabi for "management" or "administrative". Part of the title of the Sikhs' main elected body, the Shiromani Gurdwara Parbandhak Committee in Amritsar and also used in the title of many Sikh organisations in the UK.

Parchar: Punjabi for "preaching".

Parivar: Punjabi for "family".

Parkash: A name meaning "light" or "manifestation".

Piri: Punjabi and Persian for "spiritual power".

Prakash: Variant Romanisation of *parkash* (see above).

Punjabi: Pertaining to the Punjab (see above). Used of a language. Also found as Panjab.

Rai: Part of the name of the seventh *Guru*, Guru Har Rai.

Raj: Punjabi for "rule" or "dominion". "*Raj karega khalsa*", meaning "the *khalsa* will rule" is a Sikh rallying cry.

Ram: A name, which in the *Guru Granth Sahib* is an epithet for God. In Hindu tradition, Ram is an incarnation of Vishnu. In Sikhism, the name is found as the first name of the fourth *Guru*, Guru Ram Das Ji.

Ramdas: Variant Romanisation of Ram Das, the name of the fourth *Guru*.

Ramgarhia: A Sikh social and occupational grouping. *Ramgarhias* took their name from Guru Ram Das and the fort called Ramgarh.

Ravi: First part of the name of a mediaeval mystic *bhagat* and poet, Ravidas, some of whose compositions are included in the *Guru Granth Sahib*.

Rup: Punjabi for "form", as in *Guru Gobind Singh's* words,"*khalsa mero rup hai khas*", meaning "the *khalsa* is my very form." Also found written as "*roop*".

Sabha: Punjabi for "assembly", often used of Sikh organisations.

Sabiacharik: Punjabi for "of civilised conduct" or "cultural".

Sacha: Punjabi for "true".

Sahib: Punjabi and Urdu honorific ending and term of respect for individuals. It is used for sites long associated with Sikh history, the *Guru Granth Sahib*, and the Sikh flag.

Samaj: Punjabi for "society", often used of organisations.

Sandesh: Punjabi for "message".

Sang: Punjabi for "association" or "company".

Sangat: Punjabi for "congregation".

Sangha: Punjabi for "group" or "union", often used of organisations.

Sanstha: Punjabi for "institution" or "organisation".

Sat: Punjabi for "true".

Seva: Punjabi for "service".

Sewa: Variant Romanisation of *seva* (see above).

Sewak: Punjabi for "one who gives voluntary service", for example in the *gurdwara*.

Shaheed: Punjabi meaning "martyr". Also found written as *shahid*.

Sharomani: Variant Romanisation of *shiromani* (see below).

Shere: Punjabi/Urdu for "lion", as for example in Sher-e-Punjab (Lion of Panjab).

Shiri: Variant Romanisation of *Shri* (see below).

Shiromani: Punjabi for "principal", as in the Shiromani Gurdwara Parbandhak Committee.

Shri: Prefix denoting respect, sometimes meaning simply "Mr", sometimes used in the title of a *Guru*, as in Shri Guru Nanak Dev.

Sri: Variant Romanisation of *Shri* (see above).

Shromani: Variant Romanisation of *shiromani* (see above).

Takht: Punjabi for "throne", quite often relating to one of the five principal Sikh "seats of authority" or centres where important decisions are made relating to Sikhism.

Tegh: Punjabi and Persian for "sword", used in the first name of the ninth *Guru*, Guru Tegh Bahadur.

Thath: Meaning "splendour", also used of some *gurdwaras*.

Udham: The name of Udham Singh who in 1940 killed Sir Michael O'Dwyer, who had praised General Dyer, the former Governor of the Punjab, following his massacre of Sikhs in 1919.

Yadgaar: Meaning "memorial".

INTRODUCING THE ZOROASTRIAN COMMUNITY

ZOROASTRIANS IN THE UNITED KINGDOM

Origins

The first Zoroastrian known to have visited the United Kingdom came in 1723. The first Indian firm to open for business in Britain was run by a *Parsi* (see section on *Parsis* below) family called Cama and Company and began in 1855. The Zoroastrian community is thus a long-established community in Britain. It was from its *Parsi* members, who made up the majority of the early Zoroastrian settlers, that the first three Asian British Members of Parliament came. The first of these was the Liberal MP, Dadabhai Naoroji, elected in 1892.

Migration

The founders of the community initially settled in Britain in the nineteenth century and the first community organisation was formally established in 1861. Other *Parsis* came from India in the 1950s, immediately following Indian independence and later, prior to the introduction in the 1960s of tighter immigration controls on migration from New Commonwealth countries. There were also Indian origin *Parsis* who came from Aden and from East Africa (mainly Zanzibar, Kenya and Uganda), following the introduction in the late 1960s and early 1970s of Africanisation policies in these newly independent states. Iranian Zoroastrians came to Britain from Iran largely after the downfall of the Pahlavi dynasty in 1979.

There are currently around 5,000-10,000 Zoroastrians in the UK. There is only one Zoroastrian place of worship in the UK recorded in the directory, namely a designated room for worship within Zoroastrian House. Globally, there are approximately 120-150,000 Zoroastrians, mainly in Iran, India (particularly Bombay and Gujarat state), Pakistan, Britain, North America, Australia and New Zealand.

Languages

Zoroastrians with family roots in India, whether directly from India or via East Africa, have Parsi Gujarati as their tongue of daily conversation. Zoroastrians with an Iranian family background, have Persian or Farsi as their mother tongue, although very many of the young generation are fluent in English. Zoroastrian prayers are said in the ancient Iranian languages of Avestan and Pahlavi.

ORIGINS AND DEVELOPMENT OF ZOROASTRIANISM

Zarathushtra

The term Zoroastrianism comes from the Greek form (Zoroaster) of the name Zarathushtra, who was the founder of the religion. The religion is also known as *Zarathushtrianism* from the Iranian form of the founder's name, or as *Mazdayasni Zarthushti/ Zartoshti* (*Mazdayasni* means worshipper of God).

There is considerable debate about the precise dates of Zarathushtra's life. Some within the Zoroastrian community argue for a date as early as 6,000BCE, while other Zoroastrians and many academics external to the community argue for a date around 1,200BCE. Whatever his precise date of birth, it is generally agreed that Zarathushtra lived in North Eastern Iran.

Zoroastrians believe that Zarathushtra's life was threatened by evil forces from infancy onwards. At a young age he went to live a solitary life of meditation in the countryside and it is believed that his first vision came to him at the age of thirty. His personal visionary experiences inspired him to infuse the traditional Iranian religion in which he functioned as a *zaotar* or (priest), with a personal, experiential dimension.

He spent the following forty-seven years of his life spreading a prophet's message in which he denounced the *daevas* (the former gods of some of the Iranians, which Zarathushtra saw as demonic spirits); proclaimed the worship of Ahura Mazda (the Wise Lord) as the source of *asha* (truth, righteousness, order, justice) and *vohu manah* (good mind); and called people to the threefold ethic of *humata* (good thoughts), *hukhta* (good words) and *hvarshta* (good deeds).

Zarathushtra's teaching was accepted by the then king Vishtaspa of the Kayanian dynasty, but he faced considerable opposition from supporters of the existing polytheistic religious structures.

History and Influence

Zoroastrianism eventually became the imperial religion of three successive Iranian empires. Precisely how this occured is uncertain, although just prior to the Achaemenid period, the *Magi*, whom the historian Herodotus identifies as a priestly grouping of the Medes in the North West of Iran, seem to have adopted Zoroastrian beliefs and to have played a part in developing the religion's unifying role within the Empire.

In various forms of development Zoroastrianism became, successively, the religion of the Achaemenids (559-331BCE), the Parthians (mid second century BCE - 224CE) and the Sasanians (224-652CE). In various ways it is thought to have influenced post-exilic Judaism, Christianity, Islam, Greek philosophers such as Plato, Pythagoras and Aristotle and also *Mahayana* Buddhism in the East.

The Parsis in India and the Zoroastrians in Iran

In the ninth century CE some Zoroastrians from Khorasan, a province in north-eastern Iran, left Iran following the Arab conquest, seeking religious and economic freedom. They settled at Sanjan in Gujarat, North West India, in 936CE. This community became known as the *Parsis* or *Parsees*, from Pars the name of the province of north east Iran from which they had first set out. Over the next thousand years many more Zoroastrians emigrated to India due to religious persecution in Iran. Because of this, many Zoroastrians consider India as their adopted homeland, although a significant community also remained in Iran.

SOURCES OF ZOROASTRIAN BELIEFS AND PRACTICES

The Avesta

The main body of Zoroastrian scripture is known as the *Avesta*. It originally consisted of twenty-one books, the contents of which were orally transmitted for many centuries from generation to generation and then written down in the fifth or sixth century CE in a specially composed Avestan alphabet. Only about one quarter of these texts survive in their original form. In their present form, the Zoroastrian scriptures may be classified into five divisions:

Yasna and Gathas

The *Yasna* is concerned with acts of worship, praise, prayer, supplication and religious devotion. It is divided into seventy-two chapters, which include the seventeen *Gathas*. The *Gathas* are *The Divine Hymns of Zarathushtra* and are metrical compositions written in the ancient Avestan language. They are difficult to translate today since some words in the *Gathas* only appear in these sources and nowhere else. Sometimes, therefore, one can only gain an approximate sense of their meaning.

The Yashts (hymns)

The *Yashts* (*Yashti* meaning "homage" in Avestan) are prose and verse hymns addressed to individual *yazatas/yazads* (adorable beings worthy of adoration). In all, there are twenty-one *Yashts*, some of which are thought to be very ancient.

The Vendidad (or Videvdat)

The word *Vendidad* is the present form of the ancient Avestan word *Vidaeva-data*, meaning rules and regulations to oppose *daeva* or evil. It is not read as a prayer book, but it specifies in detail the laws of purity and also contains diverse material such as the account of creation; the geography of *Airyana Vaeja* (the known limits of the Aryan world); the legend of a golden age; legal matters; and the revelation received by Zarathushtra.

Visperad

Visperad (meaning "Service of all the Masters") is a collection of materials supplementary to the *Yasna*. These are never recited independently, but are usually recited at the six religious festivals known as *gahanbars* (see below) and they contain invocations and offerings of homage to "all the Lords or heavenly powers" (*Vispe Ratavo*).

Khordeh Avesta

The *Khordeh Avesta* is a short extract from the *Avesta* containing: *Nyayeshes*, which are praises to the elements – *Khorshed* (sun), *Mehr* (the heavenly light), *Mahabokhta* (the moon), *Avan* (water) and *Adar* (fire); the *Afrinagan* and *Afrins*, which are blessings; the *Gahs*, which are prayers to the five parts into which a day is divided; and the *Sirozah*, which contains twenty-two *Yashts*, invoking the *Yazatas*.

Later Texts

In addition to the *Avesta* there are many texts written in *Pazand* (a mixture of Pahlavi and Persian), mostly in the ninth century CE, which reflect the later growth of the religion and its encounter with Judaism, Christianity, Islam and Buddhism, and include some translations and summaries of otherwise lost ancient sources.

KEY ZOROASTRIAN BELIEFS

Ahura Mazda

Zarathushtra taught that Ahura Mazda (the Wise Lord or the Lord of Wisdom) is to be seen as the One Supreme, All-Powerful, All-Knowing, All-Wise, uncreated, eternally Good and Perfect, ever-present, Creator of *Asha* and *Vohu Manah* (Good Mind). Ahura Mazda is present everywhere, and is seen as a friend to all, never to be feared by human beings. According to the teaching of Zarathushtra, Ahura Mazda alone is worthy of absolute worship.

Zoroastrians believe that Zarathushtra identified, for the first time in human history, the importance of the *Vohu Manah* (Good Mind). His ethical *monotheism* taught human beings to think and reflect with a clear, rational mind, in order to dispel ignorance and blind faith.

Spenta Mainyu (The Holy Spirit) and Angra Mainyu (The Destructive Spirit)

The classical Zoroastrian teaching is that Ahura Mazda did not create evil: a perfect, All-Wise and Good God could, by definition, not create evil. Rather, evil is seen as the work of *Angra Mainyu* (the Destructive Spirit). The characteristics of *Angra Mainyu* are anger, greed, jealousy and destruction. In this present world, the forces of evil attack and afflict Ahura Mazda's creations, adopting a kind of parasitic existence and eating away at the good creation, bringing chaos, violence and destruction in opposition to the force of *Spenta Mainyu* (the Holy Spirit). Human beings are seen as *hamkar* (fellow-workers) with Ahura Mazda in bringing about the ultimate defeat of evil.

Whilst all Zoroastrians share the conviction that evil will be overcome by Ahura Mazda, Zoroastrianism is a complex and living tradition that has evolved over the centuries. Its richness has therefore included differing emphases and accounts of how evil will be overcome. For example, in a Pahlavi text of the 9th century, the world is represented as a trap into which evil is ensnared, in order that evil may ultimately be destroyed. Some Zoroastrians, however, assign sole authority to the *Gathas* (see above) and in their interpretation of the *Gathas* emphasise the absolute power of Ahura Mazda over evil.

The "Seven Good Creations" and Their Guardians

The sky, waters, earth, plants, cattle, humans, and fire are the seven primary creations which make up the world. Zoroastrians believe that Ahura Mazda fashioned this world with the aid of spiritual forces which he created as guardians of the seven creations. They collectively came to be known as the *Amesha Spentas* (Bounteous Immortals). They are also believed, in their turn, to have brought forth the *yazatas* (see below) which are referred to as the "adorable ones".

Amesha Spentas

The virtues of the *Amesha Spentas* reflect the attributes of Ahura Mazda although some Zoroastrians see them more as symbolic ideals. In either case, they set the ethical framework for human kind.

Vohu Manah (Good Mind) is the guardian of cattle; Asha Vahishta (Best Order/Truth and Righteousness) is the guardian of fire; Kshathra Vairya (Divine Kingdom/ Dominion) is the guardian of sky; Spenta Armaiti (Bounteous Devotion) is the guardian of earth; Haurvatat (Wholeness) is the guardian of water; Ameretat (Immortality) is the guardian of plants.

The *Amesha Spentas* all have Pahlavi names as well, where Vohu Manah is known as Bahman; Asha Vahishta as Ardibehesht; Kshathre Vairya as Shahrevar; Spenta Armaiti as Aspandarmad; Haurvatat as Khordad; and Ameretat as Amardad. Each of these forces is symbolically represented in important rituals and when invoked with devotion and purity are believed to be powerfully present.

Yazatas

Next in rank to the *Amesha Spentas* come the *Yazatas/Yazads* (or "adorable ones"). They are seen neither as gods nor angels. They came to be understood as beings which assist the *Amesha Spentas* and further the well-being of the seven good creations of Ahura Mazda. Thus, for example, Asha Vahishta, the guardian of fire, is helped by Adar Yazad who is the *Yazata* for fire and Haurvatat, the guardian of the waters, is assisted by Tir Yazad who is the *Yazata* for the rains. Each Amesha Spenta is assisted by three or four Yazatas and the Yazatas have a particular role in helping human beings to realise the inherent nature of Ahura Mazda and to achieve an all-embracing happiness rooted in recognising the nature of Wisdom. Many Zoroastrians say that this makes them like angels.

The Role of Humanity

In Zoroastrian teaching, the first human was the hermaphrodite, Gayomard who had both male and female offspring. Of all the beings created by Ahura Mazda, humans are the most able to come to understand the Good Mind (*Vohu Manah*). They have been given a *Fravashi* (guardian angel).

This immaterial essence and directing principle operates through wisdom, innate reason, intellect, will and conscience to enable them to make genuine choices between good and evil thoughts, words and deeds. Ahura Mazda has given humanity this freedom to choose between the forces of good and evil. Human beings, therefore, are the makers of their own destiny according to the choices they make. The *Fravashi* is believed to operate on the basis of wisdom, innate reason, intellect and will, all of which are understood to be filtered through conscience.

The Concept of Death and Afterlife

In Zoroastrianism, death is seen as the separation of body and soul. On the morning after the fourth day after death, it is believed that the *urvan* (soul) is judged at the *Chinvat Bridge* (*Bridge of the Separator*). Its good thoughts, words and deeds are weighed in the balance against the evil and the *urvan* either ascends to the *House of Song* (heaven) or falls from the bridge into the abyss of the *House of Deceit* (hell) which, in Zoroastrian texts, is pictured as cold and dark.

Saoshyant, The End Time, Resurrection, Last Judgement and Frasho-keriti

There is some contemporary debate about the details of these beliefs but, in classical Zoroastrian belief, the soul was believed to continue to exist after death in heaven or hell until the end of time. It was believed that, at the end of time the forces of evil would be completely destroyed by the good and the *Saoshyant* (Saviour) would raise the dead and initiate judgement.

Everyone was believed to pass through "an ocean of molten metal" in which the good would feel the "molten metal" as "cool milk", while the imperfect would be cleansed before

joining the blessed. Time would cease to exist and the world would return to its original perfect state of total goodness and harmony known to Zoroastrians as *Frasho-keriti* (Making Wonderful).

ZOROASTRIAN LIFE

Zoroastrian Ethics

Asha (truth/righteousness) is the central principle of Zoroastrian ethics. It is related to *Vohu Manah* and includes within it all virtues. Among the choices which confront human beings in the cosmic battle between good and evil are those between good thoughts, good words and good deeds and bad thoughts, bad words and bad deeds; between happiness and despair; between optimism and pessimism; between joy and misery; between moderation and deficiency or excess; between truth and falsehood; between order and chaos; between light and darkness; between charity and greed; between life and death.

Zoroastrians are urged to live life to the full and to enjoy the good creation. Zoroastrians, who believe that Ahura Mazda made the whole of the material world, including plants and animals have always been very environmentally conscious. Fasting and celibacy are seen as weakening human beings and lessening their power to struggle against evil and as rejecting the divine gift of the good life. Moderation is encouraged. Zoroastrian ethics enjoin an active, industrious, honest and charitable life.

Initiation

Navjote (Gujarati for "new birth") or *Sedreh-Pushi* (Farsi for "wearing *sedreh*") are names for the initiation ceremony for the children of Zoroastrian parents. The actions of a child born of Zoroastrian parents are held to be the responsibility of its parents until the child has undergone this ceremony. Although in earlier times the ceremony took place at the age of fifteen, it now usually takes place for both males and females between the ages of seven and eleven, before puberty. Exceptionally, it can be held later on, with the permission of the officiating priest. Friends and relatives of the child attend the ceremony which combines prayer, ritual and celebration.

Before the ceremony the initiate is given a ritual purificatory bath and is then invested with the *sudreh* and *kushti* (see below) and recites the *Fravarane* which is a declaration of faith said daily by Zoroastrians. The *Fravarane* begins with the words: "Come to my aid, O Mazda! I profess myself a worshipper of Mazda, I am a Zoroastrian worshipper of Mazda." It praises good thoughts, good words and good deeds, and ends by ascribing all good things to Ahura Mazda.

Sudreh and Kushti/Koshti

The *sudreh* and *kushti* are meant to be worn at all times by Zoroastrians. The *sudreh* is always worn next to the skin and is seen as "the garment of *vohumanah* (good purpose)". It is a sacred shirt which is always white in order to symbolise purity, and is made of muslin or cotton cloth. At the bottom of its v-shaped neck there is a one inch square pocket which contains a slit. This pocket is known as the *gireban* or *kisseh-kerfeh* (pocket of good deeds) and reminds Zoroastrians that they should be filling up their lives with good deeds, but also that whatever good a person does, it is only one square inch compared to Ahura Mazda's goodness. There is also a large pouch (known as a *girdo*) at the back of the *sudreh* which represents a storehouse for future good deeds.

A small vertical dart, known as a *tiri*, comes out of the hem of the *sudreh*, the significance of which has varying interpretations. There is also a small triangular patch on the opposite side of the *tiri* which symbolises the threefold Zoroastrian teaching of good thoughts, good words and good deeds.

The *sudreh* symbolises "the advantageous path" and the *kushti* indicates the proper direction for proceeding on that path. The *kushti* is a sacred cord which is worn over the *sudreh*. It is passed three times around the waist and knotted at the front and back. It is woven from seventy-two

threads of fine lambs' wool which symbolise the seventy-two chapters of the *Yasna* (*Act of Worship*). The *kushti* is sanctified by special prayers at every stage of the weaving.

Both *sudreh* and *kushti* are seen as a protection against evil. The *sudreh-kushti* is commonly known as the armour and sword belt of the religion, worn in the battle against evil.

Gah/Geh

For devotional purposes the twenty-four hours in a day are divided into five *Gah* (times): *Havan* (from sunrise to noon); *Rapithwan* (from noon till 3.00pm); *Uziren* (from 3.00pm to sunset); *Aiwisruthrem* (from sunset to midnight); *Ushahen* (from midnight to sunrise).

To prepare for prayer Zoroastrians wash their hands, face and all uncovered parts of the body. They untie the *kushti* and stand, holding it before Ahura Mazda, focusing on the sun, fire, or even artificial light if no natural light is available, as a symbol of *asha* (truth). Prayer is then offered to Ahura Mazda and the *kushti* is retied.

The *Ashem Vohu* three line prayer is the first prayer taught to all Zoroastrian children and is concerned with *asha*. It is followed by the twenty-one word *Ahunavar* or *Ahuna Vairya*, which in the Zororastrian scriptures is said to have been recited by Ahura Mazda when He created the world. This prayer is deemed to be the most powerful instrument of prayer in warding off evil.

Death Practices

Death is seen as the work of evil. A dead body represents the apparent triumph and presence of evil and is therefore polluting. Because of this, it is believed that disposal should be carried out as quickly as possible and in a way which is least harmful to the living. Disposal into rivers or the sea is believed to pollute the water and disposal by burial could pollute the land. Therefore, in India and Pakistan, the customary system is what is argued to be the ecologically sound exposure of the body in a *dokhma*. This is a confined building, also known colloquially as the *Tower of Silence*. In this, the body is rapidly consumed by vultures and the bones are destroyed by the action of lime in a deep pit.

In accordance with purity laws professional corpse-bearers who enter the *dokhma* must regularly undergo a ritual purification bath. Only a small number are still in use in India and Pakistan, whilst in Iran this practice has been discontinued. In the UK, when bodies are not flown back to India, they are usually buried or cremated and the ashes interred at the Zoroastrian cemetery at Brookwood in Surrey, established in 1863.

Diet

There are no dietary requirements for Zoroastrians although, from personal choice or sometimes from deference to the wider religious population of Iran and India, many abstain from pork and beef and some are vegetarian.

ZOROASTRIAN WORSHIP

Places of Worship

Traditionally, Zoroastrian places of worship are known as *Fire Temples* because a consecrated fire burns perpetually inside them. A reverence for fire is found within the broader Aryan tradition and pre-dates Zarathushtra. The use of temples was introduced into Zoroastianism during the times of the Achaemenid kings in around the fifth century BCE.

Before entering the worship hall, Zoroastrian men and women must bathe, remove shoes, cover their heads when praying, and then perform the *kushti* ritual in the entrance to the place of worship. There is a consecrated chamber where the fire is housed and into which only *priests* may enter. Parsi Zoroastrian worshippers may bow before the fire and take some cold ash to place on their forehead in order to receive the divine blessing.

Fire

Fire (*Atar* or *Adur/Adar*) is used in many Zoroastrian ceremonies and many individual Zoroastrians keep an oil lamp burning in their homes. This centrality of fire in Zoroastrian worship has led some people to describe Zoroastrians as "fire worshippers". This is, however, a misunderstanding and offensive to Zoroastrians. Zoroastrians do not worship fire but worship Ahura Mazda and venerate the *Amesha Spentas* and the *Yazatas*. Fire is seen as the creation of *Asha* and is considered a sacred force because it is a source of light and warmth as well as a symbol of truth and righteousness. Fire has therefore become an icon of Zoroastrianism.

Fire energy is understood to be the source of all other energies and of life itself throughout the universe. Standing before the fire, Zoroastrians believe they are standing in the presence of Ahura Mazda. This philosophy lies behind the *Atash Nyayesh* (*Litany of Fire*).

ZOROASTRIAN CALENDARS AND FESTIVALS

Calendar

The Zoroastrian view of time is a linear one which has a specific end in view with the restoration of all things to a state of wholeness and perfection. The current Zoroastrian dating system began with the date of the coronation and designation of the last Zoroastrian monarch of Sasanian Iran, Yazdegird III, whose reign commenced in 631 CE. The letters "AY" (After Yazdegird) are used to denote the year, making 1997 CE the Zoroastrian year 1366 AY.

The annual calendar is composed of twelve months with thirty days in each month. The twelfth month, however, also has five additional *Gatha* days making a three hundred and sixty-five day annual calendar. Traditionally, one month was added every one hundred and twenty years in order to synchronise this calendar with the solar calendar consisting of three hundred and sixty-five and a quarter days.

In the Zoroastrian calendar, the names of the months correspond with the names of the *Amesha Spentas* and the *Yazatas*.

The *Shahenshahi* or *Yazdegerdi* calendar first adopted by the *Parsis* runs one month behind the Iranian *Kadmi* (ancient) calendar. Then the *Fasli* (solar) calendar was adopted by some *Parsis* in the diaspora. The *Fasli* calendar has dates which are fixed in alignment with the *Gregorian* calendar and is observed by the Iranian Zoroastrians.

There are therefore three calendars which might be found in use amongst Zoroastrians. The majority of Zoroastrians in the UK follow the *Shahenshahi* calendar, although it should be noted that very many Zoroastrians in the UK, and elsewhere in the world, tend to celebrate festivals such as New Year in all three calendars. The dates given below are in accordance with the solar calendar.

Festivals

Religious festivals, of which there are various kinds, play a central role in the devotional life of Zoroastrians.

Gahanbars (seasonal festivals)

These are a series of six festivals devoted to the *Amesha Spentas* and to the creation of sky, water, earth, plants, animals and people. These festivals traditionally last for five days each. They are holy days of obligation during which prayers are recited. On the final day a communal feast is held.

The first *gahanbar*, called *Maidyoizaremaya* or *Maidyu Zarem* (meaning "mid-Spring") is linked with the sky. The second, *Maidyoishema* or *Maidyu Shem* (meaning "mid-Summer") is linked with the waters. The third, *Paitishahya* or *Paiti Shahim* (meaning "bringing in the corn") is linked with the earth. The fourth, *Ayathrima* or *Ayathrem* (meaning "homecoming") is linked with plants. The fifth, *Maidhyairya* or *Maidyaryam* (meaning "mid-Winter") is linked with cattle, and the sixth *gahanbar*, *Hamaspathmaedaya* or *Hamas Pathmaidyam*, also known as *Fravahrs* (meaning "Feast of Heavenly Souls), is a special festival in honour of humanity's creation.

The cycle is then completed by the observance of *No-Ruz* (see below) which is the New Year festival. The dates of the *gahanbars* vary according to which calendar is used and all vary in relation to the *Gregorian* calendar. The principal observance at the *gahanbars* is the *Yasht-i-Visperad* which is a three-hours long service commencing at sunrise, giving thanks for the creations and sanctifying them with rituals and sacred words.

No-Ruz (New Year's Day – Spring Vernal Equinox) (20th/21st March)

This is one of the most important festivals signifying the imminent arrival of spring. According to popular belief, it was founded by King Jamshid of the ancient Pishdadian dynasty. It is marked by the wearing of new clothes, the holding of festivities, and the giving and receiving of presents. The *Shahenshahi No Ruz* is celebrated in August.

Khordad Sal (6th day after No-Ruz)

Celebrates the birth of the Prophet Zarathustra. Among Iranian Zoroastrians the festival is known as *Zad Rooz-e Ashoo Zartosht*.

Zarthosht no Diso (5th day, 10th month)

Marks the anniversary of Zarathushtra's death.

Muktad (25th day, 12th month)

This is the name given to the final ten days of the year observed in *Parsi* custom. Among Iranian Zoroastrians only the last five days before *No-Ruz* are observed. These days are in honour of the *Fravashis* (the heavenly selves of all people) and are usually marked by prayers and a ritual meal in honour of them. During the last five days of *Muktad*, the five *Gathas* are recited and ceremonies are performed in Zoroastrian homes and *Fire Temples*. Vases of flowers are put around homes and in *Fire Temples* to commemorate relatives who have died and prayers are recited in remembrance of them and for all human souls since it is believed that the souls of the dead pay visits at this time. The

Iranian Zoroastrians also call the first five days of this period *Panje-kas* (the Lesser Pentad) and the last five days *Panje-mas* (the Greater Pentad).

Jashans

Each day and month in the Zoroastrian calendar is dedicated to an *Amesha Spenta* or *Yazata*, except for *Farvardin* which is connected with the first month and the nineteenth day, known as *Farvardingan*, observed as a day of remembrance for departed souls. In addition to the obligatory days of observance outlined above there are other festival days when the particular days and months dedicated to the *Amesha Spentas* and the *Yazatas* coincide. Marking these days is not obligatory, but it is considered meritorious. The *Jashans* include:

Tiragan (or Tir ruz/rojand, and Tir mah)
(10th day, 4th month)
A festival devoted to Tir, the *Yazata* of rain and fertility. The festival overlaps with the second seasonal *gahanbar* and on this day, people throw water at each other in celebration of its significance.

Mehrgan (or Meher ruz/roj, or Mehr mah)
(10th day, 7th month)
An autumnal festival, dedicated to the *Yazata* Mehr, who is associated with justice and with the sun.

Ava-roj Parab (or Avaroj or Avamah)
(10th day, 8th month)
Celebrated as the birthday of the waters. Special food offerings and prayers are made on this day in which Zoroastrians go to a river or to the sea-side and give thanks for its purification and pray for the nourishment of the world.

Adar-roj Parab (or Adar-roj or Adar mah)
(9th day, 9th month)
Celebrated as the festival of fire on which, traditionally, food is not cooked in the house so that fire is allowed to rest whilst Zoroastrians give thanks for the warmth and light which come from it throughout the year. Special prayers are offered in the presence of the house fire.

Sadeh (10th day, 11th month)
An open air mid-winter festival celebrated with bonfires and held fifty days before *No-Ruz*. It celebrates the discovery of fire by Hoshang Shah, believed by Zoroastrians to have been an historical figure of the Pishdadian dynasty.

Jashan ceremonies include the representation of the sevenfold creation by means of the display of a variety of objects. The sky is represented by a piece of metal; water is contained in a beaker; the objects are placed on the carpeted ground of the earth; plant life is represented by flowers and fruits; animal life by milk; humanity by the officiating priests; and spiritual fire by physical fire, fed by sandalwood and incense. Each of these items is offered with specific prayers to their spiritual counterparts among the *Amesha Spentas* who are, in turn, by their powerful presence believed to bless the offerings which are then shared by those present.

ZOROASTRIAN ORGANISATIONS

Organisations

The first Zoroastrian organisation in the UK was established in 1861 and was known as the Religious Fund of the Zoroastrians of Europe. Later, it became The Incorporated Parsee Association of Europe and obtained rented premises for meetings and worship and in 1925 purchased a building. In 1969 this organisation, by then known as the Zoroastrian Association of Europe, purchased a centre in West Hampstead, London. Since 1978, the organisation has been known as The Zoroastrian Trust Funds of Europe.

Although there are small numbers of Zoroastrians elsewhere in Britain and Europe, the headquarters and centre of the Zoroastrian Trust Funds of Europe (Incorporated) in London is the focus for most Zoroastrian activity in the country. The building, known as Zoroastrian House, is used for worship and other community activities.

Personnel

A *Dastur* (high priest) or a *Mobed* (authorised priest) officiates at Zoroastrian ceremonies and may be helped by *Ervad Sahebs* (assistants to the high priest). When officiating, Zoroastrian priests are dressed in white and wear the traditional *padan* (piece of white cloth) over their mouths, in order not to pollute the fire while praying. The ceremony for initiation into the priesthood takes over a month and there are two grades of initiation. In the UK, the *Ervads* (priests) are members of priestly families who have been initiated in India and function here as priests on a part-time basis, as required.

FURTHER READING

Azargoshasb, A, *Festivals of Ancient Iran*, Tehran, 1970.

Boyce, M, *A History of Zoroastrianism*, Volume I, E J Brill, Leiden, 1976.

Boyce, M, *A Persian Stronghold of Zoroastrianism*, Clarendon Press, Oxford 1977.

Boyce, M, *Textual Sources for the Study of Zoroastrianism*, Manchester University Press, 1984.

Boyce, M, *Zoroastrians: Their Religious Beliefs and Practices*, Routledge and Kegan Paul, London, 1984.

Boyce, M, Grenet, F, and Beck, R, *A History of Zoroastrianism*, Volume III, E J Brill, Leiden, 1990.

Boyce, M, *Zoroastrianism: Its Antiquity and Constant Vigour*, 1985 Columbia University Iranian Lectures, 1992.

Dhalla, M N, *History of Zoroastrianism*, Ubsons, Bombay, 1985.

Davond, P (trans), *The Holy Gathas*, D J Irani, Bombay, 1924.

Hinnells, J, *Zoroastrianism and the Parsis*, Ward Lock Educational, London, 1981.

Hinnells, J, "Parsi Zoroastrians in London", in Ballard, R, *Desh Pardesh: The South Asian Presence in Britain*, Hurst and Company, London, 1994, pp. 251-271.

Hinnells, J, *Zoroastrians in Britain*, Oxford University Press, Oxford, 1996.

Kulke, E, *The Parsees in India: A Minority as Agent of Social Change*, Weltforum-Verlag, Munich, 1974.

Mehr, F, *The Zoroastrian Tradition: An Introduction to the Ancient Wisdom of Zarathustra*, Element Books, Dorset, 1991.

Mistree, K, *Zoroastrianism: An Ethnic Perspective*, Zoroastian Studies, Bombay, 1982.

Modi, J J, *Religious Ceremonies and Customs of the Parsees*, Bombay, 1986.

Writer, R, *Contemporary Zoroastrians: An Unstructured Nation*, University Press of America, Maryland, 1994.

Writer, R, "Parsee survival in India: the role of caste", in *World Faiths Encounter*, No 10, March 1995, pp. 38-47.

Zaehner, R, *The Teachings of the Magi*, Allen and Unwin, London, 1956.

Zaehner, R, *The Dawn and Twilight of Zoroastrianism*, Weidenfeld & Nicolson, London, 1961.

ZOROASTRIAN UNITED KINGDOM ORGANISATIONS

The two Zoroastrian organisations listed in this section, whilst based in the United Kingdom and having a United Kingdom role, also have a role beyond the United Kingdom itself.

World Zoroastrian Organisation
135 Tennison Road, South Norwood, London, SE25 5NF
Tel: 01279-503771 (h) **Fax:** 01279-503619
Contact: Shahpur Framroze Captain
Position: President
Activities: Umbrella, newsletters
Other Languages: Gujarati, Persian
A world body set up to establish and maintain contact between Zoroastrians worldwide; advance the Zoroastrian religious faith; establish charitable homes and provide grants for further education and medical treatment.

Zoroastrian Trust Funds of Europe (Inc)
Zoroastrian House, 88 Compayne Gardens, West Hampstead, London, NW6 3RU
Tel: 0171-328-6018 **Tel:** 0181-997-2076 (h)
Fax: 0171-625-1685
Contact: Rusi K Dalal
Position: President
Activities: Worship, resource, umbrella, visits, youth, newsletters, books, inter-faith
Social Groups: Iranian Zoroastrian, Parsi
Other Languages: Gujarati, Farsi, Hindi
Affiliations: Federation of Zoroastrian Associations of North America; Federation of Parsee Zoroastrian Anjumans of India; Inter Faith Network for the UK.
Established in 1861, it is the oldest ethnic minority organisation in the UK. Today, it represents the interests of about 7,000 Zoroastrians in Europe, with Zoroastrian House as a centre of social, cultural and religious activities.

ZOROASTRIAN REGIONAL AND LOCAL ORGANISATIONS AND COMMUNITIES

Since the Zoroastrian community in the United Kingdom is not very numerous or geographically widespread, a range of contacts are given for each local Zoroastrian community. These are organised according to the various regions into which the local sections of the directory are divided.

With regard to the Greater London region, in this chapter only, all details are under a conflated Regional Area, Borough and local section.

ENGLAND

NORTH EAST
Regional and County Bodies

North East Zoroastrian Community
37 Kingsley Avenue, Melton Park, Gosforth, Newcastle upon Tyne, NE3 5QN (h)
Tel: 0191-236-7443 (h)
Contact: Kersi Fanibunda
Position: Newcastle upon Tyne Contact

North East Zoroastrian Community
15 St Charles Road, Spennymoor, County Durham, DL16 6JY (h)
Tel: 01388-815983 (h)
Contact: Jeeroji Fiji Kotwall
Position: County Durham Contact
Social Groups: Parsi
Other Languages: Gujarati

NORTH WEST
Regional and County Bodies

North West Zoroastrian Community
5 Craigweil Avenue, Didsbury, Manchester, Greater Manchester, M20 6JQ (h)
Tel: 0161-445-7554 (h)
EMail: b.avari@mmu.ac.uk
Contact: Burjor Avari
Position: Secretary
Activities: Youth, inter-faith
Social Groups: Parsi
Other Languages: Gujarati, Farsi
Affiliations: Zoroastrian Trust Funds of Europe

North West Zoroastrian Community
32 Noris Road, Sale, Cheshire, M33 3QR (h)
Tel: 0161-973-3535 (h)
Contact: Taraneh Zomorrody
Position: Sale Contact

North West Zoroastrian Community
48 Bank Road, Stalybridge, Cheshire (h)
Tel: 01457-835486 (h)
Contact: Cyrus Jokhi
Position: Stalybridge Contact

North West Zoroastrian Community
121 Wood Lane, Timperley, Cheshire, WA15 7PG
(h)
Tel: 0161-980-1921 (h)
Contact: Shireen Khambatta
Position: Timperley Contact

Zarthusthi-Parsee-Irani Forum
11 Prospect Avenue, Darwen, Lancashire,
BB3 1JQ (h)
Tel: 01254-705306 (h)
Contact: Maneck Meher Mehta
Position: Director
Activities: Resource, media, youth, newsletters,
books, inter-faith
Social Groups: Iranian Zoroastrian, Parsi
Other Languages: Gujarati, Persian, Avesta

WEST MIDLANDS
Regional and County Bodies

Zoroastrian Community of the Midlands
15 Pickwick Grove, Birmingham, West Midlands,
BL3 9LL (h)
Tel: 0121-777-5786 (h)
Contact: Mini Pochkhanawala
Position: Birmingham Contact

Zoroastrian Community of the Midlands
1 Grange Road, Balsall Common, Coventry, West
Midlands, CV7 7AD (h)
Tel: 01676-533472 (h)
Contact: Thirty Kotwal
Position: Coventry Contact

GREATER LONDON

Harrow Zoroastrian Group
53 Norton Road, Wembley, Middlesex,
HA0 4RG (h)
Tel: 0181-903-7791 (h)
Contact: Ervad Rustom Bhedwar
Position: Chairman/Priest
Activities: Inter-faith
Social Groups: Iranian Zoroastrian, Parsi
Other Languages: Gujarati, Farsi
Affiliations: Zoroastrian Trust Funds of Europe

*North London Zoroastrian Association
(NOLZA)*
1 Salisbury Mansions, St Ann's Road, London,
N15 3JP (h)
Tel: 0181-800-3698 (h)
Contact: Faridoon Madon MBE
Position: Founder President
Activities: Resource, youth, elderly, women, inter-
faith
Social Groups: Iranian Zoroastrian, Parsi
Other Languages: Gujarati, Persian

Zoroastrians of East London
104 Mortlake Road, Ilford, Essex, IG1 2SY (h)
Tel: 0181-478-8828 (h)
Contact: Councillor Filly Maravala
Position: Secretary
Activities: Worship, resource, visits, youth, elderly,
newsletters
Social Groups: Parsi
Other Languages: Gujarati, Farsi

Zoroastrians of East London
109 Chestnut Avenue, London, E7 0JF (h)
Contact: Keki Kanga
Position: Newham Contact

Zoroastrians of South London
21 Eldertree Way, Mitcham, Surrey, CR4 1AJ (h)
Tel: 0181-648-3292 (h)
Contact: Mrs Meher Kapadia
Position: Honorary Treasurer
Activities: Youth, elderly
Social Groupings: Iranian Zoroastrians, Parsis
Other Languages: Gujarati

SOME OTHER RELIGIOUS COMMUNITIES AND GROUPS

INTRODUCTION

The directory focuses primarily on nine world religious communities. The present chapter offers some supplementary information about a number of other forms of religious life in the United Kingdom which are not dealt with in detail within the other chapters but have, in most cases, some historical or doctrinal relationship with the nine traditions which form the directory's major subject matter.

The precise nature of these relationships is often a disputed one, particularly from the perspective of the majority traditions covered in the earlier chapters. The directory does not attempt to adjudicate on these disputes, resulting as they do from conflicting and often mutually exclusive self-understandings (although placing these traditions in this section is an acknowledgment of the existence of the issues involved). The reader may, in other contexts, see one or more of these groups referred to as "New Religious Movements", although there are also many more groups, that are beyond the scope of this directory, which might also be described by that name and for information on these, the directory is referred to INFORM (Information Network on New Religious Movements) Houghton Street, London, WC2A 2AE, Tel: 0171-955-7564.

Some of the groups included in this chapter such as the Sant Nirankaris and the Sathya Sai Baba Organisation, understand themselves in universalistic terms as spiritual traditions which can include members of different religious traditions. Paganism understands itself as being entirely independent of the traditions covered in the earlier chapters. Some forms of Pagan organisation are relatively modern but Pagans in general understand themselves as in some way representing the older indigenous religious traditions of the UK. It therefore seemed important to include some information on Pagan traditions within the directory.

Because this chapter provides only brief overviews, generally speaking only a single contact point is provided for each community and grouping listed in this chapter. This does not, however, imply that there might not be other useful points of contact.

BRAHMA KUMARIS

The Brahma Kumaris World Spiritual University is a movement based upon the teachings given earlier this century by a Sindhi businessman of Hindu religious background. He was born as Dada Lekhraj and later became known by the spiritual name of Prajapita Brahma. It is believed that Prajapita Brahma received a vision that the transformation of the world as we know it will be followed by the establishment of an earthly paradise from which competition, hunger, the pain of death and inequalities (especially between men and women) will be abolished.

The movement believes in the soul as the eternal identity of the human being which uses the costume of the body to express itself. The human soul also goes through birth and rebirth, but always in human form. God is believed to be the Supreme of all souls, an unlimited source of light, love and peace. The movement sees the universe in a cyclic process of creation, degeneration and re-creation similar to the Hindu framework of *yugas* or ages. The recreation of a paradise at the end of each cycle comes about through understanding and imbibing fundamental spiritual truths that are universal to most faiths.

The movement's world headquarters are in Mount Abu, Rajasthan, India. There are local Brahma Kumari Centres throughout India and in sixty-five countries around the world. There are forty centres in the UK. Students at these centres practice *Raja Yoga* meditation, the experience of the consciousness of the soul and the awareness of the eternal relationship with the Supreme Soul. Courses are offered in meditation and spiritual understanding. Other courses and activities include Positive Thinking, Stress Management and workshops on Inter-Personal Skills. Workshops and classes are also held in hospitals, prisons, in businesses, and for other special interest groups.

Early morning meditation classes are held daily, and on Thursday mornings. Food is offered to God which is then shared with everyone who is present. Regular students of the Brahma Kumaris are vegetarian, abstain from tobacco and alcohol and are celibate. Most centres outside India are run by people who are working and who devote their free time to teaching meditation. At larger centres, some full time teachers are required who lead a "*surrendered*" spiritual life. There is no membership, but people attend centres as regular students and also help with teaching and other duties, sometimes within a few months of studying.

The Brahma Kumaris are a Non-Governmental Organisation affiliated to the United Nations and also have consultative status with the United Nations Economic and Social Council and UNICEF. In this capacity they have organised three international projects. The Million Minutes for Peace and Global Co-operation for a Better World Projects reached 129 countries. As part of their current project "Sharing Our Values for a Better World", the publication *Living Values: A Guidebook*, is in use as an educational tool in schools and community establishments in several countries. A programme is also being developed for educators entitled "Lifelong Learning: An Education in Values for the Development of Human Potential".

Brahma Kumaris World Spiritual University
Global Co-operation House,
65 Pound Lane, London, NW10 2HH
Tel: 0181-459-1400 **Fax:** 0181-451-6480
Contact: Sister Maureen
Position: Programme Co-ordinator
E-Mail: bk@bkwsugch.demon.co.uk

Bibliography

Babb, L A, *Redemptive Encounters: Three Modern Styles in the Hindu Traditions*, University of California Press, Berkeley, 1986, pp. 93-158.

Chander, J, *A Brief Biography of Brahma Baba*, Prajapita Brahma Kumaris World Spiritual University, Mount Abu, 1984.

Chander, J and Panjabi, M, *Visions of a Better World: A United Nations Peace Messenger Publication*, Brahma Kumaris World Spiritual University, London, 1994.

Kirpalani, J and Panjabi, M, *Living Values: A Guidebook*, Brahma Kumaris World Spiritual University, London, 1995.

O'Donnell, K, *Raja Yoga, New Beginnings*, Prajapita Brahma Kumaris World Spiritual University, Mount Abu, 1987.

Waling, F, "The Brahma Kumaris", in *Journal of Contemporary Religion*, Volume X, No. 1, 1995, pp. 3-28.

CHRISTIAN SCIENTISTS

The Christian Science movement was founded by Mary Baker Eddy, who was born in New Hampshire, in the United States, in 1821. The Church of Christ, Scientist, was incorporated with a charter in 1879. It sought to restore what it understood to be original Christianity and particularly the lost element of the healing ministry in contrast to reliance upon conventional medical treatment. In 1908, Mary Baker Eddy founded the daily newspaper, *The Christian Science Monitor*, which is still published today.

Christian Science understands its authority to be drawn from the *Bible*. Its complete teachings are set out in the textbook *Science and Health with Key to the Scriptures* by Mary Baker Eddy. A Christian Scientist's understanding of God and of human beings is based on the first chapter of Genesis where it is recorded that God made man in "his own image". God, Spirit, is understood to be all-powerful, ever-present Mind, the source of all good. His creation is seen as spiritual, entirely good and free from sin, suffering and death.

Christian Scientists believe they find freedom and redemption from sin by acknowledging their God-given identity. They look to Jesus Christ as the *Way-shower* and *Exemplar*, and they seek to follow his teachings and example. They understand Jesus as exemplifying the *Christ*, his God-given nature. They accept Jesus' virgin birth, *crucifixion, resurrection* and *ascension*.

The Christian Science movement thus came from the Christian community, and understands itself as within it, although this self-understanding would be disputed by many of the organisations listed in the chapter on "Introducing the Christian Community", particularly on the basis of differences in understanding the person and role of Jesus.

The movement is organised in branch churches which are each expected to maintain a *Reading Room* in which Christian Science literature may be read, borrowed or bought. On Wednesday evenings at Christian Science *churches Testimony Meetings* are held where people testify about the healings which they have experienced. The movement has *Practioners* who devote their lives full-time to practising the Church's healing methods.

Church of Christ, Scientist

Christian Science Committee on Publication,
2 Elysium Gate,
126 New Kings Road, London, SW6 4LZ
Tel: 0171-371-0060 **Fax:** 0171-371-9204
Contact: Mr Alan Grayson
Position: District Manager for Great Britain and Ireland
Internet: http://www.tfccs.com/

Bibliography

Christian Science Publishing Society, *A Century of Christian Science Healing,* The Christian Science Publishing Society, Boston, 1966.

Eddy, Mary Baker, *Science and Health with Key to the Scriptures*, First Church of Christ, Scientist, Boston, 1994.

Peel, Robert, *Spiritual Healing in a Scientific Age*, Harper and Row, Cambridge, 1988.

CHURCH OF JESUS CHRIST OF LATTER-DAY SAINTS

The *Mormons*, as they are often popularly known, are officially named The Church of Jesus Christ of Latter-day Saints. They claim to be a Christian Church and assert that there are three basic Christian positions. The first is that of the Churches claiming an unbroken line of *Apostolic Succession*, such as the *Roman Catholic* and *Eastern Orthodox* Churches. The second is that of those Churches which claim a *Reformation* was necessary to restore the doctrinal integrity of the Church. The third is the position of The Church of Jesus Christ of Latter-day Saints which believes that apostasy has led to the need for a restoration of the true Church, believing that this restoration had to be divine not human.

Mormons claim that they are that *Restored Church* in these, the *Latter-days*. They use the term *saints* in the *New Testament* sense to indicate a believer (as distinct from someone who has been *canonised* as a *saint*).

Mormons differ from other Christian Churches in a number of other ways: they do not accept the teaching of the *Trinity* and affirm that the Godhead of Father, Son and Holy Ghost are three separate and distinct Beings. They also teach that the Father and the Son have physical bodies. They believe that their Church *President* is a *prophet* who receives continuing revelation from God.

The Church was founded in Fayette, New York, USA by Joseph Smith who became its first *President*. He claimed a mandate from God, through an event in 1820 that Mormons call the *First Vision* and which they believe consisted of the appearance of God the Father and His Son, Jesus Christ to the young Smith. In 1827, Smith published *The Book of Mormon: Another Testament of Jesus Christ*. The Church uses this as scripture alongside the *Bible* in its King James version. Two other works are accepted as scripture: the *Doctrine and Covenants* and the *Pearl of Great Price*.

The Church formally came into existence in 1830. Its first foreign mission was to Britain, in 1837, and its oldest continuous branch anywhere in the world is in Preston, Lancashire. By 1996, its worldwide membership was 9,500,000, with 170,000 British members.

The worldwide governing body of the Church is the *First Presidency* (the *President* and two *Counsellors*). They are assisted by *The Council of the Twelve Apostles* and by *The Councils of the Seventy*. Worldwide, the Church is organised into *stakes* (the equaivalent of a *diocese*), *wards* (organised local units), and *branches* (embryonic *wards*). Government is through *priesthood*, with two orders: the *Aaronic Priesthood* (for males aged twelve and upwards and judged worthy) and the *Melchizedek Priesthood* (a higher order for men aged eighteen and over).

The Church is well known for its *missionary* work. Many members (usually nineteen to twenty-one year old men) dedicate two years of their lives to serve as unpaid *missionaries* wherever they are sent. Members are encouraged to live by a health code known as *The Word of Wisdom*. This encourages healthy living and discourages the use of stimulants such as alcohol, tea and coffee.

The Church has *chapels* for regular public worship, but its *temples* are reserved for *sacred ordinances* and are entered only by members in good standing. *Temples* exist throughout the world. There is one in Lingfield, Surrey and another is under construction in Chorley, Lancashire.

The family is viewed as of critical importance and its ultimate expression is believed to be found in *temple ordinances* for both the living and the dead. These *ordinances* include a course of instruction on the *gospel*. This course is known as an *endowment*. It is accompanied by a rite known as *sealing*, in which husbands and wives, who will previously have been married in a civil ceremony, extend their vows beyond this life to "time and all eternity".

In a similar ceremony parents are also *sealed* to their children and any existing children would be brought in, after the *sealing* of the couple, and *sealed* to them at that point. Any future children are automatically *sealed* to their parents and do not need to be *sealed* to them by an additional ceremony as they are deemed to be born "under the *covenant*".

Mormons believe that *temple* blessings may be offered to those of their family who have died. They practice *baptism* and, following genealogical research, they extend the offer of *baptism* through what they understand as *New Testament*-style proxy *baptisms* (I Corinthians 15 v 29). Proxy *sealings* are also performed. Throughout, though, the right to choose remains. Deceased ancestors have the full right to accept or reject *ordinances* performed on their behalf. Such *baptisms* are not recorded on membership records. Mormons refer to this proxy work as a "labour of love", offered freely, without compulsion.

The Church believes in good inter-faith relationships and co-operates with other Churches in worthwhile social and humanitarian projects designed to relieve suffering and uphold Christian values. Because of what it perceives to be its unique position as the divinely-inspired restored Church it does not, however, participate in *ecumenical* councils, believing that *ecumenism* can lead to doctrinal compromise.

Church of Jesus Christ of Latter-day Saints

751 Warwick Road, Solihull, West Midlands, B91 3DQ
Tel: 0121-711-2244, Ext 202
Fax: 0121-709-0180
Contact: Mr Bryan J Grant
Position: Director of Public Affairs

Bibliography

Arrington, L J and Britton D, *The Mormon Experience: A History of the Latter-day Saints*, Allen and Unwin, London, 1979.

Hinckley, Gordon B, *Truth Restored, The Church of Jesus Christ of Latter-day Saints*, 1979.

Ludlow, D H (editor), *Encyclopaedia of Mormonism*, Macmillan, New York, 1992.

Smith, J F, *Essentials in Church History*, Deseret News Press, Salt Lake City, 1942.

JEHOVAH'S WITNESSES

The Jehovah's Witness movement was founded by Charles Taze Russell, who was born into a Presbyterian Christian family in Pennsylvania, North America, in 1852. After a period of religious scepticism, between 1870 and 1875 he became deeply engaged in the study of the Bible with a group of six people. He issued a pamphlet entitled *The Object and Manner of the Lord's Return*, arguing for the spiritual nature of Christ's second coming.

In 1879, Russell founded *Zion's Watch Tower and Herald of Christ's Presence*. The Zion's Watch Tower Society was established in 1881 and, in 1884, the Society was granted a legal charter for "the dissemination of *Bible* truths in various languages" by means of publications.

Russell then produced a seven volume series of doctrinal works now known as *Studies in the Scriptures*. At a convention of the Society in 1931, a motion was adopted that the Society should from then on be known as Jehovah's Witnesses. The emphasis of the movement's activity moved increasingly towards witness in the streets and on the doorsteps of people's homes. In seeking to share their faith with others, where the *New World* translation of the *Bible* is available in the language of the people concerned this is used in preference to other translations, since it is understood to be a literal translation from the original biblical languages of Hebrew, Aramaic and Greek.

The local units of the Jehovah's Witness organisation are the *congregations* which meet in what are known as *Kingdom Halls* and are organised under the direction of a body of *elders*. The *congregations* are linked together into *circuits*. These, in turn, are grouped in *districts*. Worldwide, their work is overseen by a small governing body.

Jehovah's Witnesses base their religious authority upon an appeal to the *Bible*. For Jehovah's Witnesses, Jesus is viewed as God's Son, but not as "Jehovah God". He is seen as the first creation of Jehovah. The holy spirit is seen as the active force of Jehovah and Jehovah's Witnesses therefore reject the doctrine of the Trinity held by the historic Christian Churches.

Jehovah's Witnesses are not supposed to hold political office, vote, or salute the flag of any nation. In times of war they adopt strict neutrality and eschew even non-combatant military service. This position of non-involvement in secular affairs of state is rooted in their belief that the only true government is that of Jehovah who rules in heaven alongside Jesus Christ and 144,000 individuals who were once earthly humans. Jehovah's Witnesses believe that, in the near future, Jehovah will replace all human government with his own. The earth will become again like Eden and the righteous of all the ages of the earth will be resurrected to live in harmony under Jehovah's rule.

To become a Jehovah's Witness involves a period of study of the *Bible* with other Jehovah's Witnesses. Then the person dedicates himself or herself formally to witnessing to, and serving, Jehovah God and is fully immersed in baptismal water to mark this new life of witness. Jehovah's Witnesses see witnessing to Jehovah's work and divine plan as essential in their faith. Door to door witnessing is part of this.

Jehovah's Witnesses
Watch Tower House, The Ridgway,
London, NW7 1RN   **Tel:** 0181-906-2211
Fax: 0181-906-3938

Bibliography

Beckford, J, *The Trumpet of Prophecy: A Sociological Study of Jehovah's Witnesses*, Basil Blackwell, Oxford, 1975.

Watchtower Bible and Tract Society, *Jehovah's Witnesses in the Divine Purpose*, Watchtower and Bible Tract Society, 1959.

NAMDHARI SIKH COMMUNITY

All Namdhari Sikhs are *Amritdhari* (initiated) and adhere strictly to the teachings of all the Sikh *Gurus* and believe in a continuing succession of living *Gurus* starting with the founder *Satguru* Nanak Dev. They believe with equal reverence in the Sikh scriptures of the *Adi Granth Sahib* and the *Dasam Granth Sahib*.

It is their fundamental belief that the tenth *Guru, Satguru* Gobind Singh did not pass away at Nander (Maharastra) in 1708 as Sikhs generally believed, but actually lived until 1812. The Namdharis further believe that the *Guruship* still continues with the successive living *Gurus* rather than that it has been conferred on the *Adi Granth*. For Namdharis, there has been no change in the status of the *Adi Granth* since the time of the fifth *Guru, Satguru* Guru Arjan Dev. In their understanding, the institution of scripture and of *Guruship* continue side by side, and do not coincide.

The Namdhari Sikhs believe that the eleventh Namdhari *Guru*, Satguru Balak Singh (1785-1862), was installed to *Guruship* by *Satguru* Gobind Singh. The twelfth Namdhari *Guru*, *Satguru* Ram Singh (born 1816 and exiled to Burma in 1872) was succeeded by *Satguru* Hari Singh (1819-1906) who, in turn, passed the *Guruship* to *Satguru* Partap Singh (1890-1959). The present supreme spiritual head of over 2.5 million Namdhari Sikhs world wide is His Holiness Sri *Satguru* Jagjit Singh ji Maharaj who was born in 1920 and attained *Guruship* in 1959. It is this principle of a continuous succession and presence of a supreme spiritual authority forever in a living *Satguru* which distinguishes the Namdharis.

Satguru Ram Singh revived and reformed the Sikh principles laid down by earlier Sikh *Gurus* by challenging the distortions which many saw as having crept into the Sikh community over the years. As a sign of the restoration of the Sikh code of ethics and their social, moral, religious and political spirit, *Satguru* Ram Singh unfurled a white triangular Flag on the day of the *Baisakhi* Festival on 12 April 1857, symbolising freedom, truth, unity, love, purity, simplicity and peace. On this day the Namdhari *Panth* (*Sant Khalsa*) was inaugurated. In India's political records, Namdharis are also known as *Kukas* ("shouters", in their state of mystical ecstasy). They were pioneers in the struggle for the freedom of India from the British Raj and hold an honourable place in the history of the independence of India.

Namdharis are initiated by their living *Satguru* (True Guru) with the sacred *Nam* known as *Gurmantar* (God's Holy word), whispered into their ears secretly. The practice of *Nam* was originated by the *Satguru* Nanak and is used for silent recitation with meditation for the purpose of spiritual realisation, under the direct guidance and grace of their living *Satguru*.

Namdhari Sikhs are strict vegetarians and totally abstain from all intoxicating drinks containing drugs and any foods which contain animal products. Namdharis can easily be recognised from their white turbans tied horizontally across their forehead and the white woollen *mala* or rosary (made with 108 knots) used in their meditation and prayer. Namdharis are pacifists. They are also widely known for their very simple mass marriage ceremonies in the presence of their *Satguru*. Namdharis also have an intense love for devotional and traditional Indian classical music.

Namdharis are found in many countries all over the world. Their international headquarters is at Sri Bhaini Sahib, Ludhiana District in Punjab, India. It is estimated that there are around 10,000 Namdhari Sikhs in the UK.

National Organisation

Namdhari Sangat UK (The Sant Khalsa Spiritual Institute of the Namdhari Sikh Community in the UK)

Contact can be made through the General Secretary:
Mr Ranjit Singh Flora
60 Ring Road, Leicester, Leicestershire, LE2 3RR

Tel: 0116-270-0197 **Fax:** 0116-270-0197
Tel: 0116-254-5995

or
Publicity Secretary:
Mr Vasdev Singh Bhamrah
4 Hawthorne Road, Blakenhall,
Wolverhampton, West Midlands, WV2 3EH
Tel: 01902-332964 **Fax:** 01902-332964

Namdhari Sikh Gurdwaras and Community Centres in the UK

Gurdwara Namdhari Sangat
96 Upton Lane, Forest Gate,
London, E7 9LW
Tel: 0181-257-1460

Namdhari Sikh Community Centre
Unit 6, Balfour Buss Centre, Balfour Road,
Southall, Middlesex, UB2 5BD
Tel: 0181-893-6071

**Gurdwara Namdhari Sangat &
Namdhari Sikh Community Centre**
1199 Coventry Road, Hay Mills, Birmingham,
West Midlands, B25 8DF
Tel: 0121-753-0092

Gurdwara Namdhari Sangat
61 Louis Street, Leeds, West Yorkshire
Tel: 0113-262-5095

Bibliography

Ahluwalia M M, *Kukas: The Freedom Fighters of Punjab*, Allied Publishers, New Delhi, 1965.

Bali Yogendra & Bali Kalika, *The Warriors in White: Glimpses of Kooka History*, Har Anand Publications, New Delhi, 1995.

Cole, W and Singh Sambhi, Piara, *The Sikhs: Their Religious Beliefs and Practices*, Routledge and Kegan Paul, London, 1978.

Hanspal, H, *Namdharis Before and After Independence*, Punjabi Press, New Delhi, 1989.

MacLeod, W, *Textual Sources for the Study of Sikhism*, Manchester University Press, Manchester, 1984.

Singh Bhai N & Singh Bhai K, *Rebels Against the British Rule*, Atlantic Publishers & Distributors, New Delhi, 1989.

Singh Gurmit, *Sant Khalsa*, Usha Institute of Religious Studies, Sirsa, 1978.

Singh, Jaswinder, *Kuka Movement*, Atlantic Publishing, New Delhi, 1985.

Singh, Khushwant, *A History of the Sikhs* (Volume II), Oxford University Press, New Delhi, 1977.

Singh Nahar, *Guru Ram Singh & Kuka Sikhs*, R K Printings (Vol 1, 2 and 3), New Delhi, 1966.

Singh Nihal, *Enlighteners*, Namdhari Sahit Parkashan, Sri Jiwan Nagar, 1966.

Singh Sanehi, "The Nature of Guruship According to the Namdhari Tradition", in McMullen, C (ed), *The Nature of Guruship*, Christian Institute for Sikh Studies, Batala, 1976.

Suri, V, *Ludhiana District Gazette, People - Namdhari*, Government of Punjab, Chandigarh, 1970.

Wells S & Bhamrah, V, Singh, *Meeting the Namdhari Sikhs*, Wolverhampton Inter Faith Group, Wolverhampton, 1991.

PAGANS

Paganism is not a single, structured religion. It is a nature spirituality linked to the cyclical and rhythmic patterns of nature. The Pagan vision of the Divine includes both the male and the female. Some Pagan traditions in the UK pre-date in their presence other major religous traditions. Among contemporary Pagans there are those who believe that modern Paganism is in continuity with these pre-Christian traditions. Paganism should be distinguished from *Satanism* which can be either a deliberate inversion of Christianity or else a celebration of personal power, pride and potential.

There are a number of Pagan traditions. Some Pagans follow their own inspirations whilst others are trained in particular disciplines, including *the Craft* (or *Witchcraft* for which some prefer the name *Wicca*), *Druidry*, *Odinism* (*Asatru*), *Shamanism*, *Women's Traditions*, and *Men's Traditions*. Whilst there are significant differences between these aspects of Paganism, most Pagans share in common an ecological vision and involvement that is born of Paganism's belief in the organic vitality and spirituality of the natural world.

There are an enormous variety of *Magical Groups*, with practice ranging from the folk traditions of herbalism through to the use of elaborate techniques of visualisation and high ritual drama. Alongside these specifically *Magical* groups some, although not all, Pagans engage in magic which is understood among Pagans to be "the art and science of changing reality (or consciousness) according to the Will."

The *Craft* is an initiatory path into communion with the powers of Nature and the human psyche which aims at self-transformation. Within these traditions men are intiated as *priests* and women as *priestesses*. In the UK, four main traditions of the *Craft* can be found - *Gardnerian*, *Alexandrian*, *Traditionalist* and *Hereditary*. *Gardnerians* claim lineage from Gerald Gardner who was central in the modern revival of the *Craft*; *Alexandrians* identify with Alex and Maxine Sanders who developed Gardner's ideas; *Traditionalists* claim that their methods pre-date *Wicca's* twentieth-century revival and have been passed down to them; *Hereditaries* claim traditions passed on through relations of blood and marriage in particular families. Each *Craft* tradition is formed of many local independent groups, sometimes called *covens*, but an increasing number of people celebrate alone and are known as *solitaries*.

There are over twenty Pagan *Druid Orders* although not all *Druid Orders* are Pagan. Some *Druid* groups understand themselves to be Christian; some are Celtic; others are folk in character; some are committed to religious mysteries; and others are more populist in orientation. A Council of British Druids meets to discuss matters of concern to all *Druids*. Some *Druid* groups are teaching groups based upon correspondence courses; some focus on particular sacred locations, such as Stonehenge or Glastonbury.

The *Hutta* tradition is found in many forms but is centred around the *Aesir*, which are culture deities and the *Vanir*, which are vitality and fertility deities. Both groups of deities were part of the pre-Christian traditions of Northern Europe. Some people within these north-west European traditions prefer the word *Asatru* (meaning "trust in deities"). Others, who have a particular affinity with the deity Odin, prefer the name *Odinist*.

Shamanism is extremely diverse. Today *Shamanism* often refers to the tradition of Pagans who do not belong to *Druid*, *Heathen* or *Craft* groups and who meet in relatively unstructured and very participatory gatherings without belonging to identifiable traditions or groups within Paganism. Some *Shamans* describe themselves as *Wiccan*, *Druidic* or as *Women's Mystery Shamans*. Others, however, underline the specifically *Shamanistic* nature of their path which emphasises the reality of the spirit world and the *Shaman's* role as an intermediary with this world or as a guide through it.

All Pagan traditions have been influenced in some way by feminism, with which they share many concerns. Women's spirituality is therefore respected in all Pagan traditions and Women's Spirituality groups relate to the vision of the Goddess or of Goddesses. Some Pagan women work within existing traditions whilst others have established their own traditions.

A few Men's groups have been formed to celebrate male spirituality by exploring male mysteries and initiatory cults, either ancient or modern.

Pagan Federation
BM Box 7097, London, WC1N 3XX
Tel: 01691-671066
(Media enquiries 01787 238257)
Fax: 01691-671066
Contact: Anthony Meadows
(or Peter Jennings, Media Officer)
Position: President
Internet: http://sunacm.swan.ac.uk/~paganfed/

Bibliography

Aswynn, F, *Leaves of Yggdrasil: a Synthesis of Runes, Gods, Magic, Feminine Mysteries and Folklore*, Llewellyn, 1990.

Carr-Gomm, P and Murphy-Gibb, D, *The Druid Renaissance*, Harper Collins, 1996.

Crowley, V, *Wicca: The Old Religion in the New Age*, Millenium, Thorsons, 1996.

Crowley, V, *Principles of Paganism*, Thorsons, 1996.

Dobson, B P (ed), *The Little Red Book: The International Guide to Pagan Resources and Events*, Oakleaf Circle, Preston, 1996.

Gadon, E, *The Once and Future Goddess*, Aquarian, 1990.

Harvey, G, *Listening People, Speaking Earth: Contemporary Paganism*, Hurst & Co, London, 1997.

Harvey, G and Hardman, C, (eds), *Paganism Today*, Thorsons, 1996.

House of the Goddess (ed), *The Pagan Index*, House of the Goddess, London, 1994.

Hutton, R, *The Pagan Religions of the British Isles: Their Nature and Legacy*, Blackwell, 1993.

Matthews, J (ed), *Choirs of God: Revisioning Masculinity*, Mandala Books, 1991.

Pagan Federation, *Pagan Federation Information Pack*, Pagan Federation, London, (second edition), 1992.

Starhawk, *The Spiral Dance*, Harper and Row, New York, 1989.

RASTAFARIANS

The name *Rastafarian* dervies from *Ras* (Prince) Tafari who, in 1930, became Emperor Haile Selassie I of Ethiopa, and is seen as being the 225th descendent in direct line of succession from King Solomon, having the titles *King of Kings*, *Lord of Lords* and *Conquering Lion of the Tribes of Judah*.

The origins of the contemporary Rastafarian movement are to be found in the experience of the dispossessed black people of a racially stratified Jamaica in the early part of this century. In this context, a variety of movements developed which sought to emphasise the dignity and pride of the black inheritance and promised the possibility of African political and economic independence. One of those who was significant in this regard was Marcus Garvey, who prophesied the crowning of a black king. In studying the *Bible* in the light of contemporary events, groups of people came to see Haile Selassie as the Lion of the Tribe of Judah foretold in the Book of Revelation and what Rastafraians refer to as Ras Tafari Livity came into being.

The beliefs of Rastafarians can be quite varied. However, there is a general belief that, following what Rastafarians characterise as his physical "disappearance", the presence of Haile Selassie's presence can still be accessed as *Jah*. Accordingly, Rastas use the terminology of "I and I" instead of referring to "me" or "you", and this indicates the indwelling of *Jah* within human beings. Rastas also refer to the image of *Babylon* as a symbol of the totality of the godless system of the western world which is destined to collapse. Life outside Africa is experienced in terms of exile and suffering, but with the hope of an Exodus - a return to Ethiopa. As a symbol of continous independence this stands for something far more than the present geo-graphical boundaries of the modern state of Ethiopa.

Rastafarians often have a strong emphasis on living in harmony with the natural world and, accordingly, most are vegetarians and some are vegans. Many Rastafarians abstain from alocohol and tobacco, although the use of cannabis is seen as being sanctioned by the *Bible*. The *Bible* is seen as a divine Word, interpreted by Rastafarians through collective reading, study and debate, which is known among Rastafarians as *reasoning*.

Uncut, plaited hair, known as *dreadlocks*, are found amongst most male Rastafarians. The colours of black, red, green and gold (standing, respectively, for the black race; the memory of the blood of slavery; the promised land; and a golden future) are often found in combination in the clothing of Rastafarians.

There are a whole range of Rastafarian organisations and groups in the United Kingdom. Although some Rastafarians have rejected western Christianity as a white religion, some have been baptised as members of the Ethiopian Orthodox Church. Further information and advice on Rastafarians can be obtained from:

Rastafarian Society, The
290-296 Tottenham High Road, London, N15 4AJ
Tel: 0181-808-2185   **Fax:** 0181-801-9815

Bibliography

Cashmore, E, *Rastaman: The Rastafarian Movement in England*, George Allen and Unwin, London, 1979.

Clarke, P, *Black Paradise: The Rastafarian Movement*, Aquarian Press, Wellingborough, 1986.

Plummer, J, *Movement of Jah People: The Growth of the Rastafarians*, Press Gang, Birmingham, 1978.

RAVIDASSIA

Guru Ravidass was born in Benares (Varanasi), the sacred city of the Hindu tradition, in northern India, in the first quarter of the fifteenth century CE. At this time, the religious situation in India was very complex and poor people felt greatly oppressed by the tyranny of high-caste society. Guru Ravidass was one of the prime exponents of a movement which pre-dated the emergence of Sikhism and which aimed to reform society through the preaching of *bhakti* (devotion) to God and the equality of humankind, and declared that God was accessible to all.

Against this background, Guru Ravidass struggled against the powerful in society in order to work for justice, equality and social freedom for all. Contemporary Ravidassia are inspired by his philosophy which encourages them to seek to create a classless society in which all may live with equal rights and freedom. They follow the teachings and philosophy of Guru Ravidass and worship the holy book the *Guru Granth Sahib*, within which forty-one hymns composed by Guru Ravidass are included. Ravidassia believe that these hymns were presented to Guru Nanak, the founder of the Sikh religion, at Benares and were later included the *Guru Granth Sahib*. The Ravidassia community has its own identity, religious practice and symbols.

There are nineteen Guru Ravidass *sabhas* (associations) in the UK. Each *sabha* is a charity through its membership of the Sri Guru Ravidass Sabha UK which is registered with the Charity Commission. Each local *sabha* has its own *bhawan* (temple) but all are governed by the Supreme Council of the Sri Guru Ravidass Sabha UK, which operates from its head office at the Sri Guru Ravidass Bhawan in Handsworth, Birmingham. Also affiliated to this Supreme Council are Guru Ravidass Bhawans from France, the USA and Canada.

The *sabha*, a worship place for the community, also looks after its social, educational and cultural interests. The Supreme Council produces programmes to co-ordinate and organise activities which are designed to benefit the community in its leading of a peaceful and successful life in the UK.

Ravidassia celebrate Guru Ravidass's birthday as a major event and hold celebrations on the birthdays of the Sikh *Gurus* and other prominent saints who participated in the *Bhakti* movement to reform society. The Ravidassia are committed to peace but do not participate in any political activities.

Sri Guru Ravidass Sabha UK
Shri Guru Ravidass Bhawan, Union Row,
Handsworth, Birmingham, West Midlands,
B21 9EN
Tel: 0121-554-8761 **Tel:** 0121-554-1570 (h)
Contact: Dr Charan Singh Bunger
Position: General Secretary

Bibliography

Cole, W O, and Sambhi, P Singh, *A Popular Dictionary of Sikhism*, Curzon Press, London, 1990.

Juergensmeyer M, *Religion as Social Vision: The Movement Against Untouchability in 20th Century Punjab*, University of California Press, California, 1982.

Kalsi, S Singh, *The Evolution of a Sikh Community in Britain: Religious and Social Change Among the Sikhs of Leeds and Bradford*, Community Religions Project Monograph Series, University of Leeds Department of Theology and Religious Studies, Leeds, 1992.

Nesbitt, E, "Pitfalls in Religious Taxonomy: Hindus and Sikhs, Valmikis and Ravidasis," in *Religion Today*, Volume VI, 1, 1990, pp. 9-12.

Nesbitt, E, *My Dad's Hindu, My Mum's Side are Sikh: Issues in Religious Identity*, ACE Research and Curriculum Paper, Charlbury National Foundation for the Arts Education, Warwick, 1991.

Webster, C B, *Popular Religion in the Punjab Today*, ISPCK, Delhi, 1974.

SANT NIRANKARIS

Sant Nirankaris understand themselves as a spiritual regeneration movement which originated in India and emphasises the supremacy of one God - *Nirankar*, meaning "The Formless Being". They believe in the Fatherhood of Nirankar and the brotherhood of humankind regardless of race, colour, creed or religion. They do not subscribe to casteism and believe in equality and responsible living in accordance with the guidelines given by a living *Guru* (spiritual Teacher and Guide). Baba Hardev Singh is the present living *Guru* and his international headquarters are in Delhi.

The movement is known as the Sant Nirankari Mission or Universal Brotherhood. Nirankaris are thus worshippers of Nirankar. It has respect for all religions. The movement's largest following is in India where the followers come from various religions, stations and walks of life.

In the UK the Mission is a registered charity in the name of St Nirankari Mandal UK and there are twenty-two branches.

Sant Nirankari Mandal UK
33 Broad Street, Wolverhampton, West Midlands, WV1 1HZ
Contact: Mr T S Dhillon

Bibliography

Chadha, Khem Raj, *Enlightening the World, Volumes I & II*, Sant Nirankari Mandal, Delhi, 1994.

Kalsi, S Singh, *The Evolution of a Sikh Community in Britain: Religious and Social Change Among the Sikhs of Leeds and Bradford*, Community Religions Project Monograph Series, University of Leeds Department of Theology and Religious Studies, Leeds, 1992.

Lal, Krishan, *The Mission and the Missionaries*, Sant Nirankari Mandal, Delhi, 1987.

Sargar, Kirpar, *Understanding the Sant Nirankari Mission*, Sant Nirankari Mandal, Delhi, 1994.

Satyarthi, J R D, *Gurudev Hardev*, Sant Nirankari Mandal, Delhi, 1988.

Seekree, H S, "The Sant Nirankaris", in Webster, C B, *Popular Religion in the Punjab Today*, ISPCK, Delhi, 1974, pp. 26-29.

SATHYA SAI BABA ORGANISATION

Sai Baba was born in a tiny village called Puttaparthi in southern India in 1926 and began a mission at the age of fourteen. He teaches that basic human nature is divine and that the purpose of this life is the realisation of that divinity. He states that this will occur through leading a moral life, rendering selfless service to those in need, and developing love and respect for all life.

Sai Baba says that he has not come to disturb any religion but to confirm each in his own faith so that a Christian may become a better Christian, a Muslim a better Muslim, a Hindu a better Hindu. He teachers that love is the core of all religion and that this love crosses the boundaries of religion and embraces the whole of humanity.

Sai Baba has established elementary and secondary schools, colleges, a major university, clinics, hospitals and, more recently, a speciality hospital, all of which provide services without charge.

The Satya Sai Baba organisation is global, being found in 137 countries. In the UK, there are over 145 centres and groups, consisting of people from all faiths and walks of life who practise Sai Baba's teachings through spiritual disciplines, education in human values and selfless service. The organisation understands itself as a spiritual organisation which embraces all faiths.

Sathya Sai Baba Organisation
6 Chesle Close, Portishead, Somerset, BS20 8JE
Tel: 01275-848039 **Fax:** 01275-848039
Contact: Mrs Joan Brake
Position: UK Vice President

Bibliography

Bailey, D, *Sai Baba: A Journey to Love*, Sri Sathya Sai Towers Pvt. Ltd., Prashanthi Nilayam, India.

Bowen, D, *The Sathya Sai Baba Community in Bradford: Its Origin and Development, Religious Beliefs and Practices*, Community Religions Project Monograph Series, University of Leeds, Leeds, 1988.

Hislop, J S, *Conversation with Bhagavan Sri Sathya Sai Baba*, Sri Sathya Sai Education and Publication Foundation, Bangalore, 1978.

Kasturi, N, *Sai Baba: Satyam Sivam Sundaram*, Sri Sathya Sai Books and Publications Trust, Prashanthi Nilayam, India.

Krystal, P, *Sai Baba: The Ultimate Experience*, Aura Books, Los Angeles, California.

Mason, P and Laing, R, *Sai Baba: The Embodiment of Love*, Sawbridge Enterprises, London.

Murphet, H, *Sai Baba Avatar*, Macmillan India Ltd, Madras.

Sandweiss, S, *Sai Baba The Holy Man and the Psychiatrist*, Birth Day Publishing Company, San Diego, California.

VALMIKIS

The Valmiki community derives its name from the *Maharishi* Valmiki, who is believed to have written the Hindu holy book, the *Ramayana*. Valmikis believe that they lived in India before the Aryan invasion and had a very rich and developed culture. The foundation of their social life was based upon the philosophy of *dharma*, *karma* and non-violence and the society was not divided into *castes*. Hence, Valmikis do not recognise the *caste* system as formulated in the later Hindu scriptures called the *Manusmriti*.

Valmikis focus upon the main themes of the Holy *Ramayana* as being: kingly obligations, parental authority, filial duty, wifely devotion, brotherly love, friendly loyalty, love and care for the environment and the whole creation. These are the values which are believed to reflect the spirit of the times and community to which the Holy *Ramayana* belonged. They also still form the basis of the Valmiki way of life here in the UK and all over the world.

Maharishi Valmik Sabha
2, St Luke's Road, Holbrooks, Coventry, West Midlands, CV6 4JA
Tel: 01203-688744 **Tel:** 01203-662845 (h)
Contact: Dr Davinder Prasad
Position: Vice President

Bibliography

Nesbitt, E, "Pitfalls in Religious Taxonomy: Hindus and Sikhs, Valmikis and Ravidasis," in *Religion Today*, Volume VI, 1, 1990, pp. 9-12.

Nesbitt, E "Religion and identity: The Valmiki community in Coventry", in *New Community*, Volume XVI, No. 2, pp. 261-274.

FINDING OUT MORE: SOME OTHER RELEVANT PUBLICATIONS AND RESOURCES

FINDING OUT MORE

There are many resources available for anyone who wants to find out more about any aspect of religion. Direct contact can be made with the faith community organisations listed in this directory. Some produce literature which they will be glad to send or they may have suggestions for where to go to get further information written by members of their tradition.

In addition, as a basic strategy the following sources of information can be used:

- Whitaker's *Books in Print*, which can be consulted at most bookshops, will indicate if the books you want are in print in the UK and can be ordered.

- If you do not wish to purchase the books, your local library may have the books or should be able to obtain them for you through an inter-library loan from another library in the UK.

- Other useful resources are libraries of universities with a Department of Theology, Divinity or Religious Studies, and some university collections of materials on race and ethnic relations. (Ring to ask if you can use these for reference purposes since loans are rarely possible unless you are a student or member of staff of the institution or, in some cases, can register as an external user).

- There are also useful collections of resources in Religious Education Centres. The National Society's Religious Education Centre in London at 36, Causton Street, London, SW1P 4AU can tell you if there is an RE Centre in your area.

- Electronic subject, title and key word searches of CD-ROM and on-line book and journal bibliographies and library catalogues can give you many suggestions for further reading. Ask your local library what computer search options are available through their system (there can sometimes be a charge for printing out references).

- The Internet provides a vast and growing resource for information and discussion about religions, including home pages on particular subjects, much of which is free to the user, although some is accessible only on a subscription basis. To access the Internet one needs to be able to use a computer linked to a modem and to have an EMail address and an Internet search engine.

- In using the Internet it is important to be aware that whilst there is much that will be of value, there is also a lot of material of questionable worth and also some of questionable accuracy. It is therefore a resource that should be used with discernment.

- There are electronic discussion groups on the Internet. The number and scope of these is constantly changing, but a full list of academic e-conferences is available by anonymous file transfer protocol from Diane Kovacs at ksuvxa.kent.edu, who has compiled a useful *Directory of Scholarly E-Conferences*.

- You can post a query on the Internet in an electronic conference on a relevant topic.

- Complete texts are accessible on the Internet and can be downloaded to PC and disc including, for example, parallel versions of some scriptures in different languages.

- With respect to electronic resources on the Christian Churches, ChurchNet UK http://www.churchnet.org.uk/ provides a valuable gateway into relevant information, and for Religious Education resources, there is RE-XS http://re-xs.ucsm.ac.uk (available by subscription).

- The University of Derby is currently planning MultiFaith Net as a complementary resource to ChurchNet UK, offering a subscription access gateway to other than Christian religion information on the Inernet including, it is hoped, electronic access to many of the contents of this directory, *Religions in the UK: A Multi-Faith Directory* at http://www. multifaithnet.org/

Overviews of Religions

- Look up overview articles in this book, in encyclopaedias such as the *Encylcopaedia Britannica* or one of the encyclopaedias specifically dedicated to religion such as the *Macmillan Encyclopaedia of Religion*.

- Another possibility is to consult relevant chapters in readily available general overview books on world religions (see sub-section on "World Religions: Overview" in the section on "General Texts on Religions" below). It is important to remember, however, that interpretations of a given tradition's history, beliefs and practices can vary widely, and beyond basic facts there may be many different ways of describing the tradition in question.

Special Topics

- To look at a topic across all the religions or to find out more about a particular issue in one religion, check the sub-section on "World Religions: Special Topics" in the section on "General Texts on Religions" below and the further reading at the end of most chapters in this directory.

- An electronic keyword search of the Internet, on CD-ROM bibliographies (such as *Religion Index I*, see below) or of library catalogues can provide a mine of information to follow up on particular topics.

- The further reading on each religious community in this directory includes some translations or interpretations of sacred texts (among Muslims, it is understood that the *Qu'ran* cannot be adequately "translated" from the original Arabic, but only "interpreted" into other languages). In the section on "General Texts on Religions" below, you will find suggestions of publications which bring together selections from the sacred texts of various traditions.

A Note for School Students

If working on a project, it is best to get as much help as you can directly from your teacher or your nearest RE Centre (see section on "Some Relevant Organisations" in this chapter) before contacting religious organisations or University departments. Do not be surprised if not all religious organisations answer a written enquiry. Many of them are very small and may not have the staff needed to answer all the queries which they receive, even if you have helpfully enclosed a stamped and self-addressed envelope. To increase your chance of getting an answer:

● Discuss your question with your teacher. Make sure it is not too big or too vague. Focus on a clear topic.

● Write to the organisation at least two weeks before you need the information you hope that they can send you.

● Tell the person to whom you are writing exactly what sort of information you hope they can send you.

● Enclose a large, stamped and self-addressed envelope.

● If you are sent particularly helpful information it is courteous to write back and thank the organisation – especially if someone has written you a personal letter.

GENERAL TEXTS ON RELIGIONS

This section lists a selection of the large number of useful general overviews of religious traditions which exist. Some of these provide an overview of a variety of world religious traditions. Others cover particular topics across a number of religions, such as women or prayer. Still others are bibliographical in nature. Finally, there is a section which covers books which include a variety of scriptural texts from different religions. In addition to texts on the world religious traditions, there is also a selection of texts which provide an overview of the forms of organised religious life known as "New Religious Movements."

World Religions: Overviews

Al-Faruqi, I (ed), *Historical Atlas of the Religions of the World*, Macmillan, New York, 1974.

Bishop, P (ed), *The Encyclopaedia of World Faiths*, Orbis, New York, 1987.

Bowker, J, *The Oxford Dictionary of Religions*, OUP, Oxford, 1997.

Cole, W O and Morgan, P, *Six Religions in the Twentieth Century*, Hulton Educational, London, 1984.

Eliade, M (ed), *The Encylopaedia of Religion* (sixteen volumes), Collier Macmillan, London, 1986.

Hardy, F (ed), *The World's Religions: The Religions of Asia*, Routledge, London, 1988.

Harris, I; Mews, S; Morris, P and Shepherd, J, *Contemporary Religions: A World Guide*, Longman, London, 1993.

Hinnells, J (ed), *A New Dictionary of Religions*, Blackwells, Oxford, 1995.

Hinnells, J (ed), *A New Handbook of Living Religions*, 2nd edition, Blackwells, Oxford, 1996.

Lurker, M, *Dictionary of Gods and Goddesses, Devils and Demons*, Routledge and Kegan Paul, London, 1987.

Rausch, D and Voss, C, *World Religions: A Simple Guide*, SCM Press, London, 1994.

Schumacher, S and Woerner, G (eds), *The Rider Encyclopaedia of Eastern Philosophy and Religion: Buddhism, Hinduism, Taoism, Zen*, Rider, London, 1989.

Smart, N, *The World's Religions: Old Traditions and Modern Transformations*, Cambridge University Press, Cambridge, 1989.

World Religions: Special Topics

Brosse, J, *Religious Leaders*, W & R Chambers, Edinburgh, 1991.

Carmody, D and J, *Prayer in World Religions*, Orbis, Maryknoll, New York, 1990.

Hinnells, J (ed), *Who's Who of World Religions*, Macmillan, London, 1991.

Holm, J and Bowker, J (eds), *Worship*, Pinter, London, 1994.

Holm, J and Bowker, J (eds), *Making Moral Decisions*, London, 1994.

Holm, J and Bowker, J (eds), *Myth and History*, Pinter, London, 1994.

Holm, J and Bowker, J (eds), *Attitudes to Nature*, Pinter, London, 1994.

Holm, J and Bowker, J (eds), *Human Nature and Destiny*, Pinter, London, 1994.

Holm, J and Bowker, J (eds), *Sacred Writings*, Ointer, London, 1994.

Holm, J and Bowker, J (eds), *Picturing God*, Pinter, London, 1994.

Holm, J and Bowker, J (eds), *Rites of Passage*, Pinter, London, 1994.

Holm, J and Bowker, J (eds), *Sacred Place*, Pinter, London, 1994.

Holm, J and Bowker, J (eds), *Women in Religion*, Pinter, London, 1994.

King, U, *Women in the World's Religions*, Paragon, New York, 1987.

Magida, A, *How to be a Perfect Stranger: A Guide to Etiquette in Other People's Ceremonies*, Jewish Light Publishing, Woodstock, Vermont, 1996.

Morgan, P and Lawton, C (ed), *Ethical Issues in Six Religious Traditions*, Edinburgh University Press, Edinburgh, 1996.

Prickett, J (ed), *Living Faiths: Initiation Rites*, Lutterworth, Press, London, 1978.

Prickett, J (ed), *Living Faiths: Death*, Lutterworth Press, London, 1980.

Prickett, J (ed), *Living Faiths: Marriage and the Family*, Lutterworth Press, London, 1985.

World Religions: Bibliographical Resources

American Theological Library Association, *Index to Book Reviews in Religion: An Author, Title, Reviewer, Series and Annual Classified Index to Reviews of Books Published in and of Interest to the Field of Religion*, American Theological Library Association, Evanston, Illinois, annual (since 1989 and now available on a single *Religion Index* CD-Rom).

American Theological Library Association, *Religion Index One: Periodicals*, American Theological Library Association, Evanston, Illinois, semi-annual (since 1949 and now available on a single *Religion Index* CD-Rom).

American Theological Library Association, *Religion Index Two: Multi-Author Works*, American Theological Library Association, Evanston, Illinois, annual (since 1976 and now available on a single *Religion Index* CD-Rom).

Barley, L; Field, C; Kosmin, B; and Nielsen, J, *Reviews of United Kingdom Statistical Sources, Volume XX, Religion: Recurrent Christian Sources, Non-Recurrent Christian Data, Judaism, Other Religions*, Pergamon Press, Oxford, 1987.

Daniels, T, *Millennialism: An International Bibliography*, New York, Garland, 1992.

Carman, J and Juergensmeyer, M (eds), *A Bibliographic Guide to the Comparative Study of Ethics*, Cambridge University Press, Cambridge, 1991.

Holm, J, *Keyguide to Information Sources on World Religions*, Mansell, London, 1991.

Lea, E and Jesson A (compilers), *A Guide to the Theological Libraries of Great Britain and Ireland*, Association of British Theological and Philosophical Libraries, London, 1986.

Whitaker, *Religious Books in Print: A Reference Catalogue*, Whitaker, London, annual (since 1984).

World Religions: Texts

Burke, T, *The Major Religions: An Introduction with Texts*, Blackwell, Oxford, 1996.

Comte, F, *Sacred Writings of World Religions*, W & R Chambers, Edinburgh, 1992.

Coward, H, *Sacred Word and Sacred Text: Scriptures in World Religions*, Orbis, New York, 1991.

Markham, I (ed), *A World Religions Reader*, Blackwell, Oxford, 1996.

Smart, N and Hecht, R (eds), *Sacred Texts of the World: A Universal Anthology*, Macmillan, London, 1982.

New Religious Movements

Barker, Eileen, *New Religious Movements: A Practical Introduction*, HMSO, London, 1989.

Beckford, J, *Cult Controversies: The Societal Response to the New Religious Movements*, Tavistock, London, 1985.

Clarke, P (ed), *The New Evangelists: Recruitment, Methods and Aims of New Religious Movements*, Ethnographica, London, 1987.

Dyson, A, and Barker, E (eds), *Sects and New Religious Movements*, Bulletin of the John Rylands University Library of Manchester, Manchester, 1988.

Melton, G (ed), *New Age Encyclopaedia*, Gale, Detroit, 1990.

Needleman, J, and Baker, G, *Understanding the New Religions*, The Seabury Press, New York, 1978.

Wallace, R, *The Elementary Forms of New Religious Life*, Routledge and Kegan Paul, London, 1983.

Wilson, B, *The Social Dimensions of Sectarianism: Sects and New Religious Movements in Contemporary Society*, Clarendon Press, Oxford, 1990.

DIRECTORIES OF RELIGIOUS ORGANISATIONS

This section includes details of relevant directories and handbooks on the religions covered in the directory. Some of these give less detail on particular organisations than can be found in this directory and some give more. A number are produced annually and others every few years, some on a regular and others on an irregular basis. Some of the religious community directories are now quite old, but where they have not been superseded by later editions they are included here as an historical record of the development of these communities and because some of the information in these publications remains valid and relevant.

Bahá'í

There is no generally available publication giving details of Bahá'í groups in the UK. However, the Bahá'í Community of the UK (27 Rutland Gate, London, SW7 1PD, Tel: 0171-584-2566) maintains up-to-date listings of all Spiritual Assemblies and Local Groups.

Buddhist

Parsons, R (ed), *The Buddhist Directory: Buddhist Groups and Centres and Other Related Organisations in the United Kingdom and Ireland*, 7th edition, Buddhist Society, London, 1997.

Christian

Most of the Christian Churches and some of the organisations listed in this directory have their own national and regional level directories or handbooks. At a local level many Churches Together ecumenical bodies also produce directories of their member Churches and organisations. Those listed below are therefore only those directories which cover a number of Churches or types of Christian group:

Brierley, P (ed), *UK Christian Handbook 1996/97*, Christian Research Association, London, 1996 (biennial).

Brierley, P (ed), *The Irish Christian Handbook: Lámhleabhar Chríostaí na hEireann*, 1995/96, Christian Research Association, London, 1994.

Butt, P (ed), *The Body Book: A Directory of Christian Fellowships*, 5th edition, Team Spirit Services, Romford, 1995.

Byrne, L (ed), *Directory of Women's Organisations and Groups in Churches and Ecumenical Bodies in Britain and Ireland*, Council of Churches for Britain and Ireland, London, 1992.

Centre for Caribbean Studies, *A Handbook of the Afro-West Indian United Council of Churches*, Centre for Caribbean Studies, London, 1984.

Churches Together in England, *Register of Local Ecumenical Projects and Sponsoring Bodies*, Churches Together in England, London, 1992.

Douglas, D, *The Handbook of the International Ministerial Council of Great Britain 1990*,

International Ministerial Council of Great Britain, Watford, 1990.

Gerloff, R, "Appendix 5:I, List of Black Independent and Related Churches (including Councils of Churches) in Britain" in, *A Plea for British Black Theologies: The Black Church Movement in Britain in its Transatlantic Cultural and Theological Interaction*, Volume II, Peter Lang, Frankfurt-am-Main, Germany, 1992, pp 863–1055.

National Association of Christian Communities and Networks, *Directory of Christian Groups, Communities and Networks*, 3rd edition, NACCAN, Birmingham, 1993.

Hindu

There is no generally available Hindu publication listing Hindu religious groups nationally, although lists have appeared in some general publications. The International Society for Krishna Consciousness maintains a database of Hindu groups. There are a wide range of handbooks pertaining to specific caste organisations, but these are not generally publicly available.

Jain

There are no publicly available Jain directories or handbooks. However, the Institute of Jainology (Unit 18, Silicon Business Centre, 26–28 Wandsworth Road, Greenford, Middlesex, UB6 7JZ, Tel: 0181-997-2300) aims to maintain an up-to-date database of Jain groups.

Jewish

Many local/regional Jewish Representative Councils produce their own directories of member organisations and synagogues, as do many national umbrella organisations within the Jewish community. The most comprehensive overall Jewish directory is annual and the current edition is:

Massil, S (ed), *The Jewish Year Book*, Vallentine Mitchell, London, 1997.

Muslim

Ali, M, *The Mosques in the United Kingdom and Eire and Prayer Time Table*, Ambala Sweet Centre, London, 1991.

Darr, N (ed), *Muslim Directory 1995/96*, Muslim Directory, London, 1995.

Darr, N (ed), *Muslim Directory: Midlands 1996/97*, Muslim Directory, London, 1996.

Lancashire Council of Mosques, *Directory of Mosques/Madrassahs in Lancashire, 1994/95*, Lancashire Council of Mosques, 1994.

Muslim Education Trust, *List of Mosques and Islamic Centres in Britain*, Muslim Education Trust, London, 1988.

Rahman, G (ed), *The Directory of Mosques, Islamic Centres and other Muslim Organisations in the United Kingdom and Ireland*, Council of Mosques UK and Eire, London, nd.

Sikh

Shergill, N S, *International Directory of Gurdwaras and Sikh Organisations*, N S Shergill, London, 1985.

Sikh Cultural Society of Great Britain, *The Sikh Gurdwaras (Sikh Temples) in the United Kingdom*, 5th edition, Sikh Cultural Society of Great Britain, London, 1989.

Zoroastrian

There is no generally available Zoroastrian directory or handbook. However, the Zoroastrian Trust Funds of Europe aims to maintain details of the Zoroastrian community in the UK.

New Religious Movements

Ward, G (series ed); Dandelion, B P (Associate editor for the UK); and Poggi, I (Associate Editor for Ireland), *Religions Directory International: A Comprehensive Guide to the World's Religions, Churches, Denominations, Temples, Synagogues, Religious Organisations and Spiritual Groups: Volume I: UK and Ireland*, Apogee Books, Detroit, Michigan, 1990.

National: General

In addition to handbooks and directories covering particular religions, there are a number of publications which have a more general coverage. Some are listed below:

Clarke, F (ed), *Interfaith Directory*, International Religious Foundation Incorporated, New York, 1987.

Office of Population and Censuses and Surveys, *The Official List, Part III - Certified Places of Worship*, Office of Population and Censuses and Surveys, General Register Office, London, 1981.

Local Religious: General

Many local and regional directories and listings exist. Details of these can often be obtained through local Racial Equality Councils, local Councils for Voluntary Service, or local libraries (which sometimes also have computerised listings). Examples of some of those which are published in the more permanent form of booklets and pamphlets are given below:

Aston Community Involvement Unit, *Newham Directory of Religious Groups*, Second Edition 1994-95, Aston Community Involvement Unit, London, 1994.

Birmingham City Council Department of Planning and Architecture, *Sacred Spaces: A Guide to Birmingham's Varied Religious Buildings*, Birmingham City Council Department of Planning and Architecture, Birmingham, n.d.

Bexley Directorate of Education, *Libraries and Museums, List of Local Places of Worship, 1994/95 edition*, Bexley Directorate of Education, Libraries and Museums, 1994.

Blyth, H (ed), *Places of Worship in Oxford*, Advisory Centre for Multi-Cultural Education, Oxford, 1989.

Brent Council Education Department, *Brent Religious Education, Now and Tomorrow*, Brent Council Education Department, Brent, 1988.

Capey, C (ed), *Faiths in Focus in Ipswich and Suffolk: A Collection to Celebrate the Centenary of the World's Parliament of Religions, held in Chicago in 1893*, Ipswich, 1993.

Cornwall County Council Education Department, *Religious Education Directory Cornwall*, Cornwall County Council Education Department, nd.

Faivre, D, *Glimpses of a Holy City: A Guide to Places of Worship in Southall*, Brother Daniel Faivre, Southall, 1992.

Gwent County Council Libraries and Information Services, *Religious Organisations in Gwent*, Gwent County Council Libraries and Information Services, Gwent, 1995.

Hertfordshire County Council Education Department, *Faith Communities Handbook (Hertfordshire)*, Hertfordshire County Council Education Department, Hertfordshire, 1991.

Hillingdon Standing Advisory Committee on Religious Education, *Visiting Places of Worship: A Resource Pack*, Hillingdon Standing Advisory Committee on Religious Education, Hillingdon, nd.

King, T (ed), *Places of Worship in Birmingham*, City of Birmingham Education Department and the Regional R E Centre (Midlands), Birmingham, nd.

Leeds City Council Department of Education, *Directory of Faith Communities in Leeds*, Leeds City Council Department of Education, Leeds, nd.

Lewisham Education Quality Assurance and Development Team and South London Multi-Faith Religious Education Centre, *Directory of Places of Worship in the London Borough of Southwark: For School Visits as Part of Religious Education*, Lewisham Education Quality Assurance and Development Team and Southwark Standing Advisory Council on Religious Education, 1995.

Lewisham Education Quality Assurance and Development Team and South London Multi-Faith Religious Education Centre, *Directory of Places of Worship in the London Borough of Lewisham: For School Visits as Part of Religious Education*, 2nd edition, Lewisham Education

Quality Assurance and Development Team and Southwark Standing Advisory Council on Religious Education, 1995.

Lewisham Education Quality Assurance and Development Team and South London Multi-Faith Religious Education Centre, *Directory of Places of Worship in the London Borough of Greenwich: For School Visits as Part of Religious Education*, 2nd edition, Lewisham Education Quality Assurance and Development Team and Southwark Standing Advisory Council on Religious Education, 1995.

Mason, L, *Religion in Leeds*, Alan Sutton, Stroud, 1994.

Mead, J (ed), *Visiting Places of Worship in Waltham Forest*, Multi-Cultural Development Service, Waltham Forest, nd.

Milton Keynes Justice and Peace Centre, *Milton Keynes Directory of Faiths: A Guide to the Faith Communities of Milton Keynes*, Milton Keynes Justice and Peace Centre, 1994.

Plummer, A, *Places of Worship and Clergy or Leaders' List: Borough of Greenwich*, 3rd edition, Anthony Plummer, Plumstead, 1995.

Publicity Unit of the Chief Executive's Department of the Metropolitan Borough of Trafford, *Places of Worship in the Metropolitan Borough of Trafford*, Publicity Unit of the Chief Executive's Department of the Metropolitan Borough of Trafford, Trafford, nd.

Redbridge Standing Advisory Council on Religious Education, *Redbridge Religions Directory: Handbook for Religious Education*, London Borough of Redbridge, London, 1994.

Warwickshire County Council Education Department, *A Directory of Places of Worship and Useful Contacts and Addresses for Teachers of Religious Education in Warwickshire*, Warwickshire County Council Education Department, Warwick.

Westminster Interfaith Programme, *Who is My Neighbour? Other Faiths in West London: A Directory*, Westminster Interfaith Programme, Southall, 1991.

Willows, H (ed), *A Guide to Worship in Central London*, London Central YMCA, London, 1988.

Wolverhampton Inter Faith Group and Wolverhampton Multi-Cultural Support Team, *Directory of Places of Worship in Wolverhampton*, Wolverhampton Inter Faith Group and Wolverhampton Multi-Cultural Support Team, Wolverhampton, 1989.

DIRECTORIES OF ETHNIC MINORITY ORGANISATIONS

There are a number of ethnic minority directories which are not primarily concerned to cover religious groups but do, in fact, provide useful contact information for them. At local level there are many such directories and listings, details of which can often be obtained through local Racial Equality Councils, local Councils for Voluntary Service, or local libraries. The directories listed below are restricted to some which aim to give UK-wide coverage:

Confederation of Indian Organisations (UK), *Directory of Asian Voluntary Organisations, 1994/95*, Confederation of Indian Organisations, London, 1994.

Hansib Publications, *EM: Ethnic Minorities Directory: A Commercial and Social Directoy of African, Asian and Caribbean Communities in Britain*, Hansib Publishing, London, 1993.

O'Maolain, C, *Ethnic Minority and Migrant Organisations, European Directory: 1996*, Joint Council for the Welfare of Immigrants, London, with the Centre for Research in Ethnic Relations, Warwick University, Coventry, 1996.

Patel, C B, *Who's Who of Asians in Britain*, New Life Publications, London, 1988.

Sachar, J S, *Asian Who's Who International: 1995/96*, Asian Observer Publications, Ilford, 1992.

SOME RELEVANT RESOURCE ORGANISATIONS

There are a wide range of organisations which can give further advice on the religious traditions and organisations covered in this volume. Those listed here are organisations which can provide information spanning two or more religious traditions. This section comprises a single list in alphabetical order, not split further down, unlike most chapters, into countries of the UK, regions, towns and cities.

In the chapters on the various religious communities there are a number of entries which relate to resource organisations operating on a UK and local basis with respect to particular, individual religious traditions.

Banbury Area Religious Education Centre
The Methodist Church, Marlborough Road, Banbury, Oxfordshire, OX16 8BZ
Tel: 01295-262676 **Fax:** 01925-262676
Contact: Mrs Judith Macey
Position: Administrator
Other Languages: Punjabi
An independent multifaith centre which has been established for twenty years and is run entirely by volunteers. It aims to give support, both with materials for loan to members and with training opportunities to those providing Religious Education in schools and faith communities.

Bradford Interfaith Education Centre
Listerhills Road, Bradford, West Yorkshire, BD7 1HD
Tel: 01274-731674 **Fax:** 01274-731621
Contact: David Fitch
Position: Centre Co-ordinator
Other Languages: Urdu, Panjabi, Gujarati, Hindi
Resource and training centre for Religious and Cultural Education established in 1986. Supports Religious Eduction and Collective Worship in schools and trains professional groups (nurses, police, social services) in religious and cultural awareness. Staff lead visits to places of worship and a library/loan service is available.

British & Foreign School Society
National Religious Education Centre, Brunel University, Osterley Campus, Borough Road, Isleworth, Middlesex, TW7 5DU
Tel: 0181-891-0121 **Fax:** 0181-891-8211
Contact: Maurice Lynch
Position: Director
The primary concern is to service the needs of teachers, inspectors and lecturers responsible for Religious Education. It has an annual programme of inservice courses, engages in research and curriculum development in spiritual, moral and religious education.

Centre for the Study of Islam & Christian-Muslim Relations
Selly Oak Colleges, 996 Bristol Road, Birmingham, West Midlands, B29 6LQ
Tel: 0121-472-4231 **Fax:** 0121-472-8852
Contact: Professor Jorgen Nielsen
Position: Director
Affiliations: Inter Faith Network for the UK

Centre for the Study of Judaism & Jewish-Christian Relations

Selly Oak Colleges, Central House, Birmingham, West Midlands, B29 6LQ
Tel: 0121-472-4231 **Fax:** 0121-472-3206
Contact: Mrs Elnora Ferguson
Position: Chair of Council
Affiliations: Inter Faith Network for the UK
Development of knowledge and understanding of Judaism and Jewish/Christian relations in local and community schools and in higher education through the Selly Oak Colleges with their international links and their association with the University of Birmingham.

Community Religions Project

Department of Theology and Religious Studies, University of Leeds, Leeds, West Yorkshire, LS2 9JT
Tel: 0113-233-3644 **Fax:** 0113-233-3654
Email: j.killington@leeds.ac.uk
Contact: Jill Killington
Position: Project Secretary
Affiliations: Inter Faith Network for the UK
The project focuses on the religious practices, beliefs and organisations of religious communities in Britain. One of its major aims is to encourage research and make available completed work through the publication of research papers and monographs.

Education Resource Centre

John Street Secondary School, 96 Main Street, Glasgow, Strathclyde, G40 1JP
Tel: 0141-554-3080 **Fax:** 0141-554-1233
Contact: Marie Ward
Position: Centre Manager
Providing resources and advice to teaching staff, all educationalists and pupils in Glasgow City Council schools.

Information Network Focus on Religious Movements

Houghton Street, London, WC2A 2AE
Tel: 0171-955-7654 **Fax:** 0171-955-7679
Email: inform@lse.ac.uk
Contact: Harry Coney
Position: Information Officer
INFORM helps enquirers by giving them information directly or by putting them in touch with its extensive network of experts. Its research covers the collection, analysis and publication about the diverse beliefs and practices of New Religious Movements.

Inter Faith Network for the UK

5-7 Tavistock Place, London, WC1H 9SN
Tel: 0171-388-0008 **Fax:** 0171-387-7968
The UK's national inter-faith body, linking over 80 faith community, inter-faith and educational bodies. It promotes good relations between the faiths in this country and gives information and advice on interfaith issues. For more details see pp. 11-12 on the Network.

Interfaith Resource Centre

91 Mantilla Drive, Styvechale, Coventry, West Midlands, CV3 6LG
Tel: 01203-415531
Contact: Dr C S Chan

International Consultancy on Religion Education & Culture

Manchester Metropolitan University, 799 Wilmslow Road, Manchester, Greater Manchester, M20 2RR
Tel: 0161-434-0828 **Fax:** 0161-434-8374
Contact: Martin Palmer
Position: Director
ICOREC is an interfaith, intercultural consultancy engaged in promoting greater understanding and appreciation of the variety of faiths and cultures in our world. It has a belief that religion plays a key role in shaping and giving meaning to daily life.

International Interfaith Centre

2 Market Street, Oxford, Oxfordshire, OX1 3FF
Tel: 01865-202745 **Fax:** 01865-202746
EMail: iic@interfaith-centre.org
Internet: http://www.interfaith-centre.org/oxford/
Contact: Sandy Martin
Position: Joint Co-Ordinator
A registered charity for information and research into worldwide inter-faith activity, and a support network for those engaged in this work. It arranges conferences and lectures, publishes a newsletter and offers advice on international inter-faith action.

International Sacred Literature Trust

1st Floor, 22 Northumberland Avenue, Charing Cross, London, WC2 5BH
Tel: 0171-839-0884 **Fax:** 0171-930-1437
Contact: Paul Seto
Position: Director
Activities: Newsletters, books
Established to publish, in contemporary and literary English, the teachings, stories, poetry and songs from humanity's vast spiritual heritage, thereby increasing tolerance through understanding.

National Association of SACREs
Religious Education Centre, Westhill College, Selly
Oak, Birmingham, West Midlands, B29 6LL
Tel: 0121-472-7245, Ext. 257
Contact: Mr Geoffrey Teece
Position: Secretary
Affiliations: Inter Faith Network for the UK

**National Society's Religious Education
Centre, The**
36 Causton Street, London, SW1P 4AU
Tel: 0171-932-1190 **Fax:** 0171-932-1199
Contact: Mrs Alison Seaman
Position: Deputy Director
Founded in 1811 to promote Christian values in
education and was responsible for establishing many
schools in the last century. Today its London RE
Centre supports everyone involved in Christian and
Religious Education by providing information and
advice.

Religious Education & Environment Programme
8th Floor, Rodwell House, Middlesex Street,
London, E1 7HJ
Tel: 0171-377-0604 **Fax:** 0171-247-2144
EMail: reep@globalnet.co.uk
Contact: Robert Vint
Position: Programme Administrator
Activities: Newsletters, books, inter-faith
REEP provides down-to-earth training for teachers
of Religious Education and staff responsible for
assemblies and the moral and spiritual development of
children. These events study all the major faiths using
environmental issues as a starting point.

Religious Education Council of England & Wales
CEM Royal Buildings, Victoria Street, Derby,
Derbyshire, DE1 1GW
Tel: 01332-296655 **Fax:** 01332-343253
Contact: Revd Dr Stephen Orchard
Position: Secretary
Affiliations: Inter Faith Network for the UK
Its membership is from faith communities and
nationally representative RE teacher associations. It
provides a national forum for considering matters
affecting RE in schools, and is concerned with the
promotion of the interests of RE at national level.

Religious Experience Research Centre
Westminster College, Oxford, Oxfordshire,
OX2 9AT
Tel: 01865-243006 **Fax:** 01865-201197
Contact: Peggy Morgan

Position: Director
The Centre is associated with the Alister Hardy
Society under the Alister Hardy Trust. Its purpose is
research into and advice about research procedures,
findings and related issues concerning religious,
transcendent and spiritual experiences among
individuals of any religious institution or tradition or
none.

Religious Resource & Research Centre
University of Derby, Mickleover, Derby, Derbyshire,
DE3 5GX
Tel: 01332-622222 **Fax:** 01332-514323
Email: p.g.weller@derby.ac.uk
Contact: Paul Weller
Position: Director
Affiliations: Inter Faith Network for the UK
A designated research centre of the University of
Derby. It has three principal research foci: religious
and social issues related to religious plurality; pastoral
care in a plural context; and the interaction of beliefs;
values and cultures. For more details see the display
pages on the Religious Resource and Research
Centre and the University on pp. 9-10.

St Mungo Museum of Religious Life & Art
2 Castle Street, Glasgow, Strathclyde, G4 0RH
Tel: 0141-553-2557 **Fax:** 0141-552-4744
Contact: Mark O'Neill
Position: Head of Curatorial Services
The Museum looks at the importance of religion in
shaping peoples lives from three perpectives: religion
and art, religion and the life cycle, and Scottish
religion. It hosts two temporary exhibitions on
religious themes each year.

**Scottish Joint Committee for Religious & Moral
Education**
c/o Department of Education, Church of Scotland,
121 George Street, Edinburgh, Lothian, EH2 4YN
Tel: 0131-225-5722
Contact: Revd John Stevenson
Position: Secretary

**Scottish Working Party on Religions of the World
in Education**
Department of Social Studies Education, Faculty of
Education, University of Strathclyde, 76 Southbrae
Drive, Glasgow, Strathclyde, G13 1BP
Tel: 0141-050-3393
Contact: Chris Foxon

Shap Working Party

c/o The National Society's RE Centre, 36 Causton Street, London, SW1P 4AU
Tel: 0171-932-1194 **Fax:** 0171-932-1199
Contact: Miss Lorraine McColl
Position: Administrator
Affiliations: Inter Faith Network for the UK
Shap was set up to encourage the study and teaching of world religions. Members come from a variety of religious backgrounds and all fields of education. Its publications include a calendar of religious festivals and an annual journal. See its full page display on p. 696.

Study Centre for Christian-Jewish Relations

17 Chepstow Villas, London, W11 3DZ
Tel: 0171-727-3597 (h) **Fax:** 0171-221-1556
Contact: Clare Jardine/Mary Kelly
Position: Co-Director
Affiliations: Inter Faith Network for the UK
The Centre is autonomous with no special membership framework. It aims to provide a place for the study of Judaism and the Jewish roots of Christianity. It holds lectures, short courses, welcomes visitors to the specialist library and publishes pamphlets.

Suffolk Inter-Faith Resource (SIFRE)

c/o University College Suffolk, Bolton Lane Annexe, Ipswich, Suffolk, IP4 2BT
Tel: 01473-233447 **Fax:** 01473-289360
Contact: Mrs Cynthia Capey
Position: Chair/Co-ordinator
Affiliations: Inter Faith Network for the UK
Languages: Punjabi, Bengali, Cantonese, Arabic
A resource of people seeking "to advance public knowledge and understanding of different religions and philosophies, particularly in Suffolk". A limited company, supported by, but independent of, University College, Suffolk, engaging in research, study tours, publications, lectures, and seminars. Its tutors work in schools and community groups.

Values Education Council

c/o Faculty of Education, University of Central England, Westbourne Road, Edgbaston, Birmingham, B15 3TN
Tel: 0121-753-3715
Contact: Mr David Rowse
Position: General Secretary

Welsh Association of SACREs

Curriculum Support Service, County Hall, Mold, Clwyd, CH7 6ND
Tel: 01352-704103 **Tel:** 01745-354023
Fax: 01352-754202
Contact: Mr Gavin Craigen
Position: Secretary
Other Languages: Welsh
Forum for SACREs in Wales to: discuss concerns and make representations to other bodies; enable co-operation between LEAs and their SACREs and Agreed Syllabus Conferences; facilitate the sharing of experience and expertise among SACREs; undertake other activities benefitting RE and Collective Worship in Wales.

Welsh National Centre for Religious Education

University of Wales, School of Education, Bangor, Gwynedd, LL57 2UW
Tel: 01248-382761 **Fax:** 01248-382155
Contact: Rheinallt A Thomas
Position: Director

Westhill Religious Education Centre

Westhill College, Selly Oak, Birmingham, West Midlands, B29 6LL
Tel: 0121-472-7248
Contact: Dr John A Rudge
Position: Director
The Centre provides in-service training in all aspects of Religious Education in a multi-faith context in primary and secondary schools; accredited courses by distance learning; study visits to faith communities in Birmingham; consultancies; publications.

York Religious Education Centre

University College of Ripon and York St John, Lord Mayor's Walk, York, North Yorkshire, Y03 7EX
Tel: 01904-616858 **Fax:** 01904-612512
Email: c.mercier@ucrysj.ac.uk
Contact: Carrie Mercier
Position: Centre Tutor
The centre aims to promote quality Religious Education in colleges, Churches and schools; to support teaching and research in Religious Studies and Theology; to contribute to the professional training of teachers in RE and to encourage religious dialogue.

SOME RELEVANT NEWSPAPERS AND MAGAZINES

A number of papers and magazines are published in the UK which serve particular communities. In some cases these are explicitly religious. In other cases they serve a community defined by ethnic or linguistic background but carry materials relating to faith traditions represented within their readership.

Details for other media resources such as national papers and television and radio can be found in such publications as the *Guardian Media Guide* (1997). This also gives details of the regulatory bodies dealing with the various media.

A useful resource for organisations wishing to get their activities covered by the media is Moi Ali's *DIY Guide to Public Relations for Charities, Voluntary Organisations and Community Groups*, Directory of Social Change, 1995.

Additional fields of information other than standard ones are included in organisations listed in this section covering "Religion" where the publication has an explicitly religious basis; "Communities" where it has defined its readership by religious community; and "Frequency" of publication.

Al-Sharq-al Aousat
Arab Press House, 182-184 High Holborn, London, WC1V 7AP
Tel: 0171-831-8181 **Fax:** 0171-831-2310
Communities: Arab
Frequency: Daily

Asian Times
148 Cambridge Heath Road, Bethnal Green, London, E1 5QJ
Tel: 0171-702-8012
Communities: South Asian

Baptist Times, The
P O Box 54, 129 The Broadway, Didcot, Oxfordshire, OX11 8XB
Contact: Mr John Capon
Religion: Christian (Baptist)
Frequency: Weekly

Catholic Herald, The
Herald House, Lamb's Passage, Bunhill Road, London, EC1Y 8TQ
Tel: 0171-588-3101 **Fax:** 0171-256-9728
Contact: Deborah Jones
Religion: Christian (Roman Catholic)
Frequency: Weekly

Church of England Newpaper, The
Parliamentary Communications Ltd, 10 Little College Street, Westminster, London, SW1P 3SH
Tel: 0171-976-7760 **Fax:** 0171-976-0783
Email: Letters@church.mhs.compuserve.com
Contact: C M Blakely
Position: Editor
Religion: Christian (Anglican)
Communities: Anglican.
Frequency: Weekly

Church Times, The
Church Times, 33 Upper Street, London, N1 0PN
Tel: 0171-359-4570 **Fax:** 0171-226-3073
Contact: Paul Handley
Religion: Christian (Anglican)
Communities: Church of England, Anglican Communion
Frequency: Weekly

Daily Jang
1 Sanctuary Street, London, SE1 1ED
Tel: 0171-403-5833 **Fax:** 0171-378-1653
Contact: Zahoor Niazi
Frequency: Daily

Dialogue

Al-Khoei Foundation, Stone Hall, Chevening
Road, Kilburn, London, NW6 6TN
Tel: 0171-372-4049　**Fax:** 0171-372-0694
Email: postmaster@al-khoei.demon.co.uk
Contact: Sayyed Nadeem A Kazmi
Languages: English, Arabic, French
Religion: Muslim
Communities: British; Worldwide Academics/
Diplomats, Muslim/Non-Muslim Academics.
Frequency: Monthly

English Churchman, The

English Churchman Trust Ltd, 22 Lesley Avenue,
Canterbury, Kent, CT1 3LF
Tel: 01227-781282
Contact: Dr. Napier Malcolm
Position: Editor
Religion: Christian (Anglican)
Communities: Christian, Protestant & Evangelical,
Church of England,
Frequency: Fortnightly

Evangelism Today

320 Ashley Down Road, Bristol, Greater Bristol,
B57 9BQ (h)
Tel: 0117-9241679 (h)　**Fax:** 0117-9241679
Contact: Bill Spencer
Position: Editor
Activities: Media, newsletters
Religion: Christian (Evangelical)
Frequency: Monthly

Friend, The

Drayton House, 30 Gordon Street, London,
WC1H 0BQ
Contact: Deborah Padfield
Religion: Christian (Quaker)
Frequency: Weekly

Garavi Gujarat

Garavi Gujarat Publications Ltd, 1 Silex Street,
London, SE1 0DW
Tel: 0171-928-1234　**Fax:** 0171-261-0055
Contact: Ramniklal Solanki
Position: Editor
Languages: English, Gujarati
Communities: Hindus and Muslims from the sub-
continent.
Frequency: Weekly

Gujarat Samachar

Gujarat Samachar Publications Ltd, 8/16 Coronet
Street, London, N1 6HD
Tel: 0171-729-5453　**Fax:** 0171-739-0358

Contact: Chandrakant Babubhai Patel
Languages: Gujarati, English
Communities: Hindu, Jain, Muslim, Chistian
Frequency: Weekly

Hinduism Today

1b Claverton Street, London, SW1V 3AY
Tel: 0171-630-8688
EMail: 100700.513@compuserve.com
Editor: Acharya Palaniswami
Company: Himalayan Academy, USA
Languages: English
Religion: Hindu
Communities: Hindu
Frequency: Monthly

Impact International

PO Box 2493, Suite B, 233 Seven Sisters Road,
London, N4 2BL
Contact: Mr M H Faruqi
Religion: Muslim
Frequency: Monthly

Islamic Times, The

Raza Academy, 138 Northgate Road, Edgeley,
Stockport, Cheshire, SK3 9NL
Tel: 0161-477-1595
Contact: Mr Mohammad Khetab
Languages: English, Urdu
Religion: Muslim
Communities: Muslim, Any others interested
Frequency: Monthly

Jewish Chronicle, The

Jewish Chronicle Ltd, 25 Furnival Street, London,
EC4A 1JT
Tel: 0171-415-1500　**Fax:** 0171-405-9040
Email: jcadmin@jchron.co.uk
Contact: Edward J Temko
Languages: English
Religion: Jewish
Communities: Jewish
Frequency: Weekly

Jewish Quarterly

PO Box 2978, London, W1A5 1JR
Tel: 0171-629-5004　**Fax:** 0171-629-5110
EMail: jewish.quarterly@ort.org
Contact: Mrs Elene Lappin
Religion: Jewish
Community: Jewish
Frequency: Quarterly

Lotus Realm Magazine
16-20 Turner Street, Manchester, Greater
Manchester, M4 1DZ
Tel: 0161-839-2060 **Fax:** 0161-839-4815
EMail: lotus@c-vision.demon.co.uk
Contact: Dharmacharini Kalyanaprabha
Position: Editor
Frequency: Three times a year

Manna
The Sternberg Centre for Judaism, 80 East End
Road, London, N3 2SY
Contact: Rabbi Tony Bayfield
Religion: Jewish
Frequency: Quarterly

Methodist Recorder, The
The Methodist Newspaper Co Ltd, 122 Golden
Lane, London, EC1Y 0TL
Tel: 0171-251-8414 **Fax:** 0171-608-3490
Contact: Michael Taylor
Languages: English
Religion: Christian (Methodist)
Communities: Members of the Methodist Church
and interested non-members
Frequency: Weekly

Middle Way
The Buddhist Society, 58 Eccleston Square, London,
SW1V 1PH
Contact: Dr Desmond Biddhulph
Religion: Buddhist
Frequency: Quarterly

Month, The
The Month Publications, 114 Mount Street,
London, W1Y 6AH
Tel: 0171-491-7596 **Fax:** 0171-629-6936
Email: ei17@dial.pipex.com
Contact: Revd Tim Noble
Languages: English
Religion: Christian (Roman Catholic)
Communities: Christian
Frequency: Monthly

Muslim News, The
Visitcrest Ltd, PO Box 380, Harrow, Middlesex,
HA2 6LL
Tel: 0171-831-0428 **Fax:** 0171-831-0830
Email: musnews@rmplc.co.uk
Contact: Ahmed Versi
Position: Editor
Languages: English
Communities: Muslim
Frequency: Weekly

New Moon
28 St Albans Lane, London, NW11 7QE
Tel: 0181-731-8031 **Fax:** 0181-381-4033
Religion: Jewish
Communities: Jewish

Punjab Times International
Khalsa Printers Ltd, 24 Cotton Brook Road,
Sir Francis Ley Industrial Park, Derby, Derbyshire,
DE23 8YJ
Tel: 01332-372851 **Fax:** 01332-372833
Contact: Mr R Singh Purewal
Position: Chair
Languages: Punjabi, English
Communities: Sikh, English
Frequency: Weekly

Punjabi Guardian
Soho News Building, 129 Soho Road, Handsworth,
Birmingham, West Midlands, B21 9ST
Tel: 0121-554-3995 **Fax:** 0121-507-1065
Contact: Inderjit Singh Sangha
Position: Director
Communities: Sikh
Frequency: Fortnightly

Q News International
PO Box 516, Wembley, Middlesex, HA9 7UD
Tel: 0171-734-4887 **Fax:** 0171-734-4891
Contact: Mr Faud Nahdi
Religion: Muslim
Frequency: Weekly

Sikh Messenger
43 Dorset Road, Merton Park, London, SW19 3EZ
Tel: 0181-540-4148
Contact: Mr Indarjit Singh OBE
Languages: English
Religion: Sikh
Communities: Sikh, non-Sikh
Frequency: Quarterly

Tablet, The
Great Peter Street, London, SW1P 2HB
Contact: Mr John Wilkins
Religion: Christian (Roman Catholic)
Frequency: Weekly

Universe, The
Gabriel Communications, St James's Buildings,
Oxford Street, Manchester, Greater Manchester,
M1 6FP
Contact: Mr Paulinus Barnes
Religion: Christian (Roman Catholic)
Frequency: Weekly

THE SHAP WORKING PARTY ON WORLD RELIGIONS IN EDUCATION

For over 25 years **SHAP** has promoted and supported good practice in the teaching of world religions at all levels of education; through its annual **Calendar of Religious Festivals** it also reaches a wide public readership, fostering awareness of faith traditions in the UK and beyond and providing an indispensable reference work which is second to none.

SHAP is widely known through its publications; these include:

The Shap Calendar of Religious Festivals

An annual publication appearing each year in August and covering a period of 15 months, this includes a detailed listing of the festivals of the world's religions. There are detailed notes on each festival - completely revised and updated for the 1996/7 edition - and a separate wall chart calendar, suitable for the classroom or office.

An annual journal **World Religions in Education**

Each year this explores a different issue or theme from the varying perspectives of faith traditions; recent themes have included *Exploring Loss, Grief and Change (1994), From Syllabus to Schemes - Planning and Teaching Religious Education (1995) and Exploring Conflict and Reconciliation: Issues for Religious Education (1996)*. Each issue highlights important books and other resources related to the theme; it also offers reviews of recent books on world religions and Religious Education. Back copies of the journal are often available.

SHAP has also published other key books. A new edition of its popular **Festivals in the World Religions** (Longman, 1986) is planned, whilst its most recent publication **Teaching World Religions - A Handbook for Teachers** (Heinemann, 1993) offers perceptive insights into faith traditions, imaginative approaches to teaching and extensive bibliographies, all set within a clear understanding of the place of Religious Education in schools.

Conferences and **Day Courses** are arranged by **SHAP** from time to time in different parts of the country and are advertised regionally or nationally.

Further details of **SHAP** publications and of annual subscriptions to the Journal and/or Calendar can be obtained from

SHAP Working Party Publications

36 Causton Street, London SW1P 4AU, Tel: 0171-932-1194, Fax: 0171-932-1199

ACKNOWLEDGEMENTS

INTRODUCTION

The phase of the Multi-Faith Directory Research Project which led to this 1997 edition was funded by the University of Derby and The Inter Faith Network for the United Kingdom.

Many individuals and organisations have offered assistance to the project. Of all the acknowledgements which should be made, one of the most significant must be to **Mrs Eileen Fry** who worked as the project's Research and Administrative Assistant for the two and a half years which lie behind this publication. Eileen's efficiency and dedication to the project in her attention to detail and handling of the mechanics of consultation, as well as of information collection and retrieval, have been the bedrock of the project.

Since the current edition builds upon the 1993 edition as well as extending it, acknowledgement should also be made of the contribution made by the project's previous Research Assistant, **Ms Rachelle Castle**, whose willingness to search out new avenues of information and knowledge led to the success of the first edition.

As a partnership between the University of Derby Religious Resource and Research Centre and The Inter Faith Network for the United Kingdom, special acknowledgements are also due to the staff of The Inter Faith Network for their contributions and encouragement throughout the period of the project: **Mr Brian Pearce**, the Network's Director, and to **Dr Harriet Crabtree**, its Deputy Director, for their support to the project team in Derby and their attention to detail in commenting upon drafts of the entire directory, and to **Dr Harriet Crabtree** for initial drafts of some sections of the text.

Thanks should also be recorded to **Mrs Harsha Shah** of the Network office for facilitating smooth contacts and exchange of information between the Network office and the project office in Derby. Acknowledgement should also be made of the work of **Ms Sophie Hawkins**, **Mr Anthony Padgett** and **Dr Christiana Whitehead** who commented on extensive portions of the 1993 text whilst offering voluntary help in the Network office.

Special thanks are also due to the members of the **Executive Committee** of The Inter Faith Network for the UK who, as well as commenting on the introductory materials for their own religious community, also examined the introductory materials for the chapter on "Inter-Faith Activity in the UK", as well as reading and commenting on the chapters on "Visiting Places of Worship and Hosting Visits" and "Making Contact, Organising Events and Consultations" and also the section on "Religious Statistics" in the "Religious Landscape of the United Kingdom" chapter. The names of these Committee members are recorded below within the sections covering the acknowledgements in relation to the materials on particular religious communities.

The project has, however, also depended upon the voluntary contributions of many other individuals and organisations from within the religious communities of the UK. In relation to the directory's introductory materials on the various religious communities, the keys to organisational names and the listings of organisations, consultative arrangements were established with representatives from the relevant religious communities which extended beyond the membership of the Network's Executive Committee.

Panels of consultants were formed which built upon the previous panels for the 1993 edition, but whose memberships were appropriately supplemented. The panels of consultants included both individuals from within the religious traditions concerned and a number of individuals with particular academic expertise from outside of the traditions.

These panels of consultants include the following individuals and organisations who offered their time and expertise in commenting upon and contributing to drafts of the texts for each religious community, the section on "Religious Statistics" in the "Religious Landscape of the UK" chapter and the chapters on "Visiting Places of Worship and Hosting Visits" and on "Making Contact, Organising Events and Consultations."

A number of these consultants also commented helpfully on the categories of traditions, movements, languages and other matters offered to the organisations and places of worship included in the organisational listings section of each religion, and also contributed to the checking of listings of national organisations within their religions.

CONSULTATION ON RELIGIOUS TRADITIONS AND INTER-FAITH ACTIVITIES

The Baha'i Community

Mr Hugh Adamson, Bahá'í Community of the United Kingdom; *Dr Navin Doostar*, Bahá'í representative on The Inter Faith Network for the UK Executive Committee.

The Buddhist Community

Mr Stephen Batchelor, Sharpham; *Mr Anil Goonewardene*, Buddhist Society; *Venerable Rathna Jothi*, East Midlands Buddhist Association; *Dharmachari Kulananda*, Friends of the Western Buddhist Order; *Mr Ron Maddox*, The Buddhist Society; *Revd Myokyo-ni*, The Zen Centre, London; *Dr Akong Tulku Rinpoche*, Kagyu Samye Ling; *Most Venerable Pandit Dr Vajiragnana*, London Buddhist Vihara; *Ms Dal Strutt*, The Buddhist Society; *Ms Georgina Black*, Network of Buddhist Organisations (UK) who co-ordinated wider consultation with a number of the Network of Buddhist Organisations' member organisations. Additionally consulted were *Professor Richard Gombrich*, University of Oxford; and *Dr Paul Williams*, University of Bristol. Special thanks for assistance in detailed drafting are due to *Mrs Peggy Morgan*, Westminster College, Oxford.

The Christian Community

Most Revd Father Olu Abiola, Council of African and Afro-Caribbean Churches (UK); *Mr John Adegoke*, Centre for Black and White Christian Partnership, Birmingham; *Canon David Atkinson*, Archdeacon of Lewisham; *Father Michael Barnes*, Westminster Interfaith Programme; *Ms Vida Barnett*, Shap Working Party on World Religions in Education; *Revd Esme Beswick*, Joint Council for Anglo-Caribbean Churches; *Revd Marcus Braybrooke*, World Congress of Faiths; *Revd Eric Brown*, Afro-West Indian United Council of Churches; *Mrs Jenny Carpenter*, Churches Together in England; *Revd Canon Dr Tony Chesterman*, University of Derby, Religious Resource and Research Centre Steering Committee; *Revd Maxwell Craig*, Action of Churches Together in Scotland; *Revd Dr Colin Davey*, Council of Churches for Britain and Ireland; *Revd Noel Davies*, Churches Together in Wales; *Revd S M Douglas*, International Ministerial Council of Great Britain; *Canon Michael Evans*, Tunbridge Wells; *Venerable Ian Gatford*, University of Derby, Religious Resource and Research Centre Steering Committee; *Mrs Ivy Gutridge, MBE*, Wolverhampton Inter-Faith Group; *Revd Basil Hazledine*, Epsom; *Rt Revd Charles Henderson*, Roman Catholic Committee for Other Faiths of the Bishops' Conference of England and Wales; *Revd David Heslop*, University of Derby, Religious Resource and Research Centre; *Revd Carmel Jones*, New Assembly of Churches; *Revd Canon Dr Christopher Lamb*, Churches' Commission for Inter Faith Relations, Council of Churches for Britain and Ireland; *Revd Anne McClelland*, Richmond Inter-Faith Group; *Revd Paul Quilter*, University of Derby, Religious Resource and Research Centre Steering Committee; *Revd Geoffrey Roper*, General Secretary of the Free Church Federal Council; *Sister Margaret Shepherd*, NDS, Council of Christians and Jews; *Revd David Staple OBE*, former General Secretary of the Free Church Federal Council; *Dr David Stevens*, Irish Council of Churches; *Rt Revd Roy Williamson*, Church of England Bishop of Southwark.

The Hindu Community

Mr Rameshbhai Acharya, Leicester; *Mr Vipin Aery*, National Council of Hindu Temples; *Sri Akhandadi das*, International Society for Krishna Consciousness; *Mr Raj Bali*, University of Derby, Religious Resource and Research Centre Steering Committee; *Professor Bharadwaj*, Arya Pratinidhi Sabha; *Mrs Sarawati Dave*, Vishwa Hindu Parishad (UK); *Mr A Daxini*, Shree Sanatan Mandir, Leicester; *Mr Deepak Naik*, National Council of Hindu Temples; *Dr Nandakumara*, Bharatiya Vidya Bhavan; *Mr Jitubhai Pancholi*, Swaminarayan Hindu Mission; *Mr D B Patel*, Shree Sanatan Mandir, Leicester; *Mr Navin Patel*, Swaminarayan Hindu Mission; *Rasamandala das*, ISKCON Education Service; *Dr H V Satyanarayana Sastry*, Bharatiya Vidya Bhavan; *Dr Ramanbhai Shah*, Swaminarayan Hindu Mission; *Mr Om Parkash Sharma*, National Council of Hindu Temples. Also consulted were *Dr Kim Knott*, University of Leeds; *Dr Julius Lipner*, University of Cambridge; *Dr Eleanor Nesbitt*, University of Warwick; *Dr Malory Nye*, University of Stirling. Special thanks for assistance in detailed drafting are due to **Dr Dermot Killingley**, University of Newcastle upon Tyne.

The Jain Community

Mr Nemu Chandaria, Institute of Jainology; **Professor Padminabh Jaini**, University of California, Berkeley, USA and Trustee of the Institute of Jainology; **Mr Vinod Kapashi**, Federation of Jain Organisations in the UK; **Mr Bipin Mehta**, Institute of Jainology; **Dr Natubhai Shah**, London; **Mr Ramesh Shah**, Middlesex. Also consulted were: **Dr Paul Marett**, Jain Academy; **Ms Kristi Wiley**, University of California, Berkeley, USA.

The Jewish Community

Rabbi David Goldberg, London Society of Jews and Christians; **Revd Jonathan Gorsky**, Council of Christians and Jews; the late **Rabbi Hugo Gryn CBE**, West London Synagogue of British Jews; **Rabbi Dr Julian Jacobs**, Chief Rabbi's Representative on Inter-Faith Affairs; **Mr Paul Mendel**, Council of Christians and Jews; **Professor Eric Moonman OBE**, London; **Mr Neville Nagler**, Board of Deputies of British Jews; **Mrs Rosalind Preston OBE**, Board of Deputies of British Jews; **Mr Robert Rabinowitz**, Jewish Continuity; **Mr Laurie Rosenberg**, Board of Deputies of British Jews; **Ms Marlena Schmool**, Board of Deputies of British Jews; **Rabbi Dr Norman Solomon**, Oxford Centre for Hebrew and Jewish Studies; **Rabbi Jacqueline Tabick**, West London Synagogue.

The Muslim Community

Dr Manazir Ahsan, Islamic Foundation; **Dr Bahadur Dalal**, World Ahl ul-Bayt (AS) Islamic League; **Mr Gai Eaton**, Islamic Cultural Centre, Regent's Park Mosque, London; **Mr Mohsin Jaffer**, Islamic Education Board; **Mrs Ummul Banin S Merali**, World Ahl ul-Bayt (AS) Islamic League; **Mr Abdul Hamid Qureshi**, Lancashire Council of Mosques; **Maulana Mohammad Shahid Raza**, Imams and Mosques Council, UK; **Mr Iqbal Sacranie**, UK Action Committee on Islamic Affairs; **Mr Aslam Siddiqi**, University of Derby, Religious Resource and Research Centre Steering Committee; **Dr Ataullah Siddiqui**, Islamic Foundation; **Mr Syed Syediau**, World Islamic Mission (UK). Also consulted were

Dr Jorgen Nielsen, Centre for the Study of Islam and Christian-Muslim Relations, Selly Oak Colleges, Birmingham and **Mr Ahmed Andrews**, University of Derby.

The Sikh Community

Mr Surinder Singh Attariwala, Network of Sikh Organisations (UK); **Mrs Bhupinder Kaur Bagga**, Sikh Council for Inter Faith Relations; **Mr Mohinder Singh Chana**, Bradford; **Dr Hardial Singh Dhillon**, University of Derby, Religious Resource and Research Centre Steering Committee; **Mr Surjit Singh Kalra**, Birmingham; **Mr Teja Singh Manget**, Sikh Missionary Society; **Mrs Satwant Kaur Rait**, Leeds; **Mr Gurpal Singh**, Bhatra Sikh Centre, Cardiff; **Mr Indarjit Singh, OBE, JP**, the Network of Sikh Organisations (UK); **Dr Kartar Surinder Singh**, Sikh Council for Inter Faith Relations; **Mr Darshan Singh Tatla**, Birmingham. Also consulted were **Dr Eleanor Nesbitt**, University of Warwick and **Professor Christopher Shackle**, School of Oriental and African Studies, University of London.

The Zoroastrian Community

Mr Malcolm Deboo, Zoroastrian House; **Mr Jehangir Sarosh**, London Zoroastrian Community; **Mr Shahrokh Shahrokh**, London; **Dr Rashna Writer**, Birkbeck College, London. Also consulted was **Professor John Hinnells**, School of Oriental and African Studies, University of London and Visiting Professor in Religious Studies, University of Derby.

Some Other Religious Communities and Groups

On the Brahma Kumaris, **Sister Maureen** of the Brahma Kumaris World Spiritual University; on the Church of Christ, Scientist, **Mr Alan Grayson** of the Christian Science Committee on Publication for Great Britain and Ireland; on the Church of Jesus Christ of Latter-day Saints, **Mr Bryan Grant** of the Public Affairs Office of the Church of Jesus Christ of Latter-day Saints, Europe North area; on the Jehovah's Witnesses, the **London Office of The Watch Tower Bible and Tract Society of Pennsylvania**; on the Namdharis, **Mr Vasdev Singh Bamrah, Mr Ranjit Singh Flora** and **Mrs Charanjit Ajit Singh** of the Namdhari Sangat UK; on the Sant Nirankaris, **Mr T**

S Dhillon of the Sant Nirankari Mandal UK; on Pagans, **Dr Vivianne Crowley** of the Pagan Federation, **Dr Graham Harvey** of King Alfred's College of Higher Education, Winchester and **Dr Ronald Hutton**, University of Bristol; on the Rastafarians, **Henry Nicholson** of the Rastafarian Society, London; on the Ravidassia, **Dr Charan Singh Bunger** of the Sri Guru Ravidass Sabha UK; on the Sathya Sai Baba Organisation, *Joan Brake* of the Central Council of the United Kingdom; on the Valmikis, **Dr Davinder Prasad** of the Maharishi Valmik Sabha, Coventry.

Inter-Faith Organisations

The following people active in local and national inter-faith organisations commented upon the chapter on "Inter Faith Activity in the UK" and assisted in checking local listings of religious organisations and places of worship:

Ms Cynthia Bailey, Wellingborough Multi-Faith Group; **Mr Peter Baker**, Redbridge Council of Faiths; **Dr Peter Bell**, Leeds Concord Inter-Faith Fellowship; **Mr Hugh Boulter**, Reading Inter-Faith Group; **Revd Robert Boulter**, Manchester Inter-Faith Group; **Mr Ronnie Bray**, Kirklees and Calderdale Inter-Faith Fellowship; **Revd Marcus Braybooke**, World Congress of Faiths; **Mr Paul Brocklehurst**, Peterborough Inter Faith Council; **Ms Cynthia Capey**, Suffolk Inter-Faith Resouce; **Revd Jean Clark**, Coventry Inter-Faith Group; **Mr Tom Daffern**, World Conference on Religion and Peace; **Ms Rosemary Eldridge**, Glasgow Sharing of Faiths Group; **Mr Bob Exon**, Bradford Concord Inter-Faith Society; **Ms Jo Fageant**, Reading Inter-Faith Group; **Revd Peter Godfrey**, International Association for Religious Freedom, British Members' Group; **Rabbi David Goldberg**, London Society of Jews and Christians; **Mrs Ivy Gutridge**, Wolverhampton Inter-Faith Group; **Ms Dorte Elizabeth Haarhaus**, Leeds Concord Inter Faith Fellowship; **Mrs Diana Hanmer**, World Congress of Faiths; **Mr John Hay**, Nottingham Inter-Faith Council; **Ms Jean Hobbs**, Kirklees and Calderdale Inter-Faith Fellowship; **Mr Stanley Hope**, Rochdale Interfaith Action; **Mrs Angela Jagger**, Leicester Council of Faiths; **Sister Clare Jardine**, Study Centre for Christian-Jewish Relations; **Sister Mary Kelly**, Study Centre for Christian-Jewish Relations; **Mrs Lorraine Khan**, Cardiff Interfaith Association; **Ms Judith Law**, Waltham Forest All Faiths Group; **Revd Anne**

McClelland, Richmond Inter-Faith Group; **Father Gordian Marshall**, Standing Conference of Jews, Christians and Muslims in Europe; **Mr Sirjit Singh Marway**, Medway Inter-Faith Group; **Mr Paul Mendel**, Council of Christians and Jews; **Mrs Deborah Montero**, Newham Association of Faiths; **Mrs Peggy Morgan**, Shap Working Party on World Religions in Education; **Revd Supriyo Mukherjee**, Coventry Inter Faith Group; **Mr Gulam Husein Musa**, Gloucestershire Inter Faith Association; **Mr Stuart Nimmo**, Cleveland Interfaith Group; **Mrs Gwen Palmer**, Religious Education Council; **Mrs June Ridd**, Bristol Interfaith Group; **Dr James Russell**, Edinburgh Interfaith Association; **Mr Hari Shukla**, Tyne and Wear Racial Equality Council Inter Faith Panel; **Ms Janine Shrigley**, Derby Open Centre Multi-Faith Group; **Mr Kartar Surinder Singh**, Dudley Council of Faiths; **Revd Hilary Smart**, Walsall Inter Faith Group; **Sister Isobel Smyth**, Glasgow Sharing of Faiths Group; **Ms Pat Stevens**, Harrow Inter-Faith Council; **Sister Sujata**, Birmingham Council of Faiths; **Revd Geoffrey Usher**, International Association for Religious Freedom; **Ms Caroline Wallace**, Birmingham Fellowship of Faiths; **Ms Margaret Wilkins**, Walsall Inter Faith Group; **Canon Michael Wolfe**, Merseyside Inter-Faith Group; **Ms Angela Wood**, Standing Conference on Inter-Faith Dialogue in Education; **Mr S K Vadivale**, Oxford Round Table of Religions; **Mr David Yarham**, Cambridge Inter-Faith Group.

CONSULTATION ON SPECIFIC SECTIONS AND CHAPTERS

For the chapter on "The Religious Landscape of the UK", the following people were consulted:

Professor James Beckford, University of Warwick; **Ms Kerry Bowen**, Churches and Chapels Section of the Office for National Statistics; **Dr Steve Bruce**, University of Aberdeen; **Dr. Gavin Craigen**, Welsh Association of Standing Advisory Councils on Religious Education; **Dr Grace Davie**, University of Exeter; **Dr Sophie Gilliat**, University of Warwick; *Officials of the Department of the Environment*; **Mrs Gwen Palmer**, Religious Education Council; **Dr Gerald Parsons**, Open University; **Revd. Maurice Ryan**, Stranmillis College, Belfast and Northern Ireland Inter-Faith Forum; **Dr Sebastian Poulter**, University of Southampton; **Revd. John Stevenson**, Church of Scotland Education Department.

For the section of "The Religious Landscape of the UK" chapter dealing with "Religious Statistics", together with the consultants on "The Religious Landscape of the UK" chapter and those on the individual religious traditions listed above, the project also consulted the academic advisers of the Religions and Statistics Research Project of the University of Derby's Religious Resource and Research Centre, as follows:

Ms Elizabeth Arweck, King's College, University of London; *Dr Rohit Barot*, University of Bristol; *Dr Grace Davie*, University of Exeter; *Dr Sewa Singh Khalsi*, University of Leeds; *Dr Kim Knott*, University of Leeds; *Dr Eleanor Nesbitt*, University of Warwick; *Professor Ceri Peach*, St Catherine's College, University of Oxford; *Mrs Marlena Schmool*, Board of Deputies of British Jews; *Dr Steve Vertovec*, University of Warwick; *Dr Frank Whaling*, University of Edinburgh. Additionally consulted on the section on "Religious Statistics" was *Dr Peter Brierley*, the Christian Research Association and *Dr Roger Ballard*, University of Manchester.

COLLECTION AND VERIFICATION OF DIRECTORY LISTINGS

In compiling the original contact lists which form the basis of the organisational listings in this directory, the project contacted all the organisations and places of worship contained in the 1993 edition.

It supplemented this with further research aimed at including organisations which were not uncovered by the research for the 1993 edition or did not yet exist at that time. For this research, the project acknowledges the co-operation and contributions of many individuals and organisations which have provided it with information and examined draft listings.

The individuals and organisations who gave substantial help throughout the project are individually named above. Gratitude for help and assistance should also be recorded to all the organisations which are affiliated to *The Inter Faith Network*; many local *Race Equality Councils*; many local *Councils for Voluntary Service*; many *Local Education Authority Religious Education Advisers*; many *Local Authority Planning Departments*; and many *Local Authority Library Services*, not all of whom can be named individually here but who have provided the project with valuable information upon organisations and who, in some cases, have also contributed to checking the draft listings.

Acknowledgements should also be recorded to the *editors* and *publishers* of existing handbooks and directories of religious organisations and groups (which this directory is not intended to replace, but rather to complement). The project referred to these during the process of preparing to make its own direct contact with the organisations listed in this edition which had not previously been in existence or had not been uncovered by the research for the 1993 edition. Details of some of these handbooks and directories are to be found in the "Finding Out More: Some Other Relevant Publications and Resources" chapter of this volume.

OTHER ACKNOWLEDGEMENTS

The participation and support of over 200 consultants listed above has saved the project from making a number of avoidable errors and has ensured that the directory is the product of a truly co-operative process of partnership. At the same time, the consultants are not responsible for any errors which might remain through the editing process. Having acknowledged the contributions of all those above, as Editor I should, of course, state that I take responsibility for the final product of this process and that no one other than myself should bear the responsibility for any errors or imbalances which remain.

However, the collaborative nature of the project includes the contribution of others too. It is difficult individually to acknowledge all those who have contributed in so many ways and I apologise for any whose names I have left out in error. But, thanks should at least be expressed to *Mrs Elizabeth Huddleston* for proof-reading the non-listing sections of the directory; to *Mrs Margaret Pugh* and *Mr Robbie Pugh* for the practical voluntary assistance of various kinds provided at different points throughout the project in Derby; and to *Mrs Kathleen Edwards*, for considerable help in the closing stages of the project.

The contributions of *Mr Daniel Banfield, Ms Diane Butcher, Ms Jane Cromblehome, Ms Sarah Louise Harding, Mr Richard Jenkins, Ms Sacha Mothersole, Mr Simon Penny, Ms Hayley Rafill, Ms Joanna*

Rooney, Mr Tom Sussmes, Ms Eleanor Thomas, Ms Melanie Tsugalidiu, Ms Rachel Webb, Ms Abigail Williams, Mr Simon Wilson and Ms Helen Wrigglesworth (students of the University of Derby) should also be acknowledged for their services in preparing and filling the many envelopes which this project entailed and to Mr Damian Partridge and Mr Gurdeep Sahota, General Managers of the University of Derby Student Employment Agency for arranging their employment on the project.

The support of a range of past and present University of Derby staff has also been crucial to the progress of the project. For their initial support to getting the project which led to the first edition off the ground in 1990, thanks are due to Mr David Udall, former Deputy Director (Academic); Mr Trevor Easingwood, former Deputy Director (Resources); and Mr Michael Hall, Deputy Vice-Chancellor.

For contributions to the preparation, publication and administration of the current edition the support and contributions of the following should be acknowledged: Professor Pamela Abbott, former Assistant Dean of the School of Education and Social Science and now Dean of Social Sciences at the University of Teeside; Mr Michael Wiser, Dean of School of Education and Social Science; Professor Jonathan Powers, Senior Pro Vice-Chancellor; Ms Zena Hawley of the Marketing Unit; Mrs Anne Aderogba, of the Centre for Educational Development, Methods and Media; Mrs Margaret Wagstaff and Ms Gina Hall of the Mickleover site Reception staff who process incoming and outgoing site mail and upon whose practical assistance, in processing a large amount of mail, the project has depended; Mrs Gill Speed and members of the University Finance Department who have processed orders for the director; and Mrs Susan Sadula, of the School of Education and Social Science administrative staff who helped out at a particularly difficult time for the project.

Thanks are also due to Mr Daniel Butt, Mr Kamaljeet Nijjar, Mr Davis Anighoro, and Mr David King, students of the University's School of Mathematics and Computing, for setting up a sales database as part of a student project. In addition, the support of the members of the Steering Committee of the Religious Resource and Research Centre and of colleagues at the University of Derby within the Religious Studies subject area and the Academic Resource and Research Centre.

Special thanks for their professionalism, patience and collaborative working are due to Ms Debbie Martin and Mr David Bush of the Print Department; and to Mr Neville Wells, Print and Reprographics Manager.

A final word of thanks is due to my parents Denis and Rhoda Weller for their hospitality whilst I worked through the final checks of the directory and to my mother for assisting in some of these checks; to my wife Greta Preisler-Weller who contributed to the project by designing the directory's cover used in both the 1993 edition and this edition; and to my children, David, Lisa and Katrina Weller for their patience and tolerance with me whilst I have devoted time to the project.

As with the first edition, for David, Lisa and Katrina it is my hope that this new edition of the directory will make another small contribution towards the creation of a society in which it might be possible for them to grow up discovering that people of various religions can live in creative peace and harmony with one another and with the wider world which all humankind shares.

Dr Paul Weller
Editor, *Religions in the UK* and
Project Director, Multi-Faith Directory
Research Project

Religious Resource and Research Centre,
School of Education and Social Science,
University of Derby

TOPIC INDEX

The "Topic Index" lists the page references within the general introductory chapters and the introductions to each religious community where you can find paragraphs of material on particular items. The items appearing in bold are the standard main section titles (see p.14 in the "User's Guide" which appear in the introductions to each religion. The items in normal type are the sub-sections particular to the religion concerned, and the sections in italics are more detailed and specific paragraphs within these sub-sections.

If a word which you are looking for does not appear in this index, you can also search for it in the "Significant Word Index" which gives individual page references for each word which is italicised in the text (generally, these are Romanisations of words in languages other than English, or are English language words with a specific meaning within the religion concerned: see pp. 14-15 in the "User's Guide") and also for a number of other significant words including names of religious personalities and leaders. Alternatively, the word you are looking for might be found in the "Keys to Organisation Listings" in the chapters on each religion

SIGNIFICANT WORD INDEX

This index lists all the significant words appearing within the directory's textual materials and Keys to Organisation Titles (therefore excluding the listings). These significant words include all the words appearing within the text in italics (generally, these are Romanisations of words in languages other than English, or are English language words with a specific meaning within the religion concerned: see pp. 14–15 in the "User's Guide"). But a number of other significant words are also given including names of religious personalities and leaders.

Since words in other than English and non-European languages often appear in English in a variety of Romanisations, it is always worth checking the index for other possible renderings of the word which you want to find. Whilst an attempt has been made to be consistent within the directory's textual materials, words in the Keys to Organisation Titles will often appear in variant forms, reflecting the diversity of usage among the organisations listed. Therefore once you have looked up a word initially, if other renderings are noted, it would also be worth checking the references for these within this index.

The singular form of English words in the index covers page references for both the singular and plural forms of the word. Not all instances of a word within the directory are given, but a range are included that will help users to unlock the meaning of the word or to set it in a wider context.

A

Aameen, 592
Aaronic Priesthood, 669
Aarti, 346, 355
Abad, 591
Abada, 595
Abbasid, 451
Abbots, 137
Abd, 472, 591, 595
Abdu'l-Bahá, 95-97, 99-102
Abdu'l-Bahá's Will, 96
Abel, 591
Abhidhamma-Pitaka, 126
Abi Talib, 451
Abraham, 382, 386, 443-445, 450, 453, 459
Abrahamic, 71
Abu Bakr, 450-451, 591, 593
Achaemenid, 652, 657
Acharanga Sutra, 366
Acharya Tejendraprasad Pande, 304
Acharya Umasvati, 367
Acharyas, 370
Achintya-Bhedha-Abheda, 296
Act of Supremacy, 216
Act of Uniformity, 216
Ad, 607
Adab, 591
Adam, 201, 477, 591, 597
Adar, 653-654, 657, 659
Adar Yazad, 654
Adar-roj, 659
Adar-Roj Parab, 659

Adass, 443
Adath, 443
Aden, 355, 379-380, 443, 651
Adhan, 470, 599
Adharma, 367
Adhyatmik, 355
Adi, 607-608, 614, 647
Adi Granth, 607-608, 614, 647, 672
Administrative Order, 98, 101
Adur, 657
Advaita, 293-297, 303, 305
Advaita Vedanta, 296, 305
Advaitins, 296
Advent, 212-213
Adventist, 284, 286
Aesir, 674
Afghanistan, 290
Africa, 26, 96, 196-198, 222, 450-452, 615, 676, 605-606, 651
African, 12, 26, 221-222, 289, 365, 449, 615, 676
African Churches, 222
African-Caribbean, 25-26, 196
Africanisation, 26, 289, 449, 615, 651
Afrinagan, 653
Afrins, 653
Aga Khan, 455, 591
Agama, 126, 366
Agape, 200, 206
Agency, 222, 236, 284
Aggadah, 384
Agha Khanis, 455

Agudah, 443
Agudas, 443
Ahavat, 443
Ahimsa, 61, 297, 300, 357, 367, 369-370
Ahl, 591
Ahl al-Hadith, 591
Ahl-e-Hadith, 460, 473-474, 477, 591
Ahl-i-Hadith, 454
Ahl-ul-Bait, 591, 593
Ahl-ul-Bayt, 591
Ahla, 591
Ahlebait, 591
Ahnaf, 592
Ahuna Vairya, 656
Ahunavar, 656
Airyana Vaeja, 653
Aiwisruthrem, 656
Ajit, 646-647
Akal, 607-608, 646
Akal Purakh, 608
Akal Takhat, 607
Akali, 646-647
Akasha, 367
Akhand, 613-614, 646, 648
Akhand Path, 613-614, 646
Akiva, 443
Akka, 96, 99-100
Akong Rinpoche, 135
Akshar, 296, 304, 355-356, 360
Akshar Brahman, 296
Akshar Purushottam Sanstha, 304
Akshardham, 303

UK AND NATIONAL ORGANISATION INDEX

This index includes all UK and national level organisations of the religious traditions included in the directory, together with UK and national inter-faith organisations and resource organisations, listed in alphabetical order of organisation name (with organisations having a Welsh name listed under both their English and Welsh names). For ease of reference and for clarification in cases which might otherwise be ambiguous if only the name of the organisation and not its religion were known to a directory user and there are organisations of different religions but with similar names, in each case the religion or type of organisation indexed is indicated by means of a code preceding the page references, as follows:

Ba: Bahá'í	Je: Jewish
Bu: Buddhist	M: Muslim
C: Christian	R: Resource
H: Hindu	S: Sikh
IF: Inter-Faith	So: Some other
Ja: Jain	Z: Zoroastrian

A

ACATE (Association of Centres of Adult Theological Education), C: 234

Action by Christians Against Torture, C: 234

Action of Churches Together in Scotland, C: 270

Afro-West Indian United Council of Churches, C: 227

Agency for Jewish Education, Je: 396

Agudas Harabbanim (Association of Rabbis of Great Britian), Je: 396

Agudath Hashochtim V'Hashomrim of Great Britain (Cattle Section), Je: 396

Agudath Hashochtim V'Hashomrim of Great Britain (Poultry Section), Je: 396

Ahlul-Bayt Tours Association, M: 464

Aladura International Church (UK & Overseas), C: 230

Albanian Islamic Centre & Society, M: 465

Al-Furqan Charity Trust, M: 464

Al-Furqan Islamic Heritage Foundation, M: 464

Al-Hoda Limited, M: 464

Al-Hurau Schools Trust, M: 464

Al Khoei Foundation, M: 465

Al-Muhajiroun, M: 465

Al Muntada Al Islami Trust, M: 465

Al-Muttaqiin, M: 465

Alliance of Religions and Conservation, IF: 81

All Muslim Funeral Society, M: 465

AMANA, M: 465

Amaravati Buddhist Monastery, Bu: 139

Amida Trust, Bu: 139

Amnesty International Religious Liaison Panel, IF: 81

Anglo-Jewish Association, Je: 396

Angulimala, The Buddhist Prison Chaplaincy Organisation, Bu: 139

Anjumen-e-Jamali (Dawoodi Bohra Jumaat), M: 465

Apostolic Church, The, C: 230

ApTibet (Appropriate Technology for Tibetans, Bu: 139

Armenian Apostolic Oriental Orthodox Church, C: 230

Arya Pratinidhi Sabha (UK), H: 309

Assembly of Masorti Synagogues, Je: 396

Assemblies of God in Great Britain & Ireland, C: 231

Assemblies of God in Great Britain & Ireland, Ireland Regional Council, C: 267

Assemblies of God in Great Britain & Ireland South Wales Regional Council, C: 279

Association for British Muslims, M: 466

Association for Jewish Youth, Je: 398

Association for Pastoral Care & Counselling, IF: 81

Association of Adath Yisrael Synagogues, Je: 397

Association of Interchurch Families, C: 234

Association of Jewish Communal Professionals, Je: 397

Association of Jewish Ex-Servicemen & Women, Je: 397

Association of Jewish Friendship Clubs, Je: 397

Association of Jewish Refugees in GB, Je: 397

Association of Jewish Sixth Formers, Je: 397

Association of Jewish Teachers, Je: 397

Association of Jewish Women's Organisations in UK, Je: 397

Association of Ministers (Chazanim) of Great Britain, Je: 397

Association of Muslim Researchers, M: 466

Association of Muslim Schools of UK & Eire (AMS), M: 466

Association of Muslim Youth & Community Workers, M: 466

Association of Orthodox Jewish Professionals of GB, Je: 397

Association of Reform & Liberal Mohalim, Je: 397

LOCAL GUIDE INDEX

The local guide index enables directory users to seek out organisations in an alternative way to looking up regions in each individual chapter. It gives references for the pages on which all local (or regional, in the case of Christian organisations) religious and interfaith organisations in a given place can be found. In each case the religion or type of organisation indexed is indicated by means of a code preceding the page references, as follows:

Ba: Bahá'í
Bu: Buddhist
C: Christian
H: Hindu
IF: Inter-Faith

Ja: Jain
Je: Jewish
M: Muslim
S: Sikh
Z: Zoroastrian

A

Aberdeen, Grampian, Ba:119 Bu:182 C:271-272, 275-277 Je:440 M:584
Aberystwyth, Dyfed, Bu:144, 184 M:588
Abingdon, Oxfordshire, Ba:113
Aboyne, Grampian, C:272
Accrington, Lancashire, IF:86 M:502
Acomb, North Yorkshire, C:241, 243
Airdrie, Strathclyde, C:271, 276
Alford, Grampian, Ba:119
Ambleside, Cumbria, C:247
Anglesey, Gwynedd, C:280
Annan, Dumfries and Galloway, C:276
Antrim, County Antrim, Ba:118
Ardrishaig, Highland, C:272
Argyll, Highlands and Islands, C:277
Armagh City, County Armagh, C:269
Ashburton, Devon, Bu:177
Ashford, Kent, C:258 M:571
Ashton-under-Lyne, Lancashire, H:317 M:502-503
Aylesbury, Buckinghamshire, Ba:113 Bu:171 M:571
Ayr, Strathclyde, Bu:182 C:275

B

Balby, South Yorkshire, M:483
Ballymena, County Antrim, Ba:118 C:266, 269
Banbridge, County Down, C:268
Banbury, Oxfordshire, C:259 M:571
Bangor, County Down, Ba: 118 C:268-269, 281 IF:47

Bangor, Gwynedd, Bu: 184 C:281 M:588
Barnard Castle, County Durham, Bu:149
Barnsley, West Yorkshire, Bu:151
Barrow-in-Furness, Cumbria, Bu:154
Barry, South Glamorgan, M:588
Basildon, Essex, Bu:171-172 H:349 Je:433 M:571
Basingstoke, Hampshire, Ba:113 IF:90 M:571 S:640
Bath, Somerset, C:265 IF:91 M:582
Bathgate, Lothian, C:272 M:584
Batley, West Yorkshire, IF:85 M:483-485
Beaminster, Dorset, IF:92
Beccles, Suffolk, Ba:110
Beckenham, Kent, C:263 H:348-349
Bedford, Bedfordshire, Ba:113 Bu:171-172 H:349 IF:90 M:571-572 S:640
Bedworth, Warwickshire, C:254
Belfast, County Antrim, C:235, 266-270 H:353 IF:92 Je:439 M:584
Belper, Derbyshire, Bu:159
Belsay, Northumberland, Bu:149, 183
Beverley, East Riding of Yorkshire, Bu:151
Bexhill-on-Sea, East Sussex, H:350
Bexley, Kent, Ba:113
Birkenhead, Merseyside, Bu:154 C:247, 249, 254
Birmingham, West Midlands, Ba:109 Bu:148, 161 C:233-235, 238, 252-254 H:310, 329-331 IF:88 Ja:376 Je:417-419 M:464, 467, 469, 471-476, 528-539, 541 S:617-620, 629-632, 636 Z:663
Bishop Auckland, County Durham, C:237, 241
Bishop's Stortford, Hertfordshire, C:257, 261
Blackburn, Lancashire, Bu:153-154 C:246 H:317 Je:410 M:468, 502-505 S:624
Blackpool, Lancashire, Je:410 M:505
Blaenavon, Gwent, IF:93
Bognor Regis, West Sussex, Je:433
Bolton, Lancashire, Bu:154 C:247-248 H:317-318 IF:86 M:467, 505-507, 518
Borehamwood, Hertfordshire, Je:404, 433
Boston, Lincolnshire, Bu:159
Bournemouth, Dorset, Ba:117 Bu:177 C:266 IF:92 Je:438, 439 M:582
Brackley, Northamptonshire, C:261
Bracknell, Berkshire, Ba:113 Bu:172, 175
Bradford, West Yorkshire, Ba:106 Bu:151 C:242-244 H:310, 314-316 IF:85 Je:407-408 M:465, 471, 478, 485-490 S:621-622
Bradford-upon-Avon, M:582
Brecon, Powys, C:280-281
Brentwood, Essex, C:262
Brierfield, Lancashire, IF:86 M:507

NOTES